The British
BOXING
Board of Control
YEARBOOK
1994

Edited by
Barry J. Hugman

Published by Tony Williams Publications,
24a Queen Square, North Curry, Taunton, Somerset TA3 6LE

ISBN 1 869833 81 3

Distributed by Little Red Witch Book Distribution,
Helland Cottage, Helland, North Curry, Taunton, Somerset TA3 6DU
Telephone 0823 490080, Fax 0823 490281

Typeset by Typecast (Artwork & Design), 8 Mudford Road, Yeovil, Somerset BA21 4AA
Film Origination by R. Booth (Bookbinder) Ltd
Printed & Bound by R. Booth (Bookbinder) Ltd, Antron Hill, Mabe, Penryn, Cornwall TR10 9HH
Trade Sales, Searle Association, Telephone 0753 539295

All other sales enquiries should be referred to The Little Red Witch Book Distribution Co

Contents

4

Acknowledgements

As the editor of the *British Boxing Yearbook,* now in its tenth year, I would once again like to thank all the people who have helped the current production come together in such an orderly fashion.

Since I first conceived the idea of producing a yearbook back in 1982, I have always been lucky to have the full support and co-operation of the BBBoC, first with Ray Clarke and then with his predecessor, John Morris. As the book has gone from strength to strength, my demands on the Board have increased and John Morris and his staff have always been quick to respond most positively. From the top right through the office, help is always forthcoming. I feel I must compliment John Morris (General Secretary), Simon Block (Assistant Secretary), Paula Gibson, Mary Farnan, Joanne Landers and Karyn Locke, not only for keeping me informed on a regular basis of changes applicable to the *Yearbook,* regarding boxers, managers, promoters and other licenceholders, but also in the friendly manner they deport themselves.

Once again, I would like to place on record my gratitude to my great friend and assistant editor, Ron Olver. Ron has been involved in boxing well over 40 years and without a doubt, he has been the major influence in helping to establish ex-boxers' associations. A former Assistant Editor of *Boxing News;* former Assistant Editor of *Boxing World;* British correspondent for the *Ring;* author of *The Professionals;* author of the boxing section within *Encyclopedia Britannica;* author of *Boxing,* Foyles Library Service; former co-Editor of the *Boxing News Annual;* member of the BBBoC Benevolent Fund Grant's Committee; Vice-President of many ex-boxers' associations and the writer of the Old Timers feature in *Boxing News* for well over 20 years.

This year I have leaned on Chris Kempson more than ever and he has responded brilliantly. Chris, a lifelong boxing fan, worked with *Boxing Monthly, Boxing Weekly* and *Boxing Outlook,* prior to becoming a regular contributor to the *Amateur Boxing Scene* and writing a weekly column for the *Hackney Gazette.* He has been involved with the *Yearbook* since 1987 and this year was responsible for the PBA and Team Lennox articles, along with his usual look at the amateur boxing scene. In order to produce in-depth articles, a great deal of research was required, and Chris spent much time in the company of the men who make those operations tick. A committed Lennox Lewis fan, Lorraine Blanc, must also be thanked for typing the Team Lennox article over and over again until it became the finished product, while further aid came in the shape of John Cross, the sports editor of the *Islington Gazette,* and a young man sure to make his mark among boxing writers before too long. John was kind enough to take a look across the board at the country's most promising youngsters and I am sure you will agree that his article makes interesting reading.

Derek O'Dell and O. F. Snelling, men with boxing knowledge second to none and always busy writing boxing books, as well as helping Gilbert Allnutt to produce Croydon EBA's magnificent glossy *Southern Ex-Boxer,* somehow found the time to write articles for the *Yearbook.* Derek also supplied many old-time photos and, along with David Roake, is one of the leading collectors in the country. And John Jarrett, a man who started writing for *Boxing News* in the 1940s, once again put his considerable ability to the test when recounting last season's ups-and-downs in Around British Rings During 1992-93.

The international section of the *Yearbook* is spearheaded by the A-Z of Current World Champions and Eric Armit is again to be congratulated on piecing together biographical details, plus last season's record. This section also owes much to ABC's Bob Yalen (world) and the EBU General Secretary, Mrs Enza Merchionne Jacoponi (Europe), who kept me up to date with all title bout information, including weights, scores and any other relevant data.

Among the amateurs, apart from Chris Kempson, others who helped, were: *Boxing News'* David Prior, a man who is currently in the process of writing a history of amateur boxing in this country; Frank Hendry (Scottish ABA); Terry Smyth (Welsh ABA); Miss Linda Kelly (Irish ABA) and Patrick Myler, author of *The Fighting Irish.* Patrick provides information, year after year, on the previous Irish amateur season, including full details of internationals and complete results from the senior, intermediate and junior championships.

Over the last few years, the *Yearbook* has relied heavily on Les Clark for its photos. Les, a real boxing nut from a fighting family, travels the country taking action photos at many venues, while also visiting dressing rooms and gyms for poses that can be used to good effect in the *Yearbook.* If anyone requires a picture in the book, Les can be reached at 352 Trelawney Avenue, Langley, Bucks SL3 7TS. Other photos were supplied by Chris Bevan, Belvoir House, Moss Road, Askern, Yorkshire; David Jacobs of Action Images Ltd, 74 Willoughby Lane, London N17 0SP; George Ashton of Sportapics Ltd; Pennie Cattle and Harry Goodwin, my old friend from Manchester.

Others who mustn't be forgotten are: Bernard Hart, the Managing Director of Lonsdale Sports Equipment Ltd, who through the auspices of the Lonsdale International Sporting Club, sponsors the BBBoC Awards that herald the launch of the *Yearbook;* Neil Blackburn, another good friend of mine and long-term fan, who keeps both Ron Olver and myself informed of obituaries from the world of boxing; Jean Bastin of Typecast (Artwork & Design), who diligently cares for the typesetting and John Williams of Williams-Agg-Manning Marketing, as those of you advertising within these pages will know, is the *Yearbook's* advertising manager.

Finally, I would again like to thank the publisher, Tony Williams, whose great enthusiasm and support has again made the publication of the *British Boxing Yearbook* possible.   B. J. Hugman (Editor)

"Europe's Number One"

10 Western Road
Romford
Essex
RM1 3JT

Tel: (0708) 730480 (Office)
(0708) 724023 (Gym) Freddie King
Fax: (0708) 723425

Introduction

Welcome to the tenth edition of the *British Boxing Board of Control Yearbook,* a book which has hopefully kept apace with the rise of British boxing throughout the 1980s right up to the present time.

The biggest single change in this edition is the move to revert back to full records for all British-based boxers who have been active since 1 July 1992, rather than merely portraying results for the previous 18 months. This decision was taken because of the strength of opinion among the licence holders and the fact that the new format allows pictures to break the flow of continuous records.

In a season that saw Britain gain her first world heavyweight champion this century in Lennox Lewis, Chris Kempson has produced an excellent insight into how the Lewis camp operates. The reader should be able to ascertain just what it takes to look after and promote the interests of Lennox, who, in these days of multi-titleholders, holds the WBC version. Frank Maloney, the champion's manager, must be congratulated on confounding his critics and taking his fighter almost all the way. I say almost, reservedly, because there is still the hurdle that is Riddick Bowe to surmount. Assuming that Lewis overcomes Frank Bruno and Tommy Morrison, and Bowe survives the assortment of stiffs that come his way, this is the fight that the public wants in order to unify the title.

Talk about unifying titles is a pet subject for all of us who remember the days of eight champions. With four organisations, the IBF, WBA, WBC and WBO, competing among each other for its own segment of a world title, and with 17 weight divisions currently available, it is not uncommon to have 68 men claiming to be world champion at any given time. And, if you add to that figure men representing lesser organisations, such as the WBF, then there are infinitely more fighters out there who feel they have the right to be called a world champion. That they call themselves champions does not mean they are necessarily the best and for the man in the street the situation has become totally confusing.

In the days when there were only eight weights and far more active fighters plying their trade than today, many men who deserved to fight for titles were often shunned because they didn't have the right connections, while others operating at the bottom end of a weight division were extremely disadvantaged. They had two choices. Either weight reduce, or fight an opponent who could have a pull of half a stone, plus, on the night. Whether you like it or not, the extra weight divisions are here to stay, affording far more men an opportunity of winning a title at their natural weight and making the sport medically safer at the same time. Weight reduction, being one of the biggest single causes of tragedies in the ring. With the growth of much larger men in this day and age, I would even suggest that the heavyweight division eventually increases to fifteen stone, plus.

Accepting that 17 or 18 weight divisions is to the betterment of a fighter's health, it is up to the higher authorities, not television or the self made bodies, to decide who are the best men to fight for titles, if we are to have a fairer, more sensible system. Different versions of world titles are not something new, but the trend has certainly escalated now that television wishes to show fights with added status.

A far better arrangement, would be a world commission made up of representatives from the USA, EBU and other countries, determining who are the legitimate world champions, by authorising the IBF, WBA, WBC and WBO champions to box off every year. This move could satisfy everyone involved, including television companies, who would get plenty of mileage from the eliminating tournament.

Finally, on putting together Facts and Figures for 1992-93, I was pleasantly surprised to find that the number of promotions had remained at the same level as the previous year. With the recession still raging, it was not unnatural to feel that boxing might suffer further at the hands of a weak economy. That the sport survives such rigours, shows the people involved to be more than capable of fending off the anti-boxing brigade. However, opponents of boxing must never be taken lightly, and standards must continue to rise, if we are to march successfully intact into the next century. I see no reason why that cannot be achieved.

Abbreviations and Definitions

PTS	Points
CO	Count Out
RSC	Referee Stopped Contest
RTD	Retired
DIS	Disqualified
NC	No Contest
ND	No Decision

Barry J.Hugman, the founder-editor of the British Boxing Board of Control Yearbook, now in its tenth year

British Boxing Board of Control Ltd: Structure

(Members of the World Boxing Council, World Boxing Association, International Boxing Federation, World Boxing Organisation, Commonwealth Boxing Council and European Boxing Union)

PRESIDENT	Sir David Hopkin
VICE PRESIDENT	Leonard E. Read, QPM
CHAIRMAN	Sir David Hopkin
VICE CHAIRMAN	Leonard E. Read, QPM
GENERAL SECRETARY	John Morris

ADMINISTRATIVE
STEWARDS

Dr Adrian Whiteson, OBE
Dr Oswald Ross
William Sheeran
Dennis Lockton
Lincoln Crawford
Dr James Shea
Frank Butler, OBE
Tom Pendry, MP
Cliff Curvis
Bill Martin
Robert Graham
Lord Brooks of Tremorfa
Julian Critchley, MP
Gerald Woolard

STEWARDS OF APPEAL*

Robin Simpson, QC
John Mathew, QC
Nicholas Valios
Robert Harman, QC
William Tudor John
Geoffrey Finn
Judge Brian Capstick
Colin Ross Munro, QC
Peter Richards
Lord Meston

HONORARY
CONSULTANT*   Ray Clarke, OBE

HEAD OFFICE

Jack Petersen House
52a Borough High Street
London SE1 1XW
Tel. 071 403 5879
Fax. 071 378 6670
Telegrams:
BRITBOX, LONDON

* Not directors of the company

AREA COUNCILS - AREA SECRETARIES

AREA NO 1 (SCOTLAND)
Brian McAllister
11 Woodside Crescent, Glasgow G3 7UL
Telephone 041 332 0932

AREA NO 2 (NORTHERN IRELAND)
Stanley Anderson
5 Ardenlee Avenue, Ravenhill Road, Belfast,
Northern Ireland BT6 0AA
Telephone 0232 453829

AREA NO 3 (WALES)
Dai Corp
113 Hill Crest, Brynna, Llanharan, Mid Glamorgan
Telephone 0443 226465

AREA NO 4 (NORTHERN)
(Northumberland, Cumbria, Durham, Cleveland, Tyne and Wear, North Yorkshire [north of a line drawn from Whitby to Northallerton to Richmond, including these towns].)
John Jarrett
5 Beechwood Avenue, Gosforth, Newcastle
Telephone 091 2856556

AREA NO 5 (CENTRAL)
(North Yorkshire [with the exception of the part included in the Northern Area - see above], Lancashire, West and South Yorkshire, Greater Manchester, Merseyside and Cheshire, Isle of Man, North Humberside.)
Harry Warner
14 St Christopher's Road,
The 18th Fairway, Ashton under Lyme, Lancashire
Telephone 061 330 4572

AREA NO 6 (SOUTHERN)
(Bedfordshire, Berkshire, Buckinghamshire, Cambridgeshire, Channel Islands, Isle of Wight, Essex, Hampshire, Kent, Hertfordshire, Greater London, Norfolk, Suffolk, Oxfordshire, East and West Sussex.)
Simon Block
British Boxing Board of Control
Jack Petersen House, 52a Borough High Street, London SE1 1XW
Telephone 071 403 5879

AREA NO 7 (WESTERN)
(Cornwall, Devon, Somerset, Dorset, Wiltshire, Avon, Gloucestershire.)
Jim Paull
The Coach House, Clarence Court, Kent Road,
Congresbury, Bristol BS19 5BE
Telephone 0934 876036

AREA NO 8 (MIDLANDS)
(Derbyshire, Nottinghamshire, Lincolnshire, Salop, Staffordshire, Herefordshire and Worcestershire, Warwickshire, West Midlands, Leicestershire, South Humberside, Northamptonshire.)
Alec Kirby
105 Upper Meadow Road, Quinton, Birmingham B32
Telephone 021 421 1194

Foreword

by John Morris *(General Secretary, British Boxing Board of Control)*

THIS is the time of year to welcome back regular readers of the best and most comprehensive yearbook you can find in British boxing and to offer warm greetings to the new readers anxious to keep fully up-to-date at the end of a momentous period for the sport – particularly in this country, with LENNOX LEWIS reigning proudly as the World Boxing Council's heavyweight champion of the world.

Once again, editor Barry Hugman has produced a wonderful book, crammed with facts, loaded with records and as always, ringing the changes with new or up-dated features. The Yearbook's stature grows year by year, as I know only too well from my own travels around the world.

John Morris, the General Secretary of the British Boxing Board of Control   Derek Rowe (Photos) Ltd

Wherever I may be, there will be disappointment if I have not managed to squeeze in a few copies for administrators I meet at contests and conventions.

There is no doubt that the period covered by this issue is one of fascination for boxing in Britain, what may not be so readily apparent is that this is, in addition, a time of change. Certainly, there is no room in the sport for complacency, because boxing faces problems that must be resolved if we are to march into the 21st Century confident that boxing's place as a major spectator sport is assured, or even survives at all.

We have to combat the opponents, those who would like to see boxing vanish. This is not the place for a lengthy discussion of issues, but many aspects of medical and public safety must be reviewed constantly, the rights of individuals – boxers in particular – have to be treated progressively and boxing still needs to come to terms with the demands of television.

Over the years, I have called for closer liaison between the professional and amateur sides of the sport. This has never been more important after the major problems that have afflicted the English Amateur Boxing Association over the past twelve months. It has been encouraging to note that the Emergency Committee, entrusted with the task of re-shaping the amateur game in England, has already shown a willingness to talk, something I never found among those in charge over the past decades.

It has always amazed and alarmed me that they could not see that boxing is one sport with common problems, even if administered in separate sectors. Furthermore, they had for many years refused even to talk to those of us involved with professional boxing.

What I have always regarded as a complete lack of vision may, at least in part, explain why the English ABA has found itself in such an almighty mess.

People in boxing very often do not agree with each other, but if we do not meet to talk over the issues, to exchange ideas and look ahead, we really will blight our future. The BBBoC is eager to talk and to look into the future – something I hope the newly founded Professional Boxers' Association has discovered.

Whatever the issues, it will not always be possible to agree, but if we do not communicate there can only be friction and that boxing does not need and cannot afford.

The views of supporters are important too, particularly when they are coming from people well informed about every aspect of boxing. So my thanks for your interest and support for boxing – professional and amateur, and I am confident this yearbook will not only add to your enjoyment, but greatly increase your knowledge as well.

British Boxing Board of Control Awards, 1993

The Awards, inaugurated in 1984, in the form of statuettes of boxers, were originally designed by Morton T. Colver, the manufacturer of the Lonsdale Belt and the winners for 1993 were selected by an Awards Committee, comprising of John Morris, Frank Butler OBE, Bill Martin, Doctor Adrian Whiteson OBE and Barry J. Hugman, the editor of the *British Boxing Yearbook*.

British Boxer of the Year – Lennox Lewis

There were no other nominations, with Lennox Lewis a decisive winner of this prestigious award. At any other time, fighters such as Paul Weir (mini-fly), Steve Robinson (feather), Chris Pyatt (middle) and Nigel Benn (super-middle), who all picked up versions of the world title at their respective weights, would have been well in the running for the "Fighter of the Year" Award. But this was the year that Britain, in the shape of Lennox Lewis, finally got its hands on the world heavyweight crown for the first time this century.

From the moment Lennox won the world junior (1983) and then the Olympic super-heavyweight title in 1988, the drive to become heavyweight champion of the world has been his sole mission. Much has been written about him belonging to Canada, but the fact remains that he was born in England, even if he did learn to box in the land of the Maple Leaf, and he began his professional career right here in London.

The doubters have never been too far away, but he has always been a class above other British heavyweights, just ask Gary Mason and Derek Williams, and when Razor Ruddock came here to contest the right to fight for the WBC title, he stunned both sides of the Atlantic in the manner of his victory. He didn't just beat Ruddock, a man who had twice given Mike Tyson a stiff argument, he destroyed him. In just under four minutes of explosive action, the number one contender was smashed to the canvas three times before being rescued by American referee, Joe Cortez. And with the public at large licking their lips at the prospect of a contest between Riddick Bowe, who had relieved Evander Holyfield of his WBC/WBA and IBF titles, and Lennox, their hopes were

Lennox Lewis, the only nomination for the "British Boxer of the Year" Award, crushed the dangerous Canadian, Razor Ruddock, inside two rounds, prior to winning the WBC heavyweight title   Les Clark

11

dashed.

It has been well documented how Bowe, a man beaten in the Olympic final by Lewis, refused to fight his number one challenger and threw the WBC belt in a London dustbin. Picked up and dusted down by the WBC, Lennox was proclaimed their champion without having to fight. Although a highly unsatisfactory manner in which to become a world champion, it paved the way for a first defence against another Tyson victim, Tony Tucker. With Las Vegas the venue, last May, Tucker was belted to the canvas twice, but managed to go the distance as the champion became the first Brit to win a world heavyweight title fight on American soil this century. The main reason for the action not ending early, was almost certainly due to the fact that Lennox had injured his right hand prior to the contest. He later had a successful operation to repair knuckle and tendon damage.

By the time you read this, Lennox should have settled his argument with Frank Bruno and will be presumably looking towards his next challenger. There are one or two good matches to be made, even if you allow for the fact that Lewis versus Bowe will only come together when both have run completely out of challengers. But that may not be too far away, once Holyfield, Tommy Morrison and Michael Moorer have been given their opportunities.

Lennox Lewis has already proved to be the best ever British heavyweight and who would bet against him in his quest to unify the title? Whatever the future holds for him, he has made history and, Bowe apart, it is difficult at present to see where stiff competition to him is likely to come from. On top of that, he has set a great example to all youngsters wishing to become boxers by his exemplary behaviour and sportsmanship, both inside and outside the ring, and as such, fully warrants this award.

Previous winners:- 1984: Barry McGuigan. 1985: Barry McGuigan. 1986: Dennis Andries. 1987: Lloyd Honeyghan. 1988: Lloyd Honeyghan. 1989: Dennis Andries. 1990: Dennis Andries. 1991: Dave McAuley. 1992: Colin McMillan.

Best British Contest of the Year: Andy Till v Wally Swift Jnr

Other nominations: Sean Murphy v Alan McKay, Nigel Benn v Nicky Piper, Crisanto Espana v Meldrick Taylor, Robbie Regan v Salvatore Fanni.

A capacity crowd at Watford, including many standing, witnessed this, the second fight between the two men, on 17 September, 1992, and were not disappointed. Swift, defending his British light-middleweight title for the second time, was looking to make the Lonsdale Belt his own, while Till was aiming to repeat a 1989 victory over his rival, inside the distance this time, if possible. And with

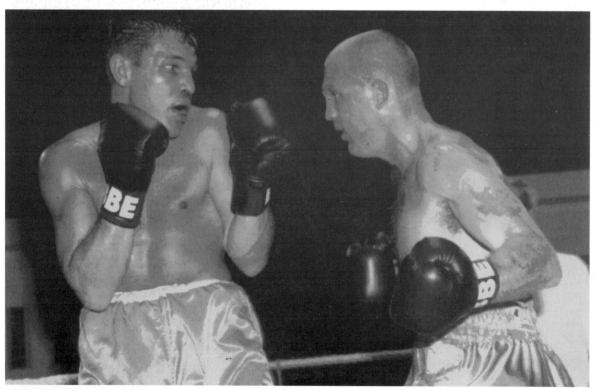

Wally Swift junior (left), defending his British light-middleweight title, faces up to the oncoming Andy Till during their first meeting of the season at Watford. This tremendous battle was voted the "Best British Contest of the Year"   Les Clark

both men promising to give it their all, the scene was set.

The contest got away to a flier, with the first three rounds among the fiercest witnessed in a British ring. Swift attacked with fast punches from both hands as Till smothered as many blows as he could and hit back with some of his own. Both fighters have proven chins, and they needed them. In the second round, Till was staggered a couple of times, while Swift was cut on the right eye and in the third there was no let up. It was already a war of attrition.

We discovered later that Wally had broken his right hand in the fourth and that certainly explained why he boxed one-handed from then on. But there was still no drop in the pace as both looked to dominate. After having a couple of difficult rounds, obviously in coming to terms with his injury, Swift got his left hand going and jabbed and hooked with regularity, while the challenger fought back strongly with both fists chugging away. By the ninth round, both men were cut; Swift above and below the left, as well as on the right, and Till under the left. But still the pace remained unabated.

Coming into the final round, it was dreadfully close. As the one-handed Swift tried to outpunch his rival, Till came back with rights and lefts over the top to finally turn the fight his way, winning on the referee's scorecard by the narrowest of margins, 118-117½.

There just had to be a return. And in April 1993, Andy Till confirmed his superiority over the brave Swift inside four rounds, while winning the Lonsdale Belt outright. However, in years to come, those fortunate enough to have been at Watford on 17 September, 1992, or to have seen the fight screened live on Sky Sports, will remember both men for their display that night.

Previous winners:- 1984: Jimmy Cable v Said Skouma. 1985: Barry McGuigan v Eusebio Pedroza. 1986: Mark Kaylor v Errol Christie. 1987: Dave McAuley v Fidel Bassa. 1988: Tom Collins v Mark Kaylor. 1989: Michael Watson v Nigel Benn. 1990: Orlando Canizales v Billy Hardy. 1991: Chris Eubank v Nigel Benn. 1992: Dennis Andries v Jeff Harding.

Best Overseas Boxer of the Year: Crisanto Espana

Other nominations: Daniel Jimenez, Ruben Palacio and Laurent Boudouani.

Before anybody says what about Goya Vargas, just remember that he beat Paul Hodkinson in Dublin, Southern Ireland, and not under the jurisdiction of the BBBoC, while Espana, a Belfast based Venezuelan, had two world title fights; one in London and the other in Belfast.

The younger brother of the former WBA lightweight champion, Ernesto, he has made steady progress since joining Barney Eastwood's stable in 1988. And clever matchmaking and good recent wins over Luis Santana, Hector Hugo Vilte, Kevin Wahley-El and David Taylor, brought him a shot at WBA welterweight champion, Meldrick Taylor in London on the Lewis v Ruddock bill.

He proved a class act that night of 31 October, 1992, and well and truly came of age, convincingly beating Taylor, a man who had come within two seconds of outpointing Julio Cesar Chavez back in March 1990. Espana's huge reach advantage and power was too much for the champion to overcome and he was pounded to defeat at 2.11 of the eighth round, having been put down heavily moments earlier.

Following the Taylor victory, he successfully defended the title in Belfast against Rodolfo Aguilar over fifteen rounds and joins six former world champions who have won the Award previously.

Previous winners:- 1984: Buster Drayton. 1985: Don Curry. 1986: Azumah Nelson. 1987: Maurice Blocker. 1988: Fidel Bassa. 1989: Brian Mitchell. 1990: Mike McCallum. 1991: Donovan Boucher.1991: Jeff Harding.

Venezuela's Crisanto Espana, who destroyed Meldrick Taylor to win the WBA welterweight title, was recognised as the "Best Overseas Boxer of the Year"

Special Award: Phil Martin

This is an Award made for services to boxing, but in the case of Phil Martin, his work reaches far beyond the sport and into the community.

A good class amateur, and fighting under his real name, Phil Adelagan, he reached the English semi-finals at light-heavy in 1974, turning professional later that year. As a pro between 1974 and 1978, he had 20 contests, winning fourteen and fought Tim Wood for the vacant British light-heavyweight title in April 1976, losing narrowly on points over fifteen rounds.

After retiring from boxing, he embarked on a four year course as a mature student at Salford College, passing out in Physiology and Sports Science. He still wasn't done with the sport, however, and following the Moss Side race riots of 1981, he set up an amateur boxing club to serve the neighbourhood. So successful did the club's boxers become that he and several of the boys turned pro together in 1987, in order to allow them all to maximise their talent.

With the professional side of the gym now named Champs Camp, Phil trained both Joey Jacobs (super-feather) and Tony Ekubia (light-welter) to British titles in 1990 and as a manager, his first champion came in the shape of Carl Thompson (cruiser) in June 1992. That victory acted as a spur to the rest of the Moss Side stable and during a nine month spell, Frank Grant (middle), Maurice Coore (light-heavy) and Paul Burke (light), all won British titles; a magnificent achievement.

Previous winners:- 1984: Doctor Adrian Whiteson. 1985:

Sportsmanship Award: Nicky Piper

Known as the MENSA (having a score of 153) man, Nicky has continued to captivate boxing audiences with his own brand of points scoring, by means of a long left-lead and good defensive skills.

After winning an ABA light-middleweight title in 1989, he turned professional and came to national prominence at the end of last year when challenging Nigel Benn for the latter's WBC super-middleweight title. Bringing a record of 16 wins in 18 contests into the fight, having lost to Carl Thompson and drawn with Maurice Coore, wasn't an outstanding one, but the clever Welshman gave Benn plenty of problems to solve before going down to defeat in round eleven.

With seven "O" and two "A" levels, Nicky doesn't have to work in the fight game for a living, but chooses too. He also brings a refreshing breath of fresh air to the industry with his honest approach and integrity and is positive about putting something back into boxing.

As chairman of the new Professional Boxers' Association, he is actively helping young fighters both inside and outside the ring. And regardless of what many people might think, there has long been a need for an organisation that can promote and protect the interests of boxers, especially in contractual and advisory matters. With men of the calibre of Nicky and Colin McMillan involved, their future is in good hands.

Harry Gibbs. 1986: Ray Clarke. 1987: Hon. Colin Moynihan. 1988: Tom Powell. 1989: Winston Burnett. 1990: Frank Bruno. 1991: Muhammad Ali. 1992: Doctor Oswald Ross.

The winner of the "Special Award", Phil Martin (centre), shown celebrating Carl Thompson's WBC International cruiserweight title win over the American, Arthur Weathers   Les Clark

Previous winners:- 1986: Frank Bruno. 1987: Terry Marsh. 1988: Pat Cowdell. 1989: Horace Notice. 1990: Rocky Kelly. 1991: Wally Swift Jnr. 1992: Duke McKenzie.

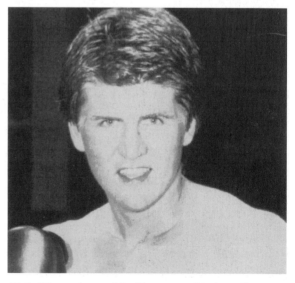

Nicky Piper, winner of the "Sportsmanship Award"
                                                    Les Clark

The Lonsdale International Sporting Club

President: The Earl Grey.
Patrons: Tom Pendry, MP (UK); Reg Gutteridge (UK); Angelo Dundee (USA); Thomas Hauser (USA); Joe Koizumi (Japan); Chris Greyvenstein (South Africa); Kepler Wessels (South Africa).
Directors: Bernard Hart; Frank Tyner; Philip Yeates.
Function Headquarters: London Marriott, Grosvenor Square, London W1.
Office: 2 Bryn Street, Ashton in Makerfield, Wigan, Lancs WN3 4EY.

Auspiciously, the Club was formed on 8 July 1992 – the birthdate of the great British bare-knuckle champion, Tom Cribb, as well as the anniversary of the last bare-knuckle heavyweight championship fight between John L. Sullivan and Jake Kilrain – at The London Marriott in Mayfair's Grosvenor Square, an address which is made famous by the fact that the United States Embassy occupies one complete side of the Square.

The first person to actually take out a membership at the Marriott, and so have the distinction of being number one founder member, was London ABA (North-West Division)

Honorary Secretary, Harry Fenner. Founder memberships were offered at £25 per annum (without the annual subscription changing during the member's lifetime) until the opening dinner/dance/cabaret function on 27 September, when the Club celebrated the centenary of the first heavyweight championship fight under Queensberry Rules. The fight actually took place on 7 September 1892, between Sullivan and James J. Corbett, and resulted in a new champion with a 21-round knockout. Appropriately, the guest of honour at this opening function was the last European world heavyweight champion, Ingemar Johansson of Sweden, who won and lost the championship to Floyd Patterson. (At the time of the dinner, Lennox Lewis had not laid claim to the WBC title).

The attendance for the opening night was just over 300, and the founder memberships stood at around that figure; from then on the membership was increased to £40, and later to £52. For this, the member receives a club tie, lapel badge, rule book, and a unique membership card featuring a montage of great fighters from the collection of the club artists, Brian and Doreen Meadows.

Among the early members were Brian London, Billy

The opening night of the Lonsdale Sporting Club: Four British heavyweights toast a former world champion. Left to right: Billy Walker, Bernard Hart (proprietor), Brian London, Ingemar Johansson, Jack Bodell and Danny McAlinden

Last year's "British Boxer of the year", Colin McMillan (left), meets one of the all-time greats of the featherweight division, Willie Pep, flanked by Bernard Hart (right)

Les Clark

Walker, Chris Finnegan, MBE, Emile Griffith and Howie Albert (USA), writers Richard and Lynda LaPlante, Frank Maloney, and book publisher, Jeremy Robson.

The second function on 25 October, saw the Club honour Floyd Patterson, who was the youngest man (at the time) to win the world heavyweight championship, and the first man to regain the title. As well as being a past Olympic gold medal winner, Patterson had also served ten years as Chairman of the New York State Athletic Commission, and mention was made of the invaluable youth work that he had performed. Lonsdale Sports presented Patterson with a jumbo-sized bag of boxing equipment for his New York club for under-privileged boys.

On 24 November, the Club were honoured to host the British Boxing Board of Control Annual Awards, together with the launch of Barry Hugman's Yearbook, an absolutely essential manual to all persons working within the sport. The guest of honour on this occasion was one of the past all-time greats, Willie Pep, the Italian-American holder of the world featherweight title during the 1940's. Willie was a brilliant guest of honour and made the award to Britain's "Boxer of the Year", Colin McMillan, who, by coincidence, lost his world featherweight championship in similar unusual circumstances to Pep, with a dislocated shoulder.

Early in the new year, the Club combined with rugby league, by presenting a night of amateur boxing at Wigan Rugby Club for the Shaun Edwards testimonial season; a capacity house enjoyed an exciting night's boxing with a large donation being made to the testimonial fund. The success of this night will result in the Club organising similar testimonial nights at several northern rugby league clubs.

The dinner season closed in May at the London Marriott with a tribute night to Herol Graham, surely Britain's best boxer of the last decade not to have won a world championship. Herol, who had lost the last of his titles to Frank Grant, is a great sportsman, who would have beaten many world champions with ease.

In between the functions, Club members visited Johannesburg for the South African Boxing Writers' Dinner, Las Vegas for Lennox Lewis' WBC heavyweight defence against Tony Tucker, New York for Emile Griffith's testimonial night in Madison Square Garden and Atlantic City for Evander Holyfield v Alex Stewart and Vinny Pazienza v Lloyd Honeyghan.

As this article is being written, the Club's new General Administrator, Philip Yeates, is opening the banqueting season at The Village Hotel, Blackpool, in September, when Brian London will spearhead a night of sporting champions in the presence of their worships, The Mayor and Mayoress of Blackpool and the Club President, The Earl Grey and Countess Grey. The Club will again host the British Boxing Awards in conjunction with Barry Hugman and the BBB of C at the London Marriott, and in addition to the amateur boxing nights mentioned, the Club are proposing to promote the annual schoolboy fixture between England and Russia in both London and Manchester in June 1994. There will be many more dinner functions, amateur boxing nights, overseas trips and special arrangements for members at the big fights and other sports events in the United Kingdom. And at just £1 per week, the Club has to be exceptional value, as the growing membership indicates. Forward to victory and greater sporting achievements!

Introducing The Professional Boxers' Association (PBA)

by Chris Kempson

On Wednesday 3 February 1993, a significant number of professional boxers in this country came together to agree upon the formation of the Professional Boxers' Association (PBA). The inaugural meeting took place at the Whitbread Brewery, Chiswell Street, London EC1.

The PBA, which is the latest and most positive attempt at introducing a "trade union" for British boxers past and present – earlier initiatives having ultimately failed – adopted the following main objectives:-

(i) to promote and protect the interests of members and former members;

(ii) to protect the rights, including contractual, and (where applicable) the employment rights of members connected with professional boxing;

(iii) to provide assistance, including legal, where the PBA in its absolute discretion deems appropriate in any matter arising out of a member's or a former member's involvement in professional boxing and

(iv) to establish and/or administer funds for the benefit of members and former members, or for such other purposes as the PBA in its absolute discretion deems appropriate.

The PBA's principal officers have impressive credentials. Barry McGuigan is the PBA President, Nicky Piper its Chairman, Colin McMillan acts as Secretary, while Jim McDonnell holds the key post as Treasurer. The Association's Patron is Henry Cooper OBE, KSG and Harry Carpenter OBE, is Vice-President.

To find out more about the new Association and its hopes and aspirations for the future, I undertook the following interview at the beginning of June 1993 with its hard-working Secretary, the former WBO featherweight champion, Colin McMillan. Colin was also the former undefeated British and Commonwealth featherweight champion. He will soon be returning to active ring combat, following a shoulder injury sustained in September 1992.

Chris Kempson. Why is there a need for the PBA?

Colin McMillan. Well, boxing was the only major sport in Britain, which did not have an association to represent its

The PBA's Management Committee: Left to right: Top Row: New pro, Kent Davis, Jim McDonnell and Mark Kaylor. Front Row: Colin McMillan (Secretary), Nicky Piper (Chairman) and Barry McGuigan (President)   Les Clark

participants. The other ten major sports in this country each have their own association of players. Why should boxing be the exception.

CK. Who really started the PBA?

CM. Barry McGuigan, ably supported by Garth Crooks the ex-Spurs' star and former Chairman of the Professional Footballers' Association (PFA), were the guiding lights for the PBA. We really owe a lot to Barry McGuigan, who was very determined to set the Association up. Barry and Garth (who is Chairman of the Institute of Professional Sport) worked very hard during 1992 to get things on the move. Peter Lawson, the General Secretary of the CCPR, has also given us considerable assistance and Legal and General Assurance Society has also helped out as well.

CK. How did you become involved with the PBA?

CM. I spoke with Barry many times about his proposals for the PBA and liked what I heard. It really seemed like a breath of fresh air for boxing in this country and I eventually decided to get involved with the PBA.

CK. Which other boxers are actively involved in the Association at present?

CM. Well, in addition to Barry, myself, Nicky Piper and Jim McDonnell, we have Chris Eubank, Mark Kaylor and Steve Collins on our Management Committee. We expect that there will also be scope and opportunities for others to help us out in the months ahead.

CK. How is the PBA financed?

CM. The PBA is a members' organisation. The members pay an annual subscription of £20. We are actively seeking commercial partners who, through sponsorship, can help us raise the financial resources that are required if we are to fulfil our objectives. We are grateful for the assistance given to us by the General Boilermakers Union (GMB) and other organisations, but are determined that we shall remain a professional Association, independent of control, other than through professional boxers themselves.

CK. Do you receive any other types of support from other organisations?

CM. Yes, we are very fortunate in this respect. The Central Council of Physical Recreation (CCPR) have very generously allowed us to use the excellent services of one of their staff, Sue Moody, for a year. Sue works full-time for us at the CCPR's office in south-west London, where we also hold our meetings.

CK. What has been the general reaction to the PBA from boxers past and present?

CM. Very positive indeed and our membership is growing all the time. We have some very high profile members, including our first world heavyweight champion this century, Lennox Lewis. When I decided to turn professional I spoke to many ex-pros and to a man they all said If they knew then what they know now they would have done things differently. Boxers haven't really gone

forward with the times and hopefully the PBA will now make this possible for them to do so.

CK. What has been the BBBoC's reaction to the Association?

CM. Very positive. They have welcomed the establishment of the PBA. Constructive dialogue has taken place between the Board and ourselves and we have quarterly meetings with them.

CK. How have the country's promoters and managers reacted to the new Association?

CM. So far, most promoters and managers have been supportive. Some individuals might feel that we will not flourish, but that seems to be a minority view. After all, we just want justice and a fair deal for boxers. We only want a decent slice of the cake, we don't want to take promoters and managers' livelihoods away. Many ex-champions have very little to show for everything they endured while they were active boxers. We want to try and ensure that in future this unfortunate type of situation does not arise.

CK. Do you think that because the leading lights of the PBA are high profile characters, many "grass roots boxers" will wonder what it can offer them?

CM. No, not at all. I think our strength is that. Most of us in the PBA have been fortunate enough to become quite successful through boxing. In a sense, we don't need the PBA for ourselves, we exist to help the vast majority of boxers, who, for whatever reason, may not make it to the top of the tree. Our concerns are first and foremost for them. They need looking after and this is what the PBA aims to do.

CK. What specific services can you offer your members?

CM. Quite a considerable number, which is very promising for a young organisation like the PBA. The most important aspect we have focused on so far must be the changes we are proposing to the boxer/manager agreement. We are working closely with the BBBoC on this. Also, we are looking very closely at the insurance arrangements for professional boxers and hope to be able to announce something positive on this in the near future.

CK. What else is on the PBA's shopping list?

CM. Naturally we are concerned about the health and safety of our members and we need to ensure that the medical back-up and protection at boxing shows is adequate. We want to enlist the help of the St John Ambulance Service if we can. Their expertise and experience will be invaluable for our members, in hopefully instructing them in basic first-aid procedures. We also provide an advisory service for our members and those youngsters who want to take up professional boxing as a career.

CK. What do you think you will be able to do to help boxers manage their finances successfully?

CM. Well, we will certainly be looking at matters of

taxation, pensions and other financial and contractual arrangements.

CK. How will the PBA be able to help boxers when their active life in the ring comes to an end?

CM. We are exploring various training possibilities, which we hope will enable our members to move successfully into another trade, or occupation, when their career in the ring is over. We will also be setting up a charitable fund to help boxers in need, particulary to help them with medical care.

CK. How does the PBA make itself known to boxers throughout the United Kingdom?

CM. Well it happens in various ways. Naturally, we talk to boxers at the various shows held up and down the country. Barry McGuigan and Nicky Piper are visiting Northern Ireland soon to spread the word there and we shall be holding a series of regional meetings in this country to get our message across. We produce a newsletter for our members and, hopefully, some non-members will be shown it by their friends and they will decide to join us as well.

CK. What can the press do to help promote the work of the PBA?

CM. Well Chris, as an established boxing journalist like yourself, you will know good publicity goes a long way

and I am very pleased to have been able to tell you about our work and our aims for the future. The press is a powerful tool and we would welcome as much publicity, good publicity that is, as we can get.

CK. Other attempts at forming "boxers unions" have failed, why do you think the PBA should succeed, therefore?

CM. Our attitude is very, very positive. We have done our homework and are making progress. The time is right for the PBA and there is a real need for an association like this. We never consider for one moment that we will fold-up, that would be negative thinking. We are an entirely positive body.

CK. Well, finally, Colin, does the PBA plan to hold social functions?

CM. Yes, indeed we do. We are staging a British Boxing Celebrity Golf Tournament at Hanbury Manor Golf and Country Club, near Ware in Hertfordshire, on 20 July 1993 and we plan to stage the inaugural dinner of the PBA in London on 21 June 1994. We certainly want to get the boxers and their families involved in our various activities.

CK. Well Colin, the PBA has certainly made a wonderful start and on behalf of the *British Boxing Yearbook,* I would like to wish you every success for the future. Thank you very much indeed for giving up your time so freely to talk to me.

Barry McGuigan, the PBA President, shown in his fighting days demolishing the Frenchman, Farid Gallouze

20

Around British Rings During 1992-93

by John Jarrett

JULY

The World Boxing Organisation may well be the least respected of the alphabet boys responsible for the current proliferation of world championships, but it looks like they are here to stay and the feeling in the fight game seems to be a case of if you can't beat them you may as well join them.

At Manchester's G-Mex Centre, Pat Barrett and Derek Angol tried to climb aboard the WBO bandwagon, but were rudely rebuffed by Manning Galloway and Tyrone Booze, respectively. Defending his welterweight title for the sixth time, Galloway held a master class in defensive boxing and came out a surprisingly easy winner against the local favourite, who was a study in frustration as he tried in vain to unload the big punches that had brought him 25 wins inside schedule. "I expected more from Barrett," smiled the champion afterwards. So did we.

Derek Angol had reigned as British and Commonwealth cruiserweight champion, was undefeated in 26 pro fights, and had to be a racing certainty in his dispute with American journeyman, Booze, for the vacant WBO title. Well, if you've ever had a few bob on a fight, this one should have cured you of the habit for life. At 32, Booze had won only one fight in the past four years and you couldn't see him winning this one, not even if Angol gave him five rounds start. But the veteran let Derek punch himself out and then flattened his rival in seven rounds!

It seems that the Dudley welterweight, Robert Wright, is one of those people who are still getting dressed when opportunity comes knocking at their front door. Not wanting to miss it, he answers the call even though he isn't ready. It was that way a few months ago when he was offered a shot at the Commonwealth title on just seven days notice.

Unfortunately for Robert, the champion happened to be the capable Canadian, Donovan Boucher, and he was stopped in eleven rounds. This time, when the call came, it was for a British title challenge against Gary Jacobs in Glasgow, being given ten days notice when official challenger John Davies pulled out with injury.

Robert took the fight. You knew he would. You also knew what would happen in that Glasgow ring with Gary Jacobs. Yet the man from Dudley gave it his best shot, as always, edging the first round and shaking the champion in round two. But Jacobs is back on the rails now after being shunted on to a branch line and by round six he was well on top when the referee led Wright back to his corner.

Another British champion in action was Fidel Castro, although his super-middleweight title was not on the line against Frank Eubanks in their Manchester meeting. That chance was already lined up for Henry Wharton, come September, and if Fidel wanted a warm-up, Eubanks made it hot enough in the early rounds, anyway. But by the sixth, Frank's eyes were banged up and his corner pulled him out.

Welsh middleweight champion, Wayne Ellis, put his title up for grabs in London against Mike Phillips, the fight being stopped in the seventh round with Phillips under fire, while down in Bristol, unbeaten Ross Hale turned in a fine performance to pick up the vacant Western Area welterweight title, stopping Julian Eavis in round eight.

Heavyweight action was quiet with only Henry Akinwande working the kinks out at Manchester, as Steve Garber became victim number 18 after just two rounds. Steve had been on the floor and his eye was cut and he was no test for the big fellow who was now looking for a title shot.

Over in France, the Barney Eastwood stable had two entries going, with Ray Close contesting the European super-middleweight title against Franck Nicotra and Crisanto Espana taking on the American, David Taylor. Close fought out of his skin and looked in front going into round eight, before the Frenchman dropped him with a left-hook. The Irishman beat the count, but couldn't beat the champion and it was stopped later in the round. Espana had a good workout and kept his number one (WBA) rating as he got his man out of there in seven rounds.

Tempting fate, the Darlington light-welterweight, Alan Hall, lost his unbeaten certificate in his second American fight as Steve Barreras stopped him inside five rounds. This Las Vegas gamble snapped Hall's run at thirteen!

AUGUST

This was the month when it seemed everyone in boxing was on holiday, with not one show scheduled in Britain, and only three of our glove-slingers finding action in foreign rings. Pride of place went to the big fellow, British, Commonwealth, and European heavyweight champion, Lennox Lewis, as he gave the Americans another opportunity to assess his ability.

Lewis took his act to Atlantic City, where he was booked for ten rounds, or less, with Mike Dixon, who figured to be no more than a warm-up for the world title eliminator against Razor Ruddock come October.

Ruddock was sitting ringside along with trainer Floyd Patterson, the former world champion, and they were suitably impressed. "He looked good," said Ruddock, while Patterson told reporters, "He's a harder puncher than I thought."

Mike Dixon could vouch for the veracity of both statements, being stopped for the first time in 16 pro fights. Referee Rudy Battle actually brought proceedings to a halt after 62 seconds of round four, with Lewis beginning to unload his heavy artillery, taking his unbeaten tally to 21 straight, 18 via the short route.

From Tennessee, now billed out of Atlanta, Georgia, Mike would rather have been in either place than sharing the ring with Lewis at Harrah's on the boardwalk at Atlantic City. A big right shook him in the first and he was rocked again by a right uppercut before the bell. He surprised Lennox with an uppercut of his own in round two and paid for his boldness, taking a hammering as the Englishman opened up in the third. Dixon was given a standing count early in the fourth before it was halted. As he left his seat, Floyd Patterson knew he would have to have his Razor honed to perfection for the face-to-face confrontation with Lennox Lewis in London.

Former British and European cruiserweight champion, Johnny Nelson, was not so fortunate in his jaunt to Ajaccio in France. The enigmatic Nelson was going in with Norbert Ekassi, the French-based Cameroon, in a fight he had to win to grab back some credibility for himself.

Johnny had turned in another abysmal showing in his second crack at a world title, this time with IBF champion, James Warring, in America, and was shaping up like a candidate for the "who needs him club." Well, for two rounds, Nelson outboxed his plodding opponent, but in the third, Ekassi set up a big attack and the referee stepped in to save an exhausted Nelson.

Any gardener worth a bag of bonemeal knows that the rose is a thing of beauty, but its thorns are lethal and command respect. Midlands Area lightweight champion, Peter Till, learned that about the "Rose of Soweto," who fights under the name of Dingaan Thobela.

The South African is a former WBO champion and as number one contender for the WBA lightweight title was looking forward to a crack at champion, Joey Gamache. A hand operation had kept him out of the ring for almost a year and Till was brought to Springs, in South Africa, to see if the rose would bloom again.

He did, staying undefeated in his 28th professional fight with a decisive ninth round stoppage of the Midlands champion. When the referee pulled him out of the fight, Till had been on the canvas five times and was throwing nothing back. But he gave the African a stiff workout and earned his purse, not to mention the admiration of the crowd.

SEPTEMBER

The new season really started with a bang and British boxers were quickly knee-deep in title bouts, both here and abroad. Biggest shock on the home front was the loss of Colin McMillan's WBO featherweight crown to a rough and ready underdog in Ruben Palacio.

The Columbian showed no respect for the silky skills of McMillan, which for some reason were not too conspicuous, anyway, and Colin's brief tenure of the title came to an end in round eight when a shoulder injury rendered him incapable of carrying on. The official verdict was a technical knockout and along with Colin's crown went a mega-payday for a unification match with WBC

Andy Till (left) keeps Wally Swift junior at bay during their bruising British light-middleweight title scrap   Les Clark

champion, Paul Hodkinson.

"Hoko" had completed the first leg of the double a fortnight previously when he turned back the gritty challenge of French tough guy, Fabrice Benichou, at Blagnac near Toulouse. Benichou fought out of his skin and was doing fine on the scorecards, despite being knocked down in the fourth and in trouble through rounds six and seven. But the scoring was rendered academic in the tenth when Benichou sustained a nasty vertical cut on his upper lip that brought an end to the fight, leaving Hodkinson the winner and still the WBC champion.

A guy who was hungry for a crack at either Hodkinson or McMillan, or both, was Geordie warrior, John Davison. At Sunderland, John finally got a crack at the British featherweight title, meeting Tim Driscoll for the vacant crown. It was a typical Davison performance. Bleeding from a cut over his left eye, he climbed off the floor in round seven to hammer Driscoll to the canvas for the full count, becoming the first Newcastle fighter to win a British championship since Seaman Tommy Watson won the same title back in 1932.

Time ran out for Herol Graham as he was beaten for the first time in fourteen years by a British fighter, Frank Grant taking his middleweight title with a ninth round stoppage at Leeds. Strength triumphed over skill in this all-southpaw battle as the unsung challenger plugged away until Graham went down in round nine. He beat the count, but he couldn't beat Grant, and the referee wrote finis to a fine chapter in British boxing history.

Graham's stablemate, Fidel Castro, was also beaten that night in a fine contest that saw his British super-middleweight title pass to the Commonwealth champion, Henry Wharton, on a decision adjudged by TV viewers as nothing less than highway robbery! Yet those at ringside were happy that Wharton had done enough to win! TV or not TV, that is the question . . .

In a battle of epic proportions at Watford, the Northolt milkman, Andy Till, had all he could handle in Wally Swift, who desperately tried to hang on to his British light-middleweight championship, despite the handicap of a damaged right hand. Swift made a glorious effort to win the fight with his left-jab and left-hook, but Till's two powerful fists made the difference at the end, finishing half a point ahead to take the title.

Always a good place for a fight on a Saturday night, Glasgow staged two WBO title bouts. The controversial Chris Eubank came through after a tough bout with American Tony Thornton and local hero Pat Clinton had his hands full with the perennial challenger, Danny Porter. In taking his unbeaten run to 33, Eubank blew hot and cold with many thinking him lucky to come out with his title intact. And while Clinton deserved his victory over Porter, his crown wobbled a few times before the final bell established Danny as a hot candidate for the lead role in "Always The Bridesmaid, Never The Bride!" He'd appear in drag, of course.

When a British fighter comes back from Italy with a draw, you know he won the fight hands down but had to settle for one of those continental decisions. Well,

Crawford Ashley finished even after twelve rounds with Yawe Davis for the vacant European light-heavyweight title, but by all accounts the verdict was spot on. So there you are! One judge actually voted for the lad from Leeds, but another saw it a draw and that's how it went into the book.

London welterweight, Mickey Hughes, had previously tried to win the Southern Area, the British, then the Commonwealth title. He came up empty every time. So Mickey moved up to light-middleweight and finally got lucky in a fight for the vacant Commonwealth crown, although many Crystal Palace patrons thought the Australian, Craig Trotter, had done enough to win.

I don't know what Phil Martin feeds his fighters on, but when I do, I'm going to order a case! At Manchester's New Century Hall, Maurice "Hard" Coore took the third British title for Martin's aptly named Champ's Camp, when he hammered out a ninth round victory over Noel Magee for the vacant light-heavyweight title. Coore joined cruiser-weight, Karl Thompson, and middleweight, Frank Grant, as Lonsdale Belt holders.

Liverpool's British and Commonwealth light-welter-weight champion, Andy Holligan, kept his titles and his unbeaten record with an awesome display of power to knock out former champion Tony Ekubia in round seven and make the Lonsdale Belt his own property.

Heavyweight action saw Herbie Hide take his unbeaten log to 17 straight, all inside the distance, with a one-sided pounding of former European champion, Jean Chanet, in front of his hometown supporters at Norwich. The French veteran was a mess when it was stopped in round seven, but he went home with his proud record of never having been knocked off his feet, still intact.

Lennox Lewis surrendered the European title he took off Chanet, after being ordered to make a defence against Henry Akinwande by 31 October. He already had a date for that night, an all-important clash with Razor Ruddock at Earls Court in a fight that would see the winner go in with new world champ, Riddick Bowe. At least that was the plan. . .

At the bottom end of the heavyweight ladder, a big lad with dreams of emulating his dad was Joe Bugner junior, and he chalked up his fifth straight pro win with a decision over Gary Williams in a four-three's preliminary bout at York Hall.

OCTOBER

There was a big explosion at Earls Court and when the smoke cleared over the ring it was seen that Donovan "Razor" Ruddock, the Jamaican-born, Canadian heavy-weight, had been completely demolished just 46 seconds into round two, and as the smoke drifted away so too did all the doubts expressed about Lennox Lewis on his climb up the heavyweight ladder.

Razor Ruddock was no has-been with hinges on his knees, he had travelled 19 tough rounds through Mike Tyson territory, yet he had barely started on his London journey when he was ambushed and ruthlessly cut down. Suddenly, big Lennox Lewis was the new gun in town!

Close-quarter action from the Frank Bruno (left) versus Pierre Coetzer fight at Wembley, which ended when the Englishman scored a stoppage win in the eighth round

Les Clark

His sensational victory and the manner in which he accomplished it sent shock waves through the American big fight business and completely eclipsed Frank Bruno's sterling stoppage of Pierre Coetzer at Wembley some two weeks previously, in a fight recognised as an IBF eliminator. The rugged South African had gone into the seventh round with Riddick Bowe last time out and he came to fight, but by round eight he was bruised, bloody, and on the deck. He managed to get up at six but had nothing left and referee Roy Francis stopped it.

Those WBO titles seemed to have found a home in Britain and Duke McKenzie collected another one when he beat tough Texan, Jesse Benavides, at Catford, to add the super-bantamweight title to the bantamweight crown he wore previously. And when you add those two titles to the IBF flyweight championship Duke won four years ago, you have to stick his name up there as the first British fighter to win world titles at three different weights. Maybe we should be calling him "King", not Duke!

With all these world titles about we have to get our share and Nigel Benn picked up his second one when he beat Mauro Galvano for the WBC super-middleweight championship, right in the Italian's backyard and much to the displeasure of the crowd. Benn had dominated the action up to the end of round three when Galvano's corner

told the referee he was unable to continue because of an eye injury, claiming Benn's head and not his fists as the contributing factor. Fortunately, for Nigel, referee Cortez ignored their pleas and Benn was declared the winner and new champion.

Glasgow's Gary Jacobs was not so lucky in Paris, when going for the vacant European welterweight championship against Ludovic Proto. With an undefeated pro record of 28 fights, the Frenchman was being touted for top honours, but he was a major disappointment in his big test. Having said that, he did win the decision and the title, thanks to two myopic judges. Even the French press agreed with the Belgian judge, Bob Logist, in calling Jacobs a winner.

France was not a happy hunting ground either for Derek Angol. Going for the European cruiserweight title against Akim Tafer, Angol turned in a fine performance, decked the champion in round two, and was heading for victory when Tafer knocked him down in the tenth. Derek beat the count but the referee waved it over much to Angol's disgust. By way of consolation the EBU ordered a rematch.

There were plenty of fights at the Albert Hall, inside and outside the ring, the night that 23-year-old Billy Schwer fulfilled his promise by taking Carl Crook's British and Commonwealth lightweight titles. The Chorley man was pulled out after nine rounds, having been decked three times and bleeding from the mouth, though his heart was okay, and he wanted to carry on.

Former undefeated British bantamweight champion, Billy Hardy, pleased his local fans at Sunderland when he captured the vacant Commonwealth featherweight title with a ten rounds stoppage of gutsy 21-year-old Australian, Ricky Rayner. At Bury, British super-featherweight champion, Michael Armstrong, tried to buck the odds when defending his title against Neil Haddock, but even the fact that the Welshman was the thirteenth challenger made no difference. Armstrong went the way of all the others and so did his title, via a sixth round stoppage.

The Johnny Nelson road-show played South Africa, but was booed out of town after a pathetic performance against heavyweight champion, Corrie Sanders, who took a unanimous decision, while in Antwerp, Herbie Hide had to climb off the canvas in the first round before stopping Australian Craig Petersen in seven rounds to retain his WBC International heavyweight title.

Veteran 33-year-old Winston Burnett put fight number 117 in the book, dropping the duke to Mark Randazzo over in the States, while two ABA champions had their professional baptism; light-flyweight Darren Fifield boxing a draw with Glyn Shepherd and lightweight Dean Amory taking a six rounds decision over Brian Hickey.

NOVEMBER

They finally figured a way to get the European flyweight title away from Salvatore Fanni. Get him out of Italy! Welsh promoters Kevin Hayde and Dai Gardiner teamed up with Barry Hearn to pay the Sardinian enough money to leave home and defend against Robbie Regan in Cardiff and it paid off as the British champion took the title with a close, but unanimous decision.

Even then it was a tough one. The way he started, you'd think Fanni was fighting at home and it wasn't until the fourth that Regan got his act together. He moved into the lead as a packed house roared him on, but the last few rounds saw the champion making a desperate bid to hang on to his laurels and just fall short as Wales welcomed her first European champion since Colin Jones.

Two other European title challengers, Dave Pierre and Paul Burke, did not enjoy Regan's home advantage and came off second best when fighting in the champ's backyard. To be fair, however, Pierre would have been up against it wherever he had fought undefeated light-welterweight champion, Valery Kayumba, who had been slated to face Darlington's Alan Hall, victor over Pierre in a British title eliminator. Dave got his big chance when Hall pulled out and faded after a good start to be knocked out in round nine.

Like Pierre, Paul Burke was in with a good champion in Jean-Baptiste Mendy, who had taken the lightweight crown from Italy's Antonio Renzo, but you couldn't blame him for taking the fight as he waited to make his challenge to the new British champion, Billy Schwer. After all he was from Phil Martin's Champs Camp in Manchester, where collecting titles had become a way of life. But Monsieur

Mendy had other ideas and his southpaw skills were always too much for Burke who, nevertheless, did well to travel the full distance. It was good experience that would not be wasted.

The three-year reign of Commonwealth welterweight champion Donovan Boucher came to an end in three rounds when he met Eamonn Loughran at Doncaster. Since defeating Gary Jacobs for the title in 1989, Boucher had beaten five challengers, including Britons, Kirkland Laing, Mickey Hughes, and Robert Wright, but he found Loughran's power too much as the Irish boy blasted him to the canvas twice before the referee called a halt.

Chris Eubank aired his WBO super-middleweight title again when he met Juan Carlos Giminez at Manchester. However, the pug from Paraguay was never in with a shout, as Eubank strutted his stuff for win number 34 and the fans went home asking when, if ever, will the Brighton enigma meet some of the iron in his division.

British and Commonwealth light-welterweight champion, Andy Holligan, gave his Liverpool fans some anxious moments before coming home in front of late substitute, Mark Smith, a tartar from Tennessee, who gave Andy more aggravation than he needed in taking his pro log to 20-0. On the undercard at the Everton Park Sports Centre, bantamweight bomber Prince Nassem Hamed had Pete Buckley on the deck in the second round, but had to be content with a points decision for the first time in six fights.

In the first round of his British title eliminator against Ensley Bingham, it looked as though fight number thirteen was going to be unlucky for the Birmingham light-middleweight, Robert McCracken, as he found himself on the canvas from a perfect left-hook. But he got up and fought his way back to put the issue beyond doubt in round ten with a smashing right that left Bingham literally out on his feet, the referee catching him before he fell.

Stepping out for the first time since his abortive challenge for Manning Galloway's WBO welterweight title, Manchester's Pat Barrett went on the road and blasted out Mexican Tomas Quinones in round one of their fight in Casino, Italy. Old Tom Collins didn't enjoy his trip abroad as he was knocked out in round two of a Johannesburg bout with Joseph Chingangu.

Doncaster veteran Dean Bramhald celebrated his 128th fight by becoming a champion, taking the Central Area lightweight title from Kevin Toomey in a good ten rounder, that saw the latter on the deck three times.

DECEMBER

An IQ of 153 may have qualified Cardiff's Nicky Piper for membership in MENSA, but it did little for him when he tried to matriculate in the school of hard knocks. The punching power of WBC super-middleweight champion, Nigel Benn, overcoming the brain power of the clever young Welshman in round eleven of their contest at Muswell Hill. Nevertheless, it was a fine effort from the underdog and his sharp boxing had him leading after ten rounds on one official scorecard and quite a few unofficial ones, beside. But it was not a ten-rounds fight, and in the eleventh, Benn dropped Nicky with a left-hook. He got up at nine, but was hit with a barrage of punches that brought the referee's intervention.

Whoever coined the phrase "good stuff comes in little bundles" could have been thinking of Bethnal Green flyweight, Francis Ampofo. At the Grosvenor House in London's Mayfair, a far cry from his birthplace in Ghana, Francis once again claimed the British title with a decisive victory over James Drummond, dropping the gallant Scot twice, en-route to a comprehensive points win. Ampofo had lost the title to Robbie Regan, who then tossed it back on the market after becoming European champion.

Big Henry Akinwande, unbeaten in 18 fights, fourteen inside schedule, looked a safe bet to become European champion when he travelled to Berlin to contest the vacant heavyweight title with Axel Schulz. Lured by a £50,000 purse, Henry was still unbeaten when he came home, but he had been fobbed off with a draw after looking a comfortable winner over the limited German. Schulz, who finished with a swollen right eye, also kept his unbeaten certificate after 16 fights, and a return was being negotiated even as the crowd filtered out of the Ice Sports Hall.

Another British fighter to come up empty on a trip abroad this month, was Fidel Castro, who boxed Italy's Vincenzo Nardiello for the vacant European super-middleweight title in Ariccia. Trying to become a champion again, after losing his British crown to Henry Wharton, Fidel found the awkward southpaw a difficult puzzle to solve and looked well beaten at the finish, becoming the 23rd British fighter in a row to fail in a European title bid on foreign soil.

At York Hall, tough man Andy Till put a second notch on his light-middleweight Lonsdale Belt when he turned back the challenge of Tony Collins. The former WBC International champion was never in with a shout and under fire when the referee stopped it in round three.

Commonwealth bantamweight champion, Johnny Armour, retained his title at Catford against Zambian veteran, Albert Musankabala, the fight being stopped in round five as the African staggered to his feet after being felled with a lovely right-hook. It was later revealed that Musankabala had broken his right hand in the third round, but the champion always looked in control.

Barry Hearn's heavyweight hope, Herbie Hide, impressed in getting rid of seasoned American James Pritchard inside two rounds on the Benn-Piper bill at the Alexandra Palace, dumping his man three times to bring the referee's intervention. Herbie took his record to 19-0, all inside schedule!

Stepping out for the first time as British and Commonwealth lightweight champion, Billy Schwer accounted for a former WBO titleholder in Mauricio Aceves of Mexico. Billy won with a third round cut eye stoppage, but not before he himself had suffered damage below his left eye.

Irish-born Patrick "Blue Boy" Gallagher, former double ABA lightweight champion (he defeated Schwer in the 1990 final), made a winning debut when he beat Karl Taylor on a cut eye stoppage in round three.

A couple of our topliners picked up some easy money for Christmas as Pat Barrett blitzed American veteran Sam Gervins in one round at San Severo in Italy to take his record to 34-2-1, while Eamonn Loughran was back in the ring just two weeks after winning his Commonwealth welterweight title, disposing of the outclassed West Indian, Desbon Seaton, in round two.

JANUARY

The WBC heavyweight championship belt, which Riddick Bowe dropped into a dustbin rather than honour an agreement to fight Lennox Lewis, was picked out, polished, and presented to Lewis at a gala boxing dinner held in London at the Marriott Hotel. Jose Sulaiman himself flew in from Mexico to make it official and for the first time since Bob Fitzsimmons in 1897, Britain had a world heavyweight champion. The first real fight for Lennox would come against the number one contender, Tony Tucker, the former IBF champion, and manager Frank Maloney said he hoped they could bring the fight to London.

It was Burns Night at the St Andrew's Sporting Club in Glasgow, but Drew Docherty had something else to celebrate. In the first defence of his British bantamweight title, he outboxed and outpunched arch rival, Donnie Hood, in an excellent contest, to come out with the decision and put a second notch on that coveted Lonsdale Belt.

That old warrior Lloyd Honeyghan is still fighting in championship class and he was just too much for Mickey Hughes when they clashed at Brentwood, with the latter's Commonwealth light-middleweight title on the line. Lloyd took the first four rounds before splitting the champion's nose in round five, forcing the referee to call a halt.

Local hero Chris Pyatt kept his fans happy at Leicester when he retained his WBC International middleweight title with a rather one-sided decision over Danny Garcia of Puerto Rico, while taking his record to 37-3 and keeping his name in the frame for a crack at one of the world titles.

The WBA Penta-Continental titles may not count for much on the world Stock Exchange but there is a lovely belt for the champion valued about £400 that he keeps forever and Welsh featherweight champion Steve Robinson was more than happy to have one strapped around his slim waist after his decisive victory over Paul Harvey at Cardiff.

Sometimes it only takes one punch. With fifteen straight wins, Bristol hero Ross Hale had set the West Country alight and, having won a British light-welterweight title eliminator, was looking for big things as the New Year got underway. Andreas Panayi ruined everything with one punch, a left-hook explosion that left Hale with a broken jaw and a busted dream.

We had a couple of winners on foreign soil, which is nice to see even if the opposition wasn't off the top shelf. Nottingham welterweight Errol McDonald journeyed to Aachen and punched out an easy four rounds stoppage over Colombian, Otero Orlando, while in France, former IBF, British and Commonwealth cruiserweight champion, Glenn McCrory, had no trouble with American veteran, Ric Lainhart, the referee stepping in after Ric was dumped for the third time in round two.

At Southwark, Commonwealth bantamweight champion, Johnny Armour, had an easy ride as his southpaw punches took care of American Ricky Romero in just 84 seconds for the Englishman's eleventh straight win. On the same bill, former European super-middleweight champion, James Cook, made it three wins since losing his crown when he beat Midlands titleholder, Carlos Christie, over eight tough rounds.

FEBRUARY

It was time to do something about it. For almost two years, 23 British challenges for European honours on foreign soil had come up empty. One of those failures, on paper at least, was Gary Jacobs, after he looked a good winner over Ludovic Proto in Paris last October.

So these two southpaws hooked up again, in Paris, but this time Mr Jacobs was taking no prisoners. It got a bit rough at times and the cuts received by Proto in the second round and Jacobs in round three were caused by heads bumping. But the hammering administered to the undefeated Frenchman was more from the Scot's vengeful fists and the Frenchman surrendered in round nine, leaving Gary Jacobs the winner and champion of Europe!

Manager Phil Martin did it again. He brought another of his fighters into a British championship ring and for the fourth time the lad went home with a Lonsdale Belt keeping his pants up! This time it was Paul Burke, who upset the odds and Billy Schwer, taking the British and Commonwealth lightweight titles with a seventh round cut eye stoppage at Wembley's Grand Hall. In one of the prelims, Martin even managed to motivate veteran heavyweight Steve Garber into spoiling the unbeaten (7-0) record of Joe Bugner junior with a sixth-round stoppage.

With number one contender Kevin Kelley (USA) sitting ringside, WBC featherweight champion, Paul Hodkinson, staged a ruthless presentation of his punching powers when he destroyed Ricardo Cepeda inside four rounds at Olympia. The Puerto Rican challenger was no match for "Hoko" as the Liverpool lad went on the rampage from round one and although Cepeda was only decked once, in the second round, he was being hammered when his cornerman got up on the ring apron to pull Paul off.

Commonwealth bantamweight champion, Johnny Armour, hung on to his title after a tough twelve-rounds with unheralded Zambian, Morgan Mpande, at Catford, coming out with the decision and a badly cut left eye for win number twelve. And in a war for the vacant British featherweight crown, Sean Murphy climbed back on the

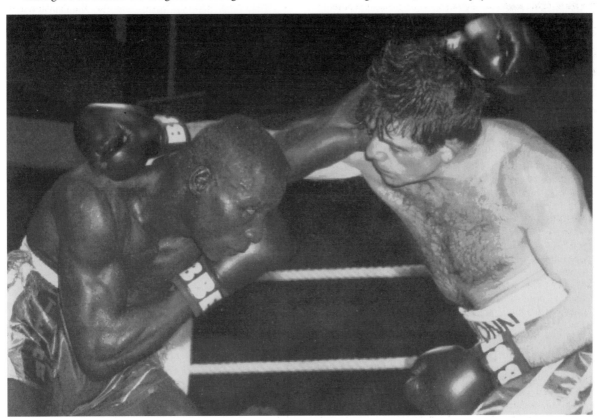

Both Eamonn Loughran (right) and Mike Benjamin miss the target, as the former successfully defended his Commonwealth welterweight title inside six rounds at Cardiff
Les Clark

throne when he stopped gutsy Alan McKay in nine gruelling rounds at Dagenham. The little guys completely outshone the big fellows on that bill when the much-hyped Herbie Hide failed to impress anyone, least of all world champion Riddick Bowe sitting at ringside, as he laboured to halt Michael Murray in five untidy rounds to claim the British heavyweight championship, which frankly has seen better days.

Chris Eubank increased his bank balance with the sixth defence of his WBO super-middleweight title, this time against former IBF champion, Lindell Holmes, at Olympia. It was another pedestrian performance from Eubank and the 35-year-old American was still there at the final bell, by which time most people were remembering what they used to do on a Saturday night. Enjoy themselves!

There was a slew of second-division titles on the line during the month as Lou Gent finally got lucky and picked up the WBC International belt at super-middle, with a decision over the Nigerian, Hunter Clay; Michael Ayers defended his WBC International lightweight title against South African, Danny Myburgh, who was stopped in five; Carl Thompson added the WBC International title to his British cruiserweight crown with an easy two rounds kayo of American Stormy Weathers; and in two fights for WBA Penta-Continental crowns, Nicky Piper punched out a decision over Miguel Maldonado at super-middle, while Birmingham's Pete Buckley had to travel to Vienna for his shot at the vacant super-bantamweight title, losing a decision to Austrian, Harald Geier.

Big punches were flying as Eamonn Loughran retained his Commonwealth welterweight title at Cardiff with a six rounds stoppage over Mike Benjamin from Guyana, and at Bradford, British middleweight champion, Frank Grant, was just too strong for game John Ashton, who was pulled out after seven rounds.

Out for almost two years, it was comeback time for Kirkland Laing and the former British and European welterweight champion breezed to a three-rounds stoppage over Bozon Haule, but at 38 you wonder what he has left. Dennis Andries was another old firehorse who answered the bell again, to punch out a decision over David Sewell, but at 39 the chances of him adding to his three WBC title wins is remote.

It was debut time for some of the graduates from the Barcelona Olympics, as Belfast bantamweight, Wayne McCullough (silver) and Robin Reid (bronze), took their vests off to punch for pay. McCullough, with American backing, stopped Alfonso Zamora in four rounds at Reseda, California, while middleweight Reid unleashed a right hand bomb to stop Mark Dawson inside one round at Dagenham. A couple of ABA finalists also joined the money ranks. Eric Noi stopped Tim Robinson in four rounds at super-middleweight in Manchester and in Madison Square Garden, under the Bowe-Dokes shambles, Adrian Stone punched out a six rounds decision over Sean Daughtry in a welterweight bout.

Let us not overlook the fine performance of Croydon heavyweight, Roger McKenzie, who pulled off an upset win over Magne Havnaa in Randers. The former WBO cruiserweight champion was blasted to the canvas twice before quitting on his stool, rather than come out for round six.

MARCH

A little guy making big news was Robbie Regan, revelling in his new title as flyweight champion of Europe. Robbie set the Welsh crowd alight at Cardiff when he took Danny Porter apart inside three rounds to keep his title. It was Danny's seventh crack at a title and once again he came up empty as Regan did in three rounds what WBO champion Pat Clinton couldn't do in twelve! Porter was ruthlessly destroyed by a new-look Regan, who added punch to his polish, dropping Danny in the third and hammering him into the ropes to bring the referee's intervention.

The return bout between WBC super-middleweight champion, Nigel Benn and Mauro Galvano, went on in Glasgow and will be remembered for one punch, a short right Italian-hook that almost knocked Benn out in the dying seconds of the final round. The bell came in the nick of time and the champion staggered across the ring into the arms of trainer, Jimmy Tibbs. Galvano was left to reflect upon what might have happened had he put more effort into clouting Benn and less into clutching him.

That same Saturday night in Paris, Midlander Mark McCreath fought the way a challenger should when going up against European light-welterweight champion, Valery Kayumba. Mark gave it a helluva shot before the referee pulled him out in round eleven and the French-based African had a cut eye and lacerated lip to take home along with his belt.

Big Henry Akinwande was successful in his bid for the vacant Commonwealth heavyweight title, but that was about all he did win after twelve dull rounds with New Zealand-born Jimmy Thunder. At 6'7", Henry is one of the tallest heavyweights in the game today, but he is a long way from being one of the best.

Another dismal performance by a British heavyweight, saw former Commonwealth and European champion, Derek Williams, beaten by Bert Cooper in Atlantic City. Cooper is rarely in shape, but he didn't have to be as he whacked his way to an easy decision.

Belfast's Ray Close went into the lion's den, Campione D'Italia, to fight Vincenzo Nardiello for his European super-middleweight title. The fight was stopped in round ten after an accidental clash of heads had left the Italian with a bad cut on the left eyebrow and Close was proclaimed the new champion, despite Nardiello's claim of a deliberate butt.

Fight night at Hartlepool saw the WBA Penta-Continental welterweight belt awarded to Argentinian, Marcelo di Croce, who upset the hopes of Darren Dyer with a fourth round stoppage. It was also a big night for local Mark Cichocki, who hammered his way to the Northern Area light-middleweight title, stopping Rob Pitters in the tenth round in only his third pro fight.

Croydon heavyweight Roger McKenzie was another unlikely winner of an area title when he took the vacant

Olympian, Adrian Dodson, made an impressive start to his pro career when he blasted Chris Mulcahy to a first round stoppage defeat
Les Clark

Southern championship with a stunning eighth round stoppage over Warren Richards at York Hall. And at Cardiff, Darron Griffiths kept his unbeaten record as he took the vacant Welsh super-middleweight title with a sixth round hammering of John Kaighin.

The much-heralded pro debut of amateur star Adrian Dodson took place at York Hall in Bethnal Green, where he had no trouble disposing of Chris Mulcahy inside the first round of a light-middleweight four-three's. Big things are expected of Dodson, just as they were of Errol Christie, once upon a time. At the Free Trade Hall in Manchester, Christie's comeback crashed in round two of a middleweight bout with Trevor Ambrose and the one-time golden boy knew it was time to hang them up for good.

APRIL
This was a month of sensations in the featherweight division. WBO champion Ruben Palacio lost his title in the north-east, but not to local hero John Davison. It was a hospital analyst who administered the KO to the Columbian when he diagnosed Palacio's mandatory blood sample as HIV positive. With three days to go, the WBO immediately stripped Palacio of the title and allowed promoters Barry Hearn and Tommy Gilmour to bring in

Steve Robinson to box Davison for the vacant championship. The Cardiff journeyman brought his 13-9-1 pro record to Washington and fought out of his skin to snatch a tight split decision from a jaded Davison, who had trained to peak fitness three times to meet the tragic South American.

Just over a week later, Paul Hodkinson suffered a crushing defeat at the lethal hands of Mexican, Goyo Vargas, who ripped the WBC crown from the Liverpool lad with a savage seventh round beating in Dublin. Vargas was a revelation as he took everything Paul threw at him and after the champion had been smashed to the canvas twice in the round, manager Eastwood and trainer Checa climbed through the ropes waving the towel in surrender. With Paul's title went prospects of a million dollar defence in New York against American, Kevin Kelley.

At the Royal Albert Hall, hard man Andy Till retained his British light-middleweight title, scoring his hat-trick over former champion, Wally Swift, with a ruthless fourth round victory that gave him a Lonsdale Belt to take home for good. Being stopped for the first time in 36 fights didn't sit well with Wally or his dad and they strongly protested Larry O'Connell's intervention. But Wally had just been rocked by two tremendous shots and only the ropes kept him on his feet.

The Frank Bruno show went on the road and a crowd of 7,500 turned up at Birmingham's National Exhibition Centre to see him fight American, Carl "The Truth" Williams, ten rounds or less. Hoping to grab pole position for a crack at Lennox Lewis, the big fellow was less than impressive, more than a little rough, and needed nine rounds, plus 20 seconds, to convince referee Dave Parris that he was the better man.

Leicester light-middleweight, Shaun Cummins, is known in the trade as "The Guvnor" and Mickey Hughes knew why after challenging Shaun for his WBA Penta-Continental crown at Brentwood. A refugee from the welterweight division, Mickey boxed well enough, but found the champion too big and too strong and took the final count on one knee in round eleven.

In another Penta-Continental title bout, Nicky Piper made hard work of retaining his super-middleweight belt against California-based Kenyan, Chris Sande, who lasted into round nine at Swansea. And while we are dealing with the "Mickey Mouse" titles flooding the fight game, Johnny Nelson managed to win the World Boxing Federation cruiserweight crown, stopping the veteran Australian,

Shaun Cummins (right) storms into Mickey Hughes during the successful defence of his WBA Penta-Continental light-middleweight title　　　　　Les Clark

Dave Russell, in eleven rounds, down under in Melbourne.

Leeds' light-heavyweight, Michael Gale, went looking for a title after putting 18 unbeaten fights (1 draw) on his record, but found Canada's Brent Kosolofski too tough in their Commonwealth title clash. Even Michael's hometown fans couldn't lift him and he was punched out when it was stopped in round nine.

If Gale couldn't win a title in his own backyard, what chance did Crawford Ashley, Carl Crook, and Michael Ayers have challenging the champions on their own patch?

Ashley was crucified by Michael Nunn's body shots when going for the WBA super-middleweight title in Memphis, taking five counts before it was stopped in round six.

Carl Crook's trip to Paris was just as painful, as he failed to take the European lightweight crown from the head of Jean-Baptiste Mendy. The former British and Commonwealth champion was making his second attempt on this title, but as against previous champion, Antonio Renzo, he was biting off more than he could chew, and was stopped in eight rounds after being decked three times by the southpaw, Italian.

Not content with sight-seeing in Rome, Michael Ayers made the mistake of challenging Giovanni Parisi for his WBO lightweight belt while he was in town. The London boy was 13-0 going in but couldn't solve the Italian puzzle, although he was still trying at the final bell.

Outside the ring, Henry Wharton handed in his British super-middleweight title to concentrate on bigger things, proof indeed that the proliferation of titles in boxing today has devalued the one-time dream of every kid who laced on a pair of gloves...to be a champion!

MAY

Lennox Lewis, Britain's very own heavyweight champion, moved ahead of Riddick Bowe in the race for credibility with a hard-earned decision over his number one contender, Tony Tucker, in Las Vegas. Awarded his title in the WBC boardroom, Lewis proved himself a

Following up his exciting victories over Wally Swift junior and Tony Collins, Andy Till stopped Wally (right) in a return match, to win a Lonsdale Belt outright　　　Les Clark

worthy champion in the ring against the former IBF title-holder, who had lost only to Mike Tyson in a 50-fight career. Tucker came to fight, but Lennox was up to his task, although the right hand that decked the American twice will require surgery before it sees the inside of a glove again.

Glasgow's Scottish Exhibition Centre was knee deep in WBO titles on the night that Chris Eubank kept his super-middleweight championship with a draw against the stubborn challenge of Ray Close. The Irishman had earned his chance by winning the European title from an Italian in Italy and he looked on the way to staging a major upset against Eubank until smashed to the canvas in round eleven with a tremendous uppercut. Ray somehow hauled himself back into the fight and defied Eubank's efforts to finish it and at the final bell many thought he had done enough to win. But that knockdown had enabled Chris to salvage a draw from the jaws of defeat and he returned to his dressing room still the WBO champion.

Pat Clinton was not so fortunate, caving in under the relentless assault of "Baby Jake" Matlala to lose his WBO flyweight title on a shocking eighth round stoppage. The tiny South African had been kayoed in an IBF challenge against Dave McAuley but was never in danger against the local favourite, who was floored three times in the eighth, before the referee called it off.

Little Paul Weir restored the balance for Scotland, lifting the vacant WBO mini-flyweight title with a seventh round cuts stoppage of tough Mexican, Fernando Martinez. How the unrated Weir, with a mere five pro fights under his belt, was eligible for a world title challenge is something only the WBO can answer, but then they already have a lot to answer for.

Over in Berlin, Henry Akinwande added the vacant European heavyweight title to his Commonwealth crown as he outboxed and outpunched Axel Schulz in their rematch. It was a replica of the first fight, only this time big Henry impressed the judges enough to give him the decision.

Sumbu Kalambay sampled what a lot of British fighters have become accustomed to when boxing in Italy, as local boy Chris Pyatt was awarded a close decision after a gruelling battle for the vacant WBO middleweight title in Leicester. The African went home claiming he had been robbed, but Pyatt deserved his win on his own workrate.

Another hometown hero was Sunderland's Commonwealth featherweight champion, Billy Hardy, who survived a knockdown and a cut eye to retain his title against the spirited challenge of Canadian, Barrington Francis.

In non-title action, European welterweight king, Gary Jacobs, forced Horace Fleary to quit after four undemanding rounds, while British and Commonwealth light-welterweight champion, Andy Holligan, made short work of Lorenzo Garcia, who was on his way back to Ohio after a couple of rounds.

As well as the British heavyweight title, Herbie Hide also holds the WBC International and Penta-Continental belts, and the latter was on the line against veteran American, Wimpy Halstead, at Norwich. With his hometown fans cheering him on, Herbie took his record to 22 straight, all inside schedule, as he pounded Wimpy to an easy fourth round defeat.

Three former champions on the comeback trail turned in fine wins. Glenn McCrory took a tough decision over Mark Young in Las Vegas, Ensley Bingham stopped Mark Kelly in five rounds at Middleton, and Del Bryan hung a right-hook on Oscar Checa's chin in round two for an upset win in Belfast.

Boxing's darker side surfaced as two fighters spent worrying nights in hospital. Liverpool's Jimmy Owen was poleaxed in 35 seconds as Floyd Churchill took the Central Area super-featherweight title, while John Ogiste collapsed after being stopped in eight rounds by W. O. Wilson for the Southern Area middleweight title. Happily, both boys survived without surgery.

JUNE

Lou Gent provided Nigel Benn with the perfect showcase for his talents and the WBC super-middleweight champion cleared the way for a million pound pay day against Chris Eubank in October, after they had met each other on a Saturday night at Olympia. Lou had won a Southern Area title and held the WBC International belt, but he had failed when challenging for major titles against Glenn McCroy, Johnny Nelson, Henry Wharton, and Fidel Castro. He failed again, as Benn turned loose a fearsome display of power punching that saw the gutsy London challenger decked five times in four sensational rounds, before the referee stopped it. But what a failure! If only Lou had the clout to go with his courage.

You spell Duke McKenzie's name C-H-A-M-P-I-O-N! British flyweight title, European championship, only British fighter to win THREE world titles, it was getting so that on fight night Duke had to look at the programme to remind himself which title was on the line. This night at the Lewisham Theatre, it was McKenzie's WBO super-bantamweight crown that was up for grabs as he left his corner to face Puerto Rican, Daniel Jimenez. They went twelve, hard rounds, with Jimenez scoring a ninth round knockdown to tip the scales his way with two of the three judges.

Tough Andy Till bit off more than he could chew when he challenged Frenchman, Laurent Boudouani, for his European light-middleweight title at Edmonton. The British champion was bleeding from cuts on both eyes and had been decked twice when manager Harry Holland pulled him out after four rounds. In London, British flyweight champion, Francis Ampofo, knocked out Albert Musankabala in three rounds with a thudding right to the head to take the vacant Commonwealth title.

Former British and Commonwealth cruiserweight champion, Derek Angol, journeyed to Ferrara in Italy to face Massimiliano Duran for the vacant European title and maybe wished he had stayed at home. Derek suffered a frightful knockout in the eleventh round of a gruelling scrap and spent a few days in hospital before being allowed home.

Lloyd Honeyghan's return to Atlantic City was far

from a happy one. The stage for his brilliant world title triumph in 1986, saw Lloyd gamely answering the bell for round ten against the exuberant Vinny Pazienza, but having nothing left. And when he was floored for the second time in the fight, Mickey Duff threw in the towel.

At 39, former British and European welterweight champion, Kirkland Laing, was left to ponder his future in the fight business on being stopped with a cut eye after five rounds by young Kevin Lueshing, who went home as the new Southern Area light-middleweight champion.

In a non-title bout at Lewisham, Commonwealth bantamweight champion, Johnny Armour, stayed unbeaten in his thirteenth pro fight with a decision over Boualem Belkif, but the Algerian gave Johnny a stiff argument and a cut right eye to think about. At Hemel Hempstead, Commonwealth featherweight titleholder, Billy Hardy, got ten good rounds under his belt against Mexican, Angel Fernandez, as he waited for news of a European title challenge.

And after racking up six straight wins in America, Olympic finalist, Wayne McCullough, came home to Belfast to give the fans a treat, swamping Conn McMullen with a million punches before the referee stopped it in round three. More quality and less quantity in his punching could see this bonny bantamweight become a big star.

Brave Andy Till (left) tried all he knew against the European light-middleweight champion, Laurent Boudouani, but was badly cut-up and outclassed in a vain title bid at Picketts Lock
Les Clark

Facts and Figures, 1992-93

There were 738 British-based boxers who were active during the period 1 July 1992 to 30 June 1993, spread over 236 promotions held in Britain, the same amount of tournamounts as the previous season. The above figure comprised 557 boxers already holding licences or having been licenced previously, five foreign-born boxers (Abel Asinamali, Steve Collins, Roland Ericsson, Bozon Haule, Dave Muhammed) who started their careers elsewhere and 176 new professionals.

Unbeaten during season (minimum qualification: 6 contests) 8: Sean Baker (1 draw), Andreas Panayi (1 draw). **7:** Shaun Anderson, Warren Stowe. **6:** Mark Baker, Marco Fattore (1 draw), Herbie Hide, Paul Lloyd, Robert McCracken, Shea Neary, John White.

Most wins during season (minimum qualification: 6 contests) 7: Shaun Anderson, Sean Baker, Martin Jolley, Andreas Panayi, Warren Stowe. **6:** Mark Baker, Herbie Hide, John Irwin, Andrew Jervis, Paul Lloyd, Robert McCracken, Shea Neary, John White.

Most contests during season (minimum qualification: 10 contests) 15: Kid McAuley. **13:** Russell Washer. **12:** Dean Bramhald, Miguel Matthews, Rick North, Steve Scott. **11:** John Kaighin, Graham McGrath. **10:** Mark Dawson, Norman Dhalie.

Most contests during career (minimum qualification: 50 contests) 136: Dean Bramhald. **115:** Shamus Casey. **93:** Des Gargano. **86:** Paul Murray. **66:** Julian Eavis. **65:** Glyn Rhodes. **62:** Ian Chantler, Miguel Matthews, Steve Pollard. **61:** Cordwell Hylton. **55:** Dennis Andries, Dave Owens. **53:** John Smith. **52:** Newton Barnett, Steve Gee, Sugar Gibiliru, Kirkland Laing, Trevor Meikle. **51:** Ray Newby.

Longest unbeaten sequence (minimum qualification: 10 contests) 36: Chris Eubank (1 draw). **23:** Lennox Lewis. **22:** Herbie Hide. **21:** Henry Akinwande (1 draw), Andy Holligan. **17:** Bradley Stone (1 draw), Robert McCracken, Henry Wharton (1 draw). **15:** Darron Griffiths (3 draws). **13:** John Armour, Glenn Campbell (1 draw), Kevin Sheeran, Tony Silkstone, Warren Stowe, Richie Woodhall. **12:** Cornelius Carr, Maurice Coore (1 draw), Gary Delaney (1 draw), Gary Logan, Clay O'Shea (2 draws), Jason Rowland. **11:** Dean Cooper, Kevin Lueshing, Carl Wright. **10:** Nigel Benn, Shaun Cummins (1 draw), Chris Pyatt.

Ron Pudney: A Man With the Fight Game in His Blood

by Derek O'Dell

Tracing the whereabouts of some fighters who plied their trade in the 1930s can be an exasperating task. Many boxed professionally as a means to an end. The game provided cash and they fought for no other reason than economics – a pressing responsibility to feed mouths at home and once they had hung up the gloves, they dropped out of the scene altogether. This phenomenon spilled over into the 1940s. Fortunately, many old-time glovemen have been re-united with their contemporaries, thanks to the formation of the ex-boxers' movement throughout Great Britain.

Some kept in touch with the game and gave their services as managers, trainers, and referees. Ron Pudney, former Croydon scrapper, is one of that ilk. I see more of him now in his present role of BBB of C Inspector than I did when he was a star middleweight from 1947 to 1953. We cross paths at various venues throughout the metropolis and we are fellow-members of the Croydon Ex-Boxers' Association.

Last summer I was watching a television broadcast of a fight between two of the world's top middleweights.

Between rounds, the camera focussed on the corner where Ron was supervising activities. I wondered how many viewers and fans realised that the bespectacled, avuncular official shown on their screens was once a highly-rated eleven-stone-six fighter. It occurred to me that in his heyday Ron would have stood a 50-50 chance of beating both the fighters who were disputing a fragmented version of the world championship. A "pseudo" championship, this one, Ron never competed for a British title, let alone a fabrication of a "world" diadem. He came up in the days of the Turpins, Albert Finch, Alby Hollister, Alex Buxton, and Vince Hawkins, and he held his own with them. But a shot at the top honours eluded him.

It was one of the Turpins who set back his championship aspirations by comprehensively outboxing him and winning by a clear margin. Dick was then British champion and, as such, was rated higher than Randolph, whose meteoric rise was to reach its pinnacle in 1951. Ron admits that he under-rated Dick's punching power. "I decided to force matters from the start, and a series of good

Ron (left) evades a sweeping left-hook from the reigning British middleweight champion, Dick Turpin. The Croydon man creditably lost on points over eight rounds in March 1950

old fashioned straight lefts broke my nose early in the first round. I tried to bustle him out of his stride, but he outjabbed me and was a comfortable winner."

It was the way Ron came back from that loss – a better man and a better boxer – that persuaded me to follow his subsequent progress. Before the year was out he had added the scalp of Bert Sanders, that tough fighter from Kilburn, to his list of victims. Sanders had been a pro fighter for ten years, and his record included most of the rated men in his division: Dick and Randolph Turpin, Albert Finch, Alby Hollister, Jimmy Davis, Bert Hyland, Reg Hoblyn, Alex Buxton and Dick Langley, etc. Bert was never easy to beat, but Ron kept his nose in front all the way. He never gave up, even when the tide of the battle was going against him.

Billy Goddard, who was in boxing before Ron turned pro, told me: "I was in Ron Pudney's corner when he fought Hoxton's Wally With at the Caledonian Road Baths. He had been a professional fighter for six months, and was showing promise. It was a hard fight – one of the hardest I've seen. With tried to rough him up. At first, it looked as if he'd get away with it, but Ron would not be intimidated. He was green, but he had guts, and fought back to match his foe punch for punch. He outgamed With and got a popular points win. I knew then that he had what it took."

Ron had started his pro career with a flourish, but when Ollie Williams stopped him most people wrote him off as being a flash-in-the-pan. Billy Goddard thought otherwise. "Outgamed" was the operative word when trying to sum up

Ron Pudney in fighting pose

Action from Earls Court in December 1951, shows Pudney (left) walking through George Dilkes' jab on his way to a sixth round victory

Ron Pudney. Billy had put his finger right on the button.

At a later date I was to see Ron outgame another good boxer in Bob Cleaver of the Borough and Attleborough. The Croydon boy had come through 1948 unbeaten, but early in 1949 Cleaver had outscored him in his first eight-rounder. When offered a return as a late substitute, Ron jumped at the chance.

It was at Bungay, during the holiday season. The crowd were restive throughout the supporting bouts and people were leaving seats while the rounds were in progress, and heading for the bar. At one stage, there were as many in the licensed area as were in the hall. However, the atmosphere changed dramatically once Cleaver and Ron squared up to each other. Nobody left his seat, and the bar emptied as the patrons rushed out to view the activities in the ring.

You could have got long odds against a Pudney victory at the end of the second round. Cleaver had kept him off with a stabbing left, and had frequently scored with accurate rights to both head and body. In the third, Ron had found a way inside Cleaver's leads and had begun to force the fight. Cleaver, a consistent boxer, fought back, but in the end he was outgamed. Ron showed, as he had already showed to Billy Goddard, that he would never give up easily. It was a popular win, and he was brought back to the Eastern Counties to take on and beat ring-wise, Ginger Sadd.

By virtue of this fine victory, he was now among the *élite* of the middleweights, and closed the year with wins over George Casson, Harry Davis, Ronnie Croad, and the tough Indian scrapper from the Nat Seller stable, Mac Joachim. He had also drawn with Jock Taylor in his rival's hometown of Sidcup.

To come up in the shadow of such notable Croydon boxers as Albert Finch and Mark Hart, and to prove worthy of being mentioned in the same breath, was no mean achievement. It was Albert Finch's father who introduced Ron to manager Jack Burns. Albert had sparred with Ron at "The Gun" gymnasium, and had picked him out as a prospect. "Snowy" Buckingham and Matt Wells were called in as trainers, and Ron got off to a fine start by knocking out Charley Golding in two rounds.

In 1951, Albert's faith was rewarded when Ron took the Southern Area middleweight title from Alex Buxton. Not only did the Croydon boy win the title that was once the property of Finch and Hart, but the victory gained him a coveted *Boxing News* Certificate of Merit. Ron had won another such certificate in 1950 with a great win over Bert Hyland at Earl's Court. To get anywhere in the middleweight division in those days you had to get past the fighting Irishman. Ron did so in a magnificently-fought eight-rounder that set the ringsiders talking.

It wasn't all honey. Ron's next fight was the set-back against Dick Turpin, and Les Allen outpointed him seven months later, but he didn't discourage easily. A series of bad decisions went against him in 1951, but he was the number one contender before the year was out. A knockout victory over Eric McQuade and wins over Wally Beckett and George Dilkes had him knocking on the championship

July 1953 and fight number 64, saw Ron (left) lose his Southern Area middleweight title to the up-and-coming, Wally Beckett

door. It had been his best year. Henry Hall, Bos Murphy, Bert Sanders, Michael Stack, and Gordon Hazell outscored him, but they were all disputed verdicts. Ron came back to hold Henry Hall to a draw, but was not expected to retain his area crown against Bedworth's Les Allen. Allen had beaten Ron once, and had marred the rise of many an aspiring middleweight. Terry Downes later found him too much of a handful, and he was to go on to beat Ron's nemesis, Bobby Dawson. Allen was talented and skilful. He ran Ron ragged for eleven rounds, but our man had great faith in himself. He came out for the final round like a rocket and decked Allen with a left-hook. Les got up, but a barrage finished him off. Ron Pudney was back on top, breathing defiance to all our middleweights.

At his best, he was a lovely boxer. He carried a heavy punch, could take it, and dish it out. He didn't know the meaning of the infinitive "to quit". Yet a defeat that finished him as a serious fighter was imminent. In 1952, the crack American, Bobby Dawson, knocked him out in eight rounds at the Albert Hall. Dawson had lost but three out of 30 bouts, and Ron's gameness was no asset that night. He refused to quit, and took a pummelling. It should have been stopped earlier, and the referee lost his licence as a result of his handling of the fight. Yet you could never tell with Ron: he had a habit of coming back after a bad spell.

Manager Jack Burns took him to Australia for a couple of fights. Ron lost them both, against men he should have beaten. Billy Goddard was there and admits: "Ron couldn't train properly. The facilities were non-existent, and there was the acclimatising problem. Also, the Aussies were marvellous hosts. There were too many late nights, and Ron put on weight in all the wrong places."

The surplus flesh caused no end of problems. Getting down to the middleweight limit impaired his stamina, and he lost his Southern Area crown to Wally Beckett on points. After one more fight Ron retired, but he kept in touch by opening a gym and taking out a trainer's licence.

Tom Powell, who is the oldest licence-holder – as timekeeper – in the country, persuaded Ron to become a Board of Control Inspector in 1975. It's a job with heavy responsibilities and not one where you can "turn a blind eye".

That figure on the TV screen knows the game thoroughly. After all, he's been in it since he was a schoolboy, and in his own words: "boxing doesn't owe me a thing, but I owe it plenty." He's the right man for the job – a square peg in a square ring.

In these days of all the show-biz glitz that surrounds the top stars, how refreshing to look upon a man, who has seen it all, still contributing to the welfare of the sport.

(This article first appeared, in a modified form, within the pages of *The Southern Ex-Boxer*. The author is indebted to that magazine's editor, Gilbert Allnutt, for permission to reprint it here.)

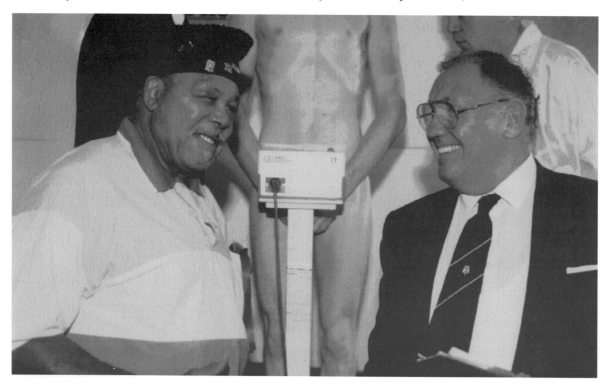

Ron (right) in his capacity as BBBoC licenced inspector, pictured with the "Old Mongoose" and all-time great, Archie Moore

Fighters Who Could Make the Grade During 1993-94

by John Cross

British boxing is bubbling with young talent once again. The sport certainly has a wealth of promising contenders who will be, given the proper time and encouragement, ready for shots at any one of the many titles that are around these days. Of course, there are plenty more than a handful of young hopefuls set for good things, but I've tried to take a look at some of the best and their chances of making it past the existing champions and title challengers at their respective weights.

The light-middleweight division is a fine example to start with. British champion, Andy Till, currently looks invincible, while former world welterweight champion, Lloyd Honeyghan, has won the Commonwealth belt after moving up, and the WBA Penta-Continental champion, Shaun Cummins, is already established at the top. But just starting out are two of Britain's most promising youngsters and they should be challenging within a couple of years.

The 1992 Olympic representatives, Adrian Dodson and Robin Reid, have both turned professional since Barcelona and their progress towards titles promises to be very exciting.

Reid, of Warrington, was chosen at light-middleweight to go to Barcelona and collected a bronze medal. He had a fine amateur record and was a regular England international, so it was no surprise when he decided to sign for Frank Warren. A couple of months later he made short work of Burton-on-Trent's Mark Dawson, who was stopped after two minutes eight seconds with a perfect right-hand counter-punch. Since then he has gone six rounds with the durable and experienced Andy Furlong, who he beat by a wide points margin. Reid, 22, has proved he can deliver a knock out punch and is a skillful boxer who can last the distance.

Islington's promising 22-year-old Dodson, has also taken an easy route so far and it is difficult to assess both him and Reid before they step up a class. But neither boxer can be blamed for getting professional experience with quick wins against opposition that lacks true class. Dodson, formerly of the Lynn and St Pancras amateur clubs, has already beaten Chris Mulcahy, Rick North, Russell Washer, and an American. The first two Englishmen caved in within two rounds, but Dodson's best performance came when he beat Greg Wallace on the undercard of Glenn McCrory's comeback in Las Vegas. Dodson's body shots looked awesome and would wear down many British title contenders even now.

We have not had the chance to see much of his boxing ability yet, but if that comes up to scratch then the Reid-Dodson battle for supremacy should be an exciting one. Together, with promising Clay O'Shea, Robert McCracken, Jamie Robinson and Kevin Sheeran, the light-middle division could be due for a shake-up.

In a match made over six rounds, the extremely talented Adrian Dodson (right), having his fourth contest, was forced to travel the full distance for the first time against Russell Washer

Les Clark

Also in Britain's Barcelona squad was flyweight Rowan Williams, who has followed Reid and Dodson and turned pro. The flyweight division is short of real competition because of a lack of true quality depth. Robbie Regan, Francis Ampofo, Pat Clinton and James Drummond are well established, while Darren Fifield and Vince Feeney look promising. But Williams has the boxing ability to take it by storm, evidenced when he beat former ABA light-flyweight champion, Nick Tooley, on his paid debut. The youngster throws lots of fast flurries and concentrates on quantity and speed rather than power.

Portsmouth's Michael Driscoll is still on course to make a challenge for the British light-welterweight title – despite being on the wrong end of an appalling points decision to former British light-welter champion, Tony McKenzie. So many people were astounded at referee Adrian Morgan's verdict, yet everyone in the game seems to have ignored that freak result. The "White Tornado" – a former England amateur international – has returned with an unconvincing win over veteran Ray Newby. The 24-year-old beat Tottenham's promising Bernard Paul on a cuts stoppage at Alexandra Palace last December and another couple of wins in similar fashion should see him back on course for a final eliminator. He can jab powerfully with either hand and has the ability to knock people out. Quite how he would get on against the outstanding British and Commonwealth champion, Andy Holligan, is another matter. But he looks a good bet, although Alan Hall, Mark McCreath and Dave Pierre make for a strong division.

Brixton's Gary Logan should be higher up the ratings in the welterweight division, but long periods of inactivity have held him back. The 24-year-old Southern Area champion was kept fairly busy by manager, Mickey Duff, in the early part of his career with 19 wins from 20 fights. The likeable Logan has a strong punch and has plenty of skill, which he showed in good points wins over Trevor Ambrose and Des Robinson in 1991. And he continued his winning ways when he beat Glyn Rhodes at the Crofton Leisure Centre in his own backyard in South London in May. The win was rather controversial – Rhodes was counted out by referee Dave Parris, but claimed he simply misjudged it and was strong enough to get up – but there was only going to be one winner. Logan, when fit and sharp, can pick opponents off with a quick jab and is capable of throwing a dangerous left-hook. Unfortunately, he sometimes seems as if he would rather not get into the ring, but if he can show stomach for the battle he should challenge for the British title. The only thing in his way is the rich talent in the welterweight class. Barry Hearn's Matchroom stable has Darren Dyer, of Islington, and Commonwealth champion, Eamonn Loughran. Both have exceptional punching power and if Dyer can put his troubles behind him then a fight with Logan would be one not to be missed.

Fellow south Londoner, Terry Dunstan, has already attracted attention, despite only having a handful of fights. The 24-year-old Dunstan, of Vauxhall, has punching power, but looks as though he is happy enough to settle for points wins in the early part of his career. He has already outboxed Steve Yorath and Steve Osborne. Perhaps he has been

Considered by many to be lucky to get a draw against Glyn Shepherd (left) on his pro debut, the former ABA champion, Darren Fifield, is still a youngster who shows plenty of promise
Les Clark

reluctant to show off his power for fear of not being matched because he looks strong and tends to stroll through fights. He took his stroll too far in his third outing against Redditch's Lee Prudden, in an untidy six-twos at Barking in March. Although he clearly believes in his ability and throws a lot of flashy shots, he often holds back on the power, which is used very occasionally. A step up in power and pace should see him rise quite rapidly. Trained by Howard Rainey at the St Monica's gym where he used to be an amateur, he has sparred with some big names, including Lennox Lewis, when he turned pro after winning gold in the 1988 Olympics. The cruiserweight division lacks strength in depth, despite having British and WBC International champion, Carl Thompson, who, if he carries on in his current vein of form, should challenge for a world title. Veteran Dennis Andries and former IBF champion, Glenn McCrory, are still in contention, but Dunstan has the ability to move into the top five within a short space of time.

One step up in weight into the glamorous heavies division is, sadly, lacking the young talent breaking through at the moment. Last year's prospect, Herbie Hide, has won British, WBC International and WBA Penta-Continental titles without having to work up too much of a sweat against some weak opponents. The 21-year-old has shown promise and the next twelve months, with challenges coming in thick and fast from European champion, Henry Akinwande, among others, should sort out his future. But any realistic talk of a match with WBA and IBF champion, Riddick Bowe, would seem very premature. And, anyway, he often comes in at around the late fourteen stone mark – a couple of stone at least behind Bowe, Lewis and Bruno.

The promising J. A. Bugner, 22, and six foot six inches tall, looked a good prospect before Christmas. But he will need a strong character to come back after losing his seven fight unbeaten record to Bradford's Steve Garber at Wembley in February, which has put a temporary halt to his rise through the ranks. Bugner lacks real power, although he is a good enough boxer. But that went against him in the defeat. He was miles ahead on Dave Parris' scorecard, but did not and could not knock his opponent out and went down to a right hand after just 43 seconds of the sixth and final round.

Meanwhile, among the lightweights, Liverpool's Nigel Wenton has taken a huge step towards getting back on track – by taking on trainer Eric Seccombe. Wenton would be the first to admit that he has shied away from hard work in the past. Although he has true boxing ability, with a vicious streak, his lack of training has often left him overweight and unable to finish the job. And he has found it difficult to settle, having been with Barney Eastwood and several trainers, before following his brother, Ritchie, a featherweight, and signing up with Frank Warren. Wenton suffered a shock defeat at the hands of Carlisle rookie, Charles Shepherd. The Liverpudlian certainly looked a good winner and even the referee admitted he was ahead on his scorecard, but he dropped points because of the use of "dirty tricks." If Wenton can put his mind to it, then there is no doubt that he has the flair to challenge for honours in a division bursting with talent. He has a lightning jab and can punch powerfully and can cut down the ring with great ease, as he showed against Telford's Davy Robb at York Hall, Bethnal Green, in December. Wenton took just three rounds to destroy Robb with a chopping right. Still very cocky, he fancies that he can take the division by storm.

British champion, Paul Burke, who dethroned Billy Schwer, looks a tough customer and will be difficult to beat. Luton's previously unbeaten Schwer should come back – he certainly sells enough tickets! But he has a big problem in that he is very prone to facial cuts – he marks up even after a series of jabs. However, he has been training hard with headgear and his cornerman, Dennie Mancini, certainly has the experience to solve the problem.

But lower down the ranks is a name which should haunt Schwer – Tottenham's Patrick Gallagher. Gallagher, 22, beat him on points in the 1990 ABA final and turned pro last autumn. The lightweight is an exceptional talent, bursting with skill, with a lethal left-hook, but in the ring he has so far lacked concentration. To date he has had two quick wins against lowly opposition. While that's fine for any youngster starting out to get experience, he has had only two contests in a year and may have to ponder on his direction and future, because he has the ability to go all the way.

Former undefeated WBC International champion, Michael Ayers, is another with title credentials. The 28-year-old from Paddington beat Australian Scott Brouwer to win his belt, which he defended successfully – despite being floored by Danny Myburgh – before challenging WBO champion, Giovanni Parisi. The fight in Rome ended in a

Although contest number thirteen produced a points defeat at the hands of Neville Brown, Paul Busby (right), seen in action against Paul Wesley, could yet prove to be a force in the middleweight division

Les Clark

brave points defeat, but he should have gained valuable experience for new challenges. He is limited defensively, but can throw the big shots.

Sidcup's Mark Baker, a former ABA finalist, is another who has yet to be given a real test, but the manner of his five wins so far suggest the 24-year-old super-middleweight can go a long way. Baker, a former Repton Cedar Street amateur, has the ability to wear opponents down with dangerous body punches. By far his most impressive performance to date was against Welsh journeyman, Karl Mumford, at Lewisham in April. Baker's awesome shot's to Mumford's stomach and chest sent him down twice before the towel came in. But he also has the ability to knock them out. Managed by the Terry Lawless–Mickey Duff camp, he should prove to be one to watch and could reach the top ten within the next 18 months or so. By then, the Chris Eubank–Nigel Benn saga may be somewhat clearer, while Ray Close, Henry Wharton and Nicky Piper should still be about.

Middlesbrough's unbeaten middleweight, Cornelius Carr, is an excellent prospect, who mixes good boxing skill, which has secured many of his 18 professional wins, with strong jabs and a dangerous left-hook. The 24-year-old came through a severe test against experienced Londoner, Stan King, in Sunderland during May. The northerner took the opening sessions and had King down in the fourth, but Carr finished battered and bruised as his opponent came back strongly in the last two of the eight rounder. Referee, Gerald Watson, gave the nod to Carr by just half a point. Having recently signed with Mickey Duff, he looks a strong contender in a division which has currently one of the strongest looking top ten in Britain.

Middleweight champion, Frank Grant, has made a successful defence of his title, but there are plenty of others in the queue to take him on. Dubliner, Steve Collins, is a fighter highly regarded on the world scene, while Chris Pyatt has fulfilled his dream and won the WBO crown. Commonwealth champion Richie Woodhall would be a strong challenger, with Neville Brown next in line. Brown beat Worcester's previously unbeaten Paul Busby, a skillful but awkward former England amateur, in a final eliminator. They were amateur rivals, but remain good friends and may meet again, because Busby will always point to the fact that he damaged a hand early in the fight.

Canning Town's featherweight, Bradley Stone, has a big following who should see him rise through the ranks within the next year or so. Anyone who saw his exciting draw with Downham's Kevin Middleton at Lewisham in October will know what I'm talking about. Their energy and determination looked an excellent reference for future title success. The pair gave everything in a superb battle. Stone looks strong and determined and has good boxing skill. However, he was given an education against experienced Chris Clarkson, who caught him with a flurry of shots in the opening sessions at Wembley in February. The south Londoner made a slow start and gradually turned the screw and sent Clarkson down in the third. Although the Hull lad deserved to lose, it was not by the 79-77½ verdict on referee Dave Parris' card. That victory extended Stone's record to unbeaten in fifteen and, at the same time, taught him some valuable lessons. He will need those qualities in a division packed with talent like Paul Hodkinson and Colin McMillan.

Let's hope that young prospects like Stone can prove to be as exciting talents in years to come as the likes of Hodkinson and McMillan.

Good luck to you all!

Making headway among the featherweights is Bradley Stone (right), seen here backing up Norman Dhalie last December

Les Clark

Team Lennox: A World Heavyweight Championship Recipe

by Chris Kempson

For so long, all of us connected with the fight game in these islands have had a dream, that one day, Britain would again have its very own world heavyweight champion. Towards the end of 1992, the dream came true, in the shape and form of Lennox Lewis. This article takes a close look at the man himself and those in "Team Lennox," who have worked long and hard to ensure that their man achieved "The Greatest Prize in Sport".

Lennox Lewis was born in east London, a breeding ground of so many great British fighters, on 2 September 1965, the year in which gas was first discovered in the North sea. Lewis is of Jamaican extraction, his parents being born there. He enjoyed life as he grew up in east London, playing with friends and generally having fun. Today, he still retains links with the area around West Ham, his birthplace, and is a keen follower of the "Hammers'" football team.

Lennox moved to the province of Ontario in Canada on a permanent basis when he was twelve years of age, to live with his mother, Violet, who he is very close to and who had been residing there for sometime. The move to the land of the Maple Leaf led directly to his involvement with boxing.

As a youngster, Lewis dabbled in most sports, notably athletics, basketball and football, but eventually he was advised by his school principal to join a boxing club. Lennox's cockney accent got him into all kinds of scrapes and fights at school and he eventually made his way to the Kitchener-Waterloo boxing club in Kitchener, Ontario, where he was able to channel his aggression more appropriately. Success in the ring was soon to follow. He won his amateur debut in November 1978, knocking out a guy called Junior Lindsay in two rounds. Two years later he was champion of Ontario Province and still only a welterweight at the age of 16, he became national junior champion of Canada.

His first major success on the international amateur stage came in November 1983 in Santo Domingo in the Dominican Republic, during the second World Junior Championships. Only just turned 18 and by now a fully blown super-heavyweight, Lennox won the gold medal. His opponent in the final was the Cuban, Pedro Quesada, who withdrew with a broken hand. By now, he was no longer just content to win trophies and maybe become a fireman, he wanted to see how far he could go in the ring.

His next big international test was to be the Los Angeles Olympics in 1984. Although the Games were boycotted by Cuba and the old Soviet Union, as well as

Men who can afford a smile. From left to right: Lennox Lewis, Dennis Lewis and Frank Maloney

Les Clark

many of the former east European countries, there were still some good super-heavies around, notably, America's Tyrell Biggs, Italy's Francesco Damiani and the useful Yugoslav, Azis Salihu. Lennox opened his Olympic campaign in fine style, stopping Pakistan's Mohammed Yousof in the final round, before coming up against Biggs in the quarter-final. The more experienced American outpointed Lewis and went on to take the gold medal at super-heavyweight. Biggs, who outpointed Damiani in the final, became the first Olympic champion in this new weight division.

Lennox paid a brief visit to the country of his birth at the end of October 1984, when he represented Canada against England in an international match held at the Bletchley Leisure Centre. He met reigning ABA champion and Olympic bronze medallist, Bobby Wells, from Kingston ABC, and duly proceeded to knock Bobby out in the third round. It was the first time the Englishman had been cleanly knocked out and the match ended in a six-all draw. Incidentally, the international was the first in this country to be staged with one team, the Canadians, wearing headguards.

In August 1985, Lennox won his first North American title in Beaumont, Texas, claiming the gold medal. Three months later he was in Seoul, South Korea, for the World Cup, where he won the silver medal, being outscored in the final by the wily and very experienced Vyacheslav Jakovlev of the Soviet Union.

Then it was back to Britain in July 1986, to Edinburgh in fact, for the Commonwealth Games. Because of the boycott by the African nations, there were just three entrants in the super-heavyweight division. ABA champion, James Oyebola, was stopped by Lennox in the second round, a similar fate which befell Welshman, Aneurin Evans, in the final. Lewis was now the Commonwealth champion and gold medallist. He scored triple gold success in 1987, winning international tournaments in Europe, in Stockholm and Saint Nazaire, and sandwiched in between was a triumph in the Canadian championships in Oromocto, in March. Approaching the Pan American Games in Indianapolis with high hopes, he advanced to the final in fine style, only to be outpointed by Cuba's Jorge Gonzalez, although the decision was debatable. The Cuban, a former world number one, had earlier outpointed Riddick Bowe on his way to the final. Lewis gained "sweet revenge" over the Cuban in the North American Championships, which were held in Toronto a week later, with a clear 3-0 unanimous verdict.

He duly won the gold medal at the prestigious annual Felix Stamm multi-nations tournament held in Warsaw in November 1987, normally the exclusive domain of the powerful former Eastern Bloc countries, and retained his Canadian title in Edmonton in March 1988, having been super-heavyweight champion since 1984. A month later, he won a silver medal in the Intercup tournament, staged in Germany. Back to Canada, Ottawa in fact, brought further gold medal success for Lennox in the annual world-rated Canada Cup competition held in May.

The September 1988 Olympics to be held in Seoul, South Korea, duly beckoned for the heir apparent to the Olympic throne. Lewis, who, by then, was sure he wanted to turn professional, was out to impress the world and the hordes of professional promoters and managers who always flock to the Games. He didn't disappoint the onlookers, as he swept majestically to the Olympic title and the gold medal.

The useful Kenyan, Odera, lasted two rounds and a "revenge" win followed in the quarter-final when he settled an old score, knocking out Ulli Kaden, of the German Democratic Republic, in the opening session. Poland's formidable Janus Zarenkiewicz withdrew from his scheduled semi-final contest with Lennox, having had a tough battle against the West German, Schnieders. The giant Canadian advanced to the final to face his heavier American rival, Riddick Bowe, whom he eventually beat with some ease. Fierce accurate shots to the head in the second round, forced the American to take two standing counts and Lennox Lewis became Olympic champion there and then, in the city where he had gained a silver medal almost three years earlier. In an amateur career spanning a decade, he was never off his feet in 109 contests and he had fought and beaten the best super-heavyweights on the planet. There was nothing left for him to win among the amateurs.

Although courted by most of the top American fight barons, Lewis' signature on professional forms was eventually secured after three-months persuasive talking by the then small-time London fight promoter/manager, Frank Maloney (more of Frank, a little later on). London has always had a special significance for Lewis and he started his paid career at the Royal Albert Hall on 22 June 1989. Before a modest, but interested audience, Midlands journeyman, Al Malcolm, was dispatched inside two rounds and Lennox was on his way. The cover page of the programme on that evening's joint Frank Maloney/Mike Barrett promotion, carried these words:- "The birth of a champion, be in at the beginning" – how prophetic they were.

Now, 22 fights later, he is the WBC heavyweight champion of the world, with a successful title defence already under his belt. On the way to the top, Lennox won the European, then the British and finally the Commonwealth titles. Only three men have gone the distance with him – Ossie Ocasio, Levi Billups and latterly, Tony "TNT" Tucker, in Lewis's initial WBC title defence. Former WBA champion, Mike Weaver, was iced in six rounds, and Tyrell Biggs, Lennox's 1984 Olympic conquerer, was crushed in three, while Donovan "Razor" Ruddock of Canada was destroyed in just 226 seconds in the WBC final eliminator staged at Earls Court in London in the early hours of 1 November 1992. Having fought in Canada and the United States on his way to the title, his record is impressive, his power awesome, and his skill and technique improve all the time.

By a strange twist of fate and curious circumstances, Lennox did not actually win his title in the ring like most champions tend to do. America's then undisputed world heavyweight kingpin, Riddick Bowe, who had been trounced by Lewis in the 1988 Olympic final in Seoul, sadly refused to defend his WBC crown against the new challenger. With that, the WBC stripped Bowe of their version of the title on 16 December 1992, with the WBC President, Jose Sulaiman, coming from Mexico to London's west-end on 14 January 1993 and presenting Lennox with his WBC belt at a gala charity dinner held at the Mariott Hotel.

The once poor boy from the mean streets of London's east-end was now the "toast of London town" and our first world heavyweight champion since British-born Bob Fitzsimmons in 1899, when Queen Victoria was on the throne, a lifetime and more away!

Well, what of Lennox Lewis outside the roped square. He is an articulate, fairly private person, with an engaging smile and a good sense of humour, although a fierce temper, slow to rise, occasionally comes to the surface. With natural charm, he has a tremendous love and affection for his mother, Violet. His likes include all types of music, reggae, rap, soul and funk, as well as classical (like Beethoven), he undertakes charity work, plays chess in his spare time and also enjoys golf, tennis and is a good cook. He now lives in Hadley Wood on the outskirts of north London, having previously resided in Kent, but often visits his mother's house back in Canada, while tending to spend most of his holidays in Jamaica.

I have known Lennox since June 1989 and have always enjoyed his company. He is easy to talk to, polite, and confident of his ability, and at the same time a true warrior and champion of the ring. Long may he reign as our heavyweight champion of the world and, at the same time, go on to fulfill his ultimate goal of unifying the title in the next year or so.

Frank Maloney, the 39-year-old managerial genius who signed up Lennox Lewis in April 1989, has come a long way from the tough streets of Peckham, his birthplace, in south-east London, to stand alongside Lennox Lewis.

Maloney has been obsessed with boxing since he was nine. He recalls, around the age of eleven, visiting the world famous Thomas A'Becket gymnasium in London's Old Kent Road, to watch fighters work out there, including our top heavyweight in those days, Henry Cooper.

He boxed for three clubs, the Fisher, Lynn, and Trinity and, as an amateur flyweight he took part in 67 contests, reaching the finals of the London Feds on two occasions. Also reached a London ABA final, being stopped by Wapping's murderous puncher, Jimmy Flint.

On leaving school, Frank tried his hand unsuccessfully at becoming an apprentice jockey for a few weeks before switching to the role of a market trader, which he found more to his liking.

Still maintaining his interest in boxing, he became a trainer and match-maker for the Hollington ABC in Camberwell, but in 1981 he left the amateur code and joined up with Frank Warren, who was beginning to make his mark as a new promoter in the pro game. In his new role, Maloney used the gymnasium at The Castle public house in Commercial Road, the heart of London's east-end, to train Warren's fighters.

Earlier, he had become involved in the restaurant and licensing trade and when the alliance with Warren finished after 18-months, Maloney took a three-year break from the game, although it remained in his blood and he continued to attend shows.

Towards the end of 1985, a young Walworth lightweight named Richie Edwards approached Frank and asked him to be his manager. He soon formed a promotional alliance with fellow south-Londoner, Vince Heckman, and they ran their first show at Lewisham Concert Theatre in May 1986. Maloney also began to add more fighters to his expanding stable and, along with Heckman, he promoted good value-for-money shows at Greenwich Borough Hall and the Crofton Leisure Centre in Catford, as well as the Lewisham Concert Theatre.

In the early part of 1987, a surprise telephone call from Mike Barrett led to Maloney becoming the matchmaker for the Mike Barrett/Micky Duff shows held at the York Hall in Bethnal Green. During this period, Frank renewed his earlier acquaintance with Terry Marsh, whom he had got to know during his days with Frank Warren, and together they formed the promotional outlet for Ambrose Mendy's newly formed World Sports Corporation. Maloney helped bring over three former world champions, "Terrible" Tim Witherspoon, John Tate, and the legendary, Roberto "Hands of Stone" Duran, for WSC promotions. At the same time, he continued to assist Mike Barrett, following the latter's promotional split from Micky Duff in 1988 and he also made matches for London promoters, Gary

Trainer, Pepe Correa   Les Clark

43

Davidson and Harry Holland.

In October 1988, Maloney teamed-up with Mike Barrett to stage the "fight of the year" at the Royal Albert Hall in London between Nigel Benn and Anthony Logan. He also had other great nights with Benn, notably at Crystal Palace, the Royal Albert Hall again and at the Kelvin Hall in Glasgow. During this time, Frank continued to run his promotions at Picketts Lock, Gloucester, Eltham and Sheppey. His final show with Benn took place in the "Supertent" at Finsbury Park on 21 May 1989, when Islington's Michael Watson knocked the "Dark Destroyer" out in six rounds.

It was during his promotional association with Nigel Benn that Maloney persuaded some members of a financial services corporation, the then Levitt Group, and Roger J. Levitt in particular, to assist him in trying to sign up Canada's Olympic super-heavyweight gold medallist, Lennox Lewis.

After much persuasion and endless trans-Atlantic telephone conversations, Lewis agreed to join Frank Maloney and signed the contract which turned him professional in April 1989. As they say "the rest is history". Later on, Roger Levitt, a keen boxing fan, acted as Lewis' commercial manager. He is no longer involved with "Team Lennox" these days, however.

Although Lennox Lewis is undoubtedly the "jewel in the Londoner's managerial and promotional crown", Frank maintains a fine stable of other talented fighters and during his association with Lewis he has continued to promote in a variety of venues up and down the country, although London has remained his clear promotional powerbase. Shows have been held in Bexleyheath, Hull, Doncaster, Gillingham and Sheffield and Maloney has also worked promotionally with Barry Hearn and Harry Holland during this period. Maloney's promotional outfit, Champion Enterprises Ltd, is certainly riding high these days on both sides of the Atlantic.

Maloney has also worked with major European promoters and has spent many years involved with American boxing. In fact, on 6 May 1993, at the Riviera Casino in Las Vegas, Maloney co-promoted a show which was billed as "The British Are Coming", with several home fighters on the under card. He and his backers work closely with Main Events, the American promotional organisation run by the famous Duva family, based in New Jersey. And for the last two years or so, Panos Eliades, a successful London chartered accountant, has been "Team Lennox'" main financial backer in this country. Eliades, is a personable and charming man of Greek-Cypriot extraction, who is not really a boxing fan as such, but seems to thrive on helping Frank Maloney set up multi-million dollar fight deals for Lennox Lewis. He has been tremendously successful so far and is a very important cog in the "Team Lennox" fight wheel. However, in the comparatively quiet early days of Lewis' professional career, successful businessman and fight entrepreneur, Stan Hoffman, looked after the American end of the operation.

Frank always acquits himself well when dealing with the high-powered "wheeler-dealer" American fight frater-

Lennox (left) on his way to a second round win over the WBC's number one contender, Razor Ruddock   Les Clark

nity and has handled Don "Only in America" King with particular skill, grace, and considerable success. The bombastic King tried to ridicule, intimidate and brow-beat Maloney, both in London and in the United States, on various occasions, in the lead-up to Lewis' title defence against Tucker on 8 May 1993. But, in the event, the "pugilistic pygmy" as King irreverently described Maloney, negotiated hard, kept his cool, and willingly took the American's money, while Lennox easily retained his title, to pile on the misery for the outrageous King. As Maloney said at the time, "Don King has made me famous across America. He is the best PR man I could have ever hired and he pays well, too, for the privilege".

So, its been a long, hard road for the former market trader from south-east London to his now familiar jet-set lifestyle, with constant trans-Atlantic trips, endless meetings and discussions with the top media and TV companies at home, like Sky and in the United States, with HBO and Pay per View, and much more besides.

Maloney once told me: "Boxing is besotted by jealousy and I have to make sure that I succeed as there are a lot of people out there who are just rubbing their hands waiting to see me fail". The bad news for them, is that he has succeeded and has brought the heavyweight championship of the world to this country for the first time this century.

Away from the glamour of the fight trade, Maloney is a quiet, calm, somewhat shy man, who it is said is troubled by dyslexia. Equally at home in either tracksuit, jeans and a tee shirt, or "booted and suited", he gets on well with all sorts of people and brings the best out of them, that's the secret of much of his success.

Frank is proud of his connections with Peckham and regularly visits the cafe's and pubs in the area to see friends and acquaintances he grew up with. He considers it important to remember where you come from.

Interested in poetry, he often reads and meditates in churches away from the hustle and bustle of his busy lifestyle and at opposite ends of the spectrum is a follower of football, being a keen supporter of Millwall. He has also shown some fascination for the occult and fortune-telling, but, really, boxing consumes him 24-hours each and every day.

Although small in stature, Frank Maloney has truly become a managerial and promotional giant, who is able to compete with and "beat" those at home and abroad. His story too, like that of Lennox Lewis, is very much one of success.

During his professional career, Lennox Lewis has had two main trainers. For his first contests, the somewhat controversial American, John Davenport, was in the saddle. Davenport, a former marine and prison officer who had worked with Carl "The Truth" Williams and Mike Tyson in his amateur days, was able to commit himself full-time and come to London to supervise Lennox's ring education. Under his guidance, Lewis won both the British and European titles. However, Davenport was not universally liked by the British boxing establishment, nor by some sections of the media, and there was some debate among the fight fraternity as to "how much" Lewis had in fact progressed under his tutelage. For my part, I got along well with him. I found him, although a man of few words, always courteous and polite. He is a man dedicated to his trade, who simply sleeps, eats and reads boxing. Davenport's role in helping Lewis to reach the heavyweight championship of the world must be fully recognised and not underplayed in anyway, in making a valuable contribution to Lennox's fistic education.

However, just prior to Lennox's contest with Derek "Sweet D" Williams at London's Royal Albert Hall on 30 April 1992, in which Lewis put up his British and European titles and Williams threw in his Commonwealth crown, Davenport was replaced by Puerto Rican born, Jose "Pepe" Correa. Although based in Maryland, Correa had known Lewis since his amateur days. Correa came into the Lewis camp with impeccable credentials, having worked successfully with the fabulous "Sugar" Ray Leonard. He is an impressive, bubbly, friendly man, confident of his ability and determined to get the very best out of Lennox Lewis. At a weigh-in he once told me, there are two ways to do it, "the easy or the hard, it's up to Lennox which one he chooses, I know which way I would take", he added with a steely smile. Correa has trained Lewis now in four contests and the WBC champion remains undefeated and the new partnership seems to be working just fine. In my view, under Pepe Correa's guidance, Lennox has become a more polished and accomplished fighter, one whose balance and movement has improved considerably.

Correa's skills have now taken Lewis to the very top of the world heavyweight scene.

The spectacled Pepe Correa is ably assisted on the training front by 29 -year-old Harold "The Shadow" Knight, a former world class super-featherweight from Plainfield, New Jersey. Knight won the USBA super-featherweight title in April 1987 and made two successful title defences, before challenging the impressive Rocky Lockeridge for his IBF world crown on 2 April 1988. The contest took place in Atlantic City and the champion handled the hitherto undefeated challenger well, out-boxing and out-punching the game Knight over fifteen rounds. Incidentally, this was the last fifteen-round world title fight to be contested. Even in defeat, "The Shadow", has left his mark on the world boxing scene, forever. His silky skills, courage, and punching power, have been used to good effect to help both improve and fine tune Lennox's true world championship class. Mention here must also be made of Jamaican born, but American-based, Courtney Shand, who is Lennox's personal conditioner. Shand is responsible for ensuring that the champion is in tip-top shape when he enters the ring to do battle. An important job and a key post in "Team Lennox" therefore falls on young Courtney's broad shoulders. He is clearly the man with the magic touch in his fingers.

Various sparring partners, too numerous to mention,

The WBC heavyweight champion, Lennox Lewis, proudly shows off the belt Les Clark

are hired and sometimes fired as they toil hard and long to get Lennox Lewis into the finest shape of his life. Former world heavyweight champions, Tony Tubbs and Mike Weaver, cruiserweight contender, Vince "Slim" Boulware, and the Texan heavyweight prospect, Mike Williams, are among the latest crop of hired helpers to face Lennox Lewis.

In the highly commercialised world of professional boxing there is a pressing need to have a legal advisor on board. John R. Hornewer, a 32-year-old lawyer from Chicago in Illinois, acts as the champion's personal attorney. John, who first met Lennox after the Seoul Olympics, represents the interests of a number of professional sportsmen. He works diligently with "Team Lennox" in advising and promoting all aspects of Lennox Lewis's commercial and boxing career. John is pretty adept too at using a camera, or video equipment, and many of his fine photographs adorn programmes, brochures, magazines, and other publications involving the many ring triumphs of Lennox Lewis.

On the domestic side of the fence, 31-year-old Dennis Lewis, the champion's older brother, acts as his personal manager, sifting through myriads of commitments and potential calls on his brother's time. Dennis remained in London while Lennox moved to Canada, but the brothers always kept in close contact with each other and he is also responsible for running and organising the Lennox Lewis Fan Club. Thus, a key role in the "Team Lennox" organisation is filled by the charming and affable, Dennis Lewis, a former leather furniture salesman and disc jockey.

The very important position of camp co-ordinator is filled by the tall and genial American, Ollie Dunlap, another former Leonard aid. Ollie, with his small white beard, comes across as a dashing figure. I first met him prior to Lewis's fight with Ruddock last autumn and he is a very cool and competent character who ensures that "Team Lennox" is in the right place at the right time and is working smoothly and efficiently. A warm and friendly man, he handles the boxing press with patience and charm and goes about his work quietly, but most effectively.

Nearly last, but by no means least, we take a look at the administrative side of Champion Enterprises Ltd, which is a key component of the "Team Lennox" organisation. Mick Williamson, who hails from Bermondsey in south-east London, has been the General Manager of Champion Enterprises Ltd for the past two years or so. Their office, which is now located in north-London, was previously situated in a fashionable part of London's west-end. The bearded, quietly spoken Williamson, affectionately known in boxing circles as "Mick the Rub", testimony to him having successfully undertaken a course in massage and physiotherapy, has been involved in boxing for much of his life.

Mick first became acquainted with Frank Maloney when they were both working for Frank Warren during the early part of the 1980s. A cuts and corner man in those days, he has held a manager's licence for a number of years and has also worked as a fight agent. Still a fine "cuts man", he undertook that particular role in the corner during the early part of Lennox's professional career. Mick remains cool, calm and collected, while the pressure builds as big fight nights approach, and he has acquitted himself well both at home and abroad in the cause of "Team Lennox".

Sophie Judkins is another very important member of the office. She fills the important role of being Frank Maloney's personal assistant, a lively, demanding, and fascinating post, which she undertakes cheerfully and effectively.

From time to time, as a big Lennox Lewis fight draws near, additional specialist help is sometimes required and personnel are drafted in to enable the administrative side of "Team Lennox" to continue to function effectively during times of enormous stress and strain. Geraldine Davies, who has a wealth of experience in arranging group or individual tours to major sporting events, proved a real asset in the run-up to the Lewis v Tucker contest in May 1993, as did Essex man, former Matchroom press officer, Andy Ayling, who made the trip to Las Vegas with the team.

But in the ring, it is up to Lennox Lewis to deliver the goods on behalf of "Team Lennox". However, the WBC heavyweight champion will be the first to admit that all the other members play a vital part and fulfil an important role in his ultimate success. "Team Lennox" is all about being successful, in fact, it is a fine world heavyweight championship recipe for success.

Well, what does the future hold in store for Lennox Lewis and how will history judge Britain's first world heavyweight champion in the fast disappearing 20th century. Now that the proposed "two-fight" package involving WBO champion, Tommy Morrison, and former undisputed world champion, Evander Holyfield, has evaporated, Lennox has been matched to fight Britain's other top heavyweight, Frank Bruno. The fight, billed as "history in the making", looks set to take place at Cardiff Arms Park, the ancestral home of Welsh rugby football, in the early hours of Saturday 2 October 1993. It will prove to be Britain's richest ever fight with, for the first time, two British-born fighters contesting the richest prize in sport. Beyond that, there is a match for the winner against Tommy Morrison and then a "unification" contest against America's Riddick Bowe, always assuming, of course, that he remains undefeated.

We must leave it up to future historians to see how they eventually judge Britain's Lennox Lewis against the great world heavyweight champions of yesteryear. For my part, I think Lennox Lewis is a very good champion, in an era of heavyweight indifference. But, one thing I am certain of, is that it has been a privilege to be a boxing journalist when BRITAIN has, at last, had a HEAVYWEIGHT CHAMPION OF THE WORLD.

In concluding, I should like to thank the many members of "Team Lennox" who have helped me produce this feature article. They are also true champions in their own right, and I am deeply grateful to them for their honesty, patience, and cheerfulness, in responding to my many enquiries.

Diary of British Boxing Tournaments, 1992-93

Tournaments are listed by date, town, venue, and promoter and cover the period 1 July 1992 - 30 June 1993

Code: SC = Sporting Club

Date	Town	Venue	Promoters
02.07.92	Middleton	Civic Hall	Tara Boxing Promotions
07.07.92	Bristol	Brunel Centre	McMahon Promotions
09.07.92	Glasgow	Scottish Exhibition Centre	National Promotions
14.07.92	Mayfair	Grosvenor House	Matchroom
18.07.92	Manchester	Free Trade Hall	Martin/National Promotions
25.07.92	Manchester	G-Mex Centre	Warren
03.09.92	Dunstable	Queensway Hall	National Promotions
03.09.92	Liverpool	Everton Park Sports Centre	Snagg
07.09.92	Bethnal Green	York Hall	National Promotions
08.09.92	Southend	Garon's Suite	Levine
08.09.92	Doncaster	Dome Leisure Centre	Rushton
08.09.92	Norwich	Sports Village	Matchroom
09.09.92	Stoke	King's Hall	Brogan
10.09.92	Sunderland	Crowtree Leisure Centre	St Andrew's SC
11.09.92	Glasgow	Marriott Hotel	Morrison
14.09.92	Bradford	Norfolk Gardens Hotel	Yorkshire Executive SC
15.09.92	Crystal Palace	National Sports Centre	Matchroom/Anglo-Swedish Promotions
15.09.92	Liverpool	Everton Park Sports Centre	National Promotions
17.09.92	Watford	Town Hall	Holland
19.09.92	Glasgow	Scottish Exhibition Centre	Matchroom/St Andrew's SC
21.09.92	Glasgow	Forte Crest Hotel	St Andrew's SC
21.09.92	Cleethorpes	Winter Gardens	Gray
23.09.92	Leeds	Elland Road	National Promotions
24.09.92	Stockport	Town Hall	Trickett
25.09.92	Liverpool	Everton Park Sports Centre	Vaughan
26.09.92	Earls Court	Olympia National Hall	Warren
28.09.92	Manchester	New Century Hall	Martin/National Promotions
29.09.92	Stoke	King's Hall	Brogan
30.09.92	Solihull	Civic Hall	Midlands SC
01.10.92	Telford	Ice Rink	National Promotions
05.10.92	Liverpool	Devonshire House Hotel	Snagg
05.10.92	Northampton	Moat House Hotel	Cox
05.10.92	Bardon	Stardust Nightclub	Griffin
05.10.92	Bristol	Rainbow Cabaret Club	McMahon Promotions
05.10.92	Manchester	Piccadilly Hotel	Trickett
07.10.92	Sunderland	Crowtree Leisure Centre	National Promotions
07.10.92	Barry	Vale of Glamorgan Leisure Centre	Dragon Boxing Promotions
07.10.92	Glasgow	Forte Crest Hotel	St Andrew's SC
12.10.92	Bradford	Norfolk Gardens Hotel	Yorkshire Executive SC
13.10.92	Bury	Castle Leisure Centre	Tara Boxing Promotions
13.10.92	Mayfair	Grosvenor House	Matchroom
13.10.92	Wolverhampton	Park Hall Hotel	Wolverhampton SC
14.10.92	Stoke	Trentham Gardens	North Staffs SC
15.10.92	Lewisham	The Theatre	National Promotions
16.10.92	Hull	The Superbowl	Edwards
17.10.92	Wembley	The Arena	National Promotions
19.10.92	Glasgow	Forte Crest Hotel	St Andrew's SC
19.10.92	Mayfair	Grosvenor House	National Promotions
21.10.92	Stoke	King's Hall	Brogan
22.10.92	Bethnal Green	York Hall	Champion Enterprises
22.10.92	Glasgow	Marriott Hotel	Morrison
23.10.92	Gateshead	Leisure Centre	Conroy

Date	Town	Venue	Promoters
23.10.92	Liverpool	Everton Park Sports Centre	Vaughan
26.10.92	Cleethorpes	Beachcomber Club	Frater
27.10.92	Leicester	Granby Halls	Matchroom
27.10.92	Cradley Heath	Haden Hill Leisure Centre	Cowdell

Albert Hall - 28 October 1992: Game Carlo Colarusso (right) never stopped trying, but was outgunned and stopped by the former world champion, Lloyd Honeyghan, in the sixth   Les Clark

Date	Town	Venue	Promoters
28.10.92	Cardiff	Star Leisure Centre	Aird
28.10.92	Kensington	Albert Hall	National Promotions
29.10.92	Bayswater	Royal Lancaster Hotel	Nordoff/Robins Trust
29.10.92	Hayes	The Stadium	Evans
29.10.92	Leeds	Town Hall	National Promotions
30.10.92	Birmingham	Metropole Hotel	Cowdell
31.10.92	Earls Court	The Arena	Champion Enterprises
02.11.92	Liverpool	Devonshire House Hotel	Snagg
02.11.92	Wolverhampton	Civic Hall	National Promotions
09.11.92	Bradford	Norfolk Gardens Hotel	Yorkshire Executive SC
10.11.92	Dagenham	Goresbrook Leisure Centre	Matchroom
12.11.92	Liverpool	Everton Park Sports Centre	National Promotions
12.11.92	Burnley	William Thompson Centre	Tara Boxing Promotions
12.11.92	Bayswater	King David Suite	Philip Green Memorial Trust
12.11.92	Stafford	Colosseum	Gray
14.11.92	Cardiff	National Ice Rink	Matchroom/Dragon Boxing Promotions
18.11.92	Solihull	Civic Hall	Midlands SC
19.11.92	Evesham	Public Halls	Evesham SC
20.11.92	Liverpool	Everton Park Sports Centre	Vaughan
23.11.92	Glasgow	Forte Crest Hotel	St Andrew's SC
23.11.92	Coventry	Leofric Hotel	Gray
24.11.92	Doncaster	Dome Leisure Centre	Matchroom
24.11.92	Wolverhampton	Park Hall Hotel	Wolverhampton SC
25.11.92	Mayfair	Hilton Hotel	Barrett
26.11.92	Hull	Royal Hotel	Hull & District SC
28.11.92	Manchester	G-Mex Centre	Matchroom
01.12.92	Liverpool	Everton Park Sports Centre	Snagg

MarketPlace	: Ebay
Order Number	: 190962311397-931389033009
Ship Method	: Hermes Tracked
Order Date	: 2014-01-14
Email	: mbut246@yahoo.co.uk

Items : 1

Qty	Item	Locator
1	The British Boxing Board of Control Yearbook	HOL-1-UJ-206-03-15
	ISBN : 1869833813	OD

RCode:

Please note:

Items are dispatched individually. If you have ordered multiple books they will

arrive in separate packages

We hope that you are completely satisfied with your purchase and ask you to leave positive feedback accordingly.

However, if you are unsatisfied with your order, please contact us by telephone or email. We will do whatever it takes to resolve the issue.

Mulberry House, Woods Way, Goring By Sea, West Sussex, BN12 4QY. Tel:+44(0)1903 507544
Email: ebay@worldofbooks.com | Twitter: @WorldofBooksltd | Web: www.worldofbooks.com

Date	Town	Venue	Promoters
01.12.92	Bristol	Rainbow Cabaret Club	McMahon Promotions
01.12.92	Hartlepool	Borough Hall	Robinson
02.12.92	Bardon	Stardust Nightclub	Griffin
03.12.92	Lewisham	The Theatre	National Promotions
04.12.92	Telford	Racquet Centre	National Promotions
07.12.92	Mayfair	Grosvenor House	National Promotions
07.12.92	Manchester	Piccadilly Hotel	Trickett
07.12.92	Birmingham	Grand Hotel	Cowdell
09.12.92	Stoke	King's Hall	Brogan
09.12.92	Stoke	Trentham Gardens	North Staffs SC
10.12.92	Bethnal Green	York Hall	Champion Enterprises
10.12.92	Glasgow	Hospitality Inn	Morrison
10.12.92	Corby	Grampian Club	K. K. Promotions
12.12.92	Muswell Hill	Alexandra Palace	Matchroom
14.12.92	Bradford	Norfolk Gardens Hotel	Yorkshire Executive SC
14.12.92	Cardiff	Star Leisure Centre	Aird
14.12.92	Cleethorpes	Winter Gardens	Gray
14.12.92	Northampton	Glenville's Club	Cox
15.12.92	Liverpool	Ferrari's Nite Spot	Vaughan
17.12.92	Wembley	Grand Hall	National Promotions
17.12.92	Barking	Broadway Theatre	Warren
22.12.92	Mayfair	Grosvenor House	Matchroom
14.01.93	Mayfair	Marriott Hotel	Champion Enterprises
19.01.93	Cardiff	National Sports Centre	Matchroom/Dragon Boxing Promotions
20.01.93	Solihull	Civic Hall	Midlands SC
20.01.93	Wolverhampton	Civic Hall	National Promotions
25.01.93	Bradford	Norfolk Gardens Hotel	Yorkshire Executive SC
25.01.93	Glasgow	Forte Crest Hotel	St Andrew's SC
26.01.93	Leicester	Granby Halls	Matchroom
27.01.93	Cardiff	Star Leisure Centre	Aird
27.01.93	Stoke	Trentham Gardens	North Staffs SC
27.01.93	Stoke	King's Hall	Brogan
28.01.93	Southwark	Elephant & Castle Leisure Centre	National Promotions
29.01.93	Glasgow	Hospitality Inn	Morrison
30.01.93	Brentwood	International Hall	Matchroom
02.02.93	Derby	Ritzy's Nightclub	Shinfield
03.02.93	Earls Court	Olympia National Hall	Warren
05.02.93	Manchester	Free Trade Hall	Martin/National Promotions
06.02.93	Cardiff	National Sports Centre	Matchroom/Dragon Boxing Promotions
09.02.93	Wolverhampton	Park Hall Hotel	Wolverhampton SC
10.02.93	Lewisham	The Theatre	National Promotions
13.02.93	Manchester	Free Trade Hall	Warren
15.02.93	Mayfair	Grosvenor House	National Promotions
15.02.93	Manchester	Piccadilly Hotel	Trickett
16.02.93	Tooting	Leisure Centre	Matchroom/Anglo-Swedish Promotions
17.02.93	Bethnal Green	York Hall	Champion Enterprises
18.02.93	Hull	Willerby Manor	Hull & District SC
20.02.93	Earls Court	Olympia National Hall	Matchroom
22.02.93	Glasgow	Forte Crest Hotel	St Andrew's SC
22.02.93	Eltham	Yorkshire Grey	Champion Enterprises
22.02.93	Birmingham	Grand Hotel	Cowdell
22.02.93	Bedworth	Civic Hall	Griffin
22.02.93	Liverpool	Devonshire House Hotel	Snagg
23.02.93	Kettering	Reflections' Night Club	K. K. Promotions
23.02.93	Doncaster	Dome Leisure Centre	Matchroom
24.02.93	Wembley	Grand Hall	National Promotions
25.02.93	Bradford	St George's Hall	National Promotions
25.02.93	Burnley	William Thompson Centre	Tara Boxing Promotions

York Hall - 17 February 1993: British cruiserweight champion, Carl Thompson (left), added the WBC International title to his collection when knocking out the American, Arthur Weathers, inside two rounds   Les Clark

Date	Town	Venue	Promoters
26.02.93	Irvine	Volunteer Rooms	St Andrew's SC
27.02.93	Dagenham	Goresbrook Leisure Centre	Warren
27.02.93	Ellesmere Port	Epic Centre	Vaughan
01.03.93	Bradford	Norfolk Gardens Hotel	Yorkshire Executive SC
03.03.93	Solihull	Civic Hall	Midlands SC
04.03.93	Glasgow	Hospitality Inn	Morrison
04.03.93	Peterborough	The Arena	K. K. Promotions
06.03.93	Glasgow	Scottish Exhibition Centre	St Andrew's SC
08.03.93	Leeds	Queen's Hotel	Treymaine
09.03.93	Hartlepool	Borough Hall	Robinson/Matchroom
09.03.93	Bristol	Rainbow Cabaret Club	McMahon Promotions
11.03.93	Walsall	Saddler's Club	Gray
16.03.93	Mayfair	Grosvenor House	Matchroom
16.03.93	Edgbaston	Tower Ballroom	Cowdell
16.03.93	Wolverhampton	Civic Hall	National Promotions
17.03.93	Stoke	King's Hall	Brogan
17.03.93	Stoke	Trentham Gardens	North Staffs SC
18.03.93	Lewisham	The Theatre	National Promotions
19.03.93	Manchester	Free Trade Hall	Martin
23.03.93	Wolverhampton	Park Hall Hotel	Wolverhampton SC
24.03.93	Belfast	Ulster Hall	McMahon Promotions
24.03.93	Cardiff	Star Leisure Centre	Aird
26.03.93	Glasgow	Hospitality Inn	Morrison
29.03.93	Glasgow	Forte Crest Hotel	St Andrew's SC
29.03.93	Liverpool	Devonshire House Hotel	Snagg
29.03.93	Mayfair	Marriott Hotel	National Promotions
30.03.93	Cardiff	National Sports Centre	Matchroom/Dragon Boxing Promotions
31.03.93	Barking	Broadway Theatre	Warren
31.03.93	Bethnal Green	York Hall	Champion Enterprises
01.04.93	Evesham	Public Halls	Evesham SC
04.04.93	Brockley	Crofton Park Leisure Centre	Champion Enterprises
07.04.93	Leeds	Town Hall	National Promotions
10.04.93	Swansea	Dillwyn Llewelyn Leisure Centre	Warren
14.04.93	Kensington	Albert Hall	Champion Enterprises

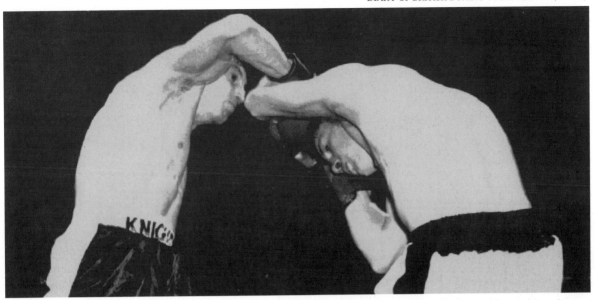

International Hall - 20 April 1993: The unbeaten Paul Knights (left) made it seven out of seven with a points win over Welshman, Phil Found
Les Clark

Date	Town	Venue	Promoters
17.04.93	Washington	Northumbria Leisure Centre	Matchroom/St Andrew's SC
19.04.93	Northampton	Moat House Hotel	Cox
19.04.93	Manchester	Piccadilly Hotel	Trickett
20.04.93	Brentwood	International Hall	Matchroom
22.04.93	Mayfair	Grosvenor House	National Promotions
22.04.93	Bury	Castle Leisure Centre	Tara Boxing Promotions
24.04.93	Birmingham	National Exhibition Centre	National Promotions
26.04.93	Manchester	New Century Hall	Martin
26.04.93	Glasgow	Forte Crest Hotel	St Andrew's SC
26.04.93	Lewisham	The Theatre	National Promotions
26.04.93	Bradford	Norfolk Gardens Hotel	Yorkshire Executive SC
26.04.93	Cleethorpes	Beachcomber Club	Frater
28.04.93	Solihull	Civic Hall	Midlands SC
29.04.93	Newcastle	Mayfair Ballroom	Fawcett
29.04.93	Mayfair	Hilton Hotel	National Promotions
29.04.93	Hayes	Stadium Leisure Centre	Evans
29.04.93	Hull	Royal Hotel	Hull & District SC
30.04.93	Glasgow	Hospitality Inn	Morrison
04.05.93	Liverpool	Ferrari's Nite Spot	Vaughan
05.05.93	Belfast	Ulster Hall	Eastwood Promotions
06.05.93	Hartlepool	Borough Hall	Robinson
06.05.93	Bayswater	Royal Lancaster Hotel	Motability Trust
06.05.93	Walsall	Saddler's Club	Gray
10.05.93	Cleethorpes	Winter Gardens	Gray
11.05.93	Norwich	Sports Village	Matchroom
12.05.93	Sheffield	Octagon Centre	Hobson
12.05.93	Stoke	Moat House Hotel	Brogan
14.05.93	Kilmarnock	Grand Hall	Morrison
15.05.93	Glasgow	Scottish Exhibition Centre	Matchroom/St Andrew's SC
18.05.93	Edgbaston	Tower Ballroom	Cowdell
18.05.93	Kettering	Reflection's Night Club	K. K. Promotions
19.05.93	Leicester	Granby Halls	Matchroom
19.05.93	Sunderland	Crowtree Leisure Centre	National Promotions
23.05.93	Brockley	Crofton Park Leisure Centre	Champion Enterprises

Date	Town	Venue	Promoters
24.05.93	Bradford	Norfolk Gardens Hotel	Yorkshire Executive SC
26.05.93	Mansfield	Leisure Centre	National Promotions
27.05.93	Bristol	Whitchurch Sports Centre	McMahon Promotions
27.05.93	Burnley	William Thompson Centre	Tara Boxing Promotions
28.05.93	Middleton	Civic Hall	Martin
29.05.93	Paisley	Ice Rink	Morrison
01.06.93	Manchester	New Century Hall	Mens' Aid Committee
07.06.93	Walsall	Town Hall	Cowdell
07.06.93	Glasgow	Forte Crest Hotel	St Andrew's SC
08.06.93	Derby	Pink Coconut Club	Shinfield
09.06.93	Lewisham	The Theatre	National Promotions
09.06.93	Liverpool	Devonshire House Hotel	Snagg
11.06.93	Gateshead	Leisure Centre	Conroy
14.06.93	Bayswater	Royal Lancaster Hotel	National Promotions
15.06.93	Hemel Hempstead	Dacorum Pavilion	National Promotions
17.06.93	Bedworth	Civic Hall	Griffin
18.06.93	Belfast	Maysfield Leisure Centre	McMahon Promotions
21.06.93	Swindon	Supermarine Sports Complex	Burrows
23.06.93	Edmonton	Picketts Lock Leisure Centre	Champion Enterprises
23.06.93	Gorleston	Ocean Rooms	Brogan
24.06.93	Watford	Leisure Centre	Holdsworth
25.06.93	Battersea	Town Hall	Gee
26.06.93	Earls Court	Olympia National Hall	Matchroom
26.06.93	Keynsham	Keynsham R.F.C.	McMahon Promotions
28.06.93	Morecambe	Carlton Club	Tara Boxing Promotions
29.06.93	Mayfair	Grosvenor House	Matchroom
29.06.93	Edgbaston	Tower Ballroom	Cowdell

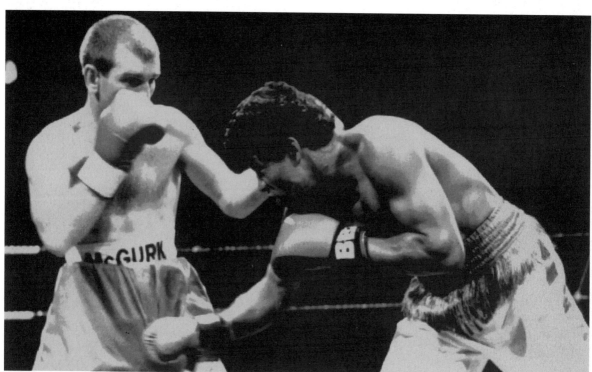

Dacorum Pavilion - 15 June 1993: the Commonwealth featherweight champion, Billy Hardy (left), had a tough workout before running out clear points winner over the late substitute from Mexico, Angel Fernandez

Les Clark

Current British-Based Champions: Career Records

Shows the complete record of all British champions, or British boxers holding international championships, who have been active between 1 July 1992 and 30 June 1993. Names in brackets are real names, where they differ from ring names. The first place name given is the boxer's domicile. Boxers are either shown as self managed, or with a named manager. This information has been supplied by the BBBoC and is in accordance with their records at the time of going to press. These records also include Derek Angol, who relinquished his British and Commonwealth cruiserweight titles during the above period.

Henry Akinwande

Lewisham. *Born* London, 12 October, 1965
European & Commonwealth Heavyweight
Champion. Ht. 6'7"
Manager M. Duff

04.10.89	Carlton Headley W CO 1 Kensington
08.11.89	Dennis Bailey W RSC 2 Wembley
06.12.89	Paul Neilson W RSC 1 Wembley
10.01.90	John Fairbairn W RSC 1 Kensington
14.03.90	Warren Thompson W PTS 6
	Kensington
09.05.90	Mike Robinson W CO 1 Wembley
10.10.90	Tracy Thomas W PTS 6 Kensington
12.12.90	Francois Yrius W RSC 1 Kensington
06.03.91	J. B. Williamson W RSC 2 Wembley
06.06.91	Ramon Voorn W PTS 8 Barking
28.06.91	Marshall Tillman W PTS 8 Nice, France
09.10.91	Gypsy John Fury W CO 3 Manchester *(Elim. British Heavyweight Title)*
06.12.91	Tim Bullock W CO 3 Dussledorf, Germany
28.02.92	Young Joe Louis W RSC 3 Issy les Moulineaux, France
26.03.92	Tucker Richards W RSC 2 Telford
10.04.92	Lumbala Tshimba W PTS 8 Carquefou, France
05.05.92	Kimmuel Odum W DIS 6 Marseille, France
18.07.92	Steve Garber W RTD 2 Manchester
19.12.92	Axel Schulz DREW 12 Berlin, Germany *(Vacant European Heavyweight Title)*
18.03.93	Jimmy Thunder W PTS 12 Lewisham *(Vacant Commonwealth Heavyweight Title)*
01.05.93	Axel Schulz W PTS 12 Berlin, Germany *(Vacant European Heavyweight Title)*

Career: 21 contests, won 20, drew 1.

Henry Akinwande   Les Clark

Francis Ampofo

Bethnal Green. *Born* Ghana, 5 June, 1967
British & Commonwealth Flyweight
Champion. Ht. 5'1½"
Manager B. Hearn

30.01.90	Neil Parry W PTS 6 Bethnal Green
06.03.90	Robbie Regan L PTS 6 Bethnal Green
29.05.90	Eric George W RSC 3 Bethnal Green
12.09.90	Eric George W CO 2 Bethnal Green
26.03.91	Ricky Beard W PTS 8 Bethnal Green
22.06.91	Neil Johnston W RSC 2 Earls Court
03.09.91	Robbie Regan W RSC 11 Cardiff *(British Flyweight Title Challenge)*

Francis Ampofo (left) storms into Welshman Robbie Regan on his way to the British flyweight title   Les Clark

53

17.12.91 Robbie Regan L PTS 12 Cardiff
(British Flyweight Title Defence)
25.02.92 Ricky Beard W PTS 8 Crystal Palace
16.06.92 Shaun Norman RSC 4 Dagenham
12.12.92 James Drummond W PTS 12 Mayfair
(Vacant British Flyweight Title)
17.02.93 Alberto Cantu W RSC 5 Bethnal Green
29.06.93 Albert Musankabala W RSC 3 Mayfair
*(Vacant Commonwealth Flyweight
·Title)*

Career: 13 contests, won 11, lost 2.

Derek Angol

Camberwell. *Born* London, 28 November,
1964
Former Undefeated British &
Commonwealth Cruiserweight Champion.
Ht. 6'3½"
Manager T. Lawless

15.12.86 Gus Mendes W RSC 3 Mayfair
22.01.87 Abner Blackstock W PTS 6 Bethnal
Green
12.03.87 Patrick Collins W CO 6 Piccadilly
09.04.87 Mick Cordon W RSC 4 Bethnal Green
08.10.87 Lennie Howard W RSC 5 Bethnal
Green
15.02.88 Abner Blackstock W RSC 6 Mayfair
14.03.88 Alek Penarski W CO 2 Mayfair
13.04.88 Jonjo Greene W PTS 6 Bethnal Green
05.05.88 Cordwell Hylton W RSC 5 Wembley
17.10.88 Roy Smith W RSC 1 Mayfair

Derek Angol   Les Clark

19.12.88 Jack Johnson W CO 1 Mayfair
18.01.89 Rick Enis W RSC 3 Kensington
08.03.89 Jamie Howe W PTS 8 Kensington
29.03.89 Teo Arvizu W RSC 3 Wembley
07.06.89 Andre Crowder W RSC 3 Wembley
04.10.89 Raymond Gonzalez W RSC 2
Kensington

30.11.89 Apollo Sweet W PTS 12 Southwark
*(Commonwealth Cruiserweight Title
Challenge)*
08.02.90 Eddie Smith W RSC 2 Southwark
14.03.90 Andy Straughn W CO 8 Kensington
*(Commonwealth Cruiserweight Title
Defence)*
04.10.90 Manfred Jassman W RSC 8 Bethnal
Green
10.01.91 Dan Murphy W RSC 9 Wandsworth
13.02.91 Dave Garside W RSC 2 Wembley
*(Vacant British Cruiserweight Title &
Commonwealth Cruiserweight Title
Defence)*
17.04.91 Yves Monsieur W RSC 2 Kensington
08.05.91 Tee Jay W RSC 3 Kensington
*(British & Commonwealth
Cruiserweight Title Defence)*
17.10.91 Dave Russell W RSC 4 Southwark
*(Commonwealth Cruiserweight Title
Defence)*
16.05.92 Robert Clevenger W CO 2 Muswell
Hill
25.07.92 Tyrone Booze L CO 7 Manchester
(Vacant WBO Cruiserweight Title)
22.10.92 Akim Tafer L RSC 10 Epernay, France
*(European Cruiserweight Title
Challenge)*
24.02.93 Steve Yorath W RSC 5 Wembley
22.06.93 Massimiliano Duran L CO 11 Ferrara,
Italy
(Vacant European Cruiserweight Title)

Career: 30 contests, won 27, lost 3.

Nigel Benn (right) seen in action hammering Iran Barkley to a first round defeat in August 1990   Chris Farina

John Armour   Les Clark

John Armour

Chatham. *Born* Chatham, 26 October, 1968
Commonwealth Bantamweight Champion.
Ht. 5'4¾"
Manager M. Duff

24.09.90	Lupe Castro W PTS 6 Lewisham
31.10.90	Juan Camero W RSC 4 Crystal Palace
21.01.91	Elijro Mejia W RSC 1 Crystal Palace
30.09.91	Pat Maher W CO 1 Kensington
29.10.91	Pete Buckley W PTS 6 Kensington
14.12.91	Gary Hickman W RSC 6 Bexleyheath
25.03.92	Miguel Matthews W PTS 6 Dagenham
30.04.92	Ndabe Dube W RSC 12 Kensington
	(Vacant Commonwealth Bantamweight Title)
17.10.92	Mauricio Bernal W PTS 8 Wembley
03.12.92	Albert Musankabala W RSC 6 Lewisham
	(Commonwealth Bantamweight Title Defence)
28.01.93	Ricky Romero W CO 1 Southwark
10.02.93	Morgan Mpande W PTS 12 Lewisham
	(Commonwealth Bantamweight Title Defence)
09.06.93	Boualem Belkif W PTS 10 Lewisham

Career: 13 contests, won 13.

Nigel Benn

Ilford. *Born* Ilford, 22 January, 1964
WBC S. Middleweight Champion. Former
WBO & Commonwealth Middleweight
Champion. Ht. 5'9½"
Manager Self

28.01.87	Graeme Ahmed W RSC 2 Croydon
04.03.87	Kevin Roper W RSC 1 Basildon
22.04.87	Bob Niewenhuizen W RSC 1 Kensington
09.05.87	Winston Burnett W RSC 4 Wandsworth
17.06.87	Reggie Marks W RSC 1 Kensington
01.07.87	Leon Morris W CO 1 Kensington
09.08.87	Eddie Smith W CO 1 Windsor
16.09.87	Winston Burnett W RSC 3 Kensington
13.10.87	Russell Barker W RSC 1 Windsor
03.11.87	Ronnie Yeo W RSC 1 Bethnal Green
24.11.87	Ian Chantler W CO 1 Wisbech
02.12.87	Reggie Miller W CO 7 Kensington
27.01.88	Fermin Chirinos W CO 2 Bethnal Green
07.02.88	Byron Prince W RSC 2 Stafford
24.02.88	Greg Taylor W RSC 2 Aberavon
14.03.88	Darren Hobson W CO 1 Norwich
20.04.88	Abdul Amoru Sanda W RSC 2 Muswell Hill
	(Vacant Commonwealth Middleweight Title)
28.05.88	Tim Williams W RSC 2 Kensington
26.10.88	Anthony Logan W CO 2 Kensington
	(Commonwealth Middleweight Title Defence)
10.12.88	David Noel W RSC 1 Crystal Palace
	(Commonwealth Middleweight Title Defence)
08.02.89	Mike Chilambe W CO 1 Kensington
	(Commonwealth Middleweight Title Defence)
28.03.89	Mbayo Wa Mbayo W CO 2 Glasgow
21.05.89	Michael Watson L CO 6 Finsbury Park
	(Commonwealth Middleweight Title Defence)
20.10.89	Jorge Amparo W PTS 10 Atlantic City, USA
01.12.89	Jose Quinones W RSC 1 Las Vegas, USA
14.01.90	Sanderline Williams W PTS 10 Atlantic City, USA
29.04.90	Doug de Witt W RSC 8 Atlantic City, USA
	(WBO Middleweight Title Challenge)
18.08.90	Iran Barkley W RSC 1 Las Vegas, USA
	(WBO Middleweight Title Defence)
18.11.90	Chris Eubank L RSC 9 Birmingham
	(WBO Middleweight Title Defence)
03.04.91	Robbie Sims W RSC 7 Bethnal Green
03.07.91	Kid Milo W RSC 4 Brentwood
26.10.91	Lenzie Morgan W PTS 10 Brentwood
07.12.91	Hector Lescano W CO 3 Manchester
19.02.92	Dan Sherry W RSC 3 Muswell Hill
23.05.92	Thulani Malinga W PTS 10 Birmingham
03.10.92	Mauro Galvano W RTD 3 Marino, Italy
	(WBC S. Middleweight Title Challenge)
12.12.92	Nicky Piper W RSC 11 Muswell Hill
	(WBC S. Middleweight Title Defence)
06.03.93	Mauro Galvano W PTS 12 Glasgow
	(WBC S. Middleweight Title Defence)
26.06.93	Lou Gent W RSC 4 Earls Court
	(WBC S. Middleweight Title Defence)

Career: 39 contests, won 37, lost 2.

Paul Burke

Preston. *Born* Preston, 25 July, 1966
British & Commonwealth Lightweight
Champion. Ht. 5'10"
Manager P. Martin

21.01.87	Steve Brown W CO 4 Stoke
30.01.87	Paul Marriott L PTS 6 Kirkby
02.03.87	Paul Marriott W PTS 6 Marton
06.04.87	Paul Marriott W PTS 6 Newcastle
30.04.87	Paul Gadney W PTS 6 Bethnal Green
01.06.87	Pat Barrett W PTS 6 Bradford

Paul Burke   Harry Goodwin

15.09.87 Marvin P. Gray L RSC 6 Batley
18.11.87 Rudy Valentino W PTS 6 Bethnal Green
15.12.87 James Jiora L PTS 4 Bradford
11.02.88 Paul Gadney DREW 8 Gravesend
25.01.89 Paul Charters W PTS 6 Bethnal Green
23.02.89 Mark Kelly L DIS 5 Stockport
07.03.89 Tony Connellan W RSC 5 Manchester
11.04.89 Billy Buchanan W RSC 4 Oldham
21.10.89 Aaron Kabi DREW 8 Middlesbrough
09.12.89 Angel Mona L RSC 3 Toulouse, France
23.04.90 Tony Richards L PTS 10 Glasgow
(Elim. British Lightweight Title)
25.09.90 Robert Harkin W PTS 8 Glasgow
21.01.91 Peter Bradley W PTS 10 Glasgow
(Elim. British Lightweight Title)
31.05.91 Art Blackmore W RSC 3 Manchester
20.09.91 Tony Richards W PTS 8 Manchester
09.02.92 Dave Andrews W PTS 6 Bradford

28.04.92 Paul Charters W RSC 7 Houghton le Spring
(Final Elim. British Lightweight Title)
28.09.92 Marcel Herbert W PTS 6 Manchester
17.11.92 Jean-Baptiste Mendy L PTS 12 Paris, France
(European Lightweight Title Challenge)
24.02.93 Billy Schwer W RSC 7 Wembley
(British & Commonwealth Lightweight Title Challenge)

Career: 26 contests, won 17, drew 2, lost 7.

Ray Close

Belfast. *Born* Belfast, 20 January, 1969
European & All-Ireland S. Middleweight Champion. Ht. 5'10"
Manager B. Eastwood

19.10.88 Steve Foster W RSC 2 Belfast

14.12.88 Kevin Roper W PTS 4 Kirkby
25.01.89 B. K. Bennett W RSC 3 Belfast
08.03.89 Andy Wright W RSC 4 Belfast
12.04.89 Dennis White W RSC 2 Belfast
19.09.89 Gary Pemberton W PTS 6 Belfast
31.10.89 Rocky McGran W RSC 7 Belfast
(Vacant All-Ireland S. Middleweight Title)
29.11.89 Shamus Casey W CO 2 Belfast
13.12.89 Denys Cronin L PTS 6 Kirkby
21.02.90 Frank Eubanks W PTS 8 Belfast
17.03.90 Denys Cronin W PTS 8 Belfast
23.05.90 Rocky McGran W RTD 1 Belfast
15.09.90 Ray Webb W PTS 8 Belfast
11.05.91 Carlos Christie W PTS 6 Belfast
07.09.91 Carlos Christie W PTS 6 Belfast
13.11.91 Simon Collins W PTS 6 Belfast
11.12.91 Terry Magee W RSC 7 Dublin
(All-Ireland S. Middleweight Title Defence)
25.04.92 Ian Chantler W RSC 1 Belfast
03.07.92 Franck Nicotra L RSC 8 Pontault Combault, France
(European S. Middleweight Title Challenge)
18.12.92 Jean-Roger Tsidjo W PTS 8 Clermont Ferra, France
17.03.93 Vincenzo Nardiello W PTS 12 Campione d'Italia, Italy
(European S. Middleweight Title Challenge)
15.05.93 Chris Eubank DREW 12 Glasgow
(WBO S. Middleweight Title Challenge)

Career: 22 contests, won 19, drew 1, lost 2.

Maurice Coore   Harry Goodwin

Maurice Coore

Manchester. *Born* Manchester, 22 June, 1965
British L. Heavyweight Champion. Ht. 6'5"
Manager P. Martin

15.01.90 Dennis Banton W PTS 6 Mayfair
03.05.90 Everton Blake W PTS 8 Kensington
22.05.90 Nicky Piper DREW 6 St Albans
22.02.91 Everton Blake W RSC 8 Manchester

Ray Close

12.04.91 Glazz Campbell W CO 2 Manchester
31.05.91 Rodney Brown W RSC 6 Manchester
29.11.91 Steve Osborne W PTS 6 Manchester
31.01.92 Denroy Bryan W RSC 1 Manchester
05.04.92 Willie Ball W RSC 3 Bradford
18.07.92 Tony Booth W PTS 6 Manchester
28.09.92 Noel Magee W RSC 9 Manchester
         (Vacant British L. Heavyweight Title)
05.02.93 Larry Prather W PTS 10 Manchester
Career: 12 contests, won 11, drew 1.

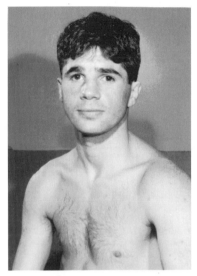

Drew Docherty   George Ashton

(Andrew) Drew Docherty

Croy. *Born* Glasgow, 29 November, 1965
British Bantamweight Champion. Ht. 5'6"
Manager T. Gilmour

14.09.89 Gordon Shaw W PTS 6 Motherwell
23.11.89 Chris Clarkson W PTS 6 Motherwell
09.05.90 Rocky Lawlor DREW 8 Solihull
03.10.90 Steve Robinson W PTS 8 Solihull
21.11.90 Pete Buckley W PTS 8 Solihull
14.11.91 Stevie Woods W RSC 1 Edinburgh
27.01.92 Neil Parry W RSC 4 Glasgow
27.04.92 Pete Buckley W PTS 8 Glasgow
01.06.92 Joe Kelly W RSC 5 Glasgow
         (British Bantamweight Title Challenge)
25.01.93 Donnie Hood W PTS 12 Glasgow
         (British Bantamweight Title Defence)
26.04.93 Russell Davison W PTS 8 Glasgow
Career: 11 contests, won 10, drew 1.

Chris Eubank

Brighton. *Born* Dulwich, 8 August, 1966
WBO S. Middleweight Champion. Former
Undefeated WBO Middleweight
Champion. Former Undefeated WBC
International Middleweight Champion. Ht.
5'10"
Manager B. Hearn

03.10.85 Tim Brown W PTS 4 Atlantic City, USA
07.11.85 Kenny Cannida W PTS 4 Atlantic City, USA
08.01.86 Mike Bragwell W PTS 4 Atlantic City, USA

Chris Eubank   Chris Bevan

25.02.86 Eric Holland W PTS 4 Atlantic City, USA
25.03.87 James Canty W PTS 4 Atlantic City, USA
15.02.88 Darren Parker W RSC 1 Copthorne
07.03.88 Winston Burnett W PTS 6 Hove
26.04.88 Michael Justin W RSC 5 Hove
04.05.88 Greg George W RSC 5 Wembley
18.05.88 Steve Aquilina W RSC 4 Portsmouth
31.01.89 Simon Collins W RSC 4 Bethnal Green
08.02.89 Anthony Logan W PTS 8 Kensington
01.03.89 Franki Moro W PTS 8 Bethnal Green
26.05.89 Randy Smith W PTS 10 Bethnal Green
28.06.89 Les Wisniewski W RSC 2 Brentwood
04.10.89 Ron Malek W RSC 5 Basildon
24.10.89 Jean-Noel Camara W RSC 2 Bethnal Green
05.11.89 Johnny Melfah W CO 4 Kensington
20.12.89 Jose da Silva W RTD 6 Kirkby
16.01.90 Denys Cronin W RSC 3 Cardiff
06.03.90 Hugo Corti W RSC 8 Bethnal Green
         (WBC International Middleweight Title Challenge)

25.04.90 Eduardo Contreras W PTS 12 Brighton
         (WBC International Middleweight Title Defence)
05.09.90 Kid Milo W RSC 8 Brighton
         (WBC International Middleweight Title Defence)
22.09.90 Reginaldo Santos W CO 1 Kensington
18.11.90 Nigel Benn W RSC 9 Birmingham
         (WBO Middleweight Title Challenge)
23.02.91 Dan Sherry W TD 10 Brighton
         (WBO Middleweight Title Defence)
18.04.91 Gary Stretch W RSC 6 Earls Court
         (WBO Middleweight Title Defence)
22.06.91 Michael Watson W PTS 12 Earls Court
         (WBO Middleweight Title Defence)
21.09.91 Michael Watson W RSC 12 Tottenham
         (Vacant WBO S. Middleweight Title)
01.02.92 Thulani Malinga W PTS 12 Birmingham
         (WBO S. Middleweight Title Defence)
25.04.92 John Jarvis W CO 3 Manchester
         (WBO S. Middleweight Title Defence)

57

27.06.92 Ronnie Essett W PTS 12 Quinta do
Lago, Portugal
(WBO S. Middleweight Title Defence)
19.09.92 Tony Thornton W PTS 12 Glasgow
(WBO S. Middleweight Title Defence)
28.11.92 Juan Carlos Giminez W PTS 12
Manchester
(WBO S. Middleweight Title Defence)
20.02.93 Lindell Holmes W PTS 12 Earls Court
(WBO S. Middleweight Title Defence)
15.05.93 Ray Close DREW 12 Glasgow
(WBO S. Middleweight Title Defence)

Career: 36 contests, won 35. drew 1.

Frank Grant   Harry Goodwin

Frank Grant

Bradford. *Born* Bradford, 22 May, 1965
British Middleweight Champion. Ht. 5'11"
Manager P. Martin

20.10.86 Lincoln Pennant L RSC 1 Bradford
01.06.87 Steve Ward W RSC 3 Bradford
10.09.87 Tony Lawrence W RSC 3
Peterborough
16.10.87 Mick Maw W PTS 6 Gateshead
29.02.88 Steve Kofi W RSC 3 Bradford
11.03.88 Gerry Richards W RSC 3 Cottingham
28.03.88 Dave Thomas W PTS 6 Bradford
24.10.88 Shaun Cummins W RTD 7
Northampton
12.12.88 Franki Moro W CO 6 Bradford
16.01.89 Mark Howell W RSC 1 Bradford
20.02.89 Franki Moro L PTS 6 Bradford
24.04.89 Peter Sorby W RSC 1 Bradford
22.05.89 Neil Munn W RSC 3 Bradford
09.11.89 Simon Collins W RTD 6 Cardiff
11.12.89 Steve Aquilina W RSC 4 Bradford
21.03.90 Kid Milo L PTS 10 Solihull
(Elim. British S. Middleweight Title)
12.04.91 Alan Richards W RSC 5 Manchester
31.05.91 Tim Dendy W PTS 8 Manchester
20.09.91 Conrad Oscar W CO 2 Manchester
29.11.91 Winston Wray W RSC 3 Manchester
09.02.92 Willie Ball W PTS 6 Bradford
05.04.92 Sammy Matos W CO 1 Bradford

23.09.92 Herol Graham W RSC 9 Leeds
(British Middleweight Title Challenge)
25.02.93 John Ashton W RTD 7 Bradford
(British Middleweight Title Defence)

Career: 24 contests, won 21, lost 3.

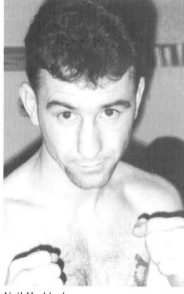

Neil Haddock   Les Clark

Neil Haddock

Llanelli. *Born* Newport, 22 June, 1964
British S. Featherweight Champion. Former
Undefeated Welsh S. Featherweight
Champion. Ht. 5'6"
Manager G. Davies

16.02.87 Mark Purcell L PTS 6 Gloucester
19.03.87 Rudy Valentino L PTS 6 Bethnal
Green
01.04.87 Gary Cass W PTS 6 Southsea
30.04.87 Carl Merrett W PTS 6 Newport
26.05.87 Joey Jacobs L PTS 8 Oldham
01.10.87 Lee Amass W RSC 4 Croydon
08.12.87 Mike Russell W PTS 8 Plymouth
17.02.88 B. F. Williams L PTS 8 Bethnal Green
24.02.88 Peter Till L PTS 8 Aberavon
08.03.88 Andrew Furlong L PTS 6 Holborn
30.03.88 Richard Adams W PTS 6 Bethnal
Green
11.04.88 Mike Durvan L RSC 4 Mayfair
01.12.88 Michael Driscoll DREW 6 Gravesend
22.03.89 Lee Amass W RSC 5 Sheppey
18.09.90 Ditau Molefyane L RTD 5
Wolverhampton
18.10.90 Mark Ramsey W RSC 5 Birmingham
19.11.90 Steve Robinson L RSC 9 Cardiff
20.11.91 Barrie Kelley W PTS 6 Cardiff
17.12.91 Andy Deabreu W RSC 3 Cardiff
11.05.92 Steve Robinson W PTS 10 Llanelli
(Vacant Welsh S. Featherweight Title)
13.10.92 Michael Armstrong W RSC 6 Bury
*(British S. Featherweight Title
Challenge)*
01.12.92 Harry Escott W PTS 10 Liverpool

Career: 22 contests, won 12, drew 1, lost 9.

Billy Hardy   Les Clark

Billy Hardy

Sunderland. *Born* Sunderland, 15
September, 1964
Commonwealth Featherweight Champion.
Former Undefeated British Bantamweight
Champion. Ht. 5'6"
Manager D. Mancini

21.11.83 Kevin Downer W PTS 6 Eltham
03.12.83 Brett Styles W PTS 6 Marylebone
27.01.84 Keith Ward W PTS 6 Longford
13.02.84 Johnny Mack W RSC 6 Eltham
01.03.84 Graham Kid Clarke W PTS 8
Queensway
27.03.84 Glen McLaggon W PTS 6 Battersea
06.04.84 Graham Kid Clarke W RSC 7 Watford
25.04.84 Anthony Brown W RSC 5 Muswell
Hill
04.06.84 Roy Webb L PTS 6 Mayfair
06.09.84 Les Walsh W PTS 6 Gateshead
10.10.84 Jorge Prentas L RSC 5 Shoreditch
12.02.85 Ivor Jones W PTS 8 Kensington
17.04.85 Ivor Jones W PTS 10 Bethnal Green
08.06.85 Valerio Nati L RSC 4 Florence, Italy
10.10.85 Keith Wallace W RSC 7 Alfreton
*(Final Elim. British Bantamweight
Title)*
02.06.86 Rocky Lawlor W PTS 8 Mayfair
19.02.87 Ray Gilbody W RSC 3 St Helens
(British Bantamweight Title Challenge)
23.04.87 Rocky Lawlor W RSC 7 Newcastle
04.06.87 Brian Holmes W PTS 10 Sunderland
17.03.88 John Hyland W CO 2 Sunderland
(British Bantamweight Title Defence)
11.05.88 Luis Ramos W RSC 2 Wembley
29.09.88 Jose Gallegos W RSC 4 Sunderland
02.11.88 Vincenzo Belcastro L PTS 12 Paolo,
Italy
*(European Bantamweight Title
Challenge)*
14.02.89 Ronnie Carroll W PTS 12 Sunderland
(British Bantamweight Title Defence)
29.03.89 Jose Soto W PTS 8 Wembley
28.06.89 Vincenzo Belcastro DREW 12 Pavia,
Italy

Herbie Hide (right) looks to open the awkward Jean Chanet's defences during their September 1992 clash at Norwich

Les Clark

(European Bantamweight Title Challenge)
10.10.89 Brian Holmes W CO 1 Sunderland
(British Bantamweight Title Defence)
24.01.90 Orlando Canizales L PTS 12 Sunderland
(IBF Bantamweight Title Challenge)
22.05.90 Miguel Pequeno W RSC 4 Stockton
29.11.90 Ronnie Carroll W RSC 8 Sunderland
(British Bantamweight Title Defence)
28.02.91 Francisco Ortiz W RSC 7 Sunderland
04.05.91 Orlando Canizales L RSC 8 Laredo, USA
(IBF Bantamweight Title Challenge)
03.03.92 Chris Clarkson W RSC 5 Houghton le Spring
07.10.92 Ricky Raynor W RSC 10 Sunderland
(Vacant Commonwealth Featherweight Title)
19.05.93 Barrington Francis W PTS 12 Sunderland
(Commonwealth Featherweight Title Defence)
15.06.93 Angel Fernandez W PTS 10 Hemel Hempstead

Career: 36 contests, won 29, drew 1, lost 6.

Herbie Hide

Norwich. *Born* Nigeria, 27 August, 1971
British, WBC International & WBA Penta-Continental Heavyweight Champion. Ht. 6'1½"

Manager B. Hearn

24.10.89 L. A. Williams W CO 2 Bethnal Green
05.11.89 Gary McCrory W RTD 1 Kensington
19.12.89 Steve Osborne W RSC 6 Bethnal Green
27.06.90 Alek Penarski W RSC 3 Kensington
05.09.90 Steve Lewsam W RSC 4 Brighton
26.09.90 Jonjo Greene W RSC 1 Manchester
17.10.90 Gus Mendes W RSC 2 Bethnal Green
18.11.90 Steve Lewsam W RSC 1 Birmingham
29.01.91 Lennie Howard W RSC 1 Wisbech
09.04.91 David Jules W RSC 1 Mayfair
14.05.91 John Westgarth W RTD 4 Dudley
03.07.91 Tucker Richards W RSC 3 Brentwood
15.10.91 Eddie Gonzalez W CO 2 Hamburg, Germany
29.10.91 Chris Jacobs W RSC 1 Cardiff
21.01.92 Conroy Nelson W RSC 2 Norwich
(Vacant WBC International Heavyweight Title)
03.03.92 Percell Davis W CO 1 Amsterdam, Holland
08.09.92 Jean Chanet W RSC 7 Norwich
06.10.92 Craig Peterson W RSC 7 Antwerp, Belgium
(WBC International Heavyweight Title Defence)
12.12.92 James Pritchard W RSC 2 Muswell Hill
30.01.93 Juan Antonio Diaz W RSC 3 Brentwood
(Vacant WBA Penta-Continental Heavyweight Title)

27.02.93 Michael Murray W RSC 5 Dagenham
(Vacant British Heavyweight Title)
11.05.93 Jerry Halstead W RSC 4 Norwich
(Penta-Continental Heavyweight Title Defence)

Career: 22 contests, won 22.

Andy Holligan

Liverpool. *Born* Liverpool, 6 June, 1967
British & Commonwealth L. Welterweight Champion. Ht. 5'5¾"

Manager M. Duff

19.10.87 Glyn Rhodes W PTS 6 Belfast
03.12.87 Jimmy Thornton W RTD 2 Belfast
27.01.88 Andrew Morgan W RSC 5 Belfast
26.03.88 Tony Richards W RSC 2 Belfast
08.06.88 David Maw W RSC 1 Sheffield
19.10.88 Lenny Gloster W PTS 8 Belfast
14.12.88 Sugar Gibiliru W PTS 8 Kirkby
16.03.89 Jeff Connors W RSC 5 Southwark
19.09.89 Billy Buchanan W RSC 5 Belfast
25.10.89 Tony Adams W RSC 3 Wembley
26.09.90 Mike Durvan W CO 1 Mayfair
31.10.90 Eric Carroyez W RTD 2 Wembley
17.04.91 Pat Ireland W RSC 2 Kensington
16.05.91 Simon Eubank W RSC 2 Liverpool
20.06.91 Tony Ekubia W PTS 12 Liverpool
(British & Commonwealth L. Welterweight Title Challenge)
28.11.91 Steve Larrimore W RSC 8 Liverpool
(Commonwealth L. Welterweight Title Defence)

59

Lloyd Honeyghan

Andy Holligan   Chris Bevan

27.02.92	Tony McKenzie W RSC 3 Liverpool
	(British & Commonwealth L.
	Welterweight Title Defence)
15.09.92	Tony Ekubia W CO 7 Liverpool
	(British & Commonwealth L.
	Welterweight Title Defence)
07.10.92	Dwayne Swift W PTS 10 Sunderland
12.11.92	Mark Smith W PTS 10 Liverpool
26.05.93	Lorenzo Garcia W RSC 2 Mansfield

Career: 21 contests, won 21.

Lloyd Honeyghan

Bermondsey. *Born* Jamaica, 22 April, 1960
Commonwealth L. Middleweight
Champion. Former WBC Welterweight
Champion. Former Undefeated WBA, IBF,
British, European, Commonwealth &
Southern Area Welterweight Champion. Ht.
5'8½"
Manager Self

08.12.80	Mike Sullivan W PTS 6 Kensington
20.01.81	Dai Davies W RSC 5 Bethnal Green
10.02.81	Dave Sullivan W PTS 6 Bethnal Green
16.11.81	Dave Finigan W RSC 1 Mayfair
24.11.81	Alan Cooper W RSC 4 Wembley
25.01.82	Dave Finigan W CO 2 Mayfair
09.02.82	Granville Allen W RSC 5 Kensington
02.03.82	Tommy McCallum W PTS 6
	Kensington
15.03.82	Derek McKenzie W RSC 3 Mayfair
23.03.82	Dave Sullivan W RSC 3 Bethnal Green
18.05.82	Kostas Petrou W PTS 8 Bethnal Green
22.09.82	Kid Murray W RSC 3 Mayfair
22.11.82	Frank McCord W CO 1 Mayfair
18.01.83	Lloyd Hibbert W PTS 10 Kensington
	(Elim. British Welterweight Title)
01.03.83	Sid Smith W CO 4 Kensington
	(Southern Area Welterweight Title
	Challenge & Elim. British
	Welterweight Title)
05.04.83	Cliff Gilpin W PTS 12 Kensington
	(Vacant British Welterweight Title)
09.07.83	Kevin Austin W RSC 10 Chicago,
	USA
24.10.83	Harold Brazier W PTS 10 Mayfair

Lloyd Honeyghan

06.12.83	Cliff Gilpin W PTS 12 Kensington
	(British Welterweight Title Defence)
05.06.84	Roberto Mendez W PTS 8 Kensington
05.01.85	Gianfranco Rosi W CO 3 Perugia, Italy
	(European Welterweight Title
	Challenge)
12.02.85	R. W. Smith W RTD 6 Kensington
06.03.85	Roger Stafford W RSC 9 Kensington
30.08.85	Danny Paul W PTS 10 Atlantic City,
	USA
01.10.85	Ralph Twinning W RSC 4 Wembley
27.11.85	Sylvester Mittee W RSC 8 Muswell
	Hill
	(European Welterweight Title Defence.
	British & Commonwealth Welterweight
	Title Challenge)
20.05.86	Horace Shufford W RSC 8 Wembley
	(Final Elim. WBC Welterweight Title)
27.09.86	Don Curry W RTD 6 Atlantic City,
	USA
	(World Welterweight Title Challenge)
22.02.87	Johnny Bumphus W RSC 2 Wembley
	(IBF Welterweight Title Defence)
18.04.87	Maurice Blocker W PTS 12
	Kensington
	(WBC Welterweight Title Defence)
30.08.87	Gene Hatcher W RSC 1 Marbella,
	Spain
	(WBC Welterweight Title Defence)
28.10.87	Jorge Vaca L TD 8 Wembley
	(WBC Welterweight Title Defence)
29.03.88	Jorge Vaca W CO 3 Wembley
	(WBC Welterweight Title Challenge)
29.07.88	Yung-Kil Chung W RSC 5 Atlantic
	City, USA
	(WBC Welterweight Title Defence)
05.02.89	Marlon Starling L RSC 9 Las Vegas,
	USA
	(WBC Welterweight Title Defence)
24.08.89	Delfino Marin W PTS 10 Tampa, USA
03.03.90	Mark Breland L RSC 3 Wembley
	(WBC Welterweight Title Challenge)
10.01.91	Mario Olmedo W RSC 4 Wandsworth
12.02.91	John Welters W RSC 1 Basildon
08.05.91	Darryl Anthony W CO 2 Kensington
22.04.92	Alfredo Ramirez W PTS 8 Wembley
13.05.92	Mick Duncan W RSC 2 Kensington
28.10.92	Carlo Colarusso W RSC 6 Kensington
30.01.93	Mickey Hughes W RSC 5 Brentwood

(Commonwealth L. Middleweight Title Challenge)
26.06.93 Vinny Pazienza L RTD 10 Atlantic City, USA

Career: 45 contests, won 41, lost 4.

Gary Jacobs   Les Clark

Gary Jacobs

Glasgow. *Born* Glasgow, 10 December, 1965
European Welterweight Champion. Former Commonwealth Welterweight Champion. Former Undefeated British, WBC International & Scottish Welterweight Champion. Ht. 5'7½"
Manager M. Duff

20.05.85 John Conlan W PTS 6 Glasgow
03.06.85 Nigel Burke W PTS 6 Glasgow
12.08.85 Mike McKenzie W PTS 6 Glasgow
07.10.85 Albert Buchanan W PTS 6 Cambuslang
11.11.85 Tyrell Wilson W CO 5 Glasgow
02.12.85 Dave Heaver W PTS 6 Glasgow
10.02.86 Courtney Phillips W RSC 5 Glasgow
10.03.86 Alistair Laurie W PTS 8 Glasgow
14.04.86 Billy Cairns W PTS 8 Glasgow
24.06.86 Dave Douglas L PTS 10 Glasgow
(Vacant Scottish Welterweight Title)
15.09.86 Jeff Connors W RSC 3 Glasgow
20.10.86 Kelvin Mortimer W RSC 5 Glasgow
27.01.87 Dave Douglas W PTS 10 Glasgow
(Scottish Welterweight Title Challenge)
24.02.87 Gary Williams W CO 7 Glasgow
06.04.87 Robert Armstrong W RTD 5 Glasgow
19.05.87 Gary Williams W RSC 3 Cumbernauld
08.06.87 Tommy McCallum W RSC 5 Glasgow
(Scottish Welterweight Title Defence)
26.11.87 Jeff Connors W PTS 8 Fulham
24.02.88 Del Bryan W PTS 10 Glasgow
(Final Elim. British Welterweight Title)
19.04.88 Wilf Gentzen W PTS 12 Glasgow
(Commonwealth Welterweight Title Challenge)
06.06.88 Juan Alonzo Villa W RSC 5 Mayfair
16.09.88 Javier Suazo W CO 10 Las Vegas, USA

(Vacant WBC International Welterweight Title)
29.11.88 Richard Rova W CO 4 Kensington
(Commonwealth Welterweight Title Defence)
14.02.89 Rocky Kelly W RTD 7 Wandsworth
(Commonwealth & WBC International Welterweight Title Defence)
05.04.89 George Collins W PTS 12 Kensington
(Commonwealth & WBC International Welterweight Title Defence)
27.06.89 Rollin Williams W RSC 1 Kensington
27.08.89 James McGirt L PTS 10 New York, USA
23.11.89 Donovan Boucher L PTS 12 Motherwell
(Commonwealth Welterweight Title Defence)
26.04.90 Pascal Lorcy W RSC 2 Wandsworth
09.05.90 Mike Durvan W CO 1 Kensington
17.10.90 Mickey Hughes L CO 8 Bethnal Green
05.03.91 Kenny Louis W CO 2 Glasgow
20.11.91 Peter Eubank W PTS 8 Kensington
20.02.92 Del Bryan W PTS 12 Glasgow
(British Welterweight Title Challenge)
25.03.92 Tommy Small W RSC 2 Kensington
22.04.92 Cirillo Nino W PTS 10 Wembley
09.07.92 Robert Wright W RSC 6 Glasgow
(British Welterweight Title Defence)
16.10.92 Ludovic Proto L PTS 12 Paris, France
(Vacant European Welterweight Title)
06.02.93 Ludovic Proto W RTD 9 Paris, France
(European Welterweight Title Challenge)
19.05.93 Horace Fleary W RTD 4 Sunderland

Career: 40 contests, won 35, lost 5.

Lennox Lewis   Les Clark

Lennox Lewis

Crayford. *Born* London, 2 September, 1965
WBC Heavyweight Champion. Former Undefeated British, European & Commonwealth Heavyweight Champion. Ht. 6'4¾"
Manager F. Maloney

27.06.89 Al Malcolm W CO 2 Kensington
21.07.89 Bruce Johnson W RSC 2 Atlantic City, USA
25.09.89 Andrew Gerrard W RSC 4 Crystal Palace
10.10.89 Steve Garber W CO 1 Hull
05.11.89 Melvin Epps W DIS 2 Kensington
18.12.89 Greg Gorrell W RSC 5 Kitchener, Canada
31.01.90 Noel Quarless W RSC 2 Bethnal Green
22.03.90 Calvin Jones W CO 1 Gateshead
14.04.90 Mike Simwelu W CO 1 Kensington
09.05.90 Jorge Dascola W CO 1 Kensington
20.05.90 Dan Murphy W RSC 6 Sheffield
27.06.90 Ossie Ocasio W PTS 8 Kensington
11.07.90 Mike Acey W RSC 2 Mississuaga, Canada
31.10.90 Jean Chanet W RSC 6 Crystal Palace
(European Heavyweight Title Challenge)
06.03.91 Gary Mason W RSC 7 Wembley
(British Heavyweight Title Challenge. European Heavyweight Title Defence)
12.07.91 Mike Weaver W CO 6 Lake Tahoe, USA
30.09.91 Glenn McCrory W CO 2 Kensington
(British & European Heavyweight Title Defence)
23.11.91 Tyrell Biggs W RSC 3 Atlanta, USA
01.02.92 Levi Billups W PTS 10 Las Vegas, USA
30.04.92 Derek Williams W RSC 3 Kensington
(British & European Heavyweight Title Defence. Commonwealth Heavyweight Title Challenge)
11.08.92 Mike Dixon W RSC 4 Atlantic City, USA
31.10.92 Razor Ruddock W RSC 2 Earls Court
(Final Elim. WBC Heavyweight Title & Commonwealth Heavyweight Title Defence)
08.05.93 Tony Tucker W PTS 12 Las Vegas, USA
(WBC Heavyweight Title Defence)

Career: 23 contests, won 23.

Eamonn Loughran   Pennie Cattle

61

Eamonn Loughran

Ballymena. *Born* Ballymena, 5 June, 1970
Commonwealth Welterweight Champion.
Ht. 5'9"
Manager B. Hearn

03.12.87	Adam Muir W DIS 4 Belfast
08.06.88	Tony Britland W RSC 1 Sheffield
25.06.88	Antonio Campbell DREW 4 Panama City, Panama
19.10.88	Stan King W PTS 6 Belfast
19.09.89	Ricky Nelson W RSC 3 Belfast
31.10.89	Mark Pearce W PTS 6 Belfast
29.11.89	Ronnie Campbell W RSC 1 Belfast
24.11.90	Parrish Johnson W RSC 2 Benalmadena, Spain
12.12.90	Mike Morrison W PTS 6 Basildon
12.02.91	Nick Meloscia W CO 1 Cardiff
05.03.91	Julian Eavis W PTS 6 Cardiff
26.03.91	Stan Cunningham W RSC 2 Bethnal Green
24.04.91	Kevin Plant W RTD 1 Preston
28.05.91	Terry Morrill W CO 1 Cardiff
03.09.91	Marty Duke W PTS 6 Cardiff
21.09.91	Glyn Rhodes W PTS 8 Tottenham
15.10.91	Juan Carlos Ortiz W PTS 8 Hamburg, Germany
13.03.92	Tony Ekubia L DIS 5 Bury *(Elim. British Welterweight Title)*
19.05.92	Kelvin Mortimer W RSC 1 Cardiff
29.09.92	Judas Clottey W PTS 8 Hamburg, Germany
24.11.92	Donovan Boucher W RSC 3 Doncaster *(Commonwealth Welterweight Title Challenge)*
18.12.92	Desbon Seaton W RSC 2 Hamburg, Germany
06.02.93	Michael Benjamin W RSC 6 Cardiff *(Commonwealth Welterweight Title Defence)*

Career: 23 contests, won 21, drew 1, lost 1.

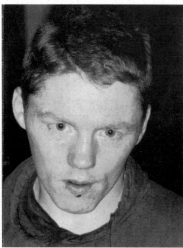

Sean Murphy   Les Clark

Sean Murphy

St Albans, *Born* St Albans, 1 December, 1964
British Featherweight Champion. Ht. 5'6"
Manager F. Warren

20.09.86	Albert Parr W PTS 6 Hemel Hempstead
09.10.86	Gordon Stobie W CO 5 Croydon
25.10.86	Simon Turner W PTS 6 Stevenage
03.12.86	Des Gargano W PTS 6 Muswell Hill
28.01.87	Keith Ward W RTD 4 Croydon
22.04.87	Kelvin Smart W CO 3 Kensington
09.05.87	Derek Amory W RSC 2 Wandsworth
01.07.87	Ray Minus L RSC 5 Kensington *(Commonwealth Bantamweight Title Challenge)*
09.08.87	Ronnie Stephenson W RSC 1 Windsor
16.09.87	David Williams W CO 1 Kensington
15.11.88	Craig Windsor W RSC 1 Norwich
01.12.88	Rocky Lawlor W RSC 2 Edmonton
31.01.89	Kid Sumali W RTD 2 Reading
07.03.89	Mike Whalley W PTS 10 Wisbech *(Elim. British Featherweight Title)*
08.05.89	Jesus Muniz W PTS 8 St Albans
19.09.89	Les Fabri W PTS 8 Millwall
24.10.89	Gerardo Castillo W RSC 1 Watford
08.03.90	Mario Lozano W PTS 8 Watford
22.05.90	John Doherty W CO 3 St Albans *(Vacant British Featherweight Title)*
25.09.90	Johnny B. Good W CO 2 Millwall *(British Featherweight Title Defence)*
05.03.91	Gary de Roux L CO 5 Millwall *(British Featherweight Title Defence)*
22.05.91	Ines Alvarado W PTS 8 Millwall
29.10.91	Colin McMillan L PTS 12 Kensington *(British Featherweight Title Challenge)*
30.04.92	Ian Honeywood W RSC 1 Kensington
27.02.93	Alan McKay W RSC 9 Dagenham *(Vacant British Featherweight Title)*

Career: 25 contests, won 22, lost 3.

Chris Pyatt   Les Clark

Chris Pyatt

Leicester. *Born* Islington, 3 July, 1963
WBO Middleweight Champion. Former
Undefeated WBC International
Middleweight Champion. Former European
L. Middleweight Champion. Former
Undefeated British & Commonwealth L.
Middleweight Champion. Ht. 5'8½"
Manager Self

01.03.83	Paul Murray W RTD 2 Kensington
05.04.83	Billy Waith W RSC 8 Kensington
28.04.83	Lee Hartshorn W RSC 3 Leicester
27.09.83	Darwin Brewster W PTS 8 Wembley
08.10.83	Tyrone Demby W RSC 2 Atlantic City, USA
22.11.83	Tony Britton W RSC 4 Wembley
22.02.84	Judas Clottey W PTS 8 Kensington
15.03.84	Pat Thomas W PTS 10 Leicester
09.05.84	Franki Moro W CO 4 Leicester
23.05.84	Alfonso Redondo W RSC 3 Mayfair
16.10.84	John Ridgman W RSC 1 Kensington
16.11.84	Brian Anderson W PTS 12 Leicester *(Final Elim. British L. Middleweight Title)*
12.02.85	Helier Custos W RSC 5 Kensington
05.06.85	Graeme Ahmed W RSC 3 Kensington
01.07.85	Mosimo Maeleke W RSC 6 Mayfair
23.09.85	Sabiyala Diavilia L RSC 4 Mayfair
19.02.86	Prince Rodney W CO 9 Kensington *(British L. Middleweight Title Challenge)*
20.05.86	Thomas Smith W RSC 1 Wembley
17.09.86	John van Elteren W RSC 1 Kensington *(Vacant European L. Middleweight Title)*
25.10.86	Renaldo Hernandez W RSC 3 Paris, France
28.01.87	Gianfranco Rosi L PTS 12 Perugia, Italy *(European L. Middleweight Title Defence)*
18.04.87	Dennis Johnson W CO 2 Kensington
26.05.87	Sammy Floyd W RSC 2 Wembley
28.10.87	Gilbert Josamu W PTS 8 Wembley
28.05.88	Jose Duarte W RSC 4 Kensington
23.11.88	Eddie Hall W RSC 2 Bethnal Green
01.12.88	Knox Brown W RSC 2 Edmonton
14.12.88	Tyrone Moore W CO 1 Bethnal Green
15.02.89	Russell Mitchell W RSC 4 Bethnal Green
17.05.89	Daniel Dominguez W RSC 10 Millwall
11.10.89	Wayne Harris W RSC 3 Millwall
25.04.90	Daniel Sclarandi W RSC 2 Millwall
23.10.90	John David Jackson L PTS 12 Leicester *(WBO L. Middleweight Title Challenge)*
05.11.91	Craig Trotter W PTS 12 Leicester *(Vacant Commonwealth L. Middleweight Title)*
01.02.92	Ambrose Mlilo W RSC 3 Birmingham *Commonwealth L. Middleweight Defence*
31.03.92	Melvyn Wynn W CO 3 Norwich
28.04.92	James Tapisha W RSC 1 Wolverhampton *(Commonwealth L. Middleweight Title Defence)*
23.05.92	Ian Strudwick W PTS 10 Birmingham
27.10.92	Adolfo Caballero W CO 5 Leicester *(Vacant WBC International Middleweight Title)*
26.01.93	Danny Garcia W PTS 12 Leicester *(WBC International Middleweight Title Defence)*
23.02.93	Colin Manners W CO 3 Doncaster
16.03.93	Paul Wesley W PTS 10 Mayfair
10.05.93	Sumbu Kalambay W PTS 12 Leicester *(Vacant WBO Middleweight Title)*

Career: 43 contests, won 40, lost 3.

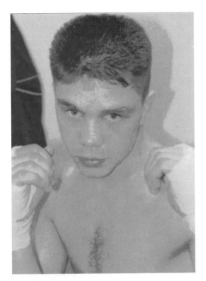

Robbie Regan   Les Clark

Steve Robinson   Les Clark

Carl Thompson   Les Clark

Robbie Regan

Cefn Forest. *Born* Caerphilly, 30 August, 1968
European Flyweight Champion. Former Undefeated British & Welsh Flyweight Champion. Ht. 5'4"
Manager D. Gardiner

19.08.89	Eric George DREW 6 Cardiff	
06.03.90	Francis Ampofo W PTS 6 Bethnal Green	
26.04.90	Kevin Downer W RSC 4 Merthyr	
20.06.90	Dave McNally DREW 6 Basildon	
19.11.90	Ricky Beard W RSC 6 Cardiff	
21.12.90	Michele Poddighe DREW 6 Sassari, Italy	
12.02.91	Kevin Jenkins W PTS 10 Cardiff	
	(Vacant Welsh Flyweight Title)	
28.05.91	Joe Kelly W PTS 12 Cardiff	
	(Vacant British Flyweight Title)	
03.09.91	Francis Ampofo L RSC 11 Cardiff	
	(British Flyweight Title Defence)	
17.12.91	Francis Ampofo W PTS 12 Cardiff	
	(British Flyweight Title Challenge)	
11.02.92	Juan Bautista W CO 1 Cardiff	
19.05.92	James Drummond W RSC 9 Cardiff	
	(British Flyweight Title Defence)	
14.11.92	Salvatore Fanni W PTS 12 Cardiff	
	(European Flyweight Title Challenge)	
30.03.93	Danny Porter W RSC 3 Cardiff	
	(European Flyweight Title Defence)	
26.06.93	Adrian Ochoa W PTS 10 Earls Court	

Career: 15 contests, won 11, drew 3, lost 1.

Steve Robinson

Cardiff. *Born* Cardiff, 13 December, 1968
WBO Featherweight Champion. Former Undefeated Welsh Featherweight Champion. Ht. 5'8"
Manager D. Gardiner

01.03.89	Alan Roberts W PTS 6 Cardiff	
13.03.89	Terry Smith W RTD 4 Piccadilly	
06.04.89	Nicky Lucas L PTS 8 Cardiff	
04.05.89	John Devine W PTS 6 Mayfair	
19.08.89	Marcel Herbert L PTS 6 Cardiff	
13.11.89	Shane Silvester W RSC 2 Brierley Hill	
10.07.90	Mark Bates L PTS 6 Canvey Island	
12.09.90	Tim Driscoll L PTS 8 Bethnal Green	
26.09.90	Russell Davison W PTS 8 Manchester	
03.10.90	Drew Docherty L PTS 8 Solihull	
22.10.90	Alan McKay L PTS 6 Mayfair	
19.11.90	Neil Haddock W RSC 9 Cardiff	
19.12.90	Brian Roche DREW 6 Preston	
24.04.91	Russell Davison W RTD 6 Preston	
28.05.91	Colin Lynch W RSC 6 Cardiff	
18.07.91	Peter Harris W PTS 10 Cardiff	
	(Welsh Featherweight Title Challenge)	
31.01.92	Henry Armstrong L PTS 6 Manchester	
11.05.92	Neil Haddock L PTS 10 Llanelli	
	(Vacant Welsh S. Featherweight Title)	
07.10.92	Edward Lloyd W RTD 8 Barry	
30.10.92	Stephane Haccoun W PTS 8 Istres, France	
01.12.92	Dennis Oakes W RTD 2 Liverpool	
19.01.93	Paul Harvey W PTS 12 Cardiff	
	(Vacant WBA Penta-Continental Featherweight Title)	
13.02.93	Medhi Labdouni L PTS 8 Paris, France	
17.04.93	John Davison W PTS 12 Washington	
	(Vacant WBO Featherweight Title)	

Career: 24 contests, won 14, drew 1, lost 9.

(Adrian) Carl Thompson

Manchester. *Born* Manchester, 26 May, 1964
British & WBC International Cruiserweight Champion. Ht. 6'0"
Manager P. Martin

06.06.88	Darren McKenna W RSC 2 Manchester	
11.10.88	Paul Sheldon W PTS 6 Wolverhampton	
13.02.89	Steve Osborne W PTS 6 Manchester	
07.03.89	Sean O'Phoenix W RSC 4 Manchester	
04.04.89	Keith Halliwell W RSC 1 Manchester	
04.05.89	Tenko Ernie W CO 4 Mayfair	
12.06.89	Steve Osborne W PTS 8 Manchester	
11.07.89	Peter Brown W RSC 5 Batley	
31.10.89	Crawford Ashley L RSC 6 Manchester	
	(Vacant Central Area L. Heavyweight Title)	
21.04.90	Francis Wanyama L PTS 6 St Amandsberg, Belgium	
07.03.91	Terry Dixon W PTS 8 Basildon	
01.04.91	Yawe Davis L RSC 2 Monaco, Monte Carlo	
04.09.91	Nicky Piper W RSC 3 Bethnal Green	
04.06.92	Steve Lewsam W RSC 8 Cleethorpes	
	(Vacant British Cruiserweight Title)	
17.02.93	Arthur Weathers W CO 2 Bethnal Green	
	(Vacant WBC International Cruiserweight Title)	
31.03.93	Steve Harvey W CO 1 Bethnal Green	

Career: 16 contests, won 13, lost 3.

Andy Till   Les Clark

Andy Till

Northolt. *Born* Perivale, 22 August, 1963
British L. Middleweight Champion. Former Undefeated WBC International & Southern Area L. Middleweight Champion. Ht. 5'9"
Manager H. Holland

63

01.09.86 Peter Reid W RSC 6 Ealing
25.09.86 Graham Jenner W PTS 6 Crystal Palace
10.11.86 Randy Henderson W PTS 6 Longford
12.01.87 Tony Lawrence W RSC 4 Ealing
18.02.87 Ian Bayliss W PTS 6 Fulham
30.04.87 Dean Scarfe L PTS 8 Wandsworth
24.09.87 Andy Wright W RSC 2 Crystal Palace
19.02.88 Geoff Sharp W RSC 5 Longford
29.11.88 W. O. Wilson W PTS 10 Battersea
01.03.89 Wally Swift Jnr W PTS 8 Bethnal Green
12.06.89 Tony Britton W RTD 8 Battersea
(Vacant Southern Area L. Middleweight Title)
10.11.89 Nigel Fairbairn W RSC 8 Battersea
14.03.90 Steve Foster W RTD 5 Battersea
06.06.90 Ensley Bingham L DIS 3 Battersea
(Final Elim. British L. Middleweight Title)
12.09.90 Alan Richards W PTS 8 Battersea
06.02.91 Alan Richards W PTS 8 Battersea
01.06.91 Terry Magee W RSC 4 Bethnal Green
15.10.91 John Davies W PTS 12 Dudley
(Vacant WBC International L. Middleweight Title)
17.09.92 Wally Swift Jnr W PTS 12 Watford
(British L. Middleweight Title Challenge)
10.12.92 Tony Collins W RSC 3 Bethnal Green
(British L. Middleweight Title Defence)
14.04.93 Wally Swift Jnr W RSC 4 Kensington
(British L. Middleweight Title Defence)
23.06.93 Laurent Boudouani L RTD 4 Edmonton
(European L. Middleweight Title Challenge)
Career: 22 contests, won 19, lost 3.

Paul Weir　　　　　　　George Ashton

Paul Weir

Irvine. *Born* Glasgow, 16 September, 1967
Flyweight. WBO M. Flyweight Champion.
Ht. 5'3"
Manager T. Gilmour

27.04.92 Eduardo Vallejo W CO 2 Glasgow
09.07.92 Louis Veitch W PTS 6 Glasgow
21.09.92 Neil Parry W RSC 4 Glasgow

23.11.92 Shaun Norman W PTS 8 Glasgow
06.03.93 Kevin Jenkins W PTS 8 Glasgow
15.05.93 Fernando Martinez W RSC 7 Glasgow
(Vacant WBO M. Flyweight Title)
Career: 6 contests, won 6.

Henry Wharton　　　　　　　Les Clark

Henry Wharton

York. *Born* Leeds, 23 November, 1967
Commonwealth S. Middleweight
Champion. Former Undefeated British S.
Middleweight Champion. Ht. 5'10½"
Manager M. Duff

21.09.89 Dean Murray W RSC 1 Harrogate
25.10.89 Mike Aubrey W PTS 6 Wembley
05.12.89 Ron Malek W RSC 1 Dewsbury
11.01.90 Guillermo Chavez W CO 1 Dewsbury
03.03.90 Joe Potts W CO 4 Wembley
11.04.90 Juan Elizondo W RSC 3 Dewsbury
18.10.90 Chuck Edwards W RSC 1 Dewsbury

31.10.90 Dino Stewart W PTS 8 Wembley
21.03.91 Francisco Lara W CO 1 Dewsbury
09.05.91 Frankie Minton W CO 7 Leeds
27.06.91 Rod Carr W PTS 12 Leeds
(Vacant Commonwealth S. Middleweight Title)
30.10.91 Lou Gent DREW 12 Leeds
(Commonwealth S. Middleweight Title Defence)
23.10.92 Nicky Walker W PTS 10 York
19.03.92 Kenny Schaefer W CO 1 York
08.04.92 Rod Carr W RSC 8 Leeds
(Commonwealth S. Middleweight Title Defence)
23.09.92 Fidel Castro W PTS 12 Leeds
(Commonwealth S. Middleweight Title Defence. British S. Middleweight Title Challenge)
07.04.93 Ray Domenge W RSC 3 Leeds
Career: 17 contests, won 16, drew 1.

Richie Woodhall

Telford. *Born* Birmingham, 17 April, 1968
Commonwealth Middleweight Champion.
Ht. 6'2"
Manager Self

18.10.90 Kevin Hayde W RSC 3 Birmingham
30.11.90 Robbie Harron W RSC 2 Birmingham
16.01.91 Chris Haydon W RSC 3 Kensington
21.02.91 Shamus Casey W RSC 3 Walsall
30.05.91 Marty Duke W RSC 4 Birmingham
29.08.91 Nigel Moore W RSC 1 Oakengates
31.10.91 Colin Pitters W PTS 8 Oakengates
04.02.92 Graham Burton W RSC 2 Alfreton
26.03.92 Vito Gaudiosi W CO 1 Telford
(Vacant Commonwealth Middleweight Title)
01.10.92 John Ashton W PTS 12 Telford
(Commonwealth Middleweight Title Defence)
04.12.92 Horace Fleary W PTS 8 Telford
16.03.93 Carlo Colarusso W PTS 8 Wolverhampton
24.04.93 Royan Hammond W PTS 10 Birmingham
Career: 13 contests, won 13.

Richie Woodhall　　　　　　　Chris Bevan

Active British-Based Boxers: Career Records

Shows the complete record for all British-based boxers, excluding current champions, who have been active between 1 July 1992 and 30 June 1993. Names in brackets are real names, where they differ from ring names. The first place name given is the boxer's domicile. Boxers are either shown as self managed, or with a named manager. This information has been supplied by the BBBoC and is in accordance with their records at the time of going to press.

Ojay Abrahams
Watford. *Born* Lambeth, 17 December, 1964
Welterweight. Ht. 5'8½"
Manager B. Hearn

21.09.91	Gordon Webster W RSC 3 Tottenham
26.10.91	Mick Reid W RSC 5 Brentwood
26.11.91	John Corcoran W PTS 6 Bethnal Green
21.01.92	Dave Andrews DREW 6 Norwich
31.03.92	Marty Duke W RSC 2 Norwich
19.05.92	Michael Smyth L PTS 6 Cardiff
16.06.92	Ricky Mabbett W PTS 6 Dagenham
13.10.92	Vince Rose L RSC 3 Mayfair
30.01.93	Vince Rose DREW 6 Brentwood
19.05.93	Ricky Mabbett L RSC 4 Leicester

Career: 10 contests, won 5, drew 2, lost 3.

Kevin Adamson
Walthamstow. *Born* Hackney, 19 February, 1968
L. Middleweight. Ht. 6'0½"
Manager Self

17.07.89	Carlton Myers W RSC 1 Stanmore
04.12.90	Darron Griffiths L RSC 4 Southend
12.11.91	Danny Shinkwin W RSC 4 Milton Keynes
30.04.92	Wayne Appleton W RSC 2 Bayswater
03.02.93	Joel Ani W RSC 6 Earls Court
27.02.93	Robert Whitehouse W RSC 1 Dagenham
31.03.93	Russell Washer W PTS 6 Barking

Career: 7 contests, won 6, lost 1.

Golfraz Ahmed
Bradford. *Born* Pakistan, 15 July, 1971
Flyweight. Ht. 5'8"
Manager J. Celebanski

26.04.93	Lyndon Kershaw L PTS 6 Bradford

Career: 1 contest, lost 1.

Tanver Ahmed (Niazi)
Glasgow. *Born* Glasgow, 25 October, 1968
Lightweight. Ht. 5'10"
Manager A. Melrose

22.10.92	John T. Kelly W PTS 6 Glasgow
01.12.92	Shaun Armstrong L PTS 6 Hartlepool
26.03.93	David Thompson W PTS 6 Glasgow
14.05.93	Dean Bramhald W PTS 6 Kilmarnock

Career: 4 contests, won 3, lost 1.

Korso Aleain (Boualem)
Leyton. *Born* Algeria, 18 October, 1962
L. Welterweight. Ht. 5'5"
Manager I. Akay

05.03.92	Everald Williams L CO 6 Battersea
30.04.92	Erwin Edwards W PTS 6 Bayswater
17.05.92	Brian Coleman W RSC 5 Harringay
26.09.92	Paul Ryan L CO 4 Earls Court

06.05.93	Joel Ani L RSC 2 Bayswater

Career: 5 contests, won 2, lost 3.

Michael Alexander   Chris Bevan

Michael Alexander
Doncaster. *Born* Doncaster, 31 August, 1971
L. Welterweight. Ht. 5'9"
Manager T. Petersen

25.01.93	Tim Hill W PTS 6 Bradford
09.03.93	J. T. Kelly L PTS 6 Hartlepool
29.04.93	Pete Roberts W RSC 2 Hull
06.05.93	Ian Noble W PTS 6 Hartlepool
28.06.93	Mick Hoban W PTS 6 Morecambe

Career: 5 contests, won 4, lost 1.

Raziq Ali
Bradford. *Born* Wakefield, 14 September, 1972
L. Middleweight. Ht. 6'0"
Manager K. Tate

08.09.92	Wayne Panayiotiou W PTS 6 Doncaster
05.10.92	Sean Baker L PTS 6 Bristol
24.05.93	David Sumner W PTS 6 Bradford

Career: 3 contests, won 2, lost 1.

Michael Alldis
Crawley. *Born* London, 25 May, 1968
Bantamweight. Ht. 5'6"
Manager B. Hearn

15.09.92	Ceri Farrell W RSC 3 Crystal Palace
10.11.92	Kid McAuley W PTS 6 Dagenham
12.12.92	Kid McAuley W CO 1 Muswell Hill

Michael Alldis   Les Clark

16.02.93	Ceri Farrell W CO 1 Tooting
29.06.93	Ady Benton L DIS 3 Mayfair

Career: 5 contests, won 4, lost 1.

Dean Allen
Swansea. *Born* Swansea, 3 August, 1967
L. Heavyweight. Ht. 6'0"
Manager M. Copp

24.01.91	Max McCracken L PTS 6 Brierley Hill
24.04.91	Paul Hanlon W PTS 6 Aberavon
13.11.91	Terry Johnson W RSC 2 Liverpool
07.09.92	Phil Soundy L RTD 4 Bethnal Green

Career: 4 contests, won 2, lost 2.

Mark Allen (Hodgson)
Denaby. *Born* Mexborough, 11 January, 1970
L. Welterweight. Ht. 5'11"
Manager J. Rushton

24.03.92	Jamie Morris L PTS 6 Wolverhampton
04.06.92	Blue Butterworth L RSC 5 Burnley
10.11.92	Bobby Guynan L RSC 2 Dagenham
09.12.92	Simon Hamblett DREW 6 Stoke
09.02.93	Simon Hamblett W PTS 6 Wolverhampton
23.02.93	Simon Hamblett L PTS 6 Doncaster
11.03.93	Jamie Morris DREW 6 Walsall
20.04.93	Paul Knights L PTS 6 Brentwood
06.05.93	Brian Coleman L PTS 6 Walsall
28.05.93	Nick Boyd L CO 2 Middleton
29.06.93	Robbie Sivyer W PTS 6 Edgbaston

Career: 11 contests, won 2, drew 2, lost 7.

Jimmy Alston

Preston. *Born* Preston, 2 February, 1967
L. Middleweight. Ht. 5'9"
Manager M. Chapman

07.12.92   Spencer Alton W PTS 6 Manchester
25.02.93   Crain Fisher L RTD 2 Burnley
22.04.93   Crain Fisher L PTS 6 Bury
Career: 3 contests, won 1, lost 2.

Spencer Alton

Derby. *Born* Derby, 4 October, 1966
L. Middleweight. Ht. 5'11"
Manager M. Shinfield

13.06.88   Ian Midwood-Tate W PTS 6
           Manchester
10.07.88   Lou Ayres L PTS 6 Eastbourne
31.08.88   Ian Midwood-Tate L PTS 6 Stoke
30.09.88   Steve West L CO 3 Battersea
19.10.88   Wil Halliday W CO 6 Evesham
31.10.88   Michael Oliver W RSC 2 Leicester
14.11.88   G. L. Booth L RSC 7 Manchester
13.12.88   Paul Dolan W RTD 4 Glasgow
20.12.88   Wayne Ellis L RTD 4 Swansea
27.01.89   Neil Patterson W CO 1 Durham
31.01.89   Brian Robinson L PTS 6 Reading
15.02.89   Mark Holden DREW 6 Stoke
06.03.89   Mark Howell L PTS 8 Manchester
21.03.89   Ricky Nelson L PTS 6 Cottingham
04.04.89   Graham Burton L RSC 3 Sheffield
09.05.89   Wayne Ellis L RSC 3 St Albans
20.06.89   Peter Vosper L PTS 6 Plymouth
06.07.89   Ian Strudwick L PTS 8 Chigwell
26.09.89   Frank Eubanks W PTS 6 Oldham
10.10.89   Terry Morrill L PTS 6 Hull
17.10.89   Peter Vosper DREW 8 Plymouth
08.11.89   Neville Brown L RSC 4 Wembley
20.12.89   Mickey Morgan W RSC 5 Swansea
15.01.90   Andy Marlow DREW 6 Northampton
30.01.90   Darren Pilling L PTS 6 Manchester
13.02.90   Colin Pitters W PTS 6 Wolverhampton
26.02.90   Antoine Tarver L PTS 4 Crystal Palace
22.03.90   Richard Carter L PTS 6
           Wolverhampton
24.05.90   Andrew Flute W RSC 1 Dudley
21.06.90   Paul Murray W PTS 6 Alfreton
10.09 92   Dave Johnson L PTS 6 Sunderland
23.10.92   Terry French L PTS 6 Gateshead
07.12.92   Jimmy Alston L PTS 6 Manchester
02.02.93   Chris Mulcahy W RSC 3 Derby
09.03.93   Mark Jay L RSC 4 Hartlepool
08.06.93   Eddie Collins W PTS 6 Derby
Career: 36 contests, won 12, drew 3, lost 21.

Trevor Ambrose

Leicester. *Born* Leicester, 8 September,
1963
Welterweight. Ht. 5'11"
Manager J. Bishop

19.02.90   Ian Thomas L RSC 3 Kettering
06.04.90   Colin Pitters W PTS 6 Telford
24.04.90   Barry Messam W RSC 4 Stoke
14.05.90   Gordon Blair L CO 5 Northampton
12.09.90   Dave Fallon W CO 3 Battersea
23.10.90   David Lake W PTS 6 Leicester
04.11.90   Eddie King W RSC 3 Doncaster
21.11.90   Andreas Panayi W RSC 5 Solihull
14.02.91   Adrian Riley W CO 6 Southampton
28.03.91   Richard O'Brien W RSC 1 Alfreton
25.04.91   Gary Logan L PTS 8 Mayfair
03.07.91   Darren Dyer L PTS 6 Brentwood

24.09.91   Willie Beattie L PTS 8 Glasgow
11.03.92   John Davies L RSC 5 Cardiff
19.05.92   Paul Jones L PTS 6 Cardiff
19.03.93   Errol Christie W CO 2 Manchester
Career: 16 contests, won 9, lost 7.

Dean Amory

Birmingham. *Born* Marston Green, 2 July,
1969
Lightweight. Ht. 5'7"
Manager W. Swift

21.10.92   Brian Hickey W PTS 6 Stoke
20.01.93   Dean Bramhald W PTS 6 Solihull
28.04.93   Elvis Parsley W PTS 6 Solihull
19.05.93   Neil Smith W PTS 6 Leicester
Career: 4 contests, won 4.

Derek Amory

Birmingham. *Born* Birmingham, 12
January, 1966
S. Featherweight. Ht. 5'5"
Manager Self

25.09.86   Roy Williams W CO 2 Wolverhampton
23.10.86   Shane Porter DREW 6 Birmingham
03.11.86   Mark Bignell W RSC 1 Edgbaston
18.11.86   Carl Parry L PTS 6 Swansea
26.01.87   Tony Heath W PTS 8 Nottingham
10.03.87   Mike Whalley L RSC 2 Manchester
09.05.87   Sean Murphy L RSC 2 Wandsworth
30.09.87   Lambsy Kayani DREW 8 Solihull
18.11.87   Carl Parry W PTS 8 Solihull
07.12.87   Graham O'Malley W PTS 8
           Birmingham
14.12.87   Craig Windsor L PTS 6 Edgbaston
20.01.88   Lambsy Kayani W PTS 8 Solihull
24.02.88   Tony Heath W PTS 8 Leicester
17.06.88   John Hyland W RSC 2 Edgbaston
28.09.88   Colin Lynch L PTS 10 Solihull
           *(Vacant Midlands Area Featherweight
           Title)*
27.10.88   Dave George W PTS 8 Birmingham
15.11.88   Joe Donohoe L PTS 8 Piccadilly
23.11.88   Patrick Kamy L RSC 2 Solihull
25.01.89   Russell Davison L PTS 8 Solihull
01.03.89   Henry Armstrong L PTS 8 Stoke
10.05.89   Peter English L PTS 8 Solihull
04.10.89   Mark Holt L PTS 10 Solihull
           *(Midlands Area Featherweight Title
           Challenge)*
30.04.90   Peter Judson W PTS 6 Brierley Hill
03.09.90   Miguel Matthews W PTS 6 Dudley
24.09.90   Noel Carroll L PTS 8 Manchester
08.10.90   James Drummond W PTS 8
           Cleethorpes
15.10.90   Jamie McBride W RTD 4 Brierley Hill
13.12.90   Darren Elsdon L PTS 6 Hartlepool
29.01.91   Carl Roberts W PTS 4 Stockport
18.03.91   Joe Donohoe L PTS 8 Piccadilly
17.06.91   Kelton McKenzie L RSC 6 Edgbaston
07.10.91   Ervine Blake L PTS 6 Birmingham
22.01.92   J. T. Williams L PTS 6 Cardiff
11.02.92   Jimmy Clark L PTS 6 Barking
09.05.92   Luis Ramon Rolon L CO 7 Madrid,
           Spain
28.10.92   Barrie Kelley L PTS 6 Cardiff
29.01.93   Edward Cook W PTS 6 Glasgow
20.02.93   Tim Driscoll L PTS 8 Earls Court
04.03.93   Edward Cook W RSC 4 Glasgow
26.04.93   Henry Armstrong L PTS 6 Manchester
Career: 40 contests, won 16, drew 2, lost 22.

Colin Anderson

Leicester. *Born* Leicester, 7 June, 1962
Welterweight. Ht. 5'9"
Manager J. Griffin

30.09.83   Wayne Trigg W PTS 4 Leicester
14.02.84   Peter Bowen W PTS 6 Wolverhampton
20.02.84   Nicky Day DREW 6 Mayfair
15.03.84   Wayne Trigg L RSC 2 Leicester
01.10.84   Joey Morris L PTS 6 Leicester
02.12.92   Chris Mulcahy L PTS 6 Bardon
26.04.93   Warren Bowers L RSC 5 Cleethorpes
Career: 7 contests, won 2, drew 1, lost 4.

Dave Anderson

Bellahouston. *Born* Glasgow, 23 December,
1966
Lightweight. Ht. 5'8"
Manager Self

25.09.90   Junaido Musah W RSC 3 Glasgow
09.10.90   Alan Peacock W RSC 3 Glasgow
10.12.90   Chris Bennett W RSC 7 Glasgow
11.02.91   Steve Pollard W PTS 6 Glasgow
15.04.91   Tony Foster W PTS 8 Glasgow
24.09.91   Ian Honeywood W PTS 8 Glasgow
28.11.91   Pete Roberts W RSC 3 Glasgow
11.09.92   Kevin Toomey W PTS 8 Glasgow
22.10.92   Kevin McKenzie W RSC 3 Glasgow
Career: 9 contests, won 9.

Shaun Anderson

Maybole. *Born* Girvan, 20 September, 1969
Bantamweight. Ht. 5'5"
Manager Self

29.05.92   Tucker Thomas W RSC 1 Glasgow
11.09.92   Mark Hargreaves W PTS 6 Glasgow
10.12.92   Graham McGrath W PTS 6 Glasgow
29.01.93   Graham McGrath W PTS 6 Glasgow
26.03.93   Dave Campbell W RSC 5 Glasgow
30.04.93   Paul Kelly W RSC 5 Glasgow
14.05.93   Kid McAuley W PTS 8 Kilmarnock
29.05.93   Ronnie Stephenson W PTS 6 Paisley
Career: 8 contests, won 8.

(Alfie) Bullit Andrews

Birmingham. *Born* Birmingham, 29 April,
1964
L. Middleweight. Ht. 5'10"
Manager Self

11.10.88   Mohammed Ayub W PTS 6
           Wolverhampton
22.11.88   Frank Graham L RSC 6
           Wolverhampton
01.03.89   Peter Reid L RSC 2 Stoke
08.05.89   Ernie Loveridge L PTS 6 Edgbaston
02.10.89   Paul Walters L RSC 5 Hanley
13.11.89   Andre Wharton L PTS 6 Brierley Hill
05.02.90   Andre Wharton L RSC 4 Brierley Hill
04.06.90   Dave Whittle L PTS 6 Edgbaston
08.10.90   Tony Booth L RSC 3 Cleethorpes
13.11.90   Wayne Appleton L RSC 5 Edgbaston
15.04.91   Scott Newman L RSC 1
           Wolverhampton
30.05.91   Darren Morris L RSC 3 Birmingham
21.05.92   Warren Stephens W PTS 6 Cradley
           Heath
30.10.92   Warren Stephens W PTS 6
           Birmingham
04.03.93   Kevin Mabbutt L PTS 6 Peterborough
29.03.93   Andrew Jervis L PTS 6 Liverpool

19.04.93 Steve Levene L PTS 6 Northampton
26.04.93 Steve McNess L RSC 3 Lewisham
07.06.93 Gary Osborne L RSC 1 Walsall
Career: 19 contests, won 3, lost 16.

Dennis Andries

Hackney. *Born* Guyana, 5 November, 1953
Cruiserweight. Former WBC L.
Heavyweight Champion. Former
Undefeated WBC Continental L.
Heavyweight Champion. Former
Undefeated British & Southern Area L.
Heavyweight Champion. Ht. 5'11"
Manager E. Steward

16.05.78 Ray Pearce W CO 2 Newport
01.06.78 Mark Seabrook W RSC 1 Heathrow
20.06.78 Bonny McKenzie L PTS 8 Southend
18.09.78 Ken Jones W PTS 6 Mayfair
31.10.78 Neville Estaban W PTS 6 Barnsley
14.11.78 Les McAteer DREW 8 Birkenhead
22.11.78 Glen McEwan W RSC 7 Stoke
04.12.78 Tom Collins W PTS 8 Southend
22.01.79 Bunny Johnson L PTS 10
Wolverhampton
30.01.79 Tom Collins W CO 6 Southend
05.04.79 Francis Hand W RSC 8 Liverpool
06.06.79 Bonny McKenzie W PTS 8 Burslem
17.09.79 Johnny Waldron W RTD 10 Mayfair
*(Southern Area L. Heavyweight Title
Challenge)*
27.02.80 Bunny Johnson L PTS 15 Burslem
*(British L. Heavyweight Title
Challenge)*
17.04.80 Mustafa Wasajja L PTS 8 Copenhagen,
Denmark
18.06.80 Chris Lawson W RSC 8 Burslem
23.03.81 Shaun Chalcraft W PTS 10 Mayfair
*(Southern Area L. Heavyweight Title
Challenge)*
16.09.81 Liam Coleman W RSC 6 Burslem
12.10.81 David Pearce L RSC 7 Bloomsbury
23.11.81 Alek Penarski W PTS 10 Chesterfield
15.03.82 Tom Collins L PTS 15 Bloomsbury
(Vacant British L. Heavyweight Title)
10.08.82 Keith Bristol W PTS 10 Strand
*(Southern Area L. Heavyweight Title
Defence)*
28.02.83 Karl Canwell W CO 4 Strand
*(Southern Area L. Heavyweight Title
Defence & Elim. British L.
Heavyweight Title)*
19.05.83 Chris Lawson W CO 4 Queensway
22.09.83 Keith Bristol W CO 4 Strand
*(Southern Area L. Heavyweight Title
Defence & Elim. British L.
Heavyweight Title)*
26.01.84 Tom Collins W PTS 12 Strand
*(British L. Heavyweight Title
Challenge)*
06.04.84 Tom Collins W PTS 12 Watford
(British L. Heavyweight Title Defence)
10.10.84 Devon Bailey W CO 12 Shoreditch
(British L. Heavyweight Title Defence)
23.03.85 Jose Seys W RSC 3 Strand
07.05.85 Jeff Meacham W CO 4 New Orleans,
USA
25.05.85 Tim Broady W RSC 5 Atlantic City,
USA
06.06.85 Marcus Dorsey W CO 3 Lafayette,
USA
11.12.85 Alex Blanchard DREW 12 Fulham

*(European L. Heavyweight Title
Challenge)*
13.02.86 Keith Bristol W RSC 6 Longford
(British L. Heavyweight Title Defence)
30.04.86 J. B. Williamson W PTS 12 Edmonton
(WBC L. Heavyweight Title Challenge)
10.09.86 Tony Sibson W RSC 9 Muswell Hill
*(WBC & British L. Heavyweight Title
Defence)*
07.03.87 Thomas Hearns L RSC 10 Detroit,
USA
(WBC L. Heavyweight Title Defence)
06.10.87 Robert Folley W PTS 10 Phoenix,
USA
20.02.88 Jamie Howe W PTS 10 Detroit, USA
22.05.88 Bobby Czyz W PTS 10 Atlantic City,
USA
10.09.88 Tony Harrison W RTD 7 Detroit, USA
17.10.88 Paul Maddison W RSC 4 Tucson, USA
21.02.89 Tony Willis W RSC 5 Tucson, USA
(Vacant WBC L. Heavyweight Title)
24.06.89 Jeff Harding L RSC 12 Atlantic City,
USA
(WBC L. Heavyweight Title Defence)
26.10.89 Art Jimmerson W PTS 10 Atlantic
City, USA
20.01.90 Clarismundo Silva W RSC 7 Auburn
Hills, USA
*(Vacant WBC Continental L.
Heavyweight Title)*
28.07.90 Jeff Harding W CO 7 Melbourne,
Australia
(WBC L. Heavyweight Title Challenge)
10.10.90 Sergio Merani W RTD 4 Kensington
(WBC L. Heavyweight Title Defence)
19.01.91 Guy Waters W PTS 12 Adelaide,
Australia
(WBC L. Heavyweight Title Defence)
11.09.91 Jeff Harding L PTS 12 Hammersmith
(WBC L. Heavyweight Title Defence)
15.11.91 Ed Neblett W RSC 4 Tampa, USA
11.12.91 Paul Maddison W RTD 8 Duluth, USA
27.02.92 Akim Tafer L PTS 12 Beausoleil,
France
(Vacant European Cruiserweight Title)
27.02.93 David Sewell W PTS 10 Dagenham
31.03.93 Willie Jake W RTD 6 Barking
Career: 55 contests, won 43, drew 2, lost 10.

Joel Ani

Hackney. *Born* Nigeria, 6 February, 1972
Welterweight. Ht. 5'7½"
Manager F. Maloney

22.10.92 Danny Quacoe W CO 1 Bethnal Green
03.02.93 Kevin Adamson L RSC 6 Earls Court
29.03.93 George Wilson W PTS 6 Mayfair
06.05.93 Korso Aleain W RSC 2 Bayswater
23.06.93 Steve McGovern L PTS 6 Edmonton
Career: 5 contests, won 3, lost 2.

Mark Antony (Brooks)

Doncaster. *Born* Worksop, 24 January,
1968
Welterweight. Ht. 5'8"
Manager J. Rushton

16.11.87 Robbie Bowen L CO 5 Stratford on
Avon
22.03.88 Paul Bowen L RSC 3 Wolverhampton
14.11.88 Phil Lashley W RSC 2 Stratford on
Avon

Mark Antony Les Clark

21.11.88 Paul Chedgzoy W CO 2 Leicester
01.12.88 Andrew Robinson W PTS 6 Stafford
14.12.88 Paul Bowen L PTS 6 Evesham
02.02.89 Shaun Cooper L CO 3 Wolverhampton
20.04.89 Andrew Brightman W PTS 6 Weston
super Mare
17.05.89 Mark Tibbs L PTS 6 Millwall
29.05.89 Mike Close L PTS 6 Liverpool
04.09.89 Warren Bowers L PTS 6 Grimsby
04.10.89 Karl Taylor L CO 2 Stratford
06.12.89 Peter Bowen L PTS 6 Stoke
13.02.90 Peter Bowen W RSC 1
Wolverhampton
07.03.90 Stuart Rimmer W RSC 1 Doncaster
21.03.90 Nick Hall L PTS 6 Solihull
27.03.90 Shaun Cogan L CO 1 Wolverhampton
21.05.90 Tony Feliciello L RTD 2 Grimsby
21.06.90 Andrew Robinson W PTS 6 Alfreton
31.10.90 Billy Schwer L RSC 2 Wembley
03.12.90 Nigel Senior W RSC 3 Cleethorpes
12.12.90 Richard Woolgar L RSC 5 Basildon
05.03.91 Jim Moffat L PTS 6 Glasgow
12.03.91 Wayne Windle L CO 1 Mansfield
12.11.91 Shaun Cooper L CO 1 Wolverhampton
20.01.92 Jamie Morris W RSC 5 Coventry
11.02.92 Billy Robinson L RSC 5
Wolverhampton
11.03.92 Simon Hamblett W CO 1 Stoke
11.05.92 Pat Delargy L PTS 6 Coventry
04.06.92 Darren Powell W CO 2 Burnley
23.11.92 Darren McInulty L PTS 6 Coventry
07.12.92 Spencer McCracken L CO 1
Birmingham
30.04.93 Colin Wallace L PTS 6 Glasgow
18.05.93 Steve Levene W RSC 1 Edgbaston
29.05.93 Steve Boyle L PTS 6 Paisley
17.06.93 Darren McInulty W CO 2 Bedworth
26.06.93 Ross Hale L RSC 1 Keynsham
Career: 37 contests, won 13, lost 24.

Nick Appiah

Hayes. *Born* Ghana, 29 November, 1968
Welterweight. Ht. 5'9"
Manager D. Gunn

29.10.92 Michael Dick W PTS 6 Hayes
24.06.93 Danny Shinkwin W PTS 6 Watford
Career: 2 contests, won 2.

Wayne Appleton
Pontefract. *Born* Hemsworth, 9 November, 1967
L. Middleweight. Ht. 5'10"
Manager Self

13.11.90	Bullit Andrews W RSC 5 Edgbaston
26.11.90	Stuart Good W CO 4 Lewisham
10.12.90	Wayne Timmins W CO 4 Birmingham
15.03.91	Andre Wharton L RSC 7 Willenhall
14.11.91	Dave Hindmarsh W RSC 8 Edinburgh
30.04.92	Kevin Adamson L RSC 2 Bayswater
01.03.93	Hughie Davey W PTS 6 Bradford
12.05.93	Richard O'Brien W RTD 2 Sheffield

Career: 8 contests, won 6, lost 2.

Lee Archer
Dudley. *Born* West Bromwich, 3 January, 1971
L. Heavyweight. Ht. 6'2"
Manager C. Flute

12.11.91	Paul Murray W PTS 6 Wolverhampton
24.03.92	Darryl Ritchie W PTS 6 Wolverhampton
28.04.92	Carl Smallwood L PTS 6 Wolverhampton
18.05.92	Marc Rowley W PTS 6 Bardon
05.10.92	Paul Murray W PTS 6 Bardon
13.10.92	Paul Murray W PTS 6 Wolverhampton
23.10.92	Ian Henry L RTD 1 Gateshead
24.11.92	Zak Chelli L PTS 6 Wolverhampton
09.02.93	Zak Goldman W CO 3 Wolverhampton
22.02.93	Carl Smallwood W PTS 8 Bedworth
17.03.93	Ian Henry W PTS 6 Stoke
06.05.93	Tony Behan DREW 6 Walsall

Career: 12 contests, won 8, drew 1, lost 3.

(Kevin) Henry Armstrong (Morris)
Manchester. *Born* Manchester, 10 December, 1967
S. Featherweight. Ht. 5'6"
Manager P. Martin

09.12.87	Sean Hogg W PTS 6 Stoke
28.03.88	Steve Bowles W RSC 5 Stoke
20.04.88	Dean Lynch L PTS 6 Stoke
03.05.88	Paul Charters W PTS 4 Stoke
16.05.88	Dean Dickinson W PTS 6 Manchester
09.08.88	Dean Dickinson L RSC 4 St Helier
20.09.88	Jimmy Vincent W PTS 6 Stoke
10.10.88	Jimmy Vincent W PTS 6 Manchester
12.12.88	Les Walsh L DIS 3 Manchester
25.01.89	Nigel Senior W PTS 8 Stoke
01.03.89	Derek Amory W PTS 8 Stoke
15.04.89	Keith Wallace L CO 7 Salisbury
20.09.89	Gary de Roux W PTS 8 Stoke
16.10.89	Graham O'Malley W PTS 8 Manchester
13.11.89	Gary Maxwell W PTS 8 Stratford on Avon
14.03.90	Mark Holt W PTS 8 Stoke
19.04.90	Gary de Roux L CO 8 Oldham
12.12.90	Colin Lynch W RSC 3 Stoke
12.04.91	Ray Newby W PTS 8 Manchester
31.01.92	Steve Robinson W PTS 6 Manchester
02.03.92	Jyrki Vierela DREW 6 Helsinki, Finland
15.09.92	Dean Lynch W RSC 5 Liverpool
26.04.93	Derek Amory W PTS 6 Manchester

Career: 23 contests, won 17, drew 1, lost 5.

Michael Armstrong (Morris)
Stoke. *Born* Moston, 18 December, 1968
Former British S. Featherweight Champion.
Ht. 5'4"
Manager J. Trickett

27.01.88	John Hales W RSC 1 Stoke
02.03.88	Gypsy Johnny W RSC 2 Stoke
20.04.88	Pepe Webber W PTS 6 Stoke
16.05.88	Steve Bowles W RSC 3 Manchester
13.06.88	Tony Heath W PTS 6 Manchester
09.08.88	G. G. Corbett W DIS 6 St Helier
20.09.88	Darren Weller W PTS 8 Stoke
26.10.88	Gary King DREW 8 Stoke
07.12.88	Mark Holt L PTS 8 Stoke
15.02.89	Gerry McBride W RSC 5 Stoke
19.04.89	Russell Davison W PTS 8 Stoke
24.05.89	Anthony Barcla W PTS 8 Hanley
04.09.89	Steve Pollard W PTS 8 Hull
06.12.89	Russell Davison L PTS 8 Stoke
06.03.90	Russell Davison W PTS 10 Stoke
18.09.90	Modest Napunyi L CO 9 Stoke *(Commonwealth Featherweight Title Challenge)*
14.10.91	Barrie Kelley W CO 4 Manchester
07.12.91	Mark Holt W RSC 4 Manchester
21.01.92	Darren Elsdon W RSC 1 Stockport *(Final Elim. British S. Featherweight Title)*
25.04.92	John Doherty W RSC 7 Manchester *(British S. Featherweight Title Challenge)*
25.07.92	Karl Taylor W RSC 3 Manchester
13.10.92	Neil Haddock L RSC 6 Bury *(British S. Featherweight Title Defence)*

Career: 22 contests, won 17, drew 1, lost 4.

Neil Armstrong
Paisley. *Born* Glasgow, 19 June, 1970
Flyweight. Ht. 5'5"
Manager A. Melrose

31.01.92	Mark Robertson W RSC 6 Glasgow
04.03.92	Des Gargano W PTS 6 Glasgow
12.03.92	Louis Veitch W PTS 6 Glasgow
10.04.92	Shaun Norman DREW 8 Glasgow
11.09.92	Louis Veitch W PTS 6 Glasgow
10.12.92	L. C. Wilson W PTS 6 Glasgow
29.01.93	Louis Veitch W PTS 6 Glasgow
04.03.93	Shaun Norman W RSC 8 Glasgow
26.03.93	Conn McMullen L RSC 5 Glasgow
29.05.93	Louis Veitch W PTS 10 Paisley

Career: 10 contests, won 8, drew 1, lost 1.

Shaun Armstrong
Hartlepool. *Born* Hartlepool, 22 September, 1968
Lightweight. Ht. 5'8"
Manager G. Robinson

05.10.92	Shea Neary L RSC 6 Liverpool
01.12.92	Tanver Ahmed W PTS 6 Hartlepool

Career: 2 contests, won 1, lost 1.

Graham Arnold
Bury St Edmonds. *Born* Fulford, 29 June, 1968
Heavyweight. Ht. 6'3"
Manager G. Holmes

24.09.91	John Palmer W CO 2 Basildon
26.10.91	Gary Charlton L RSC 1 Brentwood

Graham Arnold   Les Clark

21.01.92	Steve Yorath L PTS 6 Norwich
31.03.92	Steve Yorath W PTS 6 Norwich
08.09.92	Steve Stewart L RSC 3 Norwich
23.05.93	Julius Francis L RSC 5 Brockley

Career: 6 contests, won 2, lost 4.

(Gary) Crawford Ashley (Crawford)
Leeds. *Born* Leeds, 20 May, 1964
Former Undefeated British & Central Area
L. Heavyweight Champion. Ht. 6'3"
Manager B. Eastwood

26.03.87	Steve Ward W RSC 2 Merton
29.04.87	Lee Woolis W RSC 3 Stoke
14.09.87	Glazz Campbell L PTS 8 Bloomsbury
07.10.87	Joe Frater W RSC 5 Burnley
28.10.87	Ray Thomas W RSC 1 Stoke
03.12.87	Jonjo Greene W RSC 7 Leeds
04.05.88	Johnny Nelson L PTS 8 Solihull
15.11.88	Richard Bustin W CO 3 Norwich
22.11.88	Cordwell Hylton W CO 3 Basildon
24.01.89	John Foreman W RSC 4 Kings Heath
08.02.89	Lavell Stanley W CO 1 Kensington
28.03.89	Blaine Logsdon L RSC 2 Glasgow
10.05.89	Serg Fame W RTD 7 Solihull
31.10.89	Carl Thompson W RSC 6 Manchester *(Vacant Central Area L. Heavyweight Title)*
24.01.90	Brian Schumacher W RSC 3 Preston *(Central Area L. Heavyweight Title Defence)*
25.04.90	Dwain Muniz W RSC 1 Brighton
26.11.90	John Williams W RSC 1 Mayfair
12.02.91	Melvin Ricks W CO 1 Belfast
01.03.91	Graciano Rocchigiani L PTS 12 Dusseldorf, Germany *(Vacant European L. Heavyweight Title)*
25.07.91	Roy Skeldon W RSC 7 Dudley *(Vacant British L. Heavyweight Title)*
30.01.92	Jim Peters W RSC 1 Southampton *(British L. Heavyweight Title Defence)*
25.04.92	Glazz Campbell W RSC 8 Belfast *(British L. Heavyweight Title Defence)*
23.09.92	Yawe Davis DREW 12 Campione

68

d'Italia, Italy
(Vacant European L. Heavyweight Title)
23.04.93 Michael Nunn L RSC 5 Memphis, USA
(WBA S. Middleweight Title Challenge)
Career: 24 contests, won 18, drew 1, lost 5.

John Ashton

Alfreton. *Born* Somercotes, 22 June, 1961
Middleweight. Former Undefeated Midlands Area Middleweight & L. Middleweight Champion. Ht. 6'0¾"
Manager M. Shinfield

13.03.86 Steve Yorath W CO 3 Alfreton
25.03.86 Newton Barnett W PTS 8 Wandsworth
12.04.86 Denys Cronin L RSC 5 Isle of Man
30.05.86 Paul Smith W PTS 8 Stoke
15.09.86 Wim Thijssen L RSC 5 Scheidam, Holland
16.12.86 Mickey Lerwill W PTS 8 Alfreton
17.02.87 John Elliott DREW 6 Alfreton
02.03.87 Ian Chantler L RSC 4 Birmingham
30.03.87 Wally Swift Jnr L PTS 8 Birmingham
20.10.87 Wally Swift Jnr W PTS 8 Stoke
07.02.88 Kid Milo W PTS 10 Stafford
(Vacant Midlands Area L. Middleweight Title)
12.04.88 Derek Wormald L RSC 4 Oldham
(Elim. British L. Middleweight Title)
07.10.89 Andrea Magi L PTS 6 Pesaro, Italy
24.01.90 Kesem Clayton W PTS 10 Solihull
(Vacant Midlands Area Middleweight Title)
22.03.90 Paul Wesley W PTS 10 Wolverhampton
(Midlands Area Middleweight Title Defence)
21.06.90 Franki Moro W PTS 8 Alfreton
17.01.91 Graham Burton W PTS 10 Alfreton
28.03.91 Tony Burke W PTS 10 Alfreton
(Elim. British Middleweight Title)
24.08.91 Sumbu Kalambay L RTD 6 Pesaro, Italy
(Vacant European Middleweight Title)
10.12.91 Herol Graham L RSC 6 Sheffield
(British Middleweight Title Challenge)
26.03.92 Marvin O'Brien W PTS 8 Telford
01.10.92 Richie Woodhall L PTS 12 Telford
(Commonwealth Middleweight Title Challenge)
25.02.93 Frank Grant L RTD 7 Bradford
(British Middleweight Title Challenge)
Career: 23 contests, won 12, drew 1, lost 10.

Abel Asinamali

Tooting. *Born* USA, 20 March, 1964
L. Heavyweight. Ht. 5'10½"
Manager F. Maloney

08.01.90 Vince Durham W PTS 5 Los Angeles, USA
04.02.90 Vince Durham L PTS 6 Los Angeles, USA
26.04.90 Ken Johnson DREW 4 Irvine, USA
09.10.90 Billy Lewis L PTS 6 San Diego, USA
16.10.90 Jerome Hill W PTS 6 Albuquerque, USA
29.11.90 Paul Vega TD 1 Irvine, USA
06.12.90 Erik Brown L CO 2 Modesto, USA
23.04.92 Jason McNeill W CO 3 Eltham

10.12.92 Russell Washer L PTS 6 Bethnal Green
Career: 9 contests, won 3, drew 1, TD 1, lost 4.

Richard Atkinson

Dewsbury. *Born* Dewsbury, 25 February, 1973
L. Heavyweight. Ht. 6'1"
Manager K. Tate

27.04.92 Greg Scott-Briggs W PTS 6 Bradford
12.11.92 Carl Smallwood L PTS 6 Stafford
Career: 2 contests, won 1, lost 1.

Richard Atkinson   Chris Bevan

Michael Ayers

Tooting. *Born* London, 26 January, 1965
Former Undefeated WBC International & Southern Area Lightweight Champion. Ht. 5'8"

Manager Self

16.05.89 Young Joe Rafiu W RSC 5 Wandsworth
27.06.89 Greg Egbuniwe W CO 1 Kensington
15.11.89 Mille Markovic W RSC 2 Lewisham
05.12.89 Darren Mount W RSC 2 Catford
26.04.90 Nick Hall W CO 3 Wandsworth
04.06.91 Stuart Rimmer W CO 1 Bethnal Green
22.06.91 Wayne Weekes W RSC 6 Earls Court
(Vacant Southern Area Lightweight Title)
21.09.91 Peter Till W RSC 5 Tottenham
(Elim. British Lightweight Title)
28.01.92 Jorge Pompey W PTS 8 Hamburg, Germany
19.02.92 Rudy Valentino W RSC 7 Muswell Hill
(Southern Area Lightweight Title Defence. Elim. British Lightweight Title)
27.06.92 Sugar Gibiliru W RSC 6 Quinta do Lago, Portugal
13.10.92 Scott Brouwer W RSC 4 Mayfair
(Vacant WBC International Lightweight Title)

Michael Ayers   Pennie Cattle

20.02.93 Danny Myburgh W RSC 5 Earls Court
(WBC International Lightweight Title Defence)
16.04.93 Giovanni Parisi L PTS 12 Rome, Italy
(WBO Lightweight Title Challenge)
Career: 14 contests, won 13, lost 1.

Mossa Azward

Hackney. *Born* Kings Cross, 11 August, 1962
L. Middleweight. Ht. 5'10½"
Manager H. Holland

17.05.92 Adrian Haughton L DIS 1 Harringay
05.10.92 Paul Vache L RSC 2 Bristol
Career: 2 contests, lost 2.

Kevin Bailey

Sheffield. *Born* Sheffield, 24 March, 1970
L. Heavyweight. Ht. 5'10"
Manager R. Jones

12.05.93 Jimmy Tyers L PTS 6 Sheffield
Career: 1 contest, lost 1.

Ian Baillie

Corby. *Born* Highgate, 23 July, 1966
Flyweight. Ht. 5'2"
Manager K. Whitney

10.12.92 Tiger Singh L PTS 6 Corby
23.02.93 Graham McGrath L PTS 6 Kettering
Career: 2 contests, lost 2.

Mark Baker

Sidcup. *Born* Farnborough, 14 July, 1969
S. Middleweight. Ht. 5'9½"
Manager M. Duff

07.09.92 Jason McNeill W RSC 2 Bethnal Green
15.10.92 Graham Jenner W RTD 4 Lewisham
03.12.92 Adrian Wright W RSC 1 Lewisham
10.02.93 Paul Hanlon W RSC 2 Lewisham

69

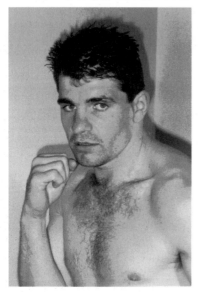

Mark Baker   Les Clark

26.04.93   Karl Mumford W CO 1 Lewisham
15.06.93   Alan Baptiste W PTS 6 Hemel
           Hempstead

Career: 6 contests, won 6.

Sean Baker

Bristol. *Born* Bristol, 21 February, 1969
Welterweight. Ht. 5'10"
Manager C. Sanigar

08.09.92   Delwyn Panayiotiou W RSC 2
           Southend
05.10.92   Raziq Ali W PTS 6 Bristol
01.12.92   Wayne Panayiotiou W RSC 3 Bristol
27.01.93   Danny Harper W PTS 6 Cardiff
09.03.93   Rick North W PTS 8 Bristol
24.03.93   Steve Levene DREW 6 Belfast
27.05.93   Gavin Lane W PTS 8 Bristol
26.06.93   David Lake W PTS 4 Keynsham

Career: 8 contests, won 7, drew 1.

Phil Ball

Doncaster. *Born* Doncaster, 23 May, 1968
S. Middleweight. Ht. 6'0½"
Manager J. Rushton

24.11.92   Martin Jolley DREW 6 Doncaster
23.02.93   Martin Jolley L RSC 5 Doncaster
01.04.93   Chris Nurse DREW 6 Evesham
29.05.93   Alan Smiles L PTS 6 Paisley
07.06.93   Justin Clements L PTS 6 Walsall
17.06.93   Mark Smallwood L RSC 1 Bedworth

Career: 6 contests, drew 2, lost 4.

Tony Banks

Leeds. *Born* Leeds, 20 June, 1967
L. Welterweight. Ht. 5'8"
Manager T. Callighan

13.11.86   Kevin Spratt DREW 6 Huddersfield
24.11.86   Tony Connellan L PTS 6 Leicester
02.03.87   Dean Eshelby DREW 6 Huddersfield
08.02.88   Barry North W RSC 3 Nottingham
18.04.88   Roy Doyle W RSC 1 Manchester
17.11.88   Pete Roberts W PTS 6 Stockport

17.02.89   Jim Moffat W PTS 6 Irvine
31.05.89   Sugar Gibiliru L CO 5 Manchester
21.09.89   Kid Sumali W RSC 1 Harrogate
28.11.89   Ludovic Proto L PTS 6 Paris, France
26.02.90   Paul Gadney L PTS 8 Crystal Palace
24.02.92   Rob Stewart DREW 6 Bradford
21.11.92   Charles Baou L CO 1 Echirolles,
           France

Career: 13 contests, won 5, drew 3, lost 5.

Alan Baptiste

Luton. *Born* Luton, 17 October, 1960
S. Middleweight. Ht. 6'1"
Manager Self

29.10.84   Terry Gilbey W PTS 6 Lewisham
26.11.84   Sean O'Phoenix DREW 6 Sheffield
23.01.85   Tony Meszaros W PTS 6 Solihull
04.02.85   Oscar Angus L RSC 5 Lewisham
18.04.85   Paul Gamble W PTS 6 Mayfair
30.04.85   Karl Barwise DREW 8 Merton
16.06.85   John Graham L PTS 8 Bethnal Green
22.07.85   Dennis Boy O'Brien W PTS 6
           Longford
10.10.85   Karl Barwise L PTS 8 Merton
21.10.85   Sean O'Phoenix L PTS 8 Nottingham
28.10.85   Gary Tomlinson W PTS 8 Stoke
19.11.85   Karl Barwise W PTS 6 Battersea
03.02.86   Paul Gamble W CO 8 Dulwich
17.03.86   Tony Meszaros W RSC 6 Birmingham
17.04.86   Tony Britton W PTS 8 Piccadilly
22.09.86   Tony Meszaros W RSC 7 Edgbaston
04.11.86   Michael Watson L PTS 8 Wembley
15.12.86   John Graham L PTS 8 Mayfair
23.03.87   T.P. Jenkins W RSC 3 Mayfair
07.05.87   Johnny Melfah L CO 1 Bayswater
26.10.87   John Graham L PTS 8 Piccadilly
03.11.87   Blaine Logsdon L RSC 3 Bethnal
           Green
29.11.88   Simon Harris L RSC 4 Battersea
07.02.89   Richard Bustin L PTS 6 Southend
16.02.89   Roland Ericsson L RSC 5 Battersea
03.10.89   Richard Bustin L PTS 6 Southend
30.04.90   Antonio Fernandez L PTS 6 Brierley
           Hill
14.05.90   Chris Walker L PTS 6 Leicester
08.10.90   Joe Frater DREW 6 Cleethorpes
12.11.90   Richard Bustin L RSC 1 Norwich
27.02.91   Gil Lewis L RSC 1 Wolverhampton
19.04.91   Tony Lawrence W RSC 5
           Peterborough
02.05.91   Kevin Morton L RSC 2 Northampton
15.06.93   Mark Baker L PTS 6 Hemel
           Hempstead

Career: 34 contests, won 12, drew 3, lost 19.

Nicky Bardle

Ealing. *Born* Ware, 30 January, 1972
Welterweight. Ht. 5'9½"
Manager H. Holland

07.11.91   Michael Clynch W RSC 4
           Peterborough
12.02.92   Steve Hearn W RSC 1 Watford
30.04.92   James Campbell L CO 1 Watford
17.09.92   Brian Coleman W RSC 4 Watford

Career: 4 contests, won 3, lost 1.

Jason Barker

Sheffield. *Born* Sheffield, 1 June, 1973
L. Welterweight. Ht. 6'0"
Manager B. Ingle

30.01.92   Nicky Lucas W PTS 6 Southampton

12.02.92   Roger Hunte L RTD 4 Wembley
29.04.92   Dave Lovell L PTS 6 Stoke
03.06.92   John O'Johnson L PTS 6 Newcastle
           under Lyne
07.07.92   Patrick Loughran L PTS 6 Bristol
21.10.92   Brian Coleman L PTS 6 Stoke
02.11.92   Shea Neary L RSC 3 Liverpool
09.12.92   John O'Johnson L PTS 8 Stoke
28.01.93   Jason Beard L RSC 3 Southwark
22.04.93   Marco Fattore L PTS 6 Mayfair
12.05.93   Shaba Edwards W PTS 6 Stoke
14.06.93   Delroy Leslie L RTD 3 Bayswater

Career: 12 contests, won 2, lost 10.

Newton Barnett

Camberwell. *Born* Jamaica 19 October,
1959
L. Middleweight. Ht. 6'0"
Manager Self

03.10.83   Ian Martin L PTS 6 Eltham
21.11.83   Ian Martin L PTS 6 Eltham
30.11.83   Kevin Webb L PTS 6 Piccadilly
06.02.84   Cliff Eastwood W PTS 6 Mayfair
01.03.84   Tony Rabbetts DREW 6 Queensway
14.03.84   Danny Sullivan L PTS 6 Mayfair
17.04.84   Danny Sullivan L PTS 6 Merton
17.09.84   Rocky McGran L CO 3 Brighton
29.10.84   Tony Baker W PTS 6 Lewisham
20.11.84   Karl Barwise L PTS 6 Merton
30.11.84   Karl Barwise W PTS 6 Longford
30.04.85   Tony Rabbetts W PTS 8 Merton
02.09.85   Shamus Casey DREW 8 Coventry
14.11.85   Ian Martin W RSC 8 Merton
02.12.85   Shamus Casey DREW 8 Dulwich
09.12.85   Victor Carvalho W PTS 6 Wandsworth
24.02.86   Charlie Watson L PTS 6 Bradford
25.03.86   John Ashton L PTS 8 Wandsworth
19.05.86   Lee Woolis W PTS 8 Nottingham
04.09.86   Steve Davies L PTS 8 Merton
03.10.86   John Mortensen L CO 2 Copenhagen,
           Denmark
16.11.87   Paul McCarthy L PTS 8 Southampton
14.12.87   Gerry Richards W PTS 6 Piccadilly
29.01.88   Mark Howell L PTS 8 Holborn
22.04.88   Joao Cabreiro L PTS 6 Lisbon,
           Portugal
11.05.88   Dave Thomas L PTS 6 Greenwich
25.05.88   Leigh Wicks DREW 8 Hastings
30.09.88   Mark Howell L PTS 8 Gillingham
26.10.88   Ian Strudwick L PTS 6 Kensington
23.11.88   Tony Britton L PTS 8 Piccadilly
08.02.89   Terry Morrill L PTS 6 Kensington
20.02.89   Tony Britton L PTS 8 Mayfair
01.03.89   Winston Wray L PTS 6 Bethnal Green
21.03.89   R. W. Smith W RTD 5 Wandsworth
05.04.89   Carlton Warren L PTS 8 Kensington
21.05.89   Winston May L PTS 4 Finsbury Park
03.06.89   Alfonso Redondo L RSC 3 Madrid,
           Spain
18.09.89   Chris Haydon W PTS 8 Mayfair
25.09.89   Winston May L PTS 6 Crystal Palace
25.10.89   Derek Grainger L PTS 8 Wembley
14.03.90   W. O. Wilson L RSC 1 Kensington
26.04.90   Paul Jones L PTS 8 Mayfair
09.05.90   Derek Grainger L RSC 4 Wembley
22.09.90   Damien Denny W RSC 6 Kensington
06.02.91   Damien Denny L PTS 8 Bethnal Green
13.02.91   Derek Grainger L RSC 3 Wembley
13.07.91   Genaro Leon L CO 2 Forges les Eaux,
           France
07.09.91   Crisanto Espana L RTD 4 Belfast
31.10.91   Robert McCracken L DIS 2
           Oakengates

30.04.92 Kevin Lueshing L PTS 6 Kensington
27.06.92 Carlo Colarusso L RTD 5 Quinta do Lago, Portugal
31.03.93 Kirkland Laing L PTS 8 Bethnal Green
Career: 52 contests, won 11, drew 4, lost 37.

Pat Barrett

Manchester. *Born* Manchester, 22 July, 1967
Welterweight. Former Undefeated British, European & Central Area L. Welterweight Champion. Ht. 5'9"
Manager Self

01.05.87 Gary Barron W RSC 6 Peterborough
18.05.87 Jim Moffat W RSC 1 Glasgow
01.06.87 Paul Burke L PTS 6 Bradford
13.06.87 Eamonn Payne W RSC 3 Great Yarmouth
01.07.87 Iskender Savas W CO 1 Interlaken, Switzerland
03.08.87 Mike Russell W PTS 6 Stoke
20.10.87 Michael Howell W PTS 4 Stoke
08.02.88 Oliver Henry W RSC 2 Manchester
01.03.88 Sugar Gibiliru DREW 8 Manchester
22.03.88 Donnie Parker W PTS 6 Baltimore, USA
12.04.88 Stanley Jones W RSC 2 Cardiff
04.05.88 Lenny Gloster W PTS 8 Solihull
08.06.88 Dave McCabe W RSC 2 Glasgow
10.10.88 Dave Haggarty W RSC 7 Glasgow
01.11.88 Jeff Connors W RSC 5 Glasgow
29.11.88 Kevin Plant W PTS 10 Manchester
(Vacant Central Area L. Welterweight Title)
06.03.89 Dean Bramhald W RSC 7 Glasgow
28.03.89 Marc Delfosse W CO 1 Glasgow
11.04.89 Sugar Gibiliru W CO 8 Oldham
(Central Area L. Welterweight Title Defence)
09.05.89 Tony Willis W CO 9 St Albans
(Vacant British L. Welterweight Title)
07.06.89 John Rafuse W CO 6 Wembley
27.06.89 Roberto Trevino W CO 2 Glasgow
19.09.89 Dana Roston W RSC 4 Millwall

Pat Barrett   Harry Goodwin

24.10.89 Robert Harkin W PTS 12 Wolverhampton
(British L. Welterweight Title Defence)
21.11.89 Joey Ferrell W RSC 6 Glasgow
02.06.90 Juan Nunez W RSC 1 Manchester
24.08.90 Efren Calamati W CO 4 Salerno, Italy
(European L. Welterweight Title Challenge)
04.10.90 Dwayne Swift W PTS 10 Bethnal Green
15.11.90 Eduardo Jacques W RSC 1 Oldham
16.01.91 Jimmy Harrison W RTD 1 Kensington
13.02.91 Salvatore Nardino W CO 6 Wembley
(European L. Welterweight Title Defence)
17.04.91 Mark McCreath W RSC 6 Kensington
(European L. Welterweight Title Defence)
09.10.91 Racheed Lawal W RSC 4 Manchester
(European L. Welterweight Title Defence)
19.12.91 Mike Johnson W RSC 2 Oldham
25.07.92 Manning Galloway L PTS 12 Manchester
(WBO L. Welterweight Title Challenge)
20.11.92 Tomas Quinones W RSC 1 Casino, Italy
19.12.92 Sam Gervins W RSC 1 San Severo, Italy
13.02.93 Juan Gonzalez W PTS 8 Manchester
Career: 38 contests, won 35, drew 1, lost 2.

(Garrett) Gary Barron

Peterborough. *Born* Peterborough, 21 December, 1964
L. Welterweight. Ht. 5'10"
Manager Self

19.02.87 Tim O'Keefe W PTS 6 Peterborough
01.05.87 Pat Barrett L RSC 6 Peterborough
14.02.88 Andrew Pybus W CO 1 Peterborough
24.02.88 Kevin Plant DREW 6 Leicester
03.11.88 James Hunter W PTS 6 Leicester
14.02.89 Tony Feliciello ND 8 Wolverhampton
01.03.89 Brian Cullen L PTS 6 Stoke
17.04.89 Frankie Lake W CO 4 Birmingham
11.09.89 Darren Mount DREW 8 Manchester
04.10.89 Oliver Harrison W PTS 8 Solihull
23.10.89 Lyn Davies L CO 2 Nottingham
24.01.90 Guillermo Zuniga L CO 1 Trapani, Italy
14.12.90 Paul Charters W RSC 3 Peterborough
13.02.91 Robert McCracken L RTD 2 Wembley
19.04.91 Tony Swift DREW 8 Peterborough
14.11.91 Paul Charters L RSC 4 Gateshead
12.02.92 Carlos Chase L RSC 5 Watford
25.03.92 Donald Stokes L RSC 2 Dagenham
30.04.92 Mark McCreath L RSC 5 Mayfair
18.06.92 Marcel Herbert W PTS 6 Peterborough
09.07.92 Peter Bradley L PTS 8 Glasgow
07.12.92 Mark McCreath L RSC 5 Mayfair
26.04.93 Tony Ekubia L RSC 4 Manchester
Career: 23 contests, won 7, drew 3, lost 12, no decision 1.

Karl Barwise

Tooting. *Born* London, 19 September, 1965
S. Middleweight. Ht. 5'11"
Manager Self

18.09.84 John Hargin W PTS 6 Merton
23.10.84 Tony Baker DREW 6 Battersea

20.11.84 Newton Barnett W PTS 6 Merton
30.11.84 Newton Barnett L PTS 6 Longford
19.12.84 Rocky McGran W RSC 6 Belfast
24.01.85 Paul Allen W CO 2 Streatham
11.02.85 Tony Baker W PTS 8 Dulwich
26.02.85 Mark Mills L PTS 6 Battersea
01.04.85 Dalton Jordan W PTS 8 Dulwich
30.04.85 Alan Baptiste DREW 8 Merton
10.10.85 Alan Baptiste W PTS 8 Merton
29.10.85 Christophe Tiozzo L PTS 8 Paris, France
19.11.85 Alan Baptiste L PTS 6 Battersea
30.01.86 Steve Ward W PTS 6 Merton
19.02.86 Michael Watson L RSC 3 Kensington
15.04.86 Neil Munn W PTS 6 Merton
22.04.86 Sammy Storey L PTS 6 Belfast
04.09.86 Dennis Boy O'Brien W RSC 2 Ealing
16.10.86 John Graham L PTS 6 Merton
29.10.86 Nicky Thorne DREW 6 Muswell Hill
05.09.90 Sean Heron L PTS 6 Brighton
22.09.90 Errol Christie L RTD 7 Kensington
20.03.91 Lester Jacobs L PTS 6 Wandsworth
03.04.91 Ali Forbes L RTD 4 Bethnal Green
26.04.91 Benji Good L RSC 3 Crystal Palace
30.05.91 Ray Webb L PTS 8 Mayfair
16.10.91 Andrew Flute W RSC 8 Stoke
22.10.91 Tony McCarthy W PTS 6 Wandsworth
13.11.91 Sammy Storey L PTS 6 Belfast
07.12.91 Pietro Pellizzaro L PTS 6 Rossano Calabro, Italy
12.05.92 Roland Ericsson L PTS 6 Crystal Palace
08.09.92 Richard Bustin L PTS 6 Norwich
15.09.92 Lou Gent L RSC 6 Crystal Palace
04.12.92 Neville Brown L RSC 6 Telford
04.03.93 Stefan Wright W RTD 5 Peterborough
18.03.93 James Cook L RSC 6 Lewisham
26.04.93 Eric Noi L PTS 6 Manchester
28.05.93 Eric Noi L RSC 4 Middleton
Career: 38 contests, won 13, drew 3, lost 22.

Jason Beard   Les Clark

Jason Beard

Beckton. *Born* Whitechapel, 24 April, 1967
L. Welterweight. Ht. 5'8½"
Manager D. Mancini

03.12.92 Robert Whitehouse W RSC 3 Lewisham
28.01.93 Jason Barker W RSC 3 Southwark
24.02.93 Michael Dick W RSC 5 Wembley
26.04.93 Brian Coleman W PTS 6 Lewisham
09.06.93 Phil Found W PTS 6 Lewisham
Career: 5 contests, won 5.

Ricky Beard
Dagenham. *Born* Hackney, 1 March, 1963
Flyweight. Ht. 5'7½"
Manager B. Hearn

02.05.89 Ged Goodwin W RSC 1 Chigwell
06.06.89 Ged Goodwin W RTD 1 Chigwell
19.09.89 Eric George L PTS 6 Bethnal Green
04.10.89 Gordon Shaw L PTS 6 Basildon
03.10.90 Neil Johnston DREW 6 Basildon
19.11.90 Robbie Regan L RSC 6 Cardiff
26.03.91 Francis Ampofo L PTS 8 Bethnal Green
30.09.91 Mickey Cantwell L PTS 8 Kensington
25.02.92 Francis Ampofo L PTS 8 Crystal Palace
14.04.92 Prince Nassem Hamed L CO 2 Mansfield
20.04.93 Tim Yeates L PTS 6 Brentwood
11.05.93 Mickey Bell W RSC 2 Norwich
29.06.93 James Drummond W PTS 8 Mayfair
Career: 13 contests, won 4, drew 1, lost 8.

Willie Beattie
Glasgow. *Born* Glasgow, 25 October, 1967
Scottish Welterweight Champion. Ht. 5'7½"
Manager Self

13.12.88 John Mullen W PTS 6 Glasgow
06.03.89 Calum Rattray W RSC 3 Glasgow
28.03.89 Ian Honeywood W PTS 4 Glasgow
08.05.89 Mick Harkin W DIS 5 Edgbaston
12.06.89 Ernie Noble W PTS 6 Glasgow
27.06.89 Calum Rattray W RSC 2 Glasgow
12.10.89 Quinn Paynter W PTS 8 Glasgow
21.11.89 Darren Mount W PTS 8 Glasgow
18.12.89 Dave Worthington W RTD 4 Glasgow
27.02.90 Humphrey Harrison L RSC 2 Manchester
01.05.90 Glyn Rhodes W RSC 5 Oldham
29.05.90 Kevin Plant W PTS 8 Glasgow
02.12.90 Antoine Fernandez L RSC 4 Elancourt, France
11.02.91 Des Robinson W PTS 8 Glasgow
24.09.91 Trevor Ambrose W PTS 8 Glasgow
31.01.92 Gordon Blair W RSC 3 Glasgow
(Vacant Scottish Welterweight Title)
10.04.92 Tony Swift L PTS 10 Glasgow
(Elim. British Welterweight Title)
07.11.92 Godfrey Nyakana L CO 1 Differdange, France
Career: 18 contests, won 14, lost 4.

Chris Beck
Cwmavon. *Born* Birmingham, 18 December, 1972
L. Heavyweight. Ht. 6'1"
Manager C. Breen

07.10.92 Karl Mumford L PTS 6 Barry
Career: 1 contest, lost 1.

Tony Behan
Birmingham. *Born* Birmingham, 5 March, 1967

L. Heavyweight. Ht. 6'0"
Manager Self

22.09.86 W.O. Wilson L CO 2 Mayfair
18.03.87 Paul Hanlon W PTS 4 Stoke
06.04.87 Jim Peters L PTS 4 Southampton
03.08.87 Darren Hobson L PTS 6 Stoke
19.11.87 Darren McKenna L RSC 1 Ilkeston
14.03.88 Richard Bustin L RSC 3 Norwich
25.04.88 Ted Cofie W RTD 4 Birmingham
03.05.88 Peter Elliott L PTS 6 Stoke
10.05.88 Floyd Davidson W PTS 6 Edgbaston
23.05.88 John Ellis DREW 6 Mayfair
22.09.88 Richard Carter L PTS 6 Wolverhampton
17.10.88 Steve Kofi DREW 6 Birmingham
05.04.89 Ian Strudwick L PTS 6 Kensington
19.04.89 Peter Elliott DREW 6 Stoke
08.05.89 Ian Vokes W PTS 6 Grimsby
16.05.89 Ian Strudwick L PTS 8 Wandsworth
02.10.89 Peter Elliott L PTS 10 Hanley
(Vacant Midlands Area S. Middleweight Title)
04.03.91 Paul Hanlon W PTS 6 Birmingham
13.05.91 Nigel Rafferty L DIS 7 Birmingham
23.05.91 Joey Peters L PTS 6 Southampton
02.12.91 Darryl Ritchie W RSC 1 Birmingham
20.01.92 Gil Lewis L PTS 8 Coventry
28.04.93 Trevor Small L PTS 6 Solihull
06.05.93 Lee Archer DREW 6 Walsall
23.06.93 Tony Booth L PTS 6 Gorleston
Career: 25 contests, won 6, drew 4, lost 15.

Leo Beirne
Llanelli. *Born* Galway, 2 December, 1966
Bantamweight. Ht. 5'6½"
Manager G. Davies

01.12.92 Graham McGrath L PTS 6 Liverpool
Career: 1 contest, lost 1.

Mickey Bell
Yarmouth. *Born* Gorleston, 17 May, 1965
Bantamweight. Ht. 5'4½"
Manager G. Holmes

11.05.93 Ricky Beard L RSC 2 Norwich
Career: 1 contest, lost 1.

Mervyn Bennett   Les Clark

Mervyn Bennett
Cardiff. *Born* Cardiff, 20 February, 1960
Welsh Lightweight Champion. Ht. 5'6½"
Manager Self

06.01.81 Geoff Smart W RSC 6 Bethnal Green
26.01.81 Paddy McGuire W RSC 2 Edgbaston
07.04.81 Philip Morris W PTS 6 Newport
25.09.81 Alec Irvine W PTS 6 Nottingham
12.10.81 Richie Foster W PTS 8 Bloomsbury
19.11.81 Don George L PTS 10 Ebbw Vale
(Vacant Welsh Featherweight Title)
26.10.82 Mike Rowley L PTS 8 Newport
24.11.82 Jimmy Duncan L PTS 8 Stoke
17.02.83 Kevin Pritchard L RSC 5 Coventry
18.04.83 Keith Foreman L RSC 6 Bradford
17.02.86 Dave Smith W PTS 8 Mayfair
10.04.86 Dave Pratt W CO 6 Leicester
29.10.86 Keith Parry L RSC 3 Ebbw Vale

Making his pro debut, Mickey Bell (right) found the experienced Ricky Beard a tough handful and was stopped inside two rounds
Les Clark

19.01.87	John Mullen W CO 1 Glasgow
16.02.87	Ray Newby L CO 8 Glasgow
19.05.92	Edward Lloyd L RSC 5 Cardiff
28.10.92	Mike Morrison W PTS 6 Cardiff
14.12.92	Mike Morrison W PTS 6 Cardiff
27.01.93	Carl Hook W PTS 10 Cardiff
	(Vacant Welsh Lightweight Title)

Career: 19 contests, won 11, lost 8.

(Adrian) Ady Benton

Bradford. *Born* Dewsbury, 26 August, 1973
Bantamweight. Ht. 5'6"
Manager K. Tate

27.04.92	Mark Hargreaves W PTS 6 Bradford
29.10.92	Vince Feeney DREW 6 Bayswater
09.11.92	Stevie Woods W PTS 6 Bradford
25.01.93	Neil Parry W RSC 6 Bradford
26.02.93	James Drummond DREW 6 Irvine
08.03.93	Dave Campbell W PTS 6 Leeds
29.06.93	Michael Alldis W DIS 3 Mayfair

Career: 7 contests, won 5, drew 2.

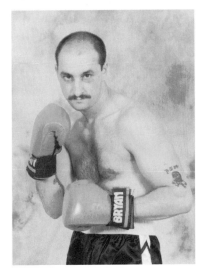

Dennis Berry   Chris Bevan

Dennis Berry

Alfreton. *Born* Birmingham, 4 April, 1967
Welterweight. Ht. 5'8"
Manager M. Shinfield

01.04.93	Lee Renshaw W RSC 3 Evesham
08.06.93	David Sumner W PTS 6 Derby

Career: 2 contests, won 2.

Ensley Bingham

Manchester. *Born* Manchester, 27 May,
1963
L. Middleweight. Ht. 5'8½"
Manager P. Martin

20.11.86	Steve Ward W CO 5 Bredbury
16.12.87	Tony Britland W CO 1 Manchester
23.02.88	Franki Moro W PTS 6 Oldham
01.03.88	Kelvin Mortimer W PTS 8 Manchester
26.04.88	Clinton McKenzie L PTS 8 Bethnal Green
18.10.88	Kostas Petrou L RSC 7 Oldham

22.03.89	Gary Cooper L PTS 8 Reading
26.09.89	Wally Swift Jnr W PTS 10 Oldham
	(Elim. British L. Middleweight Title)
28.03.90	Fernando Alanis L RSC 3 Manchester
06.06.90	Andy Till W DIS 3 Battersea
	(Final Elim. British L. Middleweight Title)
19.03.91	Wally Swift Jnr L RSC 4 Birmingham
	(Vacant British L. Middleweight Title)
29.11.91	Russell Washer W RSC 4 Manchester
29.05.92	Graham Jenner W CO 5 Manchester
18.07.92	Gordon Blair W CO 2 Manchester
02.11.92	Robert McCracken L RSC 10 Wolverhampton
	(Elim. British L. Middleweight Title)
28.05.93	Mark Kelly W RSC 5 Middleton

Career: 16 contests, won 10, lost 6.

Darren Blackford

Brixton. *Born* London, 1 December, 1966
L. Middleweight. Ht. 5'10½"
Manager F. Maloney

22.02.93	Chris Vassiliou W RSC 1 Eltham
23.05.93	Russell Washer L PTS 6 Brockley

Career: 2 contests, won 1, lost 1.

Gordon Blair

Glasgow. *Born* Glasgow, 26 February,
1969
Welterweight. Ht. 5'10"
Manager Self

21.11.89	Gavin Fitzpatrick W RSC 3 Glasgow
18.12.89	John Ritchie W PTS 4 Glasgow
19.02.90	Trevor Meikle W PTS 6 Glasgow
26.02.90	Jim Conley W RSC 3 Bradford
26.04.90	Kid Sylvester L PTS 6 Halifax
14.05.90	Trevor Ambrose W CO 5 Northampton
25.09.90	Calum Rattray W RSC 3 Glasgow
22.10.90	Shamus Casey W RSC 3 Glasgow
06.11.90	Leigh Wicks L PTS 8 Mayfair
10.12.90	Quinn Paynter W PTS 6 Glasgow
25.01.91	Danny Quigg W PTS 6 Shotts
18.02.91	Gary Logan L CO 1 Mayfair
15.04.91	Rob Pitters L PTS 6 Glasgow
31.05.91	Paul King W PTS 8 Glasgow
20.06.91	Delroy Waul W CO 2 Liverpool
24.09.91	Bozon Haule W RSC 8 Glasgow
19.11.91	Tony McKenzie L RSC 5 Norwich
31.01.92	Willie Beattie L RSC 3 Glasgow
	(Vacant Scottish Welterweight Title)
12.03.92	Mark Jay DREW 8 Glasgow

Ensley Bingham   Harry Goodwin

73

29.05.92	Ossie Maddix L PTS 6 Manchester	
18.07.92	Ensley Bingham L CO 2 Manchester	
27.10.92	Howard Clarke W RSC 4 Cradley Heath	
24.11.92	Errol McDonald L RSC 5 Doncaster	
29.01.93	Mark Cichocki L PTS 8 Glasgow	
15.02.93	Lindon Scarlett L CO 4 Mayfair	
25.06.93	Gary Logan L RSC 6 Battersea	

Career: 26 contests, won 13, drew 1, lost 12.

Everton Blake

Luton. *Born* Luton, 18 November, 1963
Former Southern Area Cruiserweight Champion. Ht. 6'3½"
Manager Self

06.04.89	Steve Conway W RSC 3 Stevenage	
04.05.89	Dave Furneaux W RSC 3 Mayfair	
22.06.89	Rebuen Thurley W RSC 5 Stevenage	
13.11.89	John Foreman L PTS 6 Brierley Hill	
06.04.90	Dave Owens W RSC 6 Stevenage	
03.05.90	Maurice Coore L PTS 8 Kensington	
14.09.90	Jason Baxter W PTS 6 Telford	
26.11.90	Gypsy Carman W PTS 6 Bethnal Green	
22.02.91	Maurice Coore L RSC 8 Manchester	
22.04.91	Terry Dixon W RSC 8 Mayfair	
14.11.91	John Graham W PTS 10 Bayswater *(Southern Area Cruiserweight Title Challenge)*	
29.10.92	Gypsy Carman W RSC 4 Hayes *(Southern Area Cruiserweight Title Defence)*	
25.11.92	John Graham L PTS 10 Mayfair *(Southern Area Cruiserweight Title Defence)*	

Career: 13 contests, won 9, lost 4.

Andrew Bloomer

Ynysbwl. *Born* Pontypridd, 26 September, 1964
Bantamweight. Ht. 5'8½"
Manager D. Gardiner

30.06.91	Leigh Williams L PTS 6 Southwark	
03.09.91	Alan Ley L PTS 6 Cardiff	
02.10.91	Bradley Stone L PTS 6 Barking	
17.10.91	Leigh Williams L PTS 6 Southwark	
04.11.91	Ceri Farrell L PTS 6 Merthyr	
20.11.91	Ceri Farrell L PTS 6 Cardiff	
28.11.91	Chris Morris L PTS 6 Liverpool	
24.02.92	Alex Docherty L PTS 6 Glasgow	
08.04.92	Jacob Smith L PTS 6 Leeds	
30.04.92	Tony Falcone L PTS 6 Mayfair	
16.05.92	Bradley Stone L PTS 6 Muswell Hill	
23.05.92	Prince Nassem Hamed L RSC 2 Birmingham	
05.10.92	Tony Falcone L PTS 8 Bristol	
12.11.92	Marcus Duncan L PTS 6 Burnley	
29.03.93	Vince Feeney L PTS 6 Mayfair	
26.04.93	Mark Bowers L PTS 6 Lewisham	
04.05.93	Paul Lloyd L PTS 6 Liverpool	

Career: 17 contests, lost 17.

Gareth Boddy

Newport. *Born* Newport, 21 May, 1969
L. Middleweight. Ht. 5'9"
Manager A. Blackstock

14.12.92	Jerry Mortimer L PTS 6 Cardiff	
27.02.93	Kevin Sheeran L RSC 1 Dagenham	

Career: 2 contests, lost 2.

Tony Booth

Sheffield. *Born* Hull, 30 January, 1970
L. Heavyweight. Ht. 5'11¾"
Manager B. Ingle

08.03.90	Paul Lynch L PTS 6 Watford	
11.04.90	Mick Duncan W PTS 6 Dewsbury	
26.04.90	Colin Manners W PTS 6 Halifax	
16.05.90	Tommy Warde W PTS 6 Hull	
05.06.90	Gary Dyson W PTS 6 Liverpool	
05.09.90	Shaun McCrory L PTS 6 Stoke	
08.10.90	Bullit Andrews W RSC 3 Cleethorpes	
23.01.91	Darron Griffiths DREW 6 Stoke	
06.02.91	Shaun McCrory L PTS 6 Liverpool	
06.03.91	Billy Brough L PTS 6 Glasgow	
18.03.91	Billy Brough W PTS 6 Glasgow	
28.03.91	Neville Brown L PTS 6 Alfreton	
17.05.91	Glenn Campbell L RSC 2 Bury *(Central Area S. Middleweight Title Challenge)*	
25.07.91	Paul Murray W PTS 6 Dudley	
01.08.91	Nick Manners DREW 8 Dewsbury	
11.09.91	Jim Peters L PTS 8 Hammersmith	
28.10.91	Eddie Smulders L RSC 6 Arnhem, Holland	
09.12.91	Steve Lewsam L PTS 8 Cleethorpes	
30.01.92	Serg Fame W PTS 6 Southampton	
12.02.92	Tenko Ernie W RSC 4 Wembley	
05.03.92	John Beckles W RSC 6 Battersea	
26.03.92	Dave Owens W PTS 6 Hull	
08.04.92	Michael Gale L PTS 8 Leeds	
13.05.92	Phil Soundy W PTS 6 Kensington	
02.06.92	Eddie Smulders L RSC 1 Rotterdam, Holland	
18.07.92	Maurice Coore L PTS 6 Manchester	
07.09.92	James Cook L PTS 8 Bethnal Green	
30.10.92	Roy Richie DREW 6 Istrees, France	
18.11.92	Tony Wilson DREW 8 Solihull	
25.12.92	Francis Wanyama L PTS 6 Izegem, Belgium	
09.02.93	Tony Wilson W PTS 8 Wolverhampton	
01.05.93	Ralf Rocchigiani DREW 8 Berlin, Germany	
03.06.93	Victor Cordoba L PTS 8 Marseille, France	
23.06.93	Tony Behan W PTS 6 Gorleston	

Career: 34 contests, won 14, drew 5, lost 15.

Tony Booth   Les Clark

John Bosco (Waigo)

Mitcham. *Born* Uganda, 16 July, 1967
L. Middleweight. Ht. 5'8½"
Manager M. Duff

05.12.91	Tony Kosova W CO 2 Peterborough	
17.02.92	Gilbert Jackson W PTS 6 Mayfair	
03.09.92	Russell Washer W RSC 2 Dunstable	
19.10.92	Steve Goodwin W RSC 2 Mayfair	
07.12.92	Griff Jones W RSC 1 Mayfair	
28.01.93	Jerry Mortimer W RSC 4 Southwark	
15.02.93	Mark Dawson W PTS 6 Mayfair	
29.03.93	Winston May W RSC 3 Mayfair	

Career: 8 contests, won 8.

Mark Bowers

Lock Heath. *Born* Fareham, 19 October, 1970
Featherweight. Ht. 5'5"
Manager M. Duff

13.05.92	Hamid Moulay W CO 1 Kensington	
17.10.92	Miguel Matthews W PTS 6 Wembley	
17.12.92	Chris Lyons W CO 2 Wembley	
26.04.93	Andrew Bloomer W PTS 6 Lewisham	
09.06.93	Kurt Griffiths W RSC 1 Lewisham	

Career: 5 contests, won 5.

Warren Bowers   Chris Bevan

Warren Bowers

Grimsby. *Born* Grimsby, 14 January, 1971
Welterweight. Ht. 5'7"
Manager L. Slater

08.05.89	Andrew Brightman W CO 5 Grimsby	
04.09.89	Mark Antony W PTS 6 Grimsby	
14.05.90	Barry North W RSC 4 Cleethorpes	
02.03.91	Andy Kent L PTS 6 Cleethorpes	
25.11.91	John Baxter L RSC 3 Cleethorpes	
04.06.92	Peter Reid L RSC 2 Cleethorpes	
26.04.93	Colin Anderson W RSC 5 Cleethorpes	

Career: 7 contests, won 4, lost 3.

Nick Boyd

Bolton. *Born* Bolton, 11 October, 1966
Lightweight. Ht. 5'10"
Manager P. Martin

05.02.93 Mark O'Callaghan W PTS 6 Manchester
28.05.93 Mark Allen W CO 2 Middleton

Career: 2 contests, won 2.

Steve Boyle

Glasgow. *Born* Glasgow, 28 November, 1962
Former Undefeated WBC International, British & Scottish Lightweight Champion. Ht. 5'7"
Manager Self

19.05.83 Shaun Dooney W RSC 3 Sunderland
06.06.83 Frankie Lake W RTD 3 Piccadilly
13.06.83 Mike McKenzie W PTS 6 Glasgow
19.09.83 Craig Walsh W PTS 6 Glasgow
17.10.83 Johnny Grant W PTS 6 Southwark
28.11.83 Robert Lloyd L PTS 6 Rhyl
07.12.83 Gary Lucas DREW 6 Stoke
27.02.84 Willie Wilson W RSC 3 Nottingham
26.03.84 Rocky Mensah DREW 8 Glasgow
11.06.84 Dave Haggarty W RSC 1 Glasgow
17.09.84 Gary Williams W CO 2 Glasgow
19.11.84 Jimmy Bunclark W RSC 2 Glasgow
21.01.85 Rory Burke W RSC 3 Glasgow
25.03.85 Peter Eubank W PTS 8 Glasgow
03.06.85 Dave Savage W RSC 7 Glasgow
          (Vacant Scottish Lightweight Title)
16.09.85 Junaido Musah W CO 4 Glasgow
14.10.85 Stanley Jones W CO 1 Glasgow
24.02.86 Mickey Baker W RSC 2 Glasgow
          (Final Elim. British Lightweight Title)
24.05.86 Tony Willis L RSC 9 Manchester
          (British Lightweight Title Challenge)
11.12.86 Simon Eubank W RSC 6 Livingston
03.03.87 Mike Durvan W PTS 10 Livingston
          (Elim. British Lightweight Title)
21.09.87 Billy Buchanan W RSC 7 Glasgow
          (Scottish Lightweight Title Defence & Final Elim. British Lightweight Title)
16.11.87 Muhammad Lovelock W PTS 8 Glasgow
24.02.88 Alex Dickson W CO 2 Glasgow
          (British Lightweight Title Challenge. Scottish Lightweight Title Defence)
19.04.88 Mark Brannon W RSC 4 Glasgow
01.11.88 Joey Jacobs W CO 8 Glasgow
          (British Lightweight Title Defence)
30.01.89 Pedro Gutierrez W PTS 12 Glasgow
          (Vacant WBC International Lightweight Title)
17.10.89 Colin Morgan W RSC 2 Cardiff
16.11.89 Policarpo Diaz L PTS 12 Madrid, Spain
          (European Lightweight Title Challenge)
14.02.90 Mark Fernandez L RSC 6 Millwall
27.04.91 Antonio Renzo L RTD 7 Rossano Calabro, Italy
          (Vacant European Lightweight Title)
05.05.92 Carl Crook L RSC 7 Preston
          (British & Commonwealth Lightweight Title Challenge)
29.05.93 Mark Antony W PTS 6 Paisley

Career: 33 contests, won 25, drew 2, lost 6.

Robert Braddock

Bolton on Dearne. *Born* Mexborough, 14 January 1971
Featherweight. Ht. 5'7"
Manager K. Tate

03.04.89 Ronnie Stephenson L CO 4 Manchester
13.10.89 Dave McNally L PTS 6 Preston
23.10.89 John Whitelaw W PTS 6 Hull
30.10.89 Pete Buckley L PTS 6 Birmingham
28.06.90 Pete Buckley L RSC 5 Birmingham
10.06.91 Tony Smith DREW 6 Manchester
23.09.91 Al Garrett DREW 6 Glasgow
07.10.91 Glyn Shepherd DREW 6 Bradford
13.11.91 Chris Morris L RSC 5 Liverpool
16.12.91 Carl Roberts L PTS 6 Manchester
28.04.92 Chip O'Neill L PTS 6 Houghton le Spring
01.06.92 Alex Docherty L PTS 6 Glasgow
08.09.92 Chris Lyons W CO 5 Doncaster
05.10.92 Karl Morling L PTS 6 Northampton
09.11.92 Chip O'Neill W RSC 3 Bradford
23.11.92 Ian McLeod DREW 6 Glasgow
07.12.92 Gary White L PTS 6 Manchester

Career: 17 contests, won 3, drew 4, lost 10.

Nigel Bradley

Sheffield. *Born* Sheffield, 24 February, 1968
L. Welterweight. Ht. 5'8"
Manager B. Ingle

14.12.87 Lee Amass L RSC 4 Piccadilly
29.01.88 John Townsley L PTS 6 Durham
23.03.88 Darren Darby W RSC 1 Sheffield
28.03.88 Adam Muir NC 4 Glasgow
18.04.88 Mark Kelly L PTS 6 Manchester
08.06.88 Mike Russell W PTS 6 Sheffield
09.09.88 David Bacon W RSC 5 Doncaster
26.10.88 Dean Dickinson W PTS 6 Sheffield
23.02.89 Chris Mulcahy W RSC 2 Stockport
09.03.89 Michael McDermott W RSC 5 Glasgow
04.04.89 John Mullen W RSC 6 Sheffield
08.10.90 John Townsley DREW 8 Glasgow
14.11.90 B. F. Williams W CO 2 Sheffield
29.01.91 Sugar Gibiliru L PTS 8 Stockport
11.02.92 Dean Hollington L PTS 6 Barking
18.03.92 Kris McAdam W CO 2 Glasgow
14.04.92 Dave Whittle W CO 3 Mansfield
29.09.92 Tony Swift L PTS 8 Stoke

Career: 18 contests, won 10, drew 1, lost 6, no contest 1.

Peter Bradley

Glasgow. *Born* Glasgow, 14 November, 1963
L. Welterweight. Ht. 5'8½"
Manager Self

18.02.85 Ian Murray W PTS 6 Mayfair
01.04.85 Tommy Frankham L RSC 2 Mayfair
01.07.85 Willie Wilson W PTS 6 Mayfair
23.09.85 Gary Flear W PTS 6 Mayfair
21.10.85 Andy Mayers L RTD 6 Mayfair
02.12.85 Paul Downie W PTS 8 Glasgow
10.02.86 Edward Lloyd W PTS 8 Glasgow
10.03.86 Dean Bramhald W PTS 8 Glasgow
02.06.86 Dean Bramhald W PTS 8 Glasgow
06.05.87 Dean Bramhald W RSC 4 Livingston
24.09.87 Marvin P. Gray L PTS 8 Glasgow

02.12.87 Graham Kid Clarke W PTS 8 Piccadilly
29.02.88 Karl Taylor W PTS 8 Birmingham
09.03.88 Steve Pollard W PTS 8 Wembley
25.04.88 Kid Sumali W PTS 8 Birmingham
26.09.88 Tony Foster W PTS 8 Piccadilly
17.01.89 Steve Pollard W PTS 8 Chigwell
08.03.89 Kid Sumali W PTS 8 Kensington
10.04.89 George Jones W RSC 4 Mayfair
18.09.89 Chubby Martin W PTS 8 Mayfair
11.12.89 Kid Sumali W RSC 3 Bayswater
19.02.90 Alberto Alicia W RSC 2 Mayfair
27.03.90 Rudy Valentino W PTS 8 Mayfair
22.10.90 Andy Deabreu W RSC 3 Mayfair
21.01.91 Paul Burke L PTS 10 Glasgow
          (Elim. British Lightweight Title)
16.09.91 Tony Borg W PTS 8 Mayfair
30.03.92 Alan Peacock W PTS 8 Glasgow
09.07.92 Gary Barron W PTS 8 Glasgow
04.09.92 Soren Sondergaard L CO 4 Copenhagen, Denmark
29.10.92 Phil Holliday L RSC 6 Morula, South Africa
29.03.93 Rob Stewart W RSC 5 Glasgow

Career: 31 contests, won 25, lost 6.

Dean Bramhald

Doncaster. *Born* Balby, 25 May, 1963
L. Welterweight. Former Central Area Lightweight Champion. Ht. 5'7½"
Manager Self

25.01.84 Wayne Trigg L CO 3 Stoke
22.02.84 Andy Deabreu L PTS 6 Evesham
27.02.84 Billy Joe Dee W PTS 6 Nottingham
19.03.84 Billy Joe Dee L PTS 6 Bradford
27.03.84 Neville Fivey DREW 6 Wolverhampton
04.04.84 Peter Bowen L PTS 6 Evesham
12.04.84 Andy Deabreu L PTS 6 Piccadilly
09.05.84 Wayne Trigg DREW 4 Leicester
21.05.84 Doug Munro L PTS 6 Aberdeen
11.06.84 Glenn Tweedie L PTS 6 Glasgow
06.08.84 Andy Williams L PTS 6 Aintree
21.09.84 Clinton Campbell W PTS 6 Alfreton
02.10.84 John Doherty L PTS 6 Leeds
10.10.84 Rocky Lawler W RSC 5 Stoke
22.10.84 John Maloney DREW 6 Mayfair
29.10.84 Ray Newby L PTS 6 Nottingham
19.11.84 Dave Adam L PTS 6 Glasgow
27.11.84 Mickey Markie DREW 6 Wolverhampton
05.12.84 Neville Fivey W PTS 6 Stoke
17.12.84 John Maloney W PTS 6 Mayfair
18.01.85 Mark Reefer L RSC 8 Bethnal Green
20.02.85 Stuart Carmichael DREW 6 Stafford
01.03.85 Craig Windsor DREW 6 Glasgow
13.03.85 Dave Adam L PTS 8 Stoke
25.03.85 Michael Marsden W PTS 8 Huddersfield
05.04.85 Bobby McDermott L PTS 8 Glasgow
18.04.85 John Doherty L PTS 8 Halifax
04.06.85 Pat Doherty L CO 6 Streatham
31.07.85 Robert Dickie L RSC 7 Porthcawl
23.09.85 Kevin Taylor L RSC 1 Bradford
21.10.85 Kevin Taylor L PTS 6 Bradford
21.11.85 Russell Jones L PTS 8 Blaenavon
30.11.85 Floyd Havard L RSC 3 Cardiff
20.01.86 Paul Downie L PTS 8 Glasgow
06.02.86 Stuart Carmichael W PTS 8 Doncaster
20.02.86 Floyd Havard L PTS 6 Halifax
10.03.86 Peter Bradley L PTS 8 Glasgow
17.03.86 Paul Downie L CO 5 Glasgow

27.04.86 Andrew Pybus W PTS 6 Doncaster
20.05.86 Eamonn McAuley L PTS 6 Wembley
02.06.86 Peter Bradley L PTS 8 Mayfair
13.06.86 Peppy Muire L RSC 7 Gloucester
30.07.86 Steve James L PTS 8 Ebbw Vale
17.11.86 Jim Moffat L PTS 6 Glasgow
25.11.86 Joey Joynson L PTS 8 Wolverhampton
03.12.86 Steve Brown L PTS 6 Stoke
15.12.86 Rocky Lester W PTS 6 Loughborough
26.01.87 Tony Swift L PTS 8 Birmingham
09.02.87 Peter Crook L PTS 8 Manchester
16.02.87 Nigel Senior L PTS 8 Glasgow
04.03.87 Tony Swift L RSC 5 Dudley
06.04.87 Drew Black L PTS 8 Glasgow
27.04.87 Kevin Spratt L PTS 8 Bradford
06.05.87 Peter Bradley L RSC 4 Livingston
04.06.87 David Maw L PTS 6 Sunderland
13.06.87 Michael Betts DREW 6 Great Yarmouth
04.09.87 David Maw L PTS 6 Gateshead
14.09.87 John Bennie W PTS 6 Glasgow
07.10.87 Tony Swift L PTS 8 Stoke
19.10.87 Peter Till L PTS 8 Birmingham
11.11.87 Ron Shinkwin W PTS 8 Stafford
24.11.87 Peter Till L PTS 8 Wolverhampton
02.12.87 Tony Swift L PTS 8 Stoke
14.12.87 Ron Shinkwin L PTS 8 Bradford
20.01.88 Davy Robb L PTS 8 Stoke
29.01.88 Frankie Lake L PTS 8 Torquay
07.02.88 Damien Denny L PTS 4 Stafford
24.02.88 David Lake W PTS 6 Southend
09.03.88 Mickey Vern W CO 5 Stoke
23.03.88 Frankie Lake DREW 8 Evesham
13.04.88 Davy Robb W RSC 5 Wolverhampton
25.04.88 Nigel Senior W PTS 8 Nottingham
16.05.88 Ronnie Campbell L RSC 7 Wolverhampton
16.06.88 Mark Dinnadge W PTS 8 Croydon
26.09.88 Dave Croft DREW 4 Bradford
06.10.88 Ronnie Campbell W RSC 6 Dudley
17.10.88 Dave Griffiths L RSC 5 Mayfair
17.11.88 Tony Feliciello L PTS 8 Weston super Mare
29.11.88 Neil Foran L PTS 6 Manchester
16.12.88 Brian Sonny Nickels L PTS 6 Brentwood
26.01.89 George Baigrie W PTS 6 Newcastle
14.02.89 Steve Hogg W PTS 6 Wolverhampton
06.03.89 Pat Barrett L RSC 2 Manchester
03.04.89 Brian Cullen W RSC 3 Manchester
19.04.89 Calum Rattray W PTS 6 Doncaster
26.04.89 Michael Driscoll L RSC 2 Southampton
29.05.89 Peter Hart L RSC 2 Liverpool
25.09.89 Ian Honeywood L RTD 4 Crystal Palace
25.10.89 Oliver Henry L PTS 6 Doncaster
28.11.89 Shaun Cooper L CO 2 Wolverhampton
17.01.90 Peter Bowen W PTS 6 Stoke
24.01.90 Paul Bowen L PTS 8 Solihull
07.03.90 Andrew Robinson L PTS 6 Doncaster
14.03.90 Shaun Cogan L PTS 6 Stoke
04.04.90 Dave Croft W PTS 6 Stafford
26.04.90 Seamus O'Sullivan L PTS 6 Wandsworth
21.05.90 Brendan Ryan DREW 6 Grimsby
05.06.90 Billy Couzens L PTS 6 Nottingham
22.06.90 Mark Dinnadge L PTS 6 Gillingham
14.11.90 Jim Lawlor DREW 8 Cleethorpes
13.12.90 Andrew Morgan DREW 8 Cleethorpes
10.12.90 Colin Sinnott W PTS 6 Bradford
17.12.90 Sugar Gibiliru L PTS 8 Manchester
17.01.91 Richard Burton L RTD 1 Alfreton
05.03.91 Charlie Kane L RSC 6 Glasgow

10.04.91 Ronnie Campbell W PTS 6 Wolverhampton
24.04.91 Dave Jenkins L PTS 8 Aberavon
13.05.91 Andrew Robinson L RTD 1 Birmingham
17.06.91 Malcolm Melvin L PTS 6 Edgbaston
04.07.91 Shane Sheridan L PTS 6 Alfreton
10.09.91 Mark Elliot L CO 5 Wolverhampton
08.10.91 Colin Sinnott L PTS 8 Wolverhampton
21.10.91 Colin Sinnott W PTS 6 Cleethorpes
20.11.91 Rocky Feliciello L PTS 6 Solihull
04.12.91 Ron Shinkwin W PTS 8 Stoke
22.01.92 Ray Newby L PTS 8 Solihull
30.01.92 Ron Shinkwin L PTS 6 Southampton
11.02.92 Ray Newby L RSC 7 Wolverhampton
11.03.92 Andreas Panayi W PTS 8 Stoke
24.03.92 Richard Swallow L PTS 8 Wolverhampton
06.04.92 Richard Swallow L PTS 6 Northampton
28.04.92 Darren McInulty L PTS 6 Wolverhampton
11.05.92 Darren McInulty L PTS 6 Coventry
12.06.92 Carl Wright L PTS 6 Liverpool
15.09.92 Mike Morrison W PTS 6 Crystal Palace
30.09.92 Barrie Kelley L PTS 6 Solihull
13.10.92 Bernard Paul DREW 6 Mayfair
26.11.92 Kevin Toomey W PTS 10 Hull
(Central Area Lightweight Title Challenge)
12.12.92 Mark Tibbs L PTS 6 Muswell Hill
20.01.93 Dean Amory L PTS 6 Solihull
18.02.93 Kevin Toomey L PTS 10 Hull
(Central Area Lightweight Title Defence)
23.03.93 Alan Peacock W PTS 6 Wolverhampton
01.04.93 Shane Sheridan W PTS 6 Evesham
30.04.93 Alan McDowall L PTS 6 Glasgow
14.05.93 Tanver Ahmed L PTS 6 Kilmarnock
07.06.93 Howard Clarke L RTD 2 Walsall
Career: 136 contests, won 31, drew 14, lost 91.

Paul Braxton (Johnson)
Grimsby. *Born* Grimsby, 19 August, 1970
L. Middleweight. Ht. 5'10"
Manager L. Slater

26.04.93 Tony Trimble L RSC 2 Cleethorpes
Career: 1 contest, lost 1.

Tony Britland
Barmouth. *Born* Dolgellau, 26 November, 1960
Welterweight. Ht. 5'7"
Manager Self

12.01.87 Mark Dinnadge L RSC 3 Ealing
18.03.87 Jimmy Ward W PTS 6 Queensway
15.04.87 Kevin Hayde W PTS 6 Carmarthen
07.05.87 Simon Paul L PTS 6 Bayswater
09.06.87 Ossie Maddix L PTS 6 Manchester
17.09.87 Ian John-Lewis L PTS 6 Gravesend
24.09.87 Martin Smith DREW 6 Crystal Palace
19.10.87 Ossie Maddix L PTS 6 Manchester
30.11.87 Barry Messam L PTS 6 Nottingham
16.12.87 Ensley Bingham L CO 1 Manchester
13.04.88 Martin Smith L RSC 2 Gravesend
08.06.88 Eamonn Loughran L RSC 1 Sheffield
25.10.88 Pat Dunne W PTS 6 Pontardawe
15.11.88 Tony Gibbs DREW 6 Piccadilly
23.11.88 John Corcoran DREW 8 Solihull
07.12.88 Michael Oliver L RSC 2 Aberavon

25.01.89 John Corcoran L PTS 8 Solihull
28.02.89 Ronnie Campbell DREW 6 Dudley
16.03.89 Leigh Wicks L PTS 8 Southwark
11.04.89 Adrian Din L PTS 6 Aberavon
17.04.89 Wayne Timmins DREW 6 Birmingham
24.04.89 Adrian Din W PTS 6 Nottingham
10.05.89 Gary Logan L CO 1 Kensington
19.08.89 Jimmy Farrell L PTS 6 Cardiff
09.11.89 Jimmy Farrell L RSC 4 Cardiff
11.12.89 Alan Richards L RSC 7 Birmingham
23.04.90 Wayne Timmins L PTS 8 Birmingham
24.05.90 Wayne Timmins L PTS 8 Dudley
11.06.90 Des Robinson L PTS 8 Manchester
16.11.90 Robert Wright L RSC 3 Telford
21.02.91 Shaun Cogan L PTS 6 Walsall
06.03.91 Robert McCracken L RSC 2 Wembley
12.04.91 Darren Morris W PTS 6 Willenhall
14.05.91 Wayne Timmins L PTS 6 Dudley
03.10.91 John Corcoran W RSC 5 Burton
21.10.91 Leigh Wicks L RSC 3 Mayfair
02.12.91 Richard O'Brien L RSC 2 Birmingham
18.05.93 Spencer McCracken L CO 1 Edgbaston
29.06.93 James Campbell L PTS 6 Edgbaston
Career: 39 contests, won 6, drew 5, lost 28.

Mark Brogan
Leicester. *Born* Leicester, 24 May, 1964
Welterweight. Ht. 5'8"
Manager J. Griffin

03.03.86 Mike Breen DREW 4 Leicester
10.04.86 Wil Halliday L PTS 4 Leicester
15.12.86 Oliver Henry L CO 2 Loughborough
22.02.93 Dave Maj L RSC 5 Liverpool
Career: 4 contests, drew 1, lost 3.

Mike Anthony Brown   Les Clark

Mike Anthony Brown
Brixton. *Born* Jamaica, 8 February, 1970
Lightweight. Ht. 5'8"
Manager F. Maloney

23.05.93 Norman Dhalie L PTS 4 Brockley
25.06.93 G.G. Goddard W CO 2 Battersea
Career: 2 contests, won 1, lost 1.

Neville Brown
Burton. *Born* Burton, 26 February, 1966
Middleweight. Ht. 5'10"
Manager M. Duff

08.11.89   Spencer Alton W RSC 4 Wembley
10.01.90   Colin Ford W RTD 4 Kensington
27.03.90   Jimmy McDonagh W RSC 2 Mayfair
09.05.90   William Pronzola W RSC 3 Wembley
13.09.90   Anthony Campbell W RSC 2 Watford
10.10.90   Nigel Moore W CO 1 Kensington
13.12.90   Chris Richards W RSC 2 Dewsbury
17.01.91   Shamus Casey W RSC 4 Alfreton
13.02.91   Jimmy Thornton W RSC 1 Wembley
28.03.91   Tony Booth W PTS 6 Alfreton
12.04.91   Winston Wray W RSC 1 Willenhall
04.07.91   Paul Wesley L RSC 1 Alfreton
29.08.91   Paul Smith W RSC 3 Oakengates
03.10.91   Paul Wesley W PTS 8 Burton
21.11.91   Colin Pitters W RSC 3 Burton
26.03.92   Paul Murray W CO 3 Telford
01.10.92   Ernie Loveridge W CO 4 Telford
02.11.92   Horace Fleary W PTS 8
           Wolverhampton
04.12.92   Karl Barwise W RSC 6 Telford
20.01.93   Graham Burton W CO 4
           Wolverhampton
16.03.93   Paul Busby W PTS 10 Wolverhampton
           (Elim. British Middleweight Title)
Career: 21 contests, won 20, lost 1.

Denzil Browne

Leeds. *Born* Leeds, 21 January, 1969
Cruiserweight. Ht. 6'2½"
Manager M. Duff

18.10.90   Mark Bowen W PTS 6 Dewsbury
29.11.90   R. F. McKenzie L PTS 6 Sunderland
13.12.90   Gary Railton W RSC 2 Dewsbury
21.02.91   Mark Bowen W PTS 6 Walsall
21.03.91   R. F. McKenzie W PTS 6 Dewsbury
09.05.91   Darren McKenna W PTS 6 Leeds
27.06.91   Steve Yorath W PTS 6 Leeds
01.08.91   Tony Colclough W RSC 1 Dewsbury
09.10.91   R. F. McKenzie L PTS 6 Manchester
30.10.91   Gus Mendes W RSC 6 Leeds
23.01.92   Darren McKenna W PTS 6 York
19.03.92   Ian Bulloch W PTS 8 York
23.09.92   Steve Yorath W PTS 8 Leeds
29.10.92   Sean O'Phoenix W RSC 4 Leeds
25.02.93   Cordwell Hylton W PTS 8 Bradford
22.04.93   Dave Muhammed W PTS 8 Mayfair
Career: 16 contests, won 14, lost 2.

Frank Bruno

Wandsworth. *Born* Hammersmith, 16
November, 1961
Former Undefeated European Heavyweight
Champion. Ht. 6'3½"
Manager Self

17.03.82   Lupe Guerra W CO 1 Kensington
30.03.82   Harvey Steichen W RSC 2 Wembley
20.04.82   Tom Stevenson W CO 1 Kensington
04.05.82   Ron Gibbs W RSC 4 Wembley
01.06.82   Tony Moore W RSC 2 Kensington
14.09.82   George Scott W RSC 1 Wembley
23.10.82   Ali Lukasa W CO 2 Berlin, Germany
09.11.82   Rudi Gauwe W CO 2 Kensington
23.11.82   George Butzbach W RTD 1 Wembley
07.12.82   Gilberto Acuna W RSC 1 Kensington
18.01.83   Stewart Lithgo W RTD 4 Kensington
08.02.83   Peter Mulendwa W CO 3 Kensington
01.03.83   Winston Allen W RSC 2 Kensington
05.04.83   Eddie Neilson W RSC 3 Kensington
03.05.83   Scott Ledoux W RSC 3 Wembley
31.05.83   Barry Funches W RSC 5 Kensington
09.07.83   Mike Jameson W CO 2 Chicago, USA

Frank Bruno

27.09.83   Bill Sharkey W CO 1 Wembley
11.10.83   Floyd Cummings W RSC 7
           Kensington
06.12.83   Walter Santemore W CO 4 Kensington
13.03.84   Juan Figueroa W CO 1 Wembley
13.05.84   James Smith L CO 10 Wembley
25.09.84   Ken Lakusta W CO 2 Wembley
           (Elim. Commonwealth Heavyweight
           Title)
06.11.84   Jeff Jordan W RSC 3 Kensington
27.11.84   Phil Brown W PTS 10 Wembley
26.03.85   Lucien Rodriguez W RSC 1 Wembley
01.10.85   Anders Eklund W CO 4 Wembley
           (European Heavyweight Title
           Challenge)
04.12.85   Larry Frazier W CO 2 Kensington
04.03.86   Gerrie Coetzee W CO 1 Wembley
           (Final Elim. WBA Heavyweight Title)
19.07.86   Tim Witherspoon L RSC 11 Wembley
           (WBA Heavyweight Title Challenge)
24.03.87   James Tillis W RSC 5 Wembley
27.06.87   Chuck Gardner W CO 1 Cannes,
           France
30.08.87   Reggie Gross W RSC 8 Marbella,
           Spain
24.10.87   Joe Bugner W RSC 8 Tottenham
25.02.89   Mike Tyson L RSC 5 Las Vegas, USA
           (WBC Heavyweight Title Challenge)
20.11.91   John Emmen W CO 1 Kensington
22.04.92   Jose Ribalta W CO 2 Wembley
17.10.92   Pierre Coetzer W RSC 8 Wembley
           (Elim. IBF Heavyweight Title)
24.04.93   Carl Williams W RSC 10 Birmingham
Career: 39 contests, won 36, lost 3.

(Delroy) Del Bryan

Birmingham. *Born* Nottingham, 16 April,
1967
Former British Welterweight Champion.
Former Undefeated Midlands Area
Welterweight Champion. Ht. 5'8"
Manager W. Swift

21.04.86   Wil Halliday W PTS 6 Birmingham
15.05.86   Gary Sommerville L PTS 6 Dudley

28.05.86   Trevor Hopson W RTD 4 Lewisham
26.06.86   Gary Sommerville L PTS 8 Edgbaston
26.09.86   Gary Cass W PTS 6 Swindon
06.10.86   Gary Sommerville W PTS 8
           Birmingham
14.10.86   Mickey Lerwill W PTS 8
           Wolverhampton
04.11.86   George Collins L RSC 4 Oldham
16.12.86   Ray Golding W PTS 6 Alfreton
08.01.87   Darren Dyer W PTS 6 Bethnal Green
17.02.87   Tommy Shiels L RSC 2 Alfreton
30.09.87   Peter Ashcroft W PTS 8 Solihull
26.10.87   Gary Sommerville W RSC 7
           Birmingham
           (Vacant Midlands Area Welterweight
           Title)
03.12.87   Mickey Hughes W PTS 8 Southend
15.12.87   Lloyd Christie W PTS 8 Bradford
24.02.88   Gary Jacobs L PTS 10 Glasgow
           (Final Elim. British Welterweight Title)
09.03.88   Michael Justin DREW 8 Wembley
20.04.88   Kelvin Mortimer W RSC 4 Stoke
04.05.88   Gary Sommerville W PTS 8 Solihull
09.08.88   Jimmy Thornton W PTS 6 St Helier
28.09.88   Ossie Maddix W PTS 8 Solihull
12.12.88   Michael Justin W RSC 8 Nottingham
           (Midlands Area Welterweight Title
           Defence)
22.03.89   Lenny Gloster W PTS 8 Solihull
10.05.89   Crisanto Espana L PTS 8 Kensington
19.08.89   Javier Castillejos W PTS 8 Benidorm,
           Spain
04.09.89   Joni Nyman L PTS 8 Helsinki, Finland
30.01.90   Simon Eubank W PTS 6 Battersea
16.02.90   Arvey Castro W RSC 1 Bilbao, Spain
17.04.90   Damien Denny W PTS 10 Millwall
           (Final Elim. British Welterweight Title)
30.09.90   Phumzile Madikane L RSC 6
           Capetown, South Africa
16.01.91   Kirkland Laing W PTS 12
           Wolverhampton
           (British Welterweight Title Challenge)
16.04.91   Anthony Ivory W PTS 10 Nottingham
26.11.91   Mickey Hughes W RSC 3 Bethnal Green
           (British Welterweight Title Defence)

77

20.02.92 Gary Jacobs L PTS 12 Glasgow
(British Welterweight Title Challenge)
12.05.92 Darren Dyer L RSC 10 Crystal Palace
29.09.92 Chris Peters W PTS 10 Stoke
Career: 36 contests, won 25, drew 1, lost 10.

Denroy Bryan

Swindon. *Born* Birmingham, 15 November, 1959
Heavyweight. Ht. 5'11¼"
Manager W. Burnett

16.09.83 Michael Armstrong W RSC 1 Swindon
14.11.83 Michael Armstrong W RSC 4 Nantwich
22.02.84 Glenn McCrory L PTS 8 Kensington
30.04.84 Dave Garside L PTS 8 Mayfair
25.01.85 Noel Quarless L RSC 1 Liverpool
22.04.85 Ralph Irving W PTS 6 Southwark
30.05.85 Carl Gaffney L RSC 1 Halifax
12.09.85 Ian Priest W RSC 7 Swindon
01.10.85 Dave Garside L RSC 3 Wembley
14.11.85 Paul Lister L PTS 8 Newcastle
19.02.86 Gary Mason L CO 1 Kensington
01.04.87 Barry Ellis DREW 8 Southsea
12.10.87 John Emmen L PTS 8 Hertogenbosch, Holland
09.02.88 James Oyebola L RSC 6 Bethnal Green
29.03.88 Keith Ferdinand L RSC 2 Bethnal Green
16.05.88 Al Malcolm L PTS 10 Wolverhampton
(Midlands Area Heavyweight Title Challenge)
28.10.88 Jess Harding L RSC 4 Brentwood
05.12.88 David Jules DREW 6 Dudley
18.01.89 David Jules L RSC 2 Stoke
23.10.89 John Williams DREW 6 Mayfair
10.11.89 Barry Ellis W RSC 3 Battersea
05.12.89 Adam Fogerty L RSC 3 Dewsbury
03.02.90 Gary McConnell L RSC 9 Bristol
06.03.90 Manny Burgo L PTS 8 Newcastle
20.03.90 Paul Lister L PTS 8 Hartlepool
25.05.90 Cesare di Benedetto L RSC 5 Avezzano, Italy
29.11.90 Adam Fogerty L RSC 2 Sunderland
12.11.91 J. A. Bugner L PTS 4 Milton Keynes
11.12.91 Joe Egan W RSC 4 Dublin
31.01.92 Maurice Coore L RSC 1 Manchester
05.10.92 Damien Caesar L RSC 5 Bristol
01.12.92 Barry Ellis W PTS 6 Bristol
02.01.93 Godfrey Nyakana L PTS 8 Differdange, France
22.02.93 Warren Richards L CO 4 Eltham
10.04.93 Dermot Gascoyne L PTS 6 Swansea
11.05.93 Scott Welch L RSC 4 Norwich
Career: 36 contests, won 7, drew 3, lost 26.

Mark Buck

Nottingham. *Born* Nottingham, 7 October, 1964
L. Heavyweight. Ht. 5'7"
Manager M. Shinfield

02.02.93 Peter Flint W CO 2 Derby
19.04.93 Jimmy Tyers L RSC 4 Manchester
Career: 2 contests, won 1, lost 1.

Wayne Buck

Nottingham. *Born* Nottingham, 31 August, 1966
Heavyweight. Ht. 5'10¾"
Manager M. Shinfield

Wayne Buck   Chris Bevan

26.03.90 Tucker Richards W CO 1 Nottingham
30.04.90 Chris Hubbert L CO 4 Nottingham
04.06.92 Gary Charlton W PTS 6 Cleethorpes
08.09.92 David Jules W RSC 3 Doncaster
12.11.92 Gary Charlton W PTS 8 Stafford
02.02.93 John Harewood L RSC 3 Derby
11.03.93 Vance Idiens W PTS 8 Walsall
Career: 7 contests, won 5, lost 2.

Pete Buckley

Birmingham. *Born* Birmingham, 9 March, 1969
Midlands Area S. Featherweight Champion. Ht. 5'8"
Manager Self

04.10.89 Alan Baldwin DREW 6 Stafford
10.10.89 Ronnie Stephenson L PTS 6 Wolverhampton
30.10.89 Robert Braddock W PTS 6 Birmingham
14.11.89 Neil Leitch W PTS 6 Evesham
22.11.89 Peter Judson W PTS 6 Stafford
11.12.89 Stevie Woods W PTS 6 Bradford
21.12.89 Wayne Taylor W PTS 6 Kings Heath
10.01.90 John O'Meara W PTS 6 Kensington
19.02.90 Ian McGirr L PTS 6 Birmingham
27.02.90 Miguel Matthews DREW 6 Evesham
14.03.90 Ronnie Stephenson DREW 6 Stoke
04.04.90 Ronnie Stephenson L PTS 8 Stafford
23.04.90 Ronnie Stephenson W PTS 6 Birmingham
30.04.90 Chris Clarkson L PTS 8 Mayfair
17.05.90 Johnny Bredahl L PTS 6 Aars, Denmark
04.06.90 Ronnie Stephenson W PTS 8 Birmingham
28.06.90 Robert Braddock W RSC 5 Birmingham
01.10.90 Miguel Matthews W PTS 8 Cleethorpes
09.10.90 Miguel Matthews L PTS 8 Wolverhampton
17.10.90 Tony Smith W PTS 6 Stoke
29.10.90 Miguel Matthews W PTS 8 Birmingham

21.11.90 Drew Docherty L PTS 8 Solihull
10.12.90 Neil Leitch W PTS 8 Birmingham
10.01.91 Duke McKenzie L RSC 5 Wandsworth
18.02.91 Jamie McBride L PTS 8 Glasgow
04.03.91 Brian Robb W RSC 7 Birmingham
26.03.91 Neil Leitch DREW 8 Wolverhampton
01.05.91 Mark Geraghty W PTS 8 Solihull
05.06.91 Brian Robb W PTS 10 Wolverhampton
(Vacant Midlands Area S. Featherweight Title)
09.09.91 Mike Deveney L PTS 8 Glasgow
24.09.91 Mark Bates W RTD 5 Basildon
29.10.91 John Armour L PTS 6 Kensington
14.11.91 Mike Deveney L PTS 6 Edinburgh
28.11.91 Craig Dermody L PTS 6 Liverpool
19.12.91 Craig Dermody L PTS 6 Oldham
18.01.92 Alan McKay DREW 8 Kensington
20.02.92 Brian Robb W RSC 10 Oakengates
(Midlands Area S. Featherweight Title Defence)
27.04.92 Drew Docherty L PTS 8 Glasgow
15.05.92 Ruben Condori L PTS 10 Augsburg, Germany
29.05.92 Donnie Hood L PTS 8 Glasgow
07.09.92 Duke McKenzie L RTD 3 Bethnal Green
12.11.92 Prince Nassem Hamed L PTS 6 Liverpool
19.02.93 Harald Geier L PTS 12 Vienna, Austria
(Vacant WBA Penta-Continental S. Bantamweight Title)
26.04.93 Bradley Stone L PTS 8 Lewisham
18.06.93 Eamonn McAuley L PTS 6 Belfast
Career: 45 contests, won 18, drew 5, lost 22.

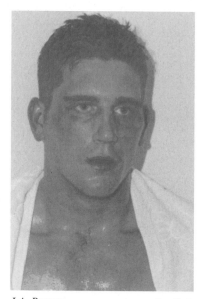

J.A. Bugner   Les Clark

(Joe) J. A. Bugner

St Ives. *Born* St Ives, 12 August, 1970
Heavyweight. Ht. 6'6"
Manager A. Smith

12.11.91 Denroy Bryan W PTS 4 Milton Keynes
06.02.92 Gary Railton W CO 3 Peterborough
05.03.92 John Harewood W PTS 4 Battersea
22.04.92 Gary McCrory W PTS 4 Wembley

07.09.92　Gary Williams W PTS 4 Bethnal Green
17.10.92　Steve Gee W PTS 6 Wembley
17.12.92　Chris Coughlan W RSC 3 Wembley
24.02.93　Steve Garber L RSC 6 Wembley
Career: 8 contests, won 7, lost 1.

Ian Bulloch

Bolsover. *Born* Bolsover, 25 January, 1965
Cruiserweight. Ht. 6'0"
Manager J. Gaynor

24.03.87　Danny Hassan W RSC 4 Nottingham
09.04.87　Patrick Collins W PTS 6 Weston super
　　　　　Mare
29.04.87　Gus Mendes W PTS 6 Stoke
09.06.87　Steve Osborne W PTS 6 Manchester
03.08.87　Ray Thomas W PTS 8 Stoke
06.10.87　Sean Daly W RSC 4 Manchester
10.11.87　Gary Railton W PTS 6 Batley
12.01.88　Abner Blackstock W PTS 8 Cardiff
07.03.88　Danny Lawford W PTS 8 Hove
09.05.88　Roy Smith L PTS 10 Nottingham
　　　　　*(Midlands Area Cruiserweight Title
　　　　　Challenge)*
15.11.88　Noel Magee DREW 10 Hull
13.12.88　Yawe Davis L RSC 6 San Pellegrino,
　　　　　Italy
03.06.89　Dave Garside W PTS 10 Stanley
　　　　　(Elim. British Cruiserweight Title)
02.10.89　Johnny Nelson L CO 2 Hanley
　　　　　(British Cruiserweight Title Challenge)
02.03.90　Fabrice Tiozzo L PTS 6 Nice, France
12.05.90　Francis Wanyama L RSC 5
　　　　　Waasmunster, Belgium
18.09.90　Gary McCrory L PTS 8 Stoke
02.03.91　Roy Smith L PTS 10 Cleethorpes
　　　　　*(Midlands Area Cruiserweight Title
　　　　　Challenge)*
24.06.91　Pedro van Raamsdonk L PTS 8
　　　　　Rotterdam, Holland
13.10.91　Przemyslaw Saleta L RSC 8 Warsaw,
　　　　　Poland
19.03.92　Denzil Browne L PTS 8 York
27.04.92　Terry Dixon L RSC 4 Mayfair
26.10.92　Art Stacey W PTS 6 Cleethorpes
Career: 23 contests, won 11, drew 1, lost 11.

(Emmanuel) Manny Burgo

North Shields. *Born* North Shields, 15
June, 1961
Heavyweight. Ht. 6'1"
Manager Self

07.03.88　Tee Lewis W PTS 3 Northampton
07.03.88　Ian Nelson W PTS 6 Northampton
22.04.88　Steve Garber W PTS 6 Gateshead
18.06.88　Tony Hallett W RSC 3 Gateshead
22.11.88　Dave Garside W PTS 8 Marton
29.03.89　Chris Jacobs W PTS 8 Bethnal Green
06.03.90　Denroy Bryan W PTS 8 Newcastle
20.03.90　Neil Malpass W RSC 3 Hartlepool
15.05.90　Al Malcolm W PTS 6 South Shields
23.01.91　Steve Gee W PTS 6 Brentwood
29.04.93　Gary Charlton W PTS 6 Newcastle
Career: 11 contests, won 11.

Vince Burns

Battersea. *Born* Paddington, 27 July, 1970
S. Featherweight. Ht. 5'7"
Manager P. Healy

29.04.93　Jason Hutson W RSC 1 Hayes
Career: 1 contest, won 1.

Garry Burrell　　　　　　　　Chris Bevan

Garry Burrell

Kirkcaldy. *Born* Musselburgh, 9 July, 1965
Lightweight. Ht. 5'7½"
Manager T. Gilmour

21.09.92　Alan Graham W PTS 6 Glasgow
09.11.92　Alan Graham W PTS 6 Bradford
22.02.93　Tim Hill L PTS 6 Glasgow
23.03.93　Yusuf Vorajee L PTS 6
　　　　　Wolverhampton
26.04.93　Robbie Sivyer W PTS 6 Glasgow
Career: 5 contests, won 3, lost 2.

Graham Burton

Sheffield. *Born* Chesterfield, 16 June, 1964
S. Middleweight. Ht. 5'10"
Manager B. Ingle

10.10.88　Frank Mobbs W RSC 3 Manchester
03.11.88　Terry French W RSC 3 Manchester
16.01.89　Dave Andrews W PTS 6 Northampton
04.04.89　Spencer Alton W RSC 3 Sheffield
06.12.89　Dave Brosnan W RSC 6 Stoke
29.01.90　Darren McKenna W PTS 4 Hull
23.04.90　Stevie R. Davies W PTS 6 Bradford
05.06.90　Nick Gyaamie W PTS 6 Eltham
18.09.90　Wayne Timmins W PTS 6
　　　　　Wolverhampton
17.01.91　John Ashton L PTS 10 Alfreton
12.03.91　Peter Gorny W PTS 6 Mansfield
13.06.91　Michael Gale L CO 4 Hull
12.11.91　Paul Busby L RSC 3 Wolverhampton
04.02.92　Richie Woodhall L RSC 2 Alfreton
17.03.92　Andrew Flute L PTS 8 Wolverhampton
13.10.92　Richard Carter DREW 8
　　　　　Wolverhampton
24.11.92　Nigel Rafferty L PTS 8
　　　　　Wolverhampton
20.01.93　Neville Brown L CO 4
　　　　　Wolverhampton
24.04.93　Cornelius Carr L PTS 6 Birmingham
26.05.93　Jason McNeill W RSC 3 Mansfield
Career: 20 contests, won 11, drew 1, lost 8.

Kevin Burton

Doncaster. *Born* Doncaster, 20 June, 1965
L. Heavyweight. Ht. 5'10½"
Manager J. Rushton

10.05.93　Pat McNamara W RSC 2 Cleethorpes
07.06.93　Tony Colclough W PTS 6 Walsall
Career: 2 contests, won 2.

Paul Burton

Sheffield. *Born* Chesterfield, 26 February,
1963
S. Middleweight. Ht. 6'0½"
Manager Self

11.02.86　Paul Boyce W RSC 1 Wolverhampton
17.04.86　Trevor Grant L PTS 6 Piccadilly
15.09.86　John Davies L CO 6 Coventry
25.11.86　Malcolm Davies W RSC 6
　　　　　Wolverhampton
17.02.87　Frank Graham W CO 1 Alfreton
22.09.87　Cornelius Carr L RSC 5 Bethnal Green
09.11.87　Lee Hartshorn W PTS 6 Leicester
30.11.87　Darren Parker L RSC 6 Manchester
11.03.88　David Heath W PTS 6 Cottingham
22.04.88　Rob Thomas L RSC 2 Lisbon, Portugal
14.11.88　Darren Pilling W RSC 2 Manchester
01.12.88　Mark White W RSC 4 Gravesend
14.09.89　Carlo Colarusso L RSC 5 Basildon
21.03.90　Sean Heron L CO 1 Preston
27.11.90　Andrew Flute W PTS 6 Stoke
10.12.90　Chris Walker L RSC 4 Nottingham
18.02.91　Max McCracken L RTD 3
　　　　　Birmingham
15.04.91　David Radford W RTD 1
　　　　　Wolverhampton
23.04.91　Simon McDougall W PTS 8 Evesham
18.05.91　Cornelius Carr L RSC 3 Verbania,
　　　　　Italy
14.11.91　Paul Hitch L CO 2 Gateshead
23.10.92　Paul Hitch L RSC 5 Gateshead
Career: 22 contests, won 10, lost 12.

Richard Burton

Manchester. *Born* Jamaica, 7 November,
1970
Central Area L. Welterweight Champion.
Ht. 5'11"
Manager J. Doughty

18.09.89　Calum Rattray W RSC 4 Glasgow
25.09.89　Lee Ahmed W RSC 4 Birmingham
11.10.89　Mike Morrison W PTS 6 Stoke
13.12.89　Tomas Arguelles DREW 6 Kirkby
15.11.90　Michael Howell W RSC 5 Oldham
17.01.91　Dean Bramhald W RTD 1 Alfreton
31.01.91　Mike Morrison W PTS 6 Bredbury
16.05.91　Chris Saunders W PTS 6 Liverpool
20.06.91　Jim Lawlor L PTS 6 Liverpool
21.11.91　John Smith W PTS 6 Burton
19.12.91　John Smith W PTS 6 Oldham
27.02.92　Chris Saunders W PTS 10 Liverpool
　　　　　*(Vacant Central Area L. Welterweight
　　　　　Title)*
02.07.92　Ray Newby W PTS 6 Middleton
24.09.92　Rob Stewart W PTS 10 Stockport
　　　　　*(Central Area L. Welterweight Title
　　　　　Defence)*
Career: 14 contests, won 12, drew 1, lost 1.

Paul Busby

Worcester. *Born* Worcester, 20 April, 1966
Middleweight. Ht. 5'11½"
Manager B. Hearn

18.11.90	Carlos Christie W PTS 6 Birmingham
04.12.90	Marty Duke W PTS 6 Bury St Edmunds
23.01.91	Tony Wellington W RSC 2 Brentwood
27.02.91	Paul Murray W PTS 6 Wolverhampton
19.03.91	Paul Smith W PTS 6 Leicester
10.09.91	Nigel Rafferty W RSC 2 Wolverhampton
12.11.91	Graham Burton W RSC 3 Wolverhampton
17.12.91	Paul Murray W CO 3 Cardiff
01.02.92	John Kaighin W PTS 4 Birmingham
23.05.92	Stinger Mason W RSC 2 Birmingham
14.11.92	Paul Wesley W PTS 8 Cardiff
19.01.93	Stan King W PTS 8 Cardiff
16.03.93	Neville Brown L PTS 10 Wolverhampton
	(Elim. British Middleweight Title)

Career: 13 contests, won 12, lost 1.

Rick Bushell

Herne Bay. *Born* Bridge, 1 March, 1965
Lightweight. Ht. 5'8"
Manager P. Byrne

11.12.89	Denzil Goddard W RSC 2 Bayswater
15.01.90	Carl Brasier W CO 1 Mayfair
11.04.90	James Jiora W PTS 6 Dewsbury
26.04.90	Andy Deabreu L PTS 6 Mayfair
21.05.90	Vaughan Carnegie W PTS 6 Mayfair
12.09.90	Eamonn McAuley L RSC 4 Battersea
10.01.91	Mike Morrison W PTS 6 Wandsworth
07.02.91	B. F. Williams W RTD 2 Watford
18.02.91	Robert Smyth W PTS 6 Mayfair
28.02.91	Marvin P. Gray L PTS 6 Sunderland
10.04.91	Vaughan Carnegie W RSC 3 Newport
18.04.91	Felix Kelly L PTS 6 Earls Court
22.06.91	Felix Kelly W PTS 6 Earls Court
23.10.91	Mark Tibbs L RSC 4 Bethnal Green
11.12.91	Mark Tibbs L RSC 2 Basildon
02.03.92	Jose Tuominen DREW 4 Helsinki, Finland
14.03.92	Soren Sondergaard L CO 3 Copenhagen, Denmark
16.05.92	Dean Hollington L RSC 2 Muswell Hill
31.10.92	A. M. Milton DREW 4 Earls Court
17.12.92	Paul Ryan L RSC 1 Barking
17.02.93	A. M. Milton L RSC 1 Bethnal Green

Career: 21 contests, won 9, drew 2, lost 10.

Richard Bustin

Norwich. *Born* Norwich, 9 October, 1964
S. Middleweight. Ht. 5'9"
Manager G. Holmes

15.02.88	Roger Silsby L PTS 6 Copthorne
14.03.88	Tony Behan W RSC 3 Norwich
05.04.88	Steve Conway W RSC 4 Basildon
28.05.88	Winston Burnett W PTS 6 Kensington
17.10.88	Dennis Banton W RSC 5 Mayfair
15.11.88	Crawford Ashley L CO 3 Norwich
07.02.89	Alan Baptiste W PTS 6 Southend
15.05.89	Alex Romeo L RSC 2 Northampton
03.10.89	Alan Baptiste W PTS 6 Southend
17.10.89	Mick Maw W CO 2 Cardiff
14.03.90	Paul McCarthy L RSC 7 Battersea
	(Vacant Southern Area S. Middleweight Title)
12.11.90	Alan Baptiste W RSC 1 Norwich

29.01.91	Simon Harris L RSC 3 Wisbech
18.04.91	John Foreman W PTS 8 Earls Court
11.06.91	Gary Ballard L PTS 8 Leicester
19.11.91	Glazz Campbell L CO 7 Norwich
	(Vacant Southern Area L. Heavyweight Title)
31.01.92	Bobbi Joe Edwards L PTS 6 Manchester
31.03.92	Gypsy Carman L PTS 6 Norwich
27.06.92	Dariusz Michalczewski L RSC 4 Quinta do Lago, Portugal
08.07.92	Karl Barwise W PTS 6 Norwich
17.04.93	Paul Hitch W PTS 6 Washington

Career: 21 contests, won 11, lost 10.

(Barrie) Blue Butterworth

Burnley. *Born* Lambeth, 5 October, 1970
L. Welterweight. Ht. 5'8½"
Manager J. Doughty

31.03.92	Brian Coleman W PTS 6 Stockport
04.06.92	Mark Allen W RSC 5 Burnley
14.09.92	Lee Soar W CO 4 Bradford
12.11.92	Dave Madden W RSC 2 Burnley
25.02.93	Ian Thomas W PTS 6 Burnley
27.05.93	Brian Coleman W PTS 6 Burnley

Career: 6 contests, won 6.

Dave Buxton

Redcar. *Born* Saltburn, 22 March, 1962
Featherweight. Ht. 5'4¾"
Manager Self

10.10.89	Dominic McGuigan L PTS 6 Sunderland
13.11.89	Ronnie Stephenson W RTD 2 Bradford
20.11.89	Des Gargano W PTS 6 Leicester
29.11.89	Kruga Hydes L RSC 4 Marton
30.01.90	Noel Carroll L PTS 6 Manchester
23.02.90	Edward Cook L RTD 1 Irvine
26.04.90	Steve Armstrong W PTS 6 Manchester
14.05.90	Neil Leitch L PTS 6 Northampton
22.05.90	Edward Cook W PTS 6 Stockton
17.12.90	Russell Davison L PTS 8 Manchester
25.01.91	Donnie Hood L RSC 5 Shotts
10.04.91	J. T. Williams L PTS 8 Newport
01.08.91	Tony Silkstone L PTS 6 Dewsbury
22.04.93	Alan Graham L PTS 6 Bury
29.05.93	Mike Deveney L PTS 6 Paisley

Career: 15 contests, won 4, lost 11.

Sean Byrne

Northampton. *Born* Manchester, 20 September, 1966
Middleweight. Ht. 6'0"
Manager J. Cox

06.04.92	Martin Jolley W RSC 6 Northampton
28.04.92	John McKenzie W RSC 6 Corby
05.10.92	Russell Washer W PTS 6 Northampton

Career: 3 contests, won 3.

Damien Caesar

Stepney. *Born* Stepney, 2 October, 1965
Heavyweight. Ht. 6'5"
Manager T. Lawless

22.04.91	Larry Peart W RSC 2 Mayfair
30.05.91	Tony Colclough W RSC 1 Mayfair
17.02.92	Steve Stewart W RSC 5 Mayfair
27.04.92	Gary Williams W RSC 4 Mayfair
05.10.92	Denroy Bryan W RSC 5 Bristol

Career: 5 contests, won 5.

Geoff Calder

Kidderminster. *Born* Kidderminster, 21 April, 1967
L. Middleweight. Ht. 6'2½"
Manager Self

06.11.85	Wayne Goult W PTS 6 Evesham
14.11.85	Mark Poultney L PTS 6 Dudley
04.12.85	Rocky Lester W RSC 3 Stoke
27.01.86	Gary Sommerville L PTS 6 Dudley
13.02.86	Mark Broome W PTS 6 Bedworth
24.02.86	Paul Seddon L PTS 6 Dudley
12.03.86	Young Ian Daly L PTS 6 Stoke
17.03.86	Dean Murray L CO 3 Birmingham
29.04.86	Trevor Grant L RSC 3 Piccadilly
08.10.86	Mike McKenzie W RTD 1 Stoke
14.10.86	Roy Callaghan L PTS 6 Wolverhampton
10.11.86	Graeme Griffin W RSC 5 Birmingham
21.11.86	Geoff Sharp L PTS 6 Maidenhead
03.12.86	Wil Halliday DREW 6 Stoke
19.02.87	Steve Hogg W PTS 6 St Helens
09.03.87	Mark Howell L PTS 6 Mayfair
24.03.87	Steve Kiernan DREW 6 Wolverhampton
18.04.87	Darren Dyer L RSC 2 Kensington
03.09.87	Levi Stevenson DREW 6 Piccadilly
30.09.87	Keith Scott W RSC 3 Mayfair
13.10.87	Rocky Feliciello L PTS 8 Wolverhampton
15.12.87	Tony Collins L RSC 2 Cardiff
24.02.88	Tony Collins L RSC 3 Aberavon
16.05.88	Steve West L RSC 4 Piccadilly
19.10.88	Paul Murray NC 2 Evesham
31.10.88	Peter Sorby L RSC 4 Leicester
24.09.92	Darren Pilling L RSC 5 Stockport
27.10.92	Andre Wharton L PTS 4 Cradley Heath

Career: 28 contests, won 7, drew 3, lost 17, no contest 1.

Albert Call

Grimsby. *Born* Grimsby, 17 April, 1967
Cruiserweight. Ht. 6'2"
Manager L. Billany

21.09.92	John Pierre W PTS 6 Cleethorpes
14.12.92	Art Stacey W PTS 6 Cleethorpes
22.02.93	Kenny Sandison W PTS 6 Liverpool

Career: 3 contests, won 3.

Dave Campbell

Middlesbrough. *Born* South Shields, 13 December, 1968
Bantamweight. Ht. 5'4½"
Manager J. Spensley

11.09.91	Mark Hargreaves L RSC 4 Stoke
14.11.91	Dave Martin W PTS 6 Bayswater
27.11.91	Shaun Norman W PTS 6 Marton
18.05.92	Glyn Shepherd W RSC 1 Marton
23.09.92	Tony Silkstone L PTS 4 Leeds
08.03.93	Ady Benton L PTS 6 Leeds
26.03.93	Shaun Anderson L RSC 5 Glasgow

Career: 7 contests, won 3, lost 4.

Glenn Campbell

Bury. *Born* Bury, 22 April, 1970
Central Area S. Middleweight Champion. Ht. 5'10"
Manager J. Doughty

19.04.90	Ian Vokes W CO 1 Oldham
01.05.90	Stevie R. Davies W RSC 2 Oldham

21.05.90   Andy Marlow W RSC 6 Hanley
11.06.90   Stinger Mason W RTD 5 Manchester
26.09.90   Tony Kosova W RSC 2 Manchester
22.10.90   Simon McDougall W RSC 4
            Manchester
26.11.90   Sean O'Phoenix W RSC 4 Bury
            (Vacant Central Area S. Middleweight
            Title)
28.02.91   Simon McDougall W PTS 10 Bury
            (Central Area S. Middleweight Title
            Defence)
17.05.91   Tony Booth W RSC 2 Bury
            (Central Area S. Middleweight Title
            Defence)
21.01.92   Nigel Rafferty W RSC 6 Stockport
10.03.92   Carlos Christie DREW 8 Bury
05.05.92   Ian Henry W RSC 1 Preston
22.04.93   Paul Wright W RSC 4 Bury
            (Elim. British S. Middleweight Title &
            Central Area S. Middleweight Title
            Defence)
Career: 13 contests, won 12, drew 1.

James Campbell

Birmingham. *Born* Birmingham, 2 July,
1967
Welterweight. Ht. 5'10"
Manager Self

21.10.91   Dean Carr W RSC 5 Cleethorpes
26.11.91   Julian Eavis L PTS 8 Wolverhampton
20.02.92   Peter Reid W PTS 6 Oakengates
30.04.92   Nicky Bardle W CO 1 Watford
17.09.92   B. F. Williams L PTS 6 Watford
30.10.92   Steve Scott W PTS 6 Birmingham
23.11.92   James McGee DREW 6 Coventry
14.12.92   Barry Thorogood L RSC 4 Cardiff
22.02.93   Steve Scott W PTS 6 Birmingham
19.04.93   Kevin Mabbutt L PTS 6 Northampton
29.06.93   Tony Britland W PTS 6 Edgbaston
Career: 11 contests, won 6, drew 1, lost 4.

Jason Campbell

Brighton. *Born* Northampton, 12
November, 1970
L. Welterweight. Ht. 5'8"
Manager F. Maloney

06.05.93   Adrian Chase L CO 2 Bayswater
Career: 1 contest, lost 1.

Martin Campbell

Wishaw. *Born* Wishaw, 2 December, 1966
L. Welterweight. Ht. 5'9"
Manager Self

08.06.88   Mark Jackson W RSC 4 Glasgow
22.09.88   Robert Wright L RSC 5
            Wolverhampton
14.05.93   Colin Wallace L PTS 6 Kilmarnock
Career: 3 contests, won 1, lost 2.

Mickey Cantwell

Eltham. *Born* London, 23 November, 1964
Southern Area Flyweight Champion. Ht.
5'2½"
Manager M. Duff

21.01.91   Eduardo Vallejo W RSC 4 Crystal
            Palace
26.03.91   Mario Alberto Cruz W PTS 6 Bethnal
            Green

30.09.91   Ricky Beard W PTS 8 Kensington
23.10.91   Carlos Manrigues W RSC 5 Bethnal
            Green
14.12.91   Shaun Norman W PTS 8 Bexleyheath
16.05.92   Louis Veitch W PTS 6 Muswell Hill
10.02.93   Louis Veitch DREW 8 Lewisham
14.04.93   Darren Fifield W PTS 10 Kensington
            (Vacant Southern Area Flyweight Title)
Career: 8 contests, won 7, drew 1.

(George) Gypsy Carman

Ipswich. *Born* Wisbech, 23 November,
1964
Cruiserweight. Ht. 6'0"
Manager Self

30.01.84   Dave Mowbray W PTS 6 Manchester
16.02.84   Lennie Howard L RTD 1 Basildon
03.04.84   Gordon Stacey W PTS 6 Lewisham
07.06.84   Deka Williams L PTS 6 Dudley
29.10.84   Wes Taylor W PTS 6 Streatham
04.02.85   Lee White L PTS 6 Lewisham
20.02.85   Charlie Hostetter L PTS 6 Muswell
            Hill
27.03.85   Glenn McCrory L PTS 8 Gateshead
09.05.85   Barry Ellis L PTS 8 Acton
10.06.85   Chris Jacobs DREW 6 Cardiff
02.09.85   Barry Ellis L PTS 8 Coventry
31.10.85   Tee Jay L PTS 6 Wandsworth
15.03.86   Mick Cordon W PTS 8 Norwich
24.03.86   Chris Harbourne W PTS 6 Mayfair
13.09.86   Tee Jay L RSC 4 Norwich
            (Vacant Southern Area Cruiserweight
            Title)
20.11.86   Lou Gent L CO 1 Merton
12.01.87   Patrick Collins W PTS 8 Glasgow
19.01.87   Johnny Nelson L PTS 6 Mayfair
19.02.87   Danny Lawford L PTS 6 Peterborough
04.03.87   Tommy Taylor L PTS 8 Dudley
24.11.87   Tommy Taylor W PTS 8 Wisbech
14.03.88   Blaine Logsdon L RSC 8 Norwich
25.04.88   Gerry Storey L PTS 6 Bethnal Green
15.09.89   Carlton Headley W PTS 6 High
            Wycombe
22.02.90   Lou Gent L PTS 10 Wandsworth
            (Southern Area Cruiserweight Title
            Challenge)
07.05.90   Eddie Smulders L RSC 4 Arnhem,
            Holland
26.11.90   Everton Blake L PTS 6 Bethnal Green
22.10.91   Tenko Ernie W PTS 6 Wandsworth
21.01.92   Dave Lawrence W PTS 6 Norwich
31.03.92   Richard Bustin W PTS 6 Norwich
27.10.92   Everton Blake L RSC 4 Hayes
            (Southern Area Cruiserweight Title
            Challenge)
29.04.93   Paul McCarthy W PTS 6 Hayes
Career: 32 contests, won 13, drew 1, lost 18.

Ian Carmichael

Preston. *Born* Preston, 7 October, 1965
Cruiserweight. Ht. 6'2"
Manager M. Chapman

13.06.87   Montague Butler W PTS 6 Great
            Yarmouth
15.09.87   Randy B. Powell W PTS 6 Kensington
01.12.88   Steve Lewsam L CO 2 Stafford
24.02.92   Dene Josham W PTS 6 Bradford
13.02.93   Mark Hulstrom L RSC 4 Randers,
            Denmark
Career: 5 contests, won 3, lost 2.

Vaughan Carnegie

Newport. *Born* Newport, 16 December,
1964
L. Welterweight. Ht. 5'11½"
Manager Self

16.01.90   Dave Jenkins W PTS 6 Cardiff
03.02.90   Dave Jenkins L PTS 6 Bristol
14.02.90   Benny Collins L PTS 6 Millwall
20.02.90   Mick Moran W RSC 3 Brentford
19.03.90   Shaun Cooper L PTS 8 Brierley Hill
25.04.90   Benny Collins L PTS 6 Millwall
14.05.90   Brendan Ryan W PTS 6 Leicester
21.05.90   Rick Bushell L PTS 6 Mayfair
06.06.90   Stuart Good L PTS 6 Battersea
12.02.91   Jason Rowland L CO 6 Basildon
07.03.91   Jason Rowland L CO 2 Basildon
10.04.91   Rick Bushell L RSC 3 Newport
14.12.92   Lee Taylor W RSC 2 Cardiff
22.02.93   Shea Neary L RSC 1 Liverpool
Career: 14 contests, won 4, lost 10.

(John) Cornelius Carr

Middlesbrough. *Born* Middlesbrough, 9
April, 1969
Middleweight. Ht. 5'9½"
Manager M. Duff

22.09.87   Paul Burton W RSC 5 Bethnal Green
28.11.87   Dave Heaver W RSC 2 Windsor
12.01.88   Shamus Casey W RSC 6 Cardiff
27.01.88   Kesem Clayton W RSC 6 Bethnal
            Green
29.03.88   Darren Parker W RSC 1 Bethnal Green
12.04.88   Franki Moro W PTS 6 Cardiff
10.05.88   Andy Catesby W RSC 5 Tottenham
15.11.88   Skip Jackson W CO 1 Norwich
20.12.88   Kevin Hayde W PTS 6 Swansea
22.03.89   Bocco George L RSC 3 Reading
24.10.89   Carlo Colarusso W RTD 4 Watford
20.02.90   Peter Gorny W RSC 4 Millwall
21.04.90   Franki Moro W PTS 8 Sunderland
26.09.90   John Maltreaux W CO 1 Metairie,
            USA
27.10.90   Jerry Nestor W CO 1 Greenville, USA
16.02.91   Frank Eubanks W RSC 5 Thornaby
02.03.91   Carlo Colarusso W PTS 8 Darlington
18.05.91   Paul Burton W RSC 3 Verbania, Italy
06.09.91   Marvin O'Brien W RSC 7 Salemi,
            Italy
29.10.92   Alan Richards W PTS 8 Bayswater
24.04.93   Graham Burton W PTS 6 Birmingham
19.05.93   Stan King W PTS 8 Sunderland
Career: 22 contests, won 21, lost 1.

Dean Carr

Doncaster. *Born* Doncaster, 29 June, 1967
Welterweight. Ht. 5'10½"
Manager J. Rushton

29.04.91   Mick Reid L RSC 1 Cleethorpes
16.09.91   Michael Byrne W PTS 6 Cleethorpes
01.10.91   Darren McInulty L PTS 6 Bedworth
21.10.91   James Campbell L RSC 5 Cleethorpes
26.11.91   Steve Bricknell W PTS 4
            Wolverhampton
04.12.91   Rob Stewart L RTD 5 Stoke
19.11.92   Billy McDougall L PTS 6 Evesham
07.12.92   Billy McDougall L PTS 6 Birmingham
Career: 8 contests, won 2, lost 6.

Richard Carter

Wolverhampton. *Born* Wolverhampton, 3
September, 1970

Middleweight. Ht. 5'10"
Manager R. Gray

22.09.88	Tony Behan W PTS 6 Wolverhampton	
05.12.88	Paul Murray W PTS 6 Dudley	
12.12.88	Andy Catesby W PTS 6 Birmingham	
13.04.89	Dean Murray W PTS 6 Wolverhampton	
24.10.89	Graeme Watson W CO 2 Wolverhampton	
22.03.90	Spencer Alton W PTS 6 Wolverhampton	
15.10.90	Shaun McCrory W PTS 8 Brierley Hill	
15.03.91	Alan Pennington W CO 6 Willenhall	
05.06.91	Colin Manners L CO 1 Wolverhampton	
10.09.91	Paul Hanlon W RSC 3 Wolverhampton	
05.12.91	Paul Murray W PTS 8 Cannock	
13.10.92	Graham Burton DREW 8 Wolverhampton	

Career: 12 contests, won 10, drew 1, lost 1.

Shamus Casey (West)

Alfreton. *Born* Pinxton, 13 January, 1960
Middleweight. Ht. 5'11"
Manager Self

25.01.84	Tony Burke L CO 1 Solihull
16.04.84	Ronnie Fraser L RSC 3 Nottingham
05.07.84	Craig Edwards L PTS 6 Prestatyn
21.09.84	Dave Foley W PTS 6 Alfreton
28.09.84	Dennis Boy O'Brien L PTS 6 Longford
11.10.84	Terry Gilbey L PTS 6 Barnsley
22.10.84	Dave King W PTS 6 South Shields
09.11.84	Reuben Thurley W CO 4 Alfreton
16.11.84	Tucker Watts L PTS 6 Leicester
26.11.84	Terry Gilbey L RSC 1 Liverpool
14.01.85	Mark Walker L PTS 6 Manchester
24.01.85	Tommy Campbell L PTS 8 Manchester
11.02.85	Paul Smith W PTS 6 Manchester
18.02.85	John Graham L PTS 6 Mayfair
01.03.85	Dennis Sheehan W PTS 6 Mansfield
11.03.85	Sean O'Phoenix L PTS 6 Manchester
20.03.85	Sean O'Phoenix L PTS 6 Stoke
15.04.85	Ronnie Tucker L PTS 6 Manchester
14.05.85	Dennis Sheehan L PTS 10 Mansfield
	(Midlands Area L. Middleweight Title Challenge)
05.06.85	Gary Stretch L RSC 2 Kensington
02.09.85	Newton Barnett DREW 8 Coventry
12.09.85	Cliff Curtis W RSC 7 Swindon
23.09.85	Danny Quigg L PTS 8 Glasgow
10.10.85	Davey Cox W PTS 6 Alfreton
22.10.85	Mick Mills L RSC 3 Hull
02.12.85	Newton Barnett DREW 8 Dulwich
09.12.85	Steve Ward L PTS 6 Nottingham
16.12.85	Robert Armstrong W PTS 6 Bradford
20.01.86	Billy Ahearne L PTS 6 Mayfair
06.02.86	Denys Cronin L RSC 6 Doncaster
10.03.86	Neil Munn L PTS 8 Cardiff
20.03.86	Andy Wright L RSC 4 Merton
22.04.86	Franki Moro L PTS 8 Carlisle
29.04.86	John Graham L PTS 8 Piccadilly
08.05.86	Randy Henderson L PTS 8 Bayswater
19.05.86	Joe Lynch W RSC 3 Plymouth
28.05.86	Andy Wright L PTS 6 Lewisham
15.09.86	Gerry Sloof L PTS 6 Scheidam, Holland
23.09.86	Derek Wormald L PTS 8 Batley
06.10.86	David Scere L PTS 6 Leicester
21.10.86	David Scere W PTS 8 Hull
29.10.86	Peter Elliott W PTS 6 Stoke
25.11.86	Steve Foster L PTS 8 Manchester
15.12.86	Tucker Watts DREW 6 Loughborough
13.01.87	Robert Armstrong L PTS 6 Oldham

26.01.87	Richard Wagstaff W PTS 8 Bradford
05.02.87	Neil Patterson L PTS 6 Newcastle
20.02.87	Dennis Boy O'Brien L PTS 8 Maidenhead
02.03.87	Roddy Maxwell L PTS 6 Glasgow
24.03.87	Ian Chantler L PTS 8 Nottingham
07.04.87	Richard Wagstaff L PTS 8 Batley
28.04.87	Sean Leighton DREW 8 Manchester
05.05.87	Dave Owens L PTS 6 Leeds
12.05.87	Jason Baxter L PTS 6 Alfreton
23.06.87	Terry Magee L CO 6 Swansea
	(Vacant All-Ireland L. Middleweight Title)
31.07.87	Cyril Jackson L RSC 5 Wrexham
22.09.87	Brian Robinson L PTS 6 Bethnal Green
28.09.87	Sean Leighton L PTS 8 Bradford
19.10.87	Sammy Storey L PTS 6 Belfast
10.11.87	Peter Brown L PTS 8 Batley
19.11.87	Kid Murray W PTS 6 Ilkeston
26.11.87	Trevor Smith L CO 4 Fulham
12.01.88	Cornelius Carr L RSC 6 Cardiff
15.02.88	Leigh Wicks L PTS 6 Copthorne
25.02.88	R. W. Smith L RSC 3 Bethnal Green
28.03.88	Tony Britton L PTS 8 Birmingham
13.06.88	Jim Kelly L PTS 6 Glasgow
25.06.88	Wayne Ellis L PTS 6 Luton
12.09.88	Shaun Cummins L CO 3 Northampton
17.10.88	Jim Kelly L PTS 6 Glasgow
01.11.88	Brian Robinson L PTS 6 Reading
17.11.88	Mark Howell L CO 1 Ilkeston
16.12.88	Conrad Oscar L PTS 6 Brentwood
25.01.89	Tony Velinor L RTD 3 Basildon
22.02.89	Mickey Murray DREW 6 Doncaster
01.03.89	Nigel Fairbairn L PTS 6 Stoke
21.03.89	Dave Thomas L PTS 6 Cottingham
29.03.89	W. O. Wilson L RSC 5 Wembley
08.05.89	Antonio Fernandez L PTS 6 Edgbaston
31.05.89	Ossie Maddix L CO 3 Manchester
11.09.89	Terry French W PTS 6 Nottingham
18.09.89	Skip Jackson W PTS 6 Northampton
26.09.89	Theo Marius L PTS 8 Chigwell
05.10.89	Val Golding L PTS 6 Stevenage
17.10.89	Carl Harney L PTS 4 Oldham
13.11.89	Ian Vokes W RSC 5 Bradford
29.11.89	Ray Close L CO 2 Belfast
21.06.90	Skip Jackson W PTS 6 Alfreton
04.09.90	Pete Bowman W PTS 6 Southend
14.09.90	Chris Richards L PTS 6 Telford
08.10.90	Billy Brough W PTS 6 Leicester
22.10.90	Gordon Blair L RSC 3 Glasgow
22.11.90	Jimmy Thornton W PTS 6 Ilkeston
14.12.90	Stefan Wright L PTS 6 Peterborough
17.01.91	Neville Brown L RSC 4 Alfreton
21.02.91	Richie Woodhall L RSC 3 Walsall
28.03.91	Pete Bowman W PTS 6 Alfreton
12.04.91	Martin Rosamond W PTS 6 Willenhall
13.05.91	Paul King W PTS 6 Northampton
04.07.91	Dave Hall W PTS 6 Alfreton
11.09.91	Clay O'Shea L PTS 6 Hammersmith
10.10.91	Dave Johnson L PTS 6 Gateshead
17.10.91	Tyrone Eastmond L PTS 6 Mossley
14.11.91	Dave Johnson L PTS 6 Gateshead
28.11.91	Ian Vokes W PTS 6 Hull
07.12.91	Steve Foster L PTS 8 Manchester
17.03.92	Gary Osborne L RSC 5 Wolverhampton
	(Vacant Midlands Area L. Middleweight Title)
28.05.92	Mark Jay L PTS 8 Gosforth
25.07.92	Warren Stowe L CO 2 Manchester
16.10.92	Terry Morrill L PTS 6 Hull
23.10.92	Fran Harding L PTS 6 Liverpool
12.11.92	Gypsy Johnny Price L PTS 6 Burnley
14.12.92	Peter Wauby L PTS 6 Cleethorpes

22.02.93	Lee Ferrie L CO 3 Bedworth
07.06.93	Stephen Wilson L PTS 6 Glasgow

Career: 115 contests, won 25, drew 5, lost 85.

Fidel Castro (Smith)

Sheffield. *Born* Nottingham, 17 April, 1963
Former British S. Middleweight Champion.
Former Undefeated Central Area
Middleweight Champion. Ht. 5'9"
Manager P. Martin

06.04.87	Ian Bayliss W RSC 5 Newcastle
28.04.87	Nick Gyaamie W RSC 2 Newcastle
29.04.87	Leigh Wicks L PTS 6 Hastings
11.05.87	Steve Foster W PTS 8 Manchester
23.09.87	Ian Jackson W PTS 6 Stoke
11.11.87	Denys Cronin W PTS 8 Usk
24.02.88	Ian Bayliss W RSC 6 Sheffield
	(Central Area Middleweight Title Challenge)
09.05.88	Franki Moro W RSC 2 Nottingham
18.05.88	Chris Galloway W PTS 6 Gillingham
23.05.88	Sean Heron W RSC 4 Mayfair
08.07.88	Francesco dell' Aquila L DIS 3 San Remo, Italy
19.11.88	Paul Tchoue W RSC 3 Chateau Thierry, France
23.01.89	Andre Mongalema L PTS 8 Paris, France
22.06.89	Denys Cronin W RSC 7 Stevenage
27.01.90	Thomas Covington W PTS 8 Sheffield
12.03.90	Darren McKenna W PTS 6 Hull
20.05.90	Nigel Fairbairn W RSC 7 Sheffield
20.08.90	Elvis Parks W PTS 6 Helsinki, Finland
29.10.90	Dave Owens W PTS 6 Birmingham
24.11.90	Johnny Melfah W RSC 4 Benalmadena, Spain
24.09.91	Ian Strudwick W RSC 6 Basildon
	(Vacant British S. Middleweight Title)
01.10.91	Johnny Melfah W RSC 7 Sheffield
25.02.92	Lou Gent W PTS 12 Crystal Palace
	(British S. Middleweight Title Defence)
18.07.92	Frank Eubanks W RTD 6 Manchester
23.09.92	Henry Wharton L PTS 12 Leeds
	(British S. Middleweight Title Defence. Commonwealth S. Middleweight Title Challenge)
16.12.92	Vincenzo Nardiello L PTS 12 Arricia, Italy
	(Vacant European S. Middleweight Title)

Career: 26 contests, won 21, lost 5.

Glenn Catley

Bristol. *Born* Sodbury, 15 March, 1972
L. Middleweight. Ht. 5'8"
Manager C. Sanigar

27.05.93	Rick North W PTS 4 Bristol
26.06.93	Chris Vassiliou W CO 2 Keynsham

Career: 2 contests, won 2.

Ian Chantler (Ashton)

St Helens. *Born* St Helens, 13 June, 1960
Middleweight. Ht. 6'0"
Manager Self

21.06.82	Elvis Morton W RSC 3 Liverpool
30.06.82	Kid Murray W PTS 6 Liverpool
23.09.82	Tony Brown L PTS 8 Liverpool
05.10.82	Tony Brown W PTS 8 Liverpool
18.10.82	Billy Ahearne W RSC 3 Blackpool
06.12.82	Lee Hartshorn L PTS 8 Manchester

20.01.83 Robert Armstrong W RTD 1 Birkenhead
28.01.83 Geoff Pegler L PTS 8 Swansea
14.02.83 Billy Ahearne W RSC 6 Liverpool
04.03.83 Danny Garrison W CO 5 Queensferry
25.03.83 Martin Patrick L PTS 8 Bloomsbury
29.04.83 Paul Mitchell L PTS 8 Liverpool
17.10.83 Gavin Stirrup L PTS 8 Manchester
06.12.83 Rocky Kelly L RSC 7 Kensington
06.04.84 Jim McIntosh L DIS 3 Edinburgh
12.06.84 Ray Murray W RSC 2 St Helens
12.11.84 Franki Moro L PTS 8 Nantwich
05.12.84 Paul Kelly W CO 3 Stoke
14.12.84 John Ridgman L RSC 8 Wembley
01.02.85 Cliff Domville W PTS 8 Warrington
01.04.85 Mark Mills L DIS 2 Dulwich
10.04.85 Alistair Laurie W RSC 8 Leeds
09.05.85 John Ridgman W RSC 8 Warrington
31.05.85 Franki Moro W PTS 8 Liverpool
19.07.85 Steve Davies W PTS 6 Colwyn Bay
12.09.85 Steve Watt L PTS 8 Merton
03.10.85 Wayne Crolla W RSC 3 Liverpool
04.11.85 Jim Kelly W PTS 8 Motherwell
06.12.85 Tony Brown L RSC 7 Liverpool
(Central Area Welterweight Title Challenge)
27.01.86 Charlie Watson L RSC 4 Bradford
23.04.86 Judas Clottey L PTS 8 Stoke
25.09.86 Sammy Sampson W PTS 8 Preston
23.10.86 Mickey Hughes L RSC 6 Basildon
03.12.86 Wally Swift Jnr L PTS 8 Stoke
19.01.87 Michael Watson L RTD 4 Mayfair
02.03.87 John Ashton W RSC 4 Birmingham
11.03.87 Dean Barclay W PTS 8 Kensington
24.03.87 Shamus Casey W PTS 8 Nottingham
09.04.87 Johnny Williamson W RSC 4 Bethnal Green
26.05.87 Mick Courtney W RTD 5 Wembley
05.10.87 Marc Ruocco L PTS 8 Paris, France
08.11.87 Romeo Kensmil W CO 6 Amsterdam, Holland
24.11.87 Nigel Benn L CO 1 Wisbech
09.02.88 George Collins L PTS 8 Bethnal Green
04.03.88 Mbayo Wa Mbayo L PTS 8 Villeurbanne, France
19.03.88 Edip Secovic L CO 4 Vienna, Austria
28.04.88 Ossie Maddix W RSC 3 Manchester
07.05.88 Giovanni de Marco L PTS 6 Roseto, Italy
09.01.89 Gilbert Dele L RSC 3 Noget sur Marne, France
15.03.89 Kesem Clayton W CO 4 Stoke
06.09.89 Wayne Ellis L RSC 4 Aberavon
22.11.89 Kesem Clayton L PTS 8 Solihull
02.06.90 Steve Foster DREW 6 Manchester
12.09.90 Tony Velinor W RSC 4 Bethnal Green
27.10.90 Santo Colombo L PTS 8 Rimini, Italy
12.12.90 Kevin Hayde W PTS 8 Basildon
23.01.91 Shaun Cummins L PTS 10 Brentwood
15.05.91 Silvio Branco L RSC 2 Montichiari, Italy
17.03.92 Stan King L CO 3 Mayfair
25.04.92 Ray Close L RSC 1 Belfast
25.11.92 Richard Okumu L RSC 2 Mayfair
03.02.93 Kevin Lueshing L RSC 2 Earls Court
Career: 62 contests, won 27, drew 1, lost 34.

Gary Charlton
Leeds. *Born* Leeds, 6 April, 1968
Heavyweight. Ht. 6'0"
Manager Self

10.10.91 John Pierre L PTS 6 Gateshead

26.10.91 Graham Arnold W RSC 1 Brentwood
11.11.91 Gary Railton L PTS 6 Bradford
23.04.92 Wayne Llewelyn L RSC 4 Eltham
04.06.92 Wayne Buck L PTS 6 Cleethorpes
07.10.92 John Harewood L PTS 6 Sunderland
12.11.92 Wayne Buck L PTS 8 Stafford
17.12.92 Kevin McBride DREW 6 Barking
23.02.93 Scott Welch W RSC 3 Doncaster
26.03.93 Mark Hulstrom L DIS 5 Copenhagen, Denmark
29.04.93 Manny Burgo L PTS 6 Newcastle
Career: 11 contests, won 2, drew 1, lost 8.

Paul Charters   Chris Bevan

Paul Charters
Newcastle. *Born* North Shields, 14 June, 1964
Northern Area L. Welterweight Champion. Former Undefeated Northern Area Lightweight Champion.. Ht. 5'7"
Manager T. Conroy

10.03.88 John Naylor L PTS 6 Croydon
11.04.88 Jim Moffat L PTS 8 Glasgow
22.04.88 Tony Foster W PTS 6 Gateshead
03.05.88 Henry Armstrong L PTS 4 Stoke
16.05.88 Shaun Cooper L PTS 6 Wolverhampton
18.06.88 Darrin Jackson W RSC 6 Gateshead
29.06.88 Steve Griffith W PTS 8 Basildon
06.12.88 Oliver Henry L CO 1 Southend
25.01.89 Paul Burke L PTS 6 Bethnal Green
28.02.89 Chris Bennett W PTS 6 Marton
29.03.89 B. F. Williams L PTS 6 Bethnal Green
14.09.89 Nick Hall L PTS 6 Motherwell
25.09.89 Paul Bowen W PTS 8 Birmingham
09.10.89 Kris McAdam W PTS 8 Glasgow
23.10.89 Dave Pratt W RTD 3 Nottingham
14.11.89 Robert Smyth W PTS 8 Evesham
05.12.89 James Jiora W RSC 4 Dewsbury
15.01.90 Tomas Arguelles L PTS 8 Mayfair
05.03.90 Marvin P. Gray W PTS 10 Nottingham
(Vacant Northern Area Lightweight Title)
15.05.90 Brian Cullen W RSC 5 South Shields

05.06.90 Paul Gadney W RSC 1 Eltham
13.11.90 John Smith W RSC 4 Hartlepool
14.12.90 Gary Barron L RSC 3 Peterborough
21.02.91 Peter Till W RSC 6 Walsall
10.05.91 Kevin Spratt W RSC 2 Gateshead
14.08.91 Antonio Renzo L CO 11 Alcamo, Italy
(European Lightweight Title Challenge)
14.11.91 Gary Barron W RSC 4 Gateshead
03.03.92 John Smith W PTS 8 Houghton le Spring
28.04.92 Paul Burke L RSC 7 Houghton le Spring
(Final Elim. British Lightweight Title)
10.09.92 Steve Pollard W RTD 5 Sunderland
23.10.92 Colin Sinnott W RTD 4 Gateshead
27.11.92 Racheed Lawal L CO 6 Randers, Denmark
17.04.93 Kevin McKenzie W RSC 4 Washington
(Vacant Northern Area L. Welterweight Title)
Career: 33 contests, won 20, lost 13.

Adrian Chase   Les Clark

Adrian Chase
Watford. *Born* St Albans, 18 October, 1968
L. Welterweight. Ht. 5'9"
Manager H. Holland

06.05.93 Jason Campbell W CO 2 Bayswater
24.06.93 Delwyn Panayiotiou W CO 1 Watford
Career: 2 contests, won 2.

(Ivan) Carlos Chase
Bushey. *Born* Watford, 10 August, 1966
L. Welterweight. Ht. 5'6¾"
Manager H. Holland

28.09.89 Tony Gibbs W PTS 6 Wandsworth
12.12.89 Carl Brasier W PTS 6 Brentford
30.01.90 Barry North W RSC 1 Battersea
14.03.90 Trevor Meikle W PTS 6 Battersea
03.04.91 Seamus O'Sullivan W PTS 8 Bethnal Green
01.06.91 Marcel Herbert W PTS 6 Bethnal Green

12.11.91	Tony Swift L PTS 6 Milton Keynes
12.02.92	Gary Barron W RSC 5 Watford
30.04.92	Dave Pierre L RSC 7 Watford
	(Southern Area L. Welterweight Title Challenge)
17.09.92	Felix Kelly W RSC 2 Watford
14.04.93	Ian Honeywood W RSC 1 Kensington

Career: 11 contests, won 9, lost 2.

Zak Chelli

Leicester. *Born* Tunisia, 2 May, 1968
L. Heavyweight. Ht. 6'3"
Manager K. Squires

24.11.92	Lee Archer W PTS 6 Wolverhampton
26.01.93	Karl Mumford W PTS 6 Leicester
22.02.93	John J. Cooke DREW 6 Bedworth
19.05.93	Nigel Rafferty W RSC 3 Leicester

Career: 4 contests, won 3, drew 1.

(Martin) Marty Chestnut (Concannon)

Birmingham. *Born* Birmingham, 8 March, 1968
S. Featherweight. Ht. 5'8"
Manager N. Nobbs

29.04.93	Fred Reeve L PTS 6 Hull
07.06.93	Ian McGirr L PTS 6 Glasgow

Career: 2 contests, lost 2.

(Peter) Carlos Christie

Birmingham. *Born* Birmingham, 17 August, 1966
Midlands Area S. Middleweight Champion. Ht. 6'0"
Manager R. Gray

04.06.90	Roger Wilson L PTS 6 Birmingham
17.09.90	John Kaighin W PTS 6 Cardiff
27.09.90	Colin Manners W PTS 6 Birmingham
29.10.90	Paul Murray W PTS 6 Birmingham
18.11.90	Paul Busby L PTS 6 Birmingham
27.11.90	Nigel Rafferty W PTS 8 Wolverhampton
06.12.90	Nigel Rafferty W PTS 6 Wolverhampton
10.01.91	Ray Webb L PTS 6 Wandsworth
28.01.91	Gil Lewis W PTS 8 Birmingham
04.03.91	Nigel Rafferty W PTS 8 Birmingham
14.03.91	Michael Gale L PTS 8 Middleton
01.05.91	Peter Elliott W RSC 9 Solihull
	(Vacant Midlands Area S. Middleweight Title)
11.05.91	Ray Close L PTS 6 Belfast
07.09.91	Ray Close L PTS 6 Belfast
20.11.91	Nicky Piper L CO 6 Cardiff
10.03.92	Glenn Campbell DREW 8 Bury
15.09.92	Roland Ericsson W RSC 4 Crystal Palace
28.01.93	James Cook L PTS 8 Southwark
28.04.93	Sammy Storey L RSC 8 Dublin

Career: 19 contests, won 9, drew 1, lost 9.

Errol Christie

Coventry. *Born* Leicester, 29 June, 1963
Middleweight. Ht. 5'10"
Manager Self

18.11.82	Terry Matthews W RTD 3 Coventry
09.12.82	Jimmy Ellis W RSC 3 Bloomsbury
17.02.83	Harlein Holden W RSC 1 Coventry

21.04.83	Sam Leonard W CO 1 Stevenage
18.05.83	Lino Cajins W RSC 1 Bloomsbury
13.06.83	Vince Gajny W RSC 2 Coventry
24.09.83	Robert Thomas W PTS 6 Totowa, USA
28.09.83	Fred Reed W RSC 3 Detroit, USA
15.10.83	Doug James W RSC 4 Coventry
01.02.84	Joel Bonnetaz W RSC 3 Bloomsbury
23.02.84	Dexter Bowman W RSC 2 Digbeth
25.04.84	Stacey McSwain W RSC 5 Muswell Hill
15.06.84	Stan White W RSC 5 Las Vegas, USA
19.09.84	Jose Seys L RSC 1 Shoreditch
01.11.84	Bobby Rico Hoye W RSC 1 Halifax
15.11.84	Cecil Pettigrew W RSC 1 Manchester
16.01.85	Gonzalo Montes W RSC 3 Shoreditch
02.02.85	Nestor Flores W CO 2 Darlington
07.03.85	Ignacio Zavala W RSC 1 Nottingham
30.05.85	Vincent Mayes W RSC 1 Halifax
18.09.85	Barry Audia W RSC 2 Muswell Hill
05.11.85	Mark Kaylor L CO 8 Wembley
	(Final Elim. British Middleweight Title)
16.04.86	Hunter Clay W PTS 10 Holborn
28.05.86	Carlton Warren W RSC 4 Muswell Hill
20.09.86	Adam George W PTS 10 Hemel Hempstead
29.10.86	Sean Mannion W PTS 10 Muswell Hill
03.12.86	Charlie Boston L RSC 8 Muswell Hill
17.06.87	Tyrone McKnight W RSC 5 Kensington
16.09.87	Rafael Corona W RSC 1 Kensington
28.11.87	Jose Quinones L RSC 4 Windsor
30.03.88	Andy Wright W CO 2 Bethnal Green
28.09.88	Joe McKenzie W RSC 3 Edmonton
26.10.88	Winston Burnett W PTS 8 Kensington
31.01.89	James Cook L RSC 5 Bethnal Green
24.10.89	Martin Camara W PTS 8 Bethnal Green
09.05.90	Thomas Covington W RSC 4 Kensington
20.06.90	Ian Strudwick L PTS 8 Basildon
22.09.90	Karl Barwise W RTD 7 Kensington
18.10.90	Stan King DREW 8 Wandsworth
18.11.90	Michael Watson L RSC 3 Birmingham
19.03.93	Trevor Ambrose L CO 2 Manchester

Career: 41 contests, won 32, drew 1, lost 8.

Floyd Churchill

Kirkby. *Born* Liverpool, 19 January, 1969
Central Area S. Featherweight Champion. Ht. 5'4"
Manager C. Moorcroft

29.04.92	T. J. Smith W RSC 2 Liverpool
14.05.92	Jamie Davidson W RSC 4 Liverpool
12.06.92	Kevin McKillan L PTS 6 Liverpool
26.09.92	Richie Wenton W RSC 2 Earls Court
12.11.92	Brian Hickey W CO 1 Liverpool
04.05.93	Jimmy Owens W CO 1 Liverpool
	(Vacant Central Area S. Featherweight Title)

Career: 6 contests, won 5, lost 1.

Cliff Churchward

Bournemouth. *Born* Weymouth, 7 June, 1966
L. Middleweight. Ht. 5'11"
Manager Self

04.10.89	Tony White L RSC 5 Basildon
14.11.89	Trevor Meikle L PTS 6 Evesham
22.11.89	Trevor Meikle L PTS 6 Stafford
11.12.89	Ernie Loveridge L PTS 6 Birmingham

27.02.90	Mickey Lerwill L PTS 6 Evesham
07.03.90	Eddie King L CO 6 Doncaster
28.06.90	Gary Simkiss DREW 6 Birmingham
08.12.90	Martin Rosamond L PTS 6 Bristol
23.01.91	Ernie Loveridge L PTS 6 Solihull
04.02.91	Andreas Panayi L PTS 6 Leicester
08.05.91	Kevin Sheeran L PTS 6 Millwall
20.05.91	James McGee L PTS 6 Leicester
05.06.91	Ernie Loveridge L PTS 8 Wolverhampton
17.06.91	Eddie King L PTS 6 Edgbaston
12.02.92	B. F. Williams L PTS 6 Watford
30.04.92	Danny Shinkwin W PTS 6 Watford
05.10.92	Kevin Mabbutt L PTS 6 Northampton
01.12.92	Andrew Jervis L PTS 6 Liverpool
10.12.92	Sean Metherell L PTS 6 Corby
16.03.93	Ernie Locke DREW 6 Edgbaston
07.04.93	David Larkin L RSC 4 Leeds

Career: 21 contests, won 1, drew 2, lost 18.

Mark Cichocki (Weatherill)

Hartlepool. *Born* Hartlepool, 18 October, 1967
Northern Area L. Middleweight Champion. Ht. 5'7"
Manager G. Robinson

01.12.92	Tony Trimble W PTS 6 Hartlepool
29.01.93	Gordon Blair W PTS 8 Glasgow
09.03.93	Rob Pitters W RSC 10 Hartlepool
	(Vacant Northern Area L. Middleweight Title)
06.05.93	Mick Duncan W RSC 7 Hartlepool
	(Northern Area L. Middleweight Title Defence)
12.05.93	Glyn Rhodes L PTS 6 Sheffield

Career: 5 contests, won 4, lost 1.

Howard Clarke

Warley. *Born* London, 23 September, 1967
Welterweight. Ht. 5'10"
Manager Self

15.10.91	Chris Mylan W PTS 4 Dudley
09.12.91	Claude Rossi W RSC 3 Brierley Hill
04.02.92	Julian Eavis W PTS 4 Alfreton
03.03.92	Dave Andrews W RSC 3 Cradley Heath
21.05.92	Richard O'Brien W CO 1 Cradley Heath
29.09.92	Paul King W PTS 6 Stoke
27.10.92	Gordon Blair L RSC 4 Cradley Heath
16.03.93	Paul King W PTS 6 Edgbaston
07.06.93	Dean Bramhald W RTD 2 Walsall
29.06.93	Paul King W PTS 6 Edgbaston

Career: 10 contests, won 9, lost 1.

Chris Clarkson

Hull. *Born* Hull, 15 December, 1967
Central Area Bantamweight Champion.
Former Undefeated Central Area Featherweight Champion. Ht. 5'4"
Manager Self

18.03.85	Gypsy Johnny L PTS 4 Bradford
09.04.85	Terry Allen W PTS 4 South Shields
30.04.85	Terry Allen W PTS 4 Chorley
30.05.85	Gypsy Johnny L PTS 4 Blackburn
17.10.85	Tony Heath W PTS 4 Leicester
13.02.86	Glen Dainty L PTS 4 Longford
17.03.86	Jamie McBride L PTS 4 Glasgow
03.11.86	Gerry McBride DREW 6 Manchester
13.11.86	Gordon Stobie W RSC 4 Huddersfield

01.12.86 Nigel Crook L RSC 6 Nottingham
27.01.87 Donnie Hood L PTS 6 Glasgow
23.02.87 Dave Boy Mallaby W PTS 4 Bradford
02.03.87 Dave Boy Mallaby W CO 3 Nottingham
16.03.87 Pepe Webber W PTS 6 Glasgow
24.03.87 Nigel Crook W PTS 6 Hull
06.04.87 Joe Kelly L PTS 8 Glasgow
14.04.87 Jamie McBride L PTS 6 Cumbernauld
28.04.87 John Green L RSC 6 Manchester
13.06.87 Ronnie Stephenson W PTS 8 Great Yarmouth
23.09.87 Mitchell King L PTS 6 Loughborough
15.11.88 Gordon Shaw W PTS 6 Hull
29.11.88 Des Gargano L PTS 6 Manchester
14.12.88 Dave George L PTS 6 Evesham
16.02.89 Johnny Bredahl L PTS 6 Copenhagen, Denmark
09.03.89 Mark Geraghty L PTS 6 Glasgow
20.03.89 George Bailey W PTS 6 Bradford
11.07.89 Des Gargano W PTS 6 Batley
11.10.89 Gerry McBride W PTS 10 Hull
 (Vacant Central Area Bantamweight Title)
23.11.89 Drew Docherty L PTS 6 Motherwell
15.03.90 Noel Carroll W PTS 6 Manchester
19.04.90 Gerry McBride W DIS 5 Oldham
 (Vacant Central Area Featherweight Title)
30.04.90 Pete Buckley W PTS 8 Mayfair
19.11.90 James Drummond W PTS 8 Glasgow
02.03.91 Francesco Arroyo L RSC 4 Darlington
 (Vacant IBF Intercontinental Bantamweight Title)
04.04.91 Duke McKenzie L RSC 5 Watford
09.10.91 Mark Geraghty L PTS 6 Glasgow
21.10.91 Ian McGirr DREW 6 Glasgow
16.12.91 Noel Carroll L PTS 6 Manchester
03.03.92 Billy Hardy L RSC 5 Houghton le Spring
14.12.92 David Ramsden W PTS 4 Bradford
24.02.93 Bradley Stone L PTS 8 Wembley
Career: 41 contests, won 18, drew 2, lost 21.

Justin Clements

Birmingham. *Born* Birmingham, 25 September, 1971
S. Middleweight. Ht. 5'11½"
Manager Self

02.12.91 Adrian Wright W PTS 6 Birmingham
03.03.92 Andy Manning DREW 6 Cradley Heath
16.03.93 Paul McCarthy W PTS 6 Edgbaston
18.05.93 Lee Sara W PTS 6 Edgbaston
07.06.93 Phil Ball W PTS 6 Walsall
Career: 5 contests, won 4, drew 1.

Pat Clinton

Croy. *Born* Croy, 4 April, 1964
Former WBO Flyweight Champion.
Former Undefeated British, European & Scottish Flyweight Champion. Ht. 5'3½"
Manager T. Gilmour

10.10.85 Gordon Stobie W PTS 6 Alfreton
11.11.85 Tony Rahman W PTS 6 Glasgow
24.02.86 Tony Rahman W PTS 6 Glasgow
29.04.86 Des Gargano W PTS 6 Manchester
09.06.86 George Bailey W CO 2 Glasgow
20.10.86 Ginger Staples W RSC 2 Glasgow
17.11.86 Gypsy Johnny W RSC 5 Glasgow
19.01.87 Sean Casey W CO 6 Glasgow

16.02.87 Des Gargano W PTS 6 Glasgow
14.04.87 Jose Manuel Diaz W RSC 8 Cumbernauld
19.05.87 Miguel Pequeno W CO 4 Cumbernauld
22.09.87 Joe Kelly W RSC 2 Bethnal Green
 (Final Elim. British Flyweight Title. Vacant Scottish Flyweight Title)
09.03.88 Joe Kelly W PTS 12 Bethnal Green
 (Vacant British Flyweight Title. Scottish Flyweight Title Defence)
16.02.89 Eyup Can L PTS 12 Copenhagen, Denmark
 (Vacant European Flyweight Title)
24.10.89 Danny Porter W RSC 5 Watford
 (British Flyweight Title Defence)
19.12.89 David Afan-Jones W RSC 6 Gorleston
 (British Flyweight Title Defence)
03.08.90 Salvatore Fanni W PTS 12 Cagliari, Italy
 (Vacant European Flyweight Title)
09.09.91 Armando Tapia W PTS 8 Glasgow
18.11.91 Alberto Cantu W PTS 8 Glasgow
18.03.92 Isidro Perez W PTS 12 Glasgow
 (WBO Flyweight Title Challenge)
19.09.92 Danny Porter W PTS 12 Glasgow
 (WBO Flyweight Title Defence)
15.05.93 Jacob Matlala L RSC 8 Glasgow
 (WBO Flyweight Title Defence)
Career: 22 contests, won 20, lost 2.

Shaun Cogan

Birmingham. *Born* Birmingham, 7 August, 1967
L. Welterweight. Ht. 5'8"
Manager Self

25.09.89 Peter Bowen W RSC 1 Birmingham
24.10.89 Gary Quigley W RSC 2 Wolverhampton
06.12.89 George Jones W PTS 6 Stoke
14.03.90 Dean Bramhald W PTS 6 Stoke
27.03.90 Mark Antony W CO 1 Wolverhampton
23.04.90 Mike Morrison W PTS 8 Birmingham
21.02.91 Tony Britland W PTS 6 Walsall
19.03.91 Rocky Lawlor W RSC 2 Birmingham
25.07.91 David Thompson W CO 1 Dudley

05.12.91 Steve Pollard W PTS 6 Oakengates
27.11.92 Soren Sondergaard L PTS 6 Randers, Denmark
16.03.93 Malcolm Melvin L PTS 10 Edgbaston
 (Vacant All-Ireland L. Welterweight Title & Midlands Area L. Welterweight Title Challenge)
18.05.93 Seth Jones W RSC 2 Edgbaston
Career: 13 contests, won 11, lost 2.

Carlo Colarusso

Llanelli. *Born* Swansea, 11 February, 1970
Welsh L. Middleweight Champion. Ht. 5'7"
Manager Self

14.09.89 Paul Burton W RSC 5 Basildon
11.10.89 Lindon Scarlett L PTS 8 Stoke
24.10.89 Cornelius Carr L RTD 4 Watford
22.11.89 Lindon Scarlett L PTS 8 Solihull
01.03.90 Kevin Hayde W RTD 3 Cardiff
14.03.90 Kevin Plant W PTS 8 Stoke
21.03.90 Sammy Sampson W RSC 3 Preston
06.04.90 Ray Webb W PTS 6 Telford
19.11.90 Gary Pemberton W RSC 3 Cardiff
29.11.90 Nigel Moore L PTS 6 Bayswater
24.01.91 Gary Pemberton W RSC 8 Gorseinon
 (Vacant Welsh L. Middleweight Title)
02.03.91 Cornelius Carr L PTS 8 Darlington
11.05.92 Russell Washer W RSC 5 Llanelli
 (Welsh L. Middleweight Title Defence)
27.06.92 Newton Barnett W RTD 5 Quinta do Lago, Portugal
28.10.92 Lloyd Honeyghan L RSC 6 Kensington
16.03.93 Richie Woodhall L PTS 8 Wolverhampton
30.03.93 Tony Velinor W RSC 3 Cardiff
Career: 17 contests, won 10, lost 7.

Tony Colclough

Birmingham. *Born* Birmingham, 9 May, 1960
L. Heavyweight. Ht. 6'0"
Manager Self

15.04.91 Steve Yorath L PTS 6 Wolverhampton
30.05.91 Damien Caesar L RSC 1 Mayfair

Carlo Colarusso (right) was too powerful for Tony Velinor and stopped him in the third round

Les Clark

01.08.91 Denzil Browne L RSC 1 Dewsbury
07.10.91 Karl Guest DREW 6 Birmingham
15.10.91 Jason McNeill W PTS 6 Dudley
02.12.91 Carl Guest W RSC 2 Birmingham
03.03.92 Greg Scott-Briggs L RSC 2 Cradley Heath
21.05.92 Mark Hale DREW 6 Cradley Heath
01.06.92 Mark Hale W PTS 6 Solihull
27.11.92 Mark Hulstrom L RSC 2 Randers, Denmark
27.02.93 Kenley Price L RSC 5 Ellesmere Port
26.04.93 Greg Scott-Briggs L RSC 4 Glasgow
07.06.93 Kevin Burton L PTS 6 Walsall
Career: 13 contests, won 3, drew 2, lost 8.

Brian Coleman

Birmingham. *Born* Birmingham, 27 July, 1969
Welterweight. Ht. 5'11"
Manager Self

21.11.91 Jamie Morris DREW 6 Stafford
11.12.91 Craig Hartwell DREW 6 Leicester
22.01.92 John O'Johnson L PTS 6 Stoke
20.02.92 Davy Robb L PTS 6 Oakengates
31.03.92 Blue Butterworth L PTS 6 Stockport
17.05.92 Korso Aleain L RSC 5 Harringay
17.09.92 Nicky Bardle L RSC 4 Watford
21.10.92 Jason Barker W PTS 6 Stoke
10.12.92 A. M. Milton DREW 4 Bethnal Green
31.03.93 A. M. Milton L PTS 4 Bethnal Green
26.04.93 Jason Beard L PTS 6 Lewisham
06.05.93 Mark Allen W PTS 6 Walsall
18.05.93 Sean Metherell DREW 6 Kettering
27.05.93 Blue Butterworth L PTS 6 Burnley
23.06.93 Jonathan Thaxton L PTS 8 Gorleston
Career: 15 contests, won 2, drew 4, lost 9.

Eddie Collins

Peterborough. *Born* London, 13 October, 1968
Middleweight. Ht. 5'8¼"
Manager Self

26.05.87 Terry Vosper L RSC 3 Plymouth
10.09.87 Dave Kettlewell W PTS 6 Peterborough
13.10.87 Kevin Thompson L CO 1 Wolverhampton
18.11.87 Andy Catesby W PTS 6 Peterborough
26.11.87 Peter Crook L PTS 6 Horwich
15.12.87 Jim Conley L PTS 4 Bradford
14.02.88 Andy Catesby W RSC 1 Peterborough
24.02.88 Nick Riozzi L PTS 6 Leicester
07.03.88 Humphrey Harrison L RSC 2 Manchester
17.04.88 John Corcoran W PTS 6 Peterborough
10.07.88 Jimmy McDonagh L PTS 8 Eastbourne
09.09.88 Mickey Murray L RSC 2 Doncaster
10.10.88 Paul Dolan L PTS 6 Glasgow
12.12.88 Jim Conley L RSC 2 Bradford
06.03.89 Dave Maxwell L PTS 6 Leicester
04.12.89 Carl Watson W PTS 6 Grimsby
19.02.90 Matt Sturgess L PTS 6 Nottingham
08.03.90 Gary Dyson W PTS 6 Peterborough
19.03.90 Matt Sturgess DREW 6 Leicester
05.04.90 Gary Dyson L PTS 6 Liverpool
22.10.90 Joe Kilshaw W PTS 6 Peterborough
12.11.90 Terry French L PTS 6 Bradford
14.12.90 Ian Henry L PTS 6 Peterborough
19.04.91 Dave Lawrence L PTS 6 Peterborough
10.05.91 Terry French L PTS 6 Gateshead
08.09.92 Earl Ling L PTS 6 Norwich

04.03.93 Steve Scott L RSC 1 Peterborough
18.05.93 Martin Rosamond L PTS 6 Kettering
08.06.93 Spencer Alton L PTS 6 Derby
Career: 29 contests, won 7, drew 1, lost 21.

Hugh Collins

Stirling. *Born* Stirling, 17 August, 1969
Lightweight. Ht. 5'6"
Manager T. Gilmour

29.03.93 Tim Hill W PTS 6 Glasgow
Career: 1 contest, won 1.

Simon Collins

Merthyr. *Born* Merthyr, 16 February, 1967
L. Heavyweight. Ht. 5'9"
Manager Self

01.10.85 Tony Stevens W PTS 6 Piccadilly
14.10.85 Malcolm Davies W PTS 6 Birmingham
04.12.85 Malcolm Melvin W PTS 6 Stoke
21.04.86 Paul Smith DREW 6 Birmingham
29.04.86 Deano Wallace L PTS 6 Piccadilly
19.07.86 Michael Watson L CO 1 Wembley
23.10.86 W.O. Wilson L PTS 8 Birmingham
03.06.87 Andy Wright DREW 6 Southwark
24.11.87 Paul McCarthy DREW 8 Southampton
01.12.88 Tony Collins L PTS 6 Edmonton
20.12.88 Paul McCarthy L DIS 3 Swansea
31.01.89 Chris Eubank L RSC 4 Bethnal Green
01.03.89 Darryl Ritchie W RSC 1 Cardiff
13.03.89 Dennis Banton W RSC 5 Piccadilly
17.04.89 Nigel Fairbairn L PTS 8 Birmingham
08.07.89 Willie Monroe NC 5 Paris, France
19.08.89 Antoine Tarver W RSC 3 Cardiff
05.10.89 Kid Milo L PTS 8 Stevenage
09.11.89 Frank Grant L RTD 6 Cardiff
02.02.90 Roland Ericsson L PTS 8 Geneva, Switzerland
17.03.90 Sammy Storey L CO 7 Belfast
26.04.90 Steve Johnson L PTS 6 Merthyr
11.05.91 Noel Magee L PTS 8 Belfast
13.11.91 Ray Close L PTS 6 Belfast

14.07.92 Lou Gent L RSC 5 Mayfair
30.01.93 Gary Delaney L PTS 8 Brentwood
30.03.93 Bobbi Joe Edwards L PTS 6 Cardiff
Career: 27 contests, won 6, drew 3, lost 17, no contest 1.

Steve Collins

Dublin. *Born* Dublin, 21 July, 1964
All-Ireland Middleweight Champion.
Former Undefeated USBA Middleweight
Champion. Ht. 5'11"
Manager Self

24.10.86 Julio Mercado W RSC 3 Lowell, USA
26.11.86 Mike Bonislawski W PTS 4 Dorchester, USA
20.12.86 Richard Holloway W RSC 2 Dorchester, USA
10.10.87 Jim Holmes W CO 1 Attleboro, USA
29.10.87 Harold Souther W PTS 8 Lowell, USA
20.11.87 Mike Williams W PTS 6 Atlantic City, USA
09.12.87 Benny Sims W PTS 8 Atlantic City, USA
18.03.88 Sammy Storey W PTS 10 Boston, USA
(Vacant All-Ireland Middleweight Title)
26.05.88 Lester Yarborough W PTS 10 Boston, USA
30.07.88 Mike Dale W PTS 8 Brockton, USA
22.10.88 Muhammad Shabbaz W RSC 4 Salem, USA
10.12.88 Jesse Lanton W PTS 10 Salem, USA
07.02.89 Paul McPeek W RSC 9 Atlantic City, USA
09.05.89 Kevin Watts W PTS 12 Atlantic City, USA
(USBA Middleweight Title Challenge)
16.07.89 Tony Thornton W PTS 12 Atlantic City, USA
(USBA Middleweight Title Defence)
21.11.89 Roberto Rosiles W RSC 9 Las Vegas, USA

All-Ireland middleweight champion, Steve Collins (left), now fighting out of this country, on his way to a third round stoppage win over Johnny Melfah Les Clark

03.02.90	Mike McCallum L PTS 12 Boston, USA
	(WBA Middleweight Title Challenge)
16.08.90	Fermin Chirino W RSC 6 Boston, USA
24.11.90	Eddie Hall W PTS 10 Boston, USA
11.05.91	Kenny Snow W RSC 3 Belfast
22.05.91	Jean-Noel Camara W CO 3 Brest, France
11.12.91	Danny Morgan W RSC 3 Dublin
22.04.92	Reggie Johnson L PTS 12 East Rutherford, USA
	(Vacant WBA Middleweight Title)
22.10.92	Sumbu Kalambay L PTS 12 Verbania, Italy
	(European Middleweight Title Challenge)
06.02.93	Johnny Melfah W RSC 3 Cardiff
20.02.93	Ian Strudwick W RSC 7 Kensington
26.06.93	Gerhard Botes W RSC 7 Kensington

Career: 27 contests, won 24, lost 3.

(Elton) Tom Collins

Leeds. *Born* Curacao, 1 July, 1955
Cruiserweight. Former European L.
Heavyweight Champion. Former
Undefeated British & Central Area L.
Heavyweight Champion. Ht. 5'11"
Manager T. Callighan

17.01.77	Ginger McIntyre W RSC 2 Birmingham
16.05.77	Mick Dolan W PTS 6 Manchester
01.06.77	Johnny Cox W CO 3 Dudley
23.11.77	George Gray W RSC 3 Stoke
19.01.78	Clint Jones W RSC 3 Merton
21.03.78	Joe Jackson W PTS 8 Luton
09.05.78	Harald Skog L PTS 8 Oslo, Norway
17.07.78	Karl Canwell L RSC 6 Mayfair
28.11.78	Carlton Benoit W CO 1 Sheffield
04.12.78	Dennis Andries L PTS 8 Southend
30.01.79	Dennis Andries L CO 6 Southend
22.10.79	Danny Lawford W RSC 7 Nottingham
28.11.79	Eddie Smith W PTS 8 Solihull
25.02.80	Greg Evans W RSC 1 Bradford
	(Vacant Central Area L. Heavyweight Title)
15.04.80	Chris Lawson W RSC 4 Blackpool
04.12.80	Mustafa Wasajja L PTS 8 Randers, Denmark
09.03.81	Karl Canwell W PTS 10 Bradford
	(Elim. British L. Heavyweight Title)
15.03.82	Dennis Andries W PTS 15 Bloomsbury
	(Vacant British L. Heavyweight Title)
26.05.82	Trevor Cattouse W CO 4 Leeds
	(British L. Heavyweight Title Defence)
07.10.82	John Odhiambo L RSC 5 Copenhagen, Denmark
09.03.83	Antonio Harris W RSC 6 Solihull
	(British L. Heavyweight Title Defence)
09.04.83	Alex Sua W PTS 12 Auckland, New Zealand
	(Elim. Commonwealth L. Heavyweight Title)
17.12.83	Leslie Stewart L PTS 10 Trinidad, West Indies
26.01.84	Dennis Andries L PTS 12 STRAND
	(British L. Heavyweight Title Defence)
06.04.84	Dennis Andries L PTS 12 Watford
	(British L. Heavyweight Title Challenge)
21.09.84	Alek Penarski L PTS 8 Alfreton
24.01.85	Jonjo Greene W RSC 7 Manchester

30.03.85	Chisanda Mutti L PTS 10 Dortmund, Germany
18.04.85	Andy Straughn L CO 1 Halifax
14.10.85	Harry Cowap W CO 4 Southwark
29.11.85	Ralf Rocchigiani L PTS 8 Frankfurt, Germany
20.12.85	Pierre Kabassu DREW 8 Forbach, France
01.04.86	Winston Burnett W PTS 8 Leeds
19.04.86	Yawe Davis W CO 3 San Remo, Italy
01.12.86	Alex Blanchard L PTS 10 Arnhem, Holland
11.03.87	John Moody W RSC 10 Kensington
	(Vacant British L. Heavyweight Title)
11.11.87	Alex Blanchard W CO 2 Usk
	(European L. Heavyweight Title Challenge)
11.05.88	Mark Kaylor W CO 9 Wembley
	(European L. Heavyweight Title Defence)
07.09.88	Pedro van Raamsdonk L RSC 7 Reading
	(European L. Heavyweight Title Defence)
22.03.89	Tony Wilson W RSC 2 Reading
	(British L. Heavyweight Title Challenge)
24.10.89	Jeff Harding L RTD 2 Brisbane, Australia
	(WBC L. Heavyweight Title Challenge)
11.08.90	Eric Nicoletta W CO 9 Cap d'Agde, France
	(European L. Heavyweight Title Challenge)
18.10.90	Frank Winterstein L PTS 10 Paris, France
21.12.90	Christophe Girard W CO 2 Romorantin, France
	(European L. Heavyweight Title Defence)
09.05.91	Leonzer Barber L RTD 5 Leeds
	(Vacant WBO L. Heavyweight Title)
06.12.91	Henry Maske L RSC 8 Dusseldorf, Germany
18.03.92	Glazz Campbell L PTS 10 Glasgow
	(Final Elim. British L. Heavyweight Title)
26.10.92	Steve Lewsam DREW 8 Cleethorpes
21.11.92	Joseph Chingangu L CO 2 Johannesburg, South Africa

Career: 49 contests, won 26, drew 2, lost 21.

Tony Collins

Yateley. *Born* London, 11 May, 1970
Former WBC International L.
Middleweight Champion. Ht. 5'10"
Manager F. Warren

01.07.87	Terry Vosper W RSC 1 Kensington
16.09.87	Willie MacDonald W RSC 1 Kensington
13.10.87	Bernardo Matthews W PTS 4 Windsor
28.11.87	Kevin Hayde W PTS 4 Windsor
15.12.87	Geoff Calder W RSC 2 Cardiff
27.01.88	Robert Armstrong W CO 1 Bethnal Green
24.02.88	Geoff Calder W RSC 3 Aberavon
29.03.88	Rob Thomas W PTS 4 Bethnal Green
12.04.88	Steve Foster W PTS 4 Muswell Hill
12.04.88	Rocky Reynolds W PTS 4 Cardiff
20.04.88	Steve Foster W PTS 4 Muswell Hill
10.05.88	Ollie Hutchinson W RSC 1 Tottenham
28.05.88	Chris Richards W RSC 3 Kensington

25.06.88	Franki Moro W PTS 6 Luton
01.11.88	Jose Bezerra de Lima W RSC 6 Reading
01.12.88	Simon Collins W PTS 6 Edmonton
20.12.88	Russell Mitchell L RSC 3 Swansea
31.01.89	Willie Montana W RSC 4 Reading
17.05.89	Don Johnson W PTS 8 Millwall
14.09.89	B. K. Bennett W RSC 1 Basildon
11.10.89	Gary Pemberton W CO 1 Millwall
15.11.89	Antonio Guerra W CO 3 Reading
19.12.89	Roger Silsby W CO 5 Gorleston
20.02.90	Joe Hernandez W CO 1 Millwall
26.05.90	Hugo Marinangeli W PTS 12 Reading
	(Vacant WBC International L. Middleweight Title)
10.10.90	Ricardo Nunez W PTS 12 Millwall
	(WBC International L. Middleweight Title Defence)
08.05.91	Ricardo Nunez W PTS 12 Millwall
	(WBC International L. Middleweight Title Defence)
03.07.91	Wally Swift Jnr L PTS 12 Reading
	(British L. Middleweight Title Challenge)
29.10.91	Paul Wesley DREW 8 Kensington
18.06.92	Russell Washer W RSC 2 Peterborough
22.10.92	Curtis Summit L RSC 7 Bethnal Green
	(Vacant WBC International L. Middleweight Title)
10.12.92	Andy Till L RSC 3 Bethnal Green
	(British L. Middleweight Title Challenge)

Career: 32 contests, won 27, drew 1, lost 4.

Edward Cook

Larkhall. *Born* Lanark, 30 November, 1967
Featherweight. Ht. 5'4¼"
Manager A. Melrose

17.05.89	Joe Mullen L PTS 8 Glasgow
14.09.89	Steve Walker W PTS 6 Motherwell
04.11.89	Steve Walker L PTS 4 Eastbourne
23.11.89	Ian McGirr L PTS 6 Motherwell
23.02.90	Dave Buxton W RTD 1 Irvine
19.03.90	Jamie McBride W PTS 6 Glasgow
26.03.90	Ian McGirr W PTS 6 Glasgow
22.05.90	Dave Buxton L PTS 6 Stockton
04.06.90	Neil Leitch W PTS 8 Glasgow
19.11.90	Ian McGirr W PTS 6 Glasgow
02.03.91	Ian McGirr W PTS 6 Irvine
15.04.91	Darren Elsdon DREW 4 Glasgow
24.10.91	Des Gargano W RSC 5 Glasgow
31.01.92	Des Gargano W PTS 6 Glasgow
20.02.92	Miguel Matthews W PTS 6 Glasgow
08.04.92	Tony Silkstone L PTS 8 Leeds
29.01.93	Derek Amory L PTS 6 Glasgow
04.03.93	Derek Amory L RSC 4 Glasgow

Career: 18 contests, won 10, drew 1, lost 7.

James Cook

Peckham. *Born* Jamaica, 17 May, 1959
Former European S. Middleweight
Champion. Former Undefeated British S.
Middleweight Champion. Former
Undefeated Southern Area Middleweight
Champion. Ht. 6'2"
Manager M. Duff

20.10.82	Mick Courtney W PTS 6 Strand
01.11.82	Gary Gething W RSC 2 Piccadilly
19.01.83	Paul Shell W PTS 8 Birmingham
03.02.83	Jimmy Price L PTS 6 Bloomsbury

09.03.83 Willie Wright W PTS 8 Solihull
14.04.83 Dudley McKenzie W PTS 8 Basildon
16.05.83 Eddie Smith W RSC 8 Manchester
23.11.83 Vince Gajny W RTD 6 Solihull
05.06.84 T. P. Jenkins W RSC 9 Kensington
          *(Vacant Southern Area Middleweight
          Title & Elim. British Middleweight
          Title)*
25.09.84 Jimmy Price L CO 2 Wembley
          (Elim. British Middleweight Title)
04.05.85 Conrad Oscar W PTS 10 Queensway
          *(Southern Area Middleweight Title
          Defence)*
02.10.85 Tony Burke L CO 2 Solihull
          *(Southern Area Middleweight Title
          Defence)*
01.03.86 Graciano Rocchigiani L PTS 8
          Cologne, Germany
26.03.86 Jan Lefeber L CO 3 Amsterdam,
          Holland
20.05.86 Michael Watson W PTS 8 Wembley
13.02.87 Mbayo Wa Mbayo L PTS 8
          Villeurbanne, France
02.10.87 Willie Wilson W CO 6 Perugia, Italy
26.10.87 Tarmo Uusivirta L PTS 10 Jyvaskyla,
          Finland
05.04.88 Cliff Curtis W RSC 4 Basildon
08.06.88 Herol Graham L RSC 5 Sheffield
          (Vacant British Middleweight Title)
31.01.89 Errol Christie W RSC 5 Bethnal Green
28.09.89 Brian Schumacher W RSC 5
          Wandsworth
          *(Final Elim. British S. Middleweight
          Title)*
30.10.90 Sammy Storey W RSC 10 Belfast
          *(British S. Middleweight Title
          Challenge)*
10.03.91 Frank Winterstein W CO 12 Paris,
          France
          *(Vacant European S. Middleweight
          Title)*
01.06.91 Mark Kaylor W RTD 6 Bethnal Green
          *(European S. Middleweight Title
          Defence)*
22.10.91 Tarmo Uusivirta W RTD 7
          Wandsworth
          *(European S. Middleweight Title
          Defence)*
03.04.92 Franck Nicotra L CO 1 Vitrolles,
          France
          *(European S. Middleweight Title
          Defence)*
07.09.92 Tony Booth W PTS 8 Bethnal Green
17.10.92 Terry Magee W RSC 5 Wembley
28.01.93 Carlos Christie W PTS 8 Southwark
18.03.93 Karl Barwise W RSC 6 Lewisham
Career: 31 contests, won 22, lost 9.

John J. Cooke

Coventry. *Born* Coventry, 22 January, 1966
Midlands Area L. Heavyweight Champion.
Ht. 5'10"
Manager J. Griffin

05.10.92 Paul Hanlon W RSC 1 Bardon
23.11.92 Paul Murray W CO 1 Coventry
02.12.92 Nigel Rafferty W PTS 6 Bardon
22.02.93 Zak Chelli DREW 6 Bedworth
17.06.93 Gil Lewis W RSC 9 Bedworth
          *(Vacant Midlands Area L. Heavyweight
          Title)*
Career: 5 contests, won 4. drew 1.

Dean Cooper

Bristol. *Born* Southampton, 5 August, 1969
Western Area L. Middleweight Champion.
Ht. 6'0"
Manager R. Porter

15.09.90 Russell Washer W PTS 6 Bristol
08.10.90 Brian Keating W PTS 6 Bradford
29.10.90 Peter Reid W RSC 1 Nottingham
06.11.90 Tony Wellington W PTS 6 Southend
08.12.90 Lee Farrell W PTS 6 Bristol
04.02.91 Mike Phillips W PTS 6 Leicester
18.02.91 Andre Wharton W PTS 8 Birmingham
22.10.91 Nick Meloscia W PTS 6 Wandsworth
09.03.93 Winston May W PTS 8 Bristol
27.05.93 Robert Peel W PTS 6 Bristol
26.06.93 Julian Eavis W PTS 10 Keynsham
          *(Vacant Western Area L. Middleweight
          Title)*
Career: 11 contests, won 11.

Chris Coughlan

Swansea. *Born* Swansea, 21 May, 1963
Cruiserweight. Ht. 6'2½"
Manager C. Breen

03.10.89 Ahcene Chemali L RSC 1 Southend
03.12.89 John Foreman L RSC 2 Birmingham
10.03.90 Mark Langley W PTS 6 Bristol
28.03.90 Phil Soundy L PTS 6 Bethnal Green
05.06.90 Trevor Barry L PTS 6 Liverpool
17.09.90 Steve Yorath L PTS 6 Cardiff
06.11.90 Art Stacey L RSC 4 Southend
08.12.90 Gary McConnell L PTS 6 Bristol
16.01.91 Phil Soundy L PTS 6 Kensington
15.02.91 Neils H. Madsen L RSC 3 Randers,
          Denmark
04.11.91 Nick Howard W CO 3 Merthyr
11.12.91 Ray Kane L PTS 6 Dublin
18.01.92 Wayne Llewelyn L RSC 3 Kensington
17.12.92 J. A. Bugner L RSC 3 Wembley
Career: 14 contests, won 2, lost 12.

Lee Crocker

Swansea. *Born* Swansea, 9 May, 1969
Middleweight. Ht. 6'0"
Manager M. Copp

31.01.91 Colin Manners L PTS 6 Bredbury
12.02.91 Paul Evans W RSC 2 Cardiff
04.04.91 Johnny Pinnock W RSC 5 Watford
30.06.91 Andrew Furlong DREW 6 Southwark
30.09.91 Fran Harding L RSC 3 Kensington
11.03.92 Russell Washer W PTS 6 Cardiff
30.04.92 Winston May W RSC 2 Bayswater
23.09.92 Nick Manners L CO 1 Leeds
17.12.92 Jamie Robinson L RTD 2 Barking
20.01.93 Ernie Loveridge W PTS 6
          Wolverhampton
28.01.93 Clay O'Shea L RSC 1 Southwark
14.06.93 Gilbert Jackson L RSC 2 Bayswater
Career: 12 contests, won 5, drew 1, lost 6.

Con Cronin

Watford. *Born* Willesden, 27 August, 1962
Lightweight. Ht. 5'7½"
Manager D. Mancini

01.05.84 Steve Cooke DREW 6 Maidstone
09.05.84 Nicky Day DREW 6 Mayfair
17.09.84 Mark Simpson L RSC 6 Brighton
01.11.84 Mickey Hull L PTS 6 Basildon
01.03.85 Steve Friel L RSC 3 Longford
04.05.85 Nicky Day DREW 6 Queensway
25.05.85 Kenny Watson W PTS 6 Longford

22.07.85 Gary King DREW 6 Longford
07.11.85 Nicky Day L PTS 6 Tottenham
25.04.88 Wayne Goult W CO 3 Bethnal Green
26.05.88 Steve Taggart W PTS 6 Bethnal Green
14.06.88 Shaun Cooper L PTS 6 Dudley
17.09.92 Jason Lepre W PTS 6 Watford
Career: 13 contests, won 4, drew 4, lost 5.

Carl Crook

Chorley. *Born* Bolton, 10 November, 1963
Former British & Commonwealth
Lightweight Champion. Former Undefeated
Central Area Lightweight Champion. Ht.
5'10"
Manager Self

16.12.85 George Jones W PTS 6 Bradford
27.01.86 Russell Jones W RSC 4 Bradford
24.03.86 Doug Munro W CO 2 Bradford
17.04.86 Muhammad Lovelock W CO 6
          Bradford
22.05.86 George Jones W RSC 1 Horwich
22.09.86 Sugar Gibiliru W PTS 6 Bradford
04.11.86 Brian Roche DREW 10 Oldham
          *(Vacant Central Area Lightweight
          Title)*
15.12.86 Sugar Gibiliru W PTS 8 Bradford
27.01.87 Dean Marsden W RSC 1 Manchester
23.02.87 Muhammad Lovelock W PTS 10
          Bradford
          *(Vacant Central Area Lightweight
          Title)*
28.04.87 George Baigrie W PTS 8 Manchester
09.06.87 Tony Richards W PTS 8 Manchester
22.09.87 Joey Jacobs L PTS 10 Oldham
          *(Central Area Lightweight Title
          Defence)*
07.10.87 Marvin P. Gray W PTS 8 Burnley
26.11.87 Marvin P. Gray W PTS 8 Horwich
26.04.88 Keith Parry W PTS 10 Bradford
          (Elim. British Lightweight Title)
25.10.88 Patrick Kamy W PTS 8 Hartlepool
14.02.89 Steve Topliss W RTD 5 Manchester
14.04.89 Nedrie Simmons W RSC 8 Manchester
31.05.89 Steve Pollard W RSC 4 Manchester
13.10.89 Mohammed Ouhmad W PTS 8 Preston
24.01.90 Joel Dulys W RSC 3 Preston
21.03.90 Najib Daho W PTS 12 Preston
          *(Commonwealth Lightweight Title
          Challenge)*
14.11.90 Tony Richards W PTS 12 Sheffield
          *(Vacant British Lightweight Title.
          Commonwealth Lightweight Title
          Defence)*
19.12.90 Ian Honeywood W RSC 4 Preston
          *(British & Commonwealth Lightweight
          Title Defence)*
24.04.91 Najib Daho W RSC 10 Preston
          *(British & Commonwealth Lightweight
          Title Defence)*
22.06.91 Brian Roche W CO 10 Earls Court
          *(British & Commonwealth Lightweight
          Title Defence)*
07.12.91 Antonio Renzo L RSC 6 Rossano
          Calabro, Italy
          *(European Lightweight Title
          Challenge)*
05.05.92 Steve Boyle W RSC 7 Preston
          *(British & Commonwealth Lightweight
          Title Defence)*
28.10.92 Billy Schwer L RTD 9 Kensington
          *(British & Commonwealth Lightweight
          Title Defence)*

29.04.93   Jean-Baptiste Mendy L RSC 8
           Levallois Perret, France
           *(European Lightweight Title
           Challenge)*
Career: 31 contests, won 26, drew 1, lost 4.

Kevin Cullinane
Liverpool. *Born* Liverpool, 5 November,
1970
Heavyweight. Ht. 5'11"
Manager D. Isaaman

29.03.93   Gary Williams L RSC 2 Liverpool
Career: 1 contest, lost 1.

Mario Culpeper
Manchester. *Born* Manchester, 8
December, 1970
S. Featherweight. Ht. 5'6"
Manager P. Martin

25.09.90   Graham O'Malley W PTS 6 Glasgow
26.04.93   Mark Hargreaves W PTS 6 Manchester
28.05.93   Dougie Fox W RSC 3 Middleton
Career: 3 contests, won 3.

Shaun Cummins
Leicester. *Born* Leicester, 8 February, 1968
WBA Penta-Continental L. Middleweight
Champion. Ht. 6'1"
Manager F. Warren

29.09.86   Michael Justin W PTS 6
           Loughborough
24.11.86   Gary Pemberton W RSC 6 Cardiff
09.02.87   Rob Thomas W PTS 8 Cardiff
23.09.87   Chris Richards W PTS 6
           Loughborough
07.03.88   Antonio Fernandez W PTS 6
           Northampton
12.09.88   Shamus Casey W CO 3 Northampton
24.10.88   Frank Grant L RTD 7 Northampton
01.03.89   Gary Pemberton W CO 2 Cardiff
05.04.89   Efren Olivo W RSC 1 Kensington
04.10.89   Kesem Clayton L RSC 6 Solihull
31.01.90   Tony Velinor W PTS 8 Bethnal Green
20.02.90   Brian Robinson W RSC 5 Millwall
26.04.90   Wally Swift Jnr L PTS 10 Merthyr
           *(Vacant Midlands Area L.
           Middleweight Title & Elim. British L.
           Middleweight Title)*
18.09.90   Paul Wesley W RSC 1 Wolverhampton
31.10.90   Terry Morrill W RSC 1 Crystal Palace
23.01.91   Ian Chantler W PTS 10 Brentwood
19.03.91   Martin Smith DREW 8 Leicester
07.11.91   Jason Rowe W RSC 2 Peterborough
05.12.91   Winston May W RSC 2 Peterborough
18.06.92   Leroy Owens W RSC 2 Peterborough
26.09.92   John Kaighin W RTD 4 Earls Court
28.11.92   Steve Foster W PTS 12 Manchester
           *(Vacant WBA Penta-Continental L.
           Middleweight Title)*
20.04.93   Mickey Hughes W CO 11 Brentwood
           *(WBA Penta-Continental L.
           Middleweight Title Defence)*
Career: 23 contests, won 19, drew 1, lost 3.

Derrick Daniel
Leyton. *Born* Bethnal Green, 3 April, 1963
L. Welterweight. Ht. 5'9½"
Manager B. Hearn

06.03.90   John Marshall W RSC 5 Bethnal Green

09.05.90   Gavin Fitzpatrick W RSC 1
           Kensington
12.09.90   Ross Hale L PTS 6 Bethnal Green
26.03.91   Mick O'Donnell DREW 6 Bethnal
           Green
11.05.92   Carl Hook W PTS 6 Piccadilly
16.06.92   Carl Hook L RSC 2 Dagenham
16.02.93   George Wilson L PTS 6 Tooting
Career: 7 contests, won 3, drew 1, lost 3.

Hughie Davey
Newcastle. *Born* Wallsend, 27 January,
1966
Welterweight. Ht. 5'8"
Manager T. Conroy

30.03.92   Wayne Shepherd W PTS 6 Bradford
28.04.92   Benji Joseph W RSC 4 Houghton le
           Spring
10.09.92   Darren McInulty W PTS 6 Southwark
21.09.92   Rick North DREW 6 Cleethorpes
23.10.92   Richard O'Brien W PTS 6 Gateshead
01.03.93   Wayne Appleton L PTS 6 Bradford
29.04.93   Paul King L PTS 6 Newcastle
11.06.93   Wayne Shepherd W PTS 6 Gateshead
Career: 8 contests, won 5, drew 1, lost 2.

(David) Jamie Davidson (Prescott)
Liverpool. *Born* Liverpool, 1 April, 1970
L. Welterweight. Ht. 6'0"
Manager Self

18.11.91   Ty Zubair W PTS 6 Manchester
10.02.92   Kevin McKillan W PTS 6 Liverpool
11.03.92   Kevin McKillan DREW 6 Stoke
28.04.92   Micky Hall W PTS 6 Houghton le
           Spring
14.05.92   Floyd Churchill L RSC 4 Liverpool
21.06.93   George Wilson L RSC 4 Swindon
Career: 6 contests, won 3, drew 1, lost 2.

Paul Davies
Swansea. *Born* Swansea, 18 October, 1968
L. Welterweight. Ht. 5'8"
Manager C. Breen

30.03.93   Phil Found L PTS 6 Cardiff
Career: 1 contest, lost 1.

Stevie R. Davies
Newcastle. *Born* Consett, 27 August, 1965
S. Middleweight. Ht. 6'3"
Manager Self

04.04.89   Sean Stringfellow L RSC 2 Manchester
22.05.89   Ian Vokes W PTS 6 Bradford
29.05.89   Trevor Barry W RSC 4 Liverpool
20.03.90   Terry French L PTS 6 Hartlepool
23.04.90   Graham Burton L PTS 6 Bradford
01.05.90   Glenn Campbell L RSC 2 Oldham
08.10.90   Sean Stringfellow W PTS 6 Leicester
22.10.90   Tony Lawrence W PTS 8 Peterborough
22.11.90   Tony Lawrence W PTS 6 Ilkeston
13.12.90   Terry French L PTS 10 Hartlepool
           *(Vacant Northern Area L. Heavyweight
           Title)*
28.02.91   Kevin Morton L RSC 3 Bury
29.04.93   Martin Langtry L RSC 2 Newcastle
Career: 12 contests, won 5, lost 7.

John Davison
Newcastle. *Born* Newcastle, 30 September,
1958

Former Undefeated British & WBC
International Featherweight Champion.
Former Undefeated WBC International S.
Bantamweight Champion. Ht. 5'5"
Manager T. Conroy

22.09.88   Des Gargano W PTS 8 Newcastle
29.09.88   Des Gargano W PTS 8 Sunderland
10.10.88   Gary Maxwell W RSC 1 Nottingham
22.11.88   James Hunter W PTS 6 Marton
12.12.88   Gary Maxwell L PTS 8 Nottingham
14.02.89   Nigel Senior W RSC 8 Sunderland
11.09.89   Colin Lynch W RSC 2 Nottingham
23.10.89   Andre Seymour W PTS 8 Glasgow
06.12.89   Karl Taylor W PTS 8 Leicester
19.02.90   Bruce Flippens W RSC 6 Glasgow
20.03.90   Srikoon Narachawat W CO 5
           Hartlepool
           *(WBC International Featherweight
           Title Challenge)*
15.05.90   Bang Saen Yodmuaydang W RSC 5
           South Shields
           *(WBC International Featherweight
           Title Defence)*
13.11.90   Jae-Hyun Hwang W RSC 5 Hartlepool
           *(WBC International Featherweight
           Title Defence)*
25.05.91   Fabrice Benichou L PTS 12 Brest,
           France
           (Vacant European Featherweight Title)
09.08.91   Richard Savage W RSC 6 Juan les
           Pins, France
22.10.91   Sakda Sorpakdee W PTS 12 Hartlepool
           *(WBC International S. Bantamweight
           Title Challenge)*
29.05.92   Fabrice Benichou L PTS 12 Amneville,
           France
           *(European Featherweight Title
           Challenge)*
10.09.92   Tim Driscoll W CO 7 Sunderland
           (Vacant British Featherweight Title)
17.04.93   Steve Robinson L PTS 12 Washington
           (Vacant WBO Featherweight Title)
Career: 19 contests, won 15, lost 4.

Russell Davison
Salford. *Born* Salford, 2 October, 1961
Former Central Area Featherweight
Champion. Ht. 5'7"
Manager J. Trickett

22.05.86   Nigel Crook L PTS 6 Horwich
09.06.86   Gary Maxwell L PTS 6 Manchester
25.09.86   Nigel Crook L PTS 6 Preston
14.10.86   Davey Hughes W PTS 6 Manchester
25.11.86   Carl Gaynor W PTS 6 Manchester
10.12.86   Davey Hughes W PTS 8 Stoke
27.01.87   Nigel Senior DREW 8 Manchester
04.03.87   Tim Driscoll W PTS 8 Oldham
31.03.87   Stuart Carmichael W PTS 8 Oldham
26.05.87   Kevin Taylor L PTS 10 Oldham
           *(Central Area S. Featherweight Title
           Challenge)*
06.10.87   Gary Maxwell L PTS 8 Manchester
16.12.87   Mike Whalley W PTS 8 Manchester
16.03.88   Gary de Roux L PTS 8 Solihull
03.05.88   Rocky Lawlor L PTS 8 Stoke
29.11.88   Mike Whalley L RSC 7 Manchester
           *(Vacant Central Area Featherweight
           Title)*
25.01.89   Derek Amory W PTS 8 Solihull
19.04.89   Michael Armstrong L PTS 8 Stoke

06.12.89	Michael Armstrong W PTS 8 Stoke
23.12.89	Kevin Kelley L PTS 8 Hoogvleit, Holland
06.03.90	Michael Armstrong L PTS 10 Stoke
26.09.90	Steve Robinson L PTS 8 Manchester
19.11.90	Peter Judson W PTS 8 Manchester
17.12.90	Dave Buxton W PTS 8 Manchester
29.01.91	Peter Judson W PTS 10 Stockport
	(Vacant Central Area Featherweight Title)
05.03.91	Colin McMillan L PTS 6 Millwall
24.04.91	Steve Robinson L RTD 6 Preston
09.09.91	Jimmy Owens W PTS 10 Liverpool
	(Central Area Featherweight Title Defence)
29.02.92	Moussa Sangaree L RSC 5 Gravelines, France
13.10.92	Craig Dermody L PTS 10 Bury
	(Central Area Featherweight Title Defence)
24.03.93	Eamonn McAuley L PTS 6 Belfast
26.04.93	Drew Docherty L PTS 8 Glasgow
15.05.93	Alan Levene L PTS 6 Bradford
24.05.93	David Ramsden L PTS 6 Bradford

Career: 33 contests, won 11, drew 1, lost 21.

Mark Dawson   Les Clark

Mark Dawson (Lee)

Burton. *Born* Burton, 26 February, 1971
L. Middleweight. Ht. 5'8"
Manager W. Swift

03.06.92	Rick North W PTS 6 Newcastle under Lyme
09.09.92	Jimmy Vincent W PTS 6 Stoke
29.09.92	Steve Goodwin L RSC 1 Stoke
28.10.92	Steve McNess W RSC 2 Kensington
07.12.92	Steve Goodwin W PTS 6 Mayfair
27.01.93	Rick North W PTS 8 Stoke
15.02.93	John Bosco L PTS 6 Mayfair
27.02.93	Robin Reid L RSC 1 Dagenham
30.03.93	Matthew Turner L PTS 6 Cardiff
12.05.93	Steve Goodwin L PTS 10 Stoke
	(Vacant Midlands Area L. Middleweight Title)

27.05.93	Derek Wormald L RTD 5 Burnley

Career: 11 contests, won 5, lost 6.

Gary Delaney

West Ham. *Born* Newham, 12 August, 1970
L. Heavyweight. Ht. 6'3"
Manager B. Hearn

02.10.91	Gus Mendes W RSC 1 Barking
23.10.91	Joe Frater W RSC 1 Bethnal Green
13.11.91	John Kaighin W PTS 6 Bethnal Green
11.12.91	Randy B. Powell W RSC 1 Basildon
11.02.92	Simon Harris DREW 8 Barking
12.05.92	John Williams W PTS 6 Crystal Palace
16.06.92	Nigel Rafferty W CO 5 Dagenham
15.09.92	Gil Lewis W CO 2 Crystal Palace
06.10.92	Simon McDougall W PTS 8 Antwerp, Belgium
10.11.92	John Oxenham W CO 5 Dagenham
12.12.92	Simon McDougall W PTS 8 Muswell Hill
30.01.93	Simon Collins W PTS 8 Brentwood

Career: 12 contests, won 11, drew 1.

(Allan) John Dempsey (McCann)

Leeds. *Born* Leeds, 9 October, 1973
Middleweight. Ht. 5'9½"
Manager P. Coleman

22.02.93	Mark Smallwood L CO 1 Bedworth

Career: 1 contest, lost 1.

Damien Denny

Belfast. *Born* Lisburn, 20 April, 1966
L. Middleweight. Ht. 5'9"
Manager Self

01.07.87	Manny Romain W CO 1 Kensington
09.08.87	Joe Lynch W RSC 1 Windsor
16.09.87	Billy Cairns W PTS 8 Kensington
13.10.87	Chris Richards W PTS 6 Windsor
27.01.88	Simon Lee W CO 7 Bethnal Green
07.02.88	Dean Bramhald W PTS 4 Stafford
09.03.88	Jimmy Thornton W PTS 8 Bethnal Green
25.06.88	Martin Smith NC 5 Luton
15.11.88	Tommy McCallum W RSC 2 Norwich
01.12.88	Kelvin Mortimer W RSC 1 Edmonton
28.03.89	Mickey Lloyd W RSC 4 Bethnal Green
11.04.89	Winston May W RSC 3 Aberavon
19.09.89	Mark Holden W RSC 2 Millwall
17.04.90	Del Bryan L PTS 10 Millwall
	(Final Elim. British Welterweight Title)
06.07.90	Parrish Johnson W RSC 4 Brentwood
22.09.90	Newton Barnett L RSC 6 Kensington
06.02.91	Newton Barnett W PTS 8 Bethnal Green
09.04.91	Jason Rowe L CO 7 Mayfair
01.12.92	Bozon Haule W PTS 6 Bristol
24.03.93	James McGee W CO 2 Belfast
	(Elim. All-Ireland L. Middleweight Title)
18.06.93	Rob Pitters W RSC 3 Belfast

Career: 21 contests, won 17, lost, no contest 1.

Paul Denton (Ramsey)

Walthamstow. *Born* Birmingham, 12 April, 1970
Welterweight. Ht. 5'10"
Manager B. Ingle

18.03.93	Mark O'Callaghan W RSC 4 Lewisham

29.04.93	Dave Maj DREW 6 Mayfair

Career: 2 contests, won 1, drew 1.

Craig Dermody

Manchester. *Born* Manchester, 11 September, 1970
Central Area Featherweight Champion. Ht. 5'6"
Manager F. Warren

31.01.91	Karl Morling W RSC 5 Bredbury
14.03.91	Kelton McKenzie W RSC 3 Middleton
16.04.91	Miguel Matthews W PTS 6 Nottingham
16.05.91	Andrew Robinson W PTS 6 Liverpool
20.06.91	Gary Hickman W RSC 2 Liverpool
01.08.91	James Hunter W RSC 2 Dewsbury
21.11.91	Miguel Matthews W PTS 6 Burton
28.11.91	Pete Buckley W PTS 6 Liverpool
19.12.91	Pete Buckley W PTS 6 Oldham
27.02.92	Miguel Matthews W PTS 6 Liverpool
02.07.92	Alan Smith W RSC 3 Middleton
13.10.92	Russell Davison W PTS 10 Bury
	(Central Area Featherweight Title Challenge)
13.02.93	Karl Taylor W RSC 5 Manchester
31.03.93	Karl Taylor L PTS 6 Barking

Career: 14 contests, won 13, lost 1.

Gary de Roux

Peterborough. *Born* Manchester, 4 November, 1962
S. Featherweight. Former British Featherweight Champion. Former Undefeated Southern Area Featherweight Champion. Ht. 5'6"
Manager Self

25.09.86	Tony Carter W RSC 2 Peterborough
20.10.86	Nigel Lawrence W RSC 1 Nottingham
28.11.86	Geoff Sillitoe W RTD 1 Peterborough
15.12.86	Tim Driscoll L PTS 6 Eltham
19.02.87	Gary King W PTS 6 Peterborough
01.05.87	Nigel Senior W PTS 8 Peterborough
10.09.87	Colin Lynch W RSC 3 Peterborough
18.11.87	Steve Pollard DREW 8 Peterborough
23.02.88	Joe Duffy W RSC 2 Bedford
16.03.88	Russell Davison W PTS 8 Solihull
05.05.88	Patrick Kamy L RSC 4 Bayswater
26.11.88	Gianni di Napoli L RSC 3 Forli, Italy
20.09.89	Henry Armstrong L PTS 8 Stoke
29.11.89	James Hunter W CO 2 Marton
13.03.90	John Green W RSC 2 Bristol
19.04.90	Henry Armstrong W CO 8 Oldham
14.12.90	Alan McKay W RSC 5 Peterborough
	(Vacant Southern Area Featherweight Title)
05.03.91	Sean Murphy W CO 5 Millwall
	(British Featherweight Title Challenge)
22.05.91	Colin McMillan L RSC 7 Millwall
	(British Featherweight Title Defence)
13.11.91	Alan McKay L RSC 8 Bethnal Green
	(Vacant Southern Area Featherweight Title)
06.05.93	Juan Castaneda L RSC 6 Las Vegas, USA

Career: 21 contests, won 13, drew 1, lost 7.

Mike Deveney

Paisley. *Born* Elderslie, 14 December, 1965
S. Featherweight. Ht. 5'5"
Manager N. Sweeney

Mike Deveney   Chris Bevan

Norman Dhali   Les Clark

Michael Dick   Les Clark

18.02.91	John George W PTS 6 Glasgow
18.03.91	Frankie Ventura W PTS 6 Piccadilly
22.04.91	Neil Leitch W PTS 6 Glasgow
09.09.91	Pete Buckley W PTS 8 Glasgow
19.09.91	Noel Carroll L PTS 6 Stockport
14.11.91	Pete Buckley W PTS 6 Edinburgh
28.01.92	Graham O'Malley L RSC 1 Piccadilly
28.02.92	Gary Hickman W PTS 6 Irvine
14.09.92	David Ramsden L PTS 6 Bradford
07.10.92	Mark Hargreaves L RSC 7 Glasgow
07.12.92	Carl Roberts W PTS 6 Manchester
27.01.93	Barry Jones L PTS 6 Cardiff
26.02.93	Alan Graham W PTS 6 Irvine
23.03.93	Colin Lynch W PTS 6 Wolverhampton
29.05.93	Dave Buxton W PTS 6 Paisley

Career: 15 contests, won 10, lost 5.

Eunan Devenney

Bushey. *Born* Donegal, 2 February, 1968
S. Featherweight. Ht. 5'5"
Manager J. Barclay

04.09.91	Alan Smith W CO 1 Bethnal Green
26.09.91	Kevin Lowe L CO 2 Dunstable
28.11.91	Greg Upton L PTS 6 Evesham
30.03.92	David Ramsden L RSC 2 Bradford
06.02.93	Russell Rees L RSC 3 Cardiff

Career: 5 contests, won 1, lost 4.

Norman Dhalie

Birmingham. *Born* Birmingham, 24 March, 1971
Lightweight. Ht. 5'7"
Manager Self

06.04.92	Karl Morling L PTS 6 Northampton
27.04.92	Wilson Docherty L RSC 2 Glasgow
02.07.92	John White L RSC 6 Middleton
29.09.92	Gary Marston DREW 6 Stoke
07.10.92	Jacob Smith W PTS 6 Sunderland
03.12.92	Bradley Stone L CO 4 Lewisham
26.01.93	Neil Smith L PTS 4 Leicester
13.02.93	John White L CO 2 Manchester
20.04.93	Bobby Guynan L PTS 6 Brentwood

29.04.93	Kevin Toomey L PTS 6 Hull
23.05.93	Mike Anthony Brown W PTS 4 Brockley
09.06.93	Joey Moffat L RTD 4 Liverpool

Career: 12 contests, won 2, drew 1, lost 9.

Harry Dhami   Les Clark

(Hardip) Harry Dhami

Gravesend. *Born* Gravesend, 17 April, 1972
L. Middleweight. Ht. 5'10"
Manager P. Healy

29.10.92	Johnny Pinnock W PTS 6 Hayes

Career: 1 contest, won 1.

Michael Dick

Aylesbury. *Born* Aylesbury, 29 October, 1964
L. Welterweight. Ht. 5'7"
Manager K. Sanders

29.10.92	Nick Appiah L PTS 6 Hayes
24.02.93	Jason Beard L RSC 5 Wembley
29.04.93	Steve McGovern L PTS 6 Hayes
23.05.93	Maurice Forbes L RSC 1 Brockley
24.06.93	B. F. Williams L RTD 3 Watford

Career: 5 contests, lost 5.

Terry Dixon

West Ham. *Born* London, 29 July, 1966
Cruiserweight. Ht. 5'11"
Manager T. Lawless

21.09.89	Dave Mowbray W RSC 1 Southampton
30.11.89	Brendan Dempsey W RSC 8 Barking
08.03.90	Cordwell Hylton W PTS 8 Watford
06.04.90	Prince Rodney W RSC 7 Stevenage
23.10.90	Dennis Bailey W PTS 6 Leicester
07.03.91	Carl Thompson L PTS 8 Basildon
22.04.91	Everton Blake L RSC 8 Mayfair
25.03.92	Mark Bowen W RTD 1 Kensington
27.04.92	Ian Bulloch W RSC 4 Mayfair
17.10.92	Darren McKenna L RSC 3 Wembley

Career: 10 contests, won 7, lost 3.

Alex Docherty

Craigneuk. *Born* Motherwell, 5 June, 1972
Bantamweight. Ht. 5'5"
Manager T. Gilmour

24.02.92	Andrew Bloomer W PTS 6 Glasgow
01.06.92	Robert Braddock W PTS 6 Glasgow
19.09.92	Kid McAuley W PTS 6 Glasgow
26.02.93	Des Gargano L RSC 4 Irvine

Career: 4 contests, won 3, lost 1.

Wilson Docherty

Croy. *Born* Glasgow, 15 April, 1968

Featherweight. Ht. 5'6"
Manager T. Gilmour

27.04.92	Norman Dhalie W RSC 2 Glasgow
09.07.92	Graham McGrath W RSC 4 Glasgow
26.04.93	Des Gargano W PTS 6 Glasgow
07.06.93	Chris Jickells W RSC 5 Glasgow

Career: 4 contests, won 4.

Adrian Dodson   Les Clark

Adrian Dodson

St Pancras. *Born* Georgetown, 20
September, 1970
L. Middleweight. Ht. 5'10"
Manager J. Ryan

31.03.93	Chris Mulcahy W RSC 1 Bethnal Green
14.04.93	Rick North W RTD 1 Kensington
06.05.93	Greg Wallace W RSC 3 Las Vegas, USA
23.06.93	Russell Washer W PTS 6 Edmonton

Career: 4 contests, won 4.

(Karl) Carlos Domonkos

Doncaster. *Born* Doncaster, 13 May, 1966
Lightweight. Ht. 5'7½"
Manager T. Petersen

| 19.10.92 | Marco Fattore L RTD 4 Mayfair |

Career: 1 contest, lost 1.

Darrit Douglas

Hove. *Born* USA, 13 January, 1968
S. Middleweight. Ht. 5'11½"
Manager B. Hearn

| 27.10.92 | Cyril Jackson W RSC 3 Leicester |
| 22.12.92 | John Kaighin L PTS 6 Mayfair |

Career: 2 contests, won 1, lost 1.

Barry Downes

Northampton. *Born* Northampton, 27
September, 1966
L. Heavyweight. Ht. 5'10½"
Manager J. Cox

18.09.89	Hugh Fury L RSC 1 Northampton
12.12.90	Ian Vokes W PTS 6 Leicester
18.02.91	Ian Vokes L PTS 6 Derby
27.02.91	Lee Prudden L PTS 6 Wolverhampton
05.10.92	Paul McCarthy L PTS 6 Northampton
14.12.92	Ian Vokes W PTS 6 Northampton

Career: 6 contests, won 2, lost 4.

Tony Doyle (Dodson)

Sheffield. *Born* Rotherham, 26 December,
1962
Lightweight. Ht. 5'10"
Manager Self

27.03.90	Martin Evans W RSC 3 Leicester
06.04.90	Stewart Fishermac L RSC 5 Telford
16.05.90	Des Gargano L PTS 6 Hull
10.09.90	Finn McCool W PTS 6 Northampton
01.10.90	Finn McCool W PTS 6 Cleethorpes
19.11.90	Mark Geraghty L PTS 8 Glasgow
10.12.90	Peter Campbell L PTS 6 Nottingham
23.01.91	Richard Joyce L CO 6 Stoke
13.03.91	Bobby Beckles L PTS 6 Stoke
12.04.91	Roy Doyle DREW 6 Manchester
23.04.91	Barry North W PTS 6 Evesham
17.06.91	Scott Doyle L PTS 6 Edgbaston
17.10.91	Paul Hughes L PTS 6 Mossley
21.11.91	Brian Hickey W PTS 6 Ilkeston
05.12.91	Davy Robb L PTS 6 Oakengates
10.02.92	Joey Moffat L RSC 3 Liverpool
04.04.92	Andy Kent W RSC 5 Cleethorpes
16.10.92	Tony Foster L PTS 8 Hull

Career: 18 contests, won 6, drew 1, lost 11.

Michael Driscoll

Portsmouth. *Born* Portsmouth, 18 May,
1969
L. Welterweight. Ht. 5'10¼"
Manager M. Fawcett

16.06.88	Dave Pierre L PTS 6 Croydon
10.07.88	David Bacon W PTS 6 Eastbourne
30.08.88	Mike Russell W CO 2 Kensington
15.09.88	Ricky Maxwell DREW 6 High Wycombe

Darrit Douglas   Chris Bevan

26.10.88	Mick O'Donnell W RSC 2 Kensington
01.12.88	Neil Haddock DREW 6 Gravesend
02.02.89	Dave Croft W RSC 2 Croydon
26.04.89	Dean Bramhald W RSC 2 Southampton
31.10.89	Steve Foran DREW 6 Manchester
22.02.90	B. F. Williams W CO 2 Wandsworth
06.03.90	Billy Couzens W CO 2 Bethnal Green
26.11.90	Wayne Windle W RSC 3 Bethnal Green
02.05.91	Andrew Morgan W PTS 6 Kensington
22.06.91	Steve Foran W RSC 4 Earls Court
01.02.92	Peter Till W RSC 3 Birmingham
25.04.92	Alan Hall L PTS 6 Manchester
27.10.92	Marvin P. Gray W PTS 8 Leicester
12.12.92	Bernard Paul W RSC 2 Muswell Hill
26.01.93	Tony McKenzie L PTS 10 Leicester
	(Elim. British L. Welterweight Title)
16.03.93	Errol McDonald W PTS 10 Mayfair
	(Elim. British L. Welterweight Title)
19.05.93	Ray Newby W RTD 2 Leicester

Career: 21 contests, won 15, drew 3, lost 3.

Tim Driscoll

Bermondsey. *Born* London, 15 May, 1964
Former Southern Area Featherweight
Champion. Ht. 5'7¼"
Manager B. Hearn

08.09.86	Andrew Pybus W RSC 4 Dulwich
13.10.86	Nigel Lawrence W PTS 6 Dulwich
17.11.86	Mike Russell W PTS 6 Dulwich
15.12.86	Gary de Roux W PTS 6 Eltham
04.03.87	Russell Davison W PTS 8 Stoke
01.12.87	Kid Sumali W PTS 8 Bow
14.12.87	Shane Silvester W RSC 2 Bedford
21.01.88	Patrick Kamy W PTS 8 Wandsworth
10.03.88	Johnny B. Good W PTS 10 Croydon
	(Vacant Southern Area Featherweight Title)
06.06.88	Russell Jones L PTS 8 Northampton
02.02.89	Johnny B. Good L PTS 10 Croydon
	(Southern Area Featherweight Title Defence)
24.10.89	Alan McKay W PTS 6 Bethnal Green
31.01.90	Graham O'Malley W PTS 8 Bethnal Green
14.04.90	Rocky Lawlor W PTS 6 Kensington
29.05.90	Johnny B. Good L PTS 10 Bethnal Green
	(Southern Area Featherweight Title Challenge)
12.09.90	Steve Robinson W PTS 8 Bethnal Green
06.02.91	Des Gargano W PTS 6 Bethnal Green
18.04.91	Aldrich Johnson W PTS 8 Earls Court
22.06.91	Ruben Aguirre W PTS 8 Earls Court
09.11.91	Maurizio Stecca L RTD 9 Campione d'Italia, Italy
	(WBO Featherweight Title Challenge)
10.09.92	John Davison L CO 7 Sunderland
	(Vacant British Featherweight Title)
20.02.93	Derek Amory W PTS 8 Earls Court

Career: 22 contests, won 17, lost 5.

James Drummond

Kilmarnock. *Born* Kilmarnock, 11
February, 1969
Flyweight. Ht. 5'6"
Manager T. Gilmour

| 18.09.89 | Tony Smith W RSC 1 Glasgow |
| 09.10.89 | Kruga Hydes W RSC 3 Glasgow |

James Drummond Les Clark

22.01.90 Kevin Jenkins L PTS 6 Glasgow
08.03.90 Kevin Jenkins W RSC 5 Glasgow
19.03.90 Neil Parry W RSC 4 Glasgow
08.10.90 Derek Amory L PTS 8 Cleethorpes
19.11.90 Chris Clarkson L PTS 8 Glasgow
18.03.91 Stewart Fishermac W RSC 8 Piccadilly
07.05.91 Des Gargano W PTS 8 Glasgow
01.06.91 Mercurio Ciaramitaro DREW 6
  Ragusa, Italy
15.11.91 Salvatore Fanni L PTS 12 Omegna,
  Italy
  (European Flyweight Title Challenge)
19.05.92 Robbie Regan L RSC 9 Cardiff
  (British Flyweight Title Challenge)
22.12.92 Francis Ampofo L PTS 12 Mayfair
  (Vacant British Flyweight Title)
26.02.93 Ady Benton DREW 6 Irvine

John Duckworth Chris Bevan

Marty Duke (left) under pressure against the undefeated Kevin Lueshing Les Clark

29.06.93 Ricky Beard L PTS 8 Mayfair
Career: 15 contests, won 6, drew 2, lost 7.

John Duckworth

Burnley. *Born* Burnley, 25 May, 1971
L. Middleweight. Ht. 6'2"
Manager N. Basso

04.04.92 Warren Stephens W RSC 5
  Cleethorpes
13.04.92 Steve Goodwin L PTS 6 Manchester
04.06.92 Phil Foxon W RSC 4 Burnley
05.10.92 Dave Maj DREW 6 Manchester
29.10.92 Tony Massey W RTD 4 Leeds
20.01.93 James McGee W PTS 6 Solihull
25.02.93 Tony Trimble W PTS 6 Burnley
31.03.93 Jamie Robinson L RSC 3 Barking
27.05.93 Warren Stephens W RSC 5 Burnley
Career: 9 contests, won 6, drew 1, lost 2.

Marty Duke

Yarmouth. *Born* Yarmouth, 19 June, 1967
L. Middleweight. Ht. 5'9"
Manager Self

16.05.88 Wayne Timmins L PTS 6
  Wolverhampton
06.09.88 Tony Cloak W PTS 6 Southend
26.09.88 Tony Cloak L RSC 2 Bedford
27.10.88 Matthew Jones L PTS 6 Birmingham
06.12.88 Peter Mundy W PTS 6 Southend
25.01.89 Tony Hodge W RSC 2 Basildon
07.02.89 Dennis White L PTS 6 Southend
04.04.89 Tony Cloak W RSC 5 Southend
27.04.89 Steve West L RSC 1 Southwark
03.10.89 Colin Ford L PTS 6 Southend
23.10.89 Andy Catesby W PTS 6 Mayfair
19.12.89 Mike Jay DREW 6 Gorleston
08.02.90 Dean Lake L RSC 4 Southwark
14.03.90 Ahmet Canbakis L RSC 6 Battersea
12.11.90 Chris Haydon W PTS 6 Norwich
04.12.90 Paul Busby L PTS 6 Bury St Edmunds
29.01.91 Paul Smith L PTS 6 Wisbech
15.04.91 James McGee W PTS 6 Leicester
08.05.91 Martin Rosamond DREW 8 Millwall
16.05.91 Danny Shinkwin L PTS 6 Battersea

30.05.91 Richie Woodhall L RSC 4 Birmingham
04.07.91 Robert McCracken L RSC 1 Alfreton
03.09.91 Eamonn Loughran L PTS 6 Cardiff
26.09.91 Adrian Riley L PTS 6 Dunstable
05.11.91 Tony McKenzie L RSC 7 Leicester
31.03.92 Ojay Abrahams L RSC 2 Norwich
08.09.92 Ricky Mabbett DREW 6 Norwich
14.11.92 Vince Rose L PTS 6 Cardiff
26.01.93 Ricky Mabbett W CO 1 Leicester
14.04.93 Kevin Lueshing L RSC 2 Kensington
23.06.93 Billy McDougall W PTS 6 Gorleston
Career: 31 contests, won 9, drew 3, lost 19.

Marcus Duncan

Lancaster. *Born* Blackpool, 9 January, 1971
Bantamweight. Ht. 5'6"
Manager J. Doughty

12.11.92 Andrew Bloomer W PTS 6 Burnley
22.04.93 Chris Lyons W RSC 2 Bury
27.05.93 Neil Swain L PTS 6 Burnley
28.06.93 Neil Parry L RSC 2 Morecambe
Career: 4 contests, won 2, lost 2.

Mick Duncan

Newcastle. *Born* Newcastle, 24 August,
1969
L. Middleweight. Ht. 5'11"
Manager Self

29.09.88 Skip Jackson L RSC 3 Sunderland
13.03.89 Richard Thompson W PTS 6 Mayfair
22.03.89 B. K. Bennett L PTS 6 Sheppey
19.05.89 John Tipping W PTS 6 Gateshead
15.06.89 Paul Abercromby L RSC 2 Glasgow
12.10.89 Steve West L RSC 5 Southwark
06.03.90 Paul King L PTS 6 Newcastle
11.04.90 Tony Booth L PTS 6 Dewsbury
16.05.90 Chris Richards W PTS 6 Hull
11.06.90 Tommy Warde W PTS 6 Manchester
15.10.90 Andre Wharton L PTS 6 Brierley Hill
26.11.90 Rob Pitters DREW 6 Bury
13.12.90 Richard O'Brien W PTS 6 Hartlepool
18.02.91 Tommy Milligan L PTS 6 Glasgow
06.03.91 Danny Quigg L PTS 6 Glasgow
18.03.91 Allan Grainger W PTS 6 Glasgow

93

10.05.91	Rob Pitters L RSC 3 Gateshead
23.09.91	Danny Quigg DREW 6 Glasgow
07.10.91	Tyrone Eastmond L RSC 5 Bradford
18.11.91	Allan Grainger W PTS 6 Glasgow
25.11.91	Willie Yeardsley W PTS 6 Liverpool
12.12.91	Dave Johnson L PTS 6 Hartlepool
20.01.92	Mark Jay L PTS 6 Bradford
20.02.92	Leigh Wicks W PTS 8 Glasgow
06.03.92	Oleg Chalajew W PTS 8 Berlin, Germany
13.05.92	Lloyd Honeyghan L RSC 2 Kensington
27.06.92	Reiner Gies L CO 7 Halle, Germany
15.10.92	Gary Logan L PTS 8 Lewisham
06.05.93	Mark Cichocki L RSC 7 Hartlepool
	(Northern Area L. Middleweight Title Challenge)

Career: 29 contests, won 10, drew 2, lost 17.

Stuart Dunn

Leicester. *Born* Leicester, 19 January, 1970
L. Middleweight. Ht. 5'10½"
Manager J. Baxter

15.10.91	Spencer McCracken DREW 6 Dudley
09.12.91	Wayne Panayiotiou W CO 4 Brierley Hill
23.01.92	Charlie Moore L RSC 3 York
27.10.92	Andy Peach W RSC 3 Leicester
28.04.93	Barry Thorogood W RSC 2 Solihull
19.05.93	Matthew Turner W RSC 3 Leicester

Career: 6 contests, won 4, drew 1, lost 1.

Terry Dunstan

Hackney. *Born* London, 21 October, 1968
Cruiserweight. Ht. 6'3"
Manager A. Urry

12.11.92	Steve Osborne W PTS 6 Bayswater
25.11.92	Steve Yorath W PTS 8 Mayfair
31.03.93	Lee Prudden W PTS 6 Barking

Career: 3 contests, won 3.

Darren Dyer

Islington. *Born* London, 31 July, 1966
Welterweight. Ht. 5'7½"
Manager B. Hearn

20.11.86	Trevor Grant W RSC 2 Bethnal Green
08.01.87	Del Bryan L PTS 6 Bethnal Green
26.02.87	Kid Murray W CO 3 Bethnal Green
18.04.87	Geoff Calder W RSC 2 Kensington
07.09.87	Kelvin Mortimer L RSC 1 Mayfair
25.02.88	Donald Gwynn W CO 1 Bethnal Green
13.04.88	Kent Acuff W CO 2 Bethnal Green
16.05.88	Thomas Garcia W RSC 2 Piccadilly
02.11.88	Harlein Holden W CO 2 Southwark
07.12.88	Jean-Marc Phenieux W RSC 3 Piccadilly
12.01.89	Anthony Travers W RSC 6 Southwark
29.03.89	Mario Coronado W RSC 1 Wembley
04.10.89	Efrom Brown W RSC 4 Kensington
11.01.90	Fernando Segura W CO 2 Dewsbury
14.03.90	Jorge Maysonet L RSC 2 Kensington
03.07.91	Trevor Ambrose W PTS 6 Brentwood
26.10.91	Kelvin Mortimer W RSC 2 Brentwood
26.11.91	Robert Wright W RSC 3 Bethnal Green
19.02.92	Ian John-Lewis W RSC 2 Muswell Hill
12.05.92	Del Bryan W RSC 10 Crystal Palace
10.11.92	Chris Peters W RSC 9 Dagenham
09.03.93	Marcelo Domingo di Croce L RSC 4 Hartlepool
	(Vacant WBA Penta-Continental Welterweight Title)

Career: 22 contests, won 18, lost 4.

Paul Dyer

Portsmouth. *Born* Portsmouth, 11 July, 1970
Welterweight. Ht. 5'11½"
Manager Self

24.09.91	Mick Reid W PTS 6 Basildon
19.11.91	Dave Andrews W PTS 6 Norwich
23.02.93	Kevin Mabbutt L PTS 6 Kettering

Career: 3 contests, won 2, lost 1.

Julian Eavis

Yeovil. *Born* Bourton, 3 December, 1965
Welterweight. Ht. 5'7¾"
Manager Self

12.10.88	Noel Rafferty W PTS 6 Stoke
17.10.88	Steve Taggart W PTS 6 Birmingham
17.11.88	Young Gully W PTS 6 Weston super Mare
07.12.88	Adrian Din L PTS 6 Stoke
14.12.88	Young Gully L PTS 6 Evesham
30.01.89	Frank Harrington W PTS 6 Leicester
06.02.89	Young Gully L RSC 4 Nottingham
15.03.89	Steve Taggart W PTS 6 Stoke
21.03.89	Steve Hogg W PTS 6 Wolverhampton
15.04.89	Andy Tonks W PTS 6 Salisbury
09.05.89	Mark Purcell L RSC 5 Plymouth
	(Western Area Welterweight Title Challenge)
25.09.89	Wayne Timmins L PTS 6 Birmingham
04.10.89	Barry Messam W PTS 8 Stafford
10.10.89	Robert Wright L PTS 8 Wolverhampton
30.10.89	Wayne Timmins L PTS 8 Birmingham
14.11.89	Bobby McGowan W PTS 6 Evesham
22.11.89	Ronnie Campbell W PTS 8 Solihull
06.12.89	Lindon Scarlett L PTS 8 Stoke
10.01.90	Gary Logan L PTS 8 Kensington
24.01.90	Kevin Plant L PTS 6 Solihull
06.02.90	Tony Connellan L PTS 8 Oldham
13.02.90	Kevin Thompson L PTS 8 Wolverhampton
27.02.90	Ernie Loveridge L PTS 6 Evesham
07.03.90	Kevin Plant L PTS 8 Doncaster
22.03.90	Wayne Timmins L PTS 8 Wolverhampton
26.04.90	Leigh Wicks DREW 8 Mayfair
24.05.90	Gary Osborne L PTS 6 Dudley
04.06.90	Paul Wesley L PTS 8 Birmingham
17.09.90	Dave Andrews L PTS 6 Cardiff
01.10.90	Kevin Plant L PTS 8 Cleethorpes
09.10.90	Ronnie Campbell DREW 6 Wolverhampton
17.10.90	Paul Wesley L PTS 6 Stoke
31.10.90	Mickey Lloyd L PTS 8 Wembley
14.11.90	Glyn Rhodes L RSC 5 Sheffield
12.12.90	Barry Messam L PTS 6 Leicester
19.12.90	Carl Wright L PTS 6 Preston
16.01.91	Gary Logan L RSC 5 Kensington
05.03.91	Eamonn Loughran L PTS 6 Cardiff
20.03.91	Kevin Plant L PTS 6 Solihull
10.04.91	Ernie Loveridge DREW 8 Wolverhampton
01.05.91	Humphrey Harrison L PTS 6 Solihull
28.05.91	Darren Liney L PTS 6 Cardiff
05.06.91	Wayne Timmins L PTS 6 Wolverhampton
11.06.91	James McGee L PTS 6 Leicester
03.07.91	Benny Collins L PTS 6 Reading
03.09.91	Michael Smyth L PTS 6 Cardiff
01.10.91	Lee Ferrie L PTS 6 Bedworth
23.10.91	Kevin Lueshing L RSC 2 Bethnal Green
26.11.91	James Campbell W PTS 8 Wolverhampton
04.12.91	Peter Reid W PTS 6 Stoke
11.12.91	James McGee DREW 6 Leicester
17.12.91	Michael Smyth L PTS 6 Cardiff
15.01.92	Robert Wright L PTS 8 Stoke
04.02.92	Howard Clarke L PTS 4 Alfreton
11.02.92	Jamie Robinson L PTS 6 Barking
24.02.92	Lee Ferrie L PTS 8 Coventry
11.03.92	Rob Pitters L PTS 6 Solihull
11.05.92	James McGee L RSC 3 Coventry
07.07.92	Ross Hale L RSC 8 Bristol
	(Vacant Western Area Welterweight Title)
05.10.92	James McGee W PTS 6 Bardon
28.11.92	Warren Stowe L RSC 6 Manchester
27.01.93	Mark Kelly L PTS 8 Stoke
22.02.93	James McGee L PTS 6 Bedworth

Darren Dyer (right) tears into the South African, Chris Peters, prior to winning on a ninth round cut eye stoppage   Les Clark

06.03.93 Robin Reid L RSC 2 Glasgow
10.05.93 Peter Waudby L PTS 6 Cleethorpes
26.06.93 Dean Cooper L PTS 10 Keynsham
(Vacant Western Area L. Middleweight Title)
Career: 66 contests, won 13, drew 4, lost 49.

(Clive) Bobbi Joe Edwards

Manchester. *Born* Jamaica, 25 December, 1957
L. Heavyweight. Ht. 5'10"
Manager Self

09.10.90 Doug McKay W RSC 1 Glasgow
26.11.90 Keith Inglis W RSC 1 Mayfair
22.02.91 Cordwell Hylton L RTD 6 Manchester
29.11.91 David Brown W RSC 4 Manchester
31.01.92 Richard Bustin W PTS 6 Manchester
29.05.92 John Foreman L RSC 4 Manchester
29.10.92 Michael Gale L PTS 10 Leeds
(Vacant Central Area L. Heavyweight Title)

Bobbie Joe Edwards

Harry Goodwin

30.03.93 Simon Collins W PTS 6 Cardiff
Career: 8 contests, won 5, lost 3.

Erwin Edwards

Clapham. *Born* Barbados, 31 October, 1966
L. Welterweight. Ht. 5'11"
Manager D. Powell

26.09.88 Mark Jackson W PTS 6 Bedford
26.10.88 Brian Cullen L PTS 6 Stoke
15.11.88 Tony Whitehouse W PTS 6 Piccadilly
29.11.88 Danny Ellis L PTS 6 Battersea
07.02.89 Muhammad Shaffique L PTS 6 Southend
20.02.89 Pat Delargy L PTS 6 Birmingham
28.02.89 Terry Collins L PTS 6 Chigwell
07.04.92 B. F. Williams L PTS 6 Southend
30.04.92 Korso Aleain L PTS 6 Bayswater
07.07.92 George Wilson W RSC 4 Bristol
08.09.92 George Wilson W RSC 3 Southend
12.11.92 Mark O'Callaghan W RSC 6 Bayswater
03.03.93 Gary Hiscox L PTS 6 Solihull
24.06.93 Dave Fallon W RSC 3 Watford
Career: 14 contests, won 6, lost 8.

Renny Edwards

Haverfordwest. *Born* Haverfordwest, 10 February, 1968
Lightweight. Ht. 5'3½"
Manager Self

07.12.88 Des Gargano W PTS 6 Aberavon
06.02.89 Dave George L PTS 6 Swansea
10.03.89 Jimmy Clark W PTS 6 Brentwood
19.08.89 Ian Johnson W PTS 6 Cardiff
10.11.89 Greg Egbuniwe W RSC 4 Battersea
29.08.91 Brian Robb L PTS 6 Oakengates
30.10.91 Tony Silkstone L PTS 6 Leeds
15.12.92 George Naylor W RSC 5 Liverpool
Career: 8 contests, won 5, lost 3.

Shaba Edwards

Clapham. *Born* Clapham, 29 April, 1966
L. Welterweight. Ht. 5'7½"
Manager H. Burgess

12.05.93 Jason Barker L PTS 6 Stoke
23.06.93 Steve Howden L RSC 1 Gorleston
Career: 2 contests, lost 2.

Tony Ekubia

Manchester. *Born* Nigeria, 6 March, 1960
Former British & Commonwealth L. Welterweight Champion. Former Undefeated Central Area Lighweight & Welterweight Champion. Ht. 5'8"
Manager J. Trickett

18.11.86 Dean Eshelby L PTS 6 Doncaster
02.12.86 Danny Cooper W RSC 4 Southend
13.01.87 Paul McKenzie W CO 3 Oldham
18.03.87 Simon Eubank W PTS 8 Solihull
13.04.87 Tommy Farrell W RSC 5 Manchester
12.05.87 Jimmy Thornton W PTS 6 Alfreton
28.09.87 Mike Russell W RSC 3 Manchester
17.11.87 Mike McKenzie W CO 2 Manchester
03.12.87 Richard Wagstaff W RSC 2 Leeds
(Vacant Central Area Welterweight Title)
23.02.88 Lenny Gloster W RTD 6 Oldham
12.04.88 Jimmy Thornton W RSC 5 Oldham
18.10.88 Mark Kelly W RSC 7 Oldham
(Vacant Central Area Lightweight Title)
14.04.89 Humphrey Harrison W RSC 5 Manchester
(Central Area Welterweight Title Defence)
26.09.89 Steve Larrimore W PTS 12 Oldham
(Commonwealth L. Welterweight Title Challenge)
28.03.90 Victor Belcher L RSC 8 Manchester
26.09.90 Alex Dickson W CO 11 Manchester
(Vacant British L. Welterweight Title & Commonwealth L. Welterweight Title Defence)
19.11.90 David Chibuye W RSC 5 Cardiff
(Commonwealth L. Welterweight Title Defence)
29.01.91 Juma Kutonda W RTD 6 Stockport
(Commonwealth L. Welterweight Title Defence)

20.06.91 Andy Holligan L PTS 12 Liverpool
(British & Commonwealth L. Welterweight Title Defence)
10.03.92 Eamonn Loughran W DIS 5 Bury
(Elim. British Welterweight Title)
31.03.92 Verdell Smith W RSC 2 Stockport
15.09.92 Andy Holligan L CO 7 Liverpool
(British & Commonwealth L. Welterweight Title Challenge)
05.02.93 Glyn Rhodes W RSC 6 Manchester
19.03.93 Marvin P. Gray W RSC 2 Manchester
26.04.93 Gary Barron W RSC 4 Manchester
Career: 25 contests, won 21, lost 4.

Mark Elliot

Telford. *Born* Telford, 2 February, 1966
L. Welterweight. Ht. 5'9"
Manager M. Duff

10.09.91 Dean Bramhald W CO 5 Wolverhampton
12.11.91 John Smith W PTS 6 Wolverhampton
05.12.91 Mick Mulcahy W RSC 2 Cannock
17.03.92 Andrew Morgan W PTS 6 Wolverhampton
20.01.93 Wayne Windle W CO 3 Wolverhampton
16.03.93 Chris Saunders W PTS 6 Wolverhampton
Career: 6 contests, won 6.

Barry Ellis

Clapham. *Born* Islington, 25 October, 1957
Heavyweight. Ht. 6'3"
Manager Self

22.09.83 Mark Cleverly W PTS 6 Strand
03.10.83 Alan Douglas W PTS 6 Eltham
12.12.83 Phil Simpson W CO 3 Bedworth
06.02.84 Glenn McCrory L RSC 1 Mayfair
01.03.84 Michael Armstrong W PTS 6 Queensway
17.04.84 Bob Young DREW 8 Merton
18.09.84 Bob Young W CO 1 Merton
29.10.84 Dave Garside L CO 8 Streatham
11.02.85 Derek Williams L RSC 2 Dulwich
09.05.85 Gypsy Carman W PTS 8 Acton
22.07.85 Ron Ellis L RSC 3 Longford
02.09.85 Gypsy Carman W PTS 8 Coventry
09.12.85 Jess Harding L PTS 8 Wandsworth
01.03.86 Michael Simwelu L RTD 4 Cologne, Germany
01.10.86 Daniel T. Moul W PTS 6 Lewisham
12.01.87 Ivan Joseph L PTS 8 Ealing
05.02.87 Paul Lister L PTS 8 Newcastle
18.02.87 Glenn McCrory L PTS 8 Fulham
02.03.87 Patrick Collins W PTS 6 Longford
01.04.87 Denroy Bryan DREW 8 Southsea
17.05.87 Siza Makhatini L PTS 8 Durban, South Africa
16.11.87 Ramon Voorn W RSC 1 Arnhem, Holland
20.01.88 Jess Harding L RSC 2 Hornsey
14.03.88 John Emmen L RSC 4 Arnhem, Holland
25.04.88 Chris Jacobs L PTS 8 Bethnal Green
23.05.88 Ivan Joseph L RSC 5 Mayfair
10.05.89 Michael Murray L RSC 3 Solihull
10.11.89 Denroy Bryan L RSC 3 Battersea
10.03.90 Gary McConnell W RSC 4 Bristol
02.06.90 Biagio Chianese L RSC 3 Rome, Italy
15.09.90 Gary McConnell L PTS 8 Bristol

07.12.90 Axel Schulz L PTS 6 Berlin, Germany
01.05.92 Mario Guedes L RSC 6 Aachen, Germany
01.12.92 Denroy Bryan L PTS 6 Bristol
Career: 34 contests, won 11, drew 2, lost 21.

Wayne Ellis   Les Clark

Wayne Ellis

Cardiff. *Born* Cardiff, 18 July, 1968
Welsh Middleweight Champion. Ht. 6'0"
Manager B. Hearn

25.06.88 Shamus Casey W PTS 6 Luton
07.09.88 Kevin Hayde W PTS 6 Reading
01.11.88 Dennis White W CO 2 Reading
20.12.88 Spencer Alton W RTD 4 Swansea
11.04.89 Mark Howell W PTS 6 Aberavon
09.05.89 Spencer Alton W RSC 3 St Albans
06.09.89 Ian Chantler W RSC 4 Aberavon
14.02.90 Lindon Scarlett DREW 6 Millwall
22.05.90 Paul Jones W PTS 6 St Albans
10.10.90 Frank Eubanks W PTS 6 Millwall
05.03.91 Johnny Melfah W RSC 2 Cardiff
03.09.91 Colin Manners L RSC 1 Cardiff
11.02.92 Alan Richards W PTS 10 Cardiff
(Vacant Welsh Middleweight Title)
14.07.92 Mike Phillips W RSC 7 Mayfair
(Welsh Middleweight Title Defence)
Career: 14 contests, won 12, drew 1, lost 1.

Darren Elsdon

Hartlepool. *Born* Hartlepool, 16 February, 1971
Former Northern Area S. Featherweight Champion. Ht. 5'5½"
Manager Self

13.11.90 Peter Campbell W PTS 4 Hartlepool
13.12.90 Derek Amory W PTS 6 Hartlepool
06.04.91 Harry Escott W RSC 2 Darlington
15.04.91 Edward Cook DREW 4 Glasgow
22.10.91 Frankie Foster W RSC 7 Hartlepool
(Northern Area S. Featherweight Title Challenge)
12.12.91 Ian McGirr W CO 4 Hartlepool
21.01.92 Michael Armstrong L RSC 1 Stockport
(Final Elim. British S. Featherweight Title)
10.09.92 Frankie Foster L PTS 10 Sunderland
(Northern Area S. Featherweight Title Defence)
Career: 8 contests, won 5, drew 1, lost 2.

(Enison) Smokey Enison (Garber)

Leeds. *Born* Sierra Leone, 29 June, 1967
Middleweight. Ht. 6'0"
Manager P. Coleman

19.03.93 Eric Noi L RSC 5 Manchester
Career: 1 contest, lost 1.

Phil Epton (Hampton)

Doncaster. *Born* Doncaster, 14 June, 1968
Welterweight. Ht. 5'8"
Manager Self

18.10.90 Mark Jay W PTS 6 Dewsbury
15.11.90 Paul King L PTS 6 Oldham
07.02.91 Pat Durkin W PTS 6 Watford
21.03.91 Paul King L PTS 6 Dewsbury
13.06.91 Willie Yeardsley W RSC 3 Hull
23.01.92 Carl Hook W PTS 6 York
19.03.92 Ricky Mabbett L RSC 3 York
23.09.92 Jimmy Vincent L RSC 6 Leeds
Career: 8 contests, won 4, lost 4.

Roland Ericsson

Mayfair. *Born* Sweden, 15 February, 1962
S. Middleweight. Ht. 5'11"
Manager Self

09.10.87 Dragan Komazec W CO 1 Aosta, Finland
26.10.87 Tommy Beckett W RSC 1 Jyvaskyla, Finland
07.02.88 Derek Myers W PTS 6 Laukka, Finland
13.02.88 Russell Barker W RSC 6 Helsingor, Finland
11.09.88 Sid Conteh W PTS 6 Laukka, Finland
16.02.89 Alan Baptiste W RSC 5 Battersea
26.04.89 Abdul Amoru Sanda W RSC 5 Battersea
22.06.89 Cliff Curtis W CO 4 Stevenage
02.02.90 Simon Collins W PTS 8 Geneva, Switzerland
22.02.90 Sean Stringfellow W RSC 4 Wandsworth
06.06.90 Cliff Curtis W RSC 2 Battersea
24.11.90 Thomas Covington W RSC 6 Benalmadena, Spain
20.03.91 Mark Kaylor L RSC 4 Wandsworth
16.05.91 Johnny Melfah L RSC 4 Battersea
22.10.91 Frank Eubanks L RSC 3 Wandsworth
13.12.91 Marian Rudi W CO 3 Minden, Germany
25.02.92 Peter Vosper W RSC 6 Crystal Palace
04.04.92 Jan Franek W RSC 5 Minden, Germany
12.05.92 Karl Barwise W PTS 6 Crystal Palace
15.09.92 Carlos Christie L RSC 4 Crystal Palace
27.11.92 Terry Magee W PTS 8 Randers, Denmark
26.03.93 Simon McDougall L RSC 5 Copenhagen, Denmark
11.06.93 Rocky Reynolds W PTS 6 Randers, Denmark
Career: 23 contests, won 18, lost 5.

Harry Escott

Sunderland. *Born* West Germany, 17 October, 1969
S. Featherweight. Ht. 5'8"
Manager P. Byrne

26.02.87 Kenny Walsh W RSC 4 Hartlepool

06.04.87	Gypsy Finch W PTS 4 Newcastle
23.04.87	Gypsy Finch W PTS 4 Newcastle
30.04.87	Craig Windsor W RSC 3 Washington
22.05.87	Ginger Staples W RSC 1 Peterlee
04.06.87	Barry Bacon W RSC 2 Sunderland
04.09.87	Kevin Plant L RSC 2 Gateshead
26.01.88	Michael Howell W RSC 4 Hartlepool
17.03.88	Ian Honeywood W RSC 4 Sunderland
25.04.88	Les Walsh W PTS 8 Bradford
23.05.88	Tony Foster L RSC 6 Bradford
22.09.88	Dave Kettlewell W PTS 6 Newcastle
14.11.88	John Townsley W RSC 3 Southwark
30.01.89	Tony Dore DREW 8 Glasgow
14.02.89	Kevin Pritchard W RSC 3 Sunderland
13.03.89	Young Joe Rafiu W PTS 8 Glasgow
11.04.89	Muhammad Lovelock W PTS 6 Oldham
05.06.89	Gary Maxwell W PTS 8 Glasgow
11.09.89	Gary Maxwell W PTS 8 Nottingham
19.10.89	Rudy Valentino W RTD 4 Manchester
07.12.89	Joey Jacobs W PTS 6 Manchester
24.01.90	Tomas Arguelles W PTS 6 Sunderland
15.05.90	Kevin Pritchard L PTS 8 South Shields
13.11.90	Brian Roche L RSC 3 Hartlepool
02.03.91	Steve Walker DREW 6 Darlington
06.04.91	Darren Elsdon L RSC 2 Darlington
06.07.91	Jackie Gunguluza L CO 6 Imperia, Italy
20.09.91	Steve Walker DREW 6 Manchester
04.02.92	Neil Smith W PTS 8 Alfreton
17.03.92	Floyd Havard L RSC 7 Mayfair
27.05.92	Wilson Rodriguez L PTS 10 Cologne, Germany
07.10.92	Dominic McGuigan W RTD 5 Sunderland
30.10.92	Eugene Speed L PTS 8 Istres, France
01.12.92	Neil Haddock L PTS 10 Liverpool
18.06.93	Medhi Labdouni L PTS 8 Fontenay Sous Bois, France

Career: 35 contests, won 21, drew 3, lost 11.

Frank Eubanks

Manchester. *Born* Manchester, 25 June, 1969
S. Middleweight. Ht. 5'10½"
Manager Self

26.09.89	Spencer Alton L PTS 6 Oldham
04.11.89	Antoine Tarver L PTS 4 Eastbourne
10.11.89	Carlton Myers W RSC 5 Battersea
30.11.89	Steve West W RSC 3 Southwark
21.02.90	Ray Close L PTS 8 Belfast
07.09.90	Alan Pennington W RSC 2 Liverpool
10.10.90	Wayne Ellis L PTS 6 Millwall
24.10.90	Roger Wilson W PTS 6 Stoke
27.11.90	Franki Moro W RSC 6 Liverpool
12.12.90	Adrian Wright W PTS 6 Stoke
16.02.91	Cornelius Carr L RSC 5 Thornaby
12.04.91	Peter Vosper W RSC 1 Manchester
24.06.91	Marvin O'Brien W PTS 6 Liverpool
22.10.91	Roland Ericsson W RSC 3 Wandsworth
22.01.92	Nicky Piper L PTS 10 Cardiff *(Elim. British S. Middleweight Title)*
18.07.92	Fidel Castro L RTD 6 Manchester

Career: 16 contests, won 9, lost 7.

(Antonio) Tony Falcone

Chippenham. *Born* Chippenham, 15 October, 1966
Featherweight. Ht. 5'6"
Manager Self

22.10.90	Karl Morling L PTS 6 Mayfair
21.11.90	Barrie Kelley L PTS 6 Chippenham
18.02.91	Barrie Kelley W PTS 6 Windsor
28.02.91	Paul Wynn W PTS 6 Sunderland
21.03.91	Tony Silkstone L PTS 6 Dewsbury
22.04.91	Alan Smith L RSC 5 Mayfair
30.05.91	Alan Smith W PTS 6 Mayfair
11.12.91	Dennis Adams W RTD 4 Basildon
30.04.92	Andrew Bloomer W PTS 6 Mayfair
07.07.92	Miguel Matthews W PTS 6 Bristol
05.10.92	Andrew Bloomer W PTS 8 Bristol

Career: 11 contests, won 7, lost 4.

Dave Fallon   Les Clark

Dave Fallon

Watford. *Born* Watford, 22 June, 1967
Welterweight. Ht. 6'0"
Manager Self

12.09.90	Trevor Ambrose L CO 3 Battersea
14.02.91	Richard Swallow L RSC 4 Southampton
12.11.91	Tim Harmey W PTS 6 Milton Keynes
05.12.91	Sean Cave W PTS 6 Peterborough
06.05.93	Noel Henry W PTS 6 Bayswater
24.06.93	Erwin Edwards L RSC 3 Watford

Career: 6 contests, won 3, lost 3.

Joe Fannin

Birmingham. *Born* Birmingham, 18 May, 1970
Lightweight. Ht. 5'7"
Manager Self

05.10.92	Craig Murray W RSC 1 Manchester
27.10.92	Richard Woolgar L PTS 6 Leicester
20.02.93	Patrick Gallagher L RTD 1 Earls Court
20.04.93	Alan Levene L CO 1 Brentwood

Career: 4 contests, won 1, lost 3.

Ceri Farrell

Swansea. *Born* Swansea, 27 October, 1967
Bantamweight. Ht. 5'7"
Manager Self

14.05.90	Kruga Hydes L PTS 6 Cleethorpes
06.06.90	Conn McMullen L RSC 5 Battersea
03.10.90	Tim Yeates L PTS 6 Basildon
05.12.90	Paul Dever W RSC 2 Stafford
12.12.90	Tim Yeates L PTS 6 Basildon
19.12.90	Mercurio Ciaramitaro DREW 6 Rimini, Italy
24.01.91	Kevin Jenkins L PTS 6 Gorseinon
07.02.91	Mark Tierney L PTS 6 Watford
06.03.91	Mark Tierney L PTS 6 Wembley
25.04.91	Mark Loftus L RSC 3 Basildon
04.11.91	Andrew Bloomer W PTS 6 Merthyr
20.11.91	Andrew Bloomer W PTS 6 Cardiff
29.11.91	John Green L RTD 4 Manchester
08.01.92	Miguel Matthews L PTS 6 Burton
22.01.92	Alan Ley L PTS 6 Cardiff
09.02.92	Peter Judson L PTS 6 Bradford
15.09.92	Michael Alldis L RSC 3 Crystal Palace
16.02.93	Michael Alldis L CO 1 Tooting

Career: 18 contests, won 3, drew 1, lost 14.

Marco Fattore   Les Clark

Marco Fattore

Watford. *Born* Italy, 17 October, 1968
Lightweight. Ht. 5'8"
Manager D. Mancini

03.09.92	Jason White W RSC 1 Dunstable
19.10.92	Carlos Domonkos W RTD 4 Mayfair
07.12.92	Steve Patton W RSC 6 Mayfair
15.02.93	Jason Hutson W PTS 6 Mayfair
29.03.93	T. J. Smith DREW 6 Mayfair
22.04.93	Jason Barker W PTS 6 Mayfair

Career: 6 contests, won 5, drew 1.

Vince Feeney

Sligo. *Born* Sligo, 12 May, 1973
Bantamweight. Ht. 5'4"
Manager Self

29.10.92	Ady Benton DREW 6 Bayswater
04.02.93	Kevin Jenkins W PTS 6 Cardiff
29.03.93	Andrew Bloomer W PTS 6 Mayfair
29.04.93	Neil Swain L PTS 6 Mayfair

Career: 4 contests, won 2, drew 1, lost 1.

Antonio Fernandez (Golding)

Birmingham. *Born* Birmingham, 3 January, 1965
Midlands Area Middleweight Champion. Ht. 5'11¼"
Manager Self

10.03.87	David Heath W RSC 5 Manchester
29.04.87	Darren Hobson L PTS 6 Stoke
18.11.87	Tony White W PTS 6 Solihull
19.01.88	Malcolm Melvin W RSC 4 Kings Heath
07.03.88	Shaun Cummins L PTS 6 Northampton
10.10.88	Chris Richards W PTS 6 Edgbaston
23.11.88	Chris Richards W PTS 8 Solihull
24.01.89	Paul Murray W PTS 6 Kings Heath
08.05.89	Shamus Casey W PTS 6 Edgbaston
13.11.89	Cyril Jackson W PTS 8 Brierley Hill
03.12.89	Steve Foster L PTS 8 Birmingham
06.03.90	Paul Jones L PTS 8 Stoke
30.04.90	Alan Baptiste W PTS 6 Brierley Hill
04.06.90	Chris Richards W PTS 6 Edgbaston
13.11.90	Chris Walker W PTS 6 Edgbaston
24.01.91	Franki Moro W PTS 6 Brierley Hill
07.10.91	Paul Murray W RSC 7 Birmingham
09.12.91	Paul McCarthy W PTS 8 Brierley Hill
03.03.92	Paul Wesley W PTS 10 Cradley Heath
	(Vacant Midlands Area Middleweight Title)
28.10.92	Darron Griffiths L PTS 10 Cardiff
	(Elim. British Middleweight Title)
18.05.93	Ernie Loveridge W PTS 8 Edgbaston

Career: 21 contests, won 16, lost 5.

(Robert) Rocky Ferrari (Ewing)

Glasgow. *Born* Glasgow, 27 October, 1972
Lightweight. Ht. 5'7"
Manager A. Morrison

25.01.91	James Hunter W CO 1 Stoke
11.02.91	Sol Francis W RSC 5 Glasgow
05.03.91	Chris Saunders W PTS 4 Glasgow
11.09.92	Mick Mulcahy W PTS 6 Glasgow

Career: 4 contests, won 4.

Lee Ferrie

Coventry. *Born* Coventry, 10 July, 1964
L. Middleweight. Ht. 5'11"
Manager J. Griffin

01.10.91	Julian Eavis W PTS 6 Bedworth
05.11.91	Trevor Meikle W PTS 6 Leicester
11.12.91	Noel Henry W RSC 5 Leicester
20.01.92	Martin Rosamond W RSC 2 Coventry
24.02.92	Julian Eavis W PTS 8 Coventry
25.03.92	Mick Reid W RSC 3 Hinckley
22.02.93	Shamus Casey W CO 3 Bedworth

Career: 7 contests, won 7.

Darren Fifield

Henley. *Born* Wantage, 9 October, 1969
Flyweight. Ht. 5'2"
Manager F. Maloney

22.10.92	Glyn Shepherd DREW 4 Bethnal Green
10.12.92	Anthony Hanna W RSC 6 Bethnal Green
14.01.93	Graham McGrath W PTS 4 Mayfair
17.02.93	Kevin Jenkins DREW 6 Bethnal Green
14.04.93	Mickey Cantwell L PTS 10 Kensington
	(Vacant Southern Area Flyweight Title)

Career: 5 contests, won 2, drew 2, lost 1.

Crain Fisher

Rochdale. *Born* Littleborough, 28 February, 1966
L. Middleweight. Ht. 5'9"
Manager J. Doughty

22.10.90	Richard O'Brien W CO 3 Manchester
28.02.91	Rob Pitters L RSC 6 Bury
21.10.91	James McGee W RSC 4 Bury
13.04.92	Trevor Meikle W PTS 6 Manchester
05.05.92	Frank Harrington W RSC 4 Preston
13.10.92	Robert Riley L PTS 4 Bury
25.02.93	Jimmy Alston W RTD 2 Burnley

A tough little battle saw the then unbeaten Darren Fifield (left) appear fortunate to scrape a six round draw against Kevin Jenkins   Les Clark

22.04.93	Jimmy Alston W PTS 6 Bury

Career: 8 contests, won 6, lost 2.

Simon Fisher

Coventry. *Born* Coventry, 21 December, 1965
Welterweight. Ht. 5'10"
Manager P. Byrne

21.09.92	Peter Waudby L RSC 2 Cleethorpes
23.11.92	Warren Stephens L PTS 6 Coventry
04.03.93	Sean Metherell L RSC 1 Peterborough

Career: 3 contests, lost 3.

Stewart Fishermac

Luton. *Born* Ulverston, 26 April, 1964
Featherweight. Ht. 5'6"
Manager Self

14.10.85	Simon Turner W PTS 6 Birmingham
07.11.85	Glen Dainty L PTS 6 Tottenham
27.11.85	George Bailey L RSC 3 Bradford
03.02.86	Terry Ashman W RTD 5 Dulwich
17.03.86	Gary Peynado W PTS 6 Birmingham
10.04.86	Billy Barton DREW 6 Weston super Mare
15.05.86	Gary Peynado L PTS 6 Dudley
22.09.86	Donnie Hood L PTS 6 Glasgow
09.11.86	Gary Peynado L PTS 8 Solihull
19.01.87	Albert Parr L RSC 2 Mayfair
07.04.87	Roy Deeble DREW 6 Ilford
29.04.87	Mitchell King L PTS 6 Loughborough
16.11.87	Nigel Lawrence W RSC 1 Southampton
01.12.87	Steve King W PTS 6 Southend
14.12.87	Mark Goult L PTS 6 Bedford
11.02.88	Mark Fairman L PTS 8 Gravesend
01.03.88	Billy Barton L RSC 2 Southend
30.09.88	Wull Strike L PTS 4 Gillingham
08.03.90	Neil Leitch DREW 6 Peterborough
27.03.90	John Whitelaw W PTS 4 Chester le Street
06.04.90	Tony Doyle W RSC 5 Telford
23.04.90	Neil Leitch L PTS 6 Bradford
14.05.90	Tony Smith W PTS 6 Leicester
11.12.90	Des Gargano L PTS 8 Evesham
12.02.91	Bradley Stone L PTS 6 Basildon
18.03.91	James Drummond L RSC 8 Piccadilly
03.03.93	Yusuf Vorajee L RSC 2 Solihull

Career: 27 contests, won 8, drew 3, lost 16.

Horace Fleary

Huddersfield. *Born* Huddersfield, 22 April, 1961
L. Middleweight. Former Undefeated German International L. Middleweight Champion. Ht. 5'10½"
Manager Self

04.07.87	Salvador Yanez L RSC 3 Helmstedt, Germany
17.10.87	Harald Schulte W PTS 6 Gifhorn, Germany
31.10.87	Niyazi Aytekin L PTS 6 Paderborn, Germany
23.11.87	Mourad Louati L RSC 3 The Hague, Holland
09.01.88	Yurder Demircan L RSC 4 Helmstedt, Germany
14.03.88	Henk van den Tak L PTS 6 Arnhem, Holland
12.05.88	Mike Wissenbach W PTS 6 Berlin, Germany

29.06.88 Silvio Mieckley DREW 4 Hamburg, Germany
02.07.88 Zelkjo Seslek W RSC 4 Helmstedt, Germany
16.09.88 Jose Varela L PTS 8 Berlin, Germany
28.10.88 Zelkjo Seslek W RSC 5 Braunschweig, Germany
08.11.88 Ferdinand Pachler L PTS 8 Vienna, Austria
12.11.88 Josef Kossmann W PTS 8 Oberkassel, Germany
16.11.88 Mike Wissenbach L PTS 6 Berlin, Germany
25.02.89 Paddy Pipa L PTS 8 Hamburg, Germany
16.09.89 Josef Rajic W CO 1 Wiener Neustadt, Germany
30.09.89 Owen Reece L PTS 6 Hamburg, Germany
13.10.89 Frederic Seillier L CO 1 Sete, France
10.11.89 Jean-Paul Roux L DIS 8 St Quentin, France
27.11.89 Franck Nicotra L DIS 6 Nogent, France
01.12.89 Andy Marks L PTS 8 Berlin, Germany
09.12.89 Hamedidi Maimoun L RSC 3 Grande Synthe, France
12.10.90 Joseph Kossmann W CO 8 Gelsenkirchen, Germany
04.01.91 Andreas Schweiger W CO 9 Supplingen, Germany
20.03.91 Paul Wesley W RSC 5 Solihull
04.04.91 Juergen Broszeitt W CO 2 Bielfeld, Germany
22.06.91 Said Skouma L PTS 8 Paris, France
13.09.91 Nelson Alves L CO 7 Dusseldorf, Germany
(Vacant German International S. Middleweight Title)
20.11.91 Kevin Sheeran L RSC 2 Cardiff
10.01.92 Teddy Jansen W CO 2 Aachen, Germany
28.02.92 Thomas Mateoi W RSC 2 Supplingen, Germany
(Vacant German International L. Middleweight Title)
04.04.92 Jan Mazgut W RSC 4 Minden, Germany
01.05.92 Trpmir Jandrek W RSC 2 Aachen, Germany
12.05.92 Adrian Strachan L PTS 6 Crystal Palace
19.09.92 Andy Marks W PTS 8 Kassel, Germany
01.10.92 Robert McCracken L PTS 8 Telford
02.11.92 Neville Brown L PTS 8 Wolverhampton
04.12.92 Richie Woodhall L PTS 8 Telford
16.04.93 Silvio Branco L PTS 6 Rome, Italy
19.05.93 Gary Jacobs L RTD 4 Sunderland
Career: 40 contests, won 15, drew 1, lost 24.

Peter Flint

Sheffield. *Born* Sheffield, 3 July, 1973
L. Heavyweight. Ht. 6'1"
Manager H. Carnall

02.02.93 Mark Buck L CO 2 Derby
08.06.93 Greg Scott-Briggs L RSC 1 Derby
Career: 2 contests, lost 2.

Andrew Flute

Tipton. Born Wolverhampton, 5 March, 1970
Middleweight. Ht. 6'1"
Manager Self

24.05.89 Stinger Mason W PTS 6 Hanley
24.10.89 Paul Murray W RSC 4 Wolverhampton
22.03.90 Dave Maxwell W RSC 5 Wolverhampton
24.05.90 Spencer Alton L RSC 1 Dudley
18.09.90 Tony Hodge W CO 2 Wolverhampton
24.10.90 Nigel Rafferty W CO 6 Dudley
27.11.90 Paul Burton L PTS 6 Stoke
13.03.91 Robert Peel W PTS 6 Stoke
10.04.91 Russell Washer W PTS 6 Wolverhampton
14.05.91 Alan Richards W PTS 8 Dudley
16.10.91 Karl Barwise L RSC 8 Stoke
05.12.91 Richard Okumu DREW 8 Cannock
17.03.92 Graham Burton W PTS 8 Wolverhampton
28.04.92 Paul Smith W RSC 5 Wolverhampton
20.01.93 Glen Payton W RSC 4 Wolverhampton
16.03.93 Mark Hale W RSC 2 Wolverhampton
24.04.93 Steve Thomas W RSC 1 Birmingham
Career: 17 contests, won 13, drew 1, lost 3.

Steve Foran   Les Clark

Steve Foran

Liverpool. *Born* Liverpool, 19 October, 1967
L. Welterweight. Ht. 5'8"
Manager Self

29.11.88 John Mullen DREW 6 Manchester
16.12.88 Dean Dickinson W PTS 6 Brentwood
02.05.89 Danny Ellis W RSC 3 Chigwell
06.06.89 Jim Talbot L PTS 8 Chigwell
28.06.89 David Lake W RSC 1 Brentwood
26.09.89 David Maw W PTS 8 Chigwell
31.10.89 Michael Driscoll DREW 6 Manchester
21.03.90 Mike Morrison W PTS 6 Preston
05.06.90 Glyn Rhodes DREW 6 Nottingham
17.10.90 Darren Mount W RSC 6 Bethnal Green
24.04.91 Wayne Windle W CO 3 Preston
22.06.91 Michael Driscoll L RSC 4 Earls Court
23.10.92 Robert Whitehouse W RSC 2 Liverpool
20.11.92 Kevin McKillan W PTS 6 Liverpool

27.02.93 Tony Foster DREW 6 Ellesmere Port
Career: 15 contests, won 9. drew 4. lost 2.

Ali Forbes   Chris Bevan

Ali Forbes

Sydenham. *Born* London, 7 March, 1961
S. Middleweight. Ht. 5'9"
Manager H. Holland

16.02.89 David Haycock W RSC 4 Battersea
22.06.90 Andy Marlow W RTD 4 Gillingham
26.09.90 Peter Vosper W PTS 6 Mayfair
06.02.91 Adrian Wright W PTS 6 Battersea
03.04.91 Karl Barwise W RTD 4 Bethnal Green
16.05.91 Quinn Paynter DREW 6 Battersea
01.06.91 Paul McCarthy W CO 2 Bethnal Green
11.03.92 Ian Strudwick L PTS 10 Solihull
(Southern Area S. Middleweight Title Challenge)
29.10.92 Nick Manners W RSC 3 Leeds
Career: 9 contests, won 7, drew 1, lost 1.

Maurice Forbes

Brixton. *Born* Jamaica, 24 June, 1968
Welterweight. Ht. 5'10½"
Manager F. Maloney

23.05.93 Michael Dick W RSC 1 Brockley
25.06.93 Kenny Scott W RSC 2 Battersea
Career: 2 contests, won 2.

Simon Ford

Shrewsbury. *Born* Wolverhampton, 8 February, 1971
L. Welterweight. Ht. 5'4"
Manager D. Nelson

03.09.92 Shea Neary L RSC 1 Liverpool
Career: 1 contest, lost 1.

Hugh Forde

Birmingham. *Born* Birmingham, 7 May, 1964
Lightweight. Former British &

Commonwealth S. Featherweight
Champion. Former Undefeated Midlands
Area S. Featherweight Champion. Ht. 5'9"
Manager M. Duff

13.05.86	Little Currie W PTS 6 Digbeth
26.06.86	Carl Cleasby W RSC 3 Edgbaston
22.09.86	Carl Gaynor W PTS 6 Edgbaston
25.10.86	Tony Graham W PTS 6 Stevenage
03.11.86	John Bennie W RSC 3 Edgbaston
08.12.86	Darren Connellan W PTS 6 Edgbaston
21.01.87	Craig Walsh W PTS 8 Solihull
07.04.87	Gary Maxwell W PTS 8 West Bromwich
24.04.87	Lambsy Kayani W PTS 8 Liverpool
14.12.87	Patrick Kamy W PTS 8 Edgbaston
19.01.88	Billy Cawley W PTS 8 Kings Heath
05.04.88	Rudy Valentino W RSC 2 Birmingham
17.06.88	Gary Maxwell W RSC 2 Edgbaston *(Vacant Midlands Area S. Featherweight Title)*
10.10.88	Wayne Weekes W RSC 7 Edgbaston
28.11.88	Brian Cullen W RTD 4 Edgbaston
08.05.89	Paul Bowen W RSC 4 Edgbaston
31.10.89	Brian Roche W RSC 2 Manchester *(Final Elim. British S. Featherweight Title)*
14.02.90	Harold Warren W PTS 8 Brentwood
25.04.90	Delfino Perez W RSC 2 Brighton
18.09.90	Joey Jacobs W RSC 11 Wolverhampton *(British S. Featherweight Title Challenge)*
24.10.90	Kevin Pritchard L CO 4 Dudley *(British S. Featherweight Title Defence)*
27.02.91	Tony Pep L RSC 9 Wolverhampton
14.05.91	Richard Joyce W RTD 5 Dudley
10.09.91	Thunder Aryeh W PTS 12 Wolverhampton *(Commonwealth S. Featherweight Title Challenge)*
12.11.91	Paul Harvey L RSC 3 Wolverhampton *(Commonwealth S. Featherweight Title Defence)*
02.11.92	Karl Taylor W PTS 6 Wolverhampton

Career: 26 contests, won 23, lost 3.

John Foreman

Birmingham. *Born* Birmingham, 6
November, 1967
L. Heavyweight. Ht. 6'0"
Manager Self

26.10.87	Randy B. Powell W RSC 1 Birmingham
18.11.87	Dave Owens L RSC 5 Solihull
16.03.88	John Fairbairn W PTS 6 Solihull
05.04.88	David Jono W CO 1 Birmingham
11.04.88	Byron Pullen W PTS 6 Northampton
17.06.88	Gus Mendes W RSC 5 Edgbaston
28.11.88	Dave Owens W CO 1 Edgbaston
24.01.89	Crawford Ashley L RSC 4 Kings Heath
13.11.89	Everton Blake W PTS 6 Brierley Hill
03.12.89	Chris Coughlin W RSC 2 Birmingham
19.03.90	Abner Blackstock W PTS 8 Brierley Hill
04.06.90	Brian Schumacher W RSC 4 Edgbaston
03.09.90	Roy Skeldon L RTD 6 Dudley *(Midlands Area L. Heavyweight Title Challenge)*
18.04.91	Richard Bustin L PTS 8 Earls Court
22.06.91	Gil Lewis DREW 6 Earls Court
16.12.91	Steve McCarthy L PTS 8 Southampton

26.01.92	Fabrice Tiozzo L RSC 6 Saint-Ouen, France
29.05.92	Bobbi Joe Edwards W RSC 4 Manchester
06.10.92	Eddie Smulders L RSC 4 Antwerp, Belgium
20.03.93	Anthony Hembrick L RSC 6 Dusseldorf. Germany

Career: 20 contests, won 11, drew 1, lost 8.

Jason Fores

Worksop. *Born* Worksop, 27 November,
1970
L. Middleweight. Ht. 5'8"
Manager K. Richardson

26.01.89	Seamus Sheridan L RSC 1 Newcastle
09.12.92	Andy Peach L PTS 6 Stoke
25.02.93	Nick Manners L RSC 2 Bradford

Career: 3 contests, lost 3.

Frankie Foster   Chris Bevan

Frankie Foster

Newcastle. *Born* Newcastle, 25 May, 1968
Northern Area S. Featherweight Champion.
Ht. 5'6"
Manager T. Conroy

22.09.88	Mick Mulcahy W PTS 6 Newcastle
29.09.88	Paul Chedgzoy W PTS 6 Sunderland
07.11.88	Pete Roberts W PTS 4 Bradford
01.12.88	Peter English L PTS 8 Manchester
26.01.89	James Jiora W PTS 6 Newcastle
09.03.89	John Townsley W PTS 8 Glasgow
03.04.89	Jose Tuominen L PTS 4 Helsinki, Finland
24.04.89	Jim Moffat L PTS 8 Glasgow
21.06.89	Paul Gadney L PTS 6 Eltham
02.10.89	Shaun White DREW 6 Bradford
11.10.89	Lester James W PTS 6 Stoke
21.10.89	Chad Broussard L PTS 6 Middlesbrough
13.11.89	Steve Winstanley L PTS 6 Bradford
24.01.90	Kid Sumali W PTS 6 Sunderland
05.02.90	Muhammad Shaffique L PTS 6

Brierley Hill

20.03.90	Dominic McGuigan DREW 4 Hartlepool
26.04.90	Les Walsh W PTS 8 Manchester
04.06.90	Stuart Rimmer W PTS 6 Glasgow
18.10.90	Nigel Senior W CO 2 Hartlepool *(Vacant Northern Area S. Featherweight Title)*
19.11.90	Sugar Gibiliru DREW 8 Manchester
22.04.91	John Doherty L PTS 10 Glasgow *(Elim. British S. Featherweight Title)*
14.08.91	Gianni di Napoli L PTS 8 Alcamo, Italy
22.10.91	Darren Elsdon L RSC 7 Hartlepool *(Northern Area S. Featherweight Title Defence)*
31.03.92	Sugar Gibiliru L PTS 8 Stockport
10.09.92	Darren Elsdon W PTS 10 Sunderland *(Northern Area S. Featherweight Title Challenge)*

Career: 25 contests, won 11, drew 3, lost 11.

Steve Foster

Manchester. *Born* Salford, 28 December,
1960
L. Middleweight. Ht. 5'8½"
Manager P. Martin

09.02.81	Pat McCarthy W RSC 3 Manchester
16.03.81	Dave Dunn L PTS 6 Manchester
26.03.81	John Lindo L RSC 1 Newcastle
28.11.85	Malcolm Melvin DREW 6 Ilkeston
06.03.86	Taffy Morris L PTS 6 Manchester
17.04.86	Martin Kielty W RSC 4 Wolverhampton
25.11.86	Shamus Casey W PTS 8 Manchester
28.04.87	Cyril Jackson W RSC 7 Manchester
11.05.87	Fidel Castro L PTS 8 Manchester
19.10.87	Cyril Jackson W RTD 3 Manchester
14.12.87	Sean Leighton L PTS 8 Bradford
27.01.88	Sammy Storey L RSC 4 Belfast
20.04.88	Tony Collins L PTS 4 Muswell Hill
19.10.88	Ray Close L RSC 2 Belfast
14.12.88	Fran Harding L PTS 6 Kirkby
01.03.89	Dario Deabreu W RSC 2 Cardiff
06.03.89	Steve Aquilina W PTS 6 Manchester
03.12.89	Antonio Fernandez W PTS 8 Birmingham
06.02.90	Sean O'Phoenix W RSC 4 Oldham
14.03.90	Andy Till L RTD 5 Battersea
02.06.90	Ian Chantler DREW 4 Manchester
22.02.91	Kesem Clayton W CO 6 Manchester
20.09.91	Colin Pitters W RTD 5 Manchester
07.12.91	Shamus Casey W PTS 8 Manchester
10.03.92	Mike Phillips W RSC 4 Bury
25.04.92	Mark Jay W RSC 7 Manchester
28.11.92	Shaun Cummins L PTS 12 Manchester *(Vacant WBA Penta-Continental L. Middleweight Title)*

Career: 27 contests, won 14, drew 2, lost 11.

Tony Foster

Hull. *Born* Hull, 9 July, 1964
Lightweight. Ht. 5'7"
Manager Self

04.09.87	Paul Kennedy L PTS 6 Gateshead
17.09.87	Ian Hosten L PTS 6 Gravesend
28.09.87	Steve Winstanley L PTS 6 Bradford
06.10.87	Roy Doyle L PTS 6 Manchester
03.11.87	Darren Darby L PTS 6 Cottingham
25.11.87	Kevin McCoy W RSC 4 Cottingham
02.12.87	Alan Roberts W RSC 5 Piccadilly
11.12.87	Mitchell King DREW 8 Coalville

11.01.88 Paul Chedgzoy W PTS 6 Manchester
25.01.88 Johnny Walker L PTS 6 Glasgow
01.02.88 Sean Hogg W PTS 6 Manchester
11.02.88 Lee Amass L RSC 6 Gravesend
28.03.88 Darryl Pettit W PTS 6 Bradford
22.04.88 Paul Charters L PTS 6 Gateshead
09.05.88 Gary Maxwell L PTS 6 Nottingham
17.05.88 Warren Slaney W PTS 6 Leicester
23.05.88 Harry Escott W RSC 6 Bradford
26.09.88 Peter Bradley L PTS 8 Piccadilly
17.10.88 John Townsley L PTS 8 Glasgow
15.11.88 Steve Pollard W RSC 3 Hull
12.12.88 Mark Kelly W PTS 6 Nottingham
08.02.89 Paul Gadney W PTS 6 Kensington
03.04.89 Jari Gronroos W PTS 4 Helsinki,
          Finland
15.04.89 Paul Moylett W PTS 6 Salisbury
27.06.89 Ian Honeywood L PTS 6 Kensington
10.10.89 Steve Pollard W RSC 3 Hull
16.11.89 Sugar Gibiliru W PTS 8 Manchester
30.11.89 Joey Jacobs L CO 4 Oldham
30.01.90 Sugar Gibiliru L PTS 10 Manchester
          (Vacant Central Area Lightweight
          Title)
21.04.90 Marvin P. Gray DREW 6 Sunderland
22.05.90 Marvin P. Gray L PTS 6 Stockton
15.06.90 Marcel Herbert L RSC 4 Telford
15.02.91 Jimmy Bredahl L PTS 6 Randers,
          Denmark
05.03.91 Floyd Havard L PTS 8 Millwall
15.04.91 Dave Anderson L PTS 8 Glasgow
12.05.91 Alain Simoes W PTS 8 Voiron, France
11.09.91 Billy Schwer L PTS 8 Hammersmith
21.11.91 Giovanni Parisi L RSC 6 Perugia, Italy
31.01.92 Angel Mona L PTS 8 Esch,
          Luxembourg
30.03.92 Ian Honeywood L RSC 4 Eltham
13.06.92 Pierre Lorcy L PTS 8 Levallois Perret,
          France
16.10.92 Tony Doyle W PTS 8 Hull
31.10.92 Dingaan Thobela L PTS 8 Earls Court
14.01.93 Alan Hall L PTS 6 Mayfair
27.02.93 Steve Foran DREW 6 Ellesmere Port
Career: 45 contests, won 16, drew 3, lost 26.

Phil Found
Hereford. *Born* Hereford, 9 June, 1967
L. Welterweight. Ht. 5'9"
Manager D. Gardiner

30.03.93 Paul Davies W PTS 6 Cardiff
29.04.93 Delroy Leslie L PTS 6 Mayfair
09.06.93 Jason Beard L PTS 6 Lewisham
26.06.93 Paul Knights L PTS 4 Earls Court
Career: 4 contests, won 1, lost 3.

Dougie Fox
Worksop. *Born* Worksop, 5 November,
1972
Featherweight. Ht. 5'7"
Manager K. Richardson

28.05.93 Mario Culpeper L RSC 3 Middleton
Career: 1 contest, lost 1.

Lee Fox
Chesterfield. *Born* Chesterfield, 20 January,
1970
S. Featherweight. Ht. 5'3¾"
Manager Self

13.11.89 Steve Armstrong W PTS 6 Manchester
06.12.89 Steve Armstrong W PTS 6 Stoke

Simon Frailing (right started his pro career off with a six round draw against fellow debutant, Bruce Ruegg

Les Clark

05.02.90 Neil Leitch L PTS 6 Brierley Hill
25.04.90 Bernard McComiskey L RTD 3
          Brighton
15.06.90 Chris Cooper W PTS 6 Telford
05.09.90 Nicky Lucas DREW 6 Brighton
03.10.90 Nicky Lucas L RTD 2 Basildon
26.11.90 Bobby Guynan W PTS 6 Bethnal
          Green
12.12.90 Mark Bates L PTS 6 Basildon
06.02.91 Bobby Guynan L PTS 6 Bethnal Green
12.03.91 Charlie Coke W PTS 6 Mansfield
26.03.91 Bobby Guynan W RTD 3 Bethnal
          Green
11.06.91 Neil Smith L PTS 6 Leicester
16.08.91 Felix Garcia Losada L CO 3 Marbella,
          Spain
21.01.92 Richard Woolgar L PTS 6 Norwich
19.02.92 Mark Bates L PTS 6 Muswell Hill
27.02.92 Wayne Rigby W PTS 6 Liverpool
14.04.92 Dean Lynch L PTS 6 Mansfield
29.04.92 Andrew Robinson W PTS 6 Stoke
29.05.92 Danny Connelly L PTS 6 Glasgow

19.10.92 Dave McHale L RSC 3 Glasgow
15.02.93 Carl Roberts L PTS 6 Manchester
16.03.93 Gareth Jordan L RSC 3
          Wolverhampton
14.06.93 Yifru Retta L RTD 3 Bayswater
Career: 24 contests, won 8, drew 1, lost 15.

Simon Frailing
Hayes. *Born* London, 13 June, 1966
S. Featherweight. Ht. 5'7"
Manager D. Gunn

29.04.93 Bruce Ruegg DREW 6 Hayes
15.06.93 Bruce Ruegg L PTS 6 Hemel
          Hempstead
Career: 2 contests, drew 1, lost 1.

Chris Francis
Stepney. *Born* London, 23 October, 1968
S. Featherweight. Ht. 5'6"
Manager M. Brennan

02.10.91   Rick Dimmock W PTS 6 Barking
11.02.92   Paul Donaghey L CO 2 Barking
17.02.93   Jason Lepre W RSC 2 Bethnal Green
31.03.93   Steve Patton W CO 4 Bethnal Green
Career: 4 contests, won 3, lost 1.

Julius Francis   Les Clark

Julius Francis

Woolwich. *Born* Peckham, 8 December, 1964
Heavyweight. Ht. 6'2"
Manager F. Maloney

23.05.93   Graham Arnold W RSC 5 Brockley
23.06.93   Joey Paladino W CO 4 Edmonton
Career: 2 contests, won 2.

Joe Frater

Grimsby. *Born* Jamaica, 30 April, 1961
L. Heavyweight. Ht. 6'1"
Manager L. Slater

06.02.80   Nigel Savery L RSC 3 Liverpool
31.03.80   John Stone W RSC 1 Cleethorpes
14.04.80   Paul Heatley W RSC 5 Manchester
12.05.80   Chuck Hirschmann DREW 4 Manchester
16.06.80   Joe Dean W PTS 6 Manchester
09.09.80   Nigel Savery L CO 6 Mexborough
08.10.80   Steve Fox W PTS 4 Stoke
05.11.80   Willie Wright W PTS 6 Evesham
08.12.80   Steve Fenton L PTS 6 Nottingham
12.02.81   Paul Heatley W PTS 6 Bolton
30.03.81   Steve Fenton L RSC 1 Cleethorpes
21.09.81   Chris Thorne W PTS 6 Nottingham
11.11.81   Steve Babbs L PTS 6 Evesham
01.02.82   P. T. Grant W PTS 8 Newcastle
10.05.82   Devon Bailey L CO 2 Copthorne
07.06.82   Jonjo Greene L PTS 6 Manchester
21.06.82   Geoff Rymer W PTS 8 Hull
04.09.82   Andy Straughn L RSC 3 Marylebone
02.03.87   Ray Thomas L PTS 6 Birmingham
07.10.87   Crawford Ashley L RSC 5 Burnley
09.11.87   Tucker Watts L PTS 6 Leicester
22.03.88   Darren Jones L PTS 6 Wolverhampton

22.09.88   Wayne Hawkins L PTS 6 Wolverhampton
27.10.88   Dave Lawrence W PTS 6 Birmingham
10.11.88   Wayne Hawkins L RSC 3 Wolverhampton
08.05.89   Deka Williams L CO 5 Grimsby
04.09.89   Nigel Rafferty W PTS 6 Grimsby
04.12.89   Tony Lawrence W PTS 6 Grimsby
14.05.90   Dave Owens L PTS 6 Cleethorpes
08.10.90   Alan Baptiste DREW 6 Cleethorpes
11.12.90   Tony Lawrence W PTS 6 Evesham
02.03.91   Nick Vardy W RSC 1 Cleethorpes
23.04.91   Dave Owens L PTS 6 Evesham
23.10.91   Gary Delaney L RSC 1 Bethnal Green
04.06.92   Greg Scott-Briggs W PTS 6 Cleethorpes
26.10.92   Dave Owens L PTS 6 Cleethorpes
Career: 36 contests, won 15, drew 2, lost 19.

Terry French

Newcastle. *Born* Newcastle, 15 January, 1967
Northern Area L. Heavyweight Champion.
Ht. 5'9½"
Manager T. Conroy

10.10.88   Adrian Din L PTS 6 Nottingham
03.11.88   Graham Burton L RSC 3 Manchester
07.12.88   Anthony Lawrence W PTS 6 Stoke
13.03.89   Paul Abercromby W RSC 4 Glasgow
11.04.89   Paul Hendrick L PTS 6 Oldham
19.04.89   Mickey Murray W PTS 6 Doncaster
12.06.89   Max Wallace L PTS 6 Battersea
11.09.89   Shamus Casey L PTS 6 Nottingham
02.10.89   Hugh Fury W PTS 6 Bradford
10.10.89   Darren Pilling L PTS 6 Sunderland
23.10.89   Chris Walker W PTS 6 Nottingham
14.11.89   Dave Maxwell W PTS 6 Evesham
11.12.89   Tony Lawrence L PTS 6 Bradford
22.01.90   George Ferrie L PTS 6 Glasgow
26.02.90   Trevor Barry W RTD 4 Bradford
20.03.90   Stevie R. Davies W PTS 6 Hartlepool
09.04.90   Sean O'Phoenix DREW 8 Manchester
21.04.90   Dave Scott W RSC 3 Sunderland
15.05.90   Simon McDougall L PTS 4 South Shields
12.11.90   Eddie Collins W PTS 6 Bradford
13.12.90   Stevie R. Davies W PTS 10 Hartlepool
(Vacant Northern Area L. Heavyweight Title)
03.04.91   Sean O'Phoenix L PTS 8 Manchester
10.05.91   Eddie Collins W PTS 6 Gateshead
10.10.91   Simon McDougall W PTS 6 Gateshead
14.11.91   Quinn Paynter L CO 6 Gateshead
03.03.92   Dave Owens L CO 1 Houghton le Spring
23.10.92   Spencer Alton W PTS 6 Gateshead
17.04.93   Simon McDougall W PTS 6 Washington
Career: 28 contests, won 15, drew 1, lost 12.

Andrew Furlong

Hammersmith. *Born* Paddington, 29 July, 1967
L. Middleweight. Ht. 5'9½"
Manager Self

14.11.85   Robert Southey W PTS 6 Merton
22.11.85   Tony Richards W PTS 6 Longford
10.01.86   Bill Smith W PTS 6 Fulham
30.01.86   Marvin P. Gray W PTS 6 Merton
27.02.86   Barry Bacon W RSC 6 Merton
15.04.86   Willie Wilson W PTS 8 Merton

28.05.86   Billy Joe Dee W RSC 2 Lewisham
04.09.86   Les Remikie W PTS 8 Merton
22.10.86   Peppy Muire L RSC 2 Greenwich
20.11.86   Chubby Martin DREW 8 Merton
12.01.87   Chubby Martin W PTS 8 Ealing
22.01.87   Brian Sonny Nickels L PTS 8 Bethnal Green
25.02.87   Mark Dinnadge DREW 8 Lewisham
18.03.87   Tony Borg W PTS 8 Queensway
01.04.87   Frankie Lake W PTS 8 Southsea
30.04.87   Andrew Prescod W PTS 8 Bethnal Green
27.05.87   Wayne Weekes L RSC 1 Lewisham
25.09.87   Oliver Henry W RTD 5 Tooting
03.12.87   Eamonn McAuley W RTD 3 Belfast
18.01.88   Ian Honeywood L PTS 8 Mayfair
08.03.88   Neil Haddock W PTS 6 Holborn
19.09.88   Tony Richards L RSC 7 Mayfair
14.11.88   Joni Nyman L RSC 2 Helsinki, Finland
16.05.89   Ian John-Lewis W RSC 3 Wandsworth
12.06.89   Rocky Kelly L RSC 5 Battersea
11.10.89   Brian Robinson L PTS 6 Millwall
02.05.91   Delroy Waul L RSC 5 Northampton
30.06.91   Lee Crocker DREW 6 Southwark
12.02.92   Gary Pemberton W PTS 6 Wembley
25.03.92   Clay O'Shea DREW 6 Kensington
13.05.92   Clay O'Shea DREW 6 Kensington
16.06.92   Mickey Hughes L CO 1 Dagenham
02.10.92   Patrick Vungbo L RSC 8 Waregem, Belgium
10.04.93   Robin Reid L PTS 6 Swansea
Career: 34 contests, won 17, drew 5, lost 12.

Carl Gaffney

Leeds. *Born* Leeds, 15 April, 1964
Heavyweight. Ht. 6'5"
Manager T. Callighan

12.05.84   Steve Abadom W RSC 3 Hanley
02.10.84   Theo Josephs W PTS 6 Leeds
23.01.85   Alphonso Forbes L CO 1 Solihull
25.03.85   Dave Madden W RSC 1 Huddersfield
30.05.85   Denroy Bryan W RSC 1 Halifax
21.11.85   Al Malcolm W PTS 8 Huddersfield
16.01.86   Joe Threlfall L CO 3 Preston
20.02.86   Chris Devine W RSC 8 Halifax
24.10.86   Damien Marignan L PTS 8 Guadalupe, FW1
01.12.86   Michael Simwelu L RSC 7 Arnhem, Holland
14.12.88   Keith Ferdinand W PTS 8 Bethnal Green
14.06.89   Rodolfo Marin L RSC 2 Madrid, Spain
25.10.89   Andrei Oreshkin L RSC 1 Wembley
02.05.91   Sean Hunter W PTS 6 Kensington
19.09.91   Michael Murray L RSC 8 Stockport
(Vacant Central Area Heavyweight Title)
09.02.92   Steve Garber W PTS 6 Bradford
13.02.93   Brian Nielson L PTS 6 Randers, Denmark
26.03.93   Mikael Lindblad L RSC 2 Copenhagen, Denmark
Career: 18 contests, won 9, lost 9.

Michael Gale

Leeds. *Born* Cardiff, 28 October, 1967
Central Area L. Heavyweight Champion.
Ht. 5'11"
Manager M. Duff

21.09.89   Dave Lawrence W RTD 4 Harrogate
13.11.89   Coco Collins W CO 1 Manchester
05.12.89   Randy B. Powell W RSC 1 Dewsbury

11.01.90	Cliff Curtis W RSC 2 Dewsbury
24.01.90	Andy Marlow W RSC 2 Sunderland
03.03.90	Peter Vosper W RSC 2 Wembley
11.04.90	Teo Arvizu W PTS 6 Dewsbury
18.10.90	Mick Queally W RSC 5 Dewsbury
15.11.90	Steve Osborne W PTS 6 Oldham
14.03.91	Carlos Christie W PTS 8 Middleton
21.03.91	David Haycock W RSC 2 Dewsbury
09.05.91	Steve Osborne W RSC 2 Leeds
13.06.91	Graham Burton W CO 4 Hull
27.06.91	Mark Bowen W PTS 8 Leeds
30.10.91	Denys Cronin DREW 8 Leeds
23.01.92	John Kaighin W PTS 8 York
08.04.92	Tony Booth W PTS 8 Leeds
29.10.92	Bobbi Joe Edwards W PTS 10 Leeds
	(Vacant Central Area L. Heavyweight Title)
07.04.93	Brent Kosolofski L RSC 9 Leeds
	(Vacant Commonwealth L. Heavyweight Title)

Career: 19 contests, won 17, drew 1, lost 1.

Patrick Gallagher

Islington. *Born* Manchester, 23 July, 1971
Lightweight. Ht. 5'7½"
Manager B. Hearn

22.12.92	Karl Taylor W RSC 3 Mayfair
20.02.93	Joe Fannin W RTD 1 Earls Court

Career: 2 contests, won 2.

Paul Gamble

Norwich. *Born* Norwich, 31 March, 1964
Middleweight. Ht. 6'2"
Manager G. Holmes

03.12.84	Rex Weaver W RSC 2 Manchester
31.01.85	John Hargin W RSC 2 Basildon
26.02.85	Dave Scott W PTS 6 Bethnal Green
01.04.85	John Graham L PTS 6 Mayfair
18.04.85	Alan Baptiste L PTS 6 Mayfair
07.09.85	Neil Munn L PTS 6 Isle of Man
06.11.85	Mickey Kidd W PTS 6 Evesham
03.02.86	Alan Baptiste L CO 8 Dulwich
15.03.86	Cliff Curtis W PTS 6 Norwich
13.09.86	Dennis Hogan W RSC 5 Norwich
08.09.92	Gilbert Jackson L RSC 1 Norwich

Career: 11 contests, won 6, lost 5.

Steve Garber

Bradford. *Born* Bradford, 20 June, 1962
Heavyweight. Ht. 6'6"
Manager P. Martin

22.04.85	Mick Cordon DREW 6 Bradford
30.05.85	Mick Cordon L PTS 6 Blackburn
02.07.85	Joe Threlfall W RSC 2 Preston
03.10.85	Dave Shelton W PTS 4 Bradford
27.11.85	Mick Cordon W PTS 6 Bradford
06.02.86	Mick Cordon L PTS 6 Doncaster
27.04.86	Mick Cordon L PTS 6 Doncaster
22.05.86	Sean Daly W PTS 6 Horwich
18.09.86	Gary McConnell L PTS 6 Weston super Mare
25.09.86	Carl Timbrell W PTS 6 Wolverhampton
22.10.86	Dave Madden W PTS 4 Bradford
01.12.86	Tony Hallett W PTS 6 Nottingham
24.02.87	Gary McConnell L CO 1 Ilford
07.10.87	Gypsy John Fury L PTS 6 Burnley
18.01.88	Mick Cordon W PTS 6 Bradford
11.02.88	John Love L CO 1 Gravesend
21.03.88	Ted Shaw W CO 1 Leicester
22.04.88	Manny Burgo L PTS 6 Gateshead

Steve Garber Harry Goodwin

23.05.88	Ted Shaw W CO 3 Bradford
26.09.88	Gifford Shillingford W RSC 4 Bradford
25.10.88	Paul Lister L PTS 6 Hartlepool
17.11.88	Michael Murray L PTS 6 Stockport
18.01.89	Peter Nyman W PTS 6 Kensington
19.05.89	Joe Threlfall W RSC 3 Gateshead
10.10.89	Lennox Lewis L CO 1 Hull
20.03.90	Chris Hubbert W RSC 1 Hartlepool
05.05.90	Knut Blin L PTS 6 Hamburg, Germany
12.11.90	David Jules W RSC 6 Bradford
30.11.90	Steve Gee W PTS 6 Birmingham
19.03.91	Al Malcolm W RSC 6 Birmingham
30.04.91	Michael Murray L CO 1 Stockport
31.05.91	Axel Schulz L CO 5 Berlin, Germany
10.10.91	Paul Lister L PTS 8 Gateshead
09.02.92	Carl Gaffney L PTS 6 Bradford
05.04.92	David Jules W RSC 4 Bradford
08.05.92	Alexandr Miroshnichenko L RSC 1 Waregem, Belgium
18.07.92	Henry Akinwande L RTD 2 Manchester
24.02.93	J. A. Bugner W RSC 6 Wembley

Career: 38 contests, won 19, drew 1, lost 18.

Des Gargano (Southern)

Manchester. *Born* Brighton, 20 December, 1960
Featherweight. Ht. 5'5"
Manager Self

25.01.85	Sugar Gibiliru L PTS 4 Liverpool
18.03.85	Sugar Gibiliru L PTS 6 Liverpool
24.04.85	Glen McLaggon L PTS 6 Stoke
03.06.85	Anthony Wakefield DREW 6 Manchester
17.06.85	Anthony Wakefield W PTS 6 Manchester
03.10.85	Anthony Brown L PTS 6 Liverpool
13.10.85	Gary Maxwell L PTS 6 Sheffield
09.12.85	Robert Newbiggin W PTS 6 Nottingham
16.12.85	Gypsy Johnny W PTS 6 Bradford
24.02.86	Kevin Taylor W PTS 6 Bradford

01.04.86	Carl Cleasby L PTS 6 Leeds
07.04.86	Gerry McBride W PTS 6 Manchester
29.04.86	Pat Clinton L PTS 6 Manchester
23.09.86	David Ingram L PTS 6 Batley
24.11.86	Andrew Steadman L PTS 6 Leicester
03.12.86	Sean Murphy L PTS 6 Muswell Hill
15.12.86	Tony Heath L PTS 6 Loughborough
30.01.87	Nigel Crook L PTS 6 Kirkby
16.02.87	Pat Clinton L PTS 6 Glasgow
13.04.87	Jimmy Lee W PTS 6 Manchester
26.05.87	John Green L PTS 6 Oldham
19.10.87	John Green L PTS 6 Manchester
28.10.87	Paul Thornton W RSC 6 Stoke
09.11.87	Tony Heath L PTS 6 Leicester
26.01.88	Graham O'Malley L PTS 4 Hartlepool
23.03.88	Lambsy Kayani L PTS 6 Sheffield
29.03.88	Graham O'Malley L PTS 8 Marton
25.04.88	Ronnie Stephenson W PTS 8 Bradford
06.06.88	Darryl Pettit W PTS 6 Manchester
13.06.88	Joe Mullen L PTS 6 Glasgow
05.09.88	Wull Strike DREW 6 Glasgow
22.09.88	John Davison L PTS 8 Newcastle
29.09.88	John Davison L PTS 8 Sunderland
10.10.88	Shane Silvester L PTS 6 Edgbaston
18.10.88	Peter English L PTS 4 Oldham
28.10.88	Eyub Can L PTS 6 Copenhagen, Denmark
21.11.88	Ronnie Stephenson W PTS 6 Leicester
29.11.88	Chris Clarkson W PTS 6 Manchester
07.12.88	Renny Edwards L PTS 6 Aberavon
16.12.88	Jimmy Clark L PTS 6 Brentwood
14.02.89	Nigel Crook L PTS 10 Manchester
17.03.89	Jimmy Bredahl L PTS 6 Braedstrup, Denmark
17.04.89	Mark Priestley W PTS 8 Middleton
10.05.89	Mark Goult L PTS 8 Solihull
17.05.89	Mark Geraghty L PTS 8 Glasgow
12.06.89	Neil Parry W PTS 6 Manchester
11.07.89	Chris Clarkson L PTS 6 Batley
04.09.89	Ronnie Stephenson W PTS 6 Hull
11.09.89	Paul Dever W RSC 1 Manchester
20.09.89	Miguel Matthews W PTS 6 Stoke
05.10.89	Wayne Windle W PTS 6 Middleton
16.10.89	Wayne Windle L PTS 6 Manchester
31.10.89	Dave McNally L PTS 6 Manchester
10.11.89	Kruga Hydes L PTS 6 Liverpool
20.11.89	Dave Buxton L PTS 6 Leicester
30.11.89	Noel Carroll L PTS 6 Oldham
11.12.89	Joe Kelly L PTS 6 Bayswater
14.02.90	Danny Porter L PTS 6 Brentwood
06.03.90	Bradley Stone L PTS 6 Bethnal Green
17.03.90	John Lowey L RSC 6 Belfast
24.04.90	Jamie Morris W PTS 4 Stoke
09.05.90	Terry Collins L PTS 6 Kensington
16.05.90	Tony Doyle W PTS 6 Hull
11.06.90	Steve Armstrong W PTS 6 Manchester
05.09.90	John George L PTS 6 Stoke
01.10.90	Tony Smith W PTS 6 Cleethorpes
09.10.90	Brian Robb L PTS 6 Wolverhampton
22.10.90	John George L PTS 6 Cleethorpes
26.11.90	Tony Smith W PTS 6 Bury
03.12.90	Tony Smith W PTS 6 Cleethorpes
11.12.90	Stewart Fishermac W PTS 8 Evesham
16.01.91	Tony Smith W PTS 6 Stoke
06.02.91	Tim Driscoll L PTS 6 Bethnal Green
28.02.91	Carl Roberts W PTS 6 Bury
07.05.91	James Drummond L PTS 8 Glasgow
16.05.91	Jimmy Owens L RSC 2 Liverpool
19.08.91	Petteri Rissanen L PTS 4 Helsinki, Finland
02.10.91	Eric George L PTS 6 Solihull
24.10.91	Edward Cook L RSC 5 Glasgow
29.11.91	Harald Geier L DIS 8 Frohsdorf, Austria

103

31.01.92	Edward Cook L PTS 6 Glasgow
24.02.92	Colin Lynch L PTS 6 Coventry
04.03.92	Neil Armstrong L PTS 6 Glasgow
11.03.92	Dennis Oakes L PTS 6 Stoke
27.04.92	David Ramsden L PTS 6 Bradford
01.06.92	Mark Hargreaves L PTS 6 Manchester
08.06.92	David Ramsden L PTS 6 Bradford
07.10.92	Prince Nassem Hamed L RSC 4 Sunderland
20.11.92	Paul Lloyd L PTS 4 Liverpool
26.02.93	Alex Docherty W RSC 4 Irvine
04.04.93	Rowan Williams L PTS 4 Brockley
26.04.93	Wilson Docherty L PTS 6 Glasgow
01.06.93	Neil Parry W PTS 6 Manchester

Career: 93 contests, won 28, drew 2, lost 63.

Al Garrett (Garrity)

Glasgow. *Born* Glasgow, 21 December, 1966
Featherweight. Ht. 5'5½"
Manager T. Gilmour

23.09.91	Robert Braddock DREW 6 Glasgow
09.12.91	Chris Jickells L RSC 2 Bradford
18.11.92	Colin Innes DREW 6 Solihull

Career: 3 contests, drew 2, lost 1.

Dermot Gascoyne

Bexleyheath. *Born* Alfreton, 23 April, 1967
Heavyweight. Ht. 6'5"
Manager F. Warren

17.12.92	John Harewood W RSC 5 Barking
03.02.93	Steve Stewart W RSC 4 Earls Court

Career: 2 contests, won 2.

Steve Gee (Egege)

Birmingham. Born Bradford, 1 April, 1961
Heavyweight. Ht. 6'2"
Manager E. Cashmore

15.04.80	Mike Creasey W RSC 5 Blackpool
29.04.80	Gordon Charlesworth W RSC 2 Mayfair
14.05.80	Colin Flute W PTS 6 Burslem
22.09.80	Colin Flute W PTS 6 Birmingham
19.10.80	Jim Burns W RSC 3 Birmingham
30.10.80	Derek Simpkin DREW 6 Wolverhampton
10.11.80	Bobby Hennessey L PTS 8 Birmingham
19.01.81	Martin Lee L RSC 5 Merton
11.03.81	Rocky Burton W PTS 8 Solihull
25.03.81	Ian Scotting W PTS 8 Doncaster
28.04.81	Theo Josephs W PTS 8 Leeds
11.09.81	Jim Burns L PTS 8 Edgbaston
05.10.81	Hughroy Currie L PTS 6 Birmingham
08.11.81	Joe Christle L PTS 6 Navan
12.01.82	Martin Herdman W PTS 6 Bethnal Green
18.02.82	Noel Quarless L PTS 6 Liverpool
09.03.82	Martin Nee W PTS 8 Hornsey
30.03.82	Rudi Pika L PTS 8 Wembley
22.04.82	Joe Christle W RSC 6 Liverpool
22.06.82	Tommy Kiely W RSC 7 Hornsey
07.09.82	Stan McDermott L PTS 8 Hornsey
16.10.82	Mel Christie W RSC 6 Killarney
02.11.82	Martin Nee W RSC 5 Hornsey
14.11.82	Joe Christle DREW 6 Navan
22.11.82	Billy Aird L PTS 8 Lewisham
07.12.82	Theo Josephs W PTS 6 Southend
14.04.83	Winston Allen W PTS 8 Basildon

04.06.83	Mike Perkins L PTS 6 Atlantic City, USA
03.09.83	Pierre Coetzer L PTS 8 Johannesburg, South Africa
17.12.83	Anders Eklund L RSC 5 Mariehamn, Finland
28.01.84	Daniel Falconi L PTS 6 Marsala, Italy
04.05.84	Al Syben L PTS 8 Brussels, Belgium
01.07.85	Rudi Pika L PTS 8 Mayfair
05.11.85	Gary Mason L RSC 5 Wembley
04.12.85	Gary Mason L RSC 5 Kensington
30.01.86	Derek Williams L PTS 6 Merton
30.04.86	Andy Straughn L PTS 8 Edmonton
28.05.86	Andrew Gerrard L PTS 8 Newport
16.10.86	Paul Lister L PTS 8 Newcastle
29.11.86	Keith Ferdinand L PTS 8 Wandsworth
16.12.86	Ian Priest L PTS 6 Alfreton
22.02.87	Derek Williams L PTS 6 Wembley
30.11.90	Steve Garber L PTS 6 Birmingham
23.01.91	Manny Burgo L PTS 6 Brentwood
13.03.91	Tucker Richards L PTS 6 Stoke
06.04.91	Corrie Sanders L RSC 4 Darlington
30.05.91	Al Malcolm L PTS 6 Birmingham
13.09.91	Axel Schulz L CO 2 Dusseldorf, Germany
15.11.91	Massimo Migliaccio L PTS 6 Omegna, Italy
07.12.91	Michael Murray L RSC 7 Manchester
17.10.92	J. A. Bugner L PTS 6 Wembley
27.11.92	Brian Neilson L PTS 6 Randers, Denmark

Career: 52 contests, won 16, drew 3, lost 33.

Lou Gent

Streatham. *Born* London, 21 April, 1965
WBC International S. Middleweight
Champion. Former Undefeated Southern
Area Cruiserweight Champion. Ht. 5'10½"
Manager Self

18.09.84	Wes Taylor W PTS 6 Merton
05.02.85	Harry Andrews W PTS 6 Battersea
26.02.85	Lee White W PTS 6 Battersea

23.03.85	Simon Harris L PTS 6 Strand
30.04.85	Tee Jay DREW 6 Merton
12.09.85	Harry Andrews W RSC 2 Merton
25.10.85	Winston Burnett W PTS 6 Fulham
14.11.85	Winston Burnett W PTS 8 Merton
11.12.85	Serg Fame L RSC 2 Fulham
27.02.86	John Williams W RSC 4 Merton
20.03.86	Serg Fame L CO 2 Merton
16.06.86	Blaine Logsdon W PTS 8 Manchester
04.09.86	Chris Devine W RSC 6 Merton
16.10.86	Jerry Reed W RSC 7 Merton
20.11.86	Gypsy Carman W CO 1 Merton
29.01.87	Glazz Campbell W PTS 6 Merton
26.03.87	Danny Lawford L RSC 7 Merton
18.03.88	Abner Blackstock W RSC 5 Wandsworth
22.04.88	Glenn McCrory L RTD 8 Gateshead (*British & Commonwealth Cruiserweight Title Challenge*)
16.02.89	Lennie Howard W RSC 2 Battersea (*Vacant Southern Area Cruiserweight Title*)
26.04.89	Cyril Minnus W DIS 3 Battersea
22.02.90	Gypsy Carman W PTS 10 Wandsworth (*Southern Area Cruiserweight Title Defence*)
28.03.90	Johnny Nelson L CO 4 Bethnal Green (*British Cruiserweight Title Challenge*)
18.10.90	Jose Seys W PTS 8 Wandsworth
20.03.91	Derek Myers W RSC 7 Wandsworth (*Elim. British L. Heavyweight Title*)
16.05.91	Gus Mendes W CO 8 Battersea
30.10.91	Henry Wharton DREW 12 Leeds (*Commonwealth S. Middleweight Title Challenge*)
25.02.92	Fidel Castro L PTS 12 Crystal Palace (*British S. Middleweight Title Challenge*)
12.05.92	Johnny Melfah L RSC 3 Crystal Palace
14.07.92	Simon Collins W RSC 5 Mayfair
15.09.92	Karl Barwise W RSC 6 Crystal Palace
16.02.93	Hunter Clay W PTS 12 Tooting (*WBC International S. Middleweight Title Challenge*)

Presented with the WBC International middleweight belt following his victory over Hunter Clay, Lou Gent poses with Alex Steene (left) and Greg Steene

Les Clark

26.06.93 Nigel Benn L RSC 4 Earls Court
(WBC S. Middleweight Title Challenge)

Career: 33 contests, won 22, drew 2, lost 9.

Mark Geraghty

Glasgow. *Born* Paisley, 25 August, 1965
Scottish S. Featherweight Champion. Ht. 5'6"

Manager T. Gilmour

14.11.88 Mark Priestley W PTS 6 Glasgow
27.01.89 Gordon Stobie W PTS 6 Durham
14.02.89 Gary Hickman L PTS 6 Sunderland
09.03.89 Chris Clarkson W PTS 6 Glasgow
20.03.89 Ian Johnson L PTS 6 Nottingham
24.04.89 Sean Hogg W PTS 6 Glasgow
17.05.89 Des Gargano W PTS 8 Glasgow
09.06.89 Jimmy Bredahl L PTS 6 Aarhus, Denmark
02.10.89 Steve Winstanley L PTS 6 Bradford
20.11.89 Gordon Shaw W RSC 4 Glasgow
22.01.90 Neil Leitch W PTS 8 Glasgow
19.03.90 Joe Donohoe L RSC 3 Glasgow
17.09.90 Peter Judson L PTS 8 Glasgow
08.10.90 Peter Judson L PTS 8 Glasgow
19.11.90 Tony Doyle W PTS 8 Glasgow
27.11.90 Muhammad Shaffique L PTS 8 Glasgow
06.03.91 Neil Leitch W PTS 10 Glasgow
(Vacant Scottish S. Featherweight Title)
01.05.91 Pete Buckley L PTS 8 Solihull
03.06.91 Neil Leitch L PTS 8 Glasgow
23.09.91 Neil Leitch W PTS 10 Glasgow
(Scottish S. Featherweight Title Defence)
09.10.91 Chris Clarkson W PTS 6 Glasgow
20.11.91 Tony Feliciello L RSC 4 Solihull
24.02.92 Colin Innes W PTS 8 Glasgow
18.03.92 Barrie Kelley W PTS 8 Glasgow
19.09.92 Micky Hall W PTS 6 Glasgow
19.10.92 Kevin Lowe W PTS 8 Glasgow
28.11.92 Alan Levene L PTS 6 Manchester
02.04.93 Medhi Labdouni L PTS 8 Fontenay Sous Bois, France
07.06.93 Karl Taylor L PTS 8 Glasgow

Career: 29 contests, won 16, lost 13.

(Dramani) Sugar Gibiliru

Liverpool. *Born* Liverpool, 13 July, 1966
Former British S. Featherweight Champion. Former Undefeated Central Area S. Featherweight & Lightweight Champion. Ht. 5'5½"

Manager Self

30.11.84 Steve Benny L PTS 4 Liverpool
25.01.85 Des Gargano W PTS 4 Liverpool
04.02.85 Martin Power W RTD 3 Liverpool
18.03.85 Des Gargano L PTS 6 Liverpool
29.03.85 Craig Windsor L PTS 6 Liverpool
17.04.85 Carl Gaynor L PTS 6 Nantwich
29.04.85 Carl Gaynor L PTS 6 Liverpool
07.10.85 Martin Power W RSC 4 Liverpool
11.11.85 Nigel Senior W RSC 5 Liverpool
06.12.85 Anthony Brown L PTS 8 Liverpool
24.01.86 Floyd Havard L PTS 6 Muswell Hill
10.03.86 Brian Roche L PTS 8 Manchester
07.04.86 Muhammad Lovelock DREW 8 Manchester
24.05.86 Floyd Havard L PTS 8 Manchester
16.06.86 Brian Roche L PTS 8 Manchester

22.09.86 Carl Crook L PTS 6 Bradford
14.10.86 Muhammad Lovelock DREW 8 Manchester
17.11.86 Simon Eubank L PTS 8 Dulwich
20.11.86 Joey Jacobs L PTS 8 Bredbury
15.12.86 Carl Crook L PTS 8 Bradford
13.01.87 Edward Lloyd L PTS 8 Oldham
24.04.87 Dean Binch W CO 3 Liverpool
15.06.87 Muhammad Lovelock L PTS 8 Manchester
22.09.87 Ray Taylor L PTS 8 Oldham
16.11.87 Robert Harkin DREW 8 Glasgow
05.12.87 Glyn Rhodes L PTS 8 Doncaster
01.03.88 Pat Barrett DREW 8 Manchester
13.04.88 Peter Till L PTS 8 Wolverhampton
28.04.88 Mark Kelly L PTS 8 Manchester
10.09.88 Jean-Charles Meuret L PTS 8 Geneva, Switzerland
28.09.88 Glyn Rhodes DREW 8 Solihull
01.12.88 Mark Kelly L PTS 8 Manchester
14.12.88 Andy Holligan L PTS 8 Kirkby
25.01.89 Ray Taylor L PTS 6 Solihull
11.04.89 Pat Barrett L CO 8 Oldham
(Central Area L. Welterweight Title Challenge)
31.05.89 Tony Banks W CO 5 Manchester
21.06.89 Rudy Valentino L PTS 6 Eltham
19.09.89 Nigel Wenton L PTS 8 Belfast
16.11.89 Tony Foster L PTS 8 Manchester
30.01.90 Tony Foster W PTS 10 Manchester
(Vacant Central Area Lightweight Title)
07.03.90 Peter Gabbitus W RTD 6 Doncaster
(Vacant Central Area S. Featherweight Title)
01.05.90 Mark Reefer L RSC 5 Oldham
(Commonwealth S. Featherweight Title Challenge)
07.07.90 Kris McAdam W PTS 8 Liverpool
19.11.90 Frankie Foster DREW 8 Manchester
17.12.90 Dean Bramhall W PTS 8 Manchester
29.01.91 Nigel Bradley W PTS 8 Stockport
30.04.91 Robert Dickie W RSC 9 Stockport
(British S. Featherweight Title Challenge)
19.09.91 John Doherty L PTS 12 Stockport
(British S. Featherweight Title Defence)
07.12.91 Paul Harvey L PTS 12 Manchester
(Commonwealth S. Featherweight Title Challenge)
31.03.92 Frankie Foster W PTS 8 Stockport
27.06.92 Michael Ayers L RSC 6 Quinta do Lago, Portugal
01.12.92 Ross Hale L RSC 1 Bristol

Career: 52 contests, won 14, drew 7, lost 31.

(Godfrey) G. G. Goddard

Alfreton. *Born* Swaziland, 6 April, 1966
Lightweight. Ht. 5'7"

Manager M. Shinfield

22.11.90 Shaun Hickey W RTD 4 Ilkeston
17.01.91 Paul Chedgzoy W RSC 3 Alfreton
13.05.91 Finn McCool L PTS 6 Northampton
20.05.91 Finn McCool W PTS 6 Bradford
23.10.91 Chubby Martin L PTS 8 Stoke
04.02.92 Kevin Toomey L PTS 6 Alfreton
11.03.92 Micky Hall DREW 6 Solihull
28.04.92 Michael Clynch L RTD 4 Corby
09.07.92 Dave McHale L RTD 4 Glasgow
18.11.92 Ian McGirr L PTS 6 Solihull
23.02.93 John Irwin L RSC 8 Doncaster

25.06.93 Mike Anthony Brown L CO 2 Battersea

Career: 12 contests, won 3, drew 1, lost 8.

Ray Golding

Dulwich. *Born* Birmingham, 27 August, 1966
L. Middleweight. Ht. 6'0"

Manager B. Ingle

09.02.93 Andy Peach W PTS 6 Wolverhampton
19.05.93 David Larkin L PTS 6 Sunderland

Career: 2 contests, won 1, lost 1.

(Valentine) Val Golding

Croydon. *Born* Croydon, 9 May, 1964
Middleweight. Ht. 5'11"

Manager F. Warren

17.07.89 Robbie Harron W RSC 2 Stanmore
05.10.89 Shamus Casey W PTS 6 Stevenage
12.12.89 Neil Munn W RSC 2 Brentford
14.04.90 Ian Strudwick L PTS 6 Kensington
22.09.90 Franki Moro W RSC 6 Kensington
15.10.90 Tod Nadon L RSC 6 Lewisham
04.09.91 Russell Washer W RTD 5 Bethnal Green
29.10.91 Graham Jenner W RSC 3 Kensington
18.01.92 Quinn Paynter L RSC 7 Kensington
26.09.92 Kevin Sheeran L RSC 1 Earls Court

Career: 10 contests, won 6, lost 4.

(Robert) Zak Goldman

Doncaster. *Born* Ainwick, 19 July, 1964
Cruiserweight. Ht. 6'2"

Manager J. Rushton

07.12.92 Paul Hanlon L PTS 6 Birmingham
15.12.92 Kenley Price L RTD 2 Liverpool
09.02.93 Lee Archer L CO 3 Wolverhampton
12.05.93 Steve Loftus L PTS 6 Stoke

Career: 4 contests, lost 4.

Paul Goode

Halifax. *Born* Northampton, 8 September, 1962
Featherweight. Ht. 5'6"

Manager T. Callighan

19.04.93 Tony Smith DREW 6 Manchester
01.06.93 Tony Smith L PTS 6 Manchester

Career: 2 contests, drew 1, lost 1.

Steve Goodwin

Sheffield. *Born* Derby, 17 February, 1966
Midlands Area L. Middleweight Champion. Ht. 5'11"

Manager B. Ingle

13.04.92 John Duckworth W PTS 6 Manchester
29.04.92 John Corcoran W PTS 8 Stoke
03.09.92 Steve McNess L PTS 6 Dunstable
29.09.92 Mark Dawson W RSC 1 Stoke
19.10.92 John Bosco L RSC 2 Mayfair
09.12.92 Mark Dawson L PTS 6 Mayfair
12.02.93 Said Bennajem L PTS 6 Aubervilliers, France
12.05.93 Mark Dawson W PTS 10 Stoke
(Vacant Midlands Area L. Middleweight Title)

Career: 8 contests, won 4, lost 4.

Alan Graham

Newcastle. *Born* Newcastle, 7 October, 1973
Lightweight. Ht. 5'11"
Manager T. Conroy

21.09.92	Garry Burrell L PTS 6 Glasgow
09.11.92	Garry Burrell L PTS 6 Bradford
10.12.92	T. J. Smith W PTS 6 Corby
25.01.93	Leo Turner W PTS 6 Bradford
26.02.93	Mike Deveney L PTS 6 Irvine
22.04.93	Dave Buxton W PTS 6 Bury
06.05.93	John T. Kelly L PTS 6 Hartlepool

Career: 7 contests, won 3, lost 4.

Herol Graham

Sheffield. *Born* Nottingham, 13 September, 1959
Former British & European Middleweight Champion. Former Undefeated British, Commonwealth & European L. Middleweight Champion. Ht. 5'11"
Manager M. Duff

28.11.78	Vivian Waite W PTS 6 Sheffield
04.12.78	Curtis Marsh W RTD 1 Southend
22.01.79	Jimmy Roberts W RSC 2 Bradford
12.02.79	Dave Southwell W PTS 8 Reading
28.02.79	Dave Southwell W PTS 8 Burslem
27.03.79	George Walker W PTS 8 Southend
27.04.79	Mac Nicholson W PTS 8 Newcastle
16.05.79	Gordon George W PTS 8 Sheffield
26.09.79	Lloyd James W PTS 8 Sheffield
27.10.79	Billy Ahearne W RSC 3 Barnsley
27.11.79	Errol McKenzie W PTS 8 Sheffield
12.02.80	Glen McEwan W PTS 8 Sheffield
22.04.80	George Danahar W PTS 8 Sheffield
09.09.80	Joey Mack W PTS 8 Sheffield
30.10.80	Larry Mayes W RSC 4 Liverpool
22.01.81	Lancelot Innes W PTS 10 Liverpool
24.03.81	Pat Thomas W PTS 15 Sheffield
	(British L. Middleweight Title Challenge)
17.06.81	Prince Rodney W RSC 1 Sheffield
25.11.81	Kenny Bristol W PTS 15 Sheffield
	(Commonwealth L. Middleweight Title Challenge)
24.02.82	Chris Christian W RSC 9 Sheffield
	(British & Commonwealth L. Middleweight Title Defence)
22.04.82	Fred Coranson W PTS 10 Liverpool
30.09.82	Hunter Clay W PTS 15 Lagos, Nigeria
	(Commonwealth L. Middleweight Title Defence)
15.03.83	Tony Nelson W RTD 5 Wembley
23.05.83	Clemente Tshinza W CO 2 Sheffield
	(Vacant European L. Middleweight Title)
11.10.83	Carlos Betancourt W CO 1 Kensington
09.12.83	Germain le Maitre W RSC 8 St Nazaire, France
	(European L. Middleweight Title Defence)
22.07.84	Lindell Holmes W RSC 5 Sheffield
25.09.84	Irwin Hines W CO 2 Wembley
16.10.84	Jose Seys W RSC 6 Kensington
26.11.84	Liam Coleman W RSC 3 Sheffield
06.03.85	Jose Rosemain W CO 5 Kensington
24.04.85	Jimmy Price W CO 1 Shoreditch
	(Vacant British Middleweight Title)
16.10.85	Roberto Ruiz W RSC 2 Kensington

03.12.85	Sanderline Williams W PTS 10 Belfast
05.02.86	Ayub Kalule W RSC 10 Sheffield
	(European Middleweight Title Challenge)
23.06.86	Ernie Rabotte W RSC 1 Las Vegas, USA
04.11.86	Mark Kaylor W RTD 8 Wembley
	(European Middleweight Title Defence)
17.01.87	Charlie Boston W RTD 7 Belfast
26.05.87	Sumbu Kalambay L PTS 12 Wembley
	(European Middleweight Title Defence)
05.12.87	Ricky Stackhouse W RSC 8 Doncaster
08.06.88	James Cook W RSC 5 Sheffield
	(Vacant British Middleweight Title)
23.11.88	Johnny Melfah W RSC 5 Bethnal Green
	(British Middleweight Title Defence)
10.05.89	Mike McCallum L PTS 12 Kensington
	(Vacant WBA Middleweight Title)
25.10.89	Rod Douglas W RSC 9 Wembley
	(British Middleweight Title Defence)
11.04.90	Ismael Negron W CO 3 Dewsbury
24.11.90	Julian Jackson L CO 4 Benalmadena, Spain
	(Vacant WBC Middleweight Title)
10.12.91	John Ashton W RSC 6 Sheffield
	(British Middleweight Title Defence)
12.03.92	Sumbu Kalambay L PTS 12 Pesaro, Italy
	European Middleweight Title Challenge)
23.09.92	Frank Grant L RSC 9 Leeds
	(British Middleweight Title Defence)

Career: 49 contests, won 44, lost 5.

John Graham

Paddington. *Born* London, 12 April, 1962
Southern Area Cruiserweight Champion. Ht. 6'1"
Manager D. Powell

18.02.85	Shamus Casey W PTS 6 Mayfair
01.04.85	Paul Gamble W PTS 6 Mayfair
16.06.85	Alan Baptiste W PTS 6 Bethnal Green
28.11.85	Mickey Kidd W PTS 8 Bethnal Green
23.01.86	Bobby Williams W PTS 8 Bethnal Green
29.04.86	Shamus Casey W PTS 8 Piccadilly
16.10.86	Karl Barwise W PTS 6 Merton
15.12.86	Alan Baptiste W PTS 8 Mayfair
12.03.87	Ray Thomas W PTS 8 Piccadilly
09.04.87	Ray Thomas W PTS 8 Bethnal Green
26.10.87	Alan Baptiste W PTS 8 Piccadilly
02.12.87	Dennis Banton W PTS 8 Piccadilly
24.03.88	Chris Galloway W RSC 6 Bethnal Green
21.04.88	Derek Myers DREW 8 Bethnal Green
15.11.88	Abner Blackstock L PTS 8 Chigwell
12.12.88	Peter Brown W RSC 7 Manchester
30.01.90	Serg Fame L RSC 1 Battersea
	(Vacant Southern Area L. Heavyweight Title)
25.04.91	Mike Aubrey W PTS 10 Basildon
	(Vacant Southern Area Cruiserweight Title)
14.11.91	Everton Blake L PTS 10 Bayswater
	(Southern Area Cruiserweight Title Defence)
25.11.92	Everton Blake W PTS 10 Mayfair
	(Southern Area Cruiserweight Title Challenge)

Career: 20 contests, won 16, drew 1, lost 3.

Allan Grainger

Glasgow. *Born* Glasgow, 28 May, 1968
L. Middleweight. Ht. 6'2"
Manager R. Watt

18.03.91	Mick Duncan L PTS 6 Glasgow
09.09.91	Willie Yeardsley W PTS 6 Glasgow
24.10.91	Jim Conley W PTS 6 Glasgow
18.11.91	Mick Duncan L PTS 6 Glasgow
24.02.92	Calum Rattray W RTD 5 Glasgow
04.03.92	Steve Scott W PTS 6 Glasgow
19.10.92	Tony Trimble W PTS 6 Glasgow
29.04.93	Mark Jay L RSC 3 Newcastle

Career: 8 contests, won 5, lost 3.

Derek Grainger

Bethnal Green. *Born* London, 15 May, 1967
Welterweight. Ht. 5'7¾"
Manager T. Lawless

28.01.88	Jim Beckett W PTS 6 Bethnal Green
25.02.88	Richard Thompson W CO 3 Bethnal Green
24.03.88	Glyn Mitchell W RSC 5 Bethnal Green
05.05.88	Frank Mobbs W RSC 2 Bethnal Green
05.10.88	Gerry Beard W PTS 4 Wembley
02.11.88	Gary Dyson W RSC 4 Southwark
30.11.88	Tony Gibbs W CO 3 Southwark
16.03.89	Simon Eubank W RSC 6 Southwark
10.05.89	Ronnie Campbell W RSC 3 Kensington
12.10.89	Barry Messam W CO 1 Southwark
25.10.89	Newton Barnett W PTS 8 Wembley
06.12.89	Young Gully W RSC 3 Wembley
03.03.90	Jerry Smith W RSC 6 Wembley
14.03.90	Ray Taylor W CO 2 Kensington
09.05.90	Newton Barnett W RSC 4 Wembley
31.10.90	Kevin Plant W RSC 4 Wembley
12.12.90	Chris Peters W PTS 8 Kensington
13.02.91	Newton Barnett W RSC 3 Wembley
17.04.91	Humphrey Harrison L RSC 7 Kensington
20.11.91	Chris Blake DREW 8 Kensington
17.12.92	Bozon Haule W RSC 5 Barking
03.02.93	Trevor Meikle W RSC 6 Earls Court
31.03.93	Wayne Shepherd W RSC 4 Barking

Career: 23 contests, won 21, drew 1, lost 1.

Marvin P. Gray

Stanley. *Born* Flint Hill, 14 December, 1965
L. Welterweight. Ht. 5'9"
Manager Self

27.03.85	Kris McAdam L RSC 3 Gateshead
30.04.85	Paul Dawson L PTS 6 Merton
04.06.85	Nicky Day L PTS 6 Streatham
26.06.85	Mickey Hull L PTS 8 Basildon
03.09.85	Anthony Wakefield W RSC 4 Gateshead
10.09.85	Chubby Martin W PTS 6 Southend
08.10.85	Willie MacDonald W PTS 6 Preston
31.10.85	Mike Whalley DREW 8 Manchester
21.11.85	Patrick Loftus L PTS 6 Hartlepool
30.01.86	Andrew Furlong L PTS 6 Merton
19.03.86	Tony Richards L PTS 6 Solihull
01.04.86	Keith Parry L RSC 4 Leeds
08.05.86	Doug Munro W PTS 8 Newcastle
20.05.86	Dean Marsden L PTS 2 Huddersfield
22.09.86	Paul Timmins W PTS 6 Edgbaston
16.10.86	Willie Wilson W PTS 8 Newcastle
13.11.86	Ernie Noble W PTS 6 Huddersfield
29.11.86	Floyd Harvard L RSC 2 Wandsworth

02.03.87	Willie Wilson W PTS 8 Marton
18.03.87	Mark Pearce W PTS 8 Solihull
30.04.87	Rudy Valentino L PTS 6 Washington
28.05.87	Carl Gaynor W PTS 6 Jarrow
07.06.87	Kevin Spratt L PTS 8 Bradford
15.09.87	Paul Burke W RSC 6 Batley
24.09.87	Peter Bradley W PTS 8 Glasgow
07.10.87	Carl Crook L PTS 8 Burnley
10.11.87	James Jiora W PTS 8 Batley
26.11.87	Carl Crook L PTS 8 Horwich
15.12.87	Kevin Spratt L RSC 6 Bradford
26.01.88	Jeff Connors L PTS 10 Hartlepool
	(Vacant Northern Area L.
	Welterweight Title)
24.02.88	Glyn Rhodes L RSC 1 Sheffield
29.11.89	Chris McReedy W PTS 6 Marton
05.03.90	Paul Charters L PTS 10 Northampton
	(Vacant Northern Area Lightweight
	Title)
21.04.90	Tony Foster DREW 6 Sunderland
22.05.90	Tony Foster W PTS 6 Stockton
10.08.90	Guillermo Mosquera L PTS 6 Naples,
	Italy
24.09.90	Ian Honeywood L PTS 8 Lewisham
15.10.90	Alan Hall L RSC 2 Lewisham
29.11.90	James Jiora W PTS 8 Marton
28.02.91	Rick Bushell W PTS 6 Sunderland
10.03.91	Alain Simoes L PTS 8 Paris, France
15.05.91	Giovanni Parisi L RSC 6 Montichiari,
	Italy
25.11.91	Andreas Panayi L PTS 8 Liverpool
06.02.92	Dave Pierre L RSC 7 Peterborough
27.10.92	Michael Driscoll L PTS 8 Leicester
19.03.93	Tony Ekubia L RSC 2 Manchester

Career: 46 contests, won 17, drew 2, lost 27.

Darron Griffiths

Cardiff. *Born* Pontypridd, 11 February, 1972
Middleweight. Welsh S. Middleweight Champion. Ht. 6'0"
Manager B. Aird

26.11.90	Colin Ford DREW 6 Mayfair
04.12.90	Kevin Adamson W RSC 4 Southend
23.01.91	Tony Booth DREW 6 Stoke
06.03.91	Barry Messam W PTS 6 Croydon
10.04.91	John Kaighin W PTS 6 Newport
25.04.91	Michael Graham W RSC 2 Mayfair
02.05.91	Carlton Myers W RTD 5 Kensington
21.10.91	John Ogiste W PTS 6 Mayfair
11.12.91	Adrian Wright W PTS 6 Stoke
22.01.92	Richard Okumu W RSC 8 Solihull
17.02.92	John Ogiste W RSC 5 Mayfair
29.04.92	Colin Manners DREW 8 Solihull
30.09.92	Colin Manners W PTS 10 Solihull
	(Elim. British Middleweight Title)
28.10.92	Antonio Fernandez W PTS 10 Cardiff
	(Elim. British Middleweight Title)
24.03.93	John Kaighin W RSC 6 Cardiff
	(Vacant Welsh S. Middleweight Title)

Career: 15 contests, won 12, drew 3.

Kurt Griffiths

Gilfach Goch. *Born* Bridgend, 16 February, 1970
Featherweight. Ht. 5'7"
Manager D. Gardiner

09.06.93	Mark Bowers L RSC 1 Lewisham

Career: 1 contest, lost 1.

Bobby Guynan

East Ham. *Born* Plaistow, 4 July, 1967
Lightweight. Ht. 5'9"
Manager B. Hearn

17.10.90	John O'Meara W RTD 2 Bethnal Green
26.11.90	Lee Fox L PTS 6 Bethnal Green
06.02.91	Lee Fox W PTS 6 Bethnal Green
26.03.91	Lee Fox L RTD 3 Bethnal Green
10.11.92	Mark Allen W RSC 2 Dagenham
30.01.93	Shaun Shinkwin W PTS 6 Brentwood
20.04.93	Norman Dhalie W PTS 6 Brentwood
26.06.93	Mike Morrison L PTS 4 Earls Court

Career: 8 contests, won 5, lost 3.

Nigel Haddock　　　　　　Les Clark

Nigel Haddock

Llanelli. *Born* Llanelli, 8 August, 1966
S. Featherweight. Ht. 5'5½"
Manager G. Davies

13.02.86	Paul Timmons L PTS 6 Digbeth
26.03.86	Paul Parry W PTS 6 Swansea
10.04.86	Ginger Staples W PTS 6 Weston super
	Mare
23.04.86	Nigel Senior W PTS 6 Stoke
19.05.86	Nigel Senior DREW 6 Nottingham
03.06.86	Albert Masih W RTD 3 Fulham
30.07.86	Tony Rahman W RSC 2 Ebbw Vale
01.10.86	Wayne Weekes L PTS 6 Lewisham
29.10.86	Nigel Senior W PTS 6 Ebbw Vale
26.11.86	Mark Reefer L RTD 3 Lewisham
15.04.87	Ginger Staples W RSC 5 Carmarthen
19.10.87	Gary Maxwell L PTS 8 Nottingham
05.11.87	John Maloney W RTD 4 Bethnal
	Green
18.11.87	Richie Foster W RSC 7 Bethnal Green
20.04.88	Patrick Kamy W PTS 6 Muswell Hill
02.11.88	Freddy Cruz L PTS 8 Paola, Italy
26.11.88	Maurizio Stecca L RTD 2 Forli, Italy
11.12.89	John Naylor W RSC 5 Nottingham
14.03.90	Kevin Pritchard DREW 6 Stoke
22.04.90	Ditau Molefyane L PTS 10 Spings,
	South Africa
30.03.93	Edward Lloyd W RTD 4 Cardiff

Career: 21 contests, won 12, drew 2, lost 7.

(Kevin) Kevin Haidarah (James)

Manchester. *Born* Manchester, 24 April, 1969
S. Featherweight. Ht. 5'7"
Manager P. Martin

19.03.93	Fred Reeve L RSC 2 Manchester

Career: 1 contest, lost 1.

Mark Hale

Nuneaton. *Born* Nuneaton, 13 October, 1969
S. Middleweight. Ht. 5'11"
Manager J. Griffin

07.10.91	Andy Manning L PTS 6 Liverpool
07.11.91	Marc Rowley W PTS 6 Peterborough
15.01.92	Paul Murray W PTS 6 Stoke
25.03.92	Marc Rowley W PTS 6 Hinckley
11.05.92	Martin Jolley L PTS 6 Coventry
21.05.92	Tony Colclough DREW 6 Cradley
	Heath
01.06.92	Tony Colclough L PTS 6 Solihull
05.10.92	Martin Jolley L RSC 4 Bardon
16.03.93	Andrew Flute L RSC 2
	Wolverhampton
11.05.93	Earl Ling W RSC 2 Norwich

Career: 10 contests, won 4, drew 1, lost 5.

Ross Hale

Bristol. *Born* Bristol, 28 February, 1967
L. Welterweight. Western Area Welterweight Champion. Ht. 5'9"
Manager C. Sanigar

16.11.89	Dave Jenkins W PTS 6 Weston super
	Mare
30.11.89	Tony Gibbs W PTS 6 Mayfair
12.12.89	Chris McReedy W RSC 4 Brentford
13.03.90	Davey Hughes W RSC 3 Bristol
30.04.90	Andy Robins W RSC 4 Bristol
12.09.90	Derrick Daniel W PTS 6 Bethnal
	Green
21.11.90	Mark Kelly W PTS 8 Chippenham
29.11.90	Chris Saunders W PTS 6 Bayswater
24.10.91	Greg Egbuniwe W RSC 4 Bayswater
22.01.92	Tony Borg W PTS 6 Cardiff
30.04.92	Jason Matthews W RSC 3 Bayswater
12.05.92	John Smith W CO 1 Crystal Palace
07.07.92	Julian Eavis W RSC 8 Bristol
	(Vacant Western Area Welterweight
	Title)
05.10.92	Malcolm Melvin W PTS 10 Bristol
	(Elim. British L. Welterweight Title)
01.12.92	Sugar Gibiliru W RSC 1 Bristol
27.01.93	Andreas Panayi L RSC 3 Cardiff
26.06.93	Mark Antony W RSC 1 Keynsham

Career: 17 contests, won 16, lost 1.

Alan Hall

Darlington. *Born* Darlington, 16 November, 1969
L. Welterweight. Ht. 5'8"
Manager F. Maloney

10.10.89	Saturnin Cabanas W RSC 2 Hull
08.12.89	John Smith W RSC 2 Doncaster
22.02.90	Muhammad Lovelock W RSC 1 Hull
21.04.90	Darren Mount W PTS 6 Sunderland
09.05.90	George Jones W RSC 1 Kensington
22.05.90	Mohamed Ouhmad W PTS 6 Stockton
15.10.90	Marvin P. Gray W RSC 2 Lewisham

31.10.90 Gino de Leon W RSC 1 Crystal Palace
02.03.91 Steve Pollard W PTS 6 Darlington
06.04.91 Alan Peacock W PTS 6 Darlington
11.06.91 Abram Gumede W PTS 8 Leicester
25.04.92 Michael Driscoll W PTS 6 Manchester
25.06.92 Russell Mosley W PTS 6 San Diego, USA
11.07.92 Steve Barreras L RSC 5 Las Vegas, USA
17.09.92 Dave Pierre W PTS 10 Watford
(*Elim. British L. Welterweight Title*)
14.01.93 Tony Foster W PTS 6 Mayfair
Career: 16 contests, won 15, lost 1.

Micky Hall
Ludworth. *Born* Ludworth, 23 April, 1967
Lightweight. Ht. 5'8"
Manager T. Conroy

03.03.92 Mick Holmes W RSC 2 Houghton le Spring
11.03.92 G. G. Goddard DREW 6 Solihull
28.04.92 Jamie Davidson L PTS 6 Houghton le Spring
19.09.92 Mark Geraghty L PTS 6 Glasgow
12.10.92 Leo Turner W RSC 5 Bradford
18.11.92 Alan Ingle W RSC 3 Solihull
09.03.93 Kevin McKenzie L PTS 6 Hartlepool
17.04.93 John T. Kelly DREW 4 Washington
06.05.93 Brian Wright W PTS 6 Hartlepool
01.06.93 Kevin McKillan L PTS 6 Manchester
Career: 10 contests, won 4, drew 2, lost 4.

Simon Hamblett
Walsall. *Born* Walsall, 10 October, 1966
L. Welterweight. Ht. 5'8"
Manager W. Tyler

24.02.92 Jamie Morris DREW 6 Coventry
11.03.92 Mark Antony L CO 1 Stoke
09.12.92 Mark Allen DREW 6 Stoke
09.02.93 Mark Allen L PTS 6 Wolverhampton
23.02.93 Mark Allen W PTS 6 Doncaster
19.04.93 Kevin McKillan L CO 2 Manchester
07.06.93 Robbie Sivyer L PTS 6 Walsall
Career: 7 contests, won 1, drew 2, lost 4.

Prince Nassem Hamed
Sheffield. *Born* Sheffield, 12 February, 1974
Bantamweight. Ht. 5'3"
Manager B. Ingle

14.04.92 Ricky Beard W CO 2 Mansfield
25.04.92 Shaun Norman W RSC 2 Manchester
23.05.92 Andrew Bloomer W RSC 2 Birmingham
14.07.92 Miguel Matthews W RSC 3 Mayfair
07.10.92 Des Gargano W RSC 4 Sunderland
12.11.92 Pete Buckley W PTS 6 Liverpool
24.02.93 Alan Ley W CO 2 Wembley
26.05.93 Kevin Jenkins W RSC 3 Mansfield
Career: 8 contests, won 8.

Paul Hanlon
Birmingham. *Born* Birmingham, 25 May, 1962
L. Heavyweight. Ht. 5'11"
Manager Self

18.11.86 Kevin Roper L RTD 5 Swansea
18.03.87 Tony Behan L PTS 4 Stoke
28.06.90 David Radford L RSC 2 Birmingham

18.09.90 Gary Osborne L RTD 2 Wolverhampton
17.10.90 Mike Betts L RTD 2 Stoke
04.03.91 Tony Behan L PTS 6 Birmingham
18.03.91 Willy James W CO 1 Derby
10.04.91 Lee Prudden L PTS 6 Wolverhampton
24.04.91 Dean Allen L PTS 6 Aberavon
13.05.91 Lee Prudden L PTS 6 Birmingham
23.05.91 Lee Prudden W PTS 6 Southampton
10.06.91 Jason Frieze W RSC 2 Manchester
10.09.91 Richard Carter L RSC 3 Wolverhampton
22.01.92 Lee Prudden W RSC 4 Stoke
20.02.92 Glen Payton L PTS 6 Oakengates
27.04.92 Joey Peters L CO 2 Mayfair
21.09.92 Tim Robinson W PTS 6 Cleethorpes
05.10.92 John J. Cooke L RSC 1 Bardon
24.11.92 Chris Nurse W PTS 6 Wolverhampton
07.12.92 Zak Goldman W PTS 6 Birmingham
10.02.93 Mark Baker L RSC 2 Lewisham
08.06.93 Martin Jolley L PTS 6 Derby
Career: 22 contests, won 7, lost 15.

Anthony Hanna   Les Clark

Anthony Hanna
Birmingham. *Born* Birmingham, 22 September, 1974
Flyweight. Ht. 5'6"
Manager N. Nobbs

19.11.92 Nick Tooley L PTS 6 Evesham
10.12.92 Darren Fifield L RSC 6 Bethnal Green
11.05.93 Tiger Singh W PTS 6 Norwich
24.05.93 Lyndon Kershaw L PTS 6 Bradford
Career: 4 contests, won 1, lost 3.

Chris Harbourne
Birmingham. *Born* Birmingham, 24 November, 1962
Cruiserweight. Ht. 6'3¾"
Manager Self

10.10.84 Alex Romeo W PTS 6 Stoke
26.10.84 Alex Romeo W PTS 6 Wolverhampton
24.03.86 Gypsy Carman L PTS 6 Mayfair

10.04.86 Dave Shelton W CO 1 Leicester
17.04.86 Tommy Taylor L PTS 6 Wolverhampton
28.09.87 Gary McConnell W RSC 3 Dulwich
12.10.87 Jess Harding L RSC 4 Mayfair
15.02.88 Eric Cardouza L PTS 6 Mayfair
02.02.89 Deka Williams W PTS 6 Wolverhampton
01.05.93 Zelko Mavrovic L RSC 1 Berlin, Germany
08.06.93 Johnny Moth DREW 6 Derby
Career: 11 contests, won 5, drew 1, lost 5.

Fran Harding
Liverpool. *Born* Liverpool, 5 September, 1966
S. Middleweight. Ht. 6'0½"
Manager P. Martin

27.07.87 Johnny Taupau W PTS 6 Sydney, Australia
04.05.88 B. K. Bennett W RSC 1 Wembley
14.12.88 Steve Foster W PTS 6 Kirkby
04.05.90 Quinn Paynter W PTS 6 Liverpool
30.09.91 Lee Crocker W RSC 3 Kensington
25.09.92 Terry Magee W PTS 6 Liverpool
23.10.92 Shamus Casey W PTS 6 Liverpool
20.11.92 Marvin O'Brien W RSC 4 Liverpool
Career: 8 contests, won 8.

John Harewood
Newcastle. *Born* Ipswich, 23 February, 1964
Heavyweight. Ht. 6'3½"
Manager J. Spensley

29.11.90 Carlton Headley W RSC 5 Marton
06.04.91 Clifton Mitchell L RSC 2 Darlington
01.08.91 Clifton Mitchell L CO 1 Dewsbury
05.03.92 J. A. Bugner L PTS 4 Battersea
27.05.92 Freddy Soentgen L PTS 6 Cologne, Germany
07.10.92 Gary Charlton W PTS 6 Sunderland
30.10.92 Clement Salles W RSC 4 Istres, France
17.12.92 Dermot Gascoyne L RSC 5 Barking
02.02.93 Wayne Buck W RSC 3 Derby
20.03.93 Bernd Friedrich L RSC 4 Dusseldorf, Germany
19.05.93 Vance Idiens W CO 3 Sunderland
26.05.93 Clifton Mitchell L RSC 4 Mansfield
29.06.93 Scott Welch L RSC 5 Mayfair
Career: 13 contests, won 5, lost 8.

Mark Hargreaves
Burnley. *Born* Burnley, 13 September, 1970
Featherweight. Ht. 5'4"
Manager N. Basso

11.09.91 Dave Campbell W RSC 4 Stoke
23.10.91 Dave Martin W PTS 6 Stoke
10.02.92 Dennis Oakes L RSC 3 Liverpool
30.03.92 Ronnie Stephenson L PTS 6 Coventry
27.04.92 Ady Benton L PTS 6 Bradford
01.06.92 Des Gargano W PTS 6 Manchester
11.09.92 Shaun Anderson L PTS 6 Glasgow
07.10.92 Mike Deveney W RSC 7 Glasgow
14.10.92 Yusuf Vorajee W RSC 4 Stoke
19.11.92 Greg Upton W RSC 3 Evesham
28.11.92 John White L PTS 4 Manchester
20.01.93 John Irwin L RSC 4 Solihull
26.04.93 Mario Culpeper L PTS 6 Manchester
01.06.93 Paul Wynn W PTS 6 Manchester
Career: 14 contests, won 7, lost 7.

Carl Harney

Manchester. *Born* Manchester, 24 June, 1970
Middleweight. Ht. 6'1"

17.10.89 Shamus Casey W PTS 4 Oldham
18.10.90 Michael Clarke W PTS 6 Wandsworth
22.02.91 Mike Phillips L RSC 5 Manchester
31.05.91 Marvin OBrien L RSC 5 Manchester
29.05.92 Matthew Jones W RSC 6 Manchester
18.07.92 John Kaighin W PTS 6 Manchester
05.02.93 Gilbert Jackson L CO 3 Manchester
Career: 7 contests, won 4, lost 3.

Danny Harper

Barnsley. *Born* Barnsley, 18 October, 1967
Welterweight. Ht. 5'9½"
Manager K. Tate

14.09.92 Steve Scott DREW 6 Bradford
12.11.92 Frank Harrington W PTS 6 Burnley
27.01.93 Sean Baker L PTS 6 Cardiff
08.03.93 Chris Mulcahy W PTS 8 Leeds
Career: 4 contests, won 2, drew 1, lost 1.

Frank Harrington

Lancaster. Born Glasgow, 1 October, 1961
Welterweight. Ht. 5'7"
Manager J. Doughty

21.04.86 Michael Betts W RSC 3 Bradford
12.05.86 Steve Harwood W CO 4 Manchester
19.05.86 Eamonn Payne L CO 3 Bradford
29.09.86 Rocky Lester W PTS 6 Loughborough
26.02.87 Brian Wareing L CO 2 Hartlepool
13.06.87 Wayne Goult W PTS 6 Great Yarmouth
07.10.87 Joe Janny W RSC 3 Burnley
26.11.87 Tony Connellan L PTS 6 Horwich
16.12.87 John Reid L PTS 6 Manchester
18.01.88 Pat Durkin W PTS 4 Bradford
29.01.88 Mike McKenzie W PTS 6 Durham
09.02.88 David Binns W RSC 2 Bradford
10.03.88 Owen Smith W RSC 1 Glasgow
26.09.88 Gerry Beard L RTD 6 Leicester
30.01.89 Julian Eavis L PTS 6 Leicester
14.02.89 Dave Kettlewell W PTS 6 Sunderland
21.05.90 Trevor Meikle L PTS 6 Hanley
23.04.91 Steve McGovern L PTS 6 Evesham
05.05.92 Crain Fisher L RSC 4 Preston
12.11.92 Danny Harper L PTS 6 Burnley
28.06.93 Colin Sinnott L RSC 6 Morecambe
Career: 21 contests, won 10, lost 11.

Peter Harris

Swansea. *Born* Swansea, 23 August, 1962
Former British & Welsh Featherweight
Champion. Ht. 5'6½"
Manager C. Breen

28.02.83 Dave Pratt L PTS 6 Birmingham
25.04.83 Jim Harvey DREW 6 Aberdeen
27.05.83 Brett Styles W PTS 8 Swansea
20.06.83 Danny Knaggs W PTS 6 Piccadilly
19.12.83 Kevin Howard W PTS 8 Swansea
06.02.84 Ivor Jones W PTS 8 Swansea
27.03.84 Johnny Dorey W RSC 6 Bethnal Green
13.06.84 Keith Wallace W PTS 10 Aberavon
28.09.84 Ray Minus L PTS 10 Nassau, Bahamas
21.11.84 John Farrell L PTS 8 Solihull
20.03.85 Kid Sumali W PTS 8 Solihull
09.05.85 John Feeney L PTS 10 Warrington

09.11.85 Antoine Montero L PTS 10 Grenoble, France
26.03.86 Steve Pollard W RSC 3 Swansea
22.04.86 Roy Webb W RTD 8 Belfast
18.11.86 Kelvin Smart W PTS 10 Swansea (*Vacant Welsh Featherweight Title*)
30.04.87 Albert Parr W RSC 3 Newport
30.09.87 John Farrell W PTS 12 Solihull (*Final Elim. British Featherweight Title*)
15.12.87 Roy Williams W RSC 2 Cardiff
24.02.88 Kevin Taylor W PTS 12 Aberavon (*Vacant British Featherweight Title*)
18.05.88 Paul Hodkinson L RSC 12 Aberavon (*British Featherweight Title Defence*)
06.09.89 Paul Hodkinson L RSC 9 Aberavon (*British & European Featherweight Title Challenge*)
24.04.91 Colin Lynch W PTS 8 Aberavon
18.07.91 Steve Robinson L PTS 10 Cardiff (*Welsh Featherweight Title Defence*)
05.06.92 Stephane Haccoun L PTS 8 Marseille, France
22.12.92 Paul Harvey L PTS 8 Mayfair
Career: 26 contests, won 14, drew 2, lost 10.

Simon Harris

Hanwell. *Born* Isleworth, 26 December, 1961
L. Heavyweight. Ht. 5'11"
Manager Self

28.09.84 Douglas Isles W RSC 2 Longford
23.10.84 Ronnie Fraser W RSC 6 Battersea
20.11.84 Harry Andrews W RSC 2 Merton
30.11.84 Gordon Stacey W CO 2 Longford
05.02.85 Sean O'Phoenix W PTS 6 Battersea
23.03.85 Lou Gent W PTS 6 Strand
04.05.85 Geoff Rymer W PTS 6 Queensway
20.09.85 Dave Owens L PTS 6 Longford
10.11.86 John Williams W PTS 6 Longford
21.11.86 Lee Davis W RSC 3 Maidenhead
03.12.86 Tony Wilson L RTD 6 Muswell Hill
29.11.88 Alan Baptiste W RSC 4 Battersea
29.01.91 Richard Bustin W RSC 3 Wisbech
03.07.91 Nicky Piper L RSC 1 Reading
11.02.92 Gary Delaney DREW 8 Barking
14.04.93 Steve McCarthy W RSC 5 Kensington
Career: 16 contests, won 12, drew 1, lost 3.

Paul Harvey

Ilford. *Born* Islington, 10 November, 1964
Featherweight. Former Commonwealth S.
Featherweight Champion. Ht. 5'8"
Manager B. Hearn

04.10.89 Steve Walker DREW 6 Basildon
16.01.90 Darren Weller W RSC 6 Cardiff
06.03.90 James Milne W RSC 6 Bethnal Green
03.04.90 James Hunter W CO 2 Canvey Island
23.04.90 Marvin Stone W PTS 6 Crystal Palace
20.06.90 Brian Robb W PTS 6 Basildon
24.10.90 Brian Robb W RSC 2 Dudley
12.12.90 Miguel Matthews W PTS 6 Basildon
09.04.91 Alan McKay W RSC 4 Mayfair
24.04.91 Peter Gabbitus W RSC 5 Preston
26.10.91 Colin Lynch W RSC 1 Brentwood
12.11.91 Hugh Forde W RSC 3 Wolverhampton (*Commonwealth S. Featherweight Title Challenge*)
07.12.91 Sugar Gibiliru W PTS 12 Manchester (*Commonwealth S. Featherweight Title Defence*)

11.02.92 Tony Pep L PTS 12 Cardiff (*Commonwealth S. Featherweight Title Defence*)
02.06.92 Regilio Tuur L CO 5 Rotterdam, Holland
13.10.92 Brian Robb W RSC 2 Mayfair
22.12.92 Peter Harris W PTS 8 Mayfair
19.01.93 Steve Robinson L PTS 12 Cardiff (*Vacant WBA Penta-Continental Featherweight Title*)
19.05.93 Kelton McKenzie W RSC 7 Leicester
Career: 19 contests, won 15, drew 1, lost 3.

Bozon Haule

Woolwich. *Born* Tanzania, 4 February, 1961
L. Middleweight. Ht. 5'7"
Manager Self

03.10.87 Niyazi Aytekin DREW 6 Stukenbrock, Germany
31.10.87 Eric Taton W PTS 6 Paderborn, Germany
09.01.88 Klaus Hein W RSC 3 Helmstedt, Germany
16.01.88 Charles Small W PTS 6 Lubeck, Germany
19.02.88 Senturk Ozdemir W RTD 5 Berlin, Germany
05.03.88 Konrad Mittermeier W RSC 3 Karlsruhe, Germany
19.03.88 Antonio Nunez Diaz W RTD 4 Hamm, Germany
23.04.88 Michel Simeon W PTS 8 Korbach, Germany
29.06.88 Tony Bawa W RSC 7 Hamburg, Germany
15.10.88 Pascal Lorcy W RSC 7 St Nazaire, France
17.02.89 Ferdinand Pachler L PTS 10 Vienna, Austria
03.04.89 Joni Nyman W CO 1 Helsinki, Finland
19.12.90 Tim Burgess L PTS 12 Glasgow
11.05.91 Oscar Checa L RSC 1 Belfast
24.09.91 Gordon Blair L RSC 8 Glasgow
23.04.92 Dave Brosnan W RSC 6 Eltham
17.09.92 Danny Shinkwin DREW 6 Watford
19.10.92 Leigh Wicks L PTS 8 Mayfair
01.12.92 Damien Denny L PTS 6 Bristol
17.12.92 Derek Grainger L RSC 5 Barking
17.02.93 Kirkland Laing L RSC 3 Bethnal Green
Career: 21 contests, won 11, drew 2, lost 8.

Steve Hearn

High Wycombe. *Born* Luton, 2 December, 1966
L. Welterweight. Ht. 5'8½"
Manager Self

12.05.89 Victor Wasley L PTS 6 Broadmeadow, Australia
06.12.89 Brax Burley L RSC 5 Cardiff, Australia
26.11.90 Felix Kelly L RSC 3 Bethnal Green
06.02.91 Trevor Royal DREW 6 Battersea
01.05.91 Rick Dimmock W PTS 6 Bethnal Green
26.11.91 Paul Knights L RSC 4 Bethnal Green
12.02.92 Nicky Bardle L RSC 1 Watford
29.10.92 Shaun Shinkwin L PTS 6 Hayes
Career: 8 contests, won 1, drew 1, lost 6.

Ian Henry

Newcastle. *Born* Gateshead, 8 May, 1967
L. Heavyweight. Ht. 6'1½"
Manager T. Conroy

26.04.90	Willy James W RSC 3 Manchester	
15.05.90	Mark Whitehouse W RSC 4 South Shields	
24.09.90	Paul Hendrick L PTS 6 Manchester	
19.11.90	Shaun McCrory W PTS 6 Manchester	
14.12.90	Eddie Collins W PTS 6 Peterborough	
21.01.91	Shaun McCrory W PTS 6 Glasgow	
28.01.91	Simon McDougall L PTS 8 Bradford	
18.03.91	Ian Vokes W RSC 2 Manchester	
25.03.91	Dave Lawrence W PTS 6 Bradford	
10.05.91	Simon McDougall W PTS 6 Gateshead	
10.10.91	Chris Walker W PTS 6 Gateshead	
14.11.91	Dave Owens W PTS 8 Gateshead	
27.11.91	John Oxenham W PTS 6 Marton	
11.03.92	Simon McDougall W PTS 8 Solihull	
05.05.92	Glenn Campbell L RSC 1 Preston	
23.10.92	Lee Archer W RTD 1 Gateshead	
01.03.93	Lee Prudden W PTS 6 Bradford	
17.03.93	Lee Archer L PTS 6 Stoke	
11.06.93	Art Stacey W PTS 6 Gateshead	

Career: 19 contests, won 15, lost 4.

Noel Henry

Hinckley. *Born* Newham, 25 October, 1968
Welterweight. Ht. 5'5¾"
Manager J. Griffin

16.10.91	Eddie King W CO 2 Stoke
28.10.91	Wayne Shepherd L PTS 6 Leicester
11.12.91	Lee Ferrie L RSC 5 Leicester
29.04.93	Shaun Shinkwin L PTS 6 Hayes
06.05.93	Dave Fallon L PTS 6 Bayswater

Career: 5 contests, won 1, lost 4.

Marcel Herbert

Newport. *Born* Cardiff, 3 March, 1965
L. Welterweight. Ht. 5'8½"
Manager Self

19.08.89	Steve Robinson W PTS 6 Cardiff
06.09.89	Miguel Matthews W PTS 6 Aberavon
14.09.89	Jimmy Clark L PTS 4 Basildon
25.09.89	Mike Close W PTS 6 Leicester
11.10.89	Colin McMillan L PTS 6 Millwall
13.11.89	Jari Gronroos W RSC 6 Helsinki, Finland
01.12.89	Frankie Dewinter W PTS 6 Ostend, Belgium
27.02.90	Tony Feliciello W CO 4 Evesham
06.04.90	Dean Hollington L PTS 6 Stevenage
15.06.90	Tony Foster W RSC 4 Telford
15.12.90	Jean-Pierre Seigliano DREW 8 Vichy, France
10.04.91	Rudy Valentino L RSC 3 Newport *(Elim. British Lightweight Title)*
01.06.91	Carlos Chase L PTS 6 Bethnal Green
20.11.91	Billy Schwer L PTS 8 Kensington
18.06.92	Gary Barron L PTS 6 Peterborough
28.09.92	Paul Burke L PTS 6 Manchester
29.04.93	Carl Wright L PTS 8 Mayfair

Career: 17 contests, won 7, drew 1, lost 9.

Brian Hickey

Sheffield. *Born* Sheffield, 24 February, 1973
Lightweight. Ht. 5'9"
Manager B. Ingle

21.11.91	Tony Doyle L PTS 6 Ilkeston
06.02.92	Michael Clynch L DIS 5 Peterborough
21.10.92	Dean Amory L PTS 6 Stoke
12.11.92	Floyd Churchill L CO 1 Liverpool
27.02.93	Gary Thornhill L CO 4 Ellesmere Port

Career: 5 contests, lost 5.

Tim Hill

North Shields. *Born* North Shields, 23 January, 1974
Lightweight. Ht. 5'9"
Manager T. Conroy

09.11.92	Fred Reeve W CO 4 Bradford
25.01.93	Michael Alexander L PTS 6 Bradford
22.02.93	Garry Burrell W PTS 6 Glasgow
29.03.93	Hugh Collins L PTS 6 Glasgow

Career: 4 contests, won 2, lost 2.

Dean Hiscox

Dudley. *Born* Dudley, 15 January, 1969
Welterweight. Ht. 5'8"
Manager Self

06.10.88	Dave Croft W PTS 6 Dudley
14.05.91	Eddie King L PTS 6 Dudley
05.06.91	Eddie King L PTS 6 Wolverhampton
21.11.91	Chris Aston L PTS 6 Stafford
02.12.91	Steve Bricknell W PTS 6 Birmingham
17.03.92	Mark Legg L PTS 6 Wolverhampton
18.05.92	Craig Hartwell W PTS 6 Bardon
13.10.92	Rob Stevenson W PTS 6 Wolverhampton
12.11.92	Peter Reid L PTS 6 Stafford
02.12.92	Darren McInulty DREW 6 Bardon
03.03.93	Jonathan Thaxton L PTS 6 Solihull
17.03.93	Dave Whittle L PTS 6 Stoke

Career: 12 contests, won 4, drew 1, lost 7.

Gary Hiscox

Dudley. *Born* Dudley, 25 May, 1970
L. Welterweight. Ht. 5'7¾"
Manager C. Flute

14.10.92	Alan Ingle L PTS 6 Stoke
12.11.92	Shane Sheridan W PTS 6 Stafford
27.01.93	Dave Madden W PTS 6 Stoke
03.03.93	Erwin Edwards W PTS 6 Solihull
26.06.93	Mark Tibbs L RSC 4 Earls Court

Career: 5 contests, won 3, lost 2.

Paul Hitch

Wingate. *Born* Hartlepool, 7 May, 1968
S. Middleweight. Ht. 5'9½"
Manager T. Conroy

10.05.91	Tony Kosova W RTD 1 Gateshead
13.05.91	Terry Johnson W PTS 6 Marton
17.06.91	Max McCracken W PTS 6 Edgbaston
22.10.91	Chris Walker W PTS 6 Hartlepool
14.11.91	Paul Burton W CO 2 Gateshead
12.12.91	Doug Calderwood W PTS 6 Hartlepool
03.03.92	Simon McDougall W PTS 6 Houghton le Spring
28.04.92	Chris Walker L RSC 2 Houghton le Spring
10.09.92	Griff Jones W RSC 2 Sunderland
23.10.92	Paul Burton W RSC 5 Gateshead
06.03.93	Bobby Mack W PTS 6 Glasgow
17.04.93	Richard Bustin L PTS 6 Washington

Career: 12 contests, won 10, lost 2.

Mick Hoban (Massie)

Glasgow. *Born* Burnley, 25 July, 1967
L. Welterweight. Ht. 5'9"
Manager J. Doughty

19.04.89	Steve Booth L PTS 6 Doncaster
13.10.92	Danny Kett W PTS 6 Bury
07.12.92	Lee Soar W PTS 6 Manchester
15.02.93	Brian Wright W PTS 6 Manchester
28.06.93	Michael Alexander L PTS 6 Morecambe

Career: 5 contests, won 3, lost 2.

Paul Hodkinson

Liverpool. *Born* Liverpool, 14 September, 1965
Former WBC Featherweight Champion.
Former Undefeated British & European
Featherweight Champion. Ht 5'4"
Manager Self

19.07.86	Mark Champney W CO 2 Wembley
17.09.86	Phil Lashley W RSC 2 Kensington
29.09.86	Les Remikie W RTD 4 Mayfair
29.10.86	Craig Windsor W CO 2 Belfast
17.01.87	Steve Sammy Sims W CO 5 Belfast
26.02.87	Kamel Djadda W RSC 4 Bethnal Green
25.04.87	Russell Jones W RSC 6 Belfast
31.07.87	Tomas Arguelles DREW 8 Panama City, Panama
19.10.87	Tomas Arguelles W CO 6 Belfast
03.12.87	Marcus Smith W RSC 7 Belfast
27.01.88	Richie Foster W RSC 3 Belfast
18.05.88	Peter Harris W RSC 12 Aberavon *(British Featherweight Title Challenge)*
14.12.88	Kevin Taylor W RSC 2 Kirkby *(British Featherweight Title Defence)*
18.01.89	Johnny Carter W CO 1 Kensington
12.04.89	Raymond Armand W RSC 2 Belfast *(Vacant European Featherweight Title)*
06.09.89	Peter Harris W RSC 9 Aberavon *(British & European Featherweight Title Defence)*
13.12.89	Farid Benredjeb W RSC 8 Kirkby *(European Featherweight Title Defence)*
28.03.90	Eduardo Montoya W RSC 3 Manchester *(Elim. IBF Featherweight Title)*
02.06.90	Marcos Villasana L RSC 8 Manchester *(Vacant WBC Featherweight Title)*
31.10.90	Guy Bellehigue W RSC 3 Wembley *(European Featherweight Title Defence)*
13.11.91	Marcos Villasana W PTS 12 Belfast *(WBC Featherweight Title Challenge)*
25.04.92	Steve Cruz W RSC 3 Belfast *(WBC Featherweight Title Defence)*
12.09.92	Fabrice Benichou W RSC 10 Blagnac, France *(WBC Featherweight Title Defence)*
03.02.93	Ricardo Cepeda W RTD 4 Earls Court *(WBC Featherweight Title Defence)*
28.04.93	Gregorio Vargas L RTD 7 Dublin *(WBC Featherweight Title Defence)*

Career: 25 contests, won 22, drew 1, lost 2.

Dean Hollington

West Ham. *Born* Plaistow, 25 February, 1969
L. Welterweight. Ht. 5'9"
Manager Self

20.02.90	Dave Jenkins W PTS 4 Millwall

Dean Hollington　　　　　　　　Les Clark

06.04.90 Marcel Herbert W PTS 6 Stevenage
25.09.90 Andre Marcel Cleak W RSC 5
　　　　　Millwall
12.02.91 Andy Robins W RSC 4 Basildon
07.03.91 Dave Jenkins W PTS 6 Basildon
17.04.91 Jim Lawlor W PTS 6 Kensington
23.10.91 John Smith W PTS 6 Bethnal Green
13.11.91 Jim Lawlor W PTS 6 Bethnal Green
11.02.92 Nigel Bradley W PTS 6 Barking
02.04.92 Tony Gibbs W CO 1 Basildon
16.05.92 Rick Bushell W RSC 2 Muswell Hill
10.02.93 John O'Johnson W PTS 6 Lewisham
26.04.93 Chris Saunders L RSC 5 Lewisham
Career: 13 contests, won 12, lost 1.

Mick Holmes

Barnsley. *Born* Burnley, 15 May, 1971
L. Welterweight. Ht. 5'7"
Manager N. Basso

07.10.91 Chris Aston L RSC 2 Bradford
03.03.92 Micky Hall L RSC 2 Houghton le
　　　　　Spring
07.10.92 Alan Ingle L RSC 5 Glasgow
Career: 3 contests, lost 3.

Ian Honeywood

Bexley. *Born* Newmarket, 20 July, 1964
L. Welterweight. Former Undefeated
Southern Area Lightweight Champion. Ht.
5'7"
Manager Self

22.10.86 Wayne Weekes W PTS 6 Greenwich
10.11.86 Andrew Pybus W RTD 2 Birmingham
17.11.86 Lee West L PTS 6 Dulwich
28.11.86 Nigel Senior L RSC 5 Peterborough
01.05.87 Bill Smith W PTS 6 Peterborough
26.05.87 Jess Rundan W RTD 3 Plymouth
10.09.87 Gary Maxwell DREW 6 Peterborough
25.09.87 Doug Munro L RSC 5 Southend
18.01.88 Andrew Furlong W PTS 8 Mayfair
17.03.88 Harry Escott L RSC 4 Sunderland
19.04.88 Jim Moffat L PTS 8 Glasgow

09.05.88 Ray Newby L RSC 1 Nottingham
30.08.88 Tony Borg W PTS 6 Kensington
31.10.88 Brian Sonny Nickels L PTS 6 Bedford
01.12.88 Kid Sumali W PTS 4 Gravesend
18.01.89 Nigel Wenton L RSC 3 Kensington
18.02.89 Sonny Long W PTS 8 Budapest,
　　　　　Hungary
28.03.89 Willie Beattie L PTS 4 Glasgow
24.04.89 Nigel Senior W PTS 4 Nottingham
21.05.89 Wayne Weekes W RSC 4 Finsbury
　　　　　Park
　　　　　*(Vacant Southern Area Lightweight
　　　　　Title)*
27.06.89 Tony Foster W PTS 6 Kensington
25.09.89 Dean Bramhald W RTD 4 Crystal
　　　　　Palace
18.12.89 John Kalbhenn L PTS 8 Kitchener,
　　　　　Canada
23.04.90 Paul Gadney W PTS 10 Crystal Palace
　　　　　*(Southern Area Lightweight Title
　　　　　Defence)*
22.06.90 Martin Cruz W RSC 3 Gillingham
24.09.90 Marvin P. Gray W PTS 8 Lewisham
19.12.90 Carl Crook L RSC 4 Preston
　　　　　*(British & Commonwealth Lightweight
　　　　　Title Challenge)*
10.03.91 Pierre Lorcy L CO 5 Paris, France
24.09.91 Dave Anderson L PTS 8 Glasgow
13.11.91 Steve Walker W PTS 6 Bethnal Green
18.01.92 Steve Pollard L PTS 6 Kensington
30.03.92 Tony Foster W RSC 4 Eltham
30.04.92 Sean Murphy L RSC 1 Kensington
14.04.93 Carlos Chase L RSC 1 Kensington
Career: 34 contests, won 18, drew 1, lost 15.

Donnie Hood

Glasgow. *Born* Glasgow, 3 June, 1963
Former Undefeated WBC International &
Scottish Bantamweight Champion. Ht 5'5"
Manager Self

22.09.86 Stewart Fishermac W PTS 6 Glasgow
29.09.86 Keith Ward W PTS 6 Glasgow
08.12.86 Jamie McBride DREW 8 Glasgow
22.12.86 Keith Ward L PTS 8 Glasgow
27.01.87 Chris Clarkson W PTS 6 Glasgow
09.02.87 Danny Porter W RSC 4 Glasgow
24.02.87 Danny Lee W PTS 8 Glasgow
07.09.87 Kid Sumali W PTS 8 Glasgow
15.09.87 David Ingram L PTS 8 Batley
26.10.87 Jimmy Lee W PTS 8 Glasgow
　　　　　(Vacant Scottish Bantamweight Title)
28.03.88 Nigel Crook W CO 2 Glasgow
12.05.88 Eyup Can L PTS 8 Copenhagen,
　　　　　Denmark
17.06.88 Fransie Badenhorst L RSC 7 Durban,
　　　　　South Africa
05.09.88 Gerry McBride W RTD 7 Glasgow
25.10.88 Graham O'Malley W RSC 9 Hartlepool
　　　　　(Elim. British Bantamweight Title)
06.03.89 Francisco Paco Garcia W RSC 6
　　　　　Glasgow
28.03.89 John Vasquez W RSC 5 Glasgow
27.06.89 Ray Minus L RSC 6 Glasgow
　　　　　*(Commonwealth Bantamweight Title
　　　　　Challenge)*
22.01.90 Dean Lynch W PTS 8 Glasgow
26.03.90 Keith Wallace W RTD 8 Glasgow
　　　　　(Elim. British Bantamweight Title)
09.10.90 Samuel Duran W PTS 12 Glasgow
　　　　　*(WBC International Bantamweight
　　　　　Title Challenge)*
10.12.90 David Moreno W RSC 4 Glasgow

25.01.91 Dave Buxton W RSC 5 Shotts
05.03.91 Virgilio Openio W PTS 12 Glasgow
　　　　　*(WBC International Bantamweight
　　　　　Title Defence)*
31.05.91 Willie Richardson W PTS 8 Glasgow
24.09.91 Rocky Commey W PTS 12 Glasgow
　　　　　*(WBC International Bantamweight
　　　　　Title Defence)*
24.10.91 Vinnie Ponzio W PTS 8 Glasgow
14.03.92 Johnny Bredahl L RSC 7 Copenhagen,
　　　　　Denmark
　　　　　(Vacant European Bantamweight Title)
29.05.92 Pete Buckley W PTS 8 Glasgow
25.01.93 Drew Docherty L PTS 12 Glasgow
　　　　　(British Bantamweight Title Challenge)
Career: 31 contests, won 23, drew 1, lost 7.

Ray Hood

Crawley. *Born* Queensferry, 28 August,
1962
Former Undefeated Welsh Lightweight
Champion. Ht. 5'8"
Manager P. Dwyer

09.06.81 Alan Tombs DREW 6 Southend
29.06.81 Vince Griffin W RSC 3 Liverpool
16.09.81 Geoff Smart W RTD 4 Burslem
23.09.81 Winston Ho-Shing L PTS 6 Sheffield
06.10.81 Peter Flanagan W RSC 5 Liverpool
13.10.81 Alan Cooper DREW 6 Nantwich
28.10.81 Delroy Pearce W PTS 6 Burslem
03.11.81 Mark Crouch W CO 6 Southend
16.11.81 Winston Ho-Shing W PTS 6 Liverpool
27.01.82 Eric Wood W PTS 6 Stoke
16.02.82 Aidan Wake W CO 4 Leeds
29.03.82 Jimmy Bunclark W RSC 2 Liverpool
05.04.82 Jimmy Duncan L PTS 8 Bloomsbury
03.06.82 Delroy Pearce W PTS 8 Liverpool
30.06.82 Tommy Cook W PTS 8 Liverpool
01.11.82 Andy Thomas W PTS 8 Liverpool
04.03.83 Andy Thomas W PTS 10 Queensferry
　　　　　(Vacant Welsh Lightweight Title)
28.10.83 Jimmy Bunclark W RSC 8
　　　　　Queensferry
14.11.83 Ken Foreman L PTS 8 Nantwich
22.11.83 Najib Daho L PTS 8 Manchester
15.03.84 Kevin Pritchard L PTS 8 Kirkby
06.04.84 Ian McLeod L RSC 2 Edinburgh
05.12.84 Dave Haggarty L PTS 6 Stoke
21.06.93 Anthony Wanza W PTS 6 Swindon
Career: 24 contests, won 15, drew 2, lost 7.

Carl Hook

Swansea. *Born* Swansea, 21 November,
1969
L. Welterweight. Ht. 5'8"
Manager G. Davies

18.07.91 Jason Matthews L PTS 6 Cardiff
25.07.91 Wayne Taylor W PTS 6 Dudley
16.09.91 Nicky Lucas W PTS 6 Mayfair
26.09.91 Ron Shinkwin L PTS 8 Dunstable
24.10.91 John O'Johnson W PTS 6 Dunstable
31.10.91 Davy Robb L PTS 4 Oakengates
05.12.91 Mark Ramsey L RSC 4 Oakengates
23.01.92 Phil Epton L PTS 6 York
11.02.92 Jason Matthews L PTS 6 Cardiff
11.05.92 Derrick Daniel L PTS 6 Piccadilly
16.06.92 Derrick Daniel W RSC 2 Dagenham
14.11.92 Edward Lloyd L PTS 6 Cardiff
27.01.93 Mervyn Bennett L PTS 10 Cardiff
　　　　　(Vacant Welsh Lightweight Title)
Career: 13 contests, won 4, lost 9.

Ron Hopley

Ripon. *Born* Ripon, 3 April, 1969
L. Middleweight. Ht. 5'8½"
Manager D. Mancini

27.11.91 William Beaton W RSC 2 Marton
23.01.92 Rick North W PTS 6 York
08.04.92 Steve Howden L PTS 6 Leeds
25.02.93 Rob Stevenson DREW 6 Bradford
07.04.93 Warren Stephens W PTS 6 Leeds
Career: 5 contests, won 3, drew 1, lost 1.

Steve Howden

Sheffield. *Born* Sheffield, 4 June, 1969
Lightweight. Ht. 5'8¾"
Manager B. Ingle

08.04.92 Ron Hopley W PTS 6 Leeds
01.06.92 Kevin McKillan L RSC 2 Manchester
07.07.92 Mike Morrison L CO 3 Bristol
01.10.92 Jimmy Reynolds L RTD 2 Telford
23.06.93 Shaba Edwards W RSC 1 Gorleston
Career: 5 contests, won 2, lost 3.

Mickey Hughes

St Pancras. *Born* London, 13 June, 1962
Former Commonwealth L. Middleweight
Champion. Ht. 5'9½"
Manager Self

01.10.85 Steve Tempro W PTS 6 Wembley
16.10.85 Manny Romain W RSC 2 Kensington
29.05.86 Junaido Musah W RSC 4 Bethnal
Green
22.09.86 Cliff Domville W RSC 4 Mayfair
23.10.86 Ian Chantler W RSC 6 Basildon
20.11.86 Manny Romain W CO 4 Bethnal Green
22.01.87 Simon Paul W RSC 2 Bethnal Green
22.02.87 Mike Essett W RSC 5 Wembley
19.03.87 Andy O'Rawe W RSC 2 Bethnal Green
09.04.87 Kelvin Mortimer W RSC 6 Bethnal
Green
25.09.87 Kelvin Mortimer W PTS 8 Southend
24.10.87 David Taylor L PTS 8 Tottenham
03.12.87 Del Bryan L PTS 8 Southend
14.03.88 Paul Murray W RSC 4 Mayfair
05.10.88 Chris Blake W RSC 5 Wembley
30.11.88 Jeff Connors W RSC 3 Southwark
02.02.89 Lenny Gloster W RSC 6 Southwark
28.09.89 Trevor Smith L RSC 6 Wandsworth
*(Southern Area Welterweight Title
Challenge)*
06.03.90 Josef Rajic W CO 2 Bethnal Green
20.03.90 Robert Wright W RSC 7 Norwich
05.06.90 Parrish Johnson W RSC 3 Nottingham
10.07.90 Winston Wray W RSC 5 Canvey Island
12.09.90 Nick Meloscia W CO 1 Bethnal Green
17.10.90 Gary Jacobs W CO 8 Bethnal Green
06.02.91 Ian John-Lewis W RSC 9 Bethnal
Green
(Elim. British Welterweight Title)
04.06.91 Donovan Boucher L PTS 12 Bethnal
Green
*(Commonwealth Welterweight Title
Challenge)*
26.11.91 Del Bryan L RSC 3 Bethnal Green
(British Welterweight Title Challenge)
16.06.92 Andrew Furlong W CO 1 Dagenham
15.09.92 Craig Trotter W PTS 12 Crystal Palace
*(Vacant Commonwealth L.
Middleweight Title)*
30.01.93 Lloyd Honeyghan L RSC 5 Brentwood
*(Commonwealth L. Middleweight Title
Defence)*

20.04.93 Shaun Cummins L CO 11 Brentwood
*(WBAPenta-Continental L.
Middleweight Title Challenge)*
Career: 31 contests, won 24, lost 7.

Jason Hutson   Les Clark

Jason Hutson

Thame. *Born* London, 11 March, 1972
S. Featherweight. Ht. 5'6"
Manager W. Ball

15.02.93 Marco Fattore L PTS 6 Mayfair
29.04.93 Vince Burns L RSC 1 Hayes
Career: 2 contests, lost 2.

Cordwell Hylton

Walsall. *Born* Jamaica, 20 September, 1958
Former Midlands Area Cruiserweight
Champion. Ht. 5'11"
Manager N. Basso

22.09.80 Nigel Savery W PTS 6 Wolverhampton
30.10.80 Steve Fenton W CO 2 Wolverhampton
01.12.80 Liam Coleman L PTS 6
Wolverhampton
02.02.81 Steve Fenton W PTS 6 Nottingham
10.02.81 John O'Neill W RSC 6 Wolverhampton
16.03.81 Chris Lawson L RSC 5 Mayfair
13.04.81 Rupert Christie W RSC 5
Wolverhampton
11.05.81 Trevor Cattouse L PTS 8 Mayfair
05.10.81 Antonio Harris W PTS 8 Birmingham
30.11.81 Ben Lawlor W RSC 2 Birmingham
23.01.82 Chisanda Mutti L RSC 3 Berlin,
Germany
16.02.82 Prince Mama Mohammed L PTS 8
Birmingham
19.03.82 Devon Bailey L RSC 2 Birmingham
24.05.82 Clive Beardsley W RSC 4 Nottingham
20.09.82 Keith Bristol NC 5 Wolverhampton
05.10.82 Alex Tompkins W PTS 8 Piccadilly
23.11.82 Winston Burnett W RSC 5
Wolverhampton
13.12.82 Steve Babbs L CO 1 Wolverhampton
15.02.83 Alek Pensarski W RSC 4
Wolverhampton
23.02.83 Devon Bailey L RSC 6 Mayfair
28.03.83 Gordon Stacey W RSC 1 Birmingham
25.04.83 Alex Tompkins W PTS 8 Southwark
19.05.83 Richard Caramanolis L CO 4 Paris,
France
03.12.83 Andy Straughn L PTS 8 Marylebone
25.01.84 Romal Ambrose W RSC 3 Solihull
07.06.84 Roy Skeldon L CO 7 Dudley
01.12.84 Louis Pergaud L DIS 6 Dusseldorf,
Germany
23.02.85 Chris Reid L CO 3 Belfast
25.04.85 Harry Andrews W PTS 6
Wolverhampton
05.06.85 Tony Wilson L CO 5 Kensington
12.10.87 Ivan Joseph L CO 6 Bow
24.02.88 Johnny Nelson L RSC 1 Sheffield
29.03.88 Eric Cardouza W CO 5 Wembley
05.05.88 Derek Angol L RSC 5 Wembley
19.09.88 Mike Aubrey L PTS 6 Mayfair

*In dropping a six round points decision to Wayne Llewelyn, Cordwell Hylton (left)
lost his third fight in a row since beating the Frenchman, Jean-Marie Emebe*

Les Clark

22.11.88 Crawford Ashley L CO 3 Basildon
02.02.89 Branko Pavlovic W RSC 2 Croydon
21.03.89 Abner Blackstock W CO 2 Wolverhampton
15.04.89 Alfredo Cacciatore L DIS 6 Vasto, Italy
21.05.89 Brendan Dempsey W PTS 8 Finsbury Park
12.08.89 Paul Muyodi L RTD 4 San Sepolcro, Italy
16.12.89 Lajos Eros L RSC 5 Milan, Italy
17.01.90 Mick Cordon W PTS 6 Stoke
08.02.90 Jim Peters W RSC 4 Southwark
08.03.90 Terry Dixon L PTS 8 Watford
25.04.90 Tee Jay L RSC 1 Millwall
13.06.90 Glazz Campbell W PTS 4 Manchester
31.10.90 Henry Maske L RSC 3 Wembley
12.02.91 Steve Lewsam W RSC 8 Wolverhampton
22.02.91 Bobbi Joe Edwards W RTD 6 Manchester
20.03.91 Roy Smith W RSC 7 Solihull
 (Midland Area Cruiserweight Title Challenge)
17.05.91 Neils H. Madsen L RSC 2 Copenhagen, Denmark
22.06.91 Norbert Ekassi L CO 5 Paris, France
16.09.91 Steve Lewsam L PTS 10 Cleethorpes
 (Midlands Area Cruiserweight Title Defence)
26.11.91 Tony Wilson L PTS 8 Wolverhampton
21.02.92 Markus Bott L PTS 8 Hamburg, Germany
06.03.92 Yuri Razumov DREW 6 Berlin, Germany
27.03.92 Jean-Marie Emebe W RSC 3 Creil, France
22.10.92 Chemek Saleta L RSC 4 Bethnal Green
25.02.93 Denzil Browne L PTS 8 Bradford
23.05.93 Wayne Llewelyn L PTS 6 Brockley
Career: 61 contests, won 26, drew 1, lost 33, no contest 1.

Vance Idiens

Cannock. *Born* Walsall, 9 June, 1962
Heavyweight. Ht. 6'4"
Manager W. Tyler

24.10.89 Mick Cordon W PTS 6 Wolverhampton
28.11.89 Ted Shaw W CO 1 Wolverhampton
06.12.89 Mick Cordon W PTS 6 Stoke
19.02.90 David Jules W PTS 6 Birmingham
22.03.90 Mick Cordon W PTS 6 Wolverhampton
24.05.90 Tucker Richards L RSC 5 Dudley
28.06.90 Paul Neilson W PTS 8 Birmingham
27.09.90 Paul Neilson W PTS 8 Birmingham
14.11.90 Paul Neilson L RSC 2 Doncaster
05.12.91 David Jules W RSC 4 Cannock
06.03.92 Mario Scheisser L RSC 1 Berlin, Germany
09.12.92 David Jules W PTS 8 Stoke
11.03.93 Wayne Buck L PTS 8 Walsall
06.05.93 Joey Paladino W PTS 8 Walsall
19.05.93 John Harewood L CO 3 Sunderland
26.06.93 Justin Fortune L RSC 1 Keynsham
Career: 16 contests, won 10, lost 6.

Alan Ingle

Dunbar. *Born* Haddington, 31 August, 1968
L. Welterweight. Ht. 5'9"
Manager T. Gilmour

21.09.92 Kevin McKenzie L PTS 6 Glasgow
07.10.92 Mick Holmes W RSC 5 Glasgow
14.10.92 Gary Hiscox W PTS 6 Stoke
18.11.92 Micky Hall L RSC 3 Solihull
25.02.93 Rob Stewart L PTS 6 Burnley
Career: 5 contests, won 2, lost 3.

Colin Innes

Newcastle. *Born* Newcastle, 24 July, 1964
S. Featherweight. Ht. 5'6"
Manager Self

10.09.90 Lee Christian W RSC 5 Northampton
24.09.90 Steve Armstrong W PTS 6 Manchester
08.10.90 Ervine Blake L PTS 6 Bradford
22.10.90 Steve Armstrong W RSC 6 Manchester
26.11.90 Carl Roberts L RSC 3 Bury
11.02.91 Steve Armstrong W PTS 6 Manchester
18.02.91 Ian McGirr L PTS 6 Glasgow
02.03.91 Tommy Smith W PTS 6 Darlington
28.03.91 Darryl Pettit W RTD 3 Alfreton
30.04.91 Noel Carroll L PTS 4 Stockport
19.09.91 Carl Roberts L PTS 4 Stockport
12.12.91 Tommy Smith L PTS 6 Hartlepool
24.02.92 Mark Geraghty L PTS 8 Glasgow
30.03.92 Chris Jickells L RSC 3 Bradford
28.05.92 Tommy Smith L PTS 6 Gosforth
05.10.92 Wayne Rigby L PTS 6 Manchester
18.11.92 Al Garrett DREW 6 Solihull
Career: 17 contests, won 6, drew 1, lost 10.

John Irwin   Chris Bevan

John Irwin

Doncaster. *Born* Denaby, 31 May, 1969
All-Ireland Featherweight Champion. Ht. 5'8"
Manager J. Rushton

08.09.92 Kid McAuley W PTS 6 Doncaster
30.09.92 Miguel Matthews W PTS 6 Solihull
24.11.92 Colin Lynch W RSC 4 Doncaster
20.01.93 Mark Hargreaves W RSC 4 Solihull
23.02.93 G. G. Goddard W PTS 8 Doncaster
16.03.93 Kid McAuley W PTS 10 Mayfair
 (Vacant All-Ireland Featherweight Title)
28.04.93 Kevin Middleton L PTS 6 Solihull
Career: 7 contests, won 6, lost 1.

Cyril Jackson

Wrexham. *Born* Wrexham, 19 September, 1962
S. Middleweight. Ht. 5'11"
Manager Self

12.09.85 George Grey W RSC 4 Blaenavon
15.10.85 John Hadley W RSC 6 Leeds
06.11.85 Joey Sanders W RSC 3 Nantwich
11.12.85 John McGlynn L CO 1 Stoke
10.11.86 Dean Scarfe L RSC 3 Fulham
28.04.87 Steve Foster L RSC 7 Manchester
31.07.87 Shamus Casey W RSC 5 Wrexham
19.10.87 Steve Foster L RTD 3 Manchester
07.12.88 Rocky Reynolds W RTD 6 Aberavon
28.09.89 Cliff Curtis W RTD 3 Cardiff
13.11.89 Antonio Fernandez L PTS 8 Brierley Hill
03.02.90 Ahmet Canbakis W PTS 6 Bristol
27.10.92 Darrit Douglas L RSC 3 Leicester
Career: 13 contests, won 7, lost 6.

Gilbert Jackson (Amponsan)

Battersea. *Born* Ghana, 21 August, 1970
Middleweight. Ht. 5'10"
Manager M. Duff

17.02.92 John Bosco L PTS 6 Mayfair
05.03.92 Tony Wellington W CO 2 Battersea
22.04.92 Russell Washer W PTS 6 Wembley
08.09.92 Paul Gamble W RSC 1 Norwich
05.02.93 Carl Harney W CO 3 Manchester
14.06.93 Lee Crocker W RSC 2 Bayswater
Career: 6 contests, won 5, lost 1.

Mark Jay (Jackson)

Newcastle. *Born* Newcastle, 4 April, 1969
L. Middleweight. Ht. 5'11"
Manager N. Fawcett

29.09.88 Tony Farrell W PTS 6 Sunderland
22.11.88 Dave Whittle W PTS 6 Marton
05.04.89 Lewis Welch L PTS 6 Halifax
19.05.89 Mick Mulcahy W PTS 6 Gateshead
25.09.89 Carlton Myers W PTS 6 Piccadilly
21.10.89 Ian Thomas L RSC 5 Middlesbrough
24.04.90 Ernie Loveridge L PTS 6 Stoke
30.05.90 Trevor Meikle DREW 6 Stoke
15.06.90 Trevor Meikle L RSC 5 Telford
18.10.90 Phil Epton L PTS 6 Dewsbury
19.11.90 John Mullen DREW 6 Glasgow
29.11.90 Barry Messam L RSC 5 Sunderland
09.10.91 Willie Quinn W PTS 6 Glasgow
16.12.91 Tyrone Eastmond L PTS 6 Manchester
20.01.92 Mick Duncan W PTS 6 Bradford
24.02.92 David Radford W PTS 6 Bradford
03.03.92 Dave Johnson L PTS 6 Houghton le Spring
12.03.92 Gordon Blair DREW 8 Glasgow
02.04.92 Jamie Robinson L PTS 6 Basildon
25.04.92 Steve Foster L RSC 7 Manchester
28.05.92 Shamus Casey W PTS 8 Gosforth
24.09.92 Derek Wormald L RSC 5 Stockport
01.12.92 Neil Patterson W PTS 6 Hartlepool
17.12.92 Clay O'Shea L CO 1 Wembley
09.03.93 Spencer Alton W RSC 4 Hartlepool
29.04.93 Allan Grainger W RSC 3 Newcastle
11.06.93 Tony Trimble W RSC 1 Gateshead
Career: 27 contests, won 12, drew 3, lost 12.

113

Kevin Jenkins

Ammanford. *Born* Glanamman, 9
December, 1970
Bantamweight. Ht. 5'2½"
Manager Self

21.12.89	Neil Parry W PTS 6 Kings Heath
22.01.90	James Drummond W PTS 6 Glasgow
03.02.90	Kruga Hydes DREW 6 Bristol
08.03.90	James Drummond L RSC 5 Glasgow
13.09.90	Mark Tierney L PTS 6 Watford
01.10.90	Antti Juntumaa L PTS 4 Helsinki, Finland
10.10.90	Mark Tierney L PTS 6 Kensington
17.10.90	Tim Yeates L PTS 6 Bethnal Green
24.01.91	Ceri Farrell W PTS 6 Gorseinon
12.02.91	Robbie Regan L PTS 10 Cardiff *(Vacant Welsh Flyweight Title)*
19.03.91	Danny Porter L RSC 7 Leicester
09.10.91	Stevie Woods DREW 8 Glasgow
19.11.91	Danny Porter L RSC 2 Norwich
18.03.92	Joe Kelly L PTS 8 Glasgow
05.05.92	Noel Carroll L PTS 7 Preston
06.02.93	Vince Feeney L PTS 6 Cardiff
17.02.93	Darren Fifield DREW 6 Bethnal Green
06.03.93	Paul Weir L PTS 8 Glasgow
26.05.93	Prince Nassem Hamed L RSC 3 Mansfield

Career: 19 contests, won 3, drew 3, lost 13.

Graham Jenner

Hastings. *Born* Hastings, 13 May, 1962
S. Middleweight. Ht. 6'0"
Manager D. Harris

10.10.85	Gary Tomlinson L PTS 6 Merton
14.11.85	George Mac W PTS 6 Merton
05.12.85	Jason Baxter L PTS 6 Digbeth
21.01.86	Tony Stevens W PTS 6 Tunbridge Wells
25.03.86	Dave Furneaux W PTS 6 Tunbridge Wells
08.04.86	Darryl Ritchie W RSC 3 Southend
16.09.86	Tommy Becket W CO 2 Southend
25.09.86	Andy Till L PTS 6 Crystal Palace
29.10.91	Val Golding L RSC 3 Kensington
08.01.92	Paul McCarthy W PTS 6 Burton
29.02.92	Paul McCarthy W PTS 8 St Leonards
29.05.92	Ensley Bingham L CO 5 Manchester
15.10.92	Mark Baker L RTD 4 Lewisham
12.11.92	John Kaighin L RSC 5 Bayswater
03.02.93	Sammy Storey L RSC 4 Earls Court
05.05.93	Terry Magee L PTS 6 Belfast

Career: 16 contests, won 7, lost 9.

Andrew Jervis

Liverpool. *Born* Liverpool, 28 June, 1969
L. Middleweight. Ht. 5'11"
Manager M. Atkinson

05.10.92	Rick North W PTS 6 Liverpool
02.11.92	Shaun Martin W CO 2 Liverpool
01.12.92	Cliff Churchward W PTS 6 Liverpool
27.01.93	Mark Ramsey L PTS 6 Stoke
22.02.93	Alan Williams W PTS 6 Liverpool
29.03.93	Bullit Andrews W PTS 6 Liverpool
09.06.93	Chris Mulcahy W PTS 6 Liverpool

Career: 7 contests, won 6, lost 1.

In a fight that was close enough to go either way, Welshman, Kevin Jenkins (left), lost over six rounds to Irishman, Vince Feeney   Les Clark

Chris Jickells   Chris Bevan

Chris Jickells

Brigg. *Born* Scunthorpe, 26 March, 1971
S. Featherweight. Ht. 5'5"
Manager K. Tate

18.11.91	Tony Smith W RSC 4 Manchester
09.12.91	Al Garrett W RSC 2 Bradford
15.01.92	Ronnie Stephenson L PTS 6 Stoke
30.03.92	Colin Innes W RSC 3 Bradford
29.04.92	Kevin Middleton W RSC 6 Solihull
01.06.92	Dave McHale L RSC 4 Glasgow
12.10.92	Ian McGirr W RSC 3 Bradford
10.02.93	Kevin Middleton L CO 1 Lewisham

07.06.93 Wilson Docherty L RSC 5 Glasgow
Career: 9 contests, won 5, lost 4.

Dave Johnson

Sunderland. *Born* Boldon, 10 August, 1972
Middleweight. Ht. 5'10"
Manager T. Conroy

13.05.91 Rocky Tyrell W PTS 6 Manchester
20.05.91 Griff Jones W PTS 6 Bradford
10.06.91 Tyrone Eastmond W PTS 6 Manchester
10.10.91 Shamus Casey W PTS 6 Gateshead
14.11.91 Shamus Casey W PTS 6 Gateshead
25.11.91 Mike Phillips L PTS 6 Liverpool
12.12.91 Mick Duncan W PTS 6 Hartlepool
03.03.92 Mark Jay W PTS 6 Houghton le Spring
28.04.92 Shaun McCrory DREW 6 Houghton le Spring
10.09.92 Spencer Alton W PTS 6 Sunderland
23.10.92 Griff Jones W PTS 6 Gateshead
17.04.93 Mike Phillips W PTS 6 Washington
11.06.93 Robert Riley W PTS 8 Gateshead
Career: 13 contests, won 11, drew 1, lost 1.

Julian Johnson

Swansea. *Born* Swansea, 4 October, 1967
L. Heavyweight. Ht. 5'10½"
Manager C. Breen

20.11.91 Nigel Rafferty DREW 6 Cardiff
22.01.92 Paul McCarthy DREW 6 Cardiff
29.02.92 Johnny Uphill W CO 3 St Leonards
11.03.92 Nicky Wadman L PTS 6 Cardiff
11.05.92 Andy Manning L PTS 6 Llanelli
25.11.92 Eddie Knight W RSC 2 Mayfair
10.04.93 Jason McNeill W PTS 6 Swansea
Career: 7 contests, won 3, drew 2, lost 2.

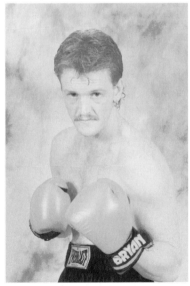

Martin Jolley   Chris Bevan

Martin Jolley

Alfreton. *Born* Chesterfield, 22 November, 1967
S. Middleweight. Ht. 5'11½"

Manager M. Shinfield

10.03.92 Gypsy Johnny Price W RSC 3 Bury
06.04.92 Sean Byrne L RSC 6 Northampton
11.05.92 Mark Hale W PTS 6 Coventry
08.09.92 Brian McGloin W PTS 6 Doncaster
05.10.92 Mark Hale W RSC 4 Bardon
14.10.92 Carl Smallwood W PTS 6 Stoke
02.11.92 Bobby Mack L PTS 6 Wolverhampton
24.11.92 Phil Ball DREW 6 Doncaster
02.02.93 Mark McBiane W RSC 5 Derby
23.02.93 Phil Ball W RSC 5 Doncaster
12.05.93 Marvin O'Brien W PTS 6 Sheffield
08.06.93 Paul Hanlon W PTS 6 Derby
Career: 12 contests, won 9, drew 1, lost 2.

Barry Jones

Cardiff. *Born* Cardiff, 3 May, 1974
Featherweight. Ht. 5'7"
Manager B. Aird

28.10.92 Conn McMullen W PTS 6 Cardiff
14.12.92 Miguel Matthews W PTS 6 Cardiff
27.01.93 Mike Deveney W PTS 6 Cardiff
24.03.93 Greg Upton W RSC 2 Mayfair
28.04.93 Kid McAuley W PTS 8 Solihull
Career: 5 contests, won 5.

(Ken) Griff Jones (Griffin)

Leeds. *Born* Leeds, 26 July, 1970
Middleweight. Ht. 6'0"
Manager T. Miller

21.01.91 David Radford W PTS 6 Leeds
28.02.91 Jon Stocks L PTS 6 Sunderland
20.05.91 Dave Johnson L PTS 6 Bradford
01.06.91 Gary Booker L PTS 6 Bethnal Green
05.11.91 Chad Strong W PTS 6 Leicester
07.12.91 Warren Stowe L RSC 6 Manchester
10.09.92 Paul Hitch L RSC 2 Sunderland
16.10.92 Tim Robinson W RSC 3 Hull
23.10.92 Dave Johnson L PTS 6 Gateshead
07.12.92 John Bosco L RSC 1 Mayfair
Career: 10 contests, won 3, lost 7.

Paul Jones

Sheffield. *Born* Sheffield, 19 November, 1966
Former Undefeated Central Area L. Middleweight Champion. Ht. 6'0"
Manager B. Hearn

08.12.86 Paul Gillings W PTS 6 Liverpool
28.10.87 Pat Durkin W PTS 4 Sheffield
10.11.87 David Binns L PTS 6 Batley
11.01.88 Humphrey Harrison L PTS 8 Manchester
27.09.88 George Sponagle DREW 8 Halifax, Canada
07.12.88 Jimmy Thornton W PTS 6 Stoke
23.01.89 Donovan Boucher L DIS 6 Toronto, Canada
13.03.89 Dale Moreland W PTS 6 Toronto, Canada
30.03.89 Benoit Boudreau W PTS 10 Moncton, Canada
19.04.89 Tony Collier W CO 3 Toronto, Canada
06.06.89 George Sponagle L PTS 8 Halifax, Canada
06.09.89 Kid Ford W PTS 6 Mississouga, Canada
13.11.89 Ian Midwood-Tate W RSC 4 Manchester
08.12.89 Antoine Tarver L PTS 4 Doncaster

06.03.90 Antonio Fernandez W PTS 8 Stoke
22.03.90 Darren Pilling W RTD 7 Gateshead
26.04.90 Newton Barnett W PTS 8 Mayfair
20.05.90 Jim Beckett W CO 1 Sheffield
22.05.90 Wayne Ellis L PTS 6 St Albans
14.11.90 Jason Rowe W PTS 10 Sheffield *(Central Area L. Middleweight Title Challenge)*
12.03.91 Tony Velinor W PTS 8 Mansfield
16.08.91 Hugo Marinangelli L CO 2 Marbella, Spain
01.10.91 Simon Eubank W CO 6 Sheffield
14.04.92 Paul Lynch W RSC 3 Mansfield
19.05.92 Trevor Ambrose W PTS 6 Cardiff
02.06.92 Patrick Vungbo W PTS 10 Rotterdam, Holland
19.09.92 Ernie Loveridge W PTS 6 Glasgow
24.11.92 Paul Wesley L RSC 2 Doncaster
Career: 28 contests, won 19, drew 1, lost 8.

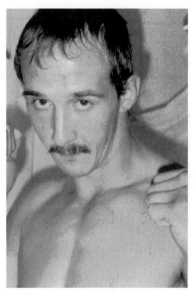

Seth Jones   Les Clark

Seth Jones

Dyffryn. *Born* St Asaph, 9 February, 1968
L. Welterweight. Ht. 5'8¾"
Manager D. Davies

29.08.91 John O'Johnson L DIS 1 Oakengates
19.09.91 Ricky Sackfield L RSC 1 Stockport
20.11.91 Jess Rundan W CO 4 Cardiff
09.12.91 Spencer McCracken L RSC 2 Brierley Hill
19.02.92 Paul Knights L RSC 5 Muswell Hill
31.03.92 Danny Kett W CO 1 Norwich
16.06.92 Paul Knights L PTS 6 Dagenham
26.09.92 Dave Lovell L RSC 4 Earls Court
01.12.92 Kevin McKenzie W RSC 3 Hartlepool
10.02.93 Jason Rowland L RSC 2 Lewisham
18.05.93 Shaun Cogan L RSC 2 Edgbaston
Career: 11 contests, won 3, lost 8.

Cham Joof

Brixton. *Born* London, 19 November, 1968
Lightweight. Ht. 5'8"
Manager T. Haynes

Cham Joof   Les Clark

22.02.93	Chris Saunders W PTS 4 Eltham	
04.04.93	Anthony Wanza W RSC 2 Brockley	
14.04.93	Mike Morrison W PTS 4 Kensington	
23.05.93	Charles Shepherd L PTS 4 Brockley	
25.06.93	Scott Smith W RTD 2 Battersea	

Career: 5 contests, won 4, lost 1.

Gareth Jordan

Monmouth. *Born* Usk, 19 December, 1971
Lightweight. Ht. 5'6¾"
Manager M. Duff

02.11.92	Con Cronin W RSC 2 Wolverhampton
04.12.92	Jason White W RSC 2 Telford
16.03.93	Lee Fox W RSC 3 Wolverhampton
26.05.93	Mark O'Callaghan W RSC 3 Mansfield

Career: 4 Contests, won 4.

Peter Judson

Keighley. *Born* Keighley, 14 January, 1970
S. Featherweight. Ht. 5'7"
Manager P. Martin

24.04.89	Darryl Pettit DREW 6 Bradford
11.07.89	Neil Leitch W PTS 6 Batley
18.09.89	Phil Lashley W PTS 6 Mayfair
02.10.89	Stevie Woods L PTS 6 Bradford
22.11.89	Pete Buckley L PTS 6 Stafford
19.02.90	Phil Lashley W CO 6 Nottingham
08.03.90	Wayne Goult L PTS 6 Peterborough
19.03.90	Andrew Robinson W PTS 6 Grimsby
26.03.90	Wayne Marston W PTS 6 Nottingham
30.04.90	Derek Amory L PTS 6 Brierley Hill
09.05.90	Brian Robb W PTS 6 Solihull
04.06.90	Jamie McBride L PTS 8 Glasgow
17.09.90	Mark Geraghty W PTS 8 Glasgow
26.09.90	Carl Roberts W PTS 6 Manchester
08.10.90	Mark Geraghty L PTS 8 Glasgow
19.11.90	Russell Davison L PTS 8 Manchester
27.11.90	Rocky Lawlor W PTS 8 Wolverhampton
29.01.91	Russell Davison L PTS 10 Stockport
	(Vacant Central Area Featherweight Title)
21.02.91	Noel Carroll W PTS 8 Leeds

20.03.91	Colin Lynch W RTD 5 Solihull
01.05.91	Jimmy Owens L PTS 6 Liverpool
28.05.91	Scott Durham W PTS 6 Cardiff
24.09.91	Ian McGirr L PTS 6 Glasgow
11.11.91	Miguel Matthews W PTS 6 Stratford upon Avon
18.11.91	Jamie McBride DREW 6 Glasgow
09.02.92	Ceri Farrell W PTS 6 Bradford
05.04.92	Barrie Kelley W PTS 6 Bradford
14.11.92	J. T. Williams DREW 6 Cardiff
25.02.93	Dominic McGuigan DREW 6 Bradford

Career: 29 contests, won 15, drew 4, lost 10.

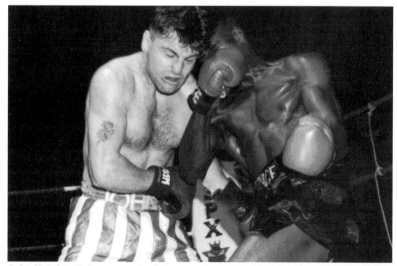

David Jules   Chris Bevan

David Jules

Doncaster. *Born* Doncaster, 11 July, 1965
Heavyweight. Ht. 6'2"
Manager Self

12.06.87	Carl Timbrell W CO 5 Leamington
07.10.87	Carl Timbrell L RSC 3 Stoke
17.03.88	Peter Fury W RTD 2 Sunderland
21.03.88	Jess Harding L RSC 2 Bethnal Green
29.09.88	Gary McCrory L PTS 6 Sunderland
22.11.88	Gary McCrory L PTS 6 Marton
05.12.88	Denroy Bryan DREW 6 Dudley
18.01.89	Denroy Bryan W RSC 2 Stoke
22.02.89	Tony Hallett W RSC 1 Doncaster
19.04.89	Rocky Burton L RSC 3 Doncaster
11.11.89	Jimmy di Stolfo W RSC 1 Rimini, Italy
30.11.89	Biagio Chianese L RSC 2 Milan, Italy
19.02.90	Vance Idiens L PTS 6 Birmingham
07.05.90	Ramon Voorn L RSC 3 Arnhem, Holland
12.11.90	Steve Garber L RSC 6 Bradford
09.04.91	Herbie Hide L RSC 1 Mayfair
05.12.91	Vance Idiens L RSC 4 Cannock
24.02.92	Rocky Burton W CO 1 Coventry
05.04.92	Steve Garber L RSC 4 Bradford
08.09.92	Wayne Buck L RSC 3 Doncaster
09.12.92	Vance Idiens L PTS 8 Stoke
10.05.93	Steve Lewsam L CO 6 Cleethorpes

Career: 22 contests, won 6, drew 1, lost 15.

John Kaighin

Swansea. *Born* Brecknock, 26 August, 1967
S. Middleweight. Ht. 5'11¾"
Manager Self

17.09.90	Carlos Christie L PTS 6 Cardiff
24.09.90	James F. Woolley L PTS 6 Lewisham
15.10.90	Max McCracken L PTS 6 Brierley Hill
22.10.90	Stefan Wright L PTS 6 Peterborough
15.11.90	Tony Wellington W PTS 6 Oldham
13.12.90	Nick Manners L CO 3 Dewsbury
24.01.91	Robert Peel L PTS 6 Gorseinon
12.02.91	Robert Peel W PTS 6 Cardiff
15.03.91	Max McCracken DREW 6 Willenhall
10.04.91	Darron Griffiths L PTS 6 Newport
24.04.91	Paul Murray W PTS 6 Aberavon
08.05.91	Benji Good W RSC 3 Kensington
15.05.91	Robert Peel W PTS 8 Swansea
06.06.91	Peter Vosper DREW 6 Barking

John Kaighin (left, a man who fights any time, any place, was knocked down twice and stopped inside three rounds by Mark Prince, the son of the former middleweight star, Clarence Prince   Les Clark

30.06.91 John Ogistie L PTS 6 Southwark
29.08.91 Adrian Wright W PTS 6 Oakengates
09.09.91 Terry Johnson W RTD 2 Liverpool
11.09.91 Lester Jacobs L RSC 2 Hammersmith
22.10.91 Andy Wright DREW 6 Wandsworth
13.11.91 Gary Delaney L PTS 6 Bethnal Green
20.11.91 Keith Inglis W RSC 1 Kensington
23.01.92 Michael Gale L PTS 8 York
01.02.92 Paul Busby L PTS 4 Birmingham
25.02.92 Andy Wright L PTS 6 Crystal Palace
05.03.92 Lester Jacobs L RSC 1 Battersea
27.04.92 Bruce Scott L CO 4 Mayfair
18.07.92 Carl Harney L PTS 6 Manchester
15.09.92 Paul Wright L DIS 5 Liverpool
26.09.92 Shaun Cummins L RTD 4 Earls Court
28.10.92 Joey Peters DREW 4 Kensington
12.11.92 Graham Jenner W RSC 5 Baywater
01.12.92 Peter Vosper W RSC 4 Bristol
22.12.92 Darrit Douglas W PTS 6 Mayfair
14.01.93 Ole Klemetsen L RTD 3 Mayfair
24.03.93 Darron Griffiths L RSC 6 Cardiff
        (Vacant Welsh S. Middleweight Title)
28.04.93 Ray Kane L PTS 6 Dublin
23.05.93 Mark Prince L RSC 3 Brockley
Career: 37 contests, won 11, drew 4, lost 22.

Charlie Kane
Clydebank. *Born* Glasgow, 2 July, 1968
L. Welterweight. Ht. 5'10½"
Manager J. Creswell

05.03.91 Dean Bramhald W RSC 6 Glasgow
21.10.91 James Jiora W PTS 6 Glasgow
24.02.92 Karl Taylor W PTS 8 Glasgow
10.12.92 Mick Mulcahy W RSC 2 Glasgow
Career: 4 contests, won 4.

Ray Kane
Belfast. *Born* Dublin, 4 June, 1968
L.Heavyweight. Ht. 6'0"
Manager B. Eastwood

07.09.91 R. F. McKenzie W PTS 4 Belfast
11.12.91 Chris Coughlan W PTS 6 Dublin
28.04.93 John Kaighin W PTS 6 Dublin
05.05.93 Johnny Uphill W CO 2 Belfast
Career: 4 contests, won 4.

Barrie Kelley
Llanelli.*Born* Llanelli, 14 February, 1972
Welsh S. Featherweight Champion. Ht. 5'6"
Manager Self

16.10.90 Ervine Blake W PTS 6 Evesham
21.11.90 Tony Falcone W PTS 6 Chippenham
29.11.90 John O'Meara W RSC 5 Bayswater
24.01.91 Martin Evans W PTS 6 Gorseinon
18.02.91 Tony Falcone L RSC 6 Mayfair
26.03.91 Dennis Adams W PTS 6 Bethnal Green
18.07.91 Robert Smyth DREW 6 Cardiff
16.09.91 Dominic McGuigan DREW 6 Mayfair
14.10.91 Michael Armstrong L CO 4
        Manchester
20.11.91 Neil Haddock L PTS 6 Cardiff
03.02.92 Noel Carroll L PTS 8 Manchester
18.03.92 Mark Geraghty L PTS 8 Glasgow
05.04.92 Peter Judson L PTS 6 Bradford
30.09.92 Dean Bramhald W PTS 6 Solihull
28.10.92 Derek Amory W PTS 6 Cardiff
19.01.93 Edward Lloyd W PTS 10 Cardiff
        (Vacant Welsh S. Featherweight Title)
Career: 16 contests, won 18, drew 2, lost 6.

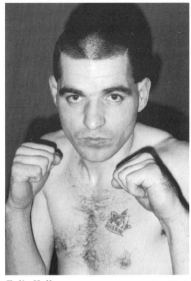

Felix Kelly   Les Clark

Felix Kelly
Paddington. *Born* Sligo, 6 June, 1965
Southern Area Lightweight Champion. Ht. 5'7"
Manager I. Akay

18.10.90 Tony Gibbs DREW 6 Wandsworth
26.11.90 Steve Hearn W RSC 3 Bethnal Green
04.12.90 Frankie Ventura W PTS 6 Southend
06.02.91 Wayne Windle W PTS 6 Bethnal
        Green
18.02.91 Trevor Royal W RSC 4 Windsor
26.03.91 Chris Saunders W PTS 6 Bethnal
        Green
18.04.91 Rick Bushell W PTS 6 Earls Court
22.06.91 Rick Bushell L PTS 6 Earls Court
26.09.91 Billy Schwer L RSC 2 Dunstable
20.11.91 Tony Borg L PTS 6 Cardiff
25.03.92 Mark Tibbs DREW 8 Dagenham
17.09.92 Carlos Chase L RSC 2 Watford
07.11.92 Didier Hughes W PTS 6 Differdange,
        France
02.01.93 Brian Kulen W PTS 6 Differdange,
        France
13.02.93 Soren Sondergaard L CO 4 Randers,
        Denmark
24.03.93 Patrick Loughran L PTS 6 Belfast
03.04.93 James Osansedo L RTD 5 Vienna,
        Austria
14.05.93 Angel Mona L RTD 2 Dijon, France
23.06.93 A.M.Milton W CO 8 Edmonton
        *(Vacant Southern Area Lightweight
        Title)*
Career: 19 contests, won 9, drew 2 , lost 8.

John T. Kelly
Hartlepool. *Born* Hartlepool, 12 June, 1970
Lightweight. Ht. 5'7"
Manager G. Robinson

22.10.92 Tanver Ahmed L PTS 6 Glasgow
02.11.92 Kevin Lowe W PTS 6 Liverpool
01.12.92 Wayne Rigby W PTS 6 Hartlepool
15.02.93 Kevin McKillan L PTS 6 Manchester
09.03.93 Michael Alexander W PTS 6
        Hartlepool

17.04.93 Micky Hall DREW 4 Washington
06.05.93 Alan Graham W PTS 6 Hartlepool
Career: 7 contests, won 4, drew1, lost 2.

Mark Kelly
Doncaster. *Born* Denaby, 15 July, 1968
Welterweight. Ht. 5'7"
Manager Self

19.10.87 Rocky Lester W CO 4 Nottingham
02.11.87 Roy Doyle W PTS 6 Manchester
25.11.87 Darren Darby W PTS 6 Cottingham
11.01.88 Oliver Harrison L RSC 1 Manchester
21.03.88 Warren Slaney W RSC 1 Leicester
18.04.88 Nigel Bradley W PTS 6 Manchester
28.04.88 Sugar Gibiliru DREW 6 Manchester
10.05.88 George Jones DREW 8 Edgbaston
13.06.88 Brian Cullen W PTS 8 Manchester
26.09.88 George Baigrie W PTS 8 Bradford
18.10.88 Tony Ekubia L RSC 7 Oldham
        *(Vacant Central Area Lightweight
        Title)*
01.12.88 Sugar Gibiliru W PTS 6 Manchester
12.12.88 Tony Foster L PTS 6 Nottingham
24.01.89 John Smith W PTS 8 Kings Heath
07.02.89 Philip Nurse L PTS 8 Manchester
23.02.89 Paul Burke W DIS 5 Stockport
06.03.89 Tony Richards L PTS 8 Leicester
03.04.89 Jan Nyholm L CO 1 Helsinki, Finland
24.01.90 Kevin Spratt L RSC 9 Solihull
        *(Central Area L.Welterweight Title
        Challenge)*
10.04.90 Brendan Ryan W PTS 6 Doncaster
14.05.90 Chris Mulcahy W PTS 8 Cleethorpes
22.10.90 John Ritchie L RSC 4 Glasgow
21.11.90 Ross Hale L PTS 8 Chippenham
06.06.91 Roy Rowland L RSC 4 Barking
25.11.91 Trevor Meikle L PTS 8 Cleethorpes
11.12.91 Andreas Panayi DREW 8 Stoke
21.05.92 Malcolm Melvin L PTS 8 Cradley
        Heath
01.06.92 Darren Morris L PTS 8 Solihull
15.12.92 Andreas Panayi L PTS 6 Liverpool
27.01.93 Julian Eavis W PTS 8 Stoke
28.05.93 Ensley Bingham L RSC 5 Middleton
29.06.93 Malcolm Melvin L PTS 6 Edgbaston
Career: 32 contests, won 13, drew 3, lost 16.

Paul Kelly (Nettleship)
Doncaster. *Born* Mexborough, 18 May, 1968
Featherweight. Ht. 5'7"
Manager J. Rushton

21.05.92 Graham McGrath L RSC 2 Cradley
        Heath
13.10.92 Chris Lyons L PTS 6 Wolverhampton
30.10.92 Chris Lyons L CO 1 Birmingham
Career: 3 contests, lost 3.

Lyndon Kershaw
Halifax. *Born* Halifax, 17 September, 1972
Bantamweight. Ht. 5'6"
Manager T. Callighan

19.10.92 Stevie Woods W PTS 6 Glasgow
14.12.92 Louis Veitch DREW 6 Bradford
26.04.93 Golfraz Ahmed W PTS 6 Bradford
24.05.93 Anthony Hanna W PTS 6 Bradford
Career: 4 contests, won 3 , drew 1.

Danny Kett Chris Bevan

Danny Kett

Norwich. *Born* Norwich, 8 October, 1970
L. Welterweight. Ht. 5'8"
Manager G. Holmes

21.01.92	Barry Glanister W RSC 1 Norwich
31.03.92	Seth Jones L CO 1 Norwich
13.10.92	Mick Hoban L PTS 6 Bury

Career: 3 contests, won 1, lost 2.

Paul King

Newcastle. *Born* Newcastle, 3 June, 1965
Welterweight. Ht. 5'8½"
Manager Self

04.09.87	Willie MacDonald W PTS 6 Gateshead
03.11.87	Mick Mason L PTS 6 Sunderland
24.11.87	Mick Mason L PTS 6 Marton
31.01.89	Jim Larmour W RTD 4 Glasgow
27.02.90	Ian Thomas W PTS 6 Marton
06.03.90	Mick Duncan W PTS 6 Newcastle
15.11.90	Phil Epton W PTS 6 Oldham
28.02.91	Dave Kettlewell W RSC 1 Sunderland
21.03.91	Phil Epton W PTS 6 Dewsbury
13.05.91	Shamus Casey L PTS 6 Northampton
31.05.91	Gordon Blair L PTS 8 Glasgow
09.10.91	Delroy Waul L RSC 6 Manchester
29.09.92	Howard Clarke L PTS 6 Stoke
16.03.93	Howard Clarke L PTS 6 Edgbaston
29.04.93	Hughie Davey W PTS 6 Newcastle
29.06.93	Howard Clarke L PTS 6 Edgbaston

Career: 16 contests, won 8, lost 8.

Stan King (Hibbert)

Forest Hill. *Born* Jamaica, 25 April, 1964
Middleweight. Ht. 5'10½"
Manager Self

05.11.87	Steve West W PTS 6 Bethnal Green

18.11.87	Max Wallace W PTS 6 Holborn
18.01.88	Chris Richards L CO 5 Mayfair
12.03.88	Rob Thomas L PTS 6 Lisbon, Portugal
29.03.88	Brian Robinson L PTS 6 Bethnal Green
10.05.88	Rocky Reynolds L PTS 6 Southend
19.10.88	Eamonn Loughran L PTS 6 Belfast
14.11.88	Hannu Vuorinen L CO 5 Helsinki, Finland
08.05.89	B. K. Bennett L RSC 5 Piccadilly
30.11.89	John Ogiste DREW 6 Mayfair
02.02.90	Bernard Bonzon L PTS 6 Geneva, Switzerland
14.03.90	Max Wallace W PTS 6 Battersea
24.04.90	Jimmy Farrell W RSC 2 Eltham
08.05.90	David Brown W PTS 6 Eltham
16.06.90	Miodrag Perunovic L PTS 8 Pitograd, Yugloslavia
18.10.90	Errol Christie DREW 8 Wandsworth
29.11.90	Ian Strudwick W RSC 2 Baywater
03.04.91	Ian Strudwick L RSC 8 Bethnal Green
24.06.91	Gilbert Hallie L PTS 8 Rotterdam, Holland
17.03.92	Ian Chantler W CO 3 Mayfair
31.03.92	Kesem Clayton W RSC 4 Norwich
11.05.92	Tony Velinor W RSC 3 Piccadilly
14.07.92	Colin Manners L PTS 8 Mayfair
19.01.93	Paul Busby L PTS 8 Cardiff
19.05.93	Cornelius Carr L PTS 8 Sunderland

Career: 25 contests, won 9, drew 2, lost 14.

Eddie Knight

Ashford. *Born* Ashford, 4 October, 1966
L. Heavyweight. Ht. 5'11"
Manager M. Barrett

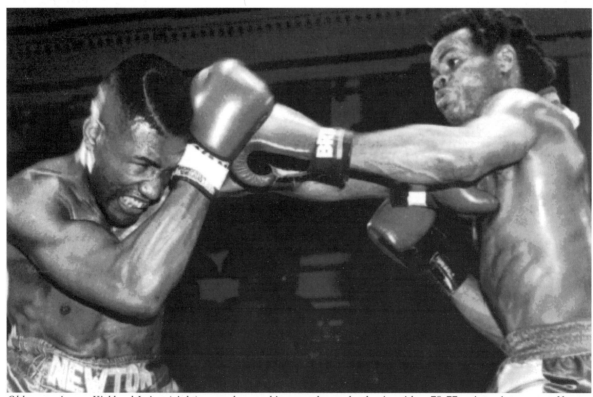

Old campaigner, Kirkland Laing (right), moved on to his second comeback win with a 79-77 points victory over Newton Barnett

Les Clark

05.10.92 Shaun McCrory L PTS 6 Bristol
29.10.92 Adrian Wright L PTS 6 Bayswater
25.11.92 Julian Johnson L RSC 2 Mayfair
Career: 3 contests, lost 3.

Paul Knights

Redhill. *Born* Redhill, 5 February, 1971
L. Welterweight. Ht. 5'10"
Manager Self

26.11.91 Steve Hearn W RSC 4 Bethnal Green
19.02.92 Seth Jones W RSC 5 Muswell Hill
16.06.92 Seth Jones W PTS 6 Dagenham
10.11.92 Alex Moffatt W CO 3 Dagenham
30.01.93 Dave Lovell W PTS 6 Brentwood
20.04.93 Mark Allen W PTS 6 Brentwood
26.06.93 Phil Found W PTS 4 Earls Court
Career: 7 contests, won 7.

Kirkland Laing

Nottingham. *Born* Jamaica, 20 June, 1954
Former British & European Welterweight
Champion. Ht. 5'9"
Manager Self

14.04.75 Joe Hannaford W CO 2 Nottingham
12.05.75 Liam White W PTS 8 Nottingham
29.09.75 Derek Simpson W PTS 8 Nottingham
25.11.75 Oscar Angus W PTS 6 Kensington
19.01.76 Terry Schofield W PTS 8 Nottingham
12.03.76 Charlie Cooper W PTS 8 Southend
13.04.76 Mike Manley W PTS 8 Southend
17.05.76 John Laine W RSC 3 Nottingham
22.09.76 Harry Watson W RSC 5 Mayfair
11.10.76 Jim Moore W RSC 2 Nottingham
22.11.76 Jim Montague W DIS 7 Birmingham
11.01.77 John Smith W PTS 10 Wolverhampton
08.03.77 Peter Morris DREW 10
Wolverhampton
16.11.77 Peter Morris W RSC 5 Solihull
27.09.78 Achille Mitchell W PTS 12 Solihull
(*Final Elim. British Welterweight Title*)
04.04.79 Henry Rhiney W RSC 10 Birmingham
(*British Welterweight Title Challenge*)
06.11.79 Des Morrison W PTS 8 Kensington
22.01.80 Salvo Nuciforo W RSC 6 Kensington
19.02.80 Colin Ward W RSC 5 Kensington
01.04.80 Colin Jones L RSC 9 Wembley
(*British Welterweight Title Defence*)
08.05.80 George Walker W PTS 8 Solihull
03.06.80 Curtis Taylor W RSC 7 Kensington
26.11.80 Joey Singleton W PTS 12 Solihull
(*Final Elim. British Welterweight Title*)
28.04.81 Colin Jones L RSC 9 Kensington
(*British Welterweight Title Challenge*)
18.11.81 Cliff Gilpin W PTS 12 Solihull
(*Final Elim. British Welterweight Title*)
09.02.82 Reg Ford L PTS 10 London
05.05.82 Joey Mack W CO 7 Solihull
04.09.82 Roberto Duran W PTS 10 Detroit, USA
10.09.83 Fred Hutchings L CO 10 Atlantic City,
USA
27.11.84 Darwin Brewster W RSC 7 Wembley
12.02.85 Mosimo Maeleke W PTS 10
Kensington
14.03.85 Wo Lamani Wo W RSC 6 Leicester
16.06.85 Franki Moro W PTS 8 Bethnal Green
05.07.85 Brian Janssen L RTD 5 Brisbane,
Australia
16.05.86 Mike Picciotti W PTS 10 Atlantic City,
USA

17.09.86 Harry Theodossiadis W RSC 4
Kensington
14.03.87 Silvester Mittee W RSC 5 Southwark
(*Vacant British Welterweight Title*)
26.05.87 Marvin McDowell W RSC 1 Wembley
26.11.87 Rocky Kelly W RSC 5 Fulham
(*British Welterweight Title Defence*)
29.03.88 Sammy Floyd W PTS 8 Wembley
15.04.89 Nino la Rocca L PTS 12 Vasto, Italy
(*Vacant European Welterweight Title*)
15.11.89 George Collins W RSC 5 Reading
(*British Welterweight Title Defence*)
10.01.90 Buck Smith L RSC 7 Kensington
27.03.90 Trevor Smith W RSC 6 Mayfair
(*British Welterweight Title Defence*)
09.05.90 Antoine Fernandez W CO 2 Wembley
(*European Welterweight Title
Challenge*)
10.10.90 Rocky Berg W RSC 2 Kensington
14.11.90 Patrizio Oliva L PTS 12 Campione
d'Italia, Italy
(*European Welterweight Title Defence*)
16.01.91 Del Bryan L PTS 12 Kensington
(*British Welterweight Title Defence*)
16.04.91 Donovan Boucher L CO 9 Nottingham
(*Commonwealth Welterweight Title
Challenge*)
17.02.93 Bozon Haule W RSC 3 Bethnal Green
31.03.93 Newton Barnett W PTS 8 Bethnal
Green
23.06.93 Kevin Lueshing L RSC 5 Edmonton
(*Vacant Southern Area L.
Middleweight Title*)
Career: 52 contests, won 40, drew 1, lost 11.

David Lake (Noonan)

Herne Bay. *Born* London, 31 January, 1964
Welterweight. Ht. 5'8"
Manager Self

04.11.87 Lee West L RSC 6 Gravesend
11.02.88 Mark Pellat W RSC 4 Gravesend
24.02.88 Dean Bramhald L PTS 6 Southend
08.03.88 Tony Gibbs L PTS 6 Holborn
13.04.88 Tony Gibbs L RSC 1 Gravesend
06.09.88 Shane Tonks W PTS 6 Southend
26.09.88 Steve Taggart W PTS 6 Piccadilly
04.10.88 Shane Tonks W RSC 4 Southend
24.10.88 Carl Brasier W RSC 1 Windsor
14.11.88 Jan Nyholm L PTS 4 Helsinki, Finland
06.04.89 Ian Hosten W PTS 6 Stevenage
09.05.89 Paul Day L RSC 6 St Albans
28.06.89 Steve Foran L RSC 1 Brentwood
23.10.90 Trevor Ambrose L PTS 6 Leicester
05.03.91 Benny Collins L RSC 4 Millwall
07.10.92 Michael Smyth L CO 2 Barry
26.06.93 Sean Baker L PTS 4 Keynsham
Career: 17 contests, won 6, lost 11.

Gavin Lane (Keeble)

Paignton. *Born* Rainham, 14 July, 1971
Welterweight. Ht. 5'11¼"
Manager J. Gaynor

28.11.91 Dewi Roberts W PTS 6 Coventry
30.03.92 Razza Campbell L PTS 6 Coventry
27.05.93 Sean Baker L PTS 8 Bristol
Career: 3 contests, won 1, lost 2.

Martin Langtry

Lincon. *Born* Hampstead, 22 May, 1964
Cruiserweight. Ht. 5'10"
Manager K. Tate

29.04.93 Stevie R. Davies W RSC 2 Newcastle
12.05.93 Simon McDougall W PTS 6 Sheffield
Career: 2 contests, won 2.

David Larkin

Leeds. *Born* Pontefract, 26 April, 1972
L. Middleweight. Ht. 5'10½"
Manager M. Duff

29.10.92 Rick North W PTS 6 Leeds
07.04.93 Cliff Churchward W RSC 4 Leeds
19.05.93 Ray Golding W PTS 6 Sunderland
Career: 3 contests, won 3.

Phil Lashley

Birmingham. *Born* Birmingham, 1 May,
1965
S. Featherweight. Ht. 5'5"
Manager Self

27.04.86 Ronnie Stephenson L PTS 4 Doncaster
30.05.86 David Beech L PTS 6 Stoke
10.09.86 Gypsy Johnny W RSC 1 Stoke
17.09.86 Paul Hodkinson L RSC 2 Kensington
10.11.86 Roy Williams W CO 1 Birmingham
18.11.86 Dean Lynch L PTS 6 Swansea
08.12.86 Frank Monkhouse L RSC 4
Birmingham
28.01.87 Shane Porter L RSC 1 Dudley
03.03.87 John Carlin L PTS 6 Livingston
24.03.87 John Carlin W RSC 1 Wolverhampton
08.04.87 Gary King L CO 1 Evesham
13.10.87 Mick Greenwood L PTS 6
Wolverhampton
09.11.87 Ronnie Stephenson DREW 4
Birmingham
24.11.87 Mark Goult L CO 1 Wisbech
14.02.88 Steve Pike L CO 1 Peterborough
21.03.88 Dean Lynch L PTS 6 Bethnal Green
13.04.88 Paul Bowen W RSC 1 Wolverhampton
20.04.88 Chris Cooper W PTS 6 Torquay
23.05.88 Roy Williams W RSC 2 Mayfair
09.09.88 Ronnie Stephenson W PTS 6 Doncaster
29.09.88 Peter Gabbitus L CO 2 Stafford
14.11.88 Mark Antony L RSC 2 Stratford upon
Avon
02.02.89 Lester James L PTS 4 Wolverhampton
28.02.89 Lester James L PTS 6 Dudley
15.03.89 Andrew Robinson L PTS 6 Stoke
17.04.89 Lester James L RSC 5 Birmingham
28.06.89 Jamie Morris L RSC 1 Kenilworth
18.09.89 Peter Judson L PTS 6 Mayfair
04.10.89 Craig Garbutt L PTS 6 Stafford
16.10.89 Neil Leitch L RSC 6 Manchester
30.10.89 Gary Hickman L RSC 4 Piccadilly
28.11.89 Neil Leitch L PTS 6 Wolverhampton
04.12.89 Neil Leitch L PTS 6 Grimsby
12.12.89 John O'Meara L CO 3 Brentford
08.02.90 Jason Primera L PTS 6 Southwark
19.02.90 Peter Judson L CO 6 Nottingham
19.03.90 Neil Leitch L PTS 6 Grimsby
27.03.90 Ronnie Stephenson W PTS 6
Wolverhampton
21.05.90 Ronnie Stephenson L PTS 6 Grimsby
04.06.90 Elvis Parsley L RSC 3 Birmingham
23.01.91 Mark Bates L RTD 3 Brentwood
04.03.91 Dave Annis W CO 2 Birmingham
01.05.91 Mark Bates L PTS 6 Bethnal Green
04.06.91 Paul Donaghey L CO 1 Bethnal Green
21.10.91 Ronnie Stephenson L PTS 6
Cleethorpes

21.11.91 Ronnie Stephenson L PTS 6 Stafford
30.03.92 Jamie McBride L RSC 1 Glasgow
05.10.92 Chip O'Neill L PTS 6 Manchester
12.05.93 Gary Marston L RSC 2 Stoke
Career: 49 contests, won 9, drew 1, lost 39.

Jim Lawlor   Chris Bevan

Jim Lawlor
Birmingham. *Born* Birmingham, 1 March, 1961
Welterweight. Ht. 5'9"
Manager Self

17.06.88 Michael Oliver DREW 6 Edgbaston
10.10.88 Michael Oliver L RSC 4 Edgbaston
28.11.88 B. F. Williams W PTS 6 Edgbaston
21.06.90 Richard O'Brien DREW 6 Alfreton
03.10.90 Trevor Meikle W PTS 6 Solihull
09.10.90 Stuart Rimmer L CO 2 Wolverhampton
14.11.90 Dean Bramhald DREW 8 Doncaster
21.11.90 Trevor Meikle W PTS 6 Solihull
06.12.90 Ronnie Campbell DREW 8 Wolverhampton
05.03.91 Mark Pearce W PTS 6 Cardiff
17.04.91 Dean Hollington L PTS 6 Kensington
20.06.91 Richard Burton W PTS 6 Liverpool
07.09.91 Abram Gumede L PTS 6 Belfast
13.11.91 Dean Hollington L PTS 6 Bethnal Green
05.12.91 Ernie Loveridge L PTS 8 Cannock
20.02.92 Wayne Timmins L PTS 6 Oakengates
21.10.92 Rick North L PTS 6 Stoke
12.11.92 Carl Wright L RSC 3 Liverpool
Career: 18 contests, won 5, drew 4, lost 9.

Mark Legg
Newcastle. *Born* South Shields, 25 March, 1970
L. Welterweight. Ht. 5'9½"
Manager Self

28.02.92 Chris Aston W RSC 5 Irvine
17.03.92 Dean Hiscox W PTS 6 Wolverhampton
18.05.92 Charles Shepherd L PTS 6 Marton
24.09.92 Ricky Sackfield W PTS 6 Stockport
Career: 4 contests, won 3, lost 1.

Jason Lepre
Portsmouth. *Born* Portsmouth, 11 July, 1969
Lightweight. Ht. 5'10"
Manager H. Holland

26.04.89 Alan Roberts W RTD 1 Southampton
09.05.89 Hugh Ruse W PTS 6 Southend
21.09.89 Darren Weller L RSC 3 Southampton
30.10.89 Steve Walker L CO 2 Piccadilly
23.05.91 Miguel Matthews W PTS 6 Southampton
16.12.91 Mark Loftus W PTS 6 Southampton
22.01.92 Kevin Simons W PTS 6 Cardiff
17.09.92 Con Cronin L PTS 6 Watford
29.10.92 Jason White L PTS 6 Hayes
17.02.93 Chris Francis L RSC 2 Bethnal Green
Career: 10 contests, won 5, lost 5.

Mickey Lerwill
Telford. *Born* Telford, 6 April, 1965
Welterweight. Ht. 5'5"
Manager G. Hayward

23.06.83 Mickey Bird W RSC 5 Wolverhampton
27.09.83 Mick Harkin DREW 6 Stoke
10.10.83 Graeme Griffin L PTS 6 Birmingham
18.01.84 Rocky Mensah L PTS 6 Stoke
30.01.84 Hugh Kelly L PTS 6 Glasgow
12.09.84 Jaswant Singh Ark L PTS 6 Stoke
20.02.85 Mark Sperin W PTS 6 Wolverhampton
26.03.85 Steve Craggs W RSC 3 Chorley
25.04.85 Dave Heaver W RSC 5 Wolverhampton
29.08.85 Mauro Martelli L PTS 6 Geneva, Switzerland
15.10.85 Kid Milo L PTS 6 Wolverhampton
19.11.85 Lenny Gloster L PTS 8 Stafford
27.01.86 Lenny Gloster W PTS 6 Dudley
25.03.86 Steve Tempro W PTS 6 Wolverhampton
17.04.86 Gary Sommerville DREW 6 Wolverhampton
14.10.86 Del Bryan L PTS 8 Wolverhampton
16.12.86 John Ashton L PTS 8 Alfreton
27.02.90 Cliff Churchward W PTS 6 Evesham
14.03.90 Ernie Loveridge L PTS 6 Stoke
04.04.90 Eddie King W PTS 6 Stafford
24.05.90 Ernie Loveridge DREW 6 Dudley
14.09.90 Trevor Meikle DREW 8 Telford
10.04.91 Gary Osborne L PTS 10 Wolverhampton
(Vacant Midlands Area Welterweight Title)
29.08.91 John McGlynn L PTS 6 Oakengates
12.11.91 Ernie Loveridge L PTS 6 Wolverhampton
05.12.91 Trevor Meikle W PTS 6 Oakengates
04.12.92 Kevin Thompson L PTS 6 Telford
Career: 27 contests, won 9, drew 4, lost 14.

Delroy Leslie
Wallington, *Born* Jamaica, 22 February, 1970
L. Welterweight. Ht. 5'11½"
Manager M. Duff

29.04.93 Phil Found W PTS 6 Mayfair
14.06.93 Jason Barker W RTD 3 Bayswater
Career: 2 contests, won 2.

Alan Levene   Les Clark

Alan Levene
Liverpool. *Born* Liverpool, 26 February, 1968
Lightweight. Ht. 5'7½"
Manager B. Hearn

13.10.89 Mike Chapman W PTS 6 Preston
20.12.89 Finn McCool W RSC 2 Kirkby
24.01.90 Steve Winstanley DREW 6 Preston
17.10.90 Sugar Free Somerville DREW 6 Bethnal Green
05.05.92 Steve Winstanley W RSC 2 Preston
28.11.92 Mark Geraghty W PTS 6 Manchester
20.04.93 Joe Fannin W CO 1 Brentwood
15.05.93 Russell Davison W PTS 6 Glasgow
Career: 8 contests, won 6, drew 2.

Steve Levene
Birmingham. *Born* Birmingham, 23 August, 1969
L. Middleweight. Ht. 5'8½"
Manager P. Cowdell

27.10.92 Steve Scott L RSC 1 Cradley Heath
07.12.92 Warren Stephens W CO 2 Birmingham
16.03.93 Alan Williams W RSC 1 Edgbaston
24.03.93 Sean Baker DREW 6 Belfast
19.04.93 Bullit Andrews W PTS 6 Northampton
18.05.93 Mark Antony L RSC 1 Edgbaston
career: 6 contests, won 3, drew 1, lost 2.

(Gilbert) Gil Lewis
Willenhall. *Born* Coventry, 29 July, 1965
L. Heavyweight. Ht. 5'10½"
Manager Self

22.11.89 Gus Mendes W RSC 2 Solihull
17.01.90 Nigel Rafferty W PTS 6 Stoke

21.03.90 Lee Woolis W PTS 6 Solihull
24.05.90 Coco Collins W PTS 6 Dudley
21.06.90 Jimmy Ellis W PTS 6 Alfreton
06.12.90 Dave Owens W CO 2 Wolverhampton
28.01.91 Carlos Christie L PTS 8 Birmingham
27.02.91 Alan Baptiste W RSC 1 Wolverhampton
22.06.91 John Foreman DREW 6 Earls Court
01.10.91 Lee Prudden DREW 8 Bedworth
21.11.91 Art Stacey W RSC 4 Stafford
20.01.92 Tony Behan W PTS 8 Coventry
01.02.91 Ginger Tshabalala L RSC 4 Birmingham
15.09.92 Gary Delaney L CO 2 Crystal Palace
17.06.93 John J. Cooke L RSC 9 Bedworth
(Vacant Midlands Area L. Heavyweight Title)
Career: 15 contests, won 9, drew 2, lost 4.

Steve Lewsam

Grimsby. *Born* Cleethorpes, 8 September, 1960
Midlands Area Cruiserweight Champion.
Ht. 6'2"
Manager Self

22.11.82 Winston Wray W PTS 4 Liverpool
07.11.83 Wes Taylor W PTS 6 Birmingham
22.11.83 Jerry Golden L RSC 5 Manchester
27.10.88 Paul Sheldon W PTS 6 Birmingham
01.12.88 Ian Carmichael W CO 2 Stafford
07.12.88 Chris Little W RSC 1 Stoke
16.02.89 Dave Lawrence W PTS 6 Stafford
08.05.89 Abner Blackstock DREW 8 Grimsby
04.09.89 Mick Cordon W PTS 8 Grimsby
04.12.89 Abner Blackstock W PTS 8 Grimsby
09.03.90 Dennis Bailey DREW 8 Grimsby
21.05.90 Dennis Bailey W PTS 8 Grimsby
05.09.90 Herbie Hide L RSC 4 Brighton
18.11.90 Herbie Hide L RSC 1 Birmingham
12.02.91 Cordwell Hylton L RSC 8 Wolverhampton
29.04.91 Dave Muhammed L PTS 8 Cleethorpes
16.09.91 Cordwell Hylton W PTS 10 Cleethorpes
(Midlands Area Cruiserweight Title Challenge)
09.12.91 Tony Booth W PTS 8 Cleethorpes
04.06.92 Carl Thompson L RSC 8 Cleethorpes
(Vacant British Cruiserweight Title)
26.10.92 Tom Collins DREW 8 Cleethorpes
03.12.92 Eddie Smulders L CO 4 Rotterdam, Holland
26.04.93 Steve Osborne L PTS 6 Cleethorpes
10.05.93 David Jules W CO 6 Cleethorpes
Career: 23 contests, won 12, drew 3, lost 8.

Alan Ley

Newport. *Born* Newport, 29 December, 1968
Bantamweight. Ht. 5'6"
Manager A. Blackstock

03.09.91 Andrew Bloomer W PTS 6 Cardiff
22.01.92 Ceri Farrell W PTS 6 Cardiff
17.02.92 Leigh Williams W PTS 6 Mayfair
19.10.92 Shaun Norman W PTS 6 Mayfiar
24.02.93 Prince Nassem Hamed L CO 2 Wembley
Career: 5 contests, won 4, lost 1.

Earl Ling

Norwich. *Born* Kings Lynn, 9 March, 1972

S. Middleweight. Ht. 5'10"
Manager G. Holmes

08.09.92 Eddie Collins W PTS 6 Norwich
11.05.93 Mark Hale L RSC 2 Norwich
Career: 2 contests, won 1, lost 1.

Wayne Llewelyn   Les Clark

Wayne Llewelyn

Deptford. *Born* Greenwich, 20 April, 1970
Heavyweight. Ht. 6'3½"
Manager B. Paget

18.01.92 Chris Coughlan W RSC 3 Kensington
30.03.92 Steve Stewart W RSC 4 Eltham
23.04.92 Gary Charlton W RSC 4 Eltham
10.12.92 Gary McCrory W RSC 2 Glasgow
23.05.93 Cordwell Hylton W PTS 6 Brockley
Career: 5 Contests, won 5.

Edward Lloyd

Rhyl. *Born* St Asaph, 23 April, 1963
S. Featherweight. Ht. 5'7½"
Manager Self

07.02.83 Stan Atherton W PTS 6 Liverpool
14.02.83 Sammy Rodgers W RSC 4 Manchester
21.02.83 Paul Cook L RSC 1 Mayfair
27.04.83 Bobby Welburn W PTS 6 Rhyl
09.05.83 Jimmy Thornton L RSC 1 Manchester
16.09.83 Jim Paton L PTS 6 Rhyl
28.11.83 John Murphy L PTS 8 Rhyl
06.02.84 Paul Keers W PTS 6 Liverpool
06.03.84 Gary Felvus L PTS 8 Stoke
12.06.84 Mickey Brooks L RSC 6 St Helens
06.08.84 Henry Arnold W RSC 6 Aintree
15.10.84 Steve Griffith L RTD 4 Liverpool
05.12.84 Jaswant Singh Ark W RSC 2 Stoke
01.02.85 Andy Williams DREW 6 Warrington
29.03.85 Billy Laidman W RSC 2 Liverpool
10.04.85 Brian Roche L RSC 7 Leeds
20.05.85 Gary Flear L PTS 8 Nottingham
19.07.85 Stanley Jones DREW 10 Colwyn Bay
(Vacant Welsh Lightweight Title)
10.02.86 Peter Bradley L PTS 8 Glasgow
06.03.86 Najib Daho L PTS 8 Manchester

24.11.86 Keith Parry L PTS 8 Cardiff
13.01.87 Sugar Gibiliru W PTS 8 Oldham
09.02.87 Craig Windsor W RSC 1 Cardiff
24.02.87 Alonzo Lopez W RTD 1 Marbella, Spain
31.10.87 Abdeselan Azowague W PTS 6 Marbella, Spain
30.11.87 Gary Maxwell L PTS 8 Nottingham
01.02.88 Colin Lynch L RTD 4 Northampton
11.02.92 Dewi Roberts W RSC 1 Cardiff
19.05.92 Mervyn Bennett W RSC 5 Cardiff
07.10.92 Steve Robinson L RTD 8 Barry
14.11.92 Carl Hook W PTS 6 Cardiff
19.01.93 Barrie Kelley L PTS 10 Cardiff
(Vacant Welsh S. Featherweight Title)
30.03.93 Nigel Haddock L RTD 4 Cardiff
05.05.93 Francisco Arroyo L RTD 3 Belfast
Career: 34 contests, won 14, drew 2, lost 18.

Paul Lloyd

Ellesmere Port. *Born* Bebington, 7 December, 1968
Bantamweight. Ht. 5'7"
Manager Self

25.09.92 Graham McGrath W RSC 3 Liverpool
23.10.92 Kid McAuley W PTS 4 Liverpool
20.11.92 Des Gargano W PTS 4 Liverpool
15.12.92 Glyn Shepherd W RSC 1 Liverpool
27.02.93 Miguel Matthews W PTS 6 Ellesmere Port
04.05.93 Andrew Bloomer W PTS 6 Liverpool
Career: 6 contests, won 6.

Robert Lloyd

Rhyl. *Born* Prestatyn, 4 August, 1960
L. Welterweight. Ht. 5'9"
Manager N. Basso

17.02.83 Bobby McGowan W RSC 1 Morley
04.03.83 Ron Atherton W CO 1 Queensferry
22.03.83 Mo Hussein L PTS 6 Bethnal Green
27.04.83 Dave Heaver DREW 6 Rhyl
09.05.83 Terry Welch W PTS 6 Manchester
25.05.83 Kevin Sheeran W RSC 5 Rhyl
09.11.83 Glyn Rhodes L PTS 8 Sheffield
28.11.83 Steve Boyle W PTS 6 Rhyl
28.01.84 Mick Harkin L PTS 6 Hanley
06.02.84 George Schofield DREW 8 Liverpool
06.03.84 Lee Roy L PTS 6 Stoke
31.07.87 Steve Hogg L PTS 6 Wrexham
09.03.92 Mike Calderwood L RSC 1 Manchester
22.10.92 Alan McDowall L RTD 4 Glasgow
15.02.93 Ricky Sackfield L RSC 4 Manchester
Career: 15 contests, won 5, drew 2, lost 8.

Ernie Locke

Cradley Heath. *Born* Warley, 1 September, 1966
Welterweight. Ht. 5'8"
Manager P. Cowdell

22.02.93 Billy McDougall L PTS 6 Birmingham
16.03.93 Cliff Churchward DREW 6 Edgbaston
Career: 2 contests, drew 1, lost 1.

Steve Loftus

Stoke. *Born* Stoke, 10 October, 1971
L. Heavyweight. Ht. 6'2½"
Manager P. Brogan

29.09.92 Bobby Mack L PTS 6 Stoke

21.10.92	Paul Murray W PTS 6 Stoke
09.12.92	Lee Prudden L PTS 6 Stoke
17.03.93	Chris Nurse L PTS 6 Stoke
12.05.93	Zak Goldman W PTS 6 Stoke

Career: 5 contests, won 2, lost 3.

Gary Logan   Les Clark

Gary Logan

Brixton. *Born* Lambeth, 10 October, 1968
Southern Area Welterweight Champion. Ht.
5'8¾"
Manager Self

05.10.88	Peppy Muire W RTD 3 Wembley
02.11.88	Tony Gibbs W PTS 6 Southwark
07.12.88	Pat Dunne W PTS 6 Piccadilly
12.01.89	Mike Russell W CO 1 Southwark
20.02.89	Dave Griffiths W RSC 5 Mayfair
29.03.89	Ronnie Campbell W PTS 6 Wembley
10.05.89	Tony Britland W CO 1 Kensington
07.06.89	Davey Hughes W CO 1 Wembley
24.08.89	Mike English W CO 2 Tampa, USA
04.10.89	Simon Eubank W PTS 6 Kensington
12.10.89	Jimmy Thornton W PTS 6 Southwark
08.11.89	Chris Blake L PTS 8 Wembley
10.01.90	Julian Eavis W PTS 8 Kensington
03.03.90	Anthony Joe Travis W CO 5 Wembley
09.05.90	Joseph Alexander W PTS 8 Wembley
13.09.90	Manuel Rojas W PTS 8 Watford
16.01.91	Julian Eavis W RSC 5 Kensington
18.02.91	Gordon Blair W CO 1 Mayfair
25.04.91	Trevor Ambrose W PTS 8 Mayfair
17.10.91	Des Robinson W PTS 8 Southwark
15.10.92	Mick Duncan W PTS 8 Lewisham
17.12.92	Roy Rowland W RSC 4 Wembley
	(Vacant Southern Area Welterweight Title)
23.05.93	Glyn Rhodes W CO 3 Brockley
25.06.93	Gordon Blair W RSC 6 Battersea

Career: 24 contests, won 23, lost 1.

Patrick Loughran

Ballymena. *Born* Ballymena, 15 September, 1972
L. Welterweight. Ht. 5'6"
Manager P. Brogan

11.09.91	Kevin Lowe W PTS 6 Stoke
11.12.91	Keith Hardman W PTS 6 Stoke
11.03.92	Rick North W PTS 6 Stoke
07.07.92	Jason Barker W PTS 6 Bristol
24.03.93	Felix Kelly W PTS 6 Belfast

Career: 5 contests, won 5.

Dave Lovell

Birmingham. *Born* Birmingham, 15 April, 1962
Welterweight. Ht. 5'7½"
Manager E. Cashmore

25.03.92	Billy Robinson L PTS 6 Hinckley
29.04.92	Jason Barker W PTS 6 Stoke
26.09.92	Seth Jones W RSC 4 Earls Court
27.10.92	Spencer McCracken L PTS 4 Cradley Heath
18.11.92	Alan Peacock L PTS 6 Solihull
30.01.93	Paul Knights L PTS 6 Brentwood
22.02.93	Alan Peacock L PTS 8 Glasgow
01.04.93	Richard O'Brien L PTS 6 Evesham

Career: 8 contests, won 2, lost 6.

Ernie Loveridge   Les Clark

Ernie Loveridge

Wolverhampton. *Born* Bromsgrove, 7 July, 1970
L. Middleweight. Former Undefeated Midlands Area Welterweight Champion. Ht. 5'10"
Manager Self

06.02.89	Ricky Nelson L RSC 6 Nottingham
17.04.89	Martin Robinson L PTS 4 Birmingham
08.05.89	Bullit Andrews W PTS 6 Edgbaston
05.06.89	Alan Richards L PTS 6 Birmingham
28.06.89	Barry Messam L PTS 6 Kenilworth
10.10.89	Matt Sturgess W RSC 1 Wolverhampton
25.10.89	Darren Mount L PTS 6 Stoke
11.12.89	Cliff Churchward W PTS 6 Birmingham
27.02.90	Julian Eavis W PTS 6 Evesham
14.03.90	Mickey Lerwill W PTS 6 Stoke

27.03.90	Eddie King W PTS 6 Wolverhampton
24.04.90	Mark Jay W PTS 6 Stoke
24.05.90	Mickey Lerwill DREW 6 Dudley
18.09.90	Ronnie Campbell W PTS 6 Wolverhampton
24.10.90	Trevor Meikle W PTS 6 Dudley
23.01.91	Cliff Churchward W PTS 6 Solihull
27.02.91	Ronnie Campbell W PTS 8 Wolverhampton
13.03.91	John Corcoran W RSC 4 Stoke
10.04.91	Julian Eavis DREW 8 Wolverhampton
14.05.91	Paul Murray W PTS 8 Dudley
05.06.91	Cliff Churchward W PTS 8 Wolverhampton
10.09.91	Gary Osborne W RSC 1 Wolverhampton
	(Midlands Area Welterweight Title Challenge)
12.11.91	Mickey Lerwill W PTS 6 Wolverhampton
05.12.91	Jim Lawlor W PTS 8 Cannack
01.02.92	Michael Oliver W PTS 8 Birmingham
19.09.92	Paul Jones L PTS 6 Glasgow
01.10.92	Neville Brown L CO 4 Telford
20.01.93	Lee Crocker L PTS 5 Wolverhampton
17.02.93	Robert McCracken L CO 4 Bethnal Green
31.03.93	Kevin Lueshing L RSC 5 Bethnal Green
18.05.93	Antonio Fernandez L PTS 8 Edgbaston

Career: 31 contests, won 18, drew 2, lost 11.

Kevin Lowe

Sheffield. *Born* Sheffield, 24 August, 1964
Lightweight. Ht. 5'6"
Manager Self

11.09.91	Patrick Loughran L PTS 6 Stoke
26.09.91	Eunan Devenney W CO 2 Dunstable
14.10.91	Carl Roberts L PTS 6 Manchester
22.10.91	Tommy Smith L RSC 4 Hartlepool
28.11.91	Joey Moffat L PTS 6 Liverpool
10.12.91	Richard Woolgar L PTS 6 Sheffield
27.02.92	Joey Moffat L PTS 6 Liverpool
30.03.92	Dave McHale L RSC 5 Glasgow
30.04.92	Dominic McGuigan L RSC 6 Mayfair
19.10.92	Mark Geraghty L PTS 8 Glasgow
02.11.92	John T. Kelly L PTS 6 Liverpool
12.11.92	Dominic McGuigan L RSC 2 Liverpool

Career: 12 contests, won 1, lost 11.

Kevin Lueshing

Beckenham. *Born* Beckenham, 17 April, 1968
Welterweight. Southern Area L. Middleweight Champion. Ht. 5'11"
Manager Self

30.09.91	John McGlynn W RSC 2 Kensington
23.10.91	Julian Eavis W RSC 2 Bethnal Green
14.12.91	Trevor Meikle W CO 3 Bexleyheath
18.01.92	Simon Eubank W CO 4 Kensington
25.03.92	Tracy Jocelyn W RSC 3 Dagenham
30.04.92	Newton Barnett W PTS 6 Kensington
03.02.93	Ian Chantler W RSC 2 Earls Court
17.02.93	Leigh Wicks W PTS 6 Bethnal Green
31.03.93	Ernie Loveridge W RSC 5 Bethnal Green
14.04.93	Marty Duke W RSC 2 Kensington
23.06.93	Kirkland Laing W RSC 5 Edmonton
	(Vacant Southern Area L. Middleweight Title)

Career: 11 contests, won 11.

Colin Lynch

Coventry. *Born* Coventry, 9 November, 1961

Former Midlands Area Featherweight Champion. Ht. 5'6"

Manager P. Byrne

26.01.87	John Devine W RSC 1 Leamington
18.03.87	Shane Porter L RSC 3 Stoke
	(Vacant Midlands Area Featherweight Title)
12.06.87	Stuart Carmichael W RSC 6 Leamington
10.09.87	Gary de Roux L RSC 3 Peterborough
18.11.87	Karl Taylor L RSC 4 Solihull
01.02.88	Edward Lloyd W RTD 4 Northampton
22.03.88	George Jones W CO 7 Wolverhampton
25.04.88	Steve Pollard L PTS 8 Birmingham
28.09.88	Derek Amory W PTS 10 Solihull
	(Vacant Midlands Area Featherweight Title)
23.11.88	Dean Lynch W PTS 8 Solihull
25.01.89	John Naylor W CO 1 Solihull
25.03.89	Freddy Cruz L PTS 8 Paestum, Italy
10.05.89	Mark Holt L RSC 7 Solihull
	(Midlands Area Featherweight Title Defence)
11.09.89	John Davison L RSC 2 Nottingham
20.12.89	Robert Dickie L RSC 1 Swansea
21.02.90	Regilio Tuur L RSC 3 Rotterdam, Holland
12.12.90	Henry Armstrong L RSC 3 Stoke
22.02.91	John Green L RSC 6 Manchester
20.03.91	Peter Judson L RTD 5 Solihull
24.04.91	Peter Harris L PTS 8 Aberavon
28.05.91	Steve Robinson L RSC 6 Cardiff
01.10.91	Paul Forrest W PTS 6 Sheffield
26.10.91	Paul Harvey L RSC 1 Brentwood
10.12.91	Paul Forrest L PTS 6 Sheffield
22.01.92	Kelton McKenzie L RSC 5 Solihull
24.02.92	Des Gargano W PTS 6 Coventry
02.03.92	Bradley Stone L RSC 3 Basildon
03.09.92	Dennis Oakes L RSC 1 Liverpool
24.11.92	John Irwin L RSC 4 Doncaster
23.03.93	Mike Deveney L PTS 6 Wolverhampton
09.06.93	Bradley Stone L RTD 1 Lewisham

Career: 31 contests, won 9, lost 22.

Dean Lynch

Swansea. *Born* Swansea, 21 November, 1964

S. Featherweight. Ht. 5'6"

Manager Self

18.09.86	Billy Barton L PTS 6 Weston super Mare
06.10.86	Paddy Maguire W PTS 6 Birmingham
18.11.86	Phil Lashley W PTS 6 Swansea
01.03.88	Gary King L PTS 6 Southend
21.03.88	Phil Lashley W PTS 6 Bethnal Green
09.04.88	John Knight L PTS 6 Bristol
20.04.88	Henry Armstrong W PTS 6 Stoke
13.05.88	Raymond Armand L PTS 8 Hyeres, France
23.11.88	Colin Lynch L PTS 8 Solihull
12.04.89	James Hunter L RSC 4 Swansea
	(Vacant Welsh S. Featherweight Title)
12.05.89	Valerio Nati L RSC 6 Lodi, Italy
22.01.90	Donnie Hood L PTS 8 Glasgow
19.02.90	Regilio Tuur L PTS 6 Arnhem, Holland

10.03.90	Freddy Cruz L RSC 4 Lamezia Terme, Italy
14.04.92	Lee Fox W PTS 6 Mansfield
15.09.92	Henry Armstrong L RSC 5 Liverpool
14.12.92	Karl Morling W RSC 4 Northampton
07.04.93	Tony Silkstone L PTS 8 Leeds
28.04.93	Francisco Arroyo L PTS 6 Dublin

Career: 19 contests, won 6, lost 13.

Paul Lynch

Swansea. *Born* Swansea, 27 December, 1966

L. Middleweight. Ht. 5'11"

Manager Self

23.10.89	Darren Burford W PTS 6 Mayfair
16.11.89	Robbie Harron W PTS 6 Weston super Mare
20.12.89	Peter Reid W RSC 4 Swansea
08.03.90	Tony Booth W PTS 6 Watford
04.12.90	Ernie Noble W RSC 3 Southend
12.02.91	Roy Rowland W RTD 4 Basildon
01.10.91	Peter Manfredo L PTS 8 Providence, USA
12.02.92	Robert McCracken L RSC 4 Wembley
14.04.92	Paul Jones L RSC 3 Mansfield
16.02.93	Tony Velinor W PTS 8 Tooting
31.03.93	Kevin Sheeran L RSC 1 Barking

Career: 11 contests, won 7, lost 4.

Chris Lyons

Birmingham. *Born* Birmingham, 2 September, 1972

Featherweight. Ht. 5'9"

Manager Self

02.12.91	Ronnie Sephenson L PTS 6 Birmingham
09.12.91	Ronnie Stephenson L PTS 6 Cleethorpes
22.01.92	Dennis Oakes L RSC 3 Stoke
17.05.92	Dave Martin DREW 6 Harringay
08.09.92	Robert Braddock L CO 5 Doncaster
13.10.92	Paul Kelly W PTS 6 Wolverhampton
30.10.92	Paul Kelly W CO 1 Birmingham
17.12.92	Mark Bowers L CO 2 Wembley
08.03.93	Chip O'Neill L PTS 6 Leeds
22.04.93	Marcus Duncan W RSC 2 Bury
26.06.93	Tim Yeates L PTS 4 Earls Court

Career: 11 contests, won 3, drew 1, lost 7.

Ricky Mabbett

Leicester. *Born* Leicester, 27 November, 1971

Welterweight. Ht. 5'9"

Manager K. Squires

19.03.92	Phil Epton W RSC 3 York
16.06.92	Ojay Abrahams L PTS 6 Dagenham
08.09.92	Marty Duke DREW 6 Norwich
27.10.92	Steve McGovern DREW 6 Leicester
26.01.93	Marty Duke L CO 1 Leicester
16.03.93	Spencer McCracken L PTS 6 Edgbaston
26.04.93	Darren McInulty W CO 3 Cleethorpes
19.05.93	Ojay Abrahams W RSC 4 Leicester

Career: 8 Contests, won 3, drew 2, lost 3.

Kevin Mabbutt

Northampton. *Born* Northampton, 23 February, 1969

Welterweight. Ht. 5'8¾"

Manager J. Cox

06.04.92	Peter Reid L PTS 6 Northampton
28.04.92	Sean Cave W PTS 6 Corby
05.10.92	Cliff Churchward W PTS 6 Northampton
14.12.92	Billy McDougall W RTD 4 Northampton
23.02.93	Paul Dyer W PTS 6 Kettering
04.03.93	Bullit Andrews W PTS 6 Northampton
19.04.93	James Campbell W PTS 6 Northampton

Career: 7 contests, won 6, lost 1.

Kris McAdam

Glasgow. *Born* Glasgow, 1 January, 1964

Scottish Lightweight Champion. Ht. 5'9½"

Manager T. Gilmour

15.10.84	Bobby Welburn DREW 6 Glasgow
25.02.85	Denzil Goddard W RSC 1 Glasgow
27.03.85	Marvin P. Gray W RSC 3 Gateshead
10.05.85	Dave Smith L PTS 6 Glasgow
16.09.85	Russell Jones L PTS 6 Glasgow
09.10.89	Paul Charters L PTS 8 Glasgow
29.11.89	Chris Bennett L CO 3 Marton
19.02.90	Martin Reilly W PTS 6 Glasgow
19.03.90	Martin Reilly W RSC 8 Glasgow
26.03.90	Jim Moffat W PTS 8 Glasgow
07.09.90	Sugar Gibiliru L PTS 8 Liverpool
22.10.90	Jim Moffat W RSC 5 Glasgow
	(Scottish Lightweight Title Challenge)
22.01.91	John Smith W PTS 6 Glasgow
22.04.91	Brian Roche L RSC 2 Glasgow
	(Elim. British Lightweight Title)
18.11.91	Colin Sinnott W PTS 6 Glasgow
27.01.92	Pete Roberts W CO 2 Glasgow
18.03.92	Nigel Bradley L CO 2 Glasgow
22.02.93	Dave Madden W PTS 8 Glasgow

Career: 18 contests, won 10, drew 1, lost 7.

Eamonn McAuley

Belfast. *Born* Belfast, 4 January, 1966

S. Featherweight. Ht. 5'7"

Manager B. Hearn

20.05.86	Dean Bramhald W PTS 6 Wembley
29.10.86	Les Remikie W RSC 2 Belfast
17.01.87	Les Remikie W RTD 2 Belfast
26.02.87	George Jones W PTS 6 Bethnal Green
25.04.87	Tony Borg W RSC 4 Belfast
19.10.87	Nicky Lucas W RTD 3 Belfast
03.12.87	Andrew Furlong L RTD 3 Belfast
28.09.89	Greg Egbuniwe W PTS 6 Wandsworth
12.09.90	Rick Bushell W RSC 4 Battersea
24.03.93	Russell Davison W PTS 6 Belfast
18.06.93	Pete Buckley W PTS 6 Belfast

Career: 11 contests, won 10, lost 1.

(Colin) Kid McAuley

Liverpool. *Born* Liverpool, 6 June, 1968

Featherweight. Ht. 5'6"

Manager J. Rushton

08.09.92	John Irwin L PTS 6 Doncaster
19.09.92	Alex Docherty L PTS 6 Glasgow
30.09.92	Yusuf Vorajee W PTS 6 Solihull
13.10.92	John White L PTS 4 Bury
23.10.92	Paul Lloyd L PTS 4 Liverpool
10.11.92	Michael Alldis L PTS 6 Dagenham
24.11.92	Miguel Matthews W PTS 6 Doncaster
12.12.92	Michael Alldis L CO 1 Muswell Hill

Twice beaten by Michael Alldis during the season, Kid McAuley (right) misses with a right-hander at Dagenham   Les Clark

27.01.93 Yusuf Vorajee L RSC 5 Stoke
03.03.93 Kevin Middleton L PTS 8 Solihull
16.03.93 John Irwin L PTS 10 Mayfair
(Vacant All-Ireland Featherweight Title)
28.04.93 Barry Jones L PTS 8 Solihull
14.05.93 Shaun Anderson L PTS 8 Kilmarnock
29.05.93 James Murray L PTS 6 Paisley
28.06.93 Carl Roberts W PTS 6 Morecambe
Career: 15 contests, won 3, lost 12.

Mark McBiane

Skegness. *Born* Leamington Spa, 6 April, 1970
L. Heavyweight. Ht. 5'11"
Manager J. Gaynor

28.11.91 Jason McNeill L PTS 6 Evesham
04.02.92 Greg Scott-Briggs L PTS 6 Alfreton
23.04.92 Nicky Wadman L RSC 1 Eltham
08.06.92 Simon McDougall L PTS 6 Bradford
02.02.93 Martin Jolley L RSC 4 Derby
Career: 5 contests, lost 5.

Kevin McBride

Clones. *Born* Monaghan, 10 May, 1973
Heavyweight. Ht. 5'6"
Manager F. Warren

17.12.92 Gary Charlton DREW 6 Barking
13.02.93 Gary Williams W PTS 4 Manchester
Carrer: 2 contests, won 1, drew 1

Paul McCarthy

Southampton. *Born* London, 24 March, 1961
L. Heavyweight. Former Southern Area S. Middleweight Champion. Ht. 6'0"
Manager J. Bishop

29.01.87 Eddie Brooks L PTS 6 Merton
03.03.87 Jim Beckett W CO 1 Southend
06.04.87 Gary Pemberton L RSC 4 Southampton
26.05.87 Neil Simpson W CO 1 Plymouth
25.09.87 Spencer Cummings W CO 3 Tooting
16.11.87 Newton Barnett W PTS 8 Southampton
09.12.87 Rocky Bourkriss W CO 1 Greenwich
14.12.87 Andy Wright L CO 3 Piccadilly
14.03.88 Mark Howell W RSC 2 Mayfair
21.04.88 Steve Aquilina W PTS 6 Bethnal Green
18.05.88 Joe McKenzie W RSC 3 Portsmouth
31.08.88 Denys Cronin L RSC 4 Stoke
24.11.88 Simon Collins DREW 8 Southampton
20.12.88 Simon Collins W DIS 3 Swansea
25.01.89 Brendan Dempsey W PTS 6 Bethnal Green
02.03.89 Cliff Curtis W RTD 7 Southampton
04.04.89 Chris Galloway W RSC 4 Southend
26.04.89 Terry Duffus W PTS 8 Southampton

09.05.89 Derek Myers L PTS 6 Southend
02.10.89 Noel Magee L CO 2 Hanley
30.11.89 Dave Lawrence W PTS 6 Southwark
14.03.90 Richard Bustin W RSC 7 Battersea
(Vacant Southern Area S. Middleweight Title)
26.05.90 Keith Halliwell W RSC 3 Reading
15.10.90 Derek Myers L PTS 8 Lewisham
23.10.90 Nicky Piper L RSC 3 Leicester
08.02.91 Fabrice Tiozzo L CO 2 Villeurbanne, France
20.03.91 Andy Wright L CO 5 Wandsworth
(Southern Area S. Middleweight Title Defence)
16.05.91 Lester Jacobs L PTS 6 Battersea
01.06.91 Ali Forbes L CO 2 Bethnal Green
19.11.91 Dave Lawrence DREW 6 Norwich
19.12.91 Antonio Fernandez L PTS 8 Brierley Hill
16.12.91 Peter Vosper W PTS 6 Southampton
08.01.92 Graham Jenner L PTS 6 Burton
22.01.92 Julian Johnson DREW 6 Cardiff
29.02.92 Graham Jenner L PTS 8 St Leonards
11.03.92 Jason McNeill L PTS 6 Cardiff
30.04.92 Hussain Shah L RTD 4 Kensington
05.10.92 Barry Downes W PTS 6 Northampton
10.12.92 Stefan Wright L PTS 6 Corby
15.02.93 Bruce Scott L PTS 6 Mayfair
16.03.93 Justin Clements L PTS 6 Edgbaston
29.04.93 Gypsy Carman L PTS 6 Hayes
Career: 42 contests, won 18, drew 3, lost 21.

Steve McCarthy

Southampton. *Born* East Ham, 30 July, 1962
Former Undefeated British & Southern Area L. Heavyweight Champion. Ht. 5'11½"
Manager H. Holland

05.02.87	Russell Barnett W CO 1 Southampton
03.03.87	B. K. Bennett W CO 3 Southend
06.04.87	Winston Burnett W PTS 8 Southampton
06.10.87	Jason Baxter DREW 6 Southend
16.11.87	Paul Wesley W CO 8 Southampton
03.02.88	Andy Wright W RSC 4 Wembley
18.05.88	Mike Aubrey W RSC 4 Portsmouth
24.11.88	Serg Fame W PTS 10 Southampton
	(Southern Area L. Heavyweight Title Challenge)
02.03.89	Yves Monsieur W PTS 8 Southampton
26.04.89	Johnny Held W PTS 8 Southampton
21.09.89	Tony Wilson L RTD 3 Southampton
	(Elim. British L. Heavyweight Title)
25.10.90	Serg Fame W PTS 12 Battersea
	(Vacant British L. Heavyweight Title)
16.12.91	John Foreman W PTS 8 Southampton
04.04.92	Henry Maske L DIS 9 Dusseldorf, Germany
29.09.92	Dariusz Michalczewski L DIS 3 Hamburg, Germany
14.04.93	Simon Harris L RSC 5 Kensington

Career: 16 contests, won 11, drew 1, lost 4.

Joe McCluskey

Croy. *Born* Glasgow, 13 March, 1970
L. Heavyweight. Ht. 6'0"
Manager T. Gilmour

27.04.92	John Oxenham W PTS 4 Glasgow
09.07.92	Lee Prudden W PTS 6 Glasgow
25.01.93	Andy Manning W PTS 6 Glasgow

Career: 3 contests, won 3.

Bernard McComiskey

Banbridge. *Born* Banbridge, 9 June, 1971
L. Welterweight. Ht. 5'7"
Manager Self

25.04.90	Lee Fox W RTD 3 Brighton
27.06.90	Stuart Rimmer W PTS 6 Kensington
22.09.90	Wayne Windle L PTS 6 Kensington
11.05.91	Sean Casey W RTD 3 Belfast
24.03.93	Trevor Royal W RSC 6 Belfast
18.06.93	Brian Wright W PTS 6 Belfast

Career: 6 contests, won 5, lost 1.

Robert McCracken

Birmingham. *Born* Birmingham, 31 May, 1968
L. Middleweight. Ht. 6'0"
Manager M. Duff

24.01.91	Mick Mulcahy W RSC 1 Brierley Hill
13.02.91	Gary Barron W RTD 2 Wembley
06.03.91	Tony Britland W RSC 2 Wembley
12.04.91	Dave Andrews W RSC 4 Willenhall
08.05.91	Tony Gibbs W CO 1 Kensington
30.05.91	Paul Murray W RSC 2 Birmingham
04.07.91	Marty Duke W RSC 1 Alfreton
25.07.91	John Smith W RTD 1 Dudley
31.10.91	Newton Barnett W DIS 2 Oakengates
28.11.91	Michael Oliver W RSC 3 Liverpool

Robert McCracken   Les Clark

12.02.92	Paul Lynch W RSC 4 Wembley
01.10.92	Horace Fleary W PTS 8 Telford
02.11.92	Ensley Bingham W RSC 10 Wolverhampton
	(Elim. British L. Middleweight Title)
20.01.93	Leigh Wicks W PTS 8 Wolverhampton
17.02.93	Ernie Loveridge W CO 4 Bethnal Green
24.04.93	Martin Smith W RSC 10 Birmingham
	(Final Elim. British L. Middleweight Title)
29.06.93	Steve Langley W RSC 4 Edgbaston

Career: 17 contests, won 17.

Spencer McCracken

Birmingham. *Born* Birmingham, 8 August, 1969
Welterweight. Ht. 5'9"
Manager Self

15.10.91	Stuart Dunn DREW 6 Dudley
09.12.91	Seth Jones W RSC 2 Brierley Hill
27.10.92	Dave Lovell W PTS 4 Cradley Heath
07.12.92	Mark Antony W CO 1 Birmingham
22.02.93	Rick North W PTS 8 Birmingham
16.03.93	Ricky Mabbett W PTS 6 Edgbaston
18.05.93	Tony Britland W CO 1 Edgbaston

Career: 7 contests, won 6, drew 1.

Mark McCreath

Lincoln. *Born* Bradford, 30 May, 1964
L. Welterweight. Former Undefeated Benelux Welterweight Champion. Ht. 5'8½"
Manager M. Duff

11.05.89	Tom Heiskonen W RSC 6 Tallin, Estonia
01.11.89	Bianto Baekelandt W CO 2 Izegem, Belgium
29.11.89	Abdel Lahjar W RTD 4 Paris, France
09.12.89	Pierre Conan W RSC 4 Toul, France
10.02.90	Josef Rajic W PTS 6 Roulers, France
26.03.90	Eric Capoen W RSC 1 Nogent sur Marne, France

19.05.90	Mohammed Berrabah W RSC 6 Montpelier, France
11.08.90	Mohamed Oumad W RTD 5 Le cap d'Agde, France
05.09.90	Mehmet Demir W RSC 5 Belgrade, Yugoslavia
05.10.90	Patrick Vungbo L PTS 10 Waregem, Belgium
	(Vacant Belgium Welterweight Title)
17.04.91	Pat Barrett L RSC 6 Kensington
	(European L. Welterweight Title Challenge)
21.06.91	Freddy Demeulenaere W RSC 5 Waregem, Belgium
	(Vacant Benelux Welterweight Title)
30.04.92	Gary Barron W RSC 5 Mayfair
01.10.92	Chris Saunders W RSC 4 Telford
07.12.92	Gary Barron W RSC 5 Mayfair
06.03.93	Valery Kayumba L RSC 11 Levallois Perret, France
	(European L. Welterweight Title Challenge)
26.05.93	Peter Till W PTS 8 Mansfield

Career: 17 contests, won 14, lost 3.

Gary McCrory

Annfield Plain. *Born* Blackhill, 20 October, 1960
Heavyweight. Ht. 6'2"
Manager Self

29.09.88	David Jules W PTS 6 Sunderland
22.11.88	David Jules W PTS 6 Marton
28.02.89	Rocky Burton L PTS 6 Marton
28.04.89	Jimmy di Stolfo L RTD 4 Milan, Italy
21.10.89	Doug McKay W PTS 6 Middlesbrough
05.11.89	Herbie Hide L RTD 1 Kensington
24.01.90	Doug McKay W PTS 6 Sunderland
19.02.90	Mike Aubrey L PTS 8 Mayfair
18.09.90	Ian Bulloch W PTS 8 Stoke
18.02.91	Pedro van Raamsdonk L PTS 8 Valkenswaard, Holland
05.04.91	Markus Bott L PTS 8 Hamburg, Germany
06.03.92	Axel Schulz L RSC 2 Berlin, Germany
22.04.92	J. A. Bugner L PTS 4 Wembley
10.12.92	Wayne Llewelyn L RSC 2 Glasgow

Career: 14 contests, won 5, lost 9.

Glenn McCrory

Annfield Plain. *Born* Stanley, 23 September, 1964
Former IBF Cruiserweight Champion. Former Undefeated British & Commonwealth Cruiserweight Champion. Ht. 6'4"
Manager Self

06.02.84	Barry Ellis W RSC 1 Mayfair
22.02.84	Denroy Bryan W PTS 6 Kensington
21.03.84	Steve Abadom W PTS 6 Mayfair
30.04.84	Frank Robinson W PTS 6 Mayfair
09.05.84	Frank Robinson W RSC 4 Mayfair
13.06.84	Andrew Gerrard W PTS 6 Aberavon
06.09.84	Andrew Gerrard W PTS 8 Gateshead
27.10.84	Tony Velasco W PTS 8 Gateshead
24.11.84	Mike Perkins W PTS 8 Gateshead
19.01.85	Nate Robinson W RSC 2 Birmingham
20.02.85	Alex Williamson W PTS 8 Muswell Hill
27.03.85	Gypsy Carman W PTS 8 Gateshead
28.05.85	Alphonso Forbes W CO 1 Muswell Hill

03.09.85	John Westgarth L CO 4 Gateshead
10.12.85	Roy Skeldon W PTS 8 Gateshead
09.04.86	Rudi Pika L PTS 8 Kensington
18.04.86	Anders Eklund L PTS 8 Randers, Denmark
17.06.86	Dave Garside L RSC 7 Blackpool
07.10.86	Hughroy Currie L RSC 2 Oldham
25.11.86	Joe Adams W PTS 6 Louisville, USA
08.01.87	Calvin Sherman W CO 1 Houston, USA
05.12.87	Danny Lawford W PTS 8 Newcastle
18.02.87	Barry Ellis W PTS 8 Fulham
31.03.87	Andy Straughn W RSC 10 Oldham *(Elim. British Cruiserweight Title)*
04.09.87	Chisanda Mutti W PTS 12 Gateshead *(Commonwealth Cruiserweight Title Challenge)*
21.01.88	Tee Jay W PTS 12 Wandsworth *(British Cruiserweight Title Challenge. Commonwealth Cruiserweight Title Defence)*
22.04.88	Lou Gent W RTD 8 Gateshead *(British & Commonwealth Cruiserweight Title Defence)*
01.11.88	Ron Warrior W CO 4 Oklahoma City, USA
15.11.88	Lorenzo Boyd W CO 2 Metairie, USA
28.02.89	Steve Mormino W PTS 10 Marton
03.06.89	Patrick Lumumba W PTS 12 Stanley *(Vacant IBF Cruiserweight Title)*
21.10.89	Siza Makhatini W CO 11 Middlesbrough

	(IBF Cruiserweight Title Defence)
22.03.90	Jeff Lampkin L CO 3 Gateshead *(IBF Cruiserweight Title Defence)*
16.02.91	Terry Armstrong W CO 2 Thornaby
30.09.91	Lennox Lewis L CO 2 Kensington *(British & European Heavyweight Title Challenge)*
26.09.92	Mohamed Bouchiche DREW 8 Paris, France
20.01.93	Ric Lainhart W RSC 2 Avoriaz, France
06.05.93	Mark Young W PTS 10 Las Vegas, USA

Career: 38 contests, won 30, drew 1, lost 7.

Shaun McCrory

Stanley, *Born* Shotley Bridge, 13 June, 1969
S. Middleweight. Ht. 6'2"
Manager Self

03.06.89	Hugh Fury W PTS 6 Stanley
10.10.89	Mick Maw L PTS 4 Sunderland
27.02.90	Ian Vokes W PTS 6 Marton
06.03.90	Benny Simmons W RSC 6 Newcastle
23.03.90	Mark Spencer W RSC 2 Chester le Street
21.04.90	Sean Stringfellow W PTS 6 Sunderland
05.06.90	Alan Pennington L PTS 8 Liverpool
05.09.90	Tony Booth W PTS 6 Stoke
15.10.90	Richard Carter L PTS 8 Brierley Hill
19.11.90	Ian Henry L PTS 6 Manchester
21.01.91	Ian Henry L PTS 6 Glasgow

06.02.91	Tony Booth L PTS 6 Liverpool
13.05.91	John Oxenham W PTS 6 Marton
03.08.91	Ron Collins L PTS 8 Selvino, Italy
13.04.92	Paul Wright L PTS 6 Manchester
28.04.92	Dave Johnson DREW 6 Houghton le Spring
05.10.92	Eddie Knight W PTS 6 Bristol

Career: 17 contests, won 8, drew 1, lost 8.

Errol McDonald

Nottingham. *Born* Nottingham, 11 March, 1964
L. Welterweight. Ht. 5'10"
Manager B. Hearn

21.10.85	Dave Heaver W CO 1 Mayfair
05.11.85	Robert Armstrong W RSC 4 Wembley
20.01.86	Lenny Gloster W PTS 8 Mayfair
17.02.86	Kid Milo DREW 6 Mayfair
27.02.86	Gary Flear W RSC 5 Bethnal Green
09.04.86	Lenny Gloster W PTS 6 Kensington
29.10.86	Gerry Beard W RSC 4 Piccadilly
19.01.87	Mark Simpson W CO 5 Mayfair
30.08.87	Jose Maria Castillo W RSC 3 Marbella, Spain
30.09.87	Roy Callaghan W RSC 4 Mayfair
18.11.87	Billy Cairns W RTD 3 Bethnal Green
03.02.88	Mike English W RSC 2 Wembley
29.03.88	Ramon Nunez W RSC 3 Wembley
21.04.88	Nick Meloscia W PTS 8 Bethnal Green
26.09.88	Jimmy Thornton W RTD 2 Piccadilly
05.10.88	Alfredo Reyes W CO 2 Wembley

Errol McDonald stands over Peter Till, who got up to go the distance in their Tooting battle

Les Clark

30.11.88	Sammy Floyd W RSC 3 Southwark	
18.01.89	Nick Meloscia W RSC 1 Kensington	
19.12.89	Mick Mulcahy W RSC 3 Bethnal Green	
27.01.90	Joe Hernandez W PTS 8 Sheffield	
28.03.90	Robert Lewis W RSC 4 Bethnal Green	
25.04.90	Mario Lopez W CO 1 Brighton	
05.06.90	Steve Larrimore W RSC 9 Nottingham	
18.11.90	Ray Taylor W RTD 3 Birmingham	
23.02.91	Juan Rondon W RSC 7 Brighton	
08.06.91	Patrizio Oliva L DIS 12 La Spezia, Italy *(European Welterweight Title Challenge)*	
10.12.91	Jose Luis Saldivia W PTS 8 Sheffield	
10.03.92	Robert Wright L CO 3 Bury	
24.11.92	Gordon Blair W RSC 5 Doncaster	
12.01.93	Otero Orlando W RSC 4 Aachen, Germany	
16.02.93	Peter Till W PTS 8 Tooting	
16.03.93	Michael Driscoll L PTS 10 Mayfair *(Elim. British L. Welterweight Title)*	

Career: 32 contests, won 28, drew 1, lost 3.

Billy McDougall

Birmingham. *Born* Birmingham, 11 October, 1965
Welterweight. Ht. 5'10"
Manager N. Nobbs

02.11.92	Jimmy Reynolds L PTS 6 Wolverhampton
19.11.92	Dean Carr W PTS 6 Evesham
07.12.92	Dean Carr W PTS 6 Birmingham
14.12.92	Kevin Mabbutt L RTD 4 Northampton
27.01.93	Jamie Morris W PTS 6 Stoke
22.02.93	Ernie Locke W PTS 6 Birmingham
29.04.93	Rob Stevenson DREW 6 Hull
06.05.93	Andy Peach W PTS 6 Walsall
23.06.93	Marty Duke L PTS 6 Gorleston

Career: 9 contests, won 5, drew 1, lost 3.

Simon McDougall

Blackpool. *Born* Manchester, 11 July, 1968
L. Heavyweight. Ht. 5'10½"
Manager Self

14.11.88	Andrew Bravardo W CO 4 Manchester
16.01.89	Steve Osborne L PTS 6 Bradford
25.01.89	Steve Osborne L PTS 6 Stoke
20.02.89	Willie Connell W RSC 4 Bradford
04.04.89	Lee Woolis L PTS 6 Manchester
12.10.89	George Ferrie W PTS 6 Glasgow
30.11.89	Jimmy Cropper W PTS 6 Oldham
07.12.89	Sean O'Phoenix L PTS 6 Manchester
07.04.90	Eddie Smulders L PTS 6 Eindhoven, Holland
15.05.90	Terry French W PTS 4 South Shields
12.10.90	Ray Alberts L PTS 6 Cayenne, France
22.10.90	Glenn Campbell L RSC 4 Manchester
10.12.90	Morris Thomas W RSC 2 Bradford
28.01.91	Ian Henry W PTS 8 Bradford
28.02.91	Glenn Campbell L PTS 10 Bury *(Central Area S. Middleweight Title Challenge)*
23.04.91	Paul Burton L PTS 8 Evesham
10.05.91	Ian Henry L PTS 6 Gateshead
30.09.91	Doug Calderwood W RSC 4 Liverpool
10.10.91	Terry French L PTS 6 Gateshead
19.10.91	Andrea Magi L RSC 5 Terni, Italy
03.03.92	Paul Hitch L PTS 6 Houghton le Spring
11.03.92	Ian Henry L PTS 8 Solihull
30.03.92	Nigel Rafferty L PTS 8 Coventry

Simon McDougall Chris Bevan

08.06.92	Mark McBiane W PTS 6 Bradford
06.10.92	Gary Delaney L PTS 8 Antwerp, Belgium
12.12.92	Gary Delaney L PTS 8 Muswell Hill
04.03.93	Alan Smiles L PTS 6 Glasgow
26.03.93	Roland Ericsson W RSC 5 Copenhagen, Denmark
17.04.93	Terry French L PTS 6 Washington
12.05.93	Martin Langtry L PTS 6 Sheffield

Career: 30 contests, won 10, lost 20.

Alan McDowall

Renfrew. *Born* Renfrew, 29 September, 1967
Lightweight. Ht. 5'10"
Manager A. Melrose

24.09.91	Johnny Patterson W PTS 4 Glasgow
28.11.91	Johnny Patterson W PTS 6 Glasgow
31.01.92	Charles Shepherd W RSC 3 Glasgow
20.02.92	Mark O'Callaghan W PTS 6 Glasgow
12.03.92	James Jiora W CO 2 Glasgow
29.05.92	Karl Taylor W PTS 6 Glasgow
22.10.92	Robert Lloyd W RTD 4 Glasgow
30.04.93	Dean Bramhald W PTS 6 Glasgow
29.05.93	Rob Stewart DREW 6 Paisley

Career: 9 contests, won 8, drew 1.

James McGee

Bedworth. *Born* Nuneaton, 9 May, 1968
L. Middleweight. Ht. 6'1"
Manager J. Griffin

19.03.91	Adrian Din W PTS 6 Leicester
15.04.91	Marty Duke L PTS 6 Leicester
20.05.91	Cliff Churchward W PTS 6 Leicester
11.06.91	Julian Eavis W PTS 6 Leicester
01.10.91	Trevor Meikle L PTS 6 Bedworth
21.10.91	Crain Fisher L RSC 4 Bury
11.12.91	Julian Eavis DREW 6 Leicester
11.02.92	Chris Mulcahy W PTS 6 Wolverhampton
25.03.92	Darren Morris DREW 6 Hinckley
11.05.92	Julian Eavis W RSC 3 Coventry
05.10.92	Julian Eavis L PTS 6 Bardon

23.11.92	James Campbell DREW 6 Coventry
20.01.93	John Duckworth L PTS 6 Solihull
22.02.93	Julian Eavis W PTS 6 Bedworth
24.03.93	Damien Denny L CO 2 Belfast *(Elim. All-Ireland L. Middleweight Title)*

Career: 15 contests, won 6, drew 3, lost 6.

Ian McGirr

Clydebank. *Born* Clydebank, 14 April, 1968
S. Featherweight. Ht. 5'6¼"
Manager T. Gilmour

23.11.89	Edward Cook W PTS 6 Motherwell
18.12.89	James Milne W PTS 6 Glasgow
19.02.90	Pete Buckley W PTS 6 Birmingham
26.03.90	Edward Cook L PTS 6 Glasgow
09.10.90	Steve Walker L RSC 4 Glasgow
19.11.90	Edward Cook L PTS 6 Glasgow
18.02.91	Colin Innes W PTS 6 Glasgow
18.03.91	Noel Carroll L PTS 6 Manchester
22.03.91	Edward Cook L PTS 6 Irvine
24.09.91	Peter Judson L PTS 6 Glasgow
08.10.91	Tony Feliciello L PTS 8 Wolverhampton
21.10.91	Chris Clarkson DREW 6 Glasgow
12.12.91	Darren Elsdon L CO 4 Hartlepool
21.09.92	Chip O' Neill W PTS 6 Glasgow
12.10.92	Chris Jickells L RSC 3 Bradford
18.11.92	G.G.Goddard W PTS 6 Solihull
13.02.93	Jyrki Vierela L PTS 6 Randers, Denmark
25.02.93	Carl Roberts W PTS 6 Burnley
07.06.93	Marty Chestnut W PTS 6 Glasgow

Career: 19 contests, won 9, drew 1, lost 9.

Brian McGloin

Doncaster. *Born* Glasgow, 20 March, 1964
S. Middleweight. Ht. 5'7½"
Manager J. Rushton

11.12.91	Marc Rowley W PTS 6 Leicester
18.05.92	Chad Strong DREW 6 Bardon
08.09.92	Martin Jolley L PTS 6 Doncaster

Career: 3 contests, won 1, drew 1, lost 1.

Steve McGovern

Bembridge. *Born* Newport, IOW, 17 April, 1969
Welterweight. Ht. 5'9"
Manager H. Holland

21.09.89	Mike Morrison W PTS 6 Southampton
17.04.90	Justin Graham W PTS 6 Millwall
21.01.91	Mark Dinnadge W PTS 6 Crystal Palace
23.02.91	Tim Harmey W PTS 6 Brighton
23.04.91	Frank Harrington W PTS 6 Evesham
08.05.91	A.M.Milton W PTS 6 Millwall
16.12.91	Chris Mylan W PTS 8 Southampton
03.03.92	Tony Swift L RSC 4 Cradley Heath
27.10.92	Ricky Mabbett DREW 6 Leicester
29.04.93	Michael Dick W PTS 6 Hayes
23.06.93	Joel Ani W PTS 6 Edmonton

Career: 11 contests, won 9, drew 1, lost 1.

Graham McGrath

Warley. *Born* West Bromwich, 31 July, 1962
Bantamweight. Ht. 5'4"
Manager Self

21.05.92	Paul Kelly W RSC 2 Cradley Heath
01.06.92	Greg Upton L PTS 6 Solihull
09.07.92	Wilson Docherty L RSC 4 Glasgow
25.09.92	Paul Lloyd L RSC 3 Liverpool
02.11.92	Dennis Oakes L PTS 4 Liverpool
01.12.92	Leo Beirne W PTS 6 Liverpool
10.12.92	Shaun Anderson L PTS 6 Glasgow
14.01.93	Darren Fifield L PTS 4 Mayfair
21.01.93	Shaun Anderson L PTS 6 Glasgow
23.02.93	Ian Baillie W PTS 6 Kettering
29.03.93	Ian McLeod L PTS 6 Glasgow
19.04.93	Karl Morling L RSC 6 Northampton
23.06.93	Rowan Williams L PTS 4 Edmonton

Career: 13 contests, won 3, lost 10.

Dominic McGuigan   Chris Bevan

Dominic McGuigan

Newcastle. *Born* Hexham, 13 June, 1963
S. Featherweight. Ht. 5'6"
Manager D. Mancini

10.10.89	Dave Buxton W PTS 6 Sunderland
24.01.90	John Milne DREW 6 Sunderland
20.03.90	Frankie Foster DREW 4 Hartlepool
21.04.90	Chris Bennett W PTS 6 Sunderland
22.05.90	Lester James L PTS 6 Stockton
16.09.91	Barrie Kelley DREW 6 Mayfair
28.11.91	John Milne L RTD 3 Glasgow
30.04.92	Kevin Lowe W RSC 6 Mayfair
15.05.92	Rene Walker L PTS 8 Augsburg, Germany
07.10.92	Harry Escott L RTD 5 Sunderland
12.11.92	Kevin Lowe W RSC 2 Liverpool
25.02.93	Peter Judson DREW 6 Bradford
27.03.93	Giorgio Campanella L RSC 3 Evian, France
19.05.93	J.T.Williams W PTS 6 Sunderland
03.06.93	Eugene Speed L CO 1 Marseille, France

Career: 15 contests, won 5, drew 4, lost 6.

Dave McHale

Glasgow. *Born* Glasgow, 29 April, 1967
S. Featherweight. Ht. 5'7"
Manager T. Gilmour

08.10.90	Sol Francis W RSC 2 Glasgow
25.11.91	Eddie Garbutt W RSC 1 Liverpool
30.03.92	Kevin Lowe W RSC 5 Glasgow
01.06.92	Chris Jickells W RSC 4 Glasgow
09.07.92	G. G. Goddard W RTD 4 Glasgow
19.10.92	Lee Fox W RSC 3 Glasgow
23.11.92	Karl Taylor W PTS 8 Glasgow
15.05.93	Miguel Matthews W RSC 4 Glasgow

Career: 8 contests, won 8.

Darren McInulty

Nuneaton. *Born* Coventry, 10 November, 1970
Welterweight. Ht. 5'11"
Manager J.Griffin

20.05.91	Derek Binsteed DREW 6 Leicester
01.10.91	Dean Carr W PTS 6 Bedworth
11.11.91	Rick North W PTS 6 Stratford upon Avon
20.01.92	Chris Mulcahy W PTS 6 Coventry
04.02.92	Richard O'Brien L PTS 4 Alfreton
11.03.92	Eddie King W RSC 1 Stoke
25.03.92	Robert Riley L PTS 6 Hinckley
28.04.92	Dean Bramhald W PTS 6 Wolverhampton
11.05.92	Dean Bramhald W PTS 6 Coventry
10.09.92	Hughie Davey L PTS 6 Sunderland
23.11.92	Mark Antony W PTS 6 Coventry
02.12.92	Dean Hiscox DREW 6 Bardon
27.02.93	Andreas Panayi L PTS 6 Ellesmere Port
24.03.93	Barry Thorogood L PTS 6 Cardiff
26.04.93	Ricky Mabbett L CO 3 Cleethorpes
17.06.93	Mark Antony L CO 2 Bedworth

Career: 16 contests, won 7, drew 2, lost 7.

Bobby Mack (McKenzie)

Birmingham. *Born* Birmingham, 12 April, 1968
L. Heavyweight. Ht. 5'11"
Manager N. Nobbs

29.09.92	Steve Loftus W PTS 6 Stoke
02.11.92	Martin Jolley W PTS 6 Wolverhampton
03.12.92	Joey Peters L PTS 6 Lewisham
06.03.93	Paul Hitch L PTS 6 Glasgow
04.04.93	Mark Prince L RSC 2 Brockley

Career: 5 contests, won 2, lost 3.

Alan McKay

Willesden. *Born* Watford, 1 June, 1967
Former Southern Area Featherweight Champion. Ht. 5'6"
Manager Self

19.09.88	Mike Chapman W PTS 6 Mayfair
15.11.88	Mark Holt W PTS 6 Piccadilly
12.01.89	Jamie Hind W RSC 3 Southwark
31.01.89	Colin McMillan W RSC 3 Bethnal Green
01.03.89	Jeff Dobson W PTS 6 Bethnal Green
27.04.89	Tony Dore W PTS 6 Southwark
26.05.89	Nicky Lucas W PTS 6 Bethnal Green
04.09.89	Jari Gronroos DREW 6 Helsinki, Finland
24.10.89	Tim Driscoll L PTS 6 Bethnal Green
28.11.89	Steve Walker DREW 6 Battersea
03.05.90	Gary Hickman W PTS 8 Kensington
22.10.90	Steve Robinson W PTS 6 Mayfair
14.12.90	Gary de Roux L RSC 5 Peterborough *(Vacant Southern Area Featherweight Title)*

09.04.91	Paul Harvey L RSC 4 Mayfair
13.11.91	Gary de Roux W RSC 8 Bethnal Green *(Vacant Southern Area Featherweight Title)*
18.01.92	Pete Buckley DREW 8 Kensington
27.10.92	Kelton McKenzie W PTS 10 Cradley Heath *(Elim. British Featherweight Title)*
27.06.93	Sean Murphy L RSC 9 Dagenham *(Vacant British Featherweight Title)*

Career: 18 contests, won 11, drew 3, lost 4.

Darren McKenna

Alfreton. *Born* Sheffield, 21 December, 1962
Cruiserweight. Ht. 5'11"
Manager B. Ingle

19.11.87	Tony Behan W RSC 1 Ilkeston
24.11.87	Calvin Hart L PTS 4 Wisbech
02.12.87	Darren Jones L RSC 3 Stoke
20.01.88	Darren Jones L PTS 6 Stoke
27.01.88	Sean Stringfellow L CO 3 Stoke
07.03.88	David Jono W DIS 3 Manchester
08.03.88	Peter Brown L PTS 6 Batley
29.03.88	Russell Barker L RSC 4 Marton
17.05.88	Tucker Watts W RSC 2 Leicester
06.06.88	Carl Thompson L RSC 2 Manchester
05.09.88	Russell Barker L RSC 3 Manchester
07.11.88	Morris Thomas L CO 4 Bradford
24.05.89	Peter Elliott L PTS 8 Hanley
05.10.89	Jimmy Cropper L PTS 4 Middleton
23.10.89	Sean Stringfellow W RSC 8 Hull
29.01.90	Graham Burton L PTS 4 Hull
06.03.90	Peter Elliott L PTS 8 Stoke
12.03.90	Fidel Castro L PTS 6 Hull
05.04.90	Allan Millett W RSC 2 Liverpool
17.04.90	Nicky Piper L RTD 4 Millwall
12.09.90	Steve Aquilina DREW 8 Stafford
08.10.90	Dave Owens L PTS 6 Leicester
09.05.91	Denzil Browne L PTS 6 Leeds
24.06.91	Johnny Held L PTS 8 Rotterdam, Holland
23.01.92	Denzil Browne L PTS 6 York
03.06.92	Morris Thomas W RSC 2 Newcastle under Lyme
17.10.92	Terry Dixon W RSC 3 Wembley
27.01.93	Steve Osborne W PTS 6 Stoke

Career: 28 contests, won 8, drew 1, lost 19.

Duke McKenzie

Croydon. *Born* Croydon, 5 May, 1963
Former WBO S. Bantamweight & Bantamweight Champion. Former IBF Flyweight Champion. Former Undefeated British & European Flyweight Champion. Ht. 5'7"
Manager Self

23.11.82	Charlie Brown W RSC 1 Wembley
24.01.83	Andy King W RSC 2 Mayfair
27.02.83	Dave Pierson W RSC 1 Las Vegas, USA
03.03.83	Gregorio Hernandez W RSC 3 Los Angeles, USA
19.03.83	Lupe Sanchez W CO 2 Reno, USA
18.10.83	Jerry Davis W RSC 2 Atlantic City, USA
22.11.83	Alain Limarola W PTS 6 Wembley
15.01.84	David Capo W PTS 4 Atlantic City, USA

23.05.84	Gary Roberts W CO 1 Mayfair
06.03.85	Julio Guerrero W PTS 8 Kensington
05.06.85	Danny Flynn W RSC 4 Kensington
16.10.85	Orlando Maestre W PTS 8 Kensington
19.02.86	Sonny Long W PTS 10 Kensington
20.05.86	Charlie Magri W RTD 5 Wembley
	(British Flyweight Title Defence &
	European Flyweight Title Challenge)
19.11.86	Lee Cargle W PTS 10 Atlantic City, USA
17.12.86	Piero Pinna W PTS 12 Acqui Terme, Italy
	(European Flyweight Title Defence)

24.03.87	Jose Manuel Diaz W PTS 8 Wembley
02.12.87	Juan Herrera W PTS 10 Wembley
09.03.88	Agapito Gomez W CO 2 Wembley
	(European Flyweight Title Defence)
04.05.88	Jose Gallegos W PTS 10 Wembley
05.10.88	Rolando Bohol W CO 11 Wembley
	(IBF Flyweight Title Challenge)
30.11.88	Artemio Ruiz W PTS 10 Southwark
08.03.89	Tony de Luca W RSC 4 Kensington
	(IBF Flyweight Title Defence)
07.06.89	Dave Boy McAuley L PTS 12 Wembley
	(IBF Flyweight Title Defence)
12.10.89	Dave Moreno W PTS 10 Southwark

08.11.89	Memo Flores W PTS 8 Wembley
30.09.90	Thierry Jacob L PTS 12 Calais, France
	(Vacant European Bantamweight Title)
10.01.91	Pete Buckley W RSC 5 Wandsworth
07.02.91	Julio Blanco W RSC 7 Watford
04.04.91	Chris Clarkson W RSC 5 Watford
30.06.91	Gaby Canizales W PTS 12 Southwark
	(WBO Bantamweight Title Challenge)
12.09.91	Cesar Soto W PTS 12 Wandsworth
	(WBO Bantamweight Title Defence)
25.03.92	Wilfredo Vargas W RSC 8 Kensington
	(WBO Bantamweight Title Defence)
13.05.92	Rafael del Valle L CO 1 Kensington
	(WBO Bantamweight Title Defence)
07.09.92	Pete Buckley W RTD 3 Bethnal Green
15.10.92	Jesse Benavides W PTS 12 Lewisham
	(WBO S. Bantamweight Title Challenge)
09.06.93	Daniel Jimenez L PTS 12 Lewisham
	(WBO S. Bantamweight Title Defence)

Career: 37 contests, won 33, lost 4.

Joe McKenzie

Newport. *Born* Newport, 6 October, 1966
L. Heavyweight. Ht. 6'0"
Manager Self

24.09.87	Russell Barker L RSC 5 Glasgow
08.12.87	Neil Simpson W RSC 1 Plymouth
17.02.88	Sugar Ray Thompson L PTS 6 Bethnal Green
30.03.88	Keith Halliwell W RSC 2 Bethnal Green
09.04.88	Paul Wesley L RSC 6 Bristol
18.05.88	Paul McCarthy L RSC 3 Portsmouth
28.09.88	Errol Christie L RSC 3 Edmonton
07.04.93	Nick Manners L RSC 2 Leeds

Career: 8 contests, won 2, lost 6.

Kelton McKenzie

Nottingham. *Born* Leicester, 18 September, 1968
Midlands Area Featherweight Champion. Ht. 5'7"
Manager Self

18.10.90	Tony Silkstone L PTS 6 Dewsbury
29.11.90	Neil Leitch DREW 6 Marton
11.12.90	Sylvester Osuji W PTS 6 Evesham
21.01.91	J. T. Williams DREW 6 Crystal Palace
14.03.91	Craig Dermody L RSC 3 Middleton
01.05.91	Tim Yeates W PTS 6 Bethnal Green
17.06.91	Derek Amory W RSC 6 Edgbaston
05.11.91	Richard Woolgar W RSC 5 Leicester
22.01.92	Colin Lynch W RSC 5 Solihull
26.03.92	Brian Robb W RSC 4 Telford
29.04.92	Elvis Parsley W RSC 5 Solihull
	(Vacant Midlands Area Featherweight Title)
18.07.92	Steve Walker W CO 2 Manchester
27.10.92	Alan McKay L PTS 10 Cradley Heath
	(Elim. British Featherweight Title)
28.04.93	Richie Wenton L PTS 8 Dublin
19.05.93	Paul Harvey L RSC 7 Leicester

Career: 15 contests, won 8, drew 2, lost 5.

Kevin McKenzie

Hartlepool. *Born* Hartlepool, 18 October, 1968
L. Welterweight. 5'7½"
Manager G. Robinson

Duke McKenzie   Les Clark

08.06.92   Jason Brattley W RTD 3 Bradford
21.09.92   Alan Ingle W PTS 6 Glasgow
22.10.92   Dave Anderson L RSC 3 Glasgow
01.12.92   Seth Jones L RSC 3 Hartlepool
09.03.93   Micky Hall W PTS 6 Hartlepool
17.04.93   Paul Charters L RSC 4 Washington
           *(Vacant Northern Area L.Welterweight
           Title)*

Career: 6 contests, won 3, lost 3.

R.F. McKenzie   Les Clark

(Roger) R. F. McKenzie

Croydon. *Born* Croydon, 3 October, 1965
Southern Area Heavyweight Champion. Ht.
6'2"
Manager P. Byrne

31.01.89   Gerry Storey W PTS 6 Bethnal Green
24.09.90   Mark Bowen L RSC 1 Mayfair
29.11.90   Denzil Browne W PTS 6 Sunderland
12.02.91   Noel Magee L PTS 6 Belfast
21.03.91   Denzil Browne L PTS 6 Dewsbury
28.05.91   Steve Yorath L PTS 6 Cardiff
07.09.91   Ray Kane L PTS 4 Belfast
09.10.91   Denzil Browne W PTS 6 Manchester
28.10.91   Pedro van Raamsdonk W CO 7
           Arnhem, Holland
12.12.91   Norbert Ekassi L RSC 3 Massy, France
14.03.92   Neils H. Madsen L PTS 6 Copenhagen,
           Denmark
25.04.92   Noel Magee L PTS 8 Belfast
31.10.92   Warren Richards DREW 6 Earls Court
13.02.93   Magne Havnaa W RTD 5 Randers,
           Denmark
31.03.93   Warren Richards W RSC 8 Bethnal
           Green
           *(Vacant Southern Area Heavyweight
           Title)*

Career: 15 contests, won 6, drew 1, lost 8.

Tony McKenzie

Leicester. *Born* Leicester, 4 March, 1963
Former British L. Welterweight Champion.
Ht. 5'9"
Manager B. Hearn

22.11.83   Albert Buchanan W CO 3
           Wolverhampton
07.12.83   Peter Flanagan W PTS 6 Stoke
30.01.84   Vince Bailey W RSC 1 Birmingham
27.02.84   David Irving W RSC 3 Birmingham
15.03.84   Johnny Grant W RSC 4 Leicester
16.04.84   Danny Shinkwin L RSC 1 Birmingham
09.05.84   Ray Price W PTS 8 Leicester
03.10.84   Michael Harris L PTS 8 Solihull
10.10.84   Manny Romain W CO 5 Stoke
29.10.84   Peter Flanagan W RSC 8 Nottingham
16.11.84   Lenny Gloster W PTS 8 Leicester
14.03.85   Tony Laing L RSC 8 Leicester
           *(Vacant Midlands Area L.
           Welterweight Title)*
07.09.85   Tony Adams W PTS 8 Isle of Man
20.11.85   Rocky Feliciello W RSC 6 Solihull
19.03.86   Simon Eubank W RSC 4 Solihull
07.05.86   Michael Harris W PTS 10 Solihull
           (Elim. British L. Welterweight Title)
20.09.86   Clinton McKenzie W RSC 3 Hemel
           Hempstead
           (Vacant British L. Welterweight Title)
25.10.86   Michael Harris W CO 10 Stevenage
           (British L. Welterweight Title Defence)
29.11.86   Ford Jennings W RSC 5 Wandsworth
28.01.87   Lloyd Christie L RSC 3 Croydon
           (British L. Welterweight Title Defence)
12.05.87   Dave Griffiths W RSC 3 Alfreton
03.11.87   Kelvin Mortimer W RSC 3 Bethnal
           Green
24.02.88   Jeff Connors W RSC 2 Leicester
03.11.88   Abdelatif Lofti Ben Sayel L RSC 2
           Leicester
27.01.90   Benji Marquez DREW 8 Sheffield
20.03.90   Benji Marquez W PTS 8 Norwich
05.06.90   Art Blackmore W RSC 4 Nottingham
19.03.91   King Zaka W RSC 1 Leicester
11.06.91   Alberto Machong W CO 3 Leicester
           *(Elim. Commonwealth L. Welterweight
           Title)*
05.11.91   Marty Duke W RSC 7 Leicester
19.11.91   Gordon Blair W RSC 5 Norwich
27.02.92   Andy Holligan L RSC 3 Liverpool
           *(British & Commonwealth L.
           Welterweight Title Challenge)*
26.01.93   Michael Driscoll W PTS 10 Leicester
           (Elim. British L. Welterweight Title)

Career: 33 contests, won 26, drew 1, lost 6.

Kevin McKillan

Manchester. *Born* Belfast, 1 March, 1969
L. Welterweight. Ht. 5'8"
Manager N. Basso

28.10.91   Michael Byrne W PTS 6 Leicester
13.11.91   Barry Glanister W PTS 6 Liverpool
22.01.92   Sugar Boy Wright W PTS 6 Solihull
10.02.92   Jamie Davidson L PTS 6 Liverpool
11.03.92   Jamie Davidson DREW 6 Stoke
01.06.92   Steve Howden W RSC 2 Manchester
12.06.92   Floyd Churchill W PTS 6 Liverpool
25.09.92   John Smith W PTS 6 Liverpool
07.10.92   J. T. Williams L PTS 6 Barry
20.11.92   Steve Foran L PTS 6 Liverpool
15.02.93   John T. Kelly W PTS 6 Manchester
19.04.93   Simon Hamblett W CO 2 Manchester
26.04.93   Steve Walker DREW 8 Manchester
01.06.93   Micky Hall W PTS 6 Manchester

Career: 14 contests, won 9, drew 2, lost 3.

Ian McLeod

Kilmarnock. *Born* Edinburgh, 11 June,
1969
Featherweight. Ht. 5'9"
Manager T. Gilmour

23.11.92   Robert Braddock DREW 6 Glasgow
29.03.93   Graham McGrath W PTS 6 Glasgow

Career: 2 contests, won 1, drew 1.

Colin McMillan

Barking. *Born* London, 12 February, 1966
Former WBO Featherweight Champion.
Former Undefeated British &
Commonwealth Featherweight Champion.
Ht. 5'5¼"
Manager Self

29.11.88   Mike Chapman W PTS 6 Battersea
10.12.88   Aldrich Johnson W PTS 6 Crystal
           Palace
31.01.89   Alan McKay L RSC 3 Bethnal Green
12.06.89   Miguel Matthews W RSC 3 Battersea
19.09.89   Graham O'Malley W PTS 8 Millwall
11.10.89   Marcel Herbert W PTS 6 Millwall
30.11.89   Sylvester Osuji W RSC 4 Barking
14.02.90   Vidal Tellez W RSC 2 Millwall
17.04.90   Jesus Muniz W PTS 8 Millwall
03.05.90   Steve Walker W PTS 6 Kensington
05.07.90   Tyrone Miller W CO 2 Greensville,
           USA
17.07.90   Malcolm Rougeaux W CO 1 Lake
           Charles, USA
25.09.90   Darren Weller W RSC 2 Millwall
10.10.90   Graham O'Malley W PTS 6 Millwall
12.11.90   Mark Holt W PTS 8 Norwich
05.03.91   Russell Davison W PTS 6 Millwall
26.04.91   Willie Richardson W PTS 8 Crystal
           Palace
22.05.91   Gary de Roux W RSC 7 Millwall
           (British Featherweight Title Challenge)
03.07.91   Herbie Bivalacqua W RSC 3 Reading
04.09.91   Kevin Pritchard W RSC 7 Bethnal
           Green
           (British Featherweight Title Defence)
29.10.91   Sean Murphy W PTS 12 Kensington
           (British Featherweight Title Defence)
18.01.92   Percy Commey W PTS 12 Kensington
           *(Vacant Commonwealth Featherweight
           Title)*
25.03.92   Tommy Valdez W CO 6 Dagenham
16.05.92   Maurizio Stecca W PTS 12 Muswell
           Hill
           (WBO Featherweight Title Challenge)
26.09.92   Ruben Palacio L RSC 8 Earls Court
           (WBO Featherweight Title Defence)

Career: 25 contests, won 23, lost 2.

Conn McMullen

Acton. *Born* Larne, 21 June, 1967
Bantamweight. Ht. 5'6"
Manager Self

06.06.90   Ceri Farrell W RSC 5 Battersea
04.12.90   Neil Parry W RSC 2 Southend
12.11.91   Mark Loftus W PTS 6 Milton Keynes
28.10.92   Barry Jones L PTS 6 Cardiff
26.03.93   Neil Armstrong W RSC 5 Glasgow
05.05.93   Miguel Matthews DREW 6 Belfast
18.06.93   Wayne McCullough L RSC 3 Belfast

Career: 7 contests, won 4, drew 1, lost 2

Pat McNamara

Leeds. *Born* Bradford, 2 June, 1967
L. Heavyweight. Ht. 6'2"
Manager P. Coleman

10.05.93 Kevin Burton L RSC 2 Cleethorpes
Career: 1 contest, lost 1.

Jason McNeill

Swansea. *Born* Bristol, 12 August, 1971
L. Heavyweight. Ht. 6'1"
Manager D. Davies

03.10.91 Mark Pain L PTS 6 Burton
15.10.91 Tony Colclough L PTS 6 Dudley
28.11.91 Mark McBiane W PTS 6 Evesham
21.01.92 Gypsy Johnny Price L PTS 4 Stockport
11.03.92 Paul McCarthy W PTS 6 Cardiff
23.04.92 Abel Asinamali L CO 3 Eltham
07.09.92 Mark Baker L RSC 2 Glasgow
23.10.92 Paul Wright L RSC 1 Liverpool
06.02.93 Karl Mumford L PTS 6 Cardiff
22.02.93 Kenny Nevers L RSC 1 Eltham
10.04.93 Julian Johnson L PTS 6 Swansea
26.05.93 Graham Burton L RSC 3 Mansfield
Career: 12 contests, won 2, lost 10.

Steve McNess   Les Clark

Steve McNess

Bethnal Green. *Born* Bow, 17 November, 1969
L. Middleweight. Ht. 5'10½"
Manager M. Duff

22.04.92 Rick North W PTS 6 Wembley
13.05.92 Mark Verikios L RSC 5 Kensington
03.09.92 Steve Goodwin W PTS 6 Dunstable
28.10.92 Mark Dawson L RSC 2 Kensington
28.01.93 Steve Scott W PTS 6 Southwark
26.04.93 Bullit Andrews W RSC 3 Lewisham
15.06.93 Martin Rosamond L RSC 5 Hempstead
Career: 7 contests, won 4, lost 3.

Dave Madden

Birmingham. *Born* Birmingham, 18 June, 1967
L. Welterweight. Ht. 5'10"
Manager N. Nobbs

12.11.92 Blue Butterworth L RSC 2 Burnley
27.01.93 Gary Hiscox L PTS 6 Stoke
22.02.93 Kris McAdam L PTS 8 Glasgow
Career: 3 contests, lost 3.

Noel Magee

Belfast. *Born* Belfast, 16 December, 1965
L. Heavyweight. Ht. 6'1"
Manager Self

22.05.85 Nigel Prickett W CO 1 Stoke
12.09.85 Dave Furneaux W RSC 3 Swindon
28.10.85 Eddie Chatterton W RSC 1 Stoke
06.11.85 Winston Burnett W PTS 8 Nantwich
11.12.85 Winston Burnett W PTS 8 Stoke
22.01.86 Blaine Logsdon W PTS 8 Stoke
20.02.86 Barry Ahmed W PTS 8 Newcastle
05.03.86 Winston Burnett W PTS 8 Stoke
23.04.86 Barry Ahmed W RSC 7 Stoke
30.05.86 Geoff Rymer W CO 1 Stoke
13.10.86 Jimmy Ellis W PTS 8 Dulwich
17.11.86 Serg Fame W PTS 8 Dulwich
24.02.87 Lennie Howard W RSC 1 Ilford
03.08.87 Jimmy Ellis W RSC 6 Stoke
20.10.87 Johnny Held L PTS 8 Stoke
13.02.88 Rufino Angulo DREW 8 Paris, France
03.05.88 Mike Brothers W CO 6 Stoke
15.11.88 Ian Bulloch DREW 10 Hull
15.02.89 Yves Monsieur L RSC 5 Stoke
02.10.89 Paul McCarthy W CO 2 Hanley
29.11.89 Sammy Storey L RSC 9 Belfast
          (British S. Middleweight Title Challenge)
15.09.90 Glazz Campbell W PTS 8 Belfast
30.10.90 Johnny Melfah W PTS 6 Belfast
12.02.91 R. F. McKenzie W PTS 6 Belfast
11.05.91 Simon Collins W PTS 8 Belfast
13.11.91 Frankie Minton W RSC 3 Belfast
11.12.91 Tony Wilson W RSC 3 Dublin
25.04.92 R. F. McKenzie W RSC 8 Belfast
28.09.92 Maurice Coore L RSC 9 Manchester
          (Vacant British L. Heavyweight Title)
Career: 29 contests, won 23, drew 2, lost 4.

Terry Magee

Ammanford. *Born* Belfast, 1 November, 1964
S. Middleweight. Former Undefeated All-Ireland L. Middleweight Champion. Ht. 5'10½"
Manager Self

29.11.82 Robbie Turner W PTS 6 Brighton
08.12.82 Tony Baker W PTS 6 Piccadilly
07.02.83 Alex Romeo L PTS 6 Piccadilly
21.02.83 Tony Burke L PTS 6 Piccadilly
16.09.83 David Scere W PTS 6 Rhyl
28.11.83 Winston Wray W PTS 6 Rhyl
06.02.84 Craig Edwards W RSC 3 Liverpool
03.03.84 Lou Johnson W RSC 2 Stoke
12.05.84 Cornelius Chisholm W RTD 3 Hanley
12.09.84 Phil O'Hare W PTS 8 Stoke
24.10.84 Nick Riozzi W RSC 5 Stoke
05.12.84 Harry Watson W RSC 3 Stoke
20.03.85 Gary Tomlinson DREW 8 Stoke
17.04.85 Gary Pearce W PTS 8 Nantwich
25.09.85 Franki Moro W PTS 10 Stoke

11.12.85 Gerry Sloof W RSC 6 Stoke
07.05.86 Gary Stretch L RSC 7 Kensington
23.06.87 Shamus Casey W CO 6 Swansea
          (Vacant All-Ireland L. Middleweight Title)
01.11.87 Charles Oosthuizen L RSC 8 Johannesburg, South Africa
26.03.88 Chris Richards W PTS 8 Belfast
14.06.88 Tony Britton W PTS 6 Birmingham
28.09.88 Wally Swift Jnr W PTS 8 Solihull
07.12.88 Kevin Hayde W PTS 8 Aberavon
12.04.89 Tony Britton W PTS 8 Swansea
16.11.89 Jimmy Gourad W PTS 8 Weston super Mare
26.03.90 Gilbert Dele L RTD 3 Paris, France
          (European L. Middleweight Title Challenge)
01.06.91 Andy Till L RSC 4 Bethnal Green
11.12.91 Ray Close L RSC 7 Dublin
          (All-Ireland S. Middleweight Title Challenge)
25.09.92 Fran Harding L PTS 6 Liverpool
17.10.92 James Cook L RSC 5 Wembley
27.11.92 Roland Ericsson L PTS 8 Randers, Denmark
05.05.93 Graham Jenner W PTS 6 Belfast
Career: 32 contests, won 21, drew 1, lost 10.

Dave Maj (Majekodunmi)

Liverpool. *Born* Liverpool, 21 November, 1964
Welterweight. Ht. 5'10¼"
Manager J. Trickett

24.06.91 Benji Joseph W RSC 4 Liverpool
09.09.91 Mark Verikios L PTS 6 Liverpool
14.10.91 David Maw L PTS 6 Manchester
16.12.91 Wayne Shepherd DREW 6 Manchester
03.02.92 Wayne Shepherd W PTS 6 Manchester
09.03.92 Willie Yeardsley W RSC 1 Manchester
13.04.92 Peter Reid W CO 1 Manchester
14.05.92 Andreas Panayi L CO 6 Liverpool
05.10.92 John Duckworth DREW 6 Manchester
12.11.92 Mark Verikios L PTS 6 Liverpool
22.02.93 Mark Brogan W RSC 5 Liverpool
29.04.93 Paul Denton DREW 6 Mayfair
21.06.93 Chris Peters L RSC 4 Swindon
Career: 13 contests, won 5, drew 3, lost 5.

Mohammed Malik

Burnley. *Born* Burnley, 24 February, 1973
L. Middleweight. Ht. 5'11"
Manager N. Basso

14.12.92 Tim Robinson L RSC 3 Cleethorpes
Career: 1 contest, lost 1.

Colin Manners

Leeds. *Born* Leeds, 4 July, 1962
Middleweight. Ht. 5'10"
Manager J. Rushton

26.04.90 Tony Booth L PTS 6 Halifax
27.09.90 Carlos Christie L PTS 6 Birmingham
18.10.90 Carlton Myers W CO 2 Dewsbury
25.10.90 Colin Ford L PTS 6 Bayswater
12.12.90 Tony Kosova W PTS 6 Leicester
31.01.91 Lee Crocker W PTS 6 Bredbury
18.02.91 John Ogiste L PTS 6 Mayfair
14.03.91 John Ogiste L PTS 8 Middleton
01.05.91 Darren Parker W CO 2 Solihull
05.06.91 Richard Carter W CO 1 Wolverhampton
03.09.91 Wayne Ellis W RSC 1 Cardiff

Colin Manners   Les Clark

29.04.92	Darron Griffiths DREW 8 Solihull	
14.07.92	Stan King W PTS 8 Mayfair	
30.09.92	Darron Griffiths L PTS 10 Solihull	
	(Elim. British Middleweight Title)	
23.02.93	Chris Pyatt L CO 3 Doncaster	

Career: 15 contests, won 7, drew 1, lost 7.

Nick Manners

Leeds. *Born* Leeds, 23 November, 1966
S. Middleweight. Ht. 6'2"
Manager M. Duff

18.10.90	Paul Murray W PTS 6 Dewsbury
13.12.90	John Kaighin W CO 3 Dewsbury
31.01.91	Terry Duffus W RSC 1 Bredbury
21.03.91	Marvin O'Brien W CO 2 Dewsbury
09.05.91	Peter Gorny W RSC 1 Leeds
27.06.91	Peter Vosper W RSC 1 Leeds
01.08.91	Tony Booth DREW 8 Dewsbury
30.10.91	Kevin Morton L PTS 8 Leeds
23.09.92	Lee Crocker W CO 1 Leeds
29.10.92	Ali Forbes L RSC 3 Leeds
25.02.93	Jason Fores W RSC 2 Bradford
01.04.93	Joe McKenzie W RSC 2 Leeds

Career: 12 contests, won 9, drew 1, lost 2.

Andy Manning

Warrington. *Born* Sheffield, 1 June, 1970
L. Heavyweight. Ht. 5'7½"
Manager R. Jones

07.10.91	Mark Hale W PTS 6 Liverpool
04.11.91	Steve Thomas L PTS 6 Merthyr
02.12.91	Marc Rowley W PTS 6 Liverpool
03.03.92	Justin Clements DREW 6 Cradley Heath
18.03.92	Willie Quinn L PTS 6 Glasgow
29.04.92	Adrian Wright W PTS 6 Stoke
11.05.92	Julian Johnson W PTS 6 Llanelli
18.05.92	John Oxenham L PTS 6 Marton
25.01.93	Joe McCluskey L PTS 6 Glasgow

Career: 9 contests, won 4, drew 1, lost 4.

Gary Marston

Stoke. *Born* Taunton, 11 December, 1966
Featherweight. Ht. 5'4"
Manager P. Brogan

29.09.92	Norman Dhalie DREW 6 Stoke
17.03.93	Jason Morris L PTS 6 Stoke
12.05.93	Phil Lashley W RSC 2 Stoke

Career: 3 contests, won 2, drew 1

Dean Martin

Birmingham. *Born* Birmingham, 28
November, 1967
Lightweight. Ht. 5'10½"
Manager E. Cashmore

30.10.92	George Naylor L PTS 6 Birmingham
18.05.93	T. J. Smith L RSC 3 Kettering

Career: 2 contests, lost 2.

Shaun Martin

Scunthorpe. *Born* Gainsborough, 1 April,
1971
L. Middleweight. Ht. 5'10½"
Manager K. Tate

02.11.92	Andrew Jervis L CO 2 Liverpool

Career: 1 contest, lost 1.

(Paul) Stinger Mason

Sheffield. *Born* Sheffield, 27 February,
1964
Middleweight. Ht. 5'8"
Manager Self

19.04.89	Sean Stringfellow W PTS 6 Stoke
24.05.89	Andrew Flute L PTS 6 Hanley
16.11.89	Tony Lawrence DREW 4 Ilkeston
27.01.90	Ian Vokes W PTS 6 Sheffield
28.03.90	Cliff Curtis W PTS 6 Bethnal Green
20.05.90	Tony Hodge W CO 2 Sheffield
11.06.90	Glenn Campbell L RTD 5 Manchester
12.11.90	Adrian Wright L RSC 4 Stratford upon Avon
13.03.91	Mike Phillips DREW 6 Stoke
13.05.91	Doug Calderwood L CO 3 Manchester
23.10.91	Roger Wilson DREW 6 Stoke
11.11.91	Russell Washer W PTS 4 Stratford upon Avon
23.05.92	Paul Busby L RSC 2 Birmingham
28.09.92	Quinn Paynter L CO 1 Manchester

Career: 14 contests, won 5, drew 3, lost 6.

Tony Massey

Leeds. *Born* Leeds, 24 January, 1968
L. Middleweight. Ht. 5'10"
Manager Self

19.03.92	Phil Foxon W RSC 1 York
28.09.92	Alan Williams W RSC 3 Manchester
29.10.92	John Duckworth L RTD 4 Leeds

Career: 3 contests, won 2, lost 1.

(Nicholas) Miguel Matthews

Ystalfera. *Born* Glanamman, 22 December,
1965
Featherweight. Ht. 5'7"
Manager Self

21.09.88	Terry Collins L PTS 6 Basildon
28.09.88	Eugene Maloney DREW 6 Edmonton
25.10.88	Hugh Ruse L PTS 6 Pontadawe
15.11.88	Tommy Bernard W RSC 2 Chigwell
14.12.88	Richie Wenton L CO 2 Kirkby
14.02.89	Brian Robb W RSC 2 Wolverhampton
06.03.89	Mickey Markie L PTS 8 Northampton
21.03.89	Ronnie Stephenson DREW 6 Wolverhampton
11.04.89	Hugh Ruse W PTS 6 Aberavon
05.06.89	Lester James DREW 6 Birmingham
12.06.89	Colin McMillan L RSC 3 Battersea
06.09.89	Marcel Herbert L PTS 6 Aberavon
20.09.89	Des Gargano L PTS 6 Stoke
28.09.89	Steve Walker L PTS 6 Cardiff
17.10.89	Alan Roberts W PTS 6 Cardiff
24.10.89	Jimmy Clark L PTS 6 Watford
06.11.89	Mickey Markie DREW 8 Northampton
03.12.89	Johnny Bredahl L PTS 6 Copenhagen, Denmark
19.02.90	Mickey Markie L PTS 8 Kettering
27.02.90	Pete Buckley DREW 6 Evesham
21.03.90	Rocky Lawlor L PTS 8 Solihull
03.09.90	Derek Amory L PTS 6 Dudley
01.10.90	Pete Buckley L PTS 8 Cleethorpes
09.10.90	Pete Buckley W PTS 8 Wolverhampton
29.10.90	Pete Buckley L PTS 8 Birmingham
21.11.90	Jason Primera L PTS 8 Solihull
12.12.90	Paul Harvey L PTS 6 Basildon
19.12.90	Paul Forrest L PTS 6 Preston
07.03.91	Bradley Stone L RSC 4 Basildon
04.04.91	Mark Tierney L PTS 6 Watford
16.04.91	Craig Dermody L PTS 6 Nottingham
25.04.91	Bradley Stone L PTS 6 Basildon
23.05.91	Jason Lepre L PTS 6 Southampton
31.05.91	Danny Connelly L PTS 8 Glasgow
13.06.91	Tony Silkstone L PTS 6 Hull
24.06.91	Jimmy Owens L PTS 6 Liverpool
09.09.91	Moussa Sangare L RSC 5 Forges les Eux, France
09.10.91	Mark Loftus DREW 6 Manchester
24.10.91	Kevin Middleton L PTS 6 Dunstable
31.10.91	Brian Robb DREW 6 Oakengates
11.11.91	Peter Judson L PTS 6 Stratford on Avon
21.11.91	Craig Dermody L PTS 6 Burton
28.11.91	Dave Hardie L PTS 6 Glasgow
11.12.91	Jimmy Clark L PTS 6 Basildon
08.01.92	Ceri Farrell W PTS 6 Burton
31.01.92	John Green DREW 6 Manchester
20.02.92	Edward Cook L PTS 6 Glasgow
27.02.92	Craig Dermody L PTS 6 Liverpool
25.03.92	John Armour L PTS 6 Dagenham
01.06.92	Danny Porter L PTS 6 Glasgow
07.07.92	Tony Falcone L PTS 6 Bristol
14.07.92	Prince Nassem Hamed L RSC 3 Mayfair
30.09.92	John Irwin L PTS 6 Solihull
17.10.92	Mark Bowers L PTS 6 Wembley
24.11.92	Kid McAuley L PTS 6 Doncaster
14.12.92	Barry Jones L PTS 6 Cardiff
30.01.93	Tim Yeates L PTS 6 Brentwood
27.02.93	Paul Lloyd L PTS 6 Ellesmere Port
18.03.93	Kevin Middleton L PTS 6 Lewisham
17.04.93	Fabian Zavattini L PTS 6 Lausanne, Switzerland
05.05.93	Conn McMullen DREW 6 Belfast
15.05.93	Dave McHale L RSC 4 Glasgow

Career: 62 contests, won 6, drew 9, lost 47.

Winston May

West Ham. *Born* London, 21 November,
1962
L. Middleweight. Ht. 5'10½"
Manager Self

29.11.88	Pat Dunne W PTS 6 Battersea
10.12.88	Mark Howell W PTS 6 Crystal Palace

31.01.89	Sammy Sampson W RSC 4 Bethnal Green
16.02.89	Martin Smith DREW 6 Battersea
11.04.89	Damien Denny L RSC 3 Aberavon
21.05.89	Newton Barnett W PTS 4 Finsbury Park
25.09.89	Newton Barnett W PTS 6 Crystal Palace
26.02.90	Alan Richards L PTS 6 Crystal Palace
17.04.90	Paul Wesley DREW 8 Millwall
03.05.90	Dusty Miller W PTS 6 Kensington
06.11.90	Brian Robinson L RSC 4 Mayfair
05.12.91	Shaun Cummins L RSC 2 Peterborough
30.04.92	Lee Crocker L RSC 2 Bayswater
09.03.93	Dean Cooper L PTS 8 Bristol
29.03.93	John Bosco L RSC 3 Mayfair

Career: 15 contests, won 6, drew 2, lost 7.

Trevor Meikle

Scunthorpe. *Born* Scunthorpe, 29 January, 1967
Welterweight. Ht. 5'9"
Manager K. Tate

16.05.89	Lewis Welch DREW 6 Halifax
12.06.89	Chris Mulcahy L PTS 6 Manchester
19.06.89	Anthony Lawrence L PTS 6 Manchester
11.07.89	Chris Mulcahy L PTS 6 Batley
10.10.89	Steve Hardman DREW 6 Manchester
23.10.89	Mick Mulcahy W PTS 6 Cleethorpes
06.11.89	Ian Thomas W PTS 6 Northampton
14.11.89	Cliff Churchward W PTS 6 Evesham
22.11.89	Cliff Churchward W PTS 6 Stafford
11.12.89	Barry Messam L CO 5 Nottingham
05.02.90	Malcolm Melvin L PTS 6 Brierley Hill
19.02.90	Gordon Blair L PTS 6 Glasgow
27.02.90	Dave Whittle DREW 8 Marton
14.03.90	Carlos Chase L PTS 6 Battersea
27.03.90	Barry Messam W PTS 6 Leicester
30.04.90	Young Gully L PTS 6 Brierley Hill
21.05.90	Frank Harrington W RSC 5 Hanley
30.05.90	Mark Jay DREW 6 Stoke
15.06.90	Mark Jay W RSC 5 Telford
14.09.90	Mickey Lerwill DREW 8 Telford
03.10.90	Jim Lawlor L PTS 6 Solihull
09.10.90	Pat Durkin W DIS 3 Liverpool
24.10.90	Ernie Loveridge L PTS 6 Dudley
06.11.90	Stuart Good L PTS 6 Southend
21.11.90	Jim Lawlor L PTS 6 Solihull
29.11.90	Dave Whittle L PTS 6 Marton
10.12.90	Kevin Spratt L PTS 6 Bradford
11.02.91	Steve Hardman L PTS 6 Manchester
21.02.91	Colin Sinnott W PTS 6 Leeds
27.02.91	Andreas Panayi W PTS 6 Wolverhampton
03.04.91	Mick Mulcahy W PTS 6 Manchester
10.04.91	Wayne Timmins L PTS 6 Wolverhampton
22.04.91	Nick Cope W RSC 2 Glasgow
01.05.91	Tommy Milligan L PTS 6 Liverpool
09.05.91	Tod Riggs L PTS 6 Leeds
03.06.91	Tommy Milligan L PTS 6 Glasgow
10.06.91	Chris Mulcahy DREW 6 Manchester
14.08.91	Efren Calamati L RSC 4 Alcamo, Italy
23.09.91	Alan Peacock W PTS 6 Glasgow
01.10.91	James McGee W PTS 6 Bedworth
05.11.91	Lee Ferrie L PTS 6 Leicester
25.11.91	Mark Kelly W PTS 8 Cleethorpes
05.12.91	Mickey Lerwill L PTS 6 Oakengates
14.12.91	Kevin Lueshing L CO 3 Bexleyheath
28.01.92	Alan Peacock L PTS 8 Piccadilly

29.02.92	Andre Kimbu L RTD 5 Gravelines, France
13.04.92	Crain Fisher L PTS 6 Manchester
30.04.92	B. F. Williams L PTS 6 Watford
14.09.92	Kevin Spratt W RSC 4 Bradford
23.10.92	Andreas Panayi L PTS 6 Liverpool
26.11.92	Willie Yeardsley W PTS 6 Hull
03.02.93	Derek Grainger L RSC 6 Earls Court

Career: 52 contests, won 17, drew 6, lost 29.

Johnny Melfah

Gloucester. *Born* Gloucester, 14 December, 1960
S. Middleweight. Ht. 5'9½"
Manager Self

08.09.86	Winston Wray L RSC 3 Dulwich
13.10.86	Andy Sumner W CO 3 Dulwich
17.11.86	Graeme Ahmed W PTS 6 Dulwich
15.12.86	Mark Mills W CO 5 Eltham
07.05.87	Alan Baptiste W CO 1 Bayswater
30.09.87	Cliff Gilpin W PTS 8 Solihull
12.10.87	Tony Burke W RSC 2 Bow
21.01.88	Carl Penn W CO 1 Wandsworth
18.03.88	Reggie Miller W RTD 5 Wandsworth
23.11.88	Herol Graham L RSC 5 Bethnal Green *(British Middleweight Title Challenge)*
08.02.89	Mustapha Cole W RTD 5 Kensington
22.03.89	Winston Wray W RSC 6 Gloucester
27.06.89	Kid Milo L CO 7 Kensington
05.11.89	Chris Eubank L CO 4 Kensington
30.10.90	Noel Magee L PTS 6 Belfast
24.11.90	Fidel Castro L RSC 4 Benalmadena, Spain
23.02.91	Sean Heron W PTS 8 Brighton
05.03.91	Wayne Ellis L RSC 2 Cardiff
16.05.91	Roland Ericsson W RSC 4 Battersea
07.09.91	Sammy Storey L PTS 8 Belfast
01.10.91	Fidel Castro L RSC 7 Sheffield
12.05.92	Lou Gent W RSC 3 Crystal Palace
25.07.92	Nicky Piper L RSC 5 Manchester *(Elim. British S. Middleweight Title)*
06.02.93	Steve Collins L RSC 3 Cardiff

Career: 24 contests, won 13, lost 11.

Malcolm Melvin

Birmingham. *Born* Birmingham, 5 February, 1967
All-Ireland & Midlands Area L. Welterweight Champion. Ht. 5'7"
Manager Self

29.11.85	Steve Foster DREW 6 Ilkeston
04.12.85	Simon Collins L PTS 6 Stoke
24.03.86	Rocky McGran L PTS 6 Mayfair
10.04.86	Lincoln Pennant W PTS 6 Leicester
21.04.86	Malcolm Davies W PTS 6 Birmingham
07.05.86	Julian Monville W PTS 6 Solihull
19.01.88	Antonio Fernandez L RSC 4 Kings Heath
07.03.88	John Ellis L PTS 6 Piccadilly
03.12.89	Dave Jenkins W PTS 6 Birmingham
05.02.90	Trevor Meikle W PTS 6 Brierley Hill
22.02.90	Chris Saunders L PTS 4 Hull
19.03.90	Barry North W PTS 6 Brierley Hill
30.04.90	Andy Kent W RSC 5 Brierley Hill
04.06.90	Brendan Ryan L RSC 7 Edgbaston
03.09.90	Dave Jenkins W PTS 8 Dudley
13.11.90	Brendan Ryan W PTS 10 Edgbaston *(Vacant Midlands Area L. Welterweight Title)*
18.03.91	Carl Brasier W PTS 6 Piccadilly
17.06.91	Dean Bramhald W PTS 6 Edgbaston

21.05.92	Mark Kelly W PTS 8 Cradley Heath
05.10.92	Ross Hale L PTS 10 Bristol *(Elim. British L. Welterweight Title)*
17.11.92	Tusikoleta Nkalankete DREW 8 Paris, France
16.03.93	Shaun Cogan W PTS 10 Edgbaston *(Vacant All-Ireland L. Welterweight Title & Midlands Area L. Welterweight Title Defence)*
29.06.93	Mark Kelly W PTS 6 Edgbaston

Career: 23 contests, won 14, drew 2, lost 7.

Sean Metherell

Kettering. *Born* Kettering, 29 March, 1966
Welterweight. Ht. 5'9"
Manager Self

10.12.92	Cliff Churchward W PTS 6 Corby
23.02.93	George Wilson L PTS 6 Kettering
04.03.93	Simon Fisher W RSC 1 Peterborough
18.05.93	Brian Coleman DREW 6 Kettering

Career: 4 contests, won 2, drew 1, lost 1.

Kevin Middleton

Downham. *Born* Deptford, 5 July, 1968
Featherweight. 5'7"
Manager B.Aird

24.10.91	Miguel Matthews W PTS 6 Dunstable
07.04.92	Pat Maher W CO 4 Southend
29.04.92	Chris Jickells L RSC 6 Solihull
15.10.92	Bradley Stone L PTS 6 Lewisham
04.12.92	Brian Robb W RSC 1 Telford
10.02.93	Chris Jickells W CO 1 Lewisham
03.03.93	Kid McAuley W PTS 8 Solihull
18.03.93	Miguel Matthews W PTS 6 Lewisham
28.04.93	John Irwin W RSC 6 Solihull

Career: 9 contests, won 7, lost 2.

(Alkis) A. M. Milton (Alkiviadov)

Streatham. *Born* London, 5 May, 1965
Lightweight. Ht. 5'3¾"
Manager Self

24.10.84	Kenny Watson L PTS 6 Mayfair
24.01.85	John Wilder W RTD 3 Streatham
04.02.85	John Faulkner L PTS 6 Lewisham

A.M. Milton   Les Clark

30.04.85	Kenny Watson W PTS 6 Merton
28.11.85	Brian Sonny Nickels L CO 4 Bethnal Green
04.09.86	Kevin Spratt DREW 6 Merton
19.11.87	Lee West L PTS 6 Wandsworth
10.05.88	Peter Hart L RSC 1 Tottenham
06.12.88	Shane Tonks W PTS 6 Southend
03.04.90	Dave Jenkins L PTS 6 Southend
25.09.90	Ray Newby W PTS 6 Millwall
12.11.90	Darren Morris W PTS 6 Norwich
08.05.91	Steve McGovern L PTS 6 Millwall
08.01.92	Darren Morris L PTS 6 Burton
31.10.92	Rick Bushell DREW 4 Earls Court
10.12.92	Brian Coleman DREW 4 Bethnal Green
17.02.93	Rick Bushell W RSC 1 Bethnal Green
31.03.93	Brian Coleman W PTS 4 Bethnal Green
23.06.93	Felix Kelly L CO 8 Edmonton
	(Vacant Southern Area Lightweight Title)

Career: 19 contests, won 7, drew 3, lost 9.

Clifton Mitchell

Sheffield. *Born* Derby, 29 October, 1965
Heavyweight. Ht. 6'2½"
Manager B. Ingle

06.04.91	John Harewood W RSC 2 Darlington
01.08.91	John Harewood W CO 1 Dewsbury
03.10.91	Tucker Richards W PTS 6 Burton
21.11.91	Tucker Richards W RSC 6 Burton
14.04.91	Michael Murray W RSC 8 Mansfield
16.03.93	Vivian Schwalger W CO 1 Wolverhampton
26.05.93	John Harewood W RSC 4 Mansfield

Career: 7 contests, won 7.

Joey Moffat

Liverpool. *Born* Liverpool, 14 February, 1964
L. Welterweight. Ht. 5'8"
Manager C.Moorcroft

10.03.90	Dave Jenkins L PTS 6 Bristol
13.11.91	Paul Hughes W RTD 4 Liverpool
28.11.91	Kevin Lowe W PTS 6 Liverpool
10.02.92	Tony Doyle W RSC 3 Liverpool
27.01.92	Kevin Lowe W PTS 6 Liverpool
29.04.92	Pete Roberts W RSC 3 Liverpool
14.05.92	Scott Doyle W RSC 8 Liverpool
15.09.92	Carl Tilley W PTS 6 Liverpool
09.06.93	Norman Dhalie W RTD 4 Liverpool

Career: 9 contests, won 8, lost 1.

Alex Moffatt

Doncaster. *Born* Burnley, 11 November, 1965
L. Welterweight. Ht. 5'8"
Manager J. Rushton

10.11.92	Paul Knights L CO 3 Dagenham
09.12.92	Shane Sheridan L CO 6 Stoke

Career: 2 contests, lost 2.

Karl Morling

Northampton. *Born* Douglas, IOM, 26 December, 1970
Featherweight. Ht. 5'4"
Manager J. Cox

15.10.90	Lee Christian W RSC 2 Kettering
22.10.90	Tony Falcone W PTS 6 Mayfair

31.01.91	Craig Dermody L RSC 5 Bredbury
02.05.91	Sol Francis W RSC 3 Northampton
13.05.91	Paul Wynn W RSC 2 Northampton
06.04.92	Norman Dhalie W PTS 6 Northampton
05.10.92	Robert Braddock W PTS 6 Northampton
14.12.92	Dean Lynch L RSC 4 Northampton
19.04.93	Graham McGrath W RSC 6 Northampton

Career: 9 contests, won 7, lost 2.

Terry Morrill

Hull. *Born* Hull, 2 February, 1965
Middleweight. Former Central Area L. Middleweight Champion. Ht. 5'10¼"
Manager Self

10.12.88	Chris Richards W PTS 6 Crystal Palace
08.02.89	Newton Barnett W PTS 6 Kensington
28.03.89	Skip Jackson L RSC 5 Glasgow
27.06.89	Mark Howell W PTS 6 Kensington
10.10.89	Spencer Alton W PTS 6 Hull
15.11.89	Davey Hughes DREW 4 Lewisham
08.12.89	Tony Baker W PTS 6 Doncaster
22.02.90	Mark Holden W RSC 7 Hull
	(Central Area L. Middleweight Title Challenge)
10.04.90	Ernie Noble W RSC 7 Doncaster
20.05.90	Jason Rowe L CO 6 Sheffield
	(Central Area L. Middleweight Title Defence)
31.10.90	Shaun Cummins L RSC 1 Crystal Palace
14.03.91	Delroy Waul DREW 8 Middleton
28.05.91	Eamonn Loughran L CO 1 Cardiff
16.10.92	Shamus Casey W PTS 6 Hull

Career: 14 contests, won 8, drew 2, lost 4.

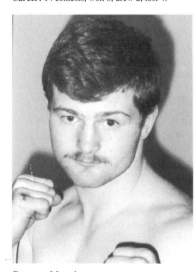

Darren Morris   Les Clark

Darren Morris

Birmingham. *Born* Birmingham, 26 May, 1966
Welterweight. Ht. 5'6½"
Manager Self

03.09.90	Joel Forbes DREW 6 Dudley
12.09.90	Keith Hardman W PTS 6 Stafford
30.10.90	Mike Betts L PTS 6 Solihull

29.10.90	Neil Porter W PTS 6 Birmingham
12.11.90	A. M. Milton L PTS 6 Norwich
27.11.90	Neil Porter L PTS 6 Stoke
06.12.90	Gary Osborne L PTS 8 Wolverhampton
21.02.91	Richard O'Brien L PTS 6 Walsall
05.03.91	Mick Mulcahy W PTS 6 Leicester
12.04.91	Tony Britland L PTS 6 Willenhall
24.04.91	Andreas Panayi DREW 6 Stoke
30.05.91	Bullit Andrews W RSC 3 Birmingham
04.07.91	Barry Messam L PTS 6 Alfreton
23.10.91	Andreas Panayi L PTS 6 Stoke
31.10.91	John O'Johnson L PTS 6 Oakengates
02.12.91	Chris Mylan L PTS 8 Birmingham
08.01.92	A. M. Milton W PTS 6 Burton
17.03.92	Wayne Timmins DREW 6 Wolverhampton
25.03.92	James McGee DREW 6 Hinckley
30.04.92	Leigh Wicks DREW 6 Mayfair
01.06.92	Mark Kelly W PTS 8 Solihull
28.09.92	Des Robinson L PTS 6 Manchester
28.10.92	Roy Rowland L RSC 2 Kensington

Career: 23 contests, won 6, drew 5, lost 12.

Jamie Morris

Nuneaton. *Born* Nuneaton, 15 February, 1970
L. Welterweight. Ht. 5'9"
Manager J. Griffin

28.06.89	Phil Lashley W RSC 1 Kenilworth
05.09.89	Carl Brasier L RSC 3 Southend
10.10.89	Andrew Robinson L PTS 6 Wolverhampton
06.12.89	Wayne Taylor L RSC 5 Leicester
17.01.90	Lee Ahmed L PTS 6 Stoke
05.02.90	Lee Ahmed W PTS 6 Leicester
27.02.90	Lee Ahmed W PTS 6 Evesham
06.03.90	George Bailey W PTS 6 Bradford
06.04.90	Rick Dimmock L PTS 6 Stevenage
24.04.90	Des Gargano L PTS 4 Stoke
30.04.90	Neil Leitch L PTS 6 Nottingham
14.05.90	Tony Heath L PTS 6 Leicester
01.10.91	Michael Byrne DREW 4 Bedworth
16.10.91	Michael Byrne W PTS 6 Stoke
11.11.91	Mitchell Barney DREW 6 Stratford upon Avon
21.11.91	Brian Coleman DREW 6 Stafford
04.12.91	Sugar Boy Wright L PTS 6 Stoke
20.01.92	Mark Antony L RSC 5 Coventry
24.02.92	Simon Hamblett DREW 6 Coventry
11.03.92	Razza Campbell L PTS 6 Stoke
24.03.92	Mark Allen W PTS 6 Wolverhampton
27.01.93	Billy McDougall L PTS 6 Stoke
11.03.93	Mark Allen DREW 6 Walsall
17.06.93	Chris Pollock L RSC 1 Bedworth

Career: 24 contests, won 6, drew 5, lost 13.

Jason Morris

Birmingham. *Born* Birmingham, 28 May, 1972
Bantamweight. Ht. 5'2"
Manager E. Cashmore

08.09.92	Jacob Smith L PTS 6 Manchester
22.02.93	Stevie Woods W CO 4 Glasgow
17.03.93	Gary Marston L PTS 6 Stoke

Career: 3 contests, won 1, lost 2.

Mike Morrison

Pembroke. *Born* Prestatyn, 24 February, 1963
Lightweight. Ht. 5'7"
Manager Self

14.09.89   Paul Day L PTS 6 Basildon
21.09.89   Steve McGovern L PTS 6 Southampton
28.09.89   Mark Atkins W PTS 6 Cardiff
11.10.89   Richard Burton L PTS 6 Stoke
15.11.89   Jason Rowland L PTS 6 Reading
30.11.89   Mo Hussein L PTS 8 Barking
20.12.89   Nigel Dobson L PTS 6 Kirkby
16.01.90   B. F. Williams L PTS 6 Cardiff
24.01.90   Carl Wright L PTS 6 Preston
01.03.90   Russell Jones L PTS 6 Cardiff
13.03.90   Nick Meloscia L PTS 6 Bristol
21.03.90   Steve Foran L PTS 6 Preston
10.04.90   Chris Saunders L PTS 6 Doncaster
23.04.90   Shaun Cogan L PTS 8 Birmingham
30.04.90   Shaun Cooper L PTS 6 Brierley Hill
22.05.90   Jason Rowland L PTS 6 St Albans
05.09.90   Tim Harmey L PTS 6 Brighton
12.09.90   Jimmy Harrison L PTS 6 Battersea
25.09.90   Mark Tibbs L PTS 6 Millwall
03.10.90   Nick Hall L PTS 8 Solihull
10.10.90   Benny Collins L PTS 6 Millwall
12.12.90   Eamonn Loughran L PTS 6 Basildon
10.01.91   Rick Bushell L PTS 6 Wandsworth
24.01.91   Andy Williams L PTS 8 Gorseinon
31.01.91   Richard Burton L PTS 6 Bredbury
06.03.91   Mark Tibbs L RSC 4 Wembley
02.05.91   Richard Swallow L PTS 6 Northampton
23.05.91   Martin Rosamond L PTS 6 Southampton
18.07.91   Michael Smyth L RSC 2 Cardiff
07.07.92   Steve Howden W CO 3 Bristol
15.09.92   Dean Bramhald L PTS 6 Crystal Palace
28.10.92   Mervyn Bennett L PTS 6 Cardiff
14.12.92   Mervyn Bennett L PTS 6 Cardiff
27.02.93   Paul Ryan L PTS 6 Dagenham
09.03.93   Trevor Royal W PTS 6 Bristol
14.04.93   Cham Joof L PTS 4 Kensington
26.06.93   Bobby Guynan W PTS 4 Earls Court
Career: 37 contests, won 4, lost 33.

Jerry Mortimer

Clapham. *Born* Mauritius, 22 June, 1962
Middleweight. Ht. 5'9"
Manager B. Aird

21.10.91   Steve Thomas L PTS 6 Mayfair
12.02.92   Darren Murphy W PTS 6 Watford
02.03.92   Lee Farrell W PTS 6 Merthyr
28.04.92   Stefan Wright L RSC 4 Corby
08.09.92   Robert Whitehouse W RSC 3 Southend
15.10.92   Russell Washer W RSC 5 Lewisham
14.12.92   Gareth Boddy W PTS 6 Cardiff
28.01.93   John Bosco L RSC 4 Southwark
09.03.93   Paul Smith W PTS 6 Bristol
Career: 9 contests, won 6, lost 3.

Kevin Morton

Leicester. *Born* Leicester, 17 April, 1969
S. Middleweight. Ht. 6'0"
Manager W. Swift

06.02.91   Dennis Afflick W PTS 6 Liverpool
28.02.91   Stevie R. Davies W RSC 3 Bury
04.04.91   Johnny Uphill W CO 1 Watford
02.05.91   Alan Baptiste W RSC 2 Northampton
30.10.91   Nick Manners W PTS 8 Leeds
03.06.92   Mark Pain W PTS 6 Newcastle under Lyme
09.09.92   Adrian Wright W PTS 6 Stoke
Career: 7 contests, won 7.

Johnny Moth (Buck)

Nottingham. *Born* Nottingham, 10 October, 1967
Cruiserweight. Ht. 5'9"
Manager M. Shinfield

08.06.93   Chris Harbourne DREW 6 Derby
Career: 1 contest, drew 1.

(Dawuda) Dave Muhammed

Eastbourne. *Born* Ghana, 2 March, 1960
Cruiserweight. Ht. 5'9¾"
Manager T. Miller

13.09.88   Thomas Henry W RSC 3 Battersea
31.10.88   Tenko Ernie W RSC 6 Bedford
16.02.89   Magne Havnaa L RSC 6 Copenhagen, Denmark
22.03.89   Mike Aubrey W RSC 5 Sheppey
22.04.89   Anaclet Wamba L RSC 4 St Brieuc, France
11.08.89   Luigi Gaudiano L RSC 6 Montorio Voman, Italy
28.11.89   Andy Straughn W PTS 8 Battersea
29.04.91   Steve Lewsam W PTS 8 Cleethorpes
12.10.91   Axel Schulz L PTS 8 Halle, Germany
27.03.92   Norbert Ekassi L RSC 3 Creil, France
22.04.93   Denzil Browne L PTS 8 Mayfair
Career: 11 contests, won 5, lost 6.

Chris Mulcahy

Manchester. *Born* Rochdale, 18 June, 1963
Welterweight. Ht. 6'0"
Manager N. Basso

11.10.88   Robbie Bowen W PTS 6 Wolverhampton
25.10.88   Dave Croft W PTS 6 Cottingham
03.11.88   Pat Durkin W RSC 2 Manchester
21.11.88   Ian Midwood-Tate L CO 1 Leicester
23.02.89   Nigel Bradley L RSC 2 Stockport
17.04.89   Dave Kettlewell W PTS 6 Middleton
24.04.89   Kevin Toomey W PTS 6 Bradford
19.05.89   Dave Whittle W PTS 6 Gateshead
25.05.89   Martin Ogilvie L PTS 6 Dundee
12.06.89   Trevor Meikle W PTS 6 Manchester
11.07.89   Trevor Meikle W PTS 6 Batley
03.10.89   Banco Bell W RSC 1 Cottingham
23.10.89   Karl Ince L CO 5 Cleethorpes
20.11.89   Ian Thomas W PTS 6 Middleton
14.05.90   Mark Kelly L PTS 8 Cleethorpes
11.06.90   Alan Peacock L RSC 3 Manchester
05.03.91   Pat Durkin L PTS 6 Leicester
03.04.91   Willie Yeardsley L PTS 6 Manchester
10.06.91   Trevor Meikle DREW 6 Manchester
02.10.91   Robert Wright L RSC 1 Solihull
21.11.91   Richard O'Brien L RSC 2 Ilkeston
20.01.92   Darren McInulty L PTS 6 Coventry
11.02.92   James McGee L PTS 6 Wolverhampton
04.04.92   Rob Stevenson W PTS 8 Cleethorpes
01.06.92   Rob Stevenson W PTS 6 Manchester
03.09.92   John Smith DREW 6 Liverpool
16.10.92   Peter Waudby L RSC 4 Hull
24.11.92   Richard Swallow L PTS 6 Wolverhampton
02.12.92   Colin Anderson W PTS 6 Bardon
02.02.93   Spencer Alton L RSC 3 Derby
08.03.93   Danny Harper L PTS 8 Leeds
31.03.93   Adrian Dodson L RSC 1 Bethnal Green

01.06.93   Tony Trimble L PTS 6 Manchester
09.06.93   Andrew Jervis L PTS 6 Liverpool
Career: 34 contests, won 14, drew 2, lost 18.

Mick Mulcahy

Manchester. *Born* Rochdale, 9 May, 1966
L. Welterweight. Ht. 5'8"
Manager N. Basso

06.06.88   Nick Langley W RSC 5 Manchester
05.09.88   Johnny Walker W PTS 4 Glasgow
22.09.88   Frankie Foster L PTS 6 Newcastle
02.10.88   Niel Leggett DREW 6 Peterborough
25.10.88   Wayne Windle W PTS 6 Cottingham
03.11.88   Peter English L RSC 4 Manchester
12.12.88   Steve Taggart L PTS 6 Birmingham
25.01.89   Mark Tibbs L CO 1 Bethnal Green
23.02.89   Sean Conn W CO 1 Stockport
13.03.89   Dean Dickinson W PTS 6 Liecester
17.04.89   Neil Leitch W RSC 2 Middleton
19.05.89   Mark Jay L PTS 6 Mayfair
29.05.89   George Kerr L PTS 6 Dundee
12.06.89   Muhammad Shaffique L RSC 2 Manchester
11.09.89   Dave Croft W PTS 4 Manchester
19.09.89   Billy Couzens L PTS 6 Bethnal Green
03.10.89   Kevin Toomey W CO 5 Cottingham
13.10.89   Carl Wright L PTS 6 Preston
23.10.89   Trevor Meikle L PTS 6 Cleethorpes
31.10.89   Carl Wright L PTS 6 Manchester
10.11.89   Chris McReedy L PTS 6 Liverpool
20.11.89   Brendan Ryan L PTS 6 Leicester
04.12.89   Brian Cullen L PTS 8 Manchester
19.12.89   Errol McDonald L RSC 3 Bethnal Green
24.04.90   Brian Cullen L PTS 8 Stoke
22.10.90   Wayne Windle L PTS 4 Cleethorpes
12.11.90   Richard Joyce L RSC 6 Stratford upon Avon
12.12.90   Neil Porter DREW 6 Stoke
24.01.91   Robert McCracken L RSC 1 Brierley Hill
05.03.91   Darren Morris L PTS 6 Leicester
03.04.91   Trevor Meikle L PTS 6 Manchester
15.04.91   Andreas Panayi L RSC 2 Leicester
10.06.91   Mike Calderwood L PTS 6 Manchester
18.11.91   Benji Joseph L PTS 6 Manchester
28.11.91   B. K. Bennett L PTS 6 Evesham
05.12.91   Mark Elliot L RSC 2 Cannock
17.03.92   Bernard Paul L PTS 6 Mayfair
04.04.92   Michael Byrne W RSC 4 Cleethorpes
01.06.92   Jason Brattley L PTS 6 Manchester
11.09.92   Rocky Ferrari L PTS 6 Glasgow
25.09.92   Carl Wright L PTS 6 Liverpool
10.12.92   Charlie Kane L RSC 2 Glasgow
02.02.93   Shane Sheridan L PTS 6 Derby
19.03.93   Steve Walker L RSC 6 Manchester
01.06.93   Wayne Windle W PTS 6 Manchester
Career: 45 contests, won 10, drew 2, lost 33.

Karl Mumford

Hengoed. *Born* Hengoed, 26 February, 1963
L. Heavyweight. Ht. 6'0"
Manager D. Gardiner

07.10.92   Chris Beck W PTS 6 Barry
14.11.92   Darryl Ritchie W PTS 6 Cardiff
26.01.93   Zak Chelli L PTS 6 Leicester
06.02.93   Jason McNeill W PTS 6 Cardiff
10.04.93   Rocky Reynolds W PTS 6 Swansea
26.04.93   Mark Baker L CO Lewisham
Career: 6 contests, won 4, lost 2.

Craig Murray

Rochdale. *Born* Rochdale, 23 January, 1971
S. Featherweight. Ht. 5'7"
Manager N. Basso

01.06.92	Tony Smith W RSC 2 Manchester
05.10.92	Joe Fannin L RSC 1 Manchester

Career: 2 contests, won 1, lost 1.

James Murray

Newmains. *Born* Lanark, 7 December, 1969
Bantamweight. Ht. 5'4"
Manager A. Melrose

26.03.93	L. C. Wilson W RSC 4 Glasgow
30.04.93	Dave Campbell W PTS 6 Glasgow
29.05.93	Kid McAuley W PTS 6 Paisley

Career: 3 contests, won 3.

Michael Murray   Harry Goodwin

Michael Murray

Manchester. *Born* Preston, 3 September,
1964
Central Area Heavyweight Champion. Ht.
6'1"
Manager J. Trickett

23.02.88	Gypsy John Fury L PTS 6 Oldham
28.04.88	Ian Nelson W RSC 6 Manchester
17.11.88	Steve Garber W PTS 6 Stockport
07.02.89	Rocky Burton W PTS 6 Manchester
10.05.89	Barry Ellis W RSC 3 Solihull
08.09.89	Noel Quarless L PTS 8 Liverpool
17.10.89	John Westgarth W RTD 4 Oldham
06.02.90	Al Malcolm W RSC 5 Oldham
02.06.90	Gypsy John Fury L RTD 6 Manchester
30.04.91	Steve Garber W CO 1 Stockport
19.09.91	Carl Gaffney W RSC 8 Stockport
	(Vacant Central Area Heavyweight Title)
15.10.91	Markus Bott W RSC 7 Hamburg, Germany
07.12.91	Steve Gee W RSC 7 Manchester
14.04.92	Clifton Mitchell L RSC 8 Mansfield
28.11.92	Ricky Sekorski W PTS 8 Manchester
27.02.93	Herbie Hide L RSC 5 Dagenham
	(Vacant British Heavyweight Title)

Career: 16 contests, won 11, lost 5.

Paul Murray

Birmingham. *Born* Birmingham, 8 January,
1961
L. Heavyweight. Ht. 5'9"
Manager P. Byrne

04.09.80	Gerry White W PTS 6 Morecambe
11.09.80	Graeme Ahmed L PTS 6 Hartlepool
29.09.80	Richard Wilson L PTS 6 Bedworth
08.10.80	Carl North W CO 2 Stoke
14.10.80	Steve McLeod W PTS 6 Wolverhampton
20.10.80	Steve Davies DREW 6 Birmingham
30.10.80	John Wiggins W PTS 6 Wolverhampton
07.11.80	Archie Salman L PTS 6 Cambuslang
18.11.80	John Wiggins L PTS 6 Shrewsbury
26.11.80	Mike Clemow L PTS 8 Stoke
08.12.80	John Wiggins L PTS 6 Nottingham
26.01.81	Errol Dennis W PTS 6 Edgbaston
16.03.81	Dennis Sheehan DREW 6 Nottingham
15.04.81	Nigel Thomas DREW 8 Evesham
28.05.81	Martin McGough L PTS 6 Edgbaston
09.07.81	Roger Guest L CO 8 Dudley
21.09.81	Gary Buckle DREW 6 Wolverhampton
07.10.81	Kostas Petrou W RSC 5 Solihull
13.10.81	Gary Buckle L PTS 6 Wolverhampton
24.11.81	Nick Riozzi W PTS 6 Wolverhampton
25.01.82	Martin McGough L RSC 4 Wolverhampton
21.02.82	Gary Buckle L PTS 8 Nottingham
10.03.82	Ron Pearce L PTS 8 Solihull
23.03.82	Errol Dennis L PTS 6 Wolverhampton
29.03.82	Tony Brown L PTS 6 Liverpool
07.04.82	Dennis Sheehan W PTS 6 Evesham
28.04.82	Lee Roy W CO 3 Burslem
17.05.82	Paul Costigan L PTS 8 Manchester
24.05.82	Dennis Sheehan DREW 6 Nottingham
07.06.82	Kostas Petrou L PTS 6 Edgbaston
13.09.82	Paul Costigan W PTS 6 Manchester
18.10.82	Kostas Petrou L RSC 5 Edgbaston
15.02.83	Bert Myrie L PTS 6 Wolverhampton
21.02.83	Steve Tempro L DIS 3 Edgbaston
01.03.83	Chris Pyatt L RTD 2 Kensington
17.05.83	T. P. Jenkins L PTS 6 Bethnal Green
23.06.83	Wayne Hawkins L PTS 6 Wolverhampton
19.09.83	Bert Myrie W PTS 8 Nottingham
26.10.83	Steve Henty L PTS 6 Stoke
14.11.83	Kid Sadler L PTS 8 Manchester
14.12.83	John Andrews L PTS 6 Stoke
19.03.84	Wayne Barker L PTS 8 Manchester
27.03.84	Rocky Kelly L RTD 5 Battersea
08.10.84	Gavin Stirrup L PTS 6 Manchester
26.01.87	Chris Walker L PTS 4 Bethnal Green
10.02.87	Chris Walker W PTS 4 Wolverhampton
16.02.87	Chris Galloway W PTS 6 Mayfair
24.02.87	Nicky Thorne L PTS 6 Wandsworth
03.08.87	Peter Elliott L PTS 6 Stoke
07.09.87	Dusty Miller L RTD 4 Mayfair
25.01.88	Paul Wesley L PTS 8 Birmingham
29.02.88	Paul Wesley DREW 8 Birmingham
14.03.88	Mickey Hughes L RSC 4 Mayfair
19.10.88	Geoff Calder NC 6 Evesham
26.10.88	Franki Moro L PTS 6 Stoke
05.12.88	Richard Carter L PTS 6 Dudley
24.01.89	Antonio Fernandez L PTS 6 Kings Heath
24.10.89	Andrew Flute L RSC 4 Wolverhampton
21.06.90	Spencer Alton L PTS 6 Alfreton
13.09.90	Nigel Rafferty L PTS 6 Watford
27.09.90	Nigel Rafferty DREW 6 Birmingham

09.10.90	Nigel Rafferty L PTS 6 Wolverhampton
18.10.90	Nick Manners L PTS 6 Dewsbury
29.10.90	Carlos Christie L PTS 6 Birmingham
16.12.90	Wayne Hawkins L PTS 6 Wolverhampton
28.01.91	Lee Prudden L PTS 6 Birmingham
06.02.91	Paul Walters DREW 6 Liverpool
27.02.91	Paul Busby L PTS 6 Wolverhampton
13.03.91	Lee Prudden DREW 6 Stoke
24.04.91	John Kaighin L PTS 6 Aberavon
14.05.91	Ernie Loveridge L PTS 8 Dudley
30.05.91	Robert McCracken L RSC 2 Birmingham
25.07.91	Tony Booth L PTS 6 Dudley
07.10.91	Antonio Fernandez L RSC 7 Birmingham
12.11.91	Lee Archer L PTS 6 Wolverhampton
05.12.91	Richard Carter L PTS 8 Cannock
17.12.91	Paul Busby L CO 3 Cardiff
15.01.92	Mark Hale L PTS 6 Stoke
06.02.92	John McKenzie L PTS 6 Peterborough
19.02.92	James F. Woolley W CO 4 Muswell Hill
26.03.92	Neville Brown L CO 3 Telford
05.10.92	Lee Archer L PTS 6 Bardon
13.10.92	Lee Archer L PTS 6 Wolverhampton
21.10.92	Steve Loftus L PTS 6 Stoke
23.11.92	John J. Cooke L CO 1 Coventry
17.06.93	Carl Smallwood L PTS 6 Bedworth

Career: 86 contests, won 14, drew 9, lost 62, no
contest 1.

Ashley Naylor

Huddersfield. *Born* Halifax, 24 March,
1968
Heavyweight. Ht. 6'3"
Manager T. Miller

01.03.93	Gary Williams DREW 6 Bradford
26.04.93	Gary Williams L PTS 6 Bradford

Career: 2 contests, drew 1, lost 1.

George Naylor

Liverpool. *Born* Liverpool, 4 September,
1968
Lightweight. Ht. 5'7"
Manager Self

25.09.92	Charles Shepherd L RSC 4 Liverpool
30.10.92	Dean Martin W PTS 6 Birmingham
20.11.92	Emlyn Rees W PTS 6 Liverpool
15.12.92	Renny Edwards L RSC 5 Liverpool

Career: 4 contests, won 2, lost 2.

(Jimmy) Shea Neary

Liverpool. *Born* Liverpool, 18 May, 1968
L. Welterweight. Ht. 5'7½"
Manager B. Devine

03.09.92	Simon Ford W RSC 1 Liverpool
05.10.92	Shaun Armstrong W RSC 6 Liverpool
02.11.92	Jason Barker W RSC 3 Liverpool
01.12.92	Chris Saunders W PTS 6 Liverpool
22.02.93	Vaughan Carnegie W RSC 1 Liverpool
29.03.93	John Smith W PTS 6 Liverpool

Career: 6 contests, won 6.

Johnny Nelson

Sheffield. *Born* Sheffield, 4 January, 1967
WBF Cruiserweight Champion. Former
Undefeated British, European & Central
Area Cruiserweight Champion. Ht. 6'2"
Manager B. Ingle

18.03.86	Peter Brown L PTS 6 Hull	
15.05.86	Tommy Taylor L PTS 6 Dudley	
03.10.86	Magne Havnaa L PTS 4 Copenhagen, Denmark	
20.11.86	Chris Little W PTS 6 Bredbury	
19.01.87	Gypsy Carman W PTS 6 Mayfair	
02.03.87	Doug Young W PTS 6 Huddersfield	
10.03.87	Sean Daly W RSC 1 Manchester	
28.04.87	Brian Schumacher L PTS 8 Halifax	
03.06.87	Byron Pullen W RSC 3 Southwark	
14.12.87	Jon McBean W RSC 6 Edgbaston	
01.02.88	Dennis Bailey L PTS 8 Northampton	
24.02.88	Cordwell Hylton W RSC 1 Sheffield	
25.04.88	Kenny Jones W CO 1 Liverpool	
04.05.88	Crawford Ashley W PTS 8 Solihull	
06.06.88	Lennie Howard W CO 2 Mayfair	
31.08.88	Andrew Gerrard W PTS 8 Stoke	
26.10.88	Danny Lawford W RSC 2 Sheffield	
	(Vacant Central Area Cruiserweight Title)	
04.04.89	Steve Mormino W RSC 2 Sheffield	
21.05.89	Andy Straughn W CO 8 Finsbury Park	
	(British Cruiserweight Title Challenge)	
02.10.89	Ian Bulloch W CO 2 Hanley	
	(British Cruiserweight Title Defence)	
27.01.90	Carlos de Leon DREW 12 Sheffield	
	(WBC Cruiserweight Title Challenge)	
14.02.90	Dino Homsey W RSC 7 Brentwood	
28.03.90	Lou Gent W CO 4 Bethnal Green	
	(British Cruiserweight Title Defence)	
27.06.90	Arthur Weathers W RSC 2 Kensington	
05.09.90	Andre Smith W PTS 8 Brighton	
14.12.90	Markus Bott W RSC 12 Karlsruhe, Germany	
	(Vacant European Cruiserweight Title)	
12.03.91	Yves Monsieur W RTD 8 Mansfield	
	(European Cruiserweight Title Defence)	

16.05.92	James Warring L PTS 12 Fredericksburg, USA	
	(IBF Cruiserweight Title Challenge)	
15.08.92	Norbert Ekassi L RSC 3 Ajaccio, France	
29.10.92	Corrie Sanders L PTS 10 Morula, South Africa	
30.04.93	Dave Russell W RSC 11 Melbourne, Australia	
	(WBF Cruiserweight Title Challenge)	

Career: 31 contests, won 22, drew 1, lost 8.

Kenny Nevers

Hackney. *Born* Hackney, 10 August, 1967
L. Heavyweight. Ht. 5'11"
Manager B. Lynch

10.12.92	Hussain Shah L PTS 4 Bethnal Green	
22.02.93	Jason McNeill W RSC 1 Eltham	
04.04.93	Hussain Shah W RSC 4 Brockley	

Career: 3 contests, won 2, lost 1.

Ray Newby

Nottingham. *Born* Sunderland, 16
December, 1963
L. Welterweight. Former Midlands Area
Lightweight Champion. Ht. 5'7"
Manager J. Griffin

20.09.84	Rocky Lawlor DREW 6 Dudley	
10.10.84	Jess Rundan W RSC 3 Evesham	
29.10.84	Dean Bramhald W PTS 6 Nottingham	
07.11.84	Gary Flear L PTS 6 Evesham	
21.11.84	Glenn Tweedie W PTS 6 Solihull	
10.12.84	Wayne Trigg W RSC 6 Nottingham	
04.02.85	Peter Bowen W PTS 8 Nottingham	
07.03.85	Steve Cooke L PTS 8 Nottingham	
25.09.85	Billy Laidman W RSC 2 Stoke	
03.10.85	John Faulkner W PTS 8 Nottingham	
21.11.85	Michael Marsden L PTS 6 Huddersfield	
20.01.86	Steve Griffith L RSC 3 Mayfair	
24.02.86	Ian Harrison W PTS 6 Coventry	
05.03.86	Mark Pearce DREW 6 Stoke	
25.03.86	Paul Dawson W RSC 3 Wandsworth	

During 1992-93, Ray Newby (right) twice drew with the once highly touted Bernard Paul

Les Clark

07.04.86	Wayne Cooper W RSC 2 Nottingham	
14.04.86	Les Remikie L PTS 6 Mayfair	
03.06.86	Peter Till W PTS 10 Wolverhampton	
	(Vacant Midlands Area Lightweight Title)	
15.09.86	George Baigrie W PTS 8 Coventry	
06.10.86	Muhammad Lovelock W PTS 8 Leicester	
29.10.86	Andy Williams L PTS 8 Ebbw Vale	
01.12.86	George Baigrie W DIS 1 Nottingham	
11.12.86	Ian McLeod L PTS 8 Livingston	
16.02.87	Mervyn Bennett W CO 8 Glasgow	
24.03.87	Joey Joynson L PTS 8 Wembley	
07.04.87	Mark Pearce L PTS 8 West Bromwich	
14.04.87	Floyd Havard L RSC 7 Cumbernauld	
12.10.87	Brian Sonny Nickels L PTS 8 Mayfair	
19.10.87	Tony Borg L PTS 8 Nottingham	
11.12.87	Billy Joe Dee W PTS 8 Coalville	
17.02.88	Wayne Weekes W PTS 8 Bethnal Green	
08.03.88	Darren Connellan W RSC 7 Batley	
10.04.88	Aladin Stevens L PTS 8 Eldorado Park, South Africa	
09.05.88	Ian Honeywood W RSC 1 Nottingham	
14.06.88	Peter Till L RSC 10 Dudley	
	(Midlands Area Lightweight Title Defence)	
31.08.88	Les Remikie W PTS 8 Leicester	
11.11.88	Madjid Mahdjoub L PTS 8 Venissieux, France	
25.09.90	A. M. Milton L PTS 6 Millwall	
12.11.90	Brian Cullen W PTS 6 Stratford upon Avon	
30.11.90	Peter Till L PTS 8 Birmingham	
12.04.91	Henry Armstrong L PTS 8 Manchester	
22.01.92	Dean Bramhald W PTS 8 Solihull	
11.02.92	Dean Bramhald W RSC 7 Wolverhampton	
24. 03.92	Ron Shinkwin W PTS 8 Wolverhampton	
18.05.92	Ron Shinkwin W RSC 5 Bardon	
02.07.92	Richard Burton L PTS 6 Middleton	
10.11.92	Bernard Paul DREW 6 Dagenham	
20.01.93	Richard Swallow L PTS 8 Solihull	
03.03.93	Richard Swallow W PTS 8 Solihull	
20.04.93	Bernard Paul DREW 6 Brentwood	
19.05.93	Michael Driscoll L RTD 2 Leicester	

Career: 51 contests, won 26, drew 4, lost 21.

Dale Nixon

Taunton. *Born* Exeter, 11 May, 1970
S. Middleweight. Ht. 6'2"
Manager C. Sanigar

09.03.93	Ian Vokes W RSC 2 Bristol	
27.05.93	Chris Nurse W RSC 2 Bristol	
26.06.93	Tim Robinson W RSC 2 Keynsham	

Career: 3 contests, won 3.

Ian Noble

Blackhall. *Born* Easington, 24 August,
1971
L. Welterweight. Ht. 5'7"
Manager G. Robinson

06.05.93	Michael Alexander L PTS 6 Hartlepool	

Career: 1 contest, lost 1.

Eric Noi

Manchester. *Born* Manchester, 12 May,
1967
S. Middleweight. Ht. 5'11"
Manager P. Martin

Eric Noi Harry Goodwin

05.02.93	Tim Robinson W RSC 4 Manchester
19.03.93	Smokey Enison W RSC 5 Manchester
26.04.93	Karl Barwise W PTS 6 Manchester
28.05.93	Karl Barwise W RSC 4 Middleton

Career: 4 contests, won 4.

Shaun Norman

Leicester. *Born* Leicester, 1 April, 1970
Flyweight. Ht. 5'3"
Manager W. Swift

11.11.91	Louis Veitch W RSC 5 Bradford
27.11.91	Dave Campbell L PTS 6 Marton
14.12.91	Mickey Cantwell L PTS 8 Bexley Heath
20.02.92	Dave Hardie L PTS 6 Glasgow
10.04.92	Neil Armstrong DREW 8 Glasgow
25.04.92	Prince Nassem Hamed L RSC 2 Manchester

Shaun Norman Les Clark

16.06.92	Francis Ampofo L RSC 4 Dagenham
19.10.92	Alan Ley L PTS 6 Mayfair
23.11.92	Paul Weir L PTS 8 Glasgow
04.03.93	Neil Armstrong L RSC 8 Glasgow

Career: 10 contests, won 1, drew 1, lost 8.

Rick North

Grimsby. *Born* Grimsby, 2 February, 1968
Welterweight. Ht. 5'8½"
Manager B. Ingle

28.05.91	Michael Smyth L RSC 1 Cardiff
16.09.91	Eddie King W RSC 5 Cleethorpes
21.01.91	Steve Bricknell W PTS 6 Cleethorpes
11.11.91	Darren McInulty L PTS 6 Stratford upon Avon
09.12.91	Michael Byrne W RSC 2 Cleethorpes
23.01.92	Ron Hopley L PTS 6 York
19.02.92	Bernard Paul L PTS 6 Muswell Hill
11.03.92	Patrick Loughran L PTS 6 Stoke
22.04.92	Steve McNess L PTS 6 Wembley
03.06.92	Mark Dawson L PTS 6 Newcastle under Lyme
03.09.92	Andreas Panayi DREW 6 Liverpool
21.09.92	Hughie Davey DREW 6 Cleethorpes
05.10.92	Andrew Jervis L PTS 6 Liverpool
21.10.92	Jim Lawlor W PTS 6 Stoke
29.10.92	David Larkin L PTS 6 Leeds
20.11.92	Andreas Panayi L PTS 6 Liverpool
14.12.92	Lee Soar W PTS 6 Cleethorpes
27.01.93	Mark Dawson L PTS 8 Stoke
22.02.93	Spencer McCracken L PTS 8 Birmingham
09.03.93	Sean Baker L PTS 8 Bristol
14.04.93	Adrian Dodson L RTD 1 Kensington
27.05.93	Glenn Catley L PTS 4 Brisol

Career: 22 contests, won 5, drew 2, lost 15.

Chris Nurse

Birmingham. *Born* Birmingham, 17 May, 1968
L. Heavyweight. Ht. 6'1"
Manager E. Cashmore

24.11.92	Paul Hanlon L PTS 6 Wolverhampton
17.03.93	Steve Loftus W PTS 6 Stoke
01.04.93	Phil Ball DREW 6 Evesham
27.05.93	Dale Nixon L RSC 2 Bristol

Career: 4 contests, won 1, drew 1, lost 2.

Dennis Oakes

Liverpool. *Born* Prescot, 16 June, 1966
Featherweight. Ht. 5'6"
Manager M. Atkinson

22.01.92	Chris Lyons W RSC 3 Stoke
10.02.92	Mark Hargreaves W RSC 3 Liverpool
11.03.92	Des Gargano W PTS 6 Stoke
03.09.92	Colin Lynch W RSC 1 Liverpool
02.11.92	Graham McGrath W PTS 4 Liverpool
01.12.92	Steve Robinson L RTD 2 Liverpool

Career: 6 contests, won 5, lost 1.

(David) Marvin O'Brien (Powell)

Leeds. *Born* Leeds, 3 September, 1966
S. Middleweight. Ht. 5'11"
Manager T. Callighan

31.01.90	Tony Hodge L RSC 3 Bethnal Green
04.04.90	Gary Osborne L CO 2 Stafford
07.09.90	Mike Phillips L RSC 1 Liverpool
12.11.90	Mike Phillips W PTS 6 Liverpool
17.01.91	Barry Messam L PTS 6 Alfreton

21.02.91	Russell Washer DREW 6 Walsall
02.03.91	Quinn Paynter DREW 6 Irvine
21.03.91	Nick Manners L CO 2 Dewsbury
31.05.91	Carl Harney W RSC 5 Manchester
24.06.91	Frank Eubanks L PTS 6 Liverpool
06.09.91	Cornelius Carr L RSC 7 Salemi, Italy
02.03.92	John Oxenham L PTS 6 Marton
26.03.92	John Ashton L PTS 8 Telford
05.04.92	Quinn Paynter L PTS 6 Bradford
17.05.92	Lester Jacobs L PTS 6 Harringay
20.11.92	Fran Harding L RSC 4 Liverpool
16.02.93	Andy Wright L PTS 6 Tooting
12.05.93	Martin Jolley L PTS 6 Sheffield

Career: 18 contests, won 2, drew 2, lost 14.

Richard O'Brien Chris Bevan

Richard O'Brien

Alfreton. *Born* Chesterfield, 29 October, 1971
Welterweight. Ht. 5'10"
Manager M. Shinfield

14.05.90	Finn McCool W RSC 3 Northampton
21.05.90	Andy Rowbotham W RSC 5 Bradford
21.06.90	Jim Lawlor DREW 6 Alfreton
15.10.90	Richard Swallow W RTD 1 Kettering
22.10.90	Crain Fisher L CO 3 Manchester
13.12.90	Mick Duncan L PTS 6 Hartlepool
17.01.91	Steve Hardman L PTS 6 Alfreton
11.02.91	Neil Porter W RSC 4 Manchester
21.02.91	Darren Morris W PTS 6 Walsall
28.03.91	Trevor Ambrose L RSC 1 Alfreton
21.10.91	Tony Connellan L PTS 8 Bury
21.11.91	Chris Mulcahy W RSC 2 Ilkeston
02.12.91	Tony Britland W RSC 2 Birmingham
04.02.92	Darren McInulty W PTS 4 Alfreton
03.03.92	Scott Doyle L PTS 4 Cradley Heath
21.05.92	Howard Clarke L CO 1 Cradley Heath
23.10.92	Hughie Davey L PTS 6 Gateshead
11.03.93	Andy Peach W PTS 6 Walsall
01.04.93	Dave Lovell W PTS 6 Evesham
12.05.93	Wayne Appleton L RTD 2 Sheffield

Career: 20 contests, won 10, drew 1, lost 9.

Mark O'Callaghan

Tunbridge Wells. *Born* Tunbridge Wells, 17 January, 1969

Mark O'Callaghan   Chris Bevan

Lightweight. Ht. 5'7"
Manager Self

03.10.91	Chris Mylan DREW 6 Burton
24.10.91	Nicky Lucas W PTS 6 Dunstable
11.12.91	Richard Joyce L RSC 3 Stoke
20.02.92	Alan McDowall L PTS 6 Glasgow
12.11.92	Erwin Edwards L RSC 6 Bayswater
20.01.93	Sugar Boy Wright W CO 1 Wolverhampton
05.02.93	Nick Boyd L PTS 6 Manchester
18.03.93	Paul Denton L RSC 4 Lewisham
22.04.93	Trevor Royal W PTS 6 Mayfair
26.05.93	Gareth Jordan L RSC 3 Mansfield

Career: 10 contests, won 3, drew 1, lost 6.

John Ogiste

Islington. *Born* London, 16 July, 1965
Middleweight. Ht. 5'9"
Manager Self

07.12.88	Robert Gomez L RSC 4 Piccadilly
08.05.89	Dean Murray W RSC 4 Piccadilly
25.09.89	Jimmy McDonagh W RSC 4 Piccadilly
30.11.89	Stan King DREW 6 Mayfair
30.04.90	David Brown DREW 6 Mayfair
06.06.90	Martin Smith L RSC 2 Battersea
18.02.91	Colin Manners W PTS 6 Mayfair
14.03.91	Colin Manners W PTS 8 Middleton
30.06.91	John Kaighin W PTS 6 Southwark
21.10.91	Darron Griffiths L PTS 6 Mayfair
17.02.92	Darron Griffiths L RSC 5 Mayfair
18.05.92	William Krijnen L PTS 8 Valkenswaard, Holland
15.09.92	Quinn Paynter L PTS 6 Liverpool
06.05.93	W. O. Wilson L RSC 8 Bayswater *(Vacant Southern Area Middleweight Title)*

Career: 14 contests, won 5, drew 2, lost 7.

(Paul) John O'Johnson (Johnson)

Nottingham. *Born* Nottingham, 2
November, 1969
L. Welterweight. Ht. 5'5"
Manager W. Swift

29.08.91	Seth Jones W DIS 1 Oakengates

John O'Johnson   Les Clark

09.10.91	James Jiora W PTS 6 Manchester
24.10.91	Carl Hook L PTS 6 Dunstable
31.10.91	Darren Morris W PTS 6 Oakengates
26.11.91	Bernard Paul L PTS 6 Bethnal Green
22.01.92	Brian Coleman W PTS 6 Stoke
30.01.92	Chris Saunders W PTS 6 Southampton
20.02.92	Alan Peacock W PTS 6 Glasgow
09.03.92	Ricky Sackfield W PTS 6 Manchester
26.03.92	Davy Robb L PTS 6 Telford
03.06.92	Jason Barker W PTS 6 Newcastle under Lyme
09.09.92	Chris Saunders DREW 6 Stoke
05.10.92	Andreas Panayi L RTD 1 Liverpool
09.12.92	Jason Barker W PTS 6 Stoke
10.02.93	Dean Hollington L PTS 6 Lewisham
17.03.93	Jonathan Thaxton L PTS 6 Stoke

Career: 16 contests, won 9, drew 1, lost 3.

Chris Okoh

Camberwell. *Born* Carshalton, 18 April,
1969
Cruiserweight. Ht. 6'2"
Manager B. Hearn

16.03.93	Lee Prudden W PTS 6 Mayfair

Career: 1 contest, won 1.

Richard Okumu

Tottenham. *Born* Uganda, 18 December,
1970
L. Middleweight. Ht. 6'0"
Manager M. Barrett

04.02.91	Benji Joseph W PTS 6 Leicester
18.02.91	Colin Pitters L PTS 6 Birmingham
05.03.91	Kevin Sheeran W RSC 2 Millwall
24.10.91	Benji Good W CO 6 Bayswater
05.12.91	Andrew Flute DREW 8 Cannock
22.01.92	Darron Griffiths L PTS 8 Solihull
22.10.92	Robert Welin W RSC 2 Bethnal Green
25.11.92	Ian Chantler W RSC 2 Mayfair

Career: 8 contests, won 5, drew 1, lost 2.

(Mike) Chip O'Neill

Sunderland. *Born* Sunderland, 10
December, 1963

Featherweight. Ht. 5'6½"
Manager T. Conroy

28.06.82	Charlie Brown L PTS 6 Bradford
20.09.82	Danny Flynn L RSC 2 Glasgow
07.03.83	Charlie Brown L RSC 3 Glasgow
28.04.92	Robert Braddock W PTS 6 Houghton le Spring
10.09.92	Vince Wilson W RSC 1 Sunderland
21.09.92	Ian McGirr L PTS 6 Glasgow
05.10.92	Phil Lashley W PTS 6 Manchester
09.11.92	Robert Braddock L RSC 3 Bradford
19.01.93	Russell Rees L RSC 1 Cardiff
08.03.93	Chris Lyons W PTS 6 Leeds
29.04.93	Paul Wynn L PTS 6 Newcastle

Career: 11 contests, won 4, lost 7.

(John) Sean O'Phoenix (Phoenix)

Sheffield. *Born* Glossop, 16 September,
1963
L. Heavyweight. Ht. 6'1"
Manager B. Ingle

26.11.84	Alan Baptiste DREW 6 Sheffield
05.12.84	Tucker Watts W RSC 1 Stoke
05.02.85	Simon Harris L PTS 6 Battersea
11.03.85	Shamus Casey W PTS 6 Manchester
20.03.85	Shamus Casey W PTS 6 Stoke
15.04.85	Gary Tomlinson W PTS 6 Manchester
29.04.85	Tucker Watts W RSC 3 Nottingham
14.05.85	Gary Tomlinson DREW 6 Mansfield
03.06.85	David Scere W PTS 6 Manchester
14.10.85	Shaun West W RTD 2 Leicester
21.10.85	Alan Baptiste W PTS 8 Nottingham
06.12.85	Sammy Brennan L PTS 6 Liverpool
05.02.86	Sammy Storey L PTS 6 Sheffield
18.03.86	Mark Walker DREW 8 Hull
14.04.86	T. P. Jenkins L PTS 8 Mayfair
16.06.86	Mike Farghaly W RSC 6 Manchester
15.09.86	Dave Mowbray W DIS 3 Manchester
27.10.86	Blaine Logsdon L CO 3 Liverpool
26.11.86	Tommy Taylor L RSC 3 Wolverhampton
18.03.87	Harry Cowap L RSC 8 Queensway *(All-Ireland L. Heavyweight Title Challenge)*
07.03.89	Carl Thompson L RSC 4 Manchester
19.10.89	Tony Lawrence W PTS 6 Manchester
07.12.89	Simon McDougall W PTS 6 Manchester
06.02.90	Steve Foster L RSC 4 Oldham
09.04.90	Terry French DREW 8 Manchester
01.05.90	Ahmet Canbakis DREW 4 Oldham
24.09.90	Dave Owens W PTS 8 Manchester
26.11.90	Glenn Campbell L RSC 4 Bury *(Vacant Central Area S. Middleweight Title)*
18.03.91	Tony Lawrence W PTS 8 Manchester
03.04.91	Terry French W PTS 8 Manchester
29.10.92	Denzil Browne L RSC 4 Leeds
09.12.92	Trevor Small L PTS 6 Stoke
22.04.93	Bruce Scott L RSC 3 Mayfair

Career: 33 contests, won 15, drew 5, lost 13.

Gary Osborne

Walsall. *Born* Bloxwich, 24 August, 1963
Former Undefeated Midlands Area L.
Middleweight Champion. Former Midlands
Area Welterweight Champion. Ht. 5'10"
Manager R. Gray

08.05.89	Peter Reid W CO 5 Edgbaston
22.03.90	Peter Reid W CO 1 Wolverhampton

04.04.90 Marvin O'Brien W CO 2 Stafford
24.05.90 Julian Eavis W PTS 6 Dudley
18.09.90 Paul Hanlon W RTD 2 Wolverhampton
17.10.90 Chris Richards W PTS 8 Stoke
06.12.90 Darren Morris W PTS 8 Wolverhampton
10.04.91 Mickey Lerwill W PTS 10 Wolverhampton
(Vacant Midlands Area Welterweight Title)
10.09.91 Ernie Loveridge L RSC 1 Wolverhampton
(Midlands Area Welterweight Title Defence)
17.03.92 Shamus Casey W RSC 5 Wolverhampton
(Vacant Midlands Area L. Middleweight Title)
28.04.92 Gary Pemberton W CO 3 Wolverhampton
07.06.93 Bullit Andrews W RSC 1 Walsall
Career: 12 contests, won 11, lost 1.

Steve Osborne

Nottingham. *Born* Nottingham, 27 June, 1965
Cruiserweight. Ht. 5'9"
Manager W. Swift

28.05.87 Gary Railton L PTS 6 Jarrow
09.06.87 Ian Bulloch L PTS 6 Manchester
24.09.87 Bobby Frankham L PTS 6 Glasgow
05.10.87 Ray Thomas L RSC 8 Piccadilly
14.12.87 Branko Pavlovic L RSC 3 Bedford
16.01.89 Simon McDougall W PTS 6 Bradford
25.01.89 Simon McDougall W PTS 6 Stoke
02.02.89 Dave Furneaux W CO 4 Southwark
13.02.89 Carl Thompson L PTS 8 Manchester
06.03.89 Jimmy Cropper W PTS 6 Manchester
05.04.89 Jimmy Cropper L PTS 6 Halifax
16.05.89 Henry Brewer W PTS 6 Halifax
12.06.89 Carl Thompson L PTS 6 Manchester
16.11.89 Dave Lawrence W PTS 6 Ilkeston
19.12.89 Herbie Hide L RSC 6 Bethnal Green
05.02.90 Dave Lawrence W PTS 8 Piccadilly
20.02.90 Rob Albon L PTS 6 Brentwood
03.03.90 Darren Westover L RSC 6 Wembley
15.11.90 Michael Gale L PTS 6 Oldham
08.12.90 Neils H. Madsen L RSC 6 Aalborg, Denmark
16.04.91 Art Stacey DREW 6 Nottingham
09.05.91 Michael Gale L RSC 2 Leeds
11.11.91 Art Stacey L PTS 6 Bradford
21.11.91 Bruce Scott L PTS 6 Burton
29.11.91 Maurice Coore L PTS 6 Manchester
12.02.92 Phil Soundy L PTS 6 Wembley
12.11.92 Terry Dunstan L PTS 6 Bayswater
10.12.92 Ole Klemetsen L RSC 1 Bethnal Green
27.01.93 Darren McKenna L PTS 6 Stoke
22.02.93 Nicky Wadman L PTS 6 Eltham
26.04.93 Steve Lewsam W PTS 6 Cleethorpes
Career: 31 contests, won 8, drew 1, lost 22.

Clay O'Shea

Islington. *Born* London, 3 November, 1966
L. Middleweight. Ht. 6'0"
Manager Self

20.02.90 Carlton Myers W RSC 1 Brentford
14.03.90 Tony Grizzle W RSC 1 Kensington
04.10.90 Benji Good W CO 2 Bethnal Green
31.10.90 Remy Duverger W PTS 6 Wembley
04.04.91 Robert Peel W PTS 6 Watford
11.09.91 Shamus Casey W PTS 6 Hammersmith
26.09.91 Tony Wellington W CO 1 Dunstable

25.03.92 Andrew Furlong DREW 6 Kensington
13.05.92 Andrew Furlong DREW 6 Kensington
15.10.92 Steve Thomas W PTS 6 Lewisham
17.12.92 Mark Jay W CO 1 Wembley
28.01.93 Lee Crocker W RSC 1 Southwark
Career: 12 contests, won 10, drew 2.

Dave Owens

Castleford. *Born* Castleford, 11 December, 1954
L. Heavyweight. Former Undefeated Central Area Middleweight Champion. Ht. 6'1"
Manager Self

12.05.76 Steve Heavisides W RSC 2 Bradford
08.06.76 Joe Jackson W PTS 4 Bradford
10.09.76 Carl McCarthy W CO 2 Digbeth
21.09.76 Steve Fenton W RSC 3 Bethnal Green
27.09.76 Neville Estaban DREW 6 Piccadilly
30.11.76 Owen Robinson W PTS 6 Leeds
20.04.77 Billy Hill W RSC 2 Manchester
27.04.77 Jim Moore W PTS 8 Bradford
15.05.77 Howard Mills W RSC 8 Manchester
10.07.77 Pat Brogan W RSC 9 Birmingham
(Vacant Central Area Middleweight Title)
13.03.78 Paul Shutt W RSC 2 Nottingham
08.05.78 Howard Mills L RTD 4 Nottingham
04.09.78 Glen McEwan L CO 1 Wakefield
07.12.78 Torben Anderson L PTS 6 Copenhagen, Denmark
12.03.79 Romal Ambrose L PTS 8 Manchester
20.09.79 Dave Davies W CO 3 Liverpool
17.10.79 Jimmy Pickard W RSC 4 Piccadilly
(Central Area Middleweight Title Defence)
29.04.80 Eddie Smith L CO 1 Stockport
12.08.80 Doug James L PTS 8 Gowerton
13.10.80 Earl Edwards L RSC 3 Windsor
03.09.85 Barry Ahmed DREW 6 Gateshead
20.09.85 Simon Harris W PTS 6 Longford
25.10.85 Nye Williams W PTS 8 Fulham
20.01.86 Tony Wilson L RSC 2 Mayfair
01.12.86 Pedro van Raamsdonk L CO 1 Arnhem, Holland
02.03.87 Peter Brown L PTS 8 Huddersfield
05.05.87 Shamus Casey W PTS 6 Leeds
18.11.87 John Foreman W RSC 5 Solihull
05.12.87 Darryl Ritchie L DIS 7 Doncaster
07.02.88 Brian Schumacher L CO 1 Stafford
28.11.88 John Foreman L CO 1 Edgbaston
31.01.89 Adam Cook DREW 6 Reading
13.03.89 James Wray L PTS 6 Glasgow
01.05.89 Jose Seys L RSC 6 Waregem, Belgium
20.11.89 Steve Williams DREW 6 Glasgow
19.12.89 Nicky Piper L CO 1 Gorleston
06.04.90 Everton Blake L RSC 6 Stevenage
14.05.90 Joe Frater W PTS 6 Cleethorpes
24.09.90 Sean O'Phoenix L PTS 8 Manchester
08.10.90 Darren McKenna W PTS 6 Leicester
29.10.90 Fidel Castro L PTS 6 Birmingham
18.11.90 Sean Heron L PTS 8 Birmingham
06.12.90 Gil Lewis L CO 2 Wolverhampton
17.02.91 Anton Josipovic L PTS 8 Prijedor, Yugoslavia
24.03.91 Christophe Girard L RSC 7 Vichy, France
23.04.91 Joe Frater W PTS 6 Evesham
27.05.91 Eddie Smulders L RSC 1 Rotterdam, Holland
14.11.91 Ian Henry L PTS 8 Gateshead
03.03.92 Terry French W CO 1 Houghton le Spring

26.03.92 Tony Booth L PTS 6 Hull
14.04.92 Martin Smith L PTS 6 Mansfield
26.10.92 Joe Frater W PTS 6 Cleethorpes
04.12.92 Bernard Bonzon L RSC 5 Geneva, Switzerland
06.03.93 Stephen Wilson L RSC 2 Glasgow
15.05.93 Willie Quinn L PTS 6 Glasgow
Career: 55 contests, won 21, drew 4, lost 30.

Jimmy Owens

Liverpool. *Born* Liverpool, 15 February, 1966
S. Featherweight. Ht. 5'6½"
Manager Self

29.01.90 Greg Egbuniwe W PTS 6 Hull
06.03.90 Steve Armstrong W PTS 4 Stoke
04.05.90 Martin Evans W RSC 2 Liverpool
21.05.90 Kruga Hydes W PTS 6 Hanley
07.09.90 Nigel Senior W PTS 6 Liverpool
12.11.90 Martin Evans W RSC 3 Liverpool
01.05.91 Peter Judson W PTS 6 Liverpool
16.05.91 Des Gargano W RSC 2 Liverpool
24.06.91 Miguel Matthews W PTS 6 Liverpool
09.09.91 Russell Davison L PTS 10 Liverpool
(Central Area Featherweight Title Challenge)
14.05.92 Graham O'Malley W PTS 6 Liverpool
04.05.93 Floyd Churchill L CO 1 Liverpool
(Vacant Central Area S. Featherweight Title)
Career: 12 contests, won 10, lost 2.

John Oxenham

Doncaster. *Born* Doncaster, 11 June, 1968
L. Heavyweight. Ht. 6'0½"
Manager H. Hayes

04.09.90 Benji Good W RSC 6 Southend
13.05.91 Shaun McCrory L PTS 6 Marton
09.10.91 Dennis Afflick W DIS 4 Marton
24.10.91 Morris Thomas W RSC 6 Glasgow
27.11.91 Ian Henry L PTS 6 Marton
02.03.92 Marvin O'Brien W PTS 6 Marton
27.04.92 Joe McCluskey L PTS 4 Glasgow
18.05.92 Andy Manning W PTS 6 Marton
03.09.92 Joey Peters L PTS 6 Dunstable
10.11.92 Gary Delaney L CO 5 Dagenham
14.06.93 Bruce Scott L RSC 1 Bayswater
Career: 11 contests, won 5, lost 6.

Mark Pain (Leslie)

Wolverhampton. *Born* Wolverhampton, 7 April, 1972
L. Heavyweight. Ht. 5'9½"
Manager B. Crooks

03.10.91 Jason McNeill W PTS 6 Burton
12.02.92 Vic Wright W RSC 1 Watford
03.06.92 Kevin Morton L PTS 6 Newcastle under Lyme
09.09.92 Glyn Rhodes L PTS 6 Stoke
03.12.92 Bruce Scott L RSC 5 Lewisham
Career: 5 contests, won 2, lost 3.

Charlie Paine (Bird)

Liverpool. *Born* Liverpool, 27 August, 1970
L. Welterweight. Ht. 5'7"
Manager B. Snagg

09.06.93 Delwyn Panayiotiou W PTS 6 Liverpool
Career: 1 contest, won 1.

Joey Paladino

St Helens. *Born* Whiston, 29 August, 1965
Heavyweight. Ht. 6'6"
Manager R. Gray

06.05.93　Vance Idiens L PTS 8 Walsall
23.06.93　Julius Francis L CO 4 Edmonton
Career: 2 contests, lost 2.

Andreas Panayi

St Helens. *Born* Cyprus, 14 July, 1969
Welterweight. Ht. 5'6"
Manager Self

21.11.90　Trevor Ambrose L RSC 5 Solihull
04.02.91　Cliff Churchward W PTS 6 Leicester
12.02.91　Eddie King W CO 2 Wolverhampton
27.02.91　Trevor Meikle L PTS 6 Wolverhampton
15.04.91　Mick Mulcahy W RSC 2 Leicester
24.04.91　Darren Morris DREW 6 Stoke
11.09.91　Robert Riley W PTS 6 Stoke
30.09.91　Steve Hardman W RSC 5 Liverpool
23.10.91　Darren Morris W PTS 6 Stoke
25.11.91　Marvin P. Gray W PTS 8 Liverpool
11.12.91　Mark Kelly DREW 8 Stoke
11.03.92　Dean Bramhald L PTS 8 Stoke
14.05.92　Dave Maj W CO 6 Liverpool
03.09.92　Rick North DREW 6 Liverpool
05.10.92　John O'Johnson W RTD 1 Liverpool
23.10.92　Trevor Meikle W PTS 6 Liverpool
20.11.92　Rick North W PTS 6 Liverpool
15.12.92　Mark Kelly W PTS 6 Liverpool
27.01.93　Ross Hale W RSC 3 Cardiff
27.02.93　Darren McInulty W PTS 6 Ellesmere Port
04.05.93　Jimmy Thornton W CO 2 Liverpool
Career: 21 contests, won 15, drew 3, lost 3.

Delwyn Panayiotiou

Llanelli. *Born* Morriston, 26 September, 1967
Welterweight. Ht. 5'8"
Manager M. Copp

Delwyn Panayiotiou　　　　Les Clark

08.09.92　Sean Baker L RSC 2 Southend
09.06.93　Charlie Paine L PTS 6 Liverpool
24.06.93　Adrian Chase L CO 1 Watford
Career: 3 contests, lost 3.

Wayne Panayiotiou　　　　Chris Bevan

Wayne Panayiotiou

Llanelli. *Born* Llanelli, 19 October, 1965
L. Middleweight. Ht. 5'11"
Manager Self

16.10.90　Russell Washer L RSC 2 Evesham
24.01.91　Russell Washer L RSC 4 Gorseinon
09.12.91　Stuart Dunn L CO 4 Brierley Hill
08.09.92　Raziq Ali L PTS 6 Doncaster
15.09.92　Carl Wright L RSC 2 Liverpool
01.12.92　Sean Baker L RSC 3 Bristol
Career: 6 contests, lost 6.

Neil Parry

Middlesbrough. *Born* Middlesbrough, 21 June, 1969
Bantamweight. Ht. 5'5"
Manager Self

12.06.89　Des Gargano L PTS 6 Manchester
21.12.89　Kevin Jenkins L PTS 6 Kings Heath
31.01.90　Francis Ampofo L PTS 6 Bethnal Green
12.03.90　Paul Dever W PTS 6 Hull
19.03.90　James Drummond L RSC 4 Glasgow
27.11.90　Stevie Woods W PTS 6 Glasgow
04.12.90　Conn McMullen L RSC 2 Southend
21.01.91　Stevie Woods L PTS 8 Glasgow
06.02.91　Paul Dever W PTS 6 Liverpool
05.03.91　Tony Smith DREW 6 Leicester
24.04.91　Paul Dever DREW 6 Stoke
17.05.91　Gary White L PTS 6 Bury
03.06.91　Stevie Woods W RSC 2 Glasgow
20.06.91　Tony Smith W PTS 6 Liverpool
12.09.91　Mark Tierney L PTS 6 Wandsworth
21.10.91　Neil Johnston L PTS 8 Glasgow
27.01.92　Drew Docherty L RSC 4 Glasgow
28.02.92　Stevie Woods W PTS 6 Irvine
11.05.92　Tim Yeates L PTS 6 Piccadilly

21.09.92　Paul Weir L RSC 4 Glasgow
27.11.92　Eyup Can L PTS 6 Randers, Denmark
25.01.93　Ady Benton L RSC 6 Bradford
29.03.93　Louis Veitch L PTS 6 Glasgow
01.06.93　Des Gargano L PTS 6 Manchester
28.06.93　Marcus Duncan W RSC 2 Morecambe
Career: 25 contests, won 7, drew 2, lost 16.

Elvis Parsley

Bloxwich. *Born* Walsall, 6 December, 1962
Lightweight. Ht. 5'7½"
Manager Self

04.06.90　Phil Lashley W RSC 3 Birmingham
20.06.90　Mark Bates L CO 1 Basildon
27.09.90　Andrew Robinson W RTD 3 Birmingham
10.12.90　Karl Taylor W PTS 6 Birmingham
18.02.91　Peter Campbell W RSC 3 Derby
01.05.91　Neil Leitch W CO 2 Solihull
20.05.91　Neil Smith L RSC 5 Leicester
02.10.91　Muhammad Shaffique W CO 1 Solihull
29.04.92　Kelton McKenzie L RSC 5 Solihull
(Vacant Midlands Area Featherweight Title)
28.04.93　Dean Amory L PTS 6 Solihull
Career: 10 contests, won 6, lost 4.

Patrick Parton

Telford. *Born* Shifnal, 5 September, 1965
Lightweight. Ht. 5'11"
Manager D. Nelson

23.02.93　T. J. Smith L PTS 6 Kettering
24.06.93　Shaun Shinkwin DREW 6 Watford
Career: 2 contests, drew 1, lost 1.

Neil Patterson

Darlington. *Born* Sedgefield, 21 April, 1962
L. Middleweight. Ht. 5'11¾"
Manager G. Robinson

22.03.84　Gary Champion L PTS 6 Maidenhead
30.04.84　Alistair Laurie L PTS 6 Glasgow
11.10.84　Chris McReedy W PTS 6 Barnsley
04.12.84　John Faulkner W PTS 6 Southend
02.02.85　Andy O'Rawe W PTS 6 Darlington
23.02.85　Peppy Muire L PTS 6 Belfast
13.04.85　Nicky Day W PTS 6 Darlington
03.10.85　Young Tony Carroll W PTS 6 Liverpool
21.11.85　Ken Foreman L PTS 10 Hartlepool
(Vacant Northern Area Welterweight Title)
24.02.86　Billy Buchanan L PTS 6 Glasgow
20.03.86　Karl Ince L PTS 6 Blackpool
05.02.87　Shamus Casey W PTS 6 Newcastle
26.02.87　Robert Armstrong L CO 4 Hartlepool
30.04.87　John Mullen W PTS 6 Washington
22.05.87　Mike McKenzie W RSC 5 Peterlee
23.09.87　Mark Holden W RSC 4 Stoke
08.10.87　John Andrews W RSC 4 Bethnal Green
24.11.87　Ossie Maddix L RSC 6 Marton
26.01.88　Ken Foreman L RSC 6 Hartlepool
(Vacant Northern Area L. Middleweight Title)
27.01.89　Spencer Alton L CO 1 Durham
01.12.92　Mark Jay L PTS 6 Hartlepool
Career: 21 contests, won 10, lost 11.

Steve Patton

Wembley. *Born* Ballyshannon, 3 August, 1970

Lightweight. Ht. 6'0"

Manager H. Holland

12.02.92 Jas Dip Singh W RSC 1 Watford
07.12.92 Marco Fattore L RSC 6 Mayfair
31.03.93 Chris Francis L CO 4 Bethnal Green
Career: 3 contest, won 1, lost 2.

Bernard Paul

Tottenham. *Born* Mauritius, 22 October, 1965

L. Welterweight. Ht. 5'7½"

Manager B. Hearn

01.05.91 Trevor Royal W CO 1 Bethnal Green
04.06.91 Dave Jenkins W RSC 1 Bethnal Green
24.09.91 Pat Delargy W RSC 5 Basildon
26.10.91 Gordon Webster W RSC 4 Brentwood
26.11.91 John O'Johnson W PTS 6 Bethnal Green

Quinn Paynter   Harry Goodwin

19.02.92 Rick North W PTS 6 Muswell Hill
17.03.92 Mick Mulcahy W PTS 6 Mayfair
16.06.92 Brendan Ryan W CO 6 Dagenham
13.10.92 Dean Bramhald DREW 6 Mayfair
10.11.92 Ray Newby DREW 6 Dagenham
12.12.92 Michael Driscoll L RSC 2 Muswell Hill
20.04.93 Ray Newby DREW 6 Brentwood
Career: 12 contests, won 8, drew 3, lost 1.

Quinn Paynter

Manchester. *Born* Bermuda, 19 August, 1965

Middleweight. Ht. 5'9"

Manager P. Martin

12.10.89 Willie Beattie L PTS 8 Glasgow
19.10.89 Paul Hendrick W RSC 5 Manchester
11.01.90 Tommy McCallum W RSC 2 Dewsbury
15.01.90 Benji Good W PTS 6 Mayfair
23.02.90 Mike Paul W RTD 4 Irvine
08.03.90 Graeme Watson W PTS 6 Glasgow
26.03.90 George Ferrie W RSC 6 Glasgow
04.05.90 Fran Harding L PTS 6 Liverpool
17.08.90 Hector Rosario L PTS 8 Hamilton, Bermuda
10.12.90 Gordon Blair L PTS 6 Glasgow
21.01.91 W. O. Wilson W PTS 8 Crystal Palace
02.03.91 Marvin O'Brien DREW 6 Irvine
16.05.91 Ali Forbes DREW 6 Battersea
14.11.91 Terry French W CO 6 Gateshead
18.01.92 Val Golding W RSC 7 Kensington
05.04.92 Marvin O'Brien W PTS 6 Bradford
18.07.92 Chris Richards W RSC 6 Manchester
15.09.92 John Ogiste W PTS 6 Liverpool
28.09.92 Stinger Mason W CO 1 Manchester
Career: 19 contests, won 13, drew 2, lost 4.

Glen Payton (Kennedy)

Telford. *Born* Gateshead, 15 May, 1964

Middleweight. Ht. 5'11"

Manager Self

31.10.91 Wilf McGee W RSC 6 Oakengates
05.12.91 John Baxter W CO 3 Oakengates
20.02.92 Paul Hanlon W PTS 6 Oakengates
26.03.92 Chris Richards L PTS 6 Telford
20.01.93 Andrew Flute L RSC 4 Wolverhampton
Career: 5 contests, won 3, lost 2.

Andy Peach

Bloxwich. *Born* Bloxwich, 1 August, 1971

Welterweight. Ht. 5'8"

Manager W. Tyler

27.10.92 Stuart Dunn L RSC 3 Leicester
09.12.92 Jason Fores W PTS 6 Stoke
09.02.93 Ray Golding L PTS 6 Wolverhampton
11.03.93 Richard O'Brien L PTS 6 Walsall
06.05.93 Billy McDougall L PTS 6 Walsall
Career: 5 contests, won 1, lost 4.

Alan Peacock

Cumbernauld. *Born* Glasgow, 17 February, 1969

L. Welterweight. Ht. 5'7"

Manager T. Gilmour

23.02.90 Gary Quigley W PTS 6 Irvine
08.03.90 Gary Quigley W PTS 6 Glasgow
29.05.90 John Ritchie W PTS 6 Glasgow
11.06.90 Chris Mulcahy W RSC 3 Manchester
17.09.90 John Ritchie W PTS 6 Glasgow
09.10.90 Dave Anderson L RSC 3 Glasgow
27.11.90 Stuart Rimmer W RSC 4 Glasgow
11.02.91 Oliver Harrison L RSC 6 Glasgow
18.03.91 Darren Mount W PTS 8 Glasgow
27.03.91 Giovanni Parisi L PTS 6 Mestre, Italy
06.04.91 Alan Hall L PTS 6 Darlington
25.05.91 Giorgio Campanella L CO 1 Trezzano, Italy
23.09.91 Trevor Meikle L PTS 6 Glasgow
27.11.91 Dave Whittle L PTS 6 Marton
28.01.92 Trevor Meikle W PTS 8 Piccadilly
20.02.92 John O'Johnson L PTS 6 Glasgow
04.03.92 Rob Stewart DREW 8 Glasgow
12.03.92 Dave Whittle DREW 8 Glasgow
30.03.92 Peter Bradley L PTS 8 Glasgow
07.10.92 John Smith DREW 6 Glasgow
18.11.92 Dave Lovell W PTS 6 Solihull
22.02.93 Dave Lovell W PTS 8 Glasgow
23.03.93 Dean Bramhald L PTS 6 Wolverhampton
Career: 23 contests, won 10, drew 3, lost 10.

Mark Pearce

Cardiff. *Born* Cardiff, 29 June, 1963
L. Welterweight. Ht. 5'7"
Manager Self

16.05.83	Young Yousuf W PTS 6 Birmingham
23.05.83	Dave Pratt W PTS 6 Mayfair
22.09.83	Dave Pratt DREW 6 Cardiff
01.12.83	Mark Reefer L PTS 6 Basildon
10.12.83	Mike Wilkes W PTS 6 Swansea
30.01.84	Dave Pratt L PTS 8 Birmingham
31.03.84	Steve Topliss L PTS 8 Derby
15.06.84	Joey Joynson L PTS 8 Liverpool
10.10.84	Alec Irvine DREW 8 Evesham
06.11.84	Pat Doherty L RSC 4 Kensington
18.01.85	Steve Griffith L PTS 8 Bethnal Green
12.02.85	Kenny Walsh W PTS 8 Wolverhampton
06.03.85	Alex Dickson L PTS 6 Kensington
21.03.85	Muhammad Lovelock L PTS 8 Manchester
21.10.85	Paul Downie L PTS 8 Glasgow
21.11.85	Andy Williams L PTS 8 Blaenavon
05.03.86	Ray Newby DREW 6 Stoke
28.04.86	Andy Williams L PTS 10 Cardiff
	(Vacant Welsh Lightweight Title)
29.10.86	Russell Jones L PTS 10 Ebbw Vale
	(Vacant Welsh S. Featherweight Title)
24.11.86	Tony Borg W PTS 8 Cardiff
18.03.87	Marvin P. Gray L PTS 8 Solihull
07.04.87	Ray Newby W PTS 8 West Bromwich
12.05.87	Najib Daho L RSC 2 Alfreton
28.10.87	Mike Russell DREW 6 Swansea
02.12.87	Rudy Valentino L PTS 6 Piccadilly
18.01.88	Dave Griffiths L PTS 10 Cardiff
	(Vacant Welsh L. Welterweight Title)
05.05.88	Tony Gibbs W RSC 4 Bethnal Green
25.01.89	Nigel Wenton L PTS 6 Belfast
12.05.89	Stefano Cassi L RTD 4 Lodi, Italy
19.08.89	Dave Griffiths L PTS 10 Cardiff
	(Welsh L. Welterweight Title Challenge)
31.10.89	Eamonn Loughran L PTS 6 Belfast
05.03.91	Jim Lawlor L PTS 6 Cardiff
29.10.91	Mick Meloscia W RTD 2 Cardiff
20.02.93	Mark Tibbs L PTS 6 Earls Court

Career: 34 contests, won 8, drew 4, lost 22.

Robert Peel

Llandovery. *Born* Birmingham, 11 January, 1969
L. Middleweight. Ht. 5'10"
Manager D. Davies

24.01.91	John Kaighin W PTS 6 Gorseinon
12.02.91	John Kaighin L PTS 6 Cardiff
13.03.91	Andrew Flute L PTS 6 Stoke
04.04.91	Clay O'Shea L PTS 6 Watford
12.04.91	Adrian Wright L RSC 6 Willenhall
15.05.91	John Kaighin L PTS 6 Swansea
29.10.91	Jason Matthews L RSC 6 Cardiff
03.02.92	Warren Stowe L PTS 6 Manchester
02.03.92	Steve Thomas DREW 6 Merthyr
11.05.92	Steve Thomas L PTS 6 Llanelli
04.06.92	Darren Pilling L PTS 6 Burnley
28.10.92	Barry Thorogood L PTS 6 Cardiff
24.03.93	Russell Washer W PTS 6 Cardiff
27.05.93	Dean Cooper L PTS 6 Bristol

Career: 14 contests, won 2, drew 1, lost 11.

Gary Pemberton

Cardiff. *Born* Cardiff, 15 May, 1960

L. Middleweight. Ht. 5'10"
Manager Self

10.09.86	Johnny Nanton W RSC 4 Muswell Hill
20.10.86	Alex Mullen L RSC 4 Glasgow
24.11.86	Shaun Cummins L RSC 6 Cardiff
28.01.87	Tommy Shiels L CO 1 Croydon
06.04.87	Paul McCarthy W RSC 4 Southampton
23.06.87	Shaun West L RSC 2 Swansea
28.09.87	Simon Paul W RSC 1 Dulwich
06.10.87	Danny Shinkwin W RSC 2 Southend
28.10.87	Mark Howell W PTS 6 Swansea
19.11.87	Steve Huxtable W RSC 4 Weston super Mare
01.03.88	Alex Romeo L RSC 3 Southend
14.04.88	Tony Britton DREW 8 Piccadilly
07.06.88	Winston Wray L PTS 6 Southend
04.10.88	Tony Cloak W RSC 1 Southend
25.10.88	Kevin Hayde L CO 4 Pontardawe
14.12.88	Crisanto Espana L RTD 1 Kirkby
01.03.89	Shaun Cummins L CO 2 Cardiff
19.08.89	Alan Richards W PTS 6 Cardiff
19.09.89	Ray Close L PTS 6 Belfast
25.09.89	Steve Craggs W CO 1 Leicester
11.10.89	Tony Collins L CO 1 Millwall
06.12.89	Jimmy McDonagh L RSC 2 Wembley
16.01.90	Jimmy Farrell L RSC 2 Cardiff
15.06.90	Chris Richards L RTD 1 Telford
13.09.90	B. K. Bennett W RSC 4 Watford
04.10.90	Brian Robinson L PTS 6 Bethnal Green
29.10.90	Tony Kosova W RSC 1 Nottingham
19.11.90	Carlo Colarusso L RSC 3 Cardiff
24.01.91	Carlo Colarusso L RSC 8 Gorseinon
	(Vacant Welsh L Middleweight Title)
10.04.91	Colin Pitters L RSC 3 Newport
01.10.91	Adrian Strachan L RSC 2 Sheffield
12.02.92	Andrew Furlong L PTS 6 Wembley
28.04.92	Gary Osborne L CO 3 Wolverhampton
22.10.92	Jamie Robinson L RSC 3 Bethnal Green
11.05.93	Vince Rose L PTS 6 Norwich
25.06.93	Miodrag Perunovic L RSC 4 Belgrade, Yugoslavia

Career: 36 contests, won 11, drew 1, lost 24.

Joey Peters

Southampton. *Born* Southampton, 10 December, 1971
L. Heavyweight. Ht. 5'9½"
Manager T. Lawless

25.04.91	Dennis Afflick W PTS 6 Basildon
23.05.91	Tony Behan W PTS 6 Southampton
04.07.91	Randy B. Powell W PTS 6 Alfreton
17.10.91	Lee Prudden W PTS 6 Southwark
25.03.92	Terry Duffus W RSC 1 Kensington
27.04.92	Paul Hanlon W CO 2 Mayfair
03.09.92	John Oxenham W PTS 6 Dunstable
28.10.92	John Kaighin DREW 6 Kensington
03.12.92	Bobby Mack W PTS 6 Lewisham

Career: 9 contests, won 8, drew 1.

Mike Phillips

Warrington. *Born* Wells, 15 July,1964
Middleweight. Ht. 5'9¼"
Manager R. Jones

07.09.90	Marvin O'Brien W RSC 1 Liverpool
18.09.90	Paul Walters DREW 6 Stoke
08.10.90	Stephen Welford W RSC 2 Bradford
22.10.90	Tommy Warde W RSC 5 Cleethorpes
29.10.90	Matt Mowatt W PTS 6 Birmingham
12.11.90	Marvin O'Brien L PTS 6 Liverpool

Mike Phillips   Les Clark

27.11.90	Darren Parker W CO 5 Stoke
05.12.90	Paul Walters L PTS 6 Stafford
12.12.90	Paul Walters W PTS 6 Stoke
23.01.91	Matt Mowatt W RSC 6 Stoke
04.02.91	Dean Cooper L PTS 6 Leicester
22.02.91	Carl Harney W RSC 5 Manchester
13.03.91	Stinger Mason DREW 6 Stoke
30.04.91	Rocky McGran W RSC 2 Stockport
17.05.91	Rob Pitters W PTS 8 Bury
01.10.91	Martin Smith L PTS 6 Sheffield
22.10.91	Rob Pitters L RSC 4 Hartlepool
25.11.91	Dave Johnson W PTS 6 Liverpool
10.03.92	Steve Foster L RSC 4 Bury
14.07.92	Wayne Ellis L RSC 7 Mayfair
	(Welsh Middleweight Title Challenge)
24.09.92	Warren Stowe L RSC 1 Stockport
25.01.93	Willie Quinn L PTS 6 Glasgow
06.02.93	Steve Thomas DREW 6 Cardiff
17.03.93	Glyn Rhodes L RSC 2 Stoke
17.04.93	Dave Johnson L PTS 6 Washington

Career: 25 contests, won 11, drew 3, lost 11.

Dave Pierre

Peterborough. *Born* Peterborough, 10 September, 1964
Southern Area L. Welterweight Champion. Ht. 5'7½"
Manager Self

28.11.86	Steve Tempro W RSC 5 Peterborough
19.02.87	Tony Whitehouse W RSC 1 Peterborough
01.05.87	Peter Bowen W RSC 2 Peterborough
06.06.88	Michael Oliver L PTS 6 Northampton
16.06.88	Michael Driscoll W PTS 6 Croydon
02.10.88	George Jones W DIS 5 Peterborough
19.10.88	Crisanto Espana L PTS 6 Belfast
28.06.89	Pat Delargy W RTD 2 Kenilworth
26.09.89	Jim Talbot L PTS 6 Oldham
05.10.89	Philip Nurse L PTS 6 Middleton
30.11.89	John Smith W PTS 6 Mayfair
08.12.89	Mark Ramsey W RSC 2 Doncaster
05.02.90	Dave Griffiths W RSC 6 Piccadilly
08.03.90	John Smith W PTS 6 Peterborough
29.05.90	Alex Dickson L PTS 8 Glasgow

14.12.90	Seamus O'Sullivan W PTS 10 Peterborough
	(Vacant Southern Area L. Welterweight Title)
19.04.91	Oliver Harrison W PTS 8 Peterborough
06.02.92	Marvin P. Gray W RSC 7 Peterborough
30.04.92	Carlos Chase W RSC 7 Watford
	(Southern Area L. Welterweight Title Defence)
17.09.92	Alan Hall L PTS 10 Watford
	(Elim. British L. Welterweight Title)
09.11.92	Valery Kayumba L CO 9 Differdange, France
	(European L. Welterweight Title Challenge)
04.03.93	Mark Ramsey W PTS 8 Peterborough
29.04.93	Tusikoleta Nkalankete L CO 4 Levallois Perret, France

Career: 23 contests, won 15, lost 8.

(Warren) John Pierre

Newcastle. *Born* Newcastle, 22 April, 1966
Cruiserweight. Ht. 6'0"
Manager G. McCrory

10.10.91	Gary Charlton W PTS 6 Gateshead
20.01.92	Art Stacey L PTS 6 Bradford
21.09.92	Albert Call L PTS 6 Cleethorpes

Career: 3 contests, won 1, lost 2.

Darren Pilling

Burnley. *Born* Burnley, 18 January, 1967
L. Middleweight. Ht. 5'8½"
Manager J. Doughty

03.09.88	Malcolm Davies W RSC 5 Bristol
06.10.88	Paul Hendrick L PTS 6 Manchester
26.10.88	Mark Holden L PTS 6 Sheffield
14.11.88	Paul Burton L RSC 2 Manchester
10.10.89	Terry French W PTS 6 Sunderland
16.11.89	Carl Watson W PTS 6 Ilkeston
30.01.90	Spencer Alton W PTS 6 Manchester
05.03.90	Alan Richards W PTS 8 Northampton
22.03.90	Paul Jones L RTD 7 Gateshead
04.06.92	Robert Peel W PTS 6 Burnley
24.09.92	Geoff Calder W RSC 5 Stockport
12.11.92	Robert Riley L PTS 6 Burnley

Career: 12 contests, won 7, lost 5.

Johnny Pinnock

High Wycombe. *Born* Hornsey, 21 August, 1968
L. Middleweight. Ht. 5'10½"
Manager D. Gunn

04.04.91	Lee Crocker L RSC 5 Watford
01.06.91	Darren Murphy L PTS 6 Bethnal Green
29.10.92	Harry Dhami L PTS 6 Hayes
29.04.93	Danny Shinkwin W RSC 3 Hayes

Career: 4 contests, won 1, lost 3.

Nicky Piper

Cardiff. *Born* Cardiff, 5 May, 1966
WBA Penta-Continental S. Middleweight
Champion. Ht. 6'3"
Manager F. Warren

06.09.89	Kevin Roper W CO 2 Aberavon
17.10.89	Gus Mendes W RSC 3 Cardiff
19.12.89	Dave Owens W CO 1 Gorleston
17.04.90	Darren McKenna W RTD 4 Millwall
22.05.90	Maurice Coore DREW 6 St Albans
23.10.90	Paul McCarthy W RSC 3 Leicester

12.11.90	John Ellis W CO 1 Norwich
05.03.91	Johnny Held W RSC 3 Millwall
08.05.91	Serge Bolivard W RSC 1 Millwall
22.05.91	Martin Lopez W CO 1 Millwall
03.07.91	Simon Harris W RSC 1 Reading
04.09.91	Carl Thompson L RSC 3 Bethnal Green
29.10.91	Franki Moro W RSC 4 Kensington
20.11.91	Carlos Christie W CO 6 Cardiff
22.01.92	Frank Eubanks W PTS 10 Cardiff
	(Elim. British S. Middleweight Title)
11.03.92	Ron Amundsen W PTS 10 Cardiff
16.05.92	Larry Prather W PTS 8 Muswell Hill
25.07.92	Johnny Melfah W RSC 5 Manchester
	(Elim. British S. Middleweight Title)
12.12.92	Nigel Benn L RSC 11 Muswell Hill
	(WBC S. Middleweight Title Challenge)
13.02.93	Miguel Maldonado W PTS 12 Manchester
	(Vacant WBA Penta-Continental S. Middleweight Title)
10.04.93	Chris Sande W RSC 9 Swansea
	(WBA Penta-Continental S. Middleweight Title Defence)

Career: 21 contests, won 18, drew 1, lost 2.

Rob Pitters

Gateshead. *Born* Birmingham, 28 May, 1960
L. Middleweight. Ht. 6'1"
Manager Self

26.09.90	Neil Porter DREW 6 Manchester
08.10.90	Colin Sinnott W PTS 6 Bradford
15.10.90	Mickey Costello W RSC 4 Kettering
26.11.90	Mick Duncan DREW 6 Bury
13.12.90	Karl Ince W RSC 5 Hartlepool
21.02.91	Martin Rosamond W RSC 2 Walsall
28.02.91	Crain Fisher W RSC 6 Bury
15.04.91	Gordon Blair W PTS 6 Glasgow
10.05.91	Mick Duncan W RSC 3 Gateshead
17.05.91	Mike Phillips L PTS 8 Bury
22.10.91	Mike Phillips W PTS 4 Hartlepool
11.03.92	Julian Eavis W PTS 6 Solihull
04.06.92	Warren Stowe L PTS 8 Burnley
09.03.93	Mark Cichocki L RSC 10 Hartlepool
	(Vacant Northern Area L. Middleweight Title)

Johnny Pinnock   Les Clark

18.06.93	Damien Denny L RSC 3 Belfast

Career: 15 contests, won 9, drew 2, lost 4.

Steve Pollard

Hull. *Born* Hull, 18 December, 1957
Lightweight. Former Central Area
Featherweight Champion. Ht. 5'7"
Manager Self

28.04.80	Bryn Jones W PTS 6 Piccadilly
27.05.80	Pat Mallon W PTS 6 Glasgow
02.06.80	Andy Thomas W PTS 6 Piccadilly
02.10.80	Eddie Glass W PTS 6 Hull
03.11.80	Rocky Bantleman W CO 2 Piccadilly
01.12.80	Chris McCallum W PTS 6 Hull
17.02.81	Billy Laidman W PTS 6 Leeds
02.03.81	Bryn Jones W RSC 5 Glasgow
30.03.81	John Sharkey L RSC 6 Glasgow
27.04.81	Ian McLeod L PTS 8 Piccadilly
01.06.81	Gary Lucas L PTS 8 Piccadilly
11.06.81	John Sharkey W PTS 8 Hull
08.03.82	Brian Hyslop DREW 8 Hamilton
22.04.82	Rocky Bantleman W RSC 8 Piccadilly
10.05.82	Lee Graham DREW 8 Piccadilly
26.05.82	Alan Tombs DREW 8 Piccadilly
23.09.82	Pat Doherty L PTS 8 Merton
26.10.82	Lee Halford L PTS 8 Hull
25.11.82	Kevin Howard L PTS 6 Sunderland
10.02.83	Keith Foreman L PTS 8 Sunderland
29.03.83	Steve Farnsworth W RSC 2 Hull
	(Central Area Featherweight Title Challenge)
18.06.83	Andre Blanco W PTS 8 Izegem, Belgium
04.10.83	Jim McDonnell L RSC 5 Bethnal Green
22.11.83	Joey Joynson L PTS 8 Wembley
22.01.84	Jean-Marc Renard L PTS 8 Izegem, Belgium
13.11.84	Jim McDonnell L RSC 6 Bethnal Green
17.12.84	John Doherty L PTS 10 Bradford
	(Central Area Featherweight Title Defence)
12.03.85	Mike Whalley L RSC 8 Manchester
20.01.86	Alex Dickson L RSC 7 Glasgow
10.03.86	Dave Savage L PTS 8 Glasgow
26.03.86	Peter Harris L RSC 3 Swansea
13.11.86	Dean Marsden L CO 7 Huddersfield
07.04.87	Darren Connellan W PTS 8 Batley
15.04.87	Paul Gadney L PTS 8 Lewisham
30.04.87	Gary Nickels L RSC 1 Wandsworth
22.09.87	Kevin Taylor L PTS 8 Oldham
18.11.87	Gary de Roux DREW 8 Peterborough
11.12.87	Gary Maxwell L PTS 8 Coalville
28.01.88	John Bennie L PTS 6 Bethnal Green
24.02.88	Craig Windsor L PTS 8 Glasgow
09.03.88	Peter Bradley L PTS 8 Bethnal Green
30.03.88	Scott Durham W PTS 8 Bethnal Green
25.04.88	Colin Lynch W PTS 8 Birmingham
18.05.88	John Bennie W PTS 8 Lewisham
30.08.88	Mike Chapman W PTS 8 Kensington
15.11.88	Tony Foster L RSC 3 Hull
17.01.89	Peter Bradley L PTS 8 Chigwell
31.05.89	Carl Crook L RSC 4 Manchester
04.09.89	Michael Armstrong L PTS 8 Hull
10.10.89	Tony Foster L RSC 3 Hull
22.03.90	Chris Bennett W PTS 4 Gateshead
07.04.90	Frankie Dewinter L PTS 6 St Elois Vyve, Belgium
20.05.90	Mark Ramsey L PTS 6 Sheffield
30.11.90	Shaun Cooper L PTS 6 Birmingham
11.02.91	Dave Anderson L PTS 6 Glasgow

02.03.91 Alan Hall L PTS 6 Darlington
05.12.91 Shaun Cogan L PTS 6 Oakengates
18.01.92 Ian Honeywood L PTS 6 Kensington
30.03.92 J. T. Williams W PTS 6 Eltham
30.04.92 Jason Rowland L RSC 2 Kensington
10.09.92 Paul Charters L RTD 5 Sunderland
16.10.92 Kevin Toomey L RSC 7 Hull
Career: 62 contests, won 19, drew 4, lost 39.

Chris Pollock

Bedworth. *Born* Coventry, 2 October, 1972
Welterweight. Ht. 5'10½"
Manager P. Byrne

17.06.93 Jamie Morris W RSC 1 Bedworth
Career: 1 contest, won 1.

Danny Porter

Hitchin. *Born* Biggleswade, 27 April, 1964
Flyweight. Ht. 5'3"
Manager B. Hearn

09.11.86 Antti Juntumaa L PTS 4 Vasa, Finland
09.02.87 Donnie Hood L RSC 4 Glasgow
08.04.87 Pepe Webber W CO 5 Evesham
07.03.88 David Afan-Jones W RSC 4 Piccadilly
10.05.88 Phil Dicks W RSC 4 Southend
30.09.88 Gordon Shaw W RSC 1 Gillingham
15.11.88 Mark Goult L PTS 6 Norwich
07.12.88 Paul Dever W CO 1 Stoke
06.04.89 Francisco Paco Garcia W PTS 8 Stevenage
22.06.89 Amon Neequaye W RSC 7 Stevenage
24.10.89 Pat Clinton L RSC 5 Watford
(British Flyweight Title Challenge)
14.02.90 Des Gargano W PTS 6 Brentwood
20.03.90 Mark Goult L PTS 10 Norwich
(Vacant Southern Area Bantamweight Title)
06.07.90 Alfred Kotei L PTS 12 Brentwood
(Commonwealth Flyweight Title Challenge)
31.10.90 Pablo Salazar W RSC 7 Crystal Palace
19.03.91 Kevin Jenkins W RSC 7 Leicester
12.06.91 Salvatore Fanni L RSC 9 Sassari, Italy
(European Flyweight Title Challenge)
19.11.91 Kevin Jenkins W RSC 2 Norwich
12.02.92 Salvatore Fanni DREW 12 Sarno, Italy
(European Flyweight Title Challenge)
01.06.92 Miguel Matthews W PTS 6 Glasgow
19.09.92 Pat Clinton L PTS 12 Glasgow
(WBO Flyweight Title Challenge)
30.03.93 Robbie Regan L RSC 3 Cardiff
(European Flyweight Title Challenge)
Career: 22 contests, won 12, drew 1, lost 9.

Gypsy Johnny Price

Bolton. *Born* Wigan, 10 April, 1973
S. Middleweight. Ht. 5'10"
Manager J. Doughty

21.10.91 Graham Wassell W RSC 5 Bury
21.01.92 Jason McNeill W PTS 4 Stockport
10.03.92 Martin Jolley L RSC 3 Bury
12.11.92 Shamus Casey W PTS 6 Burnley
09.03.93 Cliff Taylor W RSC 6 Hartlepool
19.04.93 Graham Wassell W RSC 1 Manchester
Career: 6 contests, won 5, lost 1.

Kenley Price

Liverpool. *Born* Liverpool, 30 December, 1965
Cruiserweight. Ht. 6'1½"
Manager S. Vaughan

15.12.92 Zak Goldman W RTD 2 Liverpool
27.02.93 Tony Colclough W RSC 5 Ellesmere Port
Career: 2 contests, won 2.

Ray Price

Swansea. *Born* Swansea, 16 July, 1961
Middleweight. Former Welsh L. Welterweight Champion. Ht. 5'10"
Manager C. Breen

30.04.79 Gerry Howland DREW 4 Barnsley
17.09.79 Tim Moloney L PTS 4 Mayfair
24.09.79 Bonnet Bryan W PTS 4 Mayfair
16.10.79 Kid Curtis W CO 2 West Bromwich
22.10.79 Bill Smith DREW 6 Mayfair
30.10.79 Phillip Morris DREW 6 Caerphilly
06.11.79 Neil Brown W PTS 6 Stafford
21.11.79 Neil Brown W PTS 6 Evesham
28.11.79 Shaun Durkin DREW 6 Doncaster
03.12.79 Tim Moloney L PTS 6 Marylebone
11.12.79 Young John Daly L PTS 6 Milton Keynes
17.03.80 Terry Parkinson W PTS 6 Mayfair
19.05.80 Colin Wake L PTS 6 Piccadilly
26.03.81 Billy Vivian L PTS 8 Ebbw Vale
07.04.81 Tyrell Wilson W PTS 6 Newport
11.05.81 Barry Price W PTS 8 Copthorne
08.06.81 John Lindo W RSC 2 Bradford
13.10.81 Robbie Robinson L CO 1 Blackpool
22.03.82 Geoff Pegler W PTS 10 Swansea
(Vacant Welsh L. Welterweight Title)
25.10.82 Willie Booth L PTS 8 Airdrie
09.11.82 Tony Adams L RSC 1 Kensington
02.03.83 Lee Halford W PTS 6 Evesham
21.03.83 Gunther Roomes L RSC 1 Mayfair
27.05.83 Geoff Pegler NC 1 Swansea
(Welsh L. Welterweight Title Defence)
04.10.83 Mo Hussein L PTS 8 Bethnal Green
19.12.83 Geoff Pegler L RTD 8 Swansea
(Welsh L. Welterweight Title Defence)
30.01.84 Steve Tempro W PTS 8 Birmingham
14.03.84 Ken Foreman L PTS 6 Mayfair
09.05.84 Tony McKenzie L PTS 8 Leicester
13.06.84 Michael Harris L PTS 10 Aberavon
(Vacant Welsh L. Welterweight Title)
30.06.84 David Irving L RSC 4 Belfast
08.12.84 Franki Moro L PTS 8 Swansea
04.02.85 Claude Rossi W RSC 6 Nottingham
18.09.85 George Collins L PTS 4 Muswell Hill
02.12.85 Steve Ellwood L RSC 5 Dulwich
07.10.92 Steve Thomas W PTS 6 Barry
10.04.93 Russell Washer L RSC 4 Swansea
Career: 37 contests, won 13, drew 4, lost 1, no contest 1.

Mark Prince

Tottenham. *Born* London, 10 March, 1969
L. Heavyweight. Ht. 6'1"
Manager T. Haynes

04.04.93 Bobby Mack W RSC 2 Brockley
23.05.93 John Kaighin W RSC 3 Brockley
25.06.93 Art Stacey W CO 2 Battersea
Career: 3 contests, won 3.

Lee Prudden

Redditch. *Born* Birmingham, 3 December, 1968
L. Heavyweight. Ht. 6'0"
Manager Self

Lee Prudden   Les Clark

28.01.91 Paul Murray W PTS 6 Birmingham
27.02.91 Barry Downes W PTS 6 Wolverhampton
13.03.91 Paul Murray DREW 6 Stoke
26.03.91 Nigel Rafferty L PTS 6 Wolverhampton
10.04.91 Paul Hanlon W PTS 6 Wolverhampton
13.05.91 Paul Hanlon W PTS 6 Birmingham
23.05.91 Paul Hanlon L PTS 6 Southampton
05.06.91 Nigel Rafferty L PTS 6 Wolverhampton
03.07.91 James F. Woolley W PTS 6 Brentwood
21.09.91 James F. Woolley W PTS 6 Tottenham
01.10.91 Gil Lewis DREW 8 Bedworth
17.10.91 Joey Peters L PTS 6 Southwark
22.01.92 Paul Hanlon L RSC 4 Stoke
22.04.92 Phil Soundy L RSC 5 Wembley
09.07.92 Joe McCluskey L PTS 6 Glasgow
07.09.92 Bruce Scott L PTS 6 Bethnal Green
23.11.92 Stephen Wilson L PTS 6 Glasgow
09.12.92 Steve Loftus W PTS 6 Stoke
01.03.93 Ian Henry L PTS 6 Bradford
08.03.93 Art Stacey DREW 6 Leeds
16.03.93 Chris Okoh L PTS 6 Mayfair
31.03.93 Terry Dunston L PTS 6 Barking
Career: 22 contests, won 7, drew 3, lost 12.

Darren Pullman

Swansea. *Born* Swansea, 11 January, 1974
Middleweight. Ht. 5'10"
Manager C. Breen

10.04.93 Steve Thomas DREW 6 Swansea
Career: 1 contest, drew 1.

Danny Quacoe

Horsham. *Born* Hammersmith, 30 December, 1965
Welterweight. Ht. 5'10"
Manager H. Holland

22.10.92 Joel Ani L CO 1 Bethnal Green
Career: 1 contest, lost 1.

145

Willie Quinn

Haddington. *Born* Edinburgh, 17 February, 1972
Middleweight. Ht. 5'11½"
Manager T. Gilmour

09.10.91	Mark Jay L PTS 6 Glasgow
27.01.92	Hugh Fury W RSC 3 Glasgow
18.03.92	Andy Manning W PTS 6 Glasgow
30.03.92	John McKenzie W RSC 4 Glasgow
19.09.92	Martin Rosamond W RSC 4 Glasgow
25.01.93	Mike Phillips W PTS 6 Glasgow
06.03.93	Steve Thomas W RSC 4 Glasgow
15.05.93	Dave Owens W PTS 6 Glasgow

Career: 8 contests, won 7, lost 1.

Nigel Rafferty

Wolverhampton. *Born* Wolverhampton, 29 December, 1967
L. Heavyweight. Ht. 5'11"
Manager Self

05.06.89 Carl Watson L PTS 6 Birmingham
28.06.89 Tony Hodge L PTS 6 Brentwood
06.07.89 Tony Hodge W PTS 6 Chigwell
04.09.89 Joe Frater L PTS 6 Grimsby
24.10.89 Paul Wesley W PTS 6 Wolverhampton
22.11.89 Paul Wesley W PTS 8 Stafford
28.11.89 Paul Wesley W PTS 6 Wolverhampton
04.12.89 Dean Murray W PTS 6 Grimsby
20.12.89 Paul Wright DREW 6 Kirkby
17.01.90 Gil Lewis L PTS 6 Stoke
31.01.90 Antoine Tarver L PTS 4 Bethnal Green
19.02.90 Paul Wesley W PTS 8 Birmingham
19.03.90 Terry Gilbey W PTS 6 Grimsby
01.05.90 Sean Heron L RSC 2 Oldham
13.09.90 Paul Murray W PTS 6 Watford
27.09.90 Paul Murray DREW 6 Birmingham
09.10.90 Paul Murray W PTS 6 Wolverhampton
24.10.90 Andrew Flute L CO 6 Dudley
27.11.90 Carlos Christie L PTS 6 Wolverhampton
06.12.90 Carlos Christie L PTS 6 Wolverhampton
28.01.91 Alan Richards DREW 8 Birmingham
04.03.91 Carlos Christie L PTS 8 Birmingham
26.03.91 Lee Prudden W PTS 6 Birmingham
13.05.91 Tony Behan W DIS 7 Birmingham
05.06.91 Lee Prudden L PTS 6 Wolverhampton
10.09.91 Paul Busby L RSC 2 Wolverhampton
20.11.91 Julian Johnson DREW 6 Cardiff
02.12.91 Kesem Clayton W PTS 8 Birmingham
21.01.92 Glenn Campbell L RSC 6 Stockport
30.03.92 Simon McDougall W PTS 8 Coventry
25.04.92 Sammy Storey L RSC 3 Belfast
16.06.92 Gary Delaney L CO 5 Dagenham
24.11.92 Graham Burton W PTS 8 Wolverhampton
02.12.92 John J. Cooke L PTS 6 Bardon
23.03.93 Stephen Wilson W RSC 3 Wolverhampton
14.04.93 Ole Klemetsen L RSC 2 Kensington
19.05.93 Zak Chelli L RSC 3 Leicester

Career: 37 contests, won 16, drew 4, lost 17.

Gary Railton

Burnopfield. *Born* Consett, 15 July, 1966
Heavyweight. Ht. 6'2"
Manager Self

30.04.87 Mamadou N'Diaye W RSC 2 Washington
28.05.87 Steve Osborne W PTS 6 Jarrow

04.09.87 Mick Cordon W PTS 6 Gateshead
10.11.87 Ian Bulloch L PTS 6 Batley
14.12.87 Eric Cardouza L CO 2 Piccadilly
13.12.90 Denzil Browne L RSC 2 Dewsbury
11.11.91 Gary Charlton W PTS 6 Bradford
06.02.92 J. A. Bugner L CO 3 Peterborough
12.02.93 Mikael Lindblad L RSC 2 Randers, Denmark

Career: 9 contests, won 4, lost 5.

David Ramsden

Bradford. *Born* Bradford, 22 January, 1970
Featherweight. Ht. 5'4"
Manager J. Celebanski

20.01.92 Glyn Shepherd W RSC 1 Bradford
30.03.92 Eunan Devenney W RSC 2 Bradford
27.04.92 Des Gargano W PTS 6 Bradford
08.06.92 Des Gargano W PTS 6 Bradford
14.09.92 Mike Deveney W PTS 6 Bradford
14.12.92 Chris Clarkson L PTS 4 Bradford
24.05.93 Russell Davison W PTS 6 Bradford

Career: 7 contests, won 6, lost 1.

Mark Ramsey

Small Heath. *Born* Birmingham, 24 January, 1968
L. Welterweight. Ht. 5'7½"
Manager B. Ingle

15.11.89 Mick O'Donnell W RSC 1 Lewisham
08.12.89 Dave Pierre L RSC 2 Doncaster
22.02.90 Karl Taylor W RSC 4 Hull
10.04.90 George Jones W RSC 6 Doncaster
20.05.90 Steve Pollard W PTS 6 Sheffield
18.10.90 Neil Haddock L RSC 5 Birmingham
30.05.91 Colin Sinnott W PTS 6 Birmingham
05.12.91 Carl Hook W RSC 5 Oakengates
27.01.93 Andrew Jervis W PTS 6 Stoke
12.02.93 Reymond Deva W PTS 6 Aubervilliers, France
04.03.93 Dave Pierre L PTS 8 Peterborough
01.05.93 Vyacheslav Ianowski L PTS 8 Berlin, Germany

Career: 12 contests, won 8, lost 4.

Emlyn Rees

Tonypandy. *Born* Rhondda, 19 November, 1965
Lightweight. Ht. 5'7"
Manager D. Gardiner

20.11.92 George Naylor L PTS 6 Liverpool

Career: 1 contest, lost 1.

Russell Rees

Gilfach Goch. *Born* Pontypridd, 4 October, 1974
S. Featherweight. Ht. 5'7"
Manager D. Gardiner

19.01.93 Chip O'Neill W RSC 1 Cardiff
06.02.93 Eunan Devenney W RSC 3 Cardiff
30.03.93 Ian Reid W PTS 6 Cardiff

Career: 3 contests, won 3.

Fred Reeve

Hull. *Born* Hull, 14 April, 1969
S. Featherweight. Ht. 5'5½"
Manager M. Toomey

09.11.92 Tim Hill L CO 4 Bradford
14.12.92 Leo Turner L RSC 2 Bradford

Fred Reeve   Les Clark

19.03.93 Kevin Haidarah W RSC 2 Manchester
29.04.93 Marty Chestnut W PTS 6 Hull

Career: 4 contests, won 2, lost 2.

Ian Reid

Balham. *Born* Lambeth, 30 August, 1972
S. Featherweight. Ht. 5'2"
Manager C. McKenzie

30.03.93 Russell Rees L PTS 6 Cardiff

Career: 1 contest, lost 1.

Peter Reid

Alfreton. *Born* Derby, 19 February, 1966
Welterweight. Ht. 5'10½"
Manager M. Shinfield

01.09.86 Andy Till L RSC 6 Ealing
10.10.86 John Davies L RSC 2 Gloucester
12.12.88 Mark Holden L RSC 4 Manchester
16.01.89 Steve Kiernan W PTS 6 Bradford
27.01.89 Frank Mobbs W PTS 4 Durham
22.02.89 Frank Mobbs W PTS 4 Bradford
01.03.89 Bullit Andrews W RSC 2 Stoke
08.05.89 Gary Osborne L CO 5 Edgbaston
26.09.89 Jim Beckett L PTS 8 Chigwell
13.11.89 Martin Robinson L PTS 6 Brierley Hill
20.12.89 Paul Lynch L RSC 4 Swansea
10.03.90 Martin Rosamond W RSC 6 Bristol
22.03.90 Gary Osborne L CO 1 Wolverhampton
18.10.90 Andrew Tucker L PTS 6 Hartlepool
29.10.90 Dean Cooper L RSC 1 Nottingham
21.11.91 Robert Riley W PTS 6 Ilkeston
04.12.91 Julian Eavis L PTS 6 Stoke
20.02.92 James Campbell L PTS 6 Oakengates
06.04.92 Kevin Mabbutt W PTS 6 Northampton
13.04.92 Dave Maj L CO 1 Manchester
04.06.92 Warren Bowers W RSC 2 Cleethorpes
12.11.92 Dean Hiscox W PTS 6 Stafford

Career: 22 contests, won 9, lost 13.

Robin Reid

Warrington. Liverpool, 19 February, 1972
L. Middleweight. Ht. 5'9"
Manager F. Warren

27.02.93 Mark Dawson W RSC 1 Dagenham
06.03.93 Julian Eavis W RSC 2 Glasgow
10.04.93 Andrew Furlong W PTS 6 Swansea
Career: 3 contests, won 3.

Lee Renshaw

Sheffield. *Born* Sheffield, 4 May, 1975
Welterweight. Ht. 5'9"
Manager H. Carnall

01.04.93 Dennis Berry L RSC 3 Evesham
Career: 1 contest, lost 1.

Yifru Retta

Canning Town. *Born* Ethiopia, 24
September, 1971
S. Featherweight. Ht. 5'8½"
Manager T. Lawless

14.06.93 Lee Fox W RTD 3 Bayswater
Career: 1 contest, won 1.

Jimmy Reynolds

Birmingham. *Born* Birmingham, 25 June,
1970
L. Welterweight. Ht. 5'10"
Manager Self

25.09.89 Delroy Waul L RSC 4 Birmingham
11.12.89 Dave Jenkins L PTS 6 Birmingham
01.10.92 Steve Howden W RTD 2 Telford
02.11.92 Billy McDougall W PTS 6
Wolverhampton
Career: 4 contests, won 2, lost 2.

(Richard) Rocky Reynolds

Swansea. *Born* Swansea, 13 July, 1968
L. Heavyweight. Ht. 5'8¾"
Manager Self

16.09.86 Danny St Claire W RSC 1 Southend
06.10.86 Kesem Clayton L PTS 6 Birmingham
18.11.86 Johnny Stone W PTS 6 Swansea
28.11.86 Nigel Fairbairn L PTS 6 Peterborough
08.01.87 Roy Horn L PTS 6 Bethnal Green
30.04.87 Kevin Hayde W PTS 6 Newport
19.11.87 Michael Justin W PTS 6 Weston super
Mare
01.03.88 Tony Baker W PTS 6 Southend
12.04.88 Tony Collins L PTS 4 Cardiff
10.05.88 Stan King W PTS 6 Southend
18.05.88 Mark Hibbs W PTS 6 Aberavon
07.06.88 Jimmy McDonagh W PTS 6 Southend
04.10.88 Geoff Sharp W PTS 6 Southend
07.12.88 Cyril Jackson L RTD 6 Aberavon
10.04.93 Karl Mumford L PTS 6 Swansea
11.06.93 Roland Ericsson L PTS 6 Randers,
Denmark
Career: 16 contests, won 9, lost 7.

Glyn Rhodes

Sheffield. *Born* Sheffield, 22 October, 1959
Welterweight. Former Central Area
Lightweight Champion. Ht. 5'11"
Manager B. Ingle

15.11.79 John Lindo L PTS 6 Liverpool
28.11.79 Mark Osbourne W PTS 4 Doncaster
10.12.79 Mike Clemow L PTS 6 Torquay
09.01.80 Steve Sammy Sims W RSC 6 Burslem

25.01.80 Shaun Durkin W PTS 6 Hull
05.02.80 John Cooper W PTS 6 Southend
12.02.80 Bill Smith W PTS 4 Sheffield
03.03.80 Kevin Sheehan L CO 1 Nottingham
24.03.80 Derek Groarke W RSC 4 Bradford
21.04.80 John Henry W RSC 5 Bradford
29.04.80 Jackie Turner L PTS 8 Mayfair
28.07.80 Bill Hay DREW 6 Fivemiletown
04.09.80 Jarvis Greenidge W RSC 8 Morecambe
15.09.80 Gary Ball DREW 6 Mayfair
07.10.80 Ceri Collins W RSC 8 Piccadilly
30.10.80 Jimmy Bunclark L RSC 7 Liverpool
01.12.80 Bobby Welburn L CO 1 Hull
22.01.81 Brian Snagg L PTS 8 Liverpool
09.03.81 Jimmy Brown W PTS 8 Mayfair
24.03.81 Eric Wood L PTS 8 Sheffield
29.04.81 Doug Hill W RTD 6 Burslem
11.05.81 Jackie Turner W RSC 2 Mayfair
17.06.81 Paul Keers W RSC 1 Sheffield
26.10.81 Lance Williams DREW 8 Mayfair
12.01.82 Vernon Vanriel L CO 2 Bethnal Green
05.05.82 Lance Williams L RSC 7 Solihull
03.06.82 Brian Snagg W RTD 4 Liverpool
22.11.82 Kevin Pritchard W CO 5 Liverpool
*(Vacant Central Area Lightweight
Title)*
14.03.83 Jimmy Bunclark L PTS 10 Sheffield
*(Central Area Lightweight Title
Defence)*
09.11.83 Robert Lloyd W PTS 8 Sheffield
13.01.84 Frederic Geoffrey L RSC 5 Nemours,
France
11.04.84 Mo Hussein L RSC 1 Kensington
29.10.84 Willie Wilson W RTD 3 Nottingham
13.10.85 Muhammad Lovelock L CO 10
Sheffield
*(Vacant Central Area Lightweight
Title)*
19.10.87 Andy Holligan L PTS 6 Belfast
05.12.87 Sugar Gibiliru W PTS 8 Doncaster
24.02.88 Marvin P. Gray W RSC 1 Sheffield
23.03.88 Nigel Senior W PTS 8 Sheffield
22.04.88 Chris Blake L PTS 6 Lisbon, Portugal
28.09.88 Sugar Gibiliru DREW 8 Solihull
26.10.88 George Baigrie W RSC 2 Sheffield
22.12.88 Habib Hammani L DIS 5 Milan, Italy
09.03.89 George Baigrie W RSC 5 Glasgow
04.04.89 Kid Sylvester L PTS 6 Sheffield
25.09.89 Jeff Connors W PTS 6 Piccadilly
05.10.89 Tony Connellan L PTS 6 Middleton
21.11.89 Louie Antuna W PTS 8 Glasgow
04.12.89 Barry Messam W PTS 6 Manchester
27.01.90 Billy Couzens L PTS 6 Sheffield
13.03.90 Paul Moylett W RSC 4 Bristol
01.05.90 Willie Beattie L RSC 5 Oldham
05.06.90 Steve Foran DREW 6 Nottingham
05.09.90 Tony Swift W RSC 7 Stoke
14.11.90 Julian Eavis W RSC 5 Sheffield
29.01.91 Simon Eubank W RSC 3 Wisbech
23.02.91 Neil Foran W RSC 2 Brighton
18.05.91 Itoro Mkpanam L RSC 5 Verbania,
Italy
29.06.91 Antoine Fernandez L CO 2 Le
Touquet, France
21.09.91 Eamonn Loughran L PTS 8 Tottenham
26.12.91 Jean-Charles Meuret L CO 2 Berne,
Switzerland
09.09.92 Mark Pain W PTS 6 Stoke
05.02.93 Tony Ekubia L RSC 6 Manchester
17.03.93 Mike Phillips W RSC 2 Stoke
12.05.93 Mark Cichocki W PTS 6 Sheffield
23.05.93 Gary Logan L CO 3 Brockley
Career: 65 contests, won 33, drew 5, lost 27.

Alan Richards

Barry. *Born* Cardiff, 9 April, 1965
Middleweight. Ht. 5'9"
Manager Self

22.05.89 Tony Grizzle W PTS 6 Mayfair
05.06.89 Ernie Loveridge W PTS 6 Birmingham
19.08.89 Gary Pemberton L PTS 6 Cardiff
22.11.89 Martin Robinson W RSC 2 Stafford
28.11.89 Jim Beckett W RSC 2 Wolverhampton
11.12.89 Tony Britland W RSC 7 Birmingham
21.12.89 Colin Pitters L PTS 6 Kings Heath
26.02.90 Winston May W PTS 6 Crystal Palace
05.03.90 Darren Pilling L PTS 8 Northampton
27.03.90 Colin Pitters W PTS 8 Wolverhampton
09.05.90 Paul Wesley L PTS 8 Solihull
06.06.90 Trevor Smith L RSC 7 Battersea
12.09.90 Andy Till L PTS 8 Battersea
24.10.90 Wayne Timmins W CO 4 Dudley
21.11.90 Wally Swift Jnr L PTS 8 Solihull
28.01.91 Nigel Rafferty DREW 8 Birmingham
06.02.91 Andy Till L PTS 8 Battersea
12.04.91 Frank Grant L RSC 5 Manchester
14.05.91 Andrew Flute L PTS 8 Dudley
20.11.91 Russell Washer W PTS 6 Cardiff
11.02.92 Wayne Ellis L PTS 10 Cardiff
(Vacant Welsh Middleweight Title)
29.10.92 Cornelius Carr L PTS 8 Bayswater
Career: 22 contests, won 9, drew 1, lost 12.

Chris Richards

Nottingham. *Born* Nottingham, 4 April,
1964
Middleweight. Ht. 5'5¼"
Manager W. Swift

07.09.87 Darren Bowen W RSC 1 Mayfair
23.09.87 Shaun Cummins L PTS 6
Loughborough
13.10.87 Damien Denny L PTS 6 Windsor
03.11.87 Brian Robinson L PTS 6 Bethnal
Green
18.01.88 Stan King W CO 5 Mayfair
29.01.88 Lou Ayres W RSC 3 Holborn
26.03.88 Terry Magee L PTS 8 Belfast
28.05.88 Tony Collins L RSC 3 Kensington
10.10.88 Antonio Fernandez L PTS 6 Edgbaston
23.11.88 Antonio Fernandez L PTS 6 Solihull
12.12.88 Terry Morrill L PTS 6 Crystal Palace
16.01.89 Mark Holden L DIS 3 Northampton
24.01.89 Ian Strudwick L PTS 6 Wandsworth
13.02.89 G. L. Booth W RSC 8 Manchester
10.03.89 Theo Marius L RSC 2 Brentwood
08.05.89 G. L. Booth W RSC 2 Manchester
22.05.89 B. K. Bennett L PTS 8 Mayfair
16.05.90 Mick Duncan L PTS 6 Hull
04.06.90 Antonio Fernandez L PTS 8 Edgbaston
15.06.90 Gary Pemberton W RTD 1 Telford
14.09.90 Shamus Casey W PTS 6 Telford
17.10.90 Gary Osborne L PTS 8 Stoke
13.11.90 Andrew Tucker W RSC 2 Hartlepool
13.12.90 Neville Brown L RSC 2 Dewsbury
13.02.91 Delroy Waul L PTS 6 Wembley
16.04.91 Paul Smith DREW 6 Nottingham
24.04.91 Colin Pitters L RSC 6 Stoke
26.11.91 Adrian Strachan L PTS 6 Bethnal
Green
26.03.92 Glen Payton W PTS 6 Telford
18.06.92 Stefan Wright L PTS 6 Peterborough
18.07.92 Quinn Paynter L RSC 6 Manchester
Career: 31 contests, won 9, drew 1, lost 21.

Warren Richards

Eltham. *Born* London, 10 July, 1964
Heavyweight. Ht. 6'3"
Manager Self

24.04.90	Mark Langley W RSC 2 Eltham
26.05.90	Mick Cordon W CO 1 Reading
24.10.90	Sean Hunter L RSC 3 Stoke
21.03.91	Joe Adams W CO 4 Meridan, USA
12.04.91	Johnny Wright W CO 2 Greenville, USA
30.03.92	John Westgarth DREW 6 Eltham
23.04.92	Newbirth Mukosi W CO 1 Eltham
31.10.92	R. F. McKenzie DREW 6 Earls Court
22.02.93	Denroy Bryan W CO 4 Eltham
31.03.93	R. F. McKenzie L RSC 8 Bethnal Green
	(Vacant Southern Area Heavyweight Title)

Career: 10 contests, won 6, drew 2, lost 2.

Wayne Rigby

Manchester. *Born* Manchester, 19 July, 1973
S. Featherweight. Ht. 5'6"
Manager Self

27.02.92	Lee Fox L PTS 6 Liverpool
08.06.92	Leo Turner W PTS 6 Bradford
02.07.92	Leo Turner W CO 5 Middleton
05.10.92	Colin Innes W PTS 6 Manchester
01.12.92	John T. Kelly L PTS 6 Hartlepool

Career: 5 contests, won 3, lost 2.

Robert Riley Chris Bevan

Robert Riley

Sheffield. *Born* Sheffield, 22 June, 1965
Middleweight. Ht. 5'11¾"
Manager Self

04.02.85	Alan Williams W PTS 6 Liverpool
13.10.85	Wayne Hall W PTS 6 Sheffield
10.03.86	Mick Kane W PTS 6 Manchester
31.03.87	Ossie Maddix L RSC 3 Oldham
11.09.91	Andreas Panayi L PTS 6 Stoke
21.11.91	Peter Reid L PTS 6 Ilkeston
19.12.91	Charlie Moore L PTS 6 Oldham

25.03.92	Darren McInulty W PTS 6 Hinckley
13.10.92	Crain Fisher W PTS 4 Bury
12.11.92	Darren Pilling W PTS 6 Burnley
25.02.93	Warren Stowe L DIS 4 Burnley
	(Vacant Central Area L. Middleweight Title)
11.06.93	Dave Johnson L PTS 8 Gateshead

Career: 12 contests, won 6, lost 6.

Darryl Ritchie (Jones)

Rhyl. *Born* Rhyl, 26 April, 1963
L. Heavyweight. Ht. 6'0½"
Manager Self

08.04.86	Graham Jenner L RSC 3 Southend
04.03.87	Jimmy Cropper W RSC 2 Stoke
18.03.87	Paul Wesley DREW 4 Stoke
07.04.87	Peter Brown L PTS 6 Batley
23.09.87	Sean Stringfellow W RSC 1 Stoke
28.09.87	Terry Gilbey W PTS 6 Manchester
25.11.87	Terry Gilbey W RSC 7 Cottingham
05.12.87	Dave Owens W DIS 7 Doncaster
26.04.88	Adam Cook L RSC 5 Bethnal Green
01.03.89	Simon Collins L RSC 1 Cardiff
08.06.89	Dario Deabreu W RSC 6 Cardiff
02.12.91	Tony Behan L RSC 1 Birmingham
24.03.92	Lee Archer L PTS 6 Wolverhampton
14.11.92	Karl Mumford L PTS 6 Cardiff

Career: 14 contests, won 6, drew 1, lost 7.

Brian Robb

Telford. *Born* Liverpool, 5 April, 1967
S. Featherweight. Ht. 5'6"
Manager Self

14.02.89	Miguel Matthews L RSC 2 Wolverhampton
27.03.90	Neil Leitch W PTS 6 Wolverhampton
09.05.90	Peter Judson L PTS 6 Solihull
22.05.90	Nicky Lucas W PTS 6 Canvey Island
20.06.90	Paul Harvey L PTS 6 Basildon
09.10.90	Des Gargano W PTS 6 Wolverhampton
24.10.90	Paul Harvey L RSC 2 Dudley
23.01.91	Jason Primera L RSC 7 Solihull
04.03.91	Pete Buckley L RSC 7 Birmingham
05.06.91	Pete Buckley L PTS 10 Wolverhampton
	(Vacant Midlands Area S. Featherweight Title)
29.08.91	Renny Edwards W PTS 6 Oakengates
31.10.91	Miguel Matthews DREW 6 Oakengates
05.12.91	Neil Leitch W CO 2 Oakengates
20.02.92	Pete Buckley L RSC 10 Oakengates
	(Midlands Area S. Featherweight Title Challenge)
26.03.92	Kelton McKenzie L RSC 4 Telford
13.10.92	Paul Harvey L RSC 2 Mayfair
04.12.92	Kevin Middleton L RSC 1 Telford

Career: 17 contests, won 5, drew 1, lost 11.

Davy Robb

Telford. *Born* Liverpool, 14 August, 1964
L. Welterweight. Ht. 5'10"
Manager Self

09.11.87	Steve Phillips W PTS 6 Birmingham
24.11.87	Andrew Morgan L PTS 6 Wolverhampton
02.12.87	Peter Bowen W PTS 6 Stoke
20.01.88	Dean Bramhald W PTS 8 Stoke
24.02.88	Mark Reefer L RSC 1 Southend
13.04.88	Dean Bramhald L RSC 5 Wolverhampton

06.10.88	Steve Phillips W PTS 8 Dudley
10.11.88	Oliver Henry W PTS 8 Wolverhampton
14.12.88	Frankie Lake W RSC 3 Evesham
02.02.89	Darren Mount L RSC 5 Wolverhampton
26.05.89	Neil Foran L RSC 4 Bethnal Green
31.10.91	Carl Hook W PTS 4 Oakengates
05.12.91	Tony Doyle W PTS 6 Oakengates
20.02.92	Brian Coleman W PTS 6 Oakengates
26.03.92	John O'Johnson W PTS 6 Telford
10.12.92	Nigel Wenton L RSC 3 Bethnal Green

Career: 16 contests, won 10, lost 6.

Carl Roberts

Blackburn. *Born* Blackburn, 19 March, 1970
S. Featherweight. Ht. 5'7"
Manager Self

26.09.90	Peter Judson L PTS 6 Manchester
22.10.90	Shaun Hickey W CO 4 Manchester
26.11.90	Colin Innes W RSC 3 Bury
17.12.90	Trevor Royal W PTS 6 Manchester
29.01.91	Derek Amory L PTS 4 Stockport
28.02.91	Des Gargano L PTS 6 Bury
03.04.91	Neil Leitch L RSC 6 Manchester
19.09.91	Colin Innes W PTS 4 Stockport
14.10.91	Kevin Lowe W PTS 6 Manchester
16.12.91	Robert Braddock W PTS 6 Manchester
10.03.92	Graham O'Malley L PTS 6 Bury
07.12.92	Mike Deveney L PTS 6 Manchester
15.02.93	Lee Fox W PTS 6 Manchester
25.02.93	Ian McGirr L PTS 6 Burnley
28.06.93	Kid McAuley L PTS 6 Morecambe

Career: 15 contests, won 7, lost 8.

Pete Roberts

Hull. *Born* Liverpool, 15 July, 1967
L. Welterweight. Ht. 5'4"
Manager M. Toomey

25.10.88	Mark Jackson W CO 2 Hartlepool
07.11.88	Frankie Foster L PTS 4 Bradford
17.11.88	Tony Banks L PTS 6 Stockport
20.03.89	Brendan Ryan L PTS 6 Nottingham
05.04.90	Mike Close W CO 1 Liverpool
23.04.90	Brendan Ryan L PTS 6 Bradford
04.05.90	John Smith W PTS 6 Liverpool
09.10.90	John Smith L PTS 8 Liverpool
25.02.91	Peter Crook W RSC 6 Bradford
13.06.91	Wayne Windle L RSC 7 Hull
	(Vacant Central Area Lightweight Title)
07.10.91	John Smith W PTS 8 Liverpool
28.11.91	Dave Anderson L RSC 3 Glasgow
27.01.92	Kris McAdam L CO 2 Glasgow
29.04.92	Joey Moffat L RSC 3 Liverpool
29.04.93	Michael Alexander L RSC 2 Hull

Career: 15 contests, won 5, lost 10.

Des Robinson

Manchester. *Born* Manchester, 5 January, 1969
Welterweight. Ht. 5'9"
Manager P. Martin

26.09.89	Carl Watson W RTD 2 Oldham
05.10.89	Tommy Warde W RSC 2 Middleton
19.10.89	Martin Smith L PTS 4 Manchester
10.11.89	Richard Adams DREW 6 Battersea
16.11.89	David Heath W RSC 3 Manchester
03.12.89	Colin Pitters W PTS 6 Birmingham
27.02.90	Ricky Nelson W RSC 6 Manchester

15.03.90 Jim Talbot W PTS 8 Manchester
26.03.90 Tony Baker W PTS 8 Bradford
26.04.90 Rocky Bryan W PTS 6 Wandsworth
22.05.90 Jimmy Harrison W PTS 6 St Albans
11.06.90 Tony Britland W PTS 6 Manchester
25.10.90 Razor Addo L PTS 8 Bayswater
11.02.91 Willie Beattie L PTS 8 Glasgow
19.03.91 Lindon Scarlett L RSC 4 Birmingham
17.10.91 Gary Logan L PTS 8 Southwark
28.09.92 Darren Morris W PTS 6 Manchester
14.11.92 Michael Smyth L PTS 6 Cardiff
Career: 18 contests, won 11, drew 1, lost 6.

Jamie Robinson
West Ham. *Born* London, 12 September, 1968
L. Middleweight. Ht. 5'9"
Manager F. Warren

17.08.90 Duke de Palma W PTS 4 Las Vegas, USA
04.10.90 Rodney Knox L RSC 1 Atlantic City, USA
23.10.91 Dave Whittle W RSC 4 Bethnal Green
13.11.91 Michael Oliver W PTS 6 Bethnal Green
11.02.92 Julian Eavis W PTS 6 Barking
02.04.92 Mark Jay W PTS 6 Basildon
22.10.92 Gary Pemberton W RSC 3 Bethnal Green
17.12.92 Lee Crocker W RTD 2 Barking
27.02.93 Russell Washer W PTS 6 Dagenham
31.03.93 John Duckworth W RSC 3 Barking
Career: 10 contests, won 9, lost 1.

Tim Robinson
Grimsby. *Born* Cleethorpes, 28 June, 1968
S. Middleweight. Ht. 5'10"
Manager Self

21.09.92 Paul Hanlon L PTS 6 Cleethorpes
16.10.92 Griff Jones L RSC 3 Hull
14.12.92 Mohammed Malik W RSC 3 Cleethorpes
14.01.93 Hussain Shah L PTS 4 Mayfair
05.02.93 Eric Noi L RSC 4 Manchester
10.05.93 Mark Smallwood L RSC 4 Cleethorpes
26.06.93 Dale Nixon L RSC 2 Keynsham
Career: 7 contests, won 1, lost 6.

Martin Rosamond
Southampton. *Born* Cyprus, 10 March, 1969
L. Middleweight. Ht. 5'10"
Manager Self

02.03.89 Andy Tonks W RSC 2 Southampton
04.04.89 B. K. Bennett L PTS 6 Southend
26.04.89 Johnny Stone L RSC 3 Southampton
21.09.89 Tony Grizzle W RSC 5 Southampton
28.09.89 Max Wallace L RSC 1 Wandsworth
08.02.90 Darren Burford L PTS 6 Southwark
10.03.90 Peter Reid L RSC 6 Bristol
21.05.90 Tony Grizzle W RSC 2 Mayfair
22.06.90 Jimmy McDonagh W RSC 6 Gillingham
18.10.90 Matthew Jones W PTS 6 Birmingham
06.11.90 Kid Sylvester L RSC 3 Mayfair
08.12.90 Cliff Churchward W PTS 6 Bristol
21.02.91 Rob Pitters L RSC 2 Walsall
12.04.91 Shamus Casey L PTS 6 Willenhall
23.04.91 Barry Messam L PTS 6 Evesham
08.05.91 Marty Duke DREW 8 Millwall
23.05.91 Mike Morrison W PTS 6 Southampton

04.06.91 Adrian Strachan L PTS 6 Bethnal Green
03.07.91 Kevin Sheeran L CO 1 Reading
24.09.91 Adrian Strachan L PTS 6 Basildon
20.01.92 Lee Ferrie L RSC 2 Coventry
19.09.92 Willie Quinn L RSC 4 Glasgow
18.05.93 Eddie Collins W PTS 6 Kettering
15.06.93 Steve McNess W RSC 5 Hemel Hempstead
Career: 24 contests, won 9, drew 1, lost 14.

Vince Rose   Pennie Cattle

Vince Rose
Tottenham. *Born* London, 9 July, 1968
L. Middleweight. Ht. 5'8"
Manager B. Hearn

13.10.92 Ojay Abrahms W RSC 3 Mayfair
14.11.92 Marty Duke W PTS 6 Cardiff
30.01.93 Ojay Abrahams DREW 6 Brentwood
11.05.93 Gary Pemberton W PTS 6 Norwich
Career: 4 contests, won 3, drew 1.

Jason Rowland
West Ham. *Born* London, 6 August, 1970
L. Welterweight. Ht. 5'9¾"
Manager Self

19.09.89 Terry Smith W RSC 1 Millwall
15.11.89 Mike Morrison W PTS 6 Reading
14.02.90 Eamonn Payne W RSC 1 Millwall
17.04.90 Dave Jenkins W CO 1 Millwall
22.05.90 Mike Morrison W PTS 6 St Albans
12.02.91 Vaughan Carnegie W PTS 6 Basildon
07.03.91 Vaughan Carnegie W CO 2 Basildon
11.12.91 Brian Cullen W RSC 4 Basildon
30.04.92 Steve Pollard W RSC 2 Kensington
17.12.92 Jimmy Vincent W PTS 6 Wembley
10.02.93 Seth Jones W RSC 2 Lewisham
18.03.93 John Smith W PTS 6 Lewisham
Career: 12 contests, won 12.

Roy Rowland
West Ham. *Born* London, 19 May, 1967
Welterweight. Ht. 5'10"
Manager Self

29.10.86 Nick Lucas W PTS 6 Muswell Hill
03.12.86 Nick Meloscia W PTS 6 Muswell Hill
13.01.87 Ray Golding W PTS 6 Oldham
04.03.87 Andy Cox W RSC 3 Basildon
22.09.87 Brian Wareing W CO 1 Bethnal Green
03.11.87 Wil Halliday W RSC 1 Bethnal Green
02.12.87 Roy Callaghan W PTS 6 Kensington
09.03.88 Dave Haggarty W RSC 1 Bethnal Green
29.03.88 Nick Meloscia L RSC 1 Bethnal Green
07.09.88 Kelvin Mortimer W PTS 6 Reading
01.11.88 Kevin Hayde W PTS 6 Reading
25.01.89 Andy Tonks W RTD 1 Bethnal Green
15.02.89 Mike Russell W RSC 2 Bethnal Green
28.03.89 Paul Seddon W RSC 3 Bethnal Green
14.09.89 John Smith W RSC 3 Basildon
15.11.89 Lloyd Lee W PTS 8 Reading
25.04.90 Peter Eubank W RSC 8 Millwall
12.02.91 Paul Lynch L RTD 4 Basildon
06.06.91 Mark Kelly W RSC 4 Barking
02.10.91 Peter Eubank W PTS 8 Barking
25.03.92 Humphrey Harrison W CO 7 Dagenham
28.10.92 Darren Morris W RSC 2 Kensington
17.12.92 Gary Logan L RSC 4 Wembley
(Vacant Southern Area Welterweight Title)
Career: 23 contests, won 20, lost 3.

Trevor Royal   Les Clark

Trevor Royal
Bristol. *Born* Bristol, 8 May, 1962
S. Featherweight. Ht. 5'7"
Manager Self

15.09.90 Dave Jenkins L RSC 4 Bristol
29.10.90 Peter Campbell L PTS 6 Nottingham
21.11.90 Gavin Fitzpatrick W PTS 6 Chippenham
08.12.90 Gavin Fitzpatrick W RSC 1 Bristol
17.12.90 Carl Roberts L PTS 6 Manchester
06.02.91 Steve Hearn DREW 6 Battersea
18.02.91 Felix Kelly L RSC 4 Windsor
03.04.91 Terry Riley W RTD 4 Bethnal Green
10.04.91 Robert Smyth L PTS 6 Newport
22.04.91 Kevin Toomey L PTS 6 Bradford
01.05.91 Bernard Paul L CO 1 Bethnal Green
10.06.91 Bobby Beckles L PTS 6 Manchester

09.03.93 Mike Morrison L PTS 6 Bristol
24.03.93 Bernard McComiskey L RSC 6 Belfast
22.04.93 Mark O'Callaghan L PTS 6 Mayfair
27.05.93 Greg Upton L CO 2 Bristol
(Vacant Western Area S. Featherweight Title)
Career: 16 contests, won 3, drew 1, lost 12.

Bruce Ruegg   Les Clark

Bruce Ruegg

Bournemouth. *Born* Wimborne, 31 July, 1970
S. Featherweight. Ht. 5'5"
Manager J. Bishop

29.04.93 Simon Frailing DREW 6 Hayes
18.05.93 Nicky Towns L PTS 6 Kettering
15.06.93 Simon Frailing W PTS 6 Hemel Hempstead
Career: 3 contests, won 1, drew 1, lost 1.

Lee Ryan

Northampton. *Born* Northampton, 26 July, 1971
Lightweight. Ht. 5'9"
Manager R. Gray

11.03.93 Scott Smith L PTS 6 Walsall
19.04.93 T. J. Smith L RSC 2 Northampton
Career: 2 contests, lost 2.

Paul Ryan

Hackney. *Born* South Ockenham, 2 February, 1965
Lightweight. Ht. 5'8"
Manager A. Urry

26.09.91 Chris Mylan W PTS 6 Dunstable
18.01.92 Alex Sterling W RSC 4 Kensington
25.03.92 Michael Clynch W RSC 4 Dagenham
16.05.92 Greg Egbuniwe W RSC 4 Muswell Hill
26.09.92 Korso Aleain W CO 4 Earls Court
17.12.92 Rick Bushell W RSC 1 Barking
03.02.93 Neil Smith W RSC 1 Earls Court
27.02.93 Mike Morrison W PTS 6 Dagenham
Career: 8 contests, won 8.

Ricky Sackfield

Salford. *Born* Birmingham, 11 April, 1967
L. Welterweight. Ht. 5'7"
Manager J. Trickett

30.04.91 Willie Yeardsley W PTS 4 Stockport
19.09.91 Seth Jones W RSC 1 Stockport
21.10.91 Rob Stewart L PTS 6 Bury
21.01.92 David Thompson W CO 1 Stockport
03.02.92 Scott Doyle W PTS 6 Manchester
09.03.92 John O'Johnson L PTS 6 Manchester
31.03.92 Carl Wright L RSC 1 Stockport
24.09.92 Mark Legg L PTS 6 Stockport
15.02.93 Robert Lloyd W RSC 4 Manchester
26.03.93 Soren Sondergaard L RSC 2 Copenhagen, Denmark
Career: 10 contests, won 5, lost 5.

Kenny Sandison

Liverpool. *Born* Liverpool, 30 July, 1966
Heavyweight. Ht. 6'3"
Manager B. Devine

01.12.92 Gary Williams L PTS 6 Liverpool
27.01.93 Gary Williams DREW 6 Stoke
22.02.93 Albert Call L PTS 6 Liverpool
Career: 3 contests, drew 1, lost 2.

Lee Sara (Thomas)

Carmarthen. *Born* Carmarthen, 30 January, 1970
S. Middleweight. Ht. 5'11"
Manager D. Davies

18.05.93 Justin Clements L PTS 6 Edgbaston
Career: 1 contest, lost 1.

Chris Saunders

Barnsley. *Born* Barnsley, 15 August, 1969
L. Welterweight. Ht. 5'8"
Manager B. Ingle

22.02.90 Malcolm Melvin W PTS 4 Hull
10.04.90 Mike Morrison W PTS 6 Doncaster
20.05.90 Justin Graham W RSC 3 Sheffield
29.11.90 Ross Hale L PTS 6 Bayswater
05.03.91 Rocky Ferrari L PTS 4 Glasgow
19.03.91 Richard Woolgar W RSC 3 Leicester
26.03.91 Felix Kelly L PTS 6 Bethnal Green
17.04.91 Billy Schwer L RSC 1 Kensington
16.05.91 Richard Burton L PTS 6 Liverpool
06.06.91 Mark Tibbs W RSC 6 Barking
30.06.91 Billy Schwer L RSC 3 Southwark
01.08.91 James Jiora W PTS 6 Dewsbury
03.10.91 Gary Flear L PTS 6 Burton
24.10.91 Ron Shinkwin W PTS 6 Dunstable
21.11.91 Jason Matthews L RSC 4 Burton
30.01.92 John O'Johnson L PTS 6 Southampton
11.02.92 Eddie King W RSC 4 Wolverhampton
27.02.92 Richard Burton L PTS 10 Liverpool
(Vacant Central Area L. Welterweight Title)
09.09.92 John O'Johnson DREW 6 Stoke
01.10.92 Mark McCreath L RSC 4 Telford
01.12.92 Shea Neary L PTS 6 Liverpool
22.02.93 Cham Joof L PTS 4 Eltham
16.03.93 Mark Elliot L PTS 6 Wolverhampton
26.04.93 Dean Hollington W RSC 5 Lewisham
Career: 24 contests, won 9, drew 1, lost 14.

Lindon Scarlett   Chris Bevan

Lindon Scarlett

Dudley. *Born* Dudley, 11 January, 1967
Welterweight. Ht. 5'10"
Manager M. Duff

22.04.87 Tommy Shiels L PTS 6 Kensington
07.05.87 Dusty Miller W PTS 6 Bayswater
09.11.87 Sean Heron L PTS 6 Glasgow
20.01.88 Simon Paul W PTS 6 Solihull
12.04.88 Ted Kershaw L RSC 7 Oldham
11.10.89 Carlo Colarusso W PTS 8 Stoke
22.11.89 Carlo Colarusso W PTS 8 Solihull
06.12.89 Julian Eavis W PTS 8 Stoke
14.02.90 Wayne Ellis DREW 6 Millwall
13.03.90 Romolo Casamonica L PTS 8 Milan, Italy
08.05.90 Mickey Lloyd L RSC 2 Brentford
18.10.90 Kevin Spratt W RSC 2 Birmingham
16.11.90 Tony Gibbs W PTS 6 Telford
19.03.91 Des Robinson W RSC 4 Birmingham
24.10.91 Razor Addo W PTS 8 Bayswater
22.01.92 Kelvin Mortimer W RSC 1 Solihull
08.02.92 Javier Castillejos L PTS 8 Madrid, Spain
23.05.92 Chris Peters DREW 8 Birmingham
15.02.93 Gordon Blair W CO 4 Mayfair
Career: 19 contests, won 11, drew 2, lost 6.

Billy Schwer

Luton. *Born* Luton, 12 April, 1969
Former British & Commonwealth Lightweight Champion. Ht. 5'8½"
Manager M. Duff

04.10.90 Pierre Conan W RSC 1 Bethnal Green
31.10.90 Mark Antony W RSC 2 Wembley
12.12.90 Sean Casey W RSC 1 Kensington
16.01.91 Dave Jenkins W PTS 6 Kensington
07.02.91 John Smith W RSC 2 Watford
06.03.91 Chubby Martin W RSC 3 Wembley
04.04.91 Andy Robins W RSC 2 Watford
17.04.91 Chris Saunders W RSC 1 Kensington
02.05.91 Karl Taylor W RSC 2 Northampton
30.06.91 Chris Saunders W RSC 3 Southwark
11.09.91 Tony Foster W PTS 8 Hammersmith

26.09.91	Felix Kelly W RSC 2 Dunstable
24.10.91	Patrick Kamy W CO 1 Dunstable
20.11.91	Marcel Herbert W PTS 8 Kensington
12.02.92	Tomas Quinones W CO 8 Wembley
25.03.92	Bobby Brewer W RSC 4 Kensington
03.09.92	Wayne Windle W CO 1 Dunstable
28.10.92	Carl Crook W RTD 9 Kensington
	(British & Commonwealth Lightweight Title Challenge)
17.12.92	Mauricio Aceves W RSC 3 Wembley
24.02.93	Paul Burke L RSC 7 Wembley
	(British & Commonwealth Lightweight Title Defence)
15.06.93	Farid Benredjeb W PTS 8 Hemel Hempstead

Career: 21 contests, won 20, lost 1.

Bruce Scott

Hackney. *Born* Jamaica, 16 August, 1969
L. Heavyweight. Ht. 5'9½"
Manager M. Duff

25.04.91	Mark Bowen L PTS 6 Mayfair
16.09.91	Randy B. Powell W RSC 5 Mayfair
21.11.91	Steve Osborne W PTS 6 Burton
27.04.92	John Kaighin W CO 4 Mayfair
07.09.92	Lee Prudden W PTS 6 Bethnal Green
03.12.92	Mark Pain W RSC 5 Lewisham
15.02.93	Paul McCarthy W PTS 6 Mayfair
22.04.93	Sean O'Phoenix W RSC 3 Mayfair
14.06.93	John Oxenham W RSC 1 Bayswater

Career: 9 contests, won 8, lost 1.

Kenny Scott　　　　　　　　Chris Bevan

Kenny Scott

Chesterfield. *Born* Chesterfield, 23 April, 1967
Welterweight. Ht. 6'1"
Manager M. Shinfield

25.06.93	Maurice Forbes L RSC 2 Battersea

Career: 1 contest, lost 1.

Steve Scot

Chorley. *Born* Fulwood, 20 January, 1966
L. Middleweight. Ht. 5'11"
Manager J. McMillan

04.03.92	Allan Grainger L PTS 6 Glasgow
26.03.92	Rob Stevenson L PTS 6 Hull
14.09.92	Danny Harper DREW 6 Bradford
27.10.92	Steve Levene W RSC 1 Cradley Heath
30.10.92	James Campbell L PTS 6 Birmingham
26.11.92	Rob Stevenson W PTS 6 Hull
14.12.92	Kevin Spratt L PTS 6 Bradford
28.01.93	Steve McNess L PTS 6 Southwark
22.02.93	James Campbell L PTS 6 Birmingham
04.03.93	Eddie Collins W RSC 1 Peterborough
26.03.93	Colin Wallace L PTS 6 Glasgow
26.04.93	John Stronach L PTS 6 Bradford
29.05.93	Colin Wallace L PTS 6 Paisley
11.06.93	Dave Whittle L PTS 6 Gateshead

Career: 14 contests, won 3, drew 1, lost 10.

Greg Scott-Briggs　　　　　　　　Chris Bevan

Greg Scott-Briggs

Chesterfield. *Born* Swaziland, 6 February, 1966
L. Heavyweight. Ht. 6'1"
Manager M. Shinfield

04.02.92	Mark McBiane W PTS 6 Alfreton
03.03.92	Tony Colclough W RSC 2 Cradley Heath
30.03.92	Carl Smallwood L PTS 6 Coventry
27.04.92	Richard Atkinson L PTS 6 Bradford
28.05.92	Steve Walton W PTS 6 Gosforth
04.06.92	Joe Frater L PTS 6 Cleethorpes
30.09.92	Carl Smallwood L PTS 6 Solihull
17.03.93	Carl Smallwood L PTS 8 Stoke
26.04.93	Tony Colclough W RSC 4 Glasgow
08.06.93	Peter Flint W RSC 1 Derby

Career: 10 contests, won 5, lost 5.

Hussain Shah

Crayford. *Born* Pakistan, 1 June, 1964
L. Heavyweight. Ht. 6'0"
Manager F. Maloney

30.04.92	Paul McCarthy W RTD 4 Kensington
26.09.92	Nicky Wadman W RSC 4 Earls Court

Hussain Shah　　　　　　　　Les Clark

10.12.92	Kenny Nevers W PTS 4 Bethnal Green
14.01.93	Tim Robinson W PTS 4 Mayfair
28.02.93	George Allison W PTS 6 Georgetown, Guyana
04.04.93	Kenny Nevers L RSC 4 Brockley

Career: 6 contests, won 5, lost 1.

Kevin Sheeran

Crawley. *Born* Redhill, 10 August, 1971
L. Middleweight. Ht. 6'0"
Manager F. Warren

05.03.91	Richard Okumu L RSC 2 Millwall
08.05.91	Cliff Churchward W PTS 6 Millwall
22.05.91	Stuart Good W PTS 6 Millwall
03.07.91	Martin Rosamond W CO 1 Reading
04.09.91	Clive Dixon W RSC 4 Bethnal Green
29.10.91	Dave Hall W RSC 1 Kensington
20.11.91	Horace Fleary W RSC 2 Cardiff
02.04.92	Mike Russell W RSC 2 Basildon
30.04.92	Tracy Jocelyn W RSC 3 Kensington
26.09.92	Val Golding W RSC 1 Earls Court
03.02.93	Russell Washer W PTS 6 Earls Court
27.02.93	Gareth Boddy W RSC 1 Dagenham
31.03.93	Paul Lynch W RSC 1 Barking
28.04.93	Danny Juma W RSC 8 Dublin

Career: 14 contests, won 13, lost 1.

Charles Shepherd

Carlisle. *Born* Burnley, 28 June, 1970
Lightweight. Ht. 5'4"
Manager N. Basso

28.10.91	Chris Aston W PTS 6 Leicester
31.01.92	Alan McDowall L RSC 3 Glasgow
18.05.92	Mark Legg W PTS 6 Marton
25.09.92	George Naylor W RSC 4 Liverpool
22.10.92	Didier Hughes L PTS 4 Bethnal Green
13.02.93	Nigel Wenton W PTS 8 Manchester
23.05.93	Cham Joof W PTS 4 Brockley

Career: 7 contests, won 5, lost 2.

Glyn Shepherd

Carlisle. *Born* Whiston, 30 May, 1963

151

Bantamweight. Ht. 5'4"
Manager N. Basso

07.10.91	Robert Braddock DREW 6 Bradford	
28.10.91	Tony Smith W PTS 6 Leicester	
20.01.92	David Ramsden L RSC 1 Bradford	
18.05.92	Dave Campbell L RSC 1 Marton	
22.10.92	Darren Fifield DREW 4 Bethnal Green	
15.12.92	Paul Lloyd L RSC 1 Liverpool	

Career: 6 contests, won 1, drew 1, lost 3.

Wayne Shepherd

Carlisle. *Born* Whiston, 3 June, 1959
Welterweight. Ht. 5'6"
Manager N. Basso

07.10.91	Benji Joseph W PTS 6 Bradford
28.10.91	Noel Henry W PTS 6 Leicester
16.12.91	Dave Maj DREW 6 Manchester
03.02.92	Dave Maj L PTS 6 Manchester
30.03.92	Hughie Davey L PTS 6 Bradford
18.05.92	Dave Whittle W PTS 6 Marton
14.10.92	Richard Swallow L PTS 8 Stoke
31.10.92	George Scott L RSC 6 Earls Court
13.02.93	Delroy Waul L RSC 5 Manchester
31.03.93	Derek Grainger L RSC 4 Barking
11.06.93	Hughie Davey L PTS 6 Gateshead

Career: 11 contests, won 3, drew 1, lost 7.

Shane Sheridan   Chris Bevan

Shane Sheridan

Derby. *Born* Reading, 5 November, 1968
L. Welterweight. Ht. 5'9"
Manager M. Shinfield

28.03.91	David Thompson W CO 5 Alfreton
04.07.91	Dean Bramhald W PTS 6 Alfreton
21.11.91	Scott Doyle L PTS 6 Ilkeston
12.11.92	Gary Hiscox L PTS 6 Stafford
09.12.92	Alex Moffatt W PTS 6 Stoke
02.02.93	Mick Mulcahy W PTS 6 Derby
01.04.93	Dean Bramhald L PTS 6 Evesham

Career: 7 contests, won 4, lost 3.

Danny Shinkwin

Boreham Wood. *Born* Watford, 25
November, 1961

Welterweight. Ht. 5'9¼"
Manager J. Barclay

01.04.82	Mark Crouch W PTS 6 Walthamstow
19.04.82	Gary Petty W PTS 6 Bristol
27.04.82	Eric Purkis L PTS 6 Southend
04.09.82	Dan Myers W PTS 6 Piccadilly
06.04.84	Elvis Morton L PTS 6 Watford
16.04.84	Tony McKenzie W RSC 1 Birmingham
19.05.84	Colin Neagle L PTS 6 Bristol
05.06.84	David Irving L CO 2 Kensington
25.09.87	Eddie Brooks L PTS 6 Tooting
06.10.87	Gary Pemberton L RSC 2 Southend
11.11.87	Kevin Thompson L CO 4 Stafford
20.01.88	Martin Smith L PTS 6 Hornsey
16.05.91	Marty Duke W PTS 6 Battersea
12.11.91	Kevin Adamson L RSC 4 Milton Keynes
12.02.92	Mike Russell W PTS 6 Watford
30.04.92	Cliff Churchward L PTS 6 Watford
17.09.92	Bozon Haule DREW 6 Watford
29.04.93	Johnny Pinnock L RSC 3 Hayes
24.06.93	Nick Appiah L PTS 6 Watford

Career: 19 contests, won 6, drew 1, lost 12.

Shaun Shinkwin   Les Clark

Shaun Shinkwin

Boreham Wood. *Born* Watford, 30
November, 1962
Lightweight. Ht. 5'9½"
Manager J. Barclay

01.04.82	Billy Ruzgar L PTS 4 Walthamstow
19.04.82	Vince Vahey L PTS 4 Bristol
10.05.82	Kevin Hay W PTS 6 Copthorne
08.06.82	Eugene Maloney W PTS 4 Southend
14.06.82	Eddie Morgan L PTS 6 Mayfair
13.10.82	Joe Donohoe L PTS 6 Walthamstow
22.11.82	Allen Terry W PTS 4 Lewisham
29.11.82	Carl Gaynor W PTS 6 Southwark
06.12.82	Eddie Morgan DREW 6 Bristol
24.01.83	Steve King W RSC 5 Mayfair
31.01.83	Carl Gaynor L PTS 6 Southwark
21.02.83	Dave Pratt W PTS 6 Mayfair
09.03.83	Eddie Morgan L PTS 6 Solihull
17.03.83	Chris Harvey W PTS 6 Marylebone
16.04.83	Michael Harris L PTS 6 Bristol

12.02.92	Greg Egbuniwe L DIS 1 Watford
29.10.92	Steve Hearn W PTS 6 Hayes
30.01.93	Boby Guynan L PTS 6 Brentwood
29.04.93	Noel Henry W PTS 6 Hayes
24.06.93	Patrick Parton DREW 6 Watford

Career: 20 contests, won 10, drew 2, lost 8.

Tony Silkstone

Leeds. *Born* Leeds, 2 March, 1968
Bantamweight. Ht. 5'5"
Manager M. Duff

11.04.90	Andrew Robinson W PTS 6 Dewsbury
26.04.90	Andrew Robinson W PTS 6 Halifax
18.10.90	Kelton McKenzie W PTS 6 Dewsbury
15.11.90	Sean Casey W PTS 6 Oldham
13.12.90	Neil Smith W PTS 6 Dewsbury
21.03.91	Tony Falcone W PTS 6 Dewsbury
09.05.91	Alan Smith W PTS 6 Leeds
13.06.91	Miguel Matthews W PTS 6 Hull
01.08.91	Dave Buxton W PTS 6 Dewsbury
30.10.91	Renny Edwards W PTS 6 Leeds
08.04.92	Edward Cook W PTS 8 Leeds
23.09.92	Dave Campbell W RSC 4 Leeds
07.04.93	Dean Lynch W PTS 8 Leeds

Career: 13 contests, won 13.

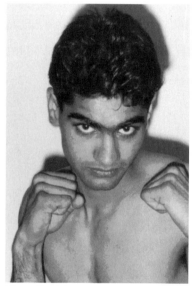

Tiger Singh   Les Clark

(Sukhdarshan) Tiger Singh (Mahal)

Peterborough. *Born* India, 28 October, 1970
Flyweight. Ht. 5'8"
Manager G. Holmes

10.12.92	Ian Baillie W PTS 6 Corby
11.05.93	Anthony Hanna L PTS 6 Norwich

Career: 2 contests, won 1, lost 1.

Colin Sinnott

Preston. *Born* Preston, 10 September, 1965
Welterweight. Ht. 5'8"
Manager M. Chapman

26.03.90	Barry North W CO 6 Nottingham
08.10.90	Rob Pitters L PTS 6 Bradford
16.10.90	Andy Robins W PTS 6 Evesham
01.11.90	David Thompson W PTS 6 Hull

10.12.90	Dean Bramhald L PTS 6 Bradford
28.01.91	Dave Kettlewell W RSC 3 Bradford
21.02.91	Trevor Meikle L PTS 6 Leeds
22.04.91	J. B. Chadwick W CO 3 Bradford
30.05.91	Mark Ramsey L PTS 6 Birmingham
08.10.91	Dean Bramhald W PTS 8 Wolverhampton
21.10.91	Dean Bramhald L PTS 6 Cleethorpes
18.11.91	Kris McAdam L PTS 6 Glasgow
23.10.92	Paul Charters L RTD 4 Gateshead
28.06.93	Frank Harrington W RSC 6 Morecambe

Career: 14 contests, won 7, lost 7.

Robbie Sivyer
Alfreton. *Born* Chesterfield, 22 September, 1973
Lightweight. Ht. 5'9"
Manager J. Gaynor

26.04.93	Garry Burrell L PTS 6 Glasgow
07.06.93	Simon Hamblett W PTS 6 Walsall
29.06.93	Mark Allen L PTS 6 Edgbaston

Career: 3 contests, won 1, lost 2.

Trevor Small
Birmingham. *Born* Solihull, 26 February, 1968
Cruiserweight. Ht. 6'0"
Manager W. Swift

09.12.92	Sean O'Phoenix W PTS 6 Stoke
20.01.93	Art Stacey W PTS 6 Solihull
28.04.93	Tony Behan W PTS 6 Solihull

Career: 3 contests, won 3.

Carl Smallwood
Atherstone. *Born* Nuneaton, 15 April, 1973
L. Heavyweight. Ht. 6'1¼"
Manager R. Gray

30.03.92	Greg Scott-Briggs W PTS 6 Coventry
28.04.92	Lee Archer W PTS 6 Wolverhampton
30.09.92	Greg Scott-Briggs W PTS 6 Solihull
14.10.92	Martin Jolley L PTS 6 Stoke
12.11.92	Richard Atkinson W PTS 6 Stafford
22.02.93	Lee Archer L PTS 8 Bedford
17.03.93	Greg Scott-Briggs W PTS 8 Stoke
17.06.93	Paul Murray W PTS 6 Bedworth

Career: 8 contests, won 6, lost 2.

Mark Smallwood
Atherstone. *Born* Nuneaton, 30 January, 1975
Middleweight. Ht. 6'2"
Manager R. Gray

22.02.93	John Dempsey W CO 1 Bedworth
17.03.93	Sean Smith W RSC 1 Stoke
10.05.93	Tim Robinson W RSC 4 Cleethorpes
17.06.93	Phil Ball W RSC 1 Bedworth

Career: 4 contests, won 4.

Alan Smiles
Edinburgh. *Born* Leith, 9 March, 1965
Cruiserweight. Ht. 6'0"
Manager A. Melrose

29.01.93	Nicky Wadman W PTS 6 Glasgow
04.03.93	Simon McDougall W PTS 6 Glasgow
29.05.93	Phil Ball W PTS 6 Paisley

Career: 3 contests, won 3.

Alan Smith
Swansea. *Born* Pembroke Dock, 15 September, 1964
Featherweight. Ht. 5'7"
Manager D. Davies

13.03.91	Mitchell Barney W PTS 6 Stoke
22.04.91	Tony Falcone W RSC 5 Mayfair
09.05.91	Tony Silkstone L PTS 6 Leeds
30.05.91	Tony Falcone L PTS 6 Mayfair
04.09.91	Eunan Devenney L CO 1 Bethnal Green
27.02.92	John White L RSC 1 Liverpool
02.07.92	Craig Dermody L RSC 3 Middleton

Career: 7 contests, won 2, lost 5.

Jacob Smith
Darlington. *Born* Darlington, 30 January, 1974
Bantamweight. Ht. 5'6¼"
Manager M. Duff

08.04.92	Andrew Bloomer W PTS 6 Leeds
28.09.92	Jason Morris W PTS 6 Manchester
07.10.92	Norman Dhalie L PTS 6 Sunderland

Career: 3 contests, won 2, lost 1.

John Smith
Liverpool. *Born* Liverpool, 13 October, 1959
L. Welterweight. Ht. 5'9"
Manager Self

26.06.86	Ray Golding W PTS 6 Edgbaston
22.09.86	John Townsley W PTS 6 Edgbaston
06.11.86	Robert Harkin L PTS 8 Glasgow
20.11.86	John Best L PTS 6 Bredbury
08.12.86	Gary Sommerville DREW 8 Edgbaston
18.03.87	John Best L RSC 2 Solihull
24.04.87	Brian Wareing L PTS 8 Liverpool
24.09.87	John Dickson L PTS 6 Glasgow
01.02.88	Peter Crook L PTS 6 Manchester
17.03.88	Mick Mason DREW 8 Sunderland
29.03.88	Paul Seddon W RSC 4 Marton
17.06.88	Gary Sommerville W RSC 5 Edgbaston
28.11.88	Gary Sommerville L PTS 8 Edgbaston
24.01.89	Mark Kelly L PTS 8 Kings Heath
22.03.89	John Davies L PTS 8 Solihull
17.07.89	Richard Adams W RSC 3 Stanmore
08.09.89	Muhammad Lovelock W PTS 6 Liverpool
14.09.89	Roy Rowland L RSC 3 Basildon
17.10.89	Jim Talbot L PTS 6 Oldham
25.10.89	Kevin Plant L PTS 6 Doncaster
10.11.89	Seamus O'Sullivan L PTS 6 Battersea
30.11.89	Dave Pierre L PTS 6 Mayfair
08.12.89	Alan Hall L RSC 2 Doncaster
29.01.90	Darren Mount L PTS 8 Liverpool
08.03.90	Dave Pierre L PTS 6 Peterborough
19.03.90	Brendan Ryan L PTS 6 Leicester
05.04.90	Darren Mount L PTS 8 Liverpool
04.05.90	Pete Roberts L PTS 6 Liverpool
24.09.90	Mark Dinnadge W RTD 2 Lewisham
09.10.90	Pete Roberts W PTS 8 Liverpool
13.11.90	Paul Charters L RSC 4 Hartlepool
21.01.91	Kris McAdam L PTS 6 Glasgow
07.02.91	Billy Schwer L PTS 6 Watford
26.03.91	Andrew Morgan L RSC 4 Wolverhampton
24.04.91	Andrew Morgan L PTS 6 Aberavon
16.05.91	Kevin Toomey L PTS 6 Liverpool
13.06.91	Kevin Toomey L PTS 6 Hull
25.07.91	Robert McCracken L RTD 1 Dudley
07.10.91	Pete Roberts L PTS 8 Liverpool
23.10.91	Dean Hollington L PTS 6 Bethnal Green
12.11.91	Mark Elliot L PTS 6 Wolverhampton
21.11.91	Richard Burton L PTS 6 Burton
02.12.91	Mike Calderwood DREW 8 Liverpool
19.12.91	Richard Burton L PTS 6 Oldham
01.02.92	George Scott L RSC 3 Birmingham
03.03.92	Paul Charters L PTS 8 Houghton le Spring
12.05.92	Ross Hale L CO 1 Crystal Palace
03.09.92	Chris Mulcahy DREW 6 Liverpool
25.09.92	Kevin McKillan L PTS 6 Liverpool
07.10.92	Alan Peacock L PTS 6 Glasgow
12.11.92	Mark Tibbs L RSC 6 Bayswater
18.03.93	Jason Rowland L PTS 6 Lewisham
29.03.93	Shea Neary L PTS 6 Liverpool

Career: 53 contests, won 8, drew 5, lost 40.

Martin Smith
Tottenham. *Born* London, 16 August, 1967
L. Middleweight. Ht. 6'0"
Manager B. Ingle

24.09.87	Tony Britland DREW 6 Crystal Palace
20.01.88	Danny Shinkwin W PTS 6 Hornsey
10.03.88	Cecil Branch W PTS 6 Croydon
13.04.88	Tony Britland W RSC 2 Gravesend
11.05.88	Simon Paul W RTD 5 Greenwich
28.05.88	Oliver Henry W PTS 6 Kensington
25.06.88	Damien Denny NC 5 Luton
16.02.89	Winston May DREW 6 Battersea
14.09.89	Brian Robinson L PTS 6 Basildon
19.10.89	Des Robinson W PTS 4 Manchester
13.11.89	Joni Nyman L PTS 8 Helsinki, Finland
25.11.89	Andre Kimbu L PTS 8 Gravelines, France
22.02.90	Robbie Harron W PTS 6 Hull
15.03.90	James Collins W PTS 6 Manchester
06.06.90	John Ogiste W RSC 2 Battersea
12.02.91	Rex Kortram W PTS 6 Rotterdam, Holland
19.03.91	Shaun Cummins DREW 8 Leicester
07.05.91	Danny Quigg W PTS 6 Glasgow
01.10.91	Mike Phillips W PTS 6 Sheffield
28.10.91	Gilbert Hallie DREW 8 Arnhem, Holland
10.01.92	Said Skouma W PTS 8 Vitrolles, France
14.04.92	Dave Owens W PTS 6 Mansfield
08.05.92	Freddie Demeulenaere DREW 8 Waregem, Belgium
24.04.93	Robert McCracken L RSC 10 Birmingham *(Final Elim. British L. Middleweight Title)*

Career: 24 contests, won 14, drew 5, lost 4, no contest 1.

Neil Smith
Leicester. *Born* Leicester, 15 January, 1972
S. Featherweight. Ht. 6'1½"
Manager Self

13.12.90	Tony Silkstone L PTS 6 Dewsbury
06.02.91	Dennis Adams L PTS 6 Bethnal Green
14.03.91	John Naylor W RSC 6 Middleton
20.05.91	Elvis Parsley W RSC 5 Leicester
11.06.91	Lee Fox W PTS 6 Leicester
05.11.91	Neil Leitch W RSC 1 Leicester
04.02.92	Harry Escott L PTS 8 Alfreton

26.01.93 Norman Dhalie W PTS 4 Leicester
03.02.93 Paul Ryan L RSC 1 Earls Court
19.05.93 Dean Amory L PTS 6 Leicester
Career: 10 contests, won 5, lost 5.

Paul Smith   Les Clark

Paul Smith

Sheffield. *Born* Sheffield, 14 July, 1960
S. Middleweight. Ht. 5'10"
Manager Self

03.10.83 David Scere L PTS 6 Liverpool
17.10.83 David Scere L PTS 6 Manchester
09.11.83 Billy Ahearne L PTS 6 Sheffield
05.12.83 Billy Ahearne DREW 8 Manchester
30.01.84 Billy Ahearne W RSC 5 Manchester
12.03.84 Mike Farghaly L PTS 8 Manchester
09.04.84 Mike Farghaly L RSC 3 Manchester
22.07.84 Malcolm Davies W RTD 4 Sheffield
11.02.85 Shamus Casey L PTS 6 Manchester
01.03.85 Gary Tomlinson L PTS 6 Mansfield
14.03.85 Tucker Watts L RSC 4 Leicester
17.04.85 Nigel Pearce W PTS 6 Nantwich
29.04.85 Robert Armstrong W RSC 6
Nottingham
13.10.85 Seb Soloman W RSC 3 Sheffield
03.12.85 Rocky McGran L PTS 6 Belfast
05.02.86 Kevin Hughes W RSC 5 Sheffield
15.02.86 Rocky McGran L PTS 6 Dublin
21.04.86 Simon Collins DREW 6 Birmingham
30.05.86 John Ashton L PTS 8 Stoke
10.09.86 Cliff Domville W DIS 2 Stoke
26.09.86 Johnny Williamson L RSC 7 Swindon
06.04.87 Shaun West W PTS 6 Leicester
30.04.87 Mickey Ould W PTS 6 Wandsworth
03.06.87 Dennis Boy O'Brien W RSC 2
Southwark
28.10.87 Ian Bayliss L RSC 3 Sheffield
(Vacant Central Area Middleweight Title)
08.03.88 Dave Thomas L PTS 6 Batley
04.04.89 Peter Mundy W RTD 1 Sheffield
29.01.91 Marty Duke W PTS 6 Wisbech
06.03.91 Benji Good L PTS 6 Croydon
19.03.91 Paul Busby L PTS 6 Leicester

16.04.91 Chris Richards DREW 6 Nottingham
29.08.91 Neville Brown L RSC 3 Oakengates
28.04.92 Andrew Flute L RSC 5
Wolverhampton
25.01.93 Stephen Wilson L RSC 1 Glasgow
09.03.93 Jerry Mortimer L PTS 6 Bristol
Career: 35 contests, won 12, drew 3, lost 20.

Scott Smith

Birmingham. *Born* Birmingham, 11 July, 1969
L. Welterweight. Ht. 5'8"
Manager N. Nobbs

09.12.92 Jonathan Thaxton L PTS 6 Stoke
11.03.93 Lee Ryan W PTS 6 Walsall
25.06.93 Cham Joof L RTD 2 Battersea
Career: 3 contests, won 1, lost 2.

Sean Smith

Hull. *Born* Hull, 5 January, 1967
Middleweight. Ht. 5'11"
Manager Self

16.10.92 Graham Wassell L RSC 2 Hull
05.02.93 Paul Wright L RSC 2 Manchester
17.03.93 Mark Smallwood L RSC 1 Stoke
Career: 3 contests, lost 3.

(Terry) T. J. Smith

Kettering. *Born* Kettering 17 October, 1967
Lightweight. Ht. 5'7½"
Manager C. Hall

29.04.92 Floyd Churchill L RSC 2 Liverpool
10.12.92 Alan Graham L PTS 6 Corby
23.02.93 Patrick Parton W PTS 6 Kettering
29.03.93 Marco Fattore DREW 6 Mayfair
19.04.93 Lee Ryan W RSC 2 Northampton
18.05.93 Dean Martin W RSC 3 Kettering
Career: 6 contest, won 3, drew 1, lost 2.

Tommy Smith

Darlington. *Born* Darlington, 18 December, 1970
S. Featherweight. Ht. 5'7"
Manager G. Robinson

10.12.90 Danny Connelly L PTS 6 Glasgow
16.02.91 Johnny Patterson W PTS 6 Thornaby
02.03.91 Colin Innes L PTS 6 Darlington
06.04.91 Paul Wynn W PTS 6 Darlington
22.10.91 Kevin Lowe W RSC 4 Hartlepool
12.12.91 Colin Innes W PTS 6 Hartlepool
28.05.92 Colin Innes W PTS 6 Gosforth
06.05.93 Paul Wynn L PTS 6 Hartlepool
Career: 8 contests, won 5, lost 3.

Tony Smith

Burnley. *Born* Burnley, 4 May, 1969
Featherweight. Ht. 5'5"
Manager N. Basso

18.05.87 Gordon Shaw L PTS 6 Glasgow
07.09.87 Gordon Shaw W PTS 6 Glasgow
14.09.87 Gordon Shaw L PTS 6 Glasgow
07.10.87 John Hales W RSC 4 Burnley
26.10.87 Wull Strike L RSC 5 Glasgow
07.12.87 Joe Mullen L RSC 6 Glasgow
25.01.88 Mark Robertson L RSC 1 Glasgow
25.04.88 John Hales W RSC 5 Nottingham
08.06.88 Gordon Shaw L PTS 6 Glasgow
18.06.88 Mark Priestley W RSC 6 Gateshead

05.09.88 Paul Dever W PTS 6 Manchester
12.09.88 Mickey Markie DREW 6 Northampton
06.10.88 Gordon Stobie W PTS 6 Manchester
29.10.88 Salvatore Fanni L RSC 1 Milan, Italy
16.01.89 Mickey Markie L RSC 2 Northampton
05.04.89 George Bailey W PTS 6 Halifax
17.04.89 Seamus Tuohy DREW 6 Middleton
18.09.89 James Drummond L RSC 1 Glasgow
30.11.89 Seamus Tuohy L PTS 6 Oldham
29.01.90 Billy Proud W PTS 6 Bradford
27.02.90 Billy Proud L RSC 2 Marton
14.05.90 Stewart Fishermac L PTS 6 Leicester
21.05.90 Stevie Woods L RSC 6 Bradford
17.10.90 Pete Buckley L PTS 6 Stoke
24.10.90 Paul Dever W PTS 8 Stoke
26.11.90 Des Gargano L PTS 8 Bury
03.12.90 Des Gargano L PTS 6 Cleethorpes
16.01.91 Des Gargano L PTS 6 Stoke
05.03.91 Neil Parry DREW 6 Leicester
18.03.91 Gary White L PTS 6 Manchester
07.05.91 Stevie Woods L RTD 2 Glasgow
10.06.91 Robert Braddock DREW 6 Manchester
20.06.91 Neil Parry L PTS 6 Liverpool
01.10.91 Des Gargano L PTS 6 Cleethorpes
28.10.91 Glyn Shepherd L PTS 6 Leicester
18.11.91 Chris Jickells L RSC 4 Manchester
01.06.92 Craig Murray L RSC 2 Manchester
19.04.93 Paul Goode DREW 6 Manchester
01.06.93 Paul Goode L PTS 6 Manchester
Career: 39 contests, won 10, drew 5, lost 24.

Michael Smyth

Barry. *Born* Caerphilly, 22 February, 1970
Welterweight. Ht. 5'9¾"
Manager D. Gardiner

02.05.91 Carl Brasier W RSC 2 Kensington
28.05.91 Rick North W RSC 1 Cardiff
18.07.91 Mike Morrison W RSC 2 Cardiff
03.09.91 Julian Eavis W PTS 6 Cardiff
20.11.91 Mike Russell W RSC 3 Cardiff
17.12.91 Julian Eavis W PTS 6 Cardiff
19.05.92 Ojay Abrahams W PTS 6 Cardiff
07.10.92 David Lake W CO 2 Barry
14.11.92 Des Robinson W PTS 6 Cardiff
Career: 9 contests, won 9.

Lee Soar

Barnsley. *Born* Barnsley, 12 October, 1970
L. Welterweight. Ht. 5'10"
Manager K. Tate

25.11.91 Mark Broome W PTS 6 Cleethorpes
28.01.92 Steve Bricknell W PTS 6 Piccadilly
14.09.92 Blue Butterworth L CO 4 Bradford
07.12.92 Mick Hoban L PTS 6 Manchester
14.12.92 Rick North L PTS 6 Cleethorpes
Career: 5 contests, won 2, lost 3.

Phil Soundy

Benfleet. *Born* Benfleet, 24 October, 1966
Cruiserweight. Ht. 5'11½"
Manager T. Lawless

04.10.89 Coco Collins W RSC 2 Basildon
24.10.89 Trevor Barry W RSC 1 Bethnal Green
14.02.90 Andy Balfe W RSC 3 Brentwood
28.03.90 Chris Coughlan W PTS 6 Bethnal
Green
22.05.90 Cliff Curtis W PTS 6 Canvey Island
06.07.90 Steve Yorath W CO 3 Brentwood
12.09.90 Rob Albon W RSC 1 Bethnal Green
03.10.90 Steve Yorath W PTS 6 Basildon
12.12.90 David Haycock W RSC 3 Kensington

Phil Soundy (left) slams into a defenceless Dean Allen, before stopping his man in the fourth   Les Clark

16.01.91	Chris Coughlan W PTS 6 Kensington
12.02.91	Gus Mendes W RSC 3 Basildon
07.03.91	Terry Duffus W RSC 2 Basildon
24.04.91	Steve Yorath L PTS 6 Basildon
11.09.91	Gus Mendes L RSC 3 Hammersmith
12.02.92	Steve Osborne W PTS 6 Wembley
22.04.92	Lee Prudden W RSC 5 Wembley
13.05.92	Tony Booth L PTS 6 Kensington
07.09.92	Dean Allen W RTD 4 Bethnal Green
28.10.92	Des Vaughan W RTD 4 Kensington

Career: 19 contests, won 16, lost 3.

Kevin Spratt

Bradford. *Born* Leeds, 22 March, 1966
Welterweight. Former Undefeated Central
Area L. Welterweight Champion. Ht. 5'6"
Manager Self

19.05.86	Wayne Goult W RSC 5 Bradford
17.06.86	Barry Bacon W PTS 6 Blackpool
04.09.86	A. M. Milton DREW 6 Merton
22.09.86	Kevin Plant W PTS 6 Bradford
06.10.86	Rocky Lester W PTS 6 Leicester
20.10.86	Kevin Plant W RSC 4 Bradford
13.11.86	Tony Banks DREW 6 Huddersfield
26.01.87	Brian Murphy W PTS 6 Bradford
10.02.87	Darren Connellan L PTS 8 Batley
06.04.87	David Bacon W PTS 6 Nottingham
27.04.87	Dean Bramhald W PTS 8 Bradford
07.06.87	Marvin P. Gray W PTS 8 Bradford
16.10.87	David Maw W PTS 8 Gateshead
15.12.87	Marvin P. Gray W RSC 6 Bradford

09.02.88	Darren Connellan W PTS 6 Bradford
10.03.88	Jim Moffat L PTS 8 Glasgow
26.04.88	Oliver Harrison W RSC 7 Bradford
12.10.88	Steve Hogg W PTS 8 Stoke
27.02.89	Calvin Meeks L RSC 3 Reseda, USA
22.05.89	David Bacon L RSC 6 Bradford
13.10.89	Peter Crook W RSC 3 Preston
	(Vacant Central Area L. Welterweight Title)
24.01.90	Mark Kelly W RSC 9 Solihull
	(Central Area L. Welterweight Title Defence)
09.05.90	Kevin Plant W PTS 10 Solihull
	(Central Area L. Welterweight Title Defence)
18.10.90	Lindon Scarlett L RSC 2 Birmingham
10.12.90	Trevor Meikle W PTS 6 Bradford
18.03.91	John Townsley W RTD 6 Glasgow
10.05.91	Paul Charters L RSC 2 Gateshead
14.09.92	Trevor Meikle L RSC 4 Bradford
14.12.92	Steve Scott W PTS 6 Bradford

Career: 29 contests, won 20, drew 2, lost 7.

(Mick) Art Stacey

Leeds. *Born* Leeds, 26 September, 1964
Cruiserweight. Ht. 6'0½"
Manager K. Tate

09.10.90	Trevor Barry DREW 6 Liverpool
06.11.90	Chris Coughlan W RSC 4 Southend
27.11.90	Allan Millett W PTS 6 Liverpool
21.02.91	Tony Lawrence W PTS 6 Leeds

18.03.91	Paul Gearon W RSC 1 Derby
16.04.91	Steve Osborne DREW 6 Nottingham
03.06.91	Dennis Afflick W PTS 6 Glasgow
11.11.91	Steve Osborne W PTS 6 Bradford
21.11.91	Gil Lewis L RSC 4 Stafford
20.01.92	John Pierre W PTS 8 Bradford
26.10.92	Ian Bulloch L PTS 6 Cleethorpes
27.11.92	Neils H. Madsen L PTS 8 Randers, Denmark
14.12.92	Albert Call L PTS 6 Cleethorpes
20.01.93	Trevor Small L PTS 6 Solihull
08.03.93	Lee Prudden DREW 6 Leeds
11.06.93	Ian Henry L PTS 6 Gateshead
25.06.93	Mark Prince L CO 2 Battersea

Career: 17 contests, won 7, drew 3, lost 7.

Warren Stephens

Birmingham. *Born* Birmingham, 18 May,
1970
L. Middleweight. Ht. 6'0"
Manager Self

04.04.92	John Duckworth L RSC 5 Cleethorpes
21.05.92	Bullit Andrews L PTS 6 Cradley Heath
30.10.92	Bullit Andrews L PTS 6 Birmingham
23.11.92	Simon Fisher W PTS 6 Coventry
07.12.92	Steve Levene L CO 2 Birmingham
18.02.93	Rob Stevenson L PTS 6 Hull
07.04.93	Ron Hopley L PTS 6 Leeds
27.05.93	John Duckworth L RSC 5 Burnley

Career: 8 contests, won 1, lost 7.

Ronnie Stephenson   Chris Bevan

Ronnie Stephenson

Doncaster. *Born* Doncaster, 18 November, 1960
Featherweight. Ht. 5'8"
Manager Self

22.01.86 Paddy Maguire W PTS 4 Stoke
10.03.86 Jamie McBride L PTS 4 Glasgow
27.04.86 Phil Lashley W PTS 4 Doncaster
03.06.86 Billy Cawley L PTS 6 Wolverhampton
15.09.86 Gerry McBride W PTS 6 Manchester
22.09.86 Bobby McDermott DREW 6 Manchester
24.11.86 Gerry McBride L PTS 8 Leicester
10.03.87 Gerry McBride L RSC 7 Manchester
  (Vacant Central Area Bantamweight Title)
06.05.87 Joe Kelly L PTS 8 Livingston
13.06.87 Chris Clarkson L PTS 8 Great Yarmouth
09.08.87 Sean Murphy L RSC 1 Windsor
14.09.87 Bobby McDermott L RSC 2 Glasgow
09.11.87 Phil Lashley DREW 4 Birmingham
24.11.87 Chris Cooper W RSC 4 Wolverhampton
14.12.87 Nigel Crook L PTS 6 Bradford
29.01.88 Chris Cooper W PTS 6 Torquay
24.02.88 Chris Cooper W PTS 6 Southend
14.03.88 Mark Goult L RSC 4 Norwich
11.04.88 Joe Mullen L PTS 8 Glasgow
25.04.88 Des Gargano L PTS 8 Bradford
14.05.88 Andre Hoeffler L PTS 6 Anderlecht, Belgium
26.05.88 Glen Dainty L RSC 6 Bethnal Green
09.09.88 Phil Lashley L PTS 6 Doncaster
19.10.88 Chris Cooper W PTS 6 Evesham
14.11.88 Mike Close L PTS 4 Stratford upon Avon
21.11.88 Des Gargano L PTS 6 Leicester
07.12.88 Mark Walker W RSC 6 Stoke
14.02.89 Alan Roberts W PTS 6 Wolverhampton
06.03.89 Mark Walker W RTD 5 Leicester
21.03.89 Miguel Matthews DREW 6 Wolverhampton
03.04.89 Robert Braddock W CO 4 Manchester

04.09.89 Des Gargano L PTS 6 Hull
10.10.89 Pete Buckley W PTS 6 Wolverhampton
13.11.89 Dave Buxton L RTD 2 Bradford
14.03.90 Pete Buckley DREW 6 Stoke
27.03.90 Phil Lashley L PTS 6 Wolverhampton
04.04.90 Pete Buckley W PTS 8 Stafford
23.04.90 Pete Buckley L PTS 6 Birmingham
21.05.90 Phil Lashley W PTS 6 Grimsby
04.06.90 Pete Buckley L PTS 8 Birmingham
03.12.90 Dave Annis L PTS 6 Cleethorpes
21.10.91 Phil Lashley W PTS 6 Cleethorpes
21.11.91 Phil Lashley W PTS 6 Stafford
02.12.91 Chris Lyons W PTS 6 Birmingham
09.12.91 Chris Lyons W PTS 6 Cleethorpes
15.01.92 Chris Jickells W PTS 6 Stoke
30.03.92 Mark Hargreaves W PTS 6 Coventry
25.07.92 John White L PTS 6 Manchester
29.05.93 Shaun Anderson L PTS 6 Paisley
Career: 49 contests, won 20, drew 4, lost 25.

Rob Stevenson   Chris Bevan

Rob Stevenson

Hull. *Born* Hull, 16 March, 1971
L. Middleweight. Ht. 5'9"
Manager M. Toomey

28.11.91 Matt Mowatt L PTS 6 Hull
26.03.92 Steve Scott W PTS 6 Hull
04.04.92 Chris Mulcahy L PTS 8 Cleethorpes
29.04.92 Alan Williams W PTS 6 Liverpool
01.06.92 Chris Mulcahy L PTS 6 Manchester
13.10.92 Dean Hiscox L PTS 6 Wolverhampton
26.11.92 Steve Scott L PTS 6 Hull
18.02.93 Warren Stephens W PTS 6 Hull
25.02.93 Ron Hopley DREW 6 Bradford
29.04.93 Billy McDougall DREW 6 Hull
Career: 10 contests, won 3, drew 2, lost 5.

Rob Stewart

Darwen. *Born* Blackburn, 17 January, 1965
L. Welterweight. Ht. 5'8¼"
Manager J. McMillan

14.10.91 Gary Pagden W PTS 6 Manchester
21.10.91 Ricky Sackfield W PTS 6 Bury
04.12.91 Dean Carr W RTD 5 Stoke

21.01.92 Chris Aston W RSC 4 Stockport
24.02.92 Tony Banks DREW 6 Bradford
04.03.92 Alan Peacock DREW 8 Glasgow
31.03.92 Mike Calderwood W PTS 4 Stockport
24.09.92 Richard Burton L PTS 10 Stockport
  (Central Area L. Welterweight Title Challenge)
25.02.93 Alan Ingle W PTS 6 Burnley
29.03.93 Peter Bradley L RSC 5 Glasgow
29.05.93 Alan McDowall DREW 6 Paisley
Career: 11 contests, won 6, drew 3, lost 2.

Steve Stewart

Clapham. *Born* Luton, 10 August, 1967
Heavyweight. Ht. 6'5"
Manager M. Hill

17.02.92 Damien Caesar L RSC 5 Mayfair
30.03.92 Wayne Llewelyn L RSC 4 Eltham
08.09.92 Graham Arnold W RSC 3 Norwich
03.02.93 Dermot Gascoyne L RSC 4 Earls Court
Career: 4 contests, won 1, lost 3.

Bradley Stone

Canning Town. *Born* Mile End, 27 May, 1970
Featherweight. Ht. 5'5¾"
Manager M. Duff

06.03.90 Des Gargano W PTS 6 Bethnal Green
28.03.90 Stevie Woods W RSC 2 Bethnal Green
14.04.90 Kruga Hydes W PTS 6 Kensington
29.05.90 Gary Hickman DREW 6 Bethnal Green
10.07.90 Andrew Robinson W PTS 6 Canvey Island
10.10.90 Gary Jones W RSC 3 Millwall
12.02.91 Stewart Fishermac W PTS 6 Basildon
07.03.91 Miguel Matthews W RSC 4 Basildon
25.04.91 Miguel Matthews W PTS 6 Basildon
02.10.91 Andrew Bloomer W PTS 6 Barking
02.04.92 Colin Lynch W RSC 3 Basildon
16.05.92 Andrew Bloomer W PTS 6 Muswell Hill
15.10.92 Kevin Middleton W PTS 6 Lewisham
03.12.92 Norman Dhalie W CO 4 Lewisham
24.02.93 Chris Clarkson W PTS 8 Wembley
26.04.93 Pete Buckley W PTS 8 Lewisham
09.06.93 Colin Lynch W RTD 1 Lewisham
Career: 17 contests, won 16, drew 1.

Sammy Storey

Belfast. *Born* Belfast, 9 August, 1963
Former British S. Middleweight Champion.
Former All-Ireland Middleweight Champion. Ht. 6'0"
Manager Self

03.12.85 Nigel Shingles W RSC 6 Belfast
05.02.86 Sean O'Phoenix W PTS 6 Sheffield
22.04.86 Karl Barwise W PTS 6 Belfast
29.10.86 Jimmy Ellis W RSC 5 Belfast
25.04.87 Rocky McGran W PTS 10 Belfast
  (Vacant All-Ireland Middleweight Title)
19.10.87 Shamus Casey W PTS 6 Belfast
05.12.87 Paul Mitchell W PTS 6 Doncaster
27.01.88 Steve Foster W RSC 4 Belfast
18.03.88 Steve Collins L PTS 10 Boston, USA
  (All-Ireland Middleweight Title Defence)
19.10.88 Tony Lawrence W RSC 3 Belfast
07.12.88 Darren Hobson W RSC 6 Belfast
25.01.89 Abdul Amoru Sanda W RSC 8 Belfast

08.03.89　Kevin Roper W RSC 3 Belfast
19.09.89　Tony Burke W PTS 12 Belfast
　　　　　(Vacant British S. Middleweight Title)
29.11.89　Noel Magee W RSC 9 Belfast
　　　　　(British S. Middleweight Title Defence)
17.03.90　Simon Collins W CO 7 Belfast
30.10.90　James Cook L RSC 10 Belfast
　　　　　(British S. Middleweight Title Defence)
31.05.91　Saldi Ali L PTS 8 Berlin, Germany
07.09.91　Johnny Melfah W PTS 8 Belfast
13.11.91　Karl Barwise W PTS 6 Belfast
25.04.92　Nigel Rafferty W RSC 3 Belfast
03.02.93　Graham Jenner W RSC 4 Earls Court
28.04.93　Carlos Christie W RSC 8 Dublin
Career: 23 contests, won 20, lost 3.

Warren Stowe
Burnley. *Born* Burnley, 30 January, 1965
Central Area L. Middleweight Champion.
Ht. 5'8"
Manager J. Doughty

21.10.91　Matt Mowatt W RSC 3 Bury
07.12.91　Griff Jones W RSC 6 Manchester
03.02.92　Robert Peel W PTS 6 Manchester
10.03.92　B. K. Bennett W PTS 6 Bury
25.04.92　David Radford W RSC 3 Manchester
04.06.92　Rob Pitters W PTS 8 Burnley
25.07.92　Shamus Casey W CO 2 Manchester
24.09.92　Mike Phillips W RSC 1 Stockport
12.11.92　Steve Thomas W RSC 1 Burnley
28.11.92　Julian Eavis W RSC 6 Manchester
25.02.93　Robert Riley W DIS 4 Burnley
　　　　　(Vacant Central Area L. Middleweight
　　　　　Title)
22.04.93　Leigh Wicks W PTS 6 Bury
27.05.93　Peter Waudby W PTS 6 Burnley
Career: 13 contests, won 13.

John Stronach
Keighley. *Born* Middlesbrough, 14
October, 1969
Welterweight. Ht. 5'10"
Manager J. Celebanski

26.04.93　Steve Scott W PTS 6 Bradford
Career: 1 contest, won 1.

Ian Strudwick
Hockley. *Born* Orsett, 1 April, 1964
Middleweight. Former Southern Area
Middleweight Champion. Ht. 5'10½"
Manager Self

26.10.88　Newton Barnett W PTS 6 Kensington
29.11.88　Mark Howell W PTS 6 Kensington
24.01.89　Chris Richards W PTS 6 Wandsworth
05.04.89　Tony Behan W PTS 6 Kensington
16.05.89　Tony Behan W PTS 8 Wandsworth
28.06.89　Robert Armstrong W CO 1 Brentwood
06.07.89　Spencer Alton W PTS 4 Chigwell
05.12.89　Paul Wesley W PTS 6 Catford
14.02.90　Thomas Covington W PTS 8
　　　　　Brentwood
14.04.90　Val Golding W PTS 6 Kensington
20.06.90　Errol Christie W PTS 8 Basildon
25.10.90　Tony Burke L PTS 10 Bayswater
　　　　　(Southern Area Middleweight Title
　　　　　Challenge)
29.11.90　Stan King L RSC 2 Bayswater
03.04.91　Stan King W RSC 8 Bethnal Green
24.09.91　Fidel Castro L RSC 6 Basildon
　　　　　(Vacant British S. Middleweight Title)

11.12.91　Ray Webb W CO 8 Basildon
　　　　　(Vacant Southern Area S.
　　　　　Middleweight Title)
11.03.92　Ali Forbes W PTS 10 Solihull
　　　　　(Southern Area S. Middleweight Title
　　　　　Defence)
23.05.92　Chris Pyatt L PTS 10 Birmingham
29.10.92　Paul Wesley L RSC 1 Bayswater
20.02.93　Steve Collins L RSC 7 Earls Court
23.06.93　W. O. Wilson L RSC 8 Edmonton
　　　　　(Southern Area Middleweight Title
　　　　　Challenge)

Career: 21 contests, won 14, lost 7.

David Sumner
Preston. *Born* Preston, 24 August, 1964
L. Middleweight. Ht. 5'8¾"
Manager M. Chapman

24.05.93　Raziq Ali L PTS 6 Bradford
08.06.93　Dennis Berry L PTS 6 Derby
Career: 2 contests, lost 2.

Neil Swain
Gilfach Goch. *Born* Pontypridd, 4
September, 1971
Flyweight. Ht. 5'5"
Manager D. Gardiner

29.04.93　Vince Feeney W PTS 6 Mayfair
27.05.93　Marcus Duncan W PTS 6 Burnley
Career: 2 contests, won 2.

Richard Swallow
Northampton. *Born* Northampton, 10
February, 1970
L. Welterweight. Ht. 5'8"
Manager R. Gray

15.10.90　Richard O'Brien L RTD 1 Kettering
14.02.91　Dave Fallon W RSC 4 Southampton
06.03.91　Carl Brasier W PTS 6 Croydon
02.05.91　Mike Morrison W PTS 6 Northampton
24.03.92　Dean Bramhald W PTS 8
　　　　　Wolverhampton
06.04.92　Dean Bramhald W PTS 6 Northampton
29.04.92　Chris Aston W RSC 3 Solihull
14.10.92　Wayne Shepherd W PTS 8 Stoke
24.11.92　Chris Mulcahy W PTS 6
　　　　　Wolverhampton
20.01.93　Ray Newby W PTS 8 Solihull
03.03.93　Ray Newby L PTS 8 Solihull
11.06.93　Soren Sondergaard L RTD 3 Randers,
　　　　　Denmark

Career: 12 contests, won 9, lost 3.

Tony Swift
Birmingham. *Born* Solihull, 29 June, 1968
Welterweight. Ht. 5'10"
Manager W. Swift

25.09.86　Barry Bacon W PTS 6 Wolverhampton
06.10.86　Wil Halliday W PTS 6 Birmingham
23.10.86　Patrick Loftus W PTS 6 Birmingham
26.11.86　Adam Muir W PTS 6 Wolverhampton
08.12.86　George Baigrie W PTS 6 Birmingham
26.01.87　Dean Bramhald W PTS 8 Birmingham
04.03.87　Dean Bramhald W RSC 5 Dudley
25.03.87　Peter Bowen W PTS 8 Stafford
22.06.87　Peter Bowen W PTS 8 Stafford
07.10.87　Dean Bramhald W PTS 8 Stoke
19.10.87　Kevin Plant W PTS 8 Birmingham

02.12.87　Dean Bramhald W PTS 8 Stoke
16.03.88　Ron Shinkwin W PTS 8 Solihull
04.05.88　Kevin Plant DREW 8 Solihull
28.09.88　Kevin Plant DREW 8 Solihull
23.11.88　Lenny Gloster L PTS 8 Solihull
12.06.89　Humphrey Harrison W PTS 8
　　　　　Manchester
28.11.89　Seamus O'Sullivan W RSC 1 Battersea
16.02.90　Ramses Evilio W PTS 6 Bilbao, Spain
30.05.90　Darren Mount W PTS 8 Stoke
05.09.90　Glyn Rhodes L RSC 7 Stoke
25.10.90　Jimmy Harrison L PTS 8 Battersea
19.04.91　Gary Barron DREW 8 Peterborough
12.11.91　Carlos Chase W PTS 6 Milton Keynes
03.03.92　Steve McGovern W RSC 4 Cradley
　　　　　Heath
10.04.92　Willie Beattie W PTS 10 Glasgow
　　　　　(Elim. British Welterweight Title)
29.09.92　Nigel Bradley W PTS 8 Stoke
Career: 27 contests, won 21, drew 3, lost 3.

Wally Swift Jnr
Birmingham. *Born* Nottingham, 17
February, 1966
Former British L. Middleweight Champion.
Former Undefeated Midlands Area L.
Middleweight Champion. Ht. 5'7"
Manager W. Swift

25.09.85　John Conlan W RTD 3 Stoke
11.11.85　Steve Craggs W RTD 4 Birmingham
09.12.85　Steve Tempro W RSC 4 Birmingham
22.01.86　Teddy Anderson W RSC 6 Solihull
03.02.86　Frankie Lake W PTS 8 Birmingham
24.03.86　Paul Cook W PTS 8 Mayfair
02.06.86　Gerry Beard W PTS 8 Mayfair
08.09.86　Steve Ellwood W PTS 8 Dulwich
13.10.86　Dean Barclay DREW 8 Dulwich
19.11.86　Franki Moro W PTS 8 Solihull
03.12.86　Ian Chantler W PTS 8 Stoke
22.01.87　Dave Dent L PTS 8 Bethnal Green
10.02.87　Granville Allen W RSC 4
　　　　　Wolverhampton
24.02.87　Dave McCabe L PTS 8 Glasgow
30.03.87　John Ashton W PTS 8 Birmingham
20.10.87　John Ashton L PTS 8 Stoke
20.01.88　Tommy McCallum W PTS 8 Solihull
28.03.88　Ossie Maddix L PTS 8 Stoke
04.05.88　Chris Blake W PTS 8 Solihull
28.09.88　Terry Magee L PTS 8 Solihull
25.01.89　Kevin Hayde W PTS 8 Solihull
01.03.89　Andy Till L PTS 8 Bethnal Green
13.03.89　Tony Britton W PTS 8 Mayfair
08.04.89　Alfonso Redondo W PTS 8 Madrid,
　　　　　Spain
19.08.89　Suzuki Miranda W PTS 6 Benidorm,
　　　　　Spain
26.09.89　Ensley Bingham L PTS 10 Oldham
　　　　　(Elim. British L. Middleweight Title)
26.04.90　Shaun Cummins W PTS 10 Merthyr
　　　　　(Vacant Midlands Area L.
　　　　　Middleweight Title & Elim. British L.
　　　　　Middleweight Title)
18.09.90　Mark Holden W RSC 3 Stoke
21.11.90　Alan Richards L PTS 8 Solihull
23.01.91　Paul Wesley W PTS 10 Solihull
　　　　　(Midlands Area L. Middleweight Title
　　　　　Defence)
19.03.91　Ensley Bingham W RSC 4 Birmingham
　　　　　(Vacant British L. Middlweight Title)
03.07.91　Tony Collins W PTS 12 Reading
　　　　　(British L. Middleweight Title Defence)
08.01.92　Randy Williams W PTS 10 Burton

18.04.92	Jean-Claude Fontana L PTS 12 Hyeres, France
	(European L. Middleweight Title Challenge)
17.09.92	Andy Till L PTS 12 Watford
	(British L. Middleweight Title Defence)
14.04.93	Andy Till L RSC 4 Kensington
	(British L. Middleweight Title Challenge)

Career: 36 contests, won 25, drew 1, lost 10.

Cliff Taylor

Wheatley Hill. *Born* Hartlepool, 13 October, 1961
S. Middleweight. Ht. 6'0"
Manager G. Robinson

01.12.92	Graham Wassell L PTS 6 Hartlepool
18.02.93	Ian Vokes W PTS 6 Hull
09.03.93	Gypsy Johnny Price L RSC 6 Hartlepool

Career: 3 contests, won 1, lost 2.

Karl Taylor   Les Clark

Karl Taylor

Birmingham. *Born* Birmingham, 5 January, 1966
Lightweight. Ht. 5'5"
Manager Self

18.03.87	Steve Brown W PTS 6 Stoke
06.04.87	Paul Taylor L PTS 6 Southampton
12.06.87	Mark Begley W RSC 1 Leamington
18.11.87	Colin Lynch W RSC 4 Solihull
29.02.88	Peter Bradley L PTS 8 Birmingham
04.10.89	Mark Antony W CO 2 Stafford
30.10.89	Tony Feliciello L PTS 8 Birmingham
06.12.89	John Davison L PTS 8 Leicester
23.12.89	Regilio Tuur L RSC 2 Hoogvliet, Holland
22.02.90	Mark Ramsey L RSC 4 Hull
29.10.90	Steve Walker DREW 6 Birmingham
10.12.90	Elvis Parsley L PTS 6 Birmingham
16.01.91	Wayne Windle W PTS 8 Stoke
02.05.91	Billy Schwer L RSC 2 Northampton

25.07.91	Peter Till L RSC 4 Dudley
	(Midlands Area Lightweight Title Challenge)
24.02.92	Charlie Kane L PTS 8 Glasgow
28.04.92	Richard Woolgar W PTS 6 Wolverhampton
29.05.92	Alan McDowall L PTS 6 Glasgow
25.07.92	Michael Armstrong L RSC 3 Manchester
02.11.92	Hugh Forde L PTS 6 Wolverhampton
23.11.92	Dave McHale L PTS 8 Glasgow
22.12.92	Patrick Gallagher L RSC 3 Mayfair
13.02.93	Craig Dermody L RSC 5 Manchester
31.03.93	Craig Dermody W PTS 6 Barking
07.06.93	Mark Geraghty W PTS 8 Glasgow

Career: 25 contests, won 8, drew 1, lost 16.

Lee Taylor

Cardiff. *Born* Haverfordwest, 8 September, 1973
L. Welterweight. Ht. 5'7"
Manager W. Aird

14.12.92	Vaughan Carnegie L RSC 2 Cardiff

Career: 1 contest, lost 1.

Jonathan Thaxton

Norwich. *Born* Norwich, 10 September, 1974
L. Welterweight. Ht. 5'6"
Manager B. Ingle

09.12.92	Scott Smith W PTS 6 Stoke
03.03.93	Dean Hiscox W PTS 6 Solihull
17.03.93	John O'Johnson W PTS 6 Stoke
23.06.93	Brian Coleman W PTS 8 Gorleston

Career: 4 contests, won 4.

Ian Thomas

Leeds. *Born* Leeds, 31 March, 1966
Welterweight. Ht. 5'11"
Manager T. Miller

03.06.89	Dave Whittle L PTS 6 Stanley
19.06.89	Ernie Loveridge DREW 6 Manchester
21.10.89	Mark Jay W RSC 5 Middlesbrough
06.11.89	Trevor Meikle L PTS 6 Northampton
13.11.89	Jim Conley W RSC 5 Bradford
20.11.89	Chris Mulcahy L PTS 6 Leicester
13.12.89	Dave Whittle L PTS 6 Kirkby
19.02.90	Trevor Ambrose W RSC 3 Kettering
10.09.90	Mickey Costello W PTS 6 Northampton
25.02.93	Blue Butterworth L PTS 6 Burnley
27.02.93	Paul King L PTS 6 Marton

Career: 11 contests, won 4, drew 1, lost 6.

Steve Thomas

Merthyr. *Born* Merthyr, 13 June, 1970
Middleweight. Ht. 6'0"
Manager D. Gardiner

21.10.91	Jerry Mortimer W PTS 6 Mayfair
04.11.91	Andy Manning W PTS 6 Merthyr
02.03.92	Robert Peel DREW 6 Merthyr
08.04.92	Charlie Moore L RSC 3 Leeds
11.05.92	Robert Peel W PTS 6 Llanelli
07.10.92	Ray Price L PTS 6 Barry
15.10.92	Clay O'Shea L PTS 6 Lewisham
12.11.92	Warren Stowe L RSC 1 Burnley
19.01.93	Matthew Turner L PTS 6 Cardiff
06.02.93	Mike Phillips DREW 6 Cardiff
06.03.93	Willie Quinn L RSC 4 Glasgow

Steve Thomas   Les Clark

10.04.93	Darren Pullman DREW 6 Swansea
24.04.93	Andrew Flute L RSC 1 Birmingham

Career: 13 contests, won 3, drew 3, lost 7.

David Thompson

Hull. *Born* Hull, 14 March, 1969
L. Welterweight. Ht. 5'8"
Manager M. Toomey

26.03.90	Mark Conley W PTS 4 Bradford
09.04.90	Andy Rowbotham W PTS 6 Manchester
26.04.90	Andy Rowbotham DREW 6 Manchester
21.05.90	Johnny Walker L CO 1 Bradford
01.11.90	Colin Sinnott L PTS 6 Hull
16.11.90	Carl Tilley L CO 1 Telford
17.12.90	Eddie King W PTS 6 Manchester
18.02.91	Barry North W PTS 6 Birmingham
25.02.91	Steve Winstanley W RTD 4 Bradford
28.03.91	Shane Sheridan L CO 5 Alfreton
17.05.91	Jason Brattley DREW 6 Bury
13.06.91	James Jiora DREW 6 Hull
30.06.91	Nicky Lucas W PTS 6 Southwark
25.07.91	Shaun Cogan L CO 1 Dudley
13.11.91	Mark Tibbs L PTS 6 Bethnal Green
28.11.91	Kevin Toomey L PTS 6 Hull
09.12.91	Chris Aston L PTS 6 Bradford
21.01.92	Ricky Sackfield L CO 1 Stockport
30.03.92	Jason Brattley L PTS 6 Bradford
26.03.93	Tanver Ahmed L PTS 6 Glasgow

Career: 20 contests, won 6, drew 3, lost 11.

Kevin Thompson

Birmingham. *Born* Wolverhampton, 11 February, 1967
Welterweight. Ht. 6'0"
Manager Self

09.04.87	Roy Horn W PTS 6 Piccadilly
13.10.87	Eddie Collins W CO 1 Wolverhampton
26.10.87	Dusty Miller W PTS 4 Piccadilly
11.11.87	Danny Shinkwin W CO 4 Stafford
09.12.87	Wil Halliday W PTS 6 Evesham
12.01.88	Frank McCord W RSC 6 Cardiff

09.03.88	Robert Armstrong W RSC 6 Stoke
15.09.89	Mickey Lloyd L CO 7 High Wycombe
02.12.89	Patrick Vungbo L PTS 8 Brussels, Belgium
13.02.90	Julian Eavis W PTS 8 Wolverhampton
14.02.91	Leigh Wicks L PTS 8 Southampton
04.12.92	Mickey Lerwill W PTS 6 Telford

Career: 12 contests, won 9, lost 3.

Gary Thornhill

Liverpool. *Born* Liverpool, 11 February, 1968
S. Featherweight. Ht. 5'6½"
Manager S. Vaughan

27.02.93	Brian Hickey W CO 4 Ellesmere Port

Career: 1 contest, won 1.

Jimmy Thornton

Sheffield. *Born* Sheffield, 22 September, 1964
Middleweight. Ht. 5'8"
Manager Self

25.11.82	Stuart Carmichael W PTS 6 Morley
14.12.82	Seamus McGuinness L PTS 6 Belfast
09.05.83	Edward Lloyd W RSC 1 Manchester
12.05.83	Colin Roscoe W RSC 2 Morley
23.05.83	Peter Flanagan W RSC 3 Sheffield
13.06.83	Gary Williams W RTD 5 Doncaster
12.09.83	Lee Halford L PTS 8 Leicester
29.02.84	Ray Murray W PTS 6 Sheffield
12.03.84	Lenny Gloster L PTS 6 Manchester
09.04.84	Dave Haggarty L PTS 8 Glasgow
06.06.84	Peter Bowen W PTS 6 Sheffield
22.07.84	Peter Bowen W RSC 2 Sheffield
25.10.84	Dan Myers W PTS 6 Birmingham
26.11.84	Ron Shinkwin W RSC 2 Sheffield
10.12.84	Ray Murray W RSC 4 Nottingham
04.02.85	Steve Tempro W RSC 4 Birmingham
20.03.85	Mickey Bird W PTS 6 Stoke
10.04.85	Ricky Richards L PTS 6 Leeds
31.05.85	Rocky Feliciello L PTS 8 Liverpool
24.03.87	Kelvin Mortimer W PTS 6 Nottingham
13.04.87	Peter Ashcroft L PTS 6 Manchester
12.05.87	Tony Ekubia L PTS 6 Alfreton
09.08.87	George Collins L PTS 6 Windsor
03.12.87	Andy Holligan L RTD 2 Belfast
09.03.88	Damien Denny L PTS 8 Bethnal Green
12.04.88	Tony Ekubia L RSC 5 Oldham
09.08.88	Del Bryan L PTS 6 St Helier
26.09.88	Errol McDonald L RTD 2 Piccadilly
07.12.88	Paul Jones L PTS 6 Stoke
06.03.89	Dave Andrews L PTS 6 Northampton
21.04.89	Roy Callaghan W RSC 3 Bethnal Green
19.05.89	Ray Taylor L PTS 8 Gateshead
06.07.89	Jim Beckett L PTS 8 Chigwell
12.10.89	Gary Logan L PTS 6 Southwark
29.01.90	Tony Baker W PTS 6 Bradford
22.11.90	Shamus Casey L PTS 6 Ilkeston
13.02.91	Neville Brown L RSC 1 Wembley
02.03.92	Dave Whittle W PTS 6 Marton
02.07.92	Delroy Waul L RSC 6 Middleton
04.05.93	Andreas Panayi L CO 2 Liverpool

Career: 40 contests, won 17, lost 23.

Barry Thorogood

Cardiff. *Born* Cardiff, 1 December, 1972
L. Middleweight. Ht. 6'0"
Manager W. Aird

28.10.92	Robert Peel W PTS 6 Cardiff

14.12.92	James Campbell W RSC 4 Cardiff
27.01.93	Russell Washer W PTS 6 Cardiff
24.03.93	Darren McInulty W PTS 6 Cardiff
28.04.93	Stuart Dunn L RSC 2 Solihull

Career: 5 contests, won 4, lost 1.

Mark Tibbs

West Ham. *Born* London, 7 May, 1969
Lightweight. Ht. 5'10"
Manager B. Hearn

15.11.88	Mike Chapman W PTS 6 Norwich
23.11.88	Shane Tonks W PTS 6 Bethnal Green
14.12.88	G. G. Corbett W PTS 6 Bethnal Green
25.01.89	Mick Mulcahy W CO 1 Bethnal Green
15.02.89	Jamie Hind W RSC 1 Bethnal Green
05.04.89	Steve Taggart W CO 1 Kensington
17.05.89	Mark Antony W PTS 6 Millwall
19.09.89	Hugh Ruse W RSC 3 Millwall
11.10.89	Dave Croft W RSC 5 Millwall
20.02.90	Mark Fairman W CO 2 Millwall
25.04.90	Eddie King W CO 1 Millwall
25.09.90	Mike Morrison W PTS 6 Millwall
06.03.91	Mike Morrison W RSC 4 Wembley
06.06.91	Chris Saunders L RSC 6 Barking
23.10.91	Rick Bushell W RSC 4 Bethnal Green
13.11.91	David Thompson W PTS 6 Bethnal Green
11.12.91	Rick Bushell W RSC 2 Basildon
25.03.92	Felix Kelly DREW 8 Dagenham
12.11.92	John Smith W RSC 6 Bayswater
12.12.92	Dean Bramhald W PTS 6 Muswell Hill
20.02.93	Mark Pearce W PTS 6 Earls Court
06.03.93	Jimmy Vincent L PTS 6 Glasgow
26.06.93	Gary Hiscox W RSC 4 Earls Court

Career: 23 contests, won 20, drew 1, lost 2.

Peter Till

Walsall. *Born* Walsall, 19 August, 1963
L. Welterweight. Midlands Area
Lightweight Champion. Ht. 5'6"
Manager Self

25.04.85	Clinton Campbell W CO 1 Wolverhampton
23.05.85	J. J. Mudd W PTS 6 Dudley
17.10.85	Patrick Loftus W PTS 6 Leicester
14.11.85	Paul Wetter W RSC 3 Dudley
27.01.86	George Jones W PTS 8 Dudley
17.04.86	Tyrell Wilson W CO 5 Wolverhampton
15.05.86	Les Remikie W PTS 6 Dudley
03.06.86	Ray Newby L PTS 10 Wolverhampton *(Vacant Midlands Area Lightweight Title)*
25.09.86	Gerry Beard DREW 8 Wolverhampton
26.11.86	Gerry Beard W CO 4 Wolverhampton
28.01.87	George Baigrie W PTS 8 Dudley
04.03.87	Carl Merrett W PTS 8 Dudley
30.03.87	Tony Richards L PTS 8 Birmingham
19.07.87	Aladin Stevens L CO 4 Johannesburg, South Africa
19.10.87	Dean Bramhald W PTS 8 Birmingham
24.11.87	Dean Bramhald W PTS 8 Wolverhampton
07.02.88	Michael Marsden W CO 1 Stafford
24.02.88	Neil Haddock W PTS 8 Aberavon
13.04.88	Sugar Gibiliru W PTS 8 Wolverhampton
14.06.88	Ray Newby W PTS 10 Dudley *(Midlands Area Lightweight Title Challenge)*
22.09.88	Jim Moffat W RSC 4 Wolverhampton

10.11.88	George Jones W RSC 8 Wolverhampton *(Midlands Area Lightweight Title Defence)*
02.02.89	Camel Touati W RSC 3 Wolverhampton
13.04.89	Phillipe Binante W RSC 3 Wolverhampton
21.12.89	Tony Richards L CO 8 Kings Heath
18.10.90	Nick Hall W PTS 6 Birmingham
30.11.90	Ray Newby W PTS 8 Birmingham
21.02.91	Paul Charters L RSC 6 Walsall
31.05.91	Valery Kayumba L RSC 3 Grenoble, France
25.07.91	Karl Taylor W RSC 4 Dudley *(Midlands Area Lightweight Title Defence)*
21.09.91	Michael Ayers L RSC 5 Tottenham *(Elim. British Lightweight Title)*
09.12.91	Scott Doyle W CO 3 Brierley Hill
01.02.92	Michael Driscoll L RSC 3 Birmingham
17.03.92	Mark Reefer W RSC 3 Mayfair
04.06.92	Racheed Lawal L RSC 1 Randers, Denmark
15.08.92	Dingaan Thobela L RSC 9 Springs, South Africa
16.02.93	Errol McDonald L PTS 8 Tooting
26.05.93	Mark McCreath L PTS 8 Mansfield

Career: 38 contests, won 25, drew 1, lost 12.

Carl Tilley　　　　　　　　Les Clark

Carl Tilley

Doncaster. *Born* Doncaster, 4 October, 1967
Lightweight. Ht. 5'6½"
Manager Self

04.09.90	Stuart Good W RSC 5 Southend
16.11.90	David Thompson W CO 1 Telford
13.05.91	Steve Winstanley W RTD 4 Marton
09.10.91	Bobby Beckles W RSC 4 Marton
02.03.92	James Jiora W PTS 6 Marton
30.04.92	Greg Egbuniwe L PTS 6 Kensington
15.09.92	Joey Moffat L PTS 6 Liverpool

Career: 7 contests, won 5, lost 2.

Nick Tooley
Teignmouth. *Born* Exeter, 19 December, 1970
Flyweight. Ht. 5'2"
Manager J. Gaynor

26.10.92	Louis Veitch W PTS 6 Cleethorpes
19.11.92	Anthony Hanna W PTS 6 Evesham
17.02.93	Rowan Williams L PTS 4 Bethnal Green

Career: 3 contests, won 2, lost 1.

Kevin Toomey   Chris Bevan

Kevin Toomey
Hull. *Born* Hull, 19 September, 1967
Central Area Lightweight Champion. Ht. 5'9"
Manager M. Toomey

24.04.89	Chris Mulcahy L PTS 6 Bradford
04.09.89	Andy Rowbotham W RSC 1 Grimsby
03.10.89	Mick Mulcahy L CO 5 Cottingham
01.11.90	Joel Forbes W PTS 6 Hull
12.12.90	Andy Kent DREW 6 Leicester
24.01.91	Barry North W PTS 6 Brierley Hill
18.02.91	Andy Kent L RSC 5 Derby
22.04.91	Trevor Royal W PTS 6 Bradford
16.05.91	John Smith W PTS 6 Liverpool
13.06.91	John Smith W PTS 6 Hull
30.09.91	Mike Calderwood L RSC 2 Liverpool
28.11.91	David Thompson W PTS 6 Hull
10.12.91	Wayne Windle L PTS 6 Sheffield
04.02.92	G. G. Goddard W PTS 6 Alfreton
26.03.92	Wayne Windle W DIS 8 Hull
	(Central Area Lightweight Title Challenge)
11.09.92	Dave Anderson L PTS 8 Glasgow
16.10.92	Steve Pollard W RSC 7 Hull
26.11.92	Dean Bramhald L PTS 10 Hull
	(Central Area Lightweight Title Defence)
18.02.93	Dean Bramhald W PTS 10 Hull
	(Central Area Lightweight Title Challenge)

29.04.93	Norman Dhalie W PTS 6 Hull
28.05.93	Phil Holliday L RSC 2 Johannesburg, South Africa

Career: 21 contests, won 12, drew 1, lost 8.

Nicky Towns
Kettering. *Born* Kettering, 23 May, 1970
Lightweight. Ht. 5'8"
Manager C. Hogben

18.05.93	Bruce Ruegg W PTS 6 Kettering

Career: 1 contest, won 1.

Tony Trimble
Middlesbrough. *Born* Middlesbrough, 20 March, 1960
L. Middleweight. Ht. 5'9¾"
Manager T. Callighan

19.10.92	Allan Grainger L PTS 6 Glasgow
01.12.92	Mark Cichocki L PTS 6 Hartlepool
25.02.93	John Duckworth L PTS 6 Burnley
26.04.93	Paul Braxton W RSC 2 Cleethorpes
01.06.93	Chris Mulcahy W PTS 6 Manchester
11.06.93	Mark Jay L RSC 1 Gateshead

Career: 6 contests, won 2, lost 4.

Leo Turner
Bradford. *Born* Bradford, 17 September, 1970
S. Featherweight. Ht. 5'9"
Manager J. Celebanski

08.06.92	Wayne Rigby L PTS 6 Bradford
02.07.92	Wayne Rigby L CO 5 Middleton
12.10.92	Micky Hall L RSC 5 Bradford
14.12.92	Fred Reeve W RSC 2 Bradford
25.01.93	Alan Graham L PTS 6 Bradford

Career: 5 contests, won 1, lost 4.

Matthew Turner
Rhoose. *Born* Cardiff, 20 September, 1968
L. Middleweight. Ht. 5'9"
Manager B. Hearn

19.01.93	Steve Thomas W PTS 6 Cardiff
30.03.93	Mark Dawson W PTS 6 Cardiff
19.05.93	Stuart Dunn L RSC 3 Leicester

Career: 3 contests, won 2, lost 1.

Jimmy Tyers
Spennymoor. *Born* Bishop Auckland, 23 March, 1967
L. Heavyweight. Ht. 6'0"
Manager T. Callighan

19.04.93	Mark Buck W RSC 4 Manchester
12.05.93	Kevin Bailey W PTS 6 Sheffield

Career: 2 contests, won 2.

Johnny Uphill
Hastings. *Born* Welling, 27 January, 1967
L. Heavyweight. Ht. 6'2"
Manager D. Harris

07.03.88	Keith Butler W RSC 1 Hove
26.04.88	Tony Lawrence L RSC 5 Hove
25.05.88	Benny Simmons W PTS 6 Hastings
04.04.91	Kevin Morton L CO 1 Watford
29.02.92	Julian Johnson L CO 3 St Leonards
05.05.93	Ray Kane L CO 2 Belfast

Career: 6 contests, won 2, lost 4.

Greg Upton
Teignmouth. *Born* Canada, 11 June, 1971
Western Area S. Featherweight Champion. Ht. 5'5½"
Manager J. Gaynor

28.11.91	Eunan Devenney W PTS 6 Evesham
29.04.92	Chris Morris W RSC 2 Liverpool
01.06.92	Graham McGrath W PTS 6 Solihull
19.11.92	Mark Hargreaves L RSC 3 Evesham
24.03.93	Barry Jones L RSC 2 Cardiff
27.05.93	Trevor Royal W CO 2 Bristol
	(Vacant Western Area S. Featherweight Title)

Career: 6 contests, won 4, lost 2.

Paul Vache
Bristol. *Born* London, 23 June, 1967
L. Middleweight. Ht. 5'11"
Manager B. Lynch

05.10.92	Mossa Azward W RSC 2 Bristol

Career: 1 contest, won 1.

Chris Vassiliou
Margate. *Born* Hitchin, 18 June, 1963
L. Middleweight. Ht. 5'11"
Manager P. Byrne

22.02.93	Darren Blackford L RSC 1 Eltham
26.06.93	Glenn Catley L CO 2 Keynsham

Career: 2 contests, lost 2.

Des Vaughan
Sydenham. *Born* Lewisham, 3 January, 1965
Cruiserweight. Ht. 6'4"
Manager Self

25.10.90	Coco Collins W CO 1 Battersea
18.02.91	Rob Albon L PTS 6 Windsor
05.03.92	Rocky Shelly W RSC 5 Battersea
28.10.92	Phil Soundy L RTD 4 Kensington

Career: 4 contests, won 2, lost 2.

Louis Veitch
Glasgow. *Born* Glasgow, 9 March, 1963
Flyweight. Ht. 5'2"
Manager J. McMillan

09.10.91	Tucker Thomas W RSC 4 Marton
11.11.91	Shaun Norman L RSC 5 Bradford
12.03.92	Neil Armstrong L PTS 6 Glasgow
10.04.92	Mark Robertson L PTS 6 Glasgow
16.05.92	Mickey Cantwell L PTS 6 Muswell Hill
09.07.92	Paul Weir L PTS 6 Glasgow
11.09.92	Neil Armstrong L PTS 6 Glasgow
26.10.92	Nick Tooley L PTS 6 Cleethorpes
14.12.92	Lyndon Kershaw DREW 6 Bradford
29.01.93	Neil Armstrong L PTS 6 Glasgow
10.02.93	Mickey Cantwell DREW 8 Lewisham
29.03.93	Neil Parry W PTS 6 Glasgow
29.05.93	Neil Armstrong L PTS 10 Paisley

Career: 13 contests, won 2, drew 2, lost 9.

Tony Velinor
Stratford. *Born* London, 21 December, 1964
L. Middleweight. Ht. 5'8"
Manager B. Hearn

28.10.88 Robert Armstrong W RSC 4 Brentwood
22.11.88 Andy Tonks W RTD 1 Basildon
16.12.88 Kesem Clayton L RSC 2 Brentwood
25.01.89 Shamus Casey W RTD 3 Basildon
28.03.89 Ricky Nelson W RSC 4 Chigwell
26.05.89 Skip Jackson W RSC 2 Bethnal Green
19.09.89 Mark Howell W PTS 8 Bethnal Green
31.01.90 Shaun Cummins L PTS 8 Bethnal Green
22.05.90 Trevor Grant W PTS 6 Canvey Island
12.09.90 Ian Chantler L RSC 4 Bethnal Green
12.03.91 Paul Jones L PTS 8 Mansfield
03.07.91 Jason Rowe W RSC 1 Brentwood
11.05.92 Stan King L RSC 3 Piccadilly
16.02.93 Paul Lynch L PTS 8 Tooting
30.03.93 Carlo Colarusso L RSC 3 Cardiff
Career: 15 contests, won 8, lost 7.

Mark Verikios   Les Clark

Mark Verikios

Swansea. *Born* Swansea, 31 October, 1965
Welterweight. Ht. 5'10"
Manager Self

15.05.91 Lee Farrell W RSC 5 Swansea
06.06.91 Tim Harmey W CO 4 Barking
09.09.91 Dave Maj W PTS 6 Liverpool
13.05.92 Steve McNess W RSC 5 Kensington
12.11.92 Dave Maj W PTS 6 Liverpool
Career: 5 contests, won 5.

Jimmy Vincent

Birmingham. *Born* Barnet, 5 June, 1969
L. Welterweight. Ht. 5'8"
Manager T. Petersen

19.10.87 Roy Williams W PTS 6 Birmingham
11.11.87 Mick Greenwood W PTS 6 Stafford
19.11.87 Darryl Pettit W RSC 6 Ilkeston
24.11.87 Roy Williams W PTS 6 Wolverhampton
14.02.88 Niel Leggett L PTS 6 Peterborough
29.02.88 Billy Cawley W CO 1 Birmingham
13.04.88 Dave Croft W PTS 6 Wolverhampton
16.05.88 Barry North W PTS 6 Wolverhampton

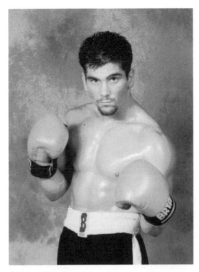

Jimmy Vincent   Chris Bevan

14.06.88 Dean Dickinson W PTS 6 Birmingham
20.09.88 Henry Armstrong L PTS 6 Stoke
10.10.88 Henry Armstrong L PTS 6 Manchester
17.10.88 Dean Dickinson W PTS 6 Birmingham
14.11.88 Peter Gabbitus L PTS 6 Stratford upon Avon
22.11.88 Barry North W RSC 4 Wolverhampton
12.12.88 Tony Feliciello L PTS 8 Birmingham
09.09.92 Mark Dawson L PTS 6 Stoke
23.09.92 Mark Epton W RSC 6 Leeds
17.12.92 Jason Rowland L PTS 6 Wembley
06.03.93 Mark Tibbs W PTS 6 Glasgow
Career: 19 contests, won 12, lost 7.

Ian Vokes

Hull. *Born* Hull, 27 March, 1966
L. Heavyweight. Ht. 6'0"
Manager M. Toomey

13.03.89 Eugene Brown L RSC 1 Leicester
24.04.89 Hugh Fury L PTS 6 Bradford
08.05.89 Tony Behan L PTS 6 Grimsby
22.05.89 Stevie R. Davies L PTS 6 Bradford
03.10.89 Andy Marlow L PTS 6 Cottingham
23.10.89 Andrew Bravardo W RSC 5 Cleethorpes
30.10.89 Tony Lawrence L PTS 6 Piccadilly
13.11.89 Shamus Casey L RSC 5 Bradford
27.01.90 Stinger Mason L PTS 6 Sheffield
13.02.90 Dave Maxwell L PTS 6 Wolverhampton
27.02.90 Shaun McCrory L PTS 6 Marton
19.04.90 Glenn Campbell L CO 1 Oldham
08.10.90 Pete Bowman W PTS 6 Cleethorpes
01.11.90 Pete Bowman W PTS 6 Hull
12.11.90 Tony Lawrence L PTS 6 Bradford
12.12.90 Barry Downes L PTS 6 Leicester
18.02.91 Barry Downes W PTS 6 Derby
18.03.91 Ian Henry L RSC 2 Manchester
22.04.91 Joe Kilshaw DREW 6 Bradford
13.05.91 Steve Truepenny L CO 2 Manchester
28.11.91 Shamus Casey L PTS 6 Hull
14.12.92 Barry Downes L PTS 6 Northampton
18.02.93 Cliff Taylor L PTS 6 Hull
09.03.93 Dale Nixon L RSC 2 Bristol
Career: 24 contests, won 4, drew 1, lost 19.

Yusuf Vorajee

Coventry. *Born* Bradford, 21 August, 1969
Featherweight. Ht. 5'5½"
Manager R. Gray

30.09.92 Kid McAuley L PTS 6 Solihull
14.10.92 Mark Hargreaves L RSC 4 Stoke
27.01.93 Kid McAuley W RSC 5 Stoke
03.03.93 Stewart Fishermac W RSC 2 Solihull
23.03.93 Garry Burrell W PTS 6 Wolverhampton
05.05.93 John White L PTS 6 Belfast
Career: 6 contests, won 3, lost 3.

Peter Vosper

Plymouth. *Born* Plymouth, 6 October,1966
S. Middleweight. Ht. 5'10"
Manager C. Sanigar

15.02.89 Mark White W PTS 6 Bethnal Green
01.03.89 Lester Jacobs L PTS 6 Bethnal Green
29.03.89 George Moody L PTS 6 Bethnal Green
09.05.89 Tony Cloak W RSC 2 Plymouth
20.06.89 Spencer Alton W PTS 6 Plymouth
17.10.89 Spencer Alton DREW 8 Plymouth
30.11.89 Ray Webb L PTS 6 Southwark
03.03.90 Michael Gale L RSC 2 Wembley
26.04.90 Michael Clarke L PTS 6 Wandsworth
21.05.90 Chris Walker W RSC 2 Mayfair
26.09.90 Ali Forbes L PTS 6 Mayfair
12.04.91 Frank Eubanks L RSC 1 Manchester
30.05.91 Russell Washer W PTS 6 Mayfair
06.06.91 John Kaighin DREW 6 Barking
27.06.91 Nick Manners L RSC 1 Leeds
16.12.91 Paul McCarthy L PTS 6 Southampton
25.02.92 Roland Ericsson L RSC 6 Crystal Palace
01.12.92 John Kaighin L RSC 4 Bristol
Career: 18 contests, won 5, drew 2, lost 11.

Nicky Wadman

Brighton. *Born* Brighton, 8 August, 1965
Cruiserweight. Ht. 6'1"
Manager Self

11.03.92 Julian Johnson W PTS 6 Cardiff
23.04.92 Mark McBiane W RSC 1 Eltham
26.09.92 Hussain Shah L RSC 4 Earls Court
29.01.93 Alan Smiles L PTS 6 Glasgow
22.02.93 Steve Osborne W PTS 6 Eltham
Career: 5 contests, won 3, lost 2.

Steve Walker

Manchester. *Born* Manchester, 25 June, 1963
S. Featherweight. Ht. 5'7"
Manager P. Martin

14.09.89 Edward Cook L PTS 6 Motherwell
28.09.89 Miguel Matthews W PTS 6 Cardiff
04.10.89 Paul Harvey DREW 6 Basildon
30.10.89 Jason Lepre W CO 2 Piccadilly
04.11.89 Edward Cook W PTS 4 Eastbourne
28.11.89 Alan McKay DREW 6 Battersea
18.12.89 John Milne DREW 6 Glasgow
23.02.90 Tommy Graham W RSC 4 Irvine
08.03.90 John Milne DREW 8 Glasgow
28.03.90 Francisco Arroyo W PTS 6 Manchester
03.05.90 Colin McMillan L PTS 6 Kensington
04.06.90 Gary Peynado W PTS 6 Edgbaston
09.10.90 Ian McGirr W RSC 4 Glasgow
29.10.90 Karl Taylor DREW 6 Birmingham

12.11.90	Muhammad Shaffique W PTS 6 Stratford upon Avon
24.01.91	Richie Foster W PTS 8 Brierley Hill
02.03.91	Harry Escott DREW 6 Darlington
19.03.91	Mark Holt W PTS 8 Birmingham
20.09.91	Harry Escott DREW 6 Manchester
13.11.91	Ian Honeywood L PTS 6 Bethnal Green
18.07.92	Kelton McKenzie L CO 2 Manchester
19.03.93	Mick Mulcahy W RSC 6 Manchester
26.04.93	Kevin McKillan DREW 8 Manchester

Career: 23 contests, won 11, drew 8, lost 4.

Colin Wallace

Cleland. *Born* Motherwell, 11 January, 1971
L. Middleweight. Ht. 5'6"
Manager A. Melrose

26.03.93	Steve Scott W PTS 6 Cardiff
30.04.93	Mark Antony W PTS 6 Glasgow
14.05.93	Martin Campbell W PTS 6 Kilmarnock
29.05.93	Steve Scott W PTS 6 Paisley

Career: 4 contests, won 4.

Anthony Wanza

Croydon. *Born* Trinidad, 15 December, 1961
Lightweight. Ht. 5'7"
Manager G. Steene

04.04.93	Cham Joof L RSC 2 Brockley
21.06.93	Ray Hood L PTS 6 Swindon

Career: 2 contests, lost 2.

Russell Washer Les Clark

Russell Washer

Swansea. *Born* Swansea, 21 January, 1962
Middleweight. Ht. 5'10"
Manager Self

15.09.90	Dean Cooper L PTS 6 Bristol
02.10.90	Nick Gyaamie W RSC 4 Eltham
16.10.90	Wayne Panayiotiou W RSC 2 Evesham

29.10.90	Chris Walker L RSC 2 Nottingham
11.12.90	Matt Mowatt W RSC 6 Evesham
24.01.91	Wayne Panayiotiou W RSC 4 Gorseinon
21.02.91	Marvin O'Brien DREW 6 Walsall
19.03.91	Tony Meszaros L PTS 6 Birmingham
10.04.91	Andrew Flute L PTS 6 Wolverhampton
30.05.91	Peter Vosper L PTS 6 Mayfair
04.09.91	Val Golding L RTD 5 Bethnal Green
11.11.91	Stinger Mason L PTS 4 Stratford on Avon
20.11.91	Alan Richards L PTS 6 Cardiff
29.11.91	Ensley Bingham L RSC 4 Manchester
11.03.92	Lee Crocker L PTS 6 Cardiff
22.04.92	Gilbert Jackson L PTS 6 Wembley
11.05.92	Carlo Colarusso L RSC 5 Llanelli *(Welsh L. Middleweight Title Challenge)*
18.06.92	Tony Collins L RSC 2 Peterborough
03.09.92	John Bosco L RSC 2 Dunstable
05.10.92	Sean Byrne L PTS 6 Northampton
15.10.92	Jerry Mortimer L RSC 5 Lewisham
28.11.92	Paul Wright L PTS 8 Manchester
10.12.92	Abel Asinamali W PTS 6 Bethnal Green

27.01.93	Barry Thorogood L PTS 6 Cardiff
03.02.93	Kevin Sheeran L PTS 6 Earls Court
27.02.93	Jamie Robinson L PTS 6 Dagenham
24.03.93	Robert Peel L PTS 6 Cardiff
31.03.93	Kevin Adamson L PTS 6 Barking
10.04.93	Ray Price W RSC 4 Swansea
23.05.93	Darren Blackford W PTS 6 Brockley
23.06.93	Adrian Dodson L PTS 6 Edmonton

Career: 31 contests, won 7, drew 1, lost 23.

Graham Wassell

Pontefract. *Born* Wakefield, 29 December, 1966
S. Middleweight. Ht. 6'4"
Manager Self

13.11.90	Alan Gandy DREW 6 Edgbaston
21.10.91	Gypsy Johnny Price L RSC 5 Bury
16.10.92	Sean Smith W RSC 2 Hull
01.12.92	Cliff Taylor W PTS 6 Hartlepool
19.04.93	Gypsy Johnny Price L RSC 1 Manchester

Career: 5 contests, won 2, drew 1, lost 2.

Delroy Waul Harry Goodwin

Peter Waudby

Hull. *Born* Hull, 18 November, 1970
L. Middleweight. Ht. 5'10½"
Manager L. Billany

21.09.92 Simon Fisher W RSC 2 Cleethorpes
16.10.92 Chris Mulcahy W RSC 4 Hull
14.12.92 Shamus Casey W PTS 6 Cleethorpes
10.05.93 Julian Eavis W PTS 6 Cleethorpes
27.05.93 Warren Stowe L PTS 6 Burnley
Career: 5 contests, won 4, lost 1.

Delroy Waul

Manchester. *Born* Manchester, 3 May, 1970
Welterweight. Ht. 6'1"
Manager F. Warren

29.05.89 Calum Rattray W PTS 6 Dundee
12.06.89 Calum Rattray W PTS 6 Glasgow
25.09.89 Jimmy Reynolds W RSC 4 Birmingham
10.10.89 David Maw W PTS 4 Sunderland
05.12.89 Richard Adams W RSC 4 Dewsbury
11.01.90 Richard Adams W RSC 3 Dewsbury
22.10.90 Jim Talbot W RTD 3 Mayfair
15.11.90 Mike Russell W CO 1 Oldham
13.12.90 Kid Sylvester W RSC 6 Dewsbury
31.01.91 Kevin Hayde W RSC 6 Bredbury
13.02.91 Chris Richards W PTS 6 Wembley
14.03.91 Terry Morrill DREW 8 Middleton
02.05.91 Andrew Furlong W RSC 5 Northampton
16.05.91 Paul Wesley W RSC 7 Liverpool
20.06.91 Gordon Blair L CO 2 Liverpool
09.10.91 Paul King W RSC 6 Manchester
19.12.91 Jason Rowe W RSC 4 Oldham
31.01.92 Patrick Vungbo L DIS 8 Waregem, Belgium
02.07.92 Jimmy Thornton W RSC 6 Middleton
13.02.93 Wayne Shepherd W RSC 5 Manchester
25.06.93 Bruno Wuestenberg L PTS 8 Brussels, Belgium
Career: 21 contests, won 17, drew 1, lost 3.

Scott Welch

Brighton. *Born* Yarmouth, 21 April, 1968
Heavyweight. Ht. 6'2"
Manager B. Hearn

08.09.92 John Williams W RSC 5 Norwich
06.10.92 Gary Williams W PTS 4 Antwerp, Belgium
23.02.93 Gary Charlton L RSC 3 Doncaster
11.05.93 Denroy Bryan W RSC 4 Norwich
29.06.93 John Harewood W RSC 5 Mayfair
Career: 5 contests, won 4, lost 1.

Nigel Wenton

Liverpool. *Born* Liverpool, 5 April, 1969
Lightweight. Ht. 5'7"
Manager F. Warren

08.06.88 Steve Taggart W RSC 2 Sheffield
25.06.88 Rafael Saez W RSC 3 Panama City, Panama
19.10.88 Niel Leggett W RTD 2 Belfast
02.11.88 Kid Sumali W RTD 3 Southwark
15.11.88 Tony Graham W RSC 3 Piccadilly
07.12.88 John Bennie W RSC 5 Belfast
14.12.88 Young Joe Rafiu W RSC 1 Kirkby
18.01.89 Ian Honeywood W RSC 3 Kensington
25.01.89 Mark Pearce W PTS 6 Belfast
08.03.89 Juan Torres W RTD 3 Belfast
12.04.89 Edwin Murillo W CO 2 Belfast
10.05.89 Nigel Senior W RSC 2 Kensington
07.06.89 Eamonn Payne W RSC 3 Wembley
28.07.89 Fabian Salazar L PTS 6 Isla Margarita, Venezuela
19.09.89 Sugar Gibiliru W PTS 8 Belfast
31.10.89 Tomas Arguelles W PTS 6 Belfast
13.12.89 Tony Dore W PTS 6 Kirkby
21.02.90 Luis Mendieta W RSC 3 Belfast
17.03.90 Scott de Pew W RSC 2 Belfast
29.04.90 Sharmba Mitchell L PTS 8 Atlantic City, USA
15.07.90 Bryant Paden DREW 10 Atlantic City, USA
07.09.91 Oliver Harrison W RTD 5 Belfast
13.11.91 Tony Richards W RSC 5 Belfast
11.12.91 Jeff Roberts W CO 2 Dublin
25.04.92 Ed Pollard W RTD 6 Belfast
10.12.92 Davy Robb W RSC 3 Bethnal Green
13.02.93 Charles Shepherd L PTS 8 Manchester
18.06.93 David Sample L PTS 10 Belfast
Career: 28 contests, won 23, drew 1, lost 4.

Richie Wenton

Liverpool. *Born* Liverpool, 28 October, 1967
Featherweight. Ht. 5'8"
Manager F. Warren

14.12.88 Miguel Matthews W CO 2 Kirkby
25.01.89 Sean Casey W PTS 4 Belfast
10.04.89 Stuart Carmichael W RSC 2 Mayfair
13.12.89 Joe Mullen W RSC 5 Kirkby
21.02.90 Ariel Cordova W PTS 6 Belfast
17.03.90 Mark Johnston W PTS 4 Belfast
28.03.90 Jose Luis Vasquez W PTS 6 Manchester
23.05.90 Graham O'Malley W PTS 6 Belfast
09.07.90 Eugene Pratt W CO 1 Miami Beach, USA
15.09.90 Graham O'Malley W PTS 6 Belfast
30.10.90 Alejandro Armenta W RSC 2 Belfast
12.02.91 Sean Casey W PTS 4 Belfast
31.03.92 Graham O'Malley W PTS 6 Stockport
25.07.92 Ramos Agare W RSC 3 Manchester

Scott Welch   Les Clark

26.09.92 Floyd Churchill L RSC 2 Earls Court
28.04.93 Kelton McKenzie W PTS 8 Dublin
Career: 16 contests, won 15, lost 1.

Paul Wesley

Birmingham. *Born* Birmingham, 2 May, 1962
Middleweight. Ht. 5'9"
Manager N. Nobbs

20.02.87 B. K. Bennett L PTS 6 Maidenhead
18.03.87 Darryl Ritchie DREW 4 Stoke
08.04.87 Dean Murray W PTS 6 Evesham
29.04.87 John Wright W PTS 4 Loughborough
12.06.87 Leon Thomas W RSC 2 Leamington
16.11.87 Steve McCarthy L CO 8 Southampton
25.01.88 Paul Murray W PTS 8 Birmingham
29.02.88 Paul Murray DREW 8 Birmingham
15.03.88 Johnny Williamson W CO 2 Bournemouth
09.04.88 Joe McKenzie W RSC 6 Bristol
10.05.88 Tony Meszaros W PTS 8 Edgbaston
21.03.89 Carlton Warren L CO 2 Wandsworth
10.05.89 Rod Douglas L CO 1 Kensington
24.10.89 Nigel Rafferty L PTS 6 Wolverhampton
22.11.89 Nigel Rafferty L PTS 8 Stafford
28.11.89 Nigel Rafferty L PTS 6 Wolverhampton
05.12.89 Ian Strudwick L PTS 6 Catford
24.01.90 Rocky Feliciello W PTS 6 Solihull
19.02.90 Nigel Rafferty L PTS 8 Birmingham
22.03.90 John Ashton L PTS 10 Wolverhampton
            (Midlands Area Middleweight Title Challenge)
17.04.90 Winston May DREW 8 Millwall
09.05.90 Alan Richards W PTS 8 Solihull
04.06.90 Julian Eavis W PTS 8 Birmingham
18.09.90 Shaun Cummins L RSC 1 Wolverhampton
17.10.90 Julian Eavis W PTS 6 Stoke
23.01.91 Wally Swift Jnr L PTS 10 Solihull
            (Midlands Area L. Middleweight Title Challenge)
20.03.91 Horace Fleary L RSC 5 Solihull
16.05.91 Delroy Waul L RSC 7 Liverpool
04.07.91 Neville Brown W RSC 1 Alfreton
31.07.91 Francesco dell'Aquila L PTS 8 Casella, Italy
03.10.91 Neville Brown L PTS 8 Burton
29.10.91 Tony Collins DREW 8 Kensington
03.03.92 Antonio Fernandez L PTS 10 Cradley Heath
            (Vacant Midlands Area Middleweight Title)
10.04.92 Jean-Charles Meuret L PTS 8 Geneva, Switzerland
03.06.92 Sumbu Kalambay L PTS 10 Salice Terme, Italy
29.10.92 Ian Strudwick W RSC 1 Bayswater
14.11.92 Paul Busby L PTS 8 Cardiff
24.11.92 Paul Jones W RSC 2 Doncaster
16.03.93 Chris Pyatt L PTS 10 Mayfair
04.06.93 Jacques le Blanc L PTS 10 Moncton, Canada
Career: 40 contests, won 14, drew 4, lost 22.

Andre Wharton

Brierley Hill. *Born* Wordsley, 16 June, 1969
L. Middleweight. Ht. 5'8"
Manager Self

13.11.89 Bullit Andrews W PTS 6 Brierley Hill
05.02.90 Bullit Andrews W RSC 4 Brierley Hill
19.03.90 Gary Dyson DREW 6 Brierley Hill
03.09.90 David Radford W RSC 5 Dudley
15.10.90 Mick Duncan W PTS 6 Brierley Hill
24.01.91 Stefan Wright W RSC 5 Brierley Hill
18.02.91 Dean Cooper L PTS 8 Birmingham
15.03.91 Wayne Appleton W RSC 7 Willenhall
27.10.92 Geoff Calder W PTS 4 Cradley Heath
Career: 9 contests, won 7, drew 1, lost 1.

Gary White

Rochdale. *Born* Littleborough, 13 April, 1971
Featherweight. Ht. 5'7"
Manager J. Doughty

28.02.91 Stevie Woods W PTS 6 Bury
18.03.91 Tony Smith W PTS 6 Manchester
17.05.91 Neil Parry W PTS 6 Bury
07.12.92 Robert Braddock W PTS 6 Manchester
Career: 4 contests, won 4.

Jason White

Thame. *Born* Aylesbury, 16 February, 1970
Lightweight. Ht. 5'4"
Manager Self

03.09.92 Marco Fattore L RSC 1 Dunstable
29.10.92 Jason Lepre W PTS 6 Hayes
04.12.92 Gareth Jordan L RSC 2 Telford
Career: 3 contests, won 1, lost 2.

John White　　　　　　　　Chris Bevan

John White

Salford. *Born* Manchester, 6 November, 1970
Featherweight. Ht. 5'6"
Manager F. Warren

27.02.92 Alan Smith W RSC 1 Liverpool
02.07.92 Norman Dhalie W RSC 6 Middleton
25.07.92 Ronnie Stephenson W PTS 6 Manchester
13.10.92 Kid McAuley W PTS 4 Bury

28.11.92 Mark Hargreaves W PTS 4 Manchester
13.02.93 Norman Dhalie W CO 2 Manchester
05.05.93 Yusuf Vorajee W PTS 6 Belfast
Career: 7 contests, won 7.

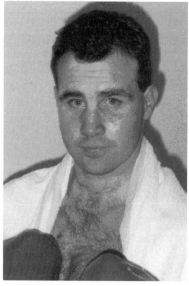

Robert Whitehouse　　　　　Les Clark

Robert Whitehouse

Swansea. *Born* Oxford, 9 October, 1965
Welterweight. Ht. 5'9"
Manager M. Copp

08.09.92 Jerry Mortimer L RSC 3 Southend
23.10.92 Steve Foran L RSC 2 Liverpool
03.12.92 Jason Beard L RSC 3 Lewisham
27.02.93 Kevin Adamson L RSC 1 Dagenham
Career: 4 contests, lost 4.

Dave Whittle

Newcastle. *Born* North Shields, 19 May, 1966
Welterweight. Ht. 5'9"
Manager T. Conroy

22.11.88 Mark Jay L PTS 6 Marton
28.02.89 Tony Farrell W PTS 6 Marton
31.03.89 Seamus Sheridan W RSC 2 Scarborough
19.05.89 Chris Mulcahy L PTS 6 Gateshead
03.06.89 Ian Thomas W PTS 6 Stanley
13.12.89 Ian Thomas W PTS 6 Kirkby
27.02.90 Trevor Meikle DREW 8 Marton
04.06.90 Bullit Andrews W PTS 6 Edgbaston
29.11.90 Trevor Meikle W PTS 6 Marton
13.05.91 Barry Messam L PTS 6 Marton
23.10.91 Jamie Robinson L RSC 4 Bethnal Green
27.11.91 Alan Peacock W PTS 6 Marton
02.03.92 Jimmy Thornton L PTS 6 Marton
12.03.92 Alan Peacock DREW 8 Glasgow
14.04.92 Nigel Bradley L CO 3 Mansfield
18.05.92 Wayne Shepherd L PTS 6 Marton
17.03.93 Dean Hiscox W PTS 6 Stoke
11.06.93 Steve Scott W PTS 6 Gateshead
Career: 18 contests, won 9, drew 2, lost 7.

Leigh Wicks

Brighton. *Born* Worthing, 29 July, 1965
Welterweight . Ht. 5'9¼"
Manager Self

29.04.87 Fidel Castro W PTS 6 Hastings
26.09.87 Jason Rowe W PTS 6 Hastings
18.11.87 Lou Ayres W PTS 6 Holborn
26.01.88 Theo Marius L PTS 8 Hove
15.02.88 Shamus Casey W PTS 6 Copthorne
26.04.88 Franki Moro DREW 8 Hove
04.05.88 Tony Britton W PTS 8 Wembley
18.05.88 Mark Howell W RSC 8 Portsmouth
25.05.88 Newton Barnett DREW 8 Hastings
22.11.88 Roy Callaghan L PTS 8 Basildon
16.03.89 Tony Britland W PTS 8 Southwark
12.10.89 Tony Gibbs W CO 2 Southwark
08.02.90 Ernie Noble W PTS 8 Southwark
26.04.90 Julian Eavis DREW 8 Mayfair
06.11.90 Gordon Blair W PTS 8 Mayfair
10.01.91 Barry Messam W PTS 6 Wandsworth
14.02.91 Kevin Thompson W PTS 8 Southampton
21.10.91 Tony Britland W RSC 3 Mayfair
20.02.92 Mick Duncan L PTS 8 Glasgow
30.04.92 Darren Morris DREW 6 Mayfair
19.10.92 Bozon Haule W PTS 8 Mayfair
20.01.93 Robert McCracken L PTS 8 Wolverhampton
17.02.93 Kevin Lueshing L PTS 6 Bethnal Green
22.04.93 Warren Stowe L PTS 6 Bury
Career: 24 contests, won 14, drew 4, lost 6.

Alan Williams

Liverpool. *Born* Liverpool, 2 August, 1962
L. Middleweight. Ht. 5'10½"
Manager C. Moorcroft

11.06.84 Bobby McGowan W DIS 1 Manchester
24.10.84 Michael Justin L RSC 6 Birmingham
30.11.84 Cliff Domville L RSC 3 Liverpool
04.02.85 Robert Riley L PTS 6 Liverpool
29.03.85 Bobby Welburn L CO 2 Liverpool
18.03.91 Stephen Welford L CO 1 Derby

Dave Whittle　　　　　　　Les Clark

29.04.92	Rob Stevenson L PTS 6 Liverpool	
28.09.92	Tony Massey L RSC 3 Manchester	
22.02.93	Andrew Jervis L PTS 6 Liverpool	
16.03.93	Steve Levene L RSC 1 Edgbaston	

Career: 10 contests, won 1, lost 9.

(Robert) B. F. Williams

Watford. *Born* Park Royal, 14 December, 1965
L. Welterweight. Ht. 5'11"
Manager R. Colson

28.05.86	Kenny Watson W RSC 5 Lewisham	
01.10.86	Andrew Prescod L RSC 4 Lewisham	
27.01.87	Jess Rundan L PTS 6 Plymouth	
18.02.87	Dave Nash W RSC 3 Fulham	
19.03.87	Les Remikie W PTS 6 Bethnal Green	
15.04.87	John Mullen L PTS 6 Lewisham	
30.04.87	Paul Kennedy W PTS 6 Washington	
18.09.87	Mike Russell W PTS 8 Swindon	
19.11.87	Ian Hosten W PTS 6 Wandsworth	
09.12.87	Chubby Martin DREW 8 Greenwich	
17.02.88	Neil Haddock W PTS 8 Bethnal Green	
28.09.88	Tony Borg L RSC 7 Edmonton	
28.11.88	Jim Lawlor L PTS 6 Edgbaston	
31.01.89	Danny Ellis W RSC 6 Bethnal Green	
29.03.89	Paul Charters W PTS 6 Bethnal Green	
26.04.89	Seamus O'Sullivan L RSC 6 Battersea	
15.09.89	Tony Gibbs W PTS 6 High Wycombe	
25.10.89	Richard Joyce W RSC 4 Stoke	
12.12.89	Steve Taggart W RSC 2 Brentford	
16.01.90	Mike Morrison W PTS 6 Cardiff	
22.02.90	Michael Driscoll L CO 2 Wandsworth	
25.10.90	Danny Cooper L PTS 6 Battersea	
14.11.90	Nigel Bradley L CO 2 Sheffield	
07.02.91	Rick Bushell L RTD 2 Watford	
12.02.92	Cliff Churchward W PTS 6 Watford	
07.04.92	Erwin Edwards W PTS 6 Southend	
30.04.92	Trevor Meikle W PTS 6 Watford	
17.09.92	James Campbell W PTS 6 Watford	
17.04.93	Jean Chiarelli L PTS 8 Gaillard, France	
24.06.93	Michael Dick W RTD 3 Watford	

Career: 30 contests, won 18, drew 1, lost 11.

Derek Williams

Battersea. *Born* Stockwell, 11 March, 1965
Former European & Commonwealth Heavyweight Champion. Ht. 6'5"
Manager Self

24.10.84	Tony Tricker W RSC 6 Mayfair	
24.01.85	Mike Creasey W RSC 3 Streatham	
11.02.85	Barry Ellis W RSC 2 Dulwich	
25.03.85	Alphonso Forbes W RSC 2 Merton	
20.09.85	Ron Ellis L PTS 8 Longford	
30.01.86	Steve Gee W PTS 6 Merton	
22.02.87	Steve Gee W PTS 6 Wembley	
24.03.87	Andrew Gerrard W PTS 6 Wembley	
25.06.87	Jess Harding W PTS 6 Bethnal Green	
08.10.87	John Westgarth W RSC 7 Bethnal Green	
28.01.88	Dave Garside W PTS 10 Bethnal Green	
18.05.88	Mark Young W CO 4 Portsmouth	
26.10.88	John Westgarth W RSC 2 Kensington	
29.11.88	Young Haumona W CO 4 Kensington	
	(Vacant Commonwealth Heavyweight Title)	
14.02.89	Noel Quarless W CO 1 Wandsworth	
05.04.89	Al Evans W RSC 2 Kensington	
24.08.89	Mark Wills L PTS 8 New York, USA	

05.12.89	Hughroy Currie W RSC 1 Catford	
	(Vacant European Heavyweight Title. Commonwealth Heavyweight Title Defence)	
03.02.90	Jean Chanet L PTS 12 St Didier, France	
	(European Heavyweight Title Defence)	
28.05.90	Jean Chanet L PTS 12 Paris, France	
	(European Heavyweight Title Challenge)	
01.05.91	Jimmy Thunder W RSC 2 Bethnal Green	
	(Commonwealth Heavyweight Title Defence)	
30.09.91	David Bey W RTD 6 Kensington	
18.01.92	Tim Anderson W RSC 1 Kensington	
30.04.92	Lennox Lewis L RSC 3 Kensington	
	(Commonwealth Heavyweight Title Defence. British & European Heavyweight Title Challenge)	
25.03.93	Bert Cooper L PTS 10 Atlantic City, USA	

Career: 25 contests, won 19, lost 6.

Gary Williams

Nottingham. *Born* Nottingham, 25 September, 1965
Heavyweight. Ht. 5'11½"
Manager W. Swift

27.04.92	Damien Caesar L RSC 4 Mayfair	
07.09.92	J. A. Bugner L PTS 4 Bethnal Green	
06.10.92	Scott Welch L PTS 4 Antwerp, Belgium	
01.12.92	Kenny Sandison W PTS 6 Liverpool	
27.01.93	Kenny Sandison DREW 6 Stoke	
13.02.93	Kevin McBride L PTS 4 Manchester	
01.03.93	Ashley Naylor DREW 6 Bradford	
29.03.93	Kevin Cullinane W RSC 2 Liverpool	
26.04.93	Ashley Naylor W PTS 6 Bradford	

Career: 9 contests, won 3, drew 2, lost 4.

(John) J. T. Williams

Cwmbran. *Born* Pontylottyn, 22 May, 1970
S. Featherweight. Ht. 5'6¾"
Manager Self

21.01.91	Kelton McKenzie DREW 6 Crystal Palace	
10.04.91	Dave Buxton W PTS 8 Newport	
28.05.91	Frankie Ventura W PTS 6 Cardiff	
18.07.91	Billy Barton W PTS 6 Cardiff	
22.01.92	Derek Amory W PTS 6 Cardiff	
30.03.92	Steve Pollard L PTS 6 Eltham	
07.10.92	Kevin McKillan W PTS 6 Barry	
14.11.92	Peter Judson DREW 6 Cardiff	
19.05.93	Dominic McGuigan L PTS 6 Sunderland	

Career: 9 contests, won 5, drew 2, lost 2.

(Kirk) John Williams (Gibbon)

Birmingham. *Born* Birmingham, 26 October, 1963
Cruiserweight. Ht. 6'2½"
Manager Self

12.02.85	Dougie Isles W RSC 5 South Shields	
14.10.85	Alex Romeo W PTS 6 Birmingham	
11.11.85	Roy Smith L RSC 2 Birmingham	
27.02.86	Lou Gent L RSC 4 Merton	
12.05.86	Blaine Logsdon L RSC 3 Manchester	
15.09.86	Steve Williams L PTS 6 Glasgow	
10.11.86	Simon Harris L PTS 6 Longford	

27.01.87	Sean Daly L RSC 2 Manchester	
19.01.88	Jon McBean W CO 3 Kings Heath	
17.02.88	Lennie Howard L RSC 5 Bethnal Green	
26.05.88	Gerry Storey W PTS 6 Bethnal Green	
28.10.88	Magne Havnaa L RTD 4 Copenhagen, Denmark	
23.10.89	Denroy Bryan DREW 6 Mayfair	
21.02.90	Joe Egan L PTS 6 Belfast	
03.03.90	Luigi Gaudiano L RSC 1 Pagani, Italy	
24.09.90	Steve Yorath W PTS 6 Mayfair	
26.11.90	Crawford Ashley L RSC 1 Mayfair	
12.05.92	Gary Delaney L PTS 6 Crystal Palace	
08.09.92	Scott Welch L RSC 5 Norwich	

Career: 19 contests, won 5, drew 1, lost 13.

Rowan Williams

Birmigham. *Born* Birmingham, 18 March, 1968
Flyweight. Ht. 5'5½"
Manager F. Maloney

17.02.93	Nick Tooley W PTS 4 Bethnal Green	
04.04.93	Des Gargano W PTS 4 Brockley	
23.06.93	Graham McGrath W PTS 4 Edmonton	

Career: 3 contests, won 3.

George Wilson

Camberwell. *Born* London, 7 April, 1966
Welterweight. Ht. 5'10"
Manager G. Steene

18.06.92	Sean Cave L PTS 6 Peterborough	
07.07.92	Erwin Edwards L RSC 4 Bristol	
08.09.92	Erwin Edwards L RSC 3 Southend	
16.02.93	Derrick Daniel W PTS 6 Tooting	
23.02.93	Sean Metherell W PTS 6 Kettering	
29.03.93	Joel Ani L PTS 6 Mayfair	
21.06.93	Jamie Davidson W RSC 4 Swindon	

Career: 7 contests, won 3, lost 4.

(Lee) L. C. Wilson

Rotherham. *Born* Rotherham, 8 July, 1972
Bantamweight. Ht. 5'7"
Manager T. Bell

10.12.92	Neil Armstrong L PTS 6 Glasgow	
26.03.93	James Murray L RSC 4 Glasgow	

Career: 2 contests, lost 2.

Stephen Wilson

Wallyford. *Born* Edinburgh, 30 March, 1971
S. Middleweight. Ht. 6'0"
Manager T. Gilmour

23.11.92	Lee Prudden W PTS 6 Glasgow	
25.01.93	Paul Smith W RSC 1 Glasgow	
06.03.93	Dave Owens W RSC 2 Glasgow	
23.03.93	Nigel Rafferty L RSC 3 Wolverhampton	
07.06.93	Shamus Casey W PTS 6 Glasgow	

Career: 5 contests, won 4, lost 1.

Tony Wilson

Wolverhampton. *Born* Wolverhampton, 25 April, 1964
Former British L. Heavyweight Champion. Ht. 5'11"
Manager Self

12.02.85	Blaine Logsdon W RSC 4 Kensington	
28.02.85	Winston Burnett W RSC 5 Wolverhampton	

05.06.85 Cordwell Hylton W CO 5 Kensington
14.11.85 Alex Romeo W RSC 2 Dudley
20.01.86 Dave Owens W RSC 2 Mayfair
04.03.86 Jonjo Greene W PTS 8 Wembley
20.05.86 Dennis Bailey W RSC 6 Wembley
03.12.86 Simon Harris W RTD 6 Muswell Hill
16.12.86 Pat Strachan W RSC 3 Alfreton
24.03.87 Keith Bristol W CO 1 Nottingham
*(Final Elim. British L. Heavyweight
Title)*
05.05.87 Jesse Shelby L RSC 2 Leeds
11.11.87 Louis Coleman W RSC 3 Usk
15.12.87 Blaine Logsdon W RSC 6 Cardiff
(Vacant British L. Heavyweight Title)
10.05.88 Brian Schumacher W RSC 6
Tottenham
(British L. Heavyweight Title Defence)
29.11.88 Randy Smith W PTS 10 Manchester
14.12.88 Tony Harrison W PTS 8 Bethnal Green
25.01.89 Brian Schumacher W RSC 3 Bethnal
Green
(British L. Heavyweight Title Defence)
22.03.89 Tom Collins L RSC 2 Reading
(British L. Heavyweight Title Defence)
21.09.89 Steve McCarthy W RTD 3
Southampton
(Elim. British L. Heavyweight Title)
21.12.89 Dave Lawrence W RSC 6 Kings Heath
30.08.90 Steve Harvey W RSC 8 Boise, USA
30.10.90 James Flowers L PTS 10 Chicago,
USA
02.10.91 Glazz Campbell L PTS 8 Solihull
26.11.91 Cordwell Hylton W PTS 8
Wolverhampton
11.12.91 Noel Magee L RSC 3 Dublin
21.03.92 Fabrice Tiozzo L PTS 8 St Denis,
France
23.05.92 Ginger Tshabalala L RSC 3
Birmingham
18.11.92 Tony Booth DREW 8 Solihull
09.02.93 Tony Booth L PTS 8 Wolverhampton
Career: 29 contests, won 20, drew 1, lost 8.

Vince Wilson

Gateshead. *Born* Gateshead, 1 December,
1960

Vince Wilson   Chris Bevan

Featherweight. Ht. 5'6"
Manager Self

08.05.86 Carl Gaynor DREW 6 Newcastle
02.06.86 John Bennie L RSC 4 Glasgow
16.10.86 Carl Gaynor L RSC 1 Newcastle
05.02.87 Gypsy Finch L RSC 4 Newcastle
28.02.89 Geoff Ward W RSC 1 Marton
18.09.89 Mickey Markie L RSC 1 Northampton
10.09.92 Chip O'Neill L RSC 1 Sunderland
Career: 7 contests, won 1, drew 1, lost 5.

(Winston) W. O. Wilson

Wandsworth. *Born* Coventry, 9 March,
1965
Southern Area Middleweight Champion.
Former Undefeated Southern Area L.
Middleweight Champion. Ht. 6'3"
Manager H. Holland

25.03.86 Floyd Davidson W RSC 3 Wandsworth
19.05.86 Steve Ward L DIS 3 Nottingham
08.09.86 Freddie James W PTS 6 Dulwich
22.09.86 Tony Behan W CO 2 Mayfair
25.09.86 Gerald McCarthy W RSC 1 Crystal
Palace
23.10.86 Simon Collins W PTS 8 Birmingham
02.03.87 Alex Mullen L PTS 8 Glasgow
01.10.87 Joao Cabreiro W PTS 6 Croydon
28.01.88 Jimmy Cable W CO 2 Bethnal Green
29.11.88 Andy Till L PTS 10 Battersea
29.03.89 Shamus Casey W RSC 5 Wembley
07.06.89 Franki Moro W RTD 4 Wembley
04.10.89 Kevin Hayde W PTS 8 Kensington
14.03.90 Newton Barnett W RSC 1 Kensington
21.01.91 Quinn Paynter L PTS 8 Crystal Palace
07.11.91 Nigel Fairbairn W RSC 8 Peterborough
*(Vacant Southern Area L.
Middleweight Title)*
06.05.93 John Ogiste W RSC 8 Bayswater
(Southern Area Middleweight Title)
23.06.93 Ian Strudwick W RSC 8 Edmonton
*(Southern Area Middleweight Title
Defence)*
Career: 18 contests, won 14, lost 4.

Wayne Windle

Sheffield. *Born* Sheffield, 18 October, 1968
Former Central Area Lightweight
Champion. Ht. 5'8"
Manager Self

25.10.88 Mick Mulcahy L PTS 6 Cottingham
17.11.88 Dave Pratt L PTS 6 Ilkeston
02.02.89 Jeff Dobson L RSC 6 Croydon
04.04.89 John Ritchie DREW 4 Sheffield
05.10.89 Des Gargano L PTS 6 Middleton
16.10.89 Des Gargano W PTS 6 Manchester
16.11.89 Noel Carroll L PTS 6 Manchester
04.12.89 Brendan Ryan DREW 6 Manchester
29.01.90 Mike Close W PTS 6 Liverpool
05.02.90 Mike Close W PTS 6 Brierley Hill
22.02.90 Bernard McComiskey W PTS 6
Kensington
12.03.90 Barry North W PTS 6 Hull
21.03.90 Neil Foran L PTS 6 Preston
29.05.90 Terry Collins L PTS 6 Bethnal Green
11.06.90 Muhammad Lovelock W PTS 6
Manchester
12.09.90 Brian Cullen W RSC 1 Stafford
08.10.90 Johnny Walker DREW 6 Leicester
22.10.90 Mick Mulcahy W PTS 4 Cleethorpes
14.11.90 Andy Robins W PTS 6 Sheffield

26.11.90 Michael Driscoll L RSC 3 Bethnal
Green
16.01.91 Karl Taylor L PTS 8 Stoke
06.02.91 Felix Kelly L PTS 6 Bethnal Green
12.03.91 Mark Antony W CO 1 Mansfield
24.04.91 Steve Foran L CO 3 Preston
13.06.91 Pete Roberts W RSC 7 Hull
*(Vacant Central Area Lightweight
Title)*
16.08.91 Aukunun L PTS 6 Marbella, Spain
21.09.91 George Scott L CO 2 Tottenham
10.12.91 Kevin Toomey W PTS 6 Sheffield
26.03.92 Kevin Toomey L DIS 8 Hull
*(Central Area Lightweight Title
Defence)*
03.09.92 Billy Schwer L CO 1 Dunstable
20.01.93 Mark Elliot L CO 3 Wolverhampton
01.06.93 Mick Mulcahy L PTS 6 Manchester
Career: 32 contests, won 12, drew 3, lost 17.

Stevie Woods

Kirkcaldy. *Born* Manchester, 3 September,
1967
Bantamweight. Ht. 5'6"
Manager T. Gilmour

18.09.89 Kevin James W RSC 4 Glasgow
02.10.89 Peter Judson W PTS 6 Bradford
23.10.89 James Milne L CO 1 Glasgow
11.12.89 Pete Buckley L PTS 6 Bradford
16.02.90 Cristobal Pascual L CO 2 Bilbao, Spain
20.03.90 Billy Proud W PTS 6 Hartlepool
28.03.90 Bradley Stone L RSC 2 Bethnal Green
21.05.90 Tony Smith W RSC 6 Bradford
27.11.90 Neil Parry L PTS 6 Glasgow
21.01.91 Neil Parry W PTS 8 Glasgow
28.02.91 Gary White L PTS 6 Bury
07.05.91 Tony Smith W RTD 2 Glasgow
03.06.91 Neil Parry L RSC 2 Glasgow
09.10.91 Kevin Jenkins DREW 8 Glasgow
14.11.91 Drew Docherty L RSC 1 Edinburgh
28.02.92 Neil Parry L PTS 6 Irvine
19.10.92 Lyndon Kershaw L PTS 6 Glasgow
09.11.92 Ady Benton L PTS 6 Bradford
22.02.93 Jason Morris L CO 4 Glasgow
Career: 19 contests, won 6, drew 1, lost 12.

Richard Woolgar

Northampton. *Born* Newport Pagnell, 29
September, 1967
Lightweight. Ht. 5'5½"
Manager B. Hearn

24.10.90 Andrew Robinson W RSC 3 Dudley
12.12.90 Mark Antony W RSC 5 Basildon
19.03.91 Chris Saunders L RSC 3 Leicester
05.11.91 Kelton McKenzie L RSC 5 Leicester
10.12.91 Kevin Lowe W PTS 6 Shefffield
21.01.92 Lee Fox W PTS 6 Norwich
28.04.92 Karl Taylor L PTS 6 Wolverhampton
27.10.92 Joe Fannin W PTS 6 Leicester
Career: 8 contests, won 5, lost 3.

Derek Wormald

Rochdale. *Born* Rochdale, 24 May, 1965
L. Middleweight. Ht. 5'10"
Manager J. Doughty

28.04.86 Dave Binsteed W RSC 2 Liverpool
20.05.86 Taffy Morris W PTS 6 Huddersfield
16.06.86 Claude Rossi W PTS 6 Manchester
23.09.86 Shamus Casey W PTS 8 Batley
16.10.86 Nigel Moore DREW 6 Merton

11.11.86	David Scere W RSC 3 Batley
25.11.86	Cliff Domville W RSC 4 Manchester
08.12.86	Martin McGough W RTD 4 Edgbaston
10.02.87	Manny Romain W CO 3 Batley
07.04.87	Tony Brown W RSC 6 Batley
28.04.87	Johnny Stone W RSC 1 Manchester
15.09.87	Sammy Sampson W PTS 10 Batley
09.02.88	Richard Wagstaff W RSC 6 Bradford
23.02.88	Judas Clottey W PTS 10 Oldham
12.04.88	John Ashton W RSC 4 Oldham
	(Elim. British L. Middleweight Title)
11.10.89	Gary Stretch L RSC 1 Millwall
	(British L. Middleweight Title Challenge)
24.09.92	Mark Jay W RSC 5 Stockport
27.05.93	Mark Dawson W RTD 5 Burnley

Career: 18 contests, won 16, drew 1, lost 1.

Adrian Wright

Wolverhampton. *Born* Wolverhampton, 8 November, 1967
L. Heavyweight. Ht. 5'9½"
Manager Self

05.09.90	Roger Wilson W PTS 4 Stoke
18.09.90	Pele Lawrence W CO 2 Stoke
12.11.90	Stinger Mason W RSC 4 Stratford upon Avon
12.12.90	Frank Eubanks L PTS 6 Stoke
06.02.91	Ali Forbes L PTS 6 Battersea
13.03.91	Chris Walker L PTS 4 Stoke
12.04.91	Robert Peel W RSC 6 Willenhall

29.08.91	John Kaighin L PTS 6 Oakengates
02.12.91	Justin Clements L PTS 6 Birmingham
11.12.91	Darron Griffiths L PTS 6 Stoke
29.04.92	Andy Manning L PTS 6 Stoke
09.09.92	Kevin Morton L PTS 6 Stoke
29.10.92	Eddie Knight W PTS 6 Bayswater
03.12.92	Mark Baker L RSC 1 Lewisham

Career: 14 contests, won 5, lost 9.

Andy Wright

Tooting. *Born* Aldershot, 20 December, 1963
Former Undefeated Southern Area S. Middleweight Champion. Ht. 5'11½"
Manager G. Steene

20.03.86	Shamus Casey W RSC 4 Merton
15.04.86	J. J. Smith L PTS 6 Merton
28.05.86	Shamus Casey W PTS 6 Lewisham
04.09.86	Kevin Roper W CO 2 Merton
20.11.86	Winston Burnett W PTS 8 Merton
24.02.87	Nick Vardy W CO 1 Wandsworth
03.06.87	Simon Collins DREW 6 Southwark
24.09.87	Andy Till L RSC 2 Crystal Palace
01.12.87	Alex Romeo W RSC 2 Southend
14.12.87	Paul McCarthy W CO 3 Piccadilly
03.02.88	Steve McCarthy L RSC 4 Wembley
30.03.88	Errol Christie L CO 2 Bethnal Green
15.11.88	Darren Hobson L RSC 3 Hull
08.03.89	Ray Close L RSC 4 Belfast
20.03.91	Paul McCarthy W CO 5 Wandsworth
	(Southern Area S. Middleweight Title

	Challenge)
22.10.91	John Kaighin DREW 6 Wandsworth
25.02.92	John Kaighin W PTS 6 Crystal Palace
16.02.93	Marvin O'Brien W PTS 6 Tooting

Career: 18 contests, won 10, drew 2, lost 6.

Brian Wright

Shildon. *Born* Northallerton, 12 December, 1969
L. Welterweight. Ht. 5'8½"
Manager G. Robinson

15.02.93	Mick Hoban L PTS 6 Manchester
06.05.93	Micky Hall L PTS 6 Hartlepool
18.06.93	Bernard McComiskey L PTS 6 Belfast

Career: 3 contests, lost 3.

Carl Wright

Liverpool. *Born* Liverpoool, 19 February, 1969
L. Welterweight. Ht. 5'7"
Manager C. Moorcroft

13.10.89	Mick Mulcahy W PTS 6 Preston
31.10.89	Mick Mulcahy W PTS 6 Manchester
24.01.90	Mike Morrison W PTS 6 Preston
19.12.90	Julian Eavis W PTS 6 Preston
31.03.92	Ricky Sackfield W RSC 1 Stockport
14.05.92	Brendan Ryan W PTS 4 Liverpool
12.06.92	Dean Bramhald W PTS 6 Liverpool
15.09.92	Wayne Panayiotiou W RSC 2 Liverpool

Former Southern Area super-middles champion, Andy Wright (left), swings into action against Marvin O'Brien on his way to a points win at Tooting

Les Clark

167

25.09.92	Mick Mulcahy W PTS 8 Liverpool
12.11.92	Jim Lawlor W RSC 3 Liverpool
29.04.93	Marcel Herbert W PTS 8 Mayfair

Career: 11 contests, won 11.

Paul Wright

Liverpool. *Born* Liverpool, 24 February, 1966
S. Middleweight. Ht. 5'9¾"
Manager C. Moorcroft

13.10.89	Andy Balfe W RSC 1 Preston
31.10.89	John Tipping W RSC 1 Manchester
20.12.89	Nigel Rafferty DREW 6 Kirkby
13.04.92	Shaun McCrory W PTS 6 Manchester
14.05.92	Chris Walker W PTS 6 Liverpool
15.09.92	John Kaighin W DIS 5 Liverpool
23.10.92	Jason McNeill W RSC 1 Liverpool
28.11.92	Russell Washer W PTS 8 Manchester
05.02.93	Sean Smith W RSC 2 Manchester
22.04.93	Glenn Campbell L RSC 4 Bury
	(Elim. British S. Middleweight Title & Central Area S. Middleweight Title Challenge)

Career: 10 contests, won 8, drew 1, lost 1.

Robert Wright   Les Clark

Robert Wright

Dudley. *Born* Dudley, 25 August, 1966
Welterweight. Ht. 5'11"
Manager Self

16.05.88	Steve Hogg W PTS 6 Wolverhampton
14.06.88	Joff Pugh W RSC 5 Dudley
22.09.88	Martin Campbell W RSC 5 Wolverhampton
13.04.89	Steve Hogg W PTS 6 Wolverhampton
05.06.89	Dean Dickinson W RSC 4 Birmingham
10.10.89	Julian Eavis W PTS 8 Wolverhampton
11.12.89	Mike Russell W CO 1 Birmingham
20.03.90	Mickey Hughes L RSC 7 Norwich
16.11.90	Tony Britland W RSC 3 Telford
02.10.91	Chris Mulcahy W RSC 1 Solihull
20.11.91	Tony Gibbs W RTD 2 Solihull
26.11.91	Darren Dyer L RSC 3 Bethnal Green

15.01.92	Julian Eavis W PTS 8 Stoke
10.03.92	Errol McDonald W CO 3 Bury
17.03.92	Donovan Boucher L RSC 11 Mayfair
	(Commonwealth Welterweight Title Challenge)
09.07.92	Gary Jacobs L RSC 6 Glasgow
	(British Welterweight Title Challenge)
05.05.93	Sidney Msutu L PTS 10 Cape Town, South Africa

Career: 17 contests, won 12, lost 5.

Stefan Wright

Peterborough. *Born* Peterborough, 23 May, 1970
S. Middleweight. Ht. 5'10"
Manager Self

22.10.90	John Kaighin W PTS 6 Peterborough
14.12.90	Shamus Casey W PTS 6 Peterborough
24.01.91	Andre Wharton L RSC 5 Brierley Hill
07.11.91	Gary Booker W PTS 6 Peterborough
28.04.92	Jerry Mortimer W RSC 4 Corby
18.06.92	Chris Richards W PTS 6 Peterborough
10.12.92	Paul McCarthy W PTS 6 Corby
04.03.93	Karl Barwise L RTD 5 Peterborough

Career: 8 contests, won 6, lost 2.

(Andrew) Sugar Boy Wright

Dudley. *Born* Dudley, 13 December, 1969
Lightweight. Ht. 5'7"
Manager Self

04.12.91	Jamie Morris W PTS 6 Stoke
22.01.92	Kevin McKillan L PTS 6 Solihull
20.01.93	Mark O'Callaghan L CO 1 Wolverhampton

Career: 3 contests, won 1, lost 2.

Paul Wynn

Newcastle. *Born* Newcastle, 23 March, 1972
S. Featherweight. Ht. 5'6"
Manager N. Fawcett

28.02.91	Tony Falcone L PTS 6 Sunderland
06.04.91	Tommy Smith L PTS 6 Darlington
13.05.91	Karl Morling L RSC 2 Northampton
29.04.93	Chip O'Neill W PTS 6 Newcastle
06.05.93	Tommy Smith W PTS 6 Hartlepool
01.06.93	Mark Hargreaves L PTS 6 Manchester

Career: 6 contests, won 2, lost 4.

Willie Yeardsley

Isle of Man. *Born* Isle of Man, 1 May, 1962
L. Middleweight. Ht. 5'10"
Manager M. Toomey

25.02.91	Pat Durkin W PTS 6 Bradford
03.04.91	Chris Mulcahy W PTS 6 Manchester
30.04.91	Ricky Sackfield L PTS 4 Stockport
13.06.91	Phil Epton L RSC 3 Hull
09.09.91	Allan Grainger L PTS 6 Glasgow
07.10.91	Dave Binsteed W PTS 6 Liverpool
25.11.91	Mick Duncan L PTS 6 Liverpool
20.01.92	Benji Joseph W PTS 6 Bradford
06.02.92	Benji Joseph W RSC 4 Peterborough
24.02.92	Matt Mowatt W PTS 6 Bradford
09.03.92	Dave Maj L RSC 1 Manchester
04.06.92	Stuart Wilson W PTS 6 Burnley
26.11.92	Trevor Meikle L PTS 6 Hull

Career: 13 contests, won 7, lost 6.

Tim Yeates   Pennie Cattle

Tim Yeates

Stanford le Hope. *Born* Worcester, 19 August, 1966
Bantamweight. Ht. 5'7"
Manager B. Hearn

03.10.90	Ceri Farrell W PTS 6 Basildon
17.10.90	Kevin Jenkins W PTS 6 Bethnal Green
12.12.90	Ceri Farrell W PTS 6 Basildon
23.01.91	Eric George W RSC 6 Brentwood
01.05.91	Kelton McKenzie L PTS 6 Bethnal Green
11.05.92	Neil Parry W PTS 6 Piccadilly
30.01.93	Miguel Matthews W PTS 6 Brentwood
20.04.93	Ricky Beard W PTS 6 Brentwood
26.06.93	Chris Lyons W PTS 4 Earls Court

Career: 9 contests, won 8, lost 1.

Steve Yorath

Cardiff. *Born* Cardiff, 8 August, 1965
Cruiserweight. Ht. 6'2"
Manager Self

21.11.85	Dai Davies L RSC 5 Blaenavon
13.03.86	John Ashton L CO 3 Alfreton
08.05.90	Rob Albon L PTS 6 Brentford
06.07.90	Phil Soundy L CO 3 Brentwood
17.09.90	Chris Coughlan W PTS 6 Cardiff
24.09.90	John Williams L PTS 6 Mayfair
03.10.90	Phil Soundy L PTS 6 Basildon
19.10.90	Neils H. Madsen L PTS 6 Skive, Denmark
15.04.91	Tony Colclough W PTS 6 Wolverhampton
24.04.91	Phil Soundy W PTS 6 Basildon
28.05.91	R. F. McKenzie W PTS 6 Cardiff
27.06.91	Denzil Browne L PTS 6 Leeds
21.01.92	Graham Arnold W PTS 6 Norwich
31.03.92	Graham Arnold L PTS 6 Norwich
18.05.92	Maro van Spaendonck L PTS 4 Valkenswaard, Holland
23.09.92	Denzil Browne L PTS 8 Leeds
25.11.92	Terry Dunstan L PTS 8 Mayfair
24.02.93	Derek Angol L RSC 5 Wembley
03.04.93	Biko Botowamungu L RSC 5 Vienna, Austria

Career: 19 contests, won 5, lost 14.

British Title Bouts, 1992-93

9 July, 1992 Gary Jacobs 10.6¾ (Scotland) W RSC 6 Robert Wright 10.7 (England), Glasgow. Welterweight Title Defence.

Coming in as a late substitute for the indisposed John Davies, Wright put up a good show early on. It was only when the body shots began to drain him in the fourth that the end looked in sight. Going to work with uppercuts, Jacobs had his man in all kinds of trouble and in the sixth a barrage of blows floored Wright who, on rising, was rescued by Roy Francis with 2.12 of the round gone. Jacobs vacated the British title after becoming European champion in February.

10 September, 1992 John Davison 9.0 (England) W CO 7 Tim Driscoll 8.13 (England), Sunderland. Vacant Featherweight Title.

Battling for the title vacated by Colin McMillan, Davison and Driscoll put on a great show for the TV cameras. Badly cut over the left eye in the third, Davison walked through the punches to break the Londoner's nose in the fifth and floored him in the sixth. Driscoll was still not done for, decking Davison early in round seven. However, Davison shrugged it off to pound Driscoll to the ground where he was counted out by Billy Rafferty at 2.57 of the round.

15 September, 1992 Andy Holligan 9.13 (England), W CO 7 Tony Ekubia 9.13 (England), Liverpool. Light-Welterweight Title Defence.

With Ekubia going well, it looked as though the fight would be as close as their previous one, but suddenly in the sixth, Holligan floored him for a nine count. Ekubia made it to the bell, but was all in. He came out for the seventh to give it a final shot, but another heavy left-hook had him over again and with 0.41 of the round gone, John Coyle completed the count.

17 September, 1992 Wally Swift Jnr 10.12 (England) L PTS 12 Andy Till 10.12½ (England), Watford. Light-Middleweight Title Defence.

In a war of attrition, Andy Till took the title from the

After being knocked down three times, Carl Crook (right) was retired at the end of round nine, leaving Billy Schwer as the British and Commonwealth lightweight champion   Les Clark

169

courageous Swift, who also suffered a suspected broken right hand. Despite a great finish by the champion, Mickey Vann scored it 118-117½ for Till, but it was close enough to have gone either way. Both men finished with cut left eyes and a third fight between the pair was eagerly awaited.

23 September, 1992 Herol Graham 11.5¾ (England) L RSC 9 Frank Grant 11.6 (England), Leeds. Middleweight Title Defence.

Having been harrassed from the opening bell, it became apparent as the contest wore on that Graham's reflexes, which had always been his major attribute, were beginning to let him down. With success in sight, the huge underdog, Grant, finally found the target in the ninth, dropping Graham twice, before Paul Thomas called a halt after 2.20 of the round had ensued.

23 September, 1992 Fidel Castro 11.13½ (England) L PTS 12 Henry Wharton 11.12¾ (England), Leeds. Super-Middleweight Title Defence.

On the same bill as Graham versus Grant, another title changed hands, but on this occasion it involved one of the most disputed decisions seen in recent years as referee, Larry O'Connell, saw Wharton as the winner by 118-117½ points. For the record, Castro boxed well, albeit spasmodically, while Wharton, although consistently forcing the action, lacked the quality of punch to be decisive. At the end of April, Wharton vacated the title in order to concentrate on the world crown.

28 September, 1992 Maurice Coore 12.6¼ (England) W RSC 9 Noel Magee 12.6¼ (Ireland), Manchester. Vacant Light-Heavyweight Title.

Dropped in the opening round, Coore came back well to blast out Magee in the ninth. The fight for the title vacated by Crawford Ashley was even until Coore's body punching began to take effect and by the ninth round the Irishman was almost defenceless as punches poured down on him from all angles. He finally toppled over and was rescued by the referee, Paul Thomas, with 2.26 of the round remaining.

13 October, 1992 Michael Armstrong 9.3¾ (England) L RSC 6 Neil Haddock 9.4 (Wales), Bury. Super-Featherweight Title Defence.

Never able to recover properly from a second round knockdown, Armstrong became the thirteenth successive champion in this weight division to lose the title in their first defence. With blood streaming from a cut over the left eye, Armstrong crumbled in the sixth, being put down twice before he was rescued by Larry O'Connell at 1.29 of the round.

28 October, 1992 Carl Crook 9.8½ (England) L RTD 9 Billy Schwer 9.8 (England), London. Lightweight Title Defence.

In one of the most exciting fights of the year, the younger Schwer dethroned a proud champion who was making his fifth defence. Having been on the floor three times in the ninth and suffering from double vision and a badly cut mouth, Crook was nearly at the end of his tether and his corner wisely called referee, John Coyle, over to retire their man at the end of the round.

10 December, 1992 Andy Till 10.13¾ (England) W RSC 3 Tony Collins 10.11 (England), London. Light-Middleweight Title Defence.

Once Till had found the range for his punches there was only one man in it, as the champion began to bull the challenger to the ropes. Slumping to the floor in the third under the weight of Till's blows, Collins, on rising, was subjected to a non-stop barrage and when not fighting back he was rescued by Dave Parris with 1.20 of the round still remaining.

22 December, 1992 Francis Ampofo 7.13¾ (England) W PTS 12 James Drummond 8.0 (Scotland), London. Vacant Flyweight Title.

The contest for the title vacated by Robbie Regan brought together two men who had both been beaten in challenges against the Welshman. While Ampofo made a good start, the taller Scot was dropped twice and cut by the left eye before he began to get back into the fight during the sixth. As Ampofo tired from his exertions, it became more interesting, but at the final bell he was clearly ahead 118½-116 on Adrian Morgan's scorecard.

25 January, 1993 Drew Docherty 8.5¼ (Scotland) W PTS 12 Donnie Hood 8.6 (Scotland), Glasgow. Bantamweight Title Defence.

In an exiting contest between boxer versus fighter, it was the champion's better boxing, especially his countering, which overcame the body punching of Hood. And, at the end of twelve well contested rounds, Dave Parris' scores of 118½-116½ in favour of Docherty, were judged to be a fair reflection by the vast majority.

24 February, 1993 Billy Schwer 9.8½ (Luton) L RSC 7 Paul Burke 9.8½ (England), Wembley. Lightweight Title Defence.

With Burke beginning to get back into the fight after a slow start, Paul Thomas brought the proceedings to a halt after 2.15 of the seventh round, due to three open cuts on Schwer's face. Burke also had damage to both eyes, but had been allowed to continue. Although Schwer was ahead at the closure, it is highly unlikely that the facial injuries would have stood up for the remainder of the contest.

25 February, 1993 Frank Grant 11.6 (England) W RTD 7 John Ashton 11.5¾ (England), Bradford. Middleweight Title Defence.

The bulldozing power of the southpaw champion proved too much for Ashton, who had to endure three counts and a badly cut left eye, prior to the seventh. After completing one more round, the referee, Dave Parris, was called over by Ashton's corner and the fight was halted, Grant having retained his title and at the same time recorded his 17th inside the distance victory.

27 February, 1993   Herbie Hide 14.12½ (England) W RSC 5 Michael Murray 16.2 (England), Dagenham. Vacant Heavyweight Title.

In a mismatch, Murray was found wanting as a British title challenger for the crown vacated by the WBC champion, Lennox Lewis, and was down four times in all before Dave Parris called it off at 2.12 of round five. Murray, who got the title match because of his good win over new WBO cruiser king, Markus Bott, was not in the best of condition, while Hide showed his inexperience when often unable to dissect the challenger's crab-like defence.

27 February, 1993   Sean Murphy 9.0 (England) W RSC 9 Alan McKay 8.13¾ (England), Dagenham. Vacant Featherweight Title.

On the same bill as Hide versus Murray, but in stark contrast, Sean Murphy captured a Lonsdale belt when Billy Rafferty stepped in at 1.53 of the ninth round to rescue his opponent, who had just risen from a nine count. Both men had fought their hearts out in a wonderful contest for the title recently vacated by John Davison. Prior to the finish, McKay appeared comfortably ahead, but was running out of gas fast, whereas Murphy, with a badly cut right eye, was running out of time.

14 April, 1993   Andy Till 11.0 (England) W RSC 4 Wally Swift Jnr 10.9¾ (England), London. Light-Middleweight Title Defence.

With only 0.24 of round four gone, Larry O'Connell jumped between the two fighters to rescue the extremely game challenger, who appeared to be defenceless on the ropes, the recipient of a chilling left-hook. Both men received eye damage in a terrific battle while it lasted, but in the end it was the coldly menacing Till who emerged the victor and winner of a Lonsdale belt outright.

British light-middleweight champion, Andy Till (left), made it a hat-trick of wins over Wally Swift junior, when he stopped the former titleholder inside four rounds last April

Les Clark

171

Lord Lonsdale Challenge Belts: Outright Winners

The original belts were donated to the National Sporting Club by Lord Lonsdale and did not bear his name, the inscription reading "The National Sporting Club's Challenge Belt." It was not until the British Boxing Board of Control was formed that the emblems were reintroduced and the belts became known as the Lord Lonsdale Challenge Belts. The first contest involving the BBBoC belt was Benny Lynch versus Pat Palmer for the flyweight title on 16 September 1936. To win a belt outright a champion must score three title match victories at the same weight, not necessarily consecutively.

Outright Winners of the National Sporting Club's Challenge Belt, 1909-1935 (20)

FLYWEIGHT	Jimmy Wilde; Jackie Brown
BANTAMWEIGHT	Digger Stanley; Joe Fox; Jim Higgins; Johnny Brown; Johnny King
FEATHERWEIGHT	Jim Driscoll; Tancy Lee; Johnny Cuthbert; Nel Tarleton
LIGHTWEIGHT	Freddie Welsh
WELTERWEIGHT	Johnny Basham; Jack Hood
MIDDLEWEIGHT	Pat O'Keefe; Len Harvey; Jock McAvoy
L. HEAVYWEIGHT	Dick Smith
HEAVYWEIGHT	Bombardier Billy Wells; Jack Petersen

Outright Winners of the BBBoC Lord Lonsdale Challenge Belts, 1936-1993 (81)

FLYWEIGHT	Jackie Paterson; Terry Allen; Walter McGowan; John McCluskey; Hugh Russell; Charlie Magri; Pat Clinton; Robbie Regan
BANTAMWEIGHT	Johnny King; Peter Keenan (2); Freddie Gilroy; Alan Rudkin; Johnny Owen; Billy Hardy
FEATHERWEIGHT	Nel Tarleton; Ronnie Clayton (2); Charlie Hill; Howard Winstone (2); Evan Armstrong; Pat Cowdell; Robert Dickie; Paul Hodkinson; Colin McMillan; Sean Murphy
S. FEATHERWEIGHT	Jimmy Anderson; John Doherty
LIGHTWEIGHT	Eric Boon; Billy Thompson; Joe Lucy; Dave Charnley; Maurice Cullen; Ken Buchanan; Jim Watt; George Feeney; Tony Willis; Carl Crook
L. WELTERWEIGHT	Joey Singleton; Colin Power; Clinton McKenzie (2); Lloyd Christie; Andy Holligan
WELTERWEIGHT	Ernie Roderick; Wally Thom; Brian Curvis (2); Ralph Charles; Colin Jones; Lloyd Honeyghan; Kirkland Laing
L. MIDDLEWEIGHT	Maurice Hope; Jimmy Batten; Pat Thomas; Prince Rodney; Andy Till
MIDDLEWEIGHT	Pat McAteer; Terry Downes; Johnny Pritchett; Bunny Sterling; Alan Minter; Kevin Finnegan; Roy Gumbs; Tony Sibson; Herol Graham
L. HEAVYWEIGHT	Randy Turpin; Chic Calderwood; Chris Finnegan; Bunny Johnson; Tom Collins; Dennis Andries; Tony Wilson; Crawford Ashley
CRUISERWEIGHT	Johnny Nelson
HEAVYWEIGHT	Henry Cooper (3); Horace Notice; Lennox Lewis

NOTES: Jim Driscoll was the first champion to win an NSC belt outright, whilst Eric Boon later became the first champion to put three notches on a BBBoC belt.

Nel Tarleton and Johnny King are the only champions to have won both belts outright.

Freddie Welsh and Johnny King, each with just two notches on an NSC Lonsdale belt, were allowed to keep their spoils after winning British Empire titles, while Walter McGowan and Charlie Magri, with one notch on a BBBoC belt, kept their awards under the three years/no available challengers ruling.

Henry Cooper holds the record number of belts won by a single fighter, three in all.

Chris and Kevin Finnegan are the only brothers to have won belts outright.

Jim Higgins holds the record for winning an NSC belt outright in the shortest time, 279 days, whilst Colin McMillan won a BBBoC belt in just 160 days.

British Champions, 1891-1993

Shows the tenure of each British champion at each weight from 1891, when the National Sporting Club was founded and championship bouts were contested under Marquess of Queensberry Rules, using gloves.

Between 1891 and 1929, the year that the BBBoC was formed, men who held general recognition are shown **in bold**, as champions, while the others are seen purely as claimants.

Champions born outside Britain, who won open titles in this country, are not shown at the risk of confusing the issue further.

Also, it must be stated that many of the champions and claimants listed below, prior to 1909, were no more than English titleholders, having fought for the "Championship of England", but for our purposes they carry the "British" label.

Prior to 1909, the year that the Lord Lonsdale Challenge Belt was introduced and weight classes subsequently standardised, poundages within divisions could vary quite substantially, thus enabling men fighting at different weights to claim the same "title" at the same time. A brief history of the weight fluctuations between 1891 and 1909, shows:

Bantamweight   Billy Plimmer was recognised as the British titleholder in 1891 at 110 lbs and became accepted as world champion when George Dixon, the number one in America's eyes, gradually increased his weight. In 1895 Pedlar Palmer took the British title at 112 lbs, but by 1900 he had developed into a 114 pounder. Between 1902 and 1904, Joe Bowker defended regularly at 116 lbs and in 1909 the NSC standardised the weight at 118 lbs, even though the USA continued for a short while to accept only 116 lbs.

Featherweight   Between 1891 and 1895, one of the most prestigious championship belts in this country was fought for at 126 lbs and although George Dixon was recognised in the USA as world featherweight champion, gradually moving from 114 to 120 lbs, no major contests took place in Britain during the above period at his weight. It was only in 1895, when Fred Johnson took the British title at 120 lbs, losing it to Ben Jordan two years later, that we came into line with the USA. Ben Jordan became an outstanding champion, who, between 1898 and 1899, was seen by the NSC as world champion at 120 lbs. However, first Harry Greenfield, then Jabez White and Will Curley, continued to claim the 126 lbs version of the British title and it was only in 1900 when Jack Roberts beat Curley, that the weight limit was finally standardised at nine stone.

Lightweight   Outstanding champions often carried their weights as they grew in size. A perfect example of this was Dick Burge, the British lightweight champion from 1891-1901, who gradually increased from 134 to 144 lbs, while still maintaining his right to the title. It was not until 1902 that Jabez White brought the division into line with the USA. Later, both White and then Goldswain, carried their weight up to 140 lbs and it was left to Johnny Summers to set the current limit of 135 lbs.

Welterweight   The presence of Dick Burge fighting from 134 to 144 lbs plus up until 1900, explains quite adequately why the welterweight division, although very popular in the USA, did not take off in this country until 1902. The championship was contested between 142 and 146 lbs in those days and was not really supported by the NSC, but by 1909 with their backing it finally became established at 147 lbs.

Note that the Lonsdale Belt notches (title bout wins) relate to NSC, 1909-1935, and BBBoC, 1936-1990.

Champions in **bold** are accorded national recognition.

*Undefeated champions.

Title Holder	Lonsdale Belt Notches	Tenure	Title Holder	Lonsdale Belt Notches	Tenure	Title Holder	Lonsdale Belt Notches	Tenure
Flyweight (112 lbs)			Teddy Gardner*	1	1952	Francis Ampofo	1	1992-
Sid Smith		1911	Terry Allen*	2	1952-1954			
Sid Smith	1	1911-1913	Dai Dower*	1	1955-1957	**Bantamweight (118 lbs)**		
Bill Ladbury		1913-1914	Frankie Jones*	2	1957-1960	**Billy Plimmer**		1891-1895
Percy Jones*	1	1914	Johnny Caldwell*	1	1960-1961	Tom Gardner		1892
Tancy Lee	1	1915	Jackie Brown*	1	1962-1963	Willie Smith		1892-1896
Joe Symonds	1	1915-1916	Walter McGowan*	1	1963-1966	Nunc Wallace		1893-1895
Jimmy Wilde*	3	1916-1923	John McCluskey*	3	1967-1977	George Corfield		1893-1895
Elky Clark*	2	1924-1927	Charlie Magri*	1	1977-1981	**Pedlar Palmer**		1895-1900
Johnny Hill*	1	1927-1929	Kelvin Smart	1	1982-1984	George Corfield		1895-1896
Jackie Brown		1929-1930	Hugh Russell*	3	1984-1985	Billy Plimmer		1896-1898
Bert Kirby	1	1930-1931	Duke McKenzie*	2	1985-1986	Harry Ware		1899-1900
Jackie Brown	3	1931-1935	Dave Boy McAuley*	1	1986-1988	**Harry Ware**		1900-1902
Benny Lynch*	2	1935-1938	Pat Clinton*	3	1988-1991	Andrew Tokell		1901-1902
Jackie Paterson	4	1939-1948	Robbie Regan	1	1991	Jim Williams		1902
Rinty Monaghan*	1	1948-1950	Francis Ampofo	1	1991	**Andrew Tokell**		1902
Terry Allen*	1	1951-1952	Robbie Regan*	2	1991-1992	Harry Ware		1902

173

Title Holder	Lonsdale Belt Notches	Tenure
Joe Bowker		1902-1910
Owen Moran		1905-1907
Digger Stanley		1906-1910
Digger Stanley	2	1910-1913
Bill Beynon	1	1913
Digger Stanley	1	1913-1914
Curley Walker*	1	1914-1915
Joe Fox*	3	1915-1917
Tommy Noble	1	1918-1919
Walter Ross*	1	1919-1920
Jim Higgins	3	1920-1922
Tommy Harrison		1922-1923
Bugler Harry Lake	1	1923
Johnny Brown*	3	1923-1928
Alf Pattenden	2	1928-1929
Johnny Brown		1928
Teddy Baldock		1928-1929
Teddy Baldock*	1	1929-1931
Dick Corbett	1	1931-1932
Johnny King	1	1932-1934
Dick Corbett*	1	1934
Johnny King	1+2	1935-1947
Jackie Paterson	2	1947-1949
Stan Rowan*	1	1949
Danny O'Sullivan	1	1949-1951
Peter Keenan	3	1951-1953
John Kelly	1	1953-1954
Peter Keenan	3	1954-1959
Freddie Gilroy*	4	1959-1963
Johnny Caldwell	1	1964-1965
Alan Rudkin	1	1965-1966
Walter McGowan	1	1966-1968
Alan Rudkin*	4	1968-1972
Johnny Clark*	1	1973-1974
Dave Needham	1	1974-1975
Paddy Maguire	1	1975-1977
Johnny Owen*	4	1977-1980
John Feeney	1	1981-1983
Hugh Russell	1	1983
Davy Larmour	1	1983
John Feeney	1	1983-1985
Ray Gilbody	2	1985-1987
Billy Hardy*	5	1987-1991
Joe Kelly	1	1992
Drew Docherty	2	1992-

Featherweight (126 lbs)

Title Holder	Lonsdale Belt Notches	Tenure
Fred Johnson		1890-1895
Billy Reader		1891
Billy Reader		1891-1892
Harry Spurden		1892-1895
Fred Johnson		1895-1897
Harry Greenfield		1896-1899
Ben Jordan*		1897-1900
Jabez White		1899-1900
Will Curley		1900-1901
Jack Roberts		1901-1902
Will Curley		1902-1903
Ben Jordan*		1902-1905
Joe Bowker*		1905
Johnny Summers		1906
Joe Bowker		1905-1906
Jim Driscoll		1906-1907
Spike Robson*		1906-1907
Jim Driscoll*	3	1907-1913
Spike Robson		1907-1910
Ted Kid Lewis*	1	1913-1914
Llew Edwards*	1	1915-1917
Charlie Hardcastle	1	1917

Title Holder	Lonsdale Belt Notches	Tenure
Tancy Lee*	3	1917-1919
Mike Honeyman	2	1920-1921
Joe Fox*	1	1921-1922
George McKenzie	2	1924-1925
Johnny Curley	2	1925-1927
Johnny Cuthbert	1	1927-1928
Harry Corbett	1	1928-1929
Johnny Cuthbert	2	1929-1931
Nel Tarleton	1	1931-1932
Seaman Tommy Watson	2	1932-1934
Nel Tarleton	2	1934-1936
Johnny McGrory*	1	1936-1938
Jim Spider Kelly	1	1938-1939
Johnny Cusick	1	1939-1940
Nel Tarleton*	3	1940-1947
Ronnie Clayton	6	1947-1954
Sammy McCarthy	1	1954-1955
Billy Spider Kelly	1	1955-1956
Charlie Hill	3	1956-1959
Bobby Neill	1	1959-1960
Terry Spinks	2	1960-1961
Howard Winstone*	7	1961-1969
Jimmy Revie	2	1969-1971
Evan Armstrong	2	1971-1972
Tommy Glencross	1	1972-1973
Evan Armstrong*	2	1973-1975
Vernon Sollas	1	1975-1977
Alan Richardson	2	1977-1978
Dave Needham	2	1978-1979
Pat Cowdell*	3	1979-1982
Steve Sims*	1	1982-1983
Barry McGuigan*	2	1983-1986
Robert Dickie*	3	1986-1988
Peter Harris	1	1988
Paul Hodkinson*	3	1988-1990
Sean Murphy	2	1990-1991
Gary de Roux	1	1991
Colin McMillan*	3	1991-1992
John Davison*	1	1992-1993
Sean Murphy	1	1993-

S. Featherweight (130 lbs)

Title Holder	Lonsdale Belt Notches	Tenure
Jimmy Anderson*	3	1968-1970
John Doherty	1	1986
Pat Cowdell	1	1986
Najib Daho	1	1986-1987
Pat Cowdell	1	1987-1988
Floyd Havard	1	1988-1989
John Doherty	1	1989-1990
Joey Jacobs	1	1990
Hugh Forde	1	1990
Kevin Pritchard	1	1990-1991
Robert Dickie	1	1991
Sugar Gibiliru	1	1991
John Doherty	1	1991-1992
Michael Armstrong	1	1992
Neil Haddock	1	1992-

Lightweight (135 lbs)

Title Holder	Lonsdale Belt Notches	Tenure
Dick Burge		1891-1897
Harry Nickless		1891-1894
Tom Causer		1894-1897
Tom Causer		1897
Dick Burge*		1897-1901
Jabez White		1902-1906
Jack Goldswain		1906-1908
Johnny Summers		1908-1909
Freddie Welsh	1	1909-1911
Matt Wells	1	1911-1912

Title Holder	Lonsdale Belt Notches	Tenure
Freddie Welsh*	1	1912-1919
Bob Marriott*	1	1919-1920
Ernie Rice	1	1921-1922
Seaman Nobby Hall		1922-1923
Harry Mason*		1923-1924
Ernie Izzard	2	1924-1925
Harry Mason		1924-1925
Harry Mason*	1	1925-1928
Sam Steward		1928-1929
Fred Webster		1929-1930
Al Foreman*	1	1930-1932
Johnny Cuthbert		1932-1934
Harry Mizler		1934
Jackie Kid Berg		1934-1936
Jimmy Walsh	1	1936-1938
Dave Crowley	1	1938
Eric Boon	3	1938-1944
Ronnie James*	1	1944-1947
Billy Thompson	3	1947-1951
Tommy McGovern	1	1951-1952
Frank Johnson*	1	1952-1953
Joe Lucy	1	1953-1955
Frank Johnson	1	1955-1956
Joe Lucy	2	1956-1957
Dave Charnley*	3	1957-1965
Maurice Cullen*	4	1965-1968
Ken Buchanan*	2	1968-1971
Willie Reilly*	1	1972
Jim Watt	1	1972-1973
Ken Buchanan*	1	1973-1974
Jim Watt*	2	1975-1977
Charlie Nash*	1	1978-1979
Ray Cattouse	2	1980-1982
George Feeney*	3	1982-1985
Tony Willis	3	1985-1987
Alex Dickson	1	1987-1988
Steve Boyle*	2	1988-1990
Carl Crook	5	1990-1992
Billy Schwer	1	1992-1993
Paul Burke	1	1993-

L. Welterweight (140 lbs)

Title Holder	Lonsdale Belt Notches	Tenure
Des Rea	1	1968-1969
Vic Andreetti*	2	1969-1970
Des Morrison	1	1973-1974
Pat McCormack	1	1974
Joey Singleton	3	1974-1976
Dave Boy Green*	1	1976-1977
Colin Power*	2	1977-1978
Clinton McKenzie	1	1978-1979
Colin Power	1	1979
Clinton McKenzie	5	1979-1984
Terry Marsh*	1	1984-1986
Tony Laing*	1	1986
Tony McKenzie	2	1986-1987
Lloyd Christie	3	1987-1989
Clinton McKenzie*	1	1989
Pat Barrett*	2	1989-1990
Tony Ekubia	1	1990-1991
Andy Holligan	3	1991-

Welterweight (147 lbs)

Title Holder	Lonsdale Belt Notches	Tenure
Charlie Allum		1903-1904
Charlie Knock		1904-1906
Curly Watson*		1906-1910
Young Joseph		1908-1910
Young Joseph	1	1910-1911
Arthur Evernden		1911-1912
Johnny Summers		1912

Title Holder	Lonsdale Belt Notches	Tenure	Title Holder	Lonsdale Belt Notches	Tenure	Title Holder	Lonsdale Belt Notches	Tenure
Johnny Summers	2	1912-1914	Harry Mason		1925-1926	Eddie Thomas	2	1949-1951
Tom McCormick		1914	Jack Hood*	3	1926-1934	Wally Thom	1	1951-1952
Matt Wells*		1914	Harry Mason		1934	Cliff Curvis*	1	1952-1953
Johnny Basham	3	1914-1920	Pat Butler*		1934-1936	Wally Thom	2	1953-1956
Matt Wells		1914-1919	Dave McCleave		1936	Peter Waterman*	2	1956-1958
Ted Kid Lewis		1920-1924	Jake Kilrain	1	1936-1939	Tommy Molloy	2	1958-1960
Tommy Milligan*		1924-1925	Ernie Roderick	5	1939-1948	Wally Swift	1	1960
Hamilton Johnny Brown		1925	Henry Hall	1	1948-1949	Brian Curvis*	7	1960-1966

After being pounded to the canvas by British light-middleweight champion, Andy Till, the challenger, Tony Collins, was halted moments later

Les Clark

Title Holder	Lonsdale Belt Notches	Tenure
Johnny Cooke	2	1967-1968
Ralph Charles*	3	1968-1972
Bobby Arthur	1	1972-1973
John H. Stracey*	1	1973-1975
Pat Thomas	2	1975-1976
Henry Rhiney	2	1976-1979
Kirkland Laing	1	1979-1980
Colin Jones*	3	1980-1982
Lloyd Honeyghan*	2	1983-1985
Kostas Petrou	1	1985
Sylvester Mittee	1	1985
Lloyd Honeyghan*	1	1985-
1986Kirkland Laing	4	1987-1991
Del Bryan	2	1991-1992
Gary Jacobs*	2	1992-1993

L. Middleweight (154 lbs)

Title Holder	Lonsdale Belt Notches	Tenure
Larry Paul	2	1973-1974
Maurice Hope*	3	1974-1977
Jimmy Batten	3	1977-1979
Pat Thomas	3	1979-1981
Herol Graham*	2	1981-1983
Prince Rodney*	1	1983-1984
Jimmy Cable	2	1984-1985
Prince Rodney	2	1985-1986
Chris Pyatt*	1	1986
Lloyd Hibbert*	1	1987
Gary Cooper	1	1988
Gary Stretch*	2	1988-1990
Wally Swift Jnr	2	1991-1992
Andy Till	3	1992-

Middleweight (160 lbs)

Title Holder	Lonsdale Belt Notches	Tenure
Ted Pritchard*		1891-1892
Ted White		1893-1896
Ted Pritchard		1894
Anthony Diamond		1898
Dido Plumb		1900
Jack Palmer		1902-1903
Charlie Allum		1905-1906
Pat O'Keefe		1906
Pat O'Keefe		1906
Tom Thomas	1	1906-1910
Jim Sullivan*	1	1910-1912
Jack Harrison*	1	1912-1913
Pat O'Keefe	2	1914-1916
Bandsman Jack Blake	1	1916-1918
Pat O'Keefe*	1	1918-1919
Ted Kid Lewis		1920-1921
Tom Gummer	1	1920-1921
Gus Platts		1921
Johnny Basham*		1921
Ted Kid Lewis	2	1921-1923
Johnny Basham		1921
Roland Todd*		1923-1925
Roland Todd		1925-1927
Tommy Milligan	1	1926-1928
Frank Moody		1927-1928
Alex Ireland		1928-1929
Len Harvey	5	1929-1933
Jock McAvoy*	3+2	1933-1944
Ernie Roderick	1	1945-1946
Vince Hawkins	1	1946-1948
Dick Turpin	2	1948-1950
Albert Finch	1	1950
Randy Turpin*	1	1950-1954
Johnny Sullivan	1	1954-1955
Pat McAteer*	3	1955-1958

Title Holder	Lonsdale Belt Notches	Tenure
Terry Downes	1	1958-1959
John Cowboy McCormack	1	1959
Terry Downes*	2	1959-1962
George Aldridge	1	1962-1963
Mick Leahy	1	1963-1964
Wally Swift	1	1964-1965
Johnny Pritchett*	4	1965-1969
Les McAteer	1	1969-1970
Mark Rowe	1	1970
Bunny Sterling	4	1970-1974
Kevin Finnegan*	1	1974
Bunny Sterling*	1	1975
Alan Minter*	3	1975-1977
Kevin Finnegan	1	1977
Alan Minter*	1	1977-1978
Tony Sibson	1	1979
Kevin Finnegan*	1	1979-1980
Roy Gumbs	3	1981-1983
Mark Kaylor	1	1983-1984
Tony Sibson*	1	1984
Herol Graham*	1	1985-1986
Brian Anderson	1	1986-1987
Tony Sibson*	1	1987-1988
Herol Graham	4	1988-1992
Frank Grant	2	1992-

S. Middleweight (168 lbs)

Title Holder	Lonsdale Belt Notches	Tenure
Sammy Storey	2	1989-1990
James Cook*	1	1990-1991
Fidel Castro	2	1991-1992
Henry Wharton*	1	1992-1993

L. Heavyweight (175lbs)

Title Holder	Lonsdale Belt Notches	Tenure
Dennis Haugh		1913-1914
Dick Smith	2	1914-1916
Harry Reeve*	1	1916-1917
Dick Smith*	1	1918-1919
Boy McCormick*	1	1919-1921
Jack Bloomfield*	1	1922-1924
Tom Berry	1	1925-1927
Gipsy Daniels*	1	1927
Frank Moody	1	1927-1929
Harry Crossley	1	1929-1932
Jack Petersen*	1	1932
Len Harvey*	1	1933-1934
Eddie Phillips		1935-1937
Jock McAvoy	1	1937-1938
Len Harvey	2	1938-1942
Freddie Mills*	1	1942-1950
Don Cockell	2	1950-1952
Randy Turpin*	1	1952
Dennis Powell	1	1953
Alex Buxton	2	1953-1955
Randy Turpin	1	1955
Ron Barton*	1	1956
Randy Turpin*	2	1956-1958
Chic Calderwood*	4	1960-1966
Young John McCormack	2	1967-1969
Eddie Avoth	2	1969-1971
Chris Finnegan	2	1971-1973
John Conteh*	2	1973-1974
Johnny Frankham	1	1975
Chris Finnegan*	1	1975-1976
Tim Wood	1	1976-1977
Bunny Johnson*	3	1977-1981
Tom Collins	3	1982-1984
Dennis Andries*	5	1984-1986

Title Holder	Lonsdale Belt Notches	Tenure
Tom Collins*	1	1987
Tony Wilson	3	1987-1989
Tom Collins*	1	1989-1990
Steve McCarthy*	1	1990-1991
Crawford Ashley*	3	1991-1992
Maurice Coore	1	1992-

Cruiserweight (190 lbs)

Title Holder	Lonsdale Belt Notches	Tenure
Sam Reeson*	1	1985-1986
Andy Straughn	1	1986-1987
Roy Smith	1	1987
Tee Jay	1	1987-1988
Glenn McCrory*	2	1988
Andy Straughn	1	1988-1989
Johnny Nelson*	3	1989-1991
Derek Angol*	2	1991-1992
Carl Thompson	1	1992-

Heavyweight (190 lbs +)

Title Holder	Lonsdale Belt Notches	Tenure
Charlie Mitchell*		1882-1894
Ted Pritchard		1891-1895
Jem Smith*		1895-1896
George Chrisp		1901
Jack Scales		1901-1902
Jack Palmer		1903-1906
Gunner Moir		1906-1909
Iron Hague		1909-1910
P.O. Curran		1910-1911
Iron Hague		1910-1911
Bombardier Billy Wells	3	1911-1919
Joe Beckett*		1919
Frank Goddard	1	1919
Joe Beckett		1919
Joe Beckett*	1	1919-1923
Frank Goddard		1923-1926
Phil Scott*		1926-1931
Reggie Meen		1931-1932
Jack Petersen	3	1932-1933
Len Harvey		1933-1934
Jack Petersen		1934-1936
Ben Foord		1936-1937
Tommy Farr	1	1937-1938
Len Harvey*	1	1938-1942
Jack London	1	1944-1945
Bruce Woodcock	2	1945-1950
Jack Gardner	1	1950-1952
Johnny Williams	1	1952-1953
Don Cockell*	1	1953-1956
Joe Erskine	2	1956-1958
Brian London	1	1958-1959
Henry Cooper*	9	1959-1969
Jack Bodell	1	1969-1970
Henry Cooper	1	1970-1971
Joe Bugner	1	1971
Jack Bodell	1	1971-1972
Danny McAlinden	1	1972-1975
Bunny Johnson	1	1975
Richard Dunn	2	1975-1976
Joe Bugner*	1	1976-1977
John L. Gardner*	2	1978-1980
Gordon Ferris	1	1981
Neville Meade	1	1981-1983
David Pearce*	1	1983-1985
Hughroy Currie	1	1985-1986
Horace Notice*	4	1986-1988
Gary Mason	2	1989-1991
Lennox Lewis*	3	1991-1993
Herbie Hide	1	1993-

British Area Title Bouts, 1992-93

Central Area

Titleholders at 30 June 1993
Fly: *vacant.* **Bantam:** Chris Clarkson. **Feather:** Craig Dermody. **S. Feather:** Floyd Churchill. **Light:** Kevin Toomey. **L. Welter:** Richard Burton. **Welter:** Ossie Maddix. **L. Middle:** Warren Stowe. **Middle:** *vacant.* **S. Middle:** Glenn Campbell. **L. Heavy:** Michael Gale. **Cruiser:** *vacant:* **Heavy:** Michael Murray.

Title Bouts (1 July 1992 - 30 June 1993)
24 September 1992   Richard Burton w pts 10 Rob Stewart, Stockport (L. Welter Defence)
13 October 1992   Craig Dermody w pts 10 Russell Davison, Bury (Feather Challenge)
29 October 1992   Michael Gale w pts 10 Bobbi Joe Edwards, Leeds (Vacant L. Heavy)
26 November 1992   Dean Bramhald w pts 10 Kevin Toomey, Hull (Light Challenge)
18 February 1993   Kevin Toomey w pts 10 Dean Bramhald, Hull (Light Challenge)
25 February 1993   Warren Stowe w dis 4 Robert Riley, Burnley (Vacant L. Middle)
22 April 1993   Glenn Campbell w rsc 4 Paul Wright, Bury (S. Middle Defence)
4 May 1993   Floyd Churchill w co 1 Jimmy Owens, Liverpool (Vacant S. Feather)

Midlands Area

Titleholders at 30 June 1993
Fly: *vacant.* **Bantam:** *vacant.* **Feather:** Kelton McKenzie. **S. Feather:** Pete Buckley. **Light:** Peter Till. **L. Welter:** Malcolm Melvin. **Welter:** *vacant.* **L. Middle:** Steve Goodwin. **Middle:** Antonio Fernandez. **S. Middle:** Carlos Christie. **L. Heavy:** John J. Cooke. **Cruiser:** Steve Lewsam. **Heavy:** *vacant.*

Title Bouts (1 July 1992 - 30 June 1993)
16 March 1993   Malcolm Melvin w pts 10 Shaun Cogan, Edgbaston (L. Welter Defence)
12 May 1993   Steve Goodwin w pts 10 Mark Dawson, Stoke (Vacant L. Middle)
17 June 1993   John J. Cooke w rsc 9 Gil Lewis, Bedworth (Vacant L. Heavy)
During the above period, Ernie Loveridge (Welter) and Gary Osborne (L. Middle) relinquished their titles. Roy Skeldon (L. Heavy) retired.

Northern Area

Titleholders at 30 June 1993
Fly: *vacant.* **Bantam:** *vacant.* **Feather:** *vacant.* **S. Feather:** Frankie Foster. **Light:** *vacant.* **L. Welter:** Paul Charters. **Welter:** *vacant.* **L. Middle:** Mark Cichocki. **Middle:** *vacant.* **S. Middle:** *vacant.* **L. Heavy:** Terry French. **Cruiser:** *vacant.* **Heavy:** Paul Lister.

Title Bouts (1 July 1992 - 30 June 1993)
10 September 1992   Frankie Foster w pts 10 Darren Elsdon, Sunderland (S. Feather Challenge)
9 March 1993   Mark Cichocki w rsc 10 Rob Pitters, Hartlepool (Vacant L. Middle)
17 April 1993   Paul Charters w rsc 4 Kevin McKenzie, Washington (Vacant L. Welter)
6 May 1993   Mark Cichocki w rsc 7 Mick Duncan, Hartlepool (L. Middle Defence)
During the above period, Paul Charters (Light) relinquished his title.

Northern Ireland Area
Titleholders at 30 June 1993 - None.

Scottish Area
Titleholders at 30 June 1993

Mickey Cantwell (right) became the first ever Southern Area flyweight champion when he outpointed Darren Fifield over ten action packed rounds

Les Clark

Fly: *vacant.* **Bantam:** *vacant.* **Feather:** Jamie McBride. **S. Feather:** Mark Geraghty. **Light:** Kris McAdam. **L. Welter:** *vacant.* **Welter:** Willie Beattie. **L. Middle:** *vacant.* **Middle:** *vacant.* **S. Middle:** *vacant.* **L. Heavy:** *vacant.* **Cruiser:** *vacant.* **Heavy:** *vacant.*

During the above period, Donnie Hood (Bantam) forfeited his title after losing to Drew Docherty in a British title fight and Robert Harkin (L. Welter) retired.

Southern Area

Titleholders at 30 June 1993
Fly: Mickey Cantwell. **Bantam:** *vacant.* **Feather:** *vacant.* **S. Feather:** *vacant.* **Light:** Felix Kelly. **L. Welter:** Dave Pierre. **Welter:** Gary Logan. **L. Middle:** Kevin Lueshing. **Middle:** W. O. Wilson. **S. Middle:** *vacant.* **L. Heavy:** Glazz Campbell. **Cruiser:** John Graham. **Heavy:** R. F. McKenzie.

Title Bouts (1 July 1992 - 30 June 1993)
29 October 1992   Everton Blake w rsc 4 Gypsy Carman, Hayes (Cruiser Defence)
25 November 1992   John Graham w pts 10 Everton Blake, London (Cruiser Challenge)
17 December 1992   Gary Logan w rsc 4 Roy Rowland, Wembley (Vacant Welter)
31 March 1993   R. F. McKenzie w rsc 8 Warren Richards, London (Vacant Heavy)
14 April 1993   Mickey Cantwell w pts 10 Darren Fifield, London (Vacant Fly)
6 May 1993   W. O. Wilson w rsc 8 John Ogiste, London (Vacant Middle)
23 June 1993   W. O. Wilson w rsc 8 Ian Strudwick, London (Middle Defence)
23 June 1993   Kevin Lueshing w rsc 5 Kirkland Laing, London (Vacant L. Middle)
23 June 1993   Felix Kelly w co 8 A. M. Milton, London (Vacant Light)
During the above period, Michael Ayers (Light) and W. O. Wilson (L. Middle) relinquished their titles. Tony Burke (Middle) retired. Alan McKay lost his belt when he was beaten by Shaun Murphy

for the vacant British featherweight title, while Ian Strudwick forfeited the super-middleweight title when he lost to W. O. Wilson in a Southern Area middleweight challenge.

Welsh Area

Titleholders at 30 June 1993
Fly: *vacant.* **Bantam:** *vacant.* **Feather:** *vacant.* **S. Feather:** Barrie Kelley. **Light:** Mervyn Bennett. **L. Welter:** *vacant.* **Welter:** John Davies. **L. Middle:** Carlo Colarusso. **Middle:** Wayne Ellis. **S. Middle:** Darron Griffiths. **L. Heavy:** *vacant.* **Cruiser:** *vacant.* **Heavy:** Chris Jacobs.

Title Bouts (1 July 1992 - 30 June 1993)
14 July 1992   Wayne Ellis w rsc 7 Mike Phillips, London (Middle Defence)
19 January 1993   Barrie Kelley w pts 10 Edward Lloyd, Cardiff (Vacant S. Feather)
27 January 1993   Mervyn Bennett w pts 10 Carl Hook, Cardiff (Vacant Light)
24 March 1993   Darron Griffiths w rsc 6 John Kaighin, Cardiff (Vacant S. Middle)
During the above period, Steve Robinson (Feather) and Neil Haddock (S. Feather) relinquished their titles.

Western Area

Titleholders at 30 June 1993
Fly: *vacant.* **Bantam:** *vacant.* **Feather:** *vacant.* **S. Feather:** Greg Upton. **Light:** *vacant.* **L. Welter:** *vacant.* **Welter:** Ross Hale. **L. Middle:** Dean Cooper. **Middle:** *vacant.* **S. Middle:** *vacant.* **L. Heavy:** *vacant.* **Cruiser:** *vacant.* **Heavy:** *vacant.*

Title Bouts (1 July 1992 - 30 June 1993)
7 July 1992   Ross Hale w rsc 8 Julian Eavis, Bristol (Vacant Welter)
27 May 1993   Greg Upton w co 2 Trevor Royal, Bristol (Vacant S. Feather)
26 June 1993   Dean Cooper w pts 10 Julian Eavis, Keynsham (Vacant L. Middle)

Following a tremendous battle of swaying fortunes, Felix Kelly (right) found a corking left-hook to kayo A.M. Milton in the eighth round of their Southern Area lightweight title fight.

Les Clark

Commonwealth Title Bouts, 1992-93

15 September, 1992   Andy Holligan 9.13 (England) W CO 7 Tony Ekubia 9.13 (England), Liverpool, England. Light-Welterweight Title Defence.

For a report see under British Title Bouts, 1992-93.

15 September, 1992   Mickey Hughes 11.0 (England) W PTS 12 Craig Trotter 10.13 (Australia), London, England. Vacant Light-Middleweight Title.

Controversially awarded a 118-117½ verdict by referee, Roy Francis, Hughes, who finished the fight cut over the left eye, finally picked himself up a title after all the years of hard work. Trotter boxed well in this, his third attempt to win a Commonwealth title, and was agrieved at not getting the decision, but it had been close. The title had been vacated by Chris Pyatt when he decided to move up a weight division.

23 September, 1992   Henry Wharton 11.12¾ (England) W PTS 12 Fidel Castro 11.13½ (England), Leeds, England. Super-Middleweight Title Defence.

For a report see under British Title Bouts, 1992-93.

1 October, 1992   Richie Woodhall 11.4¾ (England) W PTS 12 John Ashton 11.5¾ (England), Oakengates, England. Middleweight Title Defence.

In a very good competitive match, it was Woodhall's left-jab and right-cross which finally won the day. The cagey Ashton boxed well, was difficult to nail and did well on the inside, where the champion showed his inexperience. The referee, John Coyle, scored the bout 119½-115½.

7 October, 1992   Billy Hardy 8.13½ (England) W RSC 10 Rick Raynor 9.0 (Australia), Sunderland, England. Vacant Featherweight Title.

Fighting for the title vacated after Colin McMillan became WBO champion, the Australian finally began to crack under the constant pressure and with two cuts over the left eye, referee, Mickey Vann, rescued him at 1.15 of the tenth round. Hardy had been a revelation at the higher weight, picking his shots accurately with both hands and often punching his rival around the ring.

28 October, 1992   Carl Crook 9.8½ (England) L RTD 9 Billy Schwer 9.8 (England), London England. Lightweight Title Defence.

For a report see under British Title Bouts, 1992-93.

31 October, 1992   Lennox Lewis 16.3½ (England) W RSC 2 Donovan Ruddock 16.7½ (Canada), London, England. Heavyweight Title Defence.

The former Olympic champion, Lewis, was sensational as he recorded a stoppage victory at 0.46 of the second round, having blasted the feared Canadian to the canvas three times in a bout that was also a final eliminator for the WBC title. From the moment that the bemused Ruddock was in trouble, Lewis never left him alone. His hand speed was totally bewildering and the power that he exuded would have sent shock waves through the division. The bout was refereed by the American, Joe Cortez.

24 November, 1992   Donovan Boucher 10.6 (Canada) L RSC 3 Eamonn Loughran 10.6 (Ireland), Doncaster, England. Welterweight Title Defence.

Mickey Hughes (left) finally won a title after seven years as a pro when he took a narrow points verdict over Australian, Craig Trotter, to become the Commonwealth light-middleweight champion   Les Clark

Another Canadian favourite bit the dust when Eamonn Loughran wrested the title from the tried and tested Boucher. Loughran made a good start, but it was in the third round that the action really warmed up. The champion was sent to the canvas three times before the referee, Adrian Morgan, dived in to rescue him after 2.10 of the round had elapsed.

3 December, 1992   John Armour 8.5 (England) W RSC 5 Albert Musankabala 8.4 (Zambia), London, England. Bantamweight Title Defence.

After gradually imposing himself on the African during the opening four rounds, the impressive Armour stepped up another gear in the fifth when he went for the finish. The end was sudden as Musankabala walked on to a cracking short right-hook and fell face down. He climbed up at six, but the referee, Larry O'Connell, had seen enough and called a halt to the proceedings at 0.47 of the round.

30 January, 1993   Mickey Hughes 10.13 (England) L RSC 5 Lloyd Honeyghan 10.12 (England), Brentwood, England. Light-Middleweight Title Defence.

Right from the off, Hughes went looking for the former world welterweight champion, but instead of getting on top of Honeyghan he found himself on the wrong end of sharp counters. The finish came in the fifth as Honeyghan missed with the right, but caught his rival with an arcing left-hook, which opened up a cut on Hughes' nose that later required ten stitches. With a minute gone of the fifth round, Dave Parris stopped the contest to save Hughes from suffering further damage.

6 February, 1993   Eamonn Loughran 10.6¾ (Ireland) W RSC 6 Michael Benjamin 10.5½ (Guyana), Cardiff, Wales. Welterweight Title Defence.

Using body punches to break up his opponent, Loughran showed yet again that he is improving all the time. Several times on shaky legs, Benjamin tried desperately to take the fight to the Irishman, but was outpunched continually. By the sixth it was only bravery that kept the challenger going and a chopping right hand sent Benjamin collapsing to the floor. With 0.43 of the round gone, the referee, Adrian Morgan, immediately called a halt to the proceedings.

10 February, 1993   John Armour 8.4¾ (England) W PTS 12 Morgan Mpande 8.4 (Zambia), London, England. Bantamweight Title Defence.

A Gruelling distance fight saw Armour survive a knockdown and overcome a badly cut left eye to take a close 118-117 decision. The African was a hard nut to crack, but once Armour got to work downstairs, albeit receiving several warnings to keep them up from the referee, Roy Francis, he slowed his rival appreciably.

24 February, 1993   Billy Schwer 9.8½ (England) L RSC 7 Paul Burke 9.8½ (England), Wembley, England. Lightweight Title Defence.

For a report see under British Title Bouts, 1992-93.

18 March, 1993   Henry Akinwande 16.0 (England) W PTS 12 Jimmy Thunder 15.12 (New Zealand), London, England. Vacant Heavyweight Title.

Following an extremely dull contest, the referee, John Coyle, awarded Henry Akinwande a 118½-116½ points decision. The pattern of the fight was set early on, with the 6' 7" Akinwande flicking out fast jabs and retreating, while Thunder would invariably throw punches from out of range. While there was no argument as to the winner, Akinwande lacked the power to finish inside the distance and will find Lennox Lewis, who had vacated the title on becoming WBC champion, a hard act to follow.

7 April, 1993   Brent Kosolofski 12.6¼ (Canada) W RSC 9 Michael Gale 12.6½ (England), Leeds, England. Vacant Light-Heavyweight Title.

The Canadian proved a revelation as he not only put a dent in Gale's previously unbeaten record, but at the same time he captured the title that had been vacated by the Australian, Guy Waters. He rarely took a backward step and began to walk through Gale in the fifth. Although not floored, the Englishman, almost out on his feet and shipping punishment, was rescued by Mickey Vann after 2.06 of round nine.

19 May, 1993   Billy Hardy 8.13 (England) W PTS 12 Barrington Francis 9.0 (Guyana), Sunderland, England. Featherweight Title Defence.

Badly cut by the side of the left eye and dropped heavily in the second round for an eight count, where lesser men would have crumbled, the champion merely gritted his teeth and kept going. Prior the final bell, it had appeared desperately close, with Hardy needing to win the round clearly in order to remain champion and although doing so, to the surprise of many, he was awarded a clear 119½-116 decision by referee, Billy Rafferty.

29 June, 1993   Francis Ampofo 8.0 (England) W RSC 3 Albert Musankabala 7.13 (Zambia), London, England. Vacant Flyweight Title.

Fighting for the title vacated by Alfred Kotei, currently residing in the USA, Albert Musankabala was given a second chance to become a Commonwealth champion inside seven months, having earlier been defeated for the bantamweight crown by John Armour. This time he was stopped at 1.08 of the third, when referee, Larry O'Connell, decided he was in no fit state to continue. Having been floored by a tremendous right to the side of the head, he just about got to his feet at the count of nine, but with Ampofo menacing, the fight was wisely called off.

Note: Derek Angol vacated the cruiserweight title during the period, following a bad defeat when challenging for the European crown.

Commonwealth Champions, 1908-1993

Prior to 1970, the championship was contested as for the British Empire title.

COMMONWEALTH COUNTRY CODE
A = Australia; BAH = Bahamas; BAR = Barbados; BER = Bermuda; C = Canada; E = England; F = Fiji; GH = Ghana; GU = Guyana; I = Ireland; J = Jamaica; K = Kenya; N = Nigeria; NZ = New Zealand; NI = Northern Ireland; PNG = Papua New Guinea; SA = South Africa; SAM = Samoa; S = Scotland; T = Tonga; TR = Trinidad; U = Uganda; W = Wales; ZA = Zambia; ZI = Zimbabwe.

*Undefeated champions

Title Holder	Country	Tenure
Flyweight (112 lbs)		
Elky Clark*	S	1924-1927
Jackie Paterson	S	1940-1948
Rinty Monaghan*	NI	1948-1950
Teddy Gardner	E	1952
Jake Tuli	SA	1952-1954
Dai Dower*	W	1954-1957
Frankie Jones	S	1957
Dennis Adams*	SA	1957-1962
Jackie Brown	S	1962-1963
Walter McGowan*	S	1963-1969
John McCluskey	S	1970-1971
Henry Nissen	A	1971-1974
Big Jim West*	A	1974-1975
Patrick Mambwe	ZA	1976-1979
Ray Amoo	N	1980
Steve Muchoki	K	1980-1983
Keith Wallace*	E	1983-1984
Richard Clarke*	J	1986-1987
Nana Yaw Konadu*	GH	1987-1989
Alfred Kotei*	GH	1989-1993
Francis Ampofo	E	1993-
Bantamweight (118 lbs)		
Jim Higgins	S	1920-1922

Title Holder	Country	Tenure
Tommy Harrison	E	1922-1923
Bugler Harry Lake	E	1923
Johnny Brown	E	1923-1928
Teddy Baldock*	E	1928-1930
Dick Corbett	E	1930-1932
Johnny King	E	1932-1934
Dick Corbett*	E	1934
Jim Brady	S	1941-1945
Jackie Paterson	S	1945-1949
Stan Rowan	E	1949
Vic Toweel	SA	1949-1952
Jimmy Carruthers*	A	1952-1954
Peter Keenan	S	1955-1959
Freddie Gilroy*	NI	1959-1963
Johnny Caldwell	NI	1964-1965
Alan Rudkin	E	1965-1966
Walter McGowan	S	1966-1968
Alan Rudkin	E	1968-1969
Lionel Rose*	A	1969
Alan Rudkin*	E	1970-1972
Paul Ferreri	A	1972-1977
Sulley Shittu*	GH	1977-1978
Johnny Owen*	W	1978-1980
Paul Ferreri	A	1981-1986
Ray Minus*	BAH	1986-1991

Title Holder	Country	Tenure
John Armour	E	1992-
Featherweight (126 lbs)		
Jim Driscoll*	W	1908-1913
Llew Edwards*	W	1915-1917
Johnny McGrory*	S	1936-1938
Jim Spider Kelly	NI	1938-1939
Johnny Cusick	E	1939-1940
Nel Tarleton*	E	1940-1947
Tiger Al Phillips	E	1947
Ronnie Clayton	E	1947-1951
Roy Ankrah	GH	1951-1954
Billy Spider Kelly	NI	1954-1955
Hogan Kid Bassey*	N	1955-1957
Percy Lewis	TR	1957-1960
Floyd Robertson	GH	1960-1967
John O'Brien	S	1967
Johnny Famechon*	A	1967-1969
Toro George	NZ	1970-1972
Bobby Dunne	A	1972-1974
Evan Armstrong	S	1974
David Kotey*	GH	1974-1975
Eddie Ndukwu	N	1977-1980
Pat Ford*	GU	1980-1981
Azumah Nelson*	GH	1981-1985
Tyrone Downes*	BAR	1986-1988
Thunder Aryeh	GH	1988-1989
Oblitey Commey	GH	1989-1990
Modest Napunyi	K	1990-1991
Barrington Francis*	C	1991
Colin McMillan*	E	1992
Billy Hardy	E	1992-
S. Featherweight (130 lbs)		
Billy Moeller	A	1975-1977
Johnny Aba*	PNG	1977-1982
Langton Tinago	ZI	1983-1984
John Sichula	ZA	1984
Lester Ellis*	A	1984-1985
John Sichula	ZA	1985-1986
Sam Akromah	GH	1986-1987

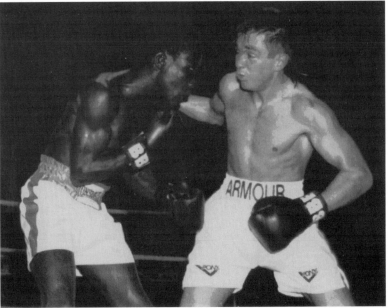

Making his first defence of the Commonwealth bantamweight title, John Armour (right) impressed with a fifth round stoppage win over the experienced Zambian, Albert Musankabala

Les Clark

COMMONWEALTH CHAMPIONS, 1908-1993

Title Holder	Country	Tenure
John Sichula	ZA	1987-1989
Mark Reefer*	E	1989-1990
Thunder Aryeh	GH	1990-1991
Hugh Forde	E	1991
Paul Harvey	E	1991-1992
Tony Pep	C	1992-

Lightweight (135 lbs)

Title Holder	Country	Tenure
Freddie Welsh*	W	1912-1914
Al Foreman	E	1930-1933
Jimmy Kelso	A	1933
Al Foreman*	E	1933-1934
Laurie Stevens*	SA	1936
Arthur King	C	1948-1951
Frank Johnson	E	1953
Pat Ford	A	1953-1954
Ivor Germain	BAR	1954
Pat Ford*	A	1954-1955
Johnny van Rensburg	SA	1955-1956
Willie Toweel	SA	1956-1959
Dave Charnley	E	1959-1962
Bunny Grant	J	1962-1967
Manny Santos*	NZ	1967
Love Allotey	GH	1967-1968
Percy Hayles*	J	1968-1975
Jonathan Dele	N	1975-1977
Lennox Blackmore	GU	1977-1978
Hogan Jimoh	N	1978-1980
Langton Tinago	ZI	1980-1981
Barry Michael	A	1981-1982
Claude Noel	T	1982-1984
Graeme Brooke	A	1984-1985
Barry Michael	A	1985-1986
Langton Tinago	ZI	1986-1987
Mo Hussein	E	1987-1989
Pat Doherty	E	1989
Najib Daho	E	1989-1990
Carl Crook	E	1990-1992
Billy Schwer	E	1992-1993
Paul Burke	E	1993-

L. Welterweight (140 lbs)

Title Holder	Country	Tenure
Joe Tetteh	GH	1972-1973
Hector Thompson	A	1973-1977
Baby Cassius Austin	A	1977-1978
Jeff Malcolm	A	1978-1979
Obisia Nwankpa	N	1979-1983
Billy Famous*	N	1983-1986
Tony Laing	E	1987-1988
Lester Ellis	A	1988-1989
Steve Larrimore	BAH	1989
Tony Ekubia	E	1989-1991
Andy Holligan	E	1991-

Welterweight (147 lbs)

Title Holder	Country	Tenure
Johnny Summers	E	1912-1914
Tom McCormick	I	1914
Matt Wells	E	1914-1919
Johnny Basham	W	1919-1920
Ted Kid Lewis	E	1920-1924
Tommy Milligan*	S	1924-1925
Eddie Thomas	W	1951
Wally Thom	E	1951-1952
Cliff Curvis	W	1952
Gerald Dreyer	SA	1952-1954
Barry Brown	NZ	1954
George Barnes	A	1954-1956
Darby Brown	A	1956
George Barnes	A	1956-1958
Johnny van Rensburg	SA	1958
George Barnes	A	1958-1960

Title Holder	Country	Tenure
Brian Curvis*	W	1960-1966
Johnny Cooke	E	1967-1968
Ralph Charles*	E	1968-1972
Clyde Gray	C	1973-1979
Chris Clarke	C	1979
Clyde Gray*	C	1979-1980
Colin Jones*	W	1981-1984
Sylvester Mittee	E	1984-1985
Lloyd Honeyghan*	E	1985-1986
Brian Janssen	A	1987
Wilf Gentzen	A	1987-1988
Gary Jacobs	S	1988-1989
Donovan Boucher	C	1989-1992
Eamonn Loughran	NI	1992-

L. Middleweight (154 lbs)

Title Holder	Country	Tenure
Charkey Ramon*	A	1972-1975
Maurice Hope*	E	1976-1979
Kenny Bristol	GU	1979-1981
Herol Graham*	E	1981-1984
Ken Salisbury	A	1984-1985
Nick Wilshire	E	1985-1987
Lloyd Hibbert	E	1987
Troy Waters*	A	1987-1991
Chris Pyatt*	E	1991-1992
Mickey Hughes	E	1992-1993
Lloyd Honeyghan	E	1993-

Middleweight (160 lbs)

Title Holder	Country	Tenure
Ted Kid Lewis	E	1922-1923
Roland Todd*	E	1923-1925
Len Johnson*	E	1926
Tommy Milligan	S	1926-1928
Alex Ireland	S	1928-1929
Len Harvey	E	1929-1933
Jock McAvoy*	E	1933-1939
Ron Richards*	A	1940-1941
Bos Murphy	NZ	1948
Dick Turpin	E	1948-1949
Dave Sands*	A	1949-1952
Randy Turpin	E	1952-1954
Johnny Sullivan	E	1954-1955
Pat McAteer	E	1955-1958
Dick Tiger	N	1958-1960
Wilf Greaves	C	1960
Dick Tiger*	N	1960-1962
Gomeo Brennan	BAH	1963-1964
Tuna Scanlon*	NZ	1964
Gomeo Brennan	BAH	1964-1966
Blair Richardson*	C	1966-1967
Milo Calhoun	J	1967
Johnny Pritchett*	E	1967-1969
Les McAteer	E	1969-1970
Mark Rowe	E	1970
Bunny Sterling	E	1970-1972
Tony Mundine*	A	1972-1975
Monty Betham	NZ	1975-1978
Al Korovou	A	1978
Ayub Kalule*	U	1978-1980
Tony Sibson*	E	1980-1983
Roy Gumbs	E	1983
Mark Kaylor	E	1983-1984
Tony Sibson*	E	1984-1988
Nigel Benn	E	1988-1989
Michael Watson*	E	1989-1991
Richie Woodhall	E	1992-

S. Middleweight (168 lbs)

Title Holder	Country	Tenure
Rod Carr	A	1989-1990

Title Holder	Country	Tenure
Lou Cafaro*	A	1990-1991
Henry Wharton	E	1991-

L. Heavyweight (175 lbs)

Title Holder	Country	Tenure
Jack Bloomfield*	E	1923-1924
Tom Berry	E	1927
Gipsy Daniels*	W	1927
Len Harvey	E	1939-1942
Freddie Mills*	E	1942-1950
Randy Turpin*	E	1952-1955
Gordon Wallace	C	1956-1957
Yvon Durelle*	C	1957-1959
Chic Calderwood*	S	1960-1966
Bob Dunlop*	A	1968-1970
Eddie Avoth	W	1970-1971
Chris Finnegan	E	1971-1973
John Conteh*	E	1973-1974
Steve Aczel	A	1975
Tony Mundine	A	1975-1978
Gary Summerhays	C	1978-1979
Lottie Mwale	ZA	1979-1985
Leslie Stewart*	TR	1985-1987
Willie Featherstone	C	1987-1989
Guy Waters*	A	1989-1993
Brent Kosolofski	C	1993-

Cruiserweight (190 lbs)

Title Holder	Country	Tenure
Stewart Lithgo	E	1984
Chisanda Mutti	ZA	1984-1987
Glenn McCrory*	E	1987-1989
Apollo Sweet	A	1989
Derek Angol*	E	1989-1993

Heavyweight (190 lbs +)

Title Holder	Country	Tenure
Tommy Burns	C	1910
P.O. Curran	I	1911
Dan Flynn	I	1911
Bombardier Billy Wells	E	1911-1919
Joe Beckett*	E	1919-1923
Phil Scott	E	1926-1931
Larry Gains	C	1931-1934
Len Harvey	E	1934
Jack Petersen	W	1934-1936
Ben Foord	SA	1936-1937
Tommy Farr*	W	1937-1938
Len Harvey*	E	1939-1942
Jack London	E	1944-1945
Bruce Woodcock	E	1945-1950
Jack Gardner	E	1950-1952
Johnny Williams	W	1952-1953
Don Cockell*	E	1953-1956
Joe Bygraves	J	1956-1957
Joe Erskine	W	1957-1958
Brian London	E	1958-1959
Henry Cooper	E	1959-1971
Joe Bugner	E	1971
Jack Bodell	E	1971-1972
Danny McAlinden	NI	1972-1975
Bunny Johnson	E	1975
Richard Dunn	E	1975-1976
Joe Bugner*	E	1976-1977
John L. Gardner*	E	1978-1981
Trevor Berbick*	C	1981-1986
Horace Notice*	E	1986-1988
Derek Williams	E	1988-1992
Lennox Lewis*	E	1992-1993
Henry Akinwande	E	1993-

European Title Bouts, 1992-93

3 July, 1992   Frank Nicotra 11.13½ (France) W RSC 8 Ray Close 11.12¼ (Ireland), Pontault Combault, France. Super-Middleweight Title Defence.

Boxing well within himself and showing great spirit, the Irishman appeared to be out in front of Nicotra, coming into the eighth, having earlier recovered from a sixth round knockdown at the hands of the heavy hitting champion. However, once the Frenchman had cracked in a tremendous right uppercut flush on the jaw, Close's days were numbered and although he got up, he had nothing left and the referee called a halt with just eleven seconds of the round remaining.

15 August, 1992   Jean-Baptiste Mendy 9.7 (France) W PTS 12 Angel Mona 9.7½ (France), Ajaccio, France. Lightweight Title Defence.

After being decked twice, and then being cut under the right eye, and carrying the added pressure of having been knocked out in one round by his rival two years earlier, Mona came roaring back in the last two sessions. Although he forced Mendy to touch down on a couple of occasions, his efforts came too late and the champion survived to take the 118-112, 117-111, 116-114 points verdict.

23 September, 1992   Yawe Davis 12.6¾ (Italy) DREW 12 Crawford Ashley 12.5¼ (England), Campione

d'Italia, Italy. Vacant Light-Heavyweight Title.

Following twelve rounds of boxing to find a champion for the title vacated by Graciano Rocchigiani, a draw was declared after the officials arrived at scores of 115-115, 114-116 for Davis and 115-112 for Ashley. Davis was the stronger of the two and commanded the centre of the ring for most of the fight, but didn't work hard enough and with neither man ever dominating, a draw was a fair result.

16 October, 1992   Ludovic Proto 10.0½ (France) W PTS 12 Gary Jacobs 10.5½ (Scotland), Paris, France. Vacant Welterweight Title.

In what appeared to be hardly an accurate reflection of how the fight had gone, the three judges awarded the title, vacated on the retirement of Patrizio Oliva, to the lucky Frenchman with scores of 116-114, 117-112, 114-118. Even allowing for a point being deducted from Jacobs' total, for holding, the Scot had warranted victory by beating his rival to the punch in eight of the twelve rounds. And although he held far too much for a man seemingly in control, he was obviously satisfied that he had done enough. Both men suffered cut eyes; Proto to his right, with Jacobs damaged on both.

22 October, 1992   Akim Tafer 13.8 (France) W RSC 10 Derek Angol 13.7¾ (England), Epernay, France.

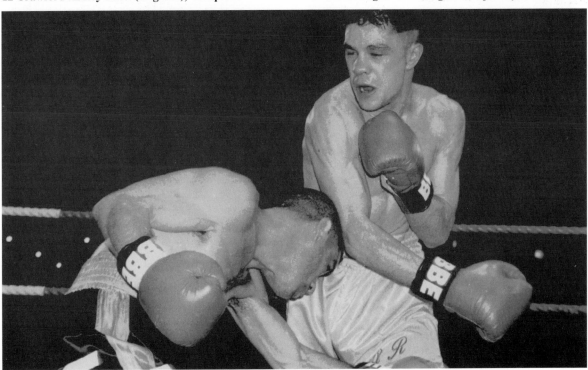

Robbie Regan (right) hits out at Salvatore Fanni on his way to the European flyweight title   Les Clark

Cruiserweight Title Defence.

With turmoil reigning, a rematch was ordered immediately, following the 2.46 tenth round stoppage that had saved Angol from further punishment. The Englishman, way out in front on points and having put the champion down heavily in the second, had been pushed out of the ring by Tafer and given only eight seconds to recover. To be fair, he had been badly hurt only moments before by solid head punches and it was doubtful whether he could have continued anyway.

22 October, 1992   Sumbu Kalambay 11.5½ (Italy) W PTS 12 Steve Collins 11.5½ (Ireland), Verbania, Italy. Middleweight Title Defence.

Although the Irishman made an excellent start, Kalambay began to peg the lead back by the halfway stage and at the final bell, had fully deserved the 117-114, 116-114, 116-116 majority points decision. A dreadful eighth round for Collins, culminating in him being cut over the right eye, was probably the turning point, and apart from the tenth, the wily champion kept his nose in front.

7 November, 1992   Valery Kayumba 9.13¼ (France) W CO 9 Dave Pierre 9.13¾ (England), Differdange, France. Light-Welterweight Title Defence.

Pierre got away well over the early rounds, but began to fade badly as the Frenchman gradually found the range for his heavier blows. There was no real urgency from Kayumba until the ninth, when he began to realise that he could knock his man over and, after being floored three times, the challenger was counted out before the round ended.

14 November, 1992   Salvatore Fanni 7.12 (Italy) L PTS 12 Robbie Regan 7.13½ (Wales), Cardiff, Wales. Flyweight Title Defence.

In a magnificent fight, the little Welshman finally came of age as he outpointed the durable Fanni with scores of 117-114, 117-115, 117-116, showing how hard-fought it had been. The tough champion certainly hadn't come to lose and tried to match his challenger all the way. However, the younger Regan proved too fresh and too mobile and once he had made the body his target, Fanni's title began to find its way to Wales with full backing from the exhuberent, singing fans.

17 November, 1992   Jean-Baptiste Mendy 9.8 (France) W PTS 12 Paul Burke 9.8 (England), Paris, France. Lightweight Title Defence.

The Frenchman was always in control, a fact reflected by the scores of 120-112, 119-109, 118-113 in his favour, but once he had injured his right hand in the seventh, he ceased to look for a knockout win and concentrated instead on adding to his points total. Burke boxed well, after a slow start, but ultimately gave way to the champion's superior skills and technique.

29 November, 1992   Jean-Claude Fontana 10.12¾ (France) L CO 3 Laurent Boudouani 10.12½ (France), Dijon, France. Light-Middleweight Title Defence.

The former Olympic silver medallist, Boudouani, finally came good as he knocked out his fellow-Frenchman to take the title. A cracking right-hook that sent Fontana crashing into the ropes for a standing eight count in the second was the beginning of the end. The champion somehow made it through to the bell, but was then subjected to an unmerciful battering in the third until falling to the floor to be counted out.

3 December, 1992   Regilio Tuur 9.3½ (Holland) W PTS 12 Jacobin Yoma 9.3½ (France), Rotterdam, Holland. Vacant Super-Featherweight Title.

To celebrate a new era of Dutch boxing, Tuur made an excellent start against an opponent who had drawn with him three years earlier in New York and he quickly moved in front. But Yoma, although cut on the right eye in the fourth, was not done for and hit back strongly in the middle rounds, only for the former Olympian to re-assert himself and finish strongly to take a 118-115, 116-114, 115-113 (Paul Thomas) decision. The title had become vacant after Jimmy Bredahl had won the WBO version of the world championship.

16 December, 1992   Vincenzo Nardiello 11.13¼ (Italy) W PTS 12 Fidel Castro 11.12½ (England), Ariccia, Italy. Vacant Super-Middleweight Title.

Unanimously outpointed 118-113, 117-114, 116-115 by the Italian southpaw, Castro could hardly complain after not putting in the work required to lift the title, vacated by the Frenchman, Franck Nicotra, away from home. He had his chances though and in the fourth round severely rocked Nardiello, but the Italian weathered the storm and methodically boxed his way to victory.

18 December, 1992   Fabrice Benichou 8.13½ (France) L PTS 12 Maurizio Stecca 8.13½ (Italy), Clermont Ferrard, France. Featherweight Title Defence.

In winning the title from the tough Frenchman on a 113-114 (referee, John Coyle), 117-113, 114-112 majority points decision, away from home, Stecca went a long way towards reviving his career. Lucky not to be disqualified, the champion was warned several times for misuse of the head and it was headwork that split Stecca's left eye in the seventh. However, the better boxing of the Italian got him home, while Benichou had only himself to blame.

19 December, 1992   Axel Schulz 14.9 (Germany) DREW 12 Henry Akinwande 15.0½ (England), Berlin, Germany. Vacant Heavyweight Title.

Unable to turn his superior boxing ability over the plodding, one paced German, into an inside the distance victory, an indictment of his punching power, Akinwande, instead, had to rely on the judges and a majority draw by scores of 115-115, 115-115, 118-115, in his favour.

Although having a tendency to slap and flick his punches made the fight difficult to score, even allowing for that, Akinwande surely did enough to beat the limited Schulz. With Lennox Lewis pursuing his world title ambitions, he was forced to vacate the championship he had dearly wished to keep.

27 January, 1993 Vincenzo Belcastro 8.5½ (Italy) W PTS 12 Antonio Picardi 8.5¼ (Italy), Orzinuovi, Italy. Vacant Bantamweight Title.

Awarded a very close 115-114, 115-114, 116-116 points decision over his fellow-Italian, Picardi, Belcastro regained the title he had relinquished in 1990. Picardi forced the action, trying to bustle Belcastro out of it, but as the contest developed into a fast paced affair, with no knockdowns recorded, it was Belcastro's clever countering that gained him the decision. The title had become vacant after Johnny Bredahl had won the WBO version of the world championship.

28 January, 1993 Jean-Baptiste Mendy 9.7¼ (France) W RTD 3 Antonio Renzo 9.8¼ (Italy), Levallois Perret, France. Lightweight Title Defence.

Using his jab to pick up points and keep his rival at bay, Mendy controlled the fight, refereed by Larry O'Connell, from the opening bell and by round three he was beginning to take Renzo apart with good combinations. Renzo continued to come forward, but was continuously running on to punches and being banged up. Looking a sorry state, it was no surprise that he failed to answer the bell for the fourth round.

6 February, 1993 Ludovic Proto 10.6¾ (France) L RSC 9 Gary Jacobs 10.6¾ (Scotland), Paris, France. Welterweight Title Defence.

In a rematch, following the disputed decision that gave Proto the title last October, Jacobs made no mistake this time around. Both men were badly cut over their right eyes, mainly due to frequent accidental head clashes caused by the southpaw styles more than anything else, but the Scot had the resolve. After flooring the Frenchman in the second and battering him in the eighth, Jacobs immediately put his rival down at the restart of the ninth and although rising at the count of five, Proto was rescued by the referee at 0.15 of the round.

11 February, 1993 Akim Tafer 13.7½ (France) W RSC 6 Dmitri Eliseev 13.6½ (Ukrania), Romaranin, France. Cruiserweight Title Defence.

The first man from the former Soviet Union to challenge for a European title, Eliseev was rescued by the referee towards the end of the sixth round, following a second knockdown. Earlier, he had been floored in the fifth by a heavy left-uppercut, had been badly cut under the left eye, and was generally on the sharp end of the champion's power.

6 March, 1993 Valery Kayumba 9.13½ (France) W RSC 11 Mark McCreath 9.13½ (England), Levallois Perret, France. Light-Welterweight Title Defence.

Showing an ability to absorb everything the champion could throw at him, McCreath continuously marched forward, looking to bring the fight summarily to a halt. Kayumba, however, is a classy performer, and was always in front, but he could have rarely been attacked as hard. Finally, in the eleventh, as McCreath wilted from exhaustion although not being floored, the referee brought matters to a halt.

17 March, 1993 Vincenzo Nardiello 11.13½ (Italy) L RSC 10 Ray Close 11.13 (Ireland), Campione d'Italia, Italy. Super-Middleweight Title Defence.

Causing quite an upset, Close won the title in Italy when an accidental head butt brought the fight to a halt at 0.29 of round ten, when Nardiello was unable to continue due to a bad cut over his left eye. Close appeared to be marginally in front at the closure and was landing more accurate punches, while the champion was drained and had little left. There were no knockdowns.

23 March, 1993 Regilio Tuur 9.3¼ (Holland) W RTD 6 Michele la Fratta 9.3¾ (Italy), Rotterdam, Holland. Super-Featherweight Title Defence.

Retreating throughout, the Italian barely threw a punch of note, while Tuur moved forward relentlessly, finally catching up with La Fratta in the fifth and dropping him with combination punches to head and body. And, after being cut under the right eye and receiving a standing count at the end of the sixth, administered by referee, Adrian Morgan, he was wisely retired by his corner during the interval.

27 March, 1993 Maurizio Stecca 8.13¼ (Italy) L RSC 11 Herve Jacob 8.13 (France), Boulogne, France. Featherweight Title Defence.

Following an accidental clash of heads in the eleventh round, Stecca lost his title when he received a long vertical cut between both eyes and was deemed by the referee unable to continue. At the time, Jacob had a whole series of cuts, including two on the right eyebrow, himself. However, he had been allowed to fight on and was ahead on points on the scorecards, having come back into the fight from the sixth onwards after Stecca showed a reluctance to come forward.

30 March, 1993 Robbie Regan 7.13½ (Wales) W RSC 3 Danny Porter 7.13½ (England), Cardiff, Wales. Flyweight Title Defence.

Showing much improved power, Regan stopped his tough challenger at 2.37 of the third, having had him on the deck for an eight count, before pounding him without reply. The experienced Porter never stood a chance, while Regan's performance suggested that a big step up in class is just around the corner. For the record, the contest was refereed by Mickey Vann and judged by John Coyle and Paul Thomas.

3 April, 1993 Laurent Boudouani 10.12½ (France) W CO 9 Romolo Casamonica 10.12¼ (Italy), Soissons, France. Light-Middleweight Title Defence.

Outclassing his game opponent, round after round, although occasionally taking a breather, Boudouani finally opened up in the ninth with heavy body shots, followed by right-crosses to the head and floored Casamonica for the full count. The champion showed he was well worth a world rating, while the Italian can take comfort in the fact that there are few fighters around with the quality of the Frenchman.

7 April, 1993 Vincenzo Belcastro 8.5 (Italy) W PTS 12 John Miceli 8.4¼ (Belgium), Naples, Italy. Bantamweight Title Defence.

The Belgian-Sicilian, Miceli, gave Belcastro a few early problems when going on the offensive, but once the champion had sorted his style out, even though suffering from a cut eye, he opened up himself. Although dropping Miceli in the sixth, he was unable to repeat the dose and was content to box his way to an easy 118-109, 118-110, 120-108 (referee, Roy Francis) points victory.

29 April, 1993 Jean-Baptiste Mendy 9.8¼ (France) W RSC 8 Carl Crook 9.8½ (England), Levallois Perret, France. Lightweight Title Defence.

Outboxed throughout, Crook put up a brave show in front of an appreciative crowd. Knocked down three times, in the sixth, the seventh, and the eighth, and badly cut on the left cheek, the challenger showed his gameness as he continually tried to fight back. However, following the third knockdown, the referee had seen enough and brought matters to a halt.

1 May, 1993 Henry Akinwande 16.0 (England) W PTS 12 Axel Schulz 15.1 (Germany). Berlin, Germany. Vacant Heavyweight Title.

Although he continued to show a distinct lack of power needed to survive at the highest level, Akinwande made no mistakes this time and clearly outboxed the tough German in their return bout. Luckily for the new champion, Schulz is not a great puncher, either, and the elongated Britisher showed his superiority in all departments to come home with scores of 117-113, 116-114, 118-113.

12 May, 1993 Eddie Smulders 12.5 (Holland) W RSC 9 Yawe Davis 12.6 (Italy), Casino, Italy. Vacant Light-Heavyweight Title.

With Britain's Crawford Ashley not available, the Dutchman went into the lion's den to contest the vacant title against an Italian in Italy. If he was worried, it didn't show, and by the fifth round he had begun to work Davis over with a selection of heavy blows and appeared to be on his way to victory. Davis came back well, but with both men exhausted, Smulders, somehow found the strength to floor his rival and the fight was stopped at 2.13 of the ninth in his favour. Mickey Vann of England refereed.

28 May, 1993 Herve Jacob 8.13½ (France) L CO 10 Maurizio Stecca 8.13¼ (Italy), Dunkerque, France. Featherweight Title Defence.

In a return contest that wasn't going his way, Stecca, somehow found the punches, a left-right combination, to pull the fight out of the bag and kayo Jacob in the tenth round. He hadn't boxed well in an untidy contest and later admitted that he had been on the verge of retiring, but once referee, Dave Parris, had completed the count and he had regained his title, he was yet again looking to the future.

22 June, 1993 Massimiliano Duran 13.7 (Italy) W CO 11 Derek Angol 13.6¾ (England), Ferrara, Italy. Vacant Cruiserweight Title.

In a fight to decide the successor to Akim Tafer, who had recently relinquished the title, Angol more than held his own over the first eight rounds, with good left leads keeping his man unbalanced, although occasionally being wobbled himself, and he even cut Duran's right eye early on. However, once the Italian began to find the range, the writing was on the wall and Angol was dropped in the eighth. He somehow survived into the eleventh where he was belted to the floor in a bloody mess. Getting up bravely, he was again smashed to the canvas, this time to be counted out at 2.50 of the round. The end was traumatic, with Angol unconscious for a considerable period in the ring and then spending time in hospital before being allowed home a few days later.

23 June, 1993 Laurent Boudouani 10.13½ (France) W RTD 4 Andy Till 10.13¾ (England), London, England. Light-Middleweight Title Defence.

Always a fighter to the bitter end, brave Andy Till found the champion just too good. Retired in the interval between the fourth and fifth rounds, with cuts requiring 17 stitches, he had done his best, having been floored twice and consistently beaten up by a man with obvious talent. Boudouani proved to have blistering hand-speed, excellent technique and defensive ability, plus the power that makes it unnecessary to go to the scorecards.

23 June, 1993 Agostino Cardamone 11.4 (Italy) W CO 3 Francesco dell'Aquila 11.5 (Italy), Avellino, Italy. Vacant Middleweight Title.

Following the retirement of Sumbu Kalambay, the hard hitting Cardamone caused quite a sensation in an all-Italian contest against the former champion, as he blasted his way to the title with a frenzied third round attack. Dell'Aquila didn't quite know what had hit him as a left-right combination deposited on the deck for the full count. The general consensus around ringside was that the fighting carpenter was "hungry" enough to go all the way.

European Champions, 1909-1993

Prior to 1946, the championship was contested under the auspices of the International Boxing Union, re-named that year as the European Boxing Union (EBU).

EUROPEAN COUNTRY CODE
AU = Austria; BEL = Belgium; CZ = Czechoslovakia; DEN = Denmark; E = England; FIN = Finland; FR = France; GER = Germany; GRE = Greece; HOL = Holland; HUN = Hungary; ITA = Italy; LUX = Luxembourg; NI = Northern Ireland; NOR = Norway; POR = Portugal; ROM = Romania; S = Scotland; SP = Spain; SWE = Sweden; SWI = Switzerland; TU = Turkey; W = Wales; YUG = Yugoslavia.

*Undefeated champions

Title Holder	Country	Tenure	Title Holder	Country	Tenure	Title Holder	Country	Tenure
Flyweight (112 lbs)			Lucien Popescu	ROM	1930-1931	Louis Skena*	FR	1953-1954
Sid Smith	E	1913	Jackie Brown*	E	1931-1932	Nazzareno Giannelli	ITA	1954-1955
Bill Ladbury	E	1913-1914	Praxile Gyde	FR	1932-1935	Dai Dower	W	1955
Percy Jones*	W	1914	Kid David*	BEL	1935-1936	Young Martin	SP	1955-1959
Tancy Lee	S	1915-1916	Ernst Weiss	AU	1936	Risto Luukkonen	FIN	1959-1961
Jimmy Wilde*	W	1916-1923	Valentin Angelmann*	FR	1936-1938	Salvatore Burruni*	ITA	1961-1965
Michel Montreuil	BEL	1923-1925	Enrico Urbinati*	ITA	1938-1943	Rene Libeer*	FR	1965-1966
Elky Clark	S	1925-1927	Raoul Degryse	BEL	1946-1947	Fernando Atzori	ITA	1967-1972
Emile Pladner	FR	1928	Maurice Sandeyron	FR	1947-1949	Fritz Chervet*	SWI	1972-1973
Johnny Hill	S	1928-1929	Rinty Monaghan*	NI	1949-1950	Fernando Atzori	ITA	1973
Emile Pladner	FR	1929	Terry Allen	E	1950	Fritz Chervet*	SWI	1973-1974
Eugene Huat*	FR	1929	Jean Sneyers*	BEL	1950-1951	Franco Udella	ITA	1974-1979
Kid Oliva	FR	1930	Teddy Gardner*	E	1952	Charlie Magri*	E	1979-1983

Danny Porter (right) looks to find a way inside Robbie Regan's guard. The Welshman sucessfully defended his European flyweight title with a third round stoppage of Porter

Les Clark

187

Title Holder	Country	Tenure
Antoine Montero*	FR	1983-1984
Charlie Magri*	E	1984-1985
Franco Cherchi	ITA	1985
Charlie Magri	E	1985-1986
Duke McKenzie*	E	1986-1988
Eyup Can*	TU	1989-1990
Pat Clinton*	S	1990-1991
Salvatore Fanni	ITA	1991-1992
Robbie Regan	W	1992-

Bantamweight (118 lbs)

Title Holder	Country	Tenure
Joe Bowker	E	1910
Digger Stanley	E	1910-1912
Charles Ledoux	FR	1912-1921
Tommy Harrison	E	1921-1922
Charles Ledoux	FR	1922-1923
Bugler Harry Lake	E	1923
Johnny Brown*	E	1923-1924
Henry Scillie*	BEL	1925-1928
Domenico Bernasconi	ITA	1929
Carlos Flix	SP	1929-1931
Lucien Popescu	ROM	1931-1932
Domenico Bernasconi*	ITA	1932
Nicholas Biquet	BEL	1932-1935
Maurice Dubois	SWI	1935-1936
Joseph Decico	FR	1936
Aurel Toma*	ROM	1936-1937
Nicholas Biquet*	BEL	1937-1938
Aurel Toma	ROM	1938-1939
Ernst Weiss	AU	1939
Gino Cattaneo	ITA	1939-1941
Gino Bondavilli*	ITA	1941-1943
Jackie Paterson	S	1946
Theo Medina	FR	1946-1947
Peter Kane	E	1947-1948
Guido Ferracin	ITA	1948-1949
Luis Romero	SP	1949-1951
Peter Keenan	S	1951-1952
Jean Sneyers*	BEL	1952-1953
Peter Keenan	S	1953
John Kelly	NI	1953-1954
Robert Cohen*	FR	1954-1955
Mario D'Agata	ITA	1955-1958
Piero Rollo	ITA	1958-1959
Freddie Gilroy	NI	1959-1960
Pierre Cossemyns	BEL	1961-1962
Piero Rollo	ITA	1962
Alphonse Halimi	FR	1962
Piero Rollo	ITA	1962-1963
Mimoun Ben Ali	SP	1963
Risto Luukkonen*	FIN	1963-1964
Mimoun Ben Ali	SP	1965
Tommaso Galli	ITA	1965-1966
Mimoun Ben Ali	SP	1966-1968
Salvatore Burruni*	ITA	1968-1969
Franco Zurlo	ITA	1969-1971
Alan Rudkin	E	1971
Agustin Senin*	SP	1971-1973
Johnny Clark*	E	1973-1974
Bob Allotey	SP	1974-1975
Daniel Trioulaire	FR	1975-1976
Salvatore Fabrizio	ITA	1976-1977
Franco Zurlo	ITA	1977-1978
Juan Francisco Rodriguez	SP	1978-1980
Johnny Owen*	W	1980
Valerio Nati	ITA	1980-1982
Giuseppe Fossati	ITA	1982-1983
Walter Giorgetti*	ITA	1983-1984
Ciro de Leva*	ITA	1984-1986
Antoine Montero	FR	1986-1987

Title Holder	Country	Tenure
Louis Gomis*	FR	1987-1988
Fabrice Benichou	FR	1988
Vincenzo Belcastro*	ITA	1988-1990
Thierry Jacob*	FR	1990-1992
Johnny Bredahl*	DEN	1992
Vincenzo Belcastro	ITA	1993-

Featherweight (126 lbs)

Title Holder	Country	Tenure
Young Joey Smith	E	1911
Jean Poesy	FR	1911-1912
Jim Driscoll*	W	1912-1913
Ted Kid Lewis*	E	1913-1914
Louis de Ponthieu*	FR	1919-1920
Arthur Wyns	BEL	1920-1922
Eugene Criqui*	FR	1922-1923
Edouard Mascart	FR	1923-1924
Charles Ledoux	FR	1924
Henri Hebrans	BEL	1924-1925
Antonio Ruiz	SP	1925-1928
Luigi Quadrini	ITA	1928-1929
Knud Larsen	DEN	1929
Jose Girones*	SP	1929-1934
Maurice Holtzer*	FR	1935-1938
Phil Dolhem	BEL	1938-1939
Lucien Popescu	ROM	1939-1941
Ernst Weiss	AU	1941
Gino Bondavilli	ITA	1941-1945
Ermanno Bonetti*	ITA	1945-1946
Tiger Al Phillips	E	1947
Ronnie Clayton	E	1947-1948
Ray Famechon	FR	1948-1953
Jean Sneyers	BEL	1953-1954
Ray Famechon	FR	1954-1955
Fred Galiana*	SP	1955-1956
Cherif Hamia*	FR	1957-1958
Sergio Caprari	ITA	1958-1959
Gracieux Lamperti	FR	1959-1962
Alberto Serti	ITA	1962-1963
Howard Winstone*	W	1963-1967
Jose Legra*	SP	1967-1968
Manuel Calvo	SP	1968-1969
Tommaso Galli	ITA	1969-1970
Jose Legra*	SP	1970-1972
Gitano Jimenez	SP	1973-1975
Elio Cotena	ITA	1975-1976
Nino Jimenez	SP	1976-1977
Manuel Masso	SP	1977
Roberto Castanon*	SP	1977-1981
Salvatore Melluzzo	ITA	1981-1982
Pat Cowdell*	E	1982-1983
Loris Stecca*	ITA	1983
Barry McGuigan*	NI	1983-1985
Jim McDonnell*	E	1985-1987
Valerio Nati*	ITA	1987
Jean-Marc Renard*	BEL	1988-1989
Paul Hodkinson*	E	1989-1991
Fabrice Benichou	FR	1991-1992
Maurizio Stecca	ITA	1992-1993
Herve Jacob	FR	1993
Maurizio Stecca	ITA	1993-

S. Featherweight (130 lbs)

Title Holder	Country	Tenure
Tommaso Galli	ITA	1971-1972
Domenico Chiloiro	ITA	1972
Lothar Abend	GER	1972-1974
Sven-Erik Paulsen*	NOR	1974-1976
Roland Cazeaux	FR	1976
Natale Vezzoli	ITA	1976-1979
Carlos Hernandez	SP	1979
Rodolfo Sanchez	SP	1979
Carlos Hernandez	SP	1979-1982

Title Holder	Country	Tenure
Cornelius Boza-Edwards*	E	1982
Roberto Castanon	SP	1982-1983
Alfredo Raininger	ITA	1983-1984
Jean-Marc Renard	BEL	1984
Pat Cowdell*	E	1984-1985
Jean-Marc Renard*	BEL	1986-1987
Salvatore Curcetti	ITA	1987-1988
Piero Morello	ITA	1988
Lars Lund Jensen	DEN	1988
Racheed Lawal	DEN	1988-1989
Daniel Londas*	FR	1989-1991
Jimmy Bredahl*	DEN	1992
Regilio Tuur	HOL	1992-1993
Jacobin Yoma	FR	1993-

Lightweight (135 lbs)

Title Holder	Country	Tenure
Freddie Welsh	W	1909-1911
Matt Wells	E	1911-1912
Freddie Welsh*	W	1912-1914
Bob Marriott	E	1919-1920
Georges Papin	FR	1920-1921
Ernie Rice	E	1921-1922
Seaman Nobby Hall	E	1922-1923
Harry Mason*	E	1923
Fred Bretonnel	FR	1924
Lucien Vinez	FR	1924-1927
Luis Rayo*	SP	1927-1928
Aime Raphael	FR	1928-1929
Francois Sybille	BEL	1929-1930
Alf Howard	E	1930
Francois Sybille	BEL	1930-1931
Bep van Klaveren	HOL	1931-1932
Cleto Locatelli	ITA	1932
Francois Sybille	BEL	1932-1933
Cleto Locatelli*	ITA	1933
Francois Sybille	BEL	1934
Carlo Orlandi*	ITA	1934-1935
Enrico Venturi*	ITA	1935-1936
Vittorio Tamagnini	ITA	1936-1937
Maurice Arnault	FR	1937
Gustave Humery*	FR	1937-1938
Aldo Spoldi*	ITA	1938-1939
Karl Blaho	AU	1940-1941
Bruno Bisterzo	ITA	1941
Ascenzo Botta	ITA	1941
Bruno Bisterzo	ITA	1941-1942
Ascenzo Botta	ITA	1942
Roberto Proietti	ITA	1942-1943
Bruno Bisterzo	ITA	1943-1946
Roberto Proietti*	ITA	1946
Emile Dicristo	FR	1946-1947
Kid Dussart	BEL	1947
Roberto Proietti	ITA	1947-1948
Billy Thompson	E	1948-1949
Kid Dussart	BEL	1949
Roberto Proietti*	ITA	1949-1950
Pierre Montane	FR	1951
Elis Ask	FIN	1951-1952
Jorgen Johansen	DEN	1952-1954
Duilio Loi*	ITA	1954-1959
Mario Vecchiatto	ITA	1959-1960
Dave Charnley*	E	1960-1963
Conny Rudhof*	GER	1963-1964
Willi Quatuor	GER	1964-1965
Franco Brondi	ITA	1965
Maurice Tavant	FR	1965-1966
Borge Krogh	DEN	1966-1967
Pedro Carrasco*	SP	1967-1969
Miguel Velazquez	SP	1970-1971
Antonio Puddu	ITA	1971-1974

Title Holder	Country	Tenure	Title Holder	Country	Tenure	Title Holder	Country	Tenure
Ken Buchanan*	S	1974-1975	Gilbert Lavoine	FR	1953-1954	Hans-Henrik Palm	DEN	1982
Fernand Roelandts	BEL	1976	Wally Thom	E	1954-1955	Colin Jones*	W	1982-1983
Perico Fernandez*	SP	1976-1977	Idrissa Dione	FR	1955-1956	Gilles Elbilia*	FR	1983-1984
Jim Watt*	S	1977-1979	Emilio Marconi	ITA	1956-1958	Gianfranco Rosi	ITA	1984-1985
Charlie Nash*	NI	1979-1980	Peter Waterman*	E	1958	Lloyd Honeyghan*	E	1985-1986
Francisco Leon	SP	1980	Emilio Marconi	ITA	1958-1959	Jose Varela	GER	1986-1987
Charlie Nash	NI	1980-1981	Duilio Loi*	ITA	1959-1963	Alfonso Redondo	SP	1987
Joey Gibilisco	ITA	1981-1983	Fortunato Manca*	ITA	1964-1965	Mauro Martelli*	SWI	1987-1988
Lucio Cusma	ITA	1983-1984	Jean Josselin	FR	1966-1967	Nino la Rocca	ITA	1989
Rene Weller	GER	1984-1986	Carmelo Bossi	ITA	1967-1968	Antoine Fernandez	FR	1989-1990
Gert Bo Jacobsen*	DEN	1986-1988	Fighting Mack	HOL	1968-1969	Kirkland Laing	E	1990
Rene Weller*	GER	1988	Silvano Bertini	ITA	1969	Patrizio Oliva*	ITA	1990-1992
Policarpo Diaz*	SP	1988-1990	Jean Josselin	FR	1969	Ludovic Proto	FR	1992-1993
Antonio Renzo	ITA	1991-1992	Johann Orsolics	AU	1969-1970	Gary Jacobs	S	1993-
Jean-Baptiste Mendy	FR	1992-	Ralph Charles	E	1970-1971			
			Roger Menetrey	FR	1971-1974	**L. Middleweight (154 lbs)**		
L. Welterweight (140 lbs)			John H. Stracey*	E	1974-1975	Bruno Visintin	ITA	1964-1966
Olli Maki*	FIN	1964-1965	Marco Scano	ITA	1976-1977	Bo Hogberg	SWE	1966
Juan Sombrita-Albornoz	SP	1965	Jorgen Hansen	DEN	1977	Yolande Leveque	FR	1966
Willi Quatuor*	GER	1965-1966	Jorg Eipel	GER	1977	Sandro Mazzinghi*	ITA	1966-1968
Conny Rudhof	GER	1967	Alain Marion	FR	1977-1978	Remo Golfarini	ITA	1968-1969
Johann Orsolics	AU	1967-1968	Jorgen Hansen	DEN	1978	Gerhard Piaskowy	GER	1969-1970
Bruno Arcari*	ITA	1968-1970	Josef Pachler	AU	1978	Jose Hernandez	SP	1970-1972
Rene Roque	FR	1970-1971	Henry Rhiney	E	1978-1979	Juan Carlos Duran	ITA	1972-1973
Pedro Carrasco*	SP	1971-1972	Dave Boy Green	E	1979	Jacques Kechichian	FR	1973-1974
Roger Zami	FR	1972	Jorgen Hansen*	DEN	1979-1981	Jose Duran	SP	1974-1975
Cemal Kamaci	TU	1972-1973						
Toni Ortiz	SP	1973-1974						
Perico Fernandez*	SP	1974						
Jose Ramon Gomez-Fouz	SP	1975						
Cemal Kamaci*	TU	1975-1976						
Dave Boy Green*	E	1976-1977						
Primo Bandini	ITA	1977						
Jean-Baptiste Piedvache	FR	1977-1978						
Colin Power	E	1978						
Fernando Sanchez	SP	1978-1979						
Jose Luis Heredia	SP	1979						
Jo Kimpuani*	FR	1979-1980						
Giuseppe Martinese	ITA	1980						
Antonio Guinaldo	SP	1980-1981						
Clinton McKenzie	E	1981-1982						
Robert Gambini	FR	1982-1983						
Patrizio Oliva*	ITA	1983-1985						
Terry Marsh*	E	1985-1986						
Tusikoleta Nkalankete	FR	1987-1989						
Efren Calamati	ITA	1989-1990						
Pat Barrett*	E	1990-1992						
Valery Kayumba	ITA	1992-						

Welterweight (147 lbs)

Title Holder	Country	Tenure
Young Joseph	E	1910-1911
Georges Carpentier*	FR	1911-1912
Albert Badoud*	SWI	1915-1919
Johnny Basham	W	1919-1920
Ted Kid Lewis*	E	1920
Piet Hobin*	BEL	1921-1925
Mario Bosisio*	ITA	1925-1928
Alf Genon	BEL	1928-1929
Gustave Roth	BEL	1929-1932
Adrien Aneet	BEL	1932-1933
Jack Hood*	E	1933
Gustav Eder*	GER	1934-1936
Felix Wouters	BEL	1936-1938
Saverio Turiello	ITA	1938-1939
Marcel Cerdan*	FR	1939-1942
Ernie Roderick	E	1946-1947
Robert Villemain*	FR	1947-1948
Livio Minelli	ITA	1949-1950
Michele Palermo	ITA	1950-1951
Eddie Thomas	W	1951
Charles Humez*	FR	1951-1952

Andy Till (right) gamely fights back during his European light-middleweight title attempt, but found the power of champion, Laurent Boudouani, too much to handle and was retired at the end of the fourth round

Les Clark

189

Title Holder	Country	Tenure
Eckhard Dagge	GER	1975-1976
Vito Antuofermo	ITA	1976
Maurice Hope*	E	1976-1978
Gilbert Cohen	FR	1978-1979
Marijan Benes	YUG	1979-1981
Louis Acaries	FR	1981
Luigi Minchillo*	ITA	1981-1983
Herol Graham*	E	1983-1984
Jimmy Cable	E	1984
Georg Steinherr*	GER	1984-1985
Said Skouma*	FR	1985-1986
Chris Pyatt	E	1986-1987
Gianfranco Rosi*	ITA	1987
Rene Jacquot*	FR	1988-1989
Edip Secovic	AU	1989
Giuseppe Leto	ITA	1989
Gilbert Dele*	FR	1989-1990
Said Skouma	FR	1991
Mourad Louati	HOL	1991
Jean-Claude Fontana	FR	1991-1992
Laurent Boudouani	FR	1992-

Middleweight (160 lbs)

Title Holder	Country	Tenure
Georges Carpentier*	FR	1912-1918
Ercole Balzac	FR	1920-1921
Gus Platts	E	1921
Johnny Basham	W	1921
Ted Kid Lewis	E	1921-1923
Roland Todd	E	1923-1924
Bruno Frattini	ITA	1924-1925
Tommy Milligan*	S	1925
Rene Devos*	BEL	1926-1927
Mario Bosisio	ITA	1928
Leone Jacovacci	ITA	1928-1929
Marcel Thil	FR	1929-1930
Mario Bosisio	ITA	1930-1931
Poldi Steinbach	AU	1931
Hein Domgoergen*	GER	1931-1932
Ignacio Ara*	SP	1932-1933
Gustave Roth	BEL	1933-1934
Marcel Thil	FR	1934-1938
Edouard Tenet	FR	1938
Bep van Klaveren	HOL	1938
Anton Christoforidis	GRE	1938-1939
Edouard Tenet*	FR	1939
Josef Besselmann*	GER	1942-1943
Marcel Cerdan	FR	1947-1948
Cyrille Delannoit	BEL	1948
Marcel Cerdan*	FR	1948
Cyrille Delannoit	BEL	1948-1949
Tiberio Mitri*	ITA	1949-1950
Randy Turpin	E	1951-1954
Tiberio Mitri	ITA	1954
Charles Humez	FR	1954-1958
Gustav Scholz*	GER	1958-1961
John Cowboy McCormack	S	1961-1962
Chris Christensen	DEN	1962
Laszlo Papp*	HUN	1962-1965
Nino Benvenuti*	ITA	1965-1967
Juan Carlos Duran	ITA	1967-1969
Tom Bogs	DEN	1969-1970
Juan Carlos Duran	ITA	1970-1971
Jean-Claude Bouttier*	FR	1971-1972
Tom Bogs*	DEN	1973
Elio Calcabrini	ITA	1973-1974
Jean-Claude Bouttier	FR	1974
Kevin Finnegan	E	1974-1975
Gratien Tonna*	FR	1975
Bunny Sterling	E	1976
Angelo Jacopucci	ITA	1976

Title Holder	Country	Tenure
Germano Valsecchi	ITA	1976-1977
Alan Minter	E	1977
Gratien Tonna*	FR	1977-1978
Alan Minter*	E	1978-1979
Kevin Finnegan	E	1980
Matteo Salvemini	ITA	1980
Tony Sibson*	E	1980-1982
Louis Acaries	FR	1982-1984
Tony Sibson*	E	1984-1985
Ayub Kalule	DEN	1985-1986
Herol Graham	E	1986-1987
Sumbu Kalambay*	ITA	1987
Pierre Joly	FR	1987-1988
Christophe Tiozzo*	FR	1988-1989
Francesco dell' Aquila	ITA	1989-1990
Sumbu Kalambay*	ITA	1990-1993
Agostino Cardamone	ITA	1993-

S. Middleweight (168 lbs)

Title Holder	Country	Tenure
Mauro Galvano	ITA	1990-1991
James Cook	E	1991-1992
Franck Nicotra*	FR	1992
Vincenzo Nardiello	ITA	1992-1993
Ray Close	NI	1993-

L. Heavyweight (175 lbs)

Title Holder	Country	Tenure
Georges Carpentier	FR	1913-1922
Battling Siki	FR	1922-1923
Emile Morelle	FR	1923
Raymond Bonnel	FR	1923-1924
Louis Clement	SWI	1924-1926
Herman van T'Hof	HOL	1926
Fernand Delarge	BEL	1926-1927
Max Schmeling*	GER	1927-1928
Michele Bonaglia*	ITA	1929-1930
Ernst Pistulla*	GER	1931-1932
Adolf Heuser*	GER	1932
John Andersson*	SWE	1933
Martinez de Alfara	SP	1934
Marcel Thil*	FR	1934-1935
Merlo Preciso	ITA	1935
Hein Lazek	AU	1935-1936
Gustave Roth	BEL	1936-1938
Adolf Heuser*	GER	1938-1939
Luigi Musina*	ITA	1942-1943
Freddie Mills*	E	1947-1950
Albert Yvel	FR	1950-1951
Don Cockell*	E	1951-1952
Conny Rux*	GER	1952
Jacques Hairabedian	FR	1953-1954
Gerhard Hecht	GER	1954-1955
Willi Hoepner	GER	1955
Gerhard Hecht	GER	1955-1957
Artemio Calzavara	ITA	1957-1958
Willi Hoepner	GER	1958
Erich Schoeppner*	GER	1958-1962
Giulio Rinaldi	ITA	1962-1964
Gustav Scholz*	GER	1964-1965
Giulio Rinaldi	ITA	1965-1966
Piero del Papa	ITA	1966-1967
Lothar Stengel	GER	1967-1968
Tom Bogs*	DEN	1968-1969
Yvan Prebeg	YUG	1969-1970
Piero del Papa	ITA	1970-1971
Conny Velensek	GER	1971-1972
Chris Finnegan	E	1972
Rudiger Schmidtke	GER	1972-1973
John Conteh*	E	1973-1974
Domenico Adinolfi	ITA	1974-1976
Mate Parlov*	YUG	1976-1977
Aldo Traversaro	ITA	1977-1979
Rudi Koopmans	HOL	1979-1984

Title Holder	Country	Tenure
Richard Caramonolis	FR	1984
Alex Blanchard	HOL	1984-1987
Tom Collins	E	1987-1988
Pedro van Raamsdonk	HOL	1988
Jan Lefeber	HOL	1988-1989
Eric Nicoletta	FR	1989-1990
Tom Collins*	E	1990-1991
Graciano Rocchigiani*	GER	1991-1992
Eddie Smulders	HOL	1993-

Cruiserweight (190 lbs)

Title Holder	Country	Tenure
Sam Reeson*	E	1987-1988
Angelo Rottoli	ITA	1989
Anaclet Wamba*	FR	1989-1990
Johnny Nelson*	E	1990-1992
Akim Tafer*	FR	1992-1993
Massimiliano Duran	ITA	1993-

Heavyweight (190 lbs +)

Title Holder	Country	Tenure
Georges Carpentier	FR	1913-1922
Battling Siki*	FR	1922-1923
Erminio Spalla	ITA	1923-1926
Paolino Uzcudun*	SP	1926-1928
Pierre Charles	BEL	1929-1931
Hein Muller	GER	1931-1932
Pierre Charles	BEL	1932-1933
Paolino Uzcudun	SP	1933
Primo Carnera*	ITA	1933-1935
Pierre Charles	BEL	1935-1937
Arno Kolblin	GER	1937-1938
Hein Lazek	AU	1938-1939
Adolf Heuser	GER	1939
Max Schmeling*	GER	1939-1941
Olle Tandberg	SWE	1943
Karel Sys*	BEL	1943-1946
Bruce Woodcock*	E	1946-1949
Joe Weidin	AU	1950-1951
Jack Gardner	E	1951
Hein Ten Hoff	GER	1951-1952
Karel Sys	BEL	1952
Heinz Neuhaus	GER	1952-1955
Franco Cavicchi	ITA	1955-1956
Ingemar Johansson*	SWE	1956-1959
Dick Richardson	W	1960-1962
Ingemar Johansson*	SWE	1962-1963
Henry Cooper*	E	1964
Karl Mildenberger	GER	1964-1968
Henry Cooper*	E	1968-1969
Peter Weiland	GER	1969-1970
Jose Urtain	SP	1970
Henry Cooper	E	1970-1971
Joe Bugner	E	1971
Jack Bodell	E	1971
Jose Urtain	SP	1971-1972
Jurgen Blin	GER	1972
Joe Bugner*	E	1972-1975
Richard Dunn	E	1976
Joe Bugner*	E	1976-1977
Jean-Pierre Coopman	BEL	1977
Lucien Rodriguez	FR	1977
Alfredo Evangelista	SP	1977-1979
Lorenzo Zanon*	SP	1979-1980
John L. Gardner*	E	1980-1981
Lucien Rodriguez	FR	1981-1984
Steffen Tangstad	NOR	1984-1985
Anders Eklund	SWE	1985
Frank Bruno*	E	1985-1986
Steffen Tangstad*	NOR	1986
Alfredo Evangelista	SP	1987
Anders Eklund	SWE	1987
Francesco Damiani*	ITA	1987-1989
Derek Williams	E	1989-1990
Jean Chanet	FR	1990
Lennox Lewis*	E	1990-1992
Henry Akinwande	E	1993-

A-Z of Current World Champions

by Eric Armit

Shows the record since 1 July 1992, and a career summary for all the IBF/WBA/WBC/WBO champions as 30 June 1993. The author has also produced a synopsis of the fighter's career and has shown all nicknames where applicable. The place name given is the boxer's domicile, not necessarily his birthplace.

Yuri (Ebihara) Arbachakov

Armenia, CIS. *Born* 22 October, 1966
WBC Flyweight Champion. Former Undefeated Japanese Flyweight Champion

As an amateur representing Russia, he collected gold medals at flyweight in both the 1989 World championships, beating Pedro Reyes in the final, and the 1989 European championships. Also won the Russian title in the same year and, as an amateur, he ended up with a total of 186 fights, winning 165 and stopping or knocking out 53 opponents. His talent was spotted by a Japanese promoter and he turned professional in Japan in February 1990. Halted the useful Mexican, Justo Zuniga, in his fifth fight and in his sixth bout, knocked out the former IBF flyweight champion, Roland Bohol, in just two rounds. Yuri collected the vacant Japanese flyweight title in July 1991, knocking out Takahiro Mizuno in the first round, but was too good for the other flyweights in Japan and relinquished the crown in December 1991. Taken the distance for the first time in March 1992 by Thai, Smanchai Chalermsri, he challenged for the WBC title in June and climbed off the canvas in the third – voted the "Most Dramatic Round of the Year" by the WBC – to knockout the tough Muangchai Kitikasem in eight rounds. Defended his title with a points victory over the aggressive South Korean, Yun-Un Chin, in October 1992, flooring his opponent three times but failing to put him away. Faced Kitikasem again in Thailand last March and, despite one round being cut short when Muangchai was in trouble, Yuri made his more accurate work pay and halted the Thai in the ninth round. A cool, upright boxer with a tight guard, he is a very hard puncher with a particularly strong right-cross. However, he is a bit stiff and lacks technique at in-fighting at

this stage. Has stopped or knocked out thirteen victims.

20.10.92	Yun-Un Chin W PTS 12 Tokyo *(WBC Flyweight Title Defence)*
20.03.93	Muangchai Kitikasem W RSC 9 Lopburi *(WBC Flyweight Title Defence)*

Career: 15 contests, won 15.

Leonzer Barber

Leonzer Barber

Detroit, USA. *Born* 18 February, 1966
WBO L. Heavyweight Champion.
Former Undefeated WBC Con Am L. Heavyweight Champion

Leonzer's father also fought as a professional and he followed in the family tradition. Despite being a Kung Fu fan, he took up boxing and is now a member of the famous Kronk team in Detroit. 6'3" tall, strong and a hard right hand puncher, he had no real amateur credentials before turning professional in December 1986. Made a stuttering start, having only one fight in 1986 and one in 1987. Was then inactive until August 1989. In dispute

with his manager, he joined the US Marines for a spell and when he returned he promptly lost on points to James Flowers. Stopped five of his seven opponents in 1990, including experienced Elvis Parks and the former world title challenger, Jim McDonald. Took the vacant WBC Continental Americas light-heavyweight title in February 1991 by halting Robert Johnson in three rounds. Kronk influence gained him a place opposite Tom Collins at Leeds in May 1991 for the vacant WBO title and Leonzer took full advantage of his chance, forcing his rival to retire at the end of the sixth round. Knocked out Tony Willis and stopped Ron Martin in non-title fights, before only just holding on to his title with a controversial split decision over Anthony Hembrick in January. In a close fight, a knockdown in the eleventh round gave Leonzer a narrow edge. Topped the bill on the first major show in China for years when he won a unanimous decision over Mike Sedillo in Beijing last February. Has eleven stoppage victories in his record to date.

03.09.92	Keith McMurray W CO 8 San Bernardino
27.02.93	Mike Sedillo W PTS 12 Beijing *(WBO L. Heavyweight Title Defence)*

Career: 18 contests, won 17, lost 1.

Nigel (Dark Destroyer) Benn

Ilford, England. *Born* 22 January, 1964
WBC S. Middleweight Champion.
Former Commonwealth & WBO Middleweight Champion

One of the most explosive fighters ever seen in a British ring, he learned his boxing with the Royal Fusiliers before joining West Ham ABC and crashing onto the scene in 1986, leaving a trail of bodies on his way to the ABA middleweight title. A year earlier he had been thwarted by leading amateur, Rod Douglas, but this time round he made no mistake, putting his rival out of the championships at the north-east London divisional stage. Under the management of Burt McCarthy, he made his professional debut in January 1987 and soon ran up 16 quick wins, with an amazing nine coming in the first round. At this juncture of his career, he was given a crack at the vacant Commonwealth middleweight title against Abdul Amoru Sanda in April 1988 and demolished his rival in the second round. He defended the title three more times against Anthony Logan, David Noel and Mike Chilambe, before losing it in May 1989 at the hands of Michael Watson, when he was counted out in the sixth round. However, the warning signs had always been there. Although all 22 earlier contests had ended inside the distance, in his favour, the defence against Logan saw Nigel floored in the first round and close to being stopped in the second, only to pull out a tremendous left-hook to send the Jamaican crashing for the full count. His repatriation started in October 1989 under the watchful eye of former British champion, Vic Andreetti, having broken free from former trainer, Brian Lynch, and he went the distance for the first time, outpointing Jorge Amparo in Atlantic City. Following two more solid wins in America against Jose Quinones and Sanderline Williams, he challenged Doug de Witt for his WBO middleweight title in April 1990 and scored a good victory when the referee came to the champion's rescue in the eighth round. Retained his title in explosive fashion, when he destroyed Iran Barkley in the first stanza, under the three knockdown ruling in Las Vegas, but then came unstuck against Chris Eubank, who took Nigel's best punches and came back with more of his own for a ninth round stoppage victory at Manchester in November 1990. Away from the ring for nearly six months, he came back to beat Robbie Sims, Kid Milo, Lenzie Morgan, Hector Lescano, Dan Sherry

and Thulani Malinga, before getting a crack at Mauro Galvano's WBC super-middleweight title and becoming champion at the end of the third round. During the period between the third and fourth rounds, with the Italian badly cut, his corner decided to pull their man out of the contest and appeal for a disqualification. Luckily, the referee would have none of it and awarded Nigel a sensational retirement victory, instead. Three indifferent title defences, an eleventh round stoppage of Nicky Piper, a low key points win against Galvano, and a storming fourth round victory over Lou Gent, set up a return match against deadly rival, Eubank, due to be held later this year. At 5'9½" tall, he has always been an exciting two fisted slugger, but more recently, especially under the tutelage of Jimmy Tibbs, he has extended his repertoire, being able to pace himself better and has added a little more variety to his work.

Note: Full record will be found in the Current British-Based Champions: Career Records' section.

Julio Cesar (Navajo) Borboa
Guaymas, Mexico. *Born* 12 August, 1969
IBF S. Flyweight Champion

A real surprise package, who went from prelim fighter to world champion in the space of two fights, Julio is one of eight children and started boxing in 1984. He was runner-up in the 1986 Mexican amateur championships and won the flyweight title in 1987. Turned professional in February 1988 and his first 16 fights all ended inside the distance, with Julio winning fourteen, despite often giving away weight and being stopped by Pablo Valenzuela and Cuauhtemoc Gomez. He moved his base to Los Angeles in 1991, under the management of Frank Espinosa, but made a bad start with a six rounds points loss to Francis Vivish in September. A victory over Elio Dominguez was followed by another points loss over six rounds and another win over the former. His record made him look a safe opponent for the unbeaten Alfred Kotei in November

1992, but Julio shocked the fans in Kotei's adopted hometown of Philadelphia by outboxing the Ghanaian boxer to earn a world rating. His next fight, last January, was a challenge for the IBF crown against the unbeaten Robert Quiroga in the champion's own back yard. Julio completed his fairy story by busting up the champion so badly that the referee halted the action in the twelfth round. The 5'3" tall Mexican, inspired by his idol, the late Gilberto Roman, has a stiff jab and is a precision puncher with good combinations who can both counterpunch or mix it. He showed his title winning effort was no fluke, with a successful defence against another unbeaten favourite, Joel Luna Zarate. In a dull fight, he easily outboxed Luna with his superior skills. Has accounted for 17 opponents inside the distance.

18.08.92	Joel Diaz L PTS 6 Phoenix
02.09.92	Elio Dominguez W CO 7 Bakersfield
17.11.92	Alfred Kotei W PTS 10 Philadelphia
16.01.93	Robert Quiroga W RSC 12 San Antonio
	(IBF S. Flyweight Title Challenge)
22.05.93	Joel Luna Zarate W PTS 12 Mexico City
	(IBF S. Flyweight Title Defence)
Career:	23 contests, won 19, lost 4.

Riddick (Big Daddy) Bowe
New York, USA. *Born* 10 August, 1967
IBF & WBA Heavyweight Champion. Former Undefeated WBC & Con Am Heavyweight Champion

Born in the same tough Brownsville area of New York as Mike Tyson. As an amateur, Riddick won a World junior title and competed in the 1988 Olympic Games, where he was stopped in the super-heavyweight final by Lennox Lewis. Claims 104 wins in 112 amateur fights. Turned professional in March 1989 and won thirteen fights in that year, stopping or knocking out twelve of his opponents. Scored eight victories in 1990, including wins over the former WBC champion, Pinklon Thomas, dangerous Bert Cooper and big Art Tucker. Registered important wins in 1991 as he halted Tyrell Biggs and Bruce Seldon and decisioned the former WBA title holder, Tony Tubbs. Also won the vacant WBC Continental Americas title in December when Elijah Tillery was disqualified in the first round for kicking, before battering Pierre Coetzer to defeat in seven rounds, in July 1992, to earn a world title shot. Won the WBC, WBA and IBF titles with a stirring points victory in a fiercely contested fight against Evander Holyfield last November. The fight was only endorsed by the WBC after Riddick agreed that if he was victorious he would defend his title against Lennox Lewis. Negotiations for the fight broke down and, when Riddick failed to agree to fight Lewis, the WBC withdrew recognition of him as champion. A farcical mismatch saw him dispose of veteran Michael Dokes in less than a round in his first defence. In his second defence, he crushed veteran Jesse Ferguson in another poor match. 6'5" tall, with fast hands and a good punch, he answered many of the questions over his heart in the fight with Holyfield, but will have to face better challengers before his real potential can be gauged. Has 29 wins inside the distance.

18.07.92	Pierre Coetzer W RSC 7 Las Vegas
13.11.92	Evander Holyfield W PTS 12 Las Vegas *(IBF, WBA & WBC Heavyweight Title Challenge)*
06.02.93	Michael Dokes W RSC 1 New York City *(IBF & WBA Heavyweight Title Defence)*
22.05.93	Jesse Ferguson W RSC 2 Washington *(WBA Heavyweight Title Defence)*

Career: 34 contests, won 34.

Jimmy Bredahl

Copenhagen, Denmark. *Born* 26 August, 1967
WBO S. Featherweight Champion. Former Undefeated European S. Featherweight Champion

Cool, stylish southpaw, with a good jab and a sound defence, his younger brother, Johnny, is the WBO super-flyweight champion. As an amateur he won four Danish titles, two at

bantamweight and two at feather-weight, and competed in the 1987 European championships. Had his first paid fight in March 1989, decisioning Des Gargano and in December knocked out Rocky Lawlor in one round. Scored a good victory at the end of 1990 as he outpointed the now world rated Dominican, Wilson Rodriguez, and wins over Tony Foster, Kevin Pritchard and the French champion, Areski Bakir, in 1991, earned him a European rating. Jimmy collected the vacant European super-featherweight title in March 1992 when he outboxed and halted the favourite, Pierre Lorcy, in eleven rounds. In his next fight, in September, he won the WBO crown with a points decision over the very experienced Frenchman, Daniel Londas. He looked a clear winner, but one official gave the decision as a draw, making it a majority verdict. On the same night, his brother won the WBO super-flyweight title in a unique family double. Not a big puncher, only five of his wins have come inside the distance.

| 04.09.92 | Daniel Londas W PTS 12 Copenhagen *(WBO S. Featherweight Title Challenge)* |
| 26.03.93 | Chuck Richards W PTS 8 Copenhagen |

Career: 14 contests, won 14.

Johnny Bredahl

Copenhagen, Denmark. *Born* 27 August, 1968
WBO S. Flyweight Champion. Former Undefeated European Bantamweight Champion

Brother of the WBO super-feather-weight champion, Jimmy. Won a bronze medal in the 1986 European junior championships and the follow-ing year did the same in the senior tournament, beating John Lyon. Competed in the 1988 Olympic Games and was Danish flyweight champion in 1987 and 1988 and also Scandinavian champion in 1988. Turned professional in December 1988, decisioning Chris Clarkson in his second fight in February 1989. And, in fact, seven of his first eight victories were British

fighters. Showed impressive form, stopping Andrea Mannai and Benito Martinez at the end of 1990. Earned a place in the European ratings with a points win over Antonio Picardi, but was considered a slight outsider when he met Donnie Hood for the vacant European title in March 1992. Johnny confirmed his potential by climbing off the floor in the third round and boxing brilliantly to halt Hood in the seventh round. He did not fight again until September, by when he had relin-quished the European title to challenge for the WBO super-flyweight crown. Picked up the WBO title in impressive style as he outboxed Jose Quirino on a night when his brother also won the WBO super-featherweight title. In his only defence to date, he easily decisioned Puerto Rican, Rafael Caban. An excellent boxer with a great jab, he is a sharp puncher as his seven stoppages illustrate, although still short on experience against really top class fighters.

04.09.92	Jose Quirino W PTS 12 Copenhagen *(WBO S. Flyweight Title Challenge)*
13.02.93	Jose de Jesus W CO 1 Randers
26.03.93	Rafael Caban W PTS 12 Copenahgen *(WBO S. Flyweight Title Defence)*

Career: 17 contests, won 17.

Il-Jung Byun

South Korea
WBC Bantamweight Champion

A good amateur, winning 109 of his 119 contests. However, he ruined his reputation when he staged an hour long sit-down in the ring at the 1988 Olympics after being adjudged the loser to Bulgarian, Alexandr Hristov, in his second bout. This act may have made him a villain elsewhere, but it made him a hero in South Korea, and he has a big following there. Turned professional in February 1990 and topped the bill in his first fight, decisioning Noel Cornelio. Did not fight again for nine months, before halting Eddie Torres in three rounds. In 1991 he knocked out Rey Parreno in three rounds and decisioned the good Venezuelan, David Marchan, but had to climb off the floor to outpoint

William Ramos. Had only two fights in 1992, halting Michael Tampani in nine rounds and showing impressive form in outclassing the Philippines super-flyweight champion, Rey Paciones, to take an easy points verdict. After halting Suksawat Tow Boonlert in January 1993, he sprang a major surprise by outpointing and outmanoeuvring the tough and experienced Mexican, Victor Rabanales, to win the WBC bantamweight title on a unanimous decision in March. Il-Jung took the early rounds and then finished strongly to put the result beyond doubt. In his first defence, he put Josefino Suarez down in the first round and confused his challenger by constantly switching leads on the way to an easy decision. He is a clever southpaw stylist, mobile and a sharp accurate hitter, but not a power puncher, and only four of his fights have ended early. A fractured thumb, suffered in the fight against Suarez, will mean an extended period of inactivity for Il-Jung.

16.08.92	Rey Paciones W PTS 10 Taegu
10.01.93	Suksawat Tow Boonlert W RSC 4 Kyongui
28.03.93	Victor Rabanales W PTS 12 Kyungju *(WBC Bantamweight Title Challenge)*
28.05.93	Josefino Suarez W PTS 12 Seoul *(WBC Bantamweight Title Defence)*

Career: 10 contests, won 10.

Josue Camacho

Guaynabo, Puerto Rico. *Born* 31 January, 1969
WBO L. Flyweight Champion. Former Undefeated Puerto Rican Flyweight Champion

Turned professional in August 1988, but after having three fights during the year, was then inactive until May 1990. He picked up some useful wins, until being halted in the twelfth and last round of a fight with Julio Cesar Acevedo, a former victim, for the vacant Puerto Rican light-flyweight crown. Fought only twice in 1991, winning the Puerto Rican flyweight title with a points victory over Miguel Santos in March, but suffering his second defeat when decisioned by the

experienced Angel Rosario. Another period of inactivity followed, with Josue not fighting until March 1992, when he retained his Puerto Rican title with a points win over Eduardo Nazario. Scored a minor win in May, decisioning Luis Ramos, but, despite his mediocre record, he was then nominated to fight for the vacant WBO light-flyweight title. The bout was a farce as the other contender was a Mexican preliminary fighter with a poor record, Eduardo Vallejo, and Josue had no trouble in knocking him out in six rounds. He is probably the weakest of all the world champions and interest in his title is so low that he has not yet made a defence of the crown.

31.07.92	Eduardo Vallejo W CO 6 San Juan *(Vacant WBO L. Flyweight Title)*
21.06.93	Carlos Rodriguez W PTS 10 Santiago

Career: 15 contests, won 13, lost 2.

Orlando Canizales

Laredo, USA. *Born* 25 November, 1965
IBF Bantamweight Champion. Former Undefeated USBA S. Flyweight Champion. Former Undefeated NABF Flyweight Champion

Comes from a fighting family, with his elder brother, Gaby, being a former WBA and WBO bantamweight champion. Orlando turned professional as an 18-year-old in August 1984 and was held to a draw in his third fight by Rogelio Leanos. In 1985 he scored a points win over future world title challenger, Armando Castro, and also halted Steve Whetstone. Suffered the only loss in his career when he was decisioned by former Olympic champion, Paul Gonzales, in a challenge for the NABF flyweight title in July 1986. Orlando had Gonzales on the floor, but lacked the experience to finish him. Had a great year in 1987, halting former world champion, Prudencio Cardona, knocking out top Mexican, Javier Lucas, taking a split decision over Alonso Gonzales and halting Armando Velasco in two rounds to lift the vacant NABF flyweight crown. Orlando moved up to

super-flyweight to collect the USBA title, stopping Louis Curtis, and then jumped straight up to bantamweight to become IBF champion, when halting Kelvin Seabrooks in round fifteen of their fight in July 1988. He made a quick defence in November, knocking out Jimmy Navarro in one round and in his only fight in 1989, halted Seabrooks again, this time in eleven rounds, in another title defence. The first fighter to take Orlando the distance in a world title fight was Billy Hardy, the Texan retaining his crown in January 1990 on a split decision. In June, Orlando gained revenge for his only defeat, disposing of Gonzales in two rounds in a title bout, and two months later knocked out Eddie Rangel in another defence. Brave Billy Hardy was crushed in eight rounds, Fernie Morales outpointed and Ray Minus stopped in eleven rounds, in title fights in 1991, and Colombian, Francisco Alvarez, and Filipino, Samuel Duran, were beaten in 1992 defences. In 1993 he turned back a determined challenge from young Clarence Adams, forcing his rival to retire in round eleven, but a May defence against Derrick Whiteboy proved a disappointment when he was cut in a clash of heads during the third round and the bout was declared a no contest. A very strong, brutal puncher, Orlando seems to have gone off the boil in recent fights, but is still a force, with 26 quick wins under his belt.

11.07.92	Fernando Ramos W CO 7 Monte Carlo
18.09.92	Samuel Duran W PTS 12 Bozeman *(IBF Bantamweight Title Defence)*
27.03.93	Clarence Adams W RTD 11 Evian les Bains *(IBF Bantamweight Title Defence)*
19.06.93	Derrick Whiteboy NC 3 Houston *(IBF Bantamweight Title Defence)*

Career: 37 contests, won 34, drew 1, lost 1, no decision 1.

Michael Carbajal

Phoenix, USA. *Born* 17 September, 1967
IBF and WBC L. Flyweight Champion. Former Undefeated NABF L. Flyweight Champion

A former top amateur, he just failed to lift the major prizes, winning silver medals in both the Olympic Games and the Pan American championships, but was 1986 National Golden Gloves champion and won the USA title in 1988. Claimed a 94-9 amateur record. 1989, his first year as a professional, saw him win ten fights, including a points victory over the experienced Pedro Feliciano. After only twelve fights, he was NABF light-flyweight champion, following a unanimous points verdict against Tony de Luca. Michael retained the title, forcing Fernando Martinez to retire in the ninth round of their fight in June, and after only 14 bouts he challenged Muangchai Kitikasem for the IBF crown in July 1990. A weight weakened Kitikasem was outclassed and stopped in seven rounds, a brilliant performance by the youngster from Arizona. Michael made the first defence of his title in December 1990, knocking out the Panamanian, Leon Salazar, in four rounds and in 1991 halted Macario Santos and outpointed Javier Varguez and Hector Luis Patri in further defences. In 1992 he had just two title bouts, decisioning Marcos Pacheco and stopping Robinson Cuestas and also won three non-title bouts. Really proved his class and his courage against the WBC champion, Humberto Gonzalez, last March. Despite being floored in the second round and down again and almost out in the fifth, he came back to show he had courage as well as class, to knock out the tough little Mexican in the seventh round, in the first million dollar fight in the division. Michael is a good stylist and a hard puncher. He is 5'5" tall and is trained and managed by his brother Danny. As a youngster he idolised Roberto Duran and the win over Gonzalez shows that Michael has the charisma to be a star in his own right. Has fifteen wins inside the distance.

13.08.92	Jose L. Roman W PTS 10 Phoenix	
14.10.92	Jose Diaz W RSC 8 Rosemont	
12.12.92	Robinson Cuestas W RSC 8 Phoenix	
	(IBF L. Flyweight Title Defence)	
13.03.93	Humberto Gonzalez W CO 7 Las Vegas	
	(IBF L. Flyweight Title Defence & WBC L. Flyweight Title Challenge)	

Career: 28 contests, won 28.

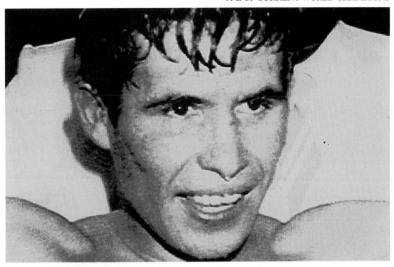
Julio Cesar Chavez

Julio Cesar (Super Star) Chavez
Ciudad Obregon, Mexico. *Born* 12 July, 1962
WBC L. Welterweight Champion. Former Undefeated IBF L. Welterweight Champion. Former Undefeated WBC & WBA Lightweight Champion. Former Undefeated WBC S. Featherweight Champion

Rated by many as the best fighter pound for pound in the world today, he set a new all-time record by going over thirteen years without a defeat. A craftsman at cutting down the ring, forcing the opponents to fight his fight, and deadly on the inside with his vicious hooks and uppercuts. Turned professional in February 1980 and spent his early years fighting in the Mexican Provinces, mainly around Tijuana and Culiacan, and did not actually appear on a card in Mexico City until after he was world champion. Was lucky to retain his unbeaten record when a loss on disqualification to Miguel Ruiz was subsequently reversed by the local Commission to a knockout victory, instead. Won the vacant WBC super-featherweight title in September 1984, stopping Mario Martinez, and made nine defences, including wins over Roger Mayweather, Ruben Castillo, Rocky Lockridge and Juan Laporte. Moved up to lightweight in 1987 and took the WBA crown by stopping Edwin Rosario and added the WBC title in October 1988 with a technical decision over fellow Mexican, Jose Luis Ramirez. Weight problems quickly forced him up to light-welterweight and he defeated his old foe Roger Mayweather on a tenth round retirement in May 1989 to become WBC light-welterweight champion. After successfully defending against Sammy Fuentes and Alberto Cortes, he won the IBF title in dramatic fashion. Outboxed by Meldrick Taylor, he needed a last round knockout to win. Somehow, he produced the punches needed to force a stoppage but, with only two seconds remaining, many criticised the referee for halting the fight at that point. Julio relinquished the IBF title in 1991 and has concentrated in defending his WBC crown. Defeated Kyung-Duk Ahn in 1990 and John Duplessis and Lonnie Smith in 1991. Took care of Angel Hernandez and Frankie Mitchell in defences in 1992 and then settled an old argument last September, when he easily outpointed Hector Camacho to prove that he was superior to the cocky Puerto Rican. Hero worshipped in Mexico, he drew the largest ever live attendance for a fight in March 1993, systematically wearing down Greg Haugen, before forcing a stoppage in the fifth round. Also had too much power for Terrence Alli and halted him in the sixth. In all, Julio has been successful in 25 world title fights and is unbeaten in 87 bouts.

01.08.92	Frankie Mitchell W RSC 4 Las Vegas *(WBC L. Welterweight Title Defence)*
12.09.92	Hector Camacho W PTS 12 Las Vegas *(WBC L. Welterweight Defence)*
31.10.92	Bruce Pearson W RSC 3 Culiacan
13.12.92	Marty Jakubowski W RSC 6 Las Vegas
20.02.93	Greg Haugen W RSC 5 Mexico City *(WBC L. Welterweight Title Defence)*
10.04.93	Silvio Rojas W KO 3 Zapotan
08.05.93	Terrence Alli W RSC 6 Las Vegas *(WBC L. Welterweight Title Defence)*

Career: 87 contests, won 87.

Juan M. (Latigo) Coggi

Santa Fe, Argentine. *Born* 19 December, 1961
WBA L. Welterweight Champion.
Former Undefeated Argentinian L. Welterweight Champion

Cool, southpaw boxer with a long reach and a hard punch, particularly with the vicious left-hook that has earned him the nickname of "The Whip". Was Argentinian amateur champion in 1980 and lost only twice in 37 fights, before turning professional in April 1982. Made his way rapidly through the ranks and won his first 22 fights, until losing on points to experienced Adolfo Arce Rossi in March 1985. He was twice held to a draw by Ramon Collado, prior to picking up the Argentinian light-welterweight title with a third round knockout of dangerous Hugo Hernandez in October 1986. Took the WBA title from Patrizio Oliva with another third round knockout in July 1987, ending the Italian's run of 48 consecutive victories. Knocked out South Korean, Sang-Ho Lee, in two rounds in his only defence in 1988 and, in 1989, decisioned the experienced Harold Brazier, the future WBA champion, Akinobu Hiranaka, and the former WBC lightweight champion, Jose Luis Ramirez. The Hiranaka fight was a tough one, with Coggi down twice and the Japanese fighter hospitalised afterwards. Lost his title to Loreto Garza on a split decision in August 1990, but fought badly and looked a clear loser. Returned to bread and butter fights in Argentina and was not particularly impressive in winning thirteen in a row. Took his big chance when it came again, flooring the less experienced WBA champion, Morris East, twice, to regain his title on an eighth round stoppage. His first defence, saw him halt the experienced Jose Rivera on a cut and his power came into play again

Juan M. Coggi

Al Cole

during his second defence, as he floored Hiroyuki Yoshino three times and put him out in the fifth round. Has stopped or knocked out 35 opponents.

14.08.92	Eduardo Jacques W CO 6 Buenos Aires	
11.09.92	Juan A. Contreras W RTD 8 Bella Vista	
13.01.93	Morris East W RSC 8 Mar del Plata *(WBA L. Welterweight Title Challenge)*	
22.02.93	Domingo Martinez W CO 3 Mar del Plata	
10.04.93	Jose Rivera W RSC 7 Mar del Plata *(WBA L. Welterweight Defence)*	
23.06.93	Hiroyuki Yoshino W CO 5 Tokyo *(WBA L. Welterweight Title Defence)*	

Career: 66 contests, won 62, drew 2, lost 2.

Al (Ice) Cole

Suffern, USA. *Born* 21 April, 1964
IBF Cruiserweight Champion. Former Unbeaten USBA Cruiserweight Champion

6'3" tall, strong with good stamina, he is a well schooled fighter. Without having previously impressed as an amateur, he came close to making the United States' team for the 1988 Olympics when he won the trials, but lost a box-off to Andrew Maynard. Turned professional in March 1989, along with fellow amateur stars, Charles Murray and Ray Mercer, forming the Triple Threat team. Scored good early wins over Aundrey Nelson, John Beckles and the Canadian light-heavyweight champion, Drake Thadzi. Remained undefeated until December 1990, when he was outsmarted by Leon Taylor and lost a split decision. Fought a return with Taylor in March 1991 and again had trouble with him, but this time took a unanimous decision to collect the vacant USBA cruiserweight crown. Retained the title in 1991 with a unanimous verdict over Nate Miller and an eleventh round stoppage of Frankie Swindell. Handed a shot at the IBF title in July 1992 against James Warring, their styles did not mix and a poor contest saw Cole forcing the action and finishing strongly to take the title. Was unimpressive in a title defence against Uriah Grant in February 1993, but a

number of postponements had probably affected his preparation. The fight was hard and close and he only really pulled it out of the fire when Grant faded in the late rounds. Although strong he is not a big puncher and has stopped only eleven victims, with all of his important fights going the distance.

30.07.92	James Warring W PTS 12 Stanhope *(IBF Cruiserweight Title Challenge)*	
28.02.93	Uriah Grant W PTS 12 Atlantic City *(IBF Cruiserweight Title Defence)*	

Career: 23 contests, won 22, lost 1.

Bobby (Chappie) Czyz

Wanaque, USA. *Born* 10 February, 1962
WBA Cruiserweight Champion.
Former IBF L. Heavyweight Champion

5'10" tall, with a 69" reach, as an amateur international, he was selected to represent the USA in Poland, but failed to made the trip and so avoided a fatal air crash that killed a number of outstanding young amateurs. Turned professional in April 1980, boxing at middleweight, and won his first 20 fights, including victories over Elisha Obed and Robbie Sims, before losing a unanimous decision to tough Mustafa Hamsho. Flirted with the super-middleweight division for a while, beating Marvin Mack and Murray Sutherland, and then won the IBF light-heavyweight title in September 1986, outpointing Slobodan Kacar. Bobby made three defences of the IBF crown, halting David Sears and Jim McDonald and knocking out Willie Edwards, but then suffered a controversial loss to Charles Williams in October 1987. Bobby had Williams down in the second and badly hurt in the third. At that point the referee gave Williams a standing count, which was not included in the IBF rules and he recovered to force Bobby to retire in the tenth round. Beaten on points by Dennis Andries in May 1988, he then lost a decision to Virgil Hill in a challenge for the WBA light-heavyweight title in March 1989. When he was stopped by Charles

Williams in June 1989, in an attempt to regain his old IBF title, it looked as though Bobby had hit a dead end. However, he refused to accept the situation and moved up to cruiser-weight, where he outpointed Robert Daniels in an upset to lift the WBA crown in March 1991. Defended the title with points victories over Bash Ali in August 1991 and Donnie Lalonde in May 1992, but injuries and postponements have kept him inactive since then. A gutsy fighter, with 26 quick wins under his belt, he has had an eventful career both inside and outside the ring.

Career: 45 contests, won 40, lost 5.

Rafael Del Valle

Santurce, Puerto Rico. *Born* 16 October, 1967
WBO Bantamweight Champion

Won a bronze medal for Puerto Rico in the 1987 Pan American Games and competed in the Central American championships, but failed to make selection for the 1988 Olympics and turned professional in May 1989. Halted his first five opponents and ran up six wins in 1990, including two points victories over useful Hector Medina. He moved up to the ten round class in 1991 and, in his eleventh fight, registered a big win when he out-pointed the former WBC super-flyweight champion, Juan Carazo. His first appearance outside Puerto Rico came in May 1992 when he faced Duke McKenzie for the WBO title. Rafael was a late substitute and a rank outsider, so it was a major surprise when he knocked out Duke in the opening round, the first time McKenzie had been stopped. Con-tractual problems kept Rafael out of the ring for ten months and in his first title defence he easily dealt with fellow Puerto Rican, Wilfredo Vargas, halting him in five rounds. In his second defence he showed he could box as well as punch, as he floored and clearly outboxed the former WBC bantamweight champion, Miguel Lora. However, Rafael is still very much an unknown force and it remains to be seen whether his knockout of

197

McKenzie was a true measure of his talent, or a one off performance. Has stopped ten opponents.

24.03.93	Wilfredo Vargas W RSC 5 Conado *(WBO Bantamweight Title Defence)*
19.06.93	Miguel Lora W PTS 12 Hato Rey *(WBO Bantamweight Title Defence)*
Career: 15 contests, won 15.	

Cristanto Espana

La Flor, Venezuela. *Born* 25 October, 1964
WBA Welterweight Champion.
Former Undefeated WBC International Welterweight Champion

He was inspired to take up boxing by the success of his elder brother, Ernesto, who won the WBA lightweight title in 1979. As an amateur, he had 64 fights, losing ten, took a gold medal in the 1981 South American championships and competed in the 1981 World Cup, before turning professional in March 1984. He had three fights that year, stopping all of his opponents, but managed only two more bouts to the end of 1987. His lucky break came when he was recommended to Barney Eastwood and moved his base to Belfast in 1988. He showed his power in 1989, with stoppage wins over Judas Clottey, Del Bryan and Lloyd Christie. Five more quick wins in 1990, earned him a WBC rating and in February 1991 he lifted their vacant International welterweight crown, following a points victory over the experienced Dominican, Luis Santana. Crisanto retained the title by halting the former South American champion, Hector Hugo Vilte, in seven rounds, in November 1991 and, after a couple of easy wins, he took the WBA title from Meldrick Taylor in London last October. Having showed coolness and determination as he ground down the faster American and halted him in eight rounds, he was less impressive in his first defence against Rodolfo Aguilar. However, he still worked his way to a points verdict against a clever opponent and currently has a 29-0 record, which includes 24 inside the distance victories.

03.07.92	David Taylor W RSC 7 Pontault
31.10.92	Meldrick Taylor W RSC 8 London *(WBA Welterweight Title Challenge)*
05.05.93	Rodolfo Aguilar W PTS 12 Belfast *(WBA Welterweight Title Defence)*
Career: 29 contests, won 29.	

Chris Eubank

Brighton, England. *Born* 8 August, 1966
WBO S. Middleweight Champion.
Former Undefeated WBO & WBC International Middleweight Champion

Never a national champion, he currently holds the record for having more successful world title wins (eleven, plus one draw) than any other British fighter, ever. Started his professional career on the mean streets of New York and downtown gyms of the south Bronx, having already had a taste of boxing with Peckham ABC. He had moved to America to join his father and studied and qualified as a word processor operator, until the call of the ring got too much for him. Had his first contest at Atlantic City in October 1985 and ran up five wins (only one inside the distance), before he came back to England. A year later he signed up with trainer, Ronnie Davies, and moved to Brighton in order to get his career on the road again. Made a good start with a first round victory over Darren Parker in February 1988 and had fourteen further wins, before being given the opportunity to challenge for the WBC International middleweight title against Hugo Corti in March 1990. He had by now come under the promotional banner of Barry Hearns and after beating the Argentinian in the eighth round he defended the title twice more, Eduardo Contrerras and Kid Milo, being the victims. For some time the drums had been beating for an assault on Nigel Benn's WBO middleweight title and following a first round kayo of Reginaldo Santos, the pair came together in November 1990. Animosity between the two men had been brewing up and in a wildly exciting "grudge" fight at the Birmingham Exhibition centre, Chris called up all

his reserves and came back strongly to force a stoppage in the ninth. After successful defences over Dan Sherry and Gary Stretch, he was matched with Benn's conqueror, Michael Watson, in June 1991. Retaining his crown with a debatable points decision, the scene was set for a return at Tottenham FC in September. However, in the meantime, Chris had relinquished the middleweight title, having struggled to make the weight, and it was the WBO supermiddleweight crown, vacated by the legendary Thomas Hearns, that was on the line. And with the title looking almost certain to go to Watson, tragedy struck. In the penultimate round, Watson floored Chris and it seemed to be over. But Eubank climbed up immediately to drop his rival, and although Watson got up and came out for the final round, the referee quickly rescued him. The rest is history, with Watson suffering severe brain damage, lucky to survive and never to box again. Chris took time out to decide whether he wanted to continue, but has since come back with successful defences over Thulani Malinga, John Jarvis, Ronnie Essett, Tony Thornton, Juan Carlos Giminez, Lindell Holmes and most recently, Ray Close. The last fight was a "Close" call for the champion. Having shown a disturbing tendancy to showboat and stall, and not picking the most dangerous of opponents, Chris was lucky to keep his title against the underrated Irishman. Indeed, it was only a knockdown in the penultimate round that allowed Chris a share of the spoils. And with the public demanding a better class of opponent, a Benn versus Eubank fight will now take place early in the new season. Strutting and arrogant, Chris is a difficult man to assess, but in the ring he has shown himself to be a fighter with a sound chin, a solid dig in both hands, and defensively sound. While he remains an enigma, he remains big box office, and if he can get past Benn, the clamour for unification fights against the Americans, Michael Nunn and James Toney, will become mouth watering possibilities.

Note: Full records will be found in the Current British-Based Champions: Career Records' section.

Nestor Giovannini

Rafaela, Argentine. *Born* 7 February, 1961
WBO Cruiserweight Champion. Former Undefeated WBC International L. Heavyweight Champion. Former Argentinian L. Heavyweight Champion

Turned professional in 1984 and promptly lost his first fight on points to Mario Melo. He won and lost in other bouts with Melo, but in August 1986 he lifted the Argentinian light-heavyweight title with a technical decision over Jorge Salgado. Faced Salgado for the South American title in December 1986, but was held to a draw and the third bout in the series, in December 1987, saw Nestor drop a points verdict and his crown. He bounced straight back with a first round knock out of Noe Cruciani in March 1988, to become WBC International champion. Retained the title in a points win over Mwehu Beya in September and then took on Jeff Harding in Australia, in May 1989, but lost on points. Faced Harding in a fight for the WBC crown in March 1990, but was floored three times and halted in round eleven. Having been out of the ring for ten months, he then met his old foe Jorge Salgado for the vacant Argentinian title and lost on points. Disappeared from the scene again at the end of 1991, but returned in February 1993, losing on a fourth round disqualification to Marcelo Dominguez for the vacant Argentinian cruiserweight title. A tough, rugged fighter, but limited in technique and, not a puncher and, despite recent poor form, he was given a shot at Markus Bott and shocked the German fans by taking the WBO title on a split decision.

20.02.93	Marcelo Dominguez L DIS 4 Buenos Aires *(Vacant Argentinian Cruiserweight Title)*	
27.03.93	Andres Anselmi W RSC 1 Villa Sarmiento	
26.06.93	Markus Bott W PTS 12 Hamburg *(WBO Cruiserweight Title Challenge)*	
Career: 44 contests, won 31, drew 3, lost 10.		

Miguel (Angel) Gonzalez

Ensenada, Mexico. *Born* 15 November, 1970
WBC Lightweight Champion. Former Undefeated WBC International Lightweight Champion

An outstanding amateur, representing Mexico in a number of international matches and competing in the 1988 Olympic Games, he claimed only two losses in 65 bouts before turning professional under Carlos Rosales in January 1989. Made good progress in Mexico, but his career really took off when he moved to Tokyo at the end of 1990. Won five fights in Japan, under the ring name of Santa Tokyo, including a victory over the tough South Korean, Tae-Jin Moon, in March 1991, which earned him a world rating. He returned to Mexico at the end of 1991 and in March 1992 won the WBC International lightweight crown by knocking out Ramon Marchena in five rounds. He was to have fought Darryl Tyson for the vacant WBC title in August 1992, but the American was injured and Miguel climbed off the floor and retired Wilfredo Rocha, who came in as a substitute, in nine rounds to take the title. He proved his right to be champion in December, with a clear unanimous decision over Tyson. Had a tougher time in his defence against fellow Mexican, Hector Lopez. Miguel was hurt and almost knocked out in the fourth, but rallied to dominate the remaining rounds and retain the title on a unanimous decision. He has a similar style to Julio Cesar Chavez and is a fine boxer with a tight defence, and is a good counter puncher. Also holds victories over Paquito Openo and Francisco Tomas Cruz, and has 24 inside the distance wins.

24.08.92	Wilfredo Rocha W RTD 9 Mexico City *(Vacant WBC Lightweight Title)*	
05.12.92	Darryl Tyson W PTS 12 Mexico City *(WBC Lightweight Title Defence)*	
11.03.93	Bruno Rabanales W PTS 10 Guadalajara	
26.04.93	Hector Lopez W PTS 12 Aguascalientes *(WBC Lightweight Title Defence)*	
Career: 29 contests, won 29.		

David Griman

Los Teques, Venezuela. *Born* 10 March, 1967
WBA Flyweight Champion. Former Undefeated Venezuelan S. Flyweight Champion

One of Venezuela's most successful amateurs, David picked up silver medals in both the World championships and the Pan American Games. He also won the Venezuelan title four times and the Simon Bolivar championship twice. Turned professional in March 1989 and, in only his seventh fight, halted Marino Tovar to win the Venezuelan super-flyweight crown. In 1990 he moved his base to Tokyo, where he began by halting Ebo Danquah in February. Divided his time between Tokyo and the Caribbean in 1990, scoring four more wins, the toughest being against South Korean, Hyun-Chul Lee, when he was badly cut and unimpressive in his points victory. Moving up the ratings gave him the opportunity to challenge Kaosai Galaxy for the WBA super-flyweight crown in July 1991. The fight was held at a crocodile farm near Bangkok and, although David started well, he found the strength of the champion too much and was floored and halted in the fifth round. Moved down to flyweight and in December 1992 challenged his fellow country-man, Aquiles Guzman, for the WBA title. After a classic boxer versus puncher match, the boxer came out on top, with David taking the crown. His first defence was a tough job in Osaka against the local hero, and former double world champion, Hiroki Ioka. David won the fight on the inside, outpunching Ioka and halting him in the eighth round. 5'7" tall, and a skilful boxer with fast hands, he has found his punching power more effective at flyweight. Has twelve wins inside the distance.

31.07.92	Edison Torres W RSC 6 Caracas	
15.12.92	Aquiles Guzman W PTS 12 Caracas *(WBA Flyweight Title Challenge)*	
21.06.93	Hiroki Ioka W RSC 8 Osaka *(WBA Flyweight Title Defence)*	
Career: 18 contests, won 17, lost 1.		

Jeff Harding   Peter Goldfield

Jeff (Hit Man) Harding

Sydney, Australia. *Born* 5 February, 1965
WBC L. Heavyweight Champion.
Former Undefeated OPBF & Australian L. Heavyweight Champion

Teak tough, pressure fighter, with an iron chin and limitless stamina. Won 32 out of 40 amateur fights before having his first professional start in November 1986. Began at super-middleweight, but, in March 1988, decisioned Apollo Sweet to take the New South Wales cruiserweight title. Won the OPBF and Australian light-heavyweight titles a month later, forcing experienced Doug Sam to retire in the fifth round of their fight and continued his good form in 1988 by stopping Jorge Salgado, Don Lee, Dean Moore and Carlos Antunes. After a couple more victories he challenged Dennis Andries for the WBC crown in June 1989. A desperate battle saw him floored and badly cut, only to come back and halt the champion for a dramatic last round victory. Jeff retained his title in a disappointing fight in October, when Tom Collins retired after only two rounds. Made one more defence, halting Nestor Giovanni in March 1990 and then lost his crown to Andries in July. Jeff was ahead on points, but his iron chin let him down and he was knocked out in the seventh

round. He fought his way back into contention and regained the title in September 1991, with a majority decision over Andries, after a bitter battle. Last year he made title defences against Christophe Tiozzo, halting him in eight rounds, and David Vedder, who was outpointed in December. Activity in 1993 has been affected by the postponement of a defence against Mike McCallum. In his early days he made the news due to his beach bum life style, but has proved to be a tough nut to crack, while halting 17 opponents.

| 03.12.92 | David Vedder W PTS 12 St Jean de Luz |
| | *(WBC L. Heavyweight Title Defence)* |

Career: 24 contests, won 23, lost 1.

Genaro (Chicanito) Hernandez

Los Angeles, USA. *Born* 10 May, 1966
WBA S. Featherweight Champion

Being 5'11" tall, with a 72" reach, gives Genaro a big advantage against most super-featherweights. In addition, he is a good tactician with a sharp jab and also has a sound chin. Trained by his Mexican-born father, Rodolfo, he followed his elder brother Rudy into the paid ranks, after winning 80 of his 90 amateur fights. Had his first professional contest in September 1984 and scored ten victories before being really tested against unbeaten Texan, Lupe Miranda, in September 1986. Genaro handled Miranda with ease, taking a unanimous decision, but was then laid up for most of 1987 with injuries. Won the Californian State super-featherweight crown in November 1988, flooring the tough Refugio Rojas twice and halting him in six rounds. Went on to beat experienced foes, Eddie Pollard and Felipe Orozco, in 1989 and, in May 1990, travelled to Tokyo to knock out the former IBF super-bantamweight title challenger, Leon Collins, in three rounds. Took on sluggers, Ben Lopez and Rodolfo Gomez, at the end of 1990 and halted them both, showing that he could outpunch the punchers when he had to. Finally landed a shot at the vacant WBA title in November 1991, facing the French veteran,

Genaro Hernandez

Daniel Londas, in France. Genaro outclassed the cagey Londas, flooring him three times and stopping him in round nine. He struggled a little in his first defence, in February 1992, against the awkward Venezuelan, Omar Catari, but won a clear points decision. Retained his title in two further defences in 1992. Hurt his right hand early in his fight against Masuaki Takeda, but still boxed his way to an easy win, and then outclassed the unbeaten Yuji Watanabe and stopped him in six rounds. His two most recent defences were against the former WBC bantamweight champion, Raul Perez. The first ended in a technical draw, when Perez was cut in the first round and, in the return, Genaro knocked his challenger out in round eight with a devastating body punch. With his height, reach, and versatile attack, he is a tough fighter to face and, with Azumah Nelson on the wane, he is probably the best fighter in the division, although he needs better opposition to prove it. Has stopped or knocked out fourteen victims.

15.07.92	Masuaki Takeda W PTS 12 Fukuoka
	(WBA S. Featherweight Title Defence)
20.11.92	Yuji Watanabe W RSC 6 Tokyo
	(WBA S. Featherweight Title Defence)
26.04.93	Raul Perez TD 1 Los Angeles
	(WBO S. Featherweight Title Defence)
28.06.93	Raul Perez W CO 8 Los Angeles
	(WBA S. Featherweight Title Defence)

Career: 29 contests, won 28, drew 1.

Virgil (Sugar) Hill

Clinton, USA. *Born* 18 January, 1964
WBA L. Heavyweight Champion.
Former Undefeated WBC
International & Con Am L.
Heavyweight Champion

Born in Clinton, Missouri, but now a big star in his adopted home in North Dakota, where he draws huge crowds. A converted southpaw, he had an outstanding amateur career, winning gold medals in the North American championships and the National Golden Gloves, and a silver medal in the 1984 Olympic Games. Claiming 250 wins and only eleven losses as an amateur, he turned professional in November 1984, but his mechanical style and lack of a big punch made his start a slow one, with only four fights in his first fourteen months. He was more active in 1986, winning his ten bouts and collecting the vacant WBC Continental Americas light-heavyweight title, following a points decision over Clarence Osby in December. Produced three consecutive knockouts in 1987 to boost his stock, but was still an outsider when he challenged Leslie Stewart for the WBA title in September. Virgil surprised the experts by flooring Stewart twice and knocking him out in round four to win the title. Made a quick defence in November, decisioning the tough Frenchman, Rufino Augulo, in Paris, and retained his title with victories over Jean-Marie Emebe, Ramzi Hassan and Willie Featherstone in 1988. If there were any doubters left, Virgil converted them in March 1989 when winning a unanimous decision over Bobby Czyz, and made two more defences in the year, halting Joe Lasisi and James Kinchen. He took his tally of defences to ten, outpointing David Vedder and Tyrone Frazier in 1990, and Mike Peak in January 1991, but then dropped his title to Thomas Hearns in June. After suffering a broken nose and being clearly outboxed by the super veteran, personal and managerial problems led to him being out of the ring for nine months. Returned to action in Australia, with a verdict over Aundrey Nelson in March 1992, and knocked out Lottie Mwale in April to take the WBC International title. He

Virgil Hill (right) seen successfully defending his WBA light-heavyweight title against Frenchman, Fabrice Tiozzo, last April

then won back his old crown with a unanimous decision over Frank Tate for the vacant WBA title last September and made heavy work of Adolpho Washington in his first title defence. He was well in front when a camera-man accidently cut Washington in the corner and forced the fight to a technical decision, which went to Virgil. Started well in his defence against Fabrice Tiozzo, putting the Frenchman down twice, but failed to finish him and had to settle for a points decision. Although not a big puncher, he has good technique and an excellent left hand, but seems to lack fire at times. However, he has still managed to halt 19 of 35 victims.

29.09.92	Frank Tate W PTS 12 Bismark *(Vacant WBA L. Heavyweight Title)*	
20.02.93	Adolpho Washington W TD 11 Fargo *(WBA L. Heavyweight Title Defence)*	
03.04.93	Fabrice Tiozzo W PTS 12 Levallois Perret *(WBA L. Heavyweight Title Defence)*	

Career: 36 contests, won 35, lost 1.

John David Jackson

Seattle, USA. *Born* 17 May, 1963

WBO L. Middleweight Champion

Born in Denver, his smooth, slick southpaw style has not really caught the attention of the fans and he has not received the attention or the rewards of other champions in this division. Has also changed management and promotional ties on numerous occasions, which has led to less exposure and forced him to fight abroad to earn decent purses. As an amateur, he claimed 206 wins in 215 fights, with his major achievement being a runner-up in the 1981 US championships. He turned professional in March 1984 and spent three years fighting on the East Coast against mediocre opposition, before coming to notice in July 1987 when he decisioned the former WBA light-middleweight champion, Davey Moore, in a big upset. That win earned him a fight with Lupe Aquino for the vacant WBO light-middleweight title in December 1988. John easily outboxed the favourite and forced him to retire in the eighth round. Defended his title in April 1989, halting Steve Little in eight rounds, but did not put his belt on the line again until February 1990. This defence, against Martin Camara in France, proved a tough one and ended in controversial fashion. John led in the early rounds, but seemed to fall apart in the eleventh and was badly hurt when the crowd invaded the ring, thinking that the fight had been stopped. In fact, the referee had halted the action due to the round having ended. It proved impossible to restart the fight and a no contest ruling enabled him to retain his title. John re-established his reputation by easily outpointing Chris Pyatt in October of that year in Leicester to retain his crown. He made only one defence in 1991, decisioning Tyrone Trice in July. In 1992 he beat Pat Lawlor on a ninth round retirement in June and then travelled to Italy in December to retire Michele Mastrodonato in ten rounds, in his last two title defences. Has halted 16 victims, but is not a heavy puncher and his lack of power and safety first style have kept him in the background. However, he remains a difficult fighter to beat.

19.09.92	Eric Martin W PTS 10 Tacoma
22.10.92	Sergio Medina W PTS 10 Irvine
19.12.92	Michele Mastrodonato W RTD 10 San Severo
	(WBO L. Middleweight Title Defence)
Career: 29 contests, won 28, no decision 1.	

Gert Bo Jacobsen

Ostrup, Denmark. *Born* 18 December, 1961
WBO Welterweight Champion.
Former Undefeated European Lightweight Champion

5'8" tall, as an amateur he won 80 of his 91 contests and competed in the 1981 European championships. Turned professional in October 1982 and remained undefeated in his first 26 fights. Became European lightweight champion in January 1986, stopping Rene Weller on a cut, and made successful defences when outpointing Alfredo Raininger and Fernando Blanco in the same year. He continued in the same vein in 1987, decisioning Jose Antonio Hernando and halting Alain Simoes and Claudio Nitto in further defences. Also won the vacant WBC International title, halting inept Colombian, Felipe Julio, in March.

Gert was stripped of the European title in 1988, when a back injury prevented him from making a defence, but he was compensated by a shot at Greg Haugen in October for the IBF title. He fought bravely, but Haugen was just too sharp and floored and stopped the Dane in the tenth round. After a lay off he returned eight months later, but was halted in six rounds by Poli Diaz, in a challenge for his old European title. Landed a second world title shot in February 1991 when he opposed Manning Galloway for the WBO welterweight crown. The Dane was badly cut in the third round and was retired by his corner after the eighth, with the cut and a severe facial swelling proving too much to overcome. He faced Galloway again in November 1992, but the fight finished as a no decision in the first round when the Dane suffered a bad cut. A third fight in February finally saw Gert emerge victorious over Galloway, but it was a very controversial verdict. A good counter puncher with the right and a good body puncher, he has halted or knocked out 23 opponents.

04.09.92	Rocky Berg W RSC 1 Copenhagen
27.11.92	Manning Galloway NC 1 Randers
	(WBO Welterweight Title Challenge)
12.02.93	Manning Galloway W PTS 12 Randers
	(WBO Welterweight Title Challenge)
26.03.93	Bobby Butters W RSC 6 Copenhagen
11.06.93	David Taylor W PTS 8 Randers
Career: 37 contests, won 34, lost 3.	

Daniel Jimenez

Camuy, Puerto Rico.
WBO S. Bantamweight Champion

Turned professional in June 1988, after an unspectacular time as an amateur, and made a poor start as a professional, losing his first fight on a stoppage to Wilfredo Vargas. He suffered another defeat in December 1988 to Jose de Jesus (not the WBO champion). He then left the ring for 16 months, but had little luck on his return in 1990, being beaten on points by Pedro Arroyo. Once again he was discouraged and did not fight again until December, when he knocked out Jose Rodriguez. Finally found some

Daniel Jimenez   Les Clark

form in 1991, beating Angel Vargas twice and Rodriguez again. The improvement continued in 1992, as he knocked out Hector Medina, stopped Dominico Monaco, and halted former contender, Tyrone Jackson, in one round, to win a high ranking from the WBO. He retained that ranking, despite a disappointing draw with Miguel Rodriguez in March 1993, and took his chance when it presented itself by winning a majority decision over Duke McKenzie in London. A hard working, but not powerful boxer, Daniel has had an easy rise to the top and may have problems holding on to his crown. He has halted five of his twelve victims.

18.07.92	Tyrone Jackson W RSC 1 San Juan
03.10.92	Dominic Monaco W RSC 6 Camuy
24.03.93	Miguel Rodriguez DREW 10 Conado
09.06.93	Duke McKenzie W PTS 12 London
	(WBO S. Bantamweight Title Challenge)
Career: 17 contests, won 12, drew 1, lost 3, no contest 1.	

Reggie (Sweet) Johnson

Houston, USA. *Born* 28 August, 1966
WBA Middleweight Champion.
Former Undefeated USBA & WBA Intercontinental Middleweight Champion

Reggie's father grew up with George Foreman in the tough 5th Ward area of Houston and wanted his son to follow

Reggie Johnson

the same road to fame. As an amateur, Reggie claimed 96 wins in 108 bouts, losing to Dennis Milton in the 1983 US championships, and was frustrated in his main ambition when he lost to Frank Tate in the US Olympic trials in 1984. Had his initial paid bout in August 1984 and scored six wins in that year. Stumbled a couple of times in 1985, losing on points to Adam George in January and drawing with Eric Williams in April, and was then inactive for 18 months from June 1985 until January 1987. A run of wins earned him a WBC rating, but he blew that in November 1988, by travelling to South Africa where he halted Charles Oosthuizen in seven rounds. Almost a year later he won the vacant WBA Intercontinental title in September 1989 with a unanimous decision over Israel Cole. Retained the title in September, following a second round stoppage of Victor Fernandez and, in February 1990, added the vacant USBA crown, halting Ismael Negron in eleven rounds. He decisioned Sanderline Williams and stopped Greg Dickson and Eddie Hall in USBA title defences in 1990, before challenging James Toney for the IBF title in June 1991. Toney retained his title, via a split decision, but was floored in the process. He bounced back in April 1992 to lift the vacant WBA title with a majority verdict over Irishman, Steve Collins. Made a good first defence last October, when he faced previously unbeaten Lamar

Parks and easily outboxed the dangerous slugger for a unanimous decision. Looked less impressive in stopping the very limited Ki-Yun Song in a second defence and disappointed when failing to stop Wayne Harris in a further defence. 5'10" tall, a skilful southpaw with an excellent jab and a strong punch, Reggie has stopped or knocked out 21 opponents.

27.10.92	Lamar Parks W PTS 12 Houston *(WBA Middleweight Title Defence)*
19.01.93	Ki-Yun Song W RSC 8 Boise *(WBA Middleweight Title Defence)*
04.05.93	Wayne Harris W PTS 12 Denver *(WBA Middleweight Title Defence)*

Career: 37 contests, won 34, lost 2, drew 1.

Tom (Boom Boom) Johnson

Evansville, USA. *Born* 15 July, 1964
IBF Featherweight Champion. Former Undefeated WBA Americas Featherweight Champion

Did not hit the heights as an amateur, although winning a number of local titles in Indiana, and had to overcome a serious eye injury suffered in a car crash in December 1985 before turning professional in Detroit in 1986. He was one of the few top boxers in the city who was not part of the Kronk outfit. Scored a points win over tough Troy Dorsey in September 1987 and collected the vacant WBA Americas featherweight title in November 1988, outpointing Gilbert Contreras. After 16 wins, he moved his base to New York and signed up with the Madison Square group. His plans suffered a set back when he was out-hustled by little Harold Warren in July 1990 and lost on a split points decision. Faced up to Troy Dorsey again, in November 1990, for the vacant NABF title and after another hard fight, one judge voted for Tom and the other two for a draw, so the majority decision of a draw left the title still vacant. Tom scored five stoppage wins and then challenged Manuel Medina for the IBF crown in November 1991. Started well, but the strong Medina was taking control with body punches when a clash of heads cut the champion. The fight went to a technical decision and Medina was given a unanimous points verdict. Scored four more wins and

then challenged Medina again in February 1993. Once again he started well, and again Medina was cut, but this time the fight was not stopped. Tom dominated all the way and floored Medina in the eleventh round, finally taking a split decision and the title. The champion is an aggressive fighter, who is growing in confidence and showed improved strength against Medina, and has stopped 20 opponents.

| 20.10.92 | Antonio Hernandez W PTS 10 Atlantic City |
| 26.02.93 | Manuel Medina W PTS 12 Melun *(IBF Featherweight Title Challenge)* |

Career: 34 contests, won 31, drew 1, lost 2.

Roy Jones

Pensacola, USA. *Born* 16 January, 1969
IBF Middleweight Champion

Learned his fighting from his father Roy, who fought as a professional against opponents such as Marvin Hagler. Started boxing at the age of six and at 17, in 1986, he won the National Golden Gloves title at light-welterweight. Moved up to light-middleweight in 1987 and captured the National Golden Gloves title again. Beat Frank Lilles in the 1988 Olympic trials and defeated Richie Woodhall in the Games' semi-finals, but was robbed of the gold medal by a disgraceful decision in the final. Turned professional under his father's management in May 1989 and beat useful Ron Amundsen and Steve Johnson in early fights. However, his father then became over cautious and Roy spent three years fighting poor opposition in Pensacola. He finally became tired of this approach and broke with his father to guide his own career. In January 1992 he showed his power with a 102 seconds stoppage of the experienced Mexican, Jorge Vaca, and, in April, knocked out Art Serwano in one round. He was taken the distance for the first time by the cagey Jorge Castro in a points win in June 1992 and then halted the previously unbeaten Glenn Thomas. A fourth round knockout of tough Percy

Harris and a first round blowout of Glenn Wolfe, earned him a match with the dangerous Bernard Hopkins for the vacant IBF crown. Roy finally realised his great potential when he won the title with a clear unanimous decision. He is a brilliant boxer, with great hand speed and a wide variety of punches, but is still learning and may find it difficult to hold his weight down to middleweight. In 22 bouts, only Castro and Hopkins have lasted the distance.

18.08.92	Glenn Thomas W RSC 8 Pensacola
05.12.92	Percy Harris W CO 4 Pensacola
13.02.93	Glenn Wolfe W RSC 1 Las Vegas
22.05.93	Bernard Hopkins W PTS 12 Washington
	(Vacant IBF Middleweight Title)

Career: 22 contests, won 22.

Jorge Elicier Julio

El Reten, Colombia. *Born* 26 April, 1969
WBA Bantamweight Champion

Had an outstanding amateur career, winning 88 of his 97 fights. He collected a number of titles, fighting under the family name of Rocha, and ended up with a bronze medal in the 1988 Olympic Games at light-fly-weight. Turned professional in March 1989 and collected six wins that year, all inside the distance. He continued his progress in 1990 and quickly gained a world rating when he halted the very good Venezuelan, Abraham Torres, in six rounds in May. Just a couple fo fights later, Torres drew with the future WBC champion, Joichiro Tatsuyoshi. Other fights in 1990, saw Jorge halt experienced Eduo Bermudez in six rounds and the durable Robert Schonning in ten. Scored three more stoppage wins in 1991 to take his total to 19 in a row, a Colombian record for consecutive inside the distance victories. He was finally taken the distance, in November 1991, when outpointing Venezuelan Manuel Ariza. Became the WBA bantamweight champion in October 1992, following a unanimous points decision over Eddie Cook. The fight had been dramatic, with both men badly cut, and Jorge required 35 stitches before the former champion was through with him. His sharp punching easily accounted for his fellow countryman,

Francisco Alvarez, in his first defence and, at 5'5" tall, he is an excellent boxer and a sharp puncher. Also holds victories over Wilson Sarabia and Jesus Flores and has scored 23 wins inside the distance.

03.07.92	Jose Portillo W CO 5 Envigado
09.10.92	Eddie Cook W PTS 12 Cartagena
	(WBA Bantamweight Title Challenge)
03.04.93	Francisco Alvarez W RTD 8 Cartagena
	(WBA Bantamweight Title Defence)

Career: 25 contests, won 25.

Lennox Lewis

Crayford, England. *Born* 2 September, 1965
WBC Heavyweight Champion. Former Undefeated British, Commonwealth & European Heavyweight Champion

The first British-World heavyweight champion this century, he was born in West Ham before emigrating to Canada with his mother when he was nine year's old. It was in Canada that he was first taught to box at the Kitchener-Waterloo ABC and he soon caught on, being a natural at most sports. Represented Canada when he was just 17 and a year later he won the gold medal at the inaugural World junior championships, held in the Dominican Republic, while his first major test came in the 1984 Olympics. Outpointed by Tyrell Biggs, a defeat he would later avenge as a pro, he went on to win the Commonwealth Games title in 1986 and then take the gold medal at the 1988 Olympic Games, stopping America's Riddick Bowe in the final. Having conquered the World as an amateur, it was now time to do the same as a professional and he created a major surprise in the industry when he signed with London-based manager, Frank Maloney. At that time, Maloney was reckoned to be merely small-time, but the boxing fraternity would soon find out that he too was made of sterner stuff. Based in England, Al Malcolm, who fell in the second, was his first victim in June 1989 and he went on to run up twelve more victories before relieving the Frenchman, Jean Chanet, of his European title in October 1990. The lead-in period was almost over. In his

very next outing he stopped Gary Mason in the seventh round to take the British title and went on to defend the crown against Glenn McCrory and Derek Williams, winning himself a Lonsdale Belt inside fourteen months. During the same period, he beat former World champion, Mike Weaver, Tyrell Biggs and Levi Billups, while the fight against Williams also saw him capture the latter's Commonwealth title. Following an impressive stoppage of Mike Dixon in the States, he was matched against the much feared Razor Ruddock in a final eliminator for the WBC title on 31 October 1992 at Olympia. It was the manner of the victory, a second round stoppage, that was so impressive and it quickly led to Riddick Bowe renouncing his newly won WBC belt, rather than defend it against Lennox. Mind you, Bowe still had the IBF and WBA titles, so·one would imagine that he thought it more profitable defending those champion-ships, rather than risk losing all three titles at once. Handed the WBC heavy-weight title on a plate, Lennox did not look for an easy option, successfully defending the title in America against Tony Tucker last May. He put the American down twice, the first man to do so in 50 contests, but could not keep him on the deck and ultimately had to be satisfied with a unanimous points victory. Whether or not Bowe and Lewis get together remains to be seen, but with big pay days in line against Frank Bruno and Tommy Morrison, Lennox has got work lined up for the next twelve months at least. Sooner or later the two top men will come together and my money will be on Lewis. At 6'4½" tall, he has an excellent punch, especially with the right, and has very fast hands, sports a great jab and is a fluent mover, either going backwards or forwards.

Note: Full record will be found in the Current British-Based Champions: Career Records' section.

Ricardo Lopez

Cuernavaca, Mexico. *Born* 25 July, 1967
WBC M. Flyweight Champion. Former Undefeated WBC Con Am M. Flyweight Champion

The class fighter of the division and one of the best Mexico has produced in recent years. Stylish boxer, with an excellent tactical sense and a great jab, he is also a sharp puncher and has good stamina. Was a feared street fighter and entered the gym for the first time at just seven years of age. Claimed 37 consecutive wins as an amateur and won the Mexican Golden Gloves title in 1984. Too young to compete in the major international tournaments, he turned professional in January 1985 when only 17. Managed by the famous Mexican, Arturo Hernandez, he halted his first eight opponents. Hernandez kept him fighting in the Provinces for a couple of years, whilst he learned the game, and then brought him to Mexico City in 1987 where he beat Alfonso Rivera and Javier Alonso. Further victories over useful opponents, such as Baldo Gonzalez and Jose Luis Zepeda, proved his quality, and Ricardo won his first title in November 1989 when he stopped the experienced Rey Hernandez in twelve rounds to become the WBC Continental Americas mini-flyweight champion. He defended his title, halting Jorge Rivera in March 1990, and that October won the WBC crown in style. Challenging Hideyuki Ohashi in front of his own fans in Tokyo, he totally outclassed the Japanese fighter. Ohashi was down three times, before being knocked out in round five. Made two defences in 1991, easily decisioning Kimio Hirano in Japan and Kyung-Yun Lee in Korea. Ricardo was cut against the former IBF champion, Lee, but finished the fight strongly to clearly outpoint his challenger. In 1992 he was again in dominant form as he toyed with Domingo Lucas on the way to a points verdict in March, and then knocked out Singprasert Kitikasem and Rocky Lim. He returned to Korea again in January 1993 to defeat the former amateur star, Kwang-Soo Oh, who was stopped on a cut in the ninth round, with Ricardo well ahead on all of the cards. He has not really been extended by any of his challengers and may soon decide to move up to light-flyweight and seek a fight with Michael Carbajal. Has stopped or knocked out 23 victims.

22.08.92	Singprasert Kitikasem W CO 5 Ciudad Madero *(WBC M. Flyweight Title Defence)*	
11.10.92	Rocky Lim W CO 2 Tokyo *(WBC M. Flyweight Title Defence)*	
31.01.93	Kwang-Soo Oh W RSC 9 Seoul *(WBC M. Flyweight Title Defence)*	

Career: 32 contests, won 32.

Gerald McClellan

Freepost, USA. *Born* 23 October, 1967
WBC Middleweight Champion.
Former Undefeated WBO
Middleweight Champion

6'0" tall, rangy fighter, with knockout punch in both hands, as his record proves. Was United States' amateur champion at 156 lbs in 1987, beating Tim Littles in the final and being voted "Amateur Fighter of the Year." The next year he was runner-up in the National Golden Gloves championships to Ray McElroy and turned professional in August 1988, after an amateur record of 72 wins and ten losses. Joined the Kronk team in Detroit and made an impressive start, halting his first ten opponents, seven in the first round and three in the second. Came down to earth with a bump in June 1989. He was outboxed by Dennis Milton and failed again in his next fight in September 1989, when he lost a points decision to tough Ralph Ward. Following that loss, he was criticised for his lack of dedication and trying to score a knockout with every punch. He showed more patience in points wins over Sanderline Williams and Charles Hollis in 1990, but was still knocking other opponents over in quick time. Most of those men were very poor quality, but his membership of Kronk and their influence, saw him nominated to meet John Mugabi for the vacant WBO title in November 1991. Proving a worthy challenger, he lifted the title in an awesome display, flooring a faded Mugabi three times and halting him in the first round. He never defended the WBO title and, after leaving the Kronk team, he relinquished the title to challenge Julian Jackson for the WBC crown in May 1993. Gerald won the battle of punchers, halting Jackson in the fifth, and only four of his 30 fights have lasted the distance, with 17 wins coming in the first round.

07.11.92	Steve Harvey W RSC 1 Lake Tahoe	
20.03.93	Tyrone Moore W RSC 2 Mexico City	
08.05.93	Julian Jackson W RSC 5 Las Vegas *(WBC Middleweight Title Challenge)*	

Career: 30 contests, won 28, lost 2.

Kennedy McKinney

Las Vegas, USA. *Born* 10 January, 1966
IBF S. Bantamweight Champion.
Former Undefeated USBA S.
Bantamweight Champion

Born Memphis, Tennessee, he is a former truck driver who made his name as an amateur whilst fighting for the US Army. Never winning a national title, he sprung a major surprise, emerging from the US trials to made the team for the 1988 Olympic Games. Proved this was no fluke when going on to take the gold medal at bantamweight, the first American ever to do so. He claimed 214 wins in 227 fights, before turning professional in February 1989 with the Las Vegas Golden Gloves team, under the promotional banner of the Top Rank organisation. After a run of four wins he fought a technical draw with David Sanchez in August 1989, when the fight was halted in the second round due to a cut. He came back to score eight victories in 1990 and another six in 1991. Collected his first professional title in February 1992, when he decisioned the former WBC super-fly-weight champion, Sugar Baby Rojas, to take the USBA super-bantamweight crown, despite having to overcome the disadvantage of a closing right eye. Successfully defended his title in March, flooring the former WBC super-bantamweight champion, Paul Banke, twice and forcing him to retire in the sixth round. He then won the IBF title in dramatic fashion from the previously unbeaten South African, Welcome Ncita, last December. Kennedy was badly hurt in the tenth round, floored in the eleventh and looked ready to surrender, when a desperation right knocked Ncita out cold. Retained his title against unbeaten Richie Duran, but had to overcome a slow start, before boxing his way to an unspectacular points victory. His rise to the top has not been without problems, having twice disappeared from the Las Vegas scene due to drug related difficulties, while Top Rank threatened to drop him if he did not kick the habit. Thankfully he appears to be on the right road now. 5'7" tall, he has good mobility and an excellent jab, but is not a big puncher, although he has fourteen stoppages.

02.12.92	Welcome Ncita W CO 11 Tortoli *(IBF S. Bantamweight Title Challenge)*
17.04.93	Richard Duran W PTS 12 Sacramento *(IBF S. Bantamweight Title Defence)*

Career: 24 contests, won 23, drew 1.

Henry Maske

Trevenbrietzen, Germany. *Born* 6 January, 1964
IBF L. Heavyweight Champion

6'3" tall, southpaw, and one of the few fighters to make a successful switch from Iron Curtain amateur star to world professional champion. Boxing for East Germany, Henry won gold medals at both the Olympic Games and World amateur championships, and was also European champion. He also collected a hat-full of other medals, before turning professional in May 1990 in a bout at Wembley, when he knocked out the poor Mexican, Teo Arvizu. Went on to defeat Jorge Salgado, Sean Mannion and Glazz Campbell, amongst others, that year. He earned a world rating in only his tenth fight, after outpointing Yawe Davis in May 1991 and cemented his position by beating Tom Collins on an eighth round stoppage in December. He continued to gain experience in 1992, as he knocked out the former WBA champion, Leslie Stewart, and decisioned the useful American, Lenzie Morgan, in a tough fight in June. The Morgan fight replaced a scheduled shot at the IBF title holder, Charles Williams, and injuries to the champion delayed the bout until March. Maske eventually won the title with a good display of southpaw

Henry Maske   Les Clark

boxing. Weathering a fast start by Williams, he earned a unanimous decision after controlling the fight with his right jab. An accurate, but not heavy puncher, he tends to stop his opponents by wearing them down. Morgan and Williams both had him hurt, but he has a sound chin, and good stamina, and has stopped eight of his victims. Also has wins over Cordwell Hylton, Rodrigo Benech and Mike Peak.

19.09.92	Frank Minton W RSC 2 Berlin
02.10.92	Samson Cohen W RTD 6 Berlin
20.03.93	Charles Williams W PTS 12 Dusseldorf *(IBF L. Heavyweight Title Challenge)*

Career: 20 contests, won 20.

Jacob (Baby Jake) Matlala

Johannesburg, South Africa. *Born* 8 January, 1962
WBO Flyweight Champion. Former Undefeated South African L. Flyweight Champion

Only 4'10" tall, he is a modern "Cinderella Man" of boxing, who has become a world champion at a time when his career was supposed to be on the wane. His father, now a television producer, was a good boxing prospect himself and encouraged Jacob to follow the sport. He was unbeaten in a short spell as an amateur, before turning professional in February 1980.

Won the South African light-flyweight title three years later, with an upset eleventh round stoppage of Mveleli Luzipho, but lost it to the same man on a disputed decision in October 1983. Challenged Luzipho in November 1985, but was again outpointed. Jacob then failed in four further attempts to win the title, losing three times to Vuyani Nene and also to Jaji Sibali, before finally regaining the crown in October 1990 with a points win over Wele Magolo for the vacant title. As a genuine light-flyweight, he was lucky to be given a shot at the IBF flyweight champion, Dave McAuley, in September 1991, but gave the Irishman a good fight before being knocked out in the tenth round. Jacob managed only one contest in 1992, and was badly cut in winning a non-title affair against Toto Hleli, only six weeks before challenging Pat Clinton for the WBO flyweight title. His power and aggression proved too much for Clinton and he won the WBO title on a stoppage in round eight. His strong points are his fitness and dedication, but his height and a poor defence have proved drawbacks. The little man from Soweto, with a diploma in accountancy, is really only a light-flyweight who could even make mini-flyweight. Has stopped or knocked out 18 opponents.

04.04.93	Toto Hleli W PTS 8 Springs
15.05.93	Pat Clinton W RSC 8 Glasgow *(WBO Flyweight Title Challenge)*

Career: 47 contests, won 37, drew 1, lost 9.

Juan (John John) Molina

Fajardo, Puerto Rico. *Born* 17 March, 1965
IBF S. Featherweight Champion. Former Undefeated WBO S. Featherweight Champion

Juan had a distinguished amateur career, representing Puerto Rico in the 1982 World championships, the 1983 World junior championships and the Pan American Games. Competed for Puerto Rico in the 1984 Olympic Games without success, but became a national hero when he won gold medals in the North American championships and the World Cup in 1985.

Ended with a record of 92 wins in 103 fights as an amateur and received a $100,000 signing on fee when he turned professional with the Main Events group in 1986. Won twelve fights in his first year, including a useful points victory over Kevin Marston. Lost his unbeaten tag in May 1987, when he was floored twice by experienced Lupe Suarez and halted in the ninth round. Challenged Tony Lopez for the IBF super-featherweight title in October 1988 and had the champion on the floor, before losing a close points decision. He won the vacant WBO title in April 1989, with a clear points verdict over Juan Laporte, but relinquished the crown to challenge Tony Lopez again in October. This time, Juan gave Tony a beating before halting him in the tenth round. In his first defence in January 1990 he gained revenge for the loss to Suarez, flooring the Texan twice and stopping him in six rounds. A third bout with Lopez was close, but Juan was dropped in the eleventh round, and lost his crown on a split decision. He marked time until February 1992, when he regained the IBF crown with ease, halting South African, Jackie Gunguluza, in four rounds. He made two undemanding defences at home in Puerto Rico, stopping Fernando Caicedo and Francisco Segura, and then registered a good win by taking a unanimous decision over the former IBF featherweight champion, Manuel Medina, in his third defence. 5'7" tall, a sharp puncher and a good boxer, Juan has halted or knocked out 23 victims.

02.07.92	Donnie Parker W RSC 7 Isla Verde
22.08.92	Fernando Caicedo W RSC 4 Bayamon *(IBF S. Featherweight Title Defence)*
13.02.93	Francisco Segura W RSC 8 Bayamon *(IBF S. Featherweight Title Defence)*
14.05.93	Tony Duran W RSC 2 Fajardo
26.06.93	Manuel Medina W PTS 12 Atlantic City *(IBF S. Featherweight Title Defence)*
Career: 35 contests, won 32, lost 3.	

Sung-Il (Korean Hands Of Stone) Moon

Yeoung-Am, South Korea. *Born* 20 July, 1963
WBC S. Flyweight Champion. Former WBA Bantamweight Champion

Capped an exciting period as an amateur by winning the bantamweight gold medal at the 1985 World championships. This was some consolation for failing to obtain a medal in the 1984 Olympics, where he stopped John Hyland and knocked out Robert Shannon, but lost in the quarter-finals. He had 127 amateur fights, winning 115 and halting 72 opponents, and his potential was such that he was paid $180,000 to turn professional in March 1987. He quickly proved his worth, winning the WBA bantamweight crown in only his seventh fight in August 1988, with a controversial technical decision over Kaokor Galaxy, after being cut. He retained his title, halting Edgar Monserrat in November and Chiaki Kobayashi in February 1989, but lost the crown to Galaxy on a unanimous decision in Thailand in July. He was a champion again in January 1990, but again in controversial circumstances. When challenging the hard punching Nana Yaw Konadu for the WBC super-bantamweight title, both fighters were on the floor and badly cut when another technical decision was called in the ninth round and Moon declared the winner on points. His first defence saw him halt the former champion, Gilberto Roman, in nine rounds in June and, in a defence in October, Moon was again cut and again took a technical decision, this time in five rounds over Kenji Matsumura. Moon settled the dispute over the Konadu match by halting his rival in four rounds in a return in March 1991 and then knocked out Ernesto Ford and stopped Torsak Pongsupa in further defences. In 1992 he outclassed and halted Armando Salazar in a title fight in July, but looked less impressive against Greg Richardson, last October. The American boxed well and gave Moon plenty of trouble, until the champion floored his rival twice in the twelfth round to clinch a majority verdict. His eighth defence in February 1993, saw him crush Hilario Zapata in one round. Moon is an aggressive fighter, but not a wild swinger, who has a tight defence and fast hands and likes to work on the inside with solid hooks. While he is very susceptible to cuts, the technical decision rules have allowed him to retain his crown, despite bleeding badly on three or four occasions. Of his 20 bouts, thirteen have been world title fights and he has stopped fifteen of his opponents.

04.07.92	Armando Salazar W RSC 8 Ichon *(WBC S. Flyweight Title Defence)*
31.10.92	Greg Richardson W PTS 12 Seoul *(WBC S. Flyweight Title Defence)*
27.02.93	Hilario Zapata W RSC 1 Seoul *(WBC S. Flyweight Title Defence)*
Career: 20 contests, won 19, lost 1.	

Tommy (The Duke) Morrison

Gravette, USA. *Born* 2 January, 1969
WBO Heavyweight Champion

Claims John Wayne as a great uncle, which explains his nickname. Born in Arkansas, but living in Kansas City, he took a leading role in the film, Rocky V, but has put any thoughts of an acting career to one side whilst he concentrates on his boxing. 6'2" tall, with a 78" reach, he is a free swinging, hard puncher, with a less than solid defence. Started in local toughman competitions, but then boxed successfully as an amateur, reaching the semifinals of the 1988 National Golden Gloves, but losing to Ray Mercer in the Olympic trials. He then turned professional in November 1988 under Bill Cayton, who had looked after Mike Tyson. Tommy looked crude, but powerful, as he mowed down a succession of nobodies and trial horses. After 24 straight wins, he faced his first name opponent in James Tillis in January 1991. Tommy came through in style, flooring Tillis three times and halting him in less than two minutes. Registered another quick win in February, when the former WBC champion, Pinklon Thomas, retired at the end of the first round of their bout, but his faults were cruelly exposed by Ray Mercer when he challenged for the WBO title in October. Tommy made all of the early running, until

Tommy Morrison

blowing up and being stopped in round five. He showed his courage in a June 1992 bout with tough Joe Hipp, as he overcame a broken jaw and an injured hand to stop his opponent in the ninth round. Two fights later he also had a war with Carl Williams, last January. Tommy was floored twice, but came back to halt Williams in round eight and when he faced George Foreman for the vacant WBO title, he showed improved skills and stamina to box his way to a points decision. It remains to be seen whether he can box as effectively against younger and more mobile opponents, and whether his still porous defence will let him down, but he is an exciting fighter with a left-hook that will hurt anyone he lands it on, with 32 wins coming inside the distance.

12.12.92	Marshall Tillman W RSC 1 Phoenix
16.01.93	Carl Williams W RSC 8 Reno
31.03.93	Dan Murphy W CO 3 Kansas City
07.06.93	George Foreman W PTS 12 Las Vegas
	(Vacant WBO Heavyweight Title)
Career: 38 contests, won 37, lost 1.	

Charles (The Natural) Murray

Rochester, USA. *Born* 18 August, 1968
IBF L. Welterweight Champion.
Former USBA L. Welterweight Champion

A member of the Triple Threat team, as an amateur he won 65 of his 70 fights and collected the United States' championship at 132 lbs in 1987, beating Skipper Kelp in the final. Came into the "box-offs" for the 1988 Olympic team as a late replacement, but lost to Todd Foster. Turned professional in February 1989 with Marc Roberts, along with other top amateurs, Ray Mercer and Al Cole, and they were named the Triple Threat. Now all three have won world professional titles. Scored ten wins in a busy 1989, without being severely tested. Showed good power in May 1990, blasting out useful Robert Guy, but then had to climb off the canvas in July to knockout Alfred Rojas. Won

Charles Murray

the vacant USBA crown in October 1990, outboxing Mickey Ward, before successfully defending it in January 1991, with a points victory against David Taylor and, again in April, with a stoppage of Bernard Gray. In May 1991, with both the USBA and the NABF titles on the line, he was beaten on a split decision by Terrence Alli. Charles rallied to take the tenth and eleventh rounds, but Alli had him out on his feet in the last to clinch the verdict. Returned with points wins over Livingston Bramble, Sammy Fuentes, and Tony Martin, and then clashed with Rodney Moore for the vacant IBF title. And, in a real test of

character, he came through with the decision to take the crown. A stand up boxer with fine skills, his power has not been consistent and in early fights he was hit too often for comfort. Has 18 wins inside the distance.

16.07.92	Sammy Fuentes W PTS 10 Atlantic City
11.09.92	Jerry Smith W RSC 5 Atlantic City
05.12.92	Juan Ramon Cruz W CO 2 Atlantic City
08.04.93	Tony Martin W PTS 10 Atlantic City
15.05.93	Rodney Moore W PTS 12 Atlantic City
	(Vacant IBF L. Welterweight Title)
Career: 30 contests, won 29, lost 1.	

Azumah Nelson

Accra, Ghana. *Born* 19 July, 1958
WBC S. Featherweight Champion.
Former Undefeated WBC Featherweight Champion. Former Undefeated Ghanaian, ABU & Commonwealth Featherweight Champion

5'5" tall, and one of the modern greats, he won Commonwealth, African and World Military titles as an amateur, losing just two of his 52 bouts, one of those being in the 1979 World Cup when he was forced to fight at light-welterweight. Turning professional in December 1979, he became the featherweight champion of Ghana in only his second fight and the African Boxing Union champion in his sixth. Won the Commonwealth title in September 1981, in his tenth bout, and made two title defences before being brought in as a late substitute to challenge Salvador Sanchez for the WBC featherweight crown in July 1982. He gave the great Sanchez a tough fight, until tiring and being halted in the fifteenth round. Azumah kept busy with six more wins and collected the WBC title at his second attempt, knocking out Wilfredo Gomez in eleven rounds in December 1984. He made two defences in 1985, halting Juvenal Ordenes in the fifth and knocking out Pat Cowdell in spectacular style in the first round. In 1986, he decisioned Marcos Villasana and stopped Danilo Cabrera and, in 1987, knocked out Mauro Gutierrez, before

Azumah Nelson

again outpointing Villasana. Relinquished the featherweight title in January 1988, due to weight problems, and in February won the vacant WBC super-featherweight title with a close victory over Mario Martinez. Azumah was on the floor in this bout and many felt that Martinez had done enough to win. The little man from Ghana then stopped Lupe Suarez and knocked out Sidnei dal Rovere in title bouts in 1988 and, in 1989, settled the business with Martinez, halting the Mexican in twelve tough rounds in February. After scoring a brutal stoppage victory over Jim McDonnell in November, he attempted to move up to lightweight in May 1990, but was clearly outpointed by Pernell Whitaker in a fight for the WBC and IBF titles. Returned to defending his super-featherweight crown and decisioned Juan Laporte in October, before finally meeting the Australian, Jeff Fenech, in a long awaited battle. Looking lucky to retain his crown on a draw, Azumah confounded the experts by outclassing Fenech in a return in March 1992, as he floored the Australian three times and halted him in round eight. He looked pedestrian when winning a decision in a title defence against Calvin Grove last November, but it was unanimous. Showed he is still a force by turning back the challenge of young Gabriel Ruelas in February 1993, with a strong finish, to take a majority decision. At 34, time must catch up with the little professor soon,

but with 19 world title fights behind him he has earned a place in boxing's Hall of Fame.

| 07.11.92 | Calvin Grove W PTS 12 Lake Tahoe *(WBC S. Featherweight Title Defence)* |
| 20.02.93 | Gabriel Ruelas W PTS 12 Mexico City *(WBC S. Featherweight Title Defence)* |

Career: 39 contests, won 36, drew 1, lost 2.

Terry Norris

Lubbock, USA. *Born* 17 June, 1967
WBC L. Middleweight Champion.
Former Undefeated NABF L. Middleweight Champion

5'8" tall, he is a stylish fighter with fast hands and real power in his punches. Started boxing at the age of nine and had a couple of hundred bouts as a schoolboy. Did not hit the heights as an amateur, with his major achievement being in the 1984 Texas Golden Gloves title. His elder brother, Orlin, turned professional first and recommended Terry to his manager, Joe Sayatovich. Had his first paid fight in August 1986 and looked to lack power, halting only one of his first seven opponents. Beat useful fighters, such as Gilbert Baptist and Nat Dryer, before losing in the Strohs Tournament to the experienced Derrick Kelly in August 1987. Suffered a second defeat in November 1987, when he was disqualified for hitting Joe Walker, who was on the canvas, in the first round of their fight. Showed his quality in August 1988, when decisioning the previously unbeaten Quincy Taylor and in December won the vacant NABF crown, knocking out Steve Little. Terry outpointed veteran Buster Drayton in a defence in March 1989, before challenging Julian Jackson for the WBA title in July. An explosive fight saw Terry hurt Jackson in the first round, only to be nailed and halted in the second. A split decision win over Jorge Vaca in October and a points verdict over Tony Montgomery in a NABF title defence in November, put him back into contention. He seized his chance at the second attempt, separating John Mugabi from his WBC crown with a devastating first round knockout in March 1990. In

Terry Norris

his first defence, he easily outpointed Rene Jacquot in July 1990, and was then inactive until February 1991, when he outclassed a faded Sugar Ray Leonard to take a clear points decision. Terry made three further defences in 1991, knocking out Don Curry, stopping Brett Lally, and outpointing Jorge Castro. In 1992 title defences, Carl Daniels gave him a good fight before being halted in the ninth, while Meldrick Taylor fell apart in four rounds. But he showed his power last February, with a second round crushing of the IBF welterweight champion, Maurice Blocker. However, a crack suddenly appeared in his invincibility, when making a defence against Troy Waters. The Australian took quite a beating, but fought gamely and caused a sensation by flooring and badly hurting Norris in the second round, before retiring at the end of the third. Terry was over-confident and careless, but now it has been shown that he can be hurt, others will be less overawed. 21 of his wins have come inside the distance.

13.12.92	Pat Lawlor W RTD 3 Las Vegas
20.02.93	Maurice Blocker W RSC 2 Mexico City *(WBC L. Middleweight Title Defence)*
19.06.93	Troy Waters W RTD 3 San Diego *(WBC L. Middleweight Title Defence)*

Career: 38 contests, won 35, lost 3.

Michael (Second To) Nunn

Davenport, USA. *Born* 14 April, 1963
WBA S. Middleweight Champion.
Former Undefeated NABF S.
Middleweight Champion. Former IBF
Middleweight Champion. Former
Undefeated NABF Middleweight
Champion

6'2" tall, and a classy boxer with fast
reflexes, he was inspired to take up
boxing after watching Sugar Ray
Leonard win the gold medal at the
1976 Olympic Games on TV. Tried to
follow in Ray's footsteps and claimed
168 wins in 174 amateur fights. Lost in
two out of three bouts with Virgil Hill,
for a spot in the United States' team
for the 1984 Olympics. Michael was
signed up after the trials by Dan
Goossen and turned professional in
December 1984, halting each of his
first eight opponents inside two
rounds. Made his mark in 1986, with
victories over Felipe Vaca and Mike
Tinley, and won the Californian State
middleweight title by decisioning Alex
Ramos in November. He continued his
winning style in 1987 and, in October,
he forced Darnell Knox to retire in the
third round to lift the vacant NABF
crown. Decisioned Kevin Watts and
knocked out Curtis Parker in title
defences early in 1988, and then won
the IBF title in impressive style in
July, outclassing and halting Frank
Tate in nine rounds. His first defence
saw him knock out the tough
Argentinian, Juan Domingo Roldan, in
eight rounds in November and, in
March 1989, he established his dominance of the division by shocking the
classy Sumbu Kalambay with a first
round knockout. Had a much tougher
defence against dangerous Iran
Barkley in August and had to settle for
a majority verdict. In his fourth and
fifth defences he beat former world
champions, winning another majority
decision over Marlon Starling and
halting Don Curry in ten rounds.
Dropped his title in May 1991, after a
run of 36 consecutive victories, when
he under-estimated the strength of
James Toney. He won the early
rounds, but crumbled from the
unrelenting pressure exerted by Toney,
and was stopped in the eleventh.
Moved up to super-middleweight in
November, knocking out Randall

Michael Nunn   Les Clark

Yonker in ten rounds to win the NABF
crown, and became a world champion
again, in September 1992, with a
controversial points win over
Panamanian, Victor Cordoba. He was
floored in the tenth round and the
margin of victory was a point deducted
from Cordoba for a low blow.
Retained his title in January by outclassing Cordoba, having been on the
floor four times from low blows. The
Panamanian had four points deducted
for these offences, but lost by a street.
Last February, he easily knocked out
poor Danny Morgan and turned on a
powerful display in April, when he
floored Crawford Ashley five times
and stopped him in six rounds, in his
third defence. Now with Don King,
and with Angelo Dundee in his corner,
he has halted 27 opponents.

12.09.92	Victor Cordoba W PTS 12 Las Vegas *(WBA S. Middleweight Title Challenge)*
30.01.93	Victor Cordoba W PTS 12 Memphis *(WBA S. Middleweight Title Defence)*
20.02.93	Danny Morgan W CO 1 Mexico City *(WBA S. Middleweight Title Defence)*
23.04.93	Crawford Ashley W RSC 6 Memphis *(WBA S. Middleweight Title Defence)*

Career: 42 contests, won 41, lost 1.

Katsuya Onizuka

Fukuoka, Japan. *Born* 12 March, 1970
WBA S. Flyweight Champion. Former
Undefeated Japanese S. Flyweight
Champion

His first name is really Takashi and, as
a former top amateur, he won 38 of his
43 fights before turning professional in
April 1988. Won the annual Japanese
tournament for novices in 1989 and
stopped fourteen of his first fifteen
opponents. Picked up the Japanese
super-flyweight title in October 1990,
when he halted the champion, Shunichi
Nakajima, in ten rounds, and retained
it in December, knocking out Tomohiko
Yokoyama in one round, before decisioning Nakajima in a return in
March 1991. Showed his power again
in June, when flooring challenger,
Suzuharu Kitazama, three times and
stopping him in round three. Faced
Thalerngsak Sitbobay for the vacant
WBA title in April 1992 and, although
the Thai won the early rounds, Katsuya
came on strong in the middle sessions.
The last rounds seemed to go to
Sitbobay, but the unanimous decision
went to Onizuka and a new champion
was crowned. His first defence in
September 1992, saw him easily
outclass Kenichi Matsumura and halt
him in round five. Next time out, he
faced a tougher opponent in Armando
Castro, but used his excellent skills to
batter the Mexican to a unanimous
points defeat. In his last fight we have
recorded, he had a close shave against
the Japanese based Korean, Jae-Shin
Lim, when he struggled to take an
unpopular split decision. The lanky,
5'8" tall, Onizuka is a talented box-
fighter, with a rapier like jab, but can
be too methodical and predictable.
However, he has accounted for 17
opponents inside the distance.

11.09.92	Kenichi Matsumura W RSC 5 Tokyo *(WBA S. Flyweight Title Defence)*
11.12.92	Armando Castro W PTS 12 Tokyo *(WBA S. Flyweight Title Defence)*
21.05.93	Jae-Shin Lim W PTS 12 Tokyo *(WBA S. Flyweight Title Defence)*

Career: 22 contests, won 22.

Zack Padilla

Azusa, USA. *Born* 15 March, 1963
WBO L. Welterweight Champion

Zack has made a remarkable come-back, after over five years out of the ring. An outstanding amateur, he won the United States championship at light-welterweight in 1983, beating Mickey Ward and Vince Pettway in the tournament. His hopes of an Olympic medal ended at the 1984 trials, where he lost to Tim Rabon, before he turned professional in May 1985 under the management of Tony Cerda, as a lightweight. Stopped six opponents and fought a draw with Ernie Landeros in 1985 and looked a great prospect. Once again his hopes were dashed, as he was given a beating by Dwayne Prim, in one of the early bouts of a ESPN Regional tournament, and halted in round two. Was then inactive until June 1991, but in his third come-back bout he showed he was serious with a points win over unbeaten James Page. He followed that up with a good victory over useful Danny Perez in March 1992, a stoppage of Jose Castro in six rounds, and then forcing the former Mexican welterweight champion, Jesus Cardenas, to retire in five. Had a tough time with Miguel Gonzalez in a December clash, surviving a bad eighth round to take a close decision. He further increased his reputation with a stoppage of Ricky Meyers in February, which earned him a crack at Roger Mayweather. In a fight, which was supposed to be a warm up for Mayweather's challenge to Carlos Gonzalez, he overcame two cuts in the first round to take a split decision over the former world champion. Instead of Mayweather going forward to challenge Gonzalez, Zack took his place and lifted the WBO crown with a points victory over the hard-punching champion, being busier and withstanding the Mexican's wild attacks. The pony tailed Californian is a stand-up boxer, who works behind an excellent jab, and has a tight defence and a good chin, but is not a big puncher. A real "Cinderella Man", he will take some beating.

24.08.92	Jesus Cardenas W RTD 5 Los Angeles
09.12.92	Miguel A. Gonzalez W PTS 10 Hollywood
05.02.93	Ricky Meyers W RSC 6 Atlantic City
24.04.93	Roger Mayweather W PTS 10 Las Vegas
07.06.93	Carlos Gonzalez W PTS 12 Las Vegas *(WBO L. Welterweight Title Challenge)*

Career: 19 contests, won 17, drew 1, lost 1.

Giovanni Parisi

Vibo Valencia, Italy. *Born* 2 December, 1967
WBO Lightweight Champion. Former Undefeated Italian Lightweight Champion

A stablemate to Gianfranco Rosi, he was outstanding as an amateur, being Italian champion in 1985 at light-weight and at featherweight in 1986. Crowned his unpaid career by winning the gold medal at featherweight in the 1988 Olympic Games. Turned professional in February 1989 and swept to victory in his first twelve fights, halting nine opponents. Over-confidence led to a match with the experienced former IBF featherweight champion, Antonio Rivera, in November 1990, at a time when Giovanni had been out for eight months with a hand injury. His world temporarily fell apart when he was floored in the first round and twice more in the third for a clean knockout loss. After more time out he came back in November 1991 to outclass former champion, Stefano Cassi, and knock him out in two rounds to win the vacant Italian lightweight title. He then relinquished the title, without making a defence, to chase a world title shot. Faced Javier Altamirano for the vacant WBO title in September 1992 and almost repeated the Rivera experience. Once again Giovanni was on the floor in the first round, twice in fact, but he fought back to floor the Mexican in the fifth and stop him in the tenth. Defended his title last April with a unanimous points win over previously unbeaten Michael Ayers, dropping the challenger in the fifth round. Parisi can box equally as well

as a southpaw or orthodox and is a fast accurate puncher with solid power. Also has wins over Marvin Gray, Rudy Valentino, Tony Foster and Mark Smith and has halted 18 opponents.

25.09.92	Javier Altamirano W RSC 10 Voghera *(Vacant WBO Lightweight Title)*
13.01.93	Mark Smith W CO 4 San Remo
16.04.93	Michael Ayers W PTS 12 Rome *(WBO Lightweight Title Defence)*

Career: 25 contests, won 24, lost 1.

Kyun-Yung Park

Seoul, South Korea. *Born* 16 August, 1967
WBA Featherweight Champion. Former Undefeated OPBF Featherweight Champion. Former Undefeated South Korean Featherweight & S. Bantamweight Champion

A rough, tough, rugged southpaw with an iron jaw, his aggressive whirlwind style made no impression in the amateur ranks. Despite this, he made quick progress as a professional and won the annual novice tournament in 1986 at super-bantamweight. He had his first title match in October 1987, but fell just short, and could only draw with the South Korean super-bantamweight champion, Jung-Woo Park. Thirteen months later he finally succeeded to the title by decisioning Jae-Won Choi. Weight problems forced him to move up to feather-weight in 1989 and he collected the vacant South Korean crown with a points victory over Yong-Man Chun. In his next bout, in January 1990, he added the OPBF title, halting Jojo Cayson in eight rounds. Park made two defences in 1990, knocking out Jimmy Sithfaidang, but struggled to a split decision over Cris Saguid. He then sprang a big surprise, lifting the WBA title from the heavily favoured Venezuelan, Antonio Esparragoza, with a points win in Kwangju in March 1991. Kyun-Yung received little credit for the victory and was not expected to hold the title for long. However, he made a defence in June, halting Masuaki Takeda in six rounds, and then turned back the challenge of the unbeaten Venezuelan, Eloy Rojas, in September. Had an active 1992, making four defences. He flattened Seiji Asakawa in nine rounds with a devastating left-hook, halted Koji Matsumoto in the eleventh, outpointed the tough Venezuelan, Giovanni Nieves, and won an all-southpaw battle on points over the unbeaten Ever Beleno. In March 1993, an easier defence against Thanomchit Kiatkriengkrai, saw him give his challenger a solid beating before the bout was halted in the fourth round. His strength and stamina make him a hard fighter to beat and he has proved a good champion. Has stopped fourteen opponents.

29.08.92	Giovanni Nieves W PTS 12 Taegu
	(WBA Featherweight Title Defence)
19.12.92	Ever Beleno W PTS 12 Changwon
	(WBA Featherweight Title Defence)
20.03.93	Thanomchit Kiatkriengkrai W RSC 4 Chejudo
	(WBA Featherweight Title Defence)

Career: 27 contests, won 25, drew 1, lost 1.

Tracy Harris Patterson

New Paltz, USA. *Born* 26 December, 1964

WBC S. Bantamweight Champion. Former Undefeated NABF S. Bantamweight Champion

Tracy Harris Patterson   Tom Casino

Born in Birmingham, Alabama, as Tracy Harris, but is now the son of the former world heavyweight champion, Floyd Patterson, being adopted when he was fourteen-years-old. As an amateur he was New York Golden Gloves champion in 1984, and turned professional in the following year. He was heavily protected in his early fights and ran up 20 easy victories, before losing on points to Jeff Franklin in October 1987. Tracy returned to a diet of easy fights again, stopping nine of his next ten victims, before being given another test in May 1989, when matched with the former world featherweight champion, Steve Cruz. Tracy found himself on the floor in the fight, but fought back hard and finally lost on a split decision. Most of his fights up to this time had been at featherweight, or higher, but late in 1989 he moved down to super-bantamweight. He won the vacant NABF title in this division by knocking out George Garcia in February 1990 and retained the title in April, halting Kenny Mitchell in round eight. Once again Tracy moved up in weight and relinquished the NABF crown. When no title shot came, he moved back down again to challenge Thierry Jacob for the WBC super-bantamweight title in June 1992. He took the crown in style, overwhelming

the Frenchman and stopping him in just two rounds. His next defence was a tough encounter against former champion, Daniel Zaragoza. The experienced Mexican looked to have outboxed Tracy in a very close fight, but the judges came up with a draw and he retained his crown. Also had a hard fight when he put the title on the line last March against the former WBO champion, Jesse Benavides, but won a close unanimous decision. A good little boxer, who punches hard with each hand, he has yet to really find his form as champion and his impressive total of 34 stoppages reflects the poor quality of much of his opposition.

15.09.92	Manuel Santiago W PTS 10 Helsinki
05.12.92	Daniel Zaragoza DREW 12 Berck sur Mer
	(WBC S. Bantamweight Title Defence)
13.03.93	Jesse Benavides W PTS 12 Poughkeepsie
	(WBC S. Bantamweight Title Defence)

Career: 50 contests, won 47, drew 1, lost 2.

Fred Pendelton

Philadelphia, USA. *Born* 5 January, 1963

IBF Lightweight Champion. Former Undefeated USBA Lightweight Champion

5'7" tall, with a 69" reach, and one of twelve children, he made a disastrous start, losing five of his first six amateur bouts. Turned professional when he was only 18-years-old in November 1981 and went one better when he only lost four of his first six fights. Due to poor management, he spent his early years fighting at short notice in the other man's back-yard and built up a patchy record as a result. He lost to good fighters, such as Jerome Coffee, Gerald Hayes, Anthony Fletcher and Hilmer Kenty, but occasionally showed his true worth and in June 1984, halted Tyrone Trice in one round. A change of management did wonders for Fred and in 1986 he stopped Roger Mayweather, beat Shelton LeBlanc, and then drew with Frankie Randall for the vacant USBA lightweight title. He also drew with the former world champion, Livingston

Bramble, in 1987 and, in 1988, stopped Sammy Fuentes in just fifteen seconds, before halting Bramble in ten to take the USBA crown. It wasn't roses all the way and he suffered a setback in November 1988, being halted in ten rounds by John Montes in the Inglewood Forum tournament. Challenged Pernell Whitaker for the IBF and WBC titles in February 1990, but was outboxed and lost a unanimous decision. After the champion moved up, Fred was matched with Tracy Spann for the vacant IBF crown in August 1992. Floored briefly in the first, a clash of heads also saw him badly cut, and the bout was declared a technical draw in the second round. Met Spann again last January for the title and this time he outboxed the dangerous southpaw to win on a unanimous decision. He is a cute fighter, with a wealth of experience and a potent right hand, but has a tendency to cut and his chin is not made of granite. His record does not look impressive, due to his early losses, but he has suffered only two defeats in his last 21 bouts, while 23 of his 34 wins have come inside the distance.

29.08.92	Tracy Spann TD 2 Reno	
	(Vacant IBF Lightweight Title)	
10.01.93	Tracy Spann W PTS 12 Atlantic City	
	(Vacant IBF Lightweight Title)	
15.05.93	Cruz Saldana W CO 2 Plantation City	
Career: 55 contests, won 34, drew 4, lost 17.		

Chana Porpaoin

Petchaboon, Thailand. *Born* 25 March, 1966
WBA M. Flyweight Champion.
Former Undefeated Thai M. Flyweight Champion

5'3" tall, he started boxing in Muay-thai style kick boxing, but turned to international style in 1988. Is a former stable-mate of Kaosai Galaxy and, like the former champion, he is one of twins. He won the vacant Thai mini-flyweight crown in only his seventh fight, but relinquished the title without ever making a defence. In June 1988 he decisioned future world champion, Falan Lukmingkwan, and faced his first imported opponent, South Korean, In-Kyu Hwang, in December 1988, winning on points. He has never faced a Thai opponent since then, as all of his victims have been foreigners. Had a scare in July 1989 when he was floored by Warlito Franco, but eventually won a clear points verdict. In June 1990 he outpointed the future world champion, Manny Melchor, but had a tough fight with Filipino, Ric Magramo, in July 1991 and had to overcome a bad cut to take the points verdict. Kept his winning run going and was rewarded with a shot at the WBA champion, Hideyuki Ohashi, in Japan. Chana took his chance in fine style and proved too fast and too busy for the heavy handed champion. The decision was not unanimous, with one official voting for a draw, but the other two judges gave it to Chana by seven and five rounds, respectively, to make him champion. He went a long way towards establishing himself in his first defence when he clearly decisioned the unbeaten Panamanian, Carlos Murillo. Chana was considered a bit methodical and one-paced in his early fights and his defence was not too sound, but against Ohashi he was quick and skilful and has shown considerable progress. He is not a heavy puncher, with only twelve opponents stopped or knocked out, and has wins over useful names such as Max Forrosuelo, Nikki Maca and Sammy Tyson.

02.11.92	Texas Gomez W RSC 6 Bangkok	
10.12.92	Ernest Rubillar W CO 4 Bangkok	
10.02.93	Hideyuki Ohashi W PTS 12 Tokyo	
	(WBA M. Flyweight Title Challenge)	
09.05.93	Carlos Murillo W PTS 12 Bangkok	
	(WBA M. Flyweight Title Defence)	
Career: 28 contests, won 28.		

Chris Pyatt

Leicester, England. *Born* 3 July, 1963
WBO Middleweight Champion.
Former Undefeated British & Commonwealth L. Middleweight Champion. Former European L. Middleweight Champion. Former Undefeated WBC International Middleweight Champion

Finally made it as a World champion, after years of trying as a light-middleweight, when he recently won the WBO version of the middleweight title. Had an illustrious career as an amateur with the Belgrave ABC, winning national schools titles in 1977 and 1979, a junior ABA title in 1980, and culminating when he became the ABA and Commonwealth champion at welterweight in 1982. With the Olympics nearly two years away, he decided to turn professional with Sam Burns and made his debut in March 1983, scoring a two round retirement win over Paul Murray. Brought along steadily, he picked up a further fourteen wins, before suffering his first defeat at the hands of Sabiyala Diavilia, being the recipient of an unfortunate cut eye defeat. No harm was done and, in his very next contest in February 1986, he knocked out Prince Rodney in the ninth round to annex the British light-middleweight title. Following three further wins, including a ridiculously easy first round stoppage over John van Elteren for the vacant European title, he defended his crown in Italy of all places and lost disappointingly on points to the very good Gianfranco Rosi in January 1987. Soon back in action, he put a further eleven victories under his belt and changed his manager, moving to Frank Warren, before being given a great opportunity to take the WBO light-middleweight title from the head of the American, John David Jackson. Once again he failed to rise to the big occasion, being outspeeded by a one-handed champion over twelve rounds, and it was back to the drawing board. Out of the ring for nearly two years, he came back under the promotional banner of Matchroom. Barry Hearn immediately went to work, organising a fight with Australian, Craig Trotter, for the vacant Commonwealth light-middleweight title, which Chris duly won on points and successfully defended twice inside the distance against Ambrose Mlilo and James Tapisha. Moved up a division when he took on and beat Ian Strudwick on points in May 1992 and in his next contest he won the vacant WBC International middleweight title, beating Adolfo Caballero on a fifth round count out. An impressive defence against Danny Garcia, followed by wins over Colin Manners (a tremendous third round count out) and Paul Wesley, brought Chris and Sumbu Kalambay together to contest the WBO middleweight title left vacant when the American, Gerald McClellan, decided he would rather have the WBC version instead. Chris rose to the occasion brilliantly, keeping on top of the veteran all night and although desperately tired, was adjudged to have done enough to deserve the verdict on the three judges' scorecards. An aggressive, all-action fighter, with a good wallop in both hands, he deserves his moment of glory and will probably look for WBO challenges rather than attempt to unify the division.

Note: Full record will be found in the Current British-Based Champions: Career Records' section.

Steve Robinson

Cardiff, Wales. *Born* 13 December, 1968
WBO Featherweight Champion.
Former Undefeated Welsh & WBA Penta-Continental Featherweight Champion

The least likely British born – World champion, Steve came from nowhere to win the WBO featherweight title and has become an inspiration to all youngsters wishing to make their way in the game. Tall for a feather, at 5'8", he started out as an amateur with the Ely Star ABC at the age of nine, but after 19 schoolboy bouts he left the game for six years until returning under the guidance of Ronnie Rush. Had five wins in eight senior amateur contests, before turning professional in March 1989. Prior to lifting the Welsh featherweight title in a surprise win over the champion, Peter Harris, in July 1991, he had won only eight and drawn one of fifteen bouts in a career that up to then had been plagued by late substitute jobs. That victory obviously gave him confidence and although losing his next two starts against Henry Armstong and a vacant Welsh super-featherweight title fight against Neil Haddock, he recorded excellent wins over Edward Lloyd (retired 8), Stephane Haccoun (points 8) in France, Dennis Oakes (retired 2) and Paul Harvey (points 12). The

Harvey fight in January 1993, brought him the WBA Penta-Continental featherweight belt with a fine victory over the former Commonwealth super-featherweight champion. A big underdog, he dominated Harvey and floored him twice to win handily on all three judges' scorecards. His next date was a trip to Paris where he lost a very close decision to the French-Algerian, Medhi Labdouni, in a fight that could have gone either way, and on his return to Wales he couldn't have possibly imagined what would be in store for him when he next stepped into the ring. A phone call from his manager, Dai Gardiner, the man who had guided Johnny Owen to an ill-fated World bantamweight title challenge over thirteen years earlier, informed Steve that his services were required in 48 hours time in order to contest the vacant WBO featherweight title against fellow Britisher, John Davison. The champion, Ruben Palacio, of Colombia, had failed an HIV medical and the promoters were desperate for the fight to go ahead. The scene was set and in one of the most dramatic fights seen in this country, he created a tremendous shock and surprised everyone in boxing by outpointing Davison in front of his own volatile fans. Now a World champion, and much respected at that, he is a fighter who never lets an opponent get set, has very fast hands and while not predominately a puncher, he works his rivals over most effectively with a steady accumulation of blows. Stop Press: Successfully defended his title on 10 July in Cardiff with a ninth round knockout of fellow Britisher, Sean Murphy.

Note: Full record will be found in the Current British-Based Champions: Career Records' section.

Giafranco Rosi

Assisi, Italy. *Born* 5 August, 1957
IBF L. Middleweight Champion.
Former WBC L. Middleweight Champion. Former Undefeated European L. Middleweight Champion. Former Undefeated Italian Welterweight Champion

Won Italian national titles at light-welterweight and welterweight as an

amateur in 1976 and 1977 and claimed 94 wins and four draws in 100 fights. Turned professional in September 1979 and has been, arguably, the most successful, if not the most popular, Italian boxer of all time. He was stopped on a cut by Nelson Gomez in only his sixth fight, but did not lose again for six years. Won the Italian welterweight title in April 1982, halting Guiseppe di Padova, and retained the title with stoppage victories over Antonio Torsello, Everaldo Costa, Pierangelo Pira and Francesco Gallo. Became the European champion in July 1984, with a decision over former world champion, Perico Fernandez, but in his first defence, in January 1985, he was knocked out in three rounds by Lloyd Honeyghan. Gianfranco then moved up to light-middleweight and won the European title by decisioning Chris Pyatt in January 1987. After successful defences against Emilio Sole and Marc Ruocco, he outpointed Lupe Aquino to win the WBC light-middleweight crown. His first defence in January 1988, saw him halt ex-champion, Duane Thomas, in seven rounds, but he lost his title to Don Curry in July, being floored five times and retired at the end of the ninth. After a couple of warm up fights he was champion again, as he upset the odds by decisioning Darrin van Horn in July 1989. Travelled outside Italy for the first time in 1989, but put van Horn down in the first and last rounds to win an easy verdict. He next outpointed Troy Waters in an October defence and in 1990, defeated Kevin Daigle, van Horn and Rene Jacquot in title fights. 1991 saw him turn back the challenges of Ron Amundsen, Glenn Wolfe and Gilbert Baptist and, in 1992, Angel Hernandez was stopped and Gilbert Dele decisioned. The Dele verdict was very controversial, with Rosi floored in the third, but finishing strongly to just save his title. They fought again last January and, although the decision for Rosi was split, he seemed to have won clearly. He holds the Italian rècord with his involvement in fourteen world title bouts and, although he is not pretty to watch, with his holding and rough tactics, he is effective and very difficult to fight against.

11.07.92	Gilbert Dele W PTS 12 Monte Carlo *(IBF L. Middleweight Title Defence)*
20.01.93	Gilbert Dele W PTS 12 Avoriaz *(IBF L. Middleweight Title Defence)*

Career: 60 contests, won 57, lost 3.

Pichit Sitbangprachan

Nakhon Chaiaphun, Thailand. *Born* 15 January, 1966
IBF Flyweight Champion

Farmer's son who started as a kick boxer in the Muay-thai style. Turned to international style boxing in November 1990, going straight into the ten round class and halting South Korean, Hee-Haun Moon, in three rounds. Has never faced a Thai fighter, all his opponents being imported and wins in 1991 over Ippo Gala from Indonesia and Filipinos, Sammy Tyson and Sugar Ray Hines, and Jae-Suk Han from Korea, earned him a IBF rating. And he showed he was worthy of the honour, with an eighth round stoppage of top Filipino, Ric Magramo, in May 1992. He was still considered an outsider when he faced Rodolfo Blanco for the IBF title in 1992, but blasted the Colombian out in the third round with a left-hook and a devastating right-cross. In a non title bout in January 1993, Pichit had to climb off the floor to decision Daniel Nietes, but he had an easy title defence in March, flooring Antonio Perez with a left-hook and stopping him in round four. Pichit is a muscular box-puncher, with a good jab and a hard left-hook, and has stopped or knocked out twelve opponents. Rodolfo Blanco had shown impressive durability in two tough fights with Dave McAuley, so Pichit's destruction of him was an impressive performance, but he now needs to meet some of his top challengers to prove his true quality.

05.07.92	Bun-Yong Kim W RSC 2 Bangkok	
04.10.92	Tarman Garzon W PTS 10 Bangkok	
29.11.92	Rodolfo Blanco W CO 3 Bangkok *(IBF Flyweight Title Challenge)*	
24.01.93	Daniel Nietes W PTS 10 Bangkok	
06.03.93	Antonio Perez W RSC 4 Utteradit *(IBF Flyweight Title Defence)*	

Career: 15 contests, won 15.

Ratanapol Sowvoraphin

Dankoonthod, Thailand. *Born* 6 June, 1973
IBF M. Flyweight Champion. Former Undefeated IBF Intercontinental M. Flyweight Champion

Like most top Thai boxers, Ratanapol first tried his hand at Muay-thai kick boxing before turning to the international style of fighting in October 1990. He struggled to adjust, being held to a draw in his second fight in November 1990 by Inseethong Sowtanikul, and suffered two defeats in 1991 against Asawin Sithlukmuang, losing on points in July for the Thai mini-flyweight title, and being stopped in three rounds in December. Came into his own in 1992, as he won the IBF Intercontinental crown in June with a fourth round knockout of the experienced Indonesian, Hunsi Ray, and retained it by knocking out Al Tarasona. He was lucky to be given the chance to challenge Manny Melchor for the IBF title in December, but took his opportunity well. His aggressive style shook the Filipino out of his stride and he had Melchor on the floor in the seventh round on the way to a split, but clear decision, the Filipino judge showing admirable patriotism. Defended the title in March by beating the former IBF champion, Nico Thomas, in seven rounds. A vicious body attack proved too much for Thomas to deal with and he was rescued by the referee. Showed the courage to take on his top contender, the unbeaten Ala Villamor in June, and proved his right to be champion by forcing his rival to retire in seven rounds. An aggressive southpaw fighter, with a good body attack but not a big puncher, he has nine inside the distance victories and is the youngest of the current world champions.

06.09.92	Al Tarasona W CO 4 Samut Prakarn *(IBF Intercontinental M. Flyweight Title Defence)*	
10.12.92	Manny Melchor W PTS 12 Bangkok *(IBF M. Flyweight Title Challenge)*	
14.03.93	Nico Thomas W RSC 7 Nakon *(IBF M. Flyweight Title Defence)*	
27.06.93	Ala Villamor W RTD 7 Bangkok *(IBF M. Flyweight Title Defence)*	

Career: 17 contests, won 14, drew 1, lost 2.

Dingaan (The Rose Of Soweto) Thobela

Johannesburg, South Africa. *Born* 24 September, 1966
WBA Lightweight Champion. Former Undefeated WBO Lightweight Champion. Former Undefeated South African S. Featherweight Champion

Dingaan was born in the Soweto township near Johannesburg, where his father taught him how to box. Had a total of 83 amateur fights in three years, winning 80, before turning professional in June 1986. He was held to a draw by Peter Mpikashe in his fourth contest in December 1986, but came to the fore in 1988 with a win over Ditau Molefyane. Collected the South African super-featherweight title in October of that year, halting Mpisekaya Mbaduli in eight rounds. That was the last time Dingaan faced a local opponent, and he spent 1989 beating imports such as Daniel Londas, Mark Fernandez and Danilo Cabrera and also fought in Puerto Rico, where he stopped Francisco Alvarez. Had his first bout in the United States in April 1990, when he halted the WBO lightweight champion, Mauricio Aceves, in eight rounds in a non-title fight. That win landed Dingaan a title shot against Aceves in September. He floored the Mexican in the second round, but tired in the 100 degree heat and had to hold off a strong finish by Aceves to lift the crown. He made two defences in 1991, decisioning Mario Martinez and Antonio Rivera, but relinquished the title in 1992 to go for a shot at the WBA crown. After almost a year out of the ring he returned and defeated Peter Till and Tony Foster in warm-ups, before challenging Tony Lopez in the champion's hometown in February 1993 for the WBA title. A close, tough battle, saw Lopez retain his title on a disputed unanimous decision, with many observers feeling that the South African deserved the nod. However, Dingaan gained revenge and the title, with a close but unanimous verdict in a return in Sun City in June. He won the early sessions and finished strongly, rocking Lopez in the last two rounds. Is a good puncher, with fast hands and a tight defence, and hopefully will receive the recognition as WBA champion that eluded him when he held the WBO crown. Has 16 quick wins to his credit.

15.08.92	Peter Till W RSC 9 Springs
31.10.92	Tony Foster W PTS 8 London
12.02.93	Tony Lopez L PTS 12 Sacramento
	(WBA Lightweight Title Challenge)
26.06.93	Tony Lopez W PTS 12 Sun City
	(WBA Lightweight Title Challenge)

Career: 31 contests, won 29, drew 1, lost 1.

James (Lights Out) Toney

Grand Rapids, USA. *Born* 24 August, 1968
IBF S. Middleweight Champion.
Former Undefeated IBF Middleweight Champion

5'10" tall, he started boxing at the age of twelve, but was not a big star as an amateur, having only 24 fights and failing to win any major titles. He turned professional in October 1988 and has remained undefeated since. Has been a fighter who likes to keep active and had twelve fights in 1989, with a decision over Ron Amundsen in November as his best result. Made an impression in March 1991 when he halted Philip Morefield in one round with body punches to take the Michigan State title. Won the IBC Americas title in June, halting Ricardo Bryant in four rounds, but in July threw away an early lead and had to settle for a draw with veteran, Sanderline Williams. Faced Williams again in October and this time won a unanimous decision. In January 1991 he floored the tough Merqui Sosa on the way to a split decision victory, to retain his IBC title, and then challenged Michael Nunn for the IBF crown in May 1991. A cocky Nunn badly underestimated Toney and paid the price, as he wilted under continual pressure and was floored and halted in a major upset in the eleventh round. Toney's first defence was a tough one against future world champion, Reggie Johnson, in June, and he had to come off the floor to win a split decision. His troubles continued in a title fight with Francesco dell 'Aquila in Monte Carlo, in October, when he failed to make the weight. Instead of being stripped of the title, the fight went ahead and he knocked out the Italian in four rounds. It got even tougher when James defended against Mike McCallum in

December, as the Jamaican built up an early lead, and he had to stage a big rally to get a draw. Things should have been easier against Dave Tiberi, in a title defence in February 1992, but Toney performed poorly and looked lucky to retain his title on a split decision. The verdict started a Senate investigation into boxing that is still going on. An unimpressive decision over Glenn Wolfe in a defence in April did James no good either, but he retained his title in the return with McCallum in August, although again it was a majority verdict in a mediocre fight. In February, he moved up to super-middleweight and crushed Iran Barkley in nine rounds to win the IBF crown. Although he seems to get up for the big fights, such as Nunn and Barkley, he has motivation problems against lesser opponents and does not live up to expectation. Managed by a woman, which is unusual in boxing, he has 25 inside the distance

James Toney   Chris Farina

29.08.92	Mike McCallum W PTS 12 Reno
	(IBF Middleweight Title Defence)
05.12.92	Doug de Witt W RTD 6 Atlantic City
13.02.93	Iran Barkley W RTD 9 Las Vegas
	(IBF S. Middleweight Title Challenge)
23.03.93	Govoner Chavers W RSC 9 Detroit
17.04.93	Ricky Thomas W RSC 10 Bushkill
06.06.93	Glenn Thomas W PTS 10 Las Vegas

Career: 39 contests, won 37, drew 2.

Felix Trinidad

Cupoy Alto, Puerto Rico. *Born* 10 January, 1973
IBF Welterweight Champion

His father, Felix, boxed as a professional in the late 1970s as a featherweight without much success, losing on a fifth round stoppage to Salvador Sanchez in Houston in 1979. Young Felix turned professional in March 1990 at the age of 17, already having had over 50 amateur fights, and his obvious talent, and some influence, gained a top 30 rating at light-welterweight from the WBC only a few months later. He boxed mainly in Puerto Rico, with a couple of visits to Miami and an appearance in Italy, halting eleven of his first fourteen opponents. Showed his potential in October 1992 against world rated Alberto Cortes in Paris. Floored in the second round, he blasted back to drop Cortes and stop him in round three. He then went back to beating mediocre opposition in Puerto Rico and was given a welterweight rating by the IBF, despite never facing a top fighter at the weight. Felix repaid their faith by destroying Maurice Blocker in two rounds in June to lift the IBF crown. He was simply too fast and hit too hard for his more experienced foe and looked like another Wilfred Benitez. Although he came to the title by an easy route, that does not mean that he is not talented, but he will need a few more fights to be properly judged. Only three of hs opponents have lasted the distance.

18.07.92	Joe Alexander W CO 1 San Juan
03.10.92	Alberto Cortes W RSC 3 Paris
20.02.93	Pedro Aguirre W RSC 4 Mexico City
13.02.93	Henry Hughes W RSC 3 San Juan
08.05.93	Terry Acker W CO 1 Condado
19.06.93	Maurice Blocker W CO 2 San Diego
	(IBF Welterweight Title Challenge)

Career: 20 contests, won 20.

Gregorio (Goyo) Vargas

Santa Maria Nativitas, Mexico. *Born* 27 October, 1970
WBC Featherweight Champion.
Former Undefeated Mexican Featherweight Champion

His father, Gregorio, also fought as a

professional, facing opponents such as Danny Lopez, and Gregorio junior was given his first pair of gloves when he was just six-years-old. Won the Mexican amateur title at flyweight at the age of 16, but was not selected for the Mexican team for the Pan American Games and promptly turned professional. Had his first paid fight in May 1988, with the former world featherweight champion, Sugar Ramos, as one of his advisers. Scored eleven wins, before being stopped in six rounds by Marco Ramirez in April 1989. He then lost a disputed points verdict in August 1989 to Jaime Fernandez, and was beaten again, in May 1990, on points by experienced Juan Carlos Salazar. Another minor blot was put on his record in the shape of a draw against Narciso Valenzuela in October 1990. Gregorio finally came through in February 1991, with a comprehensive points victory over Ulises Chong, to win the Mexican featherweight title. Made three defences during the year, all in the other man's territory. He decisioned Simon Gonzalez in April, stopped Jaime Fernandez in June, and knocked out Porfirio Hernandez in one round. Four more defences followed in 1992, as Gregorio outpointed Antonio Hernandez, knocked out former conqueror, Juan Carlos Salazar, in three, halted Elias Quiroz in eight, and stopped Juan Carlos Ortigoza in eleven. A threat of legal action landed him a shot at Paul Hodkinson and he displayed real talent, flooring Paul twice and beating him emphatically in the seventh round. His tactics for the fight showed maturity beyond his 22 years and the presence of the great Joe Medel in his corner may have helped. Exhibiting excellent boxing skills and a potent punch, he looked like a young Salvador Sanchez at times. Has halted 18 victims.

23.07.92	Elias Quiroz W RSC 8 Tulacingo *(Mexican Featherweight Title Defence)*
31.10.92	Juan Carlos Ortigoza W RSC 11 *(Mexican Featherweight Title Defence)*
28.04.93	Paul Hodkinson W RTD 7 Dublin *(WBC Featherweight Title Challenge)*
Career: 32 contests, won 28, drew 1, lost 3.	

Julio Cesar Vasquez

Santa Fe, Argentine. *Born* 13 July, 1966
WBA L. Middleweight Champion

Never won a national title as an amateur, but was unbeaten in 30 fights, winning 25 and drawing five. A 5'9" tall, hard punching southpaw, with a raw, rugged style, he turned professional as a welterweight in June 1986 and moved up to light-middleweight in 1987. Stopped a couple of experienced foes in Simon Escobar and Ramon Abeldano in 1988 to earn a national rating. Travelled to Las Vegas in November 1987 and halted world rated Troy Wortham in six rounds. A few years later he visited Britain in 1991 and halted Colombian, Anibal Miranda, in five rounds at Brighton. Showed his raw power in May 1991 when he knocked out experienced Judas Clottey in one round to extend his unbeaten score to 30. Fight 31 proved unlucky, losing to American, Vernon Phillips. Julio was floored at the end of the sixth round by a punch which his cornermen felt landed after the bell. They invaded the ring and disputed the decision. At first the bout was ruled a no decision, but later the local Commission changed it to a disqualification loss, due to the action of his seconds. Quickly re-established himself, with stoppage wins over Tyrone Trice and Louis Howard in Paris, although there was controversy over the former win when the two boxers were found to have worn different size gloves. Julio was now in line for a shot at the WBA title, but the champion, Vinny Pazienza, was badly injured in a car crash and the title declared vacant. Matched with Hitoshi Kamiyama in Buenos Aires in December 1992, for the title, he proceeded to put the Jap down three times for a stoppage after just 45 seconds of the first round. Defended the title last February with another first round blowout, this time his opponent was Panamanian, Aquilino Asprilla. He was given a much better test by Javier Castillejos and had some of his limitations exposed, as he floored but could not stop the Spaniard, and had to settle for a points victory. Very strong with a crushing left-hook, although his attack lacks variety, he has stopped or knocked out 32 victims, ten in the first.

11.07.92	Anthony Ivory W PTS 8 Monte Carlo
14.08.92	David McCluskey W DIS 2 Buenos Aires
21.12.92	Hitoshi Kamiyama W RSC 1 Buenos Aires *(Vacant WBA L. Middleweight Title)*
22.02.93	Aquilino Asprilla W CO 1 Mar del Plata *(WBA L. Middleweight Title Defence)*
27.03.93	Angel Moguea W RSC 3 Evian
24.04.93	Javier Castillejos W PTS 12 Madrid *(WBA L. Middleweight Title Defence)*
Career: 44 contests, won 43, lost 1.	

Julio Cesar Vasquez

Wilfredo Vasquez

Rio Piedras, Puerto Rico. *Born* 2 August, 1960
WBA S. Bantamweight Champion. Former WBA Bantamweight Champion. Former Undefeated Puerto Rican and IBF Intercontinental Bantamweight Champion

A professional since 1981, he has out-lasted his more famous former stable-mates, Mike Tyson and Edwin Rosario, as a world champion. Had only thirteen amateur fights before punching for pay and losing his first bout. Was held to a draw by useful Eusebio Espinal in his fourth contest,

217

Wilfredo Vasquez (right) scored two inside the distance victories over Thierry Jacob during 1992-93 in defence of his WBA super-bantamweight title

but then won his next fifteen fights under the management of Mike Jacobs and Bill Cayton. Took the Puerto Rican bantamweight title in 1984, stopping Juan Torres in four rounds, and three more quick wins saw him challenging Miguel Lora for the WBC crown. After losing a unanimous decision, he bounced back impressively, with victories over Jose Cervantes, Antonio Avelar and Juan Carazo, to land a shot at the WBA title in October 1987. He won in style, flooring Chan-Yong Park twice and halting him in the tenth round. Came through a difficult defence in January 1988, with a draw against Takuya Muguruma in Osaka, but then dropped his crown on a split verdict to Kaokor Galaxy in Bangkok in May. Lost his next fight on points to Raul Perez, but in 1989 he collected the IBF Intercontinental title with a split points win over Fernie Morales. His next setback came in June 1990, when he was knocked out in one round by the then WBO champion, Israel Contreras. Wilfredo had only one fight in 1991 and was lucky to land a shot at Raul Perez for the WBA super-bantamweight title in March 1992. However, he took his chance of revenge with both hands, flooring Perez three times and halting him in the third round. His first defence in June against Dominican, Freddy Cruz, was a hard

one and Wilfredo only held on to his crown by a majority decision. Towards the end of 1992, he retained his title with a eighth round cuts stoppage of former WBC champion, Thierry Jacob, and in March 1993 won a very controversial decision over another former champion, Luis Mendoza, in his third defence. Later, he cleared up any questions over the win against Jacob by knocking out the Frenchman in a return fight last June. An aggressive, hard puncher, particularly with the hook, who has halted 30 opponents, he has had weight problems, but seems determined to stay at super-bantamweight.

05.12.92	Thierry Jacob W RSC 8 Berck sur Mer *(WBA S. Bantamweight Title Defence)*
06.03.93	Luis Mendoza W PTS 12 Levallois-Perret *(WBA S. Bantamweight Title Defence)*
24.06.93	Thierry Jacob W CO 10 Bordeaux *(WBA S. Bantamweight Title Defence)*

Career: 46 contests, won 37, drew 3, lost 6.

Anaclet Wamba

Saint Brieuc, France. *Born* 6 January, 1960
WBC Cruiserweight Champion.
Former Undefeated European

Cruiserweight Champion

6'3" tall. Born in Luranga in the Congo, after only one year as an amateur he represented his country in the 1980 Olympic Games, losing to Australian, Geoff Pike. He turned professional in France in November 1982 and eventually took French citizenship. Starting out as a heavyweight, he beat Winston Allen and Rocky Burton in 1984. Also defeated experienced Louis Pergaud in October 1984 and in 1985 repeated the win, while also beating Andrew Gerrard and Dave Garside. He faced Horace Notice here in October 1985 and put up a good performance, although fading late and losing on points. Continued to fight at heavyweight for a while, but in 1988 moved down to cruiserweight and in 1989 won the European title with an upset majority decision over Italian, Angelo Rottoli. Did not defend the title, preferring to relinquish it and chase a world title shot instead. When facing Massimiliano Duran for the WBC crown in December 1990, he lost his temper with the spoiling tactics of the Italian and was disqualified in the twelfth round. Their return in July 1991 was just as bad tempered, but this time Anaclet came out on top and halted Duran in the eleventh round to take the title. A third bout in December 1991 saw Anaclet again halt Duran in round eleven. In 1992 he defended his title, halting the WBC

Anaclet Wamba

International champion, Andrei Rudenko, in five rounds, and then decisioned former Olympic champion, Andrew Maynard, in October, after flooring his rival in the first round. His most recent defence last March against the American, David Vedder, turned into a tame affair, almost sending the paying customers to sleep, and although he won over the distance he will be looking to step up a gear this coming season. Overall, he is a good, solid, but unspectacular boxer, with only 18 quick wins on his record.

18.07.92	John Keys W CO 2 Pointe A Pitre	
16.10.92	Andrew Maynard W PTS 12 Paris	
	(WBC Cruiserweight Title Defence)	
06.03.93	David Vedder W PTS 12 Levallois Perret	
	(WBC Cruiserweight Title Defence)	
Career: 43 contests, won 41, lost 2.		

Paul Weir

Irvine, Scotland. *Born* 16 September, 1967
WBO M. Flyweight Champion

A World champion after just six contests, and Britain's first at the weight, he did not even win an ABA title as an amateur. Boxing for the Springside ABC, he picked up three Scottish amateur light-flyweight titles between 1989 and 1991 and was a European bronze medallist at the weight, defeating Ben Haim (Israel), before going out of the competition, beaten on points by Luigi Castiglione (Italy). And as a Scottish international, he won five out of ten contests, with Mickey Cantwell (England) and Neil Swain (Wales), being among his victims. Turning professional under the management of Tommy Gilmour, he had his first contest in April 1992, knocking out Eduardo Vallejo of Mexico. The Mexican, who had also lost to Cantwell on the Englishman's pro debut over a year earlier, was somehow deemed good enough to challenge for the WBO light-flyweight title in July 1992, following the defeat at the hands of Paul. Paul's chance also came much earlier than expected. When the WBO mini-flyweight title was vacated after Rafael Torres of the

Dominican Republic was stripped for inactivity, Gilmour astutely recognised the opportunity and prepared his man for the occasion. However, beating Louis Veitch, Neil Parry, Shaun Norman and Kevin Jenkins was hardly the right build up for a world title clash but, with Paul in such great condition, it was worth the gamble. Stepping up in class to meet Fernando Martinez did not look a good idea after four rounds had been completed, but once the Mexican was cut it became a different story. With the bit between the teeth, Paul stormed forward to dominate and eventually force a seventh round stoppage on the doctor's advice, when Martinez was bleeding too badly to continue. With the WBO belt now safely in his care, the diminutive, 5'3" tall, Weir, plans a defence in Glasgow later in the year, before going on to win titles at three different weights, by capturing the light-fly and flyweight crowns. It is too early to judge the little Scot at this stage of his career, and only time will tell, but he is a decent boxer with a stiff punch, and could continue to make dramatic improvement, in keeping with his sky-high confidence.

Note: Full record will be found in the Current British-Based Champions: Career Records' section.

Pernell (Sweet Pea) Whitaker

Norfolk, USA. *Born* 2 January, 1964
WBC Welterweight Champion.
Former Undefeated IBF L. Welterweight Champion. Former Undefeated IBF, WBA & WBC Lightweight Champion. Former Undefeated NABF & USBA Lightweight Champion

A 5'9" tall, southpaw, he is an excellent boxer, with dazzling hand and foot speed, who is regarded as one of the best fighters in the world today. Outstanding amateur and the United States' champion in 1982, he won the World championships challenge and a Pan American Games gold medal in 1983. The following year, he took the gold medal at the Olympic Games and signed up with Shelly Finkel and the Main Events team, turning professional in November 1984. Showed his

Pernell Whitaker

class in 1986, with victories over John Montes, Rafael Williams, and former world champion, Alfredo Layne. Really arrived in March 1987, when he decisioned another former world champion, Roger Mayweather, to collect the vacant NABF lightweight title. Added the USBA crown in July of that year with a sixth round stoppage of Miguel Santana. Challenged for the WBC title in March 1988 and lost a disputed decision to Jose Luis Ramirez. Having swept the early rounds and despite a strong finish by Ramirez, he looked to have won clearly. Various writs flew about as his management claimed he had been robbed and said so. Back in business, he turned his attention to the IBF title and won that in February 1989 with an easy points verdict over Greg Haugen. Retained the title by halting outclassed Louie Lomeli in two rounds in April and then gained revenge with a clear decision over Ramirez, while defending his IBF title and winning the vacant WBC crown at the same time. One official had Pernell fourteen points ahead. Made successful defences of his IBF and WBC titles in 1990, with decisions over Fred Pendleton and Azumah Nelson, and then added the WBA title to his list by knocking out Juan Nazario in the first round in August. Made three defences of the lightweight title in 1991, winning on points over

Anthony Jones, Poli Diaz and Jorge Paez. Finding it more and more difficult to make 135 lbs, he moved up to light-welterweight in 1992 with a points victory over Harold Brazier and then won the IBF title with a clear decision over Colombian, Rafael Pineda. Moved on again to welterweight and decisioned James McGirt in March 1993 to become WBC champion, giving him his fifth world title. A sharp puncher, he has halted fifteen victims.

18.07.92	Rafael Pineda W PTS 12 Las Vegas *(IBF L. Welterweight Title Challenge)*
01.12.92	Benny Baez W CO 1 Virginia Beach
06.03.93	James McGirt W PTS 12 New York *(WBC Welterweight Title Challenge)*
Career: 33 contests, won 32, lost 1.	

Myung-Woo Yuh

Myung-Woo Yuh
Seoul, South Korea. *Born* 10 January, 1964
WBA L. Flyweight Champion. Former Undefeated OPBF L. Flyweight Champion

Turned professional in March 1982, after just five amateur contests, and in July won the annual Korean novice tournament. By the end of 1983 he had scored thirteen victories, every one of them on points. Scored his first knock-out in April 1984, when he put away Little Baguio in two rounds, and decisioned future IBF flyweight champion, Bi-Won Chung, in May. Became OPBF light-flyweight champion in December 1984, halting Edwin Inocencio in three rounds, and was doing his compulsory military service in December 1985 when he received the chance to challenge the WBA champion, Joey Olivo. It was a close fight, but Yuh applied steady pressure for fifteen rounds to take a split decision. His first defence against Jose de Jesus in March 1986 was also close and he had to settle for a split decision.

After knocking out Tomohiro Kiyuna in twelve rounds, a very tight points win over Mario de Marco came next, but in 1987 he left no room for doubt as he halted Eduardo Tunon and Benedicto Murillo and kayoed future IBF flyweight champion, Rodolfo Blanco, in two rounds. His four defences in 1988, saw him decision Wilibaldo Salazar, edge out Jose de Jesus, in a return, and then stop Putt Ohyuthanakorn and Bahar Udin. A clear win over de Marco and inside the distance victories against Katsumi Komiyama and Kenbun Taiho were the title defences in 1989. And in 1990 he stopped Hisashi Tokushima, earned a close split decision over Leo Gamez and won again over the same man in November. A tenth round stoppage of Kajkong Danphoothai in April 1991, saw Yuh reach 17 defences, but number 18 proved unlucky as he was lured outside Korea for the first time and lost his title in December on points to Hiroki Ioka in Osaka. He was then inactive for eleven months, but confounded the experts by taking on Ioka again in Osaka and regaining the title with a clear victory, despite the majority verdict. 5'3" tall, and baby faced, Yuh is an aggressive fighter with an excellent chin and limitless stamina, but is not a big puncher, with only thirteen wins inside the distance.

18.11.92	Hiroki Ioka W PTS 12 Osaka *(WBA L. Flyweight Title Challenge)*
Career: 38 contests, won 37, lost 1.	

World Title Bouts, 1992-93

MINI-FLYWEIGHT (7st.7lbs)
Titleholders as at 1 July, 1993
IBF – Ratanapol Sowvoraphin (Thailand)
WBA – Chana Porpaoin (Thailand)
WBC – Ricardo Lopez (Mexico)
WBO – Paul Weir (Scotland)

22 August, 1992   Ricardo Lopez 7.7 (Mexico) W CO 5 Singprasert Kitikasem 7.6¾ (Thailand), Ciudad Madero, Mexico (WBC).
All three judges had Lopez, who steadily increased his workrate, clearly ahead at the finish at 1.05 of the fifth round following a big left-hook which left the challenger prostrate on his back.

6 September, 1992   Fahlan Lukmingkwan 7.7 (Thailand) L PTS 12 Manny Melchor 7.6 (Philippines), Bangkok, Thailand (IBF).
The new champion won the title on a split 119-114, 116-112, 114-115 decision, counterpunching effectively throughout, while Lukmingkwan finished the contest with a badly cut left eye.

11 October, 1992   Ricardo Lopez 7.6¼ (Mexico) W CO 2 Rocky Lim 7.6¾ (Japan), Tokyo, Japan (WBC).
Lopez sent the challenger face down to the boards at 1.46 of the second round to record the fastest finish in the short history of the division.

14 October, 1992   Hi-Yon Choi 7.6¾ (South Korea) L PTS 12 Hideyuki Ohashi 7.6¾ (Japan), Tokyo, Japan (WBA).
After four successful defences, Choi's reign came to a halt when he was comprehensively outboxed by the challenger with the judges scores of 118-110, 116-112, 117-111, telling the story.

10 December, 1992   Manny Melchor 7.7 (Philippines) L PTS 12 Ratanapol Sowvoraphin 7.6½ (Thailand), Bangkok, Thailand (IBF).
Although finishing the contest with a cut over the right eye, the 19-year-old Sowvoraphin proved a real find, flooring Melchor in the seventh with a left-hook and boxing his way to a 115-112, 117-110, 112-115 split points decision.

31 January, 1993   Ricardo Lopez 7.6 (Mexico) W RSC 9 Kwang-Soo Oh 7.7 (South Korea), Seoul, South Korea (WBC).
Even though he received a badly cut eye in the very first round, the southpaw challenger fought aggressively and often took the play away from Lopez. Unfortunately, for him, the wound was re-opened when the champion

pounded him with solid lefts and rights in the ninth and the referee stepped in at 2.38 of the round, with the blood flowing freely.

10 February, 1993   Hideyuki Ohashi 7.7 (Japan) L PTS 12 Chana Porpaoin 7.7 (Thailand), Tokyo, Japan (WBA).
After a slow start by both men, the challenger got himself warmed up in the third and applied steady pressure from thereon, often landing well in clusters. Ohashi, although having the longer reach, boxed mainly on the retreat and failed to take advantage of any openings that came his way and went down on points, 112-117, 111-118, 114-114.

14 March, 1993   Ratanapol Sowvoraphin 7.7 (Thailand) W RSC 7 Nico Thomas 7.4¼ (Indonesia), Nakon, Thailand (IBF).
With a large weight advantage, and making his first defence, the champion had an easy payday at the expense of the experienced Thomas. The end came at 0.31 of the seventh when the Indonesian, already way behind on all three judges' scorecards, was rescued by the referee, following a burst of heavy punches.

9 May, 1993   Chana Porpaoin 7.7 (Thailand) W PTS 12 Carlos Murillo 7.6¾ (Panama), Bangkok, Thailand (WBA).
Boxing mainly at a distance in order to conserve his energy in 32 degrees, after having to visit the scales four times to make the weight, the champion kept in front to win 117-113, 117-112, 117-111 on the judges scorecards. Murillo, although occasionally going well on the inside, was always second best when it came to punching power and under different circumstances would probably have been stopped.

15 May, 1993   Paul Weir 7.6¾ (Scotland) W RSC 7 Fernando Martinez 7.7 (Mexico), Glasgow, Scotland (WBO).
With Rafael Torres being stripped of the title, having made no defences since 31 July 1990, Weir and Martinez came together in a battle for the vacant crown. The Mexican dominated the first four rounds with better quality punching, but once he was cut on the left eye his game plan went to pieces. Galvanised by the sight of blood, Weir stormed forward to open up further wounds and at 1.28 of the seventh the referee brought matters to a conclusion, with the little Scot being proclaimed champion.

27 June, 1993   Ratanapol Sowvoraphin 7.6 (Thailand) W RTD 7 Ala Villamor 7.4 (Philippines), Bangkok, Thailand (IBF).
After being floored twice, the challenger was saved from taking even more "stick" when his corner threw the towel

in at 2.01 of the seventh round. The battle had been so one-sided, with the unbeaten Villamor lacking the power to put the champion under any pressure, that it almost came as a welcome relief to the spectators when he was pulled out.

LIGHT-FLYWEIGHT (7st.10lbs)
Titleholders as at 1 July, 1993
IBF – Michael Carbajal (USA)
WBA – Myung-Woo Yuh (South Korea)
WBC – Michael Carbajal (USA)
WBO – Josue Camacho (Puerto Rico)

31 July, 1992   Josue Camacho 7.9 (Puerto Rico) W CO 6 Eduardo Vallejo 7.8 (Mexico), San Juan, Puerto Rico (WBO).

With Jose de Jesus stripped of the title for not defending since 10 November 1990, Vallejo, a man who had lost to both Paul Weir and Mickey Cantwell on their pro debuts, somehow slipped through the commision's net to gain a shot at the vacant crown. For the record, badly behind on all three judges' scorecards, he was despatched at 2.20 of the sixth, the victim of a seemingly innocuous body blow.

14 September, 1992   Humberto Gonzalez 7.10 (Mexico) W RSC 2 Napa Kiatwanchai 7.10 (Thailand), Los Angeles, USA (WBC).

The Challenger was decked four times before being rescued by the referee at 2.48 of the second after a devastating left-uppercut had left him in no position to continue, face down on the canvas.

18 November, 1992   Hiroki Ioka 7.10 (Japan) L PTS 12 Myung-Woo Yuh 7.10 (South Korea), Osaka, Japan (WBA).

In a successful bid to regain the crown he had lost to Ioka on 17 December 1991, the former champion, who had defended the title 17 times prior to that loss, collected a 119-111, 117-112, 114-114 majority verdict and looks set to extend the divisional record.

7 December, 1992   Humberto Gonzalez 7.10 (Mexico) W PTS 12 Melchor Cob Castro 7.10 (Mexico), Los Angeles, USA (WBC).

The southpaw Castro made life difficult for the champion, backing off continuously in an effort not to present an open target. In a boring fight, Gonzalez won a unanimous 117-112, 115-113, 117-111 decision. With heads often clashing, Castro was cut over the right eye in the eighth and Gonzalez picked up damage to the left eye in the eleventh.

12 December, 1992   Michael Carbajal 7.10 (USA) W RSC 8 Robinson Cuestas 7.9 (Panama), Phoenix, USA (IBF).

Following two knockdowns, one in the third and the other leading to the closure, the referee decided he had seen enough and rescued the brave and previously undefeated challenger at 2.04 of the eighth. Apart from the first round all the officials had Carbajal winning every round.

13 March, 1993   Michael Carbajal 7.9 (USA) W CO 7 Humberto Gonzalez 7.9½ (Mexico), Las Vegas, USA (IBF/WBC).

In a classic encounter and real throw-back fight, Gonzalez lost his WBC title, while Carbajal retained his IBF crown in a unification battle that will be remembered by all who saw it for a very long time. Down twice, in the second and the fifth and behind on all the scorecards, Carbajal roared back with a tremendous left-hook that smashed the Mexican to the floor where he was counted out at 2.59 of the seventh round.

FLYWEIGHT (8st)
Titleholders as at 1 July, 1993
IBF – Pichit Sitbangprachan (Thailand)
WBA – David Griman (Venezuela)
WBC – Yuri Arbachakov (Russia)
WBO – Jacob Matlala (South Africa)

19 September, 1992   Pat Clinton 8.0 (Scotland) W PTS 12 Danny Porter 7.13¾ (England), Glasgow, Scotland (WBO).

In one of the best fights seen in a British ring, Clinton, despite a cut left eye received in round one, boxed his way to a 118-113 (Roy Francis), 116-112, 118-112 points decision over an opponent who never gave up trying and was always dangerous. Dave Parris refereed.

26 September, 1992   Yong-Kang Kim 7.13¼ (South Korea) L PTS 12 Aquiles Guzman 7.13½ (Venezuela), Pohang, South Korea (WBA).

Dominating the fight from the fifth round onwards, pressuring all the way, the underdog challenger won a 116-113, 117-111, 117-112 unanimous points verdict away from home.

20 October, 1992   Yuri Arbachakov 8.0 (Russia) W PTS 12 Yun-Un Chin 8.0 (South Korea), Tokyo, Japan (WBC).

Despite being on the floor three times, the previously unbeaten Chin made quite a fight of it before going down 117-109, 115-113, 117-108.

29 November, 1992   Rodolfo Blanco 8.0 (Colombia) L CO 3 Pichit Sitbangprachan 7.13½ (Thailand), Bangkok, Thailand (IBF)

A huge upset win, saw the unheralded Sitbangprachan knock out the champion at 2.02 of the third to become Thailand's seventh world champion at the weight.

15 December, 1992   Aquiles Guzman 7.13½ (Venezuela) L PTS 12 David Griman 7.13½ (Venezuela), Caracas, Venezuela (WBA).

WBO flyweight champion, Pat Clinton (right), meets Danny Porter punch for punch during his successful title defence
Action Images

In an exciting boxer versus fighter battle between two compatriots, the classier work of the challenger saw him come out on top with a 116-113, 117-112, 116-113 unanimous points verdict. It was Guzman's first defence, while Griman, who came down a weight for this one after losing to Kaosai Galaxy for the super-flyweight title in 1991, made it second time lucky.

6 March, 1993   Pichit Sitbangprachan 8.0 (Thailand) W RSC 4 Antonio Perez 7.13 (Mexico), Uttaradit, Thailand (IBF).
After a quiet start both men got going in the fourth. With Perez looking to land heavy bombs, the champion beat him to it with a smashing left-hook and on rising and being subjected to further punishment, the Mexican was rescued by the third man at 2.50 of the round.

20 March, 1993   Yuri Arbachakov 8.0 (Russia) W RSC 9 Muangchai Kitikasem 7.13½ (Thailand), Lopburi, Thailand (WBC).
The heavier hitting Arbachakov overpowered his brave challenger to force a stoppage at 1.44 of the ninth round, having had Kitikasem on the deck three times and bleeding badly from the nose. With the Thai being battered unmercifully throughout, the referee had appeared slow in coming to his rescue.

15 May, 1993   Pat Clinton 7.13¾ (Scotland) L RSC 8 Jacob Matlala 7.12¾ (South Africa), Glasgow, Scotland (WBO).
Hardly ever using a straight punch, the diminutive Matlala battered the champion with hooks and uppercuts to head and body all night and with Clinton slumped on the canvas, the referee had seen enough at 1.57 of the eighth. The Scot had been decked three times and looked a sorry sight at the

finish, drained of all energy and badly cut and swollen around the left eye.

21 June, 1993   David Griman 8.0 (Venezuela) W RSC 8 Hiroki Ioka 8.0 (Japan), Osaka, Japan (WBA).
Bidding to win his third title at three weights, Ioka was no match for the champion and was not punching back when the referee rescued him at 2.38 of the eighth. Griman was ahead on all three scorecards at the finish, losing only the second round, and it was only a matter of time before he would have knocked his rival out.

SUPER-FLYWEIGHT (8st.3lbs)
Titleholders as at 1 July, 1993
IBF	–	Julio Cesar Borboa (Colombia)
WBA	–	Katsuya Onizuka (Japan)
WBC	–	Sung-Il Moon (South Korea)
WBO	–	Johnny Bredahl (Denmark)

4 July, 1992   Sung-Il Moon 8.3 (South Korea) W RSC 8 Armando Salazar 8.2¼ (Mexico), Inchon, South Korea (WBC).
Moon got off to a good start, cutting the challenger's left eye early on, before Salazar came blazing back in a vicious seventh round. The champion weathered the storm and then fired back with both hands to force a stoppage at 2.59 of the following round.

11 July, 1992   Robert Quiroga 8.2 (USA) W PTS 12 Jose Ruiz 8.3 (Puerto Rico), Las Vegas, USA (IBF).
Recovering well from a third round knockdown, Quiroga came back strongly with his persistence finally paying off. Although not at his best, and at times outspeeded by Ruiz, the champion's workrate was far superior to that of the

Puerto Rican's and he just about deserved the 114-113, 114-113, 114-114 points decision.

4 September, 1992   Jose Quirino 8.2 (Mexico) L PTS 12 Johnny Bredahl 8.3 (Denmark), Copenhagen, Denmark (WBO).

With Britain's Paul Thomas refereeing his first world title bout, the young inexperienced Dane showed remarkable maturity as he used a stabbing left-jab, coupled with a tight defence, to pile up the points and well earn his 118-111, 119-110, 118-110 points victory.

11 September, 1992   Katsuya Onizuka 8.3 (Japan) W RSC 5 Kenichi Matsumura 8.3 (Japan), Tokyo, Japan (WBA).

Showing greater hand speed, the champion surged into a good lead before settling down in the fourth to drop Matsumura twice. Then, with the challenger being punched to a standstill, the referee stepped in at 1.26 of the fifth round to save him from further punishment.

31 October, 1992   Sung-Il Moon 8.3 (South Korea) W PTS 12 Greg Richardson 8.2¾ (USA), Seoul, South Korea (WBC).

Although Richardson made a good start, the champion began to dominate from the fifth onwards, varying his punches from head to body as he took the initiative. Despite scoring two knockdowns in the final round, Moon had to settle for a 119-108, 116-110, 114-114 points verdict.

11 December, 1992   Katsuya Onizuka 8.3 (Japan) W PTS 12 Armando Castro 8.3 (Mexico), Tokyo, Japan (WBA).

Having to hold off a strong offensive early on, Onizuka worked his way into the fight with smart counters as the challenger missed badly with lunging attacks. The pattern of the fight was set, with Castro eventually going down 119-113, 118-111, 119-118 on the judges' scorecards.

16 January, 1993   Robert Quiroga 8.3 (USA) L RSC 12 Julio Cesar Borboa 8.3 (Mexico), San Antonio, USA (IBF).

Behind on all the judges' scorecards and unable to see out of either eye, Quiroga lost his hard won title when the doctor ordered the referee to stop the contest with just 30 seconds remaining. Neither man had bothered with the niceties of the game and both had stood within distance from the opening bell, but it was the more accurate punching of the rangy challenger that finally won the day.

27 February, 1993   Sung-Il Moon 8.2¾ (South Korea) W RSC 1 Hilario Zapata 8.2¾ (Panama), Seoul, South Korea (WBC).

Smashed to the deck early in the opener as a result of heavy body blows, Zapata got to his feet only to be rescued at

2.54 of the round, when unable to defend himself.

26 March, 1993   Johnny Bredahl 8.3 (Denmark) W PTS 12 Rafael Caban 8.2¾ (Puerto Rico), Copenhagen, Denmark (WBO).

Although the challenger pushed Bredahl all the way and often looking menacing, especially with the left-hook, the Dane boxed his way to a comprehensive 119-109, 120-108, 118-110 (Paul Thomas) points verdict. From start to finish, it was Bredahl's better technique and jab that dictated the flow of the contest.

21 May, 1993   Katsuya Onizuka 8.3 (Japan) W PTS 12 Jae-Shin Lim 8.2¾ (South Korea), Tokyo, Japan (WBA).

After making a slow start and having to come from behind, Onizuka won a 116-115, 117-113, 115-116 split points verdict over a game challenger, who finished exhausted. There were no knockdowns as the Jap recorded his 22nd straight win, with the bout being fought out in good spirit by both men.

22 May, 1993   Julio Cesar Borboa 8.2½ (Mexico) W PTS 12 Joel Luna Zarate 8.2½ (Mexico), Mexico City, Mexico (IBF).

Never in any real difficulty, Borboa boxed his way to a clear 117-111, 116-112, 115-113 points win over his fellow Mexican, a nephew of the great Carlos Zarate. However, that is where similarity with greatness ended and the challenger was too one paced and predictable to offer any real threat as the fight degenerated into a boring spectacle.

BANTAMWEIGHT (8st.6lbs)
Titleholders as at 1 July, 1993

IBF	–	Orlando Canizales (USA)
WBA	–	Jorge Elicier Julio (Colombia)
WBC	–	Il-Jung Byun (South Korea)
WBO	–	Rafael del Valle (Puerto Rico)

27 July, 1992   Victor Rabanales 8.5½ (Mexico) W PTS 12 Chang-Kyun Oh 8.6 (South Korea), Los Angeles, USA (WBC).

The judges' scores of 119-106, 117-109, 117-107, showed that the champion had unanimously outscored Oh by a wide margin in their eyes. However, it had been a tough battle, with both men finishing marked. Rabanales was cut over the right eye and Oh received damage to both eyes as heads cracked and three times the challenger had points deducted for fouls.

17 September, 1992   Victor Rabanales 8.5½ (Mexico) W RSC 9 Joichiro Tatsuyoshi 8.5¼ (Japan), Osaka, Japan (WBC).

Rabanales had initially won the vacant title after the champion, Tatsuyoshi, had vacated the crown when it was discovered that he needed an eye operation. With the operation a success, Tatsuyoshi was given an early opportunity to win back his old title from the Mexican, but was found wanting as body punches took their toll and eventually forced a stoppage at 1.19 of the ninth round.

18 September, 1992   Orlando Canizales 8.5½ (USA) W PTS 12 Samuel Duran 8.5¾ (Philippines), Bozeman, USA (IBF),

Successfully defending his title for the third time, Canizales once again proved his boxing skills as he cruised to a 116-112, 118-110, 118-110 points victory over a game opponent.

9 October, 1992   Eddie Cook 8.5¾ (USA) L PTS 12 Jorge Elicier Julio 8.5¼ (Colombia), Cartagena, Colombia (WBA).

The title changed hands after a bruising battle which left both men surveying the damage. Cook had two eye cuts and was dehydrated, while the new champion required 35 stitches spread over five cuts and also suffered bruised ribs. The judges were unanimous with scores of 114-112, 116-112, 115-112.

25 January, 1993   Victor Rabanales 8.6 (Mexico) W PTS 12 Dio Andujar 8.6 (Philippines), Los Angeles, USA (WBC).

Knowing only one way to fight, the rugged Rabanales, blood streaming from both eyes, pounded out a gruelling 118-110, 116-113, 117-111 points victory over his game Filipino opponent, who was also decidedly marked at the finish. The scoreline hardly gave a true reflection of the contest, with both men giving everything they had and more.

24 March, 1993   Rafael del Valle 8.5½ (Puerto Rico) W RSC 5 Wilfredo Vargas 8.6 (Puerto Rico), Conado, Puerto Rico (WBO).

An impressive first defence, after contractual problems had kept him out of the ring for ten months, saw del Valle easily crush a two-time challenger and the referee dived in to save Vargas at 1.59 of the fifth round.

27 March, 1993   Orlando Canizales 8.6 (USA) W RTD 11 Clarence Adams 8.5¼ (USA), Evian les Bains, France (IBF).

Trying to become the youngest world champion since Wilfred Benitez, Adams put up a terrific show before his father threw the towel in at 1.32 of the eleventh. The youngster came back well during the middle rounds, having been badly hurt earlier, to cut the champion up and was going well until being stunned again.

28 March, 1993   Victor Rabanales 8.4¾ (Mexico) L PTS 12 Il-Jung Byun 8.5¾ (South Korea), Kyungju, South Korea (WBC).

Although forcing the fight continuously, Rabanales was picked off by the smart counters of the challenger to go down by a clear

115-113, 117-112, 117-111 points verdict. Not interested in getting involved in a punch-up, the clever southpaw stayed on the outside, but had to show his mettle when the Mexican came on strong in a desperate last ditch attack.

3 April, 1993   Jorge Elicier Julio 8.5 (Colombia) W RTD 8 Francisco Alvarez 8.5½ (Colombia), Cartagena, Colombia (WBA).

Making his first defence a winning one, Julio easily defeated his compatriot, Alvarez, who was retired by his corner after being badly cut. The decision was a wise one as the cause had become hopeless, with the challenger completely outclassed and not winning a round.

28 May, 1993   Il-Jung Byun 8.5¾ (South Korea) W PTS 12 Josefino Suarez 8.4¾ (Mexico), Seoul, South Korea (WBC).

The new champion again showed fleet of foot as he outclassed his first challenger to win handsomely on a 120-104, 119-109, 120-106 points decision. The fight could have ended summarily when Suarez was dropped by a solid left to the head in the opening round, but although he survived he was never in the running.

19 June, 1993   Rafael del Valle 8.5½ (Puerto Rico) W PTS 12 Miguel Lora 8.6 (Colombia), Hato Rey, Puerto Rico (WBO).

Lora, the former WBC champion between 1985-1988 and now a 32-year-old veteran, was outboxed by the young champion, winning only three rounds on the judges' scorecards. In a contest, that it would only be fair to say was one sided, del Valle was awarded a 117-112, 117-112, 118-112 unanimous points verdict.

19 June, 1993   Orlando Canizales 8.6 (USA) NC 3 Derrick Whiteboy 8.3¾ (South Africa), Houston, USA (IBF).

A disappointing end to what promised to be an interesting bout, saw Canizales retain his crown after being badly cut over the left eye following a head butt in the third. Earlier, Whitboy had frustrated the champion, but the American appeared to be exerting his authority prior to the ending.

SUPER-BANTAMWEIGHT (8st.10lbs)
Titleholders as at 1 July, 1993

IBF	–	Kennedy McKinney (USA)
WBA	–	Wilfredo Vasquez (Puerto Rico)
WBC	–	Tracy Harris Patterson (USA)
WBO	–	Daniel Jimenez (Puerto Rico)

15 October, 1992   Jesse Benavides 8.9¾ (USA) L PTS 12 Duke McKenzie 8.9½ (England), London, England (WBO).

By winning the title on a unanimous 117-110, 115-113, 115-112 points decision, McKenzie joined a select band of

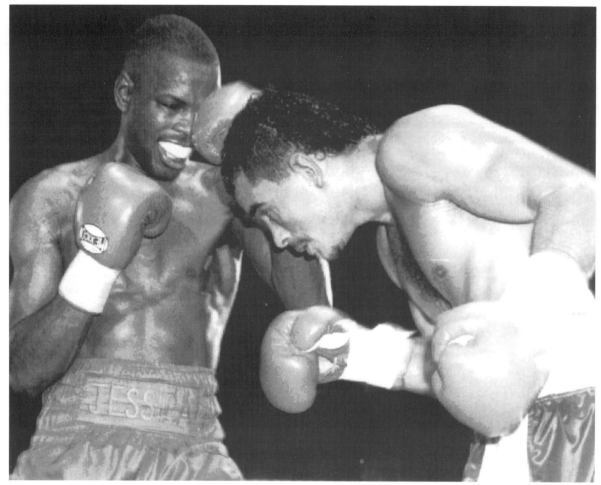

Three- time world champion, Duke McKenzie (left), appeared unlucky to lose his WBO super-bantamweight title to Daniel Jimenez last June

Les Clark

fighters who have become world champions at three different weights. An untidy scrap saw Benavides, who was also knocked down in the tenth, constantly outworked as he failed to land his heavier punches.

2 December, 1992   Welcome Nicta 8.10 (South Africa) L CO 11 Kennedy McKinney 8.9½ (USA), Tortoli, Italy (IBF).
Ahead on all three judges' (including Britain's Dave Parris) scorecards coming into the eleventh round, Nicta sent McKinney stumbling to the boards for a count of eight. It looked all over, but as the champion came in to complete the job he walked straight on to a right-cross which felled him for a count-out at 2.48 of the round.

5 December, 1992   Tracy Harris Patterson 8.9½ (USA) DREW 12 Daniel Zaragoza 8.10 (Mexico), Berck sur Mer, France (WBC).
In a very tight contest, Harris appeared lucky to hold on to

his title. The judges scored it 118-111, 114-117, 116-116, but Zaragoza had landed more cleanly, shown better defensive skills and had put Patterson down in the first.

5 December, 1992   Wilfredo Vasquez 8.10 (Puerto Rico) W RSC 8 Thierry Jacob 8.9¼ (France), Berk sur Mer, France (WBA).
On the same bill as Tracy Patterson, the man who had taken his WBC crown, Jacob's fragile features once again let him down as he attempted to win the WBA version of the title. With the contest evenly poised, the Frenchman was cut in the sixth and fought desperately to no avail, as the referee called the battle off at 0.52 of the eighth.

6 March, 1993   Wilfredo Vasquez 8.9¾ (Puerto Rico) W PTS 12 Luis Mendoza 8.9½ (Colombia), Levallois Perret, France (WBA).
In an action packed fight, that was fought out almost toe-to-toe for the entire twelve rounds, Vasquez appeared

fortunate to retain his title on a 116-114, 117-112, 115-113 unanimous points verdict. The fact that he won the last two rounds on the judges' scorecards, as Mendoza slowed, was the difference between winning and losing, while the fans certainly had value for money.

13 March, 1993   Tracy Harris Patterson 8.10 (USA) W PTS 12 Jesse Benavides 8.10 (USA), Poughkeepsie, USA (WBC).

With neither man able to impose himself totally upon the other, the contest went all the way to the final bell. Coming into the tenth round, Benavides was ahead in the scoring, but from then on Patterson let everything go, busting up the challenger's left eye and just about earning the 115-114, 117-113, 115-113 points decision.

17 April, 1993   Kennedy McKinney 8.10 (USA) W PTS 12 Richard Duran 8.10 (USA), Sacramento, USA (IBF).

Taking a far too cautious line, McKinney chose to box on the outside for most of the contest and with Duran often looking dangerous, the fans waited for the fireworks to explode. Unfortunately, apart from a few instances, Duran didn't do enough to warrant taking the title, leaving the champion to come home on a 117-111, 116-112, 116-112 points verdict.

9 June, 1993   Duke McKenzie 8.9 (England) L PTS 12 Daniel Jimenez 8.9 (Puerto Rico), London, England (WBO)

It was noticeable in the latter stages of the contest that McKenzie was being hurt by body shots, one of which put him down in the ninth for a count of nine. Prior to that, both men were even on the scorecards and although the champion recovered remarkably well to gain a share of the tenth and eleventh and won the final round, the scoring in the ninth was wide enough for the 115-115, 115-113, 115-114 decision to go Jimenez's way.

24 June, 1993   Wilfredo Vasquez 8.10 (Puerto Rico) W CO 10 Thierry Jacob 8.8¾ (France), Bordeaux, France (WBA).

The end for Jacob came when he was finally ground down in the tenth, being clubbed to the floor from a succession of heavy right hands, and counted out at 0.55. Although the Frenchman had received a badly cut right eye in the third, both men were even prior to the tenth round, but it was noticable that the champion's strength was beginning to tell.

FEATHERWEIGHT (9st.)
Titleholders as at 1 July, 1993
IBF   – Tom Johnson (USA)
WBA – Kyun Yung Park (South Korea)
WBC – Gregorio Vargas (Mexico)
WBO – Steve Robinson (Wales)

22 July, 1992   Manuel Medina 9.0 (Mexico) W RTD 10 Fabrizio Cappai 8.11¾ (Italy), Capo d'Orlando, Italy (IBF).

After holding his own with the champion for six rounds, despite being cut in the second, Cappai finally ran out of steam in the tenth and was retired by his corner.

29 August, 1992   Kyun-Yung Park 8.13½ (South Korea) W PTS 12 Giovanni Neves 8.12¾ (Venezuela), Taeju, South Korea (WBA).

In a hard fought battle, mainly at close quarters, Park proved the stronger of the two to run out a 116-113, 115-113, 116-113 points winner. There were no knockdowns, although Neves was unbalanced on several occasions.

12 September, 1992   Paul Hodkinson 8.13¾ (England) W RSC 10 Fabrice Benichou 9.0 (France), Blagnac, France (WBC).

The fight came to an end at 1.35 of the tenth round when Benichou, who had fought most courageously, sustained a terrible vertical cut to his upper lip. Prior to that, however, Hodkinson had gone forward continuously and had floored the Frenchman in the fourth round, but although ahead he somehow lacked his normal zip.

26 September, 1992   Colin McMillan 9.0 (England) L RTD 8 Ruben Palacio 8.12 (Colombia), London, England (WBO).

Making his first defence, the unfortunate McMillan dislocated his left shoulder in the eighth and was retired by his corner at 1.52 of the round. It hadn't been one of Colin's better nights, having been shaken up several times, but he was still ahead on all three judges' scorecards at the finish.

Ruben Palacio (right) takes the WBO featherweight champion, Colin McMillan, to the ropes on his way to a shock victory and the title   Action Images

23 October, 1992   Manuel Medina 8.13½ (Mexico) W PTS 12 Moussa Sangare 8.13¾ (France), Gravelines, France (IBF).

Winning by a 115-113, 116-114, 114-114 majority verdict was a fair reflection of Medina's superiority over the Mali-born challenger. Although Sangare was always looking to come inside the champion's guard, where he could throw hooks and uppercuts, he had little success, apart from the eighth onwards, being generally out of range.

19 December, 1992   Kyun-Yung Park 8.13½ (South Korea) W PTS 12 Ever Beleno 8.12¾ (Colombia), Changwon, South Korea (WBA).

In yet another hard battle, again mainly fought out at close quarters, Park retained his title when he was awarded a 117-112, 117-112, 115-114 points decision. While the champion had the power he lacked the accuracy to end the bout inside the distance.

3 February, 1993   Paul Hodkinson 8.13¾ (England) W RTD 4 Ricardo Cepeda 8.13¾ (Puerto Rico), London, England (WBC).

From the opening bell, Hodkinson kept the punches coming to outclass and eventually stop the challenger at 0.37 of the fourth round. Knocked down in the second, Cepeda never had a chance and his corner wisely threw the towel in, with the challenger in his own corner absorbing a brutal beating.

26 February, 1993   Manuel Medina 8.13¼ (Mexico) L PTS 12 Tom Johnson 8.13¾ (USA), Melun, France (IBF).

In a rematch, Johnson, although marginally ahead at the time, made sure of winning when he floored a very tired Medina for an eight count in the penultimate round. Cut over the left eye from heavy rights in the sixth, the champion finally surrendered his title on a 113-114, 115-112, 115-112 split decision.

20 March, 1993   Kyun-Yung Park 8.13¼ (South Korea) W RSC 4 Thanomchit Kiatkriengkrai 8.13¾ (Thailand), Chejudo, South Korea (WBA).

Puting his title on the line for the seventh time, the teak tough Park swarmed over his challenger in the fourth, throwing vicious punches from all angles, to record an impressive stoppage victory. Having already absorbed a solid beating and unable to defend himself, the Thai was mercifully rescued at 2.58 of the round.

17 April, 1993   Steve Robinson 8.13½ (Wales) W PTS 12 John Davison 8.12¾ (England), Washington, England (WBO).

Taking the fight at 24 hours notice, after the champion Ruben Palacio, had failed the HIV medical and had been stripped of his title, Robinson surprised almost everybody in boxing when winning a 115-114, 115-114, 114-116 split decision over Davison. With both men level coming into the twelfth, the Welshman swung it his way when he out-hit and staggered the little north-easterner to win the round and the vacant title with it.

28 April, 1993   Paul Hodkinson 8.13¼ (England) L RTD 7 Gregorio Vargas 9.0 (Mexico), Dublin, Ireland (WBC).

With Hodkinson on the verge of becoming the leading featherweight in the world, his dreams were rudely shattered by a young Mexican who had the look of a "Salvador Sanchez" about him. The champion fought well, but Vargas was better. Even as "Hoko" took up the attack and was ahead on all scorecards at the finish, one sensed that the challenger was merely biding his time. The end came at 2.27 of the seventh when the towel was thrown in after the champion had twice been smashed to the canvas and was in no condition to defend himself further.

SUPER-FEATHERWEIGHT (9st.4lbs)

Titleholders as at 1 July, 1993

IBF	–	Juan Molina (Puerto Rico)
WBA	–	Genaro Hernandez (USA)
WBC	–	Azumah Nelson (Ghana)
WBO	–	Jimmy Bredahl (Denmark)

15 July, 1992   Genaro Hernandez 9.3¼ (USA) W PTS 12 Masuaki Takeda 9.3½ (Japan), Fukuoka, Japan (WBA).

Using his reach advantage to good effect, the tall Hernandez got off to a flying start and never looked back. The judges' scores in his favour of 117-111, 119-109, 120-108, clearly emphasised his superiority over his rival who was making his second challenge for a world title.

22 August, 1992   Juan Molina 9.4 (Puerto Rico) W RSC 4 Fernando Caicedo 9.3 (Colombia), Bayamon, Puerto Rico (IBF).

Caicedo, a fourteen fight novice, was fed to the "wolves" when put in way over his head against a very good champion in Molina. The Colombian somehow lasted into the fourth where he was finally rescued at 0.38 of the round.

4 September, 1992   Daniel Londas 9.4 (France) L PTS 12 Jimmy Bredahl 9.4 (Denmark), Copenhagen, Denmark (WBO).

The challenger emulated his brother, who had won the WBO super-flyweight title earlier in the evening, when defeating the champion, Londas, by a majority 118-111, 118-111, 118-118 points verdict. Although Londas closed the range in the latter stages, with both men cut in the eleventh, Bredhal stuck to his boxing to run out a good winner. Dave Parris of Britain refereed.

7 November, 1992   Azumah Nelson 9.3 (Ghana) W PTS 12 Calvin Grove (USA), Lake Tahoe, USA (WBC).

Speeding around the ring like a racehorse, apart from being knocked down in the second round, Grove made the champion look clumsy and crude at times. Nelson tried desperately to finish his rival off, but ultimately had to settle for a 115-112, 114-113, 116-111 unanimous decision.

20 November, 1992   Genaro Hernandez 9.4 (USA) W RSC 6 Yuji Watanabe 9.3½ (Japan), Tokyo, Japan (WBA).

Apart from a brief scare in the fourth, when he was cut over the left eye, Hernandez's reach advantage made it a tough night for the challenger. Once the American had slowed his rival down with good body punches the end was ominous and Watanabe, his back to the ropes and not firing back, was rescued at 0.59 of the sixth round.

13 February, 1993   Juan Molina 9.3¾ (Puerto Rico) W RSC 8 Francisco Segura 9.2 (Mexico), Bayamon, Puerto Rico (IBF).

Pressing forward incessantly, Molina kept the challenger on the back foot throughout, with the end always in sight, especially when Segura's vision was badly impaired after being cut in the fourth. Four rounds later, a series of solid combinations forced a stoppage at 2.24 of the eighth as the Mexican finally crumbled to defeat.

20 February, 1993   Azumah Nelson 9.2 (Ghana) W PTS 12 Gabriel Ruelas 9.3 (Mexico), Mexico City, Mexico (WBC).

That the 115-114, 115-115, 115-113 points verdict went to Nelson and not the challenger was due more to experience than anything else, as Ruelas allowed himself to be kidded out of it. After making a bright start to the contest, winning the last round would have given the Mexican the title, but it was the old pro who caught the eye of the judges to retain his crown.

26 April, 1993   Genaro Hernandez 9.4 (USA) TD 1 Raul Perez 9.3¾ (Mexico), Los Angeles, USA (WBA).

Barely underway, the fight was called off at 0.28 of the first round and declared a technical draw after both men, in feinting for an opening, banged their heads together, leaving Perez with a head cut that wouldn't respond to treatment.

26 June, 1993   Juan Molina 9.3½ (Puerto Rico) W PTS 12 Manuel Medina 9.4 (Mexico), Atlantic City, USA (IBF).

A messy affair saw Molina retain his title against an extremely competent challenger, with scores of 117-111, 116-112, 115-113. Unfortunately, their styles didn't blend very well, the champion often looking to do his better work on the inside, with Medina using his height and reach to keep out of harms way, and in front an unsympathetic audience the final bell couldn't come soon enough.

28 June, 1993   Genaro Hernandez 9.4 (USA) W CO 8 Raul Perez 9.4 (Mexico), Los Angeles, USA (WBA).

Carrying a badly cut right eye from the third, Perez was able to continue but, as in their earlier meeting, it was ultimately to no avail. Continuously on the end of the champion's jab, it appeared only a matter of time before Hernandez would finish the job and in the eighth a long left to the region of the liver sent Perez crashing to be counted out at 2.11 of the round.

LIGHTWEIGHT (9st.9lbs)
Titleholders as at 1 July, 1993
IBF   –   Fred Pendleton (USA)
WBA   –   Dingaan Thobela (South Africa)
WBC   –   Miguel Gonzalez (Mexico)
WBO   –   Giovanni Parisi (Italy)

24 August, 1992   Miguel Gonzalez 9.8½ (Mexico) W RTD 9 Wilfredo Rocha 9.8½ (Colombia), Mexico City, Mexico (WBC).

In a battle for the WBC crown vacated by Pernell Whitaker, the unbeaten Gonzalez won an exciting fight when Rocha was retired on his stool at the end of the ninth. Both men had been decked, Gonzalez in the second round and Rocha in the fourth and fifth, but the former was just too strong for his rival.

29 August, 1992   Fred Pendleton 9.9 (USA) TD 2 Tracy Spann 9.8 (USA), Reno, USA (IBF).

Both men were told that they would have to start all over again some other time, after heads cracked together, leaving Pendleton with a badly cut right eye and unable to continue at 2.05 of the second round. The result of the contest, which was for the vacant IBF title relinquished by Pernell Whitaker, was deemed to be a technical draw.

25 September, 1992   Giovanni Parisi 9.7½ (Italy) W RSC 10 Javier Altamirano 9.7¾ (Mexico), Voghera, Italy (WBO).

With Dingaan Thobela forfeiting the WBO title due to his desire to contest the WBA championship, Parisi and Altamirano were brought together to contest the vacant crown. After a rocky start, Parisi, who was floored twice in the first round and hurt on several other occasions, hit back to put Altamirano down in the fifth and force his way back into the contest. The end came at 0.25 of round ten when the referee, dispensing with the count, called the fight off after the Mexican had been dropped onto his back by a cracking right to the jaw.

24 October, 1992   Joey Gamache 9.9 (USA) L RSC 11 Tony Lopez 9.8½ (USA), Portland, USA (WBA).

Out in front on two of the judges' scorecards, a badly tiring Gamache was sent crashing to the canvas in the eleventh by a crunching right hander and, after getting to his feet and staggering around, the referee immediately stepped in to rescue him with 0.40 on the clock. Lopez, who saved his best efforts for the later rounds, thus became a three-time world champion.

5 December, 1992   Miguel Gonzalez 9.9 (Mexico) W PTS 12 Darryl Tyson 9.8½ (USA), Mexico City, Mexico (WBC)

Although Tyson pressured from the off, the champion was generally in control and outboxed his rival to win by a wide 120-108, 118-110, 120-110 points margin. To his credit, Tyson, who was consistently beaten to the punch, never gave up trying.

10 January, 1993   Fred Pendleton 9.9 (USA) W PTS 12 Tracy Spann 9.9 (USA), Atlantic City, USA (IBF).

A contest of varying styles, saw the cagey veteran, Pendleton, craftily box his way to a clear 116-112, 117-111, 117-111 points decision over the aggressive Spann. This was a rematch, following a technical draw for the vacant title, and although fairly even up until the eighth it was all Pendleton from thereon as Spann had already made his big effort.

12 February, 1993   Tony Lopez 9.8¾ (USA) W PTS 12 Dingaan Thobela 9.8¾ (South Africa), Sacramento, USA (WBA).

In what appeared on the face of it an extremely harsh decision, Lopez retained his title with a 115-113, 116-114, 116-114 unanimous points verdict. Apart from suffering a dreadful cut over the right eye in the eighth, the champion looked a beaten man at the final bell, until the decision, which was followed by genuine cries from Thobela's camp for a rematch.

16 April, 1993   Giovanni Parisi 9.8 (Italy) W PTS 12 Michael Ayers 9.9 (England), Rome, Italy (WBO).

Although defiant to the end, the challenger, floored in the fifth and cut on the left eye in the eighth and outboxed in almost every round, lost by a wide 118-109, 118-110, 119-108 points margin. Ayers' courage was never in dispute, but it was never enough to beat the classy, switch-hitting Italian on his own ground.

26 April, 1993   Miguel Gonzalez 9.9 (Mexico) W PTS 12 Hector Lopez (Mexico), Aguascalientes, Mexico (WBC).

Surviving a rough fourth round, when he came close to being despatched, Gonzalez gradually got his boxing together to unanimously outpoint his compatriot with scores of 117-112, 117-111, 115-112.

26 June, 1993   Tony Lopez 9.8¾ (USA) L PTS 12 Dingaan Thobela 9.9 (South Africa), Sun City, South Africa (WBA).

In a fight refereed by John Coyle, that was a lot closer than their first, Thobela won the title on his own ground following a unanimous 116-114, 118-112, 116-114 points decision. Lopez worked the body throughout and by the sixth was well in the contest as the South African slowed considerably. However, Thobela held his boxing together, had a big eleventh round and cut the American over the left eye in the twelfth, to deservedly become the new champion.

LIGHT-WELTERWEIGHT (10st.)
Titleholders as at 1 July, 1993
IBF   –   Charles Murray (USA)
WBA   –   Juan M. Coggi (Argentine)
WBC   –   Julio Cesar Chavez (Mexico)
WBO   –   Zack Padilla (USA)

18 July, 1992   Rafael Pineda 9.13 (Colombia) L PTS 12 Pernell Whitaker 10.0 (USA), Las Vegas, USA (IBF).

The title changed hands as Pineda was knocked down in the eighth round and outboxed continuously to lose by a wide 110-116, 108-117, 108-117, margin. Whitaker's jab and move style totally bamboozled the hard hitting champion, who could not get set, often resorting to landing low blows which also proved ineffective.

1 August, 1992   Julio Cesar Chavez 10.0 (Mexico) W RSC 4 Frankie Mitchell 9.11½ (USA), Las Vegas, USA (WBC).

In an easy defence, Chavez battered the hapless American from piller to post on his way to victory. Southpaw Mitchell, blood spurting from a badly cut right eye, was floored twice in the third and again in the fourth, before the referee came to his aid with only 0.56 of the round completed.

9 September, 1992   Akinobu Hiranaka 10.0 (Japan) L RSC 11 Morris East 10.0 (Philippines), Tokyo, Japan (WBA).

A huge upset saw the inexperienced East floor and stop an extremely tired champion in the eleventh round, having got back into the fight from the sixth onwards. Prior to that, he was the one under pressure, being pinned against the ropes for long periods, but weathering the storm well.

12 September, 1992   Julio Cesar Chavez 10.0 (Mexico) W PTS 12 Hector Camacho 10.0 (Puerto Rico), Las Vegas, USA (WBC).

A fight that everybody wanted a few years back, turned into one-way traffic as Chavez hounded his rival for the full twelve rounds to win by scores of 117-111, 119-110, 120-107 (Harry Gibbs of Britain). Camacho displayed great bravery, but lacked the power to keep the champion at bay, and finished the fight with both eyes almost closed, and bleeding badly.

9 November, 1992   Carlos Gonzalez 9.12 (Mexico) W RTD 6 Lorenzo Smith 9.13 (USA), Los Angeles, USA (WBO).

The challenger put up a better fight than many expected, jabbing with fast hands and speeding around the ring where he could not be caught. Gradually, however, Gonzalez got into the action and when Smith was cut by the right eye in the fifth, he went to pieces. After racing frantically around the ring in the sixth, Smith retired on his stool at the end of the round.

14 December, 1992   Carlos Gonzalez 9.12½ (Mexico) W RSC 1 Rafael Ortiz 9.12¾ (Dominican Republic), Mexico City, Mexico (WBO).

Raising his total to 35 wins in as many fights, Gonzalez hardly raised a sweat as he pounded the limited challenger incessantly, so much so, that the referee called it off after only 1.33 of the first round had ensued.

13 January, 1993   Morris East 9.13¼ (Philippines) L RSC 8 Juan M. Coggi 9.13¾ (Argentine), Mar del Plata, Argentine (WBA).

Seeking to regain his old title, the Argentinian, Coggi, attacked the body from the off and a left-uppercut to the stomach put East down in the second. Somehow, the champion stayed in the fight until 2.50 of the eighth when the referee called a halt after he was floored, this time from head punches, and never looked likely to beat the full count.

20 February, 1993   Julio Cesar Chavez 9.13½ (Mexico) W RSC 5 Greg Haugen 10.0 (USA), Mexico City, Mexico (WBC).

Fighting in front of the largest crowd in the history of boxing, 136,000 packed into the Aztec Stadium, Chavez gave a performance worthy of the occasion. Sinking in punches to head and body, the Mexican floored his man in the first and fifth rounds and was giving the brave Haugen a remorseless beating when the referee brought matters to a halt at 2.02 of the fifth.

22 March, 1993   Carlos Gonzalez 9.13¾ (Mexico) W RSC 1 Tony Baltazar 9.13¾ (USA), Los Angeles, USA (WBO).

A sensational opening stanza saw the champion come under great pressure from the rugged Baltazar, before crashing in punches of his own that smashed the challenger to the deck. The stunned crowd watched their favourite put down twice more and stopped at 2.22 of the first round under the three-knockdown ruling.

10 April, 1993   Juan M. Coggi 10.0 (Argentine) W RSC 7 Jose Rivera 9.13¼ (Puerto Rico), Mar del Plata, Argentine (WBA).

A clash of heads in the third left the challenger reeling from a cut over the right eye and from then on Coggi made that his target. With solid lefts thumping into Rivera's face and with the damage rapidly worsening, the referee concluded matters at 2.58 of the seventh.

8 May, 1993   Julio Cesar Chavez 10.0 (Mexico) W RSC 6 Terrence Alli 9.13½ (Guyana), Las Vegas, USA (WBC).

An extremely one-sided contest was brought to a halt at 0.45 of the sixth to save a too brave for his own good, Alli, from taking further punishment at the hands of a champion who took his score to 87 straight wins. The challenger had just risen from a count of eight, after being floored by a crunching left-hook, and was being hit at will when the third man rescued him.

15 May, 1993   Charles Murray 10.0 (USA) W PTS 12 Rodney Moore 10.0 (USA), Atlantic City, USA (IBF).

Fighting for the title vacated by Pernell Whitaker, the classy Murray was too smart for a surprisingly jaded Moore and copped a 115-113, 118-110, 116-112 points decision. The contest was never much of a spectacle, with more action outside than inside, but Murray did the better work and was rarely put under too much pressure by the man from Philadelphia.

7 June, 1993   Carlos Gonzalez 10.0 (Mexico) L PTS 12 Zack Padilla 9.13 (USA), Las Vegas, USA (WBO).

In scoring a huge upset 117-111, 115-114, 117-112 (Dave Parris) points victory, Padilla merely carried on from where he had left off when beating Roger Mayweather in the eliminator. The unbeaten Gonzalez just could not fathom out Padilla's style, that had everything coming off the jab, and was never a threat. The crowd roared their appreciation throughout and at the final bell the punch counters at ringside calculated that an amazing 2,400 punches had been thrown, the majority by Padilla.

23 June, 1993   Juan M. Coggi 10.0 (Argentine) W CO 5 Hiroyuki Yoshino 10.0 (Japan), Tokyo, Japan (WBA).

Floored three times in all, the challenger, who posed no real threat throughout, was counted out at 2.15 of the fifth. The power of Coggi was just too much for his opponent and from as early as the opening round it was obvious to many shrewd ringside observers that the result would never be in question.

WELTERWEIGHT (10st. 7lbs)
Titleholders as at 1 July, 1993

IBF	– Felix Trinidad (Puerto Rico)
WBA	– Crisanto Espana (Venezuela)
WBC	– Pernell Whitaker(USA)
WBO	– Gert Bo Jacobsen (Denmark)

25 July, 1992   Manning Galloway 10.7 (USA) W PTS 12 Pat Barrett 10.4¾ (England), Manchester, England (WBO).

In scoring an easy 116-112, 119-111, 116-112 points victory, Galloway proved to be a most evasive, if light-hitting champion, while Barrett rarely caused any distress, apart from a clash of heads that left the American with damage over the left eye. Barrett continuously stalked, but when given the opportunity he relied too much on single shots to worry the champion, who dominated throughout with his flicking southpaw lead.

28 August, 1992   Maurice Blocker 10.7 (USA) W PTS 12 Luis Garcia 10.7 (Venezuela), Atlantic City, USA (IBF).

Although retaining his title on a split 115-110, 116-110, 112-115 points decision, it wasn't a confident champion on the day, but one who was content to merely hit and run for most of the contest. Apart from the fifth round when Garcia was on the floor three times and that he left the ring with a badly cut left eye, many onlookers were of the opinion he had still done enough to win.

31 October, 1992   Meldrick Taylor 10.6½ (USA) L RSC 8 Crisanto Espana 10.7 (Venezuela), London, England (WBA).

Struggling to get inside the long arms of the challenger, Taylor looked a shell of the fighter who first won a world title. He was often rocked, but somehow managed to stay upright until the eighth when he was smashed face down onto the floor. Getting up far too quickly and almost defenceless, he took more heavy blows before referee, John Coyle, rescued him at 2.11 on the clock.

27 November, 1992   Manning Galloway 10.6½ (USA) NC 1 Gert Bo Jacobsen 10.5 (Denmark), Randers, Denmark (WBO).

The fight was declared a no contest with the first round not even completed, after an accidental clash of heads left Jacobsen with blood spurting from a temple wound which could not be quelled.

12 January, 1993   James McGirt 10.7 (USA) W PTS 12 Genaro Leon 10.7 (Mexico), New York City, USA (WBC).

Carrying an injured left arm throughout the fight, McGirt still had far too much in every department for the tough Mexican who, to add to his woes, was deducted a point for holding and hitting in the third. And apart from a rocky last round, when he was forced to take more punches than at any time in the fight, McGirt was a worthy 118-113, 117-114, 117-111 points winner at the final bell.

12 February, 1993   Manning Galloway 10.6¾ (USA) L PTS 12 Gert Bo Jacobsen 10.6¾ (Denmark), Randers, Denmark (WBO).

It was a case of third time lucky when the challenger took the title with a 115-113, 115-113, 116-113 points victory, having previously twice failed to beat Galloway. This time, however, the American's hit and run style didn't impress the judges, who felt that the Dane's better quality blows, especially to the body, warranted the verdict.

6 March, 1993   James McGirt 10.7 (USA) L PTS 12 Pernell Whitaker 10.6¼ (USA), New York City, USA (WBC).

This was the fight that the division had been waiting for, a match between the best two men, McGirt and Whitaker. In the event, it fell way below the expected standard. Whitaker came home on a 117-111, 115-113, 115-114 points decision, but the expected quality was sadly missing. The "one armed" McGirt won the last two rounds almost by default, as Whitaker clowned and generally messed about and another session like that would have seen the champion retaining his title.

5 May, 1993   Crisanto Espana 10.7 (Venezuela) W PTS 12 Rodolfo Aguilar 10.5¾ (Panama), Belfast, Northern Ireland (WBA).

Against a challenger who came to defend, Espana should have done far better than merely settling for the 117-111, 120-109, 119-110 points verdict. Although he controlled the centre of the ring he never really imposed himself upon Aguilar, content to just flick out the jab and admire his work, but never prepared to cut out the space and go to work with the punching power fight crowds have come to expect of him. The contest was refereed by England's John Coyle.

19 June, 1993   Maurice Blocker 10.6 (USA) L CO 2 Felix Trinidad 10.5½ (Puerto Rico), San Diego, USA (IBF).

Right from the opening bell the signs were ominous. Blocker came out with the left-jab, while Trinidad was prepared to counter over the top. At 1.49 of the second round Blocker was counted out, having been smashed to the canvas face first by a challenger who never left his rival alone once he found that he could damage him, while not being at risk himself.

LIGHT-MIDDLEWEIGHT (11st.)
Titleholders as at 1 July, 1993

IBF	– Gianfranco Rosi (Italy)
WBA	– Julio Cesar Vasquez (Argentine)
WBC	– Terry Norris (USA)
WBO	– John David Jackson (USA)

11 July, 1992   Gianfranco Rosi 10.12½ (Italy) W PTS 12 Gilbert Dele 10.13¼ (France), Monte Carlo, Monaco (IBF).

Finishing strongly, Rosi just about did enough to warrant the 116-114, 116-111, 113-114 split decision, although a lot of his earlier work was sloppy and he had been dumped on the floor in the third. However, Dele, who made an aggressive start, began to tire in the last third of the bout and it was then that Rosi clawed his way back.

19 December, 1992   John David Jackson 10.13¼ (USA) W RTD 10 Michele Mastrodonato 10.13¼ (Italy), San Severo, Italy (WBO).

Jackson had little difficulty retaining his title against the inexperienced Italian, who sustained a steady beating throughout. With cuts below both of Mastrodonato's eyes, his corner threw the towel in at 1.14 of the tenth. Paul

Thomas of Britain, one of the judges, had the champion ahead 90-81 at the finish.

21 December, 1992   Julio Cesar Vasquez 10.12¾ (Argentine) W RSC 1 Hitoshi Kamiyama 10.12¼ (Japan), Buenos Aires, Argentine (WBA).

Fighting for the WBA crown that Vinny Pazienza was forced to abdicate following a serious car accident, the number one contender, Vasquez, won the title in the first round, via the three knockdowns in a round ruling. Kamiyama, who was never given a chance to prove himself a worthy contender, also received a bad cut over the left eye.

20 January, 1993   Gianfranco Rosi 10.13¾ (Italy) W PTS 12 Gilbert Dele 10.13½ (France), Avoriaz, France (IBF).

With Rosi behind on two of the judges' cards coming into the tenth, and having a point deducted for holding in the fifth, he made sure of the 116-111, 114-113, 112-114 points decision, when finishing strongly. Shaken badly by a heavy right in the tenth, somehow, Dele managed to hold on and survive, but had nothing left in the tank for the final two rounds as the champion tied up the verdict.

20 February, 1993   Terry Norris 10.11 (USA) W RSC 2 Maurice Blocker 10.10 (USA), Mexico City, Mexico (WBC).

Unable to make proper use of his reach advantage, the IBF welterweight champion was badly open to the left-hook and was only saved by the bell to end the first round, having taken two long counts. Tottering around the ring like a drunk in the second, Blocker's only defence was to hold on for dear life and when Norris finally broke free to hammer the challenger dazedly around the ring, the referee had no alternative other than to halt the proceedings with 0.49 of the round gone.

22 February, 1993   Julio Cesar Vasquez 11.0 (Argentine) W CO 1 Aquilino Asprilla 10.13¾ (Panama), Mar del Plata, Argentine (WBA).

With the action barely underway, the champion set up the first offensive and sent Asprilla crashing to the canvas with a corking left-hook. The challenger made it to his feet, but to no avail as Vasquez could now taste blood and chased Asprilla to the ropes where he capsized under a hail of leather and slid to the floor to be counted out at 0.47 of the round.

24 April, 1993   Julio Cesar Vasquez 10.13 (Argentine) W PTS 12 Javier Castillejos 10.12 (Spain), Madrid, Spain (WBA).

A torrid contest, excellently refereed by John Coyle, that went right down the line to a 115-114, 115-114, 120-111 points victory for the champion, proved that the hard-hitting Vasquez could take it as well as dish it out. Castillejos, after making a bright start, was put down

heavily in the sixth, but recovered well to give the champion a run for his money, firing in heavy punches of his own and against a man with less than an iron jaw he may well have won.

19 June, 1993   Terry Norris 11.0 (USA) W RTD 3 Troy Waters 10.12 (Australia), San Diego, USA (WBC).

Although the fight only lasted three rounds, those three rounds were more action packed than many contests put together. The Australian came like a lamb led to the slaughter, but left the ring a hero. Badly beaten up and downed in the first, he roared right back to blast Norris to the canvas in the second and to give the "Yank" a taste of his own medicine. It couldn't go on forever, however, and with a deep gash on his left cheek and abrasions over both eyes, Waters was retired by his corner at the end of the third after taking another heavy beating during the round.

MIDDLEWEIGHT (11st.6lbs)
Titleholders as at 1 July, 1993
IBF – Roy Jones (USA)
WBA – Reggie Johnson (USA)
WBC – Gerald McClellan (USA)
WBO – Chris Pyatt (England)

1 August, 1992   Julian Jackson 10.5 (Virgin Islands) W PTS 12 Thomas Tate 10.5 (USA), Las Vegas, USA (WBC).

Apart from suffering a fourth round knockdown at the hands of the hard-punching champion, underdog Tate surprised everyone by not only going the distance, but fighting back when hurt and often shaking up Jackson with hard punches. Jackson gained a unanimous 116-111, 117-111, 116-111 verdict, but Tate proved that he will be a real threat to all in the division.

29 August, 1992   James Toney 11.4¾ (USA) W PTS 12 Mike McCallum 11.4 (Jamaica), Reno, USA (IBF).

Although McCallum landed more punches than Toney in this re-match it was the champion who retained his title by a majority 117-110, 117-110, 114-114 points decision. In the main, however, Toney's punches were of the better quality variety and although the fight was not as exciting as the previous one, it was hard fought and totally absorbing.

27 October, 1992   Reggie Johnson 11.5¼ (USA) W PTS 12 Lamar Parks 11.5½ (USA), Houston, USA (WBA).

Wasting very few punches, Johnson gave his inexperienced rival a lesson in ringcraft throughout to take the 116-112, 116-113, 115-113 points verdict. Although he was never outclassed in a tough contest, Parks, who didn't know how to deal with a southpaw this time round, will be better prepared next time.

19 January, 1993   Reggie Johnson 11.6 (USA) W RSC 8 Ki-Yun Song 11.5 (South Korea), Boise, USA (WBA).

In a contest to decide the vacant WBO middleweight title, Chris Pyatt (left) and Sambu Kalambay swap blows during the latter stages. Pyatt showed great resolve and stamina to take a narrow points win Action Images

For an extremely limited fighter, Song did well to last as long as he did against a man of the class of Johnson, but to be fair, this was not one of the champion's better nights. However, after stumbling around for over seven rounds the challenger was finally rescued by the referee at 0.40 of the eighth, not fighting back and taking a shellacking on the ropes.

4 May, 1993   Reggie Johnson 11.6 (USA) W PTS 12 Wayne Harris 11.6 (Guyana), Denver, USA (WBA).

In opposing yet another limited fighter in Wayne Harris, a 6'3" stringbeam of a man, Johnson once again ran out of ideas and laboured to a 120-109, 120-108, 120-110 points decision. Every time the challenger was tagged, he just held or scooted backwards and with Johnson unable to solve the problems and Harris losing every round, the contest degenerated into a boring affair.

8 May, 1993   Julian Jackson 11.5 (Virgin Islands) L RSC 5 Gerald McClellan 11.6 (USA), Las Vegas, USA (WBC).

A sensational fight saw the challenger blast the title away at 2.09 of the fifth from the man considered by many to be the hardest puncher, pound-for-pound, in recent years. After a shaky first stanza, Jackson appeared to settle and although he was badly cut over the left eye from a clash of heads in the third he was still going strongly. However, in the fifth, a stunned McClellan stormed forward to blast Jackson to the canvas twice and with the champion unable

to defend himself the referee called it off.

19 May, 1993   Chris Pyatt 11.6 (England) W PTS 12 Sumbu Kalambay 11.4½ (Italy), Leicester, England (WBO).

Fighting for the title left vacant by Gerald McClellan, after he decided to challenge for the WBC crown instead, brought together the crafty veteran, Kalambay, a former champion, and the international champion, Pyatt. The Englishman made a very good start but appeared to blow-up in the latter rounds. But showing great courage and fortitude, he somehow managed to stand his ground to capture the 115-113, 116-114, 116-113 points verdict. Kalambay, who had blocked a good many punches on his arms, felt that his defensive work had won him the day, but in truth, he didn't do enough work to warrant victory.

22 May, 1993   Roy Jones 11.5 (USA) W PTS 12 Bernard Hopkins 11.5½ (USA), Washington, USA (IBF).

With James Toney moving up to super-middle, the way was cleared for the young Olympian, Roy Jones, to win his first major title, which he did with a clear 116-112, 116-112, 116-112 points verdict over the tough Philadelphian, Hopkins. With lightning reflexes and blurring handspeed, Jones certainly looks the part, having reduced such a dangerous opponent as Hopkins to merely that of a lumbering, one-paced fighter.

Nigel Benn (right) hammers Mauro Galvano to the ropes during his successful WBC super-middleweight title defence against the former champion last March

Action Images

SUPER-MIDDLEWEIGHT (12st.)

Titleholders as at 1 July, 1993

IBF – **James Toney (USA)**
WBA – **Michael Nunn (USA)**
WBC – **Nigel Benn (England)**
WBO – **Chris Eubank (England)**

2 September, 1992   Victor Cordoba 12.0 (Panama) L PTS 12 Michael Nunn 12.0 (USA), Las Vegas, USA (WBA).

Cordoba was extremely unlucky to lose his title on a 114-112, 112-114, 113-114 split decision and it was ultimately one point deducted for a low blow that was the deciding factor. However, it shoudn't have come to that as the southpaw Cordoba landed by far the heavier punches and had Nunn on the floor in the tenth and struggling to survive.

19 September, 1992   Chris Eubank 12.0 (England) W PTS 12 Tony Thornton 12.0 (USA), Glasgow, Scotland (WBO).

In his fourth defence, Chris Eubank held on to his title with scores of 115-113, 116-113, 117-112. Most ringsiders were of the opinion that Thornton gave him his toughest test to date. But though he gave of his best and hurt Eubank at times, the American was too one paced and predictable to unhinge the champion. Eubank, while often appearing infuriatingly lethargic, proved once again that he could step up a gear if required.

3 October, 1992   Mauro Galvano 12.0 (Italy) L RTD 3 Nigel Benn 11.13½ (England), Marino, Italy (WBC).

An amazing contest saw Nigel Benn declared the champion when Galvano refused to come off his stool at the end of the third round. Right from the beginning, Benn had given notice that he wasn't going to mess about as he walked through the champion, inflicting a bad cut over the left eye in the second round. However, the contest will be remembered for what happened after the fight, when the Italians tried to claim that the injury to their man had been caused by an intentional head butt. Luckily for Benn, the referee knew otherwise.

28 November, 1992   Chris Eubank 12.0 (England) W PTS 12 Juan Carlos Gimenez 12.0 (Paraguay), Manchester, England (WBO).

Controlling the action as he pleased and only working in spurts, Eubank easily retained his title by dint of a wide119-109, 118-110, 118-110 unanimous decision. Gimenez proved a tough nut to knock over, seemingly impervious to punishment, but lacked the ability to make the fight truly competitive.

12 December, 1992   Nigel Benn 11.13¾ (England) W RSC 11 Nicky Piper 11.13¾ (Wales), London, England (WBC).

Coming into the ring as a huge outsider, Nicky Piper, although beaten, could be proud of his overall performance. He had used his long reach to good effect early on and it wasn't until the latter stages that Benn began to impose himself with good punches to head and body. The body blows especially, weakened the Welshman, but it was a big left-hook to the head that put him down in the eleventh. On rising, Piper seemed to be clear-headed, but Benn gave him no respite and when a whole series of punches drove the challenger reeling to the ropes, referee Larry O'Connell decided he had seen enough and called a halt at 1.44 of the round. The judges' (all British) scorecards at the finish in Benn's favour were 98-93 (Adrian Morgan) and 96-94 (Paul Thomas), while Mickey Vann had Piper in front 95-96.

30 January, 1993   Michael Nunn 12.0 (USA) W PTS 12 Victor Cordoba 12.0 (Panama), Memphis, USA (WBA).

Giving Cordoba a steady boxing lesson and knocking the Panamanian down twice in an exciting second round almost counted for nothing, as Nunn was hit low on numerous occasions and was dropped several times from the after effects. Meanwhile, he subjected Cordoba to a steady battering throughout and it was amazing that the challenger, who also had three points deducted for low blows, was able to make it to the final bell. Somehow he did, only to lose by a wide 115-107, 117-106, 120-106 points margin.

13 February, 1993   Iran Barkley 12.0 (USA) L RTD 9 James Toney 11.13 (USA), Las Vegas, USA (IBF).

Right from the opening bell the denouement was never in doubt as Toney outspeeded and outpunched the fast fading Barkley. In what became a totally one-sided affair, it was not only a surprise that Barkley lasted so long, but that he wasn't decked, either. Finally, with his left eye almost shut and suffering from a range of cuts and with his task an impossible one, the doctor brought the bout to a halt during the interval between the eighth and ninth rounds.

20 February, 1993   Michael Nunn 12.0 (USA) W CO 1 Danny Morgan 11.13¾ (USA), Mexico City, Mexico (WBA).

A mismatch which ended at 2.59 of the first round, saw Morgan counted out, having already been decked earlier. The challenger offered nothing in the way of talent and was dispatched by Nunn, not known as a kayo expert, with maximum efficiency.

20 February, 1993   Chris Eubank 12.0 (England) W PTS 12 Lindell Holmes 11.13 (USA), London, England (WBO).

In what was just another all too familiar and frustrating spectacle, Eubank did all that was necessary to beat the 35-year-old Holmes, an opponent, in common with some of the others, who had been to the well once too often. Winning by a 116-114, 120-109, 117-112 points margin didn't prove anything, as a rematch with Benn loomed closer.

6 March, 1993   Nigel Benn 11.13¾ (England) W PTS 12 Mauro Galvano 11.13¼ (Italy), Glasgow, Scotland (WBC).

By constantly clutching and mauling his rival, the Italian was able to stay in the fight for the full twelve rounds, but as a spectacle it was "as dull as ditch water". Unfortunately, Benn couldn't change his variety and had to be content with the 118-114, 117-113, 118-112 points decision. And to make matters worse, Galvano badly stunned Benn with the last punch of the contest and could have finished it there and then if the bell hadn't come to the champion's rescue.

23 April, 1993   Michael Nunn 11.13½ (USA) W RSC 6 Crawford Ashley 11.9 (England), Memphis, USA (WBA).

Although decked five times, Ashley gave an excellent display until suffering a broken rib and being rescued by the referee at 2.59 of the sixth. There was plenty of excitement for the fans and the challenger gave as good as he got for the first three rounds, but once Nunn had found the range for his body shots, following the injury, it was merely a matter of time before Ashley would capsize.

15 May, 1993   Chris Eubank 12.0 (England) DREW 12 Ray Close 12.0 (Northern Ireland), Glasgow, Scotland (WBO).

For ten rounds it appeared that there was going to be a new champion as the underdog, Close, not fooled by Eubank's ability to give himself regular breathers, kept working to steal the points. But the difference between winning and drawing came in the eleventh round when Close was poleaxed by a tremendous uppercut. Somehow getting up at eight, Close was allowed to continue by the referee, Paul Thomas, and although fighting back strongly, he lost the round by a two point margin. This was reflected by the scorelines (Close's scores shown first) of 116-113 (Dave Parris), 112-116, 115-115 (Roy Francis).

26 June, 1993   Nigel Benn 11.13½ (England) W RSC 4 Lou Gent 12.0 (England), London, England (WBC).

Smashed to the canvas five times in four tremendous action packed rounds, Gent certainly gave great value as he stood his ground to hit back immediately and even staggered Benn on occasion. However, bravery wasn't enough and Gent was finally rescued by English referee, Larry O'Connell, at 0.35 of the fourth. The contest was judged by Adrian Morgan (Wales), Billy Rafferty (Scotland), and Mickey Vann (England).

LIGHT-HEAVYWEIGHT (12st.7lbs)
Titleholders as at 1 July, 1993

IBF   – Henry Maske (Germany)
WBA – Virgil Hill (USA)
WBC – Jeff Harding (Australia)
WBO – Leonzer Barber (USA)

29 September, 1992   Virgil Hill 12.7 (USA) W PTS 12 Frank Tate 12.7 (USA), Bismark, USA (WBA).

Fighting for the title vacated earlier in the year by Iran Barkley, Hill forced the fight throughout to gain a 116-112, 118-116, 120-109 unanimous decision. The new champion dominated with the left-jab, with the best action coming in the latter rounds when both men were staggered.

3 December, 1992   Jeff Harding 12.2¾ (Australia) W PTS 12 David Vedder 12.1¾ (USA), St Jean de Luz, France (WBC).

Behind after five rounds, Harding came winging back with good punches from both hands against the rapidly tiring challenger. Even a bad cut over the left eye failed to halt the champion as he stormed ahead of his rival to win 117-113, 116-114, 118-114 on the judges' scorecards.

20 February, 1993   Virgil Hill 12.7 (USA) W TD 11 Adolpho Washington 12.7 (USA), Fargo, USA (WBA).

Although clearly losing at the time of the finish, Washington had given the champion one hell of a tough contest, while fighting from the second round under the handicap of a badly broken nose. Forcing Hill to meet him jab-for-jab, gradually took its toll, and the challenger eventually began to ship heavy punishment. However, as a cameraman tried to get a close shot of Washington's injured left eye, while he was seated in his corner at the end of the eleventh, he accidentally smashed the damaged eye with the camera. The fight was immediately called off and Hill received the technical decision with scores of 109-99, 110-98, 109-99.

27 February, 1993   Leonzer Barber 12.7 (USA) W PTS 12 Mike Sedillo 12.6 (USA), Beijing, China (WBO).

China's first pro boxing promotion for 44 years saw two Americans in the ring for a contest that had a 400 million viewing audience. While the action didn't get off to a flying start, once Barber had resolved the problems presented by the tall challenger, he gradually took control, with his jab proving to be an effective weapon. Although there were no knockdowns, at the final bell, the champion was well worth the 116-111, 117-112, 116-111 points decision.

20 March, 1993   Charles Williams 12.6¼ (USA) L PTS 12 Henry Maske 12.6 (Germany), Dusseldorf, Germany (IBF).

Williams made a good start in an effort to make an early night of it and almost immediately cut the challenger on the left eye. However, once Maske settled, his southpaw jab was the difference between the two men. Although Williams was ever dangerous, Maske refused to get drawn in and boxed his way to a comprehensive 116-111, 118-110, 116-111 points win.

3 April, 1993   Virgil Hill 12.6 (USA) W PTS 12 Fabrice Tiozzo 12.6 (France), Levallois Perret, France (WBA).

Recovering well from two knockdowns in the first two rounds, the Frenchman came back strongly in the middle sessions, taking the fight to the champion and cutting him on the left eye and right cheek. Unfortunately for him, his efforts left him out of gas in the latter rounds and Hill kept going for a 115-112, 115-110, 113-115 points victory.

CRUISERWEIGHT (13st.8lbs)
Titleholders as at 1 July, 1993
IBF   –   Al Cole (USA)
WBA   –   Bobby Czyz (USA)
WBC   –   Anaclet Wamba (France)
WBO   –   Nestor Giovannini (Argentine)

25 July, 1992   Tyrone Booze 13.7½ (USA) W CO 7 Derek Angol 13.8 (England), Manchester, England (WBO).

Having expended his energies in the early rounds in a vain attempt to "blow" the American away, Angol also began to suffer from body punches which further drained him. The unheralded Booze, fighting to win the title that had been vacated by the Norwegian, Magne Havnaa, just kept working away downstairs until Angol's legs began to betray him. The end came at 2.32 of the seventh round as the Englishman collapsed face first to be counted out by referee Roy Francis.

30 July, 1992   James Warring 13.6 (USA) L PTS 12 Al Cole 13.8 (USA), Stanhope, USA (IBF).

By applying persistent pressure, the challenger gradually overcame a champion whose main assets were his awkwardness. Cut over the left eye in the second round, Cole did not let this inconvenience him too much as he stayed on top of Warring to run out a 116-111, 117-110, 114-113 points winner.

2 October, 1992   Tyrone Booze 13.5 (USA) W PTS 12 Ralf Rocchigiani 13.2½ (Germany), Berlin, Germany (WBO).

Booze retained his title by means of a unanimous 114-113, 116-113, 116-112 points verdict after a competitive bout. With neither fighter showing enough to win inside the distance, it was the champion's hooks and uppercuts that caught the judges' eyes.

16 October, 1992   Anaclet Wamba 13.2¾ (France) W PTS 12 Andrew Maynard 12.11¾ (USA), Paris, France (WBC).

The former Olympic champion made a great recovery to go the distance, having been floored for a long count in the early seconds. Getting back into the action from the fourth round onwards, he gave Wamba real trouble thereafter, only to eventually go down on points, 118-110, 118-112, 116-113 (Adrian Morgan). The contest was refereed by Mickey Vann of England.

13 February, 1993   Tyrone Booze 13.6 (USA) L PTS 12 Markus Bott 13.6 (Germany), Hamburg, Germany (WBO).

An interesting fight, more than an exciting one, saw the German clearly outscore Booze 117-113 (Roy Francis), 117-112 (Dave Parris), 117-112, to win the title. Bott, who took the fight to the champion, surprised a good many people with his excellent conditioning and fully deserved the verdict.

28 February, 1993   Al Cole 13.8 (USA) W PTS 12 Uriah Grant13.7 (USA), Atlantic City, USA (IBF).

Although the 116-112, 115-113, 117-111 points verdict awarded to Cole seemed a fair reflection of his work, the fans were outraged and vented their feelings loudly. There were no knockdowns and the champion certainly found the veteran a tough man to nail down, but he should have learned more from Grant than many months of sparring would have taught him.

6 March, 1993   Anaclet Wamba 13.8 (France) W PTS 12 DavidVedder 13.5½ (USA), Levallois Perret, France (WBC).

Really a pumped up light-heavy, Vedder had no realistic chance of victory and began to tire rapidly from the middle rounds onwards. And with Wamba, a fighter who only does enough to win, not stepping up the pace, the contest petered out for a 117-113, 118-111, 116-113 points win for the champion. Larry O' Connell refereed.

26 June, 1993   Marcus Bott 13.7 (Germany) L PTS 12 Nestor Giovannini 13.3½ (Argentine), Hamburg, Germany (WBO).

In a very poor championship battle, with neither man showing any class, the title changed hands when Giovannini was awarded a 114-113, 114-113, 113-114 points decision. An unfortunate clash of styles brought both men together untidily throughout and the referee, Paul Thomas, had his work cut out trying to part them. While the decision was close, there will be no great hurry to match these two men together again.

HEAVYWEIGHT (13st.8lbs +)
Titleholders as at 1 July, 1993

IBF   –   Riddick Bowe (USA)
WBA   –   Riddick Bowe (USA)
WBC   –   Lennox Lewis (England)
WBO   –   Tommy Morrison (USA)

13 November, 1992   Evander Holyfield 14.9 (USA) L PTS 12 Riddick Bowe 16.11 (USA), Las Vegas, USA (IBF/WBA/WBC).

The brave Holyfield, outweighed by 30 lbs, gave it his very best shot against the young challenger but, ultimately, it wasn't enough to save his title. Cut over the left eye in the eighth, the other eye closing fast and badly battered in the

tenth, Holyfield made a tremendous effort to fight back with the whole stadium behind him. However, the penultimate round saw the champion thoroughly spent and a left-hook dropped him for a count of three. Although Holyfield recovered well, the last round was uneventful and at the final bell Bowe became the new champion with scores of 115-112, 117-110, 117-110, in his favour.

27 February, 1993   Riddick Bowe 17.5 (USA) W RSC 1 Michael Dokes 17.6 (USA), New York City, USA (WBA/IBF).

In a fight, if you could call it that, which was over at 2.19 of the first round, the challenger hadn't even been floored when the referee leaped in to save him from further punishment. He didn't need to be, having failed to land a worthwhile punch of his own, he was being hit at will and out on his feet when rescued.

8 May, 1993   Lennox Lewis 16.9 (England) W PTS 12 Tony Tucker 16.9 (USA), Las Vegas, USA (WBC).

Handed the WBC title on a plate after Riddick Bowe refused to fight him, Lewis took on the number one challenger in Tucker, a man who had once taken Tyson the full course and a man who had never been off his feet, and proceeded to floor him twice on his way to a hard earned 117-111, 116-112 (Harry Gibbs), 118-111 (Mickey Vann) points victory. It wasn't Lewis' best ever performance, but beating opponents who matter on their own ground shows his mettle.

22 May, 1993   Riddick Bowe 17.6 (USA) W RSC 2 Jesse Ferguson 16.0 (USA), Washington, USA (WBA).

By defending the WBA version of the title (The IBF refused to sanction the bout) against Ferguson, a recent winner over Ray Mercer, Bowe further devalued the title. Flattened at the end of the first, the challenger somehow got up as the bell rang to end the round. He came out for the second and after being belted to the canvas under a torrent of well aimed blows, the referee dispensed with the formalities and called a halt to the proceedings at 0.17 of the round.

7 June, 1993   Tommy Morrison 16.2 (USA) W PTS 12 George Foreman 18.4 (USA), Las Vegas, USA (WBO).

With Michael Moorer vacating the title so that he could challenge either Lennox Lewis or Riddick Bowe, Morrison became the new champion when he outpointed Foreman with scores of 117-110, 117-110, 118-109. It was a wide margin of victory, which didn't really give the complete picture, as "Big George" continuously came forward. However, showing marked improvement, Morrison countered and moved throughout, never presenting a stationary target, while the former champion could never quite catch up with his opponent to exact any damage. That was the story of the fight and it would appear that the 45-year-old Foreman has finally reached the end of a truly remarkable career.

World Champions, 1890-1993

The following records attempt to set out by weight division every champion under Queensberry Rules since the beginning of gloves (2 oz minimum).

Boxing grew up in Great Britain and quickly spread to the USA, but it was not until the champions of these two countries came together in the latter part of the last century that it developed on an international scale. Organisations then came into existence solely for the purpose of controlling professional boxing. The National Sporting Club of Britain was formed in 1891, later to be amalgamated into the British Boxing Board of Control during 1929. By the early part of the century the sport had also begun to boom among the French, who in 1911 were instrumental in setting up the International Boxing Union to look after the interests of boxing in Europe. Following World War II the body became known as the European Boxing Union. In America many states had allowed boxing to take place, but in 1920 the New York State Athletic Commission was legally constituted under the Walker Law to govern the sport. Also, at the same time, several of the independent states of America became affiliated to form the National Boxing Association, which by 1962 was re-named the World Boxing Association. In an effort to create a balance of power, Britain supported the setting up of the World Boxing Council, formed in 1963, which brought together New York and its satellite states, with the BBBoC, the Commonwealth and the EBU. Recently the International Boxing Federation, an offshoot of the WBA, has sprung into prominence on the world boxing stage, along with the World Boxing Organisation.

Over the years many new weight divisions have been formed and original classes have been restructured. For example the bantamweight division limit, which in 1890 stood at 112 lbs, was gradually increased until it reached an internationally accepted 118 lbs in 1909. Similarly, other weight limits rose, e.g. featherweight: 1890 (118 lbs) - 1909 (126 lbs); welterweight: 1892 (142 lbs) - 1909 (147 lbs); middleweight: 1891 (154 lbs) - 1909 (160 lbs).

Championship Status Code:
AUST = Australia; CALIF = California; EBU = European Boxing Union; FR = France; GB = Great Britain; IBF = International Boxing Federation; IBU = International Boxing Union; LOUIS = Louisiana; MARY = Maryland; MASS = Massachusetts; NBA = National Boxing Association; NY = New York; PEN = Pennsylvania; USA = United States; WBA = World Boxing Association; WBC = World Boxing Council; WBO = World Boxing Organisation.

Champions in **bold** are accorded universal recognition.

* Undefeated champions.

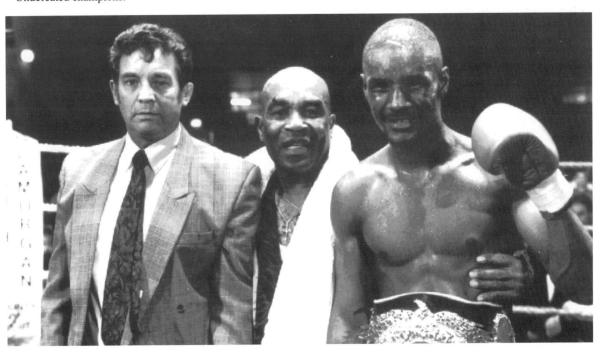

The old and the new. Former WBC featherweight champion, Howard Winstone (left), poses with the current WBO nine stone titleholder, Steve Robinson. Retired fighter, Ronnie Rush, Robinson's trainer, stands between the two Welshmen   Les Clark

Title Holder	Birthplace	Tenure	Status
M. Flyweight (105 lbs)			
Kyung-Yung Lee*	S. Korea	1987-1988	IBF
Hiroki Ioka	Japan	1987-1988	WBC
Luis Gamez*	Venezuela	1988-1989	WBA
Samuth Sithnaruepol	Thailand	1988-1989	IBF
Napa Kiatwanchai	Thailand	1988-1989	WBC
Bong-Jun Kim	S Korea	1989-1991	WBA
Nico Thomas	Indonesia	1989	IBF
Rafael Torres*	Dom Republic	1989-1992	WBO
Eric Chavez	Philippines	1989-1990	IBF
Jum-Hwan Choi	S Korea	1989-1990	WBC
Hideyuki Ohashi	Japan	1990	WBC
Fahlan Lukmingkwan	Thailand	1990-1992	IBF
Ricardo Lopez	Mexico	1990-	WBC
Hi-Yon Choi	S Korea	1991-1992	WBA
Manny Melchor	Philippines	1992	IBF
Hideyuki Ohashi	Japan	1992-1993	WBA
Ratanapol Sowvoraphin	Thailand	1992-	IBF
Chana Porpaoin	Thailand	1993-	WBA
Paul Weir	Scotland	1993-	WBO
L. Flyweight (108 lbs)			
Franco Udella*	Italy	1975	WBC
Jaime Rios	Panama	1975-1976	WBA
Luis Estaba	Venezuela	1975-1978	WBC
Juan Guzman	Dom Republic	1976	WBA
Yoko Gushiken	Japan	1976-1981	WBA
Freddie Castillo	Mexico	1978	WBC
Sor Vorasingh	Thailand	1978	WBC
Sun-Jun Kim	S Korea	1978-1980	WBC
Shigeo Nakajima	Japan	1980	WBC
Hilario Zapata	Panama	1980-1982	WBC
Pedro Flores	Mexico	1981	WBA
Hwan-Jin Kim	S Korea	1981	WBA
Katsuo Tokashiki	Japan	1981-1983	WBA
Amado Ursua	Mexico	1982	WBC
Tadashi Tomori	Japan	1982	WBC
Hilario Zapata	Panama	1982-1983	WBC
Jung-Koo Chang*	S Korea	1983-1988	WBC
Lupe Madera	Mexico	1983-1984	WBA
Dodie Penalosa*	Philippines	1983-1986	IBF
Francisco Quiroz	Dom Republic	1984-1985	WBA
Joey Olivo	USA	1985	WBA
Myung-Woo Yuh	S Korea	1985-1991	WBA
Jum-Hwan Choi	S Korea	1987-1988	IBF
Tacy Macalos	Philippines	1988-1989	IBF
German Torres	Mexico	1988-1989	WBC
Yul-Woo Lee	S Korea	1989	WBC
Muangchai Kitikasem	Thailand	1989-1990	IBF
Jose de Jesus*	Puerto Rico	1989-1992	WBO
Humberto Gonzalez	Mexico	1989-1990	WBC
Michael Carbajal*	USA	1990-1993	IBF
Rolando Pascua	Philippines	1990-1991	WBC
Melchor Cob Castro	Mexico	1991	WBC
Humberto Gonzalez	Mexico	1991-1993	WBC
Hiroki Ioka	Japan	1991-1992	WBA
Josue Camacho	Puerto Rico	1992-	WBO
Myung-Woo Yuh	S Korea	1992-	WBA
Michael Carbajal	USA	1993-	IBF/WBC
Flyweight (112 lbs)			
Sid Smith	England	1913	GB/IBU
Bill Ladbury	England	1913-1914	GB/IBU
Percy Jones*	Wales	1914	GB/IBU
Tancy Lee	Scotland	1915	GB/IBU
Joe Symonds	England	1915-1916	GB/IBU
Jimmy Wilde	Wales	1916	GB/IBU
Jimmy Wilde	Wales	1916-1923	
Pancho Villa*	Philippines	1923-1925	
Fidel la Barba*	USA	1925-1927	
Johnny McCoy	USA	1927-1928	CALIF

Title Holder	Birthplace	Tenure	Status
Frenchy Belanger	Canada	1927-1928	NBA
Izzy Schwartz	USA	1927-1929	NY
Newsboy Brown	Russia	1928	CALIF
Frankie Genaro	USA	1928-1929	NBA
Johnny Hill	Scotland	1928-1929	GB/CALIF
Emile Pladner	France	1929	NBA/IBU
Frankie Genaro	USA	1929-1931	NBA/IBU
Willie la Morte	USA	1929-1930	NY
Midget Wolgast	USA	1930-1935	NY
Young Perez	Tunisia	1931-1932	NBA/IBU
Jackie Brown	England	1932-1935	NBA/IBU
Benny Lynch*	Scotland	1935-1937	NBA
Small Montana	Philippines	1935-1937	NY/CALIF
Valentin Angelmann	France	1936-1937	IBU
Benny Lynch*	Scotland	1937	
Peter Kane	England	1938-1940	NY/IBU
Young Dado	Philippines	1938-1940	NBA/CALIF
Peter Kane	England	1940-1943	
Jackie Paterson	Scotland	1943-1947	
Jackie Paterson	Scotland	1947-1948	GB/NY
Rinty Monaghan	Ireland	1947-1948	NBA
Rinty Monaghan*	Ireland	1948-1950	
Terry Allen	England	1950	
Dado Marino	Hawaii	1950-1952	
Yoshio Shirai	Japan	1952-1954	
Pascual Perez	Argentine	1954-1960	
Pone Kingpetch	Thailand	1960-1962	
Fighting Harada	Japan	1962-1963	
Pone Kingpetch	Thailand	1963	
Hiroyuki Ebihara	Japan	1963-1964	
Pone Kingpetch	Thailand	1964-1965	
Salvatore Burruni	Italy	1965	
Salvatore Burruni	Italy	1965-1966	WBC
Horacio Accavallo*	Argentine	1966-1968	WBA
Walter McGowan	Scotland	1966	WBC
Chartchai Chionoi	Thailand	1966-1969	WBC
Efren Torres	Mexico	1969-1970	WBC
Hiroyuki Ebihara	Japan	1969	WBA
Bernabe Villacampo	Philippines	1969-1970	WBA
Chartchai Chionoi	Thailand	1970	WBC
Berkerk Chartvanchai	Thailand	1970	WBA
Masao Ohba*	Japan	1970-1973	WBA
Erbito Salavarria*	Philippines	1970-1971	WBC
Betulio Gonzalez	Venezuela	1972	WBC
Venice Borkorsor*	Thailand	1972-1973	WBC
Chartchai Chionoi	Thailand	1973-1974	WBA
Betulio Gonzalez	Venezuela	1973-1974	WBC
Shoji Oguma	Japan	1974-1975	WBC
Susumu Hanagata	Japan	1974-1975	WBA
Miguel Canto	Mexico	1975-1979	WBC
Erbito Salavarria	Philippines	1975-1976	WBA
Alfonso Lopez	Panama	1976	WBA
Guty Espadas	Mexico	1976-1978	WBA
Betulio Gonzalez	Venezuela	1978-1979	WBA
Chan-Hee Park	S Korea	1979-1980	WBC
Luis Ibarra	Panama	1979-1980	WBA
Tae-Shik Kim	S Korea	1980	WBA
Shoji Oguma	Japan	1980-1981	WBC
Peter Mathebula	S Africa	1980-1981	WBA
Santos Laciar	Argentine	1981	WBA
Antonio Avelar	Mexico	1981-1982	WBC
Luis Ibarra	Panama	1981	WBA
Juan Herrera	Mexico	1981-1982	WBA
Prudencio Cardona	Colombia	1982	WBC
Santos Laciar*	Argentine	1982-1985	WBA
Freddie Castillo	Mexico	1982	WBC
Eleoncio Mercedes	Dom Republic	1982-1983	WBC
Charlie Magri	Tunisia	1983	WBC
Frank Cedeno	Philippines	1983-1984	WBC
Soon-Chun Kwon	S Korea	1983-1985	IBF
Koji Kobayashi	Japan	1984	WBC

Title Holder	Birthplace	Tenure	Status
Gabriel Bernal	Mexico	1984	WBC
Sot Chitalada	Thailand	1984-1988	WBC
Hilario Zapata	Panama	1985-1987	WBA
Chong-Kwan Chung	S Korea	1985-1986	IBF
Bi-Won Chung	S Korea	1986	IBF
Hi-Sup Shin	S Korea	1986-1987	IBF
Fidel Bassa	Colombia	1987-1989	WBA
Dodie Penalosa	Philippines	1987	IBF
Chang-Ho Choi	S Korea	1987-1988	IBF
Rolando Bohol	Philippines	1988	IBF
Yong-Kang Kim	S Korea	1988-1989	WBC
Elvis Alvarez*	Colombia	1989	WBO
Duke McKenzie	England	1988-1989	IBF
Sot Chitalada	Thailand	1989-1991	WBC
Dave McAuley	Ireland	1989-1992	IBF
Jesus Rojas	Venezuela	1989-1990	WBA
Yul-Woo Lee	S Korea	1990	WBA
Isidro Perez	Mexico	1990-1992	WBO
Yukihito Tamakuma	Japan	1990	WBA
Muangchai Kitikasem	Thailand	1991-1992	WBC
Elvis Alvarez	Colombia	1991	WBA
Yong-Kang Kim	S Korea	1991-1992	WBA
Pat Clinton	Scotland	1992-1993	WBO
Rodolfo Blanco	Colombia	1992	IBF
Yuri Arbachakov	Russia	1992-	WBC
Aquiles Guzman	Venezuela	1992	WBA
Pichit Sitbangprachan	Thailand	1992-	IBF
David Griman	Venezuela	1992-	WBA
Jacob Matlala	S Africa	1993-	WBO

S. Flyweight (115 lbs)

Title Holder	Birthplace	Tenure	Status
Rafael Orono	Venezuela	1980-1981	WBC
Chul-Ho Kim	S Korea	1981-1982	WBC
Gustavo Ballas	Argentine	1981	WBA
Rafael Pedroza	Panama	1981-1982	WBA
Jiro Watanabe*	Japan	1982-1984	WBA
Rafael Orono	Venezuela	1982-1983	WBC
Payao Poontarat	Thailand	1983-1984	WBC
Joo-Do Chun	S Korea	1983-1985	IBF
Jiro Watanabe	Japan	1984-1986	WBC
Elly Pical	Indonesia	1985-1986	IBF
Kaosai Galaxy*	Thailand	1984-1991	WBA
Cesar Polanco	Dom Republic	1986	IBF
Gilberto Roman	Mexico	1986-1987	WBC
Elly Pical*	Indonesia	1986-1987	IBF
Santos Laciar	Argentine	1987	WBC
Tae-Il Chang	S Korea	1987	IBF
Jesus Rojas	Colombia	1987-1988	WBC
Elly Pical	Indonesia	1987-1989	IBF
Gilberto Roman	Mexico	1988-1989	WBC
Jose Ruiz	Puerto Rico	1989-1992	WBO
Juan Polo Perez	Colombia	1989-1990	IBF
Nana Yaw Konadu	Ghana	1989-1990	WBC
Sung-Il Moon	S Korea	1990-	WBC
Robert Quiroga	USA	1990-1993	IBF
Jose Quirino	Mexico	1992	WBO
Katsuya Onizuka	Japan	1992-	WBA
Johnny Bredahl	Denmark	1992-	WBO
Julio Cesar Borboa	Mexico	1993-	IBF

Bantamweight (118 lbs)

Title Holder	Birthplace	Tenure	Status
George Dixon*	Canada	1890-1892	
Billy Plimmer	England	1892-1895	
Pedlar Palmer	England	1895-1899	
Terry McGovern*	USA	1899-1900	
Dan Dougherty	USA	1900-1901	
Harry Forbes	USA	1901-1903	
Frankie Neil	USA	1903-1904	
Joe Bowker*	England	1904-1905	
Jimmy Walsh*	USA	1905-1907	
Owen Moran*	England	1907	GB

Title Holder	Birthplace	Tenure	Status
Johnny Coulon	Canada	1908-1909	USA
Monte Attell	USA	1909-1910	CALIF
Johnny Coulon	Canada	1909-1911	LOUIS
Frankie Conley	Italy	1910-1911	CALIF
Digger Stanley	England	1910-1912	GB/IBU
Johnny Coulon	Canada	1911-1914	USA
Charles Ledoux	France	1912-1913	GB/IBU
Eddie Campi	USA	1913-1914	GB/IBU
Kid Williams	Denmark	1914	GB/IBU
Kid Williams	Denmark	1914-1917	
Pete Herman	USA	1917-1920	
Joe Lynch	USA	1920-1921	
Pete Herman	USA	1921	
Johnny Buff	USA	1921-1922	
Joe Lynch	USA	1922-1923	
Joe Lynch	USA	1923-1924	NBA
Abe Goldstein	USA	1923-1924	NY
Abe Goldstein	USA	1924	
Eddie Martin	USA	1924-1925	
Charlie Rosenberg*	USA	1925-1927	
Bud Taylor*	USA	1927-1928	NBA
Teddy Baldock	England	1927	GB
Willie Smith*	S Africa	1927-1929	GB
Bushy Graham*	Italy	1928-1929	NY
Al Brown	Panama	1929-1931	NY/IBU
Pete Sanstol	Norway	1931	NBA
Al Brown	Panama	1931-1934	
Sixto Escobar	Puerto Rico	1934-1935	NBA
Al Brown	Panama	1934-1935	NY/IBU
Baltazar Sangchilli	Spain	1935-1936	NY/IBU
Lou Salica	USA	1935	NBA
Sixto Escobar	Puerto Rico	1935-1936	NBA
Tony Marino	USA	1936	NY/IBU
Sixto Escobar	Puerto Rico	1936-1937	
Harry Jeffra	USA	1937-1938	
Sixto Escobar*	Puerto Rico	1938-1939	
Lou Salica	USA	1940-1942	
Manuel Ortiz	USA	1942-1947	
Harold Dade	USA	1947	
Manuel Ortiz	USA	1947-1950	
Vic Toweel	S Africa	1950-1952	
Jimmy Carruthers*	Australia	1952-1954	
Robert Cohen	Algeria	1954-1956	NY/EBU
Raton Macias	Mexico	1955-1957	NBA
Mario D'Agata	Italy	1956-1957	NY/EBU
Alphonse Halimi	Algeria	1957	NY/EBU
Alphonse Halimi	Algeria	1957-1959	
Joe Becerra*	Mexico	1959-1960	
Alphonse Halimi	Algeria	1960-1961	EBU
Eder Jofre	Brazil	1960-1962	NBA
Johnny Caldwell	Ireland	1961-1962	EBU
Eder Jofre	Brazil	1962-1965	
Fighting Harada	Japan	1965-1968	
Lionel Rose	Australia	1968-1969	
Ruben Olivares	Mexico	1969-1970	
Chuchu Castillo	Mexico	1970-1971	
Ruben Olivares	Mexico	1971-1972	
Rafael Herrera	Mexico	1972	
Enrique Pinder	Panama	1972	
Enrique Pinder	Panama	1972-1973	WBC
Romeo Anaya	Mexico	1973	WBA
Rafael Herrera	Mexico	1973-1974	WBC
Arnold Taylor	S Africa	1973-1974	WBA
Soo-Hwan Hong	S Korea	1974-1975	WBA
Rodolfo Martinez	Mexico	1974-1976	WBC
Alfonso Zamora	Mexico	1975-1977	WBA
Carlos Zarate	Mexico	1976-1979	WBC
Jorge Lujan	Panama	1977-1980	WBA
Lupe Pintor*	Mexico	1979-1983	WBC
Julian Solis	Puerto Rico	1980	WBA
Jeff Chandler	USA	1980-1984	WBA

Title Holder	Birthplace	Tenure	Status
Albert Davila*	USA	1983-1985	WBC
Richard Sandoval	USA	1984-1986	WBA
Satoshi Shingaki	Japan	1984-1985	IBF
Jeff Fenech*	Australia	1985-1987	IBF
Daniel Zaragoza	Mexico	1985	WBC
Miguel Lora	Colombia	1985-1988	WBC
Gaby Canizales	USA	1986	WBA
Bernardo Pinango*	Venezuela	1986-1987	WBA
Takuya Muguruma	Japan	1987	WBA
Kelvin Seabrooks	USA	1987-1988	IBF
Chan-Yung Park	S Korea	1987	WBA
Wilfredo Vasquez	Puerto Rico	1987-1988	WBA
Kaokor Galaxy	Thailand	1988	WBA
Orlando Canizales	USA	1988-	IBF
Sung-Il Moon	S Korea	1988-1989	WBA
Raul Perez	Mexico	1988-1991	WBC
Israel Contrerras*	Venezuela	1989-1991	WBO
Kaokor Galaxy	Thailand	1989	WBA
Luisito Espinosa	Philippines	1989-1991	WBA
Greg Richardson	USA	1991	WBC
Gaby Canizales	USA	1991	WBO
Duke McKenzie	England	1991-1992	WBO
Joichiro Tatsuyushi*	Japan	1991-1992	WBC
Israel Contrerras	Venezuela	1991-1992	WBA
Eddie Cook	USA	1992	WBA
Victor Rabanales	Mexico	1992-1993	WBC
Rafael del Valle	Puerto Rico	1992-	WBO
Jorge Eliecer Julio	Colombia	1992-	WBA
Il-Jung Byun	S Korea	1993-	WBC

S. Bantamweight (122 lbs)

Title Holder	Birthplace	Tenure	Status
Jack Kid Wolfe*	USA	1922-1923	NY
Rigoberto Riasco	Panama	1976	WBC
Royal Kobayashi	Japan	1976	WBC
Dong-Kyun Yum	S Korea	1976-1977	WBC
Wilfredo Gomez*	Puerto Rico	1977-1983	WBC
Soo-Hwan Hong	S Korea	1977-1978	WBA
Ricardo Cardona	Colombia	1978-1980	WBA
Leo Randolph	USA	1980	WBA
Sergio Palma	Argentine	1980-1982	WBA
Leonardo Cruz	Dom Republic	1982-1984	WBA
Jaime Garza	USA	1983-1984	WBC
Bobby Berna	Philippines	1983-1984	IBF
Loris Stecca	Italy	1984	WBA
Seung-In Suh	S Korea	1984-1985	IBF
Victor Callejas*	Puerto Rico	1984-1986	WBA
Juan Meza	Mexico	1984-1985	WBC
Ji-Won Kim*	S Korea	1985-1986	IBF
Lupe Pintor	Mexico	1985-1986	WBC
Samart Payakarun	Thailand	1986-1987	WBC
Louie Espinosa	USA	1987	WBA
Seung-Hoon Lee*	S Korea	1987-1988	IBF
Jeff Fenech*	Australia	1987-1988	WBC
Julio Gervacio	Dom Republic	1987-1988	WBA
Bernardo Pinango	Venezuela	1988	WBA
Daniel Zaragoza	Mexico	1988-1990	WBC
Jose Sanabria	Venezuela	1988-1989	IBF
Juan J. Estrada	Mexico	1988-1989	WBA
Fabrice Benichou	Spain	1989-1990	IBF
Kenny Mitchell	USA	1989	WBO
Valerio Nati	Italy	1989-1990	WBO
Jesus Salud*	USA	1989-1990	WBA
Welcome Ncita	S Africa	1990-1992	IBF
Paul Banke	USA	1990	WBC
Orlando Fernandez	Puerto Rico	1990-1991	WBO
Luis Mendoza	Colombia	1990-1991	WBA
Pedro Decima	Argentine	1990-1991	WBC
Kiyoshi Hatanaka	Japan	1991	WBC
Jesse Benavides	USA	1991-1992	WBO
Daniel Zaragoza	Mexico	1991-1992	WBC
Raul Perez	Mexico	1991-1992	WBA

Title Holder	Birthplace	Tenure	Status
Thierry Jacob	France	1992	WBC
Wilfredo Vasquez	Puerto Rico	1992-	WBA
Tracy Harris Patterson	USA	1992-	WBC
Duke McKenzie	England	1992-1993	WBO
Kennedy McKinney	USA	1992-	IBF
Daniel Jimenez	Puerto Rico	1993-	WBO

Featherweight (126 lbs)

Title Holder	Birthplace	Tenure	Status
Billy Murphy	New Zealand	1890	AUST
Young Griffo*	Australia	1890-1891	AUST
George Dixon	Canada	1891-1892	USA
George Dixon	Canada	1892-1897	
Solly Smith	USA	1897-1898	
Solly Smith	USA	1898	USA
Ben Jordan	England	1898-1899	GB
Dave Sullivan	Ireland	1898	USA
George Dixon	Canada	1899-1900	USA
George Dixon	Canada	1899-1900	
Terry McGovern	USA	1900-1901	
Young Corbett II*	USA	1901-1903	
Abe Attell	USA	1903-1904	
Tommy Sullivan*	USA	1904-1905	
Abe Attell	USA	1906-1912	
Abe Attell	USA	1912	USA
Jim Driscoll*	Wales	1912-1913	GB/IBU
Johnny Kilbane	USA	1912-1913	USA
Johnny Kilbane	USA	1913-1922	
Johnny Kilbane	USA	1922-1923	NBA
Johnny Dundee*	Italy	1922-1923	NY
Eugene Criqui	France	1923	
Johnny Dundee*	Italy	1923-1924	
Kid Kaplan*	Russia	1925-1926	
Honeyboy Finnegan	USA	1926-1927	MASS
Benny Bass	Russia	1927-1928	NBA
Tony Canzoneri	USA	1927-1928	NY
Tony Canzoneri	USA	1928	
Andre Routis	France	1928-1929	
Bat Battalino*	USA	1929-1932	
Tommy Paul	USA	1932-1933	NBA
Kid Chocolate*	Cuba	1932-1933	NY
Freddie Miller	USA	1933-1936	NBA
Baby Arizmendi	Mexico	1934-1935	NY
Baby Arizmendi	Mexico	1935-1936	CALIF
Petey Sarron	USA	1936-1937	NBA
Henry Armstrong*	USA	1936-1937	CALIF
Mike Belloise	USA	1936	NY
Maurice Holtzer*	France	1937-1938	IBU
Henry Armstrong*	USA	1937-1938	NBA/NY/CALIF
Leo Rodak	USA	1938-1939	NBA
Joey Archibald	USA	1938-1939	NY
Joey Archibald	USA	1939-1940	
Joey Archibald	USA	1940	NY
Jimmy Perrin	USA	1940	LOUIS
Petey Scalzo	USA	1940-1941	NBA
Harry Jeffra	USA	1940-1941	NY
Joey Archibald	USA	1941	NY
Richie Lemos	USA	1941	NBA
Chalky Wright	Mexico	1941-1942	NY
Harry Jeffra	USA	1941-1942	MARY
Jackie Wilson	USA	1941-1943	NBA
Willie Pep	USA	1942-1946	NY
Jackie Callura	Canada	1943	NBA
Phil Terranova	USA	1943-1944	NBA
Sal Bartolo	USA	1944-1946	NBA
Willie Pep	USA	1946-1948	
Sandy Saddler	USA	1948-1949	
Willie Pep	USA	1949-1950	
Sandy Saddler*	USA	1950-1957	
Hogan Kid Bassey	Nigeria	1957-1959	
Davey Moore	USA	1959-1963	
Sugar Ramos	Cuba	1963-1964	

Title Holder	Birthplace	Tenure	Status
Vicente Saldivar*	Mexico	1964-1967	
Raul Rojas	USA	1967-1968	WBA
Howard Winstone	Wales	1968	WBC
Jose Legra	Cuba	1968-1969	WBC
Shozo Saijyo	Japan	1968-1971	WBA
Johnny Famechon	France	1969-1970	WBC
Vicente Saldivar	Mexico	1970	WBC
Kuniaki Shibata	Japan	1970-1972	WBC
Antonio Gomez	Venezuela	1971-1972	WBA
Clemente Sanchez	Mexico	1972	WBC
Ernesto Marcel*	Panama	1972-1974	WBA
Jose Legra	Cuba	1972-1973	WBC
Eder Jofre*	Brazil	1973-1974	WBC
Ruben Olivares	Mexico	1974	WBA
Bobby Chacon	USA	1974-1975	WBC
Alexis Arguello*	Nicaragua	1974-1977	WBA
Ruben Olivares	Mexico	1975	WBC
David Kotey	Ghana	1975-1976	WBC
Danny Lopez	USA	1976-1980	WBC
Rafael Ortega	Panama	1977	WBA
Cecilio Lastra	Spain	1977-1978	WBA
Eusebio Pedroza	Panama	1978-1985	WBA
Salvador Sanchez*	Mexico	1980-1982	WBC
Juan Laporte	Puerto Rico	1982-1984	WBC
Min-Keun Chung	S Korea	1984-1985	IBF
Wilfredo Gomez	Puerto Rico	1984	WBC
Azumah Nelson*	Ghana	1984-1987	WBC
Barry McGuigan	Ireland	1985-1986	WBA
Ki-Yung Chung	S Korea	1985-1986	IBF
Steve Cruz	USA	1986-1987	WBA
Antonio Rivera	Puerto Rico	1986-1987	IBF
Antonio Esparragoza	Venezuela	1987-1991	WBF
Calvin Grove	USA	1988	IBF
Jeff Fenech*	Australia	1988-1989	WBC
Jorge Paez*	Mexico	1988-1990	IBF
Maurizio Stecca	Italy	1989-1992	WBO
Louie Espinosa	USA	1989-1990	WBO
Jorge Paez*	Mexico	1990-1991	IBF/WBO
Marcos Villasana	Mexico	1990-1991	WBC
Kyun-Yung Park	S Korea	1991-	WBA
Troy Dorsey	USA	1991	IBF
Maurizio Stecca	Italy	1991-1992	WBO
Manuel Medina	Mexico	1991-1993	IBF
Paul Hodkinson	England	1991-1993	WBC
Colin McMillan	England	1992	WBO
Ruben Palacio*	Colombia	1992-1993	WBO
Tom Johnson	USA	1993-	IBF
Steve Robinson	Wales	1993-	WBO
Gregorio Vargas	Mexico	1993-	WBC

S. Featherweight (130 lbs)

Title Holder	Birthplace	Tenure	Status
Johnny Dundee	Italy	1921-1923	NY
Jack Bernstein	USA	1923	NBA/NY
Johnny Dundee	Italy	1923-1924	NBA/NY
Kid Sullivan	USA	1924-1925	NBA/NY
Mike Ballerino	USA	1925	NBA/NY
Tod Morgan	USA	1925-1929	NBA/NY
Benny Bass	Russia	1929	NBA/NY
Benny Bass	Russia	1929-1931	NBA
Kid Chocolate	Cuba	1931-1933	NBA
Frankie Klick*	USA	1933-1934	NBA
Sandy Saddler*	USA	1949-1950	OHIO
Harold Gomes	USA	1959-1960	NBA
Flash Elorde	Philippines	1960-1967	NBA
Yoshiaki Numata	Japan	1967	WBA
Hiroshi Kobayashi	Japan	1967-1971	WBA
Rene Barrientos	Philippines	1969-1970	WBC
Yoshiaki Numata	Japan	1970-1971	WBC
Alfredo Marcano	Venezuela	1971-1972	WBA
Ricardo Arredondo	Mexico	1971-1974	WBC
Ben Villaflor	Philippines	1972-1973	WBA
Kuniaki Shibata	Japan	1973	WBA
Ben Villaflor	Philippines	1973-1976	WBA
Kuniaki Shibata	Japan	1974-1975	WBC
Alfredo Escalera	Puerto Rico	1975-1978	WBC
Sam Serrano	Puerto Rico	1976-1980	WBA
Alexis Arguello*	Nicaragua	1978-1980	WBC
Yasutsune Uehara	Japan	1980-1981	WBA
Rafael Limon	Mexico	1980-1981	WBC
Cornelius Boza-Edwards	Uganda	1981	WBC
Sam Serrano	Puerto Rico	1981-1983	WBA
Roland Navarrete	Philippines	1981-1982	WBC
Rafael Limon	Mexico	1982	WBC
Bobby Chacon*	USA	1982-1983	WBC
Roger Mayweather	USA	1983-1984	WBA
Hector Camacho*	Puerto Rico	1983-1984	WBC
Rocky Lockridge	USA	1984-1985	WBA
Hwan-Kil Yuh	S Korea	1984-1985	IBF
Julio Cesar Chavez*	Mexico	1984-1987	WBC
Lester Ellis	England	1985	IBF
Wilfredo Gomez	Puerto Rico	1985-1986	WBA
Barry Michael	England	1985-1987	IBF
Alfredo Layne	Panama	1986	WBA
Brian Mitchell*	S Africa	1986-1991	WBA
Rocky Lockridge	USA	1987-1988	IBF
Azumah Nelson	Ghana	1988-	WBC
Tony Lopez	USA	1988-1989	IBF
Juan Molina*	Puerto Rico	1989	WBO
Juan Molina	Puerto Rico	1989-1990	IBF
Kamel Bou Ali	Tunisia	1989-1992	WBO
Tony Lopez	USA	1990-1991	IBF
Joey Gamache*	USA	1991	WBA
Brian Mitchell*	S Africa	1991-1992	IBF
Genaro Hernandez	USA	1991-	WBA
Juan Molina	Puerto Rico	1992-	IBF
Daniel Londas	France	1992	WBO
Jimmy Bredahl	Denmark	1992-	WBO

Lightweight (135 lbs)

Title Holder	Birthplace	Tenure	Status
Jack McAuliffe*	Ireland	1890-1895	USA
George Lavigne	USA	1896-1899	
Frank Erne	Switzerland	1899-1902	
Joe Gans*	USA	1902-1904	
Jimmy Britt	USA	1904-1905	
Battling Nelson	Denmark	1905-1906	
Joe Gans	USA	1906-1908	
Battling Nelson	Denmark	1908-1910	
Ad Wolgast	USA	1910-1912	
Willie Ritchie	USA	1912-1914	
Freddie Welsh	Wales	1914-1917	
Benny Leonard*	USA	1917-1925	
Jimmy Goodrich	USA	1925	NY
Rocky Kansas	USA	1925-1926	
Sammy Mandell	USA	1926-1930	
Al Singer	USA	1930	
Tony Canzoneri	USA	1930-1933	
Barney Ross*	USA	1933-1935	
Tony Canzoneri	USA	1935-1936	
Lou Ambers	USA	1936-1938	
Henry Armstrong	USA	1938-1939	
Lou Ambers	USA	1939-1940	
Sammy Angott*	USA	1940-1941	NBA
Lew Jenkins	USA	1940-1941	NY
Sammy Angott*	USA	1941-1942	
Beau Jack	USA	1942-1943	NY
Slugger White	USA	1943	MARY
Bob Montgomery	USA	1943	NY
Sammy Angott	USA	1943-1944	NBA
Beau Jack	USA	1943-1944	NY
Bob Montgomery	USA	1944-1947	NY
Juan Zurita	Mexico	1944-1945	NBA
Ike Williams	USA	1945-1947	NBA

Title Holder	Birthplace	Tenure	Status	Title Holder	Birthplace	Tenure	Status
Ike Williams	USA	1947-1951		Duilio Loi	Italy	1960-1962	NBA
Jimmy Carter	USA	1951-1952		Eddie Perkins	USA	1962	NBA
Lauro Salas	Mexico	1952		Duilio Loi*	Italy	1962-1963	NBA
Jimmy Carter	USA	1952-1954		Roberto Cruz	Philippines	1963	WBA
Paddy de Marco	USA	1954		Eddie Perkins	USA	1963-1965	WBA
Jimmy Carter	USA	1954-1955		Carlos Hernandez	Venezuela	1965-1966	WBA
Wallace Bud Smith	USA	1955-1956		Sandro Lopopolo	Italy	1966-1967	WBA
Joe Brown	USA	1956-1962		Paul Fujii	Hawaii	1967-1968	WBA
Carlos Ortiz	Puerto Rico	1962-1965		Nicolino Loche	Argentine	1968-1972	WBA
Ismael Laguna	Panama	1965		Pedro Adigue	Philippines	1968-1970	WBC
Carlos Oritz	Puerto Rico	1965-1968		Bruno Arcari*	Italy	1970-1974	WBC
Carlos Teo Cruz	Dom Republic	1968-1969		Alfonso Frazer	Panama	1972	WBA
Mando Ramos	USA	1969-1970		Antonio Cervantes	Colombia	1972-1976	WBA
Ismael Laguna	Panama	1970		Perico Fernandez	Spain	1974-1975	WBC
Ken Buchanan	Scotland	1970-1971		Saensak Muangsurin	Thailand	1975-1976	WBC
Ken Buchanan	Scotland	1971-1972	WBA	Wilfred Benitez*	USA	1976-1977	WBA
Pedro Carrasco	Spain	1971-1972	WBC	Miguel Velasquez	Spain	1976	WBC
Mando Ramos	USA	1972	WBC	Saensak Muangsurin	Thailand	1976-1978	WBC
Roberto Duran	Panama	1972-1978	WBA	Antonio Cervantes	Colombia	1977-1980	WBA
Chango Carmona	Mexico	1972	WBC	Wilfred Benitez*	USA	1977	NY
Rodolfo Gonzalez	Mexico	1972-1974	WBC	Sang-Hyun Kim	S Korea	1978-1980	WBC
Guts Ishimatsu	Japan	1974-1976	WBC	Saoul Mamby	USA	1980-1982	WBC
Esteban de Jesus	Puerto Rico	1976-1978	WBC	Aaron Pryor*	USA	1980-1983	WBA
Roberto Duran*	Panama	1978-1979		Leroy Haley	USA	1982-1983	WBC
Jim Watt	Scotland	1979-1981	WBC	Bruce Curry	USA	1983-1984	WBC
Ernesto Espana	Venezuela	1979-1980	WBA	Johnny Bumphus	USA	1984	WBA
Hilmer Kenty	USA	1980-1981	WBA	Bill Costello	USA	1984-1985	WBC
Sean O'Grady*	USA	1981	WBA	Gene Hatcher	USA	1984-1985	IBF
Alexis Arguello*	Nicaragua	1981-1983	WBC	Aaron Pryor*	USA	1984-1986	IBF
Claude Noel	Trinidad	1981	WBA	Ubaldo Sacco	Argentine	1985-1986	WBA
Arturo Frias	USA	1981-1982	WBA	Lonnie Smith	USA	1985-1986	WBC
Ray Mancini	USA	1982-1984	WBA	Patrizio Oliva	Italy	1986-1987	WBA
Edwin Rosario	Puerto Rico	1983-1984	WBC	Gary Hinton	USA	1986	IBF
Charlie Brown	USA	1984	IBF	Rene Arredondo	Mexico	1986	WBC
Harry Arroyo	USA	1984-1985	IBF	Tsuyoshi Hamada	Japan	1986-1987	WBC
Livingstone Bramble	USA	1984-1986	WBA	Joe Manley	USA	1986-1987	IBF
Jose Luis Ramirez	Mexico	1984-1985	WBC	Terry Marsh*	England	1987	IBF
Jimmy Paul	USA	1985-1986	IBF	Juan M. Coggi	Argentine	1987-1990	WBA
Hector Camacho*	Puerto Rico	1985-1987	WBC	Rene Arredondo	Mexico	1987	WBC
Edwin Rosario	Puerto Rico	1986-1987	WBA	Roger Mayweather	USA	1987-1989	WBC
Greg Haugen	USA	1986-1987	IBF	James McGirt	USA	1988	IBF
Vinnie Pazienza	USA	1987-1988	IBF	Meldrick Taylor	USA	1988-1990	IBF
Jose Luis Ramirez	Mexico	1987-1988	WBC	Hector Camacho	Puerto Rico	1989-1991	WBO
Julio Cesar Chavez*	Mexico	1987-1988	WBA	Julio Cesar Chavez*	Mexico	1989-1990	WBC
Greg Haugen	USA	1988-1989	IBF	Julio Cesar Chavez*	Mexico	1990-199	IBF/WBC
Julio Cesar Chavez*	Mexico	1988-1989	WBA/WBC	Loreto Garza	USA	1990-1991	WBA
Maurizio Aceves	Mexico	1989-1990	WBO	Greg Haugen*	USA	1991	WBO
Pernell Whitaker*	USA	1989	IBF	Hector Camacho*	Puerto Rico	1991-1992	WBO
Edwin Rosario	Puerto Rico	1989-1990	WBA	Edwin Rosario	Puerto Rico	1991-1992	WBA
Pernell Whitaker*	USA	1989-1990	IBF/WBC	Julio Cesar Chavez	Mexico	1991-	WBC
Juan Nazario	Puerto Rico	1990	WBA	Rafael Pineda	Colombia	1991-1992	IBF
Pernell Whitaker*	USA	1990-1992	IBF/WBC/WBA	Akinobu Hiranaka	Japan	1992	WBA
Dingaan Thobela*	S Africa	1990-1992	WBO	Carlos Gonzalez	Mexico	1992-1993	WBO
Joey Gamache	USA	1992	WBA	Pernell Whitaker*	USA	1992-1993	IBF
Giovanni Parisi	Italy	1992-	WBO	Morris East	Philippines	1992-1993	WBA
Tony Lopez	USA	1992-1993	WBA	Juan M. Coggi	Argentine	1993-	WBA
Miguel Gonzalez	Mexico	1992-	WBC	Charles Murray	USA	1993-	IBF
Fred Pendleton	USA	1993-	IBF	Zack Padilla	USA	1993-	WBO
Dingaan Thobela	S Africa	1993-	WBA				

L. Welterweight (140 lbs)

Mushy Callahan	USA	1926-1929	NBA/NY
Mushy Callahan	USA	1929-1930	NBA
Jackie Kid Berg	England	1930-1931	NBA
Tony Canzoneri	USA	1931-1932	NBA
Johnny Jadick	USA	1932-1933	NBA
Battling Shaw	Mexico	1933	NBA
Tony Canzoneri	USA	1933	NBA
Barney Ross*	USA	1933-1935	NBA
Tippy Larkin*	USA	1946-1947	MASS/NY
Carlos Oritz	Puerto Rico	1959-1960	NBA

Welterweight (147 lbs)

Mysterious Billy Smith	USA	1892-1894	
Tommy Ryan*	USA	1894-1898	
Mysterious Billy Smith	USA	1898-1900	
Matty Matthews	USA	1900-1901	
Eddie Connolly	USA	1900	
Rube Ferns	USA	1900	
Matty Matthews	USA	1900-1901	
Joe Walcott	Barbados	1901-1904	
Dixie Kid*	USA	1904-1905	
Honey Mellody	USA	1906-1907	
Mike Twin Sullivan*	USA	1907	

Title Holder	Birthplace	Tenure	Status	Title Holder	Birthplace	Tenure	Status
Mike Twin Sullivan*	USA	1907-1908	CALIF	**Sugar Ray Leonard***	USA	1981-1982	
Frank Mantell	USA	1907-1908	OHIO	Don Curry	USA	1983-1984	WBA
Harry Lewis	USA	1908-1910	OHIO	Milton McCrory	USA	1983-1985	WBC
Jimmy Gardner	USA	1908-1910	LOUIS	Don Curry	USA	1984-1985	WBA/IBF
Harry Lewis	USA	1910-1912	GB/FR	**Don Curry**	USA	1985-1986	
Jimmy Clabby	USA	1910-1912	USA/AUSTR	**Lloyd Honeyghan**	Jamaica	1986	
Waldemar Holberg	Denmark	1914	AUSTR	Lloyd Honeyghan	Jamaica	1986-1987	WBC/IBF
Tom McCormick	Ireland	1914	AUSTR	Mark Breland	USA	1987	WBA
Matt Wells	England	1914-1915	AUSTR	Marlon Starling	USA	1987-1988	WBA
Mike Glover	USA	1915	USA	Jorge Vaca	Mexico	1987-1988	WBC
Jack Britton	USA	1915	USA	Lloyd Honeyghan	Jamaica	1988-1989	WBC
Ted Kid Lewis	England	1915-1916		Simon Brown	Jamaica	1988-1991	IBF
Jack Britton	USA	1916-1917		Tomas Molinares*	Colombia	1988	WBA
Ted Kid Lewis	England	1917-1919		Mark Breland	USA	1989-1990	WBA
Jack Britton	USA	1919-1922		Marlon Starling	USA	1989-1990	WBC
Mickey Walker	USA	1922-1926		Genaro Leon*	Mexico	1989	WBO
Pete Latzo	USA	1926-1927		Manning Galloway	USA	1989-1993	WBO
Joe Dundee	Italy	1927-1929		Aaron Davis	USA	1990-1991	WBA
Joe Dundee	Italy	1929	NY	Maurice Blocker	USA	1990	WBC
Jackie Fields	USA	1929	NBA	Meldrick Taylor	USA	1991-1992	WBA
Jackie Fields	USA	1929-1930		Simon Brown	Jamaica	1991	WBC/IBF
Young Jack Thompson	USA	1930		Simon Brown	Jamaica	1991	WBC
Tommy Freeman	USA	1930-1931		Maurice Blocker	USA	1991-1993	IBF
Young Jack Thompson	USA	1931		James McGirt	USA	1991-1993	WBC
Lou Brouillard	Canada	1931-1932		Crisanto Espana	Venezuela	1992-	WBA
Jackie Fields	USA	1932-1933		Gert Bo Jacobsen	Denmark	1993-	WBO
Young Corbett III	Italy	1933		Pernell Whitaker	USA	1993-	WBC
Jimmy McLarnin	Ireland	1933-1934		Felix Trinidad	Puerto Rico	1993-	IBF
Barney Ross	USA	1934					
Jimmy McLarnin	Ireland	1934-1935		**L. Middleweight (154 lbs)**			
Barney Ross	USA	1935-1938		Denny Moyer	USA	1962-1963	WBA
Henry Armstrong	USA	1938-1940		Ralph Dupas	USA	1963	WBA
Fritzie Zivic	USA	1940-1941		Sandro Mazzinghi	Italy	1963-1965	WBA
Red Cochrane	USA	1941-1946		Nino Benvenuti	Italy	1965-1966	WBA
Marty Servo*	USA	1946		Ki-Soo Kim	S Korea	1966-1968	WBA
Sugar Ray Robinson*	USA	1946-1951		Sandro Mazzinghi*	Italy	1968-1969	WBA
Johnny Bratton	USA	1951	NBA	Freddie Little	USA	1969-1970	WBA
Kid Gavilan	Cuba	1951-1952	NBA/NY	Carmelo Bossi	Italy	1970-1971	WBA
Kid Gavilan	Cuba	1952-1954		Koichi Wajima	Japan	1971-1974	WBA
Johnny Saxton	USA	1954-1955		Oscar Albarado	USA	1974-1975	WBA
Tony de Marco	USA	1955		Koichi Wajima	Japan	1975	WBA
Carmen Basilio	USA	1955-1956		Miguel de Oliveira	Brazil	1975	WBC
Johnny Saxton	USA	1956		Jae-Do Yuh	S Korea	1975-1976	WBA
Carmen Basilio*	USA	1956-1957		Elisha Obed	Bahamas	1975-1976	WBC
Virgil Akins	USA	1958		Koichi Wajima	Japan	1976	WBA
Don Jordan	Dom Republic	1958-1960		Jose Duran	Spain	1976	WBA
Benny Kid Paret	Cuba	1960-1961		Eckhard Dagge	Germany	1976-1977	WBC
Emile Griffith	Virgin Islands	1961		Miguel Castellini	Argentine	1976-1977	WBA
Benny Kid Paret	Cuba	1961-1962		Eddie Gazo	Nicaragua	1977-1978	WBA
Emile Griffith	Virgin Islands	1962-1963		Rocky Mattioli	Italy	1977-1979	WBC
Luis Rodriguez	Cuba	1963		Masashi Kudo	Japan	1978-1979	WBA
Emile Griffith*	Virgin Islands	1963-1966		Maurice Hope	Antigua	1979-1981	WBC
Curtis Cokes	USA	1966-1967	WBA	Ayub Kalule	Uganda	1979-1981	WBA
Charley Shipes	USA	1966-1967	CALIF	Wilfred Benitez	USA	1981-1982	WBC
Curtis Cokes	USA	1967-1969		Sugar Ray Leonard*	USA	1981	WBA
Jose Napoles	Cuba	1969-1970		Tadashi Mihara	Japan	1981-1982	WBA
Billy Backus	USA	1970-1971		Davey Moore	USA	1982-1983	WBA
Jose Napoles	Cuba	1971-1975		Thomas Hearns*	USA	1982-1986	WBC
Jose Napoles	Cuba	1972-1974	WBA/WBC	Roberto Duran*	Panama	1983-1984	WBA
Hedgemon Lewis	USA	1972-1974	NY	Mark Medal	USA	1984	IBF
Jose Napoles	Cuba	1974-1975		Mike McCallum*	Jamaica	1984-1987	WBA
Jose Napoles	Cuba	1975	WBC	Carlos Santos*	Puerto Rico	1984-1986	IBF
Angel Espada	Puerto Rico	1975-1976	WBA	Buster Drayton	USA	1986-1987	IBF
John H. Stracey	England	1975-1976	WBC	Duane Thomas	USA	1986-1987	WBC
Carlos Palomino	Mexico	1976-1979	WBC	Matthew Hilton	Canada	1987-1988	IBF
Pipino Cuevas	Mexico	1976-1980	WBA	Lupe Aquino	Mexico	1987	WBC
Wilfred Benitez	USA	1979	WBC	Gianfranco Rosi	Italy	1987-1988	WBC
Sugar Ray Leonard	USA	1979-1980	WBC	Julian Jackson*	Virgin Islands	1987-1990	WBA
Roberto Duran	Panama	1980	WBC	Don Curry	USA	1988-1989	WBC
Thomas Hearns	USA	1980-1981	WBA	Robert Hines	USA	1988-1989	IBF
Sugar Ray Leonard*	USA	1980-1981	WBC	John David Jackson	USA	1988-	WBO

245

Title Holder	Birthplace	Tenure	Status
Darrin van Horn	USA	1989	IBF
Rene Jacqot	France	1989	WBC
John Mugabi	Uganda	1989-1990	WBC
Gianfranco Rosi	Italy	1989-	IBF
Terry Norris	USA	1990-	WBC
Gilbert Dele	France	1991	WBA
Vinnie Pazienza*	USA	1991-1992	WBA
Julio Cesar Vasquez	Argentine	1992-	WBA

Middleweight (160 lbs)

Title Holder	Birthplace	Tenure
Nonpareil Jack Dempsey	Ireland	1890-1891
Bob Fitzsimmons*	England	1891-1897
Kid McCoy*	USA	1897-1898
Tommy Ryan*	USA	1898-1907
Stanley Ketchel	USA	1907-1908

Title Holder	Birthplace	Tenure	Status
Billy Papke	USA	1908	
Stanley Ketchel*	USA	1908-1910	
Billy Papke	USA	1911-1912	GB
Frank Mantell	USA	1912-1913	USA
Billy Papke	USA	1912-1913	IBU
Frank Klaus	USA	1913	IBU
George Chip	USA	1913-1914	USA
Eddie McGoorty	USA	1914	AUSTR
Jeff Smith	USA	1914	AUSTR
Al McCoy	USA	1914-1917	USA
Mick King	Australia	1914	AUSTR
Jeff Smith	USA	1914-1915	AUSTR
Les Darcy*	Australia	1915-1917	AUSTR
Mike O'Dowd	USA	1917-1920	
Johnny Wilson	USA	1920-1923	

Nigel Benn, WBC super-middleweight champion and former WBO boss of the middleweights   Les Clark

Title Holder	Birthplace	Tenure	Status
Bryan Downey	USA	1922	OHIO
Dave Rosenberg	USA	1922	NY
Jock Malone	USA	1922-1923	OHIO
Mike O'Dowd*	USA	1922-1923	NY
Lou Bogash*	USA	1923	NY
Harry Greb	USA	1923-1926	
Tiger Flowers	USA	1926	
Mickey Walker*	USA	1926-1931	
Gorilla Jones	USA	1931-1932	NBA
Marcel Thil	France	1932	NBA/IBU
Marcel Thil	France	1932-1937	IBU
Ben Jeby	USA	1933	NY
Gorilla Jones*	USA	1933	NBA
Lou Brouillard	Canada	1933	NY/NBA
Vince Dundee	USA	1933-1934	NY/NBA
Teddy Yarosz	USA	1934-1935	NY/NBA
Babe Risko	USA	1935-1936	NY/NBA
Freddie Steele	USA	1936-1937	NY/NBA
Freddie Steele	USA	1937-1938	NBA
Fred Apostoli	USA	1937-1938	IBU
Fred Apostoli	USA	1937-1939	NY
Edouard Tenet	France	1938	IBU
Al Hostak	USA	1938	NBA
Solly Krieger	USA	1938-1939	NBA
Al Hostak	USA	1939-1940	NBA
Ceferino Garcia	Philippines	1939-1940	NY
Ken Overlin	USA	1940-1941	NY
Tony Zale	USA	1940-1941	NBA
Billy Soose	USA	1941	NY
Tony Zale	USA	1941-1947	
Rocky Graziano	USA	1947-1948	
Tony Zale	USA	1948	
Marcel Cerdan	Algeria	1948-1949	
Jake la Motta	USA	1949-1950	
Jake la Motta	USA	1950-1951	NY/NBA
Sugar Ray Robinson	USA	1950-1951	PEN
Sugar Ray Robinson	USA	1951	
Randy Turpin	England	1951	
Sugar Ray Robinson*	USA	1951-1952	
Randy Turpin	England	1953	EBU
Carl Bobo Olson	Hawaii	1953-1955	
Sugar Ray Robinson	USA	1955-1957	
Gene Fullmer	USA	1957	
Sugar Ray Robinson	USA	1957	
Carmen Basilio	USA	1957-1958	
Sugar Ray Robinson	USA	1958-1959	
Sugar Ray Robinson	USA	1959-1960	NY/EBU
Gene Fullmer	USA	1959-1962	NBA
Paul Pender	USA	1960-1961	NY/EBU
Terry Downes	England	1961-1962	NY/EBU
Paul Pender*	USA	1962-1963	NY/EBU
Dick Tiger	Nigeria	1962-1963	NBA
Dick Tiger	Nigeria	1963	
Joey Giardello	USA	1963-1965	
Dick Tiger	Nigeria	1965-1966	
Emile Griffith	Virgin Islands	1966-1967	
Nino Benvenuti	Italy	1967	
Emile Griffith	Virgin Islands	1967-1968	
Nino Benvenuti	Italy	1968-1970	
Carlos Monzon*	Argentine	1970-1974	
Carlos Monzon*	Argentine	1974-1976	WBA
Rodrigo Valdez	Colombia	1974-1976	WBC
Carlos Monzon*	Argentine	1976-1977	
Rodrigo Valdez	Colombia	1977-1978	
Hugo Corro	Argentine	1978-1979	
Vito Antuofermo	Italy	1979-1980	
Alan Minter	England	1980	
Marvin Hagler	USA	1980-1987	
Marvin Hagler	USA	1987	WBC/IBF
Sugar Ray Leonard*	USA	1987	WBC
Frank Tate	USA	1987-1988	IBF

Title Holder	Birthplace	Tenure	Status
Sumbu Kalambay*	Zaire	1987-1989	WBA
Thomas Hearns	USA	1987-1988	WBC
Iran Barkley	USA	1988-1989	WBC
Michael Nunn	USA	1988-1991	IBF
Roberto Duran*	Panama	1989-1990	WBC
Doug de Witt	USA	1989-1990	WBO
Mike McCallum	Jamaica	1989-1991	WBA
Nigel Benn	England	1990	WBO
Chris Eubank*	England	1990-1991	WBO
Julian Jackson	Virgin Islands	1990-1993	WBC
James Toney*	USA	1991-1993	IBF
Gerald McClellan*	USA	1991-1993	WBO
Reggie Johnson	USA	1992-	WBA
Gerald McClellan	USA	1993-	WBC
Chris Pyatt	England	1993-	WBO
Roy Jones	USA	1993-	IBF

S. Middleweight (168 lbs)

Title Holder	Birthplace	Tenure	Status
Murray Sutherland	Scotland	1984	IBF
Chong-Pal Park*	S Korea	1984-1987	IBF
Chong-Pal Park	S Korea	1987-1988	WBA
Graciano Rocchigiani*	Germany	1988-1989	IBF
Fully Obelmejias	Venezuela	1988-1989	WBA
Sugar Ray Leonard*	USA	1988-1990	WBC
Thomas Hearns*	USA	1988-1991	WBO
In-Chul Baek	S Korea	1989-1990	WBA
Lindell Holmes	USA	1990-1991	IBF
Christophe Tiozzo	France	1990-1991	WBA
Mauro Galvano	Italy	1990-1992	WBC
Victor Cordoba	Panama	1991-1992	WBA
Darrin van Horn	USA	1991-1992	IBF
Chris Eubank	England	1991-	WBO
Iran Barkley	USA	1992-1993	IBF
Michael Nunn	USA	1992-	WBA
Nigel Benn	England	1992-	WBC
James Toney	USA	1993-	IBF

L. Heavyweight (175 lbs)

Title Holder	Birthplace	Tenure	Status
Jack Root	Austria	1903	USA
George Gardner	Ireland	1903	USA
Bob Fitzsimmons	England	1903-1905	
Jack O'Brien*	USA	1905-1912	
Jack Dillon	USA	1912-1916	
Battling Levinsky	USA	1916-1920	
Georges Carpentier	France	1920-1922	
Battling Siki	Senegal	1922-1923	
Mike McTigue	Ireland	1923-1925	
Paul Berlenbach	USA	1925-1926	
Jack Delaney*	Canada	1926-1927	
Jimmy Slattery	USA	1927	NBA
Tommy Loughran*	USA	1927	NY
Tommy Loughran*	USA	1927-1929	
Jimmy Slattery	USA	1930	NY
Maxie Rosenbloom	USA	1930-1933	NY
George Nichols	USA	1932	NBA
Bob Godwin	USA	1933	NBA
Maxie Rosenbloom	USA	1933-1934	
Bob Olin	USA	1934-1935	
John Henry Lewis*	USA	1935-1938	
Tiger Jack Fox	USA	1938-1939	NY
Melio Bettina	USA	1939	NY
Len Harvey	England	1939-1942	GB
Billy Conn*	USA	1939-1940	NY/NBA
Anton Christoforidis	Greece	1941	NBA
Gus Lesnevich	USA	1941-1946	NY/NBA
Freddie Mills	England	1942-1946	GB
Gus Lesnevich	USA	1946-1948	
Freddie Mills	England	1948-1950	
Joey Maxim	USA	1950-1952	
Archie Moore*	USA	1952-1961	
Archie Moore*	USA	1961-1962	NY/EBU

Title Holder	Birthplace	Tenure	Status
Harold Johnson	USA	1961-1962	NBA
Harold Johnson	USA	1962-1963	
Willie Pastrano	USA	1963-1965	
Jose Torres	Puerto Rico	1965-1966	
Dick Tiger	Nigeria	1966-1968	
Bob Foster*	USA	1968-1971	
Bob Foster*	USA	1971-1972	WBC
Vicente Rondon	Venezuela	1971-1972	WBA
Bob Foster*	USA	1972-1974	
John Conteh*	England	1974-1977	WBC
Victor Galindez	Argentine	1974-1978	WBA
Miguel Cuello	Argentine	1977-1978	WBC
Mate Parlov	Yugoslavia	1978	WBC
Mike Rossman	USA	1978-1979	WBA
Marvin Johnson	USA	1978-1979	WBC
Victor Galindez	Argentine	1979	WBA
Matt Saad Muhammad	USA	1979-1981	WBC
Marvin Johnson	USA	1979-1980	WBA
Mustafa Muhammad	USA	1980-1981	WBA
Michael Spinks	USA	1981-1983	WBA
Dwight Muhammad Qawi	USA	1981-1983	WBC
Michael Spinks*	USA	1983-1985	
J. B. Williamson	USA	1985-1986	WBC
Slobodan Kacar	Yugoslavia	1985-1986	IBF
Marvin Johnson	USA	1986-1987	WBA
Dennis Andries	Guyana	1986-1987	WBC
Bobby Czyz	USA	1986-1987	IBF
Thomas Hearns*	USA	1987	WBC
Leslie Stewart	Trinidad	1987	WBA
Virgil Hill	USA	1987-1991	WBA
Charles Williams	USA	1987-1993	IBF
Don Lalonde	Canada	1987-1988	WBC
Sugar Ray Leonard*	USA	1988	WBC
Michael Moorer*	USA	1988-1991	WBO
Dennis Andries	Guyana	1989	WBC
Jeff Harding	Australia	1989-1990	WBC
Dennis Andries	England	1990-1991	WBC
Thomas Hearns	USA	1991-1992	WBA
Leonzer Barber	USA	1991-	WBO
Jeff Harding	Australia	1991-	WBC
Iran Barkley*	USA	1992	WBA
Virgil Hill	USA	1992-	WBA
Henry Maske	Germany	1993-	IBF

Cruiserweight (190 lbs)

Title Holder	Birthplace	Tenure	Status
Marvin Camel	USA	1979-1980	WBC
Carlos de Leon	Puerto Rico	1980-1982	WBC
Ossie Ocasio	Puerto Rico	1982-1984	WBA
S. T. Gordon	USA	1982-1983	WBC
Marvin Camel	USA	1983-1984	IBF
Carlos de Leon	Puerto Rico	1983-1985	WBC
Lee Roy Murphy	USA	1984-1986	IBF
Piet Crous	S Africa	1984-1985	WBA
Alfonso Ratliff	USA	1985	WBC
Dwight Muhammad Qawi	USA	1985-1986	WBA
Bernard Benton	USA	1985-1986	WBC
Carlos de Leon	Puerto Rico	1986-1988	WBC
Rickey Parkey	USA	1986-1987	IBF
Evander Holyfield*	USA	1986-1987	WBA
Evander Holyfield*	USA	1987-1988	WBA/IBF
Evander Holyfield*	USA	1988	
Taoufik Belbouli*	France	1989	WBA
Carlos de Leon	Puerto Rico	1989-1990	WBC
Glenn McCrory	England	1989-1990	IBF
Robert Daniels	USA	1989-1991	WBA
Boone Pultz	USA	1989-1990	WBO
Jeff Lampkin*	USA	1990-1991	IBF
Magne Havnaa*	Norway	1990-1992	WBO
Masimilliano Duran	Italy	1990-1991	WBC
Bobby Czyz	USA	1991-	WBA
Anaclet Wamba	France	1991-	WBC

Title Holder	Birthplace	Tenure	Status
James Warring	USA	1991-1992	IBF
Tyrone Booze	USA	1992-1993	WBO
Al Cole	USA	1992-	IBF
Markus Bott	Germany	1993	WBO
Nestor Giovannini	Argentine	1993-	WBO

Heavyweight (190 lbs +)

Title Holder	Birthplace	Tenure	Status
James J. Corbett	USA	1892-1897	
Bob Fitzsimmons	England	1897-1899	
James J. Jeffries*	USA	1899-1905	
Marvin Hart	USA	1905-1906	
Tommy Burns	Canada	1906-1908	
Jack Johnson	USA	1908-1915	
Jess Willard	USA	1915-1919	
Jack Dempsey	USA	1919-1926	
Gene Tunney*	USA	1926-1928	
Max Schmeling	Germany	1930-1932	
Jack Sharkey	USA	1932-1933	
Primo Carnera	Italy	1933-1934	
Max Baer	USA	1934-1935	
James J. Braddock	USA	1935-1937	
Joe Louis*	USA	1937-1949	
Ezzard Charles	USA	1949-1950	NBA
Lee Savold	USA	1950	GB/EBU
Ezzard Charles	USA	1950-1951	
Jersey Joe Walcott	USA	1951-1952	
Rocky Marciano*	USA	1952-1956	
Floyd Patterson	USA	1956-1959	
Ingemar Johansson	Sweden	1959-1960	
Floyd Patterson	USA	1960-1962	
Sonny Liston	USA	1962-1964	
Muhammad Ali*	USA	1964-1965	
Muhammad Ali*	USA	1965-1967	WBC
Ernie Terrell	USA	1965-1967	WBA
Muhammad Ali*	USA	1967	
Joe Frazier	USA	1968-1970	WBC
Jimmy Ellis	USA	1968-1970	WBA
Joe Frazier	USA	1970-1973	
George Foreman	USA	1973-1974	
Muhammad Ali	USA	1974-1978	
Leon Spinks	USA	1978	
Leon Spinks	USA	1978	WBA
Larry Holmes*	USA	1978-1983	WBC
Muhammad Ali*	USA	1978-1979	WBA
John Tate	USA	1979-1980	WBA
Mike Weaver	USA	1980-1982	WBA
Michael Dokes	USA	1982-1983	WBA
Gerrie Coetzee	S Africa	1983-1984	WBA
Tim Witherspoon	USA	1984	WBC
Pinklon Thomas	USA	1984-1986	WBC
Larry Holmes	USA	1984-1985	IBF
Greg Page	USA	1984-1985	WBA
Tony Tubbs	USA	1985-1986	WBA
Michael Spinks*	USA	1985-1987	IBF
Tim Witherspoon	USA	1986	WBA
Trevor Berbick	Jamaica	1986	WBC
Mike Tyson	USA	1986-1987	WBC
James Smith	USA	1986-1987	WBA
Mike Tyson	USA	1987	WBA/WBC
Tony Tucker	USA	1987	IBF
Mike Tyson	USA	1987-1989	
Mike Tyson	USA	1989-1990	IBF/WBA/WBC
Francesco Damiani	Italy	1989-1991	WBO
James Douglas	USA	1990	IBF/WBA/WBC
Evander Holyfield	USA	1990-1992	IBF/WBA/WBC
Ray Mercer	USA	1991-1992	WBO
Michael Moorer*	USA	1992-1993	WBO
Riddick Bowe*	USA	1992	IBF/WBA/WBC
Riddick Bowe	USA	1992-	IBF/WBA
Lennox Lewis	England	1992-	WBC
Tommy Morrison	USA	1993-	WBO

Highlights From the 1992-93 Amateur Season

by Chris Kempson

As the 1992-93 season approached our attention focused on the 19th Olympiad in Barcelona. It proved to be an immensely successful tournament for the Irish team, who won both gold and silver medals and, although England could not match Ireland's success, we did secure a satisfying bronze.

On Saturday 8 August 1992, Dublin southpaw, Michael Carruth (Irish Army and Drimnagh), won the welterweight gold medal to become the first Irish boxer ever to win an Olympic title. The 25-year-old boxed successfully three times to secure his place in the final against the hot favourite, Juan Hernandez, from Cuba. Carruth outpointed Tuifao from Western Samoa in the second series, then old German rival, Andreas Otto, in the quarter-final, before dismissing Thailand's Chenglai, to set up a final confrontation with the classy Cuban. The stocky, ginger-haired Irishman, outpointed Hernandez by 13-10 points to carve his name for ever into Irish Olympic history. It was a

magnificent victory for Carruth and for Ireland.

Team mate, Wayne McCullough, a nippy young bantamweight from the Albert Foundry Club in Belfast, also boxed his way into the Olympic final, where he met another top class Cuban in Joel Casamayor. On his way to the final, McCullough had accounted for a Ugandan, an Iraqi, a Nigerian, and a tough North Korean. The tall Cuban southpaw proved too clever and classy for the very game Belfast boy who, although going down by 8-14 points in a lively all-action final, gained a fine silver medal for his country.

Warrington Cambrian's Robin "The Grim Reaper" Reid won a satisfying bronze medal at light-middleweight for England. The 21-year-old from the north-west, knocked out Thomas from Barbados in his first series bout, before outpointing Lithuania's Maleckis and Norway's much fancied Ole Klemetsen, to enter the semi-finals. There he was outpointed 8-3 by Dutchman, Orhan Delibas, who

Heavyweight, Steve Burford (right), on the attack during his losing ABA final against Repton's Paul Lawson   Les Clark

went on to gain the silver medal. It was a notable achievement by Reid, but that elusive gold medal continues to be beyond the reach of the England team. The last Englishman to win an Olympic title was Chris Finnegan (Hayes), who triumphed at the 1968 Games in Mexico City. As matters stand, there seems to be no realistic prospect of this depressing spell being broken in the foreseeable future.

Sadly for the sport, both McCullough and Reid have decided to punch for pay, although Michael Carruth remains an amateur to the delight of his many fans, especially those in the Emerald Isle.

Another notable "event", worthy of a special mention, was the visit of HRH The Duke of Edinburgh, in his capacity as Patron of the National Association of Boys' Clubs, to the Lynn AC in south-east London, during their memorable centenary season.

When the new domestic season arrived, the ABA's AGM, held on 26 September, was stunned when the entire delegation representing both the North East and North West Counties staged a walkout in protest at the vote taken, which maintained the status quo on the ABA Council, thus preserving the continuing dominance of the system by the London ABA. This sad occasion was to herald a season of near disaster for the ABA, but more of that later.

Inside the ring, there was continued success for Ireland when their light-welterweight, Neil Sinclair, from Belfast, returned home from the World junior championships in Montreal at the beginning of October with a fine bronze medal. Sinclair went down to the eventual Russian gold medallist in a close fought semi-final. The English duo of James Branch (Repton Cedar Street) and Michael Hall (Darlington) were both eliminated in the quarter-finals.

Back in the capital, a weakened London team made a disastrous start to the new campaign, crashing to a 7-0 defeat at the hands of a very strong Berlin side at the Cafe Royal on 5 October.

However, prestige was duly restored by our promising junior boxers, when they landed a gold and two silvers in the multi-nations tournament staged in Salonica, Greece between 8-13 October. Dual junior champion, Gary Hibbert (Gallagher Boys), one of Greater Manchester's most outstanding prospects, who was making his England debut, won a magnificent gold medal at featherweight. The Repton pair of Peter Swinney, at light-welterweight, and Andrew Lowe, at middleweight, each brought home a silver medal. Southpaw Swinney was also making his England debut.

It was then the turn of our seniors to shine in the prestigious annual Tammer tournament in Tampere, Finland. Darlington's former ABA light-heavyweight champion, Anthony Todd, grabbed a silver and three bronze medals were also secured for good measure. 1992 ABA welterweight champion, Mark Santini (Birmingham City), Repton's former dual ABA light-middleweight champion, "Tiger" Tim Taylor, and the Lynn's exciting hard-punching young heavyweight prospect, Danny Williams, all boxed well to take bronze.

The inaugural Under-16 European championships,

staged in Italy between 12-17 October, proved to be a hugely successful occasion for junior boxers from England, Ireland and Wales, who captured no fewer than five of the eleven gold medals on offer. Pride of place must go to Welsh junior welterweight champion, Gary Lockett, who demolished all three opponents inside the distance to win his gold medal. Wales also won a silver and three bronze medals. Scott Gammer from Pembroke lost in an enthralling middleweight final to England's Tony Dowling, in what proved to be a classic boxing confrontation. Lee Rees, Jason Thomas and Lee Harries, all secured bronze for the Principality in the light-fly, fly and light-welterweight divisions, respectively.

Craig Spacie won a fine gold medal for England at lightweight and southpaw, Carl Wall, returned home to Merseyside with a bronze in the featherweight division. Ireland continued their magnificent run of international success by lifting two golds, a silver and a bronze. Patrick Browne became light-flyweight champion, Michael Blaney emerged victorious in the bantamweight division, while flyweight, Christopher Meredith, was just edged out in the final by Maczic of Hungary. Adrian O'Neill was stopped at the semi-final stage by Gary Lockett, but nevertheless claimed bronze, as did Brian Crowley at middleweight.

Back on the domestic scene, Young England entertained Young Norway at the Hilton Hotel in London's Mayfair on 23 November and finished up with a resounding 6-2 winning margin over their Scandinavian rivals. There were encouraging victories by three English debutants in flyweight, Colin Toohey (Gemini), welterweight, Paul Miles (Foley), and light-middle, Gary Mayor (Nottingham Golden Gloves). The Repton duo of light-welterweight, Peter Swinney, and middleweight, James Branch, both dropped points decisions, with Swinney appearing to be rather unlucky when losing out to a tight majority verdict. It was overall a very satisfying performance by England in this under-19 international.

Next it was the turn of the England senior team when they faced the mighty Irish at the Everton Park Sports Centre in Liverpool on 2 December. Puzzling decisions, rendered against the Anglos in the welter and super-heavyweight contests, made the 6-5 English victory look much tighter than it actually was. In particular, Paul Ingle, Peter Richardson, Robin Reid and Kelly Oliver, were in fine winning form. There was, however, further disappointment for the highly touted Repton prospect, James Branch, who went down to a unanimous decision in favour of Danny Ryan. In truth, Branch didn't look worthy of his record-breaking elevation from the under-19 status, just nine days earlier.

Outside the ring, the sad and premature death of Johnny Banham BEM occurred on 3 December. Banham, who was only 49, had been suffering from cancer for some months. He was both a top boxer and coach and was a superb ambassador for the police and the sport he loved. He will be sorely missed. As if that wasn't bad enough, a week later it was reported that another former English international, Brian Sandy, 50, had passed away on 8 December.

On 5 December, the ABA held an Extraordinary General Meeting in the city of London. The historic 63-29 vote at the end of the meeting meant that the composition of both the ABA Council and the National Committee would, with immediate effect, contain the same number of delegates from every Association. In essence, the vote overturned the decision taken at the ABA AGM in September to maintain the "status quo", whereby London Divisions enjoyed the same status as the provincial associations and consequently the London ABA, as a body, had much greater percentage of delegates. The times were certainly beginning to change for the ABA.

The annual clash between the "auld enemies", England and Scotland, took place at The Forum in Livingston on 28 January 1993. Once again the spoils went to England, who eventually triumphed by 7 bouts to 5, after the Scots had led 5-2 at the halfway stage. Scotland last defeated England in January 1975 in Edinburgh.

There were fine performances for the English side from Penhill light-heavyweight, Paul Rogers, veteran light-middle, "Tiger" Tim Taylor, from Repton, and reigning ABA featherweight champion, Alan Temple (Hartlepool Boys' Welfare), who is now campaigning at lightweight. ABA flyweight champion, Keith Knox (Bonnyrigg ABC), and former ABA featherweight champion, Brian Carr (Auchengeich), were the pick of the victors for the Scots.

On 8 February, Young England registered a comfortable victory by 6 bouts to 2 over their Young Australian counterparts at the Royal Lancaster Hotel in London. There were particularly impressive international debuts from lightweight, James Hare (Batley and Dewsbury), and Hunslet's welterweight, James Lowther.

Three days earlier, Ireland thumped a Great Britain representative team 8-4 in the National Stadium in Dublin to underline the immense depth of young talent in the Emerald Isle. The combined forces of England, Scotland and Wales proved to be no match for what was on paper a depleted Irish side with eight champions missing. For the visitors, only Scotland's Brian Carr and Welsh super-heavyweight star, Kevin McCormack, showed their true international class. Certainly, the Irish selectors have an enjoyable and rewarding job these days.

However, Scarborough's Paul Ingle redeemed some of England's senior pride in Berlin at the end of March when he was selected to box for Europe against a team representing North America, which contained nine Cubans. The 1991 ABA flyweight champion, who lost by a single punch to the eventual gold medallist, Choi Choi-Su, in the Barcelona Olympics last year, won his bout convincingly 18-3 against the American, Troy Porter. The match ended in a 6-6 draw.

Before we move on to take an in-depth look at the 105th ABA senior championships, which dominated the domestic season, there were two important events which we must pause over outside the ring.

First, there was the revelation made at an ABA Council meeting held in London on 13 March that the 113-year-old organisation was on the verge of bankruptcy. Honorary Treasurer, Ken Short, tendered his resignation and a motion

of no confidence in the current administration was passed by a margin of 21 votes to 16 and an Extraordinary General Meeting was arranged for 3 April in Oxford. Earlier in the month, the Sports Council had decided to withdraw their £108,000 annual grant from the ABA.

On 15 March the death occurred of east Londoner, Joe Gutteridge, arguably the country's most famous amateur referee. Born in Hackney in 1913, Joe is understood to have refereed a staggering 23,000 contests throughout his very long and distinguished career in the amateur code, covering European and Commonwealth championships, as well as countless international matches and ABA finals. His experience and knowledge will be sorely missed around the London scene, in particular, and on the national stage at large.

The domestic season was dominated, as ever, by the national senior championships, which mirrored 1991-92 in that they had a fairly new and fresh look about them due to the plethora of young stars continuing to defect to the professional ranks.

ABA champions past and present, such as Dean Amory, Peter Culshaw, Adrian Dodson, Darren Fifield, Patrick "Blue Boy" Gallagher, John Irwin, Paul Lloyd, Nick Tooley and Scott Welch "turned over", as did other young prospects, Michael Alldis and Rowan Williams. Former dual ABA light-middleweight champion, "Tiger" Tim Taylor, did not enter this season's championships, nor did the 1992 runner-up at super-heavyweight, Donovan Holness, from St Pancras. Darren McCarrick, who won the ABA light-middleweight title in 1992, was sidelined for almost a year due to medical problems and what with the retirement of Mark Edwards, who was ABA middleweight champion in 1989 and 1991, our array of senior talent has been badly denuded of late.

Now to the championships themselves, which produced their customary share of thrills, spills, and disappointments, and at the same time, ushered in the discovery of some exciting new talent.

1992 London lightweight champion, Patrick J. Gallagher, from the Angel in Islington, was outpointed in the London North-West Divisional finals and heavyweight, Mark Levy (Collyhurst & Moston), an English semi-finalist last year, lost in the East Lancashire and Cheshire finals. Repton Cedar Street's light-heavyweight, Monty Wright, unanimously outscored West Ham's Mark Delaney in the London North-East Divisional championships, in what so easily could have been an ABA final "proper", given the standing and ranking of the two men.

Reigning ABA middleweight champion from Essex, Lee Woolcock (Canvey), was bundled out of the Eastern Counties finals on a disputed majority decision, while his club mate, light-welterweight George Smith, a former ABA finalist, was outpointed by rank outsider, Gary Gates (Hastings West Hill), in the Eastern v Southern Counties zone final.

The English semi-finals held in Oxford on 3 April, proved to be a "graveyard" for a number of fancied names. Reigning champions, Patrick Mullings (St Patricks) and Mark Santini (Birmingham City), and much fancied

London light-middleweight star, Michael Scott (Islington), made their exits at this juncture, as did the former triple super-heavyweight kingpin from Wales, Kevin McCormack, who is now campaigning under the Royal Navy banner. McCormack's departure from the championships seemed questionable to say the least.

Also at Oxford, the ABA held their Extraordinary General Meeting and agreed to implement the Sports Council's proposals, namely a major reduction in members of the ABA Council, the appointment of a full-time paid administrator and the formation of a Youth Commission. The most fundamental change that was passed, was the formation of an Emergency Steering Committee – a "think tank" – under the chairmanship of Commander Rod Robertson. The Committee was charged with formulating plans for the future development of the ABA.

Later in the month, we moved up to Gateshead for the

Jason Cook (left) won the ABA featherweight crown at the expense of the highly fancied Londoner, Marcus McCrae

Les Clark

British semi-finals. Again, there were a few surprises in store. Scotland's lightweight Bradley Welsh (Leith Victoria), in what was probably the best amateur contest of the year, won a narrow and controversial decision over reigning featherweight champion, Alan Temple (Hartlepool Boys Welfare). London's middleweight hope, Jason Matthews (Crown and Manor), was destroyed inside a round by Newbridge's dual ABA champion, Joe Calzaghe, and Scottish featherweight, Carlo Melucci (Glasgow Corporation), bowed out to Marcus McCrae (Fitzroy Lodge), one of the few revelations of the season.

So, we arrived at the National Indoor Arena in Birmingham for the ABA finals on 5 May. It was only the second time in history that the finals had taken place outside of London, the other occasion being in 1944 when Manchester's Belle Vue was the venue. Bearing in mind the number of upsets which had occurred during the course of the championships, there was a grand total of 17 "first-timers" on show on finals night.

Mark Hughes (Gwent Swansea) got the proceedings off to a brisk start when he demolished Dennistoun's Michael Crossan in the first round of the light-flyweight final. The finish came with a mere two seconds left of the opening session, Crossan having had to take three standing counts, which automatically terminated the contest.

Up at flyweight, Scarborough's Paul Ingle regained the title he first won in 1991 when he stopped Scotland's Paul Shepherd (Sparta) in 1.20 of the second round. Shepherd was under pressure in the opening session, having to take two counts. In the second round, a solid left to the body forced the Scot to take another count and the referee intervened at this point.

The Midlands secured a victory in the bantamweight final when Richard Evatt (Triumph) unanimously outscored 30-year-old George Nicette (Torbay). The smooth boxing of Nicette pushed Evatt all the way, but the Midlander's pressure tactics, especially in the final round, saw him safely home.

There was a surprise victory for the hard-punching Welsh featherweight, Jason Cook (Maesteg), who bombed out the much-fancied Londoner, Marcus McCrae (Fitzroy Lodge), in the first round. McCrae was unable to cope with the raw power of Cook and had to take two standing counts, before a body shot sent him to the canvas to signal the end of the contest, without the formality of a count.

The lightweight final produced the only champion from Scotland when Bradley Welsh (Leith Victoria) stopped Vince Powell (Army) after 2.19 of the final round. The first two sessions were fairly close, but the Scot's greater firepower proved too much for the Army man to handle in the third and a strong left-hook signalled the end for Powell, following two standing counts.

Peter Richardson (Phil Thomas School of Boxing) won the lightweight crown to add to the light-welterweight title he secured in 1989. The hard-punching Richardson needed only 2.19 of the opening round to end north-easterner Rob Wileman's title dreams, following two counts. It was an impressive stoppage win for Richardson, who had been troubled by an ankle injury.

At welterweight, Chris Bessey (Army) won the all-southpaw clash with West Ham's Steve Roberts, a man who had been one of the revelations of the season and who came so close to landing an ABA title at the first time of asking. The majority verdict in Bessey's favour seemed questionable, especially as he had to take a standing count in the middle round. The Londoner is a bright prospect for the future and he will have learned much and gained valuable experience from this season's campaign.

Former multi-titled junior champion, David Starie (Hurstlea/Kerridge), was an impressive first-time winner at light-middleweight, knocking out Craig Winter from Denbigh after 0.54 of the middle round. A left-hook dropped the Welshman early in the second round and when a combination to the head decked him again he was guided back to his corner by referee Donald McNaughton. Starie, it seems, has a fine senior career ahead of him and he was certainly one of the evening's most outstanding "new" champions.

Up at middleweight, Newbridge's Joe Calzaghe became only the second boxer in the history of the ABA championships to win titles at different weights in three consecutive years. Fred Webster was the first man to do so in 1926/27/28, when he won the bantam, feather and lightweight titles. Calzaghe had become welterweight champion in 1991 and taken the light-middleweight title in 1992. This time around he unanimously outscored Bristol's Darren Dorrington (National Smelting Club) to enter into the record books. A tremendous achievement by a fine young Welsh boxer, which made his omission from the Barcelona Olympics even more unbelievable in retrospect.

Kelly Oliver (Bracebridge) retained his light-heavyweight title with a unanimous verdict over 1991 champion, southpaw, Anthony Todd, from Darlington. Oliver set up his fine points victory with a series of blistering body attacks which Todd had no answer to. It was a bad defeat for the highly regarded Todd, who had to endure no fewer than four standing counts, which should have resulted in an automatic stoppage. Oliver is certainly one to watch out for and could perhaps be our best long term bet on the international scene in future years, always assuming of course that he doesn't succumb to the lure of the professional game.

One of the discoveries of 1993, David Starie (right) picked up the senior ABA light-middleweight title with a second round kayo of Welshman, Craig Winter

Les Clark

Repton Cedar Street's, Paul Lawson, the 1991 heavy-weight champion, won his second ABA crown when he outboxed big Steve Burford from the Army. Lawson won in fine style, and with something to spare, to underline his domestic superiority over the past few years.

In the final contest of the evening, the super-heavyweight clash between Birmingham City's Mike McKenzie and Rod Allen (Preston and Fulwood) was instantly forgetable, with the majority decision going to McKenzie, in a bout devoid of any real class.

Although it had been decided earlier, for financial reasons, that England would not participate in the World senior championships in Tampere, Finland from 7-16 May, the Sports Council eventually provided some funding for this event and the ABA chose Paul Ingle, Peter Richardson, and Anthony Todd, to represent England. In the event, only Ingle made the trip. Richardson was still troubled by an ankle injury and Todd withdrew, following his bad defeat by Kelly Oliver in the ABA final at Birmingham on 5 May.

In a first series bout, Ingle met the 20-year-old Irish flyweight champion, Damaen Kelly from the Holy Trinity Club in Belfast, whom he had stopped in two rounds in December, in the England v Ireland international match in Liverpool. Kelly gained "revenge" on this occasion, squeezing home 13-12 against the new ABA champion and went on to have a fine championship. In the next round he outclassed America's Russell Roberts to win by 18 points to 6 and in the quarter-final he outpointed Igor Matveitchuk from the Ukraine. The scoring was level at 6-6, but the advantage points were subsequently awarded to the young Irishman.

In the semi-final, Kelly had to face the strong challenge of Cuba's Waldemar Font, the reigning world junior champion. Although he lost on a first round knockout to the eventual gold medallist, young Damaen, whose family I know very well, came home with a magnificent bronze medal. Indeed, Ireland finished the season as they had started, in a prominent position on the international stage. The impressive Cubans cleaned up as usual, on the medal front, winning no fewer than eight of the twelve gold medals on offer.

We continue to produce fine schoolboy and junior champions and it is to be hoped that one day soon, some of them will follow through and produce "the goods" at senior level in major international competitions, like the Olympic Games and the World championships.

The Junior ABA finals were held at Bethnal Green's York Hall on Saturday 12 December 1992 and they produced some excellent young prospects. Pick of the bunch in the Class "A" finals were Kevin Lear (West Ham), Stuart Elwell (Wednesbury) and Frankie Doherty (Angel), while Richard Sheehan (Lion), Adam Spelling (St George's), Lee Eedle (Gemini), the precocious Lynn teenager, Benny May, and Steve White (Medway Golden Gloves), caught the eye in the Class "B" finals.

Moving up to Derby's Assembly Rooms on Saturday 27 March 1993, we witnessed the thrills, spills, and upsets, of the national schools finals. Splendid performances were recorded by Sunderland's hard punching starlet, Billy Tyrrell, who retained his national title, Welsh knockout specialist, Gary Lockett (Pontypool & Panteg), Scott Rees (Gilfach Goch), Repton southpaw, Bobby Beck, West Ham's Gary Dove, Clinton Rowlands (Merlin Youth) and Unity's Ryan Rhodes. The unbeaten Doherty, southpaw Elwell, and the powerful Lear, all won schools' titles at Derby to advance to the NABC finals in May, thus setting them up for the unique championship "treble".

In the event, Doherty, Elwell and Lear, completed the fabulous treble of championship wins in the one season. Other notable performances in the NABC Class "A" finals held in Bristol on 7 May, came from Paignton's Sam Glasser, who gave a polished and skilful display of boxing, the hard-hitting Mark Walsh (Braunstone), the skilful Keith Cawley (St Pancras) and the elusive southpaw, Jonathan Jones, from Crawley.

A later week the Class "B" finals were held in Newcastle upon Tyne and it proved to be a special occasion for West Ham's Mickey Bush, who finally landed a national crown at his fifth attempt. The London duo of Benny May and Richard Sheehan excelled again and John Gallagher from Islington was also in fine form. Wednesbury's Lee Woodley and Tony Robinson (Wellington) scored spectacular inside-the-distance victories and Gary Johnson (Bracebridge) won with a wide-points margin to complete a successful season for himself and the Lincoln-based club.

The Class "C" finals which were held at the Royal Lancaster Hotel in London on 17 May, climaxed the national junior season. Fine victories came the way of the formidable West Ham "pair" of Steve Murray and Guy Wild, while the north-east foursome of Mark Smith (Hartlepool Catholic Boys), Glen Hopkins (Hylton Castle), Andrew McLean (Simonside) and Karl Maloney (The Old Vic), all won, to stamp their own particular brand of authority on the finals.

Let us hope that some of the exciting schools' and junior prospects will continue to make good progress through to the senior ranks and give us a firm base from which we can subsequently launch a successful assault on the international scene in due course.

The 1992-93 amateur boxing season has been a turbulent one in many ways. The tremendous problems surrounding the ABA, and its uncertain future, over-shadowed much of the domestic scene, which was highlighted by some fine performances at junior level, both at home and on the international scene. At senior level, we cannot seem to produce top internationals, like the Irish do with increasing regularity. The sport is now poised at a very precarious crossroad. Let us hope that those in authority will make wise decisions for the good of amateur boxing at large. The recent restoration of the ABA's annual grant by the Sports Council is a positive sign of hopefully better times ahead and the Emergency Steering Committee, which is undertaking major changes and re-structuring, will hold regular meetings with the Sports Council in an attempt to safeguard the future of amateur boxing in this country. We can only hope that they succeed.

ABA National Championships, 1992-93

Combined Services v Western Counties

Combined Services

Combined Services Championships   HMS Nelson, Portsmouth -3/4 March
L. Fly: *final:* D. Fox (RAF) w pts L. Woodcock (RN). **Fly:** O. Spensley (RAF) w pts D. Duncan (Army). **Bantam:** no entries. **Feather:** *final:* R. Basford (Army) wo. **Light:** *final:* V. Powell (Army) w co 2 D. Rudd (RAF). **L. Welter:** *final:* R. Wileman (RN) w pts J. Bhujel (Army). **Welter:** *semi-finals:* C. Bessey (Army) w pts T. French (RN), T. Gonsalves (RAF) wo; *final:* C. Bessey w pts T. Gonsalves. **L. Middle:** *final:* I. Thompson (RN) w rsc 1 L. Innes (Army). **Middle:** *final:* I. Cummins (RN) w pts J. Ollerhead (Army). **L. Heavy:** *final:* J. Gosling (RAF) w rsc 2 V. Jones (Army). **Heavy:** *final:* S. Burford w co 2 M. Humphreys (RAF). **S. Heavy:** *final:* K. McCormack (RN) w rsc 2 P. Fiske (RAF).

Western Counties

Western Counties Northern Division Championships   British Legion Hall, Penhill - 6 February
L. Fly: no entries. **Fly:** no entries. **Bantam:** *final:* R. Cross (Watchet) wo. **Feather:** *final:* A. McNally (Gloucester) w rsc 2 N. Purcell (Bronx). **Light:** *final:* M. Kane (Watchet) wo. **L. Welter:** *semi-finals:* J. Wilson (Penhill RBL) w rsc 3 D. Chatfield (Malmesbury), A. Christian (Watchet) wo; *final:* J. Wilson w pts A. Christian. **Welter:** *semi-finals:* N. Purcell (Bronx) w pts I. McDonald (Kingswood), D. Nardiello (Reckleford) w rsc 2 E. McCrae (Walcot); *final:* D. Nardiello w rtd 1 N. Purcell. **L. Middle:** *final:* G. Catley (Empire) w rsc 3 L. McCrae (Walcot). **Middle:***final:* D. Dorrington (National Smelting) w rsc 1 P. Rock (Grosvenor). **L. Heavy:** *final:* P. Rogers (Penhill RBL) w rtd 3 P. Lewis (Taunton). **Heavy:** *final:* H. Scott (Walcot) wo. **S. Heavy:** *final:* K. Oputu (St George) wo.

Western Counties Southern Division Championships   Haven Leisure Centre, Bude - 6 February
L. Fly: *final:* D. Barriball (Launceston) wo. **Fly:** *final:* D. Lawson (Devonport) wo. **Bantam:** *final:* G. Nicette (Torbay) w pts I. Dytham (Weymouth). **Feather:** *final:* N. Smith (Launceston) wo. **Light:** *semi-finals:* D. Saunders (Dawlish) w pts A. Beadman (Pisces), P. Hardcastle (Devonport) w rsc 2 J. Murdoch (Saxon); *final:* D. Saunders w dis 3 P. Hardcastle. **L. Welter:** *quarter-finals:* J. Lewis (Paignton) w pts C. Pearn (Torbay), W. Jones (Saxon) wo, J. Batten (Launceston) wo, R. Petherick (Dawlish) wo; *semi-finals:* W. Jones w rtd 1 J. Lewis, J. Batten w pts R. Petherick; *final:* W. Jones w rsc 3 J. Batten. **Welter:** *Semi-finals:* G. Edwards (Devonport) w pts H. Laidlaw (Portleven), A. Page (Poole) wo; *final:* G. Edwards w pts A. Page. **L. Middle:** *quarter-finals:* P. Herlihey (Leonis) w pts D. Norris (Paignton), S. Hennessey (Leonis) w dis 3 G. McGahey (Exeter), J. Roberts (Saxon) w rsc R. Patch (Camborne & Redruth), P. Norris (Paignton) wo; *semi-finals:* P. Herlihey w pts S. Hennessey, P. Norris w pts J. Roberts; *final:* P. Herlihey w co 1 P. Norris. **Middle:** *semi-finals:* P. LePage (Bridport) w rsc 1 A. Stables (Devonport), F. Stuart (Leonis) wo; *final:* F. Stuart w co 2 P. LePage. **L. Heavy:** *final:* L. Rousseau (Pisces) w co 2 S. Cockayne (Exmouth). **Heavy:** *semi-finals:* C. Cox (Exeter) w dis 3 D. Keenor (Barnstaple), N. Hosking (Devonport) wo; *final:* N.

Hosking w co 1 C. Cox. **S. Heavy:** *final:* P. Coleman (Ottery St Mary) w pts J. Smith (Poole).

Western Counties Finals   City Hall, Salisbury - 6 March
L. Fly: D. Barriball (Launceston) wo. **Fly:** D. Lawson (Devonport) wo. **Bantam:** G. Nicette (Torbay) w rsc 1 R. Cross (Watchet). **Feather:** A. McNally (Gloucester) w pts N. Smith (Launceston). **Light:** D. Saunders (Dawlish) w pts M. Kane (Watchet). **L. Welter:** W. Jones (Saxon) w rsc 1 A. Christian (Watchet) - replaced J. Wilson (Penhill RBL). **Welter:** D. Nardiello (Reckleford) w rsc 1 G. Edwards (Devonport). **L. Middle:** G. Catley (Empire) w rsc 2 P. Herlihey (Leonis). **Middle:** D. Dorrington (National Smelting) w pts E. Stuart (Leonis). **L. Heavy:** P. Rogers (Penhill RBL) w co 2 L. Rousseau (Pisces). **Heavy:** H. Scott (Walcot) w pts N. Hosking (Devonport). **S. Heavy:** K. Oputu (St George) w rsc 1 P. Coleman (Ottery St Mary).

Combined Services v Western Counties

Riviera Centre, Torquay - 20 March
L. Fly: D. Fox (RAF) w pts D. Barriball (Launceston). **Fly:** O. Spensley (RAF) w pts D. Lawson (Devonport). **Bantam:** G. Nicette (Torbay) wo. **Feather:** R. Basford (Army) w pts A. McNally (Gloucester). **Light:** V. Powell (Army) w pts D. Saunders (Dawlish). **L. Welter:** R. Wileman (RN) w pts W. Jones (Saxon). **Welter:** C. Bessey (Army) w pts D. Nardiello (Reckleford). **L. Middle:** G. Catley (Empire) w dis 3 I. Thompson (RN). **Middle:** D. Dorrington (National Smelting) w co 3 I. Cummins (RN). **L. Heavy:** J. Gosling (RAF) w co 3 P. Rogers (Penhill RBL). **Heavy:** S. Burford (Army) w rtd 2 H. Scott (Walcot). **S. Heavy:** K. McCormack (RN) w dis 3 K. Oputu (St George).

Eastern Counties v Home Counties v Midland Counties v Southern Counties

Eastern Counties

Essex Division   The Civic Hall, Grays - 22 January & Mersea Island - 6 February
L. Fly: no entries. **Fly:** no entries. **Bantam:** *final:* D. Dainty (Canvey Island) w pts M. Reynolds (Colchester). **Feather:** *final:* S. Rogan (Belhus Park) w co 2 R. North (Harlow). **Light:** *final:* D. Simmonds (Rayleigh) w co 2 D. Austin (Harlow). **L. Welter:** G. Smith (Canvey Island) w pts M. Saliu (Colchester). **Welter:** *semi-finals:* D. Downer (Colchester) w co 2 N. Norgate (Harlow), A. Simms (Canvey Island) w rtd 2 A. Parrish (Belhus Park); *final:* D. Downer w rsc 2 A. Simms. **L. Middle:** *final:* G. Hinch (Belhus Park) wo. **Middle:** *final:* L. Woolcock (Canvey Island) wo. **L. Heavy:** *quarter-finals:* N. Anderson (Billericay) w pts P. Sommerville (Rayleigh), M. Woodcraft (Canvey Island) wo, R. Hadley (Chelmsford) wo, P. Payton (Harlow) wo; *semi-finals:* M. Woodcraft w pts R. Hadley, N. Anderson w rsc 1 P. Payton; *final:* M. Woodcraft w pts N. Anderson. **Heavy:** *final:* G. Cox (Canvey Island) w rsc 1 P. Gorringe (Belhus Park). **S. Heavy:** no entries.

Mid-Anglia Division   The GER Club, March - 23 January
L. Fly: no entries. **Fly:** no entries. **Bantam:** no entries. **Feather:** *final:* R. Harris (March) wo. **Light:** *final:* P. Smith (Howard

Mallett) wo. **L. Welter:** *final:* J. Spurling (Cambridge) wo. **Welter:** *final:* J. Maltby (Focus) wo. **L. Middle:** *final:* L. Baxter (Chatteris) w pts S. Coulson (Focus). **Middle:** no entries. **L. Heavy:** *final:* M. Redhead (Cambridge) wo. **Heavy:** *final:* S. Whitwell (Cambridge Police) wo. **S. Heavy:** no entries.

Norfolk Division   The Ocean Rooms, Gorleston - 20 January
L. Fly: no entries. **Fly:** no entries. **Bantam:** no entries. **Feather:** *final:* A. Spenceley (Kings Lynn) wo. **Light:** *final:* M. Bell (Kingfisher) wo. **L. Welter:** no entries. **Welter:** *final:* M. Atkin (Norwich) wo. **L. Middle:** *final:* S. Smith (Kingfisher) wo. **Middle:** *final:* A. Gray (Kingfisher) w pts J. Bevis (Norwich). **L. Heavy:** *semi-finals:* D. Brunning (Norwich) w rsc 2 M. O'Brien (North Lynn), J. Estop (North Lynn) wo; *final:* D. Brunning w pts J. Estop. **Heavy:** *final:* C. Eldon (Norwich) wo. **S. Heavy:** *final:* S. Thompson (Kingfisher) w rsc 2 T. Lennox (Kings Lynn).

Suffolk Division   The Moat House, Ipswich - 13 January
L. Fly: no entries. **Fly:** no entries. **Bantam:** no entries. **Feather:** no entries. **Light:** no entries. **L. Welter:** *final:* R. Florian (Bury St Edmunds RBL) w pts M. Hawthorne (Lowestoft). **Welter:** *final:* L. Copsey (Ipswich) w rsc 1 M. Dean (Lowestoft). **L. Middle:** *final:* D. Starie (Hurstlea & Kerridge) wo. **Middle:** *final:* A. Ewen (Arcade) wo. **L. Heavy:** *final:* K. Potter (Ipswich) wo. **Heavy:** *final:* D. Brade (Ipswich) wo. **S. Heavy:** no entries.

Eastern Counties Semi-Finals & Finals   The Leisure Centre, Bury St Edmunds - 20 February
L. Fly: no entries. **Fly:** no entries. **Bantam:** *final:* D. Dainty (Canvey Island) wo. **Feather:** *semi-finals:* S. Rogan (Belhus Park) wo A. Spenceley (Kings Lynn), R. Harris (March) wo; *final:* R. Harris wo S. Rogan. **Light:** *semi-finals:* D. Simmonds (Rayleigh) wo P. Smith (Howard Mallett), M. Bell (Kingfisher) wo; *final:* D. Simmonds w rsc 1 M. Bell. **L. Welter:** *semi-finals:* G. Smith (Canvey Island) w rsc 1 J. Spurling (Cambridge), M. Hawthorne (Lowestoft) - replaced R. Florian (Bury St Edmunds RBL) wo; *final:* G. Smith w pts M. Hawthorne. **Welter:** *semi-finals:* M. Atkin (Norwich) w pts J. Maltby (Focus), D. Downer (Colchester) w co 3 L. Copsey (Ipswich); *final:* M. Atkin w pts D. Downer. **L. Middle:** *semi-finals:* D. Starie (Hurstlea & Kerridge) w co 2 L. Baxter (Chatteris), S. Smith (Kingfisher) w rsc 1 G. Hinch (Belhus Park); *final:* D. Starie w co 3 S. Smith. **Middle:** *semi-finals:* A. Ewen (Arcade) w pts L. Woolcock (Canvey Island), A. Gray (Kingfisher) wo; *final:* A. Gray w pts A. Ewen. **L. Heavy:** *semi-finals:* M. Redhead (Cambridge) w pts N. Anderson (Billericay) - replaced M. Woodcraft (Canvey Island), K. Potter (Arcade) wo D. Brunning (Norwich); *final:* M. Redhead w pts K. Potter. **Heavy:** *semi-finals:* G. Cox (Canvey Island) w co 3 C. Eldon (Norwich), D. Brade (Ipswich) w co 1 S. Whitwell (Cambridge Police); *final:* G. Cox w co 3 D. Brade. **S. Heavy:** *final:* S. Thompson (Kingfisher) wo.

Home Counties

Home Counties Championships   Molin's Recreation Club, Saunderton - 30 January & The Leisure Centre, Blackbird Leys - 13 February
L. Fly: *final:* A. Derry (Oxford YMCA) wo. **Fly:** no entries. **Bantam:** *final:* C. Feehan (Luton Boys) wo. **Feather:** *final:* J. Gynn (Stevenage) wo. **Light:** *final:* S. Dunne (Callowland) wo. **L. Welter:** *quarter-finals:* A. Tomlin (Bedford) w pts M. Flynn (Aylesbury), A. McBeal (Hitchin) w pts M. Calvert (Stevenage), T. Turner (Pinewood Starr) wo, D. Gardner (Slough) wo; *semi-finals:* A. Tomlin w pts A. McBeal, T. Turner w pts D. Gardner; *final:* T. Turner w rsc 3 A. Tomlin. **Welter:** *final:* A. Smith (St

Albans) w rsc 1 S. Ryan (Blackbird Leys). **L. Middle:** *quarter-finals:* M. Tait (Bushey) w pts R. Gray (Oxford YMCA), P. Regault (Hitchin) wo, F. Storey (Luton Boys) wo, P Evans (Willy Freund) wo; *semi-finals:* F. Storey w pts P. Evans, M. Tait w pts P. Regault; *final:* M. Tait w pts F. Storey. **Middle:** *quarter-finals:* D. Edwards (Oxford YMCA) w pts M. Hilding (Pinewood Starr), J. Waine (Blackbird Leys) wo, L. Pugh (Oxford YMCA) wo, D. McCann (Callowland) wo; *semi-finals:* L. Pugh w rsc 2 D. McCann, D. Edwards w rsc 3 J. Waine; *final:* D. Edwards w pts L. Pugh. **L. Heavy:** *semi-finals:* P. Watts (Henley) w pts P. Read (Milton Keynes), R. Baptiste (Lewsey) w pts T. Goodwin (Hitchin); *final:* P. Watts w pts R. Baptiste. **Heavy:** *final:* M. Sprott (Bulmershe) w pts T. Barnes (Henley). **S. Heavy:** *final:* M. Aspell (Mo's) wo.

Midland Counties

Derbyshire Division   Harpur Hill Social Club, Buxton - 7 January
L. Fly: no entries. **Fly:** no entries. **Bantam:** no entries. **Feather:** *final:* V. Broomhead (Buxton) wo. **Light:** *final:* L. Dunn (Chesterfield) w pts D. Ashley (Merlin). **L. Welter:** *final:* J. Dunn (Chesterfield) w pts S. Williamson (Merlin). **Welter:** *final:* G. Beardsley (Cromford) w rsc 3 M. Radford (Merlin). **L. Middle:** *semi-finals:* E. Parsons (Chesterfield) w pts M. Slater (South Normanton), K. Gibbons (Derby) wo; *final:* K. Gibbons w co 3 E. Parsons. **Middle:** *final:* A. White (Powerminster) wo. **L. Heavy:** *final:* R. Winfield (Draycott) w pts T. Watson (Royal Oak). **Heavy:** *final:* N. Akram (Derby) wo. **S. Heavy:** *final:* J. Oakes (Draycott) wo.

Leicester, Rutland & Northants Division   Heathfield Sports & Social Club, Northampton - 28 January
L. Fly: no entries. **Fly:** *final:* A. Pope (Wellingborough) wo. **Bantam:** no entries. **Feather:** no entries. **Light:** *semi-finals:* D. Kehoe (Henry Street) w co 2 D. Henderson (Venture), A. Thomas (Wellingborough) wo; *final:* D. Kehoe w pts A. Thomas. **L. Welter:** *semi-finals:* A. Bosworth (Far Cotton) w rsc 2 N. Towns (Ringstead), I. Carroll (Henry Street) wo; *final:* I. Carroll w pts A. Bosworth. **Welter:** *semi-finals:* S. Mabbett (Belgrave) w pts B. Wright (Belgrave), L. Glasgow (Venture) wo; *final:* S. Mabbett w pts L. Glasgow. **L. Middle:** *final:* C. Williams (Belgrave) wo. **Middle:** *semi-finals:* N. Hutcheon (Belgrave) w pts B. Sutton (Central), M. Thompson (Henry Street) wo; *final:* M. Thompson w co 1 N. Hutcheon. **L. Heavy:** *semi-finals:* R. Barford (Northampton) w pts T. McDonald (Venture), G. Burt (Alexton) wo; *final:* R. Barford w rsc 3 G. Burt. **Heavy:** *final:* P. Oko (Henry Street) wo. **S. Heavy:** *final:* R. McLeod (Wellingborough) wo.

Notts & Lincs Division   Phoenix Club Gym, Nottingham - 9 January
L. Fly: no entries. **Fly:** no entries. **Bantam:** no entries. **Feather:** no entries. **Light:** *semi-finals:* R. Brotherhood (Huthwaite) w rsc 3 G. Jenkinson (St Giles), J. Dillingham (Ashfield Spartan) wo; *final:* R. Brotherhood w rsc 3 J. Dillingham. **L. Welter:** *final:* S. Arter (St Giles) w pts M. Watson (Phoenix). **Welter:** *final:* M. Buxton (Radford) wo. **L. Middle:** *semi-finals:* J. Khalik (Meadows & Ruddington) w rsc 1 D. Tring (Eastwood), G. Mayor (Nottingham Golden Gloves); *final:* G. Mayor w pts J. Khalik. **Middle:** *semi-finals:* B. Exton (Bracebridge) w pts A. Shirley (Ashfield Spartan), A. Lovelace (Boston) wo; *final:* B. Exton w dis 1 A. Lovelace. **L. Heavy:** *semi-finals:* A. Kerr (Grantham) w rtd 3 D. Wood (Phoenix), K. Oliver (Bracebridge) wo; *final:* K. Oliver w rsc 3 A. Kerr. **Heavy:** *final:* M. Langtry (Bracebridge) wo. **S. Heavy:** *final:* P. Dillon (Bracebridge) wo.

Warwickshire Division   Coventry Colliery Social Club, Coventry - 23 January

L. Fly: no entries. **Fly:** *final:* G. Payne (Bell Green) wo. **Bantam:** *final:* R. Evatt (Triumph) wo. **Feather:** *final:* D. Pithie (Willenhall) wo. **Light:** *semi-finals:* K. Kearney (Triumph) w pts J. Summers (Stratford), D. Worrall (Bulkington) wo; *final:* K. Kearney w pts D. Worrall. **L. Welter:** no entries. **Welter:** no entries. **L. Middle:** *final:* S. Bendall (Triumph) wo. **Middle:** *final:* J. Twite (Triumph) w rsc 3 D. Bendall (Triumph). **L. Heavy:** no entries. **Heavy:** *final:* N. Simpson (Willenhall) wo. **S. Heavy:** no entries.

Midland Counties (North Zone) Semi-Finals   The Clifton Entertainment Centre, Nottingham - 1 February, TP Riley School, Bloxwich - 5 February & the Triumph Social Club, Coventry - 11 February

L. Fly: no entries. **Fly:** *final:* G. Payne (Bell Green) w rsc 2 A. Pope (Wellingborough). **Bantam:** *final:* R. Evatt (Triumph) wo. **Feather:** *final:* D. Pithie (Willenhall) wo V. Broomhead (Buxton). **Light:** *semi-finals:* D. Kehoe (Henry Street) w pts K. Kearney (Triumph), R. Brotherhood (Huthwaite) w co 1 L. Dunn (Chesterfield); *final:* D. Kehoe w pts R. Brotherhood. **L. Welter:** *semi-finals:* J. Dunn (Chesterfield) w pts S. Arter (St Giles), I. Carroll (Henry Street) wo; *final:* I. Carroll w rsc 2 J. Dunn. **Welter:** *semi-finals:* G. Beardsley (Cromford) w co 2 M. Buxton (Radford), S. Mabbett (Belgrave) wo; *final:* G. Beardsley w pts S. Mabbett. **L. Middle:** *semi-finals:* G. Mayor (Nottingham Golden Gloves) w pts K. Gibbons (Derby), S. Bendall (Triumph) w pts C. Williams (Belgrave); *final:* S. Bendall w pts G Mayor. **Middle:** *semi-finals:* J. Twite (Triumph) w co 1 M. Thompson (Henry Street), B. Exton (Bracebridge) wo A. White (Powerminster); *final:* J. Twite w pts B. Exton. **L. Heavy:** *semi-finals:* K. Oliver (Bracebridge) w rsc 1 R. Winfield (Draycott), R. Barford (Northampton) wo; *final:* K. Oliver w pts R. Barford. **Heavy:** *semi-finals:* N. Simpson (Willenhall) w rtd 3 P. Oko (Henry Street), M. Langtry (Bracebridge) w rsc 2 N. Akram (Derby); *final:* N. Simpson w pts M. Langtry. **S. Heavy:** *semi-finals:* J. Oakes (Draycott) w pts P. Dillon (Bracebridge), R. McLead (Wellingborough) wo; *final:* J. Oakes wo R. McLeod.

Birmingham Division   The Irish Centre, Digbeth - 10 January & Rover Exhibition Centre, Longbridge 16 January

L. Fly: no entries. **Fly:** *final:* J. Talwar (Birmingham) wo. **Bantam:** *final:* R. Bond (Coleshill) wo. **Feather:** no entries. **Light:** *final:* D. Holt (Nechells) w pts J. Martin (Birmingham). **L. Welter:** *final:* A. Maynard (Small Heath) w pts J. Scanlon (Birmingham). **Welter:** *final:* M. Santini (Birmingham) wo. **L. Middle:** *semi-finals:* A. Crosby (Small Heath) w pts M. Foulkes (Birmingham), J. Adams (Small Heath) wo; *final:* J. Adams wo A. Crosby. **Middle:** *final:* D. Sweeney (Small Heath) wo. **L. Heavy:** *final:* L. Page (Birmingham) w rtd 2 P. Fisher (Coleshill). **Heavy:** *final:* G. Douglas (Birmingham) wo. **S. Heavy:** *final:* M. McKenzie (Birmingham) wo.

South Staffs Division   The Gala Baths, West Bromwich - 22 January

L. Fly: no entries. **Fly:** *final:* D. Spencer (Pleck) wo. **Bantam:** no entries. **Feather:** *final:* M. Harris (Walsall Wood) wo. **Light:** *final:* C. Allen (Scotlands) wo. **L. Welter:** *final:* M. Richards (Wednesbury) w pts G Reid (Wolverhampton). **Welter:** *final:* P. Nightingale (Wednesbury) w pts C. Barnett (Wolverhampton). **L. Middle:** *final:* A. Houldey (Wednesbury) wo. **Middle:** *final:* S. Martin (Wolverhampton) w rsc 1 K. Halls (Bloxwich). **L. Heavy:** *final:* M. Pugh (Silver Street) wo. **Heavy:** *final:* R. Norton (Silver Street) wo. **S. Heavy:** *final:* C. Brown (Wolverhampton) w pts B. Summers (Wednesbury).

North Staffs Division   The Crafty Cockney, Smallthorne - 15 January

L. Fly: *final:* S. Cartledge (Hulton Abby) wo. **Fly:** no entries. **Bantam:** no entries. **Feather:** no entries. **Light:** *final:* M. Abbott (Hulton Abbey) wo. **L. Welter:** no entries. **Welter:** *final:* I. Swaysland (Hulton Abbey) wo. **L. Middle:** *final:* P. Stanway (The George) wo. **Middle:** *final:* J. Steele (Brownhills) wo. **L. Heavy:** *final:* D. Ashton (Brownhills) wo. **Heavy:** *semi-finals:* R. Francis (Orme) w pts P. Hulme (Burton), T. Baker (Hulton Abbey) wo; *final:* T. Baker w pts R. Francis. **S. Heavy:** *final:* T. Dunne (The George) wo.

West Mercia Division   Garrington's Social Club, Bromsgrove - 16 January

L. Fly: no entries. **Fly:** no entries. **Bantam:** no entries. **Feather:** no entries. **Light:** *final:* J. Gonzales (Warley) wo. **L. Welter:** *final:* S. Handley (Warley) wo. **Welter:** no entries. **L. Middle:** *final:* R. Doran (Shrewsbury Severnside) wo. **Middle:** *final:* I. Rogers (Shrewsbury Severnside) w pts N. Raxter (Droitwich. **L. Heavy:** no entries. **Heavy:** *final:* F. Woodrow (Hereford) wo. **S. Heavy:** no entries.

Midland Counties (South Zone) Semi-Finals & Finals   The Crafty Cockney, Smallthorne - 23 January, The Lordhill, Shrewsbury - 29 January & TP Riley School, Bloxwich - 5 February

L. Fly: *final:* S. Cartledge (Hulton Abbey) wo. **Fly:** *final:* D. Spencer (Pleck) wo J. Talwar (Birmingham). **Bantam:** *final:* R. Bond (Coleshill) wo. **Feather:** *final:* M. Harris (Walsall Wood) wo. **Light:** *semi-finals:* C. Allen (Scotlands) w pts J. Gonzales (Warley), D. Holt (Nechells) w pts M. Abbott (Hulton Abbey); *final:* D. Holt w pts C. Allen. **L. Welter:** *semi-finals:* S. Handley (Warley) w rsc 3 M. Richards (Wednesbury), A. Maynard (Small Heath) wo; *final:* A. Maynard w pts S. Handley. **Welter:** *semi-finals:* M. Santini (Birmingham) w pts I. Swaysland (Hulton Abbey), P. Nightingale wo; *final:* M. Santini w pts P. Nightingale. **L. Middle:** *semi-finals:* A. Houldey (Wednesbury) w pts R. Doran (Shrewsbury Severnside), J. Adams (Small Heath) w rtd 3 P. Stanway (The George); *final:* A. Houldey w pts J. Adams. **Middle:** *semi-finals:* D. Sweeney (Small Heath) w pts J. Steele (Brownhills), S. Martin (Wolverhampton) w pts I. Rogers (Shrewsbury Severnside); *final:* S. Martin w rsc 2 D. Sweeney. **L. Heavy:** *semi-finals:* D. Ashton (Brownhills) w pts L. Page (Birmingham), M. Pugh (Silver Street) wo; *final:* D. Ashton wo M. Pugh. **Heavy:** *semi-finals:* T. Baker (Hulton Abbey) w pts G. Douglas (Birmingham), R. Norton (Silver Street) wo F. Woodrow (Hereford); *final:* T. Baker w R. Norton. **S. Heavy:** *semi-finals:* M. McKenzie (Birmingham) w rsc 1 T. Dunne (The George), C. Brown (Wolverhampton) wo; *final:* M. McKenzie w pts C. Brown.

Midland Counties Finals   The Willenhall Social Club, Coventry - 20 February

L. Fly: S. Cartledge (Hulton Abbey) wo. **Fly:** G. Payne (Bell Green) w pts D. Spencer (Pleck). **Bantam:** R. Evatt (Triumph) wo R. Bond (Coleshill). **Feather:** D. Pithie (Willenhall) w pts M. Harris (Walsall Wood). **Light:** D. Kehoe (Henry Street) w pts D. Holt (Nechells). **L. Welter:** A. Maynard (Small Heath) w pts I. Carroll (Henry Street). **Welter:** M. Santini (Birmingham) wo G. Beardsley (Cromford). **L. Middle:** S. Bendall (Triumph) w pts A. Houldey (Wednesbury). **Middle:** J. Twite (Triumph) w rsc 1 S. Martin (Wolverhampton). **L. Heavy:** K. Oliver (Bracebridge) w pts D. Ashton (Brownhills). **Heavy:** N. Simpson (Willenhall) w co 2 T. Baker (Hulton Abbey). **S. Heavy:** M. McKenzie (Birmingham) w co 2 J. Oakes (Draycott).

Southern Counties

Southern Counties Championships   The Conyngham Cricket School, Ramsgate - 20 February & The Winter Gardens, Margate - 27 February
L. Fly: no entries. **Fly:** *final:* T. Craig (Basingstoke) wo. **Bantam:** *final:* S. Mathiot (Eastbourne) w pts A. Gunnell (Fareham). **Feather:** *semi-finals:* M. Walsh (Stacey) w rsc 2 J. Ferrar (Southampton), M. Wright (St Mary's) w pts S. Michael (Titchfield); *final:* M. Wright w pts M. Walsh. **Light:** *quarter-finals:* G. Murphy (Hove) w dis 3 M. Ghal (Keystone), J. Newton (Seaford) w rsc 1 M. Bloomfield (West Hill), M. Castleton (Titchfield) w pts A. Walsh (Stacey), R. Harrison (Faversham) w pts B. Urquhart (Westree); *semi-finals:* J. Newton w rsc 1 G. Murphy, M. Castleton w rsc 1 R. Harrison; *final:* M. Castleton w pts J. Newton. **L. Welter:** *quarter-finals:* W. Singh (Medway Golden Gloves) w pts W. Rothwell (Westree), G. Gates (West Hill) wo, K. McMahon (Woking) wo, M. Simmons (St Mary's) wo; *semi-finals:* M. Simmons w pts W. Singh, G. Gates w rsc 1 K. McMahon; *final:* G. Gates w co 1 M.Simmons. **Welter:** *prelims:* J. Bloomfield (West Hill) w pts R. Head (Westree), J. Smith (Broadstairs) wo, P. Tuckey (Cowes Medina) wo, G. Spiers (Red Ensign) wo, J. Elie (Basingstoke) wo, K. Rayment (St Mary's) wo, P. Miles (Foley) wo, S. Mallett (Southwick) wo; *quarter-finals:* P. Tuckey w pts G. Spires, K. Rayment w pts J. Elie, P. Miles w rtd 1 S. Mallett, J. Bloomfield w pts J. Smith; *semi-finals:* P. Tuckey w dis 3 K. Rayment, P. Miles w rsc 3 J. Bloomfield; *final:* P. Tuckey w pts P. Miles. **L. Middle:** *quarter-finals:* S. Sheeran (Crawley) w co 1 J. Newman (Onslow), S. Brennan (St Mary's) w pts S. Prendergast (Woking), S. Barnett (Hayling Island) w pts S. Laight (Southampton), J. Cole (Cowes Medina) w pts M. Steadman (Foley); *semi-finals:* S. Brennan w pts S. Sheeran, S. Barnett w rsc 3 J. Cole; *final:* S. Barnett w rsc 2 S. Brennan. **Middle:** *quarter-finals:* J. Fletcher (Woking) w pts J. Rice (Hove), D. Francis (Basingstoke) w co 1 D. Lowe (Southampton), J. Diggins (Foley) w rtd 2 T. Wiggins (Faversham); R. DeHara (Ashford) wo; *semi-finals:* J. Fletcher w rtd 1 R. DeHara, D. Francis w rsc 2 J. Diggins; *final:* D. Francis w pts J. Fletcher. **L. Heavy:** *quarter-finals:* C. Hart (Hove) w rsc 1 R. Sparrow (Southampton), A. Wilford (Ashford) wo, M. Snipe (Brighton) wo, L. Ramsey (Red Ensign) wo; *semi-finals:* M. Snipe w pts L. Ramsey, A. Wilford w co 2 C. Hart; *final:* M. Snipe w pts A. Wilford. **Heavy:** *semi-finals:* J. McCormack (Ramsgate) w rsc 2 E. Brown (Woking), G. Scragg (Seaford) wo; *final:* J. McCormack w pts G. Scragg. **S. Heavy:** *semi-finals:* I. Turner (Woking) w rsc 1 D. O'Connor (Seaford), D. Chilman (Orpington) w rtd 1 K. Abadom (Southampton); *final:* I. Turner w pts D. Chilman.

Regional Semi-Finals & Finals

The Willenhall Social Club, Coventry - 6 March, The Festival Hall, Basildon - 6 March & The Bletchley Leisure Centre, Milton Keynes - 20 March
L. Fly: *final:* A. Derry (Oxford YMCA) wo S. Cartledge (Hulton Abbey). **Fly:** *final:* G. Payne (Bell Green) w pts T. Craig (Basingstoke). **Bantam:** *semi-finals:* D. Dainty (Canvy Island) wo S. Mathiot (Eastbourne), R. Evatt (Triumph) wo C. Feehan (Luton Irish); *final:* R. Evatt w pts D. Dainty. **Feather:** *semi-finals:* M. Wright (St Mary's) w rsc 3 S. Rogan (Belhus Park) - replaced R. Harris (March), D. Pithie (Willenhall) w rsc 2 J. Gynn (Stevenage); *final:* D. Pithie w pts M. Wright. **Light:** *semi-finals:* M. Castleton (Titchfield) w dis 3 D. Simmonds (Rayleigh), D. Kehoe (Henry Street) wo S. Dunne (Callowland); *final:* D. Kehoe w pts M. Castleton. **L. Welter:** *semi-finals:* G. Gates (West Hill) w pts G. Smith (Canvey Island), A. Maynard (Small Heath) w pts T. Turner (Pinewood Starr); *final:* A. Maynard w pts G. Gates. **Welter:** *semi-finals:* M. Atkin (Norwich) w pts P. Tuckey (Cowes Medina), M. Santini (Birmingham) w pts A. Smith (St Albans); *final:* M. Santini w rsc 3 M. Atkin. **L. Middle:** *semi-finals:* D. Starie (Hurstlea & Kerridge) w pts S. Barnett (Hayling Island), S. Bendall (Triumph) w pts M. Tait (Bushey); *final:* D. Starie w pts S. Bendall. **Middle:** *semi-finals:* D. Francis (Basingstoke) w rsc 1 A. Gray (Kingfisher), D. Edwards (Oxford YMCA) w pts J. Twite (Triumph); *final:* D. Francis w pts D. Edwards. **L. Heavy:** *semi-finals:* M. Redhead (Cambridge) w dis 3 M. Snipe (Brighton), K. Oliver (Bracebridge) w pts P. Watts (Henley); *final:* K. Oliver w pts M. Redhead. **Heavy:** *semi-finals:* G. Cox (Canvey Island) w rsc 3 J. McCormack (Ramsgate), N. Simpson (Willenhall) w rsc 2 M. Sprott (Bulmershe); *final:* N. Simpson w pts G. Cox. **S. Heavy:** *semi-finals:* I. Turner (Woking) w co 1 S. Thompson (Kingfisher), M. McKenzie (Birmingham) wo M. Aspell (Mo's); *final:* M. McKenzie w rsc 2 I. Turner.

London

North East Division   York Hall, Bethnal Green - 18 February & Crook Log Sports Centre, Bexley Heath - 20 February
L. Fly no entries. **Fly:** *final:* J. Green (Repton) wo. **Bantam:** *final:* M. Jones (Repton) w pts D. Adams (Repton). **Feather:** *final:* M. Ward (Repton) wo. **Light:** S. Smith (Repton) wo. **L. Welter:** *semi-finals:* P. Swinney (Repton) w pts G. Turner (Hornchurch & Elm Park), T. Hennessey (West Ham) wo; *final:* P. Swinney w pts T. Hennessey. **Welter:** *quarter-finals:* S. Roberts (West Ham) w pts T. Cesay (Lion), A. Wilton (West Ham) wo, P. Wright (Repton) wo, D. Carstens (Lion) wo; *semi-finals:* S. Roberts w pts A. Wilton, P. Wright w rsc 3 D. Carstens; *final:* S. Roberts w pts P. Wright. **L. Middle:** *final:* K. Keough (Lion) w co 3 O. Jones (Repton). **Middle:** *semi-finals:* J. Matthews (Crown & Manor) w pts A. Lowe (Repton), J. Ratcliffe (Alma) wo; *final:* J. Matthews w pts L. Ratcliffe. **L. Heavy:** *quarter-finals:* M. Thomas (West Ham) w pts G. Shaw (Alma), M. Oshungburt (St Monica's) w pts D. Negus (Five Star), M. Wright Repton) wo, M. Delaney (West Ham) wo; *semi-finals:* M. Wright w pts M. Delaney, M. Oshungburt w dis 3 M. Thomas; *final:* M. Wright w co 1 M. Oshungburt. **Heavy:** *final:* P. Lawson (Repton) w rtd 1 M. Carter (County). **S. Heavy:** *final:* T. Cherubin (Repton) w dis 3 K. Fletcher (Dagenham).

North-West Division   Porchester Hall, Queensway - 4 February & London Press Centre, Holborn - 15 February
L. Fly: *final:* N. Persaud (St Pancras) wo. **Fly:** M. Horobin (St Pancras) w pts R. Ramzan (St Patrick's). **Bantam:** *final:* P. Mullings (St Patrick's) w pts J. Simpson (St Pancras). **Feather:** *final:* M. Brown (St Pancras) w rsc 2 A. Farouk (All Stars). **Light:** *quarter-finals:* D. Brown (Hayes) w pts N. King (St Pancras), I. Smith (St Pancras) wo, C. Dunne (Finchley) wo, P. J. Gallagher (Angel) wo; *semi-finals:* I. Smith w pts C. Dunne, P. J. Gallagher w pts D. Brown; *final:* I. Smith w pts P. J. Gallagher. **L. Welter:** *quarter-finals:* B. Kelly (Middle Row) w pts D. Aherne (St Pancras), J. Kilgannon (St Patrick's) w pts A. Lazarus (Hayes), A. Coker (Angel) w rsc 1 B. Patrick (St Pancras), W. Dunne (Northolt) wo; *semi-finals:* W Dunne w pts B. Kelly, A. Coker w rsc 2 J. Kilgannon; *final:* A. Coker w rsc 3 W. Dunne. **Welter:** *semi-finals:* A. Brown (Middle Row) w rsc 1 S. Vaughan (Northolt), I. Malik (Hayes) wo; *final:* I. Malik w pts A. Brown. **L. Middle:** *semi-finals:* M. Scott (Islington) w pts D. Magee (Angel), E. Giordano (Islington) w rsc 2 C. Campbell (All Stars); *final:* M. Scott w pts E. Giordano. **Middle:** *quarter-finals:* B. McDonagh (St Pancras) w dis 3 J. Waitman (Ruislip), B. Lesley (Islington) w pts G. Reyniers (St Patrick's), M. Brown (Islington) wo, O.

Newman (Hanwell) wo; *semi-finals:* B. Lesley w pts B. McDonagh, M. Brown w rsc 1 O. Newman; *final:* B. Lesley w pts M. Brown. **L. Heavy:** *quarter finals:* M. Witter (RAF Uxbridge) w co 1 P. Wiltshire (Northolt), S. Miller (Angel) wo, T. Griffiths (New Enterprise) wo, G. Foley (Islington) wo; *semi-finals:* S. Miller w rsc 2 M. Witter, T. Griffiths w pts G. Foley; *final:* T. Griffiths w rsc 3 S. Miller. **Heavy:** *semi-finals:* C. Henry (New Enterprise) w dis 2 I. Ajose (All Stars), H. Farrell (Islington) w pts G. Walters (All Stars); *final:* C. Henry w pts H. Farrell. **S. Heavy:** *final:* A. Harrison (Northolt) wo.

South-East Division   Crook Log Sports Centre, Bexleyheath - 20 February
L.Fly: no entries. **Fly:** *final:* J. Coulston (Hollington) wo. **Bantam:** *final:* D. Easton (New Addington) wo. **Feather:** *final:* M. McCrae (Fitzroy Lodge) w rtd 2 F. Rossiter (St Joseph's). **Light:** *semi-finals:* T. Rossiter (St Joseph's) w pts J. Alldis (Lynn), L. Reynolds (Fitzroy Lodge) wo; *final:* T. Rossiter w pts L. Reynolds. **L. Welter:** *semi-finals:* R. Day (Hollington) w rsc 1 L. Linguard (BKM), D. McGovern (Fitzroy Lodge) wo; *final:* R. Day w pts D. McGovern. **Welter:** *final:* M. Stupple (Fisher) wo. **L. Middle:** *semi-finals:* A. Howell (Fitzroy Lodge) w dis 2 J. Banjo (Lynn), W. Alexander (Lynn) w co 1 P. Carr (Fisher); *final:* W. Alexander w co 1 A. Howell. **Middle:** *semi-finals:* T. Banton (Lynn) w pts S. Johnson (Lynn), J. McFarlane (New Peckham) wo; *final:* T. Banton w pts J. McFarlane. **L. Heavy:** *final:* D. Archibald (Lynn) w pts K. Mitchell (Lynn). **Heavy:** *final:* D. Williams (Lynn) wo. **S. Heavy:** *semi-finals:* J. Francis (St Peter's) w pts A. Adedayo (Honour Oak), D. Watts (Lynn) w pts H. Senior (Lynn); *final:* J. Francis w pts D. Watts.

South-West Division   Town Hall, Battersea - 22 February
L. Fly: no entries. **Fly:** no entries. **Bantam:** *final:* J. Wallace (Kudos) wo. **Feather:** *final:* A. Graham (Battersea) wo. **Light:** *final:* F. Wilson (Battersea) w dis 3 D. Jones (Kudos). **L. Welter:** J. Stevens (Kingston) wo. **Welter:** no entries. **L. Middle:** *semi-finals:* B. Ellis (Kingston) w pts R. Williams (Earlsfield), H. Eastman (Battersea) wo; *final:* H. Eastman w rsc 2 B. Ellis. **Middle:** *semi-finals:* C. Campbell (Earlsfield) w rsc 2 J. Eastwood (Kingston), D. Cranston (Battersea) wo; *final:* C. Campbell w co 1 D. Cranston. **L. Heavy:** *final:* P. Forrester (Kingston) w pts R. Scott (Earlsfield). **Heavy:** *semi-finals:* N. Eastwood (Kingston) w pts B. Cornwall (Met Police), S. Hewitt (Wandsworth) w co 1 P. Thompson (Balham); *final:* N. Eastwood w pts S. Hewitt. **S. Heavy:** no entries.

London Semi-Finals & Finals   York Hall, Bethnal Green - 4 & 18 March
L. Fly: *final:* N. Persaud (St Pancras) wo. **Fly:** *semi-finals:* M. Horobin (St Pancras) wo J. Green (Repton), J. Coulston (Hollington); *final:* J. Coulston w pts M. Horobin. **Bantam:** *semi-finals:* P. Mullings (St Patrick's) w rsc 1 J. Wallace (Kudos), M. Jones (Repton) w pts D. Easton (New Addington); *final:* P. Mullings w rsc 3 M. Ward. **Feather:** *semi-finals:* M. Ward (Repton) w rsc 2 M. Brown (St Pancras), M. McCrae (Fitzroy Lodge) w pts A. Graham (Battersea); *final:* M. McCrae w pts M. Ward. **Light:** *semi-finals:* S. Smith (Repton) w pts T. Rossiter (St Joseph's), I. Smith (St Pancras) w pts F. Wilson (Battersea); *final:* S. Smith w pts I. Smith. **L. Welter:** J. Stephens (Kingston) w dis 3 A. Coker (Angel), P. Swinney (Repton) w pts R. Day (Hollington); *final:* P. Swinney w pts J. Stephens. **Welter:** *semi-finals:* S. Roberts (West Ham) w rsc 1 I. Malik (Hayes), M. Stupple (Fisher) wo; *final:* S. Roberts w rsc 2 M. Stupple. **L. Middle:** M. Scott (Islington) w pts J. Keough (Lion), H. Eastman (Battersea) w pts W. Alexander (Lynn); *final:* M. Scott w pts H. Eastman. **Middle:** *semi-finals:* J. Matthews (Crown & Manor) w

pts B. Lesley (Islington), T. Banton (Lynn) w pts C. Campbell (Earlsfield); *final:* J. Matthews w pts T. Banton. **L. Heavy:** *semi-finals:* M. Wright (Repton) w co 1 P. Forrester (Kingston), D. Archibald (Lynn) w rtd 3 G. Foley (Islington); *final:* **Heavy:** *semi-finals:* P. Lawson (Repton) w pts C. Henry (New Enterprise), D. Williams (Lynn) w co 3 N. Eastwood (Kingston); *final:* P. Lawson w pts D. Williams. **S. Heavy:** *semi-finals:* J. Francis (St Peter's) w co 3 T. Cherubin (Repton), A. Harrison (Northolt) wo; *final:* J. Francis w pts A. Harrison.

Northern Counties

North-East Counties

North-East Division   The Leisure Centre, Gateshead - 5 & 12 February
L. Fly: no entries. **Fly:** *final:* S. Parry (Lambton Street) w rsc 2 D. Noble (Ocean Road). **Bantam:** *final:* Jobie Tyers (St Cuthbert's) w pts C. Swinnerton (Phil Thomas' SOB). **Feather:** *final:* G. Newman (South Bank) wo. **Light:** *semi-finals:* A. Green (Phil Thomas' SOB) w rsc 1 I. Walker (Blyth), A. Temple (Hartlepool BW) w pts M. Hall (Darlington). **L. Welter:** *semi-finals:* P. Richardson (Phil Thomas' SOB) w pts S. Hall (Darlington), Jimmy Tyers (St Cuthbert's) wo; *final:* P. Richardson w rtd 3 Jimmy Tyers. **Welter:** *semi-finals:* J. Green (Phil Thomas' SOB) w pts D. Hassan (Hylton Castle), M. Hallimond (Shildon) w rtd 1 G. Smith (Hartlepool Catholic); *final:* M. Hallimond w rsc 2 J. Green. **L. Middle:** *quarter-finals:* D. Nixon (Elemore) w pts J. Mett (Phil Thomas' SOB), M. Lumley (Lambton Street) w rsc 1 M. Pointer (Blyth), M. Johnson (Grainger Park) wo, J. Kelsey (Hylton Castle) wo; *semi-finals:* M. Johnson w rtd 1 J. Kelsey, M. Lumley w rsc 2 D. Nixon; *final:* M. Johnson w pts M. Lumley. **Middle:** *semi-finals:* A. Exley (Grainger Park) w rsc 2 W. Bell (Aycliffe), G. Grounds (Phil Thomas' SOB) w pts I. Cooper (Hartlepool Catholic); *final:* G. Grounds w pts A. Exley. **L. Heavy:** *final:* A. Todd (Darlington) w co 1 V. Ferguson (Phil Thomas' SOB). **Heavy:** *quarter-finals:* J. Hall (Ryton) w pts G. Whitfield (Birtley), W. Pinkerton (Teams) wo, M. McGuinness (Darlington) wo, K. Duke (Sunderland) wo; *semi-finals:* K. Duke w rsc 1 J. Hall, W. Pinkerton w pts M. McGuinness; *final:* K. Duke w co 1 W. Pinkerton. **S. Heavy:** *final:* G. McGhin (Sunderland) w rsc 3 J. Brownsword (Horsley Hill).

Yorkshire & Humberside Divisions   The Civic Centre, Castleford - 12 February
L. Fly: no entries. **Fly:** *final:* P. Ingle (Scarborough) wo. **Bantam:** *semi-finals:* J. Whittaker (Halifax) w pts S. Hall (Burmantofts), Noel Wilders (Five Towns) wo; *final:* N. Wilders w pts J. Whittaker. **Feather:** *final:* L. Crosby (St Paul's) w co 2 S. Petteridge (Meanwood). **Light:** *semi-finals:* M. Fennell (Humberside Police) w rtd 1 Nicky Wilders (Five Town), R. Latibeaudiere (Meanwood) w rtd 2 R. Sampson (Heeley Bank); *final:* R. Latibeaudiere w pts M. Fennell. **L. Welter:** *semi-finals:* J. Phelan (St Paul's) w rsc 2 R. Ali (Kingston), S. Tuckett (Sharlston Colliery) w co 2 M. Johnson (Manor); *final:* J. Phelan w rsc 3 S. Tuckett. **Welter:** *semi-finals:* J. Witter (Bradford Police) w rsc 1 J. Stronach (Keighley), M. Barker (St Paul's) wo; *final:* M. Barker w pts J. Witter. **L. Middle:** *quarter-finals:* S. Stokes (Impact) w co 2 S. Hendry (Burmantofts), L. Moorhouse (St Patrick's) wo, D. Padgett (Wombwell) wo, M. Revill (Crowle) wo; *semi-finals:* S. Stokes w rsc 1 M. Revill (Crowle), L. Moorhouse w rtd 2 D. Padgett (Wombwell); *final:* L. Moorhouse w pts S. Stokes. **Middle:** *semi-finals:* J. Sharp (Sharlston Colliery) w pts R. Burton (Barnsley), J. Lumsden (Hunslet) wo; *final:* J. Sharp w pts J. Lumsden. **L. Heavy:** *semi-finals:* J. Warters (St Patrick's) w rsc 3

T. Twibill (Halifax), C. Joseph (Sedbergh) wo; *final:* C. Joseph w pts J. Warters. **Heavy:** *final:* M. Asfar (Sedbergh) w pts C. Woollas (Crowle). **S. Heavy:** *final:* B. Webb (St Paul's) w rsc 1 S. Woollas (Crowle).

North-East Counties Finals   The Pavilion, Thornaby - 26 February
L. Fly: no entries. **Fly:** P. Ingle (Scarborough) w rsc 3 D. Noble (Ocean Road) - replaced S. Parry (Lambton Street). **Bantam:** J. Tyers (St Cuthbert's) w pts N. Wilders (Five Towns). **Feather:** L. Crosby (St Paul's) wo G. Newman (South Bank). **Light:** A. Temple (Hartlepool BW) w rsc 2 R. Latibeaudiere (Meanwood). **L. Welter:** P. Richardson (Phil Thomas' SOB) w rsc 3 J. Phelan (St Paul's). **Welter:** M. Hallimond (Shildon) w pts M. Barker (St Paul's). **L. Middle:** M. Johnson (Grainger Park) w co 1 L. Moorhouse (St Patrick's). **Middle:** G. Grounds (Phil Thomas' SOB) w pts J. Sharp (Sharlston Colliery). **L. Heavy:** A. Todd (Darlington w pts C. Joseph (Sedbergh). **Heavy:** K. Duke (Sunderland) w co 2 M. Asfar (Sedbergh). **S. Heavy:** G. McGhin (Sunderland) w rsc 1 B. Webb (St Paul's).

North-West Counties

East Lancs & Cheshire Division   The Forum, Wythenshawe - 2 & 18 February
L. Fly: no entries. **Fly:** *final:* S. Bell (Bredbury) w pts G. Lewis (Arrow). **Bantam:** *semi-finals:* M. Brodie (Ancoats) w pts A. Lewis (Bury), R. Brindle (Chorley) wo; *final:* R. Brindle w rsc 3 M. Brodie. **Feather:** *final:* D. Burrows (Wythenshawe) wo. **Light:** *semi-finals:* D. Chapman (Arrow) w rsc 2 P. Hall (Workington), T. Wood (Hulton) wo; *final:* T. Wood w pts D. Chapman. **L. Welter:** *quarter-finals:* A. Davidson (Fox) w rsc 1 W. Buckley (Workington), M. Jones (Lancs Constabulary) wo, J. Barrow (Preston & Fulwood) wo, S. Walker (Boarshaw) wo; *semi-finals:* A. Davidson w co 2 M. Jones, J. Barrow w co 3 S. Walker; *final:* A. Davidson w rsc 3 J. Barrow. **Welter:** *semi-finals:* A. Ward (Louvolite) w pts M. Haslam (Moss Side), J. Wood (Chorley) w rsc 3 F. Feno (Bredbury); *final:* A. Ward w pts J. Wood. **L. Middle:** *quarter-finals:* C. Smith (West Wythenshawe) w pts P. Coe (Fox), M. Christian (Viking) wo, C. Crook (Lancs Constabulary) wo, J. Finlayson (Moss Side) wo; *semi-finals:* C. Smith w rsc 3 M. Christian, C. Crook w pts J. Finlayson; *final:* C. Smith w rsc 1 C. Crook. **Middle:** *semi-finals:* D. Muir (Droylsden) w pts R. Jones (Horizon), P. Heneghan (Moss Side) wo; *final:* P. Heneghan w rsc 2 D. Muir. **L. Heavy:** *quarter-finals:* M. Ellis (Blackpool & Fylde) w pts G. Williams (Collyhurst & Moston), C. Scaife (Bredbury) wo, P. Hazlewood (Fox) wo, D. Margiotts (Droylsden) wo; *semi-finals:* M. Ellis w pts C. Scaife, P. Hazlewood w pts D. Margiotta; *final:* M. Ellis w rsc 2 P. Hazlewood. **Heavy:** *semi-finals:* G. Wilson (Bury) w rsc 2 J. Quayson (Moss Side), M. Levy (Collyhurst & Moston) wo; *final:* G. Wilson w pts M. Levy. **S. Heavy:** *final:* R. Allen (Preston & Fulwood) w pts M. Holden (Droylsden).

West Lancs & Cheshire Division   The Everton Park Sports Centre, Liverpool - 5, 12 & 19 February
L. Fly: *final:* G. Jones (Sefton) wo. **Fly:** *final:* R. Mercer (Lowe House) wo. **Bantam:** *final:* T. Mulholland (Transport) w rsc 2 G. Talbot (Lowe House). **Feather:** *quarter-finals:* J. Heyes (Gemini) w pts C. Ainscough (Transport), A. Moon (Kirkby) wo, E. Roberts (Gemini) wo, S. Atkinson (Gemini) wo; *semi-finals:* A. Moon w rsc 2 E. Roberts, J. Heyes w pts S. Atkinson; *final:* A. Moon w pts J. Heyes. **Light:** *semi-finals:* T. Peacock (Salisbury) w rsc 2 C. Pennington (St Helens), J. Mellor (Transport) wo; *final:* T. Peacock w pts J. Mellor. **L. Welter:** *quarter-finals:* J. Vlasman

(Gemini) w pts G. Beadman (Higherside), G. Ryder (Kirkby) wo, L. Rimmer (Salisbury) wo, M. Thompson (St Helens) wo; *semi-finals:* G. Ryder w pts L. Rimmer, J. Vlasman w dis 3 M. Thompson; *final:* G. Ryder w rsc 2 J. Vlasman. **Welter:** *final:* P. Burns (Gemini) w pts J. Jones (Sefton). **L. Middle:** *final:* R. Murray (Roseheath) w rtd 3 M. Donohoe (Salisbury). **Middle:** *semi-finals:* R. Burns (Gemini) w pts P. Parr (Birkenhead), P. Stocks (Roseheath) wo; *final:* R. Burns w pts R. Stocks. **L. Heavy:** *semi-finals:* M. Ryan (Warrington) w rsc 3 G. Drew (Long Lane), P. Craig (Knowsley Vale) wo; *final:* P. Craig w pts M. Ryan. **Heavy:** *final:* D. Chubbs (Kirkby) wo. **S. Heavy:** *final:* S. Bristow (Rotunda) wo.

North-West Counties Finals   The Everton Park Sports Centre - 19 March
L. Fly: G. Jones (Sefton) wo. **Fly:** S. Bell (Bredbury) w rsc 2 R. Mercer (Lowe House). **Bantam:** R. Brindle (Chorley) w pts T. Mulholland (Transport). **Feather:** A. Moon (Kirkby) w pts D. Burrows (Wythenshawe). **Light:** T. Peacock (Salisbury) w rsc 3 D. Chapman (Arrow) - replaced T. Wood (Hulton). **L. Welter:** G. Ryder (Kirkby) w rsc 1 A. Davidson (Fox). **Welter:** P. Burns (Gemini) w rsc 3 A. Ward (Louvolite). **L. Middle:** R. Murray (Roseheath) w rsc 2 C. Smith (West Wythenshawe). **Middle:** P. Heneghan (Moss Side) w co 2 R. Burns (Gemini). **L. Heavy:** M. Ellis (Blackpool & Fylde) w rsc 1 M. Ryan (Warrington) - replaced P. Craig (Knowsley Vale). **Heavy:** G. Wilson (Bury) wo D. Chubbs (Kirkby). **S. Heavy:** R. Allen (Preston & Fulwood) wo S. Bristow (Rotunda).

Northern Counties Finals

The Everton Park Sports Centre - 19 March
L. Fly: G. Jones (Sefton) wo. **Fly:** P. Ingle (Scarborough) w pts S. Bell (Bredbury). **Bantam:** R. Brindle (Chorley) w dis 2 J. Tyers (St Cuthbert's). **Feather:** A. Moon (Kirkby) w rsc 2 L. Crosby (St Paul's). **Light:** A. Temple (Hartlepool BW) w rsc 2 T. Peacock (Salisbury). **L. Welter:** P. Richardson (Phil Thomas' SOB) w pts G. Ryder (Kirkby). **Welter:** P. Burns (Gemini) wo M. Hallimond (Shildon). **L. Middle:** R. Murray (Roseheath) w pts M. Johnson (Grainger Park). **Middle:** P. Heneghan (Moss Side) w rtd 3 G. Grounds (Phil Thomas' SOB). **L. Heavy:** A. Todd (Darlington) w rsc 1 M. Ellis (Blackpool & Fylde). **Heavy:** K. Duke (Sunderland) w pts G. Wilson (Bury). **S. Heavy:** R. Allen (Preston & Fulwood) w rsc 2 G. McGhin (Sunderland).

British ABA Quarter-Finals

English Semi-Finals   The Leisure Centre, Blackbird Leys - 3 April
L. Fly: D. Fox (RAF) w pts G. Jones (Sefton), A. Derry (Oxford YMCA) w rsc 3 N. Persaud (St Pancras). **Fly:** P. Ingle (Scarborough) w co G. Payne (Bell Green), J. Coulston (Hollington) w rsc 3 O. Spensley (RAF). **Bantam:** G. Nicette (Torbay) w pts P. Mullings (St Patrick's), R. Evatt (Triumph) w co 1 R. Brindle (Chorley). **Feather:** A. Moon (Kirkby) w rsc 2 B. Basford (Army), M. McCrae (Fitzroy Lodge) w pts D. Pithie (Willenhall). **Light:** A. Temple (Hartlepool BW) w pts S. Smith (Repton), V. Powell (Army) w pts D. Kehoe (Henry Street). **L. Welter:** R. Wileman (RN) w pts A. Maynard (Small Heath), P. Richardson (Phil Thomas' SOB) w rsc 2 J. Stephens (Kingston) - replaced P. Swinney (Repton). **Welter:** S. Roberts (West Ham) w pts M. Santini (Birmingham), C. Bessey (Army) w pts P. Burns (Gemini). **L. Middle:** D. Starie (Hurstlea & Kerridge) w pts G. Catley (Empire), R. Murray (Roseheath) w pts M. Scott

(Islington). **Middle:** D. Dorrington (National Smelting) w pts D. Francis (Basingstoke), J. Matthews (Crown & Manor) w rsc 2 P. Heneghan (Moss Side). **L. Heavy:** K. Oliver (Bracebridge) w pts M. Wright (Repton), A. Todd (Darlington) w co 1 J. Gosling (RAF). **Heavy:** P. Lawson (Repton) w pts K. Duke (Sunderland), S. Burford (Army) w rsc 2 N. Simpson (Willenhall). **S. Heavy:** M. McKenzie (Birmingham) w pts K. McCormack (RN), R. Allen (Preston & Fulwood) w pts A. Harrison (Northolt) - replaced J. Francis (St Peter's).

(Elgin), I. Longstaff (St Mary's) wo, C. McCaig (Cleland) wo, M. Neil (Osprey) wo; *semi-finals:* I. Longstaff w pts M. Neil, J. Reilly w pts C. McCaig; *final:* I. Longstaff w pts J. Reilly. **S. Heavy:** *quarter-finals:* G. Seal (Barn) w rsc 1 S. McGuire (Perth), N. McTaggart (Bellahouston) w rsc 2 B. Quinn (Bannockburn), S. McAuley (Glasgow Transport) w pts J. Akinlami (Larkhall), C. Brown (Gartcosh) w rsc 1 G. Black (Broxburn); *semi-finals:* C. Brown w co 1 S. McAuley, G. Seal w rsc 1 N. McTaggart; *final:* C. Brown w pts G. Seal.

Scottish Championships

Meadowbank Stadium, Edinburgh - 6 March, The Fairfield Social Club, Glasgow - 15 March, The Hydro Hotel, Dunblane - 19 March & The Sports Centre, Grangemouth - 25 March
L. Fly: *final:* M. Crossan (Denistoun) w pts A. Mooney (Sydney Street). **Fly:** *semi-finals:* K. Knox (Bonnyrigg) w pts P. Dignam (Bellahouston), P. Shepherd (Sparta) wo; *final:* K. Knox w pts P. Shepherd. **Bantam:** *quarter-finals:* L. Sharpe (Portobello) w pts H. McCutcheon (North West), A. McKinnon (Kingdom) w rsc 3 G. McCluskey (Forgewood), J. O'Mellon (Croy) w pts D. Rutherford (East Kilbride), R. Hanley (Bellahouston) w rsc 2 G. Mitchell (Auchengeich); *semi-finals:* A. McKinnon w pts R. Hanley, L. Sharpe w pts J. O'Mellon; *final:* A. McKinnon w pts L. Sharpe. **Feather:** *semi-finals:* B. Carr (Auchengeich) w rsc 1 M. Simpson (Astoria), C. Melucci (Glasgow Transport) w rsc 1 A. Kidd (Meadowbank); *final:* B. Carr w pts C. Melucci. **Light:** *semi-finals:* M. Gowans (Selkirk) w rsc 2 E. Barclay (Kingcorth), B. Welsh (Leith Victoria) w pts J. Docherty (Portobello); *final:* M. Gowans w pts B. Welsh. **L. Welter:** *quarter-finals:* M. Breslin (Croy) w pts M. Wood (Chirnside), S. McLevy (Clydeview) w pts W. Leckie (Haddington), J. Keating (Meadowbank) w rsc 2 P. Graham (Springhill), J. Pender (St Francis) wo; *semi-finals:* J. Pender w rsc 1 J. Keating, S. McLevy w pts M. Breslin; *final:* J. Pender w pts S. McLevy. **Welter:** *quarter-finals:* A. Wolecki (St Francis) w pts M. McArthur (Cardenden), C. McNeill (Springhill) w pts S. Magee (Rosyth), L. McBride (Elgin) w rsc 2 J. Gilheaney (Cleland), Joe Townsley (Cleland) w pts P. Munro (Lochee); *semi-finals:* Joe Townsley w rsc 2 L. McBride, A. Wolecki wo C. McNeill; *final:* Joe Townsley w pts A. Wolecki. **L. Middle:** *prelims:* W. Strachan (St Mary's) w pts R. Middlemiss (Arbroath), S. Allan (Kingdom) w rsc 2 R. Proudfoot (Dunfermline), C. Millard (Meadowbank) w rsc 2 D. Hamilton (Croy), J. Little (Larkhall) w pts N. Clark (Linnhe), B. Laidlaw (Cardenden) w 2 W. McPhee (Huntley), A. Howlett (Lochee) w pts T. Dingwall (Cleland), C. Edmonds (St Francis) wo, M. Fleming (Kingdom) wo; *quarter-finals:* C. Edmonds w pts M. Fleming, S. Allan w rsc 2 W. Strachan, J. Little w pts C. Millard, B. Laidlaw w rsc 2 A. Howlett; *semi-finals:* S. Allan (Kingdom) w pts C. Edmonds, B. Laidlaw w pts J. Little; *final:* B. Laidlaw w rsc 2 S. Allan. **Middle:** *quarter-finals:* D. Milligan (Denbeath) w pts J. McCosh (Bellahouston), Jackie Townsley (Springhill) wo, J. Metcalfe (St Francis) wo, A. Christie (Stirling) wo; *semi-finals:* D. Milligan w pts Jackie Townsley, J. Metcalfe w pts A. Christie; *final:* D. Milligan w rsc 2 J. Metcalfe. **L. Heavy:** *prelims:* L. Powliss (Arbroath) w pts J. Paton (Bruce), J. Turner (Meadowbank) w pts S. Topen (Lochee), L. Jarvis (Cardenden) w pts S. McFarlane (Cleland), A. Caulfield (St Francis) wo, M. Sangster (Bonnyrigg) wo, W. Cane (Four Isles) wo, S. Newnes (Newarthill) wo, S. Kerr (Royal Albert) wo; *quarter-finals:* J. Turner w pts L. Jarvis, A. Caulfield w pts L. Powliss, M. Sangster w pts W. Cane, S. Kerr w pts S. Newnes; *semi-finals:* A. Caulfield w pts J. Turner, M. Sangster w pts S. Kerr; *final:* A. Caulfield w pts M. Sangster. **Heavy:** *quarter-finals:* J. Reilly (Lochee) w rsc 1 A. Barron

Welsh Championships

The Afan Lido, Aberavon - 6 March, The Penylan Social Club, Swansea - 16 March, The Leisure Centre, Rhondda - 18 March & The Institute of Sport, Cardiff - 1 April
L. Fly: *final:* M. Hughes (Gwent) wo. **Fly:** *final:* H. Woods (Aberbargoed) w rsc 3 I. Turner (Heads of Valley). **Bantam:** *quarter-finals:* R. Vowles (Llanharan) w rsc 3 S. Rees (Premier), P. Crewe (Wrexham Victoria) wo, H. Jones (Pembroke) wo, K. Durham (Highfield) wo; *semi-finals:* H. Jones w dis 3 K. Durham, R. Vowles w pts P. Crewe; *final:* R. Vowles w pts H. Jones. **Feather:** *quarter-finals:* J. Cook (Maesteg) w rsc 2 S. Boyce (Pontypridd), J. Osbourne (Aberaman) w rsc 3 D. Davies (Welshpool), G. Fletcher (Newtown) w rsc 3 L. McCafferty (Colcot), L. Gooding (St Joseph's) wo; *semi-finals:* J. Cook w rsc 1 L. Gooding, G. Fletcher w pts J. Osbourne; *final:* J. Cook w rsc 2 G. Fletcher. **Light:** *quarter-finals:* G. Lawrence (Highfield) w rsc 1 V. Blackmore (Maelor), M. Newton (Coed Eva) w pts M. Allison (Preseli), M. Carruthers (Chepstow) w pts J. Cheal (Preseli), A. Robinson (Merlin Bridge) w pts S. Jones (Splott); *semi-finals:* A. Robinson w rsc 2 M. Carruthers, G. Lawrence w pts M. Newton; *final:* G. Lawrence w co 3 A. Robinson. **L. Welter:** *quarter-finals:* P. Samuels (Crindau) w co 1 W. Leamon (Chepstow), S. Evans (Idris) w pts G. Harvey (St Joseph's), J. Morgan (Cardiff YMCA) w pts J. Davies (Cwymgorse), L. Butler (Llanharran) w rsc 3 D. Hartland (Vale); *semi-finals:* J. Morgan w rsc 1 S. Evans, P. Samuels w pts L. Butler; *final:* P. Samuels w rsc 2 J. Morgan. **Welter:** *prelims:* J. Watts (Victoria Park) w pts J. Reynolds (West Hill), J. Williams (Gwent) w pts J. Clarke (Duffryn), A. Lowndes (Swansea Docks) w rsc 3 C. Davies (Croeserw), M. Bebb (Llanharran) w pts W. English (Pembroke), C. Stevens (Highfield) w pts W. Jones (Duffryn), K. Thomas (Pentwyn) wo, P. Chappel (Porthcawl & Pyle) wo, B. Pritchard (Llangefni) wo; *quarter-finals:* K. Thomas w pts P. Chappel, B. Pritchard w rsc 2 J. Watts, C. Stevens w rsc 1 M. Bebb, A. Lowndes wo J. Williams; *semi-finals:* C. Stevens w pts A. Lowndes, K. Thomas w co 1 B. Pritchard; *final:* K. Thomas w pts C. Stevens. **L. Middle:** *prelims:* C. Winter (Denbigh) w rsc 1 J. Lewis (Welshpool), P. Wynne (Prince of Wales) w pts D. Fulton (Splott), J. Robinson (Vale) w pts S. Pepperall (RAF), A. McGuire (Red Dragon) w pts C. Rees (Garw Valley), L. England (Pontypridd) wo, B. Free (Splott) wo, A. James (Heads of Valley) wo, G. Roberts (Mold) wo; *quarter-finals:* L. England w pts B. Free, A. James w pts G. Roberts, C. Winter w rtd 1 P. Wynne, J. Robinson w pts A. McGuire; *semi-finals:* C. Winter w rsc 2 J. Robinson, A. James w pts L. England; *final:* C. Winter w rsc 1 A. James. **Middle:** *quarter-finals:* S. Stradling (Rhoose) w rsc 3 D. Owen (Aberaman), J. Calzaghe (Newbridge) wo, P. Matthews (Llanelli) wo, M. Davies (Cwymgorse) wo; *semi-finals:* J. Calzaghe w rsc 1 P. Matthews, S. Stradling w rsc 1 M. Davies; *final:* J. Calzaghe w rsc 1 S. Stradling. **L. Heavy:** *prelims:* T. Brown (Idris) w pts C. Davies (Rhondda), G. Davies (Gilfach Goch) w pts M. Jones (Porthcawl & Pyle), L. Hogan (Duffryn) wo, J. Mitchell (Llandudoch) wo, D. Budden (Heads of Valley) wo, A.

Hollaway (Rhoose) wo, S. Gilheany (Bonymaen) wo, J. Allsop (Red Dragon) wo; *quarter-finals:* L. Hogan w rsc 3 J. Mitchell, D. Budden w pts A. Hollaway, S. Gilheany w pts J. Allsop, T. Brown w pts G. Davies; *semi-finals:* T. Brown w pts S. Gilheany, L. Hogan w co 1 D. Budden; *final:* T. Brown w co 3 L. Hogan. **Heavy:** *quarter-finals:* H. Hartt (Preseli) w pts E. Davies (Aberaman), R. Fenton (Pentwyn) wo, N. Harvey (Heads of Valley) wo, T. Redman (Idris) wo; *semi-finals:* T. Redman w dis 2 H. Hartt, R. Fenton w pts N. Harvey; *final:* R. Fenton w co 3 T. Redman. **S. Heavy:** *semi-finals:* A. Griffith (Trelewis) w co 1 H. Jokarzadeh (Roath), K. McCormack (Coed Eva & RN) wo; *final:* A. Griffith wo K. McCormack.

British ABA Semi-Final & Finals

The Leisure Centre, Gateshead - 13 April & The National Indoor Arena, Birmingham - 5 May
L. Fly: *semi-finals:* M. Hughes (Gwent) w rsc 2 A. Derry (Oxford YMCA), M. Crossan (Denistoun) w pts D. Fox (RAF); *final:* M. Hughes w rsc 1 M. Crossan. **Fly:** *semi-finals:* P. Shepherd (Sparta) - replaced K. Knox (Bonnyrigg) - w co 1 J. Coulston (Hollington), P. Ingle (Scarborough) wo H. Woods (Aberbargoed); *final:* P. Ingle w rsc 2 P. Shepherd. **Bantam:** *semi-finals:* G. Nicette (Torbay) w pts R. Vowles (Llanharran), R. Evatt (Triumph) w co 2 A. McKinnon (Kingdom); *final:* R. Evatt w pts G. Nicette.

Feather: *semi-finals:* M. McCrae (Fitzroy Lodge) w pts C. Melucci (Glasgow Transport) - replaced B. Carr (Auchengeich), J. Cook (Maesteg) w pts A. Moon (Kirkby); *final:* J. Cook w co 1 M. McCrae. **Light:** *semi-finals:* V. Powell (Army) wo G. Lawrence (Highfield), B. Welsh (Leith Victoria) - replaced M. Gowans (Selkirk) - w pts A. Temple (Hartlepool BW); *final:* B. Welsh w rsc 3 V. Powell. **L. Welter:** *semi-finals:* P. Richardson (Phil Thomas' SOB) w rsc 1 S. McLevy (Clydeview) - replaced J. Pender (St Francis), R. Wileman (RN) w rsc 2 P. Samuels (Crindau); *final:* P. Richardson w rsc 1 R. Wileman. **Welter:** *semi-finals:* S. Roberts (West Ham) w rsc 3 K. Thomas (Pentwyn), C. Bessey (Army) w rsc 2 J. Townsley (Cleland); *final:* C. Bessey w pts S. Roberts. **L. Middle:** *semi-finals:* C. Winter (Denbigh) w rsc 2 R. Murray (Roseheath), D. Starie (Hurstlea & Kerridge) w co 3 B. Laidlaw (Cardenden); *final:* D. Starie w co 2 C. Winter. **Middle:** *semi-finals:* D. Dorrington (National Smelting) w pts D. Milligan (Denbeath), J. Calzaghe (Newbridge) w rsc 1 J. Matthews (Crown & Manor); *final:* J. Calzaghe w pts D. Dorrington. **L. Heavy:** *semi-finals:* A. Todd (Darlington) w pts T. Brown (Idris), K. Oliver (Bracebridge) w pts M. Sangster (Bonnyrigg) - replaced A. Caulfield (St Francis); *final:* K. Oliver w pts A. Todd. **Heavy:** *semi-finals:* P. Lawson (Repton) w rsc 1 I. Longstaff (St Mary's), S. Burford (Army) wo R. Fenton (Pentwyn); *final:* P. Lawson w pts S. Burford. **S. Heavy:** *sem-finals:* R. Allen (Preston & Fulwood) w rsc 1 A. Griffith (Trelewis), M. McKenzie (Birmingham) wo C. Brown (Gartcosh); *final:* M. McKenzie w pts R. Allen.

Not even the Scottish champion, but Leith Victoria's Bradley Welsh (left) still beat Vince Powell (Army) to win the ABA lightweight title

Les Clark

Irish Championships, 1992-93

Senior Championships

The National Stadium, Dublin - 22, 23 & 29 January
L. Fly: *semi-finals:* J. Prior (Darndale, Dublin) w rsc 1 C. Moffet (Holy Family/Golden Gloves, Belfast), M. McQuillan (Holy Family, Drogheda) wo; *final:* M. McQuillan w pts J. Prior. **Fly:** quarter-finals: D. Hosford (Greenmount, Cork) w pts E. Brannigan (Dockers, Belfast), D. Kelly (Holy Trinity, Belfast) wo, D. McKenna (Holy Family, Drogheda) wo, P. McKeown (St George's/St Malachy's, Belfast) wo; *semi-finals:* D. Kelly w pts D. McKenna, D. Hosford w pts P. McKeown; *final:* D. Kelly w pts D. Hosford. **Bantam:** *semi-finals:* P. Buttimer (Sunnyside, Cork) w pts C. Notorantonio (Newhill, Belfast), T. Waite (Cairn Lodge, Belfast) w pts M. Murphy (St Paul's, Waterford); *final:* P. Buttimer w pts T. Waite. **Feather:** *semi-finals:* P. Griffin (Mount Tallant, Dublin) w pts S. Redmond (Kilmount, Dublin), P. Ireland (St George's/St Malachy's, Belfast) w pts T. Sutcliffe (Crumlin, Dublin); *final:* P. Griffin w pts P. Ireland. **Light:** *quarter finals:* E. Bolger (Wexford CBS) w pts S. Cowan (St Paul's, Waterford), G. Stephens (Drimnagh, Dublin) w pts J. Breen (St Jude's, Wexford), M. Winters (Antrim) wo, J. Blanche (St Michael's, New Ross) wo; *semi-finals:* G. Stephens w pts E. Bolger, M. Winters w pts J. Blanche; *final:* M. Winters w pts G. Stephens. **L. Welter:** *prelims:* C. McFarland (Ederney, Tyrone) w pts S. Buttimer (Togher, Louth), G. Ward (Darndale, Dublin) w pts S. McCann (Holy Family, Belfast), J. Mitchell (Cavan) w pts S. McCloskey (Dockers, Belfast), W. Walsh (St Colman's, Cork) w rsc 1 M. Kelly (Phoenix, Dublin), E. Magee (Ardoyne, Belfast) wo, G. Ormonde (Donore, Dublin) wo; F. Carruth (Drimnagh, Dublin) wo, J. Dower (St Paul's, Waterford) wo; *quarter-finals:* C. McFarland w pts G. Ward, W. Walsh w pts J. Mitchell, E. Magee w pts G. Ormonde, F. Carruth w pts J. Dower; *semi-finals:* E. Magee w pts F. Carruth, W. Walsh w pts C. McFarland; *final:* E. Magee w pts W. Walsh. **Welter:** *quarter-finals:* T. Lawlor (Kilcullen, Kildare) w pts M. McBride (Edenderry, Offaly), N. Gough (St Paul's, Waterford) wo, A. Wilton (Ledley Hall, Belfast) wo, E. Fisher (Holy Trinity, Belfast) wo; *semi-finals:* N. Gough w pts A. Wilton, E. Fisher w pts T. Lawlor; *final:* N. Gough w pts E. Fisher. **L. Middle:** *quarter-finals:* N. Reid (Donore, Dublin) w co 1 J. Murray (Ballybrack, Dublin), A. McFadden (Dunfanaghy, Donegal) w pts S. Gibson (Immaculata, Belfast), J. Webb (Holy Trinity, Belfast) wo, H. Flannery (Ennis, Clare) wo; *semi-finals:* A. McFadden w pts N. Reid, J. Webb w pts H. Flannery; *final:* J. Webb w pts A. McFadden. **Middle:** *semi-finals:* D. Galvin (Moate, Westmeath) w pts J. Rock (CIE, Dublin), D. Ryan (Raphoe, Donegal) w rsc 2 J. Mills (Crumlin, Dublin); *final:* D. Ryan w co 2 D. Galvin. **L. Heavy:** *quarter-finals:* M. Sutton (St Saviour's, Dublin) w rsc 2 D. Griffin (Drimnagh, Dublin), M. Delaney (Holy Trinity, Belfast) wo, P. Donnelly (Stoke City) wo; B. Ward (Olympic, Galway) wo; *semi-finals:* M. Delaney w co 1 P. Donnelly, M. Sutton w co 2 B. Ward; *final:* M. Sutton w pts M. Delaney. **Heavy:** *quarter-finals:* D. Cowley (St Michan's, Dublin) w pts T. Brady (Galway), P. Douglas (Holy Family/Golden Gloves, Belfast) wo, P. Doran (Phibsboro, Dublin) wo, D. Curran (CIE, Dublin) wo; *semi-finals:* P. Douglas w co 2 P. Doran, D. Curran w co 3 D. Cowley; *final:* P. Douglas w rsc 3 D. Curran. **S. Heavy:** *quarter-finals:* D. Corbett (Holy Family/Golden Gloves, Belfast) w co 2 L. Capper (Phibsboro, Dublin), G. Douglas (South Meath, Meath) wo, S. Murphy (St Michael's, Wexford) wo, W. Clyde (Ballyclare, Antrim) wo; *semi-finals:* G. Douglas w pts S. Murphy, D. Corbett w rtd 1 W. Clyde; *final:* D. Corbett w pts G. Douglas.

Intermediate Championship Finals

The National Stadium, Dublin - 27 November
L. Fly: J. Prior (Darndale, Dublin) w pts K. Moore (St Francis, Limerick). **Fly:** O. Duddy (Coleraine, Derry) w pts S. McAnee (Ring, Derry). **Bantam:** D. McAree (Immaculata, Belfast) w pts K. Towe (Clann Eireann, Armagh). **Feather:** M. Reneghan (Keady, Armagh) w pts P. Holmes (Phoenix, Dublin). **Light:** G. Stephens (Drimnagh, Dublin) w pts G. Palmer (CIE, Dublin). **L. Welter:** S. Barrett (Rylane, Cork) w co 2 H. O'Neill (Bracken, Dublin). **Welter:** N. Sinclair (Holy Family, Belfast) w pts W. Walsh (St Colman's, Cork). **L. Middle:** B. Magee (Holy Trinity, Belfast) w pts G. Rehill (Longford). **Middle:** A. Sheerin (Swinford, Mayo) w pts M. Crampton (St Broughan's, Offaly). **L. Heavy:** M. Sutton (St Saviour's, Dublin) w pts B. Devine (Dockers, Belfast). **Heavy:** P. Deane (Swinford, Mayo) w pts J. Clancy (Kilfenora, Clare). **S. Heavy:** no entries.

Junior Championship Finals

The National Stadium, Dublin - 19 March
L. Fly: P. Whelan (Neilstown, Dublin) w pts S. Donoghue (Rochfortbridge, Westmeath). **Fly:** O. Duddy (Coleraine, Derry) w pts N. Higgins (Glasnevin, Dublin). **Bantam:** A. Patterson (St Patrick's, Newry) w pts T. O'Donnell (Carrickmore, Tyrone). **Feather:** T. Carlyle (Sacred Heart, Dublin) w pts N. Monteith (Carrickmore, Tyrone). **Light:** J. Morrissey (Sunnyside, Cork) w pts M. McCartan (St Patrick's, Newry). **L. Welter:** R. Brannigan (Dockers, Belfast) w pts M. Wickham (St Patrick's, Enniscorthy). **Welter:** W. Egan (Neilstown, Dublin) w pts A. O'Neill (Coalmine, Kilkenny). **L. Middle:** B. Magee (Holy Trinity, Belfast) w pts G. Maughan (Castlerea, Roscommon). **Middle:** J. Waldron (Ballyhaunis, Mayo) w rsc 1 G. Lyons (Trim, Meath). **L. Heavy:** M. Duffy (Glin, Dublin) w rsc 3 P. Byrne (Arklow, Wicklow). **Heavy:** H. Dawson (Freshford, Kilkenny) wo. **S. Heavy:** no entries.

Irish Senior Titles: Record Championship Wins

10: Jim O'Sullivan, 1980-1990. **9:** Gerry O'Colmain, 1943-1952; Harry Perry, 1952-1962. **8:** Nick Dowling, 1968-1975; E. Smyth, 1932-1940. **7:** J. J. Chase, 1926-1932; Jim McCourt, 1963-1972. **6:** Brian Byrne, 1975-1983; Ollie Byrne, 1954-1967; M. Flanagan, 1925-1931; P. Hughes, 1929-1935; Kieran Joyce, 1983-1988; F. Kerr, 1932-1938; Mick McKeon, 1945-1951; Tommy Milligan, 1950-1955; W. J. Murphy, 1924-1932; J. O'Driscoll, 1924-1934; Ando Reddy, 1951-1961; Billy Walsh, 1983-1991. **5:** Willie Byrne, 1959-1963; Paul Fitzgerald, 1982-1988; R. Hearns, 1933-1938; Brendan McCarthy, 1967-1971; Charlie Nash, 1970-1975. **4:** Ken Beattie, 1977-1982; Paul Buttimer, 1987-1983; Michael Carruth, 1987-1992; Dave Connell, 1946-1951; Peter Crotty, 1949-1952; Gordon Ferris, 1973-1977; Dennis Galvin, 1989-1992; Joe Lawlor, 1986-1991; Eamonn McCusker, 1965-1969; Jack O'Rourke, 1963-1971; Danno Power, 1958-1962; Phil Sutcliffe, 1977-1985; Eddie Treacy, 1961-1969; T. J. Tubridy, 1912-1923.

British and Irish International Matches and Championships, 1992-93

Internationals

Wales (5) v Ireland (4)   Savvas Club, Usk - 7 October

(Welsh names first): **L. Fly:** M. Hughes w rtd 2 P. Brannigan. **Fly:** P. Crewe l rsc 2 M. McQuillan. **Bantam:** R. Vowles w pts C. Notorantonio. **Light:** P. Samuels w pts J. Branch. **L. Welter:** J. Williams w pts S. McCluskey. **Welter:** C. Thomas l pts J. McCormack. **L. Middle:** C. Winter l co 1 T. Mullen. **Middle:** J. Calzaghe w pts G. Joyce. **L. Heavy:** L. Hogan l co 3 D. Curran.

Scotland (5) v Italy (4)   Redhurst Hotel, Glasgow - 17 November

(Scottish names first): **Bantam:** J. Murray l pts V. Gigliotti. **Feather:** C. Melucci w pts S. Consoli. **Light:** J. Docherty l pts S. Usini. **L. Welter:** S. McLevy w rsc 3 S. Vetano, B. Welsh w rtd 1 C. Bocchio. **L. Middle:** J. Gilhanney l co 1 P. Donzi, A. Wright w pts D. Donato. **Middle:** J. Connelly w pts P. Farini. **L. Heavy:** W. Cane l pts V. Imparato.

Scotland (4) v Italy (4)   St Francis of Assisi Friary, Dundee - 19 November

(Scottish names first): **Bantam:** A. McKinnon w pts V. Gigliotti. **Feather:** G. Ferrie l pts S. Consoli. **Light:** M. Gowans w pts S. Usini. **Welter:** L. McBride w co 1 G. Giagnotti. **L. Middle:** A. Wolecki w pts D. Donato, B. Laidlaw l co 3 P. Donzi. **Middle:** D. Logan l pts V. Imparato. **L. Heavy:** M. Sangster l pts P. Farina.

Young England (6) v Young Norway (2)   Hilton Hotel, London - 23 November

(English names first): **Fly:** C. Toohey w pts A. Marius. **Light:** M. Hall w pts A. Marougha, D. Holt w pts O. Eggan. **L. Welter:** P. Swinney l pts K. Hegglund. **Welter:** P. Miles w rsc 1 B. Norve. **L. Middle:** D. Francis w pts J. Ludvigsen, G. Mayor w pts P. Sevel. **Middle:** J. Branch l pts T. Hansvold.

England (6) v Ireland (5)   Everton Park Sports Centre, Liverpool - 2 December

(English names first): **Fly:** P. Ingle w rsc 2 D. Kelly. **Feather:** A. Mulholland l rsc 2 P. Ireland. **Welter:** M. Santini w pts J. McCormack, P. Burns l pts E. Fisher, P. Richardson w pts M. McBride. **L. Middle:** R. Reid w rtd 2 N. Reid. **Middle:** J. Matthews l pts D. Galvin, J. Branch l pts D. Ryan. **L. Heavy:** K. Oliver w pts M. Delaney. **Heavy:** P. Lawson w pts P. Douglas. **S. Heavy:** D. Holness l pts G. Douglas.

Scotland (5) v England (7)   The Forum, Livingston - 28 January

(Scottish names first): **Fly:** K. Knox w pts M. Horobin, K. Morrison w pts S. Parry. **Bantam:** J. Murray w pts J. Murphy. **Feather:** B. Carr w pts M. Ward. **Light:** G. Hughes l pts A. Temple. **L. Welter:** S. McLevy l pts L. Rimmer, J. Pender w pts J. Scanlon. **Welter:** A. Craig l rsc 3 P. Burns. **L. Middle:** S. Morrison l rsc 3 T. Taylor. **Middle:** B. Laidlaw l pts G. Grounds.

England's number one light-heavyweight, Kelly Oliver (left), seen in action during the ABA championships   Les Clark

L. Heavy: M. Sangster l pts P. Rogers. **Heavy:** S. Aitken l rsc 1 D. Williams.

Ireland (8) v Britain (4)   National Stadium, Dublin - 5 February
(Irish names first): **L. Fly:** D. Hosford w pts K. Morrison. **Bantam:** F. Slane l pts D. Williams. **Feather:** M. Reneghan w pts G. Hibbert, S. Redmond l pts B. Carr. **Light:** G. Stephens w pts M. Newton. **L. Welter:** E. Magee w rtd 1 J. Scanlon. **Welter:** N. Gough w pts C. Thomas. **L. Middle:** N. Reid w rtd 3 T. Taylor. **Middle:** D. Ryan w pts B. Laidlaw. **L. Heavy:** M. Sutton w pts W. Cane. **Heavy:** D. Curran l pts R. Fenton. **S. Heavy:** N. Okasili l rtd 1 K. McCormack.

Young England (6) v Young Australia (2)   Royal Lancaster Hotel, London - 8 February
(English names first): **Fly:** C. Toohey l pts H. Hussain. **Bantam:** J. Murphy w pts J. Swan. **Feather:** S. White l pts T. Peden. **Light:** J. Hare w pts B. Suey. **L. Welter:** M. Jackson w pts R. Garling, M. Jones w pts A. Hill. **Welter:** J. Lowther w J. Lord, P. Miles w rsc 1 M. Nash.

Scotland (2) v Ulster (6)   Beach Leisure Centre, Aberdeen - 16 February
(Scottish names first): **Fly:** K. Morrison w pts P. McEwen, C. McCluskey l rsc 1 A. Waite. **Feather:** B. Carr w pts B. Ferris. **Light:** M. Simpson l rsc 1 J. Mitchell, E. Barclay l rsc 3 S. McCluskey, M. McConanchie l pts R. O'Connor. **Welter:** L. McBride l pts E. Fisher. **L. Heavy:** W. Cane l pts S. Kirk.

Scotland (4) v Ulster (4)   Angus Hotel, Dundee - 18 February
(Scottish names first): **Bantam:** A. McKinnon l pts A. Waite. **Feather:** C. Melucci l pts P. Ferris. **Light:** M. Gowans w pts J. Mitchell. **L. Welter:** J. Pender w pts C. McFarland, G. McLevy l rsc 2 E. Fisher. **Welter:** A. McDonald w pts S. McCluskey, A. Wolecki w pts R. O'Connor. **L. Heavy:** A. Caulfield l rsc 2 S. Kirk.

Young France (7) v Young Scotland (3)   Conflans Saint Honorine, France - 20 February
(Scottish names first): **L. Fly:** Walker l rsc 3 Tilki. **Fly:** S. Hay l rsc 2 C. Thomas. **Bantam:** R. McPhee l pts C. Laporterie, G. Murphy w pts K. Herbal. **Feather:** P. Watson l rsc 2 I. Karatay. **Light:** W. McCusker l rsc 1 G. Lecompagnon. **L. Welter:** R. Beattie l rtd 2 A. Soualmia. **Welter:** A. Wolecki l pts G. Thirpien. **L. Middle:** L. Murphy w pts S. Knecht. **L. Heavy:** A. Wright w pts F. Lefevre.

USA (4) Ireland (7)   San Jose, USA - 13 March
(Irish names first): **L. Fly:** M. McQuillan w pts A. Guardano. **Fly:** D. Kelly w pts B. Moore. **Feather:** P. Griffin w pts G. Garcia. **Light:** G. Stephens w pts D. Rios. **L. Welter:** E. Magee w pts G. Corbin. **Welter:** N. Gough l pts B. Crumb. **L. Middle:** J. Webb w pts E. Smith. **Middle:** D. Ryan l pts E. Wright. **L. Heavy:** M. Sutton l pts A. Hempstead. **Heavy:** P. Douglas w pts L. Afuhaamango. **S. Heavy:** G. Douglas l pts R. Geer.

Ireland (8) v Denmark (3)   National Stadium, Dublin - 3 April
(Irish names first): **Fly:** D. Kelly w pts J. Jensen, D. Hosford w pts M. Mollenberg. **Feather:** P. Griffin w pts D. Pedersen, P. Ireland l pts M. Eraslan. **Light:** M. Winters w pts A. Watschem. **L. Welter:** E. Magee w pts T. Damgaard. **Welter:** N. Gough w pts O. Sorensen, E. Fisher l pts H. Al. **L. Middle:** J. Webb w pts M. Rusk. **Middle:** D. Ryan w pts K. Hansen. **L. Heavy:** M. Sutton l pts B. Lentz.

Ulster (3) v England (4)   Nero's Night Club, Portstewart - 25 June

(Ulster names first): **Bantam:** E. Brannigan l pts G. Nicette. **Feather:** P. Ferris l pts A. Moon, M. Reneghan w pts G. Hibbert. **L. Welter:** C. McFarland l pts G. Ryder. **Welter:** S. Gibson w pts C. Bessey. **L. Middle:** J. Webb l co 2 D. Starie. **Middle:** D. Ryan w pts D. Dorrington.

Championships

Olympic Games   Barcelona, Spain - 26 July to 8 August
L. Fly: R. Williams (England) w pts S. Ahialey (Ghana), l pts R. Velasco (Philippines). **Fly:** P. Buttimer (Ireland) l pts M. Malagu (Nigeria); P. Ingle (England) w pts A. Baba (Ghana), l pts C-C. Su (North Korea). **Bantam:** W. McCullough (Ireland) w pts F. Muteweta (Uganda), w pts A. Ghmim (Iraq), w pts M. Sabo (Nigeria), l pts G-S. Li (North Korea), l pts J. Casamayor (Cuba). **Feather:** P. Griffin (Ireland) l rsc 2 S. Chungu (Zambia); B. Carr (Scotland) l pts F. Reyes (Spain). **Light:** A. Vaughan (England) l rsc 3 B. Irwin (Canada). **L. Welter:** P. Richardson (England) w pts V. Forrest (USA), w pts N. Alankhuyeg (Mongolia), l pts L. Doroftei (Romania). **Welter:** A. Dodson (England) w rsc 2 M. Kawakami (Japan), l pts F. Vastag (Romania); M. Carruth (Ireland) w pts M. Tuifao (Western Samoa), w pts A. Otto (Germany), w pts A. Chenglai (Thailand), w pts J. Hernandez (Cuba). **L. Middle:** R. Reid (England) w co 1 M. Thomas (Barbados), w pts L. Maleckis (Lithuania), l pts O. Klemetsen (Norway), l pts O. Delibas (Holland). **Middle:** M. Edwards (England) l pts C. Byrd (USA). **L. Heavy:** S. Wilson (Scotland) w pts M. Masoe (Samoa), l pts R. Zaulitschny (URS). **Heavy:** P. Lawson (England) l pts D. Nicholson (USA); P. Douglas (Ireland) w pts J. Pettersson (Sweden), w pts A. Tchudinov (URS), l rsc 1 A. Vanderlijde (Holland). **S. Heavy:** K. McBride (Ireland) l pts P. Hrivnak (Czechoslovakia).

World Junior Championships   Montreal, Canada - 25 September to 3 October
L. Fly: D. McKenna (Ireland) l pts R. Milhailov (Bulgaria). **Fly:** A. Patterson (Ireland) l pts R. Husseinov (Azerbaijan). **Bantam:** T. Carlyle (Ireland) l rsc 2 M. Neslan (Cuba). **Feather:** B. Jones (Wales) l pts K. Hill (Australia). **Light:** M. Hall (England) w pts F. Morales (Puerto Rico), l pts W. Fleming (Canada); G. Stephens (Ireland) w rsc 1 W. Cheng (China), l pts W. Fleming (Canada). **L. Welter:** N. Sinclair (Ireland) w pts B. Badai (Romania), w rsc 2 W-S. Park (South Korea), l pts O. Saitov (Russia). **Welter:** A. Wolecki (Scotland) l rsc 2 G. Kurbanov (Russia); B. Magee (Ireland) w rsc 3 K. Huseyin (Turkey), l pts G. Thirpien (France). **Middle:** C. Davies (Wales) l pts W. Lewis (Canada); J. Branch (England) l pts I. Arsangaliev (Russia).

World Championships   Tampere, Finland - 7 to 16 May
L. Fly: M. McQuillan (Ireland) w pts C-H. Choi (North Korea), l rsc 1 A. Guardado (USA). **Fly:** K. Knox (Scotland) l pts T. Karkkainen (Finland); P. Ingle (England) l pts D. Kelly (Ireland); D. Kelly (Ireland) w pts R. Roberts (USA), w pts I. Matveitchuk (Ukraine), l co 1 W. Font (Cuba). **Feather:** B. Carr (Scotland) w pts V. Kuosko (Sweden), l pts E. Carrion (Cuba); P. Griffin (Ireland) l pts J. Wheeler (USA). **Light:** M. Gowans (Scotland) l rtd 2 B. Wartelle (France); M. Winters (Ireland) w pts R. Balbi (Argentine), w pts J. Sefelier (Dominican Republic), l pts D. Austin (Cuba). **L. Welter:** J. Pender (Scotland) l pts O. Saitov (Russia); E. Magee (Ireland) l pts O. Urkal (Germany). **Welter:** A. Wolecki (Scotland) l rtd 1 J. Hernandez (Cuba); N. Gough (Ireland) l pts A. Otto (Germany). **Middle:** D. Ryan (Ireland) l pts R. Joval (Holland). **Heavy:** P. Douglas (Ireland) w pts P. Saat (Estonia), l pts S. Allouane (France).

265

British Junior Championship Finals, 1992-93

National Association of Boy's Clubs

Marriot Hotel, Bristol - 7 May
Class A: 42 kg: S. Conway (Batley & Dewsbury) w pts S. Green (Cheshunt). 45 kg: K. Cawley (St Pancras) w pts T. McCarthy (Transport). 48 kg: K. Lear (West Ham) w pts S. Ollerhead (Barton). 51 kg: S. Elwell (Wednesbury) w pts A. Vine (Medway). 54 kg: M. Walsh (Braunstone) w pts R. Robshaw (Dale). 57 kg: S. Glasser (Paignton) w pts B. Scott (Camberley). 60 kg: F. Doherty (Angel) wo R. Smith (Wednesbury). 67 kg: J. Jones (Crawley) w pts N. Linford (Belgrave). 71 kg: D. Coates (Highfield) w rsc 2 M. Brydon (Chester Moor).

Mayfair Suite, Newcastle - 14 May
Class B: 45 kg: R. Sheehan (Lion) w pts S. Warbrick (Gemini). 48 kg: J. Gallagher (Islington) w pts B. Ahearne (Pontypool & Panteg). 51 kg: M. Bush (West Ham) w pts L. Rees (Gilfach Goch). 54 kg: B. May (Lynn) w pts L. Eedle (Gemini). 57 kg: A. Robinson (Wellington) w rsc 1 D. Walker (Fisher). 60 kg: L. Woodley (Wednesbury) w co 3 D. Doyle (Mo's). 63.5 kg: R. Bell (Hylton Castle) w rsc 3 N. Allen (Islington). 67 kg: G. Lockett (Pontypool & Panteg) w rsc 1 P. Loughran (Luton Irish). 71 kg: M. Monaghan (Radford) w pts C. Stonestreet (Westree). 74 kg: R. Sohi (Belgrave) w pts S. Smith (Hurstleigh & Kerridge). 77 kg: G. Jonson (Bracebridge) w pts R. Taylor (Seaford).

Royal Lancaster Hotel, London - 17 May
Class C: 48 kg: N. Bell (Brighton) w rsc 2 L. Pape (Meanwood). 51 kg: D. Costello (Hollington) w pts D. Burke (Salisbury). 54 kg: S. Murray (West Ham) w pts J. Squire (Belgrave). 57 kg: T. Feehan (Coventry) w pts P. Rawling (Mo's). 60 kg: A. McLean (Simonside) w pts R. Brocklebank (Canvey Island). 63.5 kg: G. Hopkins (Hylton Castle) w pts S. Boreham (Army). 67 kg: G. Wild (West Ham) w pts D. Rhodes (Hunslet). 71 kg: J. Guest (Belgrave) w dis 2 M. Takolobighashi (Margate). 75 kg: M. Smith (Hartlepool Catholic) w pts R. Beck (Stalham & Walsham). 81 kg: C. Fry (Islington) w pts A. Dowling (St Giles). 91 kg: K. Maloney (The Old Vic) w co 1 S. Makepeace (Snodland).

Schools

Assembly Rooms, Derby - 27 March
Junior A: 32 kg: N. Loveridge (Pinewood Starr) w pts C. Nolan (Ancoats & Miles Platting). 34 kg: A. Chapman (Newham) w pts G. Rees (Newbridge). 36 kg: D. Mulholland (Transport) w pts A. Cameron (St Mary's). 39 kg: D. Carter (Hartlepool BW) w pts M. Cawley (St Pancras). 42 kg: M. Power (St Pancras) w pts G. Monahan (Llanbradach). 45 kg: A. Palmer (Chorley) w pts T. Chambers (Foley). 48 kg: M. Knowles (Bury) w pts M. Salus (West Ham). 51 kg: P. Ayres (PDC) w pts M. Davies (Slough). 54 kg: E. Maccarinelli (Bonymaen) w pts W. Hughes (Reckleford). 57 kg: A. Dodson (Gemini) w pts J. Gunn (Canvey Island).
Junior B: 36 kg: G. Steadman (West Ham) w pts D. Price (Newbridge). 39 kg: M. Woodward (Highfield) w pts T. Driscoll (Newham). 42 kg: T. Adams (Ladywood) wo D. Mannion (New Enterprise). 45 kg: S. Hodgson (Shildon) w pts B. Doherty (Dale). 48 kg: G. Wake (Hunslet) w pts M. Williams (West Ham). 51 kg: S. Swales (Phil Thomas SOB)

w pts L. Dearlove (Sparrow Farm). 54 kg: R. Beck (Repton) w rsc 3 S. Akers (Unity). 57 kg: R. Rooney (Croxteth) w pts R. O'Connor (Knowle). 60 kg: D. Mahoney (Highfield) w rsc 1 J. Bryant (Prince of Wales). 63 kg: P. Souter (Newham) w pts P. Hayes (South Normanton). 66 kg: D. Short (Berry Boys) w pts T. Kilbride (Willaston).
Intermediate: 39 kg: G. Dove (West Ham) w pts J. Booth (Radford). 42 kg: C. Williams (Merthyr) w pts S. Green (Cheshunt). 45 kg: K. Cawley (St Pancras) w pts L. Chambers (Wythenshawe). 48 kg: L. Spindley (Ridding) w pts M. McDonagh (Lynn). 51 kg: S. Elwell (Wednesbury) w pts N. Lee (Repton). 54 kg: S. Rees (Gilfach Goch) w pts W. Nurrah (Devonport). 57 kg: E. Day (Newham) w pts M. Reppion (Gemini). 60 kg: B. Ali (Birmingham) w pts G. Hutchon (Battersea). 63.5 kg: F. Doherty (Angel) w rsc 2 J. Rooney (Desborough). 66 kg: D. Frost (Leigh Park) w pts N. Linford (Belgrave). 69 kg: G. Diggins (Foley) w pts B. Ogden (South Normanton).
Senior: 42 kg: C. Rowland (Merlin) w pts J. Martin (Canvey Island). 45 kg: B. Aherne (Pontypool & Panteg) w pts R. Sheehan (Lion). 48 kg: K. Lear (West Ham) w pts R. Williams (Aberaman). 51 kg: D. Dunnion (St Joseph's) w pts M. Bush (West Ham). 54 kg: B. Scott (Camberley) w pts G. Corbyn (Phil Thomas SOB). 57 kg: J. Ravenhill (Porthcawl) w pts S. Sargent (Foley). 60 kg: W. Tyrrell (Sunderland) w co 2 L. Trott (Bronx). 63.5 kg: M. Barr (Kingston) w pts R. Bell (Hylton Castle). 67 kg: G. Lockett (Pontypool & Panteg) w rsc 1 P. Loughran (Luton Irish). 71 kg: R. Rhodes (Unity) w rsc 2 D. Doyle (Belhus Park). 75 kg: G. Johnson (Bracebridge) w rsc 1 D. Kedwell (Medway).

ABA Youth

York Hall, Bethnal Green, London - 12 December
Class A: 42 kg: C. Rowlands (Merlin) w pts C. Varley (West Ham). 45 kg: J. Nightingale (Wednesbury) w pts M. McDonagh (Lynn). 48 kg: K. Lear (West Ham) w pts L. Spindley (Ridding). 51 kg: S. Elwell (Wednesbury) w pts S. Martin (South Woodham Ferrers). 54 kg: M. Walsh (Braunstone) w pts W. Nurrah (Devonport). 57 kg: S. Sargent (Foley) w pts A. Robinson (Wellington). 60 kg: F. Doherty (Angel) w pts G. Timmins (Walsall Wood). 63.5 kg: M. Jennings (Chorley) w pts D. Frost (Leigh Park). 67 kg: L. Wainwright (Weston super Mare) w rsc 3 B. Ogden (South Normanton). 71 kg: L. Hodgkinson (Lambton Street) w pts L. Whane (Kingsteignton).
Class B: 42 kg: no entries. 45 kg: R. Sheehan (Lion) w pts K. Brown (Wallasey). 48 kg: A. Spelling (St George's) w pts W. Toohey (Gemini). 52 kg: L. Eedle (Gemini) w pts M. Bush (West Ham). 54 kg: B. May (Lynn) w pts C. Greaves (RHP). 57 kg: S. White (Medway) w co 1 C. Wall (Gemini). 60 kg: J. Hare (Batley & Dewsbury) w pts G. Robshaw (Dale). 63.5 kg: P. Larner (Bognor) w pts M. Jackson (Boarshaw). 67 kg: J. Lowther (Hunslet) w pts D. Hill (Norwich). 71 kg: R. Rhodes (Unity) w pts N. Smith (Foley). 74 kg: T. Andrews (St Monica's) w pts M. Krence (St Michael's). 77 kg: A. Dowling (St Giles) w pts R. Hayes-Scott (Brixton).

ABA Champions, 1881-1993

L. Flyweight
1971 M. Abrams
1972 M. Abrams
1973 M. Abrams
1974 C. Magri
1975 M. Lawless
1976 P. Fletcher
1977 P. Fletcher
1978 J. Dawson
1979 J. Dawson
1980 T. Barker
1981 J. Lyon
1982 J. Lyon
1983 J. Lyon
1984 J. Lyon
1985 M. Epton
1986 M. Epton
1987 M. Epton
1988 M. Cantwell
1989 M. Cantwell
1990 N. Tooley
1991 P. Culshaw
1992 D. Fifield
1993 M. Hughes

Flyweight
1920 H. Groves
1921 W. Cuthbertson
1922 E. Warwick
1923 L. Tarrant
1924 E. Warwick
1925 E. Warwick
1926 J. Hill
1927 J. Roland
1928 C. Taylor
1929 T. Pardoe
1930 T. Pardoe
1931 T. Pardoe
1932 T. Pardoe
1933 T. Pardoe
1934 P. Palmer
1935 G. Fayaud
1936 G. Fayaud
1937 P. O'Donaghue
1938 A. Russell
1939 D. McKay
1944 J. Clinton
1945 J. Bryce
1946 R. Gallacher
1947 J. Clinton
1948 H. Carpenter
1949 H. Riley
1950 A. Jones
1951 G. John
1952 D. Dower
1953 R. Currie
1954 R. Currie
1955 D. Lloyd
1956 T. Spinks
1957 R. Davies
1958 J. Brown
1959 M. Gushlow
1960 D. Lee
1961 W. McGowan

1962 M. Pye
1963 M. Laud
1964 J. McCluskey
1965 J. McCluskey
1966 P. Maguire
1967 S. Curtis
1968 J. McGonigle
1969 D. Needham
1970 D. Needham
1971 P. Wakefield
1972 M. O'Sullivan
1973 R. Hilton
1974 M. O'Sullivan
1975 C. Magri
1976 C. Magri
1977 C. Magri
1978 G. Nickels
1979 R. Gilbody
1980 K. Wallace
1981 K. Wallace
1982 J. Kelly
1983 S. Nolan
1984 P. Clinton
1985 P. Clinton
1986 J. Lyon
1987 J. Lyon
1988 J. Lyon
1989 J. Lyon
1990 J. Armour
1991 P. Ingle
1992 K. Knox
1993 P. Ingle

Bantamweight
1884 A. Woodward
1885 A. Woodward
1886 T. Isley
1887 T. Isley
1888 H. Oakman
1889 H. Brown
1890 J. Rowe
1891 E. Moore
1892 F. Godbold
1893 E. Watson
1894 P. Jones
1895 P. Jones
1896 P. Jones
1897 C. Lamb
1898 F. Herring
1899 A. Avent
1900 J. Freeman
1901 W. Morgan
1902 A. Miner
1903 H. Perry
1904 H. Perry
1905 W. Webb
1906 T. Ringer
1907 E. Adams
1908 H. Thomas
1909 J. Condon
1910 W. Webb
1911 W. Allen
1912 W. Allen
1913 A. Wye
1914 W. Allen

1919 W. Allen
1920 G. McKenzie
1921 L. Tarrant
1922 W. Boulding
1923 A. Smith
1924 L. Tarrant
1925 A. Goom
1926 F. Webster
1927 E. Warwick
1928 J. Garland
1929 F. Bennett
1930 H. Mizler
1931 F. Bennett
1932 J. Treadaway
1933 G. Johnston
1934 A. Barnes
1935 L. Case
1936 A. Barnes
1937 A. Barnes
1938 J. Pottinger
1939 R. Watson
1944 R. Bissell
1945 P. Brander
1946 C. Squire
1947 D. O'Sullivan
1948 T. Profitt
1949 T. Miller
1950 K. Lawrence
1951 T. Nicholls
1952 T. Nicholls
1953 J. Smillie
1954 J. Smillie

Mark Hughes (right) became the first Welshman to win the ABA light-flyweight title when he stopped Scotland's Michael Crossan in the first round

Les Clark

ABA champion for 1993 at bantamweight, Richard Evatt (left) had to battle all the way to beat the veteran, George Nicette, in the final

Les Clark

1955 G. Dormer	1991 D. Hardie	1912 G. Baker	1956 T. Nicholls	1992 A. Temple
1956 O. Reilly	1992 P. Mullings	1913 G. Baker	1957 M. Collins	1993 J. Cook
1957 J. Morrissey	1993 R. Evatt	1914 G. Baker	1958 M. Collins	
1958 H. Winstone		1919 G. Baker	1959 G. Judge	**Lightweight**
1959 D. Weller	**Featherweight**	1920 J. Fleming	1960 P. Lundgren	1881 F. Hobday
1960 F. Taylor	1881 T. Hill	1921 G. Baker	1961 P. Cheevers	1882 A. Bettinson
1961 P. Benneyworth	1882 T. Hill	1922 E. Swash	1962 B. Wilson	1883 A. Diamond
1962 P. Benneyworth	1883 T. Hill	1923 E. Swash	1963 A. Riley	1884 A. Diamond
1963 B. Packer	1884 E. Hutchings	1924 A. Beavis	1964 R. Smith	1885 A. Diamond
1964 B. Packer	1885 J. Pennell	1925 A. Beavis	1965 K. Buchanan	1886 G. Roberts
1965 R. Mallon	1886 T. McNeil	1926 R. Minshull	1966 H. Baxter	1887 J. Hair
1966 J. Clark	1887 J. Pennell	1927 F. Webster	1967 K. Cooper	1888 A. Newton
1967 M. Carter	1888 J. Taylor	1928 F. Meachem	1968 J. Cheshire	1889 W. Neale
1968 M. Carter	1889 G. Belsey	1929 F. Meachem	1969 A. Richardson	1890 A. Newton
1969 M. Piner	1890 G. Belsey	1930 J. Duffield	1970 D. Polak	1891 E. Dettmer
1970 A. Oxley	1891 F. Curtis	1931 B. Caplan	1971 T. Wright	1892 E. Dettmer
1971 G. Turpin	1892 F. Curtis	1932 H. Mizler	1972 K. Laing	1893 W. Campbell
1972 G. Turpin	1893 T. Davidson	1933 J. Walters	1973 J. Lynch	1894 W. Campbell
1973 P. Cowdell	1894 R. Gunn	1934 J. Treadaway	1974 G. Gilbody	1895 A. Randall
1974 S. Ogilvie	1895 R. Gunn	1935 E. Ryan	1975 R. Beaumont	1896 A. Vanderhout
1975 S. Ogilvie	1896 R. Gunn	1936 J. Treadaway	1976 P. Cowdell	1897 A. Vanderhout
1976 J. Bambrick	1897 N. Smith	1937 A. Harper	1977 P. Cowdell	1898 H. Marks
1977 J. Turner	1898 P. Lunn	1938 C. Gallie	1978 M. O'Brien	1899 H. Brewer
1978 J. Turner	1899 J. Scholes	1939 C. Gallie	1979 P. Hanlon	1900 G. Humphries
1979 R. Ashton	1900 R. Lee	1944 D. Sullivan	1980 M. Hanif	1901 A. Warner
1980 R. Gilbody	1901 C. Clarke	1945 J. Carter	1981 P. Hanlon	1902 A. Warner
1981 P. Jones	1902 C. Clarke	1946 P. Brander	1982 H. Henry	1903 H. Fergus
1982 R. Gilbody	1903 J. Godfrey	1947 S. Evans	1983 P. Bradley	1904 M. Wells
1983 J. Hyland	1904 C. Morris	1948 P. Brander	1984 K. Taylor	1905 M. Wells
1984 J. Hyland	1905 H. Holmes	1949 H. Gilliland	1985 F. Havard	1906 M. Wells
1985 S. Murphy	1906 A. Miner	1950 P. Brander	1986 P. Hodkinson	1907 M. Wells
1986 S. Murphy	1907 C. Morris	1951 J. Travers	1987 P. English	1908 H. Holmes
1987 J. Sillitoe	1908 T. Ringer	1952 P. Lewis	1988 D. Anderson	1909 F. Grace
1988 K. Howlett	1909 A. Lambert	1953 P. Lewis	1989 P. Richardson	1910 T. Tees
1989 K. Howlett	1910 C. Houghton	1954 D. Charnley	1990 B. Carr	1911 A. Spenceley
1990 P. Lloyd	1911 H. Bowers	1955 T. Nicholls	1991 J. Irwin	1912 R. Marriott

1913 R. Grace	1956 R. McTaggart	1991 P. Ramsey	1981 A. Willis
1914 R. Marriott	1957 J. Kidd	1992 D. Amory	1982 A. Adams
1919 F. Grace	1958 R. McTaggart	1993 B. Welsh	1983 D. Dent
1920 F. Grace	1959 P. Warwick		1984 D. Griffiths
1921 G. Shorter	1960 R. McTaggart	**L. Welterweight**	1985 I. Mustafa
1922 G. Renouf	1961 P. Warwick	1951 W. Connor	1986 J. Alsop
1923 G. Shorter	1962 B. Whelan	1952 P. Waterman	1987 A. Holligan
1924 W. White	1963 B. O'Sullivan	1953 D. Hughes	1988 A. Hall
1925 E. Viney	1964 J. Dunne	1954 G. Martin	1989 A. Hall
1926 T. Slater	1965 A. White	1955 F. McQuillan	1990 J. Pender
1927 W. Hunt	1966 J. Head	1956 D. Stone	1991 J. Matthews
1928 F. Webster	1967 T. Waller	1957 D. Stone	1992 D. McCarrick
1929 W. Hunt	1968 J. Watt	1958 R. Kane	1993 P. Richardson
1930 J. Waples	1969 H. Hayes	1959 R. Kane	
1931 D. McCleave	1970 N. Cole	1960 R. Day	**Welterweight**
1932 F. Meachem	1971 J. Singleton	1961 B. Brazier	1920 F. Whitbread
1933 H. Mizler	1972 N. Cole	1962 B. Brazier	1921 A. Ireland
1934 J. Rolland	1973 T. Dunn	1963 R. McTaggart	1922 E. White
1935 F. Frost	1974 J. Lynch	1964 R. Taylor	1923 P. Green
1936 F. Simpson	1975 P. Cowdell	1965 R. McTaggart	1924 P. O'Hanrahan
1937 A. Danahar	1976 S. Mittee	1966 W. Hiatt	1925 P. O'Hanrahan
1938 T. McGrath	1977 T. Marsh	1967 B. Hudspeth	1926 B. Marshall
1939 H. Groves	1978 T. Marsh	1968 E. Cole	1927 H. Dunn
1944 W. Thompson	1979 G. Gilbody	1969 J. Stracey	1928 H. Bone
1945 J. Williamson	1980 G. Gilbody	1970 D. Davies	1929 T. Wigmore
1946 E. Thomas	1981 G. Gilbody	1971 M. Kingwell	1930 F. Brooman
1947 C. Morrissey	1982 J. McDonnell	1972 T. Waller	1931 J. Barry
1948 R. Cooper	1983 K. Willis	1973 N. Cole	1932 D. McCleave
1949 A. Smith	1984 A. Dickson	1974 P. Kelly	1933 P. Peters
1950 R. Latham	1985 E. McAuley	1975 J. Zeraschi	1934 D. McCleave
1951 R. Hinson	1986 J. Jacobs	1976 C. McKenzie	1935 D. Lynch
1952 F. Reardon	1987 M. Ayers	1977 J. Douglas	1936 W. Pack
1953 D. Hinson	1988 C. Kane	1978 D. Williams	1937 D. Lynch
1954 G. Whelan	1989 M. Ramsey	1979 E. Copeland	1938 C. Webster
1955 S. Coffey	1990 P. Gallagher	1980 A. Willis	1939 R. Thomas

1944 H. Hall
1945 R. Turpin
1946 J. Ryan
1947 J. Ryan
1948 M. Shacklady
1949 A. Buxton
1950 T. Ratcliffe
1951 J. Maloney
1952 J. Maloney
1953 L. Morgan
1954 N. Gargano
1955 N. Gargano
1956 N. Gargano
1957 R. Warnes
1958 B. Nancurvis
1959 J. McGrail
1960 C. Humphries
1961 A. Lewis
1962 J. Pritchett
1963 J. Pritchett
1964 M. Varley
1965 P. Henderson
1966 P. Cragg
1967 D. Cranswick
1968 A. Tottoh
1969 T. Henderson
1970 T. Waller
1971 D. Davies
1972 T. Francis
1973 T. Waller
1974 T. Waller
1975 W. Bennett
1976 C. Jones
1977 C. Jones
1978 E. Byrne

In an all-southpaw 1993 ABA welterweight final, Chris Bessey (left won a hotly disputed verdict over Steve Roberts   Les Clark

1979 J. Frost	1890 J. Hoare	1971 A. Minter	1971 J. Conteh	1932 V. Stuart
1980 T. Marsh	1891 J. Steers	1972 F. Lucas	1972 W. Knight	1933 C. O'Grady
1981 T. Marsh	1892 J. Steers	1973 F. Lucas	1973 W. Knight	1934 P. Floyd
1982 C. Pyatt	1893 J. Steers	1974 D. Odwell	1974 W. Knight	1935 P. Floyd
1983 R. McKenley	1894 W. Sykes	1975 D. Odwell	1975 M. Heath	1936 V. Stuart
1984 M. Hughes	1895 G. Townsend	1976 E. Burke	1976 G. Evans	1937 V. Stuart
1985 E. McDonald	1896 W. Ross	1977 R. Davies	1977 C. Lawson	1938 G. Preston
1986 D. Dyer	1897 W. Dees	1978 H. Graham	1978 V. Smith	1939 A. Porter
1987 M. Elliot	1898 G. Townsend	1979 N. Wilshire	1979 A. Straughn	1944 M. Hart
1988 M. McCreath	1899 R. Warnes	1980 M. Kaylor	1980 A. Straughn	1945 D. Scott
1989 M. Elliot	1900 E. Mann	1981 B. Schumacher	1981 A. Straughn	1946 P. Floyd
1990 A. Carew	1901 R. Warnes	1982 J. Price	1982 G. Crawford	1947 G. Scriven
1991 J. Calzaghe	1902 E. Mann	1983 T. Forbes	1983 A. Wilson	1948 J. Gardner
1992 M. Santini	1903 R. Warnes	1984 B. Schumacher	1984 A. Wilson	1949 A. Worrall
1993 C. Bessey	1904 E. Mann	1985 D. Cronin	1985 J. Beckles	1950 P. Toch
	1905 J. Douglas	1986 N. Benn	1986 J. Moran	1951 A. Halsey
L. Middleweight	1906 A. Murdock	1987 R. Douglas	1987 J. Beckles	1952 E. Hearn
1951 A. Lay	1907 R. Warnes	1988 M. Edwards	1988 H. Lawson	1953 J. Erskine
1952 B. Foster	1908 W. Child	1989 S. Johnson	1989 N. Piper	1954 B. Harper
1953 B. Wells	1909 W. Child	1990 S. Wilson	1990 J. McCluskey	1955 D. Rowe
1954 B. Wells	1910 R. Warnes	1991 M. Edwards	1991 A. Todd	1956 D. Rent
1955 B. Foster	1911 W. Child	1992 L. Woolcock	1992 K. Oliver	1957 D. Thomas
1956 J. McCormack	1912 E. Chandler	1993 J. Calzaghe	1993 K. Oliver	1958 D. Thomas
1957 J. Cunningham	1913 W. Bradley			1959 D. Thomas
1958 S. Pearson	1914 H. Brown			1960 L. Hobbs
1959 S. Pearson	1919 H. Mallin	**L. Heavyweight**	**Heavyweight**	1961 W. Walker
1960 W. Fisher	1920 H. Mallin	1920 H. Franks	1881 R. Frost-Smith	1962 R. Dryden
1961 J. Gamble	1921 H. Mallin	1921 L. Collett	1882 H. Dearsley	1963 R. Sanders
1962 J. Lloyd	1922 H. Mallin	1922 H. Mitchell	1883 H. Dearsley	1964 C. Woodhouse
1963 A. Wyper	1923 H. Mallin	1923 H. Mitchell	1884 H. Dearsley	1965 W. Wells
1964 W. Robinson	1924 J. Elliot	1924 H. Mitchell	1885 W. West	1966 A. Brogan
1965 P. Dwyer	1925 J. Elliot	1925 H. Mitchell	1886 A. Diamond	1967 P. Boddington
1966 T. Imrie	1926 F. P. Crawley	1926 D. McCorkindale	1887 E. White	1968 W. Wells
1967 A. Edwards	1927 F. P. Crawley	1927 A. Jackson	1888 W. King	1969 A. Burton
1968 E. Blake	1928 F. Mallin	1928 A. Jackson	1889 A. Bowman	1970 J. Gilmour
1969 T. Imrie	1929 F. Mallin	1929 J. Goyder	1890 J. Steers	1971 L. Stevens
1970 D. Simmonds	1930 F. Mallin	1930 J. Murphy	1891 V. Barker	1972 T. Wood
1971 A. Edwards	1931 F. Mallin	1931 J. Petersen	1892 J. Steers	1973 G. McEwan
1972 L. Paul	1932 F. Mallin	1932 J. Goyder	1893 J. Steers	1974 N. Meade
1973 R. Maxwell	1933 A. Shawyer	1933 G. Brennan	1894 H. King	1975 G. McEwan
1974 R. Maxwell	1934 J. Magill	1934 G. Brennan	1895 W. E. Johnstone	1976 J. Rafferty
1975 A. Harrison	1935 J. Magill	1935 R. Hearns	1896 W. E. Johnstone	1977 G. Adair
1976 W. Lauder	1936 A. Harrington	1936 J. Magill	1897 G. Townsend	1978 J. Awome
1977 C. Malarkey	1937 M. Dennis	1937 J. Wilby	1898 G. Townsend	1979 A. Palmer
1978 E. Henderson	1938 H. Tiller	1938 A. S. Brown	1899 F. Parks	1980 F. Bruno
1979 D. Brewster	1939 H. Davies	1939 B. Woodcock	1900 W. Dees	1981 A. Elliott
1980 J. Price	1944 J. Hockley	1944 E. Shackleton	1901 F. Parks	1982 H. Hylton
1981 E. Christie	1945 R. Parker	1945 A. Watson	1902 F. Parks	1983 H. Notice
1982 D. Milligan	1946 R. Turpin	1946 J. Taylor	1903 F. Dickson	1984 D. Young
1983 R. Douglas	1947 R. Agland	1947 A. Watson	1904 A. Horner	1985 H. Hylton
1984 R. Douglas	1948 J. Wright	1948 D. Scott	1905 F. Parks	1986 E. Cardouza
1985 R. Douglas	1949 S. Lewis	1949 *Declared no contest*	1906 F. Parks	1987 J. Moran
1986 T. Velinor	1950 P. Longo	1950 P. Messervy	1907 H. Brewer	1988 H. Akinwande
1987 N. Brown	1951 E. Ludlam	1951 G. Walker	1908 S. Evans	1989 H. Akinwande
1988 W. Ellis	1952 T. Gooding	1952 H. Cooper	1909 C. Brown	1990 K. Inglis
1989 N. Brown	1953 S. Barton	1953 H. Cooper	1910 F. Storbeck	1991 P. Lawson
1990 T. Taylor	1954 K. Phillips	1954 A. Madigan	1911 W. Hazell	1992 S. Welch
1991 T. Taylor	1955 F. Hope	1955 D. Rent	1912 R. Smith	1993 P. Lawson
1992 J. Calzaghe	1956 R. Redrup	1956 D. Mooney	1913 R. Smith	
1993 D. Starie	1957 P. Burke	1957 T. Green	1914 E. Chandler	
	1958 P. Hill	1958 J. Leeming	1919 H. Brown	**S. Heavyweight**
	1959 F. Elderfield	1959 J. Ould	1920 R. Rawson	1982 A. Elliott
	1960 R. Addison	1960 J. Ould	1921 R. Rawson	1983 K. Ferdinand
Middleweight	1961 J. Caiger	1961 J. Bodell	1922 T. Evans	1984 R. Wells
1881 T. Bellhouse	1962 A. Matthews	1962 J. Hendrickson	1923 E. Eagan	1985 G. Williamson
1882 A. H. Curnick	1963 A. Matthews	1963 P. Murphy	1924 A. Clifton	1986 J. Oyebola
1883 A. J. Curnick	1964 W. Stack	1964 J. Fisher	1925 D. Lister	1987 J. Oyebola
1884 W. Brown	1965 W. Robinson	1965 E. Whistler	1926 T. Petersen	1988 K. McCormack
1885 M. Salmon	1966 C. Finnegan	1966 R. Tighe	1927 C. Capper	1989 P. Passley
1886 W. King	1967 A. Ball	1967 M. Smith	1928 J. L. Driscoll	1990 K. McCormack
1887 R. Hair	1968 P. McCann	1968 R. Brittle	1929 P. Floyd	1991 K. McCormack
1888 R. Hair	1969 D. Wallington	1969 J. Frankham	1930 V. Stuart	1992 M. Hopper
1889 G. Sykes	1970 J. Conteh	1970 J. Rafferty	1931 M. Flanagan	1993 M. McKenzie

International Amateur Champions, 1904-1993

Shows all Olympic, World, European & Commonwealth champions since 1904. British silver and bronze medal winners are shown throughout, where applicable.

Country Code

ARG = Argentine; ARM = Armenia; AUS = Australia; AUT = Austria; BEL = Belgium; BUL = Bulgaria; CAN = Canada; CEY = Ceylon (now Sri Lanka); CUB = Cuba; DEN = Denmark; DOM = Dominican Republic; ENG = England; ESP = Spain; EST = Estonia; FIJ = Fiji Islands; FIN = Finland; FRA = France; GBR = United Kingdom; GDR = German Democratic Republic; GEO = Georgia; GER = Germany (but West Germany only from 1968-1990); GHA = Ghana; GUY = Guyana; HOL = Netherlands; HUN = Hungary; IRL = Ireland; ITA = Italy; JAM = Jamaica; JPN = Japan; KEN = Kenya; MEX = Mexico; NKO = North Korea; NIG = Nigeria; NIR = Northern Ireland; NOR = Norway; NZL = New Zealand; POL = Poland; PUR = Puerto Rico; ROM = Romania; RUS = Russia; SAF = South Africa; SCO = Scotland; SKO = South Korea; STV = St Vincent; SWE = Sweden; TCH = Czechoslovakia; TUR = Turkey; UGA = Uganda; URS = USSR; USA = United States of America; VEN = Venezuela; WAL = Wales; YUG = Yugoslavia; ZAM = Zambia.

Olympic Champions, 1904-1992

St Louis, USA - 1904
Fly: G. Finnegan (USA). **Bantam:** O. Kirk (USA). **Feather:** O. Kirk (USA). **Light:** H. Spangler (USA). **Welter:** A. Young (USA). **Middle:** C. May (USA). **Heavy:** S. Berger (USA).

London, England - 1908
Bantam: H. Thomas (GBR). **Feather:** R. Gunn (GBR). **Light:** F. Grace (GBR). **Middle:** J.W.H.T. Douglas (GBR). **Heavy:** A. Oldham (GBR).
Silver medals: J. Condon (GBR), C. Morris (GBR), F. Spiller (GBR), S. Evans (GBR).
Bronze medals: W. Webb (GBR), H. Rodding (GBR), T. Ringer (GBR), H. Johnson (GBR), R. Warnes (GBR), W. Philo (GBR), F. Parks (GBR).

Antwerp, Belgium - 1920
Fly: F. Genaro (USA). **Bantam:** C. Walker (SAF). **Feather:** R. Fritsch (FRA). **Light:** S. Mossberg (USA). **Welter:** T. Schneider (CAN). **Middle:** H. Mallin (GBR). **L. Heavy:** E. Eagan (USA). **Heavy:** R. Rawson (GBR).
Silver medal: A. Ireland (GBR).
Bronze medals: W. Cuthbertson (GBR), G. McKenzie (GBR), H. Franks (GBR).

Paris, France - 1924
Fly: F. la Barba (USA). **Bantam:** W. Smith (SAF). **Feather:** J. Fields (USA). **Light:** H. Nielson (DEN). **Welter:** J. Delarge (BEL). **Middle:** H. Mallin (GBR). **L. Heavy:** H. Mitchell (GBR). **Heavy:** O. von Porat (NOR).
Silver medals: J. McKenzie (GBR), J. Elliot (GBR).

Amsterdam, Holland - 1928
Fly: A. Kocsis (HUN). **Bantam:** V. Tamagnini (ITA). **Feather:** B. van Klaveren (HOL). **Light:** C. Orlando (ITA). **Welter:** E. Morgan (NZL). **Middle:** P. Toscani (ITA). **L. Heavy:** V. Avendano (ARG). **Heavy:** A. Rodriguez Jurado (ARG).

Los Angeles, USA - 1932
Fly: I. Enekes (HUN). **Bantam:** H. Gwynne (CAN). **Feather:** C. Robledo (ARG). **Light:** L. Stevens (SAF). **Welter:** E. Flynn (USA). **Middle:** C. Barth (USA). **L. Heavy:** D. Carstens (SAF). **Heavy:** A. Lovell (ARG).

Berlin, West Germany - 1936
Fly: W. Kaiser (GER). **Bantam:** U. Sergo (ITA). **Feather:** O. Casanova (ARG). **Light:** I. Harangi (HUN). **Welter:** S. Suvio (FIN). **Middle:** J. Despeaux (FRA). **L. Heavy:** R. Michelot (FRA). **Heavy:** H. Runge (GER).

London, England - 1948
Fly: P. Perez (ARG). **Bantam:** T. Csik (HUN). **Feather:** E. Formenti (ITA). **Light:** G. Dreyer (SAF). **Welter:** J. Torma (TCH). **Middle:** L. Papp (HUN). **L. Heavy:** G. Hunter (SAF). **Heavy:** R. Iglesas (ARG).
Silver medals: J. Wright (GBR), D. Scott (GBR).

Helsinki, Finland - 1952
Fly: N. Brooks (USA). **Bantam:** P. Hamalainen (FIN). **Feather:** J. Zachara (TCH). **Light:** A. Bolognesi (ITA). **L. Welter:** C. Adkins (USA). **Welter:** Z. Chychla (POL). **L. Middle:** L. Papp (HUN). **Middle:** F. Patterson (USA). **L. Heavy:** N. Lee (USA). **Heavy:** E. Sanders (USA).
Silver medal: J. McNally (IRL).

Melbourne, Australia - 1956
Fly: T. Spinks (GBR). **Bantam:** W. Behrendt (GER). **Feather:** V. Safronov (URS). **Light:** R. McTaggart (GBR). **L. Welter:** V. Jengibarian (URS). **Welter:** N. Linca (ROM). **L. Middle:** L. Papp (HUN). **Middle:** G. Schatkov (URS). **L. Heavy:** J. Boyd (USA). **Heavy:** P. Rademacher (USA).
Silver medals: T. Nicholls (GBR), F. Tiedt (IRL).
Bronze medals: J. Caldwell (IRL), F. Gilroy (IRL), A. Byrne (IRL), N. Gargano (GBR), J. McCormack (GBR).

Rome, Italy - 1960
Fly: G. Torok (HUN). **Bantam:** O. Grigoryev (URS). **Feather:** F. Musso (ITA). **Light:** K. Pazdzior (POL). **L. Welter:** B. Nemecek (TCH). **Welter:** N. Benvenuti (ITA). **L. Middle:** W. McClure (USA). **Middle:** E. Crook (USA). **L. Heavy:** C. Clay (USA). **Heavy:** F. de Piccoli (ITA).
Bronze medals: R. McTaggart (GBR), J. Lloyd (GBR), W. Fisher (GBR).

Tokyo, Japan - 1964
Fly: F. Atzori (ITA). **Bantam:** T. Sakurai (JPN). **Feather:** S. Stepashkin (URS). **Light:** J. Grudzien (POL). **L. Welter:** J. Kulej (POL). **Welter:** M. Kasprzyk (POL). **L. Middle:** B. Lagutin (URS). **Middle:** V. Popenchenko (URS). **L. Heavy:** C. Pinto (ITA). **Heavy:** J. Frazier (USA).
Bronze medal: J. McCourt (IRL).

Mexico City, Mexico - 1968
L. Fly: F. Rodriguez (VEN). **Fly:** R. Delgado (MEX). **Bantam:** V. Sokolov (URS). **Feather:** A. Roldan (MEX). **Light:** R. Harris (USA). **L. Welter:** J. Kulej (POL). **Welter:** M. Wolke (GDR). **L. Middle:** B. Lagutin (URS). **Middle:** C. Finnegan (GBR). **L. Heavy:** D. Poznyak (URS). **Heavy:** G. Foreman (USA).

Munich, West Germany - 1972
L. Fly: G. Gedo (HUN). **Fly:** G. Kostadinov (BUL). **Bantam:** O. Martinez (CUB). **Feather:** B. Kusnetsov (BUL). **Light:** J. Szczepanski (POL). **L. Welter:** R. Seales (USA). **Welter:** E. Correa (CUB). **L. Middle:** D. Kottysch (GER). **Middle:** V. Lemeschev (URS). **L. Heavy:** M. Parlov (YUG). **Heavy:** T. Stevenson (CUB).
Bronze medals: R. Evans (GBR), G. Turpin (GBR), A. Minter (GBR).

Montreal, Canada - 1976
L. Fly: J. Hernandez (CUB). **Fly:** L. Randolph (USA). **Bantam:** Y-J. Gu (NKO). **Feather:** A. Herrera (CUB). **Light:** H. Davis (USA). **L. Welter:** R. Leonard (USA). **Welter:** J. Bachfield (GDR). **L. Middle:** J. Rybicki (POL). **Middle:** M. Spinks (USA). **L. Heavy:** L. Spinks (USA). **Heavy:** T. Stevenson (CUB).
Bronze medal: P. Cowdell (GBR).

Moscow, USSR - 1980
L. Fly: S. Sabirov (URS). **Fly:** P. Lessov (BUL). **Bantam:** J. Hernandez (CUB). **Feather:** R. Fink (GDR). **Light:** A. Herrera (CUB). **L. Welter:** P. Oliva (ITA). **Welter:** A. Aldama (CUB). **L. Middle:** A. Martinez (CUB). **Middle:** J. Gomez (CUB). **L. Heavy:** S. Kacar (YUG). **Heavy:** T. Stevenson (CUB).
Bronze medals: H. Russell (IRL), A. Willis (GBR).

Los Angeles, USA - 1984
L. Fly: P. Gonzalez (USA). **Fly:** S. McCrory (USA). **Bantam:** M. Stecca (ITA). **Feather:** M. Taylor (USA). **Light:** P. Whitaker (USA). **L. Welter:** J.

Page (USA). **Welter:** M. Breland (USA). **L. Middle:** F. Tate (USA). **Middle:** J-S. Shin (SKO). **L. Heavy:** A. Josipovic (YUG). **Heavy:** H. Tillman (USA). **S. Heavy:** T. Biggs (USA).
Bronze medal: B. Wells (GBR).

Seoul, South Korea - 1988
L. Fly: I. Hristov (BUL). **Fly:** H-S. Kim (SKO). **Bantam:** K. McKinney (USA). **Feather:** G. Parisi (ITA). **Light:** A. Zuelow (GDR). **L. Welter:** V. Yanovsky (URS). **Welter:** R. Wangila (KEN). **L. Middle:** S-H. Park (SKO). **Middle:** H. Maske (GDR). **L. Heavy:** A. Maynard (USA). **Heavy:**

R. Mercer (USA). **S. Heavy:** L. Lewis (CAN).
Bronze medal: R. Woodhall (GBR).

Barcelona, Spain - 1992
L. Fly: R. Marcelo (CUB). **Fly:** C-C. Su (NKO). **Bantam:** J. Casamayor (CUB). **Feather:** A. Tews (GER). **Light:** O. de la Hoya (USA). **L. Welter:** H. Vinent (CUB). **Welter:** M. Carruth (IRL). **L. Middle:** J. Lemus (CUB). **Middle:** A. Hernandez (CUB). **L. Heavy:** T. May (GER). **Heavy:** F. Savon (CUB). **S. Heavy:** R. Balado (CUB).
Silver medal: W. McCullough (IRL).
Bronze medal: R. Reid (GBR).

A young Muhammad Ali who, as Cassius Clay, won the 1960 Olympic light-heavyweight title. Since Floyd Patterson won an Olympic title in 1952, seven other men, Muhammad Ali, Joe Frazier, George Foreman, Leon Spinks, Michael Spinks (IBF), Ray Mercer (WBO) and Lennox Lewis (WBC), have springboarded from their gold medal successes to professional world heavyweight titles

Derek Rowe (Photos) Ltd

World Champions, 1974-1993

Havana, Cuba - 1974
L. Fly: J. Hernandez (CUB). **Fly:** D. Rodriguez (CUB). **Bantam:** W. Gomez (PUR). **Feather:** H. Davis (USA). **Light:** V. Solomin (URS). **L. Welter:** A. Kalule (UGA). **Welter:** E. Correa (CUB). **L. Middle:** R. Garbey (CUB). **Middle:** R. Riskiev (URS). **L. Heavy:** M. Parlov (YUG). **Heavy:** T. Stevenson (CUB).

Belgrade, Yugoslavia - 1978
L. Fly: S. Muchoki (KEN). **Fly:** H. Strednicki (POL). **Bantam:** A. Horta (CUB). **Feather:** A. Herrera (CUB). **Light:** D. Andeh (NIG). **L. Welter:** V. Lvov (URS). **Welter:** V. Rachkov (URS). **L. Middle:** V. Savchenko (URS). **Middle:** J. Gomez (CUB). **L. Heavy:** S. Soria (CUB). **Heavy:** T. Stevenson (CUB).

Munich, West Germany - 1982
L. Fly: I. Mustafov (BUL). **Fly:** Y. Alexandrov (URS). **Bantam:** F. Favors (USA). **Feather:** A. Horta (CUB). **Light:** A. Herrera (CUB). **L. Welter:** C. Garcia (CUB). **Welter:** M. Breland (USA). **L. Middle:** A. Koshkin (URS). **Middle:** B. Comas (CUB). **L. Heavy:** P. Romero (CUB). **Heavy:** A. Jagubkin (URS). **S. Heavy:** T. Biggs (USA).
Bronze medal: T. Corr (IRL).

Reno, USA - 1986
L. Fly: J. Odelin (CUB). **Fly:** P. Reyes (CUB). **Bantam:** S-I. Moon (SKO). **Feather:** K. Banks (USA). **Light:** A. Horta (CUB). **L. Welter:** V. Shishov (URS). **Welter:** K. Gould (USA). **L. Middle:** A. Espinosa (CUB). **Middle:** D. Allen (USA). **L. Heavy:** P. Romero (CUB). **Heavy:** F. Savon (CUB). **S. Heavy:** T. Stevenson (CUB).

Moscow, USSR - 1989
L. Fly: E. Griffin (USA). **Fly:** Y. Arbachakov (URS). **Bantam:** E. Carrion (CUB). **Feather:** A. Khamatov (URS). **Light:** J. Gonzalez (CUB). **L. Welter:** I. Ruzinkov (URS). **Welter:** F. Vastag. **L. Middle:** I. Akopokhian (URS). **Middle:** A. Kurniavka (URS). **L. Heavy:** H. Maske (GDR). **Heavy:** F. Savon (CUB). **S. Heavy:** R. Balado (CUB).
Bronze medal: M. Carruth (IRL).

Sydney, Australia - 1991
L. Fly: E. Griffin (USA). **Fly:** I. Kovacs (HUN). **Bantam:** S. Todorov (BUL). **Feather:** K. Kirkorov (BUL). **Light:** M. Rudolph (GER). **L. Welter:** K. Tsziu (URS). **Welter:** J. Hernandez (CUB). **L. Middle:** J. Lemus (CUB). **Middle:** T. Russo (ITA). **L. Heavy:** T. May (GER). **Heavy:** F. Savon (CUB). **S. Heavy:** R. Balado (CUB).

Tampere, Finland - 1993
L. Fly: N. Munchian (ARM). **Fly:** W. Font (CUB). **Bantam:** A. Christov (BUL). **Feather:** S. Todorov (BUL). **Light:** D. Austin (CUB). **L. Welter:** H. Vinent (CUB). **Welter:** J. Hernandez (CUB). **L. Middle:** F. Vastag (ROM). **Middle:** A. Hernandez (CUB). **L. Heavy:** R. Garbey (CUB). **Heavy:** F. Savon (CUB). **S. Heavy:** R. Balado (CUB).
Bronze medal: D. Kelly (NIR).

World Junior Champions, 1979-1992

Yokohama, Japan - 1979
L. Fly: R. Shannon (USA). **Fly:** P. Lessov (BUL). **Bantam:** P-K. Choi (SKO). **Feather:** Y. Gladychev (URS). **Light:** R. Blake (USA). **L. Welter:** I. Akopokhian (URS). **Welter:** M. McCrory (USA). **L. Middle:** A. Mayes (USA). **Middle:** A. Milov (URS). **L. Heavy:** A. Lebedev (URS). **Heavy:** M. Frazier (USA).
Silver medals: N. Wilshire (ENG), D. Cross (ENG).
Bronze medal: I. Scott (SCO).

Santa Domingo, Dominican Republic - 1983
L. Fly: M. Herrera (DOM). **Fly:** J. Gonzalez (CUB). **Bantam:** J. Molina (PUR). **Feather:** A. Miesses (DOM). **Light:** A. Beltre (DOM). **L. Welter:** A. Espinoza (CUB). **Welter:** M. Watkins (USA). **L. Middle:** U. Castillo (CUB). **Middle:** R. Batista (CUB). **L. Heavy:** O. Pought (USA). **Heavy:** A. Williams (USA). **S. Heavy:** L. Lewis (CAN).

Bucharest, Romania - 1985
L. Fly: R-S. Hwang (SKO). **Fly:** T. Marcelica (ROM). **Bantam:** R. Diaz (CUB). **Feather:** D. Maeran (ROM). **Light:** J. Teiche (GDR). **L. Welter:** W. Saeger (GDR). **Welter:** A. Stoianov (BUL). **L. Middle:** M. Franek (TCH). **Middle:** O. Zahalotskih (URS). **L. Heavy:** B. Riddick (USA). **Heavy:** F. Savon (CUB). **S. Heavy:** A. Prianichnikov (URS).

Havana, Cuba - 1987
L. Fly: E. Paisan (CUB). **Fly:** C. Daniels (USA). **Bantam:** A. Moya (CUB). **Feather:** G. Iliyasov (URS). **Light:** J. Hernandez (CUB). **L. Welter:** L. Mihai (ROM). **Welter:** F. Vastag (ROM). **L. Middle:** A. Lobsyak (URS). **Middle:** W. Martinez (CUB). **L. Heavy:** D. Yeliseyev (URS). **Heavy:** R. Balado (CUB). **S. Heavy:** L. Martinez (CUB).
Silver medal: E. Loughran (IRL).
Bronze medal: D. Galvin (IRL).

San Juan, Puerto Rico - 1989
L. Fly: D. Petrov (BUL). **Fly:** N. Monchai (FRA). **Bantam:** J. Casamayor (CUB). **Feather:** C. Febres (PUR). **Light:** A. Acevedo (PUR). **L. Welter:** E. Berger (GDR). **Welter:** A. Hernandez (CUB). **L. Middle:** L. Bedey (CUB). **Middle:** R. Garbey (CUB). **L. Heavy:** R. Alvarez (CUB). **Heavy:** K. Johnson (CAN). **S. Heavy:** A. Burdiantz (URS).
Silver medals: E. Magee (IRL), R. Reid (ENG), S. Wilson (SCO).

Lima, Peru - 1990
L. Fly: D. Alicea (PUR). **Fly:** K. Pielert (GDR). **Bantam:** K. Baravi (URS). **Feather:** A. Vaughan (ENG). **Light:** J. Mendez (CUB). **L. Welter:** H. Vinent (CUB). **Welter:** A. Hernandez (CUB). **L. Middle:** A. Kakauridze (URS). **Middle:** J. Gomez (CUB). **L. Heavy:** B. Torsten (GDR). **Heavy:** I. Andreev (URS). **S. Heavy:** J. Quesada (CUB).
Bronze medal: P. Ingle (ENG).

Montreal, Canada - 1992
L. Fly: W. Font (CUB). **Fly:** J. Oragon (CUB). **Bantam:** M. Neslan (CUB). **Feather:** M. Stewart (CAN). **Light:** D. Austin (CUB). **L. Welter:** O. Saitov (RUS). **Welter:** L. Brors (GER). **L. Middle:** J. Acosta (CUB). **Middle:** I. Arsangaliev (RUS). **L. Heavy:** S. Samilsan (TUR). **Heavy:** G. Kandeliaki (GEO). **S. Heavy:** M. Porchnev (RUS).
Bronze medal: N. Sinclair (IRL).

European Champions, 1924-1991

Paris, France - 1924
Fly: J. McKenzie (GBR). **Bantam:** J. Ces (FRA). **Feather:** R. de Vergnie (BEL). **Light:** N. Nielsen (DEN). **Welter:** J. Delarge (BEL). **Middle:** H. Mallin (GBR). **L. Heavy:** H. Mitchell (GBR). **Heavy:** O. von Porat (NOR).

Stockholm, Sweden - 1925
Fly: E. Pladner (FRA). **Bantam:** A. Rule (GBR). **Feather:** P. Andren (SWE). **Light:** S. Johanssen (SWE). **Welter:** H. Nielsen (DEN). **Middle:** F. Crawley (GBR). **L. Heavy:** T. Petersen (DEN). **Heavy:** B. Persson (SWE).
Silver medals: J. James (GBR), E. Viney (GBR), D. Lister (GBR).

Berlin, Germany - 1927
Fly: L. Boman (GER). **Bantam:** Dalchow (GER). **Feather:** F. Dubbers (GER). **Light:** H. Domgoergen (GER). **Welter:** R. Caneva (ITA). **Middle:** J. Christensen (NOR). **L. Heavy:** H. Muller (GER). **Heavy:** N. Ramm (SWE).

Amsterdam, Holland - 1928
Fly: A. Kocsis (HUN). **Bantam:** V. Tamagnini (ITA). **Feather:** B. van Klaveren (HOL). **Light:** C. Orlandi (ITA). **Welter:** R. Galataud (FRA). **Middle:** P. Toscani (ITA). **L. Heavy:** E. Pistulla (GER). **Heavy:** N. Ramm (SWE).

Budapest, Hungary - 1930
Fly: I. Enekes (HUN). **Bantam:** J. Szeles (HUN). **Feather:** G. Szabo (HUN). **Light:** M. Bianchini (ITA). **Welter:** J. Besselmann (GER). **Middle:** C. Meroni (ITA). **L. Heavy:** T. Petersen (DEN). **Heavy:** J. Michaelson (DEN).

Los Angeles, USA - 1932
Fly: I. Enekes (HUN). **Bantam:** H. Ziglarski (GER). **Feather:** J. Schleinkofer (GER). **Light:** T. Ahlqvist (SWE). **Welter:** E. Campe (GER). **Middle:** R. Michelot (FRA). **L. Heavy:** G. Rossi (ITA). **Heavy:** L. Rovati (ITA).

Budapest, Hungary - 1934
Fly: P. Palmer (GBR). **Bantam:** I. Enekes (HUN). **Feather:** O. Kaestner (GER). **Light:** E. Facchini (ITA). **Welter:** D. McCleave (GBR). **Middle:** S. Szigetti (HUN). **L. Heavy:** P. Zehetmayer (AUT). **Heavy:** G. Baerlund (FIN).
Bronze medal: P. Floyd (GBR).

Milan, Italy - 1937

Fly: I. Enekes (HUN). **Bantam:** U. Sergo (ITA). **Feather:** A. Polus (POL). **Light:** H. Nuremberg (GER). **Welter:** M. Murach (GER). **Middle:** H. Chmielewski (POL). **L. Heavy:** S. Szigetti (HUN). **Heavy:** O. Tandberg (SWE).

Dublin, Eire - 1939

Fly: J. Ingle (IRL). **Bantam:** U. Sergo (ITA). **Feather:** P. Dowdall (IRL). **Light:** H. Nuremberg (GER). **Welter:** A. Kolczyski (POL). **Middle:** A. Raedek (EST). **L. Heavy:** L. Musina (ITA). **Heavy:** O. Tandberg (SWE). **Bronze medal:** C. Evenden (IRL).

Dublin, Eire - 1947

Fly: L. Martinez (ESP). **Bantam:** L. Bogacs (HUN). **Feather:** K. Kreuger (SWE). **Light:** J. Vissers (BEL). **Welter:** J. Ryan (ENG). **Middle:** A. Escudie (FRA). **L. Heavy:** H. Quentemeyer (HOL). **Heavy:** G. O'Colmain (IRL).
Silver medals: J. Clinton (SCO), P. Maguire (IRL), W. Thom (ENG), G. Scriven (ENG).
Bronze medals: J. Dwyer (SCO), A. Sanderson (ENG), W. Frith (SCO), E. Cantwell (IRL), K. Wyatt (ENG).

Oslo, Norway - 1949

Fly: J. Kasperczak (POL). **Bantam:** G. Zuddas (ITA). **Feather:** J. Bataille (FRA). **Light:** M. McCullagh (IRL). **Welter:** J. Torma (TCH). **Middle:** L. Papp (HUN). **L. Heavy:** G. di Segni (ITA). **Heavy:** L. Bene (HUN).
Bronze medal: D. Connell (IRL).

Milan, Italy - 1951

Fly: A. Pozzali (ITA). **Bantam:** V. Dall'Osso (ITA). **Feather:** J. Ventaja (FRA). **Light:** B. Visintin (ITA). **L. Welter:** H. Schelling (GER). **Welter:** Z. Chychla (POL). **L. Middle:** L. Papp (HUN). **Middle:** S. Sjolin (SWE). **L. Heavy:** M. Limage (BEL). **Heavy:** G. di Segni (ITA).
Silver medal: J. Kelly (IRL).
Bronze medals: D. Connell (IRL), T. Milligan (IRL), A. Lay (ENG).

Warsaw, Poland - 1953

Fly: H. Kukier (POL). **Bantam:** Z. Stefaniuk (POL). **Feather:** J. Kruza (POL). **Light:** V. Jengibarian (URS). **L. Welter:** L. Drogosz (POL). **Welter:** Z. Chychla (POL). **L. Middle:** B. Wells (ENG). **Middle:** D. Wemhoner (GER). **L. Heavy:** U. Nietchke (GER). **Heavy:** A. Schotzikas (URS).
Silver medal: T. Milligan (IRL).
Bronze medals: J. McNally (IRL), R. Barton (ENG).

Berlin, West Germany - 1955

Fly: E. Basel (GER). **Bantam:** Z. Stefaniuk (POL). **Feather:** T. Nicholls (ENG). **Light:** H. Kurschat (GER). **L. Welter:** L. Drogosz (POL). **Welter:** N. Gargano (ENG). **L. Middle:** Z. Pietrzykowski (POL). **Middle:** G. Schatkov (URS). **L. Heavy:** E. Schoeppner (GER). **Heavy:** A. Schotzikas (URS).

Prague, Czechoslovakia - 1957

Fly: M. Homberg (GER). **Bantam:** O. Grigoryev (URS). **Feather:** D. Venilov (BUL). **Light:** K. Pazdzior (POL). **L. Welter:** V. Jengibarian (URS). **Welter:** M. Graus (GER). **L. Middle:** N. Benvenuti (ITA). **Middle:** Z. Pietrzykowski (POL). **L. Heavy:** G. Negrea (ROM). **Heavy:** A. Abramov (URS).
Bronze medals: R. Davies (WAL), J. Morrissey (SCO), J. Kidd (SCO), F. Teidt (IRL).

Lucerne, Switzerland - 1959

Fly: M. Homberg (GER). **Bantam:** H. Rascher (GER). **Feather:** J. Adamski (POL). **Light:** O. Maki (FIN). **L. Welter:** V. Jengibarian (URS). **Welter:** L. Drogosz (POL). **L. Middle:** N. Benvenuti (ITA). **Middle:** G. Schatkov (URS). **L. Heavy:** Z. Pietrzykowski (POL). **Heavy:** A. Abramov (URS).
Silver medal: D. Thomas (ENG).
Bronze medals: A. McClean (IRL), H. Perry (IRL), C. McCoy (IRL), H. Scott (ENG).

Belgrade, Yugoslavia - 1961

Fly: P. Vacca (ITA). **Bantam:** S. Sivko (URS). **Feather:** F. Taylor (ENG). **Light:** R. McTaggart (SCO). **L. Welter:** A. Tamulis (URS). **Welter:** R. Tamulis (URS). **L. Middle:** B. Lagutin (URS). **Middle:** T. Walasek (POL). **L. Heavy:** G. Saraudi (ITA). **Heavy:** A. Abramov (URS).
Bronze medals: P. Warwick (ENG), I. McKenzie (SCO), J. Bodell (ENG).

Moscow, USSR - 1963

Fly: V. Bystrov (URS). **Bantam:** O. Grigoryev (URS). **Feather:** S. Stepashkin (URS). **Light:** J. Kajdi (HUN). **L. Welter:** J. Kulej (POL). **Welter:** R. Tamulis (URS). **L. Middle:** B. Lagutin (URS). **Middle:** V. Popenchenko (URS). **L. Heavy:** Z. Pietrzykowski (POL). **Heavy:** J. Nemec (TCH).
Silver medal: A. Wyper (SCO).

Berlin, East Germany - 1965

Fly: H. Freisdadt (GER). **Bantam:** O. Grigoryev (URS). **Feather:** S. Stepashkin (URS). **Light:** V. Barranikov (URS). **L. Welter:** J. Kulej (POL). **Welter:** R. Tamulis (URS). **L. Middle:** V. Ageyev (URS). **Middle:** V. Popenchenko (URS). **L. Heavy:** D. Poznyak (URS). **Heavy:** A. Isosimov (URS).
Silver medal: B. Robinson (ENG).
Bronze medals: J. McCluskey (SCO), K. Buchanan (SCO), J. McCourt (IRL).

Rome, Italy - 1967

Fly: H. Skrzyczak (POL). **Bantam:** N. Giju (ROM). **Feather:** R. Petek (POL). **Light:** J. Grudzien (POL). **L. Welter:** V. Frolov (URS). **Welter:** B. Nemecek (TCH). **L. Middle:** V. Ageyev (URS). **Middle:** M. Casati (ITA). **L. Heavy:** D. Poznyak (URS). **Heavy:** M. Baruzzi (ITA).
Silver medal: P. Boddington (ENG).

Bucharest, Romania - 1969

L. Fly: G. Gedo (HUN). **Fly:** C. Ciuca (ROM). **Bantam:** A. Dumitrescu (ROM). **Feather:** L. Orban (HUN). **Light:** S. Cutov (ROM). **L. Welter:** V. Frolov (URS). **Welter:** G. Meier (GER). **L. Middle:** V. Tregubov (URS). **Middle:** V. Tarasenkov (URS). **L. Heavy:** D. Poznyak (URS). **Heavy:** I. Alexe (ROM).
Bronze medals: M. Dowling (IRL), M. Piner (ENG), A. Richardson (ENG), T. Imrie (SCO).

Madrid, Spain - 1971

L. Fly: G. Gedo (HUN). **Fly:** J. Rodriguez (ESP). **Bantam:** T. Badar (HUN). **Feather:** R. Tomczyk (POL). **Light:** J. Szczepanski (POL). **L. Welter:** U. Beyer (GER). **Welter:** J. Kajdi (HUN). **L. Middle:** V. Tregubov (URS). **Middle:** J. Juotsiavitchus (BUL). **L. Heavy:** M. Parlov (BUL). **Heavy:** V. Tchernishev (URS).
Bronze medals: N. McLaughlin (IRL), M. Dowling (IRL), B. McCarthy (IRL), M. Kingwell (ENG), L. Stevens (ENG).

Belgrade, Yugoslavia - 1973

L. Fly: V. Zasypko (URS). **Fly:** C. Gruescu (ROM). **Bantam:** A. Cosentino (FRA). **Feather:** S. Forster (GDR). **Light:** S. Cutov (ROM). **L. Welter:** M. Benes (YUG). **Welter:** S. Csjef (HUN). **L. Middle:** A. Klimanov (URS). **Middle:** V. Lemechev (URS). **L. Heavy:** M. Parlov (YUG). **Heavy:** V. Ulyanich (URS).
Bronze medal: J. Bambrick (SCO).

Katowice, Poland - 1975

L. Fly: A. Tkachenko (URS). **Fly:** V. Zasypko (URS). **Bantam:** V. Rybakov (URS). **Feather:** T. Badari (HUN). **Light:** S. Cutov (ROM). **L. Welter:** V. Limasov (URS). **Welter:** K. Marjaama (FIN). **L. Middle:** W. Rudnowski (POL). **Middle:** V. Lemechev (URS). **L. Heavy:** A. Klimanov (URS). **Heavy:** A. Biegalski (POL).
Bronze medals: C. Magri (ENG), P. Cowdell (ENG), G. McEwan (ENG).

Halle, East Germany - 1977

L. Fly: H. Srednicki (POL). **Fly:** L. Blazynski (POL). **Bantam:** S. Forster (GDR). **Feather:** R. Nowakowski (GDR). **Light:** A. Rusevski (YUG). **L. Welter:** B. Gajda (POL). **Welter:** V. Limasov (URS). **L. Middle:** V. Saychenko (URS). **Middle:** I. Shaposhnikov (URS). **L. Heavy:** D. Kvachadze (URS). **Heavy:** E. Gorstkov (URS).
Bronze medal: P. Sutcliffe (IRL).

Cologne, West Germany - 1979

L. Fly: S. Sabirov (URS). **Fly:** H. Strednicki (POL). **Bantam:** N. Khrapzov (URS). **Feather:** V. Rybakov (URS). **Light.** V. Demianenko (URS). **L. Welter:** S. Konakbaev (URS). **Welter:** E. Muller (GER). **L. Middle:** M. Perunovic (YUG). **Middle:** T. Uusiverta (FIN). **L. Heavy:** A. Nikolyan (URS). **Heavy:** E. Gorstkov (URS).
Bronze medal: P. Sutcliffe (IRL).

Tampere, Finland - 1981

L. Fly: I. Hristov (BUL). **Fly:** P. Lessov (BUL). **Bantam:** V. Miroschnichenko (URS). **Feather:** R. Nowakowski (GDR). **Light:** V.

Rybakov (URS). **L. Welter:** V. Shisov (URS). **Welter:** S. Konakvbaev (URS). **L. Middle:** A. Koshkin (URS). **Middle:** J. Torbek (URS). **L. Heavy:** A Krupin (URS). **Heavy:** A. Jagupkin (URS). **S. Heavy:** F. Damiani (ITA).
Bronze medal: G. Hawkins (IRL).

Varna, Bulgaria - 1983
L. Fly: I. Hristov (BUL). **Fly:** P. Lessov (BUL). **Bantam:** Y. Alexandrov (URS). **Feather:** S. Nurkazov (URS). **Light:** E. Chuprenski (BUL). **L. Welter:** V. Shishov (URS). **Welter:** P. Galkin (URS). **L. Middle:** V. Laptev (URS). **Middle:** V. Melnik (URS). **L. Heavy:** V. Kokhanovski (URS). **Heavy:** A. Jagubkin (URS). **S. Heavy:** F. Damiani (ITA).
Bronze medal: K. Joyce (IRL).

Budapest, Hungary - 1985
L. Fly: R. Breitbarth (GDR). **Fly:** D. Berg (GDR). **Bantam:** L. Simic (YUG). **Feather:** S. Khachatrian (URS). **Light:** E. Chuprenski (BUL) **L. Welter:** S. Mehnert (GDR). **Welter:** I. Akopokhian (URS). **L. Middle:** M. Timm (GDR). **Middle:** H. Maske (GDR). **L. Heavy:** N. Shanavasov (URS). **Heavy:** A. Jagubkin (URS). **S. Heavy:** F. Somodi (HUN).
Bronze medals: S. Casey (IRL). J. Beckles (ENG).

Turin, Italy - 1987
L. Fly: N. Munchyan (URS). **Fly:** A. Tews (GDR). **Bantam:** A. Hristov (BUL). **Feather:** M. Kazaryan (URS). **Light:** O. Nazarov (URS). **L. Welter:** B. Abadjier (BUL). **Welter:** V. Shishov (URS). **L. Middle:** E. Richter (GDR). **Middle:** H. Maske (GDR). **L. Heavy:** Y. Vaulin (URS). **Heavy:** A. Vanderlijde (HOL). **S. Heavy:** U. Kaden (GDR).
Bronze medal: N. Brown (ENG).

Athens, Greece - 1989
L. Fly: I. Hristov (BUL). **Fly:** Y. Arbachakov (URS). **Bantam:** S. Todorov (BUL). **Feather:** K. Kirkorov (BUL). **Light:** K. Tsziu (URS). **L. Welter:** I. Ruznikov (URS). **Welter:** S. Mehnert (GDR). **L. Middle:** I. Akopokhian (URS). **Middle:** H. Maske (GDR). **L. Heavy:** S. Lange (GDR). **Heavy:** A. Vanderlijde (HOL). **S. Heavy:** U. Kaden (GDR).
Bronze Medal: D. Anderson (SCO).

Gothenburg, Sweden - 1991
L. Fly: I. Marinov (BUL). **Fly:** I. Kovacs (HUN). **Bantam:** S. Todorov (BUL). **Feather:** P. Griffin (IRL). **Light:** V. Nistor (ROM). **L. Welter:** K. Tsziu (URS). **Welter:** R. Welin (SWE). **L. Middle:** I. Akopokhian (URS). **Middle:** S. Otke (GER). **L. Heavy:** D. Michalszewski (GER). **Heavy:** A. Vanderlijde (HOL). **S. Heavy:** E. Beloussov (URS).
Bronze medals: P. Weir (SCO). A. Vaughan (ENG).

Note: Gold medals were awarded to the Europeans who went the furthest in the Olympic Games of 1924, 1928 & 1932.

European Junior Champions, 1970-1992

Miskolc, Hungary - 1970
L. Fly: Gluck (HUN). **Fly:** Z. Kismeneth (HUN). **Bantam:** A. Levitschev (URS). **Feather:** Andrianov (URS). **Light:** L. Juhasz (HUN). **L. Welter:** K. Nemec (HUN). **Welter:** Davidov (URS). **L. Middle:** A. Lemeschev (URS). **Middle:** N. Anfimov (URS). **L. Heavy:** O. Sasche (GDR). **Heavy:** J. Reder (HUN).
Bronze medals: D. Needham (ENG), R. Barlow (ENG), L. Stevens (ENG).

Bucharest, Romania - 1972
L. Fly: A. Turei (ROM). **Fly:** Condurat (ROM). **Bantam:** V. Solomin (URS). **Feather:** V. Lvov (URS). **Light:** S. Cutov (ROM). **L. Welter:** K. Pierwieniecki (POL). **Welter:** Zorov (URS). **L. Middle:** Babescu (ROM). **Middle:** V. Lemeschev (URS). **L. Heavy:** Mirounik (URS). **Heavy:** Subutin (URS).
Bronze medals: J. Gale (ENG), R. Maxwell (ENG), D. Odwell (ENG).

Kiev, Russia - 1974
L. Fly: A. Tkachenko (URS). **Fly:** V. Rybakov (URS). **Bantam:** C. Andreikovski (BUL). **Feather:** V. Sorokin (URS). **Light:** V. Limasov (URS). **L. Welter:** N. Sigov (URS). **Welter:** M. Bychkov (URS). **L. Middle:** V. Danshin (URS). **Middle:** D. Jende (GDR). **L. Heavy:** K. Dafinoiu (ROM). **Heavy:** K. Mashev (BUL).
Silver medal: C. Magri (ENG).
Bronze medals: G. Gilbody (ENG), K. Laing (ENG).

Izmir, Turkey - 1976
L. Fly: C. Seican (ROM). **Fly:** G. Khratsov (URS). **Bantam:** M. Navros (URS). **Feather:** V. Demoianeko (URS). **Light:** M. Puzovic (YUG). **L. Welter:** V. Zverev (URS). **Welter:** K. Ozoglouz (TUR). **L. Middle:** W. Lauder (SCO). **Middle:** H. Lenhart (GER). **L. Heavy:** I. Yantchauskas (URS). **Heavy:** B. Enjenyan (URS).
Silver medal: J. Decker (ENG).
Bronze medals: I. McLeod (SCO), N. Croombes (ENG).

Dublin, Ireland - 1978
L. Fly: R. Marx (GDR). **Fly:** D. Radu (ROM). **Bantam:** S. Khatchatrian (URS). **Feather:** H. Loukmanov (URS). **Light:** P. Oliva (ITA). **L. Welter:** V. Laptiev (URS). **Welter:** R. Filimanov (URS). **L. Middle:** A. Beliave (URS). **Middle:** G. Zinkovitch (URS). **L. Heavy:** I. Jolta (ROM). **Heavy:** P. Stoimenov (BUL).
Silver medals: M. Holmes (IRL), P. Hanlon (ENG), M. Courtney (ENG).
Bronze medals: T. Thompson (IRL), J. Turner (ENG), M. Bennett (WAL), J. McAllister (SCO), C. Devine (ENG).

Rimini, Italy - 1980
L. Fly: A. Mikoulin (URS). **Fly:** J. Varadi (HUN). **Bantam:** F. Rauschning (GDR). **Feather:** J. Gladychev (URS). **Light:** V. Shishov (URS). **L. Welter:** R. Lomski (BUL). **Welter:** T. Holonics (GDR). **L. Middle:** N. Wilshire (ENG). **Middle:** S. Laptiev (URS). **L. Heavy:** V. Dolgoun (URS). **Heavy:** V. Tioumentsev (URS). **S. Heavy:** S. Kormihtsine (URS).
Bronze medals: N. Potter (ENG), B. McGuigan (IRL), M. Brereton (IRL), D. Cross (ENG).

Schwerin, East Germany - 1982
L. Fly: R. Kabirov (URS). **Fly:** I. Filchev (BUL). **Bantam:** M. Stecca (ITA). **Feather:** B. Blagoev (BUL). **Light:** E. Chakimov (URS). **L. Welter:** S. Mehnert (GDR). **Welter:** T. Schmitz (GDR). **L. Middle:** B. Shararov (URS). **Middle:** E. Christie (ENG). **L. Heavy:** Y. Waulin (URS). **Heavy:** A. Popov (URS). **S. Heavy:** V. Aldoshin (URS).
Silver medal: D. Kenny (ENG).
Bronze medal: O. Jones (ENG).

Tampere, Finland - 1984
L. Fly: R. Breitbart (GDR). **Fly:** D. Berg (GDR). **Bantam:** K. Khdrian (URS). **Feather:** O. Nazarov (URS). **Light:** C. Furnikov (BUL). **L. Welter:** W. Schmidt (GDR). **Welter:** K. Doinov (BUL). **L. Middle:** O. Volkov (URS). **Middle:** R. Ryll (GDR). **L. Heavy:** G. Peskov (URS). **Heavy:** R. Draskovic (YUG). **S. Heavy:** L. Kamenov (BUL).
Bronze medals: J. Lowey (IRL), F. Harding (ENG), N. Moore (ENG).

Brondy, Denmark - 1986
L. Fly: S. Todorov (BUL). **Fly:** S. Galotian (URS). **Bantam:** D. Drumm (GDR). **Feather:** K. Tsziu (URS). **Light:** G. Akopkhian (URS). **L. Welter:** F. Vastag (ROM). **Welter:** S. Karavayev (URS). **L. Middle:** E. Elibaev (URS). **Middle:** A. Kurnabka (URS). **L. Heavy:** A. Schultz (GDR). **Heavy:** A. Golota (POL). **S. Heavy:** A. Prianichnikov (URS).

Gdansk, Poland - 1988
L. Fly: I. Kovacs (HUN). **Fly:** M. Beyer (GDR). **Bantam:** M. Aitzanov (URS). **Feather:** M. Rudolph (GDR). **Light:** M. Shaburov (URS). **L. Welter:** G. Campanella (ITA). **Welter:** D. Konsun (URS). **L. Middle:** K. Kiselev (URS). **Middle:** A. Rudenko (URS). **L. Heavy:** O. Velikanov (URS). **Heavy:** A. Ter-Okopian (URS). **S. Heavy:** E. Belusov (URS).
Bronze medals: P. Ramsey (ENG), M. Smyth (WAL).

Usti Nad Labem, Czechoslovakia - 1990
L. Fly: Z. Paliani (URS). **Fly:** K. Pielert (GDR). **Bantam:** K. Baravi (URS). **Feather:** P. Gvasalia (URS). **Light:** J. Hildenbrandt (GDR). **L. Welter:** N. Smanov (URS). **Welter:** A. Preda (ROM). **L. Middle:** A. Kakauridze (URS). **Middle:** J. Schwank (GDR). **L. Heavy:** Iljin (URS). **Heavy:** I. Andrejev (URS). **S. Heavy:** W. Fischer (GDR).
Silver medal: A. Todd (ENG).
Bronze medal: P. Craig (ENG).

Edinburgh, Scotland - 1992
L. Fly: M. Ismailov (URS). **Fly:** F. Brennfuhrer (GER). **Bantam:** S. Kuchler (GER). **Feather:** M. Silantiev (URS). **Light:** S. Shcherbakov (URS). **L. Welter:** O. Saitov (URS). **Welter:** H. Kurlumaz (TUR). **L. Middle:** Z. Erdie (HUN). **Middle:** V. Zhirov (URS). **L. Heavy:** D. Gorbachev (URS). **Heavy:** L. Achkasov (URS). **S. Heavy:** A. Mamedov (URS).
Silver medals: M. Hall (ENG), B. Jones (WAL).
Bronze medals: F. Slane (IRL), G. Stephens (IRL), C. Davies (WAL).

Note: The age limit for the championships were reduced from 21 to 19 in 1976.

Commonwealth Champions, 1930-1990

Hamilton, Canada - 1930
Fly: W. Smith (SAF). **Bantam:** H. Mizler (ENG). **Feather:** F. Meacham (ENG). **Light:** J. Rolland (SCO). **Welter:** L. Hall (SAF). **Middle:** F. Mallin (ENG). **L. Heavy:** J. Goyder (ENG). **Heavy:** V. Stuart (ENG).
Silver medals: T. Pardoe (ENG), T. Holt (SCO).
Bronze medals: A. Lyons (SCO), A. Love (ENG), F. Breeman (ENG).

Wembley, England - 1934
Fly: P. Palmer (ENG). **Bantam:** F. Ryan (ENG). **Feather:** C. Cattarall (SAF). **Light:** L. Cook (AUS). **Welter:** D. McCleave (ENG). **Middle:** A. Shawyer (ENG). **L. Heavy:** G. Brennan (ENG). **Heavy:** P. Floyd (ENG).
Silver medals: A. Barnes (WAL), J. Jones (WAL), F. Taylor (WAL), J. Holton (SCO).
Bronze medals: J. Pottinger (WAL), T. Wells (SCO), H. Moy (ENG), W. Duncan (NIR), J. Magill (NIR), Lord D. Douglas-Hamilton (SCO).

Melbourne, Australia - 1938
Fly: J. Joubert (SAF). **Bantam:** W. Butler (ENG). **Feather:** A. Henricus (CEY). **Light:** H. Groves (ENG). **Welter:** W. Smith (AUS). **Middle:** D. Reardon (WAL). **L. Heavy:** N. Wolmarans (SAF). **Heavy:** T. Osborne (CAN).
Silver medals: J. Watson (SCO), M. Dennis (ENG).
Bronze medals: H. Cameron (SCO), J. Wilby (ENG).

Auckland, New Zealand - 1950
Fly: H. Riley (SCO). **Bantam:** J. van Rensburg (SAF). **Feather:** H. Gilliland (SCO). **Light:** R. Latham (ENG). **Welter:** T. Ratcliffe (ENG). **Middle:** T. van Schalkwyk (SAF). **L. Heavy:** D. Scott (ENG). **Heavy:** F. Creagh (NZL).
Bronze medal: P. Brander (ENG).

Vancouver, Canada - 1954
Fly: R. Currie (SCO). **Bantam:** J. Smillie (SCO). **Feather:** L. Leisching (SAF). **Light:** P. van Staden (SAF). **L. Welter:** M. Bergin (CAN). **Welter:** N. Gargano (ENG). **L. Middle:** W. Greaves (CAN). **Middle:** J. van de Kolff (SAF). **L. Heavy:** P. van Vuuren (SAF). **Heavy:** B. Harper (ENG).
Silver medals: M. Collins (WAL), F. McQuillan (SCO).
Bronze medals: D. Charnley (ENG), B. Wells (ENG).

Cardiff, Wales - 1958
Fly: J. Brown (SCO). **Bantam:** H. Winstone (WAL). **Feather:** W. Taylor (AUS). **Light:** R. McTaggart (SCO). **L. Welter:** H. Loubscher (SAF). **Welter:** J. Greyling (SAF). **L. Middle:** G. Webster (SAF). **Middle:** T. Milligan (NIR). **L. Heavy:** A. Madigan (AUS). **Heavy:** D. Bekker (SAF).
Silver medals: T. Bache (ENG), M. Collins (WAL), J. Jordan (ENG), R. Kane (SCO), S. Pearson (ENG), A. Higgins (WAL), D. Thomas (ENG).
Bronze medals: P. Lavery (NIR), D. Braithwaite (WAL), R. Hanna (NIR), A. Owen (SCO), J. McClory (NIR), J. Cooke (ENG), J. Jacobs (ENG), B. Nancurvis (WAL), R. Scott (SCO), W. Brown (WAL), J. Caiger (ENG), W. Bannon (SCO), R. Pleace (WAL).

Perth, Australia - 1962
Fly: R. Mallon (SCO). **Bantam:** J. Dynevor (AUS). **Feather:** J. McDermott (SCO). **Light:** E. Blay (GHA). **L. Welter:** C. Quartey (GHA). **Welter:** W. Coe (NZL). **L. Middle:** H. Mann (CAN). **Middle:** M. Calhoun (JAM). **L. Heavy:** A. Madigan (AUS). **Heavy:** G. Oywello (UGA).
Silver medals: R. McTaggart (SCO), J. Pritchett (ENG).
Bronze medals: M. Pye (ENG), P. Benneyworth (ENG), B. Whelan (ENG), B. Brazier (ENG), C. Rice (NIR), T. Menzies (SCO), H. Christie (NIR).

Kingston, Jamaica - 1966
Fly: S. Shittu (GHA). **Bantam:** E. Ndukwu (NIG). **Feather:** P. Waruinge (KEN). **Light:** A. Andeh (NIG). **L. Welter:** J. McCourt (NIR). **Welter:** E. Blay (GHA). **L. Middle:** M. Rowe (ENG). **Middle:** J. Darkey (GHA). **L. Heavy:** R. Tighe (ENG). **Heavy:** W. Kini (NZL).
Silver medals: P. Maguire (NIR), R. Thurston (ENG), R. Arthur (ENG), T. Imrie (SCO).

Bronze medals: S. Lockhart (NIR), A. Peace (SCO), F. Young (NIR), J. Turpin (ENG), D. McAlinden (NIR).

Edinburgh, Scotland - 1970
L. Fly: J. Odwori (UGA). **Fly:** D. Needham (ENG). **Bantam:** S. Shittu (GHA). **Feather:** P. Waruinge (KEN). **Light:** A. Adeyemi (NIG). **L. Welter:** M. Muruli (UGA). **Welter:** E. Ankudey (GHA). **L. Middle:** T. Imrie (SCO). **Middle:** J. Conteh (ENG). **L. Heavy:** F. Ayinla (NIG). **Heavy:** B. Masanda (UGA).
Silver medals: T. Davies (WAL), J. Gillan (SCO), D. Davies (WAL), J. McKinty (NIR).
Bronze medals: M. Abrams (ENG), A. McHugh (SCO), D. Larmour (NIR), S. Oglivie (SCO), A. Richardson (ENG), T. Joyce (SCO), P. Doherty (NIR), J. Rafferty (SCO), L. Stevens (ENG).

Christchurch, New Zealand - 1974
L. Fly: J. Odwori (UGA). **Fly:** D. Larmour (NIR). **Bantam:** P. Cowdell (ENG). **Feather:** E. Ndukwu (NIG). **Light:** A. Kalule (UGA). **L. Welter:** O. Nwankpa (NIG). **Welter:** M. Muruli (UGA). **L. Middle:** L. Mwale (ZAM). **Middle:** F. Lucas (STV). **L. Heavy:** W. Knight (ENG). **Heavy:** N. Meade (ENG).
Silver medals: E. McKenzie (WAL), A. Harrison (SCO).
Bronze medals: J. Bambrick (SCO), J. Douglas (SCO), J. Rodgers (NIR), S. Cooney (SCO), R. Davies (ENG), C. Speare (ENG), G. Ferris (NIR).

Edmonton, Canada - 1978
L. Fly: S. Muchoki (KEN). **Fly:** M. Irungu (KEN). **Bantam:** B. McGuigan (NIR). **Feather:** A. Nelson (GHA). **Light:** G. Hamill (NIR). **L. Welter:** W. Braithwaite (GUY). **Welter:** M. McCallum (JAM). **L. Middle:** K. Perlette (CAN). **Middle:** P. McElwaine (AUS). **L. Heavy:** R. Fortin (CAN). **Heavy:** J. Awome (ENG).
Silver medals: J. Douglas (SCO), K. Beattie (NIR), D. Parkes (ENG), V. Smith (ENG).
Bronze medals: H. Russell (NIR), M. O'Brien (ENG), J. McAllister (SCO), T. Feal (WAL).

Brisbane, Australia - 1982
L. Fly: A. Wachire (KEN). **Fly:** M. Mutua (KEN). **Bantam:** J. Orewa (NIG). **Feather:** P. Konyegwachie (NIG). **Light:** H. Khalili (KEN). **L. Welter:** C. Ossai (NIG). **Welter:** C. Pyatt (ENG). **L. Middle:** S. O'Sullivan (CAN). **Middle:** J. Price (ENG). **L. Heavy:** F. Sani (FIJ). **Heavy:** W. de Wit (CAN).
Silver medals: J. Lyon (ENG), J. Kelly (SCO), R. Webb (NIR), P. Hanlon (ENG), J. McDonnell (ENG), N. Croombes (ENG), H. Hylton (ENG).
Bronze medals: R. Gilbody (ENG), C. McIntosh (ENG), R. Corr (NIR).

Edinburgh, Scotland - 1986
L. Fly: S. Olson (CAN). **Fly:** J. Lyon (ENG). **Bantam:** S. Murphy (ENG). **Feather:** B. Downey (CAN). **Light:** A. Dar (CAN). **L. Welter:** H. Grant (CAN). **Welter:** D. Dyer (ENG). **L. Middle:** D. Sherry (CAN). **Middle:** R. Douglas (ENG). **L. Heavy:** J. Moran (ENG). **Heavy:** J. Peau (NZL). **S. Heavy:** L. Lewis (ENG).
Silver medals: M. Epton (ENG), R. Nash (NIR), P. English (ENG), N. Haddock (WAL), J. McAlister (SCO), H. Lawson (SCO), D. Young (SCO), A. Evans (WAL).
Bronze medals: W. Docherty (SCO), J. Todd (NIR), K. Webber (WAL), G. Brooks (SCO), J. Wallace (SCO), C. Carleton (NIR), J. Jacobs (ENG), B. Lowe (NIR), D. Denny (NIR), G. Thomas (WAL), A. Mullen (SCO), G. Ferrie (SCO), P. Tinney (NIR), B. Pullen (WAL), E. Cardouza (ENG), J. Oyebola (ENG).

Auckland, New Zealand - 1990
L. Fly: J. Juko (UGA). **Fly:** W. McCullough (NIR). **Bantam:** S. Mohammed (NIG). **Feather:** J. Irwin (ENG). **Light:** G. Nyakana (UGA). **L. Welter:** C. Kane (SCO). **Welter:** D. Defiagbon (NIG). **L. Middle:** R. Woodhall (ENG). **Middle:** C. Johnson (CAN). **L. Heavy:** J. Akhasamba (KEN). **Heavy:** G. Onyango (KEN). **S. Heavy:** M. Kenny (NZL).
Bronze medals: D. Anderson (SCO), M. Edwards (ENG), P. Douglas (NIR).

Directory of Ex-Boxers' Associations

by Ron Olver

BOURNEMOUTH Founded 1980. HQ: Mallard Road Bus Services Social Club, Bournemouth. Dai Dower (P); Peter Fay (C); Ken Wells (VC); Percy Singer (T); Les Smith (S), 592 Charminster Road, Bournemouth.

BRISTOL Founded 1992. HQ: British Tramways Club, Bristol. Jack Phelps (P & C); Chris Sanigar (S); Duggie Shaw (PRO), 68 Ellan Hay Road, Bradley Stoke, Bristol BS12 0HB.

CORK Founded 1973. HQ: Acra House, Maylor Street, Cork. Johnny Fitzgerald (P & C); John Cronin (VC); Eamer Coughlan (T); Tim O'Sullivan (S & PRO), Acra House, Maylor Street, Cork.

CORNWALL Founded 1989. HQ: St Austell British Legion and Redruth British Legion in alternate months. Roy Coote (P); Stan Cullis (C); Len Magee (VC); Jimmy Miller (T); John Soloman (S), 115 Albany Road, Redruth.

CROYDON Founded 1982. HQ: The Prince Of Wales, Thornton Heath. Tom Powell, BEM (P); Bill Goddard (C); Bill Curd (VC); Ralph Griffiths (T); Gilbert Allnutt (S), 25 Melrose Avenue, Norbury, London SW16 4RX.

EASTERN AREA Founded 1973. HQ: Norfolk Dumpling, Cattle Market, Hall Road, Norwich. Brian Fitzmaurice (P); Alfred Smith (C); Clive Campling (VC); Eric Middleton (T & S), 48 City Road, Norwich NR1 3AU.

IPSWICH Founded 1970. HQ: Flying Horse, Waterford Road, Ipswich. Alby Kingham (P); Frank Webb (C); Vic Thurlow (T); Nigel Wheeler (PRO); Smiler Perkins (S), 38 Cedar Avenue, Kesgrave, Suffolk.

IRISH Founded 1973. HQ: National Boxing Stadium, South Circular Road, Dublin. Maxie McCullagh (P); Gerry O' Colmain (C); Willie Duggan (VC); Tommy Butler (T); Denis Morrison (S), 55 Philipsburgh Terrace, Marino, Dublin.

KENT Founded 1967. HQ: Chatham WMC, New Road, Chatham. Teddy Bryant (P); Alf Tingley (C); Ray Lambert (PRO); Fred Atkins (T); Paul Nihill (S), 59 Balfour Road, Rochester, Kent.

LEEDS Founded 1952. HQ: North Leeds WMC, Burmantofts, Lincoln Green, Leeds 9. Johnny Durkin (P); Alan Alster (T); Les Pollard (S); Harry Hare (C); Frankie Brown (VC); Steve Butler (PRO), 107 Cambridge Street, Normanton WF6 1ES.

LEFT-HOOK CLUB Betty Faux (S), 144 Longmoor Lane, Aintree, Liverpool. No regular meetings. Formed specifically with the aim of holding functions to raise money in order to help former boxers in need.

LEICESTER Founded 1972. HQ: Belgrave WMC, Checketts Road, Leicester. Pat Butler (P); Mick Greaves (C); Mrs Rita Jones (T); Norman Jones (S), 60 Dumbleton Avenue, Leicester LE3 2EG.

LONDON Founded 1971. HQ; Finsbury Leisure Centre, London EC1. Jack Powell (P); Micky O'Sullivan (C); Andy Williamson (VC); Stephen Powell (PRO); Ray Caulfield (T); Mrs Mary Powell (S), 36 St Peters Street, Islington, London N1 8JT.

MANCHESTER Founded 1968. HQ: British Rail Social Club, Store Street, Manchester. Jackie Braddock (P); Tommy Proffit (C); Jack Edwards (VC); Eddie Lillis (T); Jackie Moran (S), 4 Cooper House, Boundry Lane, Hulme, Manchester.

MERSEYSIDE (Liverpool) Founded 1973. HQ: Queens Hotel, Derby Square, Liverpool. Johnny Cooke (P); Terry Riley (C); Jim Boyd (VC); Jim Jenkinson (T); Billy Davies (S), 7 Rockford Walk, Southdene, Kirkby, Liverpool.

NORTHAMPTONSHIRE Founded 1981. HQ: Exclusive Club, Gold Street, Northampton. Tony Perrett (P); John Cullen (C); Bill Evans (T); Winston Hughes (S), 120 Bush Hill, Westone, Northampton.

NORTHERN FEDERATION Founded 1974. Several member EBAs. Annual Gala. Eddie Monahan (S), 16 Braemar Avenue, Marshside, Southport.

NORTHERN IRELAND Founded 1970. HQ: Ulster Sports Club, Belfast. J. Bradbury (P); Gerry Smyth (C); J. Hill (VC); J. Garrett (T); Sammy Cosgrove (PRO); Al Gibson (S), 900 Crumlin Road, Belfast.

NORTH STAFFS & SOUTH CHESHIRE Founded 1969. HQ: The Saggar Makers Bottom Knocker, Market Place, Burslem, Stoke on Trent. Tut Whalley (P); Roy Simms (VC); Les Dean (S); John Greatbach (T); Billy Tudor (C & PRO), 133 Sprinkbank Road, Chell Heath, Stoke on Trent ST6 6HW.

NORWICH HQ: West End Retreat, Brown Street, Norwich. Les King (P); John Pipe (C); Jack Wakefield (T); Dick Sadd (S), 76 Orchard Street, Norwich.

NOTTINGHAM Founded 1979. HQ: The Lion Hotel, Clumber Street, Nottingham. Frank Parkes (P); Frank Hayes (C); John Kinsella (T); Jim Shrewsbury (S), 219 Rosecroft Drive, Nottingham NG5 6EL.

NOTTS & DERBY Founded 1973. Billy Strange (C); Dick Johnson (S & PRO), 15 Church Street, Pinxton, Nottingham.

PLYMOUTH Founded 1982. HQ: Exmouth Road Social Club, 11 Exmouth Road, Devonport, Plymouth. George Borg (P); Tom Pryce-Davies (C); Doug Halliday (VC); Derek Perry (T); Bruce Jones (PRO); Buck Taylor (S), 15 Greenbank Avenue, St Judes, Plymouth PL4 9BT.

PRESTON Founded 1973. HQ: County Arms Hotel, Deepdale Road, Preston. George Greenwood (P); Brian Petherwick (C); Frank Brown (T); Ted Sumner (S), 7 Kew Gardens, Penwortham, Preston PR1 0DR.

READING Founded 1977. HQ: Salisbury Club, Kings Road, Reading. Roland Dakin (P); Bob Pitman (C); Arnold Whatmore (T); Bob Sturgess (S).

ST HELENS Founded 1983. HQ: Travellers Rest Hotel, Crab Street, St Helens. George Thomas (C); Jimmy O'Keefe (VC); Tommy McNamara (T); Paul Britch (S), 40 Ashtons Green Drive, Parr, St Helens.

SCOTTISH Founded 1974. HQ: Dumbarton. Peter Keenan (P); Jackie Marshall (PRO); Bill Gardner (S).

SEFTON Founded 1975. HQ: St Benets Parochial Club, Netherton, Bootle. Alf Lunt (T); Johnny Holmes (S); 41 Higher End Park, Sefton, Bootle.

SLOUGH Founded 1973. HQ: Faraday British Legion, Slough. Charlie Knight (T); Ernie Watkins (T); Jack Bridge (C), Cowley Brick, 51 Chiltern View, Uxbridge.

SOUTHPORT Founded 1974. HQ: Mount Pleasant Hotel, Southport. John Goulborne (C); John Core (T); Eddie Monahan (S), 16 Braemar Avenue, Marshside, Southport.

SQUARE RING Founded 1978. HQ: Torquay Social Club. George Pook (P); Maxie Beech (VC); Billy Burke (S); Johnny Mudge (T); Paul King (C), 10 Pine Court Apartments, Middle Warberry Road, Torquay.

SUNDERLAND Founded 1959. HQ: Hendon Gardens, Sunderland. Bert Ingram (P); Terry Lynn (C); Billy Musgrave (T); Joe Riley (PRO); Les Simm (S), 21 Orchard Street, Pallion, Sunderland SR4 6QL.

SUSSEX Founded 1974. HQ: Brighton & Hove Sports & Social Club, Conway Street, Hove. Harry Parkinson (T); Bill Pullum (P); Bert Hollows (C); John Ford (S), 69 Moyne Close, Hove, Sussex.

SWANSEA & SOUTH WEST WALES Founded 1983. HQ: Villiers Arms, Neath Road, Hafod, Swansea. Cliff Curvis (P);

Gordon Pape (C); Ernie Wallis (T); Len Smith (S), Cockett Inn, Cockett, Swansea SA2 0GB.

TRAMORE Founded 1981. HQ: Robinson Bar, Main Street, Tramore, Co Waterford. T. Flynn (P); J. Dunne (C); C. O'Reilly (VC); W. Hutchinson (T); N. Graham (PRO); Pete Graham (S), 3 Riverstown, Tramore.

TYNESIDE Founded 1970. HQ: The Swan, Heworth. Billy Charlton (P); Maxie Walsh (C); Gordon Ginger Smith (VC); Malcolm Dinning (T); Dave McCormick Junior (S); Bill Wilkie (PRO), 60 Calderdale Avenue, Walker, Newcastle NE6 4HN.

WELSH Founded 1976. HQ: Rhydyfelin Rugby Club, Pontypridd, Mid Glamorgan. Syd Worgan (P & S); Vernon Ball (C); Howard Winstone (VC); Llew Miles (T & PRO), 7 Edward Street, Miskin, Mountain Ash, Mid Glamorgan.

WIRRAL (Birkenhead) Founded 1973. It is understood this EBA is still functioning, although no correspondence or information has been received for several years.

The above information is set at the time of going to press, and no responsibility can be taken for any changes in officers or addresses of HQs that may happen between then and publication.

ABBREVIATIONS

P - President. C - Chairman. VC - Vice Chairman. T - Treasurer. S - Secretary. PRO - Public Relations Officer.

Johnny Williams (right), a member of the Leicester EBA, seen here losing his British and British Empire heavyweight titles to Don Cockell in 1953

Obituaries

by Ron Olver

It is impossible to list everyone, but I have done my best to include final tributes for as many of the well-known boxers who passed on during the last twelve months or so, as I can. Also included are boxers who were missed in last year's edition, owing to late information. We honour them and will remember them.

ANGEL Johnny Real name Gabriel Dada. *Born* Nigeria, 1938. *Died* 22 March 1993. As a middleweight, he came to Britain in 1962 and when he retired in 1975, decided to settle here. Beat Clarence Prince, Stuart Price, Willie Fisher, Joe Bell, Henry Turkington and Nat Jacobs. Also met Sugar Ray Robinson, Wally Swift, Johnny Pritchett, Harry Scott and Bruno Visintin. Worked for British Rail.

BEYNON Len *Born* Barry, 24 April 1912. *Died* October 1992. Pro 1929-1942. Won Welsh bantamweight title by beating Terence Morgan (1932), losing it to George Williams (1933). Regained same title from Williams (1934), losing it to Mog Mason (1934). Captured the bantamweight title for the third time from Mason (1936), before relinquishing. Won Welsh featherweight title, beating Stan Jehu (1936), thus becoming the first Welsh boxer to hold titles at two different weights at the same time. Successfully defended the featherweight belt twice against George Williams in 1937 and 1938, before relinquishing. Was beaten by Jackie Brown in a final eliminator for the British bantamweight title (1936). Beat bantam champion Johnny King in a non-title fight (1939) and gave a fine display against World featherweight champion, Freddie Miller, but was outpointed (1938). Fought another world champion, flyweight, Young Perez, losing on a disputed non-title points verdict (1932). Also defeated Dave Crowley, Bert Kirby, Jim Brady, Dick Corbett and Jim Spider Kelly, all champions at one time or another. During World War II, he joined the 6th Welsh Artillery, but was later released for war work.

BROUGH Billy *Born* Whitehaven, 15 August 1971. *Died* (drowning) April 1992. Turned pro with Tommy Gilmour, having four wins in six contests between November 1989 and March 1991 and winning and losing to Tony Booth before his tragic accident. As an amateur, he boxed for Dumfries ABC and reached the semi-finals of the Scottish light-middleweight championships in 1989.

BURLEY Charley *Born* Pittsburgh, USA, 6 September 1917. *Died* 16 October 1992. Regarded by many experts and fans as the greatest middleweight who never won a World title. Boxed as a pro from 1936 until 1950 and beat Fritzie Zivic, Billy Soose, Holman Williams, Archie Moore, Cocoa Kid, Shorty Hogue, Gene Buffalo and Bert Lytell. Won the California State title by defeating Jack Chase (1944) and twice went the distance with Ezzard Charles, later to become world heavyweight champion. Considered too dangerous a test for any up and coming young white contender and in order to earn a crust, he boxed Holman Williams, another man unlucky to get a title shot, seven times.

COCHRANE Freddie "Red" *Born* Elizabeth, New Jersey, USA, 6 May 1915. *Died* January 1993. Pro 1933-1946. Known as "Red", because of the colour of his hair, he finally got a shot at the World welterweight title in July 1941, after campaigning for eight years with over 100 fights to his name, and decisioned Fritzie Zivic. Had beaten men of the calibre of Al Roth, Mickey Greb, Johnny Jadick, Jack "Kid" Berg and Norman Rubio, and although defeated on 30 odd occasions, most of his losses had been at the hands of top class ringmen. Never really got the chance to cash in on the title, due to the war, and was inactive for nearly three years after being enlisted in the US Navy. Came back in June 1945 and suffered two kayo defeats at the hands of the up-and-coming Rocky Graziano, before retiring after losing his title to Marty Servo in February 1946.

CONN Billy *Born* East Liberty, Pa., USA, 8 October 1917. *Died* 29 May 1993. Pro 1934-1948. Won World light-

Billy Conn

heavyweight title by beating Melio Bettina (1939). Successfully defended against Bettina (1939), Gus Lesnevich (1939), Lesnevich again (1940), before relinquishing title (1941). Met Joe Louis for the World heavyweight title (1941), and was comfortably ahead on points until round thirteen, when he elected to try and knock Joe out, instead of continuing to outbox him. Joe seized his chance and knocked Billy out. There was a return title fight (1946), but both men had been in the American Services, and Billy wasn't the same force, being stopped in round eight. He was known as the "Pittsburgh Kid", and elected to the Boxing Hall of Fame (1965). Beat some of the best in the business, including champions Babe Risko, Vince Dundee, Fred Apostoli, Teddy Yarosz, Fritzie Zivic, Solly Kreiger and Tony Zale.

COOPER Ron *Born* Kenfig Hill, 1927. *Died* 30 December 1992. Pro 1942-1952. Won Welsh middleweight crown by beating Bob Burniston (1952), but lost the title to Jimmy Roberts the same year. Beat Alby Hollister, Billy Carroll, Sammy Sullivan, Trevor Burt, and Harry Davis. In 1948, he stopped Joe Hart, Geoff Heath and Joe Sands in successive bouts, within two months. Also met World champion, Randy Turpin, and went the full route with champions Johnny Sullivan, Dick Turpin (three times) and Henry Hall. Worked as a miner at Newlands Colliery, doing his training after a full shift underground. In later years he became a steelworker.

DAHO Najib *Born* Morocco, 13 January 1959. *Died* 29 August 1993, following a road accident in Morocco. Pro 1977-1991. Boxed as an amateur for the Manchester YMCA and soon turned to the paid ranks, losing ten of his first 20 contests. Became Central Area champion at both super-feather and lightweight, relinquishing both titles as he moved up in class. A pro for nine years when he beat Pat Cowdell in a round to become British super-featherweight champion in May 1986, he had unsuccessful cracks at both the IBF and European crowns, before losing his title back to Cowdell in 1987. Two fights and 19 months later, he came back to lift the Commonwealth lightweight title from Pat Doherty and made a successful defence against the Canadian, John Kalbhenn. Lost the title to Carl Crook in March 1990 and after two failed championship attempts, losing to Thunder Aryeh (Commonwealth super-feather) and Crook again, for the British and Commonwealth lightweight crowns, he called it a day.

DANAHAR Arthur *Born* Bethnal Green, London, 2 June 1918. *Died* 23 November 1992. Pro 1937-1947. Won ABA lightweight title (1937). Boxed for the British lightweight title (1939), and although stopped by Eric Boon, their classic encounter went down in history, the press writing as highly of Arthur's magnificent boxing as they did of Boon's victory. They met again in a British welterweight title eliminator, Árthur winning on a stoppage (1946). Beat reigning welter champion, Ernie Roderick, in a non-title fight (1939), but was outpointed by Ernie in a title fight

(1941). Won the Southern Area welter title by beating Norman Snow (1941), successfully defending against Harry Davis (1945). Did not defend it again. Joined Irish Guards during World War II, and won the British Army professional welter crown by beating Ronnie James (1944). Also defeated Johnny Softley, Douglas Kestrell, Jim Hurst, Boyo Rees, Dave Finn, Harry Craster, George Odwell, Jake Kilrain, Jim Wellard, Jack "Kid" Berg, Harry Mizler, Frank Duffy, Lefty Flynn, and Gwyn Williams. Was kayoed by American Berry Wright (1947) and realised he was seriously ill. With both lungs affected, he was in hospital for 18 months and never boxed again. He and wife Lillian moved to Bognor Regis, and ten years later to Almeria, Spain. He paid fairly regular visits to Britain, and occasionally attended meetings of the London Ex-Boxers' Association.

DILKES George *Born* South Elmsall, 15 May 1926. *Died* April 1993. Pro 1944-1955. Won North Central Area middleweight title by beating Jimmy Bray (1948) and successfully defended against Tommy Whelan (1949), before the area was disbanded (1950). In 78 contests, he won 50 and beat good men such as Jimmy Davis, Ron Cooper, Johnny Nuttall, Duggie Myers, Jackie Jones, Des Jones, and Michael Stack. However, his best victory came in 1950 when he knocked out the former British welterweight champion, Henry Hall, in eight rounds. He also fought and lost to five other past or future British champions, in Jake Kilrain (1946), Vince Hawkins (1946), Alex Buxton (1946 and 1949), Albert Finch (1948) and Pat McAteer (1954), while losing on points in 1949 against New Zealander, Bos Murphy, the former British Empire middleweight champion.

DURANDO Ernie *Born* Bayonne, New Jersey, USA, 7 April 1926. *Died* May 1992. A pro from 1946 to 1957, he beat Rocky Castellani, Norman Hayes, Paddy Young, Jimmy Herring, Sal Belloise, and went the distance with Paul Pender and Joey Giardello. His series of five contests (one win, one draw and three defeats) with Paddy Young ended in 1953 when he was beaten over twelve rounds in an official eliminator for the American middleweight title. However, he saved his most sensational victory for October of that year when he kayoed Charles Humez of France in six rounds. Well behind on the scorecards, and in front of a hostile Parisian audience, Ernie unleashed a tremendous left-hook which put Humez down and out for the first time in his career. Only had twelve more contests and following a ten rounds points defeat at the hands of future World champion, Gene Fullmer, in 1957, he called it a day.

EDER Gustav *Born* Dortmund, Germany, 25 December 1907. *Died* 6 February 1992. Pro 1928-1939. European welterweight champion between 1934 and 1936. After defeating Nestor Charlier (Belgium) to win the vacant title, he successfully defended against Vittorio Venturi (Italy) twice, Francois Sybille (Belgium), Elnar Aggerholm (Denmark), Kid Blaho (Austria), Eduard Hrabeck (Czechoslovakia), Felix Wouters (Belgium) and Hilario

Martinez (Spain), before leaving Europe to campaign in the USA. Eventually becoming one of Germany's best ever fighters, he had failed in two previous attempts to win the title from the Belgian, Gustave Roth. Won and drew against future world champion, Anton Christoforidis, in 1938 and also listed men of the calibre of Kid Tunero, Carmelo Candel, Bep van Klaveren, Adrian Aneet, Cleto Locatelli, Jimmy Leto, Oddone Piazza, Josef Besselmann and England's Archie Sexton, among his many victims.

FLANAGAN Mickey *Born* Birkenhead, 28 November 1926. *Died* May 1992. Pro 1949-1955. Won two Boxing News Certificates of Merit within two months, after beating the champions of Scotland (Harry Hughes), Northern Ireland (Mickey O'Neill), Wales (Selwyn Evans) and British Guiana (Cliff Anderson), in consecutive fights. In October 1954, he beat Johnny Butterworth, the number one contender for the British lightweight title, but never even got a shot at an Area title. A stylish boxer with an accurate left lead and right cross, Mickey never boxed in London, which was difficult to understand, and lost just twelve of 38 contests. Became a member of the Merseyside EBA and the Wirral EBA, and was Chairman of the Northern Federation. Worked for North West Gas for 33 years.

HUGHES Harry *Born* Wishaw, 7 December 1923. *Died* September 1992. Pro 1944-1952. Won Scottish lightweight title by knocking out Danny Woods (1947) and successfully defended against Johnny Smith (1948), Don Cameron (1949), and Jim Findlay (1950), before losing it to Johnny Flannigan (1951). Averaged a fight a month throughout his career. As an amateur he won the Scottish light and welter crowns, then was struck down by illness, and at one period it was feared he would never walk again. However, he made a fine recovery. As a pro he also defeated Johnny McManus, Warren Kendall, Jimmy Green, Jim Keery, Tommy Miller, Tommy McGovern, Bert Hornby, Morry Jones and Tommy McGoldrick. He was a boilermaker and a skilled carpenter, but in his later years he worked on the oil rigs. In 1949 he beat Cliff Curvis in a final eliminator for the British lightweight title, but was beaten by Billy Thompson in a championship fight in May 1949.

KELLEHER Morty *Born* Cork, 13 January 1927. *Died* April 1993 in South Africa. Pro 1948-1954. Numbered Jackie Lucraft, Joe Carter, Kid Tanner, Gene Caffrey, Sammy Shaw, Mickey Forrester, Len Dunthorne and Johnny French, among his victims. A good class featherweight, he also drew with Teddy Peckham, while his losses came at the hands of top men such as Tommy McGovern, Luis de Santiago, Bernard Pugh and Cliff Anderson.

KINGSTON Ron *Born* Sittingbourne. *Died* 26 February 1993. Pro flyweight 1932-1947. Beat Dave Keller, Freddie Tennant, Pat Warburton and Eric Jones. Retired in 1939, but made a comeback in 1943, losing to Terry Allen. Last bout was in April 1947, when he was beaten by Bobby Boland.

LESNICK Mark *Born* Stepney, 10 December 1906. *Died* November 1992. At fourteen, he joined Brady Street BC and had 80 bouts. Won London Federation Of Boys' Clubs Junior and Senior titles at 6st. 7lb. and 7st. 0lb. Had bad eyesight at birth, and would not have been granted a licence if the Board of Control had been formed when he turned pro. By that time (1929) he had retired. Was very proud of his photo appearing on the front cover of Boxing (now Boxing News) dated 5 November 1924, with the caption "The Consistently Successful Paperweight Cyclone." Met two World flyweight champions, Johnny Hill and Jackie Brown, although weighing only 7st. 7lb. Also drew with Ernie Jarvis, who twice boxed Hill for the World title. Was never beaten inside the distance, apart from disqualifications. During World War II, he joined the Royal Army Ordnance Corps, and when asked how he passed the eyesight test replied: "They were taking anybody." But after nine months the Army found out, and he was discharged. His London home was blitzed, so he moved to Hitchin and became a market trader. In 1987 he joined the London Ex-Boxers' Association, and fascinated members with tales of his career, which he illustrated by actions. A lovely, cheeky, chirpy Cockney.

LUDLAM Eric *Born* Sheffield, 11 February 1932. *Died* 2 January 1993. One of the unluckiest boxers in the history of the sport. At birth he was classed as a weakling, and fed malt and cod liver oil. In 1939 he had rheumatoid arthritis and was wheeled around in a pram for 18 months. However, by 1943 he was pronounced fit and two years later he joined the Army Cadet Force. He won West Riding, and also ACF and NABC titles. Was a finalist in the 1949 Gold Star championships, boxing with five stitches in his hand after an accident at work. In 1951 he won Army, ISBA and ABA titles at middleweight. Turned pro the same year, beating in succession, Derek Molloy, Harry Tunney, Jack Walsh, Joe Elliott, Eric Metcalfe, Joe Odeyemi and Jack Baker. Was matched with Pat McAteer, but was in intensive care for ten days after an infection while cleaning a neighbour's drains. This was in February 1954, and he was due to get married the following month, a date that had to be postponed. On 3 April of that year he walked down the aisle on two sticks. He was never the same force again, although he did beat Dennis Fewkes, Peter Cain and Tony Dove. His scrap book was destroyed when his brothers house burned down (1955) and his wife Hilda had a miscarriage (1958). Renewed his boxing licence (1959) and kayoed Jim Lindley, but lost a few and retired for good in 1960. Was a founder-member of Sheffield EBA (1974) and appointed Secretary, later becoming Secretary of the Northern Federation. Following an accident, his walking got progressively worse. In 1986 he had a trapped nerve in his spine, was on traction for a month, and told he had osteo-arthritis. It took him eleven weeks to walk with a stick, and he couldn't manage more than 50 yards. In 1987 he had a heart attack and Hilda was in hospital seven times and underwent four operations for arterial sclerosis. His health steadily worsened in later years, but not his spirit.

McDONAGH Jimmy *Born* Hastings, 2 September 1966. *Died* (gun shot wounds) January 1992. Turned pro in September 1987 with manager Dave Harris, having been the amateur Southern Counties middleweight runner-up earlier that year, while representing West Hill ABC. Won seven and drew one of 16 professional contests and proved to be a genuine crowd pleaser, before deciding to call it a day, following a first round defeat at the hands of Nigel Fairbairn in April 1991.

MANITO Bobby Real name Peter Unwin. *Born* Kennington, 20 June 1930. Tragically killed at the hands of his own son in the summer of 1993. Turned pro in 1950, having boxed for the famous Lynn club, and had his first contest in October of that year, being knocked out by a future British title challenger, Tony Mancini, in the first round. Lost more than he won, before retiring in 1954, but was known as a crowd pleaser. Fought the infamous Reg Kray, losing on points, in the twin's professional debut and other good men he met, included Frank Cassidy, Charlie Page and George Happe. Incidentally, his last contest on 23 November 1953 was a six round points defeat by the man he started his career against, Tony Mancini. Later, he became a trainer at Brixton ABC, until taking up a similar post at the Westree club.

MASEKO Joe *Born* South Africa, 24 March 1925. *Died* 1993. Known as "jolting Joe", he first came to prominence when he won the South African (Non-European) vacant middleweight title, knocking out Henry Gordon in the first round on 7 July 1948. Successfully defended the title four times, against Wally Thompson (1950), Simon Greb (1950 and 1953) and Julius Caesar (1954), before retiring in October 1954. He also won the vacant light-heavyweight title in 1953, beating Julius Caesar, but never defended. In between times he campaigned in British rings from July 1951 until the end of 1952, defeating men of the calibre of Bob Cleaver, Michael Stack, Koffi Kiteman, Dick Langley, Alby Hollister, Billy Ellaway, Frank Duffy and Wally Beckett, prior to going home.

MORAN Nick *Born* La Barca, Jalisco, Mexico, 10 December 1923. *Died* 23 June 1993 in Mexico City. Pro 1943-1953. A good class welterweight who lost nearly as many as he won, but listed two World champions, Bob Montgomery, Jackie Wilson, as well as Tuzo Portuguez among his victims. Drew with two classy ringmen in Jesse Flores and John L. Davis, and went the distance with the ill-fated Jimmy Doyle, Ike Williams, Tippy Larkin, Kid Gavilan, Wesley Mouzon, Bernie Docusen, Kid Azteca, Charlie Salas and Bobby Dykes, before quitting the ring. Met a sorry end, dying in the gutter, the victim of heart disease and cirrhosis.

MULLER Peter *Born* Cologne, Germany, 24 February 1927. *Died* 22 June 1992. Twice fought for the European middleweight title, losing to Gustav Scholz (1959) and Laszlo Papp (1963), but was probably more famous for the fact that he was banned from boxing for several years after knocking out referee, Max Pippow, following a disqualification in a German title fight against Hans Strecht (1952). Turned pro in 1947 and took on all the best men in Europe, having over 150 contests, before dropping down a weight to unsuccessfully challenge Bruno Visintin for his European light-middleweight title in 1965, prior to retiring in 1967.

NASH Billy Real surname Woodward. *Born* 15 May 1913. *Died* 2 May 1993. Pro 1932-1939. Beat Bert Kirby, Joe Curran, Tut Whalley, Tommy Farricker, Pat McStravick, Pat Warburton, Gaston van den Bos, Frank Bonser, Willie Smith, Freddie Tennant, Tommy Pardoe, Sid Parker and Phil Milligan. Served in the Army in World War II, and later worked for a chemical company, ending up in the building trade. Was one of the best flyweights around in the 1930s, when British eight-stoners ruled the world.

PARDOE Tommy *Born* Birmingham, 1912. *Died* 7 December 1992. Pro 1933-1937. Held a unique record as an amateur, winning five ABA titles in succession between 1929-1933. Won a bronze medal in the 1932 Olympics at Los Angeles, being outpointed in the semi-final by Lou Salica of the USA, who went on to win the World professional bantamweight title. As a pro, he won the Southern Area flyweight title, beating Bert Kirby (1934), before losing it to Pat Palmer (1935). Tommy went fourteen rounds with the legendary Benny Lynch in April 1935, just two fights before the little Scot beat Jackie Brown for the world flyweight title. In recent years he had several setbacks in health, culminating in a fatal heart attack.

PASO Orlando *Born* Nigeria, 22 May 1937. *Died* 1993. Came to Britain in 1958 and stayed, beating among others, Jimmy Lynas, Alan Dean, Bill Boyd, Gerry Hassett, Malcolm Worthington, Phil Edwards, Johnny Berry and Derek Liversidge. An iron man of the ring, he was always a good test for any aspiring fighter to overcome, and stopped Young John McCormack (1965) in six rounds, two years before the Irishman became the British light-heavyweight champion. As a middleweight, he lost to three men, Mick Leahy, Wally Swift and George Aldridge, before they won British titles at the weight and also went the distance with Cowboy McCormack, a future European middles champion.

PETTENGELL Jim *Born* New Cross, London, 1 November 1905. *Died* October 1992. Boxed as an amateur and pro with varying success. In 1933, he was appointed instructor of the Mary Ward Settlement Club and one of his pupils, Danny O'Sullivan, was later to become British bantamweight champion and fight for the World title. When the Mary Ward club closed, Jim and Danny went to the Fitzroy-Lynn ABC. An electrician by trade, Jim was in a reserved occupation for three years, before joining the

Jim Pettengell with two of his champions, Dickie (left) and Danny O'Sullivan

RAF. It was while serving in Germany that he met his wife, Valerie. After the war he became a professional trainer, looking after Danny and brother Dickie, who boxed for the European flyweight crown. Among the champions he guided at some stage or other were Jack Gardner, Billy Thompson, Tommy McGovern, Albert Finch and South African heavyweight titleholder, Johnny Arthur. Eventually, he took out a manager's licence, looking after Johnny Barclay, Johnny Smith and Sammy Bonnici. He was a member of the London Ex-Boxers' Association, and in later years worked in the offices of the British Boxing Board of Control.

POWELL Dennis *Born* Llandewi, 12 December 1924. *Died* 27 May 1993. Pro 1946-1954. Won the Welsh light-heavyweight title by beating Jack Farr (1949), and successfully defended it against Doug Richards, before relinquishing. Following the Farr fight, in his very next contest he also became the Welsh heavyweight champion, beating George James (1949), before losing the title to Tommy Farr (1951). Became the British light-heavyweight champion when he defeated George Walker (1953), in what was described as one of the most gruelling and punishing fights ever seen in Britain. Seven months later he lost the crown to Alex Buxton, having just two more contests, beating Johnny Barton and losing to Ed "Polly" Smith, before hanging up his gloves. On retiring, he turned to management, looking after Tony and Maxie Smith, and Paul Brown. He and wife Olive later took over The Bell public house in Willenhall, where he was made a Freeman of the town.

POWELL Eric Real name Eric Egerton. *Born* Ashton

under Lyne. *Died* Spain 1992. Pro 1936-1949. A tough, aggressive scrapper whose career was decimated by the war years, he still made his presence felt with victories over good men such as Ben Duffy, Kid Tanner, Joe Carter, Tommy McGlinchey, Frankie Jackson and the future British, British Empire and European featherweight champion, Ronnie Clayton. Lost on points to Cliff Curvis in 1946 and had his last recorded fight in January 1949, beating Stan Parkes on points. After retiring from boxing, he owned several engineering factories and later became a dog breeder, winning Crufts with a chow named Solomon. That was his main interest and he was often to be seen in television adverts with his dogs, while also travelling the world as a judge with Crufts.

REDDINGTON Tom *Born* Salford 1919. *Died* May 1993. Pro 1934-1948. Boxed successfully at light-heavyweight and heavyweight, beating Darkie Ellis, Len Rowlands, Bob Scally, Tommy Windsor, Kid Scott, Bob Firmin, Johnny Rice, Frank Hough, George James, Gene Fowler, Ben Valentine, Arnold Hayes, Al Robinson, Ken Shaw, Alf Brown, Paddy Slavin, Gerry McDermott and the American, Bernie Reynolds. Joined the RAF in World War II, and was a Sergeant PTI. During the war he had three fights with Freddie Mills, winning one and losing two and the pair became firm friends. Enhanced his reputation when he put Bruce Woodcock on the canvas twice in round two in 1944, but ran out of gas due to lack of training and was stopped in round seven. Had two heart attacks and a stroke in the 1970s, but remained cheerful until the end.

RICHARDS Michael "Tucker" *Born* Wolverhampton, 3 June 1967. *Died* (natural causes) 28 May 1992. As an amateur he reached the Midland Counties super-heavyweight final in 1988 and eventually decided to go pro with former fighter, Bingo Crooks. Had his first contest in January 1990 and three fights later knocked out Al Malcolm in nine rounds to win the Midlands Area heavyweight title. Prior to his sudden demise, his previous four fights had been defeats at the hands of Herbie Hide, Clifton Mitchell (twice) and Henry Akinwande, with his record showing just five wins in ten contests.

RONDON Vicente Paul *Born* San Jose de Rio Chico, Venezuela, 29 July 1938. *Died* 29 December 1992. Pro 1965-1974. After 35 fights (five defeats), including wins over Bennie Briscoe and Roger Rouse, he became WBA light-heavyweight champion in 1971, beating Jimmy Dupree for the vacant title. Given his big chance when World champion, Bob Foster, was stripped by the WBA for not taking on Dupree, he went on to make successful defences against Piero del Papa, Eddie Jones, Gomeo Brennan and Doyle Baird. His reign as champion came to an end when Foster unified the title in April 1972, following a two round kayo. Came to London to fight John Conteh in 1973 and after being beaten inside nine rounds, he had just three more outings before announcing his retirement.

SMITH Billy *Born* Sunderland, 1909. *Died* November 1992. Brother of former featherweight star, Tom Smith. Pro 1924-1931. Beat Kid Kelly, Johnny Smith, Joe Myers, Douglas Parker, Benny Sharkey, Danny Veitch, Bob Lamb and Jim Bird. After retirement, he helped to train younger brother Tom. One of eight children, his father built a gym in the attic where he taught his sons to box. A popular figure, he became Vice-President of the Sunderland EBA.

URTAIN Jose Manuel Ibar *Born* Spain, 14 May 1943. *Died* 21 July 1992. Pro 1968-1977. Won European heavyweight title by beating Peter Weiland (1970) and successfully defended against Jurgen Blin (1970), before losing it to Henry Cooper (1970). Known as the "Basque Rock-Thrower", he came back to regain the title with a three knockdown, second round victory over England's Jack Bodell and reigned for just six months, until losing on points against Jurgen Blin in Madrid. From then on, although having the occasional good win over the likes of Richard Dunn and Dante Cane, it became a downhill struggle. Although he had another crack at the European title, he was knocked out in four rounds by the Belgian, Jean-Pierre Coopman, in 1977 and finally called it a day.

VALENTINE Ben *Born* Fiji. *Died* January 1993. Came to Britain in 1935 and settled here, classing Ginger Sadd, Nat Franks, Bill Hardy, Eddie Maguire, Dave McCleave, Ernie Woodman, Dai Jones, Joe Quigley, Snowey Edwards, Jack Hyams, Battling Parkin, Reg Gregory, Marcel Lauriot, Elfryn Morris, and Butcher Gascoigne, among his many victims. Was beaten by World light-heavyweight champion, Freddie Mills, having earlier returned from a short tour of America, where he defeated Mickey Snell and

Bill Muldoon, before losing to Lloyd Marshall. Ended his days in a Residential Home in West London, where the staff described him as a "lovely man" and a "model resident."

VAN KLAVEREN Bep *Born* Rotterdam, Holland, 26 September 1907. *Died* February 1992. Won an Olympic Games gold medal at featherweight (1928), before turning pro in 1928. Had a remarkable career spanning 28 years, with breaks from 1941-1946, when he was in the Dutch Army and 1949-1953, when inactive. Won the European lightweight title by beating Francois Sybille (1931) and successfully retained the crown against Harry Corbett (1931), Henri Scillie (1931), Francois Sybille (1932), before losing it to Cleto Locatelli on a last-round disqualification (1932). Immediately afterwards, he left for America, where he stayed until 1935. His victims included Frankie Petrolle, Baby Joe Gans, Ceferino Garcia, Kid Azteca and Herman Perlick. Had two fights in Australia, each time being beaten on points by Jack Carroll. Returned to Holland and won the European middleweight title by beating Edouard Tenet (1938), only to lose it four months later to Anton Christoforodis. His final amazing comeback ended at the age of 48 when he was beaten by Idrissa Dione for the European welterweight title (1955). A well known character in the bars of Rotterdam, until shortly before his death, where he regaled customers with tales of his exploits.

WOODS Danny *Born* Clydebank, 1914. *Died* 28 December 1992. Pro 1937-1950. Beat Ben Duffy, Mickey Green, Tommy McGoldrick, Tommy Miller, Jack Collins, Jimmy Stubbs and Billy Cunningham. Twice defeated in challenges for the vacant Scottish lightweight title by Joe Kerr (1943) and Harry Hughes (1947), he was never to be a national champion. However, he was good enough to draw over ten rounds in 1944 with the future British featherweight champion, Ronnie Clayton.

Ben Valentine

Leading BBBoC Licence Holders: Names and Addresses

Licensed Promoters

Billy Aird
The Golden Gloves
346 Seaside
Eastbourne
East Sussex BN22 7RJ

Michael Andrew
47 New Barn Street
Plaistow
London E13 8JY

Anglo-Swedish Promotions
Greg Steene
11 Whitcomb Street
London WC2H 7HA

Mike Barrett
PO Box 1230
London SW7 4QZ

Jack Bishop
76 Gordon Road
Fareham
Hampshire PO16 7SS

Teresa Breen
31 Penlan Road
Treboeth
Swansea

Pat Brogan
112 Crewe Road
Haslington
Crewe
Cheshire

Harry Burgess
25 Calthorpe Street
London WC1X 0JX

Bruce Burrows
126 Ferndale Road
Swindon
Wiltshire

Champion Enterprises
Frank Maloney
84 Green Lanes
London N16

Eva Christian
80 Alma Road
Plymouth
Devon PL3 4HU

Annette Conroy
144 High Street East
Sunderland
Tyne and Wear

Thomas Cooper
Pen Prys Farm
Bryn
Llanelli
Dyfed

Pat Cowdell
129a Moat Road
Oldbury
Warley
West Midlands

John Cox
11 Fulford Drive
Links View
Northampton

Dragon Boxing Promotions
Dai Gardiner &
Kevin Hayde
93 St Mary's Street
Cardiff
South Wales CF1 1DW

Eastwood Promotions
Bernard Eastwood
Eastwood House
2-4 Chapel Lane
Belfast 1
Northern Ireland

Christine Edwards
44 The Fairway
Westella
Near Hull
Humberside

James Evans
49 St Marks Crescent
Maidenhead
Berkshire

Evesham Sporting Club
Mike Goodall
Schiller
Gibbs Lane
Offenham
Evesham

Norman Fawcett
4 Wyndsak Place
Gosforth
Newcastle upon Tyne

Douglas Firkin-Flood
Stockport Road West
Bredbury
Stockport
Cheshire SK6 2AR

John Forbes
5 Durham Road
Sedgefield
Stockton on Tees
Cleveland TS21 3DW

Joe Foster
4 Denham Avenue
Fulwell
Sunderland

Joe Frater
The Cottage
Main Road
Grainthorpe
Louth
Lincolnshire

Anthony Gee
35 Greville Street
Hatton Garden
London EC1

Harold Gorton
Gorton House
4 Hollius Road
Oldham
Lancashire

Ron Gray
Ingrams Oak
19 Hatherton Road
Cannock
Staffordshire

Johnny Griffin
98 Stonehill Avenue
Birstall
Leicester

David Harris
16 Battle Crescent
St Leonards on Sea
Sussex

Brian Hearn
12 Newnham Road
Colebrook
Plymton
Devon PL7 4AW

Steve Holdsworth
85 Sussex Road
Watford
Hertfordshire
WD2 5HR

Harry Holland
12 Kendall Close
Feltham
Middlesex

Terry Holland
29/31 Orchard Road
Stevenage
Hertfordshire SG1 3HE

Alan Honniball
83 Russell Drive
Mudeford
Dorset

Hull & District Sporting Club
Mick Toomey
25 Purton Grove
Bransholme
Hull HU7 4QD

Alma Ingle
26 Newman Road
Wincobank
Sheffield S9 1LP

K K Promotions
Ken Whitney
22 Oundle Road
Weldon
Corby
Northamptonshire

Alan Lacey
Rococo House
281 City Road
London EC1V 1LA

John Levine
38 St Vincent Road
Westcliff on Sea
Essex S50 7PR

McKenzie Promotions
85-87 High Street
South Norwood
London SE25 6NA

McMahon Promotions
122 Twinnel House
Easton
Bristol

Phil Martin
79 Buckingham Road
Chorlton
Manchester M21 1QT

Matchroom
Barry Hearn
10 Western Road
Romford
Essex RM1 3TT

Midland Sporting Club
D. L. Read
Ernest & Young
Windsor House
3 Temple Row
Birmingham B2 5LA

Katherine Morrison
5 Abercromby Drive
Glasgow G40

National Promotions
Mickey Duff
National House
60-66 Wardour Street
London W1V 3HP

North Staffs Sporting Club
J Baddeley
29 Redwood Avenue
Stone
Staffordshire ST15 0DB

North-West Promotions
Pat Dwyer
93 Keir Hardie Avenue
Bootle
Liverpool 20
Merseyside

Gus Robinson
Stranton House
Westview Road
Hartlepool TS24 0BB

Christine Rushton
20 Alverley Lane
Balby
Doncaster
Yorkshire DN4 9AS

Chris Rustage
Riverside House
St Simon Street
Salford
Manchester M3 7ET

Licensed Managers

Billy Aird
The Golden Gloves
346 Seaside
Eastbourne
East Sussex BN22 7RJ

Isola Akay
129 Portnall Road
Paddington
London W9 3BN

Mike Atkinson
9 Tudor Road
Ainsdale
Southport
Lancashire PR8 2RU

Don Austin
14 Winchat Road
Broadwaters
Thamesmead
London SE28 0DZ

Billy Ball
6 Copse Close
Marlow
Buckinghamshire
SL7 2NY

Johnny Barclay
3 Newall Close
The Furlongs
Turnfurlong Lane
Aylesbury
Buckinghamshire
HP21 7FE

Mike Barrett
PO Box 1230
London SW7 4QZ

Nat Basso
38 Windsor Road
Prestwich
Lancashire M25 8FF

Bob Batey
243 Ladykirk Road
Newcastle upon Tyne
NE4 8AL

John Baxter
6 Havencrest Drive
Leicester LE5 2AG

Lance Billany
32 Beaconsfield
Carrs Meadow
Withernsea
North Humberside
HU19 2EP

Jack Bishop
76 Gordon Road
Fareham
Hampshire PO16 7SS

Abner Blackstock
23 Alice Street
Pill
Newport
Gwent
South Wales

Gerald Bousted
46 Coombe Lane
St Mary Church
Torquay
Devon

George Bowes
24 St Mawes Close
Throston Grange
Hartlepool
Cleveland

Paul Boyce
Brynamlwg
2 Pant Howell Ddu
Ynysmerdy
Briton Ferry
Neath SA11 2TU

Colin Breen
31 Penlan Road
Treboeth
Swansea
West Glamorgan

Mike Brennan
2 Canon Avenue
Chadwell Heath
Romford
Essex

Fred Britton
71 Henrietta Street
Leigh
Lancashire WN7 1LH

Pat Brogan
112 Crewe Road
Haslington
Cheshire

Michael Brooks
114 Gildane
Orchard Park Estate
Hull HU6 9AY

Dick Brownson
Armada House
Marine Parade
Instow
North Devon EX39 4JJ

Harry Burgess
25 Calthorpe Street
London WC1X 0JX

Winston Burnett
6 Faber Way
City Gardens
Sloper Road
Grangetown
Cardiff CF1 8DN

Paddy Byrne
70 Benfield Way
Portslade by Sea
Sussex BN4 2DL

Pat Byrne
11 Cadman Close
Bedworth
Warwickshire
CV12 8PD

Trevor Callighan
40 Prescott Street
Halifax
West Yorkshire
HX1 2QW

Harry Carnall
270 Hastilar Road
South Woodthorpe
Sheffield
Yorkshire S13 8EJ

Ernie Cashmore
18 North Drive
Handsworth
Birmingham
B20 8SX

John Celebanski
87 Crowtree Lane
Allerton
Bradford BD8 0AN

Michael Chapman
9 Mill Lane
Farington
Moss
Lancashire PR5 3PS

Nigel Christian
80 Alma Road
Plymouth
Devon PL3 4HU

Peter Coleman
9 Easterly Grove
Leeds
Yorkshire LS8 3AB

Roger Colson
63 Amwell Street
Roseberry Avenue
London EC1

William Connelly
72 Clincart Road
Mount Florida
Glasgow G42

Tommy Conroy
144 High Street East
Sunderland
Tyne and Wear

George Cooper
16 Robin Hood Green
St Mary Cray
Orpington
Kent

Michael Copp
62 Fleet Street
Swansea
West Glamorgan

Pat Cowdell
129a Moat Road
Oldbury
Warley
West Midlands
B68 8EE

John Cox
11 Fulford Drive
Links View
Northampton
NN2 7NX

Jimmy Cresswell
3 Williamson Street
Clydebank G81 2AS

Bingo Crooks
37 Helming Drive
Danehust Estate
Wolverhampton
West Midlands
WV1 2AF

David Davies
10 Bryngelli
Carmel
Llanelli
Dyfed SA14 7EL

Glyn Davies
63 Parc Brynmawr
Felinfoel
Llanelli
Dyfed SA15 4PG

Ronnie Davies
3 Vallensdean Cottages
Hangleton Lane
Portslade
Sussex

Brendan Devine
12 Birkdale Close
Clubmoor
Liverpool L6 0DL

Michael Donovan
8 Sefton Road
Walton
Liverpool L9 2BP

Jack Doughty
Lane End Cottage
Golden Street
Shaw
Lancashire OL2 8LY

Shaun Doyle
15 Jermyn Croft
Dodworth
Barnsley
South Yorkshire
S75 3LR

Phil Duckworth
The Shepherd
96 Pontefract Lane
Leeds
Yorkshire L59 6TG

Mickey Duff
National House
60-66 Wardour Street
London W1V 3HP

Pat Dwyer
93 Keir Hardie Avenue
Bootle
Liverpool 20
Merseyside L20 0DN

Bernard Eastwood
Eastwood House
2-4 Chapel Lane
Belfast 1
Northern Ireland

George Evans
14 Donald Street
Abercanaid
Merthyr Tydfil
Glamorgan

Greg Evans
21 Portman Road
Liverpool
Merseyside L15 2HH

Jack Evans
Morlee House
Hanbury Road
Pontypool
Monmouth

Michael Fawcett
44 Rawstone Walk
Plaistow
London E13

Norman Fawcett
4 Wyndsak Place
Gosforth
Newcastle upon Tyne

Colin Flute
84 Summerhill Road
Bilston
West Midlands
WV14 8RE

Dai Gardiner
13 Hengoed Hall
Drive
Cefn Hengoed
Hengoed
Mid Glamorgan

John Gaynor
7 Westhorne Fold
Counthill Drive
Brooklands Road
Crumpsall
Manchester
M8 6JN

Danny Gill
8 Whitehouse Street
Coseley
West Midlands
WV14 8HE

Tommy Gilmour
Forte Crest Hotel
Bothwell Street
Glasgow G2 7EN

Lee Graham
17 Felday Road
Lewisham
London SE13 7HQ

Ron Gray
Ingrams Oak
19 Hatherton Road
Cannock
Staffordshire

Johnny Griffin
98 Stonehill Avenue
Birstall
Leicestershire

Harry Griver
187 Redbridge Lane
East
Redbridge
Essex IG4 5DF

Dick Gunn
43 Moray Avenue
Hayes
Middlesex OB3 2AY

Carl Gunns
Flat 2
Heathcliffe
469 Loughborough
Road
Birstall
Leicester LE4 0DS

Clive Hall
23 Linnet Drive
Barton Seagrave
Kettering
Northamptonshire

David Harris
16 Battle Crescent
St Leonards on Sea
Sussex

Harold Hayes
16 Hyland Crescent
Warmsworth
Doncaster
South Yorkshire
DN4 9JS

Teddy Haynes
The Henry Cooper
516 Old Kent Road
London SE1 5BA

Geoff Hayward
51 Derby Avenue
Tettenhall
Wolverhampton
West Midlands
WV6 9JR

Patrick Healy
1 Cranley Buildings
Brookes Market
Holborn
London EC1

Barry Hearn
Matchroom
10 Western Road
Romford
Essex RM1 3JT

George Hill
52 Hathaway
Marton
Blackpool
Lancashire FY4 4AB

Mick Hill
35 Shenstone House
Aldrington Road
London SW16 1TL

Clive Hogben
44 Polwell Lane
Barton Seagrave
Kettering
Northamptonshire
NN15 6UA

Harry Holland
12 Kendall Close
Feltham
Middlesex

Gordon Holmes
New Cottage
Watton Road
Hingham
Norfolk NR9 4NN

Lloyd Honeyghan
22 Risborough
Deacon Way
Walworth Road
London SE17

Brendan Ingle
26 Newman Road
Wincobank
Sheffield S9 1LP

Derek Isaamen
179 Liverpool Road
South
Maghill
Liverpool L31 8AA

Mike Jacobs
"Jems"
95 Ridgeview Road
Whetstone
London N20 0HG

Colin Jones
1 Brookfield Close
Penyrheol
Gorseinon
Swansea SA4 2GW

Richard Jones
1 Churchfields
Croft
Warrington
Cheshire WA3 7JR

Duncan Jowett
Cedarhouse
Caplethill Road
Paisley
Strathclyde
Scotland

Billy Kane
17 Bamburn Terrace
Byker
Newcastle upon Tyne
NE6 2GH

Johnny Kramer
115 Crofton Road
Plaistow
London E13

Terry Lawless
4 Banyards
Off Nelmes Way
Emerson Park
Hornchurch
Essex

Buddy Lee
The Walnuts
Roman Bank
Leverington
Wisbech
Cambridgeshire

Brian Lynch
53 Hall Lane
Upminster
Essex

Pat Lynch
Gotherinton
68 Kelsey Lane
Balsall Common
Near Coventry
West Midlands

Glenn McCrory
Holborn
35 Station Road
Stanley
Co Durham DH9 0JL

Bobby McEwan
302 Langside Road
Glasgow

Clinton McKenzie
2 Wisbourgh Road
South Croydon
Surrey CR2 0DR

Jim McMillan
21 Langcliffe Road
Preston
Lancashire PR2 6UE

Frank Maloney
Champion Enterprises
84 Green Lanes
London N16

Dennie Mancini
16 Rosedew Road
Off Fulham Palace
Road
London W6 9ET

Terry Marsh
141 Great Gregorie
Basildon
Essex

Phil Martin
79 Buckingham Road
Chorlton
Manchester M21 1TQ

Gary Mason
Unit 12
Canada House
Blackburn Road
West Hampstead
London NW6

Arthur Melrose
33 Easterhill Street
Glasgow G32 8LN

Tommy Miller
128 Clapton Mount
King Cross Road
Halifax
West Yorkshire

Achille Mitchell
54 Portland Avenue
Gravesend
Kent

Carl Moorcroft
108 Stuart Road
Crosby
Liverpool 23

James Murray
87 Spean Street
Glasgow G44 4DS

David Nelson
29 Linley Drive
Stirchley Park
Telford
Shropshire
TF3 1RQ

Paul Newman
8 Teg Close
Downs Park Estate
Portslade
Sussex

Gary Nickels
11 St Andrews Drive
Highgrove Gardens
Stevenage
Hertfordshire
SG1 4UY

Norman Nobbs
364 Kings Road
Kingstanding
Birmingham
B44 0UG

Bob Paget
8 Masterman House
New Church Road
London SE5 7HU

George Patrick
84 Wooler Road
Edmonton
London N18 2JS

Billy Pearce
Flat C
36 Courtfield Gardens
South Kensington
London SW5 0PT

Terry Petersen
54 Green Leafe Avenue
Wheatley Hills
Doncaster
South Yorkshire
DN2 5RF

Steve Pollard
35 Gorthorpe
Orchard Park Estate
Hull HE6 9EY

John Pook
75 Stapley Road
Hove
Sussex

Ricky Porter
73 County Road
Swindon
Wiltshire

Dean Powell
10 Cuddington
Deacon Way
Heygate Estate
Walworth
London SE17 1SP

Dennis Read
65 Bridle Road
Shirley
Croydon
Surrey

Ken Richardson
15 East Walk
North Road Estate
Retford
Nottinghamshire
DN22 7YF

Gus Robinson
Stranton House
Westview Road
Hartlepool
TS24 0BB

John Rushton
20 Alverley Lane
Balby
Doncaster DN4 9AS

Joe Ryan
22a Glenarm Road
Clapton
London E5 0LZ

Kevin Sanders
19 Whittington
Off Parnwell Way
Peterborough
Cambridgeshire

Chris Sanigar
41 Chaplin Road
Easton
Bristol BS5 0JT

Eric Secombe
11 Joseph Trotter Close
Myddleton Street
Finsbury
London EC1

Kevin Sheehan
84 Amesbury Circus
Bells Lane Estate
Nottingham NG8 6DH

Mike Shinfield
126 Birchwood Lane
Somercotes
Derbyshire DE55 4NE

Steve Sims
The Welsh Prince
78 Commercial Street
Newport
Gwent

Len Slater
78 Sutcliffe Avenue
Nunsthorpe
Grimsby
Lincolnshire

Andy Smith
Valandra
19 St Audreys Lane
St Ives
Cambridgeshire

John Smith
6 Kildare Road
Chorlton
Manchester M21 1YR

Brian Snagg
The Princess
Princess Drive
West Derby
Liverpool L12 6QQ

Les Southey
Oakhouse
Park Way
Hillingdon
Middlesex

John Spensley
The Black Swan Hotel
Tremholme Bar
Near Stokesley
North Yorkshire
DL6 3JY

Ken Squires
27 University Close
Syston
Leicestershire LE7 8AY

Greg Steene
11 Whitcomb Street
London WC2H 7HA

Norrie Sweeney
3 Sauchill Terrace
Paisley
Scotland PA2 6SY

Wally Swift
Grove House
54 Grove Road
Knowle
Solihull
West Midlands
B93 0PJ

Amos Talbot
70 Edenfield Road
Rochdale OL11 5AE

Keith Tate
214 Dick Lane
Tyersal
Bradford BD4 8JH

Glenroy Taylor
95 Devon Close
Perivale
Middlesex

Eddie Thomas
Runnington
Penydarren Park
Merthyr Tydfil
Mid Glamorgan

Jimmy Tibbs
44 Gylingdune Gardens
Seven Kings
Essex

Terry Toole
8 Conningsby Gardens
South Chingford
London E4 9BD

Mick Toomey
25 Purton Grove
Bransholme
Hull HU7 4QD

Jack Trickett
Acton Court Hotel
189 Buxton Road
Stockport
Cheshire

Noel Trigg
Waterford
The Bridge
Bettws Lane
Newport NP9 6AB

Frankie Turner
Matchroom
10 Western Road
Essex RM1 3JT

Bill Tyler
5 Wolverhampton Road
Bloxwich
Walsall WS3 2EY

Danny Urry
26 Nella Road
Hammersmith
London W6

Stephen Vaughan
43-45 Pembroke Place
Liverpool L3 5PH

Alan Walker
47 Consett Road
Castleside
Consett
Durham DH8 9QL

Frank Warren
Centurion House
Bircherley Green
Hertford
Hertfordshire
SG14 1HP

Robert Watt
32 Dowanhill Street
Glasgow G11

Gordon White
34 Gaskell Street
London SW4 6NS

Ken Whitney
22 Oundle Road
Weldon
Northamptonshire

Mick Williamson
34a St Marys Grove
Cannonbury
London N1

Tex Woodward
Spanorium Farm
Berwick Lane
Compton Greenfield
Bristol BS12 3RX

British Boxing Yearbook: Monthly Update

<u>FULL</u> records of all active British-based boxers updated every month. Can you afford to be without a copy?

For further details please apply to Graham Grinnell, 22 East Castle Street, Bridgnorth, Shropshire WV16 4AN.
Tel. No. (0746) 765264

Licensed Matchmakers

Nat Basso
38 Windsor Road
Prestwich
Lancashire M25 8FF

Harry Burgess
25 Calthorpe Street
London WC1

Paddy Byrne
70 Benfield Way
Portslade by Sea
Sussex BN4 2DL

David Davies
10 Byrngelli
Carmel
Llanelli
Dyfed SA14 7EL

Glyn Davies
63 Parc Brynmawr
Felinfoel
Llanelli
Dyfed SA15 4PG

David Davis
179 West Heath Road
Hampstead
London NW3

Mickey Duff
National House
60-66 Wardour Street
London W1 3HP

Ernie Fossey
26 Bell Lane
Brookmans Park
Hertfordshire

John Gaynor
7 Westhorne Fold
Counthill Drive
Brooklands Road
Crumpsall
Manchester M8 6JN

Tommy Gilmour
Fort Crest Hotel
Bothwell Street
Glasgow G2 7EN

Ron Gray
Ingrams Oak
19 Hatherton Road
Cannock
Staffordshire

Patrick Healy
1 Cranley Buildings
Brookes Market
Holborn
London EC1

Steve Holdsworth
85 Sussex Road
Watford
Herts WD2 5HR

Terry Lawless
4 Banyards
Off Nelmes Way
Emerson Park
Hornchurch
Essex

Graham Lockwood
106 Burnside Avenue
Skipton
North Yorkshire
BD23 2OB

Frank Maloney
Champion Enterprises
84 Green Lanes
London N16

Dennie Mancini
16 Rosedew Road
Off Fulham Palace Road
Hammersmith
London W6 9ET

Tommy Miller
128 Clapton Mount
King Cross Road
Halifax
West Yorkshire

Chris Moorcroft
17 Cambrian Drive
Prostatyn
Clwyd LL19 9RN

Gary Nickels
11 St Andrews Drive
Highgrove Gardens
Stevenage
Hertfordshire SG1 4UY

Norman Nobbs
364 Kings Road
Kingstanding
Birmingham B44 0UG

Ricky Porter
Angelique Guest House
73 County Road
Swindon
Wiltshire

Dean Powell
10 Cuddington
Deacon Way
Heygate Estate
Walworth
London SE17 1SP

Len Slater
78 Sutcliffe Avenue
Nunsthorpe
Grimsby
Lincolnshire

Terry Toole
8 Conningsby Gardens
South Chingford
London E4 9BD

Frank Turner
Matchroom
10 Western Road
Romford
Essex RM1 3JT

Stephen Vaughan
276 Aigburth Road
Aigburth
Liverpool L17 9PJ

Winning Combination

144 High Street East, Sunderland, Tyne & Wear SK1 2BL
Tel: 091 5676871 - 0850 434457. Fax: 091 5652581
Tommy Conroy: *Manager and Trainer.*
Annette Conroy: *First North-East Lady Promoter.*
Matchmaker: Graham Lockwood.
Trainers: Micky Hitch, Charlie Armstrong, Billy Melton, Barry Norman, Malcolm Gates

SUNDERLAND BASED STABLE RECORD TO OCTOBER 1993

		C	W	L	D	
JOHN DAVISON	NEWCASTLE	19	15	4	0	WBC International Super-Bantamweight Champion
PAUL CHARTERS	NORTH SHIELDS	33	20	13	0	Northern Area Light-Welterweight Champion
FRANKIE FOSTER	NEWCASTLE	26	11	12	3	Northern Area Super-Featherweight Champion
TERRY FRENCH	DUNSTON	28	15	12	1	Northern Area Light-Heavyweight Champion
IAN HENRY	GATESHEAD	19	14	5	0	No. 1 Contender Northern Area Light-Heavyweight Title
ROB PITTERS	GATESHEAD	15	9	4	2	No. 1 Contender Northern Area Light-Middleweight Title
PAUL HITCH	WINGATE	13	11	2	0	No. 1 Contender Northern Area Middleweight Title
DAVE JOHNSON	BOLDON	14	12	1	1	Middleweight
MICKY HALL	LUDWORTH	12	6	4	2	Lightweight
CHIP O'NEIL	SUNDERLAND	8	4	4	0	Featherweight
HUGH DAVEY	WALLSEND	9	6	2	1	Welterweight
ALAN GRAHAM	NEWCASTLE	7	4	3	0	Lightweight
TIM HILL	NORTH SHIELDS	4	2	2	0	Lightweight
DAVE WHITTLE	NORTH SHIELDS	18	9	7	2	Welterweight

Licensed Referees

Class 'B'

Teddy Gardner	Southern Area
Keith Garner	Central Area
Anthony Green	Central Area
Mark Green	Southern Area
Rudi Harders	Welsh Area
Al Hutcheon	Scottish Area
David Irving	Northern Ireland
Marcus McDonnell	Southern Area
Terry O'Connor	Midlands Area
Roy Snipe	Central Area
Grant Wallis	Western Area
Gerald Watson	Northern Area

Class 'A'

Ivor Bassett	Welsh Area
Arnold Bryson	Northern Area
Phil Cowsill	Central Area
Richard Davies	Southern Area
Roddy Evans	Welsh Area
Ron Hackett	Central Area
Michael Heatherwick	Welsh Area
Brian Hogg	Central Area
Michael Jacobs	Southern Area
Wynford Jones	Welsh Area
John Keane	Midland Area
Denzil Lewis	Western Area
Len Mullen	Scottish Area
James Pridding	Midlands Area
Reg Thompson	Southern Area
Lawrence Thompson	Northern Area
Anthony Walker	Southern Area
Barney Wilson	Northern Ireland

Class 'A' Star

John Coyle	Midlands Area
Roy Francis	Southern Area
Adrian Morgan	Welsh Area
Larry O'Connell	Southern Area
Dave Parris	Southern Area
Billy Rafferty	Scottish Area
Paul Thomas	Midlands Area
Mickey Vann	Central Area

Licensed Timekeepers

Roy Bicknell	Midlands Area
Roger Bowden	Western Area
John Breward	Northern Area
Neil Burder	Welsh Area
Ivor Campbell	Welsh Area
Frank Capewell	Central Area
Robert Edgeworth	Southern Area
Harold Elliott	Northern Ireland
Harry Foxall	Midlands Area
Eric Gilmour	Scottish Area
Brian Heath	Midlands Area
Ken Honiball	Western Area

Lewis G. Hubbard	Southern Area
Winston Hughes	Midlands Area
Albert Kelleher	Northern Area
Michael McCann	Southern Area
Peter McCann	Southern Area
Norman Maddox	Midlands Area
Gordon Pape	Welsh Area
Daniel Peacock	Southern Area
Barry Pinder	Central Area
Raymond Preston	Western Area
Raymond Rice	Southern Area
Tommy Rice	Southern Area
Colin Roberts	Central Area
James Russell	Scottish Area
Nick White	Southern Area
Geoffrey Williams	Southern Area

Licensed Inspectors

Alan Alster	Central Area
Michael Barnett	Central Area
Don Bartlett	Midlands Area
Jeffrey Bowden	Western Area
John Braley	Midlands Area
Fred Breyer	Southern Area
Ray Chichester	Welsh Area
Geoff Collier	Midlands Area
John Crowe	Midlands Area
Jaswinder Dhaliwal	Midlands Area
Les Dean	Midlands Area
Robert Edgar	Central Area
Phil Edwards	Central Area
Kevin Fulthorpe	Welsh Area
David Furneaux	Northern Area
John Hall	Central Area
Richard Hingston	Western Area
Dennis Kearney	Northern Ireland
Freddie King	Southern Area
Bob Lonkhurst	Southern Area
Ken Lyas	Southern Area
Tom McElkinney	Northern Area
Stuart Meiklejohn	Central Area
David Ogilvie	Northern Area
Charlie Payne	Southern Area
Les Potts	Midlands Area
Ron Pudney	Southern Area
Ken Rimmington	Southern Area
John S. Shaw	Western Area
Bert Smith	Western Area
Charlie Thurley	Southern Area
John Toner	Northern Ireland
David Underwood	Midlands Area
David Venn	Northern Area
Ernie Wallis	Welsh Area
P. J. White	Southern Area
Billy Wilkins	Welsh Area
Geoff Williams	Midlands Area
Harry Woods	Scottish Area

Licensed Ringwhips

Robert Ainsley-Mathews	Southern Area
Robert Brazier	Southern Area
Albert Brewer	Southern Area
Steve Butler	Central Area
Theodore Christian	Western Area
Gerard Crummey	Central Area
Ernie Draper	Southern Area
Colin Gallagher	Central Area
Danny Gill	Midlands Area
Chris Gilmore	Scottish Area
Mike Goodall	Midlands Area
Peter Gray	Midlands Area
Arran Lee Grinnell	Midlands Area
David Hall	Central Area
Thomas Hallett	Northern Area
John Hardwick	Southern Area
Keith Jackson	Midlands Area
Philip Keen	Central Area
Alun Martin	Welsh Area
Tommy Miller (Jnr)	Central Area
Linton O'Brien	Northern Area
Dennis Pinching	Southern Area
Sandy Risley	Southern Area
John Vary	Southern Area
Paul Wainwright	Northern Area
James Wallace	Scottish Area
James Whitelaw	Scottish Area
John Whitelaw	Scottish Area

Dave Parris, Class "A" Star Referee
Les Clark

CHAMPS CAMP
PROMOTIONS
Manchester's No. 1 Boxing Centre

Manager:
Phil Martin
Tel: 061-881 7872 (Home)
061-226 4540 (Gym)
Fax: 061-226 3196

Correspondence:
79 Buckingham Road,
Chorlton,
Manchester
M21 1QT

Gymnasium:
139 Princess Road
Moss Side
Manchester
M14 4RE

Left to Right: Maurice Coore, Carl Thompson, Frank Grant, Paul Burke and Phil Martin

"BOXING TEAM"

STEVE GARBER HEAVY
MIKE CLAYTON HEAVY
CARL THOMPSON CRUISER (BRITISH CHAMPION)
MAURICE "HARD" COORE LIGHT-HEAVY (BRITISH CHAMPION)
FIDEL CASTRO SMITH SUPER-MIDDLE (FORMER BRITISH CHAMPION)
ERIC NOI SUPER-MIDDLE
FRAN HARDING SUPER-MIDDLE
FRANK EUBANKS SUPER-MIDDLE
FRANK "TERMINATOR" GRANT MIDDLE (BRITISH CHAMPION)
QUINN PAYNTER MIDDLE
STEVE "THE VIKING" FOSTER LIGHT-MIDDLE
ENSLEY BINGHAM LIGHT-MIDDLE
DES ROBINSON WELTER
HUMPHREY HARRISON WELTER
TONY EKUBIA LIGHT-WELTER (FORMER BRITISH & COMMONWEALTH CHAMPION)
PAUL BURKE LIGHT (BRITISH & COMMONWEALTH CHAMPION)
STEVE WALKER SUPER-FEATHER
MARIO CULPEPER SUPER-FEATHER
NICK BOYD SUPER-FEATHER
PETER JUDSON FEATHER
HENRY ARMSTRONG SUPER-BANTAM
JOHN GREEN BANTAM

Boxers' Record Index

ST. ANDREW'S SPORTING CLUB
EXCLUSIVE GENTLEMEN'S CLUB
AND
THE HOME OF SCOTTISH BOXING

1993-94 Fixture List

Monday 20th September 1993

Monday 25th October

Monday 22nd November

Monday 13th December

(Ladies Night - Dinner Dance & Cabaret)

Monday 24th January 1994

Monday 21st February

Monday 21st March

Monday 25th April

Monday 6th June

Administrative Offices and Club Room
Forte Crest,
Bothwell Street, Glasgow G2 7EN
Telephone: 041-248 5461 and 041-248 2656
Fax: 041-221 8986   Telex: 77440
DIRECTOR: TOMMY GILMOUR JNR.